# ESSENTIAL
## AS & A2 PSYCHOLOGY
### F O R   A Q A ( A )

# ESSENTIAL
## AS & A2 PSYCHOLOGY
### FOR AQA(A)

# Richard Gross & Geoff Rolls

Hodder Arnold

A MEMBER OF THE HODDER HEADLINE GROUP

To the loves of my life. R.G.

To the one and only E.J.J.M. G.R.

Orders: please contact Bookpoint Ltd, 130 Milton Park, Abingdon, Oxon OX14 4SB. Telephone: +44 (0)1235 827720. Fax: +44 (0)1235 400454. Lines are open from 9.00–5.00, Monday to Saturday, with a 24-hour message answering service. You can also order through our website www.hoddereducation.co.uk

*British Library Cataloguing in Publication Data*
A catalogue record for this title is available from the British Library

ISBN-10: 0 340 92589 2
ISBN-13: 978 0 340 92589 8

This Edition Published 2006
Impression number  10  9  8  7  6  5  4  3  2  1
Year                         2009  2008  2007  2006

Copyright © 2006 Richard Gross and Geoff Rolls

Typeset by Fakenham Photosetting Ltd, Fakenham, Norfolk.
Printed in Dubai for Hodder Arnold, an imprint of Hodder Education, a member of the Hodder Headline Group, 338 Euston Road, London NW1 3BH

# Contents

# Introduction

*Essential AS & A2 Psychology* is written for the AQA(A) specification, although it could also prove useful for students following other specifications. As the title suggests, we've included only the information you really need to be able to achieve a top grade in the AS and A2 exams – no more and no less!

However, 'Essential' in the title means something rather different in the A2 section compared with AS. With AS (Chapters 1–6), the *whole* specification has to be covered, and many particular theories and research studies that students need to know are spelled out (sometimes as 'e.g.s'). But in A2 (Chapters 8–18), there's considerable choice open to students and teachers – the specification is designed so that only a certain proportion of the content needs to be covered. So, how does this work?

Module 4 comprises five sections (Social, Physiological, Cognitive, Developmental and Comparative), each of these comprising three sub-sections (e.g. Social comprises Social Cognition, Relationships, and Pro- and Anti-Social Behaviour). The paper for this module contains three essay questions for each section, one on each sub-section (this is guaranteed). So, in the case of Social, there will definitely be one question on Social Cognition, one on Relationships, and one on Pro- and Anti-Social Behaviour. Candidates have to answer three questions, from at least two sections. This means that you could answer two questions from Social – but no more. Your other question must come from another section.

We have decided to cover Relationships (Chapter 8) and Pro- and Anti-Social Behaviour (Chapter 9). This, as with all the other chapters, is based on what we know to be the most popular topics, as reflected in the questions that candidates have answered in past examinations (as identified in the Chief Examiner's Report for each exam).

Remember, in Module 4 you only have to answer questions from two sections, which means that you can omit three sections. But experience has shown that Biological Rhythms, Sleep and Dreaming (Chapter 10) from Physiological; Cognitive Development (Chapter 11) and Social and Personality Development (Chapter 12) from Developmental; and Evolutionary Explanations of Human Behaviour (Chapter 13) from Comparative, are all popular. We haven't included any sub-sections from Cognitive.

Module 5 is very different. You *have to* answer one question from each of three sections: Individual Differences (which comprises three sub-sections), Perspectives Section B ((a) Issues, (b) Debates), and Perspectives Section C (Approaches). From Individual Differences we've included Psychopathology (Chapter 14) and Treating

Mental Disorders (Chapter 15). All the Issues (Chapter 16), Debates (Chapter 17) and Approaches (Chapter 18) are included.

Key features include:

- **Essential Study boxes (AS)**, in which the study is examined under the five headings that can be used in exam questions. These are Aims, Procedures, Findings, Conclusions and Criticisms (**APFCC**). The criticisms can be both positive (indicated by ✓ ) and negative (indicated by ✗ ). Positive and negative criticisms are of equal importance. The same format is used outside Essential Study boxes under the heading 'Evaluation of...'

- **Essential Study boxes (A2)** relate to the parts of the specification that stipulate 'research studies relating to...' (e.g. attraction and the formation of relationships, love and the breakdown of relationships, and cultural and sub-cultural differences in relationships). Usually, particular studies aren't specified (unlike AS), but candidates have to know about at least two research studies per sub-section. So, 'essential' here means 'These are studies which we think are important and which you're strongly advised to become familiar with'. Ticks and crosses are used (as in AS) to evaluate studies and theories.

- **Key Study boxes (A2 only)** highlight important studies in parts of the specification where you're *not required* to know about particular studies. Studies that might illustrate certain aspects of a topic, or certain issues, debates or approaches, are 'key' (rather than 'essential').

- **Exam Tips boxes (AS)**, which occur throughout each chapter. These are designed to provide you with pointers for answering specific Part c questions (worth 60% of your exam). These relate to both AO1 (**knowledge and understanding**) and AO2 (**analysis and evaluation**). We must stress that *there's no single correct way of answering any question*, and these boxes offer you guidelines and advice only. We also invite you to have a go at the question yourself, using our suggestions. Please note that we've included *most* of the Part c questions you could be asked in the exam, but we *haven't* tried to cover every possibility.

- **Exam Tips boxes (A2)** appear at the end of each sub-section. As in AS, they are designed to provide you with pointers for answering specific essay questions (except for the Approaches questions, which are short-answer, structured questions – see Chapter 18). Also as in AS, they relate to both AO1 and AO2. We've included only one question per sub-section and, again, haven't tried to cover every possibility.

- **Self-assessment questions (SAQs) (AS only)** appear at the end of each chapter. These are examples of Part a and Part b questions (worth 40% of your exam). These relate to AO1 only. At the end of the A2 chapters, additional essay titles are also included.

- **Sample answers (SAs)** for **AS** appear at the *end of the book*, while for **A2** they come at the *end of each chapter*. These correspond to the Exam Tips boxes. It's because there are several ways of gaining the same marks that we haven't called them 'model answers' (which implies 'this is how this question *should* be answered'). Instead, we offer you an idea of how a particular question *could* be answered.

  Please note that, in the case of **A2**, the sample answers are often longer than the number of words cited in the Exam Tips boxes. This number (600 for Module 4, 800 for Module 5 – except for Approaches) is only a *minimum* recommendation. It goes without saying that you must be sensible as to how much you write beyond this minimum (you ought to be guided by how many words you think you could write in the time allowed in the exams). But in our sample essays we've sometimes included additional material (usually AO2-relevant), which makes them quite a bit longer than the recommended minimum. Also, the length varies quite a lot from chapter to chapter, and even within the same chapter. Some topics are just easier to write a lot about than others!

- **Specification Hints boxes (A2 only)** help to interpret or 'deconstruct' the specification. They spell out exactly what the wording means (for example, how many explanations/theories of a particular behaviour you need to know), as well as suggesting links between different parts of the specification. These are related to (and sometimes combined with) **Exam Hints boxes**, which suggest what kinds of questions you could be asked and how you might answer them, based on the interpretation given in the Specification Hints boxes.

- **Chapter Summaries: Revision Schemas (AS and A2)** are key points illustrated in diagrammatic format. In most cases, there is one schematic summary for each sub-section of the chapter (in both **AS** and **A2**), but occasionally two sub-sections have been combined into one revision schema.

- **Essential Study summary boxes (AS only)** are provided at the end of each chapter. These are a useful summary, which can be used as a revision aid.

- **Essential Glossary (AS only)**. These are the terms and concepts which examiners can ask you to define or explain in Part a questions. If they don't appear in the Glossary, then they *cannot* be asked about in the exam.

- **Preparing for the AS exam** (Chapter 7). This:

  a) defines exactly what's meant by AO1 and AO2, as well as AO3 (which is assessed only in the Research Methods section)

  b) gives examples of Part a, b and c questions and how these relate to AO1/AO2/AO3.

  c) explains mark allocations for AO1 and AO2

  d) provides hints for writing evaluations (AO2)

  e) gives some examples of how to write your commentaries for AO2

  f) offers some tips on how to make the most effective use of your time both before and during the exam.

- **A2 Exams and Coursework** (Chapter 19) sets out what's included in the A2 exams. This is a vital chapter, since many examiners state that the difference between a grade A or C is not what you know but how you apply it to the particular exam question. You must ensure that you know the requirements of each of the A2 modules (PYA4, PYA5 and PYA6 (coursework)). There are important differences between the three modules and these are explained in detail. We also show how marks are allocated in each of the exams and discuss the main assessment objectives (AO1, AO2). Terms used in the exam questions are also outlined. PYA6 involves coursework. We have given guidance on how to write up your coursework and we have also given some suggestions for practicals. We've also included a useful coursework checklist for use during your write-up. There's an A2 exam summary and ten top tips for the exams which you should follow.

Much of the text is broken down into bullet points. These bite-sized chunks of information are easier to take in, whether you're working through the material for the first time, or using it for revision. We've done a lot of the selection for you. In the case of AS, this means that instead of reading through the text and deciding what's crucial and what's not, you can safely assume that *all* the material is important. However, in the A2 chapters we've sometimes provided more explanations/theories than are actually required by the specification (to give you more choice, or to give you additional AO2 possibilities: this is pointed out in the Specification Hints/Exam Tips boxes).

Sometimes, the specification refers to particular theories or areas of research, such as 'The multi-store model of memory (Atkinson and Shiffrin)' or 'Bowlby's maternal deprivation hypothesis'. The examiner can ask you specifically about these, using the same wording as used in the specification. Everything that appears in the specification in this way is covered in this book (in both AS and A2).

In other places, the names of researchers are given as 'e.g.s' in brackets. For example, 'Memory research into EWT (e.g. Loftus)' and 'Research into sources of stress, including life events (e.g. Holmes and Rahe)'. It's up to you which researchers (and therefore which studies) you choose. In most cases, these examples are the ones we've included. Also, in the second example, 'including' denotes that life events *must* be covered as one source of stress – and you could be asked specifically about them.

But, in both AS and A2, it's still important that you make your own notes and organise these in a way that suits you. We've tried to be economical in how we use language: why use several words when a few will do? You too should aim for conciseness in your exam answers.

Just as examiners use 'positive marking', so we are very much on your side. We hope you find this book easy and enjoyable to read, and that it helps you both to learn and to revise the essentials.

Good luck!

## Author acknowledgements

I would like to thank Richard Gross for his help throughout this project and for his much-valued friendship. Emma Woolf is fantastic to work with and makes the whole writing process (almost) enjoyable! Thanks Emma.

All the psychology teachers at Peter Symonds' College have, on a daily basis, provided me with AO2 feedback on the book. Indeed, any mistakes that have not been noticed can be blamed almost entirely on James Larcombe, Alex Banks, Andy Pond, Chrissie Rycroft, Kate Wright, Michelle Morgan, Katy Hyde, Naomi Klepacz and Kim Palmer!

Once again, my greatest debt is to Eve Murphy, who provides never ending support when I have to go and spend 'just another half hour' on the book.

Geoff Rolls

I would like to thank Geoff Rolls for his conscientiousness and dedication, and especially for his hands-on experience of teaching A level which is so crucial for a book such as this. I very much appreciate our personal and professional relationship.

One of the fortunate aspects of the book has been the opportunity to work yet again with Emma Woolf at Hodder Arnold, who provides just the right amount of space and encouragement to get the book finished ahead of schedule! It was also great to work again with Joanna Lincoln, whose knowledge of Psychology undoubtedly helped, as did her efficiency and expertise with the editing. Susan Millership picked up the baton at the correct moment and did a sterling job. Stewart Larking should also be mentioned for the excellent cover, and thanks to Ian West for continuing the 'AS and A2 Essential' theme with his fantastic cartoons.

Richard Gross

## Credits

The author and publishers would like to thank the following for permission to reproduce material: Pages 3, 25, 76, 85 (below), 125 and 341, CORBIS; page 4, Peterson, L.R. and Peterson, M.J. (1959), Short-term retention of individual verbal items. *Journal of Experimental Psychology*, 58, 193–198; page 8 (above), Murdock, B.B. (1962), The serial position effect in free recall. *Journal of Experimental Psychology*, 64, 482–488, page 19, Carmen Taylor/Associated Press Photo; page 34, Harlow Primate Laboratory, University of Wisconsin; page 35, Science Photo Library; page 38, Concord Films Council/Joyce Robertson; pages 62, 246, 258 (above), 499, 508, 509 (above), 548 and 554, Bettmann/CORBIS; page 67, Anthea Sieveking/Wellcome Photo Library; page 75, The Bridgeman Art Library; page 79, © Najlah Feanny/CORBIS; pages 90, 95 and 126, Rex Features; page 91, from *Psychology: Science Behaviour & Life*, 2nd edition, by Robert Crooks, permission of Holt, Rinehart & Winston; page 102, *Scientific American*; page 109 (right), from the film *Obedience*, copyright © 1965 by Stanley Milgram and distributed by Penn State Media Sales; page 109 (left), Pinter & Martin Ltd, HarperCollins Publishers Inc., New York; page 155, The Barnes Foundation, Merion Station, Pennsylvania/CORBIS; page 157 (Fig. 8.2), Saegert, Swap and Zajone (1973), Exposure content and interpersonal attraction. *Journal of Personality and Social Psychology*, 25, 234–242; page 168 (Table 8.2), based on Zeifman, D. & Hazan, C. (2000) A process model of adult attachment formation. In W. Ickes & S. Duck (eds) *The Social Psychology of Personal Relationships*. Copyright John Wiley and Sons Ltd. Reproduced with permission of the publishers and authors; page 173, Uniphoto Press International/Still Pictures; page 184 (below), BPS Visual Archive; page 184 (above), David Hartley/Rex Features; pages 185, 188, 208, 243, 448 and 462, Robert Battersby/BDI Images; page 186, Albert Bandura, Stanford University; page 190 (above), Imperial War Museum;

page 190 (below), Nathan Benn/CORBIS; page 190 (left), reprinted courtesy of ABCNEWS.com. All material copyright © 2002 ABCNEWS Internet Ventures; page 191, Lawrence Manning/CORBIS; page 191 (Fig. 9.1), Myers D.G. (1998) *Psychology* (5th edition). New York: Worth Publishers; pages 192 and 194, Philip G. Zimbardo, Inc.; page 193 (Fig. 9.2), Diener. E., Fraser, S.C., Beaman, A.L. & Kelem, R.T. (1976) Effects of deindividuating variables on stealing among Halloween trick-or-treaters. *Journal of Personality & Social Psychology*, 24, 285–290, reproduced with permission of the publishers; page 194 (Fig. 9.3), Johnson, R.D. & Downing, L.L. (1979) Deindividuation and valence of cues: Effects on prosocial and anti-social behaviour, *Journal of Personality & Social Psychology*, 37, 1532–1538, reproduced with permission of the publishers; page 197, Anderson, C.A. (1989), Temperature and aggression: Ubiquitous effects of heat on the occurrence of human aggression. *Psychological Bulletin*, 106, 74–96, Fig. 2, page 83, Fig. 3, page 85, Fig. 4, page 86; page 199 (above), Anderson, C.A. (1989), Fig. 1, page 82; page 199 (below), David Kampfner/Life File Photo Library; page 201, Patrik Giardino/CORBIS; page 202, Adrian Carroll: Eye Ubiquitous/CORBIS; page 205, Peter Hillebrecht/Associated Press Photo; page 209, Associated Press Photo; page 210, Owen Franken/CORBIS; page 214, Astier Frederik/CORBIS Sygma; page 236 (above), Baril Pascal/CORBIS; page 236 (below), Chitose Suzuki/Associated Press Photo; page 237 (above), Joe McDonald/CORBIS; page 237 (below), Martha McClintock; page 249, Mike King/CORBIS; page 250 (above middle), Alain Compost/Still Pictures; page 250 (above right), Bios/Still Pictures; page 250 (below right), Chris Davies; page 250 (above left), Kevin Schafer/Still Pictures; page 250 (below middle), Michel Gunther/Still Pictures; page 250 (below left), Mike Powles/Still Pictures; page 253 (Fig. 10.5), from Carlson, N.R. (2004) *Physiology of Behavior* 8th edition. Boston, MA: Allyn and Bacon. Copyright © 2004 by Pearson Education. Reprinted by permission of the publisher; page 257, Roland Seitre/Still Pictures; page 258 (below), Christopher Moore Ltd; page 288 (Table 11.3), reprinted with permission from Bouchard, T.J. & McGue, M. (1981) Familial studies of intelligence: A review. *Science*, 212, 1055–1059. Copyright © 1981 AAAS; page 339, David Robinson/Bubbles; page 340, David H. Wells/CORBIS; page 345 (Fig. 12.2), from Coleman, J.C. & Hendry, L. (1990) *The Nature of Adolescence* (2nd edition). Routledge. Reprinted with permission; page 358, J.J. Alcalay/Still Pictures; page 360, Dr Judith H. Langlois, University of Texas at Austin; page 364, Stephen Frink/CORBIS; page 367, S.I.N./CORBIS; page 369, Sipa Press/Rex Features; page 372, Charles Krebs/CORBIS; page 375 (left), John Cancalos/Still Pictures; page 375 (right), Margaret Wilson/Still Pictures; pages 392 and 436, Ronald Grant Archive; page 397 (Table 14.5) Rose *et al.* (1994), Heterogeneity of cognitive style among depressed inpatients. *Journal of Abnormal Psychology*, 103, 419–429; page 405 (Table 14.6), Spitzer *et al.* (1978) Symptoms of clinical depression, Research diagnostic criteria: rationale and reliability. *Archives of General Psychiatry*, 35, 773–782. Copyright © 1978, American Medical Association. All rights reserved; page 413 (Fig. 14.5), Abramson *et al.* (1978), Learned helplessness in humans: Critique and reformulation. *Journal of Abnormal Psychology*, 87, 49–74, Fig. 8; page 419 (Fig. 14.7), Saxena, S., Brody, A.L., Schwartz, J.M. & Baxter, L.R. (1998) Neuroimaging and frontal-subcortical circuitry in obsessive-compulsive disorder. *British Journal of Psychiatry*, 173 (Suppl. 35), 26–37. Reproduced by permission of the Royal College of Psychiatrists; page 436 (Fig. 15.3), *New England Journal of Medicine*; page 437 (above), British Library; page 437 (below), Geoff Tompkinson/Science Photo Library; page 442 (Fig. 15.5), copyright © 1965 Ayllon, T. and Azrin, N.H. (1965) The measurement and reinforcement of behavior of psychotics. *Journal of the Experimental Analysis of Behaviour*, 8, 357–383. Copyright © 1965 by the Society for the Analysis of Behavior, Inc.; page 460, Celia Kitzinger; pages 473 and 518 (below), AKG Images; page 496, Penfield, W. & Boldrey, E. (1937), Somatic motor and sensory representation in the cerebral cortex of man as studied by electrical stimulation. *Brain*, 60, 389–442. Reproduced by permission of Oxford University Press; page 498, Mike Walker/Rex Features; page 509 (below), Underwood & Underwood/CORBIS; page 518 (above), William Vandivert, Dennis, MA, USA/*Scientific American*; page 551, RSPCA Photolibrary; page 556, Paula Solloway/Photofusion.

Every effort has been made to obtain necessary permission with reference to copyright material. The publishers apologise if inadvertently any sources remain unacknowledged and will be glad to make the necessary arrangements at the earliest opportunity.

# AS Module 1:
## Cognitive and Developmental Psychology

# Human Memory

## What's covered in this chapter?
### You need to know about:

**Short-term and long-term memory**
- Research into the nature and structure of short-term memory (STM) and long-term memory (LTM) (e.g. encoding, capacity and duration)
- The multi-store model (MSM) of memory (Atkinson and Shiffrin)
- At least ONE alternative to the MSM model
- Working memory (Baddeley and Hitch)
- Levels of processing (Craik and Lockhart)

**Remembering and forgetting**
- Explanations of forgetting in STM (e.g. decay and displacement)
- Explanations of forgetting in LTM (e.g. retrieval failure and interference)
- The role of emotional factors in forgetting including flashbulb memories and repression (e.g. Freud)

**Critical issue: eyewitness testimony (EWT) including:**
- Research into reconstructive memory (e.g. Bartlett)
- Memory research into EWT (e.g. Loftus) including the role of leading questions

### Short-term memory (STM) and long-term memory (LTM)

The term 'memory' can mean the system of retaining information, the actual storage system or the material that has been retained. There are three memory stores: sensory memory, STM and LTM. Sensory memory is the store that contains the information received through the senses. It's the 'gate-keeper' of information, and passes material on to STM and LTM for more permanent storage.

| Encoding | Storage | Retrieval |
|---|---|---|
| Put into memory | Maintain in memory | Recover from memory |

**Figure 1.1** Three basic processes in memory

There are three basic processes in memory (see Figure 1.1):

- **Encoding:** transforming a sensory input (e.g. sound or visual image) for it to be registered in memory
- **Storage:** retaining or holding information in memory until it's required
- **Retrieval:** locating information which has been stored and extracting it from memory.

## STM

STM is a temporary place for storing information received through the senses where it receives little processing.

### ENCODING

Information arrives in sensory memory in its original form (e.g. sound, vision and so on). This information needs to be encoded in a form that STM can deal with. For example, if the input into sensory memory is the word 'banana', you could encode this visually by thinking of an image of a banana. Alternatively, you could encode it acoustically by repeating 'banana' over and over again (probably best done quietly!). Or you could encode it semantically (through meaning) by applying your pre-existing knowledge of bananas. This might involve thinking about what desserts you can make with bananas, or the time you slipped on one!

Since memory processes are often unconscious, people cannot accurately report what type of encoding they use. Substitution error studies help to examine coding in both STM and LTM. These involve participants confusing one item in a memory list with another.

Conrad (1964) presented participants with a visual list of six consonants (e.g. HBRTFS) that they then had to write down. Recall errors were mainly related to a letter's sound, not its visual appearance. For example, B was often mistaken for V, but F was hardly ever mistaken for E. These acoustic confusion errors suggest that:

- the visually presented information must have been encoded acoustically
- STM is primarily encoded on the basis of sound.

One study that examined whether encoding in STM is acoustic (sound) or semantic (meaning) was conducted by Baddeley (the Acoustic/Semantic [AS] 1966 study). In the study, participants were presented with four word lists which were either:

List A: acoustically similar (such as 'cat', 'mat', 'sat', 'sad')
List B: acoustically dissimilar (such as 'pit', 'day', 'cow')
List C: semantically similar (such as 'big', 'huge', 'tall')
List D: semantically dissimilar (such as 'hot', 'safe', 'foul')

75 participants heard one list repeated four times. Immediately after this (to test STM), they were given a list that contained all the original words but in the wrong order. Their task was to rearrange the words in the correct order. The researchers found that those participants given List A (acoustically similar) performed the worst (recall of 10%). Recall for the other lists was comparatively good (60–80%). The conclusion was that since List A was recalled the worst, it would appear that there's acoustic confusion in STM. Therefore, STM tends to be encoded on an acoustic basis.

The results of Baddeley's AS study do make 'cognitive sense'. For example, if you were asked to remember a shopping list for a short time you'd probably repeat it aloud (acoustic rehearsal) as you walked to the supermarket. However, STM is not restricted to acoustic coding. Some semantic coding has been demonstrated in STM. The small difference in recall between semantically similar (64%) and semantically dissimilar (71%) lists suggests that, at best, there's *minimal* semantic coding in STM. We can also remember visual images (e.g. faces) in STM that would be very difficult to encode on the basis of sound. For example, how would your face be encoded acoustically?

## CAPACITY

STM has a limited capacity, that is, we can only hold a small amount of information in it before it's forgotten. Serial digit span studies demonstrate this. Participants are presented with an increasingly long sequence of digits that they have to report back in order (e.g. 26478, 968423, 2975841 and so on). When they fail on 50% of the trials, they've reached their digit span capacity.

Jacobs, in his 1887 Study of Immediate Digit Span (SIDS), investigated the capacity of STM. He read aloud lists of either letters or numbers. (They had to have only one syllable, so 'w' or '7' weren't used.) He increased the length of these lists until participants could only successfully recall them 50% of the time. Jacobs used a wide age range in his sample. He found that:

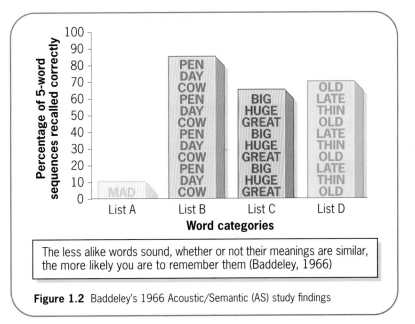

The less alike words sound, whether or not their meanings are similar, the more likely you are to remember them (Baddeley, 1966)

**Figure 1.2** Baddeley's 1966 Acoustic/Semantic (AS) study findings

- STM capacity for digits was 9, whereas for letters it was 7
- STM increased with age: 8-year-olds recalled 7 digits, whereas 19-year-olds recalled 9 digits.

Jacobs concluded that STM has a limited capacity of between 5 and 9 digits and that age does affect STM capacity, since people may improve their recall strategies with age and/or through practice. He also found that numbers were easier to recall than letters, because there were fewer of them (9) compared to letters (25 excluding 'w').

Jacobs's findings have been replicated by Miller (1956) who coined the phrase '*the magic number seven plus or minus two*' (7+/− 2) to describe the capacity of STM. However, other factors have also been shown to influence STM capacity. For example, performance is improved if items are read aloud rather than sub-vocally. Also, LTM can affect STM capacity. Indeed, the capacity of STM can be affected by mnemonic (memory improvement) techniques such as chunking (see below), or by presenting items in a rhythm. This is why we tend to group telephone numbers into chunks of three digits. It's also been found that digit span findings are culturally specific. Welsh speakers have a shorter digit span than English speakers. Because there are more syllables in Welsh words, Welsh speakers take longer to repeat the items in their STM (Ellis & Hennelly, 1980).

The longest place name in Wales – digit span this!

The capacity of STM can be increased if separate 'bits' of information are grouped together into larger 'chunks'. For example, the number 19391945 can be 'chunked' as the start and end dates of the Second World War. Reading involves chunking letters into words and words into sentences. For Miller (1956), the capacity of STM is seven plus or minus two *chunks* rather than individual pieces of information.

Simon (1974) tested his own immediate digit span. He found the length of 'chunk' affected capacity. The larger chunks were more difficult to rehearse. He consistently found his digit span to be 5 chunks.

## DURATION

You'll not be surprised that the duration of STM is short, that is, less than 30 seconds (see Essential Study 1.1).

**ESSENTIAL STUDY 1.1**

**Duration in STM** ••••••• **Peterson and Peterson** (1959) **Trigram Retention Experiment (TRE)**

### Aim (AO1)

To investigate the duration of STM when no rehearsal is allowed.

### Procedures (AO1)

Participants were read a nonsense **trigram** (three consonants which have no meaning e.g. LTB). Immediately after this, participants had to count backwards in threes starting from a very large 3-digit number (e.g. 576) for a specified time period. This time period was called the **retention interval** and varied from 3 to 18 seconds. The counting backwards task was called the **distractor task**. It was designed to prevent rehearsal of the trigrams. At the sound of a tone, participants had to recall the trigram.

### Findings (AO1)

Approximately 90% of the trigrams were recalled after a 3-second retention interval. Only about 10% were recalled after 18 seconds. Letters had to be in exactly the same place in the recalled trigram as in the original.

### Conclusion (AO1)

Without rehearsal, the duration of STM is very short indeed (less than 18 seconds).

### Criticisms (AO1/AO2)

✓ **The findings have been replicated**.

✓ **The study was highly controlled:** The use of trigrams ensured that participants couldn't impose any meaning on the material to be recalled. They all started from the same 'base level' and thus recall scores could be compared.

✗ **Low ecological validity:** The laboratory situation and the use of trigrams meant that the study was not really

**Short-term memory decay**
Unless rehearsed, verbal information may be quickly forgotten
(Peterson & Peterson, 1959)

Rapid decay with no rehearsal

Percentage who recalled trigrams

Time in seconds between presentation of trigrams and recall request (no rehearsal allowed)

**Figure 1.3** Peterson & Peterson (1959) Trigram Retention Experiment findings representative of learning in real life. When was the last time you were asked to remember complete nonsense (not including your last psychology lesson!)?

✖ **Additional cognitive task:** The counting distractor task did prevent rehearsal. But it also meant that participants had to perform an additional cognitive processing task. This may have affected their recall scores.

✖ **Interference confusion:** It was also shown that participants confused later trigrams with earlier ones. This suggests that they still had some memory of the earlier trigrams for *longer* than 18 seconds.

Despite methodological problems, researchers agree that:

* STM has a limited duration (less than 30 seconds)
* information is rapidly lost from STM if it's not rehearsed.

## LTM

LTM involves the permanent storage of information.

### ENCODING

With verbal material, coding in LTM appears to be mainly semantic. Baddeley (1966) investigated this using the same procedure as that described above in the Acoustic/Semantic (AS) STM study, except that recall of the lists wasn't immediate. There was a 20-minute retention interval, during which the 72 participants conducted another task. This ensured that recall would involve LTM. This time, those participants given List C (semantically similar) performed the worst (55% recall). Recall for the other lists was comparatively good (70–85%). Since List C was recalled the worse, it appears there's semantic confusion in LTM. Therefore, LTM tends to be encoded on a semantic basis.

Baddeley's (1966) AS LTM study is easily replicated and the findings are consistent. They also make 'cognitive sense' in everyday life. For example, try to remember a TV programme you watched a while ago. You'll remember the overall content (meaning), not the actual words (acoustic). However, there are many different types of LTM. 'Knowing how' to perform various tasks (e.g. riding a bike) is called 'procedural' memory. Autobiographical or personal memories of events or places are called 'episodic' memories. These types of LTM are rarely examined in laboratory memory studies and are arguably not encoded in the same way. In addition, songs must be encoded acoustically, and it's hard to see how smells and tastes can be encoded on the basis of meaning. LTM coding must involve a very large, long-lasting and flexible system.

### CAPACITY

The potential capacity of LTM is unlimited. Anokhin (1973) estimated that the number of possible neuronal connections in the human brain is 1 followed by 10.5 million kilometres of noughts! He concluded that '*no human yet exists who can use all the potential of his/her brain. This is why we don't accept any estimates of the limits of the human brain*'. There are no studies that you need to learn on LTM capacity.

### DURATION

A memory can last a lifetime, so the duration of LTM just depends on how long you live. Many older people love to tell (interesting?) stories from their childhood. Material in STM that's not rehearsed is quickly forgotten. This is *not* true of LTM. We couldn't keep repeating information over and over again in order to store it in our LTM. For example, you may not have ridden a bike for many years, but it's unlikely that you'll have forgotten how. The duration of LTM was demonstrated by Bahrick *et al.* (1975) – see Essential Study 1.2.

**Duration in LTM** •••••• **Bahrick *et al.* (1975) High School Yearbook Photo (HSYP) study**

**Aim** (AO1)

To investigate the existence of very long-term memories (VLTM) using real-life memories.

**Procedures** (AO1)

400 participants ranging in age from 17 to 74 were asked to remember the names of classmates from their high school (**a free recall task**). They were also shown a set of photos and a list of names, some of which were of their ex-school friends. They had to identify their ex-school friends (**a recognition task**).

**Findings** (AO1)

Those who'd left high school within the previous 15 years recalled 90% of the faces and names in the recognition task. Those who'd left 48 years previously recalled 80% of the names and 70% of the faces.

Free recall of the names was comparatively poor.

**Conclusion** (AO1)

• Recognition is easier than free recall. This suggests that we possess a lot of information in our LTM, but we need clues or cues in order to access it (see retrieval-cue forgetting, pages 15–16).

• People do possess VLTM (very long-term memories), although these decline a little over time.

**Criticisms** (AO1/AO2)

✓ **Experimental support**: These findings support those of Shepard (1967), who demonstrated people's long-term memories for adverts.

✓ **High ecological validity**: The study involved people's real-life memories rather than nonsense trigrams in the laboratory.

✗ **The study lacked some important controls.** For example, participants may have been in contact with friends or looked at the yearbook since they left high school.

✗ **Recognition, not recall:** The study only found the existence of VLTM with recognition, not recall. In addition, they were only testing one form of LTM (visual LTM).

## Summary table of STM/LTM differences

|  | STM | | LTM | |
|---|---|---|---|---|
| **Encoding** | Mainly acoustic (sound) | Baddeley (1966) (AS) study | Mainly semantic (meaning) | Baddeley (1966) (AS) study |
| **Capacity** | Small (7+/−2 chunks of information) | Jacobs (1887) (SIDS) | Unlimited | Not applicable |
| **Duration** | Short (<30 seconds) | Peterson and Peterson (1959) (TRE) study | 30 seconds to a lifetime | Bahrick *et al.* (1975) (HSYP) study |

## Multi-store model (MSM) of memory (Atkinson & Shiffrin, 1968)

### DESCRIPTION

The MSM explains how information flows from one storage system to another. The model proposes that sensory memory, STM and LTM are permanent structures of memory. We've already described some of the key characteristics of these stores. Information received through the senses (sound, sight, touch, smell) enters the sensory store. If attention is paid to it, the information is transferred and processed further by STM. If it's not attended to, the sensory information is immediately forgotten, or not even processed in the first place. If the information now in STM has been rehearsed sufficiently,

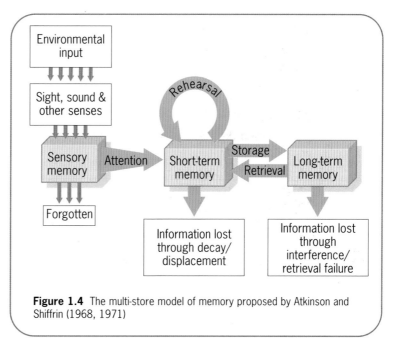

**Figure 1.4** The multi-store model of memory proposed by Atkinson and Shiffrin (1968, 1971)

it can be transferred to LTM. The greater the amount of STM rehearsal, the greater the likelihood it will transfer to LTM for more permanent storage.

Figure 1.4 above shows why it's called the multi-store model. The key processes involved are attention, rehearsal and forgetting.

### Evaluation of the MSM

✓ **Influential, useful:** The MSM was an influential, early model which psychologists still find useful.

✓ **STM/LTM differences:** There's considerable evidence that there are two distinct types of memory store, namely STM/LTM (see above).

✓ **Serial position effect:** Murdock (1962) presented participants with a list of words that they

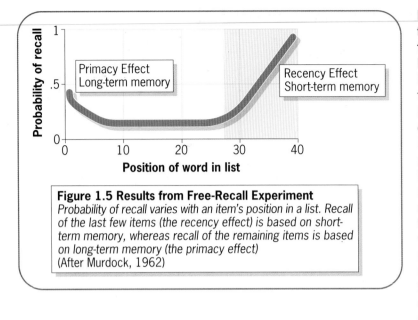

**Figure 1.5 Results from Free-Recall Experiment**
*Probability of recall varies with an item's position in a list. Recall of the last few items (the recency effect) is based on short-term memory, whereas recall of the remaining items is based on long-term memory (the primacy effect)*
(After Murdock, 1962)

had to recall in any order (a free-recall task). Murdock found that those words at the beginning and the end of the lists were recalled better than those in the middle. This is known as the serial position effect. Those words at the beginning of the list (the primacy effect) are recalled because they've been rehearsed over and over again and have been transferred to LTM. Those words from the end of the list (the recency effect) are recalled because they're still in STM. Thus, the primacy and recency effect provides support for the existence of the two separate memory stores (STM and LTM, see Figure 1.5).

✗•✓ Clinical case studies: Shallice & Warrington (1970) reported the case of KF. As a result of a motorbike accident, he had an extremely poor STM (only one or two digits). Yet his LTM for events after the accident was normal. This supports MSM. However, KF's deficit in STM was only for verbal information. His STM for visual and acoustic material was normal. This suggests the existence of more than one type of STM, not incorporated in the MSM.

✗ Mere rehearsal doesn't ensure transfer from STM to LTM: Bekerian & Baddeley (1980) found that people didn't know of the changes to BBC radio wavelengths despite hearing the information, on average, well over a thousand times.

✗ The MSM is over-simplified: It assumes a single STM and a single LTM. It's been demonstrated that there are different types of STM (see Baddeley and Hitch working memory, below) and different types of LTM (procedural, episodic and semantic memories, see page 5).

✗ The 'one-way' (linear) direction of the MSM appears to be incorrect: There is a *two-way* flow of information between STM and LTM. Morris *et al.* (1985) demonstrated how previous knowledge and interest in football could help in the recall of fictitious football scores. Participants listened to 'made-up' football results, and then had to recall them immediately (a STM task). Participants who were interested in football recalled the most. This suggests that they'd used their greater knowledge of football (LTM) to impose meaning on the results (STM). Information thus flows from LTM to STM. This isn't possible according to an earlier version of the MSM.

# EXAM tips BOX

**Outline and evaluate the multi-store model of memory. (18 marks)**

* You could structure your answer in terms of three paragraphs each about 100–130 words long. The first paragraph could involve a **description** of the MSM. You could include a diagram and describe each of the stores (AO1 worth 6 marks).

* In the second paragraph you could **analyse and evaluate** from a positive viewpoint and provide evidence that supports the model (e.g. Murdock, 1962: KF case study).

* In the final paragraph you could **analyse and evaluate** from a negative viewpoint and provide evidence that contradicts the model (Bekerian & Baddeley, 1980, Morris *et al.*, 1985: different types of STM/LTM) (AO2 worth 12 marks).

* You can choose to write an answer that concentrates entirely on the positive points or the negative points of the model – it's up to you.

Try to write out a suitable answer using about 300–350 words.

There is a sample answer at the end of the book, but try not to look at it until you've tried to answer the question yourself.

## Alternatives to the MSM Working Memory (WM) (Baddeley & Hitch, 1974)

### DESCRIPTION

Baddeley and Hitch questioned the existence of a single STM store (they weren't concerned with LTM). They argued that STM was far more complex than a mere 'stopping-off' point for transferring information to LTM. They saw STM as an 'active' store that holds several pieces of information whilst it's being worked on (hence 'working' memory). Working memory holds the information you are consciously thinking about now.

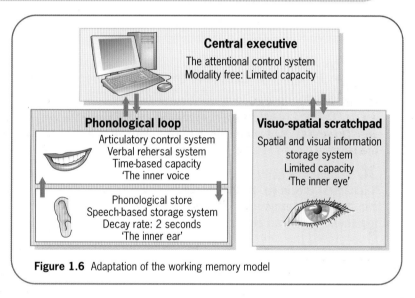

**Figure 1.6** Adaptation of the working memory model

Working memory has been compared to a computer screen, where several operations are performed on current data. To replace the single STM, Baddeley and Hitch proposed a multi-component WM (see Figure 1.6):

* The **central executive** is involved in higher mental processes such as decision-making. It allocates resources to the other slave systems depending on the task in hand. For example, sometimes it's difficult to concentrate on driving and talking at the same time. For a difficult manoeuvre, the central executive would direct your attention to the driving task, and you'd probably have to stop talking. The central executive has a limited capacity, but it's very flexible and can process information from any of the senses.
* The **articulatory loop** is a verbal rehearsal loop that holds words we're preparing to speak. Information is represented as it would be spoken (so it's called the **'inner voice'**). The capacity of the loop is about 2 seconds. There's also the phonological store or **'inner ear'**, which receives auditory information (the things you hear), and stores it in an acoustic code. This is important for language acquisition.

• The visuo-spatial scratch (or sketch) pad helps to rehearse visual or spatial information (what things look like). It uses a visual code, analysing features in terms of size, colour and shape (and so is called the 'inner eye'). It can process movements and actions, as well as static visual patterns.

Research to support the WM model has involved doing two tasks at once (the dual task method). According to WM, it should be easier to do two tasks that use different processing systems (verbal and visual) rather than two tasks that use the same 'slave' system. Baddeley (1973) got participants to follow a moving spot of light with a pointer (a tracker task). At the same time, half the participants had to describe the angles on a 'hollow' letter F. This group found the two tasks extremely difficult, because they were using the visuo-spatial sketchpad for both tasks. The other participants performed the tracking task along with a verbal task and had little difficulty performing both tasks simultaneously. They were using different 'slave' systems (verbal and visual).

## ✗✓ Evaluation of WM

✓ **Research support:** from dual task studies (Baddeley, 1973), although such laboratory studies are rather artificial. KF could remember visual but not verbal stimuli in STM, so there must be at least two systems in STM.

✓ **Importance of rehearsal?** The WM model doesn't over-emphasise the importance of rehearsal for STM retention, in contrast to the MSM.

✓ **Physiological evidence:** WM is supported by studies involving brain scans. PET (Positron Emission Tomography) scans have shown that different areas of the brain are used whilst undertaking verbal and visual tasks. These areas may correspond to the components of WM (Paulescu *et al.*, 1993).

✗ **Only STM:** WM only concerns itself with STM and so it isn't a comprehensive model of memory.

✗ **Function of central executive:** Least is known about the most important component, namely the central executive. It isn't clear how it works or what it does. This vagueness means that it can be used to explain almost any experimental results. For example, if two tasks *cannot* be done together, then it can be argued that two processing components in the model conflict or that the tasks exceed the central executive's capacity. If the two tasks *can* be done simultaneously, then it can be argued that they don't exceed the available resources. It's a circular argument ('heads I win, tails you lose'). Eysenck (1986) claimed that a single central executive might be as inaccurate as a single STM store.

✗ **The capacity of the central executive** has never been measured.

✗ **Practice or time:** The WM model doesn't explain changes in processing ability that occur as the result of practice or time.

✗ **Another store?** Recently an episodic buffer store was added to combine information from LTM with other slave systems (Baddeley, 2001). The model is getting more complicated with each new finding it cannot explain!

It's better to see STM as a number of independent components rather than a unitary STM store as the MSM suggests. However, there remain a number of problems with WM and even Baddeley stated: '*We've a long way to go before we can be sure of the details of the model*'.

## Levels of processing (LOP) (Craik & Lockhart, 1972)

DESCRIPTION

(Note: you only need to know *one* alternative model to the MSM: WM *or* LOP will do.)

Craik and Lockhart's LOP approach emphasises the processes involved in memory, rather than the storage systems. They believed that memories occur as a by-product of the processing of information. The processing of information is on a continuous dimension but can be tested at three levels:

- A superficial level analysing the basic features of a word, such as its shape ('**visual**' processing).
- An intermediate level analysing, say, the sound of a word ('**acoustic**' processing).
- A deeper level analysing the meaning of the word ('**semantic**' processing).

**Figure 1.7 Findings supporting LOP:**
Processing a word deeply - by meaning (semantic encoding) - produces better recognition of it at a later time than does shallow processing by attending to its appearance or sound (Craik & Tulving, 1975)

Craik and Lockhart argued that the deeper information is processed, the better it will be remembered. The level of the processing depends on:

- the nature of the stimulus
- the tasks to be completed
- the time available.

## EXPERIMENTAL SUPPORT FOR LOP

Craik & Tulving (1975) briefly presented participants with three different types of questions to which they had to answer 'yes' or 'no'. The questions corresponded to the three levels of processing outlined above. Examples were:

Is the word written in capital letters? DESK (testing visual processing)
Does the word rhyme with bat? Fat (testing acoustic processing)
Is the word a type of animal? Daffodil (testing semantic processing)

Participants were then given an unexpected recognition test. They had to identify the previously seen words (e.g. desk, fat, daffodil) from a list of words not previously presented. They recognised more of the words that involved deeper, semantic processing (see Figure 1.7). This supports the LOP approach.

Hyde & Jenkins (1973) got participants to perform different tasks on words. Some involved deep (semantic) processing (e.g. how often do you think this word appears in English?) and others shallow (visual) processing (e.g. how many times does the letter 'g' appear in these words?). Recall was far higher for the words that required semantic (deeper) processing. Half the participants didn't know that they would have to recall the words (incidental learning), whereas the other half did (intentional learning). Both groups actually recalled the same amount of words. This suggests that depth of processing is more important than conscious rehearsal. This study can be used as a criticism of the MSM and as support for LOP. Of course, the deliberate deception involved breaks ethical guidelines.

Craik & Watkins (1973) found that words rehearsed in a 'rote' fashion (repetition based on sound) were recalled less well than words that had been elaborated or linked with pre-existing knowledge in LTM (semantic encoding). These correspond to 'maintenance' and 'elaborative' rehearsal respectively. More information is remembered using elaborative rehearsal, again, providing support for LOP.

Evaluation of LOP

✓ **Experimental studies:** Provide support for the idea that deeper processing of information leads to greater recall (see above).

✓ **The approach was influential:** It concentrated on processes rather than structures or models.

✗ **Not just depth:** Studies have shown that factors other than depth lead to improved recall. Tyler *et al.* (1979) gave participants two sets of anagrams. One set was easy (e.g. 'doctro') and the other, using the same words, was difficult (e.g. 'rtoodc'). Participants with the difficult anagrams later recalled more. According to LOP, recall should have been the same for both lists since they involved the same level of processing. But effort and time spent on a task can also influence recall.

✗ **LOP is descriptive and not explanatory:** For example, it doesn't explain *why* deeper processing leads to better recall. But Craik and Lockhart did state that theirs wasn't a complete model of memory but *'a conceptual framework for memory research'*.

✗ **There's no independent way of measuring depth of processing:** The more deeply you process information, the better you remember it; and the better you remember something, the deeper you must have processed it (a 'circular' argument).

✓ **LOP approach was adapted:** Later, 'depth' of processing included factors such as elaboration, effort, organisation (the more organised the material the better), and distinctiveness (the more distinctive the better).

## EXAM tips BOX

**Give a brief account of ONE alternative to the multi-store model (MSM) of memory and consider its strengths and limitations. (18 marks)**

• You could choose to answer this using EITHER the Working Memory model or the Levels of Processing approach (but not both).

• You could structure your answer in terms of three paragraphs all about 100–130 words long. The first paragraph could involve a **description** of WM (or LOP) and each component (AO1 – 6 marks). A diagram of the model might help.

• In the second paragraph, you could **analyse and evaluate** from a **positive** viewpoint and provide evidence that supports WM (or LOP).

• In the final paragraph, you could **analyse and evaluate** from a **negative** viewpoint and provide arguments that don't support WM (or the LOP approach) (AO2 – 12 marks).

• You can choose to write an answer which concentrates entirely on the positive points **or** the negative points of WM (or LOP). You don't have to provide a balanced account.

Try to write out a suitable answer using about 300–350 words.

There's a sample answer for both WM and LOP approach at the end of the book, but try not to look at it until you have tried to answer the question yourself.

## Remembering and forgetting

Forgetting is the inability to recall or recognise material which was previously stored in memory. A distinction can be made between:

• material that was placed in memory and which has now disappeared (lack of availability)
• material that is still in memory but cannot be recalled (lack of accessibility).

## Forgetting in short-term memory

Forgetting in STM is usually attributed to the limited capacity (displacement) and duration (trace decay) of STM.

### Displacement

#### DESCRIPTION

*Displacement theory* explains forgetting in terms of STM capacity (7 +/−2: Miller, 1956). Once STM is full, any new information to be remembered must push out or displace old information. The old information is thus forgotten.

The displacement theory of STM

### Evaluation of displacement theory

✔ **Serial Probe Study (SPS): Waugh & Norman (1965)** presented participants with a string of 16 numbers. After this, one of the numbers was repeated (the **'probe' digit**). Participants had to recall the number that appeared immediately after the probe. The more numbers that followed the probe, the more difficult it was to recall the numbers. This was because numbers at the end had displaced the earlier numbers, making them unavailable.

For example:  3 5 2 1 8 6 5 9 8 3 4 5 6 7 9 5
If early probe (2), then recall of digit (1) is difficult (great displacement)
If later probe (7), then recall of digit (9) is easy (no displacement)

✘ **Displacement, decay and interference confusion:** The serial probe study confuses displacement with decay and interference (see variation of this study in trace decay evaluation below).

✔ **Displacement of most importance:** Shallice (1967) studied the effect of displacement and decay on STM forgetting, and concluded that displacement was the more important.

### Trace decay

#### DESCRIPTION

Trace decay theory explains why forgetting increases with time. The memory trace fades over time. When something is learnt, a structural change (the *engram*) takes place in the brain. Over time, metabolic processes break down this engram (hence 'decay') making the information unavailable. It's forgotten through disuse. Conversely, with rehearsal, this engram becomes stronger and is less likely to be forgotten.

### Evaluation of trace decay theory

✔ **Peterson and Peterson TRE study (see page 4):** Information decays rapidly from STM if rehearsal is prevented. However, their study didn't merely involve a measure of decay (the retention interval) but also introduced another task (the counting backwards). This distractor task might have led to interference or displacement of the original trigrams. The best way to study decay would be to have participants learn material and then recall it later having done *absolutely* nothing in between learning and recall. Then, if a longer time interval led to greater forgetting we could account for this through trace decay. However, it's difficult to prevent rehearsal without introducing another interference task.

✓ **Reitman (1971) musical tones distractor task:** Reitman overcame this problem by getting participants to listen to very faint musical tones during the retention interval. The attention they gave this task meant that they couldn't rehearse the information and that there'd be less interference. Results again supported trace decay.

✓ **Serial probe study (SPS) with different presentation speeds:** Waugh and Norman used the serial probe technique (above) but presented the 16 numbers at different speeds ('fast' or 'slow'). The faster the presentation rate, the less time for the numbers to decay. As predicted, participants found it easier to recall the faster lists. This supports trace decay.

✗ **Low ecological validity:** the use of nonsense trigrams and lists of numbers doesn't represent learning in everyday life and thus findings cannot be easily generalised.

STM is a fragile store where information can be easily and quickly lost. Both trace decay and displacement explanations for STM forgetting are supported. It's difficult to determine which is more important.

## Forgetting in long-term memory interference

DESCRIPTION

According to the interference explanation of forgetting, similar memories interfere, disrupt and confuse each other. The more similar the information is, the more likely interference will occur. There are two types:

- **Proactive (forward) interference:** old memories affect new memories, e.g. calling a new boyfriend by an old boyfriend's name.
- **Retroactive (backward) interference:** new memories affect old memories, e.g. after driving the college minibus I make lots of mistakes in my own car on the way home (more than usual anyway!).

Keppel & Underwood (1962) spotted something important in Peterson and Peterson's TRE studies. Participants forgot more material on later trials, suggesting that trigrams learnt on the earlier trials were interfering with later trials. Indeed, trigrams learnt on earlier trials were being recalled on later trials (see Figure 1.8). This offers strong support for proactive interference.

## EXAM tips BOX

**Consider psychological research into explanations of forgetting in short-term memory. (18 marks)**

- It may be best to think of answering this question in three paragraphs each about 100–130 words long.
- You need to include **at least two** explanations (displacement and trace decay) and describe these in the first paragraph (AO1–6 marks).
- In the second paragraph, you could **analyse and evaluate** evidence for and against displacement theory (e.g. Waugh & Norman, 1965; Shallice, 1967).
- In the final paragraph you could **analyse and evaluate** evidence for and against trace decay theory (e.g. Peterson & Peterson, 1959; Reitman, 1971). These paragraphs are worth 12 marks (AO2).

Try to write a suitable answer using about 300–350 words.

There is a sample answer at the end of the book but don't be tempted to look at it until you have tried to answer the question yourself.

Studies on interference have used the paired associate technique. Participants have to learn two word lists, with the first word the same in each case, e.g.

List A
Desk – boy
Flower – car

List B
Desk – tree
Flower – chair

When given the first word of the pairs (e.g. desk) and asked to recall List A (e.g. boy), participants often report the words from List B (e.g. tree). This is evidence for retroactive interference .

## ✗✓ Evaluation of interference theory

**✗•✓ Experimental studies** support interference (e.g. Keppel & Underwood, 1962). But many of these studies lack ecological validity.

**✓ Makes 'cognitive sense':** Most people would agree that it's more difficult to remember similar material than dissimilar material. For example, if someone was trying to remember a telephone number, you'd shout out random numbers in order to put them off.

**✗ Only one type of forgetting:** Interference is demonstrated best using the paired associate word technique, and so only explains one aspect of forgetting.

**✗ Use of meaningless word lists:** Interference is less easy to demonstrate with meaningful (semantic) material (Solso, 1995).

**✗ Not easy to demonstrate with experts:** Experts in a particular field should find it difficult to learn new information, since it should interfere with their large amount of pre-existing knowledge. This is clearly not the case, probably due to their well-organised memory.

**✗ Learning is artificially compressed in time:** Typically, participants have little time in the laboratory to learn and recall material. This artificial compression of time is more likely to cause interference. Learning in real life is more 'spread out' in time and is less affected by interference effects.

**✗ Not a popular theory:** Psychologists don't believe it's a convincing theory. Retrieval failure has recently become a more popular explanation.

Train drivers might become confused when driving home from work – an example of retroactive interference

**Figure 1.8** Recall on later trials is poorer due to interference (after Keppel & Underwood, 1962)

## Retrieval failure

### DESCRIPTION

The retrieval failure explanation of forgetting suggests that you can't remember because there aren't enough cues or clues to help recall. Memories are there in your memory (available) but cannot be accessed at that time. It's demonstrated by the 'tip of the tongue' phenomenon (TOT). People are asked questions and are certain they *know* the answer but cannot actually answer it at the time. Giving them a clue or cue, such as the first letter of the word, often helps them to retrieve it (Brown & McNeill, 1966).

Darley and Goodwin always had plenty of volunteers . . . but were the samples representative?

According to the 'encoding specificity principle', the closer the cue is to the information you're trying to remember, the more it will aid recall.

Research concentrates on two types of cues:

- **External cues: context-dependent forgetting (or remembering)**. This suggests that the context or place where material is learnt can affect recall. Godden & Baddeley (1975) got underwater divers to learn word lists either on dry land or under-water. The divers then had to recall the words in each of these places. Results showed that words learnt and recalled in the same context were remembered better. However, Fernandez & Glenberg (1985) tried to replicate such studies and never found consistent support for context-dependent effects.

- **Internal cues: state-dependent forgetting (or remembering)**. This suggests that the physiological state a person is in can affect recall. Goodwin *et al.* (1969) examined this effect with alcohol. Participants who hid money whilst drunk were more likely to remember the hiding place when they were back in their original drunken state. Darley *et al.* (1973) found similar effects for marijuana. Studies have also investigated the effect of mood on recall but results have been inconclusive. Ucros (1989) with a meta-analysis (review) of all the research concluded that there was a small state-dependent effect of mood.

## EXAM tips BOX

**Consider psychological research into explanations of forgetting in long-term memory. (18 marks)**

- Again, it may be best to think of answering this question in three paragraphs each about 100–130 words long.

- In the first paragraph, you could **describe** both proactive and retroactive interference and **very briefly** mention context- and state-dependent forgetting as supporting retrieval failure (AO1 worth 6 marks).

- In the second paragraph, you could **analyse and evaluate** studies that support or reject interference theory (e.g. Keppel & Underwood, 1962.

- In the final paragraph you could **analyse and evaluate** studies that support or reject retrieval failure (e.g. Godden & Baddeley, 1975; Goodwin *et al.,* 1969) (AO2 worth 12 marks).

Try to write out a suitable answer using about 300–350 words.

Remember, there is no single way of answering such questions. The material outlined above is designed to guide you. There's a sample answer at the end of the book but don't be tempted to look at it until you have tried to answer the question yourself.

### Evaluation of retrieval failure theory

✓ **Psychological research** supports retrieval failure forgetting (see above).

✓ **Retrieval failure theory makes 'cognitive sense':** Often sounds, smells, particular songs 'spark off' long-lost memories and provide cues for remembering. Returning to your old school may have the same effect.

✘ Impossible to disprove: We cannot disprove the idea that all memories are stored but that we lack sufficient cues to access them.

✘ Procedural memories ('knowing how') aren't explained by retrieval failure. Most procedural memories (e.g. riding a bike) aren't forgotten or affected by retrieval cues.

✘ Contextual effects not large: Contexts have to be *very* different in order to demonstrate contextual effects reliably.

Weighing up the competing explanations for forgetting, Eysenck (1998) concluded that '*it seems probable that this [retrieval failure] is the main reason for forgetting in LTM*'.

DID YOU EVER EXAGGERATE YOUR CASE STUDIES?

I FORGET

Freud was never caught out with his theory of repression

## Emotional factors in forgetting

Emotions have been shown to affect memory recall. Emotions can make memories either difficult to recall (Freud's repression theory) or unforgettable (flashbulb memories).

### Repression

#### DESCRIPTION

Freud (1901) believed that some forgetting is an unconscious, motivated process. He believed that we forget because certain memories are too psychologically painful to allow them to remain conscious. Therefore we *repress* or push the memory out of consciousness. These memories aren't 'lost'. They just remain inaccessible in our unconscious. For example, abuse experienced as a child might be repressed in memory. Repression is thus a 'defence mechanism' to protect our conscious mind. Freud developed his idea of repression whilst treating patients who were suffering from neurotic disorders (see pages 81 and 444–447).

For Freud there was no such thing as innocent forgetting. Next time you call your new boy/girlfriend by your old boy/girlfriend's name, you'd better hope they haven't read Freud! Such 'slips of the tongue' (or 'Freudian slips') are supposed to reveal something about our unconscious.

It's worth pointing out that Freud didn't believe that all forgetting could be explained through repression. Most forgetting simply involved getting rid of unwanted and unnecessary information.

One study which provided an experimental test of Freud's repression theory was conducted by Levinger & Clark (1961) in their emotionally-charged words (ECW) study. Participants were given lists of negatively-charged words (e.g. 'hate', 'anger', 'fear') and neutral words (e.g. 'window', 'cow', 'tree'). They were then asked to say exactly what came into their mind when they saw each word. This is called a free association task. During this task, the participants' galvanic skin responses (GSR) were measured. GSR detects minute traces of sweat on the fingers and is a measure of emotional response. Finally, participants were given the cue words again and asked to recall the associations they'd just reported.

Levinger and Clark found that participants took longer to think of associations to the emotional words and that GSRs were higher to the emotional words. Also, recall of the associations of the emotionally charged words was poorer than of the neutral ones.

Levinger and Clark concluded that the emotional words were more anxiety-provoking, and therefore the formation of associations or recall of these words was more difficult as a result of repression. This study is accepted as one of the best experimental demonstrations of repression. Laboratory evidence for repression is difficult to conduct, since you'd have to get participants to experience an anxiety-provoking event and this would break ethical guidelines. However, it's been claimed that arousal adversely affects STM (hence the results above), but actually *helps* LTM. Repression cannot explain this enhanced LTM effect (Eysenck & Wilson, 1973). A methodological problem with the experiment is that the emotionally-charged words were less easy to visualise and thus more difficult to form associations with. If you accept this then it might be that results had nothing to do with repression!

## Evaluation of repression theory

✓ **Experimental support:** (see Levinger & Clark ECW study below). It's reported that 20–60% of people undergoing therapy as a result of child sexual abuse report periods in their lives (often lasting several years) when they could not remember the abuse had taken place.

✓ **Case studies of amnesia:** There are reports of people who forget as a result of some deep psychological trauma. This is called 'psychogenic amnesia' or forgetting that has no physiological cause. It may help people suffering from post-traumatic stress disorder (PTSD) to cope (Parkin, 1993).

✗•✓ **'Recovered' memories:** It's also claimed that memories of child abuse have been 'recovered' from adults undergoing psychoanalytic therapy (Williams, 1994). However, this is an extremely controversial area. There's no way of independently proving whether these memories are genuine or the result of 'implanted' suggestions that fit in with Freudian theory.

✓ **'Failure feedback' tests:** Kline (1972) told people they'd failed a memory test. Their recall of the test items was much poorer than recall of participants not given the negative feedback. Presumably, 'failure feedback' made them feel anxious and caused repression of the test items.

✗ **But also 'success feedback' tests:** But a memory deficit also occurs if you give participants success feedback. The cause of the forgetting (in both cases) is the high degree of arousal, unconnected with repression.

✗ **Use of case studies:** Freud published case studies of his neurotic patients to support his ideas on repression. These have been questioned as inaccurate (even by the patients themselves!). As with all case studies, the findings cannot be generalised to a more 'normal' population.

## EXAM tips BOX

**To what extent is there psychological evidence to support the idea of repression in forgetting? (18 marks)**

- You could structure your answer in three paragraphs, each about 100–130 words long.

- The first paragraph could involve a brief description of repression (AO1 – 6 marks). With this question, it might be best to mix material that supports and rejects repression throughout the remaining two paragraphs.

- In the second paragraph you could **analyse and evaluate** Freud's evidence and that provided by cases of psychogenic amnesia. In the final paragraph you could include studies by Levinger & Clark (1961) and Kline (1972) as well as more general criticisms (AO2 – 12 marks). Remember that mere **description** of studies will not gain any AO2 marks. You must use this material as an aid to analysis and evaluation.

Try to write out a suitable answer using about 300–350 words.

There's a sample answer at the end of the book but don't be tempted to look at it until you have tried to answer the question yourself.

# Flashbulb (FB) memories

## DESCRIPTION

FB memories refer to a special kind of 'episodic' memory, which we can vividly recall in great detail (e.g. September 11th 2001 terrorist attacks in the US or Princess Diana's death). It's called a FB memory because the memory is recalled in almost photographic detail. FB memories can also be about more personal events, such as the birth of a brother or sister. For FB memories to occur, the event must be surprising, unexpected and emotionally and personally significant.

People with FB memories tend to recall the same six pieces of information surrounding the event, namely:

- Where they were
- What they were doing
- Who told them
- What they felt about it
- What others felt about it
- What happened immediately afterwards.

One recent study for **Flashbulb Memories of September 11th 2001 (FM 9/11) was conducted by Conway, Skitka, Hemmerich and Kershaw (2003).** Their **aim** was to investigate whether salient events which are accompanied by strong affect and emotion

A hijacked plane flies into one of the World Trade Centre's Twin Towers in New York on September 11th 2001. Both towers collapsed shortly after. An example of flashbulb memory?

are recalled with accuracy over a long time period or whether memory of these events is susceptible to distortion. The event in question was the World Trade Centre attacks on September 11th 2001. A random national sample of 678 participants were tested for their memory recall immediately after the attacks on the World Trade Centre and then one year later. The data was collected by a marketing company via Web-TV, which is an Internet connection via television.

**Results** showed:
- Nearly half of all Americans (+/− 3%) had a perfect flashbulb memory of 9/11
- 75% of Americans (+/− 3%) had a near-perfect recall of 9/11.

They **concluded** that:
- Flashbulb memories are more detailed, vivid and accurate than ordinary memories
- Flashbulb memories do appear to exist for particularly salient, surprising or consequential events.

There were some **criticisms** of the research. On the positive side, a nationally representative sample was obtained and the Web-TV method of data collection allows a more representative sample than Internet via computer, which is skewed toward more wealthy and educated people. It is also the first piece of research investigating flashbulb memories for 9/11, arguably the world event which will be most cited in the future as an example of FM. However, the study only tests flashbulb memories up to one year later. It remains to be seen whether flashbulb memories of 9/11 will endure.

The 9/11 study tested Americans' memories for a disaster that occurred in America. Results are supported by the 'racial relevance' research which has found that 75% of black people had a FM for the assassination of Martin Luther King (a black civil rights leader) compared to only 33% of white participants (Brown & Kulik, 1977). It seems that *personal relevance* of the event is a vital factor in FM.

**✗✓** Evaluation of FB memory research

✓ **Accurate FBs:** Conway *et al.* (1994) showed that UK participants had very accurate FB memories of Margaret Thatcher's resignation. Inaccurate FB memories involve events that weren't surprising, unexpected or of great personal significance.

✗ **The same as other memories:** FB memories are recalled in detail simply because they're repeated over and over again. This rehearsal leads to enhanced recall like any other memory.

✗ **FB memories are inaccurate:** McCloskey *et al.* (1988) found inaccurate memories of the Space Shuttle Challenger disaster. Wright (1993) found similar results for the Hillsborough tragedy involving Liverpool FC. This was despite people believing their memories to be accurate.

## EXAM tips BOX

**Briefly describe and evaluate research into the role of emotional factors in memory. (18 marks)**

* You could structure your answer in terms of three paragraphs each about 100–130 words long.

* In the first paragraph you could **briefly** describe the effects of mood, repression and/or flashbulb memories on forgetting (AO1 – 6 marks). In the final two paragraphs, you might choose to concentrate solely on repression and/or flashbulb memories.

* In the second paragraph you could **analyse and evaluate** research that supports or questions repression (e.g. Freud, 1901; Levinger & Clark, 1961; Eysenck & Wilson, 1973).

* In the final paragraph you could **analyse and evaluate** research on flashbulb memories (e.g. Conway *et al.*, 1977, 2003; Wright, 1993) (AO2 – 12 marks).

* This is a difficult question since there's so much material that could be included. There might be a 'trade-off' in your answer between breadth and depth. That is, the fewer studies you mention, the more detail required and *vice versa*. It's normally better to cover three or four studies in reasonable detail than list lots of studies and have no time to expand on them.

* You could choose to write an answer that only presents one side of the argument, that emotional factors do/don't influence forgetting.

Note: The examiners could ask you a question about FB memories alone since they're explicitly mentioned in the specification. However, we've not prepared a sample answer for several reasons. FB memories are more concerned with remembering than forgetting (the actual sub-section) and it's more likely that examiners would ask about FB memories as part of an 'emotional factors influencing forgetting' question. However, if the Chief Examiner reads this s/he may change his/her mind! You have been warned!

# Critical issue: Eyewitness testimony (EWT)

## Reconstructive memory (Bartlett)

### DESCRIPTION

Bartlett (1932) stated that memory doesn't work accurately like a camera, rather it's prone to inaccuracies and interpretations based on prior experiences, i.e. memories are reconstructed (see Essential Study 1.3).

Schemas are our ready-made expectations that help us to understand our world. We use schemas to:

* interpret the world. They help us 'fill in the gaps' in our knowledge.
* simplify the processing of information.

However, schemas can lead to memory distortions when information doesn't readily fit into existing schemas. Cultural expectations or stereotypes also influence memory.

Allport & Postman (1947) illustrated the powerful effect of schemas on memory. They asked participants to view a cartoon of a white man threatening a black man with a cut-throat razor and then describe what they'd seen. Typically, white participants reported that the black man had been holding the razor. This is a shocking finding, since white participants must have held a schema or stereotype suggesting black men were more prone to violence. It's hoped that results would be very different today.

ESSENTIAL STUDY 1.3

**Reconstructive memory** •••••• **Bartlett** (1932) **'War of the Ghosts'** (WAROG) **study**

**Aims** (AO1)

To investigate the reconstructive nature of memory by examining the effect that prior expectations and experiences have on memory recall.

**Procedures** (AO1)

A short story or drawing was shown to participants. The best known story was called 'The War of the Ghosts'. Participants had to reproduce it after different time periods (15 minutes to years later). This is called a **repeated reproduction technique**.

**Findings** (AO1)

Over time, the reproductions became shorter, more coherent, more conventional and more clichéd. The reproductions were adapted to fit the participant's own cultural expectations. Typical errors that participants made in their recall included: *Omissions*: important details were left out (e.g. 'something black came from his mouth'); *Normalisation*: the story was made more 'normal' (e.g. 'boats' instead of 'canoes'; 'fishing' instead of 'hunting seals'); *Intrusions*: extra details were added to the story in order to make more sense; *Gist recall*: participants recalled only the 'gist' or basic storyline.

**Conclusion** (AO1)

Interpretation plays a major role in remembering. Remembering is an active process of reconstruction. Bartlett called this **'effort after meaning'**, that is, making the past more coherent to fit into existing knowledge or **schemas**.

**Criticisms** (AO1/AO2)

✔ **Status of research:** This study is regarded as a 'classic' in psychology and Bartlett's work on reconstructive memory remains influential.

✔ **Other research support:** The reproductive nature of memory has been demonstrated by others (Allport & Postman, 1947) and with other formats (e.g. drawings).

✘ **Poorly controlled study:** Analysis of the reproductions was too subjective and Bartlett may have been inadvertently biased in his interpretation of the stories.

✘ **Low ecological validity:** The stories used were rather artificial and unusual. Wynn & Logie (1998) repeatedly asked undergraduates about their first week at university and memory distortions weren't evident over time. This is because they examined real-life, everyday memories.

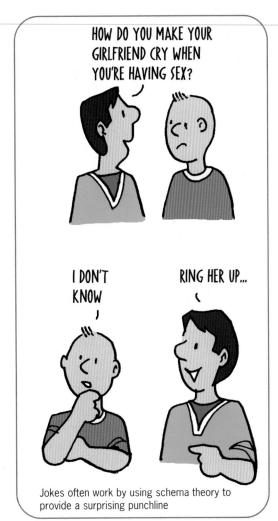

Jokes often work by using schema theory to provide a surprising punchline

Estimated speed of a car crash can be affected by the type of verb used (Loftus and Palmer, 1974)

## Evaluation of reconstructive memory

✓ Schemas do play a major part in memory recall and help to explain the reconstructive nature of memory.

✗ **Schemas are themselves influenced by memory:** Schemas can be updated and changed. It's not a one-way process whereby existing schemas lead to reconstructed memories. Experience and memories also affect our schemas.

✗ **The idea of schemas is rather vague.** What **exactly** are they? How are they acquired?

✗ **Accuracy of memory:** Schema theory over-emphasises memory inaccuracies. For example, it cannot easily explain FB memories.

### The role of leading questions (Loftus)

#### DESCRIPTION

Loftus's EWT research also illustrated the reconstructive nature of memory. Loftus showed that eyewitness memories can be affected by the wording of questions (see Essential Study 1.4). This has serious implications for the judicial system, since jurors seem to be particularly convinced by EWT.

There are two types of misleading questions which appear to affect EWT:

- *Leading questions*: a question which makes it likely that a participant's schema will influence them to give a desired answer (see Essential Study 1.4).
- *'After-the-fact information' questions*: here new misleading information is added in the question after the incident has occurred (see Loftus, 1975, below).

# EXAM tips BOX

*'There are so many factors that influence memory that we cannot be sure that any memories are not merely biased reconstructions.'* **To what extent does psychological research support this view of reconstructive memory? (18 marks)**

* Again you could structure your answer in three paragraphs, each 100–130 words long.

* In the first paragraph you could **describe** what reconstructive memory refers to, introduce Bartlett's views and refer to schemas and stereotypes (AO1 – 6 marks).

* In the second paragraph you could **analyse and evaluate** studies that support the reconstructive nature of memory (e.g. Bartlett, 1932; Allport & Postman, 1947).

* In the third paragraph you could also use eyewitness testimony research as support (see Loftus below), although criticisms of the methods employed should be mentioned. Finally, you could cite research that analyses and evaluates the reconstructive (inaccurate) nature of memory (Yuille & Cutshall, 1986). This could also include Wynn & Logie (1998) and research into flashbulb memories (AO2 – 12 marks).

Try to write out a suitable answer using about 300–350 words.

There is a sample answer at the end of the book, but try not to look at it until you've tried to answer the question yourself.

ESSENTIAL STUDY 1.4

**Unreliability of EWT** • • • • • • • **Loftus & Palmer** (1974) **'Smashed/Contacted' Car Speed study (SCCS)**

**Aim** (AO1) To investigate the effect of language (leading questions) on immediate recall.

**Procedures** (AO1) Student participants were shown slides of a two-car accident. Some were asked 'About how fast were the cars going when they **smashed into** one another?' whereas for others the verbs '**hit**', '**bumped**' '**contacted**' were used instead of '**smashed**'.

**Findings** (AO1) Estimated speed was affected by the verb used.

| Verb: | Estimated speed: | Verb: | Estimated speed: |
|---|---|---|---|
| Smashed into | 41 mph | Hit | 34 mph |
| Bumped | 38 mph | Contacted | 32 mph |

These differences were statistically significant.

**Conclusion** (AO1)

* Memory recall can be distorted by the language used.

* Participants have different interpretations of the speed and force from the use of different verbs. Leading questions do affect memory recall.

**Criticisms** (AO1/AO2)

✓ **Well controlled experiments:** The independent variable (use of verbs) is manipulated and all other variables are controlled.

✓ **Other experimental support:** There have been many studies which support Loftus.

✗ **Lacks ecological validity:** Witnessing a video clip lacks the emotional effects of watching a real-life event (see Yuille & Cutshall, 1986 below).

✗ **Sample:** Students are not representative of the wider population, so the results cannot be generalised.

✗ **Change of verb:** Did participants merely change their speed estimates due to verb change (demand characteristics) or did it actually alter their memory of the accident?

## Other EWT research studies

Two groups of participants watched a film of a car being driven through the countryside (Loftus, 1975). Group A were asked *'How fast was the white car going when it passed the 'Stop' sign while travelling along the country road?'* (there was a 'Stop' sign in the film). Group B were asked *'How fast was the white car going when it passed the barn while travelling along the country road?'* (there was no barn but the question presupposes there was one). A week later 17% of Group B reported seeing a barn compared to just 2% of Group A. The 'after-the-event' question had falsely suggested to them that there had actually been a barn. The explanation for this is source misattribution, where witnesses confuse the *actual* event itself with post-event information.

Yuille & Cutshall (1986) conducted research into a real-life crime. A thief had attempted to steal from a gun shop in Vancouver, Canada. The shop owner shot and killed the thief in front of 21 witnesses. Thirteen of the witnesses were interviewed four months later and they were asked misleading questions. However, witness accounts remained highly accurate and weren't adversely affected by the misleading information. Misleading information may not affect real-life memories to the same extent as laboratory-produced memories due to the emotions experienced at the time. This incident may have been encoded like a flashbulb memory, and so wasn't easily distorted. Also, participants had previously been interviewed by the police. Researchers only tried deliberately to mislead them four months later. Thus their memories may already have been 'fixed'.

There are a number of factors, apart from misleading questions, which influence EWT:

- **Race:** Errors are more likely to occur when the suspect and witness are racially different.
- **Clothing:** Witnesses pay more attention to transient characteristics (such as clothing) than to stable characteristics (such as height and facial shape).
- **Social influence:** People are influenced by other people's memories of events.

### EXAM tips BOX

**To what extent has psychological research shown eyewitness testimony to be unreliable? (18 marks)**

- Again you could structure your answer in three paragraphs, each 100–130 words long.
- In the first paragraph you could describe some studies that show EWT to be unreliable (e.g. Loftus & Palmer, 1974; Loftus, 1975) (AO1 – 6 marks).
- In the second paragraph you could analyse and evaluate such studies.
- In the final paragraph you could **analyse and evaluate** evidence that shows EWT to be reliable (e.g. Yuille & Cutshall, 1986; Foster *et al.,* 1994) (AO2 – 12 marks).

Try to write out a suitable answer using about 300–350 words.

There is a sample answer at the end of the book, but try not to look at it until you've attempted the question yourself.

### Evaluation of EWT research

✓ **Strong experimental support:** EWT can be affected by misleading post-event information.

✗ **Demand characteristics:** Participants in EWT studies respond to the experimental situation and provide answers they're expected to give.

✗ **Participant expectations and consequences:** Participants don't expect to be deliberately misled by university researchers, and therefore the reconstructive findings should be expected sinde they believe the researchers to be telling the truth. The consequences of inaccurate memories are minimal in a research setting compared to real-life crimes. Foster *et al.* (1994) showed that eyewitness identification was more accurate for a real-life crime as opposed to a simulation.

✖ **Deliberately misleading information:** Memory for important events isn't easily distorted when the information is obviously misleading.

✖ **Minor aspects of memory:** Misleading information only affects minor, relatively unimportant, aspects of the memory (e.g. 'barn' details above).

Does misleading information alter and replace the original memory (Loftus's view) or is the original memory merely obscured while remaining intact (McCloskey & Zaragoza, 1985)? Baddeley claimed that EWT research doesn't prove destruction of the memory trace, but merely interference with its retrieval. However, even when

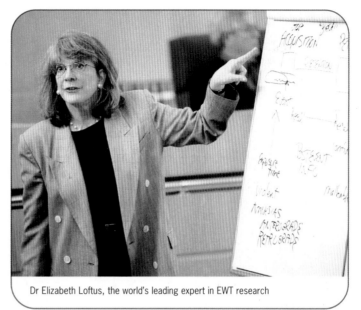

Dr Elizabeth Loftus, the world's leading expert in EWT research

participants are explicitly told about misleading information, they find it hard to ignore.

## Self-assessment questions

These are some example Part a and Part b questions (worth 40% of your exam). Part c questions (worth 60%) have been dealt with throughout the chapter in the Exam tips boxes and in the sample answers at the end of the book.

**1 a.** What is meant by the terms 'flashbulb memory' and 'eyewitness testimony'? (3 + 3 marks)

   **b.** Outline criticisms from research into the role of emotional factors in forgetting. (6 marks)

**2 a.** Describe *two* factors that influence the encoding of material in memory. (3 + 3 marks)

   **b.** Outline the main features of *one* alternative theory to the multi-store model of memory. (6 marks)

**3 a.** Explain what psychologists mean by the terms 'repression' and 'reconstructive memory'. (3 + 3 marks)

   **b.** Describe the procedures and findings of *one* study that has investigated the nature of long-term memory (LTM). (3 + 3 marks)

**4 a.** Describe the multi-store model of memory. (6 marks)

   **b.** Outline the findings of *one* study of the role of leading questions in eyewitness testimony and give *one* criticism of this study. (3 + 3 marks)

**5 a.** Outline *one* explanation of forgetting in short-term memory and give *one* criticism of this explanation. (3 + 3 marks)

   **b.** Describe *two* differences between short-term memory (STM) and long-term memory (LTM) in terms of duration and capacity. (3 + 3 marks)

| ESSENTIAL STUDY SUMMARY | | | |
|---|---|---|---|
| **Topic** | **Research study** | **Researcher date** | **Page** |
| Nature of STM | Trigram Retention Experiment (TRE) | Peterson & Peterson (1959) | 4 |
| Nature of LTM | High School Yearbook Photo (HSYP) study | Bahrick *et al.* (1975) | 6 |
| Reconstructive memory | 'War of the Ghosts' (WAROG) study | Bartlett (1932) | 21 |
| Eyewitness testimony | 'Smashed/Contacted' Car Speed (SCCS) study | Loftus & Palmer (1974) | 23 |

# CHAPTER SUMMARY: revision schema

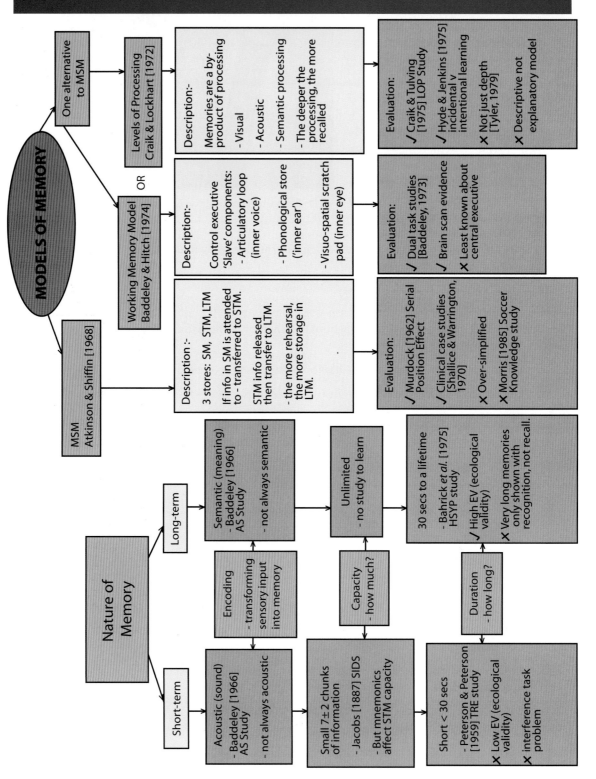

**MODELS OF MEMORY**

**One alternative to MSM**

**Levels of Processing Craik & Lockhart [1972]**

Description:-
Memories are a by-product of processing
- Visual
- Acoustic
- Semantic processing
- The deeper the processing, the more recalled

Evaluation:
✓ Craik & Tulving [1975] LOP Study
✓ Hyde & Jenkins [1975] incidental v intentional learning
✗ Not just depth [Tyler, 1979]
✗ Descriptive not explanatory model

**OR**

**Working Memory Model Baddeley & Hitch [1974]**

Description:-
Control executive
'Slave' components:
- Articulatory loop (inner voice)
- Phonological store ('inner ear')
- Visuo-spatial scratch pad (inner eye)

Evaluation:
✓ Dual task studies [Baddeley, 1973]
✓ Brain scan evidence
✗ Least known about central executive

**MSM Atkinson & Shiffin [1968]**

Description :-
3 stores: SM, STM, LTM
If info in SM is attended to - transferred to STM.
STM info released then transfer to LTM.
- the more rehearsal, the more storage in LTM.

Evaluation:
✓ Murdock [1962] Serial Position Effect
✓ Clinical case studies [Shallice & Warrington, 1970]
✗ Over-simplified
✗ Morris [1985] Soccer Knowledge study

**Nature of Memory**

**Long-term**

Semantic (meaning)
- Baddeley [1966] AS Study
- not always semantic

Unlimited
- no study to learn

30 secs to a lifetime
- Bahrick et al. [1975] HSYP study
✓ High EV (ecological validity)
✗ Very long memories only shown with recognition, not recall.

**Encoding**
- transforming sensory input into memory

**Capacity**
- how much?

**Duration**
- how long?

**Short-term**

Acoustic (sound)
- Baddeley [1966] AS Study
- not always acoustic

Small 7±2 chunks of information
- Jacobs [1887] SIDS
- But mnemonics affect STM capacity

Short < 30 secs
- Peterson & Peterson [1959] TRE study
✗ Low EV (ecological validity)
✗ interference task problem

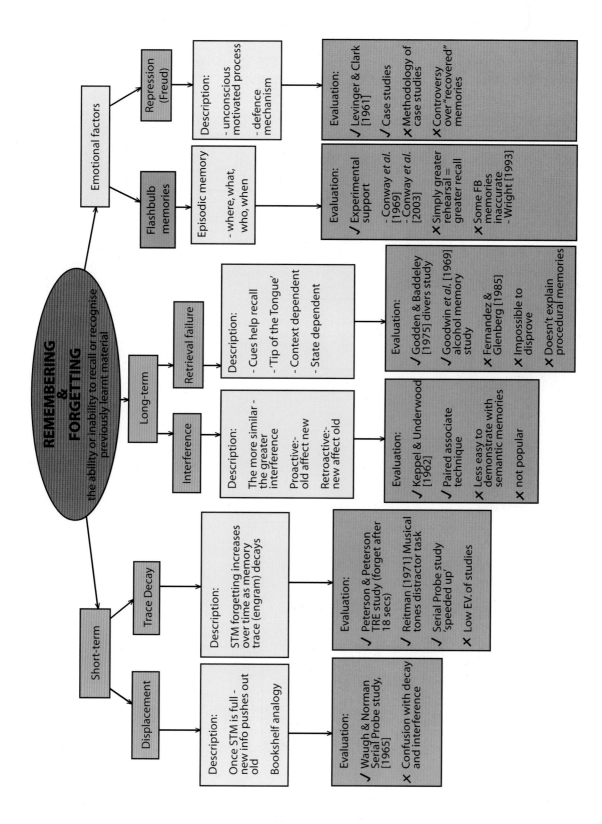

**REMEMBERING & FORGETTING**
the ability or inability to recall or recognise previously learnt material

**Emotional factors**

**Repression (Freud)**

Description:
- unconscious motivated process
- defence mechanism

Evaluation:
✓ Levinger & Clark [1961]
✓ Case studies
✗ Methodology of case studies
✗ Controversy over "recovered" memories

**Flashbulb memories**

Episodic memory
- where, what, who, when

Evaluation:
✓ Experimental support
  - Conway et al. [1969]
  - Conway et al. [2003]
✗ Simply greater rehearsal = greater recall
✗ Some FB memories inaccurate
  - Wright [1993]

**Long-term**

**Retrieval failure**

Description:
- Cues help recall
- 'Tip of the Tongue'
- Context dependent
- State dependent

Evaluation:
✓ Godden & Baddeley [1975] divers study
✓ Goodwin et al. [1969] alcohol memory study
✗ Fernandez & Glenberg [1985]
✗ Impossible to disprove
✗ Doesn't explain procedural memories

**Interference**

Description:
The more similar - the greater the interference

Proactive:-
old affect new

Retroactive:-
new affect old

Evaluation:
✓ Keppel & Underwood [1962]
✓ Paired associate technique
✗ Less easy to demonstrate with semantic memories
✗ not popular

**Short-term**

**Trace Decay**

Description:
STM forgetting increases over time as memory trace (engram) decays

Evaluation:
✓ Peterson & Peterson TRE study (forget after 18 secs)
✓ Reitman [1971] Musical tones distractor task
✓ Serial Probe study 'speeded up'
✗ Low EV. of studies

**Displacement**

Description:
Once STM is full - new info pushes out old

Bookshelf analogy

Evaluation:
✓ Waugh & Norman Serial Probe study, [1965]
✗ Confusion with decay and interference

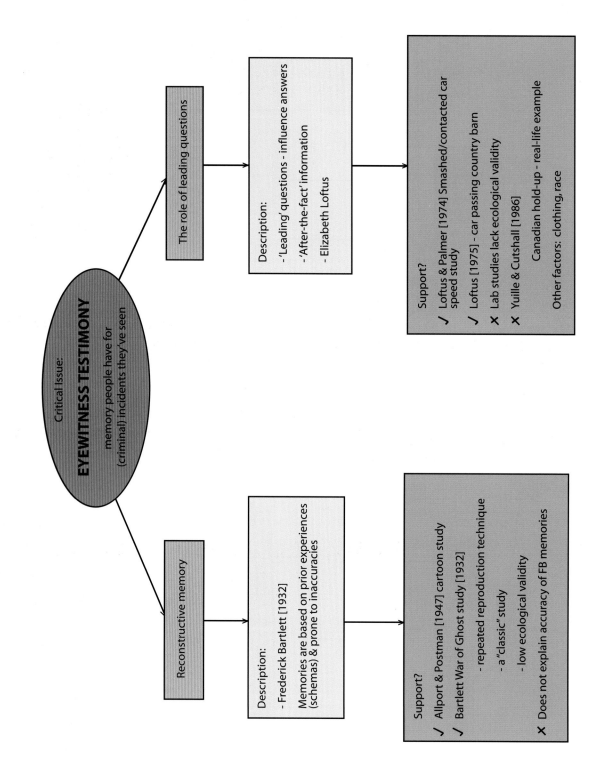

Critical Issue:

**EYEWITNESS TESTIMONY**

memory people have for (criminal) incidents they've seen

The role of leading questions

Description:
- 'Leading' questions - influence answers
- 'After-the-fact' information
- Elizabeth Loftus

Support?
✓ Loftus & Palmer [1974] Smashed/contacted car speed study
✓ Loftus [1975] - car passing country barn
✗ Lab studies lack ecological validity
✗ Yuille & Cutshall [1986]
    Canadian hold-up - real-life example

Other factors: clothing, race

Reconstructive memory

Description:
- Frederick Bartlett [1932]

Memories are based on prior experiences (schemas) & prone to inaccuracies

Support?
✓ Allport & Postman [1947] cartoon study
✓ Bartlett War of Ghost study [1932]
    - repeated reproduction technique
    - a "classic" study
    - low ecological validity
✗ Does not explain accuracy of FB memories

# AS Module 1:

# Developmental Psychology

## What's covered in this chapter?
### You need to know about:

Attachments in development
a. **The development and variety of attachments**
- The development of attachments (e.g. Schaffer). Research into individual differences, including secure and insecure attachments (e.g. Ainsworth) and cross-cultural variations
- Explanations of attachment (e.g. learning theory, Bowlby's theory)
b. **Deprivation and privation**
- Bowlby's maternal deprivation hypothesis, including evidence on which it is based
- Research into the effects of privation (e.g. studies of extreme privation and institutionalisation), including the extent to which the effects of privation can be reversed

Critical issue: day care
- The effects of day care on children's cognitive and social development

## The development and variety of attachments
### What are attachments?

According to Kagan *et al.* (1978), an attachment is:

- an intense emotional relationship specific to two people
- which endures over time, and
- in which prolonged separation from the attachment figure is accompanied by stress and sorrow.

This definition applies to attachments at any point in a person's life. But our earliest attachment serves as a *prototype* (or model) for all later attachments. The crucial first attachment is usually taken to be with our mother.

### Phases in the development of attachments

The attachment process can be divided into several phases (Schaffer, 1996):

- The **pre-attachment phase** (birth–3 months). From about six weeks, babies develop an attraction to other human beings. They prefer other people to physical objects and events. One way in which they show this preference is through smiling in response to people's faces. They direct this **social smile** to just about anyone.
- The **indiscriminate attachment phase** (3–7/8 months). Babies begin to discriminate between familiar and unfamiliar people. They smile much more at people they know, and the social smile has disappeared. But they'll still let strangers handle and look after them. They don't become visibly distressed, provided they're treated properly.
- The **discriminate attachment phase** (7/8 months onwards). Babies begin to develop specific attachments. They show this through (a) actively trying to stay close to particular people (especially the mother), and (b) becoming distressed when separated from them (*separation anxiety*). The baby can now consistently tell the difference between its mother and other people. It also understands that the mother continues to exist even when she's out of sight (*object permanence*).

  Also at this time, babies avoid close contact with unfamiliar people. Some display the *fear-of-strangers* response. This includes crying and trying to move away. It usually occurs only if the stranger tries to make contact with them.
- The **multiple attachment phase** (9 months onwards). The baby forms strong emotional ties with (a) other major caregivers (such as the father, grandparents and siblings), and (b) non-caregivers (such as other children). The fear-of-strangers response weakens. But the attachment to the mother remains the strongest.

## Individual differences in attachment

### Ainsworth *et al.'s* (1971, 1978) **Strange Situation study of Attachments** (SSoA)

#### Aims (AO1)

In 1971 and 1978, Ainsworth and her colleagues reported their findings from the Baltimore study of attachment. This was a replication (in Baltimore, US) of an earlier study Ainsworth had conducted in Uganda, Africa (1967). In that earlier study, she observed babies aged 15 weeks to two years over a nine-month period. She also interviewed their mothers. Ainsworth's main interest was in *individual differences* between mother–child pairs in the quality of their attachments.

#### Procedures (AO1)

Like the Uganda study, the Baltimore study was *longitudinal*. Ainsworth *et al.* visited 26 mother–child pairs at home every 3–4 weeks for the baby's first year of life. Each visit lasted 3–4 hours. Also like the earlier study, both interviews and naturalistic observation were used. But observation now played a much greater role.

To make sense of the vast amount of data collected for each pair, Ainsworth *et al.* needed some standard against which to compare their observations. The standard they chose was the *Strange Situation*. This comprises eight episodes (each lasting about three minutes, except for episode 1, which lasts 30 seconds), as shown in Table 2.1.

Every aspect of the participants' reactions is observed and videotaped. But most attention is given to the baby's response to the mother's return (*reunion behaviours*). In the Baltimore study, the Strange Situation was used when the babies were 12 months old. This is the age group it's designed for.

# Physiological Psychology

## What's covered in this chapter?
### You need to know about:

Stress

a. **Stress as a bodily response**

- The body's response to stressors (e.g. pituitary–adrenal system); the General Adaptation Syndrome (Selye)
- Research into the relationship between stress and cardiovascular disorders and the effects of stress on the immune system

b. **Sources of stress**

- Research into sources of stress, including life changes (e.g. Holmes & Rahe), and workplace stressors (e.g. Johansson, Marmot)
- Individual differences in modifying the effects of stressors, including the roles played by personality (e.g. Type A behaviour, hardy personality) and gender (e.g. physiological reactivity, social support)

Critical issue: stress management

- Approaches to managing the negative effects of stress, including physiological (e.g. drugs, biofeedback) and psychological methods (e.g. stress-inoculation, increasing hardiness)
- The strengths and weaknesses of methods of stress management

## Stress as a bodily response
### What do we mean by stress?

Stress can be defined in three main ways:

- stress as a **stimulus**. This refers to the characteristics of an environmental event or situation, and is basically something that happens *to* us. *Sources of stress* ('stressors') include life changes and workplace stressors.

- stress as a response. This refers to what happens *within* us as a result of environmental events or situations. In particular, it refers to the physiological/bodily responses, such as the General Adaptation Syndrome (Selye, 1956). This relates to *stress as a bodily response*.
- stress as interaction between an individual and his/her environment. We experience stress when we believe we don't have what's needed to meet the demands of a particular situation. But people differ in what makes them feel stressed, how much stress they feel, and how they try to deal with it. This relates to *stress management*.

According to Selye (1956), 'Stress is the non-specific response of the body to any demand made upon it'. Selye observed that all hospital patients display the same pattern of symptoms (or syndrome), regardless of their particular illness. These included:

- a loss of appetite
- an associated loss of weight and strength
- a loss of ambition
- a characteristic facial expression.

After examining extreme cases in more detail, Selye concluded that this non-specific response in turn reflected the *General Adaptation Syndrome* (GAS).

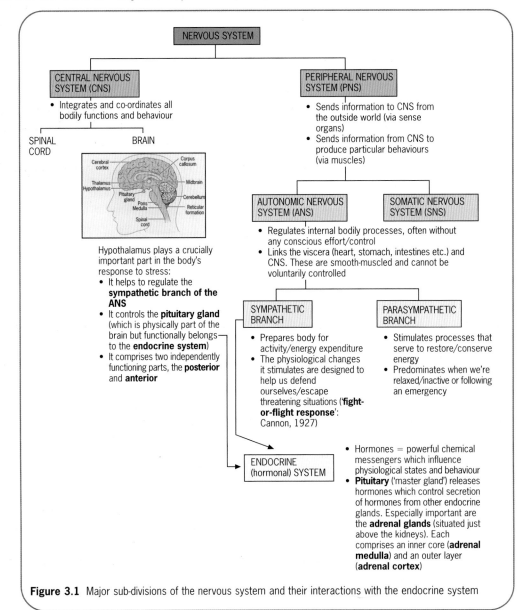

**Figure 3.1** Major sub-divisions of the nervous system and their interactions with the endocrine system

## SELYE'S GAS

According to Selye, GAS represents the body's defence against stress. The body responds in the same way to any stressor, whether it's environmental or arises from within the body itself. Environmental stressors may include insulin, excessive heat or cold, X-rays, sleep and water deprivation, and electric shock. Selye defined stress as:

> '... the individual's psychophysiological response, mediated largely by the autonomic nervous system and the endocrine system, to any demands made on the individual.'

To understand GAS, we must have a working knowledge of the nervous system and the endocrine system. We also need to understand how they *interact* with each other. These are summarised in Figure 3.1.

## THE THREE STAGES/PHASES OF GAS

### Alarm reaction

When a stimulus is perceived as a stressor, there's a brief, initial *shock phase*. Blood pressure (BP) and muscle tension drop. Resistance to the stressor is reduced. But this is quickly followed by the *countershock phase*. The hypothalamus activates the sympathetic branch of the ANS. This, in turn, stimulates the *adrenal medulla* to secrete increased levels of adrenaline and noradrenaline (*catecholamines*).

The catecholamines (or 'stress hormones'):

- mimic the activity of the sympathetic branch of the ANS, and so are called *sympathomimetics*
- trigger and maintain increased levels of physiological activity, which are collectively called the *fight-or-flight response* (FOFR) (Cannon, 1927). These changes are summarised in Table 3.1 (and see Figure 3.2).

For all these reasons, the alarm reaction is associated with the *sympatho-adrenomedullary axis* (SAA).

**Table 3.1** Major sympathetic reactions associated with the 'fight-or-flight response' (FOFR)

| Organ or function involved | Sympathetic reaction |
| --- | --- |
| Heart rate | Increases |
| Blood pressure | Increases |
| Secretion of saliva | Suppressed (dry mouth) |
| Pupils of eye | Dilate (to aid vision) |
| Limbs (and trunk) | Dilation of blood vessels of voluntary muscles (e.g. to help us run faster) |
| Peristalsis (contraction of stomach and intestines) | Slows down (we don't feel hungry in an emergency) |
| Galvanic skin response (GSR) (measure of skin's electrical resistance) | Decreases (due to increased sweating associated with increased anxiety) |
| Bladder muscles | Relax (there may be temporary loss of bladder control) |
| Breathing rate | Increases (through dilation of bronchial tubes) |
| Liver | Glucose (stored as energy) released into bloodstream to increase energy |
| Emotion | Experience of strong emotion (e.g. fear) |

### Resistance

If the stressor isn't removed, sympathetic activity *decreases*. But output from the other part of the adrenal gland (the *adrenal cortex*) *increases*. The adrenal cortex is essential for the maintenance of life, and its removal causes death. It's controlled by how much *adrenocorticotrophic hormone* (ACTH) there is in the blood. ACTH is released from the *anterior pituitary*. In turn, the anterior pituitary is controlled by the hypothalamus.

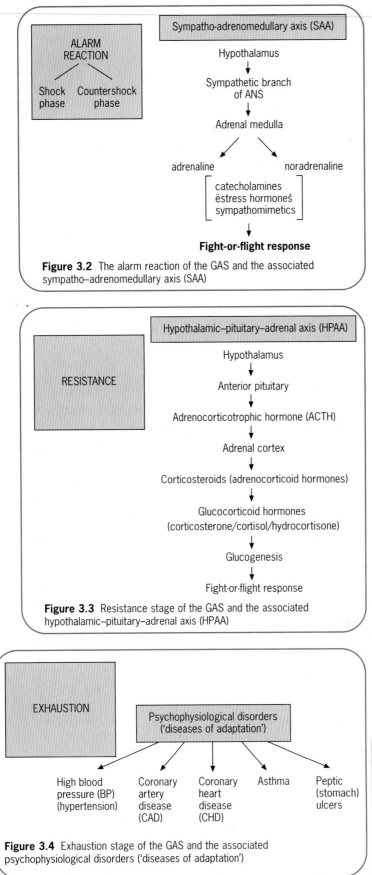

**Figure 3.2** The alarm reaction of the GAS and the associated sympatho–adrenomedullary axis (SAA)

**Figure 3.3** Resistance stage of the GAS and the associated hypothalamic–pituitary–adrenal axis (HPAA)

**Figure 3.4** Exhaustion stage of the GAS and the associated psychophysiological disorders ('diseases of adaptation')

ACTH stimulates the adrenal cortex to release *corticosteroids* (or *adrenocorticoid hormones*). One group of adrenocorticoid hormones are the *glucocorticoid hormones*, which include corticosterone, cortisol, and hydrocortisone. These regulate the amount of glucose in the blood (*glucogenesis*). This helps to resist all kinds of stress.

The glucocorticoids:

- convert protein into glucose
- make fats available for energy
- increase blood flow
- generally stimulate behavioural responsiveness.

In this way, the *hypothalamic-pituitary-adrenal axis (*HPAA) contributes to the fight-or-flight response.

**Exhaustion**

Once ACTH and corticosteroids are circulating in the bloodstream, they tend to inhibit more ACTH being released from the pituitary. If the stressor is removed during the resistance stage, blood sugar levels will gradually return to normal. But if the stressful situation continues, so will the pituitary-adrenal excitation. By this time:

- the body's resources are becoming depleted
- the adrenals can no longer function properly
- blood glucose levels drop. In extreme cases, hypoglycaemia could result in death
- *psychophysiological disorders* develop. These include high BP (hypertension), coronary artery disease (CAD), coronary heart disease (CHD), asthma, and peptic (stomach) ulcers. Selye called these the *diseases of adaptation*.

**Figure 3.5** Three stages of GAS

Evaluation of the GAS

✓ It helps account for the physiology of stress.

✗ Not all stressors produce the same pattern of physiological activity.

✗ Research into the GAS involved mainly rats' responses to stressors.

✗ Selye largely ignored the psychological aspects of stress. A stressor must first be *perceived* as a stressor before any physiological changes occur. It's almost as though he left the person out of the picture by focusing on the body's responses.

## How does stress make us ill?

### CARDIOVASCULAR DISORDERS

The GAS provides a general answer to the question: why does stress makes us ill? For more specific, detailed answers, we need to consider other research.

An evolutionary perspective:

- represents a general way of trying to understand why stress is bad for us
- provides some important links with research into the cardiovascular effects of stress (such as heart disease and circulatory disorders).

### Box 3.1. The evolutionary explanation of how stress makes us ill

The sympathetic branch of the ANS responds as a unit. This causes a state of generalised arousal, which is pretty much the same whatever the stressor might be. This was probably crucial in our evolutionary past, when our ancestors were commonly faced with life-threatening dangers. This is exactly what the FOFR is for.

For example, increased heart rate supplies more blood to the muscles, which is a good idea when faced with a hungry sabre-toothed tiger. But most everyday stressors involve a much greater *psychological* element and *aren't* life-threatening. Yet our nervous and endocrine systems have evolved in such a way that we typically react to everyday stressors as if they *were*. What may have been *adaptive*, advantageous, responses for our ancestors have become *maladaptive* today.

So what happens to all that internal, physiological activity?

- Chronic (long-term, ongoing) stress involves repeated episodes of increased heart rate and BP. This, in turn, increases plaque formation within the cardiovascular system.
- Adrenaline and noradrenaline contribute to increases in blood cholesterol levels. Cholesterol particles clump together, leading to clots in the blood and the artery walls. The arteries become thickened.
- In turn, raised heart rate is linked to a more rapid build-up of cholesterol on artery walls.
- High BP results in small lesions on the artery walls, where cholesterol gets trapped.

### Friedman and Rosenman's research

Friedman and Rosenman (two American cardiologists) concluded that some men are more prone to CHD, because they typically respond to stressful situations in a particular way. So their research is just as relevant to understanding the factors which mediate the effects of stressors (see pages 65–66).

In the late 1950s, Friedman and Rosenman found that American men were far more susceptible to CHD than American women, despite the similarity of their diets. A subsequent questionnaire study suggested that job-related stress may have been the crucial factor. They followed this up by monitoring the *blood-clotting speed* and *serum cholesterol levels* of 40 tax accountants over a period of several months. These are two warning signs of CHD. As the deadline for submitting tax returns approached, the two measures rose alarmingly. But they soon returned to normal levels following the deadline.

### Friedman and Rosenman's (1974) **Study of Type A Behaviour** (STAB)

### Aims (AO1)

Friedman and Rosenman wished to find evidence for the role of *non-physiological* factors in CHD. In particular, they were interested in the role of *individual differences* in men's ways of dealing with stressful situations.

### Procedures (AO1)

Starting in 1960–61, 3,000 American men, aged 39–59, were followed for a period of over eight years. So, it was a *longitudinal* study. They were all well when the study began.

How they dealt with stressful situations was assessed in two ways:

- a *structured interview*, which involved pre-determined, open-ended questions
- a pencil-and-paper *self-assessment* test, consisting of several multiple-choice questions.

Based on these two measures, the men were classified as displaying either Type A behaviour (TAB) or Type B (non-Type A) behaviour (TBB):

- *Type A* behaviour involves a chronic sense of time urgency, excessive competitiveness, and a generalised (but well controlled) hostility. These men are always setting themselves deadlines, suffer from 'hurry sickness', cannot bear waiting their turn (in queues), and have to do several things at once. They're also insecure about their status, and need to be admired by their peers to feel good about themselves.
- *Type B* behaviour may involve the same degree of ambition, but these men seem to be steadied by it. They're much more self-confident, relaxed and easy-going, not driven to achieve perfection, and much less hostile.

### Findings (AO1)

Type A men were more than twice as likely to develop CHD than Type B men. After taking risk factors into account (e.g. age, smoking, blood cholesterol, BP, family history of heart disease), they were still *twice* as likely to suffer heart attacks.

### Conclusions (AO1)

A man's personality can make it more likely that he will develop CHD, over and above the effects of smoking and other ('traditional') risk factors. In this sense, personality can be regarded as a risk factor.

In a more general sense, the harmful effects of stressors can be mediated through psychological factors. In other words, stressors aren't harmful *in themselves*. It's how people perceive and react to them that's (potentially) dangerous for health.

### Criticisms (AO1/AO2)

✓ **Substantial study:** It was a long-term study involving a very large sample.

✓ **Mind–body interaction:** It showed how *psychological* factors (in this case, personality) can produce *physiological effects* (CHD).

✓ **Well-designed study:** Since all the men were free of heart disease at the start, the results weren't contaminated. In other words, those who developed heart disease did so during the course of the study.

✓ **Separation of variables:** Friedman and Rosenman were able to separate out the effects of risk factors from the effects of personality.

✖ **Unreliability of measures:** The measures used to assess TAB/TBB have been criticised. For example, interviewers require special training, which is expensive and time-consuming. Also, the men's scores on one measure didn't always match their scores on the other. This means they might have been measuring *different things*.

✖ **Biased sample:** The sample was all male. Although there were good reasons for this, it means we cannot generalise the results to women.

## EXAM tips BOX

### To what extent does stress play a role in cardiovascular disorders? (18 marks)

- You could structure your answer in terms of three paragraphs, all about 100–130 words long.

- In the first paragraph you could briefly **describe** what's meant by the term stress, say what's meant by cardio-vascular disorders, and give some examples. You could then outline some of the evidence relating to the role of stress in cardiovascular disorders. This could include more general explanations (such as Selye's GAS, and the evolutionary perspective) **and/or** studies which have looked more directly at the role of stress in cardiovascular disorders. (AO1, 6 marks).

- In the second paragraph you could **analyse and evaluate** the more general explanations of the physiological effects of stress.

- In the third paragraph you could **analyse and evaluate** research that has looked more directly at the role of stress in cardiovascular disorders, such as that of Friedman and Rosenman. You need to point out some of the strengths **and** limitations of their research. *Remember, merely describing the findings of such research will only count as AO1*. (AO2, worth 12 marks).

- A word of warning: *This isn't a question about the GAS (or the evolutionary perspective). So you must emphasise only those aspects of these explanations which are relevant to the question*.

Try to write a suitable answer in about 300–350 words.

As with all questions, there's no single correct way of answering it. The above are just pointers. There's a sample answer at the end of the book. Try not to look at it until you've had a go at doing it yourself.

 Evaluation of Friedman and Rosenman's research

✔ Replication of findings: Their basic findings have been replicated in several countries (in Europe, Canada and New Zealand).

✖ Relative risks: The greater risk of CHD faced by Type As is only *relative*. The vast majority of Type As *don't* develop CHD, while many Type Bs *do*.

✖ Is TAB a distinct risk factor? Most studies have found that TAB assessed immediately following a heart attack *doesn't* predict future attacks. This suggests that it's *not* a distinct risk for CHD in those already at risk (Penny, 1996).

✖•✔ Does TAB cause CHD? Friedman and Rosenman see personality as playing a *causal* role in CHD. But their evidence is merely *correlational*. All we can say for sure is that Type A men are *more likely* to develop CHD. TAB might be a *response* to high BP and other increased physiological activity, rather than a cause. Some people may be *predisposed* to react to stressors with raised BP etc. They may learn to *cope* with these physiological changes by developing more hostile, competitive, 'driven' behaviours.

## THE EFFECTS OF STRESS ON THE IMMUNE SYSTEM

### What is the immune system?

- The *immune system* is a collection of billions of cells which travel through the bloodstream. They're produced mainly in the spleen, lymph nodes, thymus and bone marrow.
- These cells move in and out of tissues and organs, defending the body against foreign bodies or *antigens* (such as bacteria, viruses and cancerous cells).
- The major type of cell is white blood cells (*leucocytes*), of which there are many types.
- Some immune cells produce and secrete *antibodies*. These bind to antigens and destroy them.

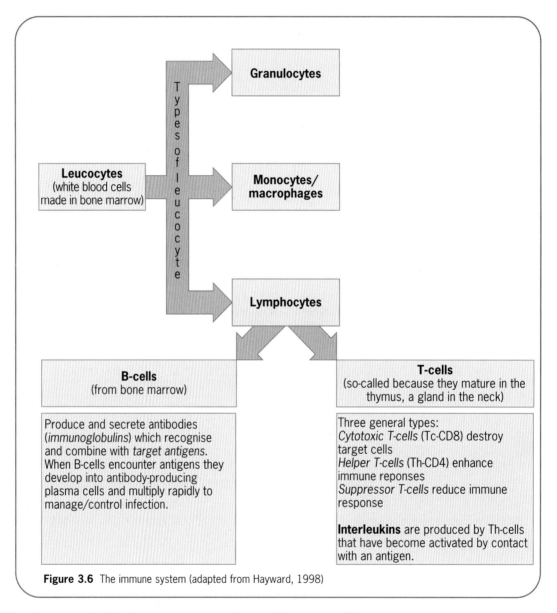

**Figure 3.6** The immune system (adapted from Hayward, 1998)

### What happens to the immune system when we're stressed?

- The immune system's ability to fight off antigens is reduced. This is why we're much more likely to pick up infections when we're 'under stress' (we often talk of being 'run down').
- But this doesn't mean that stress actually *causes* infections. Stress makes us more susceptible to infectious agents by temporarily suppressing immune function (the immunosuppressive effects of stress). Stressors that seem to have this effect include exams (e.g. Kiecolt-Glaser *et al.*, 1984: see Essential Study 3.2), and the death of a spouse (e.g. Schliefer *et al.*, 1983: see below).

- Our bodies produce more corticosteroids when we're under stress (see page x). Intermittent production of corticosteroids doesn't do much harm to the immune system. But if they're produced *continuously* (as in GAS), they can interfere with leucocyte activity and the production of antibodies.
- Stressful events have been linked to various infectious illnesses. These include influenza, herpes and the Epstein-Barr virus (associated with extreme tiredness).

### Research that demonstrates the immunosuppressive effects of stress

- Riley (1981) created stress by placing mice on a turntable rotating at 45 rpm. He found a marked decrease in their lymphocyte count over a five-hour period. In other words, their immune response was suppressed.
- In a later study, Riley studied the link between stress and tumour growth. He implanted cancer cells in two groups of mice. Group 1 had 10 minutes of rotation per hour for three days (*high-stress condition*). Group 2 had no rotation at all (*no-stress control condition*). As expected, Group 1 developed large tumours, while Group 2 showed no tumour growth.
- There are always important ethical issues raised by such experiments with non-humans. But there are scientific issues too. In particular, what can studies of mice tell us about the immunosuppressive effects of stress in humans?
- There are human studies that support Riley's findings. For example, Schliefer *et al.* (1983) investigated the immune system of men whose wives had died from breast cancer. Their immune systems functioned less well after their wives had died than before.
- Cohen *et al.* (1991) gave participants nasal drops containing cold viruses. Stress was defined as (a) the number of life changes an individual had recently experienced; and (b) how 'out of control' they felt. Those participants with the highest stress levels were almost *twice* as likely to develop colds as those with the lowest levels.
- *Interleukin-b* (see Figure 3.6, page 56) is produced soon after tissue damage. It helps to remodel connective tissue in wounds, and to form collagen (scar tissue). Kiecolt-Glaser *et al.* (1995) compared the rate of wound healing in two groups: (a) a group of 'high-stress' women, caring for relatives with Alzheimer's disease; and (b) a 'stress-free' matched control group. On average, it took 9 days longer for group (a)'s wounds to heal than (b)'s.

**ESSENTIAL STUDY 3.2**

**Kiecolt-Glaser *et al.'s* (1984) study of Immunosuppression in Medical Students** (ISMS)

#### Aims (AO1)

The researchers wanted to study the 'competence' of the immune system in people facing stressful situations (medical students facing important exams).

#### Procedures (AO1)

Kiecolt-Glaser *et al.* took blood samples from 75 first-year medical students (49 males, 26 females). They all volunteered to take part. The samples were taken (a) one month before their final exams, and (b) on the first day of the exams (after they'd sat two papers). The blood samples were analysed for the amount of leucocyte activity. Specifically, how much *natural killer cell* activity was there? These help fight off viruses and tumours.

#### Findings (AO1)

As predicted, natural killer cell activity was greatly reduced in the second sample compared with the first.

The students were also given questionnaires to assess psychiatric symptoms, loneliness and life events (all potential sources of stress: see below, pages 59–61). Immune responses were weakest of all in those students who reported feeling most lonely. It was also weakest for those who were experiencing other stressful life events and psychiatric symptoms (such as depression and anxiety).

### Conclusions (AO1)

Stress is associated with reduced immune function. That is, Kiecolt-Glaser *et al.* found evidence for the immunosuppressant effects of stress. They also showed that these effects can be increased when individuals are exposed to particular kinds of stressors.

### Criticisms (AO1/AO2)

✓ **The study was a natural experiment.** That is, the researchers didn't decide what stressors the students would be exposed to. Their exams would have happened anyway, and the researchers took the opportunity to measure their immune function in response to these stressors.

✓ **Participant variables controlled.** The students were being compared *with themselves* on the two occasions the blood samples were taken. This controls important *participant variables*, such as personality.

✗ **Not all environmental variables controlled.** Strictly, we can't be sure that it was the stressors (and only the stressors) which caused the change in immune function. Other variables which weren't controlled (as would happen in a true experiment) might have played a part.

## EXAM tips BOX

**Consider research into the effects of stress on the immune system. (18 marks)**

- You could structure your answer in terms of three paragraphs, all about 100–130 words long.

- In the first paragraph you could give a brief **description** of the immune system and briefly summarise some findings of research into the effects of stress on the immune system. (AO1, worth 6 marks).

- In the second paragraph you could look at studies of non-human animals. You could **analyse and evaluate** these in terms of (i) their relevance to human beings and (ii) their ethical acceptability.

- A word of warning: *you must address these issues in a way that's relevant to the question. If you make your points in a very general way, you'll gain very few marks*.

- A word of advice: *the question doesn't actually refer to human beings. So it would be perfectly acceptable to include studies of non-human animals (in addition to/instead of humans). But it's also acceptable for you to write just about human research*.

- In the third paragraph you could look at studies involving human beings. You could **analyse and evaluate** these in terms of (i) whether or not the evidence really shows that stress *causes* decreased immune function, (ii) how valid are the definitions/measures of stress used, and (iii) the possible practical benefits of such research. *Remember, merely describing research findings will only count as AO1*. (AO2, worth 12 marks).

Try to write a suitable answer in about 300–350 words. As with all questions, there's no single correct way of answering it. The above are just pointers. There's a sample answer at the end of the book. Try not to look at it until you've had a go at doing it yourself.

## Sources of stress

In the previous section, we've mentioned a variety of stressors. These include insulin, electric shock, excessive heat or cold, exams, and death of spouse. The last of these is an example of a major life change. In this section, we concentrate on these and workplace stressors.

## Life changes

**Holmes & Rahe's** (1967) **Social Readjustment Rating Scale** (SRRS)

### Aims (AO1)

The main aim of this study was to construct an instrument for measuring stress. Holmes and Rahe defined stress as the amount of *change* an individual has had to deal with during a particular period of time. They claimed that the degree of stress is related to both physical and psychological illness. People are more likely to show symptoms following periods of stress. The greater the stress, the more serious the illness.

### Procedures (AO1)

Holmes and Rahe examined the medical records of 5,000 patients. They also compiled a list of 43 life events, which seemed to cluster in the months prior to the onset of the patients' illness.

They told 100 people ('judges') that 'marriage' had been assigned an arbitrary value of 500. The judges then had to assign a number to each of the other life events, indicating how much readjustment they'd involve *relative to marriage*.

Death of spouse was judged (on average) to require *twice* as much readjustment as marriage. The average (mean) of the numbers assigned to each event was then divided by 10. The resulting values became the weighting (numerical value) of each life event. For example, the weighting for death of spouse was 100 (1,000 divided by 10). A sample of the 43 life events is shown in Table 3.2 on page 60.

The amount of life stress a person has experienced in a given period (say, 12 months) is measured by the total number of **life change units** (LCUs). These units are calculated by adding the mean values (in the right-hand column of Table 3.2) associated with the events the person has experienced during that time (the middle column). The ranks (left-hand column) simply denote the order in which the life events appear in the SRRS. When participants are given the SRRS, they're presented *only* with the list of life events (without mean values). They're simply asked to tick the ones that apply to them.

### Findings (AO1)

Most life events were judged to be *less* stressful than getting married. But six (including death of spouse, divorce, and personal injury or illness) were rated as *more* stressful.

Holmes and Rahe found that people with high LCU scores for the preceding year were likely to experience some sort of physical illness the following year. For example, someone scoring over 300 LCUs had about an 80% chance of becoming ill. Health problems included sudden cardiac death, non-fatal heart attacks, tuberculosis (TB), diabetes, leukaemia, accidents and sports injuries.

### Conclusions (AO1)

Holmes and Rahe concluded that stress could be measured objectively as an LCU score. This in turn predicts the person's chances of becoming ill (physically and/or mentally) following the period of stress. Stress and illness aren't just correlated. Stress actually makes us ill.

### Criticisms (AO1/AO2)

✓ **Landmark study.** This was the first major attempt to measure stress objectively and to examine its relationship to illness.

✗ **Are all changes equally stressful?** The SRRS assumes that *any* change is, by definition, stressful. But the *undesirable* aspects of events are at least as important as the fact that they change people's lives. Table 3.2 suggests that life changes have a largely *negative* feel about them (especially those with the highest LCU scores). So the SRRS may be confusing 'change' with 'negativity'.

✖ **Ambiguity.** Some of the life events are *ambiguous*. For example, those that refer to 'change in . . . ' could be positive or negative.

✖ **Missing life events.** The list of life events is *incomplete*. For example, there's no reference to the problems of old age, natural or man-made disasters (Lazarus, 1999).

✖ **Change or uncontrollable change?** It may not be change as such that's stressful, but change that's *unexpected*, and in this sense, *uncontrollable*. When people are asked to classify the undesirable life events on the SRRS as either 'controllable 'or 'uncontrollable', only the latter are correlated with later illness.

✖ **Not everyday occurrences.** By definition, most of the 43 life events aren't everyday occurrences. Kanner *et al.'s* (1981) **hassles scale** includes losing weight, traffic jams, bad weather, arguments, and financial and family worries (see below).

**Table 3.2** A selection of life events from the Social Readjustment Rating Scale (SRRS)

| Rank | Life event | Mean value |
|---|---|---|
| 1. | Death of spouse | 100 |
| 2. | Divorce | 73 |
| 3. | Marital separation | 65 |
| 4. | Jail term | 63 |
| 5. | Death of close family member | 63 |
| 6. | Personal injury or illness | 53 |
| 7. | Marriage | 50 |
| 8. | Fired at work | 47 |
| 10. | Retirement | 45 |
| 11. | Change in health of family member | 44 |
| 12. | Pregnancy | 40 |
| 13. | Sex difficulties | 39 |
| 16. | Change in financial state | 38 |
| 17. | Death of close friend | 37 |
| 18. | Change to different line of work | 36 |
| 23. | Son or daughter leaving home | 29 |
| 27. | Begin or end school | 26 |
| 38. | Change in sleeping habits | 16 |
| 42. | Christmas | 12 |
| 43. | Minor violations of the law | 11 |

 Evaluation of studies using the SRRS

✔ Support using large sample. 2,500 navy personnel from three US navy cruisers completed the SRRS before they left for a six-month tour of duty. While they were away, a health record was kept for each participant by the ships' doctors. As predicted, LCUs were positively correlated with illness (Rahe *et al.*, 1970).

✖•✔ Results open to interpretation. Instead of life events *causing* illness, it could be the other way round. Some life events (such as 8, 13, and 38: see Table 3.2) might be early signs of an illness that's already developing (Penny, 1996). This is because studies like Rahe *et al.*'s are *correlational* (see Chapter 6, page 124).

✖ Unreliable data. Many studies are *retrospective*. People are asked to *recall* both their illnesses and the stressful life events that occurred during, say, the previous 12 months. This is likely to produce unreliable data. For example, if you're under stress (for whatever reason) you may focus on minor physiological sensations and report them as 'symptoms of illness' (Davison & Neale, 2001).

✖ **Life events may mean different things to different people.** On the SRRS, particular events give a pre-determined LCU score. But individuals can experience the 'same' life event very differently. For example, divorce may mean release from an unhappy, stressful situation, and so may be a very *positive* event. (Also, what's a hassle one day may not be the next – and *vice-versa*: see below).

✖ **Hassles are more stressful.** Kanner *et al.* (1981) studied 100 men and women over a 12-month period. They confirmed their prediction that hassles were correlated with undesirable psychological symptoms. Also, hassles were a more powerful predictor of symptoms (both physiological and psychological) than the SRRS life events.

Delongis *et al.* (1982) compared the hassles scale and a life events scale as predictors of later health problems. They also wanted to study the effect of 'uplifts'. These are events that make you feel good (the opposite of hassles).

100 participants, aged 45–64, completed questionnaires, once a month, over the course of a year. Both the frequency and intensity of hassles were significantly correlated with overall health status and physical symptoms. There was *no* relationship between life events and health during the course of the study itself. But there was for the 2–3 years *prior* to the study. Daily uplifts had little effect on health.

These findings confirm Kanner *et al.*'s conclusion that daily hassles are a better predictor of health problems than life events. But this may partly reflect the time period for which life changes are recorded. In other words, it may take longer than 12 months for (certain) life events to have their effects on health.

## EXAM tips BOX

**Consider psychological research into the role of life events as a source of stress. (18 marks)**

- You could structure your answer in terms of three paragraphs, all about 100–130 words long.

- The first paragraph could include some examples of life events and a brief **description** of evidence for the role of life events as a source of stress. This is likely to focus on Holmes & Rahe's (1967) Social Readjustment Rating Scale (SRRS) study and related research. (AO1, worth 6 marks).

- In the second paragraph you could **analyse and evaluate** Holmes and Rahe's research. Remember, this was an attempt to **construct an instrument for measuring stress**. So you could consider the strengths and weaknesses of the SRRS as a way of measuring stress. You could also compare the SRRS with other attempts to measure stress.

- In the third paragraph you could **analyse and evaluate** studies which have used the SRRS and/or other measures of stress in relation to physical and/or mental illness. (AO2, worth 12 marks).

- *Remember, merely describing research findings will only count as AO1. You must evaluate (AO2) the research findings in order to answer the question.*

Try to write a suitable answer in about 300–350 words. As with all questions, there's no single correct way of answering it. The above are just pointers. There's a sample answer at the end of the book. Try not to look at it until you've had a go at doing it yourself.

## Workplace stressors

### ARE SOME OCCUPATIONS MORE STRESSFUL THAN OTHERS?

Four of the most stressful occupations are nursing, social work, teaching and the emergency services (police, ambulance, fire etc.). In *nursing*, for example, certain sources of stress are part-and-parcel of the job. These include:

- dealing constantly with patients' pain, anxiety, and death

- giving emotional support to relatives, often with little appropriate training
- having to maintain high levels of concentration for long periods (as in ITU/intensive care)
- being in the 'front line' when major disasters occur (such as the 1989 Hillsborough football disaster).

More recently, nurses and others working in healthcare have become the victims of violence.

## THE EFFECTS OF BEING IN CONTROL: GOOD OR BAD?

Executives (in industry and business organisations) are another occupational group that face above-average stress levels. They constantly have to make important decisions, and they're responsible for the outcomes. This is very stressful ('executive stress').

In a famous early study, Brady placed monkeys in 'restraining chairs' and conditioned them to press a lever. They'd receive an electric shock every 20 seconds if they didn't press the lever within that interval. But many of the monkeys died suddenly, and the experiment had to be abandoned. Post-mortem examinations showed that the monkeys had raised levels of gastrointestinal hormones. The cause of death was ulcers. Other monkeys had been restrained for up to six months without any ill effects. So the ulcers had been caused *either* by the electric shocks *or* the stress of having to press the lever to avoid them.

In a follow-up study, Brady (1958) tested the relationship between (a) high stress levels and (b) increased hormone production and the development of ulcers. He was primarily interested in the effects of stress in business executives, which is why he called his subjects 'executive monkeys'.

An 'executive monkey'

Brady tested monkeys *in pairs*. The experimental 'executive' was responsible for pressing the lever. A 'yoked control' received the shocks, but couldn't control the lever. So only the executive monkey was stressed, but both monkeys received the shocks. This occurred at 20-second intervals, for six hours at a time, over a three-week period.

The executive monkeys developed severe ulcers and eventually died. The yoked controls showed no apparent ill effects. The executive's stomach acidity was greatest during the rest period.

Brady concluded that it was stress, not the shocks, that caused the ulcers.

Other evidence suggests that people low down on the occupational ladder (that is, those who *lack* control) are most susceptible.

ESSENTIAL STUDY 3.4

### Marmot *et al.*'s (1997) Stressed Civil Servants (SCS) study

● ● ● ● ● ● ● ● ● ● ● ● ● ● ● ● ● ● ● ● ● ● ● ● ● ● ● ● ● ● ● ● ● ● ● ● ● ● ● ● ● ● ● ● ● ● ● ● ● ● ● ● ● ● ● ● ● ● ● ● ● ● ● ● ● ●

### Aims (AO1)

This was a follow-up to an earlier study of British civil servants (Marmot & Theorell, 1988: Whitehall I study). This clearly showed an inverse relationship between mortality from coronary heart disease (CHD) and grade of employment; that is, the lower the grade of employment, the more likely civil servants were to die from CHD. About 25% of this relationship could be explained by social differences in smoking, plasma cholesterol, blood pressure, obesity and physical activity. The Whitehall II study involved a new cohort (generation) of male and female civil servants, and was conducted to test the hypothesis that low control in one's job makes an important contribution to the risk of developing CHD, over and above these well-established risk factors.

**Procedures** (AO1)

All male and female civil servants aged 35–55 in 20 London-based Civil Service departments were sent an introductory letter and screening questionnaire and offered a screening examination for cardiovascular disease (1985–1988: phase 1). This represented a baseline. There was a 73% response rate and over 10,000 people were examined (almost 7000 men and over 3000 women).

They were approached again during 1989–1990 (sent a postal questionnaire: phase 2) and then again in 1991–1993 (another postal questionnaire and a screening examination: phase 3). The participation rates were 79% and 83% for phases 2 and 3 respectively. 72% participated at all three phases (over 7000 people). The average length of follow-up was 5.3 years (range of 3.7–7.6).

*Employment grades* were grouped in three categories: administrators (Unified Grade 1–7), executive officers, and clerical/office support staff. *Job control* was measured by a self-completed questionnaire at phase 1, which asked about decision authority and skill discretion. These were combined to give an index of decision latitude or control.

*CHD* was measured as (i) doctor-diagnosed ischaemia (diagnosed or suspected heart attack or angina pectoris), (ii) angina pectoris identified on the basis of a questionnaire, and (iii) severe chest pain that lasted 30 minutes or more.

**Findings** (AO1)

Compared with men in the highest grade (administrators), those in the lowest grade (clerical/office support staff) had an age-adjusted odds ratio of developing any new CHD of 1.50. In other words, after taking age into account, men in the lowest grades were *three times* more likely to develop CHD compared with those in the highest grade. The largest difference (odds ratio of 2.27) was for doctor-diagnosed ischaemia.

For women in the lowest grade, the odds ratio was 1.47 for any measure of CHD.

**Conclusions** (AO1)

As predicted, for both men and women, low control at work represented the largest contributor to the development of CHD compared with established risk factors (smoking etc.). The latter seem to account for less than half the overall risk difference between the different grades (confirming the results of Whitehall I). Although measures of social support and social networks (outside work) show less favourable patterns for those in lower grades, low control is still the greatest single risk factor. Low control is related to employment grade and appears to account for much of the grade difference in frequency of CHD in both sexes.

**Criticisms** (AO1/AO2)

✓ **Theoretical importance.** The study shows that having *too little stress* can damage your health. The commonsense view would be that it's *too much stress* that is (potentially) harmful (see below). So, the SCS study provides evidence for an important *counter-intuitive* insight into a major source of stress.

✓ **Large, well-controlled study.** An unusually large sample of both men and women was studied over a period of years (a *prospective* study). The crucial measure was the number of people at different grades who developed CHD for the first time during the course of the study (as determined at phase 1: the baseline). Because the same people were being compared with themselves (it was a *longitudinal* study), we can be reasonably sure that individual differences (such as personality, intelligence, ethnic background) didn't affect the outcome. It was employment grade that represented the crucial independent variable.

✓ **Very high response rate.** The original response rate (in phase 1) of 73% is extremely high for any kind of postal questionnaire, and the participation rates at phases 2 and 3 (79% and 83% respectively) are even higher.

✗ **Reliability/validity of CHD measures.** As Marmot *et al.* themselves recognise, two of the three measures of CHD were based either on self-reported symptoms or a questionnaire. These aren't as reliable or valid as doctor diagnosis based on a physical examination. Also, angina diagnosed by questionnaire may be a less reliable indicator of CHD in women compared with men.

✗•✔ **How typical are British civil servants?** Because we're interested in the effects of low job control in general, we'd want to apply these findings to other occupational groups. But this (albeit very large) sample of British civil servants may not be typical of either non-British civil servants or other groups of British (and non-British) workers. It's possible that 'decision latitude or control' is more relevant as a risk factor in the civil service compared with alternative occupations, where other aspects of the work itself and the work situation may have a greater influence on CHD. However, Marmot *et al.* cite a study of men in the Czech Republic which used the job control questionnaire used in Whitehall II. Low control was related to acute myocardial infarction (heart attack) in middle age, and the combination of low control and coronary risk factors accounted for the higher risk of heart attacks in men with lower education.

Brady's executive monkey experiment (EME), on the other hand, suggests that having *too much* stress damage your health (e.g. peptic ulcers). In practice, this may involve:

- having to be constantly 'in charge' and making important decisions
- being mainly or exclusively responsible for a section or department.

Weiss's (1972) replication of Brady's EME (using rats) suggests that control is harmful if it involves:

- having to be constantly vigilant.

## OTHER SOURCES OF WORKPLACE STRESS

- **Work overload/underload** can be quantitative or qualitative (see Table 3.3 below).
- **Role ambiguity** refers to an employee's confusion about his/her role in an organisation ("what exactly is my job?"). This is associated with frustration and anxiety.
- **Role conflict** occurs when an employee is asked to perform two incompatible roles or tasks. For example, s/he may have two bosses, who both want something done *now*. This is associated with cardiovascular disorders and peptic ulcers.

| Quantitative overload | Qualitative overload |
|---|---|
| Too much to do; having to be excessively quick or productive. | The work is too difficult or demands excessive attention. |
| Associated with anxiety and frustration. | Associated with anxiety and frustration. |
| **Quantitative underload** | **Qualitative underload** |
| Not having enough to do. | Under-using your skills and abilities. |
| Associated with boredom, frustration, low job satisfaction and lack of commitment. | Associated with boredom, frustration, low job satisfaction and lack of commitment. |

Table 3.3 Examples of quantitative and qualitative work overload and underload.

- **Job insecurity/redundancy** are both associated with anxiety.
- **Lack of career structure** (poor promotion opportunities) is associated with poor physical health.
- **Poor interpersonal relations/support** is associated with anxiety and low job satisfaction.
- **Bullying** and **violence** at work are associated with absenteeism and poor mental health.

## Modifying the effects of stressors: Individual differences

When discussing Friedman & Rosenman's (1974) STAB earlier in the chapter (see Essential Study 3.1, pages 54–55), several important points emerged:

- Stressors don't exist 'objectively'. Something only qualifies as a stressor if an individual perceives it as a stressor.
- So we must take psychological (and other non-physiological) factors into account if we're to understand properly what stressors are and how they affect people. (One criticism of Selye's GAS is that he focused exclusively on physiological factors: see page 53).
- One major kind of psychological factor is personality, or characteristic patterns of behaviour.
- TAB describes a typical way of reacting to life in general and work-related situations in particular. According to Friedman and Rosenman, people who display TAB have a greater chance of developing CHD than other 'types'.

But personality is only *one* way in which people differ. Other individual differences include gender and culture.

### PERSONALITY

- Recent research has focused on *specific Type A characteristics*. In particular, *hostility* seems to be the best single predictor of CHD. It's a better predictor than TAB as a whole. But this doesn't mean that hostility *causes* CHD (just as we can't claim that TAB as a whole does).
- *Type C personalities* are cancer-prone (Temoshok, 1987). They have difficulty expressing emotion, and tend to suppress or inhibit emotions (especially negative ones, such as anger). It seems likely that these personality characteristics influence the progression of cancer and patients' survival time (Weinman, 1995).
- Women diagnosed with breast cancer showed significantly more emotional suppression than those with non-life-threatening breast disease (Greer & Morris, 1975).

### EXAM tips BOX

**Consider psychological research into the effects of workplace stressors. (18 marks)**

- You could structure your answer in terms of three paragraphs, all about 100–130 words long.

- In the first paragraph you could give some examples of workplace stressors, and briefly **describe** evidence relating to the effects of workplace stressors. (AO1, worth 6 marks).

- A word of advice: **although we normally associate work with human beings, any studies involving non-human animals could be included, provided they're relevant**.

- In the second and third paragraphs you could consider what can be learned from studies of workplace stressors regarding (i) what it is about certain occupations that make them inherently more stressful; (ii) how different studies have defined and measured **control**; and (iii) why both too much and too little stress can be harmful. (AO2, worth 12 marks).

- *Remember, merely describing research findings will only count as AO1. You must analyse and evaluate (AO2) the research findings in order to answer the question*.

Try to write a suitable answer in about 300–350 words.

As with all questions, there's no single correct way of answering it. The above are just pointers. There's a sample answer at the end of the book. Try not to look at it until you've had a go at doing it yourself.

### Culture

- Western culture seems to encourage and value many of the components of TAB. For example, competitiveness and striving for achievement are common goals in capitalist societies. This is much less true of non-Western, more traditional societies (Penny, 1996).

- The SRRS has been criticised for not taking account of cultural and ethnic differences. What count as (potentially) stressful life changes differ between cultures. Even where a life event is common to all cultures (such as marriage), its meaning differs. Clearly, many of the 43 life events on the SRRS don't apply at all in many cultures. (Try to identify those life events which clearly reflect the American society of the mid-1960s in which the scale was devised.)
- Both the physical and mental health of African Americans is worse than that of whites. African Americans are especially likely to have AIDS and hypertension. This is partly caused by the direct negative effects of poverty, such as poor diet, low levels of education and poor medical care. But there are also many psychological and social stressors involved. Blacks in North America and Europe face a unique kind of stress, namely *racial discrimination* (Cooper *et al.*, 1999).

## Gender

- From a purely biological perspective, females are the stronger sex. For example, more male foetuses are spontaneously aborted, stillborn or die of birth trauma.
- This *biological vulnerability* of males persists throughout life. For example, women's average life expectancy exceeds men's by 7–8 years. Males are also more susceptible to various diseases, including convulsions, viral infections, ulcers, CHD and some kinds of cancer.
- The smaller male Y chromosome seems to account for much of this vulnerability. (Males have one X and one Y, while females have two Xs.)
- But women have higher *morbidity rates*, that is, they're more likely to suffer generalised poor health and specific diseases. For example, women have higher rates of diabetes, gastrointestinal problems and rheumatoid arthritis. They visit their GPs more often, and use more prescribed drugs.
- There's some evidence that females produce less adrenaline in response to stressors compared with males (Frankenhauser, 1983). Over the course of a lifetime, this may prove to be a protective factor.
- Women are less likely than men to display TAB. They're also less hostile than men. TAB might reflect the male gender role. This could help explain why men are more vulnerable to cardiovascular disorders.
- But the gap between the sexes for deaths from cardiovascular disorders has closed over the last 30 years or so. This could be due to *lifestyle changes*, with women smoking and drinking more than they used to (Davison & Neale, 2001).

## EXAM tips BOX

### To what extent have the effects of stressors been shown to be modified by personality? (18 marks)

- You could structure your answer in terms of three paragraphs, all about 100–130 words long.

- In the first paragraph you could briefly say what's meant by personality, then go on to **describe** briefly some relevant research into personality's influence on the effects of stress. (AO1, worth 6 marks).

- In the second and third paragraphs you should **analyse and evaluate** (some of) the research you described in the first paragraph. Here you're considering how research both supports and challenges the view that personality can modify the effects of stressors. Two important questions to bear in mind are: (i) are there any interactions between personality and other variables, such as gender? (ii) **how** is personality meant to modify the effects of stressors? (AO2, worth 12 marks).

- *Remember, merely describing research will only count as AO1. You must analyse and evaluate in order to answer the question*.

Try to write a suitable answer in about 300–350 words.

As with all questions, there's no single correct way of answering it. The above are just pointers. There's a sample answer at the end of the book. Try not to look at it until you've had a go at doing it yourself. Note: *A similar question could be asked about the modifying effects of culture and/or gender*.

# Critical issue: stress management

## Methods of managing the effects of stress

### PHYSIOLOGICAL APPROACHES

#### Psychotherapeutic drugs

- Psychotherapeutic drugs act directly on the ANS. *Anxiolytic* (anxiety-reducing) drugs are commonly used in cases of chronic stress. The *benzodiazepine* group of anxiolytics include *chlordiazepoxide* (*Librium*) and *diazepam* (*Valium*®).
- Anxiolytic drugs usually succeed in reducing the physiological effects of stress. But *side-effects* may include drowsiness and lethargy. People may also become *physically dependent* on them. If the drug is stopped, the person may experience insomnia, tremors and convulsions. These are symptoms of *withdrawal* (or *abstinence syndrome*).
- Anxiolytics are also associated with *tolerance*. That is, an increasing amount of the drug is needed to produce the same, original effect.
- Physical dependence and tolerance together constitute *drug addiction*.

#### Biofeedback

- Patients are given information (via monitors or buzzers) about BP, heart rate, muscle tension or other *autonomic functions*. These are automatically regulated by the ANS, and so we're usually unaware of them and unable to control them. But the feedback provided by the monitor or buzzer allows the patient to bring them under voluntary control. For example, a line on a TV monitor swings to the left or right depending on changes in heart rate. The person is taught to use meditation or muscle relaxation in order to control the movement of the line.
- College students suffering from muscle contraction headaches were given seven 50-minute sessions, twice weekly. They were given feedback about muscle tension (*electromyograph* (EMG) feedback). They also had to practise their newly learned skills at home when free of headaches, and at the first sign of one. A *waiting-list control group* received treatment only when the study was over. In the *placebo condition*, participants engaged in 'pseudomeditation'. Compared with both these groups, the EMG biofeedback produced significant reductions in EMG and tension headaches (in Bradley, 1995).

Biofeedback

- Biofeedback requires the use of specialised equipment. This is clearly a disadvantage compared with alternative techniques (such as *progressive muscle relaxation*), which don't. Other techniques may also be just as effective in stress reduction.
- It's unclear exactly how biofeedback works.
- Regular practice is needed if the person is to benefit, especially in the longer term.
- It may not be biofeedback itself which helps in stress reduction. Other factors, such as the person's determination to beat stress, may be crucial.
- Biofeedback is designed to treat the *symptoms* of stress, *not* to tackle the stressor itself.

### PSYCHOLOGICAL APPROACHES

#### Stress inoculation

- Stress inoculation training (SIT) is a form of cognitive restructuring. This refers to various methods of changing the way people *think* about themselves and their lives. The aim is to change their emotional responses and their behaviour.

- SIT (Meichenbaum, 1976) is an attempt to reduce stress through changing cognitions. It assumes that people sometimes find things stressful because they think about them in *catastrophising ways*. This is another (extreme) example of how stressors aren't stressful in themselves. It's how people interpret or construe events or situations that makes them stressful.
- SIT comprises three stages.

## Box 3.2  The three stages of SIT

**Stage 1: Cognitive preparation (or conceptualization)**

The therapist explores with the person how s/he thinks about and deals with stressful situations. They also discuss how successful these strategies have been. A common response to stressful situations is to make negative self-statements, such as "I can't handle this". This is a *self-defeating internal dialogue*, which makes a stressful situation even more stressful.

**Stage 2: Skill acquisition and rehearsal**

The therapist helps the person to use *preparation statements* (e.g. "Maybe what you think is anxiety is eagerness to confront it"). These are positive, coping statements that are incompatible with the negative self-statements. The person practises these preparation statements.

**Stage 3: Application and follow-through**

The therapist guides the person through more and more threatening situations. These are actual stress-producing situations (not role plays). Once the person can cope with a relatively non-threatening situation, they're presented with a more threatening one.

- Meichenbaum (1997) believes that the 'power-of-positive-thinking' approach advocated by SIT can successfully change people's behaviour. It's proved particularly successful in reducing exam-nerves and the anxiety associated with severe pain.

### Increasing hardiness

- Hardiness is really a feature of personality. That is, some people are hardy and others aren't. So hardiness can help explain individual differences in the ability to resist stress.
- According to Kobasa (1979, 1982), 'hardy' and 'non-hardy' individuals differ in three main ways:

## Box 3.3  The three Cs of hardiness

Hardy people:
- are highly committed. They're deeply involved in whatever they do, and approach life with a sense of curiosity and meaningfulness.
- view change as a challenge. They regard change (rather than stability) as normal. Change is an opportunity for personal growth and development, rather than a threat to security.
- have a strong sense of being in control. In Rotter's (1966) terms, they have a *high internal locus of control*.

- Presumably stress could be reduced if hardiness could be increased. So can a person learn to become hardier?

## Box 3.4 Three ways of increasing hardiness

- teaching people to identify the physical signs of stress (e.g. tenseness). We can't deal with a stressor unless we first identify it. Kobasa called this focusing. But identifying a stressor doesn't by itself guarantee that we'll deal with it in an appropriate or beneficial way.
- reconstructing stressful situations is an attempt to make a more realistic assessment of different stressors. This involves considering how a past stressful experience could have been dealt with more or less effectively.
- compensation through self-improvement is related to Kobasa's claim that what we believe about our abilities to bring about change has important effects on our capacity to withstand stress. When we can't avoid a stressor's effects, or deal with it in some other way, we should take on some other challenge which we *can* meet. In this way, we experience the *positive* aspects of coping with a stressor. This allows us to 'bounce back' more easily after things have gone wrong. As a result, we'll experience stressors as less stressful.

## Stress management

The term *stress management* (SM) has two main meanings:

- In a *formal* sense, SM refers to a range of techniques (both physiological and psychological) used deliberately, by professionals, to help people reduce their stress levels. These can be used singly or in combination. Major examples include *anxiolytic drugs*, *biofeedback*, *cognitive restructuring* (such as Meichenbaum's SIT*)*, and Kobasa's attempts to increase hardiness. Others include progressive muscle relaxation, meditation and hypnosis (all used to induce a state of relaxation). (See page 67.)
- In an *informal* sense, SM refers to what we all do quite spontaneously on a day-to-day basis. In this sense, we all manage our stress, more or less effectively. A major way in which we achieve this is through the use of coping strategies/mechanisms.
- These are conscious attempts to adapt to stress in a positive and constructive way. They involve cognitive and behavioural efforts to meet those external and/or internal demands which stretch our capacities and resources.
- Cohen & Lazarus (1979) classified all the coping strategies we might use into five general categories.

## Box 3.5 Cohen & Lazarus's (1979) five Categories Of Coping (COC)

- direct action response: we try to change or manipulate our relationship to the stressful situation. For example, we try to escape from it or remove it
- information seeking: we try to understand the situation better, and to predict future events associated with the stressor
- inhibition of action: we do nothing. This may be the best course of action if the stressor looks like being temporary
- intrapsychic (palliative) coping: we reassess the situation (for example, through the use of defence mechanisms) or change the 'internal environment' (through drugs, alcohol or relaxation)
- turning to others: for help and emotional support.

These categories overlap with the distinction between *problem-focused* and *emotion-focused* coping.

## Box 3.6 Lazarus & Folkman's (1984) Problem-Focused Coping (PFC) and Emotion-Focused Coping (EFC)

- problem-focused coping: taking direct action in order to solve a problem, or seeking information that's relevant to a solution
- emotion-focused coping: trying to reduce the negative emotions that are part of the experience of stress. Effective coping depends on the situation. Sometimes using *both* kinds may offer the 'best solution'.

## EXAM tips BOX

**Give a brief account of psychological methods of stress management and consider their strengths *and* limitations. (18 marks)**

- You could structure your answer in terms of three paragraphs, all about 100–130 words long.

- In the first paragraph you could briefly **describe** psychological methods of stress management. It would probably be a good idea to give a brief definition of 'stress management' and to distinguish between psychological and physiological methods. This relates to the distinction between formal and informal stress management. (AO1, worth 6 marks).

- A word of warning: *because the question says 'methods of stress management', you must describe at least two methods. As a general rule, the more methods you describe, the less detailed they need to be. The fewer you describe, the more detailed they should be.*

- In the second paragraph you could choose **one** psychological method, and look at its (potential) advantages and disadvantages/strengths and weaknesses.

- In the third paragraph you could repeat the exercise for another method.

- One way of evaluating a particular method is to compare and contrast it with one or other methods. So, for example, you could consider the strengths and limitations of coping mechanisms and stress inoculation, and each of these could be contrasted with drugs and/or biofeedback. You could also consider the strengths and limitations of psychological and physiological methods *in general*. (AO2, worth 12 marks).

Try to write a suitable answer in about 300–350 words. As with all questions, there's no single correct way of answering it. The above are just pointers. There's a sample answer at the end of the book. Try not to look at it until you've had a go at doing it yourself.

## Self-assessment questions

These are some example Part a and Part b questions (worth 40% of your exam). Part c questions (worth 60%) have been dealt with throughout the chapter in the Exam tips boxes and in the sample answers at the end of the book.

**1 a.** What is meant by the terms 'stress', 'stress management' and the 'immune system'? (2 + 2 + 2 marks)

  **b.** Outline conclusions from research into the role of personality in modifying the effects of stressors. (6 marks)

**2 a.** Describe *two* methods of managing the negative effects of stress. (3 + 3 marks)

  **b.** Outline findings from research into life changes as a source of stress. (6 marks)

**3 a.** Outline the main features of the General Adaptation Syndrome (Selye). (6 marks)

  **b.** Explain what is meant by physiological and psychological approaches to stress management and give *one* difference between them. (2 + 2 + 2 marks)

**4 a.** Describe the procedures and findings of *one* study of stress as a bodily response. (3 + 3 marks)

  **b.** Outline the findings of *one* study of the sources of stress and give *one* criticism of this study. (3 + 3 marks)

**5 a.** Describe *one* account of the body's response to stressors. (6 marks)

  **b.** Outline *two* factors that can modify the effects of stressors. (3 + 3 marks)

| ESSENTIAL STUDY SUMMARY | | | |
|---|---|---|---|
| **Topic** | **Research study** | **Researcher date** | **Pages** |
| Stress as a bodily response | Study of Type A Behaviour (STAB) | Friedman & Rosenman (1974) | 54–55 |
| | Immunosuppression in Medical Students (SMS) | Kiecolt-Glaser *et al.* (1984) | 57–58 |
| Sources of stress | Social Readjustment | Holmes & Rahe (1967) | 59–60 |
| | Stressed Civil Servants (SCS) Rating Scale (SRRS) | Marmot *et al.* (1997) | 62–63 |

# CHAPTER SUMMARY: revision schema

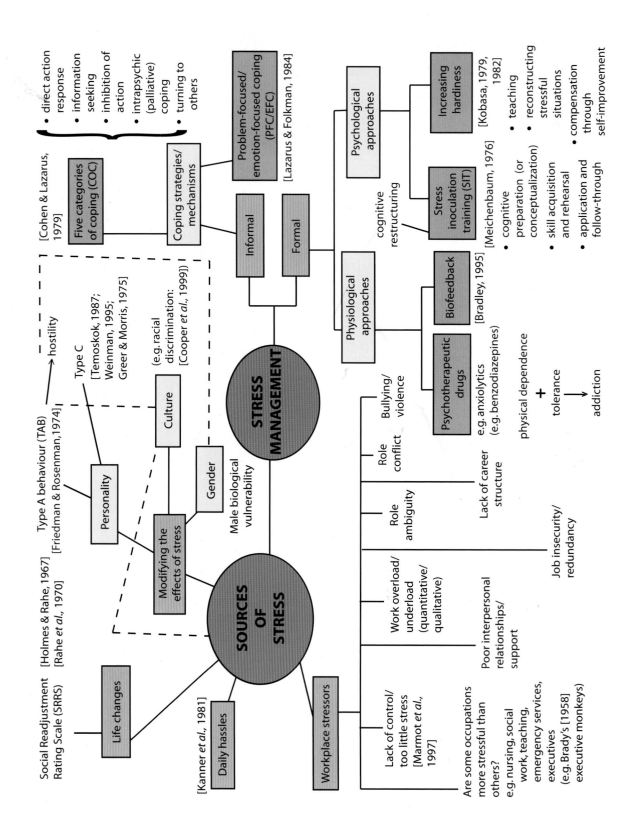

# AS Module 2:

# Abnormality

## What's covered in this chapter?

### You need to know about:

Defining psychological abnormality
- 'Statistical infrequency' definition and limitations (e.g. cultural relativism)
- 'Deviation from social norms' definition and limitations (e.g. cultural relativism)
- 'Failure to function adequately' definition and limitations (e.g. cultural relativism)
- 'Deviation from ideal mental health' definition and limitations (e.g. cultural relativism)

Biological and psychological models of abnormality
- Assumptions of biological (medical) model in terms of causes of abnormality
- Assumptions of psychodynamic model in terms of causes of abnormality
- Assumptions of behavioural model in terms of causes of abnormality
- Assumptions of cognitive model in terms of causes of abnormality

Critical issue: Eating disorders – anorexia nervosa (AN) and bulimia nervosa (BN)
- Clinical characteristics of AN and BN
- Biological models of eating disorders including relevant research studies
- Psychological models of eating disorders including relevant research studies

## Defining psychological abnormality

Abnormality is a difficult term to define, because abnormal behaviour can take many different forms and involve different features. There's no single feature that distinguishes between abnormal and normal behaviour. Despite this, attempts have been made to define abnormality.

### 'Statistical infrequency' definition

By definition, abnormality means *'deviating from the norm or average'*. Statistically infrequent behaviour is regarded as abnormal, whereas frequent behaviour is normal. Individual characteristics can be measured (e.g. mood, intelligence) and the distribution

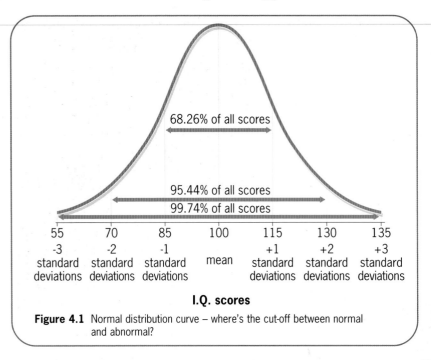

68.26% of all scores

95.44% of all scores

99.74% of all scores

| 55 | 70 | 85 | 100 | 115 | 130 | 135 |
| -3 | -2 | -1 | | +1 | +2 | +3 |
| standard deviations | standard deviations | standard deviations | mean | standard deviations | standard deviations | standard deviations |

**I.Q. scores**

**Figure 4.1** Normal distribution curve – where's the cut-off between normal and abnormal?

of these characteristics within the population can be graphed. The normal distribution curve shows the majority of people as being in the middle. These people are defined as 'normal'. Relatively few people fall at either end. These people are 'abnormal' (see normal distribution, Figure 4.1).

## LIMITATIONS

• **Fails to take account of desirable behaviour:** The term 'abnormal' is usually used in a negative sense. However, being 'abnormal' according to a statistical definition would include very gifted people (e.g. Mozart, Beckham). Such people wouldn't be classified as abnormal or as having a psychological disorder. Indeed, these people are usually respected and admired.

• **Abnormality is statistically common:** Up to 50% of the American population have a mental disorder at some time during their life (depression, anxiety and/or phobias are most common). These behaviours are therefore statistically frequent, but undesirable.

• **Not applicable to mental disorders:** The definition *can* be applied to abnormality, but not to mental disorders. Psychiatrists diagnose on the basis of symptoms, *not* the prevalence of the illness in society.

• **Gender and mental illness:** Men are less likely to consult their doctor about mental problems than females. Thus, women may be over-represented in mental illness statistics compared to men. This statistical difference doesn't accurately portray prevalence rates, merely reported rates.

• **Difficult to measure all behaviours:** Some behaviours (e.g. anxiety or mood disorders) aren't easily measured, nor do they conform to a normal distribution.

• **The 'cut-off' point?** How far from the norm (2 or perhaps 3 standard deviations?) do you have to be to be classified as abnormal? The setting of a 'cut-off' point is arbitrary. Indeed, different IQ tests have different standard deviations.

## Cultural relativism

• **Under-reporting of mental illness:** Depression is rarely reported in Asian cultures, and mental illness is rarely diagnosed in China (Rack, 1982). These contrast a lot with the American figures reported above. There are different attitudes towards reporting and diagnosing various conditions within these cultures. The 'statistically infrequent' definition cannot account for such cultural differences.

• **No universal statistical measures of behaviour:** Statistical standards are set within specific populations or cultures. These may not be appropriate for different populations or cultures. For example, Lee (1969) found that many Zulu women report screaming to themselves for days or weeks as a response to unhappiness. Such behaviours would be statistically infrequent and abnormal in our society, but entirely appropriate for Zulu women.

## 'Deviation from social norms' definition

Society sets norms or unwritten rules for acceptable behaviour. Behaviour that deviates from these norms is considered abnormal. Abnormal behaviour is therefore whatever violates social norms. This approach takes into account the *desirability of behaviour*, as social norms identify those behaviours that are desirable for both the individual and society.

## LIMITATIONS

- **Subjective:** The norms defined by society are subjective. They're often based on the opinions of elites within society rather than the majority opinion.
- **Change over time:** The norms defined by society are often related to moral standards that vary over time as social attitudes change. For example, the wearing of trousers by women and views on homosexuality.
- **Human rights abuse:** The use of this definition has allowed serious abuse of human rights. According to Szasz (1962) the term 'mental illness' is a form of social control, a subjective concept that is used to label those who don't conform to the norms of society. Those seen as abnormal are labelled and discriminated against. For example, in the Soviet Union after WW II, political dissenters were frequently classified as mentally ill and sent to mental hospitals.

Oscar Wilde (1854–1900) the Irish writer, was imprisoned for homosexuality in 1895

- **Value of breaking social norms:** It can be beneficial to break social norms. Suffragette campaigners for women's votes broke many norms and this led to electoral reform. But deviating from social norms doesn't necessarily have any consequences. For example, naturists don't harm anyone but nevertheless do break social norms.
- **'Conforming neurotics':** These are people who conform strictly to social norms, and this is their problem. They've such a fear of rejection that they adhere to all of society's norms. Such cases aren't included within this definition.

## Cultural relativism

- **Cultural differences:** Norms vary across cultures. There's no universal agreement as to what's normal or abnormal behaviour.
- **Ethnocentric bias in diagnosis:** In the West, the social norms that are adopted reflect behaviours of the majority 'white' population. Deviation from these norms by ethnic groups means that ethnic minorities are more likely to be over-represented in the mental illness statistics. This is supported by Cochrane (1977). He found that African-Caribbean immigrants are far more likely to be diagnosed as schizophrenic than whites or Asians. Of course, this might reflect the true incidence of schizophrenia in these groups. However, the high schizophrenia rate for African-Caribbean immigrants is found *only* in the UK, not in other countries. It's suggested that this reflects a cultural bias (or blindness) in diagnosis amongst British psychiatrists.

### 'Failure to function adequately' definition

This means that a person is unable to live a normal life. Such people don't experience a 'normal' range of emotions or participate in a 'normal' range of behaviours. People's behaviour is considered abnormal if it causes great distress and torment in them leading to dysfunction. That is, their behaviour disrupts their ability to work and/or conduct satisfying relationships with people. They cannot cope with day-to-day life.

Rosenhan & Seligman (1989) suggested that the concept of dysfunction includes:

- **Personal distress:** this is a key feature of abnormality. This would include depression and anxiety disorders.
- **Maladaptive behaviour:** behaviour that stops individuals from attaining satisfactory goals, both socially and occupationally.
- **Unpredictability:** behaviour that wouldn't be expected given the particular circumstances

Dr Harold Shipman: a serial killer while working as a GP

(e.g. trying to commit suicide having failed a driving test).

- **Irrationality:** behaviour that cannot be explained in a rational way.
- **Observer discomfort:** behaviour that causes distress or discomfort to others.
- **Violation of moral and ideal standards:** behaviour that doesn't fit in with society's standards.

The more of these indicators that are present, the more abnormal an individual is considered to be.

This approach does recognise the *subjective experience* of the individual.

### LIMITATIONS

- **Abnormality isn't always accompanied by dysfunction:** People with anti-social personality disorders (psychopaths) have been known to commit murders and still continue to lead a 'normal' life (e.g. Jeffrey Dahmer, Harold Shipman). Such people must be classified as abnormal in the absence of *'a failure to function adequately'*. In addition, some schizophrenics aren't aware or deny that they have a problem.
- **Subjective nature of Rosenhan and Seligman's components:** There are problems in defining some of Rosenhan and Seligman's components. For example, how is personal distress measured? People are likely to differ in their subjective experience. Similarly, there are people who experience mania (unbounded joy). Their behaviour doesn't appear to cause them distress, but would count as evidence for a psychological disorder. It would also appear to be abnormal *not* to suffer personal distress at various points during one's life, say when a close relative dies.

## Cultural relativism

**Explains higher incidence of mental illness in sub-cultures:** The 'failure to function adequately' definition might explain why certain groups or sub-groups in the population are over-represented in the mental illness statistics (see Cochrane, 1977 above). This could be due to the extra stress and pressures associated with moving to a different culture. Alternatively, it could be due to the amount of racism or prejudice experienced by such minority groups (this might include bias in psychiatric diagnosis).

## 'Deviation from ideal mental health' definition

This approach concentrates on defining the 'normal' characteristics people should possess. Abnormality is seen as a deviation from these ideals of mental health. Jahoda (1958) identified six criteria relating to ideal mental health. These factors are required for 'optimal living' (*'living life to the full'*):

- **Positive attitude towards oneself:** This is shown by having a fairly high self-regard (self-esteem).
- **Potential for growth and development:** This is shown by self-actualisation. Maslow (1968) defines this as *'becoming everything that one is capable of becoming'*. The more things you do, the healthier you are (psychologically).
- **Autonomy:** Being able to make decisions on our own and not being dependent on other people.
- **Resistance to stress:** Being able to cope with anxiety-provoking situations.
- **Accurate perception of reality:** Having an objective and realistic view of the world. For example, not being too pessimistic or optimistic.
- **Environmental mastery:** Being able to meet the demands of any situation, and being flexible enough to adapt to changing life circumstances.

The further people are from these ideals, the more abnormal they are.

## LIMITATIONS

- **Over-demanding criteria:** Most people don't meet all these ideals. For example, self-actualisation is achieved by very few people. Therefore, according to this definition, most people could be classified as abnormal. If most people are abnormal, then according to the statistical definition, abnormality would actually become the norm! In addition, Harold Shipman might also have scored highly on these six criteria!

I THINK HE'S MAD—HE SAYS HE HEARS VOICES...

YES, BUT CAN WE RELY ON THAT—HE IS MAD AFTER ALL...

Diagnosing mental health relies on patient self-reports

- **Subjective criteria:** Many of the concepts aren't clearly defined. Measuring physical health is more of an objective science using well-established methods such as X-rays and blood tests. Diagnosing mental health is far more subjective, and relies to a large extent on patient self-reports. Some of these patients may actually be mentally ill, and so may not be particularly reliable!
- **Contextual effects:** As with some of the other definitions, mental health criteria can be affected by context. Stripping naked in your Psychology lesson may be a sign of mental illness (try it and see!) whereas remaining fully clothed on a nudist beach might appear strange.
- **Changes over time:** Mental health criteria also change over time. In thirteenth-century Europe, seeing visions was a sign of religious fervour now it would be seen as a sign of schizophrenia.

## Cultural relativism

- **Mental health criteria vary across cultures:** Many studies have found that 'being mad' can vary across cultures (Berry *et al.,* 1992). For example, *Koro* refers to an acute anxiety reaction whereby a man fears his penis is retracting into his abdomen and a woman that her breasts are retracting into her body. This disorder is reported in South East Asia and is an example of a **culture-bound syndrome**. It's assumed that the Western concept of mental disorder is culture-free, but this may not be the case.
- **Collectivist societies:** Collectivist societies that emphasise co-operation amongst their members would reject the importance of individual autonomy as a criterion for mental health. Nobles (1976) claimed that African people have a sense of 'we' instead of the 'me' view common in the West. Western cultures tend to be more concerned with individual attainment and goals.

## Conclusion

It's extremely difficult to produce a culture-free definition of abnormality. What constitutes abnormal behaviour differs between cultures. This suggests that the concept of abnormality is a social construction. It's difficult enough to define abnormality *within* a culture without trying to produce one to use *between* cultures. As a result, definitions of abnormality, diagnosis and classification of mental illness must be treated with caution.

## EXAM tips BOX

**Outline and evaluate different attempts to define abnormality. (18 marks)**

- In the first paragraph you should briefly **describe at least two** different definitions of abnormality. This would take about 100–130 words (AO1–6 marks).

- In the next few paragraphs you need to **analyse and evaluate** each of the definitions. For example, with the 'statistical infrequency' definition you could state that it doesn't distinguish between desirable and undesirable behaviour or that mental illness is actually fairly common. Evaluation of the 'deviation from social norms' definition could include the claim that it is subjective, norms change over time and that it can be socially desirable to break social norms. The 'failure to function properly' definition also suffers from the problem of subjectivity and the fact that some people with mental illness still appear to function normally. This would take 200–250 words (AO2 – 12 marks).

- You could include the extent to which the definitions of abnormality have taken into account cultural factors (see Exam tips box, page 84).

There's a sample answer at the end of the book. Try not to look at it until you've had a go at doing it yourself.

# Biological and psychological models of abnormality

## The biological (medical) model

### ASSUMPTIONS/CAUSES

This is the most widely used approach to the causes and treatment of mental illness in the West. It was developed by the medical profession, hence its name.

The medical model has a number of key assumptions:

- **Similar to a disease, a physical cause:** Abnormal behaviour may be compared with a disease. It's assumed that all mental illnesses have a physiological cause related to the physical structure and/or functioning of the brain. A distinction is made between 'organic' and 'functional' disorders. Organic disorders involve obvious physical brain damage and/or disease (say, a brain tumour), whereas functional disorders don't have an obvious physiological cause (e.g. depression).
- **Symptoms:** In medicine, physical illnesses have clear-cut symptoms. Doctors diagnose using well-established criteria. Psychiatrists also use diagnostic manuals for mental illness and compare symptoms with set classifications of illnesses. There are slight differences between ICD-10 (International Classification of Diseases 10th ed, 1992) and DSM-IV (Diagnostic Statistical Manual 4th ed, 1994). Brain scans can be used to help with the diagnosis, particularly with organic disorders.
- **Genetic inheritance:** It's assumed that genes have a major effect on the likelihood of developing a mental illness. People have a genetic predisposition to certain psychological disorders. Twin and family resemblance studies have shown that some mental illnesses 'run in the family'. Kendler *et al.* (1985) found that relatives of schizophrenics were 18 times more likely to develop the illness than a matched control group.
- **Bio-chemistry:** Chemical imbalances in the brain may be involved in certain mental illnesses. Neurotransmitters (chemicals in the brain) play an important part in behaviour, and an excess of dopamine has been detected in the brains of schizophrenics. However, such findings involve correlations and don't prove cause and effect. For example, it might be the schizophrenia itself that's causing the dopamine excess, rather than the other way round.
- **Infection:** This is a common cause of physical illness, but has also been found with some mental illnesses. Barr *et al.* (1990) found increased levels of schizophrenia amongst mothers who had flu whilst they were pregnant, suggesting a possible link with the disorder.

## Assumptions of the medical model treatment of abnormality

One of the key assumptions of the medical model is that treatment involves invasive, physical intervention. It's assumed that there's a physiological cause, and so a physiological treatment is used. There are three main somatic (soma = 'body' in Greek) therapies:

A patient undergoing ECT for depression

- **Psychotherapeutic drugs (chemotherapy):** By far the most widely used treatment for mental illness. Drugs have the benefit of having been tested (for safety and effectiveness) in scientific trials. In addition, they're relatively cheap and quick to administer. However, drugs may merely reduce the symptoms and not tackle the actual cause of the disorder. Drugs can also cause side-effects, and physiological and psychological dependence. For example, the anti-depressant Prozac®, although effective in 70% of cases, can cause insomnia and headaches.
- **ECT (electro-convulsive therapy):** Here an electric current is passed through the brain to cause a small seizure or convulsion. Although the original theoretical basis for this is discredited, it's believed that it helps reset brain neurotransmitter levels. It appears to help in 75% of cases of severe depression (Fink, 2002). However, there's no agreed way to assess this success. It's even been measured as the number of patients who don't subsequently commit suicide in a set period! In 2001, there were 13,000 treatments per week in England. In about 10% of cases it's administered involuntarily (Pippard, 1992). Other ethical issues concern ECT's disputed benefits and the procedure itself (sometimes called 'barbaric').
- **Psychosurgery:** This is primarily used for severe depression. It's extremely rare in Britain, with only 7 operations in 1999 and 2 operations in 2000. Typically, electrodes are inserted into the brain and heated to destroy the brain tissue. The theoretical basis for this is unclear but it's thought that other areas of the brain may take over the function of any destroyed tissue. There are ethical concerns with psychosurgery. Some people see it as a beneficial 'last resort' for seriously ill patients, with a 75% success rate (Cobb, 1993). Others see psychosurgery as 'partially killing' the person. Of 42 patients with data available, 34 showed some improvement. However, MIND are not happy with its continued use without proper and rigorous assessment (MIND, 2002).

## Evaluation of medical approach

**Humane approach:** The medical approach attaches no blame to the mentally ill individual. People with a mental illness are just unlucky to develop it, in the same way that someone might catch an illness such as measles. This is a humane approach since mental illness, in practice, often invokes fear and stigma.

**Effective treatments:** Carefully controlled studies demonstrate the effectiveness of drugs. Possible side-effects don't outweigh the benefits. The case is less clear-cut for ECT and psychosurgery. However, patients are often pleased to have tried these 'last-ditch' treatments even if they haven't been successful.

**Physiological evidence, well-established scientific principles:** The increased use of brain scans and postmortems adds to the growing body of physiological evidence supporting the medical approach.

**Reliability of diagnosis:** Two reliability measures can be used. Different psychiatrists can be given the same patients to diagnose (*inter-rater reliability*) and the same patients can be assessed at different times by the same psychiatrist (*test-retest reliability*). Both types of reliability have increased since the introduction of the newest classification systems (post-1980). Pre-1980 diagnosis was not so accurate (see Rosenhan study below).

> 'Being sane in insane places': Rosenhan (1973) sent participants to mental hospitals where they claimed to be hearing voices. They were admitted and then behaved entirely normally. Much of their subsequent behaviour was interpreted by staff as being indicative of mental illness. Some were detained for up to 50 days. In a follow-up study, Rosenhan told hospitals in a different area that he would replicate the study to see if they could detect the sane from the insane. 41 patients were turned away in the following six months, despite the fact that Rosenhan did not send any participants! Rosenhan concluded that psychiatric diagnosis was unreliable. However, since this study diagnostic procedures have been improved, and psychiatrists don't expect to be deliberately misled or lied to by patients.

✖•✔ **Validity of diagnosis:** This refers to whether the diagnosis is measuring what it's supposed to be measuring (i.e. is there an actual underlying illness called schizophrenia?). Research shows that diagnosis is valid for the general categories of mental disorder, but not for the sub-categories of disorders. However, the same could be said of physical illness diagnosis.

✔ **Animal research support:** Many experiments carried out on animals lend weight to the biological approach to abnormal behaviour.

✖ **Reductionist approach:** The medical approach reduces the diagnosis of mental illness to lists of physical symptoms. Greater emphasis should be placed on a patient's personal feelings and experiences.

✖ **Animal studies:** Ethical and methodological issues arise with animal experiments. Is it reasonable to exploit animals for the (possible) benefit of humans (so-called 'speciesism')? In addition, researchers cannot be certain that animals that display abnormal behaviours are experiencing a mental disorder in the same way that humans do.

✖ **Responsibility denied:** People aren't held responsible for their actions or their treatment. They become 'patients'. Responsibility for the therapy is 'passed over' to the 'great expert' (the psychiatrist). Therapy works best when people take more responsibility for their treatments and behaviour. (The same is true of physical illness!)

✖ **Relies on self-report, not objective tests:** Unlike doctors, psychiatrists have few objective tests for mental illnesses. Instead, they rely on patient self-reports. This has led to cases where people have successfully pretended to be mentally ill, which challenges the accuracy of mental illness diagnosis (see Rosenhan above).

✖ **Treats symptoms, not causes:** Physiological treatments alleviate the symptoms, but don't treat the root cause. Symptoms recur when physiological treatments stop. This leads many patients to be re-admitted to hospitals, the so-called 'revolving door' syndrome. However, if the main symptom of depression is the feeling of depression, and drugs stop this, then perhaps the medical approach has succeeded. Indeed, the original cause of the depression may not be worth pursuing, since the main problem (feeling of depression) no longer exists. The root cause may also be impossible to detect.

✖ **Cause and effect problem:** It's not clear whether some physiological abnormalities are the cause of the illness or one of its effects. For example, does excess dopamine in the brain cause schizophrenia, or is it merely the effect?

✖ **Culture-bound syndromes:** Not all mental illnesses are universal. Those which occur only in particular cultures are called 'culture-bound syndromes' (as explained above). Such syndromes aren't easily explained by the medical model.

✖ **The myth of mental illness:** Szasz (1962) was a leading member of the so-called anti-psychiatry movement. He believed that since the mind doesn't exist as a physical organ, it can't be diseased. Abnormal behaviours are thus viewed as 'problems in living'. Szasz believed that diagnosis of mental illness is used as a form of 'social control'. Laing (1959) also controversially viewed mental illness as a sane response to an insane world.

**✗ Labelling and stigma:** The medical approach tends to lead to labelling of patients. Labels are definitions which when applied to people identify what they are. Mental illness terms often identify the whole person ('schizophrenics' rather than a person with schizophrenia). This doesn't occur to the same extent with physical illnesses. Labelling may lead to a *self-fulfilling prophecy*, whereby a person identified as mentally ill *actually* becomes mentally ill. Once labelling has occurred, stigma can result. Stigma is a 'mark' that sets people apart on the basis of an undesirable characteristic. The mentally ill often suffer from such stigmas.

## Psychodynamic model

### ASSUMPTIONS/CAUSES

The psychodynamic approach explains the forces or dynamics that determine behaviour. The best known example of this was proposed by Sigmund Freud. Although subsequently developed by others, there are some commonly agreed key assumptions:

The conflict between the superego and the id

- **Mental illness is psychological in origin:** The psychodynamic approach suggests that abnormality occurs as a result of psychological, not physical, problems (in contrast to the medical approach).
- **The importance of the unconscious:** Although, by definition, the unconscious isn't accessible to the conscious mind, it plays a major role in determining behaviour. The term 'dynamic unconscious' is used to explain why people don't know the reasons for their behaviour. There's an assumption that abnormal behaviours occur due to unconscious problems or forces.
- **Three components to the personality: id, ego, superego:** Freud stated that there were three components to the personality or psyche. The *id* is present at birth. This represents a person's instinctual, basic drives related to sex and aggression. Later, people are socialised into the moral standards of their culture and develop a *superego*. This represents their conscience. These two parts of the personality are in conflict and therefore need to be managed by the third part of the personality, the *ego*. When this balance isn't achieved, abnormal behaviour may result. For example, anxiety disorders may occur from an over-developed superego (conscience). Since these processes occur at an unconscious level, people aren't aware of them.
- **Importance of childhood experiences:** Freud argued that childhood experiences play a crucial part in adult development. Particularly distressing events in childhood may also become part of the unconscious. Although unconscious, they may be expressed in later abnormal behaviours.
- **Psychosexual developmental stages:** Freud argued that children pass through a number of psychosexual stages. Conflicts that occur during these stages can affect later behaviour. The stages are:
  - **Oral stage (0–1 year):** The primary source of pleasure is the mouth and sucking.
  - **Anal stage (1–3 years):** The primary source of pleasure involves the membranes of the anal region.
  - **Phallic stage (3–6 years):** The primary source of pleasure comes from the genitals.
  - **Latency stage: (6–12 years):** The development of other activities means less concentration on sexual areas.
  - **Genital stage (puberty onwards):** The primary source of pleasure is through heterosexual relationships.
    Freud believed that people can become stuck or 'fixated' at any of these stages. This will also affect later behaviour. For example, someone who smokes is described as having an 'oral' personality,

## EXAM tips BOX

**Briefly describe and evaluate the biological (medical) approach to abnormality. (18 marks)**

* Again, the three-paragraph approach could be employed. You'll have to briefly **describe** the biological (medical) approach in the first paragraph. This could include details of the assumptions of, and treatments used within the approach (AO1–6 marks).

* In the second paragraph, you could **analyse and evaluate** material that **supports** the biological approach. These include the humane nature of the approach, supporting physiological evidence, and studies that demonstrate the effectiveness of biologically based treatments.

* In the final paragraph you could analyse and evaluate material that **criticises or rejects** the approach. The validity of diagnosis, the reductionist nature of the approach, the denial of responsibility, and the treatment of symptoms could be included (AO2 – 12 marks).

* Examiners will be expecting an answer about 300–350 words long.

There's a 'sample' answer at the end of the book. Try not to look at it until you've had a go at doing it yourself.

since they gain pleasure through the mouth. Someone who is excessively tidy and obsessive might be described as having an 'anal' personality.

* **Defence mechanisms:** Childhood conflicts cause anxiety, and the ego uses a number of defence mechanisms to keep these thoughts in the unconscious. *Repression* is the major defence mechanism, whereby traumatic events are forced into the unconscious (see page 17). Defence mechanisms help to reduce anxiety, but don't resolve deep psychological problems.

## Assumptions of the psychodynamic model treatment of abnormality

One of the key assumptions of the psychodynamic model is that the main therapeutic goal is to make the 'unconscious conscious', in order to reveal the true cause of any psychological problems.

Sometimes in psychodynamic therapy, silence speaks louder than words

* Patients are encouraged to develop 'insight' (enhanced self-knowledge and understanding) in order to deal with their problems.
* Patients try to regress back to their childhood in order to re-experience feelings and conflicts.
* Therapeutic techniques to help this include:
  – Dream interpretation: Freud believed that dreams represented the disguised fulfil-ment of suppressed wishes, and that the latent (or hidden) content of dreams helped to uncover the unconscious.
  – Free association: involves the patient talking freely without prompting or interruption. Hence this therapy is often called 'the talking cure'.
* The analyst also takes note of non-verbal (or para-linguistic) communication, such as hesitations,

slips of the tongue (Freudian slips) or even silence about a particular subject. All this information provides clues about what's happening in the unconscious.

- The analyst interprets what the patient says or does and makes use of symbolism (one thing representing another). For example, a dream about 'climbing the stairs' might be interpreted as symbolic of sexual intercourse.

Psychodynamic therapies remain controversial:

- They're expensive and are usually long-term. Indeed, patients can become dependent on their therapist.
- Its effectiveness is also questioned. Eysenck (1952) reviewed 7000 cases and claimed it doesn't work and can be detrimental to patients since it might 'reveal' disturbing repressed thoughts. Such thoughts can be viewed as possible 'side-effects' of psychodynamic therapy.

 ## Evaluation of psychodynamic approach

✓ **Psychological factors:** Freud was the first to stress the importance of psychological factors causing abnormal behaviour. He argued that psychological problems can result in physical symptoms – an accepted viewpoint today. However, physiological factors are largely ignored.

✗•✓ **Importance of childhood:** Most psychologists would accept that childhood is an important, influential factor in future adult development. Indeed, many people suffering from psychological problems can recount childhood difficulties. However, the original model over-emphasised childhood influences and ignored the everyday problems faced by the adult patients. Current psychodynamic therapy recognises this.

✓ **Importance of the unconscious:** Many people would agree that unconscious processes do have an effect on human behaviour.

✓ **Influential theory:** Freud remains the best known psychologist of all time and psychoanalysis the most influential theory. His ideas appear strange to some whilst others pay for therapy based on them. Freud's ideas have found expression in many other domains including art, film, literature and so on. An unimportant theory would have been dismissed years ago. In addition, Freudian terminology has been adopted into everyday language and conversation.

✗ **Problems validating the theory:** It's impossible to test some of the model scientifically. The subtlety and complexity of the theory mean it's not suited to empirical research. The strength of the evidence remains variable. Sometimes, interpretation plays a major part in the theory. For example, if a patient 'uncovers' painful childhood memories this can be taken as a cause of any later abnormal behaviour. If they don't uncover or recall anything, it can be claimed that they still happened but remain hidden in their unconscious. Both interpretations can be used to support the model!

✗ **Poor methodology:** The dominant use of case studies in psychodynamic therapy is unscientific. Evidence produced by therapists is subjective and biased. Indeed, Freud was accused by his own patients of exaggerating the effectiveness of his therapy (Woods, 1990). Freud's patients were mainly middle class, Viennese women. Whether findings from such a sample can be generalised into a universal theory is open to question.

✗ **Over-emphasis on sexual factors:** Freud believed that sexual factors were a major cause of abnormal behaviour. Nowadays, other factors such as social relationships are recognised as important. Indeed, it's argued that inadequate inter-personal relationships can also cause sexual problems. Freud's ideas on sexual repression may be less relevant in today's sexually permissive society.

✗ **Blames parents:** Since people cannot really influence their own personality, it's assumed that people aren't to blame for their illness. However, given the importance of childhood conflicts, parents might feel the blame for any subsequent abnormal behaviour in their children. The individual is seen as the result of their parenting. Child abuse cases are cited as evidence to support this, although so-called 'recovered memory syndrome' has been questioned (see page 18).

**Figure 4.2** The apparatus used by Pavlov in his experiments on conditioned reflexes

## Behavioural model

### ASSUMPTIONS/CAUSES

The behavioural model concentrates on observable behaviour, not on physical or psychological processes. It's associated with maladaptive behaviour, not mental illness.

• **All behaviour is learnt:** All behaviour (both normal and abnormal) is learnt through the processes of classical and operant conditioning.

*Classical conditioning* is 'learning through association'. It was first proposed by Ivan Pavlov who noticed that his laboratory dogs had learnt to salivate to the sound of the footsteps of the man who fed them. They'd learnt to associate the footsteps with food. Later, Pavlov classically conditioned the dogs to salivate to the sound of a bell that he rang before giving them their food (see Figure 4.2).

*Classical conditioning* can apply to abnormal behaviour. For example, a phobia may develop when children see the fear of their parents when confronted by a spider. They learn to associate the fear with the spider.

*Operant conditioning* is 'learning through the consequences of behaviour'. If a behaviour is rewarded (reinforced) then it will be maintained or increase. If it's punished, then it will cease. Skinner investigated operant conditioning using pigeons and rats in a laboratory.

Again, operant conditioning can apply to abnormal behaviour. For example, adolescents who are criticised or ridiculed (punished) for being fat may stop eating to reduce their weight and develop an eating disorder.

• **Abnormal behaviour can be unlearnt using the same learning (conditioning) principles:** The case study of Little Albert demonstrates how a phobia can be acquired through classical conditioning.

In an experiment that would today be regarded as unethical, Watson & Rayner (1920) classically conditioned a fear response in a young child called Albert. According to Jones (1925):

'Albert, eleven months of age, was an infant with a phlegmatic disposition, afraid of nothing "under the sun" except a loud noise made by striking a steel bar. This made him cry. By striking the bar at the same time that Albert touched a white rat, the fear was transferred to the white rat. After seven combined stimulations, rat and sound, Albert not only became greatly disturbed at the sight of the rat, but this fear had spread to include a white rabbit, cotton wool, a fur coat and the experimenter's [white] hair. It did not transfer to wooden blocks and other objects very dissimilar to the rat.'

A very rare photograph of John Watson and Rosalie Rayner during the conditioning of Little Albert.

Watson & Rayner (1920) proposed to rid Little Albert of his fears through counter-conditioning. They planned to do this by pairing a pleasurable stimulus or reward (e.g. a sweet) with the sight of the rat. Unfortunately, they didn't get the chance when Albert was withdrawn from the study. The ethics of this study left a lot to be desired! (Rolls, 2005)

## Assumptions of the behaviour model treatment of abnormality

One of the key assumptions of the behavioural model is that the aim of therapy is to change maladaptive behaviour by replacing it with appropriate learnt behaviour.

- According to behaviourist theory, abnormal behaviours can be objectively measured and therapies can be planned to modify them using conditioning principles. They fit into two types:
  - **behaviour therapy** based on classical conditioning principles
  - **behaviour modification** based on operant conditioning principles.
- *Systematic desensitisation* is an example of behaviour therapy. This might involve a phobic (person with a phobia) confronting a feared object (e.g. spider) in a relaxed situation and associating these calm feelings with the object.

Arachnophobia can be successfully treated using systematic desensitisation

- *Token economies* are examples of behaviour modification. This involves the reinforcement of appropriate behaviour through the use of tokens that can be exchanged for privileges. For example, anorexics who eat all their meals might be given tokens that can be exchanged for rewards, such as home visits away from the hospital.
- Behaviourists seek to treat the symptoms, not the causes of abnormal behaviour. They believe that the symptoms are the problem, and that searching for the causes is likely to be fruitless. After all, if you can alleviate the symptoms of depression, what does it matter what the underlying causes are? Critics claim that symptoms are merely the 'tip of the iceberg', underlying causes remain, and 'symptom substitution' will occur. That is, other abnormal symptoms will replace the symptoms which have been removed.

## EXAM tips BOX

**Give a brief account of the behavioural model of abnormality and consider its strengths and limitations. (18 marks)**

- Follow the answer structure suggested with the other approaches above.
- You'll have to **describe** briefly the behavioural approach in the first paragraph (AO1 – 6 marks).
- In the second paragraph you could **analyse and evaluate** the model by outlining the strengths of the behavioural approach. In the final paragraph you could **analyse and evaluate** by presenting material that shows limitations of the model (AO2 – 12 marks).

There's a sample answer at the end of the book. Try not to look at it until you've had a go at doing it yourself.

### Evaluation of behavioural approach

✓ **Experimentally tested:** The principles of learning have been, and continue to be, tested empirically in the laboratory. The concentration on observable behaviour means it can be objectively measured.

✓ **Present, not past:** The behavioural approach concentrates on the 'here and now' rather than delving into the past. This is advantageous since many people don't know the past causes for their abnormal behaviour and it's more important to sort out present symptoms. But it's also important to try to uncover the causes, otherwise the abnormal behaviour may reappear.

✓ **Effective treatments:** Behavioural treatments are effective for certain disorders, such as obsessive-compulsive disorders and phobias. They are less effective for more serious disorders, such as schizophrenia.

✓ **Accounts for cultural differences:** The behavioural model recognises the importance of the environment in shaping behaviour. Thus it does take into account cultural differences.

✗ **Simple, mechanistic model:** The behavioural approach suggests that humans are simple mechanisms at the mercy of stimulus-response behaviours. The approach ignores people's complex thought processes. This is a reductionist, dehumanising approach.

✗ **Animal studies:** The principles of learning have been tested mainly on animals and such findings may not be totally applicable to more complex human behaviour.

✗ **Ethical treatment?** Some behavioural treatments are used without the consent of patients. In addition, certain treatments use punishments to change behaviour, and these can cause pain or discomfort to patients. Behaviourists would agree that this is undesirable, but maintain that it is necessary. Behavioural techniques can be used as a form of 'social control' to manipulate people's behaviour.

# Cognitive model

## ASSUMPTIONS/CAUSES

Inevitably, the cognitive model concentrates on the individual's thought processes. The disturbed individual is affected by disturbed thoughts. This approach sees the individual as an active processor of information. It's the way individuals perceive, anticipate and evaluate events, rather than the events themselves, which have the greatest impact on behaviour. Psychologists most associated with this approach are Beck and Ellis.

- **Cognitions affect behaviour:** Behaviour is primarily affected by an individual's thoughts and cognitions. Healthy cognitions lead to normal behaviour, whereas faulty cognitions lead to abnormal behaviour. Beck (1967b) called these irrational thoughts 'cognitive errors'.
- **Cognitive errors:** Individuals try to make sense of their world through cognitive processes. *Automatic thoughts* are thoughts that occur without thinking. People with psychological problems tend to have more negative automatic thoughts. *Attributions* refer to people's attempts to make sense of and explain their own and others' behaviour. People with psychological problems may make more inaccurate attributions. For example, they may attribute a failed relationship to their own lack of social skill. In addition, people suffering from psychological problems may have inaccurate *expectations*. For example, they may *expect* their relationships to end in failure. Such expectations will make it more likely to happen in reality – *a self-fulfilling prophecy*. In effect, people with psychological problems may lack confidence in their own ability to achieve the goals they want to in life. These illogical thoughts may not reflect reality. Nevertheless, these negative thoughts will adversely affect their behaviour.
- **Cognitive processes can be faulty in many ways:** These include:
  - (a) *Over-generalisation*: a conclusion is reached on the basis of one event or incident. For example, missing a penalty at football means you're completely useless in life.
  - (b) *Magnification and minimisation*: This involves magnifying failures and minimising successes. The glass is half-empty rather than half-full.
- **Cognitions can be monitored and altered:** It's assumed that all biased cognitions can be replaced by more appropriate ones (see treatment below).
- **Cognitive change will lead to behaviour change:** It's assumed that changing faulty thinking will lead to a change in behaviour.

## Assumptions of the cognitive model treatment of abnormality

A key assumption is that cognitive therapy involves *cognitive restructuring*. This refers to techniques used to make a patient's irrational and negative thoughts more rational and positive. The therapist's aim is to challenge the patient's thinking and to show how irrational their thoughts are. Patients are taught to monitor negative automatic thoughts and examine the evidence that supports them. In this way, patients may learn to see why they hold distorted thoughts.

Our own interpretation of events can affect future outcomes

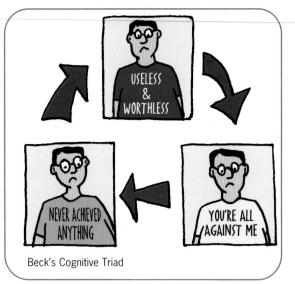

Beck's Cognitive Triad

- Cognitive therapy depends on an individual being able to talk about their thought processes lucidly. Hence, the method doesn't work for particularly severe mental disorders such as schizophrenia.
- Beck's cognitive therapy is often used for depression. Beck proposed the *cognitive triad*, where a patient has negative thoughts about themselves, about the world, and about the future (these form the triad). Therapy is a collaborative process between the patient and therapist. The first step involves identifying the problem and the desired goal. The next step involves challenging negative thoughts associated with the depression. The patient may be asked to undertake 'homework' between sessions to test these thoughts. For example, recording the number of times someone is rude to them. They may be pleasantly surprised that people aren't 'always nasty' to them as they thought. The last step involves the patient monitoring their own perceptions accurately.

## EXAM tips BOX

**Outline and evaluate the cognitive approach to abnormality. (18 marks)**

- Another straightforward question. Again, it's easiest to follow the answer structure suggested above.
- You'll have to **describe** briefly the cognitive approach in the first paragraph (AO1–6 marks).
- In the second paragraph you could **analyse and evaluate** material that supports the behavioural approach.
- In the final paragraph you could analyse and evaluate material that criticises or rejects the approach (AO2–12 marks).

There's a sample answer at the end of the book. Try not to look at it until you've had a go at doing it yourself.

### Evaluation of cognitive model

✓ **Concentrates on current cognitions:** The cognitive model doesn't delve into the past to try to sort out problems. It concentrates on the individual's current thought processes.

✓ **Research evidence:** Many people suffering from anxiety disorders and/or depression do appear to report irrational thought processes.

✓ **Influential and popular model:** Currently, the cognitive approach seems to be favoured in many fields of psychology. The cognitive approach to abnormality is no different, and many cognitive therapists practice successfully within the NHS.

✓ **Empowers the individual:** The individual is given responsibility to change their cognitions. As such, it presents a positive view of humankind.

✗ **Underplays physiological and environmental influences:** Evidence suggests that physiological factors and past events can affect an individual's behaviour. These social aspects are largely ignored with this approach. This (over-) emphasis on cognitive processes has led to criticisms that the cognitive model is reductionist and mechanistic.

❌ **Unscientific:** Since thoughts can't be observed or measured, it's been claimed that the cognitive approach is unscientific.

❌ **Cause and effect problem?** It's uncertain whether irrational beliefs cause the anxiety disorder/depression, or whether they are merely a by-product (effect) of the disorder.

❌ **Individual blame:** Since disorders result from an individual's faulty thinking, it's clear that any blame for the disorder rests with the individual. This can have the unfortunate side-effect of making the disorder worse. It might also be unfair, since factors beyond the individual's control might be seen as contributory factors to their mental disorder.

Sometimes being depressed is entirely rational

❌ **Is thinking irrational?** There are two associated problems with questioning someone's thought processes. Firstly, given some people's lives, is their thinking so irrational? Depression may be a rational response to one's (miserable) life. It's been claimed that many depressives have a more realistic view of life than 'normal' people. Viewing the world through rose-coloured spectacles might be equally irrational yet psychologically healthy! Secondly, should a therapist argue that someone is thinking irrationally when their life circumstances appear to support that pessimistic view?

# Critical issue: Eating disorders – anorexia nervosa (AN) and bulimia nervosa (BN)

Increasing numbers of sufferers from eating disorders have been reported in the last 20 years. The two most common eating disorders are anorexia nervosa (AN) and bulimia nervosa (BN).

## Clinical characteristics of anorexia nervosa (AN)

There are estimated to be 70,000 people with AN in Britain. AN literally means '*nervous loss of appetite*'.

- AN is primarily a female disorder, which usually (but not exclusively) occurs during adolescence.

Body dysmorphia: most anorexics perceive themselves to be larger than they actually are (shown by their choice of adjusted photos)

In a 1995 Panorama interview, Princess Diana admitted to being bulimic, a fact she'd managed to keep secret for many years

- There is a refusal to maintain normal body weight. Individuals have to weigh less than 85% of their normal body weight to be diagnosed as anorexics.
- Anorexics have an intense fear of being overweight. This continues even when their actual body weight is extremely low. This distorted body image is not evident to anorexics themselves.
- There's a general physical decline. This can include cessation of menstruation (amenorrhoea), low blood pressure, dry, cracking skin, constipation and insufficient sleep. Depression and low self-esteem are also common, and approximately 6% of AN cases are fatal (ANAD, 2003).

## Clinical characteristics of bulimia nervosa (BN)

BN can be viewed as a variation of AN. BN is more common than AN, affecting as much as 5% of the population. BN literally means 'ox hunger'.

- BN is characterised by periods of binge eating, frequently followed by purging. Binge eating involves the rapid consumption of large amounts of high calorific foods. Purging involves the expulsion of the food through the use of laxatives or vomiting. Sometimes coloured 'marker' foods are consumed, so the bulimic will recognise when all food has been purged.
- Bulimics have an intense fear of fatness, and are preoccupied with their body weight and shape. The discrepancy between actual body size and desired body size is considerable.
- Bulimics feel guilt about their binge/purge episodes, and are aware of their problem.
- Bulimics tend to try to keep their disorder a secret. This is often successful, since the physical effects of the disorder are less obvious than with AN.
- Physical effects of BN include: a swollen face, deterioration of tooth enamel, and digestive tract damage. These are caused by stomach acids during vomiting. Sleep problems, anxiety and depression are also common.

Summary of comparisons between AN and BN:

| | Characteristic | Anorexia nervosa | Bulimia nervosa |
|---|---|---|---|
| **DIFFERENCES** | **Weight** | Less than 85% of 'normal' weight | Fluctuating weight (under- or overweight) |
| | **Eating** | Refusal to eat | Bingeing & purging |
| | **Menstruation** | Often stops (amenorrhoea) | Irregular |
| | **Prevalence** | 1–4% (less common than BN) | 5% (more common than AN) |
| | **Appearance** | Fairly noticeable | Not so noticeable |
| | **Cognitions** | Deny disorder & hunger | Aware of disorder & hunger |
| | **Family relationships** | Deny conflict | Perceive conflict |
| | **Fatality?** | Greater likelihood of death | Less likelihood of death |
| **SIMILARITIES** | **Onset** | Usually in adolescence | Usually in adolescence |
| | **Fear** | An 'intrusive fear of fatness' | An 'intrusive fear of fatness' |
| | **Self-perception** | Unduly concerned with weight & shape | Unduly concerned with weight & shape |
| | **Gender** | Predominantly female | Predominantly female |

## Biological models of eating disorder (AN and BN)

Despite differences between AN and BN, some individuals have been known to suffer from both AN and BN at different times in their lives. Indeed, both AN and BN can be explained in a similar way:

- **Genetic influences:** Family studies have shown that first-degree relatives (e.g. siblings) of bulimics and anorexics have an increased risk of developing an eating disorder (see Essential Study 4.1 Holland *et al.* (1988) below).
- **Hypothalamic dysfunction:** The hypothalamus contains an 'on' and 'off' command for eating. The lateral zone of the hypothalamus functions as a 'hunger centre' whilst the ventromedial region operates as a 'satiety centre'. It's suggested that dysfunction of these regions can lead to eating disorders. However, much of this research has occurred in laboratory animals, as in the rat below. It's unclear whether the influences are the same for humans, although tumours in these regions have been shown to lead to excessive bingeing.
- **Neurotransmitter imbalance:** Noradrenaline has been shown to increase appetite in animals. Bulimics have been found to have low levels of serotonin. This evidence supports the finding that serotonin acts to suppress appetite. Indeed, drugs that affect serotonin activity have been helpful with eating disorders. It's unclear whether neurotransmitter levels are a cause or effect of eating disorders, although it's most likely that they are the effect of continued starvation.
- **Brain damage:** A blood-flow deficiency in the area of the brain responsible for perception and appetite could cause AN. This might explain the mismatch between sufferers' actual and perceived appearance. Brain scans have shown that cerebrospinal fluid volumes are low in anorexics, and this appears to be irreversible (Lambe *et al.*, 1997). However, postmortems have failed to record clear evidence for the brain damage hypothesis.
- **Infection:** Eagles *et al.* (2001) report that a high proportion of anorexics are born in late spring and early summer. It's suggested that an intrauterine infection during the winter months is a causative factor.

Rats who have different parts of their hypothalamus destroyed either stop eating (aphagia) or overeat (hyperphagia)

• **Protein imbalance:** Proteins are also implicated in eating disorders. For example, reduction of the protein tryptothan causes serotonin levels to drop. Bulimics deprived of tryptothan binged more violently and purged more each day.

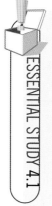

ESSENTIAL STUDY 4.1

**Biological explanations of eating disorders** (AN) •••••• **Holland** *et al.* (1988) **Study of AN Twins** (SANT)

### Aim (AO1)

To investigate genetic factors as an explanation for AN.

### Procedures (AO1)

The sample comprised identical (monozygotic – MZ) twins and non-identical (dizygotic – DZ) twins where one twin (at least) had AN. All the twins had been brought up in the same environment. Holland *et al.* measured the concordance rate for AN using questionnaires and physical measures. This is a percentage measure of the extent to which a trait in two people is in agreement or 'concord'. The higher the concordance rate in MZ twins, the higher the likelihood that AN is influenced by genetic factors (since MZ twins have identical genes).

### Findings (AO1)

They found a 56% concordance rate in MZ twins, and 5% in DZ twins brought up in the same environment. This difference was statistically highly significant (see Figure 4.3).

### Conclusion (AO1)

There is a large genetic component to AN (80% of liability to AN is explained by genetic factors). Genetic inheritance can identify a predisposition to AN. Nevertheless, other environmental factors must play a role in the development of the disorder.

### Criticisms (AO1/AO2)

✓ **Statistically significant:** The significantly higher rate found in MZs compared to DZs provides good evidence for genetic factors influencing the development of AN. But if the disorder was entirely genetic, then the MZ rate should be nearer 100%.

✗ **Twins don't just share the same genes:** They also share similar cultural and family values, and the environment for MZ twins is more similar than for DZ twins. Therefore physiological and environmental factors are confounded. Indeed, the 56% concordance rate in MZs *might* be *entirely* due to their more similar upbringing than DZs.

✗ **Small samples:** In addition, many twin studies involve a small sample size. Holland *et al.* studied only 25 MZ and 20 DZ twins, and it's estimated that 15,000 pairs would be needed for a definitive, genetic study. The low occurrence of both twin births and eating disorders make this unlikely.

✗ **Immigrant data:** Immigrants into Western society can develop eating disorders. Their relatives in non-Western societies don't suffer from eating disorders. This evidence doesn't suggest a genetic, family-based explanation for AN.

✗ **Social class:** McClelland & Crisp (2001) found a higher incidence of AN in social classes 1 and 2. They reject the idea that this is due to higher referral levels and suggest it's due to an avoidance response to adolescent conflict within such families. The biological approach cannot account for such findings.

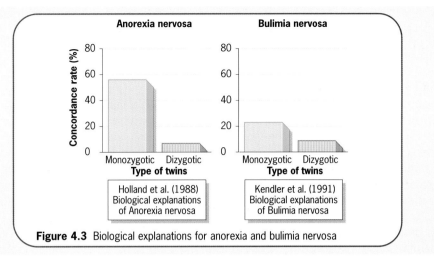

**Figure 4.3** Biological explanations for anorexia and bulimia nervosa

Another study that examined the biological explanations of eating disorders was conducted by Kendler *et al.* (1991). Their study used a similar procedure to that of Holland *et al.* (1988), but they researched BN twins and found a 23% concordance rate for MZs, and 9% for DZs. The difference was statistically significant. They concluded that there's a large genetic component to BN, although it's less evident than with AN. Again, environmental factors appear implicated in BN.

However, it's been claimed that identical twins are more likely to copy each other's behaviour, and this explains the concordance rates. This seems unlikely in a number of the cases, though, since some of the identical twins developed eating disorders while living in different countries and concealed it from the other twin. Genetic influences cannot fully explain eating disorders, since there remains a high proportion of twins where only one twin develops the disorder. Bulik *et al.* (2001) studied 30 MZ pairs (n = 60) where only one twin had BN. They found distinct developmental and personality differences, suggesting environmental factors to be of far greater importance than biological factors.

It may also be difficult to generalise these twin findings since twins may be subject to greater developmental difficulties (e.g. sense of identity) than other adolescents. Therefore such findings must be treated with caution when making comparisons with non-twins. The dramatic increase in eating disorders over the last 20 years cannot be explained by genetic factors alone. Genetic changes cannot have occurred this quickly!

## EXAM tips BOX

*'Anorexia nervosa is a biological rather than a psychological disorder.'* **Assess to what extent research supports the view that anorexia nervosa (AN) is caused by biological factors. (18 marks)**

* You could structure your answer in terms of three paragraphs, all about 100–130 words long. The question requires you to concentrate on the biological explanation of AN. The first paragraph could involve a very brief description of this (AO1–6 marks).

* In the second paragraph you could **analyse and evaluate** from a **positive** viewpoint and provide evidence that supports the biological explanation of AN. You could mention genetic influences, hypothalamic dysfunction and brain damage. The Holland *et al.* (1988) study should be included.

* In the final paragraph you could **analyse and evaluate** from a **negative** viewpoint and provide evidence that doesn't support or criticises the biological explanation of AN. This could include criticisms of the Holland *et al.* (1988) study and evidence from McClelland & Crisp (2001).

* There is no agreed explanation for AN and therefore evaluation of the biological approach **could** include reference to psychological explanations (e.g. behavioural and psychodynamic). However, marks would only be credited if the link was made <u>directly</u> to the biological explanation.

Note: The question could specifically ask about bulimia nervosa.

There's a sample answer at the end of the book. Try not to look at it until you've had a go at doing it yourself.

## Psychological models of AN & BN including relevant research studies

Although there are numerous psychological explanations for eating disorders, only two *need* be dealt with, namely, behavioural and psychodynamic.

### BEHAVIOURIST EXPLANATIONS AND RESEARCH STUDIES

- According to the behavioural approach, AN can be viewed as a learnt behaviour.
- Using classical conditioning principles, eating is associated with anxiety since it can make people overweight. Losing weight ensures the individual reduces these feelings of anxiety.
- Using operant conditioning principles, the individual avoids food to gain a reward such as feeling positive about themselves. In the early stages of the illness, individuals may even be admired or congratulated for losing weight and looking slim and 'healthy'. The refusal to eat is reinforcing and becomes a dangerous habit. In addition, the misperception of body image means that an anorexic continues to feel that they're overweight, despite physical evidence to the contrary. The anorexic may also gain the reward or satisfaction of being in control of their food intake (see Figure 4.4).
- Social learning theory (an adaptation of behaviourist theory) suggests that people imitate and copy people they admire. Young women see female role models rewarded for being slim and attractive. Today's society tends to associate being slim with being successful, fit and healthy.
- Some studies have blamed various media for this. Fashion supermodels are increasingly thin, magazine centrefolds are consistently below the average weight and even the Sindy doll has slimmed down. Impressionable adolescents may try to copy such models in the hope of gaining *vicarious reinforcement*. This is defined as reward received indirectly, by observing another person being rewarded. Indeed, if they do slim, the reinforcement will be direct!
- Groesz *et al.* (2001) support the view that the mass media portray a slender beauty ideal. A review of 25 studies showed that this ideal causes body dissatisfaction and contributes to the development of eating disorders. The effect was most marked in girls under 19 years.
- Studies have shown a high incidence of AN in occupations such as ballet dancing or modelling, where there's great pressure about appearance and a desire to remain thin (Alberge, 1999). Further support comes from the fact that eating disorders aren't so prevalent in non-Western societies (e.g. China), where fewer such role models exist. Here, pressures on women to be thin are rare. Fearn (1999) reported an increase in eating disorders in Fiji with the introduction of American television programmes which emphasise a Westernised idealised body shape.

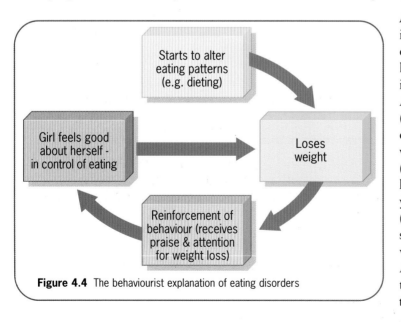

**Figure 4.4** The behaviourist explanation of eating disorders

An additional study that examined psychological explanations of eating disorders was conducted by Tyrka *et al.* (2002), where they investigated Predictors of Anorexic and Bulimic Syndromes (PABS). 157 white, 'middle class or upper-middle class' females were studied from adolescence (12–16 years) (Time 1) and followed up two (Time 2) and eight years later at young adulthood (Time 3). Questionnaire and semi-structured telephone interviews were used. Diagnoses of AN and BN were made according to DSM-IV criteria. They found that:

- Perfectionism at either Time 1 or Time 2 was a significant predictor of the onset of AN
- Low body weight was also a significant predictor of AN – this was not due to excessive dieting *prior* to the development of AN

- **Negative emotion or depressed mood** was a significant predictor of BN
- No other psychosocial characteristics were significant.

Tyrka *et al.* (2002) concluded that:

- **Psychosocial factors** can be used to predict the onset of both AN and BN
- A simple measure of body weight can help to identify girls at higher risk of developing AN
- The **measure of perfectionism** provides some support for the psychodynamic approach. Girls with such standards may shrink from the demands of adolescence.

These results are supported by other studies. Garner *et al.* (1983) found high levels of perfectionism in anorexics, and negative emotions and depression are seen in many bulimics (Bushnell *et al.*, 1994). The design of the Tyrka *et al.* study was prospective. Tracking participants over time means that there is no reliance on memory. Psychological functioning has been shown to be affected by semi-starvation or malnutrition (Keys *et al.*, 1950). Therefore, asking anorexics about their past may not be reliable. This study avoids such problems. However, the study may have been over-simplistic since it doesn't take into account any number of other factors

The fashion industry has been accused of using inappropriate role-models

that might contribute to eating disorders. For example, the biological basis of eating disorders is ignored.

In terms of bulimia, bingeing is also associated with guilt or a fear of looking fat. Purging is used to reduce this anxiety. The reduction of anxiety is reinforcing and maintains the binge/purge cycle.

---

**ESSENTIAL STUDY 4.2**

**Psychological explanations of eating disorders (BN)** •••••• **Field *et al.* (1999) Peer And Media Influences On BN** (PAMOB)

**Aim** (AO1)

To investigate prospectively the influence of peer and media influences on the development of BN.

**Procedures** (AO1)

6928 girls (9–14 years) completed questionnaires in both 1996 and 1997 (81% response rate). The questionnaires involved the assessment of self-esteem, weight concerns, attitudes and behaviour. These included specific questions related to 'importance of thinness to peers', 'teasing about weight by peers' and the influence of the media.

**Findings** (AO1)

The 74 girls who had begun purging (at least monthly) between 1996 and 1997 were distinguished by:

- the importance of their thinness to peers
- trying to look like females on TV, movies or in magazines.

Findings support the 'weight continuum theory of eating disorders'. Innocent dieting can be the first step to BN.

**Conclusion** (AO1)

- Peers and popular culture exert a strong influence on bulimics' weight-control beliefs and behaviours.
- It's possible to identify high-risk adolescent girls and develop appropriate eating disorder prevention programmes.
- Efforts should be made to persuade the media to employ role models whose weight is 'healthy', not 'underweight'.

**Criticisms** (AO1/AO2)

✓ **First prospective study:** (a study that tracks people in the future) on the influence of peer and media on development of BN. Retrospective studies of BN can be inaccurate due to their over-reliance on memory.

✓ **Large sample size:** 6928 girls were sampled, although only 74 (1%) of these actually developed BN. The sample was also restricted to American adolescents and findings may not be generalisable to other cultures.

✗ **Questionnaire methodology:** The use of questionnaires to self-report weight/height, purging and beliefs and attitudes may be unreliable due to social desirability bias. Bulimics reported trying to emulate models seen in the media. This may have been in terms of fashion or hairstyles, not weight or shape. The questions did not distinguish this!

✗ **Biological factors:** The research made no effort to investigate if any biological factors affected the 74 bulimics.

There are limitations with the behavioural explanation of eating disorders:

- Why don't all dieters carry on and become anorexic? Are anorexics really conditioned in different ways to dieters?
- Why do anorexics continue to starve themselves when they no longer receive praise and compliments about their size? It's possible that it's the attention they receive that's reinforcing.
- The behavioural model is less successful with its explanation of BN. The reward for purging is explained as the lessening of anxiety from the initial binge. But why do bulimics binge in the first place? What reward do they get from bingeing? Some suggest that bingeing represents 'comfort eating'. Bulimics binge in order to compensate for their feelings of loneliness and social inadequacy. Some bulimics may use the disorder as a way to remain the centre of attention in the family and not grow up and become independent.
- It ignores the cognitive aspects of the disorders. For example, the faulty perceptions of body image which play such a large part in eating disorders.

## PSYCHODYNAMIC EXPLANATIONS AND RESEARCH STUDIES

- Psychodynamic explanations of eating disorders suggest that adolescents don't want to grow up and separate from their parents. They become fixated at the oral stage when they were completely dependent on their parents. AN is an unconscious desire to remain dependent on their parents. In reality, this is often what happens. The adolescent struggling to cope with the disorder relies more and more on parental support.
- In Freudian terms, eating and sex are symbolically related. A refusal to eat represents a denial of sexuality. Adolescents may be unconsciously trying to prevent sexual maturity. Again, this often occurs in reality since menstruation can cease, breasts stop developing, and the link to a pre-puberty age is obvious. It is also suggested that pregnancy and a fat stomach are unconsciously linked in the anorexic mind. Thus avoidance of food can be seen as an attempt to avoid pregnancy and adult responsibilities.
- Criticisms of the psychodynamic approach focus on the lack of objective evidence. The unconscious cannot be observed or measured, and most of the claims cannot be tested or proved. However, there

are cases reported where people with AN or BN were sexually abused as children. Their desire to destroy their sexually maturing bodies may be a reaction to this.

- Romans *et al.* (2001) found evidence for a link between childhood sexual abuse and the development of eating disorders. They found that early maturation and paternal over-control were risk factors for AN and BN and that these factors are a specific concern after the experience of childhood sexual abuse.

- It's also been claimed that patients who've accepted a psychodynamic explanation for their eating disorder do so due to demand characteristics. From a desire to please their therapist, patients accept this explanation for their disorder. Finally, psychodynamic explanations cannot account for the increase in eating disorders in recent years. Surely adolescent unconscious desires couldn't have changed substantially in the last 20 years?

## EXAM tips BOX

**Outline and evaluate psychological approaches as explanations of AN. (18 marks)**

- Once again, you could structure your answer in terms of three paragraphs, all about 100–130 words long. The question requires you to concentrate on the psychological explanations of AN. The first paragraph should involve a very brief description of at least TWO of these (i.e. psychodynamic and behavioural) (AO1–6 marks).

- In the next two paragraphs you could **analyse and evaluate** each of these approaches from a **positive** and **negative** viewpoint. You should provide evidence that **supports or rejects** the psychological explanations. Analysis could include reference to the methodology employed in the research studies cited (AO2–12 marks).

Note: The question could specifically ask about BN.

There's a sample answer at the end of the book. Try not to look at it until you've had a go at doing it yourself.

## Self-assessment questions

These are some example Part a and Part b questions (worth 40% of your exam). Part c questions (worth 60%) have been dealt with throughout the chapter in the Exam tips boxes and in the sample answers at the end of the book.

**1 a.** Outline *two* attempts to define abnormality. (3 + 3 marks)

**b.** Outline *two* assumptions of the biological (medical) model in relation to the causes of abnormality. (3 + 3 marks)

**2 a.** Explain what is meant by the 'statistical infrequency' definition of abnormality and give *one* limitation of this definition. (3 + 3 marks)

**b.** Describe *three* differences in the clinical characteristics of anorexia nervosa and bulimia nervosa. (2 + 2 + 2 marks)

**3 a.** Give *two* limitations of the definition of abnormality in terms of 'deviation from ideal mental health'. (3 + 3 marks)

**b.** Outline the biological (medical) explanation of ONE eating disorder. (6 marks)

**4 a.** Outline the findings of one study into psychological explanations of eating disorders. (6 marks)

**b.** Outline *two* assumptions of the psychodynamic model in relation to the causes of abnormality. (3 + 3 marks)

| ESSENTIAL STUDY SUMMARY | | | |
|---|---|---|---|
| Topic | Research study | Researcher date | Page |
| Biological explanations of eating disorders | Study of AN Twins (SANT) | Holland *et al.* (1988) | 92 |
| Psychological explanations of eating disorders | Peer and Media influences on BN (PAMOB) | Field *et al.* (1999) | 95 |

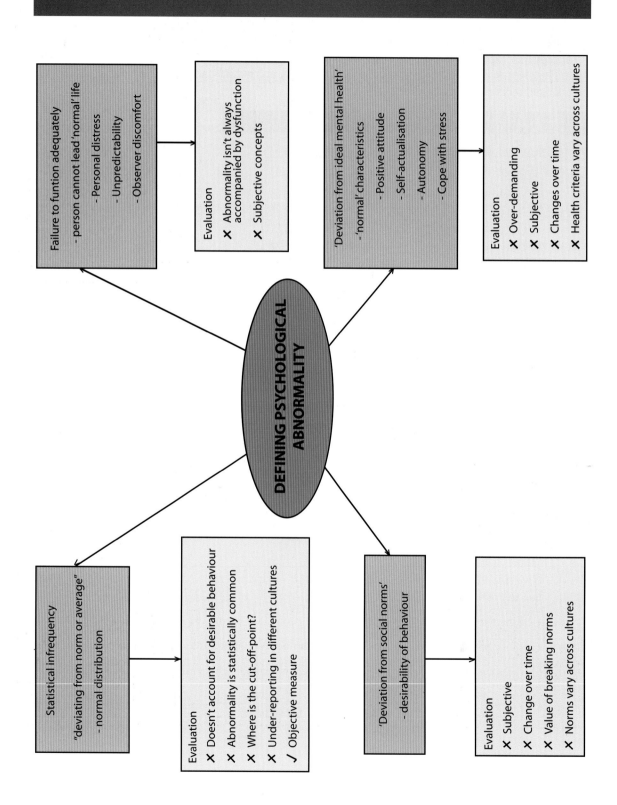

CHAPTER SUMMARY: revision schema

**DEFINING PSYCHOLOGICAL ABNORMALITY**

Failure to funtion adequately
- person cannot lead 'normal' life
- Personal distress
- Unpredictability
- Observer discomfort

Evaluation
✗ Abnormality isn't always accompanied by dysfunction
✗ Subjective concepts

'Deviation from ideal mental health'
- 'normal' characteristics
  - Positive attitude
  - Self-actualisation
  - Autonomy
  - Cope with stress

Evaluation
✗ Over-demanding
✗ Subjective
✗ Changes over time
✗ Health criteria vary across cultures

Statistical infrequency
"deviating from norm or average"
- normal distribution

Evaluation
✗ Doesn't account for desirable behaviour
✗ Abnormality is statistically common
✗ Where is the cut-off-point?
✗ Under-reporting in different cultures
✓ Objective measure

'Deviation from social norms'
- desirability of behaviour

Evaluation
✗ Subjective
✗ Change over time
✗ Value of breaking norms
✗ Norms vary across cultures

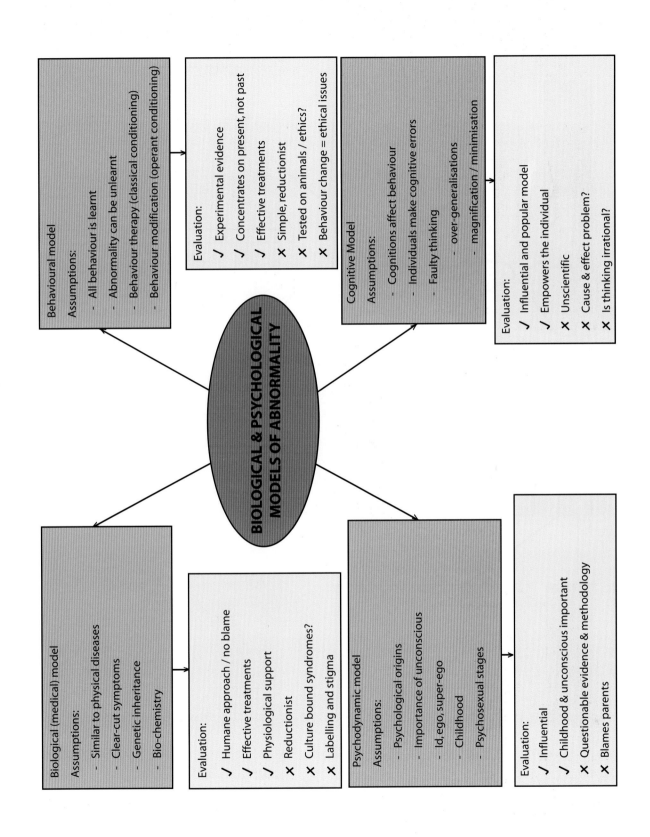

**Behavioural model**

Assumptions:
- All behaviour is learnt
- Abnormality can be unlearnt
- Behaviour therapy (classical conditioning)
- Behaviour modification (operant conditioning)

Evaluation:
- ✓ Experimental evidence
- ✓ Concentrates on present, not past
- ✓ Effective treatments
- ✗ Simple, reductionist
- ✗ Tested on animals / ethics?
- ✗ Behaviour change = ethical issues

**Cognitive Model**

Assumptions:
- Cognitions affect behaviour
- Individuals make cognitive errors
- Faulty thinking
  - over-generalisations
  - magnification / minimisation

Evaluation:
- ✓ Influential and popular model
- ✓ Empowers the individual
- ✗ Unscientific
- ✗ Cause & effect problem?
- ✗ Is thinking irrational?

**BIOLOGICAL & PSYCHOLOGICAL MODELS OF ABNORMALITY**

**Biological (medical) model**

Assumptions:
- Similar to physical diseases
- Clear-cut symptoms
- Genetic inheritance
- Bio-chemistry

Evaluation:
- ✓ Humane approach / no blame
- ✓ Effective treatments
- ✓ Physiological support
- ✗ Reductionist
- ✗ Culture bound syndromes?
- ✗ Labelling and stigma

**Psychodynamic model**

Assumptions:
- Psychological origins
- Importance of unconscious
- Id, ego, super-ego
- Childhood
- Psychosexual stages

Evaluation:
- ✓ Influential
- ✓ Childhood & unconscious important
- ✗ Questionable evidence & methodology
- ✗ Blames parents

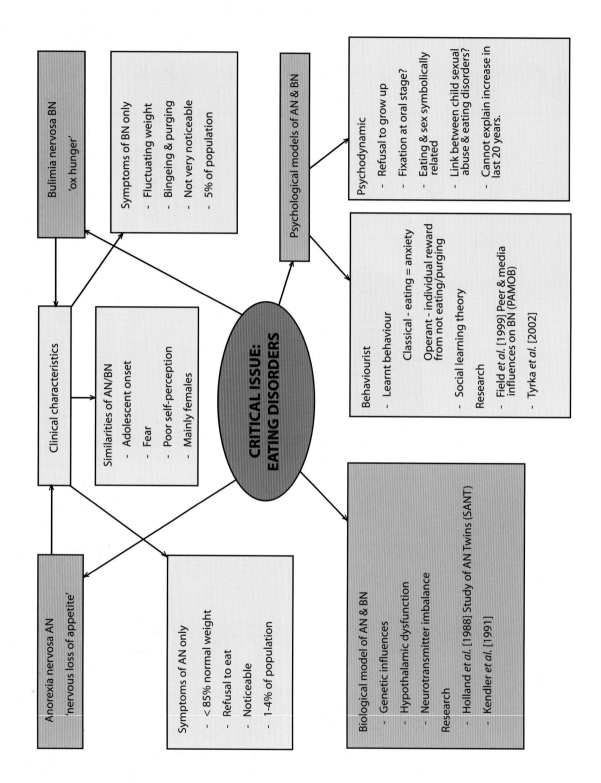

Bulimia nervosa BN
'ox hunger'

Symptoms of BN only
- Fluctuating weight
- Bingeing & purging
- Not very noticeable
- 5% of population

Psychological models of AN & BN

Psychodynamic
- Refusal to grow up
- Fixation at oral stage?
- Eating & sex symbolically related
- Link between child sexual abuse & eating disorders?
- Cannot explain increase in last 20 years.

Clinical characteristics

Similarities of AN/BN
- Adolescent onset
- Fear
- Poor self-perception
- Mainly females

CRITICAL ISSUE: EATING DISORDERS

Behaviourist
- Learnt behaviour
    Classical - eating = anxiety
    Operant - individual reward from not eating/purging
- Social learning theory
Research
- Field et al. [1999] Peer & media influences on BN (PAMOB)
- Tyrka et al. [2002]

Anorexia nervosa AN
'nervous loss of appetite'

Symptoms of AN only
- < 85% normal weight
- Refusal to eat
- Noticeable
- 1-4% of population

Biological model of AN & BN
- Genetic influences
- Hypothalamic dysfunction
- Neurotransmitter imbalance
Research
- Holland et al. [1988] Study of AN Twins (SANT)
- Kendler et al. [1991]

# Social Psychology

## What's covered in this chapter?
### You need to know about:

Social influence
a. Majority and minority influence
- Research studies into majority (conformity) and minority influence
- Explanations of why people yield to majority and minority influence
b. Obedience to authority
- Research studies into obedience to authority
- Issues of internal and external validity associated with such research
- Explanations of why people obey and how people might resist obedience

Critical issue: ethical issues in psychological research
- Ethical issues surrounding the use of deception, informed consent and the protection of participants from psychological harm, including the relevance of these issues in the context of social influence research
- Ways in which psychologists deal with these issues (e.g. through the use of ethical guidelines, ethical committees)

## Majority and minority influence
### Majority influence (conformity)

Conformity can be defined as yielding to group pressure. It's the influence a group has over an individual. This is why it's often referred to as majority influence. How you dress and the type of music you listen to are probably influenced by your peer group ('age-mates'). But this influence isn't always obvious. Authority figures might *request* or *demand* that you act in a certain way. By contrast, your peers (who are your equals) *expect* certain behaviour of you – but you may not realise it at the time.

ESSENTIAL STUDY 5.1

### Asch's (1951) Comparison-Of-Lines Experiment (COLE)

#### Aims (AO1)

Asch criticised an earlier study by Sherif (1935). Sherif claimed that when people are unsure about the answer to a question, they use others' answers to guide them. He gave his participants an *ambiguous* task. (This involved estimating how far a light moved that actually didn't move at all, as when you look at a lighted cigarette in a completely dark room.) So there couldn't be any right or wrong answers.

Asch argued that Sherif hadn't demonstrated conformity at all. The true test of conformity is to see if people will agree with others when the experimental task is *unambiguous*.

#### Procedures (AO1)

Asch showed participants two cards (as in Figure 5.1).

He then asked them to say which of the comparison lines was the same length as the standard line. This was repeated 17 times (making 18 trials altogether). On every trial, the correct answer was obvious to anyone with normal eyesight. This happened in groups of 7–9 people, but only *one* participant was naïve. The others were

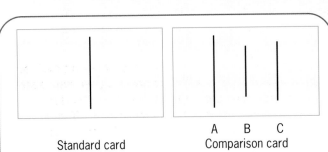

Standard card          Comparison card
**Figure 5.1** Stimulus cards used in Asch's experiment

**stooges** (or accomplices). Asch had briefed them beforehand about what answers to give on particular trials. The stooges gave their answers, in turn, and the naïve participant was the last (or last-but-one) to answer.

On the first two trials, the stooges gave the correct answer (*neutral trials*). But on the third trial, all the stooges gave the same wrong answer (*critical trial*). There were 11 more critical trials (making 12 in all), and four more neutral trials between the critical trials (six in all).

A minority of one faces a unanimous majority

#### Findings (AO1)

The crucial measure was how often naïve participants gave the same wrong answer as the stooges on the critical trials. This was a measure of conformity. Overall, there was a 32% conformity rate. In other words, participants agreed with the wrong answer on about a third of the critical trials. But there were important *individual differences*. For example, no one conformed on all the critical trials, and about 25% didn't conform even once. About 75% conformed at least once.

#### Conclusions (AO1)

Because the answers on the critical trials were obviously incorrect, Asch's study shows the impact that a majority can have on an individual. However, the majority doesn't have the same impact on every individual. In fact, Asch was interested in the social and personal conditions that help individuals *resist* group pressure.

### Criticisms (AO1/AO2)

✓ **The task was unambiguous.** Control participants who performed the line-matching task individually hardly ever made mistakes. Therefore conformity rate could be measured in an objective way.

✗ **Participants were stressed.** Some participants reported getting quite stressed when the stooges gave the wrong answer on critical trials. This could be considered unethical. Also, they were clearly deceived about what was really going on.

✗ **The artificiality of COLE.** In everyday life, we're unlikely to disagree with other people so fundamentally about the 'correct' answer. Real-life situations are rarely as clear-cut as this.

## Evaluation of Asch's conformity research

✓ **The Asch paradigm.** Asch's method for studying conformity has been adopted by many other researchers. It's a 'way of doing' conformity research.

✗ **It's uneconomical and time-consuming.** Only one naïve participant is tested at a time. Crutchfield (1954) tested participants in separate booths. Each booth had a panel of lights, which supposedly showed other participants' answers. This way, he was able to test several participants at once.

✓ **Majority size or unanimous majority?** In later experiments, Asch found that it wasn't the size of the majority that mattered. The crucial factor was whether or not the stooges agreed with each other (that is, were they *unanimous*). So, if one stooge gave a different answer from the rest (there was a *dissenter*), naïve participants were more likely to give the correct answer. That is, they were more likely to resist group pressure. The dissenting stooge seems to give the naïve participant moral support ("If he disagrees with them, why shouldn't I?").

✓ **Task difficulty.** In another experiment, Asch made the comparison lines more similar (making the task more ambiguous and consequently more difficult). This increased conformity.

✗ **Replication of Asch's findings.** Other American (and British) researchers have not always replicated Asch's findings. For example, some have found *lower* conformity rates than Asch. But others have found similar rates to Asch. This suggests that conformity in experiments may reflect current social and political conditions.

✗ **Cross-cultural studies.** Generally, people in Western cultures (such as the US and the UK) are less likely to conform than people in non-Western countries (such as Japan and Africa).

✗ **Who's the real minority and majority?** The numerical majority (the stooges) actually represent an unorthodox, unconventional (*minority*) viewpoint. The numerical minority (the naïve participants) represent the conventional, traditional (*majority*) 'truth'. This minority influenced the majority a third of the time (Moscovici & Faucheux, 1972: see Essential Study 5.2, page 104).

A famous study that is relevant to both conformity and obedience is Zimbardo *et al.*'s (1973) Prison Experiment (PE). This is discussed in Chapter 9 in relation to social psychological theories of aggression (see page 192).

## Minority influence

We usually interpret the findings from Asch's experiments as showing how a powerful majority influences an isolated individual. In other words, conformity involves majority influence (see above). But is the numerical majority always more powerful? Even in Asch's original experiment, there was *no* conformity on two-thirds of the critical trials. What's more, the numerical minority can sometimes change the views of the majority (minority influence).

### Moscovici *et al.'s* (1969) **Blue Colour Slide Experiment** (BCSE)

#### Aims (AO1)

Moscovici *et al.* were trying to demonstrate minority influence. The experimental task involved naming the colour of slides. The task was an objective one (there was a right and a wrong answer, as in Asch's experiment). Consequently, it might seem very unlikely that a minority could persuade the majority to give the wrong answer. But Moscovici *et al.* predicted that a minority could exert influence over a majority if it *consistently* called a blue slide green.

#### Procedures (AO1)

Moscovici *et al.* used groups of six participants, of whom four were naïve and two were stooges. The stooges played the role of the minority. Before the experiment began, Moscovici *et al.* tested all the participants' colour vision. They all passed the test! This meant that the naïve participants couldn't explain the stooges' wrong answers by claiming they were colour blind. All the participants gave their answers aloud. The stooges sat either in the first and second position, or first and fourth.

On 36 separate trials, a slide that was clearly blue was presented on a screen. In the *consistent condition,* the stooges called it green *every time*. In the *inconsistent condition*, they answered 'green' 24 times and 'blue' 12 times. There was also a *control condition*, where the groups consisted of six naïve participants.

#### Findings (AO1)

In the *control condition*, there were fewer than 1% green responses. This showed how obvious the correct response was. In the *inconsistent condition*, 1.25% of responses were green. In the *consistent condition*, green responses were made over 8% of the time. This was significantly more than in the other two conditions. 32% of naïve participants gave at least one green response.

Moscovici *et al.* found that there were really two types of group. In one type, nobody was influenced by the minority. In the other, several were influenced. Where the stooges sat made no difference.

#### Conclusions (AO1)

The experiment clearly showed that a consistent minority can affect the judgements made by the majority. Although the minority doesn't have a numerical advantage, their consistent behavioural style makes them influential. In conformity experiments, the influence of the majority is evident from the start. In contrast, minority influence only begins to show after a while.

#### Criticisms (AO1/AO2)

✔ **Important early study.** This was one of the first attempts to demonstrate *minority influence*.

✘ **Ethical issues.** Naïve participants couldn't give their *informed consent*. As with any study involving stooges, participants were deceived as to the true purpose of the experiment.

✘ **Artificiality.** As with Asch's experiments, the experimental task was very artificial. So, the experiment may lack *external (ecological) validity*.

No consistency; no minority influence

Consistency doesn't necessarily have to involve repeating the same response, as in the Moscovici *et al.* experiment. This was demonstrated by Nemeth *et al.* (1974).

- This was basically a replication of Moscovici *et al.*'s (1969) experiment. But Nemeth *et al.* added two conditions, in which the stooges said 'green' on half the trials and 'green-blue' on the other half.
- In the *random condition*, the green and green-blue responses were randomly distributed across the trials (there was *no* consistency in their responses). In the *correlated condition*, the stooges said green to the brighter slides and green-blue to the dimmer slides (or *vice versa*). Whether they said green or green-blue depended on the brightness of the slide. So, there was a clear *pattern* to their responses.
- Compared to a no-influence *control condition*, the *random condition* had no effect. But in the *correlated condition*, almost 21% of the responses were wrong (minority) answers. Where stooges consistently repeated the green response, there was *no* minority influence. This contrasts with Moscovici *et al.*'s findings.
- Nemeth *et al.* showed that there's *more* to minority influence than just consistency. It also matters how the majority interprets the minority's answers. They must relate to the stimulus in some predictable way. Here it was the brightness of the slide that counted.

## EXAM tips BOX

**Consider psychological research into majority influence (conformity). (18 marks)**

- You could structure your answer in terms of three paragraphs, all about 100–130 words long.
- In the first paragraph you should say what's meant by majority influence (conformity). You could then briefly *describe* some of the research findings using the *Asch paradigm*. (AO1, worth 6 marks).
- In the second paragraph you could consider some of the strengths of this research. One way of doing this is to consider replications, as well as alternative ways of investigating majority influence.
- In the third paragraph you could consider some of the limitations of this research. One way you could do this is to consider how Asch's findings have been reinterpreted by Moscovici in terms of *minority influence*. (AO2, worth 12 marks).

*Remember that here you're analysing and evaluating the findings, rather than describing them.* Try to write a suitable answer in about 300–350 words.

As with all questions, there's no single correct way of answering it. The above are just pointers. There's a sample answer at the end of the book. Try not to look at it until you've had a go at doing it yourself. Note that you could get a similar question on minority influence.

## Why do people conform?

Deutsch & Gerard (1955) distinguished between informational social influence (ISI) and normative social influence (NSI). They felt this distinction was crucial for understanding majority group influence.

### INFORMATIONAL SOCIAL INFLUENCE (ISI)

- We all have a basic need to be confident that our ideas and beliefs are correct (a need for certainty). This makes us feel in charge of our lives and in control of the world. This is the motive underlying ISI. When we're unsure about something, we tend to seek other people's opinions. If we know what they think, we're in a better position to form our own opinions. This is more likely to happen in situations we're not familiar with, or in ambiguous situations. For example, if you're voting in an election for the first time, you may be unsure which candidate to vote for. So you may ask your friends whom *they're* voting for to help you make up your own mind. This is ISI.
- The participants in Sherif's experiment were unsure how far the light moved (with good reason – it wasn't actually moving at all!). Similarly, when Asch made the comparison lines more similar the situation became more ambiguous – the correct answer was now much less obvious.

- If we conform because of ISI, it's very likely that we *really* believe the opinion we adopt. The whole point is that we're unsure what to believe, which is why we compare our own ideas with others' in the first place. So we come to share their views (we're 'converted'). When Sherif's participants were later tested individually (away from the group), they stuck to the answer they'd given while in the group. This shows that they genuinely (privately) believed that the group was correct. In other words, they said what they believed and believed what they said. This kind of conformity is called **internalisation** or **true conformity**.

- Other people help us 'define social reality'. But it also matters *who* these other people are (Brown, 1988). We're only likely to be influenced by others' opinions in an ambiguous situation if we see ourselves as sharing important characteristics with them (Abrams *et al.*, 1990). For example, you're more likely to internalise the views of other psychology students than those of, say, history students (assuming you're not doing history too).

## Normative social influence (NSI)

- The motive underlying **NSI** is the need to be accepted by other people. We want others to like and respect us, and rejection is very painful. In these ways, people have the power to reward or punish us. A way of ensuring their acceptance is to agree with them. But this doesn't necessarily mean that we truly believe in what we say.

- For example, many of Asch's participants who'd conformed on the critical trials *knew* the stooges' answer was wrong. But if they gave the correct answer, they risked being laughed at by the majority (a form of rejection). They said things like "I didn't want to look stupid" or "I didn't want to be the odd-one-out". So, what they *said* (publicly) and what they *believed* (privately) were *different.* This kind of conformity is called **compliance**. It represents a compromise in situations where we face a *conflict* between our own and others' opinions. Sherif's participants didn't face any such conflict.

- However, we only experience conflict if we disagree with others whom we see as similar to us in some relevant way. The example above of being amongst other psychology students applies here too.

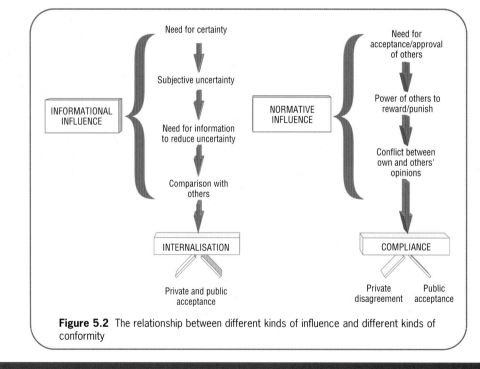

**Figure 5.2** The relationship between different kinds of influence and different kinds of conformity

## Obedience to authority

Obedience can be defined as complying with the demands or instructions of an authority figure. The authority figure has greater power and influence in that particular situation.

# EXAM tips BOX

**Give a brief account of psychological explanations of conformity and consider their strengths and limitations. (18 marks)**

- You could structure your answer in terms of three paragraphs, all about 100–130 words long.

- *A word of warning: The question asks for 'explanations of conformity', so you must include **at least two**. If you wrote about more than two, you wouldn't be expected to give as much detail as for just two.*

- In the first paragraph you could explain Deutsch & Gerard's (1955) distinction between ISI and NSI. You could also indicate how these are related to different kinds of conformity. (AO1, worth 6 marks).

- In the second paragraph you could stress the evidence supporting NSI. This is seen most clearly in Asch's experiments. You could draw on some of the limitations of Asch's research when considering the limitations of the NSI explanation. More generally, must we choose between NSI and ISI?

- In the third paragraph you could stress the evidence supporting ISI. This is seen most clearly in Sherif's experiment. In post-experimental interviews, participants said they didn't feel they'd been influenced by others' judgements. This supports Deutsch and Gerard's distinction between ISI and NSI. Again, you could draw on the limitations of Sherif's experiment when considering the limitations of the ISI explanation. (AO2, worth 12 marks).

*Remember that here you're analysing and evaluating the findings, rather than describing them.*

Try to write a suitable answer in about 300–350 words. As with all questions, there's no single correct way of answering it. The above are just pointers. There's a sample answer at the end of the book. Try not to look at it until you've had a go at doing it yourself.

---

**Table 5.1** Comparison between conformity and obedience

| Conformity | Obedience |
|---|---|
| No one tells us what to do. There's no *explicit* requirement to act in a particular way. | The authority figure orders us to do something. So there *is* an explicit requirement to act in a particular way. |
| The people who influence us are our *peers*, that is, our *equals*. They influence us by *example*, that is, we tend to behave as they do. In this way, everyone's behaviour becomes more similar. | The person who influences us has greater authority than we do in that particular situation. S/he influences us by *direction,* that is, by giving us orders or instructions. In this way, our behaviour is very different from the authority figure's. |
| We conform either because we want others to accept us, or because they provide us with important information. But we usually don't like to admit that we've been influenced by them. | We obey because we accept that society is organized in a *hierarchial* way, that is, some people have more power and influence than others. We don't mind admitting that we obey people 'in authority'. |

---

**ESSENTIAL STUDY 5.3**

### Milgram's (1963) 'Shocking Obedience Study' (SOS)

#### Aims (AO1)

Milgram set out to test the 'Germans are different' hypothesis. This claims that (a) the Germans are a highly obedient nation; and (b) Hitler couldn't have put his plans to exterminate the Jews in the 1930s and 40s into practice unless the German population had co-operated. This American experiment was meant to be a *pilot study*. He was going to carry out the 'real' experiment in Germany.

#### Procedures (AO1)

Participants volunteered for a study of memory and learning (see Figure 5.3, page 109). This was to take place at the Yale University psychology department. When they arrived, they were met by the experimenter wearing a grey lab coat. They were introduced to a Mr Wallace, who was a stooge pretending to be another participant.

The experimenter told the naïve participant and Mr Wallace that the experiment was about the effects of *punishment* on learning. One of them would be the 'teacher' and the other would be the 'learner'. Things were rigged in such a way that Mr Wallace was always the learner, and the participant the teacher.

The experimenter explained that the punishment was to take the form of electric shocks. All three then went into an adjoining room. There the experimenter strapped Mr Wallace into a chair with his arms attached to electrodes. The teacher was to deliver the shocks via a shock generator. This was situated in an adjacent room. As the photo on page 109 shows, the generator had a number of switches. Each switch was clearly marked with a voltage level (starting at 15 volts) and a verbal description ('slight shock'). Each switch gave a shock 15 volts higher than the one before. The last switch gave 450 volts.

The teacher was instructed to deliver a shock each time Mr Wallace made a mistake on a paired-associate word task. Mr Wallace indicated his answer by switching on one of four lights located above the shock generator. With each successive mistake, the teacher had to give the next highest shock (that is, 15 volts higher than the one before).

At 300 volts, Mr Wallace kicked against the wall that adjoined the two rooms. After 315 volts, he stopped kicking and also stopped responding to the teacher's questions. The teacher was instructed to keep on shocking if Mr Wallace stopped answering.

### Findings (AO1)

**Obedience rate** was defined as the percentage of participants who kept on giving shocks right up to 450 volts. Obedience rate was 65%. Many showed signs of extreme distress (such as twitching or giggling nervously, digging their nails into their flesh, and verbally attacking the experimenter). Whenever they threatened to pull out of the experiment, the experimenter would 'prod' them by saying:

- "Please continue" (or "Please go on").
- "The experiment requires that you continue."
- "It is absolutely essential that you continue."
- "You have no other choice, you *must* go on."

### Conclusions (AO1)

The 'Germans are different' hypothesis was clearly false. Milgram's participants were 40 'ordinary' Americans living in a fairly typical small town. Their high level of obedience showed that we all tend to obey people we regard as authority figures in particular situations. If we had lived in Nazi Germany in the 1930s, we might well have acted just as obediently.

### Criticisms (AO1/AO2)

✔ **Famous study:** This is one of the most famous studies in the whole of psychology.

✔ **Milgram paradigm:** It represents the first major attempt to study obedience experimentally, that is, under controlled conditions. Milgram established a basic method (a paradigm) for studying obedience in the lab. This is equivalent to Asch's paradigm for studying conformity.

✘•✔ **Pilot study:** Perhaps it's fairer (and more useful) to consider the research that it stimulated, rather than the study itself. Milgram had expected to find very *low* levels of obedience. So he conducted several further studies to determine exactly *why* his American participants were so obedient.

✘•✔ **Unethical:** It was condemned for being *unethical* (e.g. Baumrind, 1964). Milgram exposed his participants to high levels of distress, which is ethically unacceptable. This provoked a major debate within psychology about ethics in research (see **Critical Issue**, pages 112–116).

✘•✔ **Cross-cultural replications:** Milgram's experiment has been replicated in several other countries. These include Italy, Australia, the UK, Jordan and Spain. But methodological differences between these studies make it difficult to compare the results.

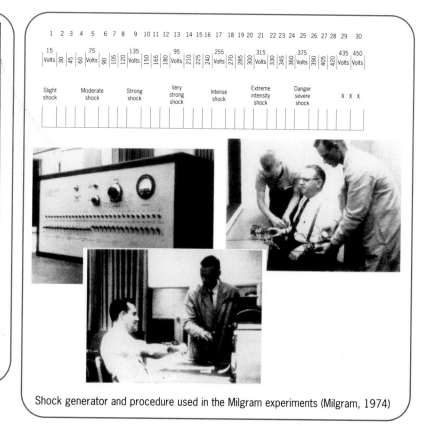

**Public Announcement**

**WE WILL PAY YOU $4.00 FOR
ONE HOUR OF YOUR TIME**

**Persons Needed for a Study of Memory**

*We will pay five hundred New Haven men to help us complete a scientific study of memory and learning. The study is being done at Yale University.

*Each person who participates will be paid $4.00 (plus 50c carfare) for approximately 1 hour's time. We need you for only one hour: there are no further obligations. You may choose the time you would like to come (evenings, weekdays, or weekends).

*No special training, education, or experience is needed. We want:

| | | |
|---|---|---|
| Factory workers | Businessmen | Construction workers |
| City employees | Clerks | Salespeople |
| Laborers | Professional people | White-collar workers |
| Barbers | Telephone workers | Others |

All persons must be between the ages of 20 and 50. High school and college students cannot be used.

*If you meet these qualifications, fill out the coupon below and mail it now to Professor Stanley Milgram, Department of Psychology, Yale University, New Haven. You will be notified later of the specific time and place of the study. We reserve the right to decline any application.

*You will be paid $4.00 (plus 50c carfare) as soon as you arrive at the laboratory.

- - - - - - - - - - - - - - - - - - - - - - - -

TO:
PROF. STANLEY MILGRAM, DEPARTMENT OF PSYCHOLOGY, YALE UNIVERSITY, NEW HAVEN, CONN. I want to take part in this study of memory and learning. I am between the ages of 20 and 50. I will be paid $4.00 (plus 50c carfare) if I participate.

NAME (Please Print).....................................

ADDRESS...............................................

TELEPHONE NO. ............... Best time to call you .......

AGE........OCCUPATION....................SEX......
CAN YOU COME:

WEEKDAYS ....... EVENINGS ......WEEKENDS.........

**Figure 5.3** Announcement in a local newspaper to recruit participants

Shock generator and procedure used in the Milgram experiments (Milgram, 1974)

## Some of Milgram's (1974) variations on his basic procedure

ESSENTIAL STUDY 5.4

### Aims (AO1)

This was basically the same in all cases, namely to change a *single* variable to see its effect on obedience rate. The *basic procedure* remained the same as in the original experiment (called the ***remote victim*** experiment).

### Procedures (AO1) and Findings (AO1)

### Voice feedback (VF)

The teacher heard a series of tape-recorded verbal responses. These were, supposedly, Mr Wallace's spontaneous reactions to the increasing shock levels. At first (75–105 volts), he made a little grunt. At 120 volts, he told the experimenter the shocks were getting painful. He then demanded to be let out, sometimes screaming in agony, sometimes refusing to give any more answers (150–315 volts). After 330 volts, there was silence! *Obedience rate* was 62.5%.

This became the new 'baseline'. In other words, in all the later experiments there was voice feedback, and some *other* variable was changed.

### Proximity (P)

The teacher was now in the same room as Mr Wallace. They sat about 1.5 ft/46 cm apart, and the teacher could see as well as hear Mr Wallace's protests and screams. *Obedience rate:* 40%.

### Touch proximity (TP)

The teacher had to help keep Mr Wallace's arms down on the arms of the chair. The electric shock supposedly came through shock plates located on the arms. *Obedience rate:* 30%.

### Remote authority (RA)

The experimenter left the room after giving the teacher the essential instructions. He gave all other instructions by phone. *Obedience rate:* 20.5%.

### Two peers rebel (TPR)

The teacher was paired with two other (stooge) teachers. One stooge read out the list of word-pairs, while the other told Mr Wallace whether his answer was right or wrong. The teacher delivered the shocks. At 150 volts, the first stooge refused to continue and moved to another part of the room. At 210 volts, the second stooge did the same. The teacher had to take over the stooges' jobs. *Obedience rate:* 10%.

### A peer administers shock (PAS)

The teacher was paired with another (stooge) teacher. It was the stooge's job to 'throw the switch'. *Obedience rate:* 92.5%.

### Conclusions (AO1)

The 62.5% obedience rate in VF is still frighteningly high. Based on P and TP, it seems easier to resist the demands of an authority figure (disobey) when you can see for yourself the effects your behaviour has on the victim. RA suggests that it's easier to follow the dictates of our conscience when the authority figure isn't around. In TPR, participants see that it's *possible* to disobey and *how* to disobey. Some participants said they didn't realise they *could*. This is a demonstration of *conformity*.

## Does Milgram's research have internal and external validity?

✗ According to Orne & Holland (1968), Milgram's experiments lacked experimental (internal) realism/validity. That is, participants didn't believe that the experimental situation they found themselves in was real. In particular, they didn't think that Mr Wallace was really receiving electric shocks. They were actually responding to the demand characteristics of the experiment. That is, they were simply picking up on the cues that showed them how they were *expected* to behave in that situation (see page 123).

✓ But there's good reason to believe that participants *did* take the situation seriously. For example, many showed signs of distress and anxiety (such as nervous laughter and digging their nails into their flesh). According to Orne and Holland, this was a 'pretence'. In post-experimental interviews, participants never indicated that they'd been pretending.

✓ Sheridan & King (1972) found high levels of obedience when participants *must* have believed the situation was real. This involved students training a puppy on a task. Whenever it made a mistake, they punished it with *actual* electric shocks. Although the shocks were small, the students could see and hear the puppy's squeals. 75% of the students delivered the maximum shock.

✓ To criticise Milgram's experiments for being unethical, you must first believe that participants *weren't* pretending. Only if you're convinced his participants were *really* stressed could you condemn Milgram for exposing them to that stress (see Critical Issue, pages 112–116).

✗ Orne and Holland also claimed that Milgram's experiments lacked mundane (external) realism (or ecological validity). That is, the findings cannot be generalised beyond the particular laboratory setting in which they were collected. So we can't learn from Milgram's research about how people behave in other situations.

However, *naturalistic studies* of obedience suggest otherwise.

• For example, Hofling *et al.* (1966) studied 22 nurses working in various US hospitals. A stooge

'Dr Smith of the psychiatric department' instructed them, by phone, to give his patient (Mr Jones) 20 mg of a drug called *Astrofen*. Dr Smith was in a desperate hurry, and he'd sign the drug authorisation form later when he came to see Mr Jones.

- *Astrofen* was actually a dummy drug (a harmless sugar pill) invented just for the experiment. The label on the box clearly stated that the maximum daily dose was 10 mg. So if the nurse obeyed Dr Smith's instructions she'd be giving twice the maximum daily dose. Also, hospital rules required that doctors sign the authorisation form before any drug was given. Another rule demanded that nurses should be absolutely sure that 'Dr Smith' was a genuine doctor.
- 21 of the 22 nurses complied without hesitation. A control group of 22 nurses were asked what they *would have done* in that situation. 21 said that they wouldn't have given the drug without written authorisation, especially as it exceeded the maximum daily dose.
- Hofling *et al.* concluded that the greater power and authority of doctors seem to influence nurses' behaviour more than those rules do. Also, what people actually *do* in a particular situation and what they say they'd do can be very different.

## Why do people obey?

According to Milgram (1974), most of us would have behaved like his obedient participants. So the explanation for such high levels of obedience lies in aspects of the situation itself, rather than in individual characteristics.

### PERCEPTION OF LEGITIMATE AUTHORITY

- Obedient participants seemed to accept the power and status of the experimenter. In the context of the Yale University psychology department, the experimenter was 'in charge'.
- When we obey, we see ourselves as the instrument or agent of the authority figure's wishes (the **agentic state**). We give up personal responsibility for our actions (the **autonomous state**) and transfer that responsibility onto the authority figure. "I was only following orders" was the most common defence given by the Nazi war criminals (including Eichmann, who ran the death camps).
- Once we come to see ourselves in this way, the specific orders are largely irrelevant. In other words, obedience always involves the same mental adjustment (the agentic state); obedience is obedience is obedience.
- Authority figures often possess highly visible symbols of their power and status. These make it much more difficult to disobey them. For example, the experimenter always wore a *grey* lab coat (a white one would have implied 'scientist' rather than 'authority figure'). Zimbardo *et al.*'s prison study (see Essential Study 9.3, page 192) also showed the impact of uniforms and other trappings of power and authority.

### PERSONAL RESPONSIBILITY

- As we've seen, the agentic and autonomous states are really two sides of a coin. Anything which detracts from the authority figure's power will increase feelings of personal responsibility. This was shown in Milgram's RA (Remote Authority) variation. When the experimenter wasn't in the same room to give his instructions in person, participants were more likely to disobey.
- This was also shown in the P (Proximity) and TP (Touch Proximity) experiments. It's much more difficult to deny responsibility if you're in the same room as Mr Wallace (instead of just hearing his screams etc.). It's even more difficult if you physically have to force him to endure the shocks. In other words, it's easier to disobey when you can see for yourself the effects of your behaviour on the victim (see Conclusions in Essential Study 5.4).
- But when someone else actually 'throws the switch' (as in PAS: A Peer Administers Shock), it's easier to *deny* personal responsibility ("*He* delivered the shock, not *me*!").

### THE 'FOOT-IN-THE-DOOR'

- Participants got 'sucked into' a situation which they found very difficult to escape from. They'd volunteered for what seemed like a 'harmless' study of learning and memory. There was no mention in the original announcement of punishment, let alone delivering electric shocks to another participant. The first they heard of it was once they'd already made the effort to get to the psychology department.

- Once they were in the experimental situation, it was more difficult to leave. The deeper in you are, the greater the effort you have to make to escape. If the original announcement had referred to punishment and/or shock, perhaps fewer volunteers would have come forward. Or perhaps they would have been a more sadistic group of people!

---

## EXAM tips BOX

**Give a brief account of psychological explanations of obedience and consider their strengths *and* limitations. (18 marks)**

- You could structure your answer in terms of three paragraphs, all about 100–130 words long.

- *A word of warning: The question asks for 'explanations of obedience', so you must give <u>at least two</u>. But if you give more than two, these won't have to be as detailed. Also, this isn't a 'Milgram question' as such, and you must avoid getting bogged down in the details of particular experiments. Try to bring other researchers into your answer.*

- The first paragraph could describe one or more of the specific factors that Milgram investigated in the variations of his original (remote victim) experiment, and/or one or more general explanations (such as personal responsibility). (AO1, worth 6 marks).

- In the second paragraph you could consider some of the strengths and limitations of the studies described in the first paragraph. *Remember, you're not* describing *the findings here. You're* evaluating *these later experiments, drawing out the conclusions, which, in turn, suggest why people obey.*

- In the third paragraph you could repeat the exercise for perhaps two examples of more general explanations of obedience. The same reminder applies here as for paragraph 2. (AO2, worth 12 marks).

Try to write a suitable answer in about 300–350 words. As with all questions, there's no single correct way of answering it. The above are just pointers. There's a sample answer at the end of the book. Try not to look at it until you've had a go at doing it yourself.

---

## How can we resist obedience?

Anything which *increases* our sense of personal responsibility will also *increase* our resistance to obey. When the experimenter said "You have no other choice, you *must* go on", many participants *stopped* obeying. It brought home to them that they *did* have a choice and *were* responsible.

Milgram himself believed that obedience could be reduced by:

- educating people about the dangers of blind obedience
- encouraging them to *question authority*
- exposing them to *disobedient models*. This is what happened in TPR. Participants were influenced more by *conformity* with the behaviour of peers than by the demands of an authority figure.

---

## Critical issue: ethical issues in psychological research

### Ethical issues arising from social influence research

- Most people would agree that it's morally unacceptable (unethical) to harm another person (physically and/or mentally) in everyday life. It may also be illegal. Similarly, if we lie or deceive someone. But until Milgram's initial obedience experiment, psychologists didn't really discuss the ethics of their research in the way they do today.
- The social influence research of Milgram, Zimbardo *et al.*, Asch and others have all been criticised for being unethical. But they have also helped to identify the crucial ethical issues that *all* psychologists must consider when planning and conducting their research. Without these social influence studies, there might not be an ethics debate at all.

## DECEPTION AND INFORMED CONSENT: MILGRAM'S RESEARCH

- There's no question that Milgram deceived his participants. The original announcement stated that the study was concerned with memory and learning. Only after volunteers were already in the experimental situation did the experimenter mention punishment and electric shock.
- Even if the study had actually been about the effects of punishment on learning, Milgram would still have been deceiving his participants. But, of course, it *wasn't.* The more serious deception was that it was really about obedience. This was never mentioned until after the experiment was over. Participants also believed that Mr Wallace was another participant. In fact, he was an actor playing the role of participant. They were also deceived about the electric shocks. Mr Wallace never actually received any!
- What all of this means is that participants couldn't give their **informed consent**. That is, they volunteered for a study without knowing its true purpose or what would happen. Had they known, they might not have volunteered in the first place. You could say that they were tricked into taking part.

## DECEPTION AND INFORMED CONSENT: ZIMBARDO *ET AL.*'S RESEARCH

- Zimbardo *et al'.*s (1973) prison experiment (see Essential Study 9.3, page 192) was advertised as a study of prison life. This was the *true* purpose of the study. In fact, Zimbardo *et al.* produced an informed consent contract. This told participants everything that was going to happen to them (as far as this could be predicted). It was signed by every participant. They gave their permission for invasion of privacy, loss of civil rights, and harassment.
- They were deceived about only one thing. They weren't told that the prisoners would be arrested by the local police force. This was partly because the police didn't give their final approval until the last minute. But Zimbardo *et al.* also wanted the arrest to come as a surprise. Zimbardo admitted that this was in breach of their own contract.

## DECEPTION AND INFORMED CONSENT: ASCH'S RESEARCH

- Asch told his participants that the experiment was concerned with perception. Since it was actually about conformity, they were clearly deceived about its true purpose.
- This means, as with Milgram, that participants couldn't give their informed consent. And also like Milgram, Asch's participants didn't realise that the other group members were, in fact, stooges.

## IS DECEPTION EVER JUSTIFIED?

- Most of Asch's participants were very enthusiastic. In post-experimental interviews, they said how they admired the elegance and significance of the experimental procedure.
- Milgram (1974) defended himself by reporting that he thoroughly *debriefed* his participants. He had a lengthy discussion with each participant individually as soon as the experiment was over (see below). He then sent them a detailed account of the procedure and results of all the experiments. He also sent them a follow-up questionnaire about their experience of taking part.
- Most participants who returned the questionnaire said they were glad or very glad they had taken part. Many said they learned something important about themselves, and there should be more research like it.
- Milgram took this to be *the* crucial justification for deceiving his participants. If *they* didn't object, why should anybody else?
- Participants had to believe they were delivering real shocks, otherwise we couldn't generalise the results to real-life obedience situations. This relates to what we said above about experimental (internal) and ecological (external) validity/realism. So deception was necessary if participants were to behave in a 'realistic' way.

## PROTECTING PARTICIPANTS FROM PSYCHOLOGICAL HARM: MILGRAM'S RESEARCH

- Baumrind (1964) accused Milgram of abusing his participants' rights and feelings. She argued that Milgram failed to protect them adequately from stress and emotional conflict.
- Milgram accepted that they did experience stress and conflict. But he argued that Baumrind's criticism assumes that the experimental outcome was *expected*. In fact, Milgram was as surprised as

anyone by the high obedience rate. The most distressed participants tended to be those who were the most obedient. So if Milgram expected very low obedience rates, he certainly didn't expect participants to experience high levels of conflict.

- But shouldn't he have stopped his research as soon as he saw how distressed participants became? Also, the whole set-up was designed to make it difficult for participants to disobey. The experimenter's prods pressurised the participant into obeying. This made withdrawal from the investigation extremely difficult. In his defence, Milgram argued that:

(a) At whatever point the participant stopped giving shocks, s/he was reunited with Mr Wallace. The participant could see he was unharmed, and was also informed that the shocks weren't real. Milgram had an extended discussion with each participant individually. He assured obedient participants that their behaviour was completely normal. He supported the disobedient ones in their resistance to the experimenter's demands. This was all part of a thorough debriefing, which Milgram had decided would take place as a matter of course. That is, it would have happened anyway, and wasn't a response to any criticisms.

(b) The experimenter *didn't* make the participant shock Mr Wallace (as Baumrind claimed). Indeed, this *couldn't* have happened. Milgram believed that people have free will, and so *choose* to obey or disobey.

---

**Table 5.2** Arguments in Milgram's defence ('for') and criticisms ('against') of his obedience experiments

| **Consent/informed consent** | |
| --- | --- |
| *For* | *Against* |
| • Participants volunteered | • They volunteered for a study of learning and memory |

| **Deception** | |
| --- | --- |
| *For* | *Against* |
| • Debriefing – as matter of course | • Debriefing only needed because of deception |
| • Participants accept it | • Prevents informed consent |
| • The end justifies the means | • Harmful to self-concept |

| **Protection of participants** | |
| --- | --- |
| *For* | *Against* |
| • Results weren't anticipated | • Participants very distressed |
| • Reunited with unharmed victim | • Debriefing only needed because of participants' distress |
| • Reassured after the experiment as part of debriefing | |
| • No evidence of long-term harm | |
| • Participants have free will | |

| **Withdrawal from the investigation** | |
| --- | --- |
| *For* | *Against* |
| • Participants free to leave at any time | • The whole situation made resistance (disobedience) difficult |
| • 37.5% disobeyed (voice-feedback condition) | |
| • 62.5% obeyed (voice-feedback condition) | |

---

## PROTECTING PARTICIPANTS FROM HARM: ZIMBARDO *ET AL.*'S RESEARCH

- Zimbardo believes that the ethical concerns are even greater in his own prison study than in Milgram's research. Volunteer prisoners suffered physical and psychological abuse over several days. Volunteer guards discovered that they enjoyed being powerful and abused this power to make other human beings suffer. Although every participant signed an informed consent form, this couldn't protect the prisoners from the guards' abuse. Nor could it protect the guards from what they learned about themselves. It took Zimbardo *et al.* six days to end the experiment that was planned to last for two weeks. Why did it take them so long?

- According to Savin (1973), the practical benefits of the prison study didn't justify the distress, mistreatment and degradation suffered by the participants. That is, the end *didn't* justify the means.

## PROTECTING PARTICIPANTS FROM HARM: ASCH'S RESEARCH

- Many of Asch's participants said they conformed only because they didn't want to be laughed at or ridiculed (see page 106). When Asch ran the experiment using several naïve participants and a single stooge, they openly ridiculed the stooge on the critical trials. Other studies have shown that participants' physiological stress levels increase on critical trials.

### EXAM tips BOX

**To what extent can use of deception in social influence research studies be justified? (18 marks)**

- You could structure your answer in terms of three paragraphs, all about 100–130 words long.

- In the first paragraph you should explain what deception involves/what it means in relation to social influence research, giving one or two examples of how deception has been used in particular experiments. (AO1, worth 6 marks).

- In the second paragraph you could show how deception and consent/informed consent are related (and explain the difference between consent/informed consent). If you refer to specific studies here, it's to *illustrate this relationship* (not to describe the study).

- You're trying to show *how/why* deception may be considered ethically unacceptable.

- In the third paragraph you could consider, say, *two or more* arguments *against* using deception (one of which is to do with consent/informed consent), then consider *two or more* arguments *in support* of its use. These arguments might centre around the *consequences* of being deceived, including (i) participants' distress, embarrassment etc., (ii) what they learn about themselves as people; (iii) the realistic nature of participants' behaviour. (AO2, worth 12 marks).

- *A word of warning: This question doesn't ask you specifically about Milgram's research, although you're likely to know a lot about it. So you're free to include other researchers' studies. The 18-mark questions don't ask you to describe the procedures of a study. So you should only do so when this is relevant.*

Try to write a suitable answer in about 300–350 words. As with all questions, there's no single correct way of answering it. The above are just pointers. There's a sample answer at the end of the book. Try not to look at it until you've had a go at doing it yourself.

## Dealing with these issues: Ethical guidelines

- An ethics committee of the American Psychological Association (APA) investigated Milgram's (1963) study soon after it was published. The committee eventually judged it to be ethically acceptable. So even at that time psychologists were aware of ethical issues involved in research with human participants. But it's generally agreed that Milgram's controversial research highlighted these issues and stimulated the ethics debate.

- The major professional bodies for psychologists are the British Psychological Society (BPS) and the APA. Both organizations have published several sets of ethical guidelines. These include the *Ethical Principles for Conducting Research with Human Participants* (BPS, 1993).

### WHY DO WE NEED ETHICAL GUIDELINES?

- The introduction to the BPS *Ethical Principles* states that:

> ' . . . for ethical reasons, some areas of human experience and behaviour may be beyond the reach of experiment, observation or other forms of psychological investigation. Ethical guidelines are necessary to clarify the conditions under which psychological research is acceptable.'

- It urges psychologists to encourage their colleagues to follow *the Ethical Principles*. They should be adopted by *anyone* conducting *any* kind of psychological research, including GCSE, and AS/A level students.

- Researchers must consider the psychological consequences of their research *for the participants*. Researchers must ensure that participants' psychological wellbeing, health, values and dignity aren't threatened in any way.

MAJOR ETHICAL PRINCIPLES

We've already considered the research of Asch, Milgram, and Zimbardo *et al.* in the light of:

- deception
- consent/informed consent
- protection of participants from psychological harm
- withdrawal from the investigation.

If the psychologist decides that deception is necessary, s/he should debrief the participants *as soon as possible* after the experiment. Debriefing is also a major means of protecting participants who've suffered emotional distress.

## EXAM tips BOX

**To what extent can ethical guidelines ensure that the major ethical issues involved in social influence research are properly dealt with? (18 marks)**

- You could structure your answer in terms of three paragraphs, each about 100–130 words long.

- *A word of warning: there's an important distinction between* ethical issues *and* ways of dealing with/trying to ensure they're dealt with properly. *Issues refer to participants' rights and psychologists' responsibilities.*

In the first paragraph you could briefly describe the major ethical issues involved in research with human participants, and *give some examples* of how these issues have been highlighted by social influence research. *Note that while there are several sets of guidelines, it's sufficient for this question just to refer to the BPS Ethical Principles.* (AO1, worth 6 marks).

- In the second paragraph you could consider the relationship between ethical codes and social influence research. For example, did such codes exist *before* this research took place, and why should social influence research be so central in the ethics debate?

- In the third paragraph you could consider who publishes ethical guidelines, their main aims and objectives, who's meant to follow the guidelines, and what they recommend psychologists should do in order to achieve the aims and objectives. For example, under what conditions, if any, is deception permissible, and what are the safeguards that help protect participants when deception is used?

- Here you're *analysing and evaluating* the use of ethical codes as ways of dealing with major ethical issues, rather than saying what they are and giving examples. (AO2, worth 12 marks).

Try to write a suitable answer in about 300–350 words. As with all questions, there's no single correct way of answering it. The above are just pointers. There's a sample answer at the end of the book. Try not to look at it until you've had a go at doing it yourself.

## Self-assessment questions

These are some example Part a and Part b questions (worth 40% of your exam). Part c questions have been dealt with throughout the chapter in the Exam tips boxes and in the sample answers at the end of the book.

1  **a.**  What is meant by the terms 'minority influence', 'ecological validity', and 'informed consent'? (2 + 2 + 2 marks)

   **b.**  Outline conclusions from research into majority influence. (6 marks)

2  **a.**  Describe *two* ways in which psychologists deal with ethical issues (such as deception, informed consent, and protecting participants from psychological harm). (3 + 3 marks)

   **b.**  Outline findings from research into minority influence. (6 marks)

3  **a.**  Outline the main features of *one* explanation of conformity. (6 marks)

**b.** Explain what is meant by the terms 'conformity' and 'obedience' and give *one* difference between them. (2 + 2 + 2 marks)

**4 a.** Describe the procedure and findings of *one* study of majority influence. (3 + 3 marks)

**b.** Outline the findings of *one* study of obedience and give one criticism of this study. (3 + 3 marks)

**5 a.** Describe explanations of why people obey. (6 marks)

**b.** Outline *two* factors that can influence obedience to authority. (3 + 3 marks)

| ESSENTIAL STUDY SUMMARY | | | |
|---|---|---|---|
| **Topic** | **Research study** | **Researcher date** | **Pages** |
| Conformity/majority influence | Comparison-Of-Lines Experiment (COLE) | Asch (1951) | 102–103 |
| Minority influence | Blue Colour Slide Experiment (BCSE) | Moscovici *et al.* (1969) | 104 |
| Obedience | Shocking Obedience Study (SOS) | Milgram (1963) | 107–109 |
| .. | Voice Feedback (VF) | .. (1974) | 109–110 |
| .. | Proximity (P) | .. .. | |
| .. | Touch Proximity (TP) | .. .. | |
| .. | Remote Authority (RA) | .. .. | |
| .. | Two Peers Rebel (TPR) | .. .. | |
| .. | A Peer Administers Shock (PAS) | .. .. | |

# CHAPTER SUMMARY: revision schema

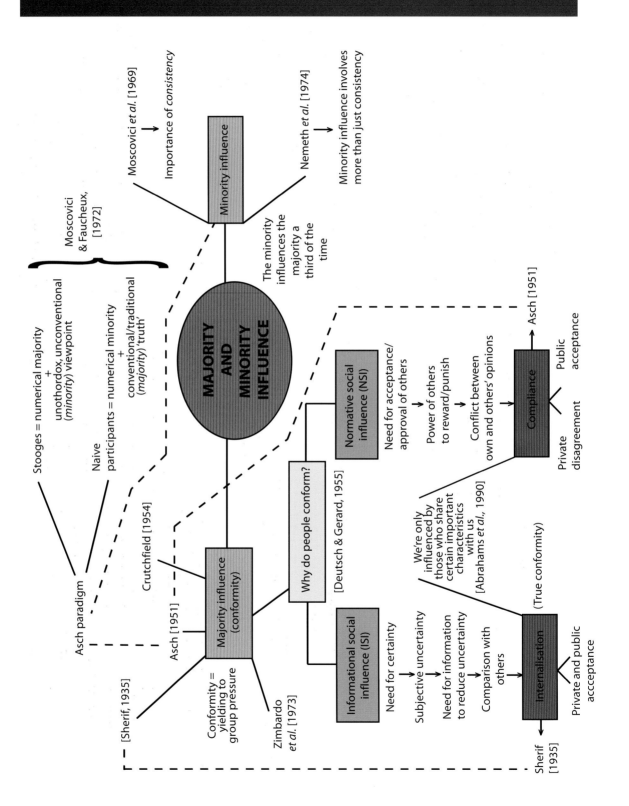

**MAJORITY AND MINORITY INFLUENCE**

**Minority influence**

Moscovici *et al.* [1969]

Importance of *consistency*

Nemeth *et al.* [1974]

Minority influence involves more than just consistency

Moscovici & Faucheux, [1972]

Stooges = numerical majority + unothordox, unconventional (*minority*) viewpoint

Naive participants = numerical minority + conventional/traditional (*majority*) 'truth'

The minority influences the majority a third of the time

Asch paradigm

Crutchfield [1954]

Asch [1951]

[Sherif, 1935]

Zimbardo *et al.* [1973]

**Majority influence (conformity)**

Conformity = yielding to group pressure

**Why do people conform?**

[Deutsch & Gerard, 1955]

**Normative social influence (NSI)**

Need for acceptance/ approval of others

Power of others to reward/punish

Conflict between own and others' opinions

**Compliance**

Public acceptance

Private disagreement

Asch [1951]

We're only influenced by those who share certain important characteristics with us [Abrahams *et al.*, 1990]

**Informational social influence (ISI)**

Need for certainty

Subjective uncertainty

Need for information to reduce uncertainty

Comparison with others

**Internalisation**

(True conformity)

Private and public accceptance

Sherif [1935]

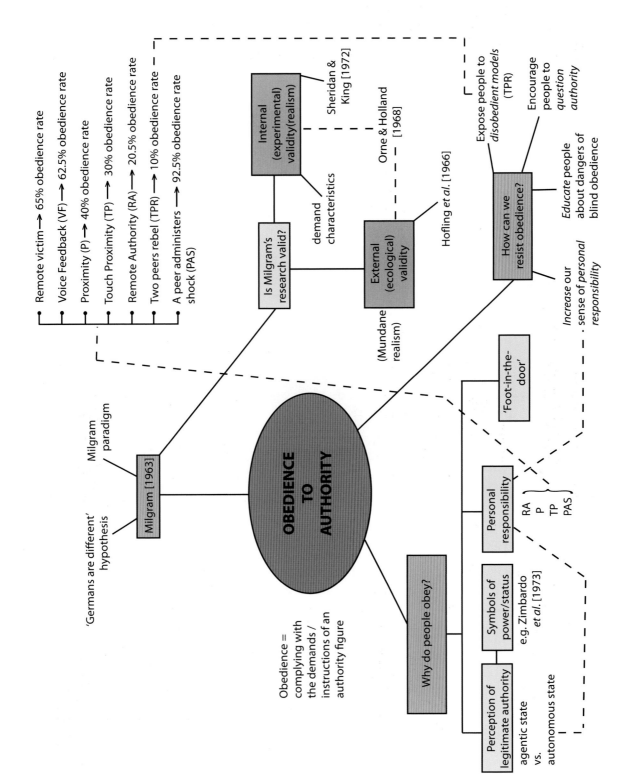

Remote victim → 65% obedience rate

Voice Feedback (VF) → 62.5% obedience rate

Proximity (P) → 40% obedience rate

Touch Proximity (TP) → 30% obedience rate

Remote Authority (RA) → 20.5% obedience rate

Two peers rebel (TPR) → 10% obedience rate

A peer administers → 92.5% obedience rate
shock (PAS)

Internal
(experimental)
validity(realism)

Sheridan &
King [1972]

Orne & Holland
[1968]

Expose people to
*disobedient models*
(TPR)

Encourage
people to
*question*
*authority*

Is Milgram's
research valid?

demand
characteristics

External
(ecological)
validity

Hofling *et al.* [1966]

How can we
resist obedience?

*Educate* people
about dangers of
blind obedience

(Mundane
realism)

*Increase* our
sense of *personal*
*responsibility*

Milgram
paradigm

Milgram [1963]

'Germans are different'
hypothesis

OBEDIENCE
TO
AUTHORITY

'Foot-in-the-
door'

Personal
responsibility

RA
P
TP
PAS

Obedience =
complying with
the demands /
instructions of an
authority figure

Why do people obey?

Symbols of
power/status

e.g. Zimbardo
*et al.* [1973]

Perception of
legitimate authority

agentic state
vs.
autonomous state

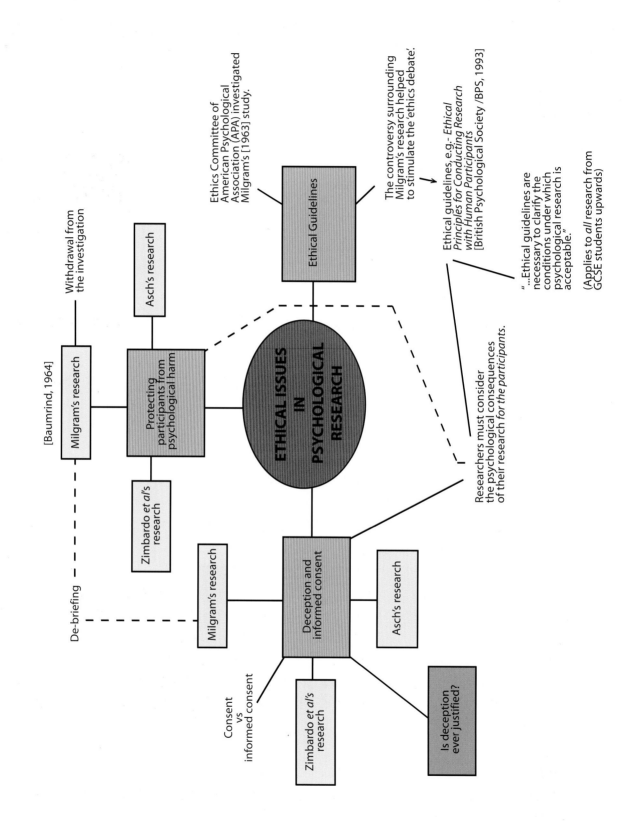

Ethics Committee of American Psychological Association (APA) investigated Milgram's [1963] study.

Ethical Guidelines

The controversy surrounding Milgram's research helped to stimulate the 'ethics debate'.

Ethical guidelines, e.g.:- *Ethical Principles for Conducting Research with Human Participants* [British Psychological Society / BPS, 1993]

"...Ethical guidelines are necessary to clarify the conditions under which psychological research is acceptable."

(Applies to *all* research from GCSE students upwards)

Withdrawal from the investigation

Asch's research

[Baumrind, 1964]

Milgram's research

Protecting participants from psychological harm

Zimbardo *et al*'s research

De-briefing

ETHICAL ISSUES IN PSYCHOLOGICAL RESEARCH

Researchers must consider the psychological consequences of their research *for the participants*.

Milgram's research

Deception and informed consent

Asch's research

Consent vs informed consent

Zimbardo *et al*'s research

Is deception ever justified?

# Research Methods

## What's covered in this chapter?
### You need to know about:

Quantitative and qualitative research methods

The nature and usage of the following research methods and their advantages and disadvantages and how they relate to the scientific nature of psychology

- Experiments (laboratory, field and natural experiments)
- Investigations using correlational analysis
- Naturalistic observations
- Questionnaires
- Interviews

The nature and usage of ethical guidelines in psychology

Research design and implementation

- Aims and hypotheses (generation of appropriate aims; the formulation of different types of the experimental/alternative hypothesis (directional and non-directional)
- Research designs: experimental (independent groups, repeated measures and matched participants) and the design of naturalistic observations, questionnaires and interviews
- Factors associated with research design, including the operationalisation of the IV/DV; conducting pilot studies; control of extraneous variables; ways of assessing and improving reliability and validity (internal and external validity); ethical issues associated with research
- The selection of participants, including random, opportunity and volunteer sampling
- The relationship between researchers and participants (including demand characteristics and investigator effects)

Data analysis

- The nature of qualitative data including strengths and weaknesses
- Measures of central tendency and dispersion (including the appropriate use and interpretation of medians, means, modes, ranges and standard deviations)
- The nature of positive and negative correlations and the interpretation of correlation coefficients
- Graphs and charts (including the appropriate use and interpretation of histograms, bar charts and scattergraphs)

## Quantitative and qualitative research methods

Quantitative research methods allow the numerical measurement of *how much* there is of something, i.e. the quantity. Qualitative research methods allow for the measurement of *what* something is like, i.e. the quality. An example of quantitative data would be the *number* of stressful incidents per day, whereas qualitative data would involve a *description* of these incidents.

There are a number of different research methods in psychology. Like the carpenter who selects the most appropriate tool for the job, psychologists choose the most appropriate method for their research. You need to know what these methods are and what their advantages and disadvantages are.

## Experiments

An experiment is a research method that helps to discover causal relationships between variables. A variable is any object, characteristic or event that changes or varies in some way. Experiments are the most widely used method in psychology.

The experimenter manipulates an independent variable (IV) to see its effect on the dependent variable (DV). The IV is the variable that is manipulated or altered by the experimenter to see its effect on the DV. The DV is the measured result of the experiment. Any change in the DV should be as a result of the manipulation of the IV. For example, alcohol consumption (IV) could be manipulated to see its effect on reaction time (the DV).

Extraneous variables are any other variables that may have an effect on the DV. Controls are employed to prevent extraneous variables spoiling the results. Any extraneous variables that aren't controlled can become confounding variables. These are so-called because they 'confound' (that is, confuse) the results.

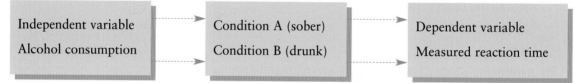

Independent variable
Alcohol consumption

Condition A (sober)
Condition B (drunk)

Dependent variable
Measured reaction time

There are several types of experiments:

### LABORATORY EXPERIMENTS

The researcher controls as many variables as possible. There's control over the 'who, what, when, where and how'. This is *usually* done in a laboratory using standardised procedures, but can be conducted anywhere provided it's in a controlled environment. Participants should also be randomly allocated to experimental groups.

**Advantages:**

✓ High degree of control: Experimenters can control all variables in the situation. This leads to greater accuracy and objectivity.

✓ Replication: Other researchers can easily repeat the experiment and check results.

✓ Cause and effect: It's possible to determine the cause and effect relationship between the IV and DV.

✓ Technical equipment: It's easier to use complicated technical equipment in a laboratory.

**Disadvantages:**

✗ Experimenter bias: Sometimes an experimenter's expectations about the study can affect results. Participants may be influenced by these expectations.

✖ **Low ecological validity:** The high degree of control can make the experimental situation artificial and not like real life. As such, it may be difficult to generalise results to other settings.

✖ **Demand characteristics:** Sometimes participants try to guess the purpose of the experiment and then act according to the 'demands' of the experiment.

## FIELD EXPERIMENTS

An experiment performed in the 'real world' rather than the laboratory. The IV is still manipulated by the experimenter.

## NATURAL EXPERIMENTS

Here the IV occurs naturally, it's not manipulated by the experimenter. The experimenter merely records the effect on the DV. An advantage here is that the effect of an IV can be studied where it would be unethical to manipulate it deliberately, e.g. family stress.

**Advantages: (can apply to both field and natural experiments)**

✓ **High ecological validity:** Due to the 'real-world' environment or naturally occurring environment, results are more likely to relate to everyday behaviour and can be generalised to other settings.

✓ **No demand characteristics:** Often participants are unaware of the experiment, and so there are no demand characteristics.

**Disadvantages:**

✖ **Less control:** It's more difficult to control extraneous variables, either 'in the field' or in naturally occurring situations.

✖ **Replication:** It's difficult to replicate field or natural experiments *precisely*.

✖ **Ethics:** There are ethical issues (e.g. informed consent, deception) when participants aren't aware of the experiment. This applies more to field experiments, since in natural experiments the independent variable naturally occurs and isn't manipulated by the experimenter.

✖ **Sample bias:** Since participants aren't randomly allocated to groups, there may be some sample bias.

| Experimental Research Methods Summary Table | | |
|---|---|---|
| **Type of experiment** | **Variable details** | **Environment** |
| Laboratory | Manipulation of IV<br>Measure DV | Controlled |
| Field | Manipulation of IV<br>Measure DV | Real-life |
| Natural | IV naturally occurs<br>Measure DV | Real-life |

## Investigations using correlational analysis

This isn't a research method as such, but a method of data analysis. It involves measuring the strength of the relationship between two or more variables (co-variables) to see if a trend or pattern exists between them.

- **A positive correlation:** one variable increases as the other variable increases, e.g. ice-cream sales increase as temperature increases.
- **A negative correlation:** one variable increases while the other variable decreases, e.g. raincoat sales decrease as temperature increases.

Correlations allow you to predict behaviour

- **A correlation coefficient:** the number that expresses the degree to which the two variables are related. The measurement ranges from +1 (perfect positive correlation) to −1 (perfect negative correlation). The closer the correlation to a perfect correlation, the stronger the relationship between the two variables. If there's no correlation, the result will be near to zero (0.0) (see scattergraphs, page 138).

## ADVANTAGES:

✓ **Allows predictions to be made:** Once a correlation has been found, we can make predictions about one variable from the other, e.g. we can predict the number of ice creams sold on hot days.

✓ **Allows quantification of relationships:** Correlations can show the strength of the relationship between two co-variables. A correlation of +0.9 means a high positive correlation, a correlation of −0.3 indicates a weak negative correlation.

✓ **No manipulation:** Correlations don't require the manipulation of behaviour, and so can be a quick and ethical method of data collection and analysis.

## DISADVANTAGES:

✗ **Cause and effect:** It cannot be assumed that one variable caused the other. Interpretation of results is made difficult, since there's no cause and effect in a correlation.

✗ **Extraneous relationships:** Other variables may influence both measured variables, e.g. most holidays are taken in the (hot?) summer and people eat ice creams on holiday. Therefore, the variable 'holiday' is related to both temperature and ice cream sales.

✗ **Only works for linear relationships:** Correlations measure only linear (straight-line) relationships. The relationship between temperature and aggression is a *curvilinear* relationship (see Figure 6.1). This would be a zero correlation, and yet there's an obvious relationship between these two variables.

## Naturalistic observations

This involves the precise (objective) measurement of naturally occurring behaviour. The observation occurs in the participant's own natural environment.

## ADVANTAGES:

✓ **High ecological validity:** Since observed behaviour takes place in the natural environment, participants behave naturally and results can be generalised to other settings.

✓ **Practical method:** It can be used in situations where deliberate manipulation

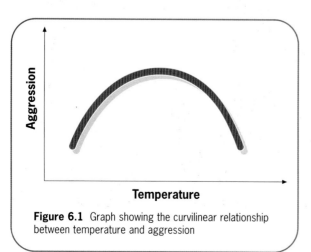

**Figure 6.1** Graph showing the curvilinear relationship between temperature and aggression

would be unethical or impractical (e.g. soccer hooliganism). It's particularly useful for studying animals or children.

✅ **Few demand characteristics:** Participants are often unaware of the observation and so there are few demand characteristics (see pages 133–134).

## DISADVANTAGES:

❌ **Cause and effect:** This cannot be inferred, since the variables are only observed, not manipulated.

❌ **Observer bias:** If observers know the purpose of the study, they may see what they want to see.

❌ **Replication:** It's difficult to check the reliability and validity (see page 131) of observations, since a lack of control means conditions can never be repeated accurately.

❌ **Ethics:** If participants are unaware of being observed, issues of invasion of privacy and informed consent arise.

## Questionnaires

Questionnaires are a written method of data collection, where respondents record their

Naturalistic observation is useful for studying animals and children

own answers to a pre-set list of questions. They're usually concerned with people's behaviour, opinions and attitudes. There are two main types of questions used:

- **Closed questions:** Responses are fixed by the researcher. They usually involve 'tick boxes' (e.g. 'yes' or 'no') or a range of fixed responses (e.g. 'always', 'usually', 'sometimes', 'never'). Such answers are easy to quantify, but restrict participants' answers.
- **Open questions:** Allow participants to answer in their own words. They're more difficult to analyse, but allow freedom of expression and obtain greater depth.

## ADVANTAGES:

✅ **Quick and cheap:** A large amount of information can be gathered in a relatively short period of time. As such, they're generally quicker and cheaper in comparison to other methods.

✅ **Large samples:** Questionnaires can be completed without the researcher present.

Victoria Beckham inadvertently revealed her husband's 'Golden Balls' nickname in a Parkinson interview on TV

Postal questionnaires can be used to gain very large samples for the cost of a stamp.

✓ **Quantitative analysis:** It's easy to analyse 'closed' questions statistically. Answers can be pre-coded on questionnaires for computer input and almost instant analysis.

✓ **Replication:** Since questionnaires use standardised questions, it's easy to replicate studies.

### DISADVANTAGES:

✗ **Misunderstanding:** Designing a questionnaire is a highly skilled job. Participants may misunderstand or misinterpret questions. For example, what do you mean when you say you 'usually' do your homework?

✗ **Biased samples:** Questionnaires are suitable only for people who are literate and willing and able to spend time filling them in.

✗ **Low response rates:** Some questionnaires have been known to obtain as little as a 5% return rate.

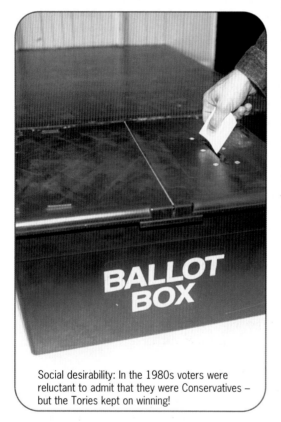

Social desirability: In the 1980s voters were reluctant to admit that they were Conservatives – but the Tories kept on winning!

✗ **Superficial issues:** Questionnaires aren't suitable for sensitive issues that require detailed understanding.

✗ **Social desirability:** Participants may present themselves in a positive light. Indeed, they may lie on sensitive issues, e.g. sexual behaviour.

## Interviews

Interviews involve researchers asking questions in a face-to-face situation. They can be very different but there are two broad types:

- **Structured (or formal) interviews:** A questionnaire is read to participants, and the interviewer writes down the responses. These interviews are identical for all participants and tend to involve simpler, quantitative questions. Interviewers don't need a lot of training, since these interviews are fairly easy to conduct.
- **Unstructured (or informal) interviews:** These are less controlled and involve an informal discussion on a particular topic. Whereas the topic is pre-determined, the direction of the interview isn't. This allows the interviewer to explore areas of greatest interest. Friendly rapport between the interviewer and respondent is important in order to gain the required level of detail and understanding. Interviewers need considerable training and expertise to conduct such interviews.

Interviews can combine these two types in semi-structured interviews.

### ADVANTAGES:

✓ **Complex issues:** Complicated or sensitive issues are best dealt with in face-to-face interviews. This is particularly true of unstructured interviews where answers can be developed.

✓ **Ease misunderstandings:** Any ambiguity or misunderstanding can be clarified within the interview.

✓ **Data analysis:** The variety and flexibility of interviews allows for the analysis of both quantitative and qualitative data.

## DISADVANTAGES:

✖ **Interviewer effects:** Interviewers may inadvertently bias the respondent's answers. This could even occur through the interviewer's appearance. For example, would a white person be less willing to admit to being racist to a black interviewer? Interviews are subject to demand characteristics and social desirability bias.

✖ **Ethical issues:** These can arise when participants don't know the true purpose of the interview. There is also a danger that participants may reveal more than they wish to.

✖ **Respondent answers:** Respondents may be unable to put into words their true feelings about a particular topic.

| Summary of ethical issues with different research methods | |
|---|---|
| **Research method** | **Ethical issues** |
| **Laboratory experiments** | • Participants **feel pressure** to act in a particular way.<br>• Reluctance of participants to exercise their **right to withdraw**.<br>• Experimental situation can be **stressful**. |
| **Field/natural experiments** | • **Informed consent** is difficult to obtain.<br>• Participants are unlikely to know of the **right to withdraw**.<br>• **Debriefing** is difficult. |
| **Naturalistic observations** | • If participants do not know they are being observed, there are issues of **informed consent, confidentiality and invasion of privacy**. |
| **Correlational analysis** | • Interpretation of results: The public may **interpret correlations incorrectly**. |
| **Interviews** | • **Confidentiality** must be maintained.<br>• **Right to withhold information** on embarrassing topics. |

# Research design and implementation

## Aims and hypotheses

An aim is a reasonably precise statement of *why* a study is taking place (e.g. to investigate the effect of alcohol on reaction times). It should include what is being studied and what the study is trying to achieve.

A hypothesis is much more precise and predicts what is expected to happen (e.g. alcohol consumption will significantly affect reaction times). Hypotheses are testable statements. There are two types:

• **Experimental (or alternative) hypothesis:** These predict significant differences in the DV as a result of manipulation of the IV. They predict that any difference or effect found will not be due to chance, e.g. there will be a significant difference in reaction times as a result of alcohol consumption. (Note: The term 'experimental hypothesis' should only be used with the experimental method. For all other methods, 'alternative hypothesis' should be used.)
• **Null hypothesis:** This is the *'hypothesis of no differences'*. It predicts that the IV will *not* affect the DV. It predicts that results will simply be due to chance, e.g. there will be no (significant) difference in reaction times as a result of alcohol consumption.

One of these hypotheses will be supported by the findings.

(Note: The inclusion of the word 'significant' in the null hypothesis is still being argued about by psychologists.)

There are also two types of experimental (alternative) hypotheses:

• **Directional (also called 'one-tailed'):** These state the direction of the results (e.g. there will be a significant increase in reaction times as a result of alcohol consumption: they'll get slower). They're called 'one-tailed' because they state one direction in which the results can go.

- **Non-directional ('two-tailed'):** These state that there will be a difference but don't state the direction of the results (e.g. there will be a significant difference in reaction times as a result of alcohol consumption). In this example, reaction times could either increase *or* decrease, and so they're called 'two-tailed'.

Directional hypotheses are used when previous research evidence suggests that it's possible to make a clear prediction, or when you're replicating a previous study that used a directional hypothesis.

## Research designs

### INDEPENDENT GROUPS DESIGN

Different participants are used in each of the conditions. Each group of participants is *independent* of the other. Participants are usually randomly allocated to each condition to try to balance out any differences.

Advantages:

✔ Order effects: There are *no* order effects (see page 129).

✔ Demand characteristics: Participants take part in one condition only. This means there's less chance of participants guessing the purpose of the study.

✔ Time saved: Both sets of participants can be tested at the same time. This saves time and money.

Disadvantages:

✘ More participants: With participants in only one condition, you need twice as many participants as repeated-measures design.

✘ Group differences: Any differences between the groups may be due to individual differences distinct from the IV. This can be minimised by the random allocation of participants to each group.

### MATCHED PARTICIPANTS (OR PAIRS) DESIGN

Different, but similar, participants are used in each of the conditions. Participants are matched across the groups on any characteristics judged to be important for that particular study. These are typically age, gender, ethnicity.

Advantages: (see advantages of independent groups design above)

✔ Group differences: Participant variables are more closely matched between conditions than independent groups design.

Disadvantages: (see disadvantages of independent groups design above)

✘ Matching is difficult: It's impossible to match all variables between participants. The one variable missed might be vitally important.

✘ Time-consuming: It takes a long time to match participants accurately on all variables.

### REPEATED MEASURES DESIGN

The same participants are tested in the two (or more) conditions. Each participant *repeats* the study in each condition.

Advantages:

✔ Group differences: The same person is measured in both conditions, there are *no* individual differences between the groups. Extraneous variables are kept constant (controlled) between the conditions.

✓ **Fewer participants:** Half as many participants are needed as for independent measures design.

## Disadvantages:

✗ **Order effects:** When participants repeat a task, results can be affected by order effects. On the second task, participants either:

- do worse due to fatigue or boredom, or

- improve through practice in the first condition. These can be controlled by *counterbalancing*, where half the participants do condition A followed by condition B and the other half do condition B, then A (ABBA).

✗ **Lost participants:** If a participant drops out of the study, they're 'lost' from both conditions.

✗ **Takes more time:** A gap may need to be given between conditions. This takes time and money.

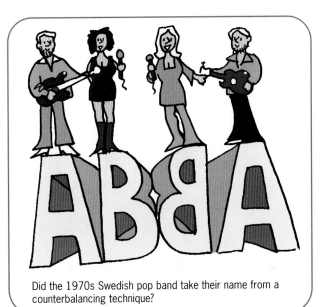

Did the 1970s Swedish pop band take their name from a counterbalancing technique?

## EXPERIMENTAL DESIGN SUMMARY:

Repeated measures: same participants

| Bob, Jane, Tom
Condition 1 | ----→ | Bob, Jane, Tom
Condition 2 |

Independent measures: different participants

| Bob, Jane, Tom
Condition 1 | ----→ | Tina, Kate, Mike
Condition 2 |

Matched pairs: matched participants

| Bob, Jane, Tom

Condition 1 | ----→ | Bob's brother, Jane's sister, Tom's brother

Condition 2 |

## Operationalisation of the IV/DV

The term 'operationalisation' means being able to define variables simply and easily in order to manipulate (IV) and measure them (DV). Sometimes this is very easily done.

For example, if we were investigating the effect of alcohol consumption on reaction times we could 'operationalise' the IV as the number of alcohol units consumed and the DV could be the speed of response to a flashing light. However, on other occasions this is more difficult.

For example, how would you 'operationalise' anger or stress levels? There isn't always a 'best way' of operationalising complex variables. The researcher has to make a judgement as to whether they're actually measuring the variables they hope to be measuring and present their arguments to support their decision. A major problem with the operationalisation of complex variables is that they measure only *one* aspect of the variable.

Both IV and DV need to be 'operationalised' accurately and objectively to maintain the integrity of any research study. Without accurate operationalisation, results may not be reliable or valid and certainly cannot be checked or replicated.

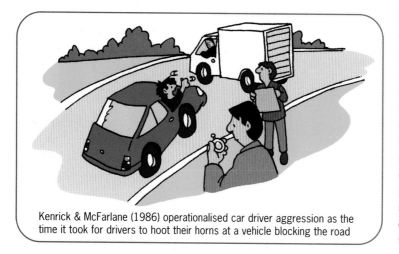

Kenrick & McFarlane (1986) operationalised car driver aggression as the time it took for drivers to hoot their horns at a vehicle blocking the road

## Pilot studies

These are small-scale 'practice' investigations, where researchers can check all aspects of their research. Changes to the design, method, analysis and so on can be made in the light of this. Pilot studies should improve the quality of the research, help avoid unnecessary work and save time and money. Participants may be able to suggest appropriate changes. For example, participants may admit that they guessed the purpose of the study and acted accordingly (demand characteristics).

## The control of variables

In any experiment, the IV is manipulated and the DV is measured. It's assumed that the IV causes any change or effect in the DV. However, there can be other variables that may affect the DV. These are called extraneous variables.

Extraneous variables must be carefully and systematically controlled so they don't vary across any of the experimental conditions or, indeed, between participants. When designing an experiment, researchers should consider three main areas where extraneous variables may arise:

- Participant variables: participants' age, intelligence, personality and so on should be controlled.
- Situational variables: the experimental setting and surrounding environment must be controlled. This may even include the temperature or noise effects.
- Experimenter variables: the personality, appearance and conduct of the researcher. Any change in these across conditions might affect the results. For example, would a female experimenter have recorded lower levels of obedience in Milgram's obedience to authority studies? (See pages 107–110.)

Extraneous variables are a problem only if they're not controlled. If they aren't carefully controlled then they may adversely affect or confound the results. They may systematically vary from one condition to another. If this happens we can no longer be sure whether any change in the DV is solely due to the manipulation of the IV or due to the presence of these other 'changing variables'. If this happens, they're called confounding variables. The presence of confounding variables minimises the value of any results and is a serious problem.

For example, if researchers wished to investigate the effect of background music (Condition 1) or silence (Condition 2) on homework performance using two classes, they'd have to control a number of possible extraneous variables. These might include age, homework difficulty and so on. If these were all successfully controlled, then the results would probably be worthwhile. However, if the researchers discovered that those in Condition 1 were considerably brighter than those in Condition 2, then intelligence would be acting as a confounding variable. The researchers could no longer be sure whether any differences in homework performance were due to the presence of the music or due to intelligence levels. Results would be confounded and worthless.

## Reliability and validity

Researchers try to produce results that are both reliable and valid. If results are reliable, they're said to be *consistent*. If a study was repeated using the same method, design and measurements, you'd expect to get similar results. If this occurs, the results can be described as reliable.

Reliability in science is essential. If results are unreliable, they cannot be trusted and so will be ignored. However, results can be reliable (i.e. consistent) but still not be accurate. Sometimes measuring instruments may be reliably producing inaccurate results! You may feel this is the case when you consistently get poor marks for your psychology homework! The teacher marks reliably but inaccurately!

Research results must also measure what they're supposed to be measuring (i.e. validity). If they do this and they're accurate, they're said to be valid. In effect, the measures can be described as 'true'. For example, is your teacher measuring your work according to exam board guidelines? If not, then their marking may be reliable but not valid!

It's possible to test both reliability and validity:

- **Internal reliability:** whether a test is consistent within itself. For example, a set of scales should measure the same weight between 50 and 100 grams as between 150 and 200 grams.
- **External reliability:** whether a test measures consistently over time. An IQ (intelligence) test should produce roughly the same measure for the same participant at different time intervals. This is called the test–retest method. Obviously you'd have to ensure that participants don't remember the answers from their previous test.

### INTERNAL VALIDITY

This refers to whether the results are valid (see above) and can be directly attributed to the manipulation of the IV. Results are internally valid if they've not been affected by any confounding variables. Are the results valid *within* the confines of the experimental setting? Various characteristics are required in order for an experiment to be internally valid. These are:

- No investigator effects (see page 134)
- No demand characteristics
- Use of standardised instructions
- Use of a random sample (see page 133).

### EXTERNAL (OR ECOLOGICAL) VALIDITY

This refers to whether the results are valid *beyond* the confines of the experimental setting. Can the results be generalised to the wider population or to different settings or different historical times? It's difficult to test whether a study has high ecological validity. It often only becomes clear when research findings are found either to apply or not apply to different situations. Field and natural experiments, and naturalistic observations, are usually regarded as being high in ecological validity. This is because the results can be more easily generalised to other real-life settings. Milgram's obedience experiments have low ecological validity on all three counts outlined above. The sample was predominantly male (cannot be generalised to females); it involved an artificial setting (Yale University laboratory), and it took place in a different historical time (1960s) to today. Bearing this in mind, are the results still valid today?

## Ethical issues associated with research

High quality research should involve good ethical practice. The British Psychological Society (BPS) publishes a code of ethics that all psychologists should follow. Much of this has been covered in the Social Influence chapter (pages 112–116):

- **Informed consent:** should be given by all participants prior to the study. Parental consent should be obtained in the case of children. Consent should also be obtained from children old enough to understand the study.
- **Avoidance of deception:** There may be occasions where some deception is unavoidable. **Presumptive consent** should then be gained from people of a similar background to the participants in the study. If they state that they'd have been willing to participate, it's likely that you'll not upset the actual participants (too much). If deception is used, participants should be told immediately afterwards and given the chance to withhold their data from the study.
- **Adequate briefing/debriefing:** All relevant details of the study should be explained to participants both before and after the study. The debrief is particularly important if deception has been used. Participants should leave the study feeling the same (or better) about themselves as when they started the study.
- **Risk or stress:** Participants should be protected from physical or psychological harm at all times.
- **Right to withdraw:** Participants should always be aware that they can leave the study at any time regardless of whether or not any payment or inducement has been offered. This can be particularly difficult during observations.
- **Privacy:** Participants' data should be treated as confidential and not disclosed to anyone. Numbers should be immediately allocated instead of names, and these should be used by the research team and in any subsequent published articles. It's easy to confuse confidentiality with anonymity. Confidentiality means that data can be traced back to names, whereas anonymous data cannot, since no names are collected by the research team. Confidential data collection is preferable in cases where participants might be followed-up later. Observations should be made only in public places where people might expect to be seen by strangers.

Good research means never having to say you're sorry!

## The selection of participants (including random, opportunity and volunteer sampling)

Psychological studies usually involve samples drawn from larger populations. Sampling is essential to avoid the need to study entire populations. The selected sample should be representative of this wider population. Representative samples *represent* the target population and should share (some of) the same important characteristics. It's called a target population because this is the group of people whom the researcher is hoping to *target* or generalise the results to. In general, the larger the sample, the better it is. However, the larger the sample, the more costly or time-consuming it is. Psychologists use a number of sampling techniques to try to obtain representative samples:

- **Random sampling:** This is the best known method. It's where every member of the population has an equal chance of being selected. The easiest way to do this is to place all names from the target population in a hat and draw out the required sample number. Computer programs can also generate random lists. This will result in a sample *selected* in an unbiased way. However, it can still result in a biased sample. For example, if 10 boys' and 10 girls' names were placed in a hat, there is a (small) chance that the first 10 names drawn from the hat could be boys. Selection would have been unbiased, but the sample would still be biased! A special form of random sampling involves the random allocation of participants to different conditions in independent groups design (see page 128).

 **Evaluation of these techniques**

✓ The sample is likely to be representative and therefore results can be generalised to the wider population.

✗ It's sometimes difficult to get details of the wider population in order to select the sample.

✗ It's sometimes difficult to decide on the appropriate layers or strata with which to select the stratified sample.

The following two techniques of sampling don't usually result in representative samples:

- **Opportunity sampling:** Involves selecting participants who are readily available and willing to take part. This could simply involve asking anybody who's passing.
- **Volunteer or self-selected sampling:** Involves people volunteering to participate. They select themselves as participants. This sampling method was used by Milgram (1963) in his Shocking Obedience Study (SOS).

 **Evaluation of these techniques**

✓ They are the easiest, most practical and cheapest ways to get large samples.

✗ The sample is likely to be biased in some (important) way. Thus the findings may not be generalised to the wider population. Volunteers may be more motivated and thus perform differently than randomly selected participants.

## The relationship between researchers and participants

Any social interaction affects people's behaviour. Conducting research is no different. It doesn't take place in a 'social vacuum', and involves some interaction between the researcher and the participant. Such interaction can therefore affect the research findings.

Orne (1962) believed that there are many features in research studies that enable the participants to guess what the study is about and what's expected of them. These demand characteristics can involve participants:

I SEE THAT OUR INTERVIEWS LASTED 3 TIMES AS LONG WITH BLONDE SINGLE WOMEN UNDER 30. COULD THIS BE DUE TO EXPERIMENTER EFFECTS...?

- guessing the purpose of the research and trying to please the researcher by giving the 'right' results
- guessing the purpose of the research and trying to annoy the researcher by giving them the wrong results. This is called the **'screw you' effect** for obvious reasons!
- acting unnaturally out of nervousness for fear of being thought 'abnormal'
- acting unnaturally in order to 'look good' (**social desirability bias**).

We've previously noted the effect of demand characteristics in different research methods.

A technique which reduces demand characteristics is the single blind procedure. This is where participants have no idea which condition of the study they're in. For example, in drug trials, they wouldn't know whether they're being given the real drug or the placebo drug ('sugar pill').

## Investigator (experimenter) effects

Investigators may inadvertently influence the results in their research. This can occur in a number of ways:

- Certain physical characteristics of the investigator may influence results. Such factors might include age, ethnicity, appearance, attractiveness and so on. For example, as mentioned earlier, white participants may be unwilling to admit their racist views to a black researcher.
- Other less obvious personal characteristics of the investigator such as accent, tone of voice or non-verbal communication (eye contact, smiling) could influence results. Participants may pick up on this and not act as they normally would.

- The investigator may also be biased in their interpretation of the data. This, of course, should never be deliberate. It is claimed that Burt (1955) made up some of his evidence on the influence of heredity on intelligence.

Qualitative and quantitative analysis of wine!

A technique which reduces investigator (experimenter) effects is the double blind procedure. This is where neither the participant nor the investigator knows which condition the participant is in. They are both 'blind' to this knowledge. This prevents the investigator from inadvertently giving the participant clues as to which condition they are in and therefore reduces demand characteristics. Obviously, there is an investigator in overall charge who is aware of the allocation to conditions.

## Data analysis

Research involves the collection of data. This data can be analysed both quantitatively and qualitatively. Psychologists are still debating the merits of each approach. Generally, qualitative studies produce subjective, detailed, less reliable data whereas quantitative studies produce objective, less detailed, more reliable data. Although all research methods can involve both types of data analysis, there are certain methods that tend to favour the qualitative approach.

| General summary of quantitative and qualitative data | |
| --- | --- |
| **Qualitative data** | **Quantitative data** |
| Subjective | Objective |
| Imprecise measures used | Precise measures used |
| Rich and detailed | Lacks detail |
| Low in reliability | High in reliability |
| Used for attitudes, opinions, beliefs | Used for behaviour |
| Collected in 'real-life' setting | Collected in 'artificial' setting |

## The Nature of Qualitative Data

Qualitative data involves people's meanings, experiences and descriptions. It is particularly good for attitudes, opinions and beliefs. Data usually consists of verbal or written descriptions. The qualitative approach suggests that information about human events and experience loses much of its meaning and value when reduced to numerical form (Coolican, 1994).

There is no one agreed way to analyse qualitative data. Each researcher has their own ideas for the best way to do it. The analysis of qualitative data is a fairly new field and new methods are emerging and developing. Some of the ways to analyse qualitative data include:

Sometimes the analysis of content can be very obvious!

- **Content analysis:** This is most commonly done within media research. Strictly speaking, it actually involves the quantification of qualitative material. That is, it analyses in a numerical way written, verbal or visual communication. It can involve the analysis of speeches, graffiti, newspapers, TV adverts and so on. Wayforth & Dunbar (1995) analysed the content of Lonely Heart columns to see if men and women were looking for the same things in life.

  Content analysis requires coding units to be developed where analysed material can be categorised, for instance, the number of times women appear as housewives in TV adverts. Analysis can involve words, themes, characters or time and space. The number of times these things do not occur can also be important.
- **Categorising:** This involves the grouping of common items together. For example, it might be possible to group students' perceptions of their Psychology course into: resources, peer/teacher relationships, teacher knowledge, delivery and so forth. It's often difficult to decide on the categories to use.
- **Quotations:** Word-for-word quotations are often used to bring the research findings to life. The quotes should 'tell it like it is'. They should typify what others have said during the research.

| Coding Units for Content Analysis | |
| --- | --- |
| **Unit** | **Examples** |
| Word | Count the number of slang words used |
| Theme | The amount of violence on TV |
| Character | The number of female bosses there are on TV programmes |
| Time and space | The amount of time (on TV) and space (in newspapers) dedicated to famine in Africa |

## Qualitative data and naturalistic observations

Observers typically give a running commentary into a tape recorder as they observe behaviour. This produces qualitative data. Such data can be coded or categorised (see above) and help to add detail to quantitative data. The diary method is another technique where observers can take notes of behaviour. This can be self-reported behaviour. The diary method has the advantage of providing genuine information in the participants' own surroundings. However, participants often find diaries difficult to complete on a long-term basis.

## Qualitative data and questionnaire surveys

Qualitative data is mainly collected from open-ended questions where participants are invited to give an answer using their own words. Such data is less likely to be biased by the interviewer's preconceived ideas. Analysis of this data can involve content analysis, categorisation or the use of quotations as described above.

## Qualitative data and interviews

Interviews have been described above. Interviews are likely to be transcribed and can then be analysed using many of the qualitative techniques described above. Unstructured interviews are most suitable for qualitative analysis. The interpretation of interview data is open to subjective interpretation. However, this lack of objectivity may be overcome by the detail that such a method allows.

## Qualitative data analysis: evaluation

Qualitative data analysis tends to be subjective, although there are methods for checking both reliability (through replication) and validity (through the use of other methods). In any case, many qualitative researchers argue that subjectivity and the personal opinion of a participant are extremely valuable and would actually strengthen any research study. Qualitative data analysis can, however, be extremely time consuming.

## Measures of central tendency and dispersion

### MEASURES OF CENTRAL TENDENCY

These are used to summarise large amounts of data into a typical value or average. They are ways of estimating the mid-point of scores. There are three averages:

The mean: where all the scores are added up and divided by the number of scores.

✓ It is a very sensitive measure.

✓ It includes all the information from the raw scores and is one of the most powerful methods.

✓ It is most appropriate with interval or ratio data. This is data measured using units of equal interval. They reflect a real difference and involve 'public' units of measurement, e.g. height, time, distance, weight – for example, the times of runners in the London Marathon.

✗ It is less useful if some of the scores are skewed, that is, if there are very large or small scores ('outliers') in the distribution of scores (the median should be used instead).

✗ Often the mean score is not one of the original scores. It may involve decimal points.

The median: This is the central score in a list of rank-ordered scores. With an odd number of scores, the median is the middle number. With an even number of scores, the median is the mid-point between the two middle scores.

✓ It is not affected by extreme scores (outliers).

✓ It is most appropriate with ordinal data. This is data that can be ranked or ordered, e.g. 1st, 2nd, 3rd. Intervals between the rankings are likely to be unequal, for example, where the runners finished in the London Marathon.

✗ It is not as sensitive as the mean, because the raw scores are not used in the calculation.

e.g    1 1 2 3 4 5 6 7 8      the median is 4

       2 3 4 6 8 9 12 13      the median is 7

**The mode:** The most common or 'popular' number in a set of scores.

✓ It is not affected by extreme scores.

✓ It sometimes makes more sense. The average number of children in a British family is better described as 2 (the mode) rather than 2.4 children (the mean).

✓ It is most appropriate with nominal data. This is frequency or category data, the simplest form of data. It merely involves counting the frequency of occurrence in each category, for example, how many runners completed the London Marathon, how many runners didn't.

The mean height of these two teams is the same but it gives a misleading impression as to how well-matched they are

✗ There can be more than one mode in a set of data,
    e.g. 2 3 6 7 7 7 9 13 15 16 16 16 20 (modes are 7 and 16).

✗ It tells us nothing about the other scores.

## MEASURES OF DISPERSION

These are measures of the variability or spread of scores. They include:

**The range:** this is calculated by taking away the lowest value from the highest value in a set of scores. *(Note: Some psychologists also add 1 to the range if the measurement is in whole numbers.)*

✓ It is easy and quick to work out.

✓ It includes extreme values, but does not incorporate individual values.

✗ It can be distorted by extreme 'freak' values and does not show whether data are clustered or evenly spread around the mean,
e.g. 2 3 4 5 5 6 7 8 9 21 and 2 5 8 9 10 12 13 15 16 18 21.
The range of these two sets of data is the same, despite the data being very different.

**Interquartile range:** shows the middle 50% of a set of scores. When the scores are in rank order, the first 'quartile' (Q1) is the first 25% of scores. The third quartile (Q3) includes the first 75% of scores. The semi-inter-quartile range is half the distance between Q1 and Q3. To obtain this, you subtract Q1 from Q3 and divide by two.

e.g.    1    2    4    6    7    8    9    12    14    16    19

                 Q1  ←—  this is the inter-quartile range  —→  Q3

Q3 − Q1 = 14 − 4 = 10. 10 divided by 2 = 5 = semi-interquartile range.

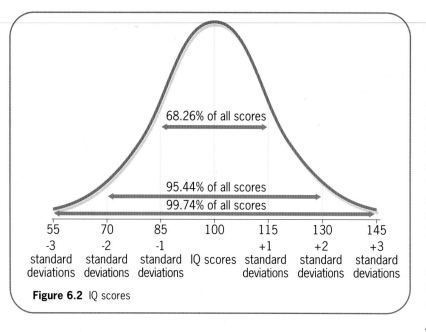

**Figure 6.2** IQ scores

68.26% of all scores

95.44% of all scores

99.74% of all scores

| 55 | 70 | 85 | 100 | 115 | 130 | 145 |
|---|---|---|---|---|---|---|
| -3 | -2 | -1 | IQ scores | +1 | +2 | +3 |
| standard deviations | standard deviations | standard deviations | | standard deviations | standard deviations | standard deviations |

✓ It is easy to calculate.

✗ It is not affected by extreme scores.

✗ It is inaccurate if there are large intervals between the scores.

Standard deviation: is a measure of the spread or variability of a set of scores from the mean. The larger the standard deviation, the larger the spread of scores.

✓ It is a more sensitive dispersion measure than the range since all scores are used in its calculation.

✓ It allows for interpretation of an individual's score. Thus In Figure 6.2, anybody with an IQ of 130+ is in the top 2.5% of the population (between +2 and +3 standard deviations of the mean).

✗ It is more complicated to calculate (you don't have to know how to do it for AS level).

✗ It is less meaningful if data aren't normally distributed.

## The nature of positive and negative correlations and the interpretation of correlation coefficients

Correlational methods have been mentioned above. Correlations can be positive, negative or showing no correlation. The stronger the correlation, the nearer it is to +1 or −1. Scattergraphs are useful techniques that show at a glance how two variables are correlated (see Figure 6.3). However, a statistical test or correlation coefficient has to be calculated to determine the exact nature of the correlation. *Again, you don't need to know how to do this at AS level.*

## Graphs and charts (including the appropriate use and interpretation of histograms, bar charts and scattergraphs)

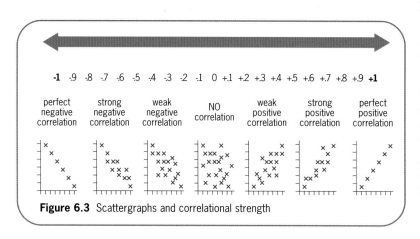

| **-1** | -.9 | -.8 | -.7 | -.6 | -.5 | -.4 | -.3 | -.2 | -.1 | 0 | +.1 | +.2 | +.3 | +.4 | +.5 | +.6 | +.7 | +.8 | +.9 | **+1** |

perfect negative correlation   strong negative correlation   weak negative correlation   NO correlation   weak positive correlation   strong positive correlation   perfect positive correlation

**Figure 6.3** Scattergraphs and correlational strength

Psychological data can be presented in a number of ways. Although psychology places the emphasis on statistical analysis, data should also be presented in a visually meaningful way. Graphs and charts enable the reader to 'eyeball' the data and help to show any patterns in the data. The use and interpretation of scattergraphs have already been dealt with. You need to know about the others. They are:

## BAR CHARTS

This shows data in the form of categories that the researcher wishes to compare, e.g. males, females. These categories should be placed on the X axis ('X is across'). The columns of bar charts should be the same widths and separated by a space. The use of a space illustrates that the variable on the X axis is not continuous. It is 'discrete' data (see Figure 6.4).

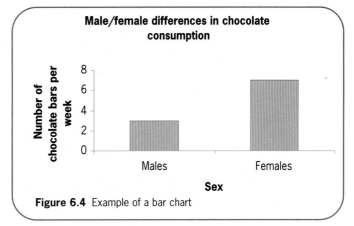

**Figure 6.4** Example of a bar chart

## HISTOGRAMS

Students often confuse histograms and bar charts. The main difference is that histograms are used for continuous data, e.g. test scores. These continuous scores or values should ascend along the X axis. The frequency of these values is shown on the Y axis. There should be no spaces between the bars since the data is continuous! The column width for each value on the X axis should be the same. Thus the area of each column is proportional to the number of cases it represents throughout the histogram (see Figure 6.5).

**Figure 6.5** Example of a histogram

## GENERAL POINTS:

- All graphs and charts must be fully labelled with an appropriate title and the X and Y axes should be accurately labelled.
- Graphs and charts look best if the Y axis height is three-quarters the X axis width.
- Only one graph or chart should be used to illustrate a set of data. Many students produce different graphs or charts of the same data!
- Use an appropriate scale on the axes. Don't mislead people by using an inappropriate scale on the axes. Political parties often do this and it's best not to follow their example.

## Self-assessment questions

## Question One:

Two teachers were interested in studying the effects of listening to music on students' revision and subsequent exam performance. Previous research suggests that listening to music whilst working has a negative effect on exam performance.

The teachers persuaded one class of students to participate. When revising for History the students listened to background music; whereas they revised for Psychology in silence (a repeated measures design).

Finally, all the participants sat a 'mock' exam in Psychology in the morning and then History in the afternoon. Each exam was marked by each class's teacher. The maximum mark was 100%. All the participants were thanked for their participation and thoroughly debriefed.

After the study, the Psychology teacher realised there were some problems with the study.

The results are shown in the table below:

**Table 1** Student exam performance against background music/silence

| Exam mark (%) against background music/ silence | |
| History mark (listening to music) | Psychology mark (silence) |
| --- | --- |
| 70 | 96 |
| 69 | 92 |
| 68 | 91 |
| 67 | 90 |
| 66 | 89 |
| 65 | 65 |
| 47 | 64 |
| 47 | 50 |
| 25 | 47 |
| 22 | 47 |
| 20 | 45 |

**(a) (i)** Give an appropriate null hypothesis for this study. (2 marks)

**(ii)** State whether your experimental/alternative hypothesis would be directional or non-directional and justify your choice. (1 + 2 marks)

**(b) (i)** Identify the type of sampling used in this study. (1 mark)

**(ii)** Explain *one* advantage and *one* disadvantage of this method of sampling. (2 marks)

**(c)** Suggest *one* advantage and *one* disadvantage of using repeated measures design in this study. (2 marks + 2 marks)

**(d)** What measure of central tendency is most suitable to describe the data in Table 1? Explain your choice of central tendency. (1 mark + 2 marks)

**(e)** Consider what the data in Table 1 seem to show about the effect of background music on exam performance. (6 marks)

**(f)** Identify *one* ethical issue that the researchers do not appear to have considered. Explain how this ethical issue could have been dealt with. (3 marks)

**(g)** Other than ethical issues, explain *two* ways in which the design of this study might have been improved. (3 + 3 marks)

## Question Two:

Some researchers wished to investigate whether intelligence is related to GCSE exam performance. Ten students were selected to participate in the study using random sampling. The students took an IQ (intelligence) test that the researchers had devised and their results were recorded. The researchers obtained the participants' GCSE results from their

**Figure 1** Relationship between intelligence (IQ) and GCSE exam performance

school. 10 points were given for a grade A, 8 points for a grade B and so on. In this way, the mean GCSE score was obtained for each student.

A correlational test was used to analyse the results. The rank order correlation coefficient was calculated as +0.83. The investigators also compared their sample's results to the wider population. The standard deviation of IQ scores in the general population is 15 with the mean being 100. The investigators concluded that their IQ score was not a valid measure of intelligence.

**(a)** Give *two* disadvantages of using correlational analysis. (2 + 2 marks)

**(b)** Write out a suitable directional (one-tailed) hypothesis for this investigation. (2 marks)

**(c)** Explain what is meant by random sampling and describe how a random sample of students could have been selected from the school registers. (1 + 2 marks)

**(d)** Describe *two* advantages of investigations using correlational analysis. (2 + 2 marks)

**(e)** Name the type of graph shown in Figure 1 above. (1 mark)

**(f)** Describe the relationship between intelligence and GCSE results in Figure 6.7. (2 marks)

**(g)** What is meant by the term 'standard deviation'? (2 marks)

**(h)** Identify *two* possible ethical issues that the investigators do not appear to have considered. Explain how the researchers might have dealt with them. (3 + 3 marks)

**(i)** Other than ethical issues, explain *two* ways in which the design of this study might have been improved. (3 + 3 marks)

# CHAPTER SUMMARY: revision schema

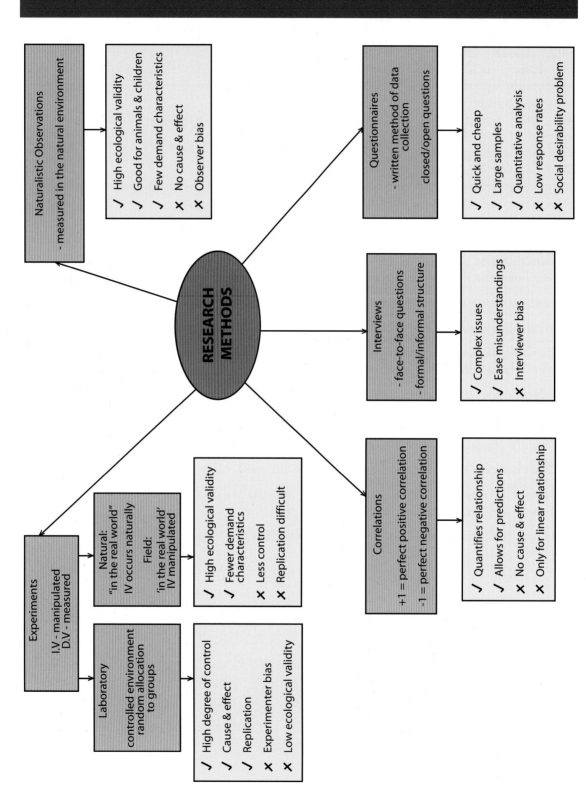

**RESEARCH METHODS**

**Naturalistic Observations**
- measured in the natural environment

✓ High ecological validity
✓ Good for animals & children
✓ Few demand characteristics
✗ No cause & effect
✗ Observer bias

**Questionnaires**
- written method of data collection
  closed/open questions

✓ Quick and cheap
✓ Large samples
✓ Quantitative analysis
✗ Low response rates
✗ Social desirability problem

**Interviews**
- face-to-face questions
- formal/informal structure

✓ Complex issues
✓ Ease misunderstandings
✗ Interviewer bias

**Correlations**
+1 = perfect positive correlation
-1 = perfect negative correlation

✓ Quantifies relationship
✓ Allows for predictions
✗ No cause & effect
✗ Only for linear relationship

**Experiments**
I.V - manipulated
D.V - measured

**Natural:**
"in the real world"
IV occurs naturally

**Field:**
"in the real world"
IV manipulated

✓ High ecological validity
✓ Fewer demand characteristics
✗ Less control
✗ Replication difficult

**Laboratory**
controlled environment
random allocation to groups

✓ High degree of control
✓ Cause & effect
✓ Replication
✗ Experimenter bias
✗ Low ecological validity

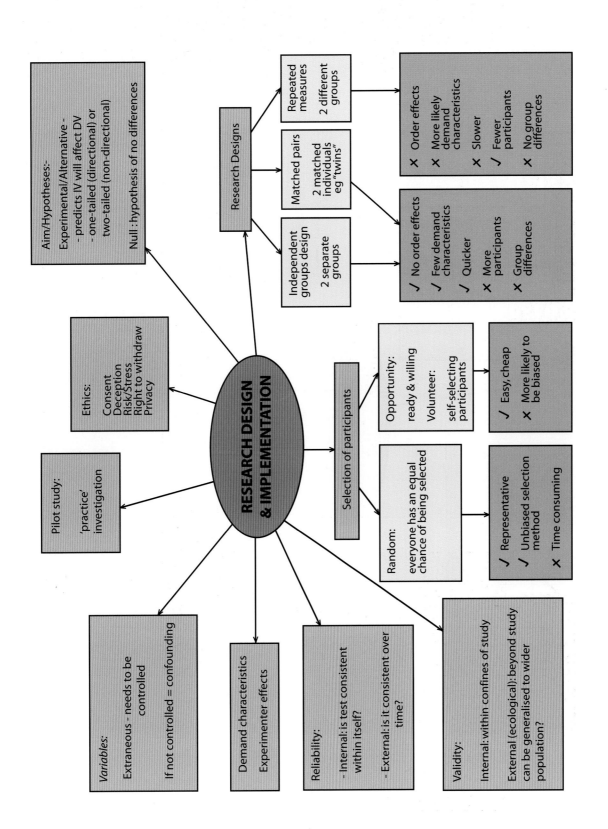

**Aim/Hypotheses:-**
Experimental/Alternative -
- predicts IV will affect DV
- one-tailed (directional) or
two-tailed (non-directional)

Null : hypothesis of no differences

**Research Designs**

Repeated measures
2 different groups

Matched pairs
2 matched individuals eg "twins"

Independent groups design
2 separate groups

✗ Order effects
✗ More likely demand characteristics
✗ Slower
✓ Fewer participants
✗ No group differences

✓ No order effects
✓ Few demand characteristics
✓ Quicker
✗ More participants
✗ Group differences

**Ethics:**
Consent
Deception
Risk/Stress
Right to withdraw
Privacy

**Pilot study:**
'practice' investigation

**RESEARCH DESIGN & IMPLEMENTATION**

**Selection of participants**

Opportunity:
ready & willing
Volunteer:
self-selecting participants

✓ Easy, cheap
✗ More likely to be biased

Random:
everyone has an equal chance of being selected

✓ Representative
✓ Unbiased selection method
✗ Time consuming

*Variables:*
Extraneous - needs to be controlled

If not controlled = confounding

Demand characteristics
Experimenter effects

**Reliability:**
- Internal: is test consistent within itself?
- External: is it consistent over time?

**Validity:**
Internal: within confines of study

External (ecological): beyond study can be generalised to wider population?

## DATA ANALYSIS

### Graphs & Charts

**Histograms:**
- Continuous data
- No spaces between bars

**Bar charts:**
- Category data
- Spaces between bars

**Scattergraphs:**
- strength of relationship between two variables
- +1 perfect positive correlation to -1 negative correlation

### Qualitative Data
- Subjective, descriptive
- Rich & detailed

e.g. content analysis

### Quantitative data
- Objective
- Numerical
- Precise

e.g. experiments

### Measures of central tendency:
- Mean - add scores and divide by numbers of scores

✓ very sensitive/interval data

- Median - central score

✓ not affected by extreme scores/ ordinal data

- Mode - most 'popular' number

✓ not affected by extreme scores/ nominal data

### Measures of dispersion:
- Range - lowest value from highest

✓ quick and easy to calculate    ✗ affected by extreme values

- Interquartile range - middle 50% of scores

✓ not affected by extreme values ✗ inaccurate, if large intervals between scores

- Standard deviation - measure of spread from the mean

✓ very sensitive measure    ✗ difficult to calculate

# 7

# Preparing for the AS Examination

Questions can be set only on material that is included in the Specification. The entire AS Specification is compulsory. You **must** learn it all. The details of the Specification are given at the start of each of the preceding chapters (1–6). Make sure you know the Specification inside out.

## The exam format

Each Exam Unit is worth 33.33% of the AS. Each of the three Exam Units is one hour long. You have to answer two questions in each Exam Unit – one on each topic. Therefore each question takes 30 minutes. Since each question is also marked out of 30, it helps to remember the '*mark-a-minute rule*'. That is, if a question is worth 6 marks, then spend 6 minutes on it and so on.

| Exam/Unit | Topic | Exam format |
|---|---|---|
| **PYA1:** | Cognitive Psychology | Answer one question from two in Cognitive Psychology. |
| | Developmental Psychology | Answer one question from two in Developmental Psychology. |
| **PYA2:** | Physiological Psychology | Answer one question from two in Physiological Psychology. |
| | Individual Differences | Answer one question from two in Individual Differences. |
| **PYA3:** | Social Psychology | Answer one question from two in Social Psychology. |
| | Research Methods | Answer the compulsory Research Methods question. |

You will be assessed on your knowledge and understanding (AO1) and on your analysis, interpretation and evaluation skills (AO2). Two marks are also given for the quality of your writing (QoWC) in each exam Unit.

## Question Structure

Apart from Research Methods, all the questions follow a similar structure. They are:

Part (a) worth 6 marks will test AO1

Part (b) worth 6 marks will test AO1

Part (c) worth 18 marks will test AO1 (6 marks) and AO2 (12 marks).

## Exam Assessment Objectives: (AO1/AO2/AO3)

There are three assessment objectives in AS:

### 1. AO1 Knowledge and understanding

You need to demonstrate knowledge and understanding of psychological theories, terminology, concepts, studies and methods in the core areas of Cognitive, Social, Developmental, Individual Differences and Physiological Psychology, Research Methods, and communicate your knowledge and understanding of Psychology in a clear and effective manner.

AO1 is assessed with reference to knowledge and understanding, range of material included (breadth), detail, accuracy, and organisation and structure.

### 2. AO2 Analyse and evaluate

You need to analyse and evaluate psychological theories, terminology, concepts, studies and methods in the core areas of Cognitive, Social, Developmental, Individual Differences and Physiological Psychology, Research Methods, and communicate your knowledge and understanding of Psychology in a clear and effective manner.

AO2 is assessed with reference to the extent of the analysis, evaluation and/or commentary offered and the degree to which material has been effectively used, appropriately selected and coherently elaborated.

### 3. AO3 Design, conduct and report

You need to be able to consider design and methodological issues, analyse and interpret data, and develop an understanding of the ethical implications of psychological investigations. This is assessed only in the PYA3 Unit, specifically the Research Methods questions that require you to refer directly to the research material given. General questions, e.g. Suggest one advantage of repeated measures design (1 mark), don't *require* you to engage with the Research material (but it might help for elaboration!).

## AO1 Exam Questions

These can be categorised into different types:

1. Terms or definitions: You must learn the Essential Glossary (see pages 604–13). This includes all the terms mentioned in the Specification. You can be asked what some of these terms mean in the exam. For example:
   – Explain what psychologists mean by the terms 'flashbulb memory' and 'repression'. (3 + 3 marks)
   – What is meant by the terms 'conformity', 'ecological validity' and 'informed consent'? (2 + 2 + 2 marks)

2. Concepts or contributory factors: This might include differences or similarities between concepts or a description of factors (i.e. ways, assumptions, limitations, implications) that might contribute to a particular concept. For example:

– Outline **two** differences between STM and LTM. (3 + 3 marks)
– Outline **two** factors that can modify the effects of stressors. (3 + 3 marks)

3. Theories or explanations: This might involve outlining or describing a particular theory, explanation or approach.
   – Outline Bowlby's maternal deprivation hypothesis. (6 marks)
   – Describe one psychological approach to stress management. (6 marks)

4. Essential (APFCC) Studies: This will involve asking a question concerning the APFCC (Aims, Procedure, Findings, Conclusions and Criticisms) of any of the Essential Studies. Examiners won't name a particular research study. They might ask for up to two criticisms of a particular study. For example:
   – Describe the aims and findings of **one** research study into obedience to authority. (3 + 3 marks)
   – Outline the findings of **one** study into eating disorders and give **two** criticisms of this study. (3 + 3 marks)

Sometimes students find it difficult to write enough for 3 marks to an APFCC question. In this case, you must try to *expand* your answer. One way of doing this would be to include brief details of, say, the Procedure if they asked about the Aim and you don't feel you have enough material to gain the 3 marks. However, you *must* relate your material to the question.

For example: Question: Outline the aim of *one* study into the capacity of STM (3 marks).

Answer: Jacobs's (1887) aim was to investigate the capacity of STM using the immediate digit span technique which involved reading aloud lists of either letters or numbers. He gradually increased the length of the lists until recall was only successful 50% of the time. Using this innovative technique, he achieved his aim of measuring how much can be stored in STM.

5. Research: This involves knowing about research (theories **and** studies) related to all areas of the Specification. Examiners might ask you to outline findings or conclusions of the research into a particular area. Knowing the Essential Studies in detail should also help here. For example:
   – Outline findings of research into the role of 'control' in stress. (6 marks)
   – Outline conclusions from research that has investigated the accuracy of eyewitness testimony. (6 marks)

## AO1 Exam Terms

| Term | Meaning |
| --- | --- |
| **Define** | You must explain what is meant by a particular term such as one used to identify a particular concept. |
| **Describe** | You must present evidence of your knowledge of the stipulated topic areas. |
| **Explain** | You must convey understanding of the stipulated topic area and make the explanation coherent and intelligible. |
| **Outline** | You must offer a summary (brief) description of the stipulated topic area. |

## Part (c) Exam Questions

Each Part (c) question is worth 18 marks and should take 18 minutes to answer. There are 6 marks for AO1 and 12 marks for AO2. The Part (c) questions can involve a combination of AO1 and AO2 terms.

### AO1 and AO2 Exam Terms

| Terms | Meaning |
|-------|---------|
| Consider 'To what extent. . .' | You must demonstrate knowledge and understanding of the stipulated topic area and an awareness of the strengths and limitations of the material presented. |

For example:

- Give a brief account of (AO1) one alternative to the multi-store model of memory and consider its strengths and limitations. (AO2) (18 marks)
- Consider (AO1 and AO2) whether the findings from social influence research can justify the methods used to obtain such findings. (18 marks)
- To what extent (AO1 and AO2) does psychological research support the view that eyewitness testimony is unreliable? (18 marks)
- Outline (AO1) some criticisms of the biological model of abnormality and consider (AO2) whether these are fair. (18 marks)

### AO2 Exam Term (this would be combined with an AO1 term such as 'Outline')

| Terms | Meaning |
|-------|---------|
| Evaluate | You must make an informed judgement regarding the value of the stipulated topic area, based on systematic analysis and examination. |

For example:

- Outline (AO1) and evaluate (AO2) one or more psychological explanation(s) of attachment. (18 marks)
- Briefly describe (AO1) and evaluate (AO2) physiological approaches to stress management. (18 marks)

## Marking allocations

The AQA Specification A exam uses a positive mark scheme which means that any irrelevant answers are ignored and only the relevant ones are marked. This occurs even if the irrelevant material comes first. The only exception to this is in the Research Methods questions where the first answer only is accepted. This means that there is no reason to cross out any (incorrect) answer except in Research Methods.

The marking allocations tend to be similar for each question with the same mark allocations. In summary, these are:

| 6 mark questions | 3 mark questions | AO1<br>Mark allocation |
|------------------|------------------|------------------------|
| 5–6 marks | 3 marks | The description is accurate and detailed. |
| 3–4 marks | 2 marks | The description is generally accurate but less detailed. |
| 1–2 marks | 1 mark | The description is lacking in detail and may be muddled and/or flawed. |
| 0 mark | 0 mark | The description is inappropriate, incorrect and/or irrelevant. |

(Note: There can also be 2 + 2 + 2 mark allocations (see 2 or 3 mark allocation below))

Exam Hint: When answering a 3-mark question, think of the following:

- **Name:** what you are going to describe using terms from the Essential Glossary
- **Explain:** exactly what the question asks for
- **Research:** try to give a research or everyday example to illustrate your answer.

| | AO2 |
|---|---|
| **12 mark questions** | **Mark allocation** |
| 11–12 marks | There is informed commentary, thorough analysis of the relevant psychological material and it has been used in a highly effective way. |
| 9–10 marks | There is informed commentary, reasonably thorough analysis of the relevant psychological material and it has been used in an effective way. |
| 7–8 marks | There is reasonable commentary, slightly limited analysis of the relevant psychological material but it has been used in an effective way. |
| 5–6 marks | There is reasonable commentary, limited analysis of the relevant psychological material but it has been used in a reasonably effective way. |
| 3–4 marks | There is superficial commentary, rudimentary analysis of the relevant psychological material and there has been minimal interpretation of this. |
| 1–2 marks | There is just discernible commentary, analysis is weak and muddled and the material presented may be irrelevant. |
| 0 marks | The commentary and any analysis is wholly irrelevant to the question. |

Most commonly with Research Methods there are 2 mark or 3 mark allocations as follows:

| **2 or 3 mark questions** | **Marking allocation** |
|---|---|
| 2–3 marks | Accurate and informed description or explanation |
| 1 mark | Brief or muddled answer |
| 0 marks | Incorrect or inappropriate answer |

*For more detailed help, refer to the document available from AQA entitled Psychology Specification A: Specimen Units and Mark schemes (www.aqa.org.uk)*

## Hints on writing evaluation (AO2 skill)

There are some general points that apply to much research. In order to develop your AO2 skills of analysis and evaluation you could consider the following:

1. **Demand characteristics:** People change their behaviour to adapt to the situation (Orne, 1962). Also 'screw you' effect (see pages 133–134).

2. **Ethics:** Does the research follow ethical guidelines? Which does it break? Could it be repeated in a more ethical way? (see page 132)

3. **Date of study** Is it very old – out of date? Was it conducted pre-ethical guidelines (BPS produced in 1975). Is the theory/study outdated?

4. **Ethnocentrism:** Does it look at people from a restricted cultural viewpoint? Why does this matter? Is the theory/study biased?

5. Sample: Many studies use a restricted sample. Many use white, middle class Psychology undergraduates. Are they representative? Sear (1986) found 75% of studies from 1980–85 used US undergraduates as participants. Can such results be generalised to other groups? Students are said to differ from the wider population in the following ways:

- Self concept not fully formed
- More egocentric
- Stronger need for peer approval
- Less stable peer relationships
- Less stable views and attitudes

6. What's the point? Miller (1969) argued that psychology should promote human welfare. Does the study do this? If not, why bother with it? Does the theory/study help to open up or extend debate? Has the research helped psychologists look at a topic in a different light?

7. Place where study occurred: Psychological research mainly involves laboratory studies which take place in an academic environment and over-emphasise cognitive aspects of behaviour at the expense of emotional ones. Typically, they also remove the participant from the support of their peers. An experiment is 'a social situation' and as such is open to all kinds of social effects.

8. External (ecological) validity: Is the study applicable to real-life experiences and can it be generalised to the wider population (e.g. sampling above) (see page 131)?

9. Coherence: What is the quality of the research argument? Is the study coherent (does it make cognitive sense)?

10. Status: What is the reputation of the researcher? e.g. Freud, Pavlov, Skinner, Piaget, Asch and Milgram. Their work has stimulated other research world-wide. Some of their ideas have been formulated into a paradigm (an approach followed by many psychologists). Have their ideas stood the test of time? Has the theory/study defined or helped to clarify the meaning of any concepts in psychology? Does the theory/study add to our understanding in this area of psychology? Is the theory/study likely to be of any use to psychologists in the future?

11. Methodological problems? Consider the methodology employed in the research. What are the advantages and disadvantages associated with them? Is the study reliable? Is the study valid? (see page 131)

12. Empirical evidence: Is the theory/study well supported by empirical evidence? Is there a lot of conflicting research? Are there other possible explanations and areas of analysis which the theory/study overlooks?

13. Operationalisation: Does the theory/study employ concepts and definitions that can be criticised?

## Some sentences which will encourage AO2 commentary:

- . . . 's study can be evaluated in a number of ways. These include . . .
- To evaluate . . . 's study it is important to consider . . .
- Further support for this argument/study can be taken from the work of . . . who found evidence to suggest that . . .
- . . . 's study is useful but . . .
- A contrasting view is that of . . . , who found that . . .
- . . . 's study does not take into account . . .
- The problem with . . . 's research, however, is that it is unreliable/ethnocentrically biased because . . .
- . . . 's research methodology can be questioned, particularly his/her use of . . .
- A conflicting view is expressed by . . . because . . .
- . . . 's study is useful/effective because . . .
- Therefore the study is not applicable because . . .

- . . . 's study lacks . . . . This is a problem because . . .
- Contrary to . . . 's research, . . . suggests that . . .
  *(adapted from Psychology Review Vol 4 No. 3 pp 8–10)*

Examiners always stress the need to elaborate your AO2 commentary. This means giving details about the evaluative point that is being made. *Why* is it a problem? For example: Why is a small sample size a problem? Why is low ecological validity a problem? and so on.

## EXAM tips BOX

1. Make a **revision timetable** and **try** to stick to it.

2. **Employ psychology:** The optimum learning time is about 20 minutes. Reward yourself at the end of your revision sessions.

3. **Active revision:** Read, condense notes, highlight essential points. Use different revision techniques. Variety beats boredom. Does your teacher use the same teaching technique for each and every lesson? Of course not!

4. **Revise with friends:** Discuss revision strategies and topics with your friends. Share your difficulties: friends might be able to solve some of your problems. This will also help their revision.

5. As a bare minimum you should ensure you've learnt the **Glossary, Essential Studies (APFCC)** and **sample answers** in this book.

6. **Start with the easiest topics:** This will give you confidence and help you move through the material more quickly.

7. **Know the Specification content.** Questions can **only** be set from the Specification. **If it's not on the Specification, it won't be in the exam.**

8. **Know the format of the exam paper.** Remember the allocation of AO1 and AO2 marks. (AO3 marks apply only to Research Methods.)

9. **Choose your questions carefully** based on the 18 mark Part (c) question. It's worth the most marks (60%) and is therefore the most important. Read the questions carefully.

10. **Answer the question:** Don't waffle. It's quality, not quantity, that counts. Make sure all of your answers are relevant.

11. **Time allocation:** Allocate your time appropriately in the exam. Don't be tempted to spend more time on your favourite answers. The first few marks are the easiest to obtain. Always answer the correct number of exam questions.

12. **'Mark-a-minute' format:** Spend the same number of minutes on a question as there are marks available. There are 30 marks available for each 30-minute question. Spend 3 minutes on a 3-mark question and so on.

13. **Practise exam questions:** 'Practice makes perfect.' With the exception of research methods questions, there are a limited number of questions that can be asked. The more past paper questions you practise, the better your examination technique will be. If you're fortunate, you may even have practised a question that comes up in the exam.

Finally, remember: examiners mark to the standard of a *'notional 17-year-old'* – they don't expect perfect answers.

The very best of luck.

# Relationships

## What's covered in this chapter?

### You need to know about:

**Attraction and the formation of relationships**

- Explanations and research studies relating to interpersonal attraction (e.g. evolutionary explanations, matching hypothesis)
- Theories relating to the formation/maintenance of relationships (e.g. reward/need satisfaction; social exchange theory)

**Love and the breakdown of relationships**

- Psychological explanations of love (e.g. triangular theory, love as attachment)
- Explanations (e.g. Lee, Duck) and research studies relating to the breakdown of relationships

**Cultural and sub-cultural differences in relationships**

- Explanations and research studies relating to the nature of relationships in different cultures (e.g. voluntary/involuntary; permanent/impermanent types of relationships)
- 'Understudied' relationships, such as gay and lesbian, and mediated relationships (e.g. relationships formed on the Internet and text [SMS] relationships)

## Attraction and the formation of relationships

In the most general sense, we're attracted to other people through the basic human need to belong and be accepted by other human beings (*affiliation*). This is one of Maslow's (1954) basic survival needs, and is also a major motive underlying conformity, namely *Normative Social Influence* (Deutsch & Gerard, 1955) (see *Essential Study* 5.1: Asch's COLE pages 102–103). Conformity can also be explained in terms of the need to evaluate our beliefs and opinions by comparing them with other people's, especially in ambiguous situations. This relates to *Informational Social Influence* and is the central idea behind Festinger's (1954) *social comparison theory*.

## Explanations of interpersonal attraction

### REWARD THEORY

A general theoretical framework for explaining initial attraction (as well as the formation/maintenance of relationships) is *reward theory* (Clore & Byrne, 1974; Lott & Lott, 1974). The basic idea is that we're attracted to individuals whose presence is rewarding for us. The more rewards someone provides us with, the more we should be attracted to them. Research has shown that a number of factors influence initial attraction through their reward value. These include:

- proximity
- exposure and familiarity
- similarity
- physical attractiveness.

### Proximity

*Proximity* (physical or geographical closeness) represents a minimum requirement for attraction: the further apart two people live, the less likely it is they'll ever meet (let alone become friends or marry each other). Related to proximity is the concept of *personal space* (Hall, 1959, 1966), which describes the human version of the 'individual distance' of zoo animals.

> **Specification Hint:** The Specification refers to 'relationships', without identifying these as friendships or romantic/sexual. While some explanations – and research studies – are more applicable to the latter, most are relevant to both types.

> **Specification Hint:** The Specification says 'Explanations ... relating to interpersonal attraction (e.g. evolutionary explanations matching hypothesis) ... ' So you need to know about at least *two explanations* (but two will do), one of which could be the matching hypothesis. This and one other are covered here.

### Box 8.1  Personal space

*Personal space* is like an invisible bubble that surrounds us. According to Hall, we learn *proxemic rules*, which prescribe:

- the amount of physical distance that's appropriate in daily interactions and
- the kinds of situations in which closeness or distance is proper.

Hall identifies four main regions or zones of personal space (see Figure. 8.1):

There are important *cultural differences* regarding proxemic rules. Each zone of personal space allows the use of different cues of touch, smell, hearing and seeing, which are more important in some cultures than others. The *caste system* in India represents a highly formalised, institutionalised set of proxemic rules.

### Exam Hint:

The question cannot ask you specifically about friendships as distinct from romantic/sexual relationships. But you need to be aware of the point in the first Box above, which can be made as part of your evaluation (AO2) of explanations and/ or research studies of attraction.

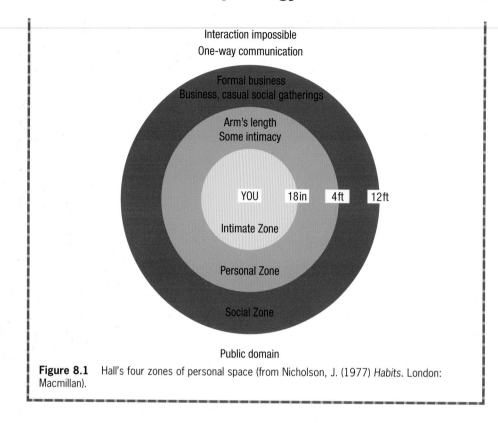

**Figure 8.1**    Hall's four zones of personal space (from Nicholson, J. (1977) *Habits*. London: Macmillan).

### Exposure and familiarity

Proximity increases the opportunity for interaction (*exposure*), which, in turn, increases *familiarity*. There's considerable evidence that familiarity breeds fondness (not contempt), that is, the better we know someone, the more we like them (see below). According to Argyle (1983), the more two people interact, the more *polarised* (extreme) their attitudes towards each other become – usually in the direction of greater liking. This, in turn, increases the likelihood of further interaction – but only if the people involved are 'equals'.

### Similarity

Evidence suggests that 'birds of a feather flock together'. The key similarities are those concerning *beliefs*, *attitudes* and *values*. According to Rubin (1973), similarity is rewarding because:

- agreement may provide a basis for engaging in joint activity
- a person who agrees with us helps us feel more confident about our own opinions. This boosts our self-esteem
- most of us are vain enough to believe that anyone who shares our views must be sensitive and praiseworthy
- people who agree about things that matter to them usually find it easier to communicate with each other
- we assume that people with similar attitudes to ourselves are going to like us, so we like them in turn (*reciprocal liking*).

### Physical attractiveness

- It often takes time to find out about other people's attitudes and values. But their physical appearance, including their attractiveness, is immediate. *Physical attractiveness* has been studied in its own right, as well as one aspect of similarity.

**Exam Hint:**

If the question asks for *one* explanation of attraction, then it's probably best to choose the matching hypothesis. We've provided most information on this explanation. But note that there's some overlap between the matching hypothesis and reward theory, the second explanation we've chosen.

- According to the *attractiveness stereotype* (e.g. Dion *et al.*, 1972), we tend to perceive attractive-looking people as also having more attractive personalities. But what makes someone attractive? Different cultures have different criteria for judging physical beauty. For example, chipped teeth, body scars, artificially elongated heads and bound feet have all been regarded as beautiful in various non-Western cultures. Definitions of beauty also change over time, as in Western culture's 'ideal' figure for women.

- Traditionally, facial beauty has been generally regarded as more important in women than men. In contrast, men's stature, especially height, plus a muscular body and (currently) a firm, round 'bum', influence how attractive women (and some other men) find them.

- In the context of personal ads and commercial dating services, the primary 'resource' (or reward) offered by females seeking a male partner is still physical attractiveness (Brehm, 1992). This matches what men actually want from a female partner. According to Buss (1989), this isn't confined to Western culture, but is a universal male preference.

- From a *sociobiological* perspective, attractive facial features may signal sexual maturity or fertility. According to Darwinian theories of human mate selection, both men and women select partners who should increase their chances of reproductive success. In other words, our mates help to ensure that our genes survive into the next generation. This is also consistent with the tendency to equate beauty with youthfulness. (The sociobiological explanation of physical attractiveness is also relevant to the formation/maintenance of relationships – see Box 8.3, page 164 and Chapter 13).

YOU'VE GOT THE SEXIEST CHIPPED TEETH I'VE EVER SEEN

## THE MATCHING HYPOTHESIS

- According to *social exchange theory* (e.g. Thibaut & Kelley, 1959: see below), people are more likely to become romantically involved if they're fairly closely matched in their ability to reward one another. This is the *matching hypothesis* (MH).

- Ideally, we'd all have the 'perfect partner' because, the theory says, we're all fundamentally selfish. But since this is impossible, we try to find a compromise. The best general 'bargain' that can be struck is a *value-match*, a subjective belief that our partner is the most rewarding we could realistically hope to find.

Ideas about what constitutes female beauty have changed over the centuries

- The findings from various tests of the MH (see below) imply that the kind of partner we'd be satisfied with is one we feel won't reject us, rather than one we positively desire. But Brown (1986) argues that the matching phenomenon results from a well-learned sense of what's 'fitting', rather than a fear of rejection. We learn to adjust our expectations of rewards in line with what we believe we have to offer others.

**Specification Hint:** You need to know *at least two research studies* relating to each explanation (but, again, two will do). Because some of the studies are quite brief, we've covered more than two. Also, because reward theory has been tested through investigation of a number of specific factors, the research studies can relate to any or all of these factors. Here we've selected proximity and familiarity.

## Research studies of reward theory

**Space invaders in the library** (SIL) (Felipe & Sommer, 1966)

- The unsuspecting participants were female university students studying at a large table (1m × 5m) with six chairs evenly spaced on either side of the table. There were at least two empty chairs on either side of each student, and one opposite.
- There were five experimental conditions in which the female experimenter:

(a) sat next to the student and moved her chair to within about 8cm of the student's (about as close as possible without actually touching). If the student moved her chair away, the experimenter would move her chair nearer

(b) sat in the chair next to the student at a normal, acceptable distance (about half a metre)

(c) sat two seats away from her (leaving one chair between them)

(d) sat three seats away

(e) sat immediately opposite her (about a metre apart).

- About 55% of the participants in condition (a) stayed in the library for longer than 10 minutes, compared with 90% in conditions (b)–(e) combined. 100% of participants in a control condition (who sat at the same-sized table, with the same number and arrangement of empty chairs, but weren't 'invaded' by the experimenter) stayed longer than 10 minutes.
- After 20 minutes, these percentages reduced to 45% in the first condition, 80% in (b)–(e) and just below 100% in the control condition.
- By the end of the 30-minute experiment, the figures were 30%, 73% and 87% respectively.
- Students were more likely to leave, move away, adjust their chair or erect barriers (such as putting a bag on the table between themselves and the 'intruder') in condition (a).
- In Hall's terms, the stranger was invading the intimate zone of the student's personal space.

 Evaluation of SIL (AO2)

✓ **High ecological validity:** The study took place in a real library (a field experiment), involving real naïve participant students. They didn't realise there was an experiment taking place, so their behaviour was 'natural'. It's reasonable to assume that these female students would have behaved similarly in, say, a train or a café.

✗ **Limited sample:** The participants were all female university students. So we can't be sure that male students, or non-students, would necessarily react to the intrusion in a similar way.

✓ **Successful replications:** However, similar results were found for male psychiatric patients and for people sitting on park benches (Felipe & Sommer, 1966).

✗ **Lack of consent:** The downside of field experiments like this is that participants aren't in a position to give their consent (they don't know there's an experiment taking place), let alone their informed consent. So a fundamental ethical principle was being breached.

✓ **Well-controlled study:** The use of a control group made this a well-designed study, especially as it was a field experiment (where control groups are often difficult to set up).

ESSENTIAL STUDY 8.2

**The Taste of Strangers experiment** (TOSE) (Saegert *et al.*, 1973)

- Female students were invited to take part in an experiment supposedly to do with the sense of taste. This involved tasting and rating various liquids.
- The experiment was designed such that each student would find herself in a closed cubicle with another student once, twice, five times, 10 times, or alone.
- At the end of the experiment, each student was asked to complete a questionnaire relating to details of the experiment. In fact, the only item of interest to the investigators was the one which asked students to assess their attraction to the person who'd shared the cubicle.
- The participants' attraction to the other student was directly related to how many interactions they'd had: the more interactions, the greater the attraction (see Figure 8.2).

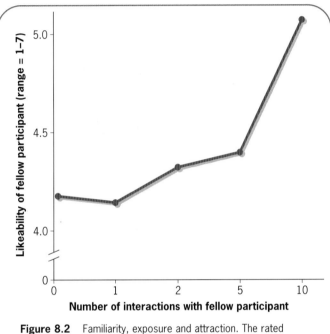

**Figure 8.2** Familiarity, exposure and attraction. The rated likeability of a fellow participant as a function of number of interactions (based on Saegert *et al.*, 1973).

 Evaluation of TOSE

✗ **Low ecological validity:** This is a highly contrived, artificial situation. People aren't usually asked to taste a number of different liquids – except as part of a market research exercise.

✗ **Use of deception:** Related to the artificiality is the use of deception. Participants believed this was a study concerned with taste, whereas it was really about how attraction is influenced by familiarity.

✗ **Limited sample:** As with SIL, the participants were female students – hardly representative of people in general.

✗ **Operationalisation of variables:** As with other experiments conducted by Zajonc and his colleagues, familiarity is defined as *the number of times* something has occurred (a *quantitative* definition). But this overlooks the importance of *qualitative* definitions. For example, how familiar we are with another person could be judged in terms of what we've learned about them (such as their attitudes and beliefs), or how well we think we could predict their behaviour.

✗✓ Evaluation of reward theory (AO2)

✓ • ✗ **Lack of coherent theory:** The basic idea of people being more or less rewarding is very simple, which is a positive aspect of the theory. But the theory is tested by investigating several unrelated factors (proximity, familiarity etc.). So the theory lacks coherence, that is, there's no attempt to integrate the different factors.

✗ **The 'magnetic metaphor':** According to Duck (1999), the 'magnetic metaphor' of attraction implies that people are unwittingly, and almost against their will, pulled towards one another's inherent, pre-existing characteristics. It's a caricature of social and personal relationships as '. . . the unthinking domain of reactive magnetism'. More recent research has looked at the *dynamics* of relationships (how they develop and unfold over time), and how they're conducted in real life (such as their inherent tensions). This shift involves fewer controlled experiments (such as SIL and TOSE), and increasing interest in previously 'understudied' relationships, such as gay and lesbian, and 'electronic' friendships (see below, pages 173–176).

# Research studies of the matching hypothesis (MH)

**The Computer Dance** (CD) **Study** (Walster *et al.*, 1966)

• 752 male and female fresher students bought tickets for a 'Welcome Week' computer dance at the University of Minnesota at the start of the new academic year.

• When they bought their ticket, they were asked to complete a detailed questionnaire about themselves. They were told that the information provided would be fed into a computer, which would then match them with their ideal date. In fact, they were assigned a partner purely randomly.

• As they completed the questionnaire, an unseen observer rated the students for physical attractiveness.

• During the intermission, the students were asked to indicate how much they liked their partner (having spent two-and-a-half hours with them).

• Physical attractiveness proved to be the single most important factor that determined how much students liked their partner, for both males and females. It was also the best single predictor of how likely the male was to ask the female out on a(nother) date – regardless of the male's attractiveness. In other words, the more attractive the partner had been rated by the observer, the more s/he was liked.

## Evaluation of CD (AO2)

✓ **High ecological validity:** The study took place in a naturalistic setting in the context of an expected – and desirable – event (the 'freshers' ball').

✗ **Use of deception:** The students were told that the questionnaire information would be used to match them with their ideal date. But the matching was purely random. They also didn't know that their attractiveness was being assessed, or that they were taking part in a study at all. So there was a lack of both consent and informed consent.

✓•✗ **Contradictory results:** The study provides strong evidence for the impact of physical attractiveness in initial attraction. This could be seen as consistent with reward theory: an attractive partner is very rewarding, and the more attractive the better! (This could also be seen as the common-sense view.) But this is actually *contrary* to what the MH predicts. If we settle for a value-match, then only those males who happened to be paired (by chance) with a date whose attractiveness level closely matched their own would have asked their female partner for a date.

✗ **Methodological problems:** Students were already guaranteed a date before meeting and interacting with their partner. According to Berscheid *et al.* (1971), a more valid test of the MH would be where we have to choose a dating partner (that is, specify *in advance* the kind of partner we'd like, including how attractive we'd like them to be). Later computer dance studies (e.g. Berscheid & Walster, 1974) used this improved methodology, and the results tended to support the MH.

**Couples' Attractiveness and Matching Photographs** (CAMP) **study** (Murstein, 1972)

- Murstein took photographs, first of 99 engaged couples, then of a separate sample of 98.
- Independent judges rated the photographs for physical attractiveness on a five-point scale without knowing who the couples were ('who belonged to whom').
- The couples had to rate their own and their partner's physical attractiveness.
- Partners received very similar ratings, and these were significantly more alike than the same ratings given to 'random couples' (that is, the actual couples' photographs randomly sorted into couples to form a control group).
- How partners rated themselves (self-concept for attractiveness) was significantly more similar than self-ratings for random couples.
- Partners' ratings of each other weren't significantly correlated.
- These findings applied more or less equally to both samples.

 Evaluation of CAMP (AO2)

✓ **Well-controlled study:** The control group was created by sorting the photographs into random couples. This allowed Murstein to calculate a difference between the correlations for the real and the random couples, making the results more interesting and more valid.

✓ **Unbiased judges:** The judges didn't know the identity or pairing of the couples when rating the photographs. This prevented any chance of a *halo effect*, that is, knowing 'who belonged to whom' would make it more likely that both partners were rated in a similar way. For example, rating the female as highly attractive would make it more likely that her partner would also be rated as highly attractive.

✗ **Limited definition of attractiveness:** In common with other similar studies, Murstein restricted his definition of physical attractiveness to facial appearance ('good-looking', 'looks' were terms used in the rating scale). But for both men and women, a 'good body' is also an important aspect of the overall rating of attractiveness (perhaps much more recently, in the case of women).

✗ **Gender differences:** Traditionally, women were regarded as a man's property, such that her beauty (however defined) increased his status and respect in the eyes of others (Sigall & Landy, 1973). But the reverse doesn't seem to apply: a man's attractiveness hasn't (at least, traditionally) enhanced a woman's standing among other women (Bar-Tal & Saxe, 1976). The study doesn't take account of such differences.

✗✓ Evaluation of the MH (AO2)

✗ **The magnetic metaphor – again:** Duck's (1999) criticism of attraction research applies here too (see above).

✓ **Supporting evidence:** As we saw above, the later computer dance studies tend to support the MH. When people are asked in advance what kinds of partner they'd like, those rated as high, low or of average attractiveness tend to ask for dates of a similar attractiveness level.

✗ **Low ecological validity of these studies:** They still only test attraction based on, at most, a few hours of interaction, and most couples don't meet under these circumstances (being paired, by computer, at a university freshers' dance).

✓ **Other supporting evidence:** There is other supporting evidence, as in Murstein's CAMP.

✓•✗ **Are relationships really like this?** We saw earlier that the MH is derived from *social* *exchange theory* (SET). According to SET, people are fundamentally selfish, and human relationships are based primarily on self-interest. Although this view shouldn't be taken too literally, our attitudes towards others are determined to a large extent by how rewarding we think they are for us (Rubin, 1973). But we're also capable of being altruistic (doing things for others without expecting anything in return), especially towards those who are closest to us.

## Theories relating to the formation/maintenance of relationships

> **Specification Hint:** You need to know about at least two '... Theories ... relating to the formation/maintenance of relationships (e.g. reward/need satisfaction, social exchange theory)'. We've discussed reward theory above, in relation to interpersonal attraction. Here we'll say some more about need satisfaction under the heading of 'Stage theories of relationships'. We've also considered above the sociobiological account of physical attractiveness.

## Stage theories of relationships

### THE FILTER MODEL (FM) (KERCKHOFF & DAVIS, 1962).

- This was based on a comparison of 'short-term couples' (together for less than 18 months) and 'long-term couples' (18 months or more) over a seven-month period.
- *Similarity of sociological* (or *demographic*) *variables* determines the likelihood of individuals meeting in the first place (the first filter). Social circumstances reduce the *'field of availables'* (Kerckhoff, 1974), that is, the range of people who are *realistically* available for us to meet (as opposed to those who are *theoretically* available). We're most likely to come into contact with people from our own ethnic, racial, religious, social class and educational groups. We tend to find these types of people most attractive initially, because similarity makes communication easier and we've something immediately in common. At this point, attraction has little to do with people's individual characteristics.
- The second filter involves individuals' *psychological* characteristics, specifically, *agreement on basic values*. Kerckhoff and Davis found this to be the best predictor of the relationship becoming more stable and permanent. For the short-term couples, the more similar their values, the stronger the relationship.

- For the long-term couples, it was the *complementarity of emotional needs* which best predicted a longer-term commitment (the third filter). This is discussed further below in relation to the maintenance of relationships.

### STIMULUS–VALUE–ROLE (SVR) THEORY (MURSTEIN, 1976, 1987)

- Intimate relationships begin with a *stimulus stage*. Here attraction is based on external attributes (such as physical attractiveness).
- In the *value stage*, similarity of values and beliefs become much more important.
- Finally, the *role stage* involves a commitment based on successful performance of relationship roles (such as husband and wife).
- All three factors play a part throughout a relationship. But each one assumes greatest significance during one particular stage (see Figure 8.3).

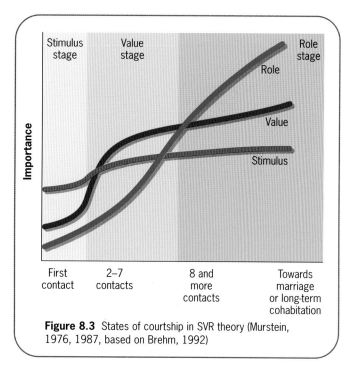

**Figure 8.3** States of courtship in SVR theory (Murstein, 1976, 1987, based on Brehm, 1992)

**Critically consider *one* explanation of interpersonal attraction. (24 marks) (30 mins) (600 words minimum) AO1/AO2**

*This essay can be split up into FOUR sections – each about 150 words long. Each section would be worth approx. 6 marks*

**Section 1:** A **description** of the matching hypothesis (MH). You should include brief details of the basic ideas involved, and say how the MH is related to social exchange theory.

AO1

**Section 2:** A **description** of research studies that test the MH. These could include:

* CD (Walster *et al.*, 1966)
* CAMP (Murstein, 1972).

AO1

*A word of warning: You should only include details that are relevant to the evaluation of these studies that comes in Section 3. The basic method and the findings are crucial.*

**Section 3:** You should **analyse and evaluate** the research studies that have tested the MH. It makes sense to begin with the studies described in Section 2, but you'll probably want to refer to other (later) research which has either supported or challenged the former.

AO2

**Section 4:** You should **analyse and evaluate** the MH. This will include reference back to some of the evaluation made of CD and CAMP in Section 3, as well as more general points, such as the underlying view of people presented in the MH and SET from which it's derived.

AO2

*Try to answer this question yourself. There's a sample answer on page 180 you can compare your answer with.*

## Evaluation of stage theories (AO2)

✓ **Consistency with personal experience:** Our own experience tells us that intimate relationships change and develop over time. If they stagnate ('this relationship isn't going anywhere'), especially romantic/sexual ones, they may be doomed to failure (Duck, 1988).

✗ **Lack of supporting evidence:** Many studies have provided only weak evidence for a fixed sequence of stages in intimate relationships (Brehm, 1992).

✗ **Do 'stages' really exist?:** 'Stages' are probably best regarded as 'phases' that occur at different times for different couples.

✓ **Relationships do change:** The claim that relationships change and develop isn't in dispute (see first bullet point), and it's useful to think of this as involving a beginning, a middle and an end. For example, how each partner understands the role of husband and wife, and how well each performs their role, are relatively late influences in a given courtship. The matching of partners' role concepts will be irrelevant to the success of the early stages of the courtship (Duck, 1999).

## SOCIAL EXCHANGE THEORY (SET)

There are different versions of SET, but all share the underlying view of people as fundamentally selfish (see above).

* According to Homans (1974), we view our feelings for others in terms of *profits* (the amount of reward obtained from a relationship minus the cost). The greater the reward and lower the cost, the greater the profit and hence the initial attraction and the longer-term wish to stay in the relationship.
* Blau (1964) argues that interactions are 'expensive': they take time, energy and commitment, and may involve unpleasant emotions and experiences. Because of this, what we get out of a relationship must exceed what we put in.
* According to Berscheid & Walster (1978), all social interactions involve an exchange of rewards (such as affection, information and status). The degree of attraction or liking will reflect how people evaluate the rewards they receive relative to those they give.

## Evaluation of SET (AO2)

✓ • ✗ **Coherent but oversimple:** The different versions of SET share a few basic ideas, such as profit and reward. The obvious link between SET and reward theory (see above) is useful, and shows the overlap between (a) explanations of initial attraction/formation of relationships and (b) the maintenance of relationships. But are we really as selfish as SET suggests, and are our relationships just about what we can get out of them for ourselves? (See Evaluation of the MH above.)

✗ **Alternative views of relationships:** Some psychologists distinguish between 'true' love and friendship, which are altruistic (the opposite of selfish), and less admirable forms based on considerations of exchange (Brown, 1986). Fromm (1962) defines true love as giving, as opposed to the false love of the 'marketing character' (expecting to have favours returned).

✗ **Empirical support for these alternative views:** Mills & Clark (1980) found support for this distinction, thus contradicting SET. They identified two kinds of intimate relationship: (a) the *communal couple,* in which each partner gives out of concern for the other; (b) the *exchange couple*, in which each keeps mental records of who's 'ahead' and who's 'behind'.

## EQUITY THEORY (ET)

- SET is really a special case of a more general account of human relationships called *equity theory* (ET). The extra component in ET that's added to reward, cost and profit is *investment*.
- According to Brown (1986):

> 'A person's investments are not just financial; they are anything at all that is believed to entitle him to his rewards, costs, and profits. An investment is any factor to be weighed in determining fair profits or losses.'

- Equity *doesn't* mean equality. Rather, it means a *constant ratio* of rewards to cost, or profit to investment. So ET involves a concern with *fairness*. It's *changes* in the ratio of what you put in and what you get out of a relationship that are likely to cause changes in how you feel about it – rather than the initial ratio. You may believe it's fair and just that you give more than you get. But if you start giving very much more than you did, and receive proportionately less, then you're likely to become dissatisfied.
- Some versions of ET (e.g. Thibaut & Kelley, 1959) actually take account of factors other than the simple and crude profit motives of SET.

**Box 8.2 The concepts of comparison level and comparison level for alternatives (Thibaut & Kelley, 1959)**

- *Comparison level* (CL) is basically the average level of rewards and costs you're used to in relationships, and is the minimum level you expect in any future relationship. So (a) if your current reward–cost ratio (RCR) falls below your CL, the relationship will be unsatisfying; (b) if it's above your CL, you'll be satisfied with it.
- *Comparison level for alternatives* (CL alt.) is basically your expectation about the RCR which *could* be obtained in other relationships. So (a) if your current RCR exceeds the CL alt., then you're doing better in the relationship than you could elsewhere. This is likely to make the relationship satisfying for you, and you'll want it to continue; (b) if the CL alt. exceeds your current RCR, then you're doing worse than you could elsewhere, the relationship is likely to be unsatisfying, and you'll not want it to continue.

✓ **Improvement on SET:** According to Duck (1988), the concept of CL alt. implies that whether or not a relationship lasts (from the perspective of one of the partners) could be due to:
   (a) the qualities of the other partner and the relationship or
   (b) the negative features of the perceived alternatives or
   (c) the perceived costs of leaving.

✓ **Usefulness of the concepts of equity/exchange:** Concern with either exchange or equity is negatively correlated with marital adjustment (Murstein *et al.,* 1977). People in close relationships don't think in terms of rewards and costs at all – until they start to feel dissatisfied (Argyle, 1987). A conscious concern with 'getting a fair deal', especially in the short term, makes *compatibility* very hard to achieve (Murstein & MacDonald, 1983). This applies to both friendships and, especially, marriage. This corresponds to Mills & Clark's *exchange couple* (see above).

✗ **Still theoretically limited:** ET still portrays people as being fundamentally selfish. Many researchers (e.g. Walster *et al.,* 1978; Duck, 1988) prefer to see people as being concerned with an equitable distribution of rewards and costs for both themselves *and* their partners.

✗ **Is equity all there is to relationships?** According to *interdependence theory* (IT) (Kelley & Thibaut, 1978), not all social interactions reflect a mutual desire for equity and fair exchange. Intimate relationships are both diverse and complex, and partners' motives can clash as well as converge. This can produce a variety of outcomes, including aggression, altruism, competition, capitulation, co-operation and intransigence ('digging your heels in'). So IT goes beyond individual partners, and considers the intersubjective harmony or conflict between the attitudes, motives, values or goals of people in various social relationships (Ickes & Duck, 2000).

## COMPLEMENTARITY

- As we saw earlier, in Kerckhoff and Davis's FM, *complementarity of needs* becomes increasingly important as relationships become long-term. This relates to the saying: 'Opposites attract'.
- Complementary behaviours take account of each other's needs, helping to make a perfect whole and the relationship feel less superficial (Duck, 1999).
- According to Winch (1958), happy marriages are often based on each partner's ability to fulfil the other's needs. For example, a domineering person could more easily satisfy a partner who needs to be dominated than one who's equally domineering. Winch found some evidence for this.
- But other evidence is sparse, and we're more likely to marry others whose needs and personalities are *similar* to ours (the *matching phenomenon*: e.g. Berscheid & Walster, 1978). In other words, 'Birds of a feather flock together'. According to Buss (1985, in Myers, 1994):

> 'The tendency of opposites to marry or mate . . . has never been reliably demonstrated, with the single exception of sex.'

- Instead of complementary needs, what about complementarity of *resources* (Brehm, 1992)? Men seem to give a universally higher priority to 'good looks' in their female partners than do women in their male partners. The reverse is true when it comes to 'good financial prospect' and 'good earning capacity'.
- Buss (1989) studied 37 cultures (including Nigeria, South Africa, Japan, Estonia, Zambia, Columbia, Poland, Germany, Spain, France, China, Palestinian Arabs, Italy and The Netherlands), involving over 10,000 people. He concluded that these sex differences '. . . appear to be deeply rooted in the evolutionary history of our species . . . '.

## Box 8.3 Do our genes dictate what we want in a mate?

- According to Buss's *sociobiological theory* (1988, 1989), men's chances of reproductive success should be increased if they mate with younger, healthy, adult females. Fertility is a function of the mother's age and health, which also affects pregnancy and her ability to care for the child.
- Men often have to rely on a woman's physical appearance to estimate her age and health, with younger, healthier women being perceived as more attractive.
- Women's mate selection depends on their need for a provider to take care of them during pregnancy and nursing. They'll be particularly attracted to men whom they see as powerful and controlling resources that contribute to her and her child's welfare.
- Buss's theory removes male–female relationships from their cultural or historical context ('mate selection' is normally used to describe non-humans).
- Women may have been forced to obtain desirable resources through men, because they've been denied direct access to political and economic power. Traditionally, a woman was regarded as a man's property: the greater her beauty, the higher his status and esteem in others' eyes (Sigall & Landy, 1973).
- Buss conveniently overlooks a major finding from his 1989 study. 'Kind' and 'intelligent' were universally ranked as *more important* than 'physically attractive' or 'good earning power' by both men and women.
- Kephart (1967) asked Americans 'If someone had all the other qualities you desire in a marriage partner, would you marry this person if you were not in love?' Well over twice as many men replied 'no' as did women. When Simpson *et al.* (1986) repeated the study, over 80% of both men and women said 'no'. Women's greater financial independence during that 20-year period had allowed them to choose marriage partners for reasons *other than* material necessity. This contradicts Buss's sociobiological explanation.
- How can Buss's theory apply to homosexual relationships, which clearly don't contribute to the survival of the species? However, homosexual relationships are subject to many of the same sociopsychological influences involved in heterosexual relationships (Brehm, 1992: see below pages 173–174).

## EXAM tips BOX

**Critically consider *one* theory of the maintenance of relationships. (24 marks) (30 mins) (600 words minimum) AO1/AO2**

*This essay can be split up into FOUR sections – each about 150 words long. Each section would be worth approx. 6 marks.*

**Section 1:** A **description** of one theory of relationship maintenance. Social exchange theory (SET) or equity theory (ET) are the most likely (but these are *only* examples).                    AO1
                                                                                                                                                                                        ↓
**Section 2:** Since the MH is derived from SET, you *could* include studies that test the MH, such as:     AO1

- CD (Walster *et al.*, 1966)
- CAMP (Murstein, 1972).

*Word of warning : If you do this, you must make it clear how these studies are relevant (this isn't a question about attraction, but about formation/maintenance of relationships).*

Alternatively/in addition, you could describe the study by Mills & Clark (1980).

**Section 3:** You should **analyse and evaluate** the research studies that are relevant to SET or ET.         AO2

**Section 4:** You should **analyse and evaluate** SET or ET. Remember that an important way of doing this is to     AO2
compare and contrast one theory with another. This can include theories covered in other parts of the chapter, such as SVR theory.

*Try to answer this question yourself. There's a sample answer on page 181 you can compare your answer with.*

# Love and the breakdown of relationships

## Psychological explanations of love

### DIFFERENT TYPES OF LOVE

- Berscheid & Walster (1978) distinguish between:
  - (a) *companionate love* ('true love' or 'conjugal love'), 'the affection we feel for those with whom our lives are deeply entwined', including very close friends and marriage partners; and
  - (b) *passionate love* (romantic love, obsessive love, infatuation, 'love-sick', or 'being in love'). Romantic love is:

  'A state of intense absorption in another ... A state of intense physiological arousal.'

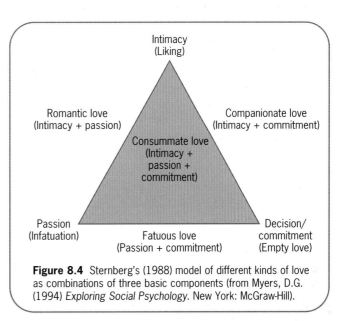

**Figure 8.4** Sternberg's (1988) model of different kinds of love as combinations of three basic components (from Myers, D.G. (1994) *Exploring Social Psychology*. New York: McGraw-Hill).

- These are *qualitatively different*, but companionate love is only a more extreme form of *liking* ('the affection we feel for casual acquaintances').
- Sternberg's *triangular model of love* (TMoL) (1988) involves three basic components (intimacy, passion and decision/commitment). These can be combined to produce *consummate love*. When only two components are combined, the resulting love is *romantic*, *companionate*, or *fatuous* (see Figure 8.4).

### Evaluation of Berscheid & Walster's, and Sternberg's, models of love (AO2)

✓ **Multidimensional:** These models identify several different kinds of love, comprising several components. These distinctions are important for understanding how intimate relationships change over time. This contrasts with, for example, Rubin's (1973) model, according to which love is a single dimension on which individuals can be ranked in terms of the strength of feelings for their partners.

✗ **Cultural differences ignored?** These models seem to support the popular ('Hollywood') view that people fall in love, and then commit themselves to each other through marriage. But in cultures where 'arranged marriages' occur, the relationship between love and marriage is reversed (see below). That is, marriage is seen as the basis on which to explore a loving relationship (Bellur, 1995). So the cultural background in which people have learned about love is important in shaping their ideas of it. (See Box 8.4).

### Box 8.4 Is romantic love unique to Western societies?

- **Moghaddam (1998) claims that the idea of people falling in love is found, in one form or another, in most human societies – even where marriages are traditionally arranged. For example, Jankowiak & Fischer (1992) analysed the songs and folklore of 166 societies, and found evidence for 'Western' romantic love in 85% of them.**
- **But Moghaddam believes that:**

> 'What is unique about romantic love in late twentieth-century Western societies is its pervasiveness: the idea that everyone should marry only when they are in love. Such an idea is fairly new historically and is still limited to Western societies.'

- **As societies become more Westernised, the percentage of people who believe that love must precede marriage increases.**
- **However, people in collectivist cultures (such as India, Pakistan and Thailand) are still less likely to believe in marrying for love than those in individualist cultures (such as England, Australia and the USA) (Levine *et al.*, 1995). (See pages 169–70 and Chapter 16.)**

## AN EVOLUTIONARY THEORY OF LOVE: LOVE-AS-ATTACHMENT

- An *evolutionary* account of love focuses on the *functions* that love evolved to meet.
- Compared with other primates, humans are dependent on their parents for an exceptionally long period of time. As length of childhood (and related brain size) increased steadily over the last million years or so of *Homo* evolution, so there were strong selection pressures toward the development of (relatively) *monogamous* (one male, one female) *pair-bonding*. In other words:

> 'Love is . . . an evolutionary device to persuade couples to stay together for long enough to give their children a good shot at making it to adulthood . . . ' (Fletcher, 2002)

- In our hunter-gatherer ancestral environment, two parents were better than one. Attachment bonds between procreative partners would have greatly enhanced the survival of the offspring (Zeifman & Hazan, 2000).
- Bowlby (1969) identified three basic behavioural systems that bond male–female pairs together: attachment, caregiving and sex. Shaver *et al.* (1996) have proposed a theory of adult romantic love in terms of these three systems. So when we say 'I love you', we can mean any or all of the following:

(a) *Love as attachment:* 'I am emotionally dependent on you for happiness, safety, and security; I feel anxious and lonely when you're gone, relieved and stronger when you're near. I want to be comforted, supported emotionally, and taken care of by you . . .'.

(b) *Love as caregiving:* 'I get great pleasure from supporting, caring for, and taking care of you; from facilitating your progress, health, growth, and happiness . . .'.

(c) *Love as sexual attraction:* 'I am sexually attracted to you and can't get you out of my mind. You excite me, "turn me on", make me feel alive . . . I want to see you, devour you, touch you, merge with you, lose myself in you, "get off on you".

- Zeifman & Hazan (2000) believe that there are four stages of adult attachments which mirror Bowlby's (1969) four phases of the infant's attachment to the mother (-figure). These are summarised in Table 8.2.

**Table 8.1** The four stages of adult attachment in relation to Bowlby's four phases of infant attachment development

| | Bowlby's phases of infant attachment | | | |
|---|---|---|---|---|
| | Pre-attachment (0–3/4 months) | Attachment-in-the-making (3/4–6/7 months) | Clear-cut attachment (6/7–12/18 months) | Goal-directed partnership (12–18 months onwards) |
| **Four stages of adult attachment** | Attraction and flirting | Falling in love | Loving | Life as usual |

Based on Zeifman & Hazan (2000)

✓ **Extension of an already influential theory:** Evolutionary theory in general, and Bowlby's attachment theory in particular, are well-established explanations of human behaviour. Extending Bowlby's theory to adults is perfectly consistent with Bowlby's own view that attachment-formation is a lifelong process.

✓ **A crucial difference between 'attachment' and 'love':** Bowlby's own theory allows for the distinction made explicit by Shaver *et al.* While love can involve sexual attraction, attachment as such doesn't (or 'love-as-attachment' is only one of its meanings). Adult–adult attachments typically involve sexual attraction (usually most intense early on in the relationship). But infants' attachments to their mothers don't!

✗ **Too biological:** Any criticisms of evolutionary theory in general will apply to extensions of it. A standard criticism is that it overemphasises biological factors, often to the exclusion of environmental, and especially *cultural*, factors. Here these include cultural and sub-cultural *differences* in relationships (see page 169).

## Explanations and research studies relating to the breakdown of relationships

### WHY DO RELATIONSHIPS GO WRONG?

> **Specification Hint:** Theories of relationship formation/maintenance also help to explain the breakdown of relationships, so it isn't necessary to know about two *additional* theories of breakdown. But we've chosen one additional theory here.

- According to Duck (2001), there's an almost infinite number of reasons why relationships break up. But they can be put into three broad categories:

1. *Pre-existing doom:* incompatibility and failure are almost pre-destined (for example, 'Schoolgirl, 17, marries her 50-year-old teacher who's already a grandfather').

2. *Mechanical failure:* two suitable people of goodwill and good nature nevertheless find they can't live together (this is the most common cause).

3. *Sudden death:* the discovery of a betrayal or infidelity can lead to the immediate termination of a romantic relationship.

- Duck believes that the 'official' reasons given to others (including the partner) to justify the break-up are far more interesting psychologically than the real reasons. The psychology of break-up involves a whole layer of individual psychological processes, group processes, cultural rules and self-presentation. But this applies mainly to romantic relationships, rather than friendships.
- When you fall out with a friend, there's usually no formal or public 'announcement'. There's no need for this, because friendships aren't exclusive relationships in the way that most sexual relationships are (it's 'normal' to have several friends at once, but not several partners!). As Duck says :

> '. . . Truly committed romantic relationships necessarily involve the foregoing of other romantic relationships and commitment to only one partner ("forsaking all others", as it says in the marriage ceremony) . . . '

- So the ending of a romantic relationship indicates that the two people are now legitimately available as partners for other relationships. This requires them to create a story for the end of the relationship that leaves them in a favourable light as potential partners. Romantic relationships are, therefore, typically ended publicly in a way that announces the ex-partners' freedom from the expectations of exclusive commitment.

**Exam Hint:**

SET and ET as accounts of relationship formation/ maintenance can be 'turned round' to explain breakdown. So if certain 'ingredients' that normally keep couples together are missing, the relationship may break down. But in your answer to an exam question on breakdown, this point would have to be made *explicitly*: you can't just assume that the examiner will draw the conclusions or make the deductions you'd like them to! (See Exam tips box on page 164.)

- Duck (2001) identifies a number of classic formats for a break-up story (such as 'X suddenly changed and I had to get out'; 'X betrayed me'; and 'We grew apart'). The crucial ingredients of such stories are those that show the speaker:

(a) is open to relationships but doesn't enter them thoughtlessly
(b) is aware of others' deficiencies but isn't overly critical
(c) is willing to work to improve a relationship or take decisive action when partners turn nasty or break the rules of relating
(d) is rational and sensible, and brings closure to relationships only after trauma, hard work, or on reasonable grounds after real effort to make things work.

## DUCK'S THEORY OF RELATIONSHIP DISSOLUTION (ToRD) (1982)

- According to Duck, breaking up (dissolution) is a personal process but one where partners have an eye on how things will look to their friends and networks. This suggests an account of relationship dissolution that has several parts. ToRD begins at the point where one of the partners has become sufficiently dissatisfied with the relationship over a long enough period of time to be seriously considering ending it.
- The four phases (*intrapsychic*, *dyadic*, *social* and *grave-dressing*), and the related thresholds are shown in Table 8.2.

**Table 8.2** A sketch of the main phases of dissolving personal relationships (based on Duck, 1982, from Duck, 1988)*

### Breakdown–dissatisfaction with relationship

**Threshold:** *'I can't stand this any more'*

### INTRAPSYCHIC PHASE

- Personal focus on partner's behaviour
- Assess adequacy of partner's role performance
- Depict and evaluate negative aspects of being in the relationship
- Consider costs of withdrawal
- Assess positive aspects of alternative relationships
- Face 'express/repress dilemma'

**Threshold:** *'I'd be justified in withdrawing'*

### DYADIC PHASE

- Face 'confrontation/avoidance dilemma'
- Confront partner
- Negotiate in 'our relationship talks'
- Attempt repair and reconciliation?
- Assess joint costs of withdrawal or reduced intimacy

**Threshold:** *'I mean it'*

### SOCIAL PHASE

- Negotiate post-dissolution state with partner
- Initiate gossip/discussion in social network
- Create publicly negotiable face-saving/blame-placing stories and accounts
- Consider and face up to implied social network effect, if any
- Call in intervention team

**Threshold:** *'It's now inevitable'*

### GRAVE-DRESSING PHASE

- 'Getting over' activity
- Retrospective; reformative postmortem attribution
- Public distribution of own version of break-up story

* Duck, S. (1998) *Relating to Others*. Milton Keynes: Open University Press/McGraw-Hill Publishing Company. Reproduced with kind permission.

Evaluation of ToRD (AO2)

✓ **Intuitively appealing:** It makes good common sense, and it's an account of relationship breakdown that we can relate to our own and/or others' experiences.

✓ **Theoretically important:** The view of relationship dissolution as a *process* (rather than an event) underlying ToRD is an important insight, which is now widely accepted. This view applies to the breakdown of friendships as well as sexual relationships (including marriages). The common and crucial factor is that the relationship is long-term and has embraced many parts of the person's emotional, communicative, leisure and everyday life (Duck, 1988). However, ToRD applies mainly to sexual relationships, because these are usually seen as exclusive in a way that friendships aren't (see above).

✓ **Taking the broader picture:** ToRD doesn't focus exclusively on the individual partner, but takes his/her social context into account. As Duck (2001) says:

> '. . . Break-up involves not only the individual who creates the break-up but the psychological sense of integrity of the person to whom it all happens . . . But a lot that happens is done with an eye on the group that surrounds the person.'

✗ **Theoretical limitations:** ToRD takes no account of why the dissatisfaction has arisen in the first place – its starting point is where dissatisfaction has already set in. To this extent, it fails to give a complete picture of dissolution.

✗ **The trouble with phases/stages:** As with all such theories, ToRD's four phases may not apply in every (or even most) case of relationship breakdown.

# Cultural and sub-cultural differences in relationships
## Explanations relating to the nature of relationships in different cultures

> **Specification Hint:** The Specification says: 'Explanations . . . relating to the nature of relationships in different cultures (e.g. voluntary/involuntary, permanent/impermanent types of relationships) . . . '. You need to know *at least two* of these, but two will do. We've included 'individualism–collectivism', which refers to a classification of cultures, where relationships (especially non-sexual ones) have a different significance. Voluntary/involuntary can most easily be interpreted as referring to 'non-arranged' and arranged marriages (which overlaps with Western and non-Western respectively).

### INDIVIDUALISM/COLLECTIVISM

- Hofstede (1980) defined culture as:

> ' . . . the collective programming of the mind which distinguishes the members of one group from another.'

- He identified four dimensions of culture, two of which are:
(a) *power distance:* the amount of respect shown by those in both superior and subordinate positions
(b) *individualism–collectivism:* whether one's identity is defined by personal choices and achievements (individualism) or by characteristics of the collective group one is more or less permanently attached to (collectivism).

- Triandis (1990), influenced by Hofstede's work, defined culture in terms of *cultural syndromes*. One of these is *individualism–collectivism*. Triandis *et al.* (1986) identified four factors related to the main construct. These are:

(a) *family integrity* ('Children should live at home with their parents until they get married')

(b) *interdependence* ('I like to live close to my good friends').

These are both features of *collectivism*.

(c) *self-reliance with hedonism* ('If the group is slowing me down, it's better to leave and work alone; the most important thing in my life is to make myself happy')

(d) *separation from in-groups* (indicated by agreement with items showing that what happens to extended family members is of little concern).

These are both features of *individualism*.

- Other 'defining attributes' are shown in Box 8.5.

### Box 8.5 Some defining attributes of collectivism–individualism (Triandis, 1990)

1. Collectivists pay much more attention to an identifiable in-group, and behave differently towards in-group compared with out-group members. The in-group is best defined in terms of the *common fate* of its members. Often it's the unit of survival, or the food community. In most cultures, the family is the main in-group. But in some, the tribal group or the work group (as in Japan) can be just as important.

2. Collectivists emphasise social hierarchy much more than individualists. Usually the father is 'head of the household' and women are generally subordinate to men.

3. For collectivists, the *self* is an extension of the in-group, whereas for individualists it's separate and distinct. In collectivist cultures, people usually belong to a small number of in-groups, which influence their behaviour greatly. This is unusual in individualist cultures, because people belong to so many groups, which often make conflicting demands on the individual.

4. In collectivist cultures, *vertical relationships* (such as parent–child) take priority over *horizontal relationships* (such as spouse–spouse) when there's a conflict between them. The reverse is true in individualist cultures.

5. Collectivists stress family integrity, security, obedience and conformity, while individualists stress achievement, pleasure and competition.

# Research studies relating to individualism/collectivism

**ESSENTIAL STUDY 8.5**

### Hofstede's (1980) 'Culture's Consequences' study (CCS)

- Hofstede had access to morale surveys conducted by IBM in 40 countries world-wide. This involved the responses of 117,000 employees, who answered questions relating to various aspects of their work experience.
- He analysed the mean scores on each questionnaire item, which resulted in his classifying the 40 countries along four dimensions. These included the two described above, namely, 'power–distance' and 'individualism–collectivism'.
- A group of mostly European and North American countries scored high on individualism, while another group of mostly South American and Asian countries scored high on collectivism.

## Evaluation of CCS (AO2)

✓ **Large and equivalent samples:** For each country, the sample size was very large. From within this overall sample, Hofstede selected respondents who all worked in servicing and marketing. This maximised the comparability of the different countries (Smith & Bond, 1998).

✗ **Predominantly male sample:** This means that the sample wasn't representative even of all IBM employees.

✗•✓ **Possible confounding variable:** IBM is a large American corporation said to have a culture of its own. But the fact that Hofstede found national culture differences *despite* this is a strength of his research (Smith & Bond, 1998).

✓ **Theoretical importance:** CCS provides us with one possible way of classifying the differences found among the 40 national cultures in his sample. Individualism–collectivism has become a widely accepted dimension within cross-cultural psychology generally.

✓•✗ **Subsequent research:** In a later study, Hofstede (1983) increased the number of countries to 50 and three 'regions' (Africa East, Africa West and Arab). The range of countries is extremely impressive. In fact, in terms of global coverage it was unrivalled – until very recently (Smith & Bond, 1998). But the former Communist bloc and most of Africa are omitted.

## Voluntary/involuntary relationships

- According to Moghaddam *et al.* (1993), interpersonal relationships in Western cultures tend to be *individualistic*, *voluntary* and *temporary*. Those in non-Western cultures are more *collectivist*, *involuntary* and *permanent*. As they say:

> 'The cultural values and environmental conditions in North America have led North American social psychologists to be primarily concerned with first-time acquaintances, friendships and intimate relationships, primarily because these appear to be the relationships most relevant to the North American urban cultural experience.'

- In other words, Western psychologists tend to equate 'relationships' with 'Western relationships' (a form of *ethnocentrism*: see Chapter 16).
- The examples given in the quote by Moghaddam *et al.* are all *voluntary*. But Western psychologists have studied a wide range of such relationships during the last 20 years or so, some of which may seem more voluntary than others. Duck (1999) gives the following examples: relationships of blended families, cross-sex non-romantic friendship, romantic or friendly relationships in the workplace, relationships between co-operative neighbours, relationships between prisoners and guards, sibling relationships, children relating to other children, and adults' relationships with their parents.

- *Marriage* is found in all known cultures (Fletcher, 2002), and is usually taken to be a voluntary relationship. But there are several reasons for asking if it really is:

(a) There are wide and important cultural variations in marital arrangements. From a Western perspective, the 'natural' form of marriage is *monogamy* (marriage to one spouse at any one time). This belief is enshrined in the law (bigamy is a criminal offence) and reflects basic Judeo–Christian doctrine. But monogamy is only one form that marriage can take. See Box 8.6.

## Box 8.6 Culture and marriage

- *Polygamy* refers to having two or more spouses at once.
- It can take the form of *polygyny* (one man having two or more wives) or (less commonly) *polyandry* (one woman with two or more husbands).
- Another arrangement is *mandatory marriage to specific relatives*, as when a son marries the daughter of his father's brother (his first cousin: Triandis, 1994).
- 84% of known cultures allow polygyny, but only 5–10% of men in such cultures actually have more than one wife (Fletcher, 2002).
- Probably fewer than 0.5% of human societies have practised polyandry as a common or preferred form of marriage (Price & Crapo, 1999). But throughout Tibet and the neighbouring Himalayan areas of India, Nepal and Bhutan, it's been common for generations. Usually, a woman marries two or more brothers (*fraternal polyandry*). This helps to keep family numbers down in order to cope with scarce resources. It also keeps brothers together. Land doesn't need to be divided between the brothers, and a single family is preserved as an economic unit.

(b) According to Duck (1999), the *choice to marry* is voluntary, presumably. But once the marriage is a few years old, it's much less voluntary than it was, since getting out of it is accompanied by a great deal of 'social and legal baggage':

> '. . . Thus when we talk about 'voluntary relationships', we need to recognize not only that the exercise of apparently free choice is always tempered by the social realities and constraints that surround us, but also that, once exercised, some choices are then disabled, and cannot be easily or straightforwardly remade. To that extent, therefore, their consequences become non-voluntary.' (Duck, 1999)

(c) When discussing Kerckhoff & Davis's (1962) *filter model* above (see page 160), we noted that our choice of potential (realistic) marriage partners is limited by *demographic variables*. To this extent, most relationships are 'arranged'. As Duck (1999) says:

> 'Many of us would perhaps not recognize – or accept – that marriages are actually "arranged" by religion, social position, wealth, class, opportunity and other things over which we have little control, even within our own culture . . . '

(d) Conversely, parentally arranged marriages in some cultures are gladly entered into, and are considered perfectly normal, natural relationships that are anticipated with pleasure (Duck, 1999).

## Research studies of arranged marriages

- Gupta & Singh (1982) found that couples in Jaipur, India who married for love reported *diminished* feelings of love if they'd been married for more than five years. By contrast, those who'd undertaken arranged marriages reported *more* love if they weren't newly-weds.
- These findings reveal that passionate love 'cools' over time, and that there's scope for love to flourish within an arranged marriage.

- In cultures where arranged marriages occur, courtship is accepted to a certain degree. But love is left to be defined and discovered *after* marriage (Bellur, 1995). This, of course, is the reverse of the 'Hollywood' picture, where love is supposed to *precede* marriage and be what marriage is all about (see Box 8.4, page 165).
- However, even in traditional cultures that practise arranged marriages, brides (and grooms) are typically given some choice in the matter (Fletcher, 2002). For example, in Sri Lanka men and women who like one another (or fall in love) usually let their parents know their choices in advance through indirect channels (de Munck, 1998). Families often use similar criteria that the individuals themselves might use if they had a free choice (including matching on attractiveness: see above). The classic example is the Jewish custom of having a *matchmaker* arrange a suitable match (Rockman, 1994).
- Arranged marriages are far more common in collectivist cultures, where the whole extended family 'marries' the other extended family. This is distinct from individualist cultures, in which the individuals marry one another (Triandis, 1994). In Japan, almost 25% of marriages are arranged (Iwao, 1993).

Traditional Japanese wedding in Kakunodate, Akita Prefecture, Japan

- In general, *divorce rates* among those who marry according to parents' wishes are much *lower* than among those who marry for love. This is an argument in favour of arranged marriages. But divorce rates among 'arranged couples' are rising, indicating that personal freedom is gaining importance and that traditional structures which define set roles for family members are becoming less valid (Bellur, 1995).

## 'Understudied relationships'

> **Specification Hint:** The Specification says 'Understudied relationships' such as gay and lesbian and mediated relationships. Since 'relationships' is plural, you need to know about *at least two* of these. 'Gay' and 'lesbian' may count as two, although you may prefer to 'pool' what you know about these under 'homosexual', and make mediated relationships (e.g. Internet relationships) the other. Note too that there's no specific reference to 'explanations' or 'research studies', but this doesn't exclude either or both of these.

### GAY AND LESBIAN RELATIONSHIPS

- The focus on long-term relationships of heterosexuals has now been supplemented with discussion of gay and lesbian relationships (Duck, 1999). This includes studies of their stability and dissolution (Kurdek, 1991, 1992). But, as yet, we know relatively little about gay and lesbian experience in serious relationships or networks of maintenance and commitment.
- Compared with same-sex friendships and cross-sex non-romantic friendships, gay and lesbian partners experience extra social burdens in terms of the influence of other people's reactions (Huston & Schwartz, 1995).
- Weston (1991) argues that 'blood-family' is often replaced for homosexuals by 'families of choice'. Gays and lesbians often aren't 'out' to blood-family, or may be estranged from their blood-families specifically because of their homosexuality. As a result, the blood-family can function very differently for gays and lesbians. Not only are they less likely to tell their parents and siblings of developing relationships; they're less likely to talk of developed intimate relationships (Huston & Schwartz, 1995).

- According to Kitzinger & Coyle (1995), psychological research into homosexuality since the mid-1970s has moved away from a 'pathology model' towards one comprising four overlapping themes:

  (a) belief in a basic, underlying similarity between homosexuals and heterosexuals

  (b) rejection of the concept of homosexuality as a central organising principle of the personality in favour of recognising the diversity and variety of homosexuals as individuals

  (c) an assertion that homosexuality is as natural, normal and healthy as heterosexuality

  (d) denial of the idea that homosexuals pose any threat to children, the nuclear family or the future of society as we know it.

- According to Bee (1994), homosexual partnerships are far more like heterosexual ones than they are different. In terms of sexual behaviour, apart from their sexual preferences, gays and lesbians don't look massively different from their heterosexual counterparts (Fletcher, 2002). Researchers have repeatedly found that many of the same gender differences between heterosexual men and women occur when comparing gays and lesbians. For example, straight men and gays have higher sex drives than straight women and lesbians, and females (straight or lesbian) are more relationship-focused than males (straight or gay). In other words:

  > ' . . . many central patterns of sexual attitudes and behaviour are more closely linked to gender than to sexual orientation. If one wants to understand gays and lesbians, a good place to start is by looking at heterosexual men and women respectively.' (Fletcher, 2002)

- But Kitzinger and Coyle argue that certain factors are omitted or distorted when homosexual relationships are assessed in terms derived from heterosexual relationships. Some of these are described in Box 8.7.

### Box 8.7  Some key differences between homosexual and heterosexual relationships

- ***Cohabitation*** (living together) is much less common for homosexuals than heterosexuals.
- ***Sexual exclusivity*** (having only one sexual partner at a time) is less common in lesbian relationships and *much* less common in gay relationships (Peplau, 1982). But the ideal of sexual exclusivity is based on an assumed heterosexual norm or 'blueprint' (Yip, 1999), which many gays and lesbians reject. Sexual infidelity may cause heterosexual couples to break up, largely because it's 'secretive'. But homosexual couples are more likely to have open relationships, and so are '. . . less likely to experience their own, or their partners' sexual affairs as signaling the end of the couple relationship' (Kitzinger & Coyle, 1995).
- Most gays and lesbians actively reject traditional (i.e. heterosexual) husband/wife or masculine/feminine sex roles as a model for enduring relationships (Peplau, 1991). Gay and lesbian couples tend to adopt 'the ethic of equality and reciprocity'. This is especially true for lesbians, who've previously been in 'unequal' heterosexual relationships (Yip, 1999).

### MEDIATED FRIENDSHIPS

- Probably one of the most unexpected uses of the Internet is the development of *online relationships* (or *cyber affairs*: Griffiths, 2000).
- In the UK, one newspaper reported that there have been over 1,000 weddings resulting from Internet meetings.
- Cyberspace is becoming another 'singles bar'. There are now many sites aimed at those looking for romance or a sexual liaison. Some are directed at singles, while others seem to encourage or facilitate virtual adultery.
- Online relationships can proceed through chat-rooms, interactive games or newsgroups. What may begin as a simple e-mail exchange, or innocent chat-room encounter, can escalate into an intense and passionate cyber affair – and eventually into face-to-face sexual encounters. Griffiths (2000) claims that '. . . electronic communication is the easiest, most disinhibiting and most accessible way to meet potential new partners'.

## Box 8.8 Three basic types of online relationship (Griffiths, 1999)

- *Purely virtual*: while these are usually sexually very explicit, the 'correspondents' never meet, just want sexual kicks, and don't consider they're being unfaithful to their actual partners.
- Increasingly sexually intense *online* contact may eventually lead to the exchange of photographs, secret telephone calls, letters and meetings. Once the individuals have met, and if practically possible, actual time spent together largely replaces online contact.
- An initial *offline* meeting will be maintained largely by an online relationship. This usually involves people living in different countries.

### Some concerns about online relationships

- The disinhibiting, anonymous nature of the Internet can make online relationships seductive and potentially addictive. As Griffiths (2000) points out:

> 'What might take months or years in an offline relationship may only take days or weeks on line ... the perception of trust, intimacy, and acceptance has the potential to encourage online users to see these relationships as a primary source of companionship and comfort.'

- According to the sociologist Taylor (in Williams, 2000):

> 'Face-to-face relationships are steadily declining. Fewer and fewer people take part in civic activities such as ... political party involvement or trade unions as the mass movement towards faceless electronic liaisons continues to increase. In the long run we will become incapable of relating to each other in person at all.'

## EXAM tips BOX

**Discuss research into cultural differences in relationships. (24 marks) (30 mins) (600 words minimum) AO1/AO2**

*This essay can be split up into FOUR sections – each about 150 words long. Each section would be worth approx. 6 marks.*

**Section 1:** A **description** of individualism/collectivism, and research studies on which these are based, such as:

- CCS – Hofstede (1980) (individualism/collectivism).

*A word of warning: You need to emphasise how individualist/collectivist cultures differ in how they value and organise relationships (the question is concerned with cultural differences in relationships, not with cultural differences in general).*

**Section 2: Analysis and evaluation of CCS** (or whatever studies cited above) and of the concept of individualism/collectivism. The latter could include (a) the general observation that identifying cultural differences helps to challenge ethnocentrism in Western psychologists' study of relationships; and (b) the observation that individualism/collectivism overlaps with/is correlated with other cultural differences, such as Western/non-Western, voluntary/involuntary relationships, and permanent/impermanent relationships.

**Section 3:** A **description** of voluntary/involuntary relationships, including research studies into arranged marriages, such as:

- Gupta & Singh (1982).

**Section 4: Analysis and evaluation** of Gupta and Singh's study, including other studies of arranged marriages. This could include consideration of the voluntariness of marriage in Western societies, and the relationship between marriage and love as understood by Western psychologists. The point that psychologists are studying an increasingly wide range of non-sexual voluntary relationships is also worth making.

*Try to answer this question yourself. There's a sample answer on page 182 that you can compare your answer with.*

AO1

↓

AO2

↓

AO1

↓

AO2

- Given the emphasis put on physical attractiveness in our image-conscious society, the disembodied, anonymous nature of online relationships may help individuals focus on the content of the message: '. . . there's no such thing as a bad hair day on the Internet . . . ' (Joinson, in Williams, 2000). For people who are normally inhibited, or those who are too cowardly to finish a romantic relationship in person, this is probably a godsend (Williams, 2000).

## PYA4: Relationships

Other possible exam questions:

- Each essay is worth 24 marks and should take 30 minutes to write
- Remember the mark scheme allocates 12 marks for AO1 (knowledge and description) and 12 marks for AO2 (analysis and evaluation).

### ATTRACTION AND FORMATION OF RELATIONSHIPS

1. Discuss research studies relating to interpersonal attraction. (24 marks)

2. Outline and evaluate two or more theories relating to the formation/maintenance of relationships. (24 marks)

### LOVE AND THE BREAKDOWN OF RELATIONSHIPS

3. Outline and evaluate research into the breakdown of relationships. (24 marks)

4. Discuss psychological explanations of love. (24 marks)

### CULTURAL AND SUB-CULTURAL DIFFERENCES IN RELATIONSHIPS

5. Critically consider the extent to which relationships have been shown to be different in different cultures. (24 marks)

6. Discuss research relating to understudied relationships (e.g. gay and lesbian relationships or mediated relationships). (24 marks)

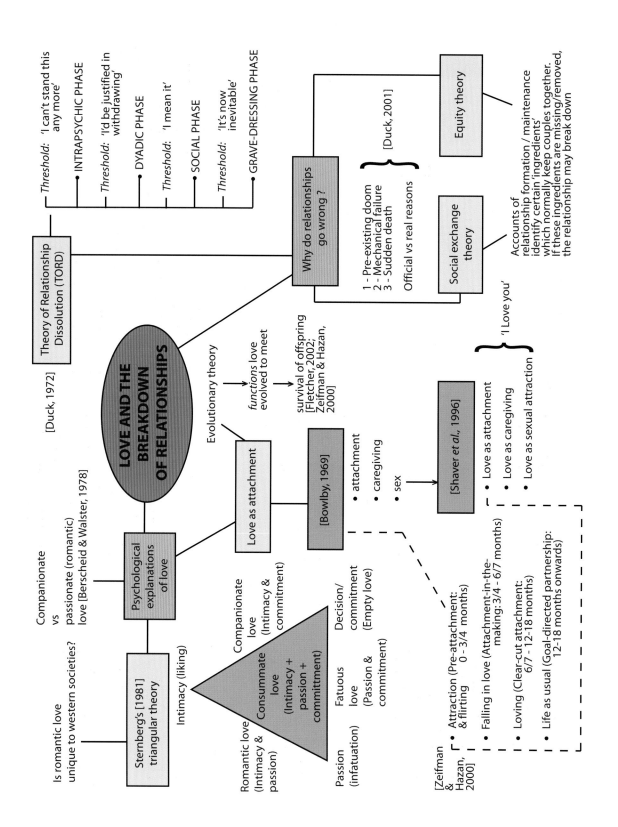

**LOVE AND THE BREAKDOWN OF RELATIONSHIPS**

Psychological explanations of love

Sternberg's [1981] triangular theory

Is romantic love unique to western societies?

Companionate vs passionate (romantic) love [Berscheid & Walster, 1978]

Intimacy (liking)

Romantic love (Intimacy & passion)

Companionate love (Intimacy & commitment)

Decision/ commitment (Empty love)

Passion (infatuation)

Fatuous love (Passion & commitment)

Consummate love (Intimacy + passion + commitment)

Love as attachment

Evolutionary theory

*functions* love evolved to meet → survival of offspring [Fletcher, 2002; Zeifman & Hazan, 2000]

[Bowlby, 1969]
- attachment
- caregiving
- sex

[Shaver *et al.*, 1996]
- Love as attachment
- Love as caregiving
- Love as sexual attraction

'I Love you'

[Zeifman & Hazan, 2000]
- Attraction (Pre-attachment: & flirting    0 - 3/4 months)
- Falling in love (Attachment-in-the-making: 3/4 - 6/7 months)
- Loving (Clear-cut attachment: 6/7 - 12-18 months)
- Life as usual (Goal-directed partnership: 12-18 months onwards)

Theory of Relationship Dissolution (TORD)

[Duck, 1972]

*Threshold:* 'I can't stand this any more'
INTRAPSYCHIC PHASE

*Threshold:* 'I'd be justified in withdrawing'
DYADIC PHASE

*Threshold:* 'I mean it'
SOCIAL PHASE

*Threshold:* 'It's now inevitable'
GRAVE-DRESSING PHASE

Why do relationships go wrong ?

1 - Pre-existing doom
2 - Mechanical failure
3 - Sudden death

Official vs real reasons

[Duck, 2001]

Social exchange theory

Equity theory

Accounts of relationship formation / maintenance identify certain 'ingredients' which normally keep couples together. If these ingredients are missing/removed, the relationship may break down

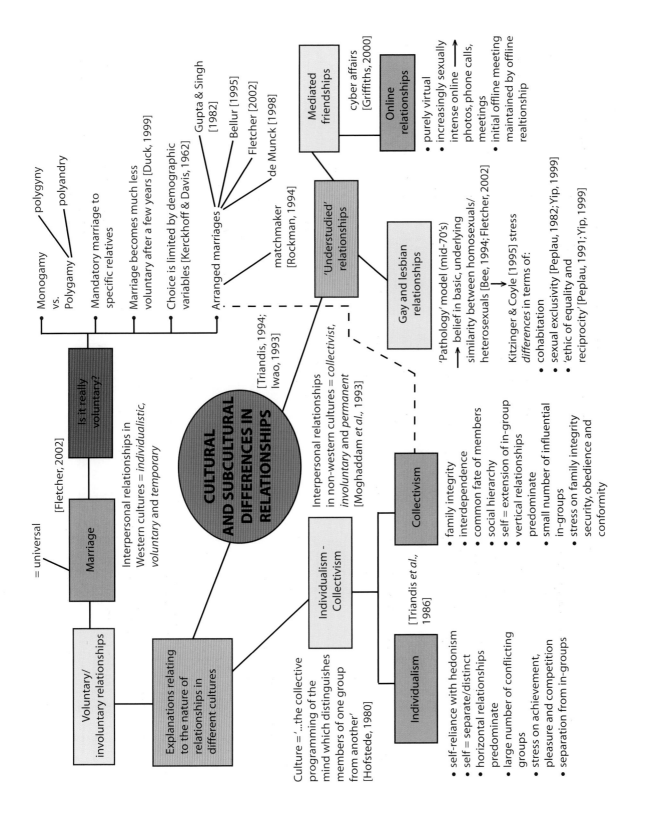

= universal

[Fletcher, 2002]

**Is it really voluntary?**

Monogamy vs. Polygamy
- polygyny
- polyandry

Mandatory marriage to specific relatives

Marriage becomes much less voluntary after a few years [Duck, 1999]

Choice is limited by demographic variables [Kerckhoff & Davis, 1962]

Arranged marriages
- Gupta & Singh [1982]
- Bellur [1995]
- Fletcher [2002]
- de Munck [1998]

matchmaker [Rockman, 1994]

**Marriage**

Interpersonal relationships in Western cultures = *individualistic, voluntary and temporary*

**Mediated friendships**

cyber affairs [Griffiths, 2000]

**Online relationships**
- purely virtual
- increasingly sexually intense online → photos, phone calls, meetings
- initial offline meeting maintained by offline realtionship

**CULTURAL AND SUBCULTURAL DIFFERENCES IN RELATIONSHIPS**

[Triandis, 1994; Iwao, 1993]

**Voluntary/ involuntary relationships**

**Explanations relating to the nature of relationships in different cultures**

Interpersonal relationships in non-western cultures = *collectivist, involuntary and permanent* [Moghaddam et al., 1993]

Culture = '...the collective programming of the mind which distinguishes members of one group from another' [Hofstede, 1980]

**Individualism - Collectivism**

[Triandis et al., 1986]

**Collectivism**
- family integrity
- interdependence
- common fate of members
- social hierarchy
- self = extension of in-group
- vertical relationships predominate
- small number of influential in-groups
- stress on family integrity security, obedience and conformity

**Individualism**
- self-reliance with hedonism
- self = separate/distinct
- horizontal relationships predominate
- large number of conflicting groups
- stress on achievement, pleasure and competition
- separation from in-groups

**'Understudied' relationships**

**Gay and lesbian relationships**

'Pathology' model (mid-70's) → belief in basic, underlying similarity between homosexuals/ heterosexuals [Bee, 1994; Fletcher, 2002]

Kitzinger & Coyle [1995] stress *differences* in terms of:
- cohabitation
- sexual exclusivity [Peplau, 1982; Yip, 1999]
- 'ethic of equality and reciprocity' [Peplau, 1991; Yip, 1999]

# SAMPLE ESSAYS

Critically consider *one* explanation of interpersonal attraction. (24 marks) (30 mins) (600 words minimum)

## Section 1:

A01

Human beings have a fundamental need for affiliation, which is the most general explanation of attraction. But this doesn't tell us why we're attracted to some people more than others (or to some and not others).

According to the matching hypothesis (MH), people are more likely to become romantically involved if they're fairly closely matched in their ability to reward one another. The MH forms part of the more general social exchange theory (SET), which is also relevant to the maintenance and dissolution of relationships. Ideally we'd all have the 'perfect' partner, because SET claims that we're all fundamentally selfish. But this is impossible, so we try to find a compromise in the form of a value-match, a subjective belief that our partner is the most rewarding we could realistically hope to find (the best general 'bargain' that can be struck).

## Section 2:

A01

The MH has been tested in a variety of ways, including the 'computer dance' method. The original study of this kind was conducted by Walster *et al.* (1966). Over 700 male and female fresher students bought tickets for a computer dance at the University of Minnesota at the start of the academic year. When they bought their ticket, they were asked to complete a detailed questionnaire about themselves. This information would be put into a computer, which would match them with their ideal date. In fact, they were assigned a partner purely randomly. While they completed the questionnaire, an unseen observer rated the students for physical attractiveness.

During the intermission, and after spending over two hours with their date, the students were asked to indicate how much they liked their partner. Physical attractiveness proved to be the single most important factor influencing how much they liked their partner – for both males and females. It was also the best single predictor of whether the male would ask the female for another date – regardless of his attractiveness. So the more attractive the partner (as rated by the observer), the more they were liked.

Murstein (1972) tested the MH by using photographs of two separate samples of engaged couples (99 and 98). Independent judges rated the photographs for physical attractiveness without knowing who belonged to whom. The couples had to rate their own and their partner's physical attractiveness. Partners received very similar ratings, and these were significantly more alike than the same ratings given to 'random couples' (the actual couples' photographs randomly sorted into couples to form a control group). How partners rated themselves was significantly more similar than self-ratings for random couples, but partners' ratings of each other weren't significantly correlated. These findings applied equally to both samples.

## Section 3:

A02

Walster *et al.*'s computer dance study had high ecological validity, taking place in a naturalistic setting in the context of an expected event. The freshers' ball would have happened anyway. But it can be criticised on ethical grounds. The students were deceived regarding how the questionnaire information would be used to match them with their ideal date – it was actually random. They also didn't know that their attractiveness was being assessed, or that they were taking part in a study at all. So there was a lack of both consent and informed consent.

The study provided strong evidence for the impact of physical attractiveness in initial attraction. This could be seen as consistent with reward theory (and with common sense!). But it's actually the opposite of what the MH predicts. If we settle for a value-match, then only those males who happened to be paired (by chance) with a date whose attractiveness level closely matched their own would have asked their female partner for a date.

Berscheid *et al.* (1971) argue that a more valid test of the MH would involve having to specify in advance the kind of partner we'd like, including how attractive we'd like them to be. Later computer dance studies (e.g. Berscheid & Walster, 1974) used this improved methodology and the results tended to support the MH.

Murstein's study was well controlled (the random couples constituted a comparison group), and the judges were unbiased (not knowing who the actual couples were prevented a halo effect). But like other similar studies, Murstein restricted his definition of physical attractiveness to facial appearance. For both sexes, a good body is also important.

## Section 4:

A02

As discussed above, the later computer dance studies tend to support the MH – unlike Walster *et al.*'s original (1966) study. When people are asked in advance what kind of partner they'd like, those rated as of high, low or average attractiveness tend to ask for dates of a similar attractiveness level.

According to Duck (1999), the 'magnetic metaphor' of attraction implies that people are unwittingly, almost against their will, pulled towards one another. This is a caricature of interpersonal relationships, and is a limitation of both the MH and reward theory. Similarly, and as mentioned earlier, the MH is derived from SET, according to which people are fundamentally selfish and human relationships are based primarily on self-interest. Although this view shouldn't be taken too literally, our attitudes towards others are determined largely by how rewarding we think they are for us (Rubin, 1973). But we're also capable of being altruistic, that is, doing things for others without expecting anything in return, especially for those who are closest to us.

*(883 words)*

Critically consider *one* theory of the formation/maintenance of relationships. (24 marks) (30 mins) (600 words minimum)

## Section 1:

A01

Social exchange theory (SET) is a major theory of the formation/maintenance of relationships. There are different versions of SET, but they all share the underlying view of people as fundamentally selfish. According to Homans (1974), we view our feelings for others in terms of profits – the amount of reward obtained from a relationship minus the cost. The greater the reward and lower the cost, the greater the profit and hence the attraction and the longer-term wish to stay in the relationship. Blau (1964) argues that interactions are 'expensive'. They take time, energy and commitment, and may involve unpleasant emotions and experiences. Because of this, what we get out of a relationship must exceed what we put in. According to Berscheid & Walster (1978), all social interactions involve an exchange of rewards (such as affection, information and status). The degree of attraction or liking will reflect how people evaluate the rewards they receive relative to those they give.

SET predicts that people are more likely to become romantically involved if they're fairly closely matched in their ability to reward one another. This is the matching hypothesis (MH). Since we cannot all have the ideal partner, we try to find a value-match, that is, a subjective belief that our partner is the most rewarding we could realistically hope to find.

## Section 2:

A01

An indirect way of testing SET is by considering studies that test the MH. The MH is more commonly discussed in the context of attraction, that is, how people get into relationships in the first place. An example is the computer dance study, starting with Walster et al. (1966). Over 700 male and female fresher students bought tickets for a computer dance at the start of the academic year. When they bought the ticket, they were asked to complete a questionnaire about themselves. This information would be fed into a computer, which would match them with their ideal date. In fact, they were assigned a partner randomly. While they completed the questionnaire, an unseen observer rated the students for physical attractiveness. After spending two hours with their partner, the students were asked to indicate how much they liked them. The more attractive the partner (as rated by the observer), the more they were liked – regardless of their own attractiveness.

Murstein's (1972) study also tested the MH, but this involved engaged couples, so this represents a more direct test of SET. In other words, the couples were in long-term relationships. Independent judges rated the photographs of two separate samples of engaged couples for physical attractiveness without knowing who belonged to whom. The couples had to rate their own and their partner's physical attractiveness. Partners received very similar ratings and these were significantly more alike than the same ratings given to 'random couples' (the actual couples' photographs randomly sorted into couples to form a control group).

## Section 3:

A02

Walster *et al.*'s study provided strong evidence for the impact of physical attractiveness in initial attraction. Although this could be seen as consistent with reward theory (and with common sense!), it's actually the opposite of what the MH predicts (and, hence, challenges the major assumption of SET that people are fundamentally selfish). Berscheid *et al.* (1971) argue that a more valid test of the MH would involve having to specify in advance the kind of partner we'd like, including how attractive we'd like them to be. Later computer dance studies (e.g. Berscheid & Walster, 1974) used this improved methodology and the results tended to support the MH.

Murstein's study was well controlled (the random couples constituted a comparison group), and the judges were unbiased (not knowing who were actual couples prevented a halo effect). But like other similar studies, Murstein restricted his definition of physical attractiveness to facial appearance. For both sexes, a good body is also important.

## Section 4:

A02

The different versions of SET share a few basic ideas, such as profit and reward. The obvious link between SET and reward theory is useful, and shows the overlap between (a) explanations of initial attraction/formation of relationships and (b) the maintenance of relationships. But are we really as selfish as SET suggests, and are our relationships just about what we can get out of them for ourselves? Although this shouldn't be taken too literally, our attitudes towards others are determined largely by how rewarding they are for us (Rubin, 1973). But we're also capable of being altruistic, that is, doing things for others without expecting anything in return – especially for those who are closest to us.

Some psychologists distinguish between 'true' love and friendship, which are altruistic (the opposite of selfish) and less admirable forms based on considerations of exchange (Brown, 1986). Fromm (1962) defines true love as giving, as opposed to the false love of the 'marketing character' (expecting to have favours returned). Mills & Clark (1980) found support for this distinction, thus contradicting SET. They identified two kinds of intimate relationship, the communal couple, where each partner gives out of concern for the other, and the exchange couple, where each partner keeps mental records of who's 'ahead' and who's 'behind'.

SET is really a special case of a more general account of human relationships called equity theory (ET). The extra component in ET that's added to reward, cost and profit is investment. Equity doesn't mean equality, but a constant ratio of rewards to costs, or profit to investment. So ET involves a concern with fairness. It's changes in the ratio of what you put in and get out of a relationship which are likely to cause changes in how you feel about it. If you start giving much more than you did, and receive proportionately less, then you're likely to become dissatisfied with the relationship.

Stage theories are also relevant here. For example, according to Murstein's stimulus-value-role (SVR) theory (1976), what's important changes as the relationship develops. SET seems completely to ignore these developmental changes.

*(983 words)*

# SAMPLE ESSAYS

# SAMPLE ESSAYS

Discuss research into cultural differences in relationships. (24 marks) (30 mins) (600 words minimum)

A01

## Section 1:

Hofstede (1980) identified four dimensions of culture, two of which are power distance (the amount of respect shown by those in both superior and subordinate positions) and individualism–collectivism. The latter refers to whether one's identity is defined by personal choices and achievements (individualism) or by characteristics of the collective group one is more or less permanently attached to (collectivism).

Hofstede had access to morale surveys conducted by IBM in 40 countries world-wide, involving the responses of 117,000 employees to questions about various aspects of their work experience. He analysed the mean scores on each questionnaire item, which resulted in his classifying the 40 countries along the four dimensions. A group of mainly European and North American countries scored high on individualism, while another group of mostly South American and Asian countries scored high on collectivism.

Triandis (1990), influenced by Hofstede's work, defined culture in terms of cultural syndromes. One of these is individualism–collectivism. Triandis et al. (1986) identified four factors related to this syndrome. Collectivists behave differently towards in-group compared with out-group members, and the in-group is best defined in terms of the common fate of its members. They also emphasise social hierarchy much more than individualists, with the father as head of the household and women as subordinate to men. Collectivists usually belong to a small number of in-groups, which have a considerable influence on their behaviour. But individualists tend to belong to a large number of groups, which often make conflicting demands on the individual. Vertical relationships (such as parent–child) take priority over horizontal relationships (such as spouse–spouse) when there's a conflict between them. The reverse is true in individualist cultures.

A02

## Section 2:

Hofstede's sample for each country was large. From within this overall sample, Hofstede selected respondents who all worked in servicing and marketing, which maximised the comparability of the different countries (Smith & Bond, 1998). But the sample was predominantly male, which means that it wasn't representative of all IBM employees. Also, IBM is a large American corporation said to have a culture of its own. But the fact that Hofstede still found national culture differences is a strength of his research (Smith & Bond, 1998). Hofstede's study has provided us with one possible way of classifying the differences found among the 40 national cultures in his sample, and individualism–collectivism has become a widely accepted dimension within cross-cultural psychology as a whole. Others, such as Triandis, have built on Hofstede's research. Identifying these cultural dimensions helps to challenge Western psychologists' ethnocentrism in their study of relationships, that is, the belief that relationships in Western culture represent a standard against which to compare those in non-Western cultures. But it's important to remember that individualism–collectivism is a dimensional, not a categorical, classification. In other words, where a particular country is placed on the scale reflects the relative importance of certain aspects of relationships. Also,

A01

voluntary/involuntary and permanent/impermanent. As Moghaddam et al. (1993) say, interpersonal relationships in Western cultures tend to be individualistic, voluntary and temporary.

## Section 3:

Despite the claim of Moghaddam et al., Western psychologists have studied a wide range of relationships during the last 20 years, some of which may seem more voluntary than others. These include cross-sex non-romantic relationships, romantic or friendly relationships in the workplace, sibling relationships, and children relating to other children (Duck, 1999). Marriage is found in all known cultures (Fletcher, 2002) and is usually taken to be a voluntary relationship. But there are wide and important cultural variations in marital arrangements. From a Western perspective, the 'natural' form of marriage is monogamy (marriage to one spouse at a time). But marriage can take the form of polygamy, which may involve one man having two or more wives (polygyny) or one woman with two or more husbands (polyandry).

Arranged marriages are far more common in collectivist cultures, where the whole extended family 'marries' the other extended family. This is distinct from individualist cultures, where only individuals marry. Gupta & Singh (1982) found that couples in Jaipur, India who married for love reported reduced feelings of love if they'd been married for more than five years. By contrast, those who'd undertaken arranged marriages reported increased love if they weren't newly-weds. These findings show that passionate love 'cools' over time, and that there's scope for love to develop within an arranged marriage. In cultures where arranged marriages occur, courtship is accepted to a certain degree. But love is left to be defined and discovered after marriage (Bellur, 1995). This is, of course, the reverse of the 'Hollywood' picture.

A02

## Section 4:

Even in traditional cultures that practise arranged marriages, brides and grooms are typically given some choice (Fletcher, 2002). For example, in Sri Lanka men and women who like one another (or fall in love) usually let their parents know their choices in advance through indirect channels (de Munck, 1998). Families often use similar criteria that the individuals themselves might use if they had a free choice (including matching on attractiveness). The classic example is the Jewish custom of having a matchmaker arrange a suitable match (Rockman, 1994).

In general, divorce rates among those who marry according to parents' wishes are much lower than among those who marry for love (an argument in favour of arranged marriages). But divorce rates among 'arranged couples' are rising, indicating that personal freedom is gaining importance and that traditional structures which define set roles for family members are becoming less valid (Bellur, 1995). But conversely, we can ask whether Western (non-arranged) marriage is really as voluntary as it's usually taken to be. According to Duck (1999), once the marriage is a few years old, it's much less voluntary than it was, since getting out of it is accompanied by a great deal of 'social and legal baggage'. Also, according to Kerckhoff & Davis's (1962) filter model, our choice of potential (realistic) marriage partners is limited by demographic variables (religion, class and so on). To this extent, most relationships are 'arranged'.

# A2 Module 4:
## Social, Physiological, Cognitive, Developmental and Comparative Psychology

# Pro- and anti-social behaviour

## What's covered in this chapter?

### You need to know about:

Nature and causes of aggression
- Social psychological theories of aggression (e.g. Social Learning Theory; deindividuation)
- Research into the effects of environmental stressors on aggressive behaviour (e.g. temperature/heat, noise)

Altruism and bystander behaviour
- Explanations (e.g. empathy–altruism; Latané & Darley's decision model) and research relating to human altruism/bystander behaviour
- Cultural differences in pro-social behaviour

Media influences on pro- and anti-social behaviour
- Explanations and research relating to media influences on anti-social behaviour
- Explanations and research relating to media influences on pro-social behaviour

## Social psychological theories of aggression (e.g. Social Learning Theory, deindividuation)

### Definitions of aggression:

Aggression can be defined as behaviour directed toward the goal of injuring or harming another living being. This applies primarily to human behaviour and can include psychological as well as physical injury (Lippa, 1994).

There are several types of aggression identified by psychologists:

- **hostile aggression:** this is generally caused by being provoked or upset and the primary purpose is to harm someone
- **instrumental aggression:** the primary goal here is to gain some kind of reward such as money. Aggression is used as a means to an end. It's not usually provoked by anger or emotion
- **pro-social aggression:** this is aggression that's performed to prevent greater harm, e.g. a police officer who shoots a terrorist

● **sanctioned aggression:** this is aggressive behaviour that's generally excused or permitted, e.g. when a person defends him/herself during a robbery.

## Social Learning Theory (SLT) of aggression

'Of the many cues that influence behaviour, at any point in time, none is more common than the actions of others.' (Bandura, 1986)

Norfolk farmer Tony Martin who shot a burglar in his home: an example of hostile and/or sanctioned aggression?

**Specification Hint:** You need to know only *two* social psychological theories of aggression. There's no need to learn more. The two we've chosen are: Social Learning Theory and Deindividuation.

**Specification Hint:** You need to know the Social Learning Theory extremely well. It can be used in other essays on pro- and anti-social behaviour and also can be one of the approaches you need to learn for Module 5: Perspectives.

### DEFINITION OF SLT

Learning behaviour that is controlled by environmental influences rather than by innate or internal forces. SLT is often called 'modelling' or 'observational learning'.

The social learning theory emphasises the importance of observing and modelling the behaviours, attitudes and emotional reactions of others.

Social Learning Theory suggests that aggression, like other forms of behaviour, is primarily learned (Bandura, 1973). Humans are not born as aggressive individuals but acquire these behaviours in the same way as other forms of social behaviour: through direct experience or by observing the actions of others.

SLT developed from Learning Theory (the Behaviourists). According to behaviourists:

Albert Bandura: the psychologist most closely associated with Social Learning Theory (SLT)

● behaviour that is reinforced (rewarded) will be repeated and learned (See Approaches: page 541)
● aggression that is associated with a reward (e.g. praise, increased self-esteem) is likely to be learned
● however, learning doesn't only occur directly; it can also occur indirectly through observing other people. This is called learning by *vicarious experience or observational learning*
● Bandura (1977b) sums this up: 'Learning would be exceedingly laborious, not to mention hazardous, if people had to rely solely on the effects of their own actions to inform them what to do.

Fortunately, most human behaviour is learned observationally through modelling: from observing others one forms an idea of how new behaviours are performed, and on later occasions this coded information serves as a guide for action.'

So observational learning occurs when individuals observe and imitate others' behaviour. There are four component processes in the theory (Attention, Retention, Production, Motivation/Reinforcement (ARPM)):

Although amateur footballers spend many years observing Premiership footballers, they're still not as good as David Beckham – perhaps they should accept they don't possess the physical capability!

1. Attention: Someone can only learn through observation if they attend to the model's behaviour. For example, children must attend to what the aggressor is doing and saying in order to reproduce the model's behaviour accurately (Allen & Santrock, 1993). (See Essential Studies 9.1 and 9.2).

2. Retention: In order to reproduce the modelled behaviour, an individual must code and remember the behaviour by placing it into long-term memory (LTM). This enables the behaviour to be retrieved. In the Bobo doll experiment (see Essential Study 9.1, page 186), the children were only able to act aggressively since this information had been stored in LTM.

3. Production: An individual must be capable of reproducing the model's behaviour. The observer must possess the physical capabilities of the modelled behaviour. In the Bobo doll study, the children possessed the physical capabilities of hitting and punching the doll.

4. Motivation or Reinforcements: An individual expects to receive positive reinforcements (rewards) for the modelled behaviour. This will help to motivate their behaviour. In the Bobo doll experiment, the children witnessed the adults gaining a reward for their aggression. Therefore the children performed the same act to achieve the same reward.

There are a number of factors that influence imitative behaviour. Individuals are more likely to copy modelled behaviour if:

- it results in outcomes (rewards) that they value
- the model is similar to the observer and is a powerful and admired role model
- the model is seen as similar to the learner, e.g. the same sex, age, and has similar interests
- the task to be imitated is neither too easy nor too difficult
- they have low self-esteem or lack confidence in their own abilities.

Bandura believed aggression reinforced by family members was the most prominent source of behaviour modelling. For example, the boy who watches his father attack his mother is more likely to become an abusive parent and husband (Siegel, 1992).

**Transmission of Aggression Through Imitation** (TATI) **study** (Bandura, Ross & Ross, 1961)

- 36 boys and 36 girls (aged between 3 and 5 years) were divided into eight experimental groups of six children. The remaining children acted as a control group.

- The children were brought individually to the experimental room where they were invited by an experimenter to play a game. In the room, there were a number of toys such as potato prints, picture stickers, a tinker toy set, a mallet and a 5-foot inflatable Bobo doll. This bounces back upright when hit. The children were guided to start playing with the picture sticker sets. An adult 'model' then entered the room and started assembling the tinker toys.

- In the non-aggressive condition, the model continued to assemble the tinker toys in a quiet manner and ignored the Bobo doll.

- In the aggressive condition, after a minute, the model started acting aggressively toward the Bobo doll. The model performed novel aggressive behaviours that might not be expected of children unless they were influenced by the model's behaviour. These included pummelling it on the head with a mallet, hurling it down, sitting on it and punching it on the nose repeatedly, kicking it across the room and flinging it in the air. It also included verbal aggression such as shouting: 'Sock him in the nose . . . '; 'Pow'; 'He keeps coming back for more . . . ' and 'He sure is a tough fella'.

- It was proposed that identical actions performed by the children would provide good evidence for observational learning. Merely hitting the Bobo doll might not be so convincing since that is what a Bobo doll is designed for.

- Prior to the subsequent test for imitation, all the children were subjected to 'mild aggression arousal'. This involved taking them to a room that contained a number of attractive toys which they were told they could play with. After two minutes of playing, they were told that they couldn't play with them after all!

- They were then taken to a further room where there were a number of aggressive (e.g. mallet, darts) and non-aggressive (e.g. crayons, dolls) toys for the children to play with. Of course, there was also a Bobo doll. The children spent 20 minutes in this room, observed through a one-way mirror.

- An experimenter rated the different levels of aggression (and non-aggression) shown by the children. This experimenter had no knowledge as to which group the children had been pre-assigned to.

- Children in the aggressive condition showed a good deal of physical and verbal aggression. Their scores were significantly higher than the children in the non-aggressive and control groups. Indeed, 70% of children in the non-aggressive or control groups had zero ratings of aggression.

- Bandura *et al.* also ensured that both male and female models were used. Their findings indicated that both boys and girls were more influenced by the male model. The tentative explanation for this was that physical aggression is typically seen as a more male sex-appropriate behaviour.

- The conclusion from the study was that observation of the behaviour of others does lead to imitative learning.

**Imitation of film-mediated aggressive models** (IF-MAM) (Bandura, Ross & Ross 1963)

- A similar method to the one above was used in this study. This time the children watched a short film in which the 'model' behaved aggressively (physically and verbally) towards the Bobo doll.

- There were three experimental conditions:

  1. 'Model-reward' condition: here the model was rewarded for abusing the doll. The model was given sweets and drinks and called a 'strong champion'.

  2. 'Model-punished': here the model was punished for abusing the doll. The model was told off for 'picking on the clown'.

  3. 'No consequences' (control) condition: here no reinforcement or punishment was given.

- After the video the children were again placed in a room with attractive toys, but they could not touch them, making them angry and frustrated.

- After this the children went to a playroom containing a Bobo doll and a number of other toys. Each child was observed for 10 minutes in the playroom.

- Children who were in the model-punished group produced significantly fewer imitative aggressive behaviours than children in either of the other two groups. There was no significant difference between the 'model-reward' and 'no consequences' groups.

- An experimenter then offered all the children a reward if they could imitate the behaviours they had earlier seen the model performing.

- Children in all three groups then performed the aggressive behaviours to the same extent. All of the children had learnt the model's aggressive behaviours.

- Bandura concluded that reinforcement (reward or punishment) is not necessary for the *learning* of new behaviours through observation – but that the expectancy of reinforcement (reward) or punishment is essential for the *performance* of these new behaviours.

- Other studies conducted by Bandura *et al.* demonstrated that children are more likely to model behaviour if they identify with and admire the model.

## Research studies on theories of aggression

### CONCLUSION

Such studies provide clear evidence for SLT and the modelling influence of both real-life and filmed aggression.

 Evaluation of research studies

✓ **Well-controlled experiments:** The experiments were well planned and executed. The inclusion of other toys in the room and the copying of specific aggressive responses clearly showed that the children had, indeed, learned behaviour from the model.

✗ **Sample characteristics:** The nursery children used were from the Stanford University Nursery. This is unlikely to be a very representative sample. In addition, these experiments involved only children as participants. Would adult learners behave in the same way? Stack (1987) reports that the highest number of suicides in New York City were recorded a few days after Marilyn Monroe's death. This suggests that adults may also learn from modelling.

✗ **Lacks ecological validity:** The artificial laboratory situation ensures that it is difficult to generalise the findings to a more realistic setting. For example, the films were only four minutes long and included no justification for the violence portrayed.

✗ **Not real aggression:** Aggression was limited to a Bobo doll. Would the children have imitated aggressive acts to a real person? Johnston *et al.* (1977) found that play aggression correlated with ratings of aggression by peers (0.76) and teachers (0.57). This suggests that play aggression *is* a worthwhile measure of real aggression.

✗ **Only adult models:** Bandura *et al.* used only adult models with children. Would the same results have been found with children as models?

✗•✓ **Demand characteristics:** Some of the children said that they felt they were expected to perform aggressively towards the doll. However, the very specific nature of the imitative aggression suggests that modelling had occurred.

✗•✓ **Short-term effects:** It's been claimed that these studies merely demonstrated short-term effects of modelling. However, Hicks (1965) found that 40% of a model's acts could be reproduced up to eight months after one showing of a 10-minute film.

✗ **Manipulation of participants:** In the Bobo doll experiment, the children were manipulated into responding to the aggressive behaviours in the film. For example, the children became frustrated because they could not play with the toys when taken into the room immediately after the film.

✗ **Unethical and morally questionable:** The experiment conducted was unethical and morally wrong because the children were encouraged to be aggressive.

✗ **Questionable operationalisation of the dependent variable:** Is the number of times a child punches a Bobo doll a valid measure of aggression? Since a Bobo doll is designed to be punched, then the number of punches is not really an adequate measure of aggression.

## EVALUATION OF SLT

✓ **Useful applications:** Social Learning Theory has numerous implications for classroom use. A discussion of the consequences of behaviour in terms of rewards and consequences can be effective in increasing appropriate behaviours and decreasing inappropriate behaviours. SLT can also be applied in other social and cultural settings.

✓ **Experimental support:** Studies such as those above (Bobo doll) provide support for SLT. Bandura *et al.* (1963) also demonstrated that viewing aggression by cartoon characters produces as much aggression as viewing live or filmed aggressive behaviour by adults. Additionally, they demonstrated that having children view pro-social behaviour can reduce displays of aggressive behaviour.

✓•✗ **Cognitive sense:** It seems obvious that environmental experiences must have an influence on the social learning of violence in children. Bandura and Ribes-Inesta (1976) reported that individuals who live in high-crime-rate areas are more likely to act violently than those who dwell in low-crime areas. However, there may be other factors that might explain this finding (e.g. unemployment, lack of educational opportunity, the fact that you are constantly getting burgled!). A straightforward observational learning explanation appears too simplistic.

✓ **Successful applications:** SLT has been applied to the development of psychological disorders (particularly phobias) (see page 439) and therapies associated with these disorders such as behaviour modification programmes (see page 442). SLT can also be used to explain the success

Do consumers identify with the personality used to advertise the brand?

of television commercials. Adverts suggest that buying a particular product will help us to be more like the people who are used to advertise the product.

**✗ Ignores biological factors:** Biological theorists argue that SLT completely ignores individuals' biological factors and the differences between individuals because of genetic, brain and learning factors (Jeffery, 1990). SLT ignores any evidence which might suggest a biological or genetic component to human aggression (Miles & Carey, 1997).

## CONCLUSION

Despite criticisms, SLT has maintained an important place in the study of aggression. In order to control aggression, Bandura believed that both the family and the mass media should provide positive role models for their children and the general public.

## Deindividuation

### DEFINITION OF DEINDIVIDUATION

The loss of a sense of individual identity and a loosening of normal inhibitions against engaging in behaviour that is inconsistent with internal standards.

### DEINDIVIDUATION THEORY OF AGGRESSION

- Deindividuation theory is a social psychological account of the individual in a group or crowd. It can be applied to aggression since the theory helps to explain how rational individuals can become aggressive hooligans in an unruly mob or crowd. Festinger suggested that there is a reduction of inner restraints or self-awareness when individuals are 'submerged in a group'. Individuals in groups fail to see the consequences of their actions and the social norms they would usually follow are forgotten.
- Although Festinger *et al.* (1952) were the first to coin the phrase 'deindividuation', Le Bon (1895) was the first to recognise how an individual's behaviour changes when in a crowd. Le Bon wrote that an individual in a crowd 'descends several rungs of the ladder of civilisation'. Le Bon proposed that there were a number of factors that lead an individual to become psychologically transformed in a crowd. The most important of these is anonymity. Le Bon proposed that the more anonymous the crowd, the greater the threat of extreme action. In short, a 'collective mindset' takes over and the crowd acts as one. The person becomes submerged into the crowd and loses self-control.
- Le Bon's idea of a collective mindset was criticised and it was proposed that anonymity leads to a release from internal restraints to produce emotional, impulsive and irrational behaviour. Zimbardo (1969) also argued that there was more to deindividuation than just anonymity in a group and suggested that reduced responsibility, increased arousal, sensory overload and altered consciousness because of drugs or alcohol play an important part.

*Exam Hint:*

If the question asks for *one* theory of aggression, then it's probably best to use the SLT and the research studies that support it. We've provided most information on this theory.

*Exam Hint:*

If the question asks for *two* social psychological theories of aggression, you do not *have* to write the same amount of material (i.e. 15 minutes worth) on each. You could decide to write slightly more on SLT (say, 20 minutes worth) and less on deindividuation (say, 10 minutes worth). In this way, you can learn slightly less material and yet still answer the question!

This ABCNEWS story uses deindividuation to explain the behaviour of crowds witnessing suicide attempts.

**Taunted to Jump?**
**Experts Examine the Impact of Groups in Emergency Situations**

*By Jenette Restivo*
*ABCNEWS*

Aug. 30 – When a 26-year-old woman stood at the edge of a Seattle bridge on Tuesday, contemplating the decision to end her life with a jump, she didn't do so in peace.

"Jump, bitch, jump!" is what she heard from the crowd of motorists at the scene. Other onlookers cursed the woman, who was distraught over a relationship. After all, she had delayed their daily commute.

"The officers that were first on the scene said there were cars that were stopping as they were going by on the freeway, and taunting her to jump," Sgt L.J. Eddy of the Seattle Police Department Crisis Intervention Team said today on ABCNEWS' *Good Morning America*. Eddy's team tried to stop the jumper, and ended up pulling her out of the water after she leaped from the bridge. (The woman is listed in serious condition at Harborview Medical Center in Seattle, with a spinal fracture and chest and abdominal injuries. She is expected to recover fully, according to Associated Press reports.)

Cruel, yes. Unusual? Experts say no.

### Losing Your Sense of Individuality

Such behavior occurs quite naturally to us in certain situations. Psychologists have a name for it: deindividuation.

Scott Plous, a professor at Wesleyan University in Connecticut, calls the mob reaction seen during the Seattle suicide attempt a classic case of deindividuation, or losing your sense of individuality. He says that being anonymous or being part of a large group will often lead to behavior that, under normal circumstances, is not socially acceptable.

Eddy concurs that this is not an unusual phenomenon.

"I have been out to incidents of jumpers on ledges in high-rises and things like that, and there is frequently someone in the crowd, I think because of that anonymity, who will yell to 'jump' or 'go ahead' or something like that," she said.

Large groups, explains Brad Bushman, a psychology professor at Iowa State University, not only dilute a sense of individuality, but also lessen accountability.

"In a large group, diffusion of responsibility occurs so the individual experiences less responsibility on their own," he said.

### Heightened Sensation

The other factor Bushman believes may have been responsible for the Seattle group's behavior is a heightened sense of arousal.

"Physiologically, the presence of other people, heat, any unpleasant event – i.e. the frustration of being delayed three hours during a rush-hour commute – can increase the likelihood of aggressive behavior," said Bushman.

The problem with this heightened sensation, he says, is it reduces our cognitive capacities – our ability to think rationally.

Dr Michael Vergare, psychology professor at the Thomas Jefferson University School of Medicine in Philadelphia, says the group's aggression may have been brought on by plain old selfishness.

"These people were feeling anger; she was getting in their way, so they distanced themselves from her dilemma," said Vergare. He called it a classic case of taking care of our needs.

Vergare says such *Lord of the Flies*-type behavior is really a defense mechanism.

"There is a certain distancing and dehumanizing of certain situations so we can master them. If we ignore the humanity, we become less humane, less civil," he said. "We depersonalize – that's how we protect ourselves."

Le Bon suggested that in large crowds people act as one!

Anonymous group behaviour ensures a reduced capability to engage in rational thinking

In the 1980s, new adaptations of deindividuation theory were proposed:

- Diener (1980) suggested that people often behave in well-scripted ways and do so without conscious awareness (this is certainly true of my teaching!). When an individual is evaluated by others or when their behaviour does not follow the script, then the individual becomes self-aware (this might occur when a student asks me a difficult question). Diener believed that crowds block the individual's capacity for self-awareness and thus the individual becomes deindividuated. However, a key factor in behaviour is social arousal. This is particularly noticeable at major sports events when fans become so involved in focusing on the game that they are no longer self-aware.

- Prentice-Dunn and Rogers (1982) suggested that there are two types of self-awareness:
  - *public self-awareness:* a concern about the impression presented to other people, knowing that you'll be evaluated by them on this basis. Public self-awareness can be reduced by: anonymity (in a crowd), diffusion of responsibility (see page 209 – a decrease in individual responsibility when in a group) and the fact that other members act as role models in a group to set the social norms or standards of behaviour which you're likely to copy. In essence, loss of public self-awareness leads to a loss of public standards of behaviour or a lowering of inhibitions.
  - *private self-awareness:* this is the concern we have for our own thoughts and feelings. This can be reduced by becoming so involved in an activity that we 'forget' ourselves. Dancing and singing (often accompanied by alcohol) at a club would be an example of this. In essence, loss of private awareness leads to a loss of internal standards and hence an over-reliance on environmental cues (others in the crowd) as to how to behave (i.e. people forget how to think for themselves).

The loss of both private and public awareness is caused by becoming immersed in a group or crowd.

Most psychologists agree that deindividuation results in disinhibited behaviour that does not follow the usual social norms (Postmes & Spears, 1998). The only difference is whether in a crowd we are controlled by someone else or whether we simply can't control our own anti-social tendencies.

A clever test of our anti-social tendencies was suggested by Dodd (1985) when he asked students to respond anonymously to the following question:

> If you could be totally invisible for 24 hours and were completely assured that you would not be detected or held responsible for your actions, what would you do?

An example of reduced private self-awareness

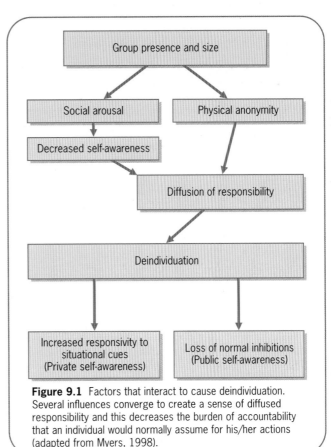

**Figure 9.1** Factors that interact to cause deindividuation. Several influences converge to create a sense of diffused responsibility and this decreases the burden of accountability that an individual would normally assume for his/her actions (adapted from Myers, 1998).

Students wrote their answers on blank sheets and they were collected and read out anonymously. The average number of anti-social responses was 36% – the same figure given by inmates at a maximum security prison where he once taught! You could try this activity in class or with friends.

## Research studies on deindividuation

ESSENTIAL STUDY 9.3

### Prison Experiment (PE) (Zimbardo *et al.,* 1973)

Deindividuation may be particularly marked in 'total institutions' (e.g. mental hospitals, prisons) where people are removed from their normal environment and stripped of their individuality. Zimbardo *et al.* investigated such a process in their simulation of a prison environment. Briefly, the details were:

- a mock (simulated) prison was deliberately created (in the basement of the Stanford University psychology department)

- 24 emotionally stable, male participants were recruited

- one group of students was assigned to the role of guards and the others were prisoners

- both the guards and prisoners were deindividuated and became anonymous members of their groups

- on arrival, the prisoners were stripped naked and issued with a loose-fitting smock. Their ID number was printed on the front and back, and they had a chain bolted around one ankle. They wore a nylon stocking to cover their hair, and were referred to by number only

- the guards wore military-style khaki uniforms and silver reflector sunglasses (making eye contact impossible). They carried clubs, whistles, handcuffs and keys to the cells. The guards had almost complete control over the prisoners, who were confined to their cells around the clock – except for meals, toilet privileges, head counts and work

- despite it being a simulation, the guards created a brutal atmosphere

- the prisoners soon began to react passively as the guards stepped up their aggression. They began to feel helpless and no longer in control of their lives. Every guard at some time or another behaved in an abusive, authoritarian way. Many seemed thoroughly to enjoy the new-found power and control that went with the uniform

- in sum, both sets of participants showed some of the classic signs of deindividuation: 'a lowered sense of personal identity, an altered state of subjective consciousness, and a host of disinhibited antisocial behaviours' (Lippa, 1994).

✓ **High ecological validity:** Both the environment and the behaviour (of guards and prisoners) were 'realistic', and the findings can be applied to real prisons. The results were especially surprising given that everyone knew it to be a 'simulation'.

✓ **Realistic measures of aggression:** Both verbal and physical aggression were measured. The guards placed 'prisoners' in physical discomfort (stood on them doing press-ups, pushed them in urinals) and verbally abused them.

✗ **Unethical?** Even Zimbardo accepted that certain aspects of the study were unethical (protection from harm, informed consent) and admitted that he became over-involved in the study.

✗ **Sample characteristics:** The sample was unrepresentative in that it included only young males.

**ESSENTIAL STUDY 9.4**

**Trick or Treater Study** (TOTS) (Diener *et al.*, 1976)

• This study tested the effects of disguise, anonymity and group membership on anti-social behaviour of young 'trick or treaters' in Seattle, USA.

• Twenty-seven women were asked to give out sweets to 1,000 'trick or treaters' during Halloween night. Half of the children who knocked at their doors were asked for their names and addresses (identifiable) whereas the others remained anonymous.

• Some of the children were on their own, while others were in groups (crowds).

• While chatting to the children, the women had to go and answer their phone and so left the children at the front door with the strict instruction to take one sweet each.

• A hidden observer recorded whether the children stole any additional sweets.

• The results are shown in Fig. 9.2 below. Children were more likely to steal in groups when they were anonymous (i.e. not identified).

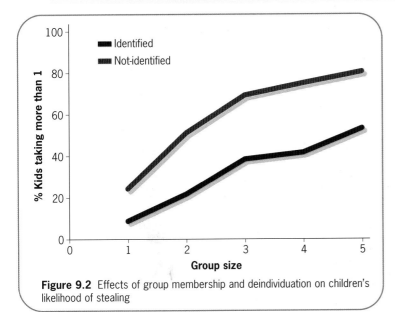

**Figure 9.2** Effects of group membership and deindividuation on children's likelihood of stealing

 **Evaluation**

✓ **High ecological validity:** The experiment took place in a real-life setting with a substantial number of children taking part.

✗ **Sample:** Despite the large sample, only children were used. Would the same findings be applicable to adults?

✗ **Operationalisation of aggression?** The study examined anti-social behaviour (stealing sweets) rather than aggression *per se*.

## ANONYMOUS LABORATORY COAT (ALC) STUDY (ZIMBARDO, 1970)

- Women were dressed in white laboratory coats and hoods in order to render them anonymous. A control group wore their ordinary clothes and had name tags prominently displayed.
- In an experimental situation similar to Milgram's study of destructive obedience, participants had to shock a victim (actually a confederate).
- The anonymous participants shocked longer (and therefore more painfully) than the identifiable participants.
- Anonymity would appear to contribute to aggressive behaviour.

Deindividuated participants in Anonymous Lab Coat Study (Zimbardo, 1970)

 Evaluation

❌ **Ku Klux Klan effect:** It was suggested that the wearing of white hoods and the subsequent association with the Klu Klux Klan may have affected the intensity of the shocks given rather than the anonymity of the participants.

❌ **Sample:** The sample were entirely women and may not be generalised to men.

❌ **Unethical?** Ethical criticisms of Milgram's study are relevant here as well (see Essential Study 5.3, page 107). These include lack of informed consent and protection from harm (i.e. stress).

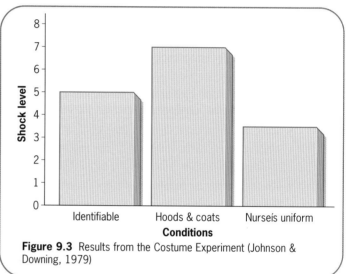

**Figure 9.3** Results from the Costume Experiment (Johnson & Downing, 1979)

## THE COSTUME EXPERIMENT (CE) (JOHNSON & DOWNING, 1979)

- This involved a variation of the ALC study above.
- Participants were made anonymous by the wearing of masks and overalls similar to the Ku Klux Klan or by means of nurses' uniforms.
- Compared with the identifiable control condition, participants shocked more when dressed in the Ku Klux Klan uniforms (i.e. hoods and coats), but they actually shocked less when dressed as nurses (see Fig. 9.3 for results).

 Evaluation

✓ **Criticism of ALC study:** The CE study demonstrated that it is not anonymity *per se* which leads to aggression but the norms associated with the social context that affects behaviour.

❌ **Artificial situation:** The study adopts a very artificial methodology and could be subject to demand characteristics.

**DARKENED ROOM AROUSAL STUDY (DRAS) (GERGEN, GERGEN & BARTON, 1973)**

- This study also showed the effects of anonymity on deindividuation.
- Both male and female students were asked to interact for an hour in an environmental chamber (a padded room). The only instruction was that there 'are no rules . . . as to what you should do together'. After the experiment, they were told that they would not interact with the other participants and would leave alone. In effect, the participants could do what they liked.
- There were two conditions: in one the lights were left on, in the other the participants were left in total darkness! This meant that participants in the dark room were anonymous, in a strange environment and deindividuated.
- Participants in the lit room found the study rather boring – no one hugged another person. In contrast, half of those in the dark room hugged another person, 89% intentionally touched others and they reported the experience to be sensuous and fun. Indeed, many volunteered to take part again.
- This study shows that deindividuation leads to the freeing of inhibitions, not necessarily aggression.

✖ **Evidence against deindividuation theory of aggression:** The DRAS demonstrated that anonymity does not always lead to aggression. Indeed, this might be an example of anonymity leading to pro-social acts. Since most participants were willing to volunteer again, they must have enjoyed the feelings of intimacy!

✖ **Low ecological validity:** Although a well-controlled study, the situation was rather artificial and involved only a small number of participants.

## CONCLUSION ON RESEARCH STUDIES

- Evidence for deindividuation theory is mixed. A meta-analysis of 60 research studies testing deindividuation theory concluded that there was insufficient support for the theory (Postmes and Spears, 1998).
- Neither disinhibition nor anti-normative behaviour is more common in large groups and crowded anonymous settings.

✖✔ **Evaluation of deindividuation theory**

✔ **Experimental support:** There is certainly some experimental support for the theory of deindividuation (see above).

✖ **Other theories:** There are other theories that can explain some aspects of human aggression (see below).

✖ **Recent analysis:** More recent social psychological research suggests that a norm-based analysis of collective behaviour is supported, i.e. people are more likely to follow local group norms if they are deindividuated.

✖ **Deindividuation does not always lead to aggression:** Sometimes there is increased conformity within a crowd and deindividuation causes increased pro-social behaviour (see DRAS, above). There is a strong feeling of belonging to the crowd (a social identity) and individuals follow the norms that may occur within the crowd (Reicher, 1987). This can explain how crowds often act on very high moral principles and do not always result in unrestrained and irrational ways. Examples would include crowd (helping) behaviour during disasters (e.g. Turkish earthquake) and Papal visits.

✖ **Analysis of football supporters' behaviour:** Ingham (1978) has shown that football supporters follow strictly ritualised rules of behaviour on the terraces and acts of violence are not the result of 'mob rule'.

## Exam Hint:

A sentence or so on competing theoretical explanations of aggression could be included as evaluation (AO2) but you *mustn't* describe them in detail. Indeed, many of them are not social–psychological explanations and therefore cannot gain any descriptive (AO1) marks.

## GENERAL EVALUATION

### Other theories

There are other theories that can explain human aggression. These include:

- **instinct theory:** the view that aggression stems from innate tendencies that are universal among members of a given species
- **biological theories:** the view that biological processes (sex hormones, neurotransmitters) influence aggression
- **drive theories:** the view that aggression stems from external conditions that arouse the motive to harm others. The frustration–aggression hypothesis is one of these.

## EXAM tips BOX

**Critically consider *one* social psychological theory of aggression. (24 marks) (30 mins) (600 words minimum) AO1/AO2**

*This essay can be split up into FOUR Sections – each about 150 words long. Each section would be worth approx. 6 marks.*

You could choose either the Social Learning Theory *or* Deindividuation. We've chosen SLT.

**Section 1:** A **description** of the Social Learning Theory (SLT) of aggression. You should include brief details of the overall approach and the four component processes (ARPM).     **AO1**

**Section 2:** You should include research studies that support the SLT. These could include:     **AO1**

- TATI – Bandura *et al.*, 1961 (page 186)
- IF-MAM – Bandura *et al.*, 1963 (page 187)

**Section 3:** You should **analyse and evaluate** the research studies that support SLT (see pages 187–188).     **AO2**

**Section 4:** You should **analyse and evaluate** the SLT approach overall (see pages 188–189).     **AO2**

*Try to answer this question yourself. There's a sample essay on page 230 with which you can compare your essay.*

## Research into the effects of environmental stressors on aggressive behaviour

- Aggression can be caused by numerous factors. These might include frustration, discomfort, personal traits, mood, hostile thoughts and feelings, misinterpretation of situations, aspects of the physical environment and situational conditions such as aggressive cues, arousal or drugs and alcohol. There are three main factors in the physical environment that are known to affect levels of aggression: crowding, temperature and noise.

Specification Hint: The Specification mentions 'the effects of environmental stressors on aggressive behaviour'. Since this is a plural, you need to know at least *two* stressors. We've decided to deal with temperature/heat and noise. The examiners could ask you about *one* or *two* stressors but not *three*. We have given more information on temperature (heat) effects so it's best to use that one if the question asks about ONE stressor only. A question will not name a specific stressor because the Specification is not specific.

### Temperature/Heat

- It's obvious that weather has an effect on behaviour. We may feel happier on sunny days and miserable when it rains. In Shakespeare's *King Lear*, the king's madness is accompanied by a violent storm. The most common weather–behaviour link is temperature to aggression. Someone who performs an aggressive act is described as having done so in 'the heat of the moment' and might be asked to 'cool down'.

- Psychologists believe that hot temperatures may increase aggression through a number of psychological and biological processes.
- Boyanowsky *et al.* (1981) researched the effects of heat on the brain and the correlation between temperature and aggression. He concluded that higher brain temperature plays a significant role in violent crime, in that temperature lowers the threshold for aggression. As temperatures go up, inhibitions diminish, causing some people to become aggressive. However, at very high temperatures, the levels of aggression diminish because, besides dealing with their mounting aggression, physiologically, people are also struggling in heat with a desire to reduce body heat.
- It's generally accepted that the relationship between aggression and temperature is an inverted U-shaped graph. Aggressive tendencies are lowest at some intermediate temperature (e.g. 65 degrees Fahrenheit) and increase as temperatures deviate from this. Such a clear relationship is not always demonstrated in field studies since people can adapt to the temperature (by wearing suitable clothing).

There are a number of models put forward to explain the temperature/aggression link:

## Negative affect escape model (NAEM) (Baron, 1979)

- Here tendencies towards aggression and escape are caused by being in a negative (bad) mood. As the bad mood increases, so does the level of aggression. However, at very high levels of negative

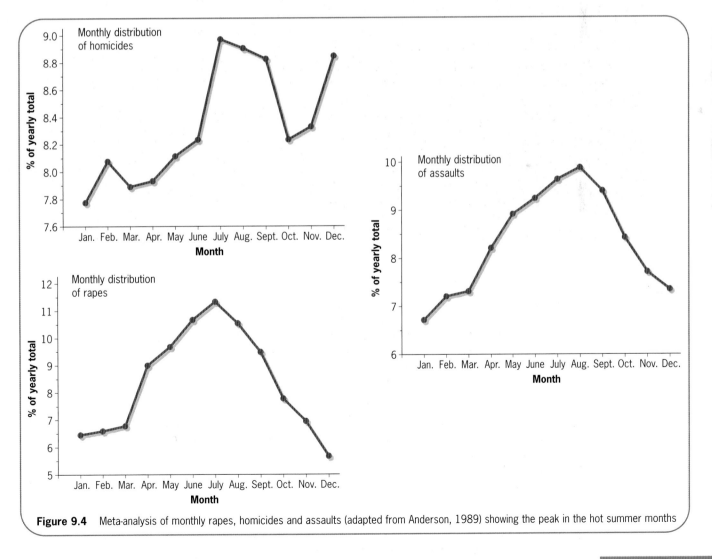

**Figure 9.4** Meta-analysis of monthly rapes, homicides and assaults (adapted from Anderson, 1989) showing the peak in the hot summer months

affect, the escape tendency becomes stronger – hence, the inverted-U relationship. It also applies to the temperature–aggression relationship. Uncomfortably cool or hot temperatures mean that escape would be a preferred option to aggression.

> **Simplified diagram of NAEM (Baron, 1979)**
>
> Discomfort (hot/cold) ——————————→ Negative mood ——→ Aggression
>
> Extreme discomfort (very hot/cold) —→ Negative mood ——→ Need to escape

✓ **This model makes cognitive sense:** faced with freezing or heat stroke, an individual would be bound to seek escape.

✗ **Aggressive behaviour or aggressive motivation?** The model does not incorporate the motivation to be aggressive. It may be that the desire to act aggressively may still be highest at extremely hot (or cold) temperatures.

## MISATTRIBUTION OF AROUSAL MODEL (MAM) (ZILLMANN, 1983)

> **Simplified diagram of MAM (Zillmann, 1983)**
>
> Discomfort
> ↓
> Increased arousal
> ↓
> misattributed to
> ↓
> Aggressive situational cue (e.g. annoying person or action)
> ↓
> Aggression

- This theory suggests that people's nervous system reactions are much the same for many different emotions. When such emotions are experienced, people link them to one obvious cause. Thus when arousal is produced by excessive temperatures, the person misattributes this anger (arousal) to some provoking cause rather than the temperature. This results in aggression.

✓ **Experimental support:** It's been shown that factors other than temperature do lead to increased arousal and that this arousal can be misattributed and lead to aggression.

## COGNITIVE NEOASSOCIATION MODEL (CONEM) (BERKOWITZ, 1983)

- Again, this theory suggests that uncomfortable temperatures cause arousal and this results in aggressive thoughts and acts, even when they are not rational or relevant. The key difference from the other model is that these temperatures cause aggressive thoughts or actions regardless of whether there are any aggressive cues in the situation. It's proposed that the dominant thoughts or cognitions surface – if they happen to be aggressive, then aggression will result.

> **Simplified diagram of CoNeM (Berkowitz, 1983)**
>
> Discomfort ——→ Increased arousal ——→ Dominant cognition ——→ Aggression

Note that all these theories predict an inverted-U-shaped relationship between temperature and aggression. A number of research studies have investigated this relationship.

## Temperature/aggression research studies

### CORRELATIONAL STUDIES

**Hot years and seasons** (HYS) (Anderson, 1987)

Anderson examined aggression related to the hotness of years. He reviewed violent and non-violent crimes in the USA between 1971 and 1980, related to the season and year. Temperature measures were taken from 240 weather stations. Violent crimes were particularly frequent in the summer and hotter years resulted in higher crime rates. These figures were particularly true of violent crimes (see Fig. 9.5).

ESSENTIAL STUDY 9.5

✓ **Other support:** Lombroso (1911) examined rapes and 'uprisings' and found they were most likely to occur in the summer months. In Europe this was July and in South America it was January. Carlsmith and Anderson (1979) reviewed 79 US cities between 1967 and 1971 and found that the hotter the temperature, the higher the likelihood of riot. These findings do appear to be consistent across eras and countries.

✗ **Correlational data:** These studies rely on correlational data. There is no definite cause and effect in a correlation. There may be other factors that explain the relationship (e.g. hotter areas of the country may be poorer or have different cultural values). Correlations between number of hot days and violence shrank to non-significance when variables indicative of the South's sub-culture of violence were statistically controlled (Rotton, 1993).

✗ **J-shaped effect?:** It's proved difficult to find evidence to show a downturn in aggression at particularly high temperatures. This may be because these particularly high temperatures are never reached or that even on hot days there is a cooler point (e.g. late at night) when much aggression takes place. If these explanations are not accepted then a J-shaped curve may be more appropriate than the inverted U-shape originally proposed.

**Figure 9.5** Quarterly and seasonal distribution of aggressive behaviour

Environmental factors may explain the relatively high incidence of violent crime in southern areas of Italy

✗ **Social Contact Hypothesis?** It's suggested that aggression increases in hotter periods because people go out more, are on holiday or congregate in larger groups during the summer. It's also been suggested that 'women's scantier clothing' may be more provocative. However, domestic violence also shows a summer increase and yet it should decrease, according to this idea, since the opportunity to get out more decreases the opportunity for it.

✗ **Uncertainty of temperature measures:** It's not always easy to ascertain the exact temperature at the time of many aggressive behaviours. Many murders committed during summer (hotter) months might have occurred on the cooler days. Alternatively, murders committed during cooler months might have been planned during hotter months. Aggressive behaviours may occur at different times to the aggressive motivation.

LAB STUDIES

## FLOOR PLAN STUDY (FPS) (BOYANOWSKY *ET AL.*, 1981)

Participants were asked to draw a series of floor plans for a building. A partner (confederate) gave negative feedback on their work. The participant was then allowed to evaluate their partner's feedback by giving them an electric shock on a scale of 1–10. There were three room conditions:

- cold (50 degrees F)
- moderate (68 degrees F)
- hot (86 degrees F).

As predicted, those in the cold and hot conditions delivered fewer shocks than those in the moderate condition.

### Evaluation

✓ **Experimental control:** Researchers have precise control over temperature levels in the laboratory situation.

✗ **Participant reactivity effects:** People do not always act naturally in the laboratory situation. It would soon become obvious in a very hot lab that the effects of temperature must be being studied. The aggression/temperature link is well known and thus the participants may react against the situation and show very low levels of aggression in hot temperatures.

✗ **Increased levels of arousal?** Participants may suffer from high levels of arousal and stress in the laboratory situation. Thus, under high temperatures, they might devote less attention to the insults of a confederate.

## FIELD STUDIES

A well known field study was conducted by Kenrick & McFarlane (1986).

**Horn honking drivers study** (HHDS) (Kenrick & McFarlane, 1986)

This study investigated horn honking in response to a confederate blocking a road junction. Three measures were recorded:

- the time it took for drivers to honk their horns
- the number of honks
- the total time spent honking.

The study took place in Phoenix, where the temperature ranged from 84 to 108 degrees F. There was a significant correlation between all three measures and temperature and this was particularly strong for drivers without air conditioning ($r = 0.76$) compared with cars with air conditioning ($r = 0.12$).

ESSENTIAL STUDY 9.6

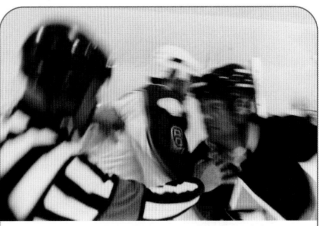

## ✗✓ Evaluation

**✗ Operationalisation of variable:** Although the study used three measures of horn honking, is horn honking actually a good measure of aggressive behaviour?

**✓ Other field study support:** Reifman *et al.* (1991) believed that being hit by a baseball pitch (throw) was a good measure of aggressive behaviour (after all, it hurts!) They also found a significant correlation: as temperature increased, there was a corresponding increase in the number of batters being hit.

Boyanowsky suggests developing cooling systems in ice hockey helmets to keep the players cool since he thinks that high temperatures lower the threshold for aggression

## ✗✓ Evaluation of temperature/aggression research

**✗ Different measures of aggression:** All the research uses different types of aggression as their measurement tool. Because there are so many forms of aggression (from 'hostile' to 'sanctioned'– see pages 183–184) it is difficult to compare much of the research on a like-for-like basis.

**✓ Consistent findings?** Generally, field and correlational studies consistently demonstrate increases in aggression at hot temperatures. Lab studies have yielded more mixed results, perhaps because of participant reactivity problems (noted above) (Anderson *et al.*, 1996).

## Noise

- Noise and sound are very different. Noise is unwanted sound and noise can put people in a very bad mood (ask your parents!). This is particularly true of loud and unpredictable noise. Indeed, extremely loud noise can lead to physiological damage.
- Aircraft noise is an obvious example of this. Chen *et al.* (1997) studied the effects of aircraft noise on residents living close to an airport in Taiwan. The residents living near the airport had greatly impaired hearing compared with a matched control group.
- Although there are physiological and psychological effects of noise, ranging from hearing impairment and sleep disturbance to mental health problems, we are concerned with research studies into the effects of noise on aggression.

I CAN'T LISTEN TO MY MUSIC BECAUSE OF ALL THE NOISE YOU'RE MAKING

Extremely loud aircraft noise has been shown to affect hearing. Growing opposition to expansion plans might lead to hostile behaviour.

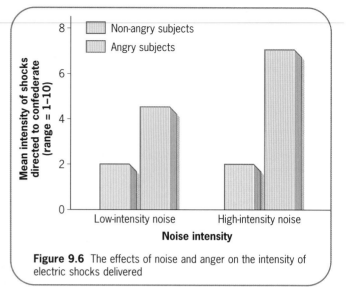

**Figure 9.6** The effects of noise and anger on the intensity of electric shocks delivered

## Noise research studies

### LAB STUDIES

**ESSENTIAL STUDY 9.7**

**Film and Noise Study** (FANS) (Geen & O'Neal, 1969)

- They examined how noise influenced aggression. They showed violent and non-violent film clips to participants.
- Participants were then told that they could evaluate the work of another person in a nearby room by giving him electric shocks (these were actually fake).
- One group gave shocks in a noisy environment, whereas the other group did so in a normal environment.
- The noisy background group who had watched the violent video gave more shocks than the other conditions.
- It would seem that only the violent film/loud noise combination caused aggression, not the noise level by itself.

**ESSENTIAL STUDY 9.8**

**Writing Essay Shock Study** (WESS) (Donnerstein & Wilson, 1976)

- Participants were asked to write an essay that was then evaluated either favourably (non-angered condition) or unfavourably (angered condition) by an assessor (actually a confederate).
- Participants could then evaluate the assessor's own essay by giving electric shocks (again fake) – this was the measure of aggression.
- However, participants were exposed to high- (95 decibels) or low-intensity (65 decibels) noise while they were delivering shocks. Those in the loud noise condition gave more intense shocks and thus were judged to be more aggressive. Those in the non-angered group were unaffected by the noise levels (see Fig. 9.6).
- Follow-up studies supported this finding. They also found that if participants believed they could control the level of noise, they were less angered by it. Control of the noise seems an important factor.

✓ **Similar findings:** Both these lab studies obtained similar findings and have demonstrated a relationship between noise and aggression.

✗ **Low ecological validity:** These are rather artificial lab studies and findings may be the result of the experimental situation. Demand characteristics may also have occurred.

✗ **Not noise in itself:** The presence of noise seems to cause aggression only when accompanied by frustration or anger. Noise in itself does not reliably lead to aggression.

## NATURAL EXPERIMENT

### AIRCRAFT NOISE ON CHILDREN (ANOC) (EVANS, HYGGE & BULLINGER, 1995; EVANS, BULLINGER & HYGGE, 1998)

- This study demonstrated the relationship between aircraft noise exposure and stress.
- Data were collected from over 200 children (9–11 years) both before and after the closure of the old Munich International Airport and before and after the opening of the new Munich airport. Control groups were used for comparison measures.
- A significant relationship between noise and stress levels was found.

 Evaluation

✓ **Well-controlled study:** This study took advantage of a naturally occurring independent variable (airport closure/opening) and was a well-designed study with control groups. It was the first longitudinal study of noise and its effects on humans.

✓ **Sample size:** The sample was fairly large but involved only a restricted age range of children.

✗ **Aggression not measured:** The study showed the effects of noise on stress (using accurate physiological measures) but not a direct link to aggression.

✗ **Not just noise:** Deficits in memory and reading ability were also found in the noisy groups. Perceived annoyance was also found to be an important factor. All of these factors could lead to increased aggression.

## NOISE AND HELPING BEHAVIOUR

Noise also seems to have an adverse reaction on helping behaviour:

- Matthews and Cannon (1975) found that participants were less willing to help someone who had 'accidentally' dropped materials when background noise levels were 85 dB than when they were 65 dB.

### Evaluation of noise/aggression research

✓•✗ **Noise does not cause aggression directly:** As the studies above have shown, noise can contribute to aggression, but only when the person is already frustrated or angered.

✓•✗ **Control of noise:** People who believe that they can control the levels of noise do not appear to become aggressive. This occurs even when they do actually experience loud noise and do not actually control it. Their belief that they can control the noise is important in reducing aggression.

## CONCLUSION

Noise may reduce helpfulness and predict aggression. Noise is not sufficient to produce aggression in itself, but in combination with provocation or pre-existing anger/hostility, it can contribute to aggression.

WHAT ARE YOU DOING?

JUST TRYING TO OVERCOME MY AGGRESSIVE TENDENCIES

Baron & Bell (1977) suggested that erotic pictures can decrease aggression.

## Other environmental influences

It's worth pointing out that there are other environmental influences that have been shown to influence aggression, including over-crowding, pollution, global warming, litter/rubbish (Baron & Byrne, 1997) and even sexual stimulation! Baron & Bell (1977) showed both men and women (separately) erotic pictures or scenery. Later, those participants shown the erotic pictures were least aggressive in giving shocks to another individual. This suggests that some erotic stimuli act to inhibit aggression. However, if the erotic material is coupled with violence then this usually causes an increase in subsequent violence.

## Altruism and bystander behaviour

### Definitions

- **Pro-social behaviour:** voluntary acts that are intended to benefit others and are positively viewed by society.
- **Helping behaviour:** a sub-category – behaviour that is intended to benefit others.
- **Altruism:** a sub-category – helping another for no reward, even at some cost to oneself. It's long been argued whether true altruism exists. So-called **egoistic helping** does result in internal rewards (feeling good, increased self-esteem, avoidance of guilt) even if there is no obvious external reward

## EXAM tips BOX

**Discuss research into the effects of *two* environmental stressors on behaviour. (24 marks) (30 mins) (600 words minimum) AO1/AO2**

*This essay can be split up into FOUR Sections – each about 150 words long. Each section would be worth approx. 6 marks.*

**Section 1:** A **description** of research into the effects of temperature on human behaviour (aggression). You could include the studies by:

- HYS – Anderson (1987)
- FPS – Boyanowsky *et al.* (1981)
- HHDS – Kenrick & McFarlane (1986).

**Section 2: Analysis and evaluation** of the research studies cited above. This might include other psychological support, problems with the methods and/or techniques used, alternative explanations for their findings or difficulties with the operationalisation of variables (e.g. aggression).

**Section 3:** A **description** of research into the effects of noise on human behaviour (aggression). You could include the studies by:

- FANS – Geen & O'Neal (1969)
- WESS – Donnerstein & Wilson (1976)
- ANOC – Evans *et al.* (1995, 1998).

**Section 4: Analysis and evaluation** of the research studies cited in Section 3. (See Section 2 for appropriate suggestions.)

*Try to answer this question yourself. There's a sample answer on page 231 you can compare your answer with.*

AO1

AO2

AO1

AO2

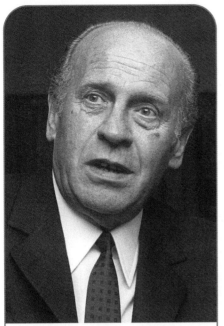

Oskar Schindler, who helped rescue Jews in Nazi Germany: an example of altruism or helping behaviour?

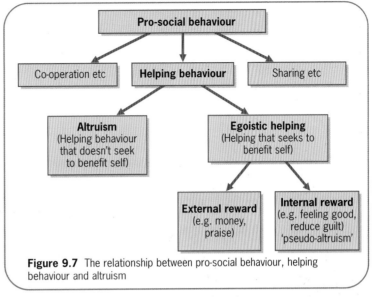

**Figure 9.7** The relationship between pro-social behaviour, helping behaviour and altruism

(money or praise). Batson (1987) labelled altruism motivated by internal reward 'pseudo-altruism'.

- **Bystander behaviour:** the tendency for others either to help or not help during emergencies when in the presence of others.

> **Specification Hint:** You need to know only a minimum of two explanations for human altruism/bystander behaviour. It's probably best to concentrate on The Empathy–Altruism Model (EAM), Batson 1987, and Latané and Darley's Cognitive Decision Model since these are mentioned in the Spec. However, we have also included brief details of the Negative State Relief Model (Cialidini *et al.*, 1987) and Piliavin's Cost–Benefit Model to give you more choice and help with evaluation.

## The Empathy–Altruism Model (EAM) (Batson, 1987)

### DESCRIPTION OF EA MODEL

Batson proposed that people do actually show true altruism to others. He suggested that when someone witnesses a distressing event, there are two kinds of upset that are experienced:

- **personal distress:** a general unpleasant feeling that the person would want to reduce as soon as possible
- **empathy:** feeling compassion and sympathy for the victim. In effect, they can see it from the victim's standpoint.

There's an important distinction to be made between the personal distress and empathy conditions. People who help to reduce personal distress could be viewed as helping for selfish or egocentric reasons, whereas

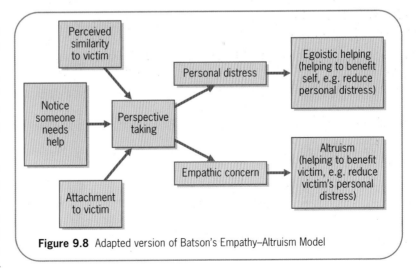

**Figure 9.8** Adapted version of Batson's Empathy–Altruism Model

those who help because of empathic concern do so for purely altruistic reasons. They want to relieve the other person's personal distress, not their own! Also important is the ease with which one can escape from the helping situation. If it's easy to escape, then this action will help to reduce feelings of personal distress but not true feelings of empathy.

According to Batson, actions based on the desire to help others result from numerous thought processes. Initially the helper takes the perspective of the person in need (this is called 'perspective taking'). Perspective taking can be stimulated by:

- perceived similarity between victim and helper
- an attachment (friendship or kinship) with the victim.

All of these factors lead to an emotional response of empathic concern. Empathic concern results in a desire to help others rather than oneself.

## RESEARCH STUDIES OF EA MODEL

ESSENTIAL STUDY 9.9

### Elaine Electric Shock (EELS) Study (Batson *et al.*, 1981)

- The aim here was to test the empathy–altruism hypothesis by trying to distinguish empathy from personal distress.
- Female participants watched a woman called Elaine (actually a confederate) on CC–TV as she received electric shocks during a learning experiment. Elaine pretended to show increasing personal distress and stated that as a child she had been hurt by an electric fence and hence was particularly distressed by the procedure.
- It was assumed at this point that all the watching participants would be feeling personal distress watching Elaine.
- The experimenters then suggested that the person watching could swap places with Elaine. By agreeing to swap places, participants were showing altruism, i.e. they helped Elaine at cost to themselves (they would now receive the shocks).
- Batson *et al.* then manipulated the degree of empathy participants felt for Elaine by saying that Elaine had either very similar (high empathy condition) or dissimilar (low empathy condition) attitudes and interests to them.
- They also manipulated the ease with which participants could escape from the experiment. Some participants were told they merely had to watch two learning trials (easy-escape condition) whereas others had to watch all 10 trials (difficult-escape condition). This made four experimental conditions.
- The results are shown in Figure 9.9. Results tend to follow a 1-versus-3 pattern, with the low-empathy/easy-escape condition resulting in low helping and fairly high helping in the other three conditions (Clarke, 1991).
- Participants in the 'difficult escape' conditions would be motivated to help by personal distress (since they *had* to keep watching). Participants in the 'easy escape' condition could reduce their personal distress by leaving and this is what happens in the 'low empathy' condition. However, in the 'easy escape/high empathy' condition, participants who felt real empathy for Elaine still helped despite the chance to reduce their personal distress by leaving. These people acted altruistically through empathic concern.

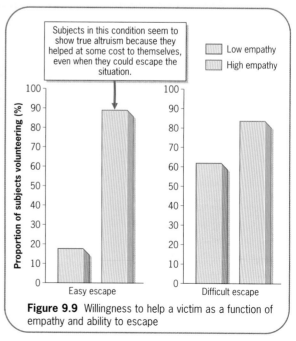

**Figure 9.9** Willingness to help a victim as a function of empathy and ability to escape

ESSENTIAL STUDY 9.10

**Follow-up to Elaine Electric Shock** (FEELS) **Study** (Batson *et al.*, 1988)

● ● ● ● ● ● ● ● ● ● ● ● ● ● ● ● ● ● ● ● ● ● ● ● ● ● ● ● ● ● ● ● ● ● ● ● ● ● ● ● ● ● ● ● ●

- This study used an identical procedure to that outlined above, except that participants were informed that they had to pass a 'maths test' before they could take Elaine's place. This gave participants the chance to fail deliberately and have a good reason to avoid getting the shocks.
- It was found that the participants who scored highest on the maths test also scored highest on subsequent empathy tests.
- It seems empathic individuals try hard to help even when they have a good excuse for not helping. They help because they have genuine concern for other people.

## Evaluation of EAM and research studies into EAM

✓ **Positive view of human behaviour:** The model proposes a positive and optimistic view of human behaviour that is not based on selfish motives.

✓ **Replicated findings:** Batson (1987) reports five different studies where the 1-versus-3 conditions findings are replicated. He also used male participants with the confederate being called Charlie.

✓•✗ **Well-controlled studies:** The research studies were lab experiments and were well controlled. However, the studies have been criticised for having low ecological validity and examining only short-term altruistic behaviour. Participants were also deceived about certain details of the studies.

✗ **Interpretation of findings?** It's unclear whether empathic participants in EELS (above) were thinking about how Elaine actually felt or about how they would feel if they were in Elaine's position. One of these positions is more altruistic than the other.

✗ **Ethical stance, not empathy?** It's possible that participants behaved in a way they felt was ethical, irrespective of whether or not they experienced empathy for the victim.

✗ **Competing concerns?** If the costs of helping are very high, it seems that egoism (concern for oneself) may be a more important factor than empathy. This finding suggests that our concern for others is a 'fragile flower, easily crushed by self-concern' (Batson (1987).

✗ **Other reasons for helping?** Even Batson has suggested that there may be reasons for helping other than the reduction of personal distress or empathic concern. These might include the relief of sadness, the desire to make oneself happy and the bolstering of self-concept. These appear to be more selfish reasons and lead on to the NSR model below. However, it's possible that people act without being aware of their sense of egoism or without feeling a sense of empathy. They just act and do what needs to be done!

## The Negative State Relief Model (NSR) (Cialdini *et al.*, 1987)

### DESCRIPTION OF NSR MODEL

In this model, Cialdini *et al.* stressed that people help others to avoid feeling sad (a negative state). People will help only to the extent that it makes them feel good about themselves. We help for selfish reasons only if:

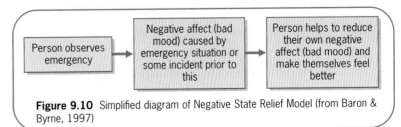

**Figure 9.10** Simplified diagram of Negative State Relief Model (from Baron & Byrne, 1997)

- there is no other way to relieve the negative state
- helping will allow us to relieve the negative state.

As they put it, 'because helping contains a rewarding component for most normally socialised adults ... it can be used instrumentally to restore mood' (Cialdini *et al.* (1987).

It doesn't matter whether the negative affect (mood) is caused by witnessing the distress of the victim or whether the helper was already in a bad mood. Either way, you help to improve your own mood.

Adults may internalise the reward of doing good deeds. Therefore adults in a bad mood may help in order to alleviate their negative state. However, if people can relieve their negative mood through some other source (such as hearing a good joke or getting some money) then they will not need to help. This is a rather pessimistic view of helping behaviour but (unfortunately) a number of experiments seem to support this view.

## CONCLUSION

The empathy–altruism hypothesis suggests that people help because someone needs help, the helper feels (empathy) for the victim and because it is satisfying to provide help. The Negative State Relief Model suggests that people help in order to reduce their own negative affect (mood) and make themselves feel better. The debate as to whether we help for altruistic or selfish reasons is ongoing.

Bierhoff (1996) concludes that 'the theoretical distinction between egoistically and altruistically motivated helping is hard to verify empirically'.

## Bystander behaviour

In 1992, in a suburb of Los Angeles, Reginald Denny was dragged from his truck and beaten nearly to death by a angry mob. This was shown live on TV. Lei Yuille watched on TV and immediately drove to the incident and along with three other bystanders in the crowd helped to save Denny's life. What led them to help?

'Bystander behaviour' refers to the behaviour of people who are present when an emergency occurs. People can choose either to help or intervene (bystander intervention) or to walk away (bystander apathy).

**Donor Card**
I would like to help someone to live after my death.

Let your relatives know your wishes, and keep this card with you at all times.

I request that after my death
*A. my *kidneys, *corneas, *heart, *lungs, *liver, *pancreas be used for transplantation, or
*B. any part of my body be used for the treatment of others
Signature *(DELETE AS APPROPRIATE)*
Date 2 2 04
Full name *ROBERT DAVID*
(BLOCK CAPITALS)
In the event of my death, if possible contact:
Name *L DAVID* Tel. 0113 857 9301

An example of altruism?

DAD, ARE YOU IN A GOOD MOOD?
YES, SON
GOOD, THEN WILL YOU DO MY PSYCHOLOGY HOMEWORK FOR ME?

Children are aware that asking for favours is best done when parents are in a good mood.

## Latané and Darley: Cognitive Decision Model (CDM) (1970)

An emergency situation is rarely encountered and it's often unclear exactly how we are meant to react. Latané and Darley proposed that bystanders go through a process of decision making; they called this the Decision Tree Model Of Helping (NERDI):

1. Notice the event

2. Recognise it as Emergency

3. Assume Responsibility

4. Decide to help

5. Intervene.

If the bystander does not answer 'Yes' at each of these stages, then they will not intervene.

There are certain factors that influence these stages. They are:

- **Preoccupation:** Darley and Batson (1973) showed that being preoccupied with other thoughts and actions can inhibit bystander intervention. The study of the Good Samaritan (see page 211) illustrates this clearly. This is most likely to affect Step 1 in the model.
- **Genuine ambiguity:** Sometimes it's not clear if the event is an emergency or whether or not people require or want help. For example, is the adult holding the hand of the crying child their parent or a stranger? This is most likely at Step 1 or 2.
- **Pluralistic ignorance:** In ambiguous situations, people look to others for help as to what to do (social reality). In an emergency situation, if all the other bystanders are also uncertain and looking for guidance, then looking to others can produce the wrong guidance, sometimes resulting in no action at all. This situation can occur in Step 2.
- **Diffusion of responsibility:** The presence of other people can influence the decision-making process. If there are lots of people present, then a diffusion of responsibility occurs whereby each person feels less responsible for dealing with the emergency. Rather surprisingly, the more bystanders there are present, the less likelihood that one of them will accept responsibility. In essence, someone else can help. This can occur in Step 3 of the model.

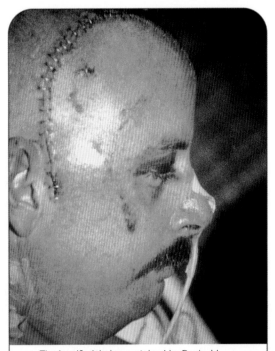

The horrific injuries sustained by Reginald Denny. His life was saved by bystander intervention.

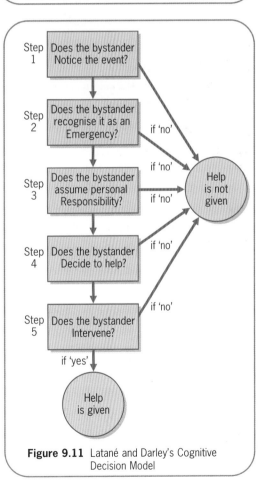

**Figure 9.11** Latané and Darley's Cognitive Decision Model

What makes some people more ready to help?

- Audience effects: The presence of others can also reduce bystander intervention because of the fear of embarrassment or ridicule. This is called *evaluation apprehension* – people are worried that they might make a fool of themselves. For these reasons, audience effects are greatest in front of strangers.

## RESEARCH STUDIES

ESSENTIAL STUDY 9.11

### Smoke-filled room (SFR) **study** (Latané and Darley, 1968)

- Students were asked to sit in a room and complete a questionnaire on the pressures of urban life.
- Smoke (actually steam) began pouring into the room through a small wall vent.
- Within four minutes, 50% had taken action and 75% had acted within six minutes, when the experiment ended.
- In groups of three participants, only one out of 24 reported the 'smoke' within four minutes and only 38% reported it within six minutes. When two confederates joined the naïve participant and answered 'dunno' to all questions, only 10% of participants reported the smoke within six minutes.
- This is a clear example of pluralistic ignorance: people didn't want to over-react and lose their cool. In the presence of others, we look to others for guidance. If they appear calm, then there must be no problem.

ESSENTIAL STUDY 9.12

### Epilepsy Study (ES) (Latané and Darley, 1970)

- Students were invited to discuss 'the personal problems faced by college students'.
- To avoid embarrassment, the students sat in separate cubicles and communicated via intercom. In turn, each student was allowed to talk for two minutes.
- During the first turn, one participant mentioned that he had seizures when stressed. On the second turn, it became obvious that this person was having a seizure.
- 85% of those persons who thought that they were alone with the seizure victim offered help. 62% of those who were in a three-person group (participant, victim and bystander) reported the seizure. Only 31% of those people in groups of six (participant, victim and four bystanders) went to help the victim (see Fig. 9.12).
- This is a clear example of diffusion of responsibility: the presence of others meant that each person felt less responsible for helping.

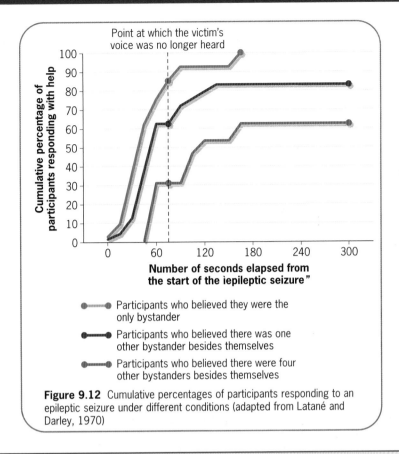

**Figure 9.12** Cumulative percentages of participants responding to an epileptic seizure under different conditions (adapted from Latané and Darley, 1970)

## Key study

### THE GOOD SAMARITAN (TGS) STUDY (DARLEY & BATSON, 1973)

- 40 religious studies students were asked to present a talk on either the parable of the Good Samaritan or their future job prospects.
- They were told that they were either ahead of schedule, on time or behind schedule.
- On their way to the talk, they met a man slumped in the doorway, groaning and coughing. He obviously needed help.
- Results showed that the topic of the talk did not affect whether or not they helped the man in distress. The important factor was the time pressures that they were under.
- 63% of those who were in no hurry helped, compared with just 10% of those behind schedule.

### Evaluation of CDM and research studies of CDM

✓ Experimental support: By 1980, there were over 50 published studies that supported these bystander effects (Latané, Nida & Wilson, 1981).

✓ Useful model applied in different setting: The CDM can be applied to many different situations, from kidney donation to stopping someone from drinking and driving.

✗ Not a full explanation: The CDM does not explain why 'no' decisions are made at each stage of the decision tree. This is particularly true after people have originally interpreted the event as an emergency. The CDM doesn't take account of emotional factors such as anxiety or fear.

✗ Results not always due to bystander apathy: Schroeder et al. (1995) suggest that the decision not to help may be based on the belief that others are better placed to help. There's no point diving in to save a drowning person and finding out you can't swim!

✗ **Presence of others does not always inhibit helping:** Bryan and Test (1967) found that male motorists were more likely to help a stranded female motorist change their flat tyre if they had seen another motorist acting the same way (58% compared with 35%). This might be explained through modelling behaviour.

✓ **Unambiguous situation:** The ES study was obviously an emergency and the presence of others could not be influencing the interpretation of the situation.

✗ **Not an emergency?** Participants in the SFR study argued that it wasn't actually an emergency situation. They claimed the smoke was 'air-conditioning vapour or smog'. In addition, nobody needed help.

✗ **Not real-life situations:** Piliavin criticised Latané and Darley for using dramatic emergencies rather than everyday helping situations.

## PILIAVIN'S COST–BENEFIT MODEL (CBM)

In contrast to the CDM, Piliavin *et al.* developed the CBM to explain the results of research studies described below. Piliavin *et al.* (1969, 1981) proposed a two-component model of emotional arousal and its reduction, as well as a cognitive appraisal of the situation in terms of costs and benefits of helping or not helping:

- **Arousal:** Emergencies are physiologically arousing and when attributed to the distress of a victim, a bystander seeks to reduce this arousal. The higher the arousal, the more likely the bystander will help. Arousal is higher if (RESCU):
  - the victim has a **Relationship** with the bystander. This is explained by the concept of 'we-ness': the closer we feel to the victim, the more likely we are to help
  - great **Empathy** is felt for the victim
  - the emergency is particularly **Severe**
  - the bystander is physically **Close** to the victim
  - the emergency is **Unambiguous**.

Arousal can be reduced by:
  - helping or seeking help
  - pluralistic ignorance: redefining the situation as one not requiring help
  - denial: leaving the scene and trying to forget it
  - diffusion of responsibility: someone else will help.

Arousal provides the motivation to help, while the cognitive component determines the most appropriate response.

- **Cognitive appraisal of cost–benefits:** This involves a weighing up of the pros and cons associated with helping or not helping (see Table 9.1).

The costs of helping include:
  - loss of time, degree of effort, danger or physical harm, embarrassment.

The costs of not helping include:
  - personal costs (guilt, self-blame) and empathy costs (knowing that the victim continued to suffer).

The rewards of helping include:
  - extrinsic (fame, money, gratitude, praise) and intrinsic reward (self-satisfaction, avoidance of guilt).

(The rewards of not helping are the opposite of the costs of helping.)

**Table 9.1** Cost–benefit analysis of helping/not helping and the likelihood of intervention.

| | | Costs of helping victim | |
| --- | --- | --- | --- |
| | | **Low** | **High** |
| **Costs of not helping victim** | **High** | Direct intervention: very likely to help | Indirect intervention (or redefine situation): fairly likely to help |
| | **Low** | Follow social norms: likely to help | Unlikely to help (denial) |

IN A SPLIT SECOND, COLIN CARRIED OUT A COST–BENEFIT ANALYSIS: THE BUSY ROAD, THE ICY RIVER, THE ESCAPED LION; OR FISH AND CHIPS FOR SUPPER WATCHING EASTENDERS

**New York Subway (NYS) Studies** (Piliavin & Piliavin, 1972; Piliavin *et al.*, 1969)

- This was a whole series of field studies carried out on the New York subway in which male students (aged 26–35) individually pretended to collapse on the trains and waited to be helped.
- Several variables were studied:
  - the presence or absence of fake bleeding (see Essential Study 9.14 below)
  - the presence or absence of a walking stick
  - the presence or absence of a bottle in a brown paper bag (i.e. whether the victim's problem appeared to be self-inflicted through alcoholism)
  - the race of the apparent victim
  - the presence or absence of a 'model' who offered help immediately or later on.
- Results showed that bystanders helped in all conditions. Indeed, often the effects of the 'model' were not tested since passengers helped so quickly. There was least helping in the 'drunk' condition, particularly where the victim was black.
- More men than women helped in proportion to the number in the train.
- Black and white passengers helped equally in proportion to the number in each train.
- In contrast to Latané & Darley's results, people helped more quickly in large groups (seven or more), than in small groups.

### Bleeding Victim (BV) Study (Piliavin & Piliavin, 1972)

- The researchers proposed that people are less likely to help a victim if they feel helping may place them in danger.
- They observed the helping behaviours of subway passengers in response to a series of 42 'staged crises' in which a confederate acting as a 'victim' with a cane feigned a collapse on a crowded train and either did not bleed (indicating a non-dangerous situation) or bled from the mouth (indicating a potentially dangerous situation).
- Passengers were less likely to help the 'bleeding' victim (65% helped compared with 95% in the no-blood condition) irrespective of how many other bystanders were present, supporting the hypothesis that the perceived danger of the situation (rather than the number of other witnesses present) determines helping behaviour. Bystanders had weighed up the costs of helping and with the blood present decided that these were too high to help.

What factors would make you more likely to help?

Using the CBM, the following interpretations of the results can be made:

- the drunk victim is helped less because the costs for not helping are low (little self-blame since it's the victim's fault)
- women help less because the costs of not helping are lower (it's not a woman's role to help)
- same-race helping occurs because the costs of not helping a victim of the same race are high.

### ✖✔ Evaluation of CBM and research studies into CBM

✔ **Experimental support:** Research shows that emergencies and crises do generate arousal and that arousal is an important causal factor in motivating helping (Dovidio *et al.*, 1991). In addition, cost–benefit analysis has helped to understand the processes involved in helping behaviour.

✔ **Non-emergency situations:** The CBM was developed to explain emergency situations. Since the 1980s, non-emergency situations have been studied and although the level of arousal is less, the CBM still appears to explain helping behaviours in these situations.

✖ **Ethics:** Was participant privacy violated? Should informed consent have been obtained for such studies? What were the potential costs of the study to science, society and those participating in the research? Were participants exposed to any potential harm? Some participants tried to pull the emergency cord to stop the train. Was there any opportunity to debrief participants?

✖ **Reductionist:** There is an implication that helping behaviour is reduced simply to an assessment of the costs and rewards.

✔ **Large sample:** A large sample was obtained (n = 4,450 men and women).

✖ **Restricted sample characteristics:** The sample involved only people travelling from Harlem to the Bronx in New York during a weekday.

✖ **Field studies but generalised findings?** Although the studies were field studies in the real world, there were special circumstances in the subway that bring into question whether the findings can be generalised. Aronson (1992) suggested that people on the subway were more likely to help because:

- they were in close proximity to the victim, with no immediate escape
- people on the subway have a feeling of sharing a 'common fate': 'I'll help you because I'm similar to you and you'd help me in this situation'.

✖ **Deterministic:** There's an assumption that helping is determined by factors beyond our control, such as our fundamental selfish tendencies.

## CONCLUSION

Helping behaviours vary enormously, from giving directions, giving small change to charities, donating blood, helping people across the road or stopping a fight, to rescuing people from fires. Some involve emergency situations; most do not. Some involve considerable costs; most do not. Sometimes the bystander knows the victim; most times, they don't. With such diversity, it's difficult to compare pro-social behaviours and the conclusions from such varied research studies.

---

## EXAM tips BOX

**Outline and evaluate *one or more* explanations of altruism and bystander behaviour in humans. (24 marks) (30 mins) (600 words minimum) AO1/AO2**

*We'll cover two explanations of altruism: the Empathy–Altruism Model (EAM) and the Negative State Relief Model (NSRM). This essay can be split up into four Sections – each about 150 words long, with each worth 6 marks.*

**Section 1: A description** of the EAM. You could include details of personal distress and empathy. It might be worth including the simple diagram of EAM but you *must* describe it fully.    **AO1**
↓

**Section 2: Analysis and evaluation** of the EAM. You could include research studies that *support* it (i.e. AO2). These include:    **AO2**

- Elaine Electric Shock (EELS) Study
- Follow-up to Elaine Electric Shock (FEELS) Study.

You could criticise any aspects of these studies and wider evaluative points concerned with the model.

**Section 3: A description** of the NSRM. It might be worth including the simple diagram of NSRM but you *must* describe it fully.    **AO1**
↓

**Section 4: Analysis and evaluation** of the NSRM. You could include research studies that *support* it (i.e. AO2). These include:    **AO2**

- Effect of Mood Enhancement (EME) Study
- Effect of Mood Fixing (EMF) Study.

You could criticise any aspects of these studies and wider evaluative points concerned with the model.

*Note: you could also have written about Latané & Darley's Cognitive Decision Model and/or Piliavin's Cost-Benefit Model if you wished.*

*Try to answer this question yourself. There's a sample answer on page 232 with which you can compare your essay.*

---

## Cultural differences in pro-social behaviour

Many psychologists assume that people are inherently selfish individualists. This may be because they have mainly explored helping behaviour in the West. Many cross-cultural studies suggest that such a universal view of human behaviour is not merited. The evidence suggests that pro-social behaviour is universal and altruism is quite commonplace.

The Ilk mountain people of Uganda have been described as the most selfish people ever studied (Turnbull, 1972). Because of scarce resources and extreme poverty, they are reported to be cruel, scheming and manipulative. It's even been reported that they steal from dying parents! In contrast, the Arapesh in New Guinea are reported as being extremely gentle and helpful (Mead, 1938–49). It would appear that there are marked cultural differences in pro-social behaviour.

Fiske (1991) outlines four different forms of social relationships. None of these involves selfishness and all appear to be universal across all cultures:

1. Communal sharing: People of all cultures share things such as food, their time, recreation areas and goods (e.g. NHS, public parks). They are generous to others without expecting anything in return.

2. Authority ranking: People provide work and goods for people of higher authority. They obey their superiors dutifully. In return, authority figures look out for their subordinates and help them out of a sense of pastoral responsibility.

3. Equality matching: People distribute things equally among peers and seek balanced exchanges with others (e.g. a baby-sitting co-op). These matched relationships are rewarding for their own sake.

4. Market pricing: People make exchanges of goods based on some ratio principle (usually involving money), i.e. 'What is it worth?'. This might involve money, other goods or labour exchanges.

Fiske (1991) argues that these types of relationship are universal in all cultures but that they are more or less prevalent in different cultures. From a purely selfish point of view, individuals would often be better off avoiding the first three social relationships; the fact that they don't is because these are rewarding for their own sake.

Different cultural values are attached to each of the four relationships. For example, market pricing is an essential part of our (Western) behaviour. We (generally) encourage and value entrepreneurial behaviour and respect people who have accumulated individual wealth, whereas in some cultures this sort of behaviour might be considered despicable and market-pricing behaviour merely occurs to benefit the communal group. This is particularly true in so-called collectivist cultures where the collective interests of the group are put ahead of individual self-interest (a contrast to individualistic societies).

The Mooshe (pronounced MOH-say) of Burkina Faso in West Africa demonstrate how the four social relationships operate in a collectivist society:

1. Communal sharing: Despite great poverty and scarce resources, the Mooshe allow free use of 'their' land to anyone. In addition, they share water from their ponds and wells that all inhabitants of the village dig and maintain.

2. Authority ranking: There's a loose network of hierarchical ranks in Mooshe society. The elders tend to direct work and do less physical work but, overall, the emphasis is on collective solidarity and sharing of both goods and work equally.

3. Equality matching (called 'tekre'): Goods that they don't produce are often swapped for other commodities. Money rarely changes hands.

4. Market pricing: When goods are purchased or craft products sold, money is used for communal benefit.

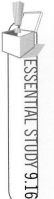

**ESSENTIAL STUDY 9.15**

### American and Hindu Helping (AHH) **Study** (Miller, Bersoff & Harwood, 1990)

- American and Hindu Indian participants read stories about people who refused to give help in different situations. The need for help varied from extreme (mouth-to-mouth resuscitation) to mild (directions to a shop). The relationship of the person also varied from relative to stranger.

- After reading the stories, participants were asked whether the person should have helped.

- Americans were much more influenced by the need for help and the relationship of the person needing help. They would give help to those in urgent need, especially if they were relatives. Hindu Indians felt obliged to give help in all situations.

- This difference was explained by America being an individualistic culture whereas India is more of a collectivist culture. Americans view helping as a form of economic exchange (see Fiske, above) and help on the basis of a cost–benefit analysis.

- People from collectivist cultures help because this is an essential part of the social roles and responsibilities implicit in their culture.

**ESSENTIAL STUDY 9.16**

### Helping Urban–Rural Differences (HURD) **Study** (Norenzayan & Levine, 1994)

- Helping behaviour tends to be more likely in rural rather than urban areas.

- Norenzayan and Levine (1994) worked out a 'helping index' based on three behaviours:

  - picking up papers dropped by a man on crutches

  - helping a blind man across the street

  - picking up a dropped pen.

- In each of the studies, persons seeking help were local nationals of the country. The exact methodology was replicated in 18 countries and the researchers found that 'cities in wealthy countries were less likely to offer help to strangers compared to cities in poor countries'.

- ✓ This is supported by Milgram's (1970) system-overload theory that people in (so-called) advanced economies screen out material that is not essential to their needs (Smith & Bond, 1998).

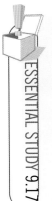

**ESSENTIAL STUDY 9.17**

### Local v Foreigner Helping (LvFH) **Studies**

- Foreigners who asked a favour in Greece receive more help than Greeks. The reverse was found in Paris and Boston (Feldman, 1967).

- In Iran, foreigners who asked directions to two real and two non-existent sites were still directed to the non-existent sites. This was because Iranians wish to show how helpful they are, even when this is not the case. After all, being given directions to a non-existent site is not actually helpful (Collett & O'Shea, 1976).

✓ **Experimental support:** There is an enormous amount of research that shows that pro-social behaviour occurs in all cultures (Whiting & Whiting, 1975). The influence of culture on helping is supported by the social learning theory view that pro-social behaviour is learned through socialisation (Moghaddam, 1998).

✗ **Biased samples:** Much of the research carried out on pro-social behaviour originates in the West and involves participants who live in America or Europe. Thus theories and explanations drawn from such research might not be universally applied – they may be culturally specific.

✗ **'Parachute' research:** There is a danger that so-called 'experts' from the West travel to non-Western societies to conduct cross-cultural research without a complete understanding of the culture that they're studying. They're said to 'parachute' in and collect their data and then leave. It's preferable to employ local people to carry out the research since they will be more aware of cultural sensitivities.

✗ **Observer bias:** There's a danger that the researchers see only what they wish to see in their research.

✗ **Contrasting methodology:** Many of the studies into pro-social behaviour in the West involve rather artificial laboratory experiments. These aren't so appropriate or feasible in many non-Western societies and thus results are difficult to compare.

✗ **Limitations of cultural norms:** Although cultural norms influence pro-social behaviour, they cannot lead to exact predictions of helping behaviour and they also lead to circular arguments. For example, why do you help someone? Because helping is a social norm. Why is it a social norm? Because people like you are seen helping others – it thus becomes the norm!

✗ **Individual differences:** There are marked differences within cultures with regard to pro-social behaviour. Different cultures may emphasise different norms but individuals are more or less affected by such norms. There's likely to be as much difference in pro-social behaviour *within* a culture as *between* cultures.

✗ **Dangers of stereotyping:** Whenever psychologists discuss cross-cultural differences there is a danger of stereotyping entire cultures. That is, Western cultures emphasise individual achievement whereas non-Western societies emphasise communal achievement. This simplistic picture does not help to explain real pro-social differences. Helping behaviour is also likely to be influenced by factors such as age, gender, skin colour and so on.

## CONCLUSION

Pro-social behaviour is universal and altruism is commonplace in all societies. As Fiske (1991) puts it: 'considering the entire human population, culture is probably the largest source of variance in altruism and other forms of helping'.

# Explanations relating to media influences on anti-social behaviour

There are a number of explanations put forward to explain the effect that media influences have on anti-social behaviour. They can be classified into two broad types:

- explanations of situational (or short-term) effects
- explanations of socialisation (or long-term) effects.

## Explanations of situational (or short-term) effects

- **Cognitive priming:** This explanation is that aggressive ideas shown in the media (particularly films) can 'spark off' other aggressive thoughts in shared memory pathways (Berkowitz, 1984). After viewing a violent film, the viewer is 'primed' to respond aggressively because the memory network involving aggression is activated. Huesmann (1982) also proposed that children may learn problem-solving scripts through observation and that aggressive scripts may be learned through observation of violent scenes. If the children find themselves in a similar situation in real life they may recall aspects of the violent script as a solution. In some ways, these echo the 'retrieval cue' theory of remembering (AS Module 1).

- **Arousal:** Bandura (1973) suggested that arousal increases the dominant behaviour in any situation. If the feeling of arousal is attributed to anger, then aggression is likely to result. Research has shown that the arousal produced by (violent) pornography facilitates aggressive behaviour (Zillman, 1983).
- **Sponsor effects:** Wood *et al.* (1991) suggest that demand characteristics are a type of 'sponsor effect'. This means that (aggressive) behaviour shown in the media is somehow portrayed as acceptable behaviour. Viewers are more likely to accept a message in the media if they think it's 'sponsored' or condoned by someone they respect and admire (see Bandura, 1973). Watching a very violent film may suggest to young people that this sort of violence is acceptable behaviour within society, especially if the film involves movie stars who are thought of as role models. Hearold (1986) showed that watching violent films was associated with both violent behaviour and general anti-social behaviour.

All of the explanations above suggest that participants 'assume a more permissive atmosphere when they are shown a violent film, and that their inhibitions about misbehaviour generally are reduced' (Felson, 1996). An important evaluation is that these explanations appear to have only short-term effects on aggressive behaviour.

- **Routine activity explanation:** This suggests that watching television is likely to *decrease* violence in society. This is because people are so busy watching television that they have less time to interact with others and actually be violent! Also, television is often a solitary occupation and therefore this decreases the time for family interaction and hence the levels of domestic violence. Messner (1986) did, indeed, find lower levels of violent and non-violent crime in cities with high levels of television viewing.

## Explanations of socialisation (or long-term) effects

- **Social Learning Theory** (Bandura, 1973; 1977b): This is easily the best-known explanation and has already been described in detail above (see pages 184–189). It's argued that television can shape behaviour through imitative learning. Watching role models perform violently may increase violent behaviour in those viewers already motivated to aggress. Television may also teach viewers the negative or positive consequences of their violence. Paik and Comstock (1994) found the effect on anti-social behaviour was greater if the actor was rewarded for their actions.
- **The cultivation effect** (Gerbner & Gross, 1976): This suggests that television creates (or cultivates) a distrust or unrealistic fear in viewers. This causes viewers to misperceive (or exaggerate) threats in real life and react in a more violent way. This is also referred to as the 'mean world' effect. The main problem with this explanation is that people who are particularly fearful are likely to avoid any threatening situations in the first place. Thus *increasing* the level of fear might actually help to *reduce* the level of violence.
- **Desensitisation:** This suggests that repeated exposure to violence in the media reduces the impact of the violence. People become 'desensitised' to the violence and it has less impact on them (habituation). They become less anxious about violence *per se* and may therefore engage in more violent behaviour. However, it could be argued that desensitised individuals might be *less* aroused by violence and therefore not be so easily provoked by real-life violence. Similarly, desensitised individuals may become indifferent to the violent message. Both of these latter possibilities would result in the desensitised individual being *less* violent, not *more*.

These explanations refer to longer-term effects on aggressive behaviour and thus may be more important processes than the situational explanations outlined above.

## Other factors affecting subsequent aggression

There are a number of other factors that have been shown to influence subsequent aggression in a viewing audience. These include:

- **Meaning and context of the communication:** It's been shown that the interpretation by the viewer of the film plays a part in subsequent feelings of aggression. Berkowitz and Alioto (1973) found that viewing American football produced an aggressive reaction in viewers only if they thought players were trying to hurt each other, rather than just professionals trying to win a game. Aggression is in the eye of the beholder and viewers impart different meanings to behaviour. The context of the behaviour can also affect meaning. Many cartoons are very violent (e.g. Tom and Jerry) but may not be interpreted as aggressive. The reality of the incident appears important in these interpretations.
- **Identification:** Several studies have shown the importance of viewers' identification with the observed aggressor. Viewers who show a high degree of identification with violent television characters tend to be more highly aggressive themselves (Berkowitz, 1985).

# Research relating to anti-social behaviour

## Laboratory studies

These occur in carefully controlled environments in the hope that a causal link can be found between watching violence and behaving aggressively.

### Imitation of film-mediated aggressive models (IF-MAM) (Bandura, Ross & Ross, 1963)

This is the best-known experimental study of observational learning and aggression. It's been covered in detail on page 187 (Essential Study 9.2) above.

ESSENTIAL STUDY 9.18

### Violent Programme Study (VPS) (Liebert & Baron, 1972)

Two groups of children were randomly assigned to either a:

- violent condition: watched a violent episode of a detective show; or a
- non-violent condition: watched an equally arousing sports event.

Afterwards, during periods of play, the violent group was assessed as behaving more aggressively than the non-violent group.

However, not all the violent-condition children acted aggressively, and aggression levels were measured quantitatively (amount), not qualitatively (type).

ESSENTIAL STUDY 9.19

**Karate Kid Study** (KKS) (Bushman, 1995)

Randomly-assigned students viewed 15 minutes of aggression from 'Karate Kid III' (experimental group) or an equally arousing non-violent clip from 'Gorillas in the Mist' (control group). After this, each participant completed a 25-trial reaction-time task against an (imaginary) opponent. If they 'won' the reaction-time trial, they could 'punish' their opponent by subjecting them to white noise. They could select the 'punishment' level (65–105 decibels) each time that they 'won' a trial. Trials were actually fixed so that they won on 50% of the trials. Participants who had watched the violent 'Karate Kid III' video clip delivered more punishment (longer duration and higher intensity) than those in the non-violent control group. It's worth noting that 'Karate Kid III' is rated as a PG by the British Board of Film Classification, suggesting that it's not particularly violent.

## Evaluation of laboratory experiments into anti-social behaviour

✗ **Ecological validity:** The lab situation is different to real life and violence within the lab is different to violence outside the confines of the lab.

✗ **Legitimised aggression:** In the lab the aggressive behaviour is legitimised by the experimental situation. Participants are told that the use of electric shocks and/or white noise is part of the experimental process.

✗ **No punishment as a consequence of actions:** Performing aggressive behaviours in the lab never results in punishment (unlike real life).

✗ **Intention to harm:** Many lab studies don't involve an intention to harm.

✓ **Applies to some aggressive individuals:** However, it may be the case that some aggressive people don't fear punishment or worry about possible consequences of their violence. Therefore lab results may be applicable to such individuals.

✗ **Demand characteristics and compliance:** The lab situation may provide clues as to how participants are expected to behave. Compliance is also likely since:
- behavioural standards expected in the situation are unclear
- the experimenter is likely to appear an influential authority figure
- participants wish to present themselves in a psychologically healthy light (Rosenberg, 1969).

## Field experiments

These involve the manipulation of the independent variable in a real-life setting.

### HOCKEY GAME STUDY (HGS) (JOSEPHSON, 1987)

Josephson showed groups of boys either a violent or a non-violent film. Later, both groups took part in a game of hockey. The boys in the violent-film condition were rated as most aggressive during the game. It was suggested that their behaviour was due to the effects of 'cognitive priming', since there were 'cues' in the violent film which mirrored aspects of the game.

## Evaluation of field experiments into anti-social behaviour

✓ **Few demand characteristics:** Since participants are often unaware of taking part in a field study, there can be no demand characteristics.

✗•✓ **Mixed findings:** Meta-analyses have failed to find clear-cut results. Wood *et al.* (1991) found in:
- 16 studies: participants acted more aggressively after watching a violent film
- 7 studies: participants in the control groups acted more aggressively
- 5 studies: no difference between control and experimental groups.

**Key study**

## NOTEL STUDY (NS) (JOY *ET AL.*, 1986)

Joy *et al.* (1986) examined the change in children's aggression after the introduction of television in a remote Canadian town (called 'Notel'). Results were compared with two other towns which already had television. Physical and verbal aggression levels increased in all three towns but were most marked in 'Notel'.

## Natural experiments

These involve a fortuitous and naturally occurring event. The independent variable is not manipulated by the experimenter.

### Evaluation

✗ **Sample:** The sample size was small (n = 45) and selective (only children aged 6–11 years).

✗ **Uncontrolled variables:** Prior to the introduction of television, the children of 'Notel' were just as aggressive as the other communities, suggesting that media effects don't explain aggressive behaviour. After all, you'd have expected the 'Notel' children to be less aggressive if television was such a powerful influence. This suggests there were other differences between the three communities.

## ST HELENA STUDY (SHS) (CHARLTON, 2000)

This study examined the effects of the introduction of television to the island of St Helena in the Atlantic. 859 children were examined and behavioural measures recorded. There was no increase in anti-social behaviour five years after the introduction of television, but pro-social behaviour had actually increased.

### Evaluation of natural experiments into anti-social behaviour

✓ **Design considerations:** Natural experiments take advantage of a naturally occurring event and as such involve no manipulation of the independent variable.

✗ **Methodological limitations:** There are many uncontrolled (confounding) variables in these natural experiments. It's therefore difficult to draw any firm conclusions about media influence on violent behaviour.

✗ **Cause and effect:** Any relationship between introduction of television and increased levels of violence may not be causal.

## Longitudinal studies

These generally use correlational analysis whereby measures of viewing behaviour are measured against levels of aggressive behaviour. In addition, participants are followed over a long period of time.

## HIGH SCHOOL STUDY (HSS) (MILAVSKY *ET AL.*, 1982)

3,200 students identified the television programmes they watched over a four-week period and then measures of aggression were obtained. This procedure was repeated over a number of years. There was little evidence of a correlation between exposure to television violence and aggressive behaviour. All the correlations were positive, but not to a statistically significant level. Support for these non-significant findings was also provided by Wiegman *et al.* (1992) in the Netherlands.

## CROSS-NATIONAL STUDY (C-NS) (HUESMANN & ERON, 1986)

This was based on earlier work where Eron *et al.* (1972) reported that amounts of television violence viewed at age eight was positively correlated to aggressive behaviour 10 years later. However, this relationship was found only for boys using peer aggressive rating scale measures. This peer rating measure included anti-social measures, not merely aggression.

Using a similar methodology, a three-year longitudinal study of primary school children in five countries reported to show some positive correlations between aggression and viewing of violence (Huesmann & Eron, 1986). However, Cumberbatch (1997) questions much of the research, suggesting that some of the correlations were not significant or actually negative! That is, the *more* television violence watched, the *less* aggressive the students were!

 Evaluation of longitudinal studies into anti-social behaviour

**✗** No consistent findings: Longitudinal studies have not shown a consistent pattern of results. There are as many negative findings as positive ones. The conclusion remains that these studies 'have not demonstrated a relationship between the amount of violence viewed on television and subsequent aggressive behaviour' (Felson, 1996). However, after Johnson *et al.* (2002) published substantive evidence (700 participants tracked over 17 years) of a correlation between viewing violence and subsequent aggressive behaviour, the American Psychiatric Association concluded that 'the debate is over . . . television violence has been shown to be a risk factor to the health and well-being of the developing child'.

**✗** No cause and effect: Even if the findings were consistent, we're still left with the major problem that correlational studies cannot prove cause and effect. There may be other variables that can explain any correlational relationship found.

## EFFECTS OF SPECIFIC MEDIA ON VIOLENCE

There is less research into these areas but there have been the following studies:

- **Music:** Barongan and Hall (1995) found that music with violent themes increased aggression.
- **Violent stories:** Some increase in aggression has been found after the reading of violent books or comics (Bushman, 2001). However, this contrasts with the low levels of aggression in Japanese society and the high levels of violence depicted in their comic books.
- **Violent news:** This appears to increase aggression, but the effect is smaller than for other programmes (Paik & Comstock, 1994).
- **Aggressive sports:** Viewing aggressive sports shows a small increase in aggression (Sachs & Chu, 2000).
- **Violent video games:** In a recent meta-analysis of 32 previous studies, Sherry (2001) concluded that the video game effect was 'less significant than the effect of television violence on aggression'. Anderson and Bushman (2001) in a similar review could explain 4% of violent behaviour measured as being due to the playing of violent video games. Effects were most noticeable in the 6–12 age range.

## EXAM tips BOX

**Critically consider explanations relating to media influences on anti-social behaviour. (24 marks) (30 mins) (600 words minimum) AO1/AO2**

*This essay can be split up into two Sections (each about 300 words per section).*

**Section 1:** A **description** of some of the explanations of media influences on anti-social behaviour. These could include:

AO1

- situational effects (cognitive priming, arousal)
- socialisation effects (Social Learning Theory, the cultivation effect, desensitisation).

**Section 2: Analysis and evaluation** of these explanations. Most criticisms will probably be associated with the Social Learning Theory explanation.

AO2

- Remember, criticisms can be both positive and negative.
- You could include research studies that support or reject the explanations you've put forward. These studies should not be *described* in detail but included as evaluative evidence of the explanations.

Note: A similar question could be asked about:

- research relating to anti-social behaviour.

*Try to answer this question yourself. There's a sample essay on page 233 with which you can compare your essay.*

### CONCLUSION

Given the evidence, it would be surprising if media effects had absolutely no influence on viewers. It's likely that there's a small effect, but it's very weak and affects only a small number of pre-disposed individuals. Nevertheless, given the large population influenced by the media, this small effect may have important consequences (Felson, 1996). Paik and Comstock (1994) suggest that violent media accounts for about 10% of the variance in societal violence, which is about the same effect of cigarettes on lung cancer rates (Wynder & Graham, 1950).

## Media influences on pro-social behaviour

> 'If violence in television causes people to be more aggressive, then shouldn't the good-hearted qualities in television cause its audience to be kinder to others?' (Cooke, 1993)

Many of the psychological processes outlined above with respect to anti-social behaviour can equally apply to pro-social behaviour. We've already seen how observation of helping behaviour encourages helping behaviour in the bystander (Bryan & Test, 1967), page 212 above).

### Explanations relating to media influences on pro-social behaviour

The following explanations have previously been addressed to anti-social behaviour but can also be applied to pro-social behaviour:

- **Cognitive priming:** Pro-social behaviours shown in the media may 'spark off' other pro-social thoughts in memory pathways. After watching pro-social acts, the viewer might be more likely to behave in helpful ways.
- **Arousal:** Watching people help others or share resources might result in heightened arousal towards pro-social behaviour. An example of this might occur when watching *Comic Relief*.
- **Sponsor effects:** Seeing others perform pro-social behaviour might suggest that this sort of behaviour is desirable behaviour. An example might include watching celebrities run the London marathon for charity.
- **Social Learning Theory:** You need to refer to pages 183–189 for a more detailed account of SLT. It seems reasonable to assume that if anti-social behaviours are learned through observational

learning, pro-social behaviours are also learnt in this way. A number of pro-social teaching packages have been developed, based on the principles of SLT (Goldstein *et al.*, 1998). Some of these are still in use today. Researchers are currently researching 'pro-social' modelling and examining whether positive modelling can result in co-operation, empathy, sharing and so forth.

## Research relating to pro-social behaviour

**ESSENTIAL STUDY 9.21**

**Good News Studies** (GNS) (Holloway *et al.*, 1977)

● ● ● ● ● ● ● ● ● ● ● ● ● ● ● ● ● ● ● ● ● ● ● ● ● ● ● ● ● ● ● ● ● ● ● ● ● ● ● ● ● ● ● ● ● ● ● ● ● ● ● ● ● ● ● ● ●

Holloway *et al.* (1977) produced support for the cognitive priming effect of the impact of good news. They invited participants into the lab for an experiment and while they were sitting in the waiting room played them a news programme over the radio. They were then asked to participate in a study involving bargaining with a fellow participant (actually a confederate). Those who had heard the pro-social news story were more likely to be co-operative in their bargaining, particularly if the news story involved an account of someone who had intentionally given help.

**ESSENTIAL STUDY 9.22**

**Good News Study Follow-up** (Blackman & Hornstein, 1977)

● ● ● ● ● ● ● ● ● ● ● ● ● ● ● ● ● ● ● ● ● ● ● ● ● ● ● ● ● ● ● ● ● ● ● ● ● ● ● ● ● ● ● ● ● ● ● ● ● ● ● ● ● ● ● ● ●

Blackman and Hornstein (1977) replicated the Holloway *et al.* study but also asked participants to rate their beliefs about human nature at the end of the study. Participants who had listened to the pro-social news report anticipated other people would be more co-operative and generally reported a higher proportion of decent and honest people in the world.

Although these findings only report short-term effects in male participants, they do illustrate how participants responded to other pro-social acts not mentioned in the news report (e.g. helpfulness, co-operation). The participants' pro-social actions were different to those on the news report. It's suggested that these related pro-social concepts were activated or 'primed' in their minds by the original pro-social news report (Berkowitz, 1985).

## 'LOST YOUR MARBLES GAME!' (SILVERMAN & SPRAFKIN, 1980)

This involved groups of three-, five- and seven-year olds watching clips of *Sesame Street*. The experimental clips were designed to teach co-operation compared with control clips which didn't. In pairs, children played a game of marbles after watching the programme clips. In order to win, the children had to co-operate with one another by taking turns. There were no differences in the levels of co-operation shown by control or experimental groups. It was suggested that these findings may have been the result of the very brief presentation of the programme clips and/or the artificial nature of the co-operation.

### ✗✓ Evaluation of research studies into pro-social behaviour

✓ **Experimental support:** Hearold (1986) conducted a review of previous pro-social research studies (a meta-analysis) and she concluded that:

'Although fewer studies exist on pro-social effects, the effect size is so much larger, holds up better under more stringent experimental conditions and is consistently higher for both boys and girls, that the potential for pro-social overrides the small but persistent negative effects of antisocial programs.'

Note: There are as many as five evaluative (A02) points contained in this quotation! Try to spot them!

✓ **Evidence for pro-social modelling:** Lovelace and Huston (1983) concluded that pro-social studies do generally produce pro-social behaviour in viewers.

✓ **Methodological advantages:** Many of the studies described above have the advantage of strict experimental control and allow the presentation of the pro-social behaviour clearly and unambiguously.

✗ **Methodological disadvantages:** However, many of the studies use brief clips from programmes some of which are specifically produced for use in the lab. In addition, measures of pro-social behaviour are conducted in an artificial situation. Generalising such findings may be difficult.

# PYA4: Pro- and anti-social possible essay questions (all 24 marks – 30 mins)

Other possible exam questions:

- each essay is worth 24 marks and should take 30 minutes to write
- remember that the mark scheme allocates 12 marks for AO1 (knowledge and description) and 12 marks for AO2 (analysis and evaluation).

## NATURE AND CAUSES OF AGGRESSION

1. **a.** Describe two social–psychological explanations of aggression (e.g. Social Learning Theory, deindividuation). (12 marks)

   **b.** Evaluate these explanations in terms of research evidence and/or alternative theories. (12 marks)

2. Describe and evaluate research into the effects of two or more environmental stressors on aggressive behaviour. (24 marks)

## ALTRUISM AND BYSTANDER BEHAVIOUR

3. Describe and evaluate psychological explanations relating to human altruism/bystander behaviour. (24 marks)

4. Describe and evaluate research into human altruism/bystander behaviour. (24 marks)

5. Critically consider cultural differences in pro-social behaviour. (24 marks)

## MEDIA INFLUENCES ON PRO- AND ANTI-SOCIAL BEHAVIOUR

6. Describe and evaluate the evidence of the influence of the media on either aggressive behaviour or pro-social behaviour. (24 marks)

7. 'What, then, can be seen as the "different" factor that has entered the lives of countless children and adolescents in recent years? This has to be recognised as the easy availability to children of gross images of violence on video.' (Newson, 1995)

   With reference to the general ideas expressed in the above quotation, discuss the view that children are adversely affected by violence on video and/or other forms of media. (24 marks)

8. Discuss the view that the media may exert a pro-social influence. (24 marks)

# CHAPTER SUMMARY: revision schema

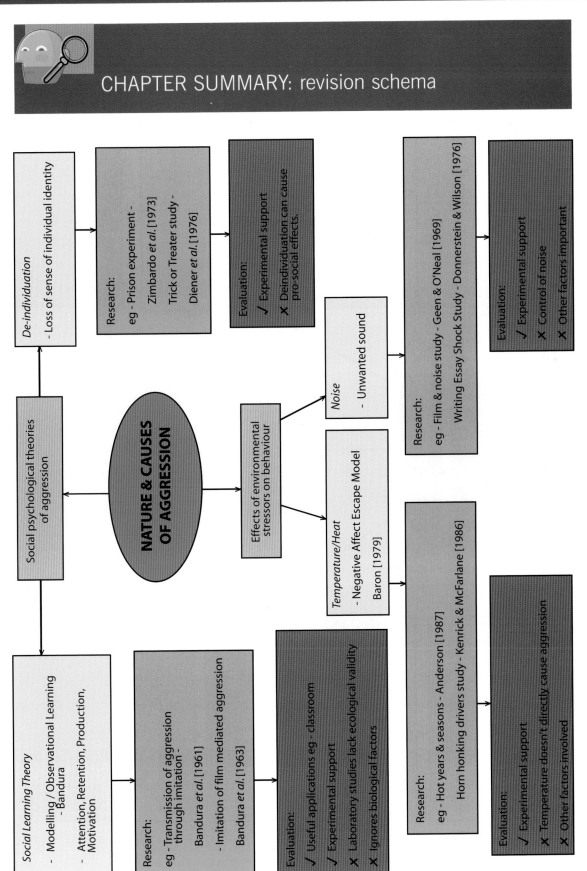

**NATURE & CAUSES OF AGGRESSION**

**Social psychological theories of aggression**

**De-individuation**
- Loss of sense of individual identity

Research:
eg - Prison experiment - Zimbardo et al. [1973]
Trick or Treater study - Diener et al. [1976]

Evaluation:
✓ Experimental support
✗ Deindividuation can cause pro-social effects.

**Social Learning Theory**
- Modelling / Observational Learning - Bandura
- Attention, Retention, Production, Motivation

Research:
eg - Transmission of aggression through imitation - Bandura et al. [1961]
- Imitation of film mediated aggression Bandura et al. [1963]

Evaluation:
✓ Useful applications eg - classroom
✓ Experimental support
✗ Laboratory studies lack ecological validity
✗ Ignores biological factors

**Effects of environmental stressors on behaviour**

**Noise** - Unwanted sound

Research:
eg - Film & noise study - Geen & O'Neal [1969]
Writing Essay Shock Study - Donnerstein & Wilson [1976]

Evaluation:
✓ Experimental support
✗ Control of noise
✗ Other factors important

**Temperature/Heat**
- Negative Affect Escape Model Baron [1979]

Research:
eg - Hot years & seasons - Anderson [1987]
Horn honking drivers study - Kenrick & McFarlane [1986]

Evaluation:
✓ Experimental support
✗ Temperature doesn't directly cause aggression
✗ Other factors involved

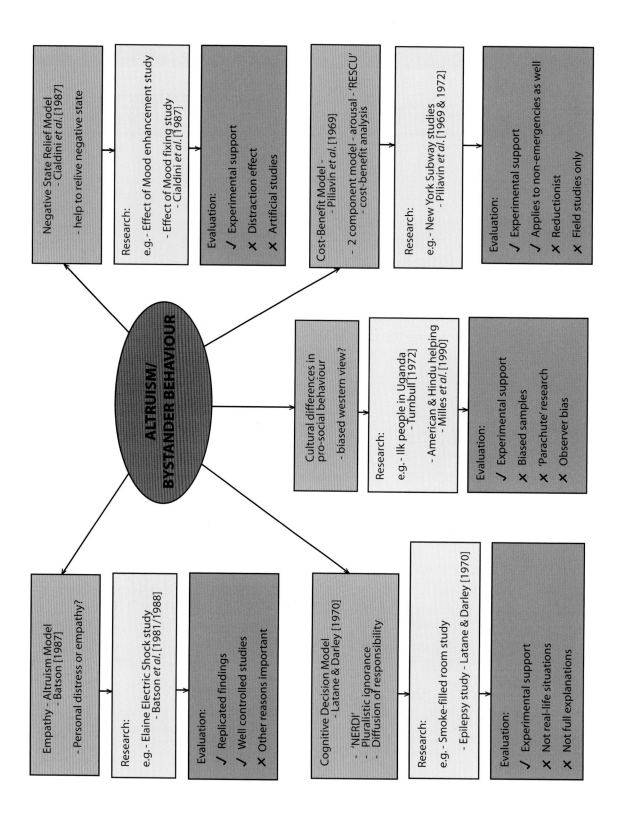

ALTRUISM/BYSTANDER BEHAVIOUR

Negative State Relief Model
- Cialdini et al. [1987]

- help to relive negative state

Research:
e.g. - Effect of Mood enhancement study
- Effect of Mood fixing study
- Cialdini et al. [1987]

Evaluation:
✓ Experimental support
✗ Distraction effect
✗ Artificial studies

Cost-Benefit Model -
- Piliavin et al. [1969]

- 2 component model - arousal - 'RESCU'
- cost-benefit analysis

Research:
e.g. - New York Subway studies
- Piliavin et al. [1969 & 1972]

Evaluation:
✓ Experimental support
✓ Applies to non-emergencies as well
✗ Reductionist
✗ Field studies only

Cultural differences in pro-social behaviour
- biased western view?

Research:
e.g. - Ilk people in Uganda
- Turnbull [1972]
- American & Hindu helping
- Milles et al. [1990]

Evaluation:
✓ Experimental support
✗ Biased samples
✗ 'Parachute' research
✗ Observer bias

Empathy - Altruism Model
- Batson [1987]

- Personal distress or empathy?

Research:
e.g. - Elaine Electric Shock study
- Batson et al. [1981/1988]

Evaluation:
✓ Replicated findings
✓ Well controlled studies
✗ Other reasons important

Cognitive Decision Model
- Latane & Darley [1970]

- 'NERDI'
- Pluralistic ignorance
- Diffusion of responsibility

Research:
e.g. - Smoke-filled room study
- Epilepsy study - Latane & Darley [1970]

Evaluation:
✓ Experimental support
✗ Not real-life situations
✗ Not full explanations

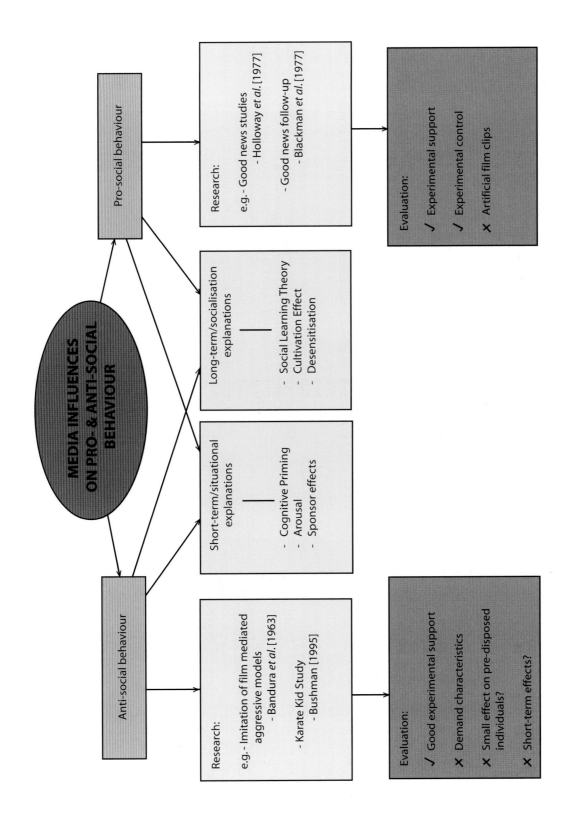

MEDIA INFLUENCES ON PRO- & ANTI-SOCIAL BEHAVIOUR

Pro-social behaviour

Anti-social behaviour

Short-term/situational explanations

- Cognitive Priming
- Arousal
- Sponsor effects

Long-term/socialisation explanations

- Social Learning Theory
- Cultivation Effect
- Desensitisation

Research:

e.g. - Good news studies
       - Holloway et al. [1977]

     - Good news follow-up
       - Blackman et al. [1977]

Evaluation:

✓ Experimental support
✓ Experimental control
✗ Artificial film clips

Research:

e.g. - Imitation of film mediated aggressive models
       - Bandura et al. [1963]

     - Karate Kid Study
       - Bushman [1995]

Evaluation:

✓ Good experimental support
✗ Demand characteristics
✗ Small effect on pre-disposed individuals?
✗ Short-term effects?

# SAMPLE ESSAYS

Critically consider *one* social psychological theory of aggression. (24 marks) (30 mins) (600 words minimum) AO1/AO2

## Section 1:

One social psychological theory of aggression is Social Learning Theory. This theory (proposed by Bandura) suggests that aggression is primarily learned through direct experience or by observing the actions of others (models). This is called learning by vicarious experience or observational learning. There are four processes involved in observational learning:

1. Attention: people have to pay attention to the modelled behaviour

2. Retention: people must retain the behaviour being modelled

3. Production: people must be capable of reproducing the model's behaviour

4. Motivation: people must expect to receive a reinforcement for copying the model's behaviour.

Behaviour is more likely to be copied if it's likely to result in positive rewards, the model shares similar characteristics to the learner and the task is moderately difficult. In terms of aggression, Bandura believed that aggression by family members was the most likely source of imitative aggression.

**AO1**

## Section 2:

Two studies that support the SLT were conducted by Bandura *et al.* (1961; 1963). In the first study, 72 boys and girls (aged three to five years) were split into two groups. The 'aggressive' group played in a room with several toys including a Bobo doll. An adult model entered the room and started to act aggressively towards the doll in very specific ways. In the 'non-aggressive' group, the adult model merely assembled toys. Children in the aggressive condition showed far higher levels of imitative (verbal and physical) aggression. The second study used a similar method except that the children watched a film in which the model acted aggressively towards the Bobo doll. In the model-rewarded condition, the adult was praised (rewarded) for abusing the doll. In the model-punished group, the adult was told off and in the 'no consequences' group, no reinforcement was given. Children in the model-punished group produced significantly fewer acts of imitative aggression. However, when all groups were asked to imitate the aggression they had previously seen, all the children were equally aggressive. This suggests that the original difference was one of performance rather than learning and that the expectancy of reinforcement (reward or punishment) is an essential feature of imitative learning.

**AO1**

## Section 3:

The Bandura *et al.* studies were well-controlled lab studies that have been replicated and clearly show evidence of observational learning of aggression. However, the sample was restricted to children and it's questionable whether adults learn aggression in the same way. The actual measure of aggression is dubious. Aggression towards a Bobo doll is not the same as aggression in real life. After all, a Bobo doll is actually designed to be hit. Some of the children felt that they were expected to act aggressively, suggesting demand characteristics may have played a part. Finally, some critics have questioned the ethical nature of the studies since they seemed to be encouraging children to imitate aggression. Nevertheless, these studies remain classics in psychology and have been extremely influential in demonstrating the effects of both real-life and filmed aggression on subsequent aggressive behaviour.

**AO2**

## Section 4:

Well-validated experiments support the SLT of aggression. It also appears to make cognitive sense that environmental experiences must play a part in influencing many forms of behaviour including aggression. However, there must be a number of other factors that lead a person to behave in an aggressive manner beyond the fact that they are copying the actions of others whom they have seen gain some reward for such actions. SLT appears over-simplistic. SLT ignores biological influences on aggression. It seems likely that genetic, biological and/or hormonal factors must play some part in influencing aggressive behaviour. The fact that SLT has been successfully applied to many behaviours and a number of different settings (e.g. advertising and therapies) suggests that it has serious merit as an explanation for human aggression but perhaps does not fully explain all facets of it. (636 words)

**AO2**

Discuss research into the effects of *two* environmental stressors on behaviour. (24 marks) (30 mins) (600 words minimum) AO1/AO2

## Section 1:

Within the multitude of theories on aggression comes the explanation that it's caused by environmental stressors. Both temperature and noise are believed to increase arousal that may lead to a negative mood or a misattribution process that increases the likelihood of aggression.

AO1

Psychologists have found an inverted U-shape link between temperature and aggression (e.g. Baron, 1979; Berkowitz, 1983). That is, as temperatures increase, aggression increases. However, at very high (or low) temperatures, the willingness to escape from the temperatures exceeds the desire to aggress. Correlational studies support this trend. Anderson (1987) found violent crimes were particularly frequent in summer months. Boyanowsky *et al.* (1981) conducted a lab study where participants were able to give electric shocks to other people who had previously evaluated their work. This procedure took place in cold, moderate or hot temperatures. Those in the cold/hot conditions delivered more shocks, supporting the temperature–aggression hypothesis. Kenrick and McFarlane (1986) in their field study of horn-honking drivers found that drivers without air conditioning were more likely to hoot a driver whose car was blocking their way.

AO1 (some AO2)

## Section 2:

The temperature/aggression hypothesis finds much experimental support. The link between temperature and aggression or riots appear consistent across eras and countries (Carlsmith & Anderson, 1979). However, these data are correlational and thus there is no definite cause and effect. Indeed, Rotton (1993) found no significant correlation between violence and temperature when the different sub-culture of Southern USA was accounted for. It's suggested that aggression increases in hotter weather simply because people go out more and hence have more 'social contact'. However, 'wife beating' also shows a summer increase which cannot be explained by the 'social contact' hypothesis. It has also proved difficult to support the predicted downturn in aggression at very high temperatures – possibly because the highest temperatures are not reached. In addition, the accuracy of the temperature measures has been questioned. Even on hot days (or months), there are cooler periods (e.g. night-time) when aggressive acts can occur. Lab studies can overcome such problems with accurate temperature measures but suffer from demand characteristics and low ecological validity.

AO2 (some AO1)

## Section 3:

Noise has been shown to cause both physiological and psychological effects. Donnerstein and Wilson (1976) got participants each to write an essay that was then evaluated by a confederate favourably (non-angered condition) or critically (angered condition). They were later allowed to evaluate the confederate's essay by giving them electric shocks. While doing this they wore headphones exposing them to either low-intensity (65 db) or high-intensity (95 db) noise. 'Angered' participants were much more likely to administer more and longer shocks in the high-intensity condition; those who were non-angered were mainly unaffected by the noise intensity. However, Geen and O'Neal (1969) showed that if a participant isn't predisposed to aggress, noise has little or no effect on aggression. Participants were divided up into two groups: one watched a violent film, the other a non-violent film. It was only those who watched the violent film who experienced an increase in aggression (measured by intensity of electric shocks that the participant administered) when exposed to high-intensity noise. In fact, those who watched the non-violent film were no more aggressive than those who were not exposed to this high-intensity noise. Evans *et al.* (1995, 1997) showed a link between aircraft noise and children's stress levels but not a direct link between noise and aggression.

AO1 (some AO2)

## Section 4:

Lab studies appear to support the link between aggression and noise. Although these involve well-controlled studies, they could be said to lack ecological validity. Results may be caused by the experimental situation and may not be generalised to more real-life situations. In addition, the presence of noise in itself does not appear to lead to aggression. Noise leads to aggression only when accompanied by frustration, anger or provocation. Furthermore, if people perceive that they have control over the noise, aggression does not seem to result.

Difficulties with the accurate operationalisation of aggression and problems with the measurement of temperature and noise suggest that the exact nature of the link between these two environmental stressors and aggression will remain unclear.

AO2

(684 words)

**SAMPLE ESSAYS**

# SAMPLE ESSAYS

Outline and evaluate *one or more* explanations of altruism/bystander behaviour in humans. (24 marks) (30 mins) (600 words minimum) AO1/AO2

## Section 1:

Batson used his Empathy–Altruism Model (EAM) to suggest that people do act altruistically. When someone witnesses a distressing event, they experience two kinds of upset:

● personal distress: a general unpleasant feeling that the person would want to reduce as soon as possible

● empathy: feeling compassion and sympathy for the victim, they see things from the victim's perspective.

Perspective taking is affected by the perceived similarity between victim and helper and any attachment (friendship or kinship) the helper has with the victim. People who help to reduce personal distress help for selfish or egocentric reasons, whereas those who help because of empathic concern do so for altruistic reasons. They want to relieve the other person's personal distress, not their own! Another factor is the ease with which one can escape from the helping situation. If it's easy to escape, then this action will help to reduce feelings of personal distress but not true feelings of empathy.

**A01**

## Section 2:

The EAM model proposes a positive and optimistic view of human behaviour that isn't based on selfish motives. Studies conducted by Batson *et al.* (1981) involved participants being offered the chance to swap places with a confederate who was receiving electric shocks as part of a learning experiment (the altruism element). They manipulated the ease of escape and the feelings of empathy participants felt towards the victim. Results supported the model in that empathic participants helped whereas low empathy–easy escape participants didn't. These research studies were lab experiments and were well controlled. However, the studies have been criticised for having low ecological validity and examining only short-term altruistic behaviour. Participants were also deceived about certain details of the studies. It's also possible that participants behaved in a way they felt was ethical, irrespective of whether or not they experienced actual empathy for the victim. Even Batson has suggested that there may be reasons for helping other than the reduction of personal distress or empathic concern. These might include the relief of sadness, the desire to make oneself happy and the bolstering of self-concept.

**A02 (some A01)**

## Section 3:

Cialdini *et al.* (1987) proposed a more selfish view of helping, stressing that people help others to avoid feeling sad (a negative state) and because it makes them feel good about themselves. This is called the Negative State Relief (NSR) Model. It doesn't matter whether the negative affect (mood) is caused by witnessing the distress of the victim or whether the helper was already in a bad mood. Either way, you help to improve your own mood. Adults may internalise the reward of doing good deeds. Therefore adults in a bad mood may help in order to alleviate their negative state. However, if people can relieve their negative mood through some other source (such as hearing a good joke or getting some money) then they will not need to help.

**A01**

## Section 4:

This is a rather pessimistic view of helping behaviour but a number of experiments seem to support this view. Cialdini *et al.* (1987) designed a study along similar lines to the Batson procedure but offered praise or payment to enhance people's mood. Help was given less often, even in the high-empathy condition, since participants no longer had to act to improve their mood. Similar selfish findings were found in a mood-fixing study. Both these studies support the NSR model. However, even Cialdini accepted that the reward procedures of EME and the fake-drug procedure of EMF might have distracted participants' attention away from their empathic emotions. Indeed, Schroeder *et al.* (1988) changed the experimental procedures to remove these distractions and found no drop in helping in the fixed-mood/high-empathy condition. They concluded their results supported EAM more than the NSR model. It's been found in numerous studies that being in a good mood results in more pro-social behaviour. Researchers have found people to be more helpful after listening to comedy, smelling pleasant odours, after finding money or by going outside on sunny days (Baron & Byrne, 1997). However, if people feel their good mood will be affected by helping (i.e. it will involve negative consequences) then they are more likely to walk away and not help.

The debate as to whether we help for altruistic or selfish reasons is ongoing.

(715 words)

**A02 (some A01)**

Critically consider explanations relating to media influences on anti-social behaviour. (24 marks) (30 mins) (600 words minimum) AO1/AO2

Section 1:

There are a number of explanations put forward to suggest that people are adversely affected by violence in the media. The cognitive priming explanation suggests that aggressive ideas shown in the media (particularly films) can 'spark off' other aggressive thoughts in memory pathways (Berkowitz, 1984). After a violent film, the viewer is 'primed' to respond aggressively because the memory network involving aggression is activated.

The arousal explanation suggests that arousal increases the dominant behaviour in any situation. If the feeling of arousal is attributed to anger, then aggression is likely to result. Research has shown that the arousal produced by (violent) pornography facilitates aggressive behaviour (Zillman, 1978).

Perhaps the best-known explanation to suggest that people are aversely affected by the media was put forward by Bandura. It's suggested here that television can shape behaviour through imitative learning. Watching role models perform violently may increase violent behaviour in those viewers already motivated to aggress. Television may also teach viewers the negative or positive consequences of their violence. Paik and Comstock (1994) did indeed find that the effect on anti-social behaviour was greater if the actor was rewarded for their actions.

The cultivation effect (Gerbner & Gross, 1976) suggests that the medium of television creates (or cultivates) a distrust or unrealistic fear in viewers. This causes viewers to misperceive (or exaggerate) threats in real life and react in a more violent way. This is also referred to as the 'mean world' effect.

Desensitisation suggests that repeated exposure to violence in the media reduces the impact of the violence. People become 'desensitised' to the violence and it has less impact on them (habituation). They become less anxious about violence *per se* and may therefore engage in more violent behaviour.

AO1

Section 2:

Evidence to support the cognitive-priming explanation was shown in the Hockey Game Study (Josephson, 1987) where boys who had been 'primed' to be aggressive through viewing an aggressive film acted more aggressively in a subsequent hockey game where relevant behavioural cues were present.

The main problem with the arousal explanation is that if arousal is attributed to factors other than anger, then arousal will not necessarily result in aggression.

There's a lot of experimental evidence to support the Social Learning Theory explanation. Bandura *et al.*'s (1963) study into the imitation of film-mediated aggressive models showed that children who observe a model behaving aggressively towards a Bobo doll subsequently behave more aggressively than those who see the model punished for their actions. This well-controlled experiment and the identification of specific learned responses provides good evidence for imitative learning. However, the sample characteristics were unrepresentative (only children from a university nursery) and the study has been criticised for lacking ecological validity. In addition, the study did not really measure real aggression (a Bobo doll is designed to be hit) and only short-term effects of the media were assessed. However, in an answer to this criticism, Hicks (1965) found that 40% of a model's acts were reproduced up to eight months after one showing of a 10-minute film. The study has also been questioned for its ethical stance, where children were encouraged to be aggressive.

The main problem with the cultivation-effect explanation is that people who are particularly fearful are likely to avoid any threatening situations in the first place. Thus increasing the level of fear might actually help to reduce the level of violence.

The desensitisation argument suffers because it could be argued that desensitised individuals might be *less* aroused by violence and therefore not be so easily provoked by real-life violence. Similarly, desensitised individuals may become indifferent to the violent message. Both of these latter possibilities would result in the desensitised individual being *less* violent, not *more*.

Given the evidence, it would be surprising if the media had no influence on anti-social behaviour. The effect is likely to be small, weak and affect only a small number of pre-disposed individuals. The exact explanations for this effect remain inconclusive.

AO2 (some AO1)

(658 words)

SAMPLE ESSAYS

# A2 Module 4:
## Social, Physiological, Cognitive, Developmental and Comparative Psychology

# Biological rhythms, sleep and dreaming

## What's covered in this chapter?

### You need to know about:

**Biological rhythms**
- Research into circadian, infradian and ultradian rhythms, including the role of endogenous pacemakers and exogenous zeitgebers
- The consequences of disrupting biological rhythms (e.g. shift work, jet lag)

**Sleep**
- Theories and research studies relating to the functions of sleep, including ecological (e.g. Meddis; Webb) and restoration (e.g. Oswald; Horne) accounts
- The implications of findings from studies of sleep deprivation for such theories

**Dreaming**
- Research findings relating to the nature of dreams (e.g. content; duration; type of dream)
- Theories of the functions of dreaming, including neurobiological (e.g. Hobson & McCarley; Crick & Mitchison) and psychological (e.g. Freud; Webb & Cartwright) accounts

## Biological rhythms

### Research studies into circadian, infradian and ultradian biological rhythms, including the role of endogenous pacemakers and exogenous zeitgebers

- A **bodily rhythm** is 'a cyclical variation over some period of time in physiological or psychological processes' (Gross *et al.*, 2001).
- Many human activities take place within a cycle of about 24 hours. These are called **circadian rhythms** ('circa' = about, 'diem' = a day).
- Rhythms which have a cycle longer than 24 hours are called **infradian rhythms**, e.g.

the human menstrual cycle. **Circannual rhythms** are yearly rhythms and are included as a sub-set of infradian rhythms.

- Cycles with shorter periods are called **ultradian rhythms**, e.g. the 90–120-minute cycle of sleep stages in humans.
- Environmental factors such as light–dark cycles, noise, clocks and so on give clues as to external cycles and are called **exogenous zeitgebers** ('zeitgeber' = German for 'time-giver').
- In the absence of any zeitgeber, behaviours which show rhythmicity are driven by internal timing devices – internal biological clocks which are referred to as **endogenous pacemakers**.

> **Specification Hint:** This is a popular section of the Specification and certainly includes some interesting material. However, many of the sub-sections overlap with each other, e.g. dreaming is a type of sleep which, in turn, is both a circadian and an ultradian rhythm. Rather than repeat material, we've dealt with it in the most appropriate section and referred to this in other sub-sections where it's also relevant. Of course, this means that there may be less material to learn (since the same information can be applied for different questions), but it's more complicated to work out exactly what is relevant for each question. In your exam, you must explicitly state how all material you present is directly relevant to the exam question and then the examiners will have to give you credit.

## Research studies on circadian rhythms

**ESSENTIAL STUDY 10.1**

### The Underground Studies (TUS) (Aschoff & Wever, 1962; Siffre 1962, 1972)

- One of the first studies into the effect of the absence of exogenous zeitgebers on human circadian rhythms was conducted by Aschoff and Wever in Munich in 1962. They isolated participants in an underground World War II bunker in the absence of environmental time cues for three to four weeks at a time. Although the participants could turn lights on and off at will, they had no external cues to provide clues as to the time of day (or night!). All the participants followed a circadian rhythm with a sleep–wake cycle of about 25 hours. Experimental changes in room temperature had no effect on their cycle.
- Michel Siffre has conducted a number of similar studies using himself as the sole participant. In 1962 he spent two months in the caves of Scarrasson in the Southern Alps. He spent 61 days underground and surfaced on 17th September, believing it to be 20th August. In 1972 he spent 205 days in 'Midnight Cave' in Texas, being monitored by NASA, and again in November 1999 he spent three months underground – missing the Millenium celebrations! Despite being aware of the results of the previous studies, each time he settled into a 24-hour, 30-minute sleep–wake cycle. Siffre reported feeling pessimistic and depressed when his clock was most out of step with the outside world.

SORRY I'M LATE SIR. I WENT TO MY BEDROOM AT THE END OF SUMMER TERM AND WITHOUT ANY EXOGENOUS ZEITGEBERS BELIEVED TODAY WAS SEPTEMBER 1st, THE START OF THE NEW TERM!

## ✗✓ Evaluation of research studies

✓ **Replicated findings:** There have been numerous sleep–wake studies and although some have reported sleep–wake cycles ranging from 13 to 65 hours, there's a fairly consistent finding of about 25 hours. Miles *et al.* (1977) report a 24.9-hour circadian rhythm for a man who had been blind from birth. Despite hearing zeitgebers to inform him of the time, he struggled to cope with a 24-hour day–night cycle and had to take stimulants and sedatives at the appropriate times in order to cope.

✗ **Cognitive sense?** It seems unlikely that humans have evolved with a faulty biological clock running every 25 hours. Animals studies show a consistent 24-hour cycle and it would make more sense for humans to follow this pattern (see Czeisler *et al.* (1999) below).

✗ **Case studies:** Many of these studies use very few participants (a single individual in the case of Siffre) and, as such, findings may not be easily generalised to a wider population. Indeed, there may be specific factors about these individuals (e.g. age, gender, personality) that also bring such results into question.

✗ **Conflicting research findings:** It's claimed that isolating participants from the environment without strictly controlling their behaviour isn't sufficient to reveal the activity of the endogenous circadian pacemaker. Czeisler *et al.* (1999) suggest that participants in earlier sleep–wake cycle studies were inadvertently affected by their exposure to high levels of artificial light which skewed their results. Czeisler *et al.* claim that allowing participants to switch on bright lights was like giving them the equivalent of a drug that reset their internal clocks. Czeisler *et al.* claim that the cycle is actually 24 hours. In their 1999 study, 24 men and women lived for a month in very low subdued light, with no clues as to the passage of time. The participants were placed on an artificial 28 hour sleep–wake cycle by the researchers. During this time, researchers monitored body chemistry and temperature signs that mark the action of the body clock. This allowed the researchers to detect when the body clock, or circadian pacemaker, was turned on. The measurements showed that the human sleep clock operates on a schedule of 24 hours, 11 minutes, not the 25 hours widely reported.

Michel Siffre is a specialist in chronobiology: the study of man's internal clock

'All of the textbooks indicate that humans have a 25-hour day instead of a 24-hour day. We now know that is wrong.': Charles Czeisler, one of the world's leading experts on sleep and shift-work patterns.

> **Specification Hint:** The Specification mentions 'research studies into circadian, infradian and ultradian rhythms' and therefore you need to know only a minimum of *two* research studies for each of these. Of course, other studies can be used for evaluation.

The magicicada of North America, which reproduces every 17 years – an extremely long infradian rhythm.

## Infradian rhythms

Infradian rhythms (longer than 24 hours) include bird migrations, hibernation, the human menstrual cycle and many reproductive cycles. Although some reproductive cycles, such as that of the 17-year magicicada genus of North America cicada, are very long infradian rhythms, we are all familiar with the yearly springtime reproduction cycle of animals. Seasonal rhythms such as this that last about a year are called circannual rhythms and are usually associated with long-lived plants and animals.

### MENSTRUAL CYCLE

- The most well-known infradian rhythm in humans is the human menstrual cycle. Through a series of complex interactions with the brain and reproductive organs, an egg is released approximately every 28 days by the ovary. During each menstrual cycle, hormones (oestrogen and progesterone) are secreted and physiological changes occur to the breasts and the reproductive organs which are prepared for possible fertilisation. Each cycle ends with menstruation unless pregnancy occurs.
- Although the menstrual cycle was identified many years ago, exactly how it's generated and how it interacts with other factors is not clearly understood. There's no doubt that it's also affected by circadian rhythms since the secretion of leuteinising hormone (which starts ovulation) occurs in the early morning hours. In addition, phase shifts which occur because of jet lag have been shown to affect menstrual cycles.

Martha McClintock was the first researcher to discover menstrual synchronisation among human females while she was still an undergraduate at Wellesley College. She's now a Professor at the University of Chicago.

## Research studies on infradian rhythms

### MCCLINTOCK'S MENSTRUAL SYNCHRONY STUDIES (MMSS) (1971, 1988) (SEE ALSO MCCLINTOCK & STERN, 1998)

ESSENTIAL STUDY 10.2

McClintock identified the synchronisation of female menstruation when she observed that the menstrual cycles among her dormitory mates became synchronised. After further research, she concluded that the synchronisation of the menstrual cycles among 135 female friends and dormitory mates (aged 17–22 years) was caused by pheromones transmitted through social interaction. Pheromones are odourless chemical substances which, when secreted by an individual into the environment, cause specific reactions in other individuals, usually of the same species. It was initially suggested that there may be a specific female pheromone that affects the timing of other female menstrual cycles (McClintock, 1971).

In 1998, McClintock and Stern began a 10-year longitudinal follow-up study that involved 29 women between the ages of 20 and 35 with a history of irregular, spontaneous ovulation. The researchers gathered samples of pheromones from nine of the women at certain points in their menstrual cycles, by placing pads of cotton under their arms. The women had previously bathed without perfumed products and then wore the cotton pads for at least eight hours. Each cotton pad was then treated with alcohol (to disguise any smell) and frozen. These pads were then wiped under the noses of the 20 other women on a daily basis!

McClintock and Stern concluded that 68% of the women responded to the pheromones. Menstrual cycles were either shortened by from one to 14 days or lengthened by from one to 12 days, dependent on when in the menstrual cycle they had been collected. The pheromones collected from the women in the early phases of their cycles shortened the cycles of the second group of women (between one and 14 days) by speeding up their pre-ovulatory surge of luteinising hormone; conversely, pheromones collected later, during ovulation, lengthened the menstrual cycles by delaying the LH surge (by one to 12 days).

It's still unclear how the pheromones trigger the menstrual-cycle changes. Because the samples were put on the participants' top lips, McClintock admits that 'we know absolutely nothing about where the chemical formula is acting, whether it's through the skin, the mucus membranes in the nose, or a pair of tiny pits in the nose' (Stern & McClintock, 1998).

## Evaluation of MMSS

✓ **Research support:** Russell *et al.* (1980), using a similar methodology to McClintock, obtained supporting results. It's unclear why this synchronisation might occur but in evolutionary terms it may have been useful for females in a social group to have their children at similar times in order to be able to share tasks such as breastfeeding or other childcare activities. This certainly appears to be the case with animals such as lionesses in the same pride.

✓·✗ **Non-human animal evidence:** The evidence for pheromonal effects in rats is very strong and in some cases the actual pheromones have been extracted and analysed. However, whether we can generalise from animal findings to humans remains controversial. Human behaviour, especially when it comes to mating behaviour, is not as straightforward as animal behaviour. An ovulating female boar, when exposed to a male boar's saliva, immediately goes into a spread-legged mating posture. Human behaviour is just not that clear-cut!

✗ **Conflicting evidence:** A study that examined a women's basketball team for an extended period of time found no correlation between the women's menstrual patterns. However, it's known that exercise, dieting and stress can each cause changes in women's menstrual patterns as well, and these may have affected any possible synchronisation effect.

✗ **Methodological errors?** It's claimed that apparent clustering of the female menstrual cycle is a myth and is no more likely than that expected by chance alone. Furthermore, many of these studies use small samples and rely on women recalling the onset date of menstruation, and this method may be inaccurate. One researcher (Wilson, 1992) has claimed that when you correct all the errors, including McClintock's, the evidence for menstrual synchrony evaporates.

In summary:

'Menstrual synchrony is a difficult phenomenon to demonstrate, its occurrence among women remains uncertain, or at least unpredictable, and if it does exist, its functional significance remains unclear.' (Cynthia A. Graham, 2002)

## Seasonal Affective Disorder (SAD)

'In the dark time of the year the soul's sap quivers.' (T.S. Eliot)

• Seasonal Affective Disorder, or SAD, is a disorder in which sufferers show seasonal changes of mood and/or behaviour. The most common mood change is depression or 'affective disorder'. Symptoms typically include depression, guilt, low self-esteem, lethargy and sleep problems.

- The exact causes of SAD are still unclear. The most common explanation is that lack of light during the night causes the *pineal gland* to secrete a chemical called *melatonin*. The increase of light at dawn tells the gland to switch off this secretion so that we can wake up. Particularly in northern countries, in the winter, some people do not seem to experience enough light. Put simply, imbalances in melatonin can lead to problems with other chemicals that may lead to depression. When it was found that exposure to bright light suppresses night-time melatonin production, it was suggested that bright artificial light could be used experimentally, and perhaps therapeutically, to manipulate the circadian sleep–wake cycle in humans (Lewy *et al.*, 1980).

## SAD STUDIES (TERMAN *ET AL.*, 1998)

- 124 participants (aged 18–65) with SAD took part in the study. Over three weeks, 85 participants received daily 30-minute exposures to bright light from a box mounted above the head. Some had light therapy in the morning, others in the evening. The remaining participants sat for 30 minutes each morning in front of an apparatus called a negative-ion generator, which emitted air ions. These treatments were placebos.
- 60% of those who received the morning light therapy showed marked improvements in SAD symptoms, compared with 30% of those in the evening light condition. Winter depression eased in only 5% of participants exposed to air ions.

 Evaluation of SAD

✓ **Replicated findings:** Other well-controlled studies by Eastman *et al.* (1998) and Winton *et al.* (1989) conducted with adequate sample sizes suggest morning bright light therapy is effective in treating SAD.

✓ **Practical treatments:** Light therapy is easy to administer in outpatient settings, lacks major side-effects (although some have questioned long-term effects of bright lights on the retina) and is cost-effective.

✗ **Not just light:** Other factors are implicated in SAD. Genetic vulnerability and stress also seem to be major factors in its causation. The exact cause of SAD remains elusive and unconfirmed.

## Ultradian rhythms

If you visit http://www.talkaboutsleep.com/sleepbasics/viewasleepstudy.htm you can view details of how a sleep study takes place at Stanford University Sleep Disorders Clinic.

- We've already mentioned how the sleep–wake cycle in humans follows a basic 24-hour cycle or circadian rhythm. However, within the sleep portion of this cycle, an ultradian rhythm exists. An ultradian rhythm is a biological rhythm that occurs with a frequency of less than 24 hours. Using a number of physiological techniques, we've learned that sleep is composed of several repetitive cycles each lasting about 90 minutes. There are three standard physiological measures of sleep. These are:
  - the **electroencephalogram (EEG)** measures brain activity. It records an average of the electrical potentials of the cells and fibres in a particular part of the brain by means of an electrode attached to the scalp. The EEG is an objective measure of brain activity and allows researchers to determine whether people are awake or asleep and to identify a number of different sleep stages

*Exam Hint:*

Seasonal Affective Disorder (SAD) can be included as either an infradian *OR* a circadian rhythm. Since the disorder occurs mainly during the winter months, it would appear to be one involving circannual rhythms which are a sub-set of infradian rhythms (more-than-24-hour rhythms). However, it's hypothesised that SAD occurs because of disruption of the body's sleep–wake cycle which is, of course, a circadian rhythm. Thus, it's possible to include SAD in either an infradian or circadian rhythm essay (or both!). However, you *must* *explicitly* state *how* SAD fits into the rhythm that you've been asked to write about.

- the **electromyogram (EMG)** measures muscle activity of the chin, specifically when muscles are tense or relaxed
- the **electrooculogram (EOG)** measures eye movements. It's been found that dreaming is usually accompanied by rapid eye movements and is thus called REM sleep. The other stages of sleep are often referred to as non-REM sleep (NREM) or slow wave sleep (SWS).

**Figure 10.1** Placement of EEG, EOG and EMG electrodes in a sleep experiment

Techniques such as these have allowed researchers to discover that infants spend about 50% of their sleep time in REM sleep, compared with adults who spend only about 20% of their sleep time in REM.

- There are distinct differences in the EEG, EMG and EOG record at each of the different sleep stages. Figure 10.2 shows the differences in the EEG, EMG and EOG during waking, REM sleep (Rapid Eye Movement Sleep) and SWS or NREM sleep.
- In REM sleep the individual undergoes a relatively brief period of vivid, erratic dreams. When the brain is monitored by EEG, the brain activity is similar to the EEG of a person in a state of wakefulness and yet it's difficult to wake people from REM sleep. Hence it's often called paradoxical sleep. Non–REM sleep is further split into four stages, each of which is identified by different electrical patterns on the EEG. Within the 90-minute sleep cycle the body begins with a cycle of non-REM sleep, followed by a shorter period of REM sleep. These cycles continue throughout the night, with the REM period getting progressively longer (see Figure 10.3). Each stage is associated with different EEG waves. Put simply, they tend to get 'bigger' as the sleep gets 'deeper'.
- The characteristics of these different stages of sleep can be summarised:
  - **Stage 1:** The period when we 'drift off'. Breathing becomes slower, heartbeat becomes irregular, blood pressure falls and blood flow is reduced. Brain waves become smaller, slower and somewhat irregular, characterised by a low-voltage fast EEG. Initially, these are called alpha waves, but gradually they slow and are called theta waves. It's easy to wake during this stage.
  - **Stage 2:** An intermediate stage of sleep that lasts about 20 minutes. The sleeper gradually goes into deeper sleep. Larger brain waves occur and occasional quick bursts of activity (sleep spindles occur and K-complexes are noted on the EEG). Bodily functions slow down and blood pressure, metabolism, secretions and cardiac activity decrease.
  - **Stage 3:** The beginning of deep sleep occurs about 35 minutes after first falling asleep. The brain waves known as delta waves are slow (at the rate of 0.5 to 4 per second) and quite large (five times the size of waves in Stage 2).
  - **Stage 4:** This is the deepest sleep stage and lasts about 40 minutes. The brain waves (called delta waves) are quite large, making a slow, jagged pattern on the EEG. It's very difficult to wake a sleeper in this stage and bodily functions sink to the deepest possible state of physical rest. The sleeper awakened

**Figure 10.2** EEG, EMG and EOG patterns of different states of consciousness

from deep sleep will probably be groggy, confused or disoriented. He or she may experience 'sleep inertia' or 'sleep drunkenness', seeming unable to function normally for quite some time. In both Stages 3 and 4, the EOG shows little movement and the EMG shows the muscles to be relaxed.

– After Stage 4, we ascend the 'sleep staircase', but instead of entering Stage 1 again, we enter REM sleep or paradoxical sleep (see Figure 10.3). During REM sleep, the EMG shows that the muscles are completely inac-

**Figure 10.3** The stages of sleep and paradoxical/REM sleep episodes after Andreasen 1994

tive whereas the eyes are extremely active (hence 'rapid eye movement') (see Fig. 10.2). Heart rate and blood pressure fluctuate and the breathing rate is higher. The end of the first REM stage marks the completion of the first ultradian cycle. See section on dreaming (pages 254–259) for more on REM sleep.

- The release of hormones also occurs in an ultradian rhythm. Human growth hormone (HGH) would be a good example of this. HGH has a pulse of hormone every three hours, yet overall its period of highest concentration is found at night.

## Research studies on ultradian rhythms

**REM and Dreaming Study** (RADS) (Dement & Kleitman, 1957)

By monitoring the EEG record during sleep, Dement and Kleitman (1957) were able to wake participants during each of the different stages of sleep. They asked the participants to report their feelings, experiences and emotions. They found that people awakened during REM sleep reported dreams 80–90% of the time. The dreams were recalled in great detail and included elaborate visual images. Only 7% of the awakenings from NREM sleep led to dream recall. Dement and Kleitman had found the point during the ultradian cycle when people dream. It's perhaps surprising that this discovery had taken so long since it's possible to detect REM simply by looking closely at a sleeping person's eyes.

**Characteristics of Dreams Study** (CODS) (Dement & Wolpert, 1958)

Using the same awakening technique during REM sleep, Dement and Wolpert (1958) identified many factors concerned with dreams and REM sleep. These included:

- All normal humans dream. People who don't report dreams merely forget their dreams. If they were woken during REM sleep and asked immediately if they were dreaming, people reported dreams.

- The length of a dream corresponds to the length of the incident that is being dreamed about. Dreams *don't* only last a second or two. However, dreams don't seem to last longer than 15 minutes and it's speculated that beyond this time people forget the beginning of the dream.

- Eye movements observed during REM sleep can correspond to a dream's content, but this isn't always the case.

- Dream content can be affected by events experienced during the day. Since it's relatively difficult to wake up during REM sleep, external stimuli can be incorporated into people's dreams. Dement and Wolpert sprayed water on their participants during REM sleep and these dreamers more often reported a dream which involved a water theme compared with a control group. This might be worth trying on a younger brother or sister – purely in the interests of science!

Evaluation of ultradian research studies

✓ ✗ Generally, Dement and Kleitman's research findings have stood the test of time and are accepted by the scientific community. However, some studies have reported figures as high as 70% for the percentage of reported dreams during NREM sleep. Foulkes (1967) attributed this difference to confusion as to what constitutes a dream. Vague dream-like experiences or muddled thoughts have sometimes been incorrectly categorised as dreams.

✗ **Lacks ecological validity?** The artificial and uncomfortable surroundings of the sleep laboratory (given all the electrodes that have to be worn) suggest that such sleep findings may lack ecological validity. Sleep in the comfort of your own bed may be of a qualitatively and/or quantitatively different nature.

## EXAM tips BOX

**Describe and evaluate research studies into infradian rhythms. (30 mins) (600 words minimum)**

This is a very specific question, asking only about infradian rhythms. You'd probably hope that the examiners would ask a more general question about 'research studies into biological rhythms', in which case you could choose to write about research studies into circadian, infradian and ultradian rhythms. However, since infradian rhythms are mentioned specifically in the Spec. they could ask you just about this type of rhythm. Be warned! You need to make sure that you are fully prepared for all possible questions. To answer this question, you have to include a minimum of two research studies.

*This essay can be split up into FOUR Sections – each about 150 words long. Each section would be worth approx. 6 marks.*

**Section 1: Define** what infradian rhythms are. You should outline the following studies:-

● MMSS (McClintock 1971; McClintock & Stern, 1998).

AO1
↓

**Section 2:** You should **analyse** and **evaluate** these research studies.

AO2

**Section 3:** You should **include** other studies into infradian rhythms. These could include:

AO1

● SAD (Terman *et al.*, 1998).

↓

**Section 4:** You should **analyse** and *evaluate* these research studies.

AO2

*Try to answer this question yourself. There's a sample essay on page 265 with which you can compare your essay.*

## The role of endogenous pacemakers

● Endogenous rhythms are rhythms that aren't imposed by the environment but are generated from within the organism. Since many of our biological cycles follow an approximate 24-hour rhythm even in the absence of external stimuli (exogenous zeitgebers), it follows that there must be some kind of internal biological clock.

● Although studies of one-cell organisms suggest the cellular nature of the system which controls circadian rhythms, the circadian pacemaker in higher organisms is located in the cells of specific structures of the organism. These include the optic and cerebral lobes of the brain in insects; the eyes in some invertebrates and vertebrates; and the pineal gland, which is

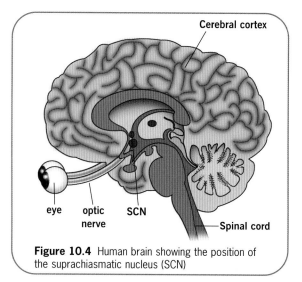

**Figure 10.4** Human brain showing the position of the suprachiasmatic nucleus (SCN)

located within the brain, in non-mammalian vertebrates. In humans and mammals, the circadian clock is located in two clusters of nerve cells called the suprachiasmatic nuclei (SCN). These are found in an area at the base of the brain called the anterior hypothalamus.

- The SCN is located just above the optic chiasm (see Figure 10.4). The optic nerve sends axons directly from the retina of the eye to the SCN. Hence in humans the SCN clock keeps to a 24-hour rhythm with inputs from the eye telling it whether it's night or day. If the SCN is damaged or removed, light can no longer reset the clock.

- Evidence for the SCN being the site of the clock comes from experiments in which the SCN was removed from rats. This led to the usual rhythmic cycles of activity and sleep being abolished (Stephan & Zucker, 1972).

- Further experiments showed that recording electrodes picked up rhythmic bursts of activity from the SCN that varied according to a 24.5-hour cycle. These rhythms persisted even when the hypothalamus was surgically isolated from the rest of the brain – a preparation known as a hypothalamic 'island' (Green & Gillette, 1982).

- Even when cells of the SCN were removed and studied *in vitro*, the 24.5-hour rhythm of neural activity continued. One group of experimenters bred a group of mutant hamsters which followed a 20-hour cycle. They transplanted SCN cells from these adult mutants into the brains of foetuses with a normal 24-hour rhythm and the recipients produced a 20-hour rhythm. When the experimenters transplanted SCNs from normal 24-hour cycle hamsters into the mutant breed, the recipients followed a 24-hour cycle within six or seven days. In each case, the recipients' rhythm no longer matched their own genes, but the genes of the SCN donors (Ralph *et al.*, 1990). This provides strong evidence for the importance of the SCN in generating and maintaining the circadian rhythm.

- Although similar experimental studies have not been conducted on humans (well, would you volunteer?), it's been shown that circadian rhythms are affected by exposure to light (Czeisler *et al.*, 1989). Anatomical studies show the presence of the SCN in humans, and Friedman *et al.* (1991) have proved the presence of a pathway (called the retinohypothalamic tract) from the retina to the SCN. There have also been a number of reported studies involving brain tumours which have damaged the region of the SCN and these have produced disorders in sleep–waking cycles (Fulton & Bailey, 1929). However, such damage is not always restricted solely to the SCN and damages a wider area of the hypothalamus, so it's uncertain that it's only the SCN damage that is critical (Carlson, 2001).

Melatonin helps to regulate the biological clock.

- Although the SCN has a rhythm of about 24 hours, it also plays a part in longer rhythms. Male hamsters have an annual rhythm of testosterone secretion and this appears to be dependent on the amount of light that occurs daily. Their breeding season begins as day length increases. Lesions (cuts) of the SCN stop these annual breeding cycles and they secrete testosterone all year.

- Although it appears to be the most important, the SCN is not the only biological clock in mammals. The pineal gland is a pea-like structure found behind the hypothalamus in humans. The pineal gland receives information indirectly from the SCN. It appears that the SCN takes the information on day length from the retina, interprets it, and passes it on to the pineal gland, which secretes the hormone melatonin in response to this message. Night-time causes melatonin secretion to rise, while daylight inhibits it. Even when light cues are absent, melatonin is still released in a cyclic manner; yet if the SCN is destroyed, circadian rhythms disappear entirely.

- In animals, melatonin acts on various structures in the brain to control hormones and physiological processes and behaviours that show seasonal variations. For example, during longer nights, more melatonin is secreted and some animals will go into the winter phase of their circannual (yearly) rhythm. The role of melatonin in humans is not clearly understood and is currently being investigated. The SCN is known to have hormone receptors for melatonin, so there may be a loop from the pineal gland back to the SCN. Researchers now use melatonin levels as an accurate marker of the circadian rhythm in humans.

- Melatonin is a natural hormone that regulates the human biological clock. Double-blind research with young adults has shown that melatonin facilitates sleep (Zhdanova *et al.*, 1995).
- The locus coeruleus is a group of cells located in the pons. When these cells are removed, REM sleep disappears. Thus it's concluded that the locus coeruleus must play an important part in activating REM sleep. The locus coeruleus produces noradrenaline and acetylcholine which are also responsible for the start of REM sleep. The NREM–REM stages of sleep are believed to operate because of an interaction between the raphe nuclei and the locus coeruleus. The raphe nuclei initiate sleep by acting on the reticular activating system (RAS).
- Recent research has found that circadian rhythms can persist in isolated lungs, livers and other tissues grown in a culture dish (i.e. *in vitro*) that were not under the control of the SCN (Yamazaki *et al.*, 2000). These findings suggest that most cells and tissues of the body may be capable of activity on a circadian basis. It's still recognised that the SCN has the key role as the major circadian pacemaker but establishes that it may co-ordinate this in collaboration with the cells, tissues and the whole organism. Although it's known that the SCN sends neural signals as well as neurohormonal signals through the blood to other organs, the specific way in which the SCN 'communicates' to the rest of the body remains unknown (see Stokkan *et al.*, 2001).
- The amount of REM sleep people experience as a percentage of total sleep decreases with age. Newborns can spend as much as 50% of their total sleep time in REM sleep whereas this percentage declines to approximately 15% by the age of 50–70 years. Thus, age appears to be an endogenous factor that affects the ultradian rhythm of sleep. There are different explanations for why this might be the case (see theories of sleep and dreaming below).
- Molecular geneticists have recently found cyclic changes in certain genes that may act as possible mechanisms underlying the internal pacemaker. This hypothesis was supported by the demonstration that a number of species required certain genes for normal circadian function to occur. Researchers produced many random mutations into the DNAs of the fruit fly, *Drosophila melanogaster*, until they found rhythm abnormalities. This 'mutant exploration' approach identified circadian clock mutants, which they called period (per) and frequency (frq, pronounced 'freak'). Using a similar process, the first mouse circadian mutation was found and called 'Clock' (see King & Takahashi, 2000).

**Exam Hint:**

Evaluation that was mentioned in relation to the circadian rhythms section can be used as evaluation of endogenous pacemakers. In addition, you should mention that much of the research on endogenous pacemakers has taken place with either non-human animals or brain-damaged patients. Such evidence is strong but it might be claimed that it's not so easily generalised to the wider population.

## Exogenous zeitgebers

An important characteristic of circadian rhythms is their ability to be synchronised by exogenous zeitgebers (external time cues) such as the light–dark cycle. Thus, although we have seen (above) that rhythms can persist in the absence of exogenous zeitgebers, normally such cues are present and the rhythms align to them. Accordingly, if a shift in external cues occurs (e.g., following travel across time zones), the rhythms become aligned to the new cues. This alignment process is called *entrainment*.

### LIGHT

- Light is the dominant environmental time cue for circadian clocks. This was not immediately recognised. As seen above, Aschoff *et al.* (1975) in their isolation studies later reported that the 'light–dark cycle seems to be of little importance for the entrainment of human circadian rhythms' (page 235). Again, as noted above, Czeisler *et al.* (1999) found out that this was in fact wrong and that the presence of strong artificial light had affected Aschoff's particpants' circadian rhythms.

A fascinating study by Campbell and Murphy (1998) is often reported as another study which demonstrates the importance of the light zeitgeber, but this time involved light that enters not through the eyes, but through the knees! Campbell and Murphy monitored the body temperatures of 15 volunteers who slept in a lab. The male and female participants were woken at different times and a light pad was shone on the back of their knees. The participants' circadian rhythms fluctuated by as much as three hours away from their normal cycle, depending on the time the light was given. The back of the knee was chosen since light applied here would not reach the participants' eyes and the blood vessels here are very near the surface. The results suggested that humans do not rely solely on the light that enters the eyes and that blood may be the messenger that carries the light signal from skin to the brain.

- Although the light–dark cycle clearly is the major zeitgeber for almost all organisms, other factors – such as social interactions, activity or exercise, and even temperature – also can modulate a cycle's phase.

### Evaluation of endogenous pacemakers and exogenous zeitgebers

- The persistence of rhythms in the absence of a dark–light cycle or other exogenous time signal (i.e. a zeitgeber) clearly seems to indicate the existence of some kind of internal time-keeping mechanism, or biological clock. However, some investigators have pointed out that the persistence of rhythmicity does not necessarily exclude the possibility that other, uncontrolled cycles generated by the Earth's revolution on its axis might be driving the rhythm (see Aschoff, 1960).
- However, the findings of Murphy and Campbell should be treated with caution. Firstly, phototransduction via the circulatory system has never been demonstrated in another organism. Researchers have failed to replicate these findings. It was suggested that, despite precautions, participants were exposed to low levels of light reaching their eyes, and even Campbell and Murphy have failed to replicate their study with sleeping participants. Despite such criticisms, there are patents pending for 'knee light pads' to help executives combat the effects of jet lag!

## The consequences of disrupting biological rhythms

- As we've seen, the synchrony of an organism with both endogenous pacemakers and exogenous zeitgebers is critical to its wellbeing and survival; without this an animal may be led into dangerous situations. For example, if a nocturnal rodent were to venture from its burrow during broad daylight, the rodent would be exceptionally easy prey for other animals. In humans, a lack of synchrony within the environment might lead to health problems in the individual, such as those associated with jet lag, shift work, and the accompanying sleep loss (e.g. impaired cognitive function, altered hormonal function and gastrointestinal complaints).

### SHIFT WORK

- Most animals follow the messages from their SCN and let it determine their circadian rhythms. Humans, however, always like to be different and often try to disobey their 'internal clock' by living a 24-hour lifestyle. The consequences of the increasing trend towards a 24/7 world are still unknown. However, the list of accidents blamed on the effects of incorrect decisions made as a result of a lack of sleep is worrying. These include the Three Mile Island and Chernobyl nuclear accidents, the Challenger Space Disaster and the Exxon Valdez oil spill. In addition, workers on night shifts have significantly higher rates of heart disease and diseases of the digestive system. It's estimated that approximately 20% of shift workers report falling asleep during work, which increases the risk of industrial accidents and decreases productivity. Ironically, shift work can diminish the economic gain it is designed to create.
- Nearly 20% of employees in industrialised countries are employed in shift work, which requires a drastic change to their sleep–wake cycles. Put simply, shift workers don't get enough sleep. Night-time shifts affect the body's natural wake–sleep pattern. This makes it difficult to stay awake during the night and difficult to sleep during the day. Daytime sleep may also be of a different quality to night-time sleep. This chronic lack of sleep harms a person's health, on-the-job safety, task

performance, memory and mood, as well as having social costs related to time spent with family and friends who follow more usual sleep–wake cycles.

There are two types of shift work:

- non-fluctuating: where workers work an unconventional but constant shift, such as 11 p.m. to 7 a.m. and

- fluctuating: where workers work eight-hour shifts (typically) that change continuously. Three different rotating eight-hour shifts enable a 'round-the-clock' operation to occur. The most common ones are 7 a.m.–3 p.m., 3 p.m.–11 p.m. and 11 p.m.–7 a.m.

The Challenger Space Disaster: It's claimed that the decision to launch was made in the early hours of the morning, when people were at their most tired.

- Each of these types of shift work produces its own set of effects. In non-fluctuating shift work, the shift in circadian rhythm remains constant once the body adapts to it. Resynchronisation may take a while, but it is possible. However, many shift workers frequently change shifts, thus intensifying the severity of circadian rhythm disturbance.

- In shift-work change, exogenous zeitgebers such as day-time and night-time are never permanently synchronised with the start and end of shifts. This means that for shift workers the sleep–wake cycle is governed by consistently mistimed circadian rhythm and alternating external cues.

- For example, a person may work the night shift for five nights in a row, followed by two days off. During the two days off, the person resumes a normal day-time (diurnal) activity with family or friends. This disrupts the person's previously adjusted circadian rhythm, and he or she must re-adjust their sleep–wake pattern when they go back to work. Without a constant pattern, biological rhythms remain continually out of synch.

- Czeisler et al. (1982) studied shift workers and found that the most preferable fluctuating shift pattern is one that rotates every 21 days in a forwards direction. This meant that workers moved to a schedule that began later in the day (phase delay) rather than earlier in the day (phase advance.) Czeisler et al. argued that a phase delay rotation pattern brings increased benefits to workers and employers, such as health improvement, fewer accidents and more production.

## JET LAG

- Jet lag (or desynchronosis), is a temporary condition that can be experienced as a result of air travel across several time zones in a short period of time. This causes the traveller's internal biological clock to be out of sync with the external environment. People experiencing jet lag have a difficult time maintaining their internal, routine sleep–wake pattern in their new location, because exogenous zeitgebers, like sunshine and local timetables, dictate a different pattern. For instance, if you fly from New York to Paris, you 'lose' hours, according to your body's clock. You'll feel tired when you get up in the morning because your body clock is telling you that it's still night-time. It might take several days for your body's rhythm to acclimatise to the new time.

- The main symptoms of jet lag are fatigue and insomnia but it can also involve anxiety, constipation or diarrhoea, dehydration, sweating and an increased susceptibility to illness.

- Passengers flying north or south in the same time zone usually don't experience jetlag since they remain in the same time zones. Passengers flying east seem to experience the greatest number of problems since they lose time. Passengers flying west still experience jet lag but seem to cope with it more easily since they gain time.

> **Specification Hint:** The Specification mentions 'the consequences of disrupting biological rhythms (e.g. shift work, jet lag)'. Since 'rhythms' here is *plural*, you need to know a minimum of two rhythms. Remember, the emphasis here is on rhythms rather than the processes that disrupt these rhythms. In addition to shiftwork, we'll deal with jet lag (which disrupts mainly circadian rhythms) *and* SAD (which disrupts both circadian and infradian rhythms), and sleep deprivation studies (e.g. Randy Gardner, Jouvet: see below) which have demonstrated the effects of circadian and ultradian rhythm disruption.

## DELAYED SLEEP PHASE SYNDROME (DSPS)

- Delayed sleep phase syndrome (DSPS) also results from a disturbance between the patient's internal biological clock and the external environment. However, although the effects are similar to jet lag, the desynchronisation isn't caused by travel or a change in external zeitgebers. Instead,

**Table 10.1** Summary table of potential essay questions

| Biological rhythms sub-section Essay Planner | | |
|---|---|---|
| | | **Content** |
| Research into: | 1. Biological rhythms<br>2. Circadian rhythms<br><br>3. Infradian rhythms<br><br>4. Ultradian rhythms | • Any from 2, 3 or 4 below<br>• TUS (Siffre, 1972)<br>• SAD (Terman *et al.*, 1998)<br>• MMSS (McClintock 1971; Stern & McClintock, 1998)<br>• SAD (Terman *et al.*, 1998)<br>• RADS (Dement & Kleitman, 1957)<br>• CODS (Dement & Wolpert, 1958) |
| Endogenous pacemakers and exogenous zeitgebers (Warning: You *could* be asked a question about either endogenous or exogenous factors on their own) | 5. Biological rhythms<br>6. Circadian rhythms<br><br><br>7. Infradian rhythms<br><br><br><br>8. Ultradian rhythms | • Any from 6, 7 or 8 below<br>• SCN, pineal gland, melatonin, molecular genes (endogenous)<br>• Light, SAD (exogenous)<br>• Melatonin seasonal variations<br>• SCN and breeding (hamsters) (endogenous)<br>• SAD, pheromones on menstrual cycle (exogenous)<br>• Hormones, locus coeruleus, age factors (endogenous)<br>• Sleep deprivation, shift work, jet lag (exogenous) |
| Consequences of disrupting biological rhythms | 9. Biological rhythms | • Shift work<br>• Jet lag<br>• SAD<br>• Delayed sleep phase syndrome<br>• Sleep deprivation studies |

DSPS is caused by a person having an internal biological rhythm that's out of phase with their environment. Typically, sufferers find it hard to go to bed before 2 a.m. and then have difficulty waking until 10 a.m. Patients who suffer from DSPS are able to get plentiful sleep; it's just postponed. Unfortunately, such a sleep–wake cycle affects various aspects of their lives such as work and family commitments. Such 'night owls' often find it difficult to meet the expectations of society and struggle to maintain jobs and friendships. DSPS is estimated to affect 7% of teenagers and to be the cause in 10% of chronic insomnia cases.

> **Specification Hint:** You need to know a minimum of *two* theories of the function of sleep (these must include the ecological and restorative theories) and at least *two* research studies associated with each.

**Exam Hint:**

If you're asked a questi[on] the 'consequences of [dis]rupting biological rhy[thms] you could include [infor]mation on SAD and stat[e] this affects both circ[adian] and circannual rhythm[s] page 238) and ma[terial] drawn from sleep [depri]vation studies (see [page] 251) would also be rel[evant] Such studies demon[strate] the consequences of [dis]rupting ultradian rhyth[ms]

# Sleep

**Theories and research studies relating to the evolution and functions of sleep, including ecological (e.g. Meddis; Webb) and restoration (e.g. Oswald; Horne) accounts.**

'If the many hours of sleep accomplish nothing, it is the greatest mistake man has ever made' (Rechtshaffen, 1999).

**Exam Hint:**

This first sub-sectio[n on] Biological rhythms [lends] itself to numerous pos[sible] exam questions. Table[s] will help to clarify v[what] questions might be a[sked] and the appro[priate] material that you coul[d use] to answer the question[s]

- Sleep is one of the last complex behaviours the exact purpose of which remains unclear. All mammals and birds sleep, and fish, reptiles and amphibians exhibit periods of quiet restfulness that we might call sleep. Since sleep is so common in the animal kingdom, it strongly suggests that it must perform some critical function. Unfortunately, scientists do not agree what that function is, and the exact purpose of sleep remains an enigma. There are countless theories proposed, but the two best-known ones are the restoration (or repair) theory and the ecological (or evolutionary) theory.

### RESTORATION AND REPAIR (R & R) THEORY OF SLEEP

- One theory of sleep is that it helps to reverse and/or restore biochemical and/or physiological processes that are progressively degraded during the day. In essence, it's suggested that being awake disrupts the homeostasis of the body in some way and sleep is required to restore it. Oswald (1980) suggested that:
  - REM sleep helps the brain to recover, hence the high levels of brain activity during REM sleep
  - slow wave sleep (mainly Stage 4) helps with body repair. There are increased levels of growth hormone during SWS.
- Many restorative processes, such as digestion, removal of waste products and protein synthesis, do indeed occur during sleep (Adam, 1980). However, many of these processes also occur during waking and some occur more so during the day. Horne (1988) concluded that sleep does not provide any repair process in humans, except for the brain. Horne referred to 'core sleep' which he believed is essential for restoration, whereas other types of sleep he called 'optional sleep' whose main purpose is for energy conservation. Stern and Morgane (1974) believe that REM sleep serves the function of allowing the brain to replenish neurotransmitters which have been used during the day. Hartmann (1973) has also suggested that REM sleep is a time for synthesising noradrenaline and dopamine to compensate for the amount used during the day.

## RESEARCH STUDIES

One way to find out how important sleep is for both brain and body restoration is to examine the effects of sleep deprivation. You should use any of the human or animal studies of total or partial sleep deprivation in the section on pages 251–254.

 **Evaluation of R & R theory**

✓ **Cognitive sense:** This restorative view of sleep function seems to make sense, especially in light of the widespread detrimental psychological and behavioural effects that we all experience with loss of sleep.

✓ **Infant REM sleep:** Babies and infants spend a far higher proportion of the day sleeping (newborns up to 18 hours), and up to 50% of this time is spent in REM sleep. It's suggested that they need this sleep to help with synaptic (brain) growth.

✓•✗ **Increased growth hormone:** Oswald (1980) proposed that protein synthesis is dependent on growth hormones that are secreted during the delta waves of slow wave sleep. However, this is not supported by the finding of a decrease rather than increase in protein synthesis of the whole body during sleep in humans. This decrease in protein synthesis is attributed to sleep being a period of overnight fasting, since protein synthesis remains constant when subjects are fed continuously via intragastric tubes throughout the 24-hour period.

✓ **Brain trauma:** Patients who have suffered brain trauma through either injury or electro-convulsive therapy spend an increased amount of time in REM sleep. Again, it's suggested that the increased blood flow during REM sleep might help in brain repair and restoration.

✓•✗ **REM rebound and length of sleep:** Sleep deprivation studies have shown that participants do make up a small proportion of the hours that they have lost on previous nights. However, they do not make up all the hours that they have lost. If sleep was so vital for repair and restoration, a far greater proportion might be expected on subsequent nights. (See total and partial sleep deprivation studies below). The REM rebound effect, whereby participants in sleep deprivation studies spend longer in REM sleep on subsequent nights, also suggests that REM sleep is particularly important to restore the brain processes. REM may help the recovery and manufacture of chemicals necessary for brain restoration.

✗ **Exercise studies:** Studies into the effects of exercise on subsequent sleep tend not to support the restoration theory. According to the theory, a marked increase in the amount of sleep would be predicted after sustained, intense physical exercise. Shapiro *et al.* (1981) examined runners who had completed a 57-mile race and found that they slept an average of only 90 minutes longer on two subsequent nights, with slightly increased levels of SWS. However, most studies of this type showed no effects on post-exercise sleep. In those studies that did show an enhancement of NREM sleep, it was concluded that the NREM sleep was a consequence of increased body temperature produced by the heating effects of the exercise. Moreover, physically-fit individuals do not have longer sleep durations or more NREM sleep than the unfit.

✗ **Non-human animal evidence:** The restorative theory

Long-distance runners have very little extra sleep on subsequent nights. Such evidence provides scant support for the restoration theory.

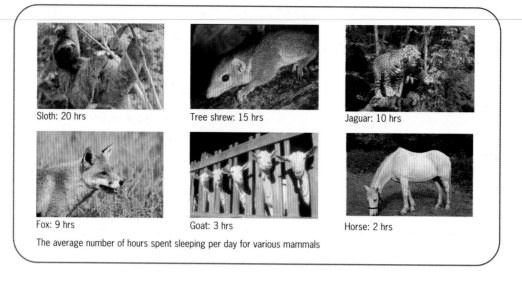

Sloth: 20 hrs

Tree shrew: 15 hrs

Jaguar: 10 hrs

Fox: 9 hrs

Goat: 3 hrs

Horse: 2 hrs

The average number of hours spent sleeping per day for various mammals

suggests that animals should differ in their sleep needs depending on the amount of energy they expend during the day. Evidence does not support this and there appears to be no correlation between a species's sleep time and energy levels. For example, giant sloths appear to expend little energy each day and spend roughly 20 hours per day sleeping.

## Ecological (or evolutionary) theory (ET) of sleep

- According to the ET of sleep, the function of sleep is similar to that of hibernation. The purpose of hibernation is to conserve energy when the environment is hostile. Similarly, the purpose of sleep is to force us to conserve energy when we would not be very efficient and to protect us at night when we might be vulnerable to predators. Sleep is thus an evolutionary-stable strategy which increases individual and, in turn, species survival. The ET predicts that animal species should vary in their sleep needs depending on how much time they need to search for food each day and how safe they are from predators when they sleep (see below).
- Therefore animals preyed upon, such as herbivores, should sleep more than carnivores since sleep would protect them from predation. However, in reality, herbivores tend to sleep much less (Oswald, 1980). The theory accounts for this seeming discrepancy with the suggestion that metabolic differences affect sleep levels. Predators or carnivores eat occasional, large meals whereas herbivores have to graze for long periods to gain sufficient energy and therefore sleep for less time. However, it still makes ecological sense for herbivores to sleep and remain inconspicuous when grazing is difficult (e.g. at night) (Green, 1987).
- Another aspect of the ecological theory suggests that the size of an animal is also related to total sleep time. Animals with high metabolic rates (e.g. shrews) expend a lot of energy and thus need more time for energy conservation and hence sleep for relatively long periods each day. Larger animals with slower metabolic rates (e.g. horses, goats) therefore sleep less. Horne (1978) proposed that energy conservation is a major function of sleep in smaller mammals such as rodents.
- For humans, in our evolutionary history, it was sensible to sleep at night when we weren't able to see to gather food and could possibly become prey for other animals. Those humans who slept in caves during the dark also conserved their energies for hunting during the day. Thus sleep is an evolutionary hangover that no longer serves much purpose.

# EXAM tips BOX

**Compare and contrast *two* theories of sleep. (24 marks)**
**(30 mins) (600 words minimum)**

'Compare and contrast' questions are far more challenging than the more usual 'describe and evaluate' format since you not only have to be able to describe two theories but also state in what ways they might be similar and in what ways they might be different.

*This essay can be split up into THREE sections. The first two could be about 150 words long (6 marks each) and the last about 300 words (12 marks).*

**Section 1:** You need to **outline** the Restoration and Repair (R & R) theory of sleep.      **A01**

**Section 2:** You need to **outline** the ecological theory (ET) of sleep.      **A01**

**Section 3:** You need to **analyse** and **evaluate** both the R & R and ET of sleep. These could be dealt with separately but it's probably better to combine them since you want to be discussing the relative merits of each in comparison with one another.      **A02**

**Note that in *every* section you must continually compare and contrast whichever theory or evaluative point you are making with the other theory.**

*Try to answer this question yourself. There's a sample essay on page 266 with which you can compare your essay.*

##  Evaluation of ET

✓ **Non-human animal evidence:** The ecological theory correctly predicts that the daily sleep time of many species is related to how vulnerable they are while asleep, how much time they must spend to feed themselves and their metabolic rates. For example, zebras sleep only two or three hours per day and graze almost continuously, whereas lions can sleep for as long as 20 hours after a kill.

✓ **Sleep deprivation studies:** These suggest that we can cope with very little sleep. There are case studies of individuals who sleep as little as one to two hours per night, seemingly with no adverse effects. Studies such as these tend to support the 'evolutionary hangover' theory of sleep.

✓•✗ **Cognitive sense?** It makes sense to suggest that sleep may have evolved to reduce the danger of predation for prey animals. However, it's not so clear why so complex a behaviour as sleep should have evolved to do this. Simple behavioural inactivity would serve the same purpose. Indeed, many animals freeze and 'play dead' when confronted by predators.

✗ **More vulnerable in sleep?** Some scientists have suggested that animals who are preyed upon may be more vulnerable to predators when asleep, given their decreased sensitivity to external stimuli. According to this view, sleep would not be an adaptive response to avoid predation. Snoring is also a difficult phenomenon to explain with this theory, since it's likely to make us more vulnerable to predation by drawing attention to ourselves sleeping (Bentley, 2000).

## The implications of findings from studies of sleep deprivation for such theories

- Everyone at some time will have experienced a certain degree of sleep deprivation and will therefore know some of its effects. Studies of sleep deprivation are helpful in order to understand the function(s) of sleep, and a greater understanding might benefit professionals who operate in sleep-deprived situations, such as shift workers, airline pilots, medics, long-distance lorry drivers and personnel in the armed forces. For example, research might identify how much sleep is needed and what kinds of sleep are most important.
- Many questions arise when studying sleep deprivation effects. 'Total sleep deprivation' refers to the situation where animals and humans are deprived of all sleep whereas 'partial sleep deprivation'

refers to the situation where humans and animals are deprived of certain types of sleep, typically REM sleep.

## TOTAL SLEEP DEPRIVATION STUDIES

### Randy Gardner (Gulevich, Dement & Johnson, 1966)

In 1965, as part of a science project, a schoolboy called Randy Gardner decided to try to break the then world record of 260 hours of wakefulness. Dement read about this in the newspaper and decided to collect some useful data during the attempt. Without the use of any stimulants (even coffee), Gardner stayed awake for exactly 264 hours 12 minutes. He did suffer the occasional hallucination, some ataxia (inability to perform co-ordinated movements), speech difficulty, visual deficits and some irritability. He was monitored closely by doctors after his ordeal and was very soon back to normal. After his sleep deprivation, Randy slept for 14 hours and very soon returned to his normal eight-hour pattern. In all, there were 67 hours of sleep which he did not 'make up'. However, the percentage of recovery sleep varied across the stages. He made up only about 7% of Stages 1 and 2, in contrast to 68% of Stage 4 sleep and 53% of REM sleep. The phenomenon whereby 'lost' REM sleep is recovered on subsequent nights is called 'REM rebound'. All in all, only 24% of total sleep loss was recovered. These findings suggest that Stage 4 and REM sleep are more important than the other stages (see Rolls, 2005, for further details).

## PARTIAL SLEEP DEPRIVATION STUDIES

### REM Sleep deprivation studies (Dement, 1960)

Eight volunteers agreed to spend a week in a sleep laboratory being deprived of REM sleep. Whenever their EEG and eye movements indicated they were entering REM sleep, they were woken up and kept awake for a few minutes. The volunteers were then allowed to go back to sleep until they entered REM sleep again. Over the course of the nights, the participants had to be woken more and more frequently. On the first night, they were woken an average of 12 times but by the last night this figure had increased to 26. During this period, participants reported mild personality changes such as irritability, anxiety and impaired concentration. When the participants were allowed to sleep normally, there was a 10% increase in the amount of time spent in REM sleep. Again, this study suggests that REM sleep is a particularly important stage of sleep.

 Evaluation

✓ **Similar findings:** Many other studies involving human participants have found similar results. Horne (1978) reviewed many studies and found little evidence that sleep deprivation either interferes with physical exercise or causes physical illness or stress. Such findings don't comprehensively support the R & R theory of sleep.

✗ **Case studies:** Many sleep-deprivation studies involve very small sample sizes and, in the case of Randy Gardner, just one participant. It's difficult to generalise findings from individual case studies although many psychologists would, nevertheless, support these findings.

✗ **Confounding variables:** There are a number of problems and confounding factors in sleep-deprivation experiments. For instance, an understanding of what occurs during sleep deprivation doesn't mean we can imply the functions of sleep. For example, there may be some important compensatory mechanism that obscures the effect of sleep deprivation.

**✗ Methodology?** Sleep-deprivation experiments are not double-blind. Participants are always aware that they're taking part in a study and this may bias results in terms of demand characteristics. Bentley (2000) reports that Dement (1960) accepted that some of his observations may have been the result of experimenter effects – he expected to see disturbances in behaviour because of lack of REM sleep and was biased in his observations. A double-blind technique could have overcome such problems. In addition, being constantly monitored may lead to an increase in stress for sleep-deprived participants. Furthermore, motivation is likely to be an important factor in people's ability to cope with a lack of sleep and participants in such experiments are likely to be highly motivated. It should also be noted that deprivation experiments typically involve more than just a loss of sleep. Usual daily routines such as work and free time are suspended and this may make results difficult to generalise to a more realistic situation.

**Future research:** Molecular biologists also study the effects of over-expressing specific genes. In the sleep research field, very few studies have been carried out to study the effects of an excess of sleep but if you hear about one, please let the authors know so we can volunteer!

## Animal studies

### TOTAL SLEEP DEPRIVATION STUDY

**Key study**

### RECHTSCHAFFEN'S RAT EXPERIMENTS (RRE) (1989)

● Rechtschaffen devised a procedure whereby a rat was placed on a turntable that rotated whenever its EEG record indicated that it was falling asleep. The turntable was placed above water which ensured that the rat had to walk in order to stop itself falling in the water. This was the experimental rat. The second rat was a 'yoked-control' rat which was forced to do the same exercise as the experimental rat but which could fall asleep on its own when the experimental rat was awake (the turntable did not revolve when the experimental rat was awake) (see Figure 10.5). This procedure ensured that both rats did the same exercise but that the experimental rat slept for only 13% of its usual sleep time and the control slept for 69% of its usual sleep time.

● The experimental rats showed an immediate decline. They appeared weak, stopped grooming and became weak and uncoordinated. Although they continued to eat, they lost weight because of a marked increase in metabolic rate. Most of the experimental rats died between 21 and 33 days later. In contrast, the control rats, although they had lost some weight, appeared to be generally healthy.

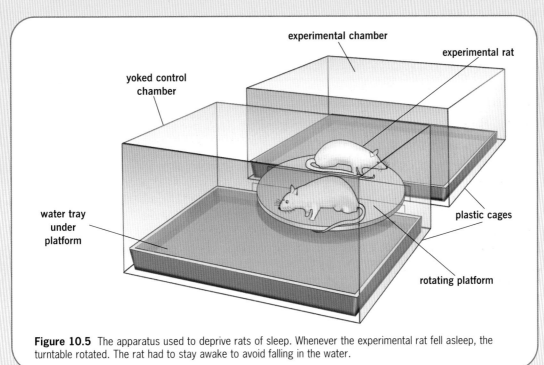

**Figure 10.5** The apparatus used to deprive rats of sleep. Whenever the experimental rat fell asleep, the turntable rotated. The rat had to stay awake to avoid falling in the water.

From Carlson, N.R., *Physiology of Behavior*, 8/e. Ally and Bacon, Boston MA. © 2004 by Pearson Education. Reprinted by permission of the publisher.

**Key study**

## FLOWERPOT CAT STUDIES (FCS) (JOUVET, 1967)

Cats have been used to examine the effects of partial sleep deprivation specifically when the animals are deprived of REM sleep. This was done using an ingenious, but cruel, method whereby cats were placed on tiny islands (upturned flowerpots) surrounded by water. When a cat enters REM sleep their postural muscles relax. This meant that the cats lost balance and fell into the water. This woke them up and they climbed back onto the flowerpots and started the sleep stage process all over again. The cats could go through all the stages of sleep except REM sleep. Interestingly, the cats became conditioned, even while asleep, to wake up when they went into REM sleep and didn't have to fall into the water each time. The cats become disturbed very quickly and died after an average of about 35 days.

 Evaluation of animal studies

**✗ Unethical:** The methods used to keep the animals awake are unethical. Many animal studies continue until the animal dies.

**✗•✓ Results cannot be generalised to humans:** Because animals cannot be persuaded to stay awake voluntarily, various methods have to be used to keep them awake. These methods usually involve causing some distress to the animal and it's claimed that it's stress that leads to the results shown, not the effect of sleep deprivation alone. In addition, human volunteers know that the experiment will end and they will soon be allowed to sleep. In contrast, animals know only that they're in an unfriendly, stressful situation and have no knowledge that the ordeal will end (Carlson, 2001). Furthermore, the physiological characteristics of animals (e.g. metabolic requirements) make them more susceptible to the damaging effects of a lack of sleep. Despite these criticisms, such studies appear to support the R & R theory of sleep.

### CONCLUSION

The sheer number of hypotheses put forward to explain the function of sleep illustrates the degree of our ignorance. From studies such as those outlined above, sleep does appear to be necessary and widespread in all animals. Psychologists have tried to identify the correct amount of sleep required for normal functioning. However, no clear pattern has emerged. There's a considerable variation in the amount of sleep reported by individuals. There appears to be no correlation between the amount of sleep and performance or intelligence. Thomas Edison and Margaret Thatcher both slept for short periods each night whereas Albert Einstein was a long sleeper. Take your pick!

# Dreaming

## Research findings relating to the nature of dreams (e.g. content, duration, relationship with the stages of sleep)

- We've already dealt with some studies and findings that relate to the nature of dreams. These include Jouvet's Flowerpot Cat studies in 1967, concerned with REM deprivation, and Dement and Wolpert's (CODS) study. The way that REM sleep fits into the 90-minute ultradian sleep rhythm and the accompanying stages of sleep has also been dealt with on pages 239–240. In terms of the content of dreams, you could use any of the theories of dreams that follow.
- It's worth pointing out that although a strong correlation between dreaming and REM sleep has been extensively demonstrated by many researchers, this does not mean that dreaming cannot occur during other sleep stages. There may be other brain areas involved in dreaming. Evidence for this comes from the fact that some dreamers do not show accompanying REM and *vice versa*.

## Theories of the functions of dreaming, including neurobiological (e.g. Hobson & McCarley; Crick & Mitchison) and psychological (e.g. Freud; Webb & Cartwright) accounts

As with sleep, there are a number of competing explanations as to why we dream. They can be summarised into two main types: neurobiological and psychological explanations. As their names suggest, neurobiological theories emphasise the role of bodily, physical processes whereas psychological theories emphasise the psychological importance of dreams.

### Neurobiological theories of dreaming

#### THE ACTIVATION–SYNTHESIS (A–S) HYPOTHESIS (HOBSON & MCCARLEY, 1977; HOBSON, 1989, 1994)

- Hobson and McCarley argued that dreams are responses to the neurophysiological events of the sleeping brain. According to their A–S Hypothesis, dreaming is caused physiologically by a 'dream state generator' located in the brain stem. It's 'on' during REM sleep, while all sensory input and motor output are blocked, and the neurons in the cerebral cortex are activated by random impulses that generate sensory information within the nervous system. Put simply, this means that the forebrain interprets the brain activity (activation) and produces it as a dream (synthesis). Basically, the brain is telling the person what is happening to the brain in code, or symbolised, in the dream. For example, if the motor system fires in such a way as to suggest running movements then this is interpreted as a dream that you are being chased.
- Originally there was no explanation given as to why the brain should try to make sense of random neural activity, although recently it's been suggested that it may play a part in memory consolidation (Hobson, 1994) by acting and testing out our brain circuits in sleep.
- Hobson and McCarley claim that in the construction of a dream 'the forebrain may be making the best of a bad job in producing even a partially coherent dream imagery from the relatively noisy signals sent up to it from the brain stem'. This implies that dreams have no emotional content since they're triggered only by sensory and motor aspects of bodily activity.

> **Specification Hint:** You need to know *two* neurobiological and *two* psychological theories of dreaming. You could, of course, be asked about one, so we've included more detail on the Activation–Synthesis Hypothesis (Hobson & McCarley, 1977) and Freud's theory of dreams. The examiners cannot specifically name the theory or theories which they want you to discuss since they're only given as e.g.s in the Specification

### ✗✓ Evaluation of the A–S Hypothesis

✓ **Sensory input and dream content:** Hobson claims that the often bizarre nature of dreams in terms of their visual imagery, emotional content and the frequent shifts of attention can be explained by the random sensory inputs that generate them. For example, people often report paralysis in dreams and this is supported by the fact that our muscles are relaxed in REM sleep (see also Jouvet Flowerpot Cat study above).

✓ The neurons responsible for taste and smell don't fire during sleep and, as predicted by the hypothesis, dreams don't contain smells or tastes.

✓ **External stimuli:** Dement and Wolpert (1958) showed that dreamers do incorporate external stimuli into their dreams, by spraying water onto their participants' sleeping faces. Dreamers incorporated water into their dreams. This suggests that other stimuli (external or internal) may affect the content of the dreams.

✓ **Dream regularity and occurrence:** Hobson and McCarley also claim that support for this hypothesis comes from the predictable regularity that is observed in the triggering of a dream state. They stress that 'the motivating force for dreaming is not *psychological* but *physiological* since the time of occurrence and duration of dreaming sleep are quite constant, suggesting a preprogrammed, neurally determined genesis'. Put simply, if dreams were caused psychologically, we'd expect a greater variety in occurrence and length of dreams.

✓ Physiological evidence: Based on our knowledge of brain physiology and PET scans of the dreaming brain, there's no doubt that the Activation–Synthesis Model is right by dismissing the Freudian notion that dreams are always instigated by a wish.

✗ Eloquent dreams: However, various evidence certainly suggests that dreaming is more than 'genetically determined'. Also, at some times we can have dreams with eloquently constructed story lines, and they actually can influence our behaviour. A famous example of this is reported by Friedrich August von Kekule who had a dream of whirling snakes and as a direct result of this dream discovered the structure of benzene – the organic chemical compound made up of a ring of carbon atoms. He reported the dream as follows:

> 'I turned my chair to the fire [after having worked on the problem for some time] and dozed. Again the atoms were gamboling before my eyes. This time the smaller groups kept modestly to the background. My mental eye, rendered more acute by repeated vision of this kind, could not distinguish larger structures, of manifold conformation; long rows, sometimes more closely fitted together; all twining and twisting in snakelike motion. But look! What was that? One of the snakes had seized hold of its own tail, and the form whirled mockingly before my eyes. As if by a flash of lighting I awoke ... Let us learn to dream, gentlemen.'
> (Weisberg, 1992)

✗ Dream coherence: People who recall their dreams would argue that dreams are often more coherent than suggested by Hobson and McCarley's hypothesis. Dreams can not only be coherent; they can be entertaining, stimulating and enjoyable! Can they really simply be the result of the random firings of electrical activity?

✗ Lucid dreaming: This is the phenomenon whereby people direct the action of their dreams. It's rare but some people are aware that they're dreaming and can deliberately direct their dream. Again, this suggests that not all dreams are the result of random firings from the brain stem.

✗•✓ Over-stated claims? McCarley and Hobson may have shown that dreams are caused by activity in the brain stem but this does not prove that wishes do not play a part in dreaming as Freud suggested. Hobson adds: 'Psychoanalysts want people to believe that they can interpret dreams and discover deep-seated meanings that are at the root of the dream process. I just don't think there is any scientific reason to believe that.' Psychoanalysts now suggest that wishes exploit – but do not cause – dreams.

✓ Furthered debate: The Activation–Synthesis Hypothesis caused an amazing amount of controversy on publication. Dream researchers, therapists and dream workers who had spent lifetimes putting dreams to practical applications could not accept that 'dreams were after all merely the senseless, random accompaniment of the autonomous electrical activity of the sleeping Central Nervous System'.

✗ One-way street: Among the psychophysiologically-minded dream researchers a major criticism of the Activation–Synthesis Model was that it was essentially a one-way street, allowing traffic to proceed only upward from brainstem to forebrain (from lower mental function to higher mental function). But the way the brain is actually put together would require a two-way street, allowing forebrain control of brain stem activation, and therefore allowing higher cortical functions such as thinking and deliberate action to influence the dream.

# CRICK & MITCHISON'S REVERSE THEORY OF LEARNING (RTOL) (1983)

Francis Crick (one of the team that cracked DNA) and Graeme Mitchison have argued that the brain's memory systems are easily overloaded and that humans experience REM sleep in order to get rid of cognitive debris. In other words, dreams are a mechanism to clear the brain of unnecessary, even harmful, memories. This theory was called 'reverse learning' since, as they put it, 'we dream to forget'.

The theory has several basic hypotheses:

The spiny anteater: an abnormally large cortex for its size. Is this because they don't dream and cannot discard unwanted information?

- the first is that the cerebral cortex as a complex network of neurons must form unwanted or mistaken connections
- the second is that these unwanted or parasitic connections may be detected and 'cleaned' during REM sleep. This process is described as the opposite (or reverse) of learning
- Without this 'unlearning' process our cortex would not function so efficiently and we would need far larger brains to perform the same tasks.

According to RToL, we should not try to recall our dreams. Crick and Mitchison suggest that dream recall might have detrimental effects and lead to disturbances, hallucinations and delusions.

## Evaluation of Reverse Theory of Learning (RToL)

✓ **Animal evidence:** There are two species who do not seem to have REM sleep. These are the echidna (spiny anteater) and two types of dolphin. According to the reverse learning theory they would need unusually large cortexes and that is indeed, what the evidence shows.

✗ **How is waste material selected?:** It's not clear how the brain chooses which material to discard in dreams. It still has to work out what is useful and what is useless and this is not fully explained in the theory.

✗ **Dream recall problems:** There's no evidence that remembering one's dreams has any effect on subsequent learning ability. People who remember almost all their dreams don't seem any more prone to 'hallucinations, delusions and obsessions' than are people who always forget their dreams.

✗ **Infant REM sleep:** RToL doesn't readily explain why newborns and foetuses have such a great proportion of REM sleep. Do they really have so much to unlearn?

✗ **No direct evidence:** There's absolutely no direct evidence for 'unlearning' during REM. Indeed, there's no evidence for 'unlearning' of *any* kind in any state, in any living organism, anywhere. 'Unlearning' appears to exist only as a hypothetical concept.

## Psychological theories of dreaming

### FREUD'S THEORY OF DREAMS

- Freud believed that dreams are the guardians of sleep. During the night, the mind protects the dreamer from being disturbed by reacting to external stimuli (noise, temperature, light and so on) and internal stimuli (emotions, fears, dissatisfaction, desires, previous day's activity) by manufacturing dreams.

- Freud's work was really concerned with internal stimuli. Essentially, for a person to continue to sleep undisturbed; strong negative emotions, forbidden thoughts and unconscious desires have to be disguised or censored in some form or another. Otherwise, confronted by these, the dreamer would become distressed and they would eventually wake up. Therefore the dream, if understood correctly, could lead to a greater understanding of the dreamer's subconscious. Dreams, he argued, provide a royal road to the understanding of the unconscious.

Freud believed a dream was composed of two parts:

- the **manifest content** refers to what the dreamer would recall on awakening. This is what they would describe as happening in the dream. Freud believed that the manifest content had no meaning; it was simply a disguised representation of the true thought underlying the dream
- the **latent content** is the true, but hidden, meaning of the dream. It involves the forbidden thoughts and the unconscious desires.

'Dream work' is the process whereby the latent content is disguised and transformed into the manifest content. This can occur in several ways, including:

- **condensation:** where a number of thoughts or wishes are combined into one dream
- **displacement:** the transference of emotion or desire toward a meaningless or unrelated object or person rather than the intended person or object
- **symbolism:** where objects in a dream are camouflaged in symbols. An image of a similar-sounding word or a similar-looking object may be used. Freud believed that many dream symbols possessed sexual meanings. For example, tree trunks, sticks (including matchsticks!), guns and so on were phallic symbols representing the penis, whereas boxes, cupboards, staircases, ovens and so on represented female genitalia.
- Freud used the method of 'dream analysis' to discover the latent content of dreams. He would ask patients to describe a dream as accurately as possible (the manifest content). They would then be told to form as many associations with the dream as they could. They had to report all their uncensored thoughts that related to the dream. The idea being that this process would allow the therapist to understand the hidden content of the dream.

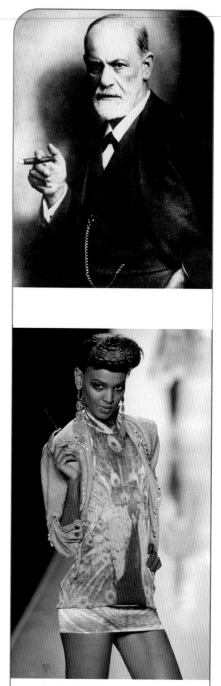

As Freud said: 'sometimes a cigar is only a cigar' . . .

## ✗✓ Evaluation of Freud's theory of dreams

✓ **Influential, long-lasting theory:** Freud proposed the most famous theory of the function of dreams and it's likely that some dreams may indeed, be disguised wishes. At the very least, some dreams may help us to 'tap' into our unconscious.

✓ **Popular, practical applications:** Dream analysis of some sort is still used today by some counselling psychologists and psychotherapists. Would such practices continue if there were no evidence to support their use?

✓ **Recent physiological evidence:** Recent developments in neuropsychology involving brain scans support the Freudian notion of a link between brain regions governing motivations and those governing dreaming. As Solms (2000) puts it:

> 'My findings suggest that dreaming is a higher mental function, generated by forebrain mechanisms. Dreams are evidently produced by motivational, emotional, memory and perceptual systems of the forebrain. It is, in short, the "wishing system", to allude back to Freud.'

✗ **Untestable:** Freud's theories have slipped out of favour with scientific psychology, principally because they're untestable and extremely subjective. Even Freud was inconsistent in his interpretation of dreams by proposing different interpretations of the same dream at different times.

✗ **Undisguised dreams:** Some dreams are not disguised. For example, some people who are worried about a sexual problem may dream about this sexual problem without any reference to symbolism. Some people may have overtly sexual dreams and 'wet dreams'. Surely such dreams have a straightforward explanation and do not involve any wish fulfilment or disguise? However, Freud might argue that sex here still represents something else!

✗ **Reductionist:** Freud's theory is reductionist in its insistence that all dreams are 'fulfilments of wishes' (see Chapter 10).

✗ **Non-human animal REM sleep:** Virtually all animals dream. Would Freud argue that they dream in order to prevent unacceptable thoughts emerging during sleep?

✗ **Nightmares:** Nightmares often do result in a person waking up. How can these be explained? They do not seem to work by protecting the waking sleeper and they do not seem to be the result of disguised wishes.

## A 'PROBLEM SOLVING' THEORY (PST): WEBB & CARTWRIGHT (1978)

- This theory suggests that dreams are a way of solving everyday problems relating to work, sex, health and so on. There are similarities with Freud's theory in that:
  - dreams are seen as a way of coping with current problems
  - dreams do occur in symbolic form but to Webb and Cartwright (1978) the manifest content is the real content and there's no need to reveal any latent content.
- One example of problem solving in dreams has already been mentioned with the case of Friedrich Kekule and his dreams of snakes that helped him solve the riddle of the molecular structure of benzene (see page 256).
- It's suggested that what may be occurring in problem-solving dreams is that they allow the dreamer to test solutions for actual problems and to compare them with solutions which have worked in the past for similar ones.
- Studies have tested the notion that people can cope better with stressful situations if they incorporate their problems into their dreams. These have involved situations as diverse as watching a horror movie or taking an IQ test (De Koninck & Koulack, 1975), to real-life settings, such as a divorce (Cartwright *et al.*, 1984), menstrual stress (Sirois-Berliss & De Koninck, 1982) and facing a natural disaster (Pagel, Vann & Altomare, 1995). The findings generally suggest that incorporation of the problem into a dream tends to be beneficial as measured by an improved mood on awakening. Divorced women who incorporated their spouse into their dreams adapted more readily to their situation than those who did not (Cartwright *et al.*, 1984).
- Delorme *et al.* (2002) conducted a study where dream diaries were kept by 35 female undergraduates for two 10-day periods. One period involved exam finals and the other was an exam-free period. A positive correlation was found between positive reappraisal in waking and active problem-solving reported in dreams.

## ❌ ✓ Evaluation of PST

✓ **Research support:** Webb and Cartwright (1978) asked participants to solve problems. The participants who were allowed an uninterrupted night's sleep proposed more realistic solutions than those deprived of REM sleep. Hartmann (1973) also reports that people who have job or family problems have proportionately more REM sleep than a control group without such problems. These studies suggest that dreams help to deal with the problems.

❌ **Non-human animal dreaming:** This theory doesn't really explain why animals have dreams. Do they have everyday life problems that need to be sorted out?

❌ **Dream recall?** If the purpose of dreams is to sort out problems in our lives, you would think that we could remember our dreams better. It's estimated that only about 5% of dreams are recalled. Does this mean that 95% of our dreams do not help with problem solving? After all, dreams are unlikely to help if we can't remember them.

❌ **Problems not solved in dreams:** Most problems are solved during our waking hours, perhaps by doing another task and then returning to the problem. If that's the case, we still have no clear idea why we dream. The problem-solving approach appears to be able to explain a very small percentage of dreams that do involve problem solving.

## EXAM tips BOX

**Describe and evaluate *one* neurobiological theory of the function of dreaming. (24 marks) (30 mins) (600 words minimum)**

*This essay can be split up into two Sections – each about 300 words long. Each section would be worth approx. 12 marks.*

**Section 1:** A **description** of the neurobiological theory chosen. In this case we've chosen the Activation–Synthesis Hypothesis of dreaming. This could include a description of any research studies which contribute to the hypothesis.

**Section 2:** A thorough **analysis** and **evaluation** of the Activation–Synthesis Hypothesis of dreaming. This could include evaluation of any research studies mentioned in Section 1. You might introduce other theories of dreaming simply as a way of evaluating the Activation–Synthesis Hypothesis.

*Try to answer this question yourself. There's a sample essay on page 267 with which you can compare your essay.*

**AO1**

↓

**AO2**

# PYA4: Biological rhythms, sleep and dreaming

Other possible exam questions:

- each essay is worth 24 marks and should take 30 minutes to write
- remember the mark scheme allocates 12 marks for AO1 (knowledge and description) and 12 marks for AO2 (analysis and evaluation).

## BIOLOGICAL RHYTHMS

1. **a.** Outline research studies into two types of biological rhythms. (12 marks)

   **b.** Assess the consequences of disrupting biological rhythms. (12 marks)

2. Critically consider the role of endogenous pacemakers and exogenous zeitgebers on biological rhythms. (24 marks)

3. Discuss the consequences of disrupting biological rhythms. (24 marks)

## SLEEP

**4.** Describe and evaluate two theories of the functions of sleep. (24 marks)

**5.** Outline and evaluate research studies relating to the ecological (e.g. Meddis; Webb) *or* restoration (e.g. Oswald, Horne) theory of sleep. (24 marks)

**6.** Explain and critically analyse the implications of findings from studies of sleep deprivation for any TWO theories of sleep. (24 marks)

## DREAMING

**7.** Critically consider research relating to the nature of dreams (e.g. content, duration, type of dream). (24 marks)

**8.** Outline and evaluate ONE neurobiological theory (e.g. Hobson & McCarley, Crick & Mitchison) and ONE psychological theory (e.g. Freud, Webb & Cartwright) of the function of dreaming. (24 marks)

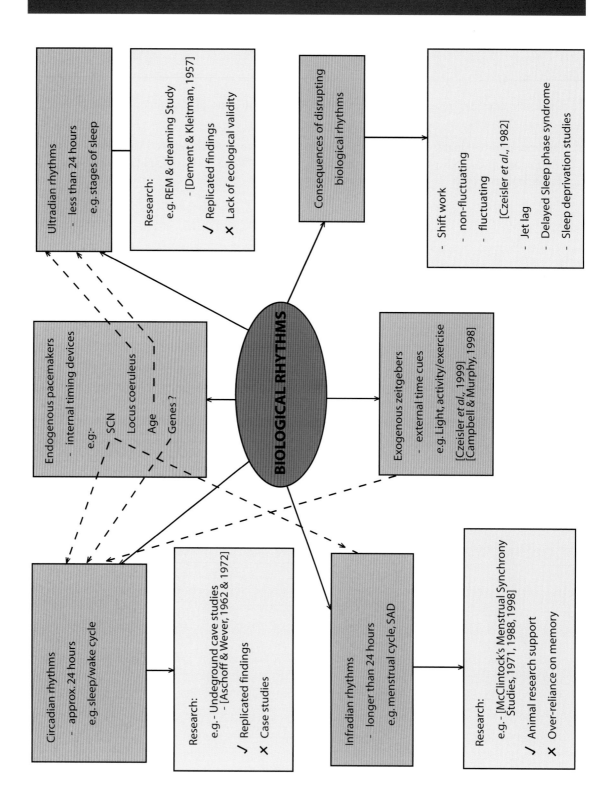

CHAPTER SUMMARY: revision schema

**BIOLOGICAL RHYTHMS**

Ultradian rhythms
- less than 24 hours
e.g. stages of sleep

Research:
e.g. REM & dreaming Study
- [Dement & Kleitman, 1957]
✓ Replicated findings
✗ Lack of ecological validity

Consequences of disrupting biological rhythms

- Shift work
  - non-fluctuating
  - fluctuating
    [Czeisler et al., 1982]
- Jet lag
- Delayed Sleep phase syndrome
- Sleep deprivation studies

Endogenous pacemakers
- internal timing devices
e.g.:-
  SCN
  Locus coeruleus
  Age
  Genes ?

Exogenous zeitgebers
- external time cues
e.g. Light, activity/exercise
[Czeisler et al., 1999]
[Campbell & Murphy, 1998]

Circadian rhythms
- approx. 24 hours
e.g. sleep/wake cycle

Research:
e.g. - Undeground cave studies
- [Aschoff & Wever, 1962 & 1972]
✓ Replicated findings
✗ Case studies

Infradian rhythms
- longer than 24 hours
e.g. menstrual cycle, SAD

Research:
e.g. - [McClintock's Menstrual Synchrony Studies, 1971, 1988, 1998]
✓ Animal research support
✗ Over-reliance on memory

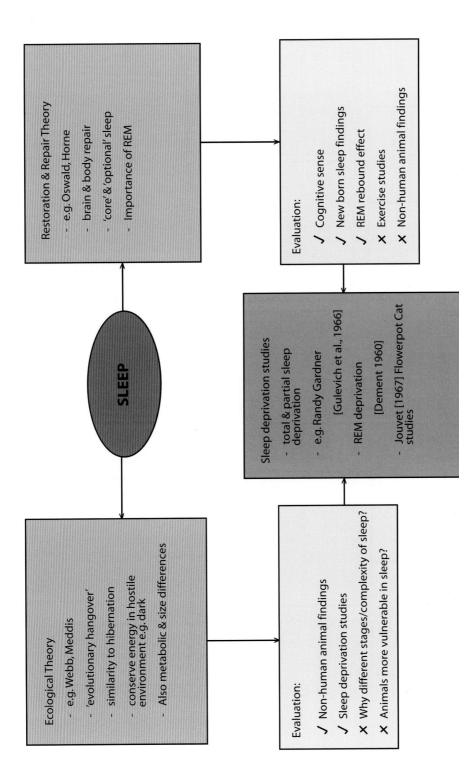

Restoration & Repair Theory
- e.g. Oswald, Horne
- brain & body repair
- 'core' & 'optional' sleep
- Importance of REM

Evaluation:
✓ Cognitive sense
✓ New born sleep findings
✓ REM rebound effect
✗ Exercise studies
✗ Non-human animal findings

SLEEP

Sleep deprivation studies
- total & partial sleep deprivation
- e.g. Randy Gardner [Gulevich et al., 1966]
- REM deprivation [Dement 1960]
- Jouvet [1967] Flowerpot Cat studies

Ecological Theory
- e.g. Webb, Meddis
- 'evolutionary hangover'
- similarity to hibernation
- conserve energy in hostile environment e.g. dark
- Also metabolic & size differrences

Evaluation:
✓ Non-human animal findings
✓ Sleep deprivation studies
✗ Why different stages/complexity of sleep?
✗ Animals more vulnerable in sleep?

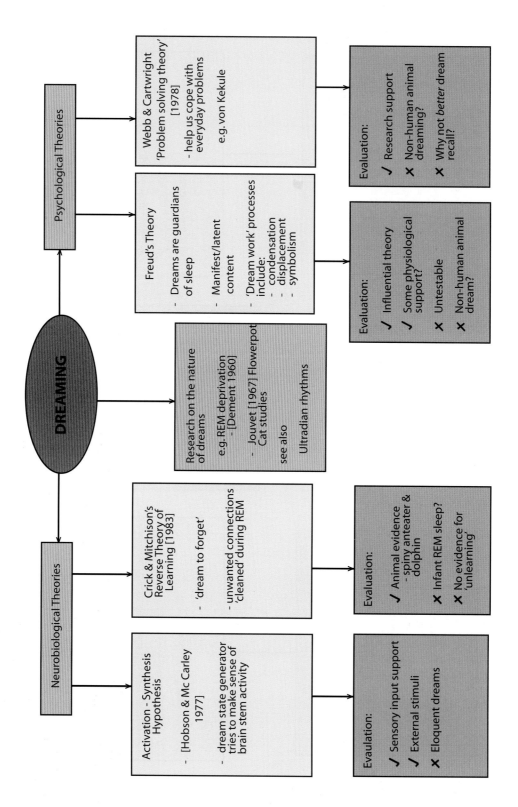

**DREAMING**

**Psychological Theories**

Webb & Cartwright 'Problem solving theory' [1978]
- help us cope with everyday problems

e.g. von Kekule

Evaluation:
✓ Research support
✗ Non-human animal dreaming?
✗ Why not better dream recall?

Freud's Theory
- Dreams are guardians of sleep
- Manifest/latent content
- 'Dream work' processes include:
  - condensation
  - displacement
  - symbolism

Evaluation:
✓ Influential theory
✓ Some physiological support?
✗ Untestable
✗ Non-human animal dream?

Research on the nature of dreams

e.g. REM deprivation
- [Dement 1960]
- Jouvet [1967] Flowerpot Cat studies

see also

Ultradian rhythms

**Neurobiological Theories**

Crick & Mitchison's Reverse Theory of Learning [1983]
- 'dream to forget'
- unwanted connections 'cleaned' during REM

Evaluation:
✓ Animal evidence
  - spiny anteater & dolphin
✗ Infant REM sleep?
✗ No evidence for 'unlearning'

Activation - Synthesis Hypothesis
- [Hobson & Mc Carley 1977]
- dream state generator tries to make sense of brain stem activity

Evaulation:
✓ Sensory input support
✓ External stimuli
✗ Eloquent dreams

Describe and evaluate research studies into infradian rhythms. (30 mins) (600 words minimum) AO1/AO2

Section 1:

Infradian rhythms are biological rhythms with cycles longer than 24 hours. The human menstrual cycle is the best-known human infradian rhythm and involves the release of an egg approximately every 28 days by the ovary. During each menstrual cycle, hormones (oestrogen and progesterone) are secreted and physiological changes occur to the breasts and the reproductive organs which are prepared for possible fertilisation. Each cycle ends with menstruation unless pregnancy occurs. McClintock (1971) first identified the synchronisation of female menstruation among her college dormitory friends. She concluded that the synchronisation of the menstrual cycles among 135 female friends (aged 17–22 years) was caused by pheromones (odourless chemicals) transmitted through social interaction. It was initially suggested that there may be a specific female pheromone that affects the timing of other female menstrual cycles. In 1988 McClintock and Stern began a 10-year longitudinal follow-up study that involved 29 women between the ages of 20 and 35 with a history of irregular, spontaneous ovulation. The researchers gathered samples of pheromones from nine of the women at certain points in their menstrual cycles by placing pads of cotton under their arms for at least eight hours. These pads were then wiped under the noses of the 20 other women on a daily basis. 68% of the women responded to the pheromones in that their menstrual cycles were either shortened by from one to 14 days or lengthened by from one to 12 days, depending on when in the menstrual cycle they had been collected. The pheromones collected from the women in the early phases of their cycles shortened the cycles of the second group of women (by between one and 14 days) by speeding up their preovulatory surge of luteinising hormone; conversely, pheromones collected later, during ovulation, lengthened the menstrual cycles by delaying the LH surge (by from one to 12 days). AO1

Section 2:

Evidence from animal studies also supports the important role of pheromones on infradian rhythms. However, these studies have typically involved rats and the problem of generalising from animals to human remains. There's also evidence that suggests that women's menstrual cycles don't become synchronised and there have been claims that methodological and statistical errors such as small samples and an over-reliance on memory recall brings into question these studies. It's suggested that if all the methodological and statistical errors inherent in the McClintock studies are addressed, the synchronisation of the menstrual cycle no longer occurs. Furthermore, there is little explanation as to why synchronisation of this infradian rhythm should occur, although it's proposed that it may have been of benefit in evolutionary terms for females to produce offspring at a similar time in order to help share the child-rearing duties. Such an explanation remains entirely speculative, although this does appear to be the case with some animals such as lions. AO2

Section 3:

Seasonal Affective Disorder (SAD) can be regarded as both an infradian and circadian rhythm. Since the disorder occurs mainly during the winter months it would appear to be a disorder involving circannual rhythms that are a sub-set of infradian rhythms. SAD is a disorder in which sufferers show seasonal changes of mood and/or behaviour. The exact causes of SAD are still unclear but it's believed that lack of light means too much melatonin is produced. Exposure to bright light suppresses night-time melatonin production and thus it's been suggested that bright, artificial light could be used experimentally, and perhaps therapeutically, to manipulate the circadian sleep wake cycle in humans (Lewy et al., 1980). Terman et al. (1998) conducted a study whereby 124 participants (aged 18 to 65) with SAD took part in the study. Over three weeks, 85 participants received daily 30-minute exposures to bright light from a box mounted above the head. Some had light therapy in the morning, others in the evening. 60% of those who received the morning light therapy showed marked improvements in SAD symptoms compared with 30% of those in the evening-light condition. AO1

Section 4:

Other well-controlled studies by Eastman et al. (1998) and Winton et al. (1989), conducted with adequate sample sizes, suggest morning bright light therapy is effective in treating SAD. Light therapy is also easy to administer in outpatient settings, lacks major side-effects (although some have questioned long-term effects of bright lights on the retina) and is cost-effective. However, other factors are implicated in SAD. Genetic vulnerability and stress also seem to be major factors in its causation. AO2

Research studies into the synchronisation of the menstrual cycle and SAD have enabled us to discover more about both these infradian rhythms even if the exact mechanisms involved remain elusive and, as yet, unconfirmed. AO2

(792 words)

# SAMPLE ESSAYS

Compare and contrast *two* theories of sleep. (24 marks) (30 mins) (600 words minimum) AO1/AO2

### Section 1:

Two theories of sleep include the Restoration and Repair (R & R) theory and the Ecological or Evolutionary theory (ET). The R & R theory suggests that sleep is essential to restore any physiological processes that are degraded through use during the day. Sleep helps to restore the homeostatic balance of the body. Oswald (1980) stated that REM sleep was necessary for brain repair and NREM sleep was for the benefit of body repair. Many restorative processes such as digestion, removal of waste products and protein synthesis do appear to occur during sleep. Horne (1988) later distinguished between 'core sleep' which he believed was essential for restoration processes and 'optional sleep' whose main purpose was for energy conservation. The R & R theory suggests different functions for the stages of sleep. For example, patients who have suffered from brain injury appear to spend more time in REM sleep than 'normal' controls. It's suggested that the increased blood flow during REM sleep may help the repair process. ET less readily explains the need for these different stages of sleep. **AO1**

### Section 2:

Like the R & R theory, ET suggests that sleep serves some restorative function as a method whereby animals can conserve energy. In this way, sleep is similar to hibernation. However, the ET goes further by stating that sleep also helps to protect us at night when we might be vulnerable to predators. Sleep is thus an evolutionary-stable strategy which increases individual and, in turn, species survival. The ET predicts that animal species should vary in their sleep needs depending on how much time they need to search for food each day and how safe they are from predators when they sleep. **AO1**

### Section 3:

The R & R theory of sleep seems to make more cognitive sense than the ET theory since we all have the experience of feeling tired prior to sleep and refreshed on awakening. With regard to the ET of sleep, it doesn't seem to make sense that as complicated a process as sleep has evolved to ensure safety from predators. Merely remaining still would surely serve the same purpose. **AO2**

Sleep deprivation studies have been cited as evidence of the R & R theory. Animal studies have shown that sleep, particularly REM sleep, is essential for proper functioning. Jouvet (1967) demonstrated that cats eventually die as a result of REM deprivation. Human studies have also demonstrated that cognitive deficits can occur as a result of total sleep deprivation, and the phenomenon of REM rebound whereby sleep-deprived participants experience more REM sleep on subsequent nights supports the R & R theory. However, such participants don't make up all the hours that they have lost, suggesting that

sleep may not be entirely a process for restoration and repair. Similarly, there are case studies of people who manage to lead perfectly 'normal' lives with very short periods of sleep each night (1–2 hours). Such studies suggest that sleep may serve some other purpose or indeed may be an 'evolutionary hangover'. **AO2**

The R & R theory can explain why babies have a far higher proportion of REM sleep. Babies and infants spend as much as 50% of their day in REM sleep. It's suggested that they need this to help with their synaptic growth. The ET, on the other hand, explains the same evidence as a time that allows parents time to recover and conserve the energy they have expended through looking after their infants. **AO2**

Findings from animal research are used with both theories. The R & R theory would predict that animals that expend a lot of energy during the day should sleep for longer periods. This does not appear to be the case. For example, giant sloths appear to exercise little during the day and yet sleep for about 20 hours per day. Such evidence is also not readily explained by the ET of sleep. According to the predation argument in the ET, animals who are likely to be preyed upon should sleep more than predators since sleep serves to hide them from predators. The ET accounts for this with the suggestion that metabolic differences affect sleep levels. Many prey species such as herbivores have to graze for long periods in order to gain sufficient nutrients and therefore have less time to sleep. Another aspect of ET is that the size of an animal is related to total sleep time. Animals with high metabolic rates (e.g. squirrels) expend a lot of energy and thus need more time for sleep. Larger animals with slower metabolic rates therefore sleep less. The second strand of this argument shares some similarities with the R & R theory. Indeed, Horne (1988) proposed that energy conservation is a major function of sleep in smaller mammals such as rodents. The animal evidence appears more readily to support the ET of sleep. **AO2**

(747 words)

Describe and evaluate *one* neurobiological theory of the function of dreaming. (24 marks) (30 mins) (600 words minimum) AO1/AO2

Section 1:

One neurobiological theory was proposed by Hobson and McCarley in 1977 and is called the Activation–Synthesis Hypothesis. Hobson and McCarley argued that dreams are responses to the neurophysiological events of the sleeping brain. According to their Activation–Synthesis Hypothesis, dreaming is caused physiologically by a 'dream state generator' located in the brain stem. It's 'on' during REM sleep, while all sensory input and motor output are blocked, and the neurons in the cerebral cortex are activated by random impulses that generate sensory information within the nervous system. Put simply, this means that the forebrain interprets the brain activity (activation) and produces it as a dream (synthesises). Basically, the brain is telling the person what is happening to the brain in code, or symbolised, in the dream. For example, if the motor system fires in such a way as to suggest running movements then this is interpreted as a dream that you are being chased. **AO1**

Originally there was no explanation given as to why the brain should try to make sense of random neural activity, although recently it's been suggested that it may play a part in memory consolidation (Hobson, 1994) by acting and testing out our brain circuits in sleep. **AO1**

Hobson and McCarley claim that in the construction of a dream 'the forebrain may be making the best of a bad job in producing even a partially coherent dream imagery from the relatively noisy signals sent up to it from the brain stem'. This implies that dreams have no emotional content since they're triggered only by sensory and motor aspects of bodily activity. **AO1**

Section 2:

Hobson claims that the often bizarre nature of dreams in terms of their visual imagery, emotional content and the frequent shifts of attention can be explained by the random sensory inputs that generate them. For example, people often report paralysis in dreams and this is supported by the fact that our muscles are relaxed in REM sleep. Hobson and McCarley also claim that support for this A–S Hypothesis comes from the predictable regularity of dreams. They stress that 'the motivating force for dreaming is not psychological but physiological since the time of occurrence and duration of dreaming sleep are quite constant, suggesting a preprogrammed, neurally determined genesis'. Put simply, if dreams were caused psychologically, we'd expect a greater variety in occurrence and length of dreams. There is excellent physiological evidence, from PET scans of the dreaming brain, that the brain stem is active during dreaming. Further evidence supporting the A–S Hypothesis comes from the fact that the neurons responsible for taste and smell don't fire during sleep and, as predicted by the hypothesis, dreams don't contain smells or tastes. **AO2**

However, various evidence certainly suggests that dreaming is more than 'genetically determined'. After all, we can have dreams with eloquently constructed story lines and they actually can influence our behaviour. A famous example of this is reported by Friedrich August von Kekule who had a dream of whirling snakes and as a direct result of this dream discovered the structure of benzene – the organic chemical compound made up of a ring of carbon atoms. Furthermore, people who recall their dreams would argue that dreams are often more coherent than suggested by Hobson and McCarley's hypothesis. Dreams can not only be coherent; they can be entertaining, stimulating and enjoyable! It seems unlikely that such dreams are nothing more than the result of random neural activity, and they are certainly not meaningless. **AO2**

The phenomenon of lucid dreaming also brings into question the A–S Hypothesis. Lucid dreaming is the process whereby people direct the action of their dreams. It's rare but some people are aware that they're dreaming and can deliberately direct their dream. Again, these dreams suggest that not all dreams are the result of random firings from the brain stem. **AO2**

The A–S Hypothesis certainly furthered debate on the function of dreaming and indeed created a good deal of controversy on publication. Dream researchers and therapists questioned the practical applications of dream analysis. **AO2**

(664 words)

**SAMPLE ESSAYS**

# Cognitive Development

## What's covered in this chapter?

### You need to know about:

Development of thinking
- Theories of cognitive development, including Piaget and Vygotsky
- Applications of these theories (e.g. to education)

Development of measured intelligence
- Research into factors associated with the development of measured intelligence, including the role of genetics and environmental factors (e.g. cultural differences)

Development of moral understanding
- Theories of moral understanding and pro-social reasoning (e.g. Kohlberg, Eisenberg), including the influence of gender (e.g. Gilligan) and cultural variations in moral understanding/pro-social reasoning

## Development of thinking

### Theories of Cognitive Development

Different theories of how the child's thinking develops (that is, cognitive development) rest on very different images of what the child is like :

- Piaget sees the child as (a) an organism *adapting to its environment*; and (b) a scientist constructing its own understanding of the world.
- For Vygotsky, by contrast, the child is a participant in an *interactive process*. Through this process, socially and culturally determined knowledge and understanding gradually become *individualised*.

### PIAGET'S THEORY

- Piaget (e.g. 1950) was interested in how *intelligence* changes as children grow (which he called *genetic epistemology*). He *wasn't* interested in why some children are more intelligent than others (see next section).
- Cognitive development occurs through the interaction of innate (inborn) capacities with environmental events.

- It involves a series of *stages*, which are:
  - (a) *hierarchical*: they build on each other, such that earlier stages are necessary for later stages to develop
  - (b) *invariant*: every child passes through the stages in the same order or sequence, and there's no regressing (going backwards) to earlier stages (except as the result of brain damage)
  - (c) *universal*: every child passes through the same stages, regardless of culture
  - (d) *qualitatively different*: each stage involves *a different type of intelligence*. We don't become more intelligent as we get older; rather, the *nature* of our intelligence changes.
  - – What underlies the stage changes are a number of *functional invariants*. These are fundamental aspects of development which remain the same, and work in the same way, through each of the stages. The crucial functional invariants are: *assimilation*, *accommodation* and *equilibration*.
  - – The major cognitive structure that changes in the course of development is the *schema* (plural = *schemas* or *schemata*).

Jean Piaget (1896–1980)

**Specification Hint:** The Specification states: 'Theories of cognitive development, including Piaget and Vygotsky'. This means (a) that you must know about *at least two* theories – but two will do; and (b) that you *must* know about both Piaget's and Vygotsky's theories. Only these two theories will be covered here.

### Schemas (or schemata)

A schema is the basic building block or unit of intelligent behaviour (see Box 11.1).

### Box 11.1  Schemas

- **Piaget saw schemas as mental structures which organise past experiences. They provide a way of understanding and predicting future experience,**
- **According to Bee (2000), schemas are more the action of categorising than actual categories.**
- **Life begins with simple schemas, largely confined to inborn reflexes (such as grasping and sucking). These operate independently, and are triggered only by particular stimuli. As the baby develops, schemas become increasingly integrated with each other.**
- **They also become less reflex and more deliberate, and under the baby's voluntary control.**

### Assimilation, accommodation and equilibration

- *Assimilation* is the process by which we incorporate new information into existing schemas. For example, babies will reflexively suck a nipple and other objects (such as a finger). But if the baby is to learn to suck from a bottle or drink from a cup, the innate sucking reflex must be modified through *accommodation*.

**Exam Hint:**

Any other theories you may know about may be used for evaluating one or other of these theories (AO2). The exam question could ask you specifically about Piaget and/or Vygotsky, but it couldn't ask you about any other theory. One way of evaluating either Piaget or Vygotsky, of course, is to compare and contrast the two theories with each other (AO2). Also, you could evaluate either in terms of its applications (such as to education, which is covered in the next section).

- When a child can deal with most, if not all, new experiences by assimilating them, it's in a state of *equilibrium* ('mental balance'). This is brought about by the process of *equilibration*.
- But if existing schemas are inadequate to cope with new situations, *cognitive disequilibrium* occurs. To restore balance, the existing schema must be 'stretched' in order to take in ('accommodate') new information or meet

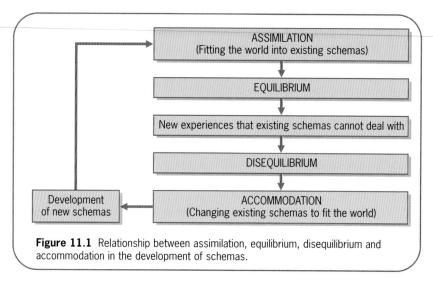

**Figure 11.1** Relationship between assimilation, equilibrium, disequilibrium and accommodation in the development of schemas.

the demands of new situations. So, for example, the baby needs to change how it sucks (including what it does with its tongue) when drinking from a cup – as well as changing the position of its head. Later on, it will drink while actually holding the cup, so different schemas will be used together in a voluntary way (see above).
- Assimilation and accommodation are necessary and complementary processes. Together, they constitute the fundamental process of *adaptation* (see Figure 11.1).

## STAGES OF COGNITIVE DEVELOPMENT

- Each of Piaget's stages represents a stage in the development of intelligence (hence 'sensorimotor intelligence', 'pre-operational intelligence' and so on).
- Each stage is also a way of summarising the various schemas a child possesses at a particular time (see Table 11.1).

**Table 11.1** Piaget's four stages of cognitive development

| Stage | Approximate age |
|---|---|
| Sensorimotor | 0–2 years |
| Pre-operational | 2–7 years |
| Concrete operational | 7–11 years |
| Formal operational | 11 years onwards |

- The ages shown in Table 11.1 are only approximate. Children move through the stages at different rates (because of both environmental and biological differences).
- Children also pass through transitional periods, in which their thinking is a mixture of two stages.
- For Piaget, development is a gradual and continuous process of change. The child moves from one stage to the next through cognitive disequilibrium.

### The sensorimotor stage

- Babies learn about the world, and interact with it, mainly (a) through their senses ('sensori') and (b) by doing ('motor').
- Based on observations of his own children, Piaget divided the sensorimotor stage into six sub-stages. A crucial development that takes place during the course of these sub-stages is *object permanence* (OP) (see Box 11.2).

1. Baby sees ball placed under cloth on her left (A).

2. She retrieves it and the sequence is repeated.

3. Baby sees ball placed under cloth on her right (B) but continues to search under cloth on her left (A).

**Figure 11.2** Piaget's demonstration of the limited object permanence of babies between eight and twelve months. They can retrieve a hidden object only from its original hiding place, not where it was last hidden. Not until about twelve months will they search under the cushion where they last saw the object hidden; they can do this even when three or four cushions are used. (Others have suggested that this ability appears as early as nine months.) (from Barnes-Gutteridge, 1974)

## Box 11.2 The development of object permanence (OP)

- In the second substage (*primary circular reactions*: 1–4 months), a baby will look where an object disappears for a few moments, but won't search for it. If the object doesn't reappear, the baby appears to lose interest ('out of sight is out of mind').
- In *secondary circular reactions* (4–10 months), the baby will reach for an object that's partially hidden. This suggests the baby realises that the rest of the object is attached to the visible part. But if the object is completely hidden, the baby makes no attempt to retrieve it.
- In the *co-ordination of secondary circular reactions* (10–12 months), a baby will search for a hidden object ('out of sight' is no longer 'out of mind'). But it will keep looking for it where it was last hidden – even when it's hidden somewhere else (see Figure 11.2).
- Between 12 and 18 months (*tertiary circular reactions*), the child will look for the object where it last saw it hidden. But object permanence isn't yet fully developed.
- The final stage (*invention of new means through mental combinations*: 18–24 months) involves the ability to *infer invisible displacements*. The child can now look for an object that's been hidden – without having actually seen this happen. For example, the child watches you place a small toy in a matchbox, which is then put under a pillow. When it's not looking, you slip the toy out of the matchbox and leave it under the pillow. When you then give the child the matchbox, it will open it, expecting to find the toy. When it sees the toy's not there, it will look for it under the pillow. Before 18 months, it would have failed to look under the pillow.

### ✗✓ Evaluation of Piaget's account of OP (AO2)

✗ **Methodological limitations:** According to Bower and Wishart (1972), how an object is made to disappear can influence the baby's response. If it's looking at an object, and reaching for it, and the lights are then turned off, it continues to search for it for up to one-and-a-half minutes (detectable through the use of infra-red cameras). This suggests that the baby does remember the object is still there – so 'out of sight' isn't 'out of mind'.

✗ **It develops earlier than Piaget claimed:** Bower and Wishart's study shows that Piaget's claims about when OP develops underestimate babies' abilities. In other words, OP develops earlier than Piaget claimed. For example, Baillargeon (1987) showed that babies as young as three-and-a-half months can display OP, and it isn't necessary for babies below six months to see the whole object in order to respond to it.

- This stage is important for the development of the general symbolic function (GSF). This refers to:
  (a) self-recognition
  (b) symbolic thought (such as language)
  (c) deferred imitation (the ability to imitate or reproduce something that's no longer present)
  (d) representational (or make-believe) play.

- The GSF involves the use of internal images (or 'interiorised' schemas). The child begins to 'think', in something like an 'adult' sense.

### The pre-operational stage

- The GSF continues to develop. But the child tends to be influenced by *how things look*, rather than by logical principles or *operations* (hence, 'pre-operational').
- Piaget sub-divided the stage into the:
  (a) *pre-conceptual sub-stage* (2–4 years) and the
  (b) *intuitive sub-stage* (4–7 years).
    - The intuitive sub-stage has probably been investigated and discussed more than any other aspect of Piaget's theory – in particular, *egocentrism* and *conservation*.
    - Both egocentrism and conservation are related to *centration*. This involves focusing on a single feature of an object or aspect of a situation. For most logical operations, the child needs to take several (or all) features into account. So the pre-operational child is *egocentric* and is also unable to *conserve*.

### Egocentrism

According to Piaget, the egocentric child:

- sees the world from his/her own standpoint
- fails to appreciate that other people might see things differently
- cannot put him/herself 'in other people's shoes' in order to appreciate that other people don't know or perceive everything they themselves do.

Phillips (1969) reported a conversation between an experimenter and a four-year-old boy:

| | |
|---|---|
| Experimenter: | 'Do you have a brother?' |
| Child: | 'Yes.' |
| Experimenter: | 'What's his name?' |
| Child: | 'Jim.' |
| Experimenter: | 'Does Jim have a brother?' |
| Child: | 'No.' |

In this case, of course, if the child could see things from Jim's point of view, he'd know that Jim has a brother – who is himself!

**The Swiss mountain scene** (SMS) **experiment** (Piaget & Inhelder, 1956)

• This involved the use of three papier-maché model mountains, as shown in Figure 11.3.

• The three mountains are of different colours. One has snow on the top, one a house, and one a red cross.

• The child walks round and explores the model, then sits on one side while a doll is placed at some different location. The child is then shown 10 pictures of different views of the model, and is asked to choose the one which represents how the doll sees it.

• Four-year-olds were completely unaware that there were perspectives other than their own. They always chose a picture which matched *their own view* of the model.

• Six-year-olds showed some awareness of other perspectives, but often chose the wrong picture.

• Only seven- and eight-year-olds consistently chose the picture that represented the *doll's view*.

• Piaget concluded that children under seven are bound by the *egocentric illusion*. They fail to understand that what they see is *relative to their own position*. Instead, they believe their own view represents 'the world as it really is'.

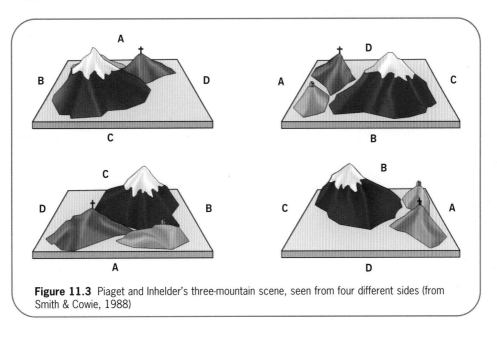

**Figure 11.3** Piaget and Inhelder's three-mountain scene, seen from four different sides (from Smith & Cowie, 1988)

## Evaluation of SMS (AO2)

**✗ Task difficulty:** Critics see the task as an unusually difficult way of presenting a problem to a young child. When the task is presented in a meaningful context (when it makes 'human sense': Donaldson, 1978), even three-and-a-half-year-olds can appreciate the world from another person's viewpoint (Borke, 1975; Hughes, in Donaldson, 1978).

**✗ Other evidence of perspective-taking:** Gelman (1979) showed that four-year-olds (a) adjust their explanations of things to make them clearer to a blindfold listener; and (b) use simpler forms of speech when talking to two-year-olds. We wouldn't expect either finding if four-year-olds are egocentric, as Piaget claims.

### Conservation

• Conservation is the understanding that any quantity (such as number, liquid quantity, length, and substance) remains the same despite physical changes in how objects are arranged.

- Piaget believed that pre-operational children cannot conserve, because their thinking is dominated by the appearance of objects ('how things look').
- A typical conservation experiment is described in Essential Study 11.2.

**Conservation of liquid quantity** (CoLQ) (Piaget, 1952)

- The child is shown two beakers of coloured liquid (A and B).
- When asked 'Is there the same amount of liquid in A and B?', the pre-operational child correctly says 'Yes'. This is called the *pre-transformation question*.
- In full view of the child, the liquid from B is poured into a taller, thinner beaker (C).
- The child is then asked 'Is there the same amount of liquid in A and C? This is the *post-transformation question*.
- The pre-operational child will now answer 'No. There's more in C'. Asked why, the child will say 'It looks more' or 'It's taller'. This is, of course, the wrong answer – despite the child agreeing that nothing's been spilled or added when liquid was poured from B into C.

- According to Piaget, the pre-operational child *centres* on just one dimension of the beaker (usually its height). It fails to take width into account. Children in the concrete operational stage understand that 'getting taller' and 'getting narrower' tend to cancel each other out (*compensation*).
- If the liquid from C is poured back into B, the pre-operational child will again say that A and B contain the same amount of liquid. But they cannot perform this operation *mentally*, that is, they lack *reversibility* (understanding that what can be done can be undone *without any gain or loss*).
- These same limitations apply to other forms of conservation, such as number and substance/quantity.

### Evaluation of Piaget's conservation experiments (AO2)

✗ **Methodological issues (a): how many questions?** Rose and Blank (1974) showed that when the pre-transformation question was dropped, six-year-olds often succeeded on the number conservation task. They also made fewer errors on the standard form of the task when tested a week later. Samuel and Bryant (1984) replicated these findings, using conservation of number, liquid quantity, and substance. The standard form of the task unwittingly 'forces' children to give the wrong answer against their better judgement. This is because they're asked the same question twice (before and after the transformation). Children believe they're expected to give a *different* answer second time ('why else would the experimenter ask me the same question twice?'). These contextual cues may override purely linguistic ones (Donaldson, 1978).

✗ **Methodological issues (b): how does the transformation happen?** According to Piaget, it shouldn't matter *who* rearranges the counters in number conservation experiments, or *how* this happens. But when 'Naughty Teddy' (a glove

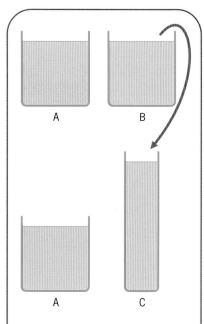

**Figure 11.4** The conservation of liquid quantity. Although the child agrees that there's the same amount of liquid in A and B, when the contents of B are poured into C, the appearance of C sways the child's judgement so that C is now judged to contain more liquid than A ('it looks more' or 'it's taller'). Although the child has seen the liquid poured from B into C and agrees that none has been spilled or added in the process (what Piaget calls 'identity'), the appearance of the higher level of liquid in the taller, thinner beaker C is compelling.

puppet operated by the experimenter) is brought out of his box and 'accidentally' re-arranges one row of counters, pre-operational children show conservation of number (and length) (McGarrigle & Donaldson, 1974; Light *et al.*, 1979). This also applies when the transformation is made by a person other than the experimenter (Hargreaves *et al.*, 1982; Light, 1986).

**✗ • ✓ Methodological issues (c): relevant or irrelevant perceptual change?** Piaget's standard procedure might convey the implicit message: 'take note of the transformation because it's relevant'. But in fact, the task involves an irrelevant perceptual change (nothing is added or taken away). By contrast, studies like the 'Naughty Teddy' experiment might imply the message: 'ignore the transformation, it makes no difference'. If children do better in this form of the task, it may be because they've failed to notice that any transformation has occurred – not that they can conserve! So, if something is actually changed (a relevant change), children should do worse in the accidental/incidental transformation condition than those tested in the standard way. This prediction has been supported in several studies (e.g. Light & Gilmour, 1983; Moore & Frye, 1986). This lends indirect support to Piaget.

## Box 11.3 Horizontal and vertical décalage

- Some types of conservation are mastered before others, and their order is invariant.
- *Liquid quantity* develops by age 6–7, *substance/quantity* and *length* by 7–8, *weight* by 8–10, and *volume* by 11–12.
- This step-by-step acquisition of new operations is called *décalage* (displacement or 'slips in the level of performance').
- In conservation, décalage is *horizontal*: there are inconsistencies *within* the same kind of ability or operation (for example, a seven-year-old can conserve number but not weight).
- *Vertical* décalage refers to inconsistencies *between* different abilities or operations (a child may have mastered all kinds of classification, but not all kinds of conservation).

### Concrete operational stage

- The child can now perform logical operations – but *only in the presence of actual objects* (hence 'concrete' operations). Conservation is an example of such an operation, which requires the ability to *decentre* (see above).
- Further examples of the child's ability to decentre include its understanding that objects can belong to more than one class or category. For example, Andrew is Bob's brother *and* Charlie's best friend.
- Children also become significantly *less egocentric*. Their viewpoint becomes increasingly *relative*, enabling them to see things from different perspectives.
- Their ability to put things in order of size (or any other dimension) (*seriation*) increases.
- But they still have difficulty with *transitivity tasks*. For example, a 7- to 11-year-old is told that 'Alan is taller than Bob, and Bob is taller than Charlie', and is then asked whether Alan or Charlie is taller. They cannot solve this problem entirely in their heads. They can usually only solve it using real (concrete) objects (such as dolls).

### Formal operational stage

- The concrete operational child is basically concerned with manipulating *things* (even if this is done mentally). These are called *first order* operations.
- By contrast, the formal operational thinker can manipulate *ideas* or *propositions*. He or she can reason solely on the basis of verbal statements (*second order* operations).
- 'Formal' here refers to the ability to follow the *form* of an argument without reference to its particular content. For example, in transitivity problems (see above), 'If A is larger than B, and B is larger than C, then A is larger than C' is a form of argument whose conclusion is logically true, *regardless* of what A, B and C might refer to.
- Formal operational thinkers can also think *hypothetically* (that is, think about what *might* be as well as what actually exists). For example, if they're asked what it would be like if people had tails, they

might say: 'Dogs would know when you were happy', or 'Lovers could hold tails in secret under the table'. Concrete operational thinkers might tell you 'not to be so silly', or say where on the body the tail might be. This would reveal their dependence on what they've actually seen (Dworetzky, 1981).

- This ability to imagine and discuss things that have never actually been encountered demonstrates the formal operational thinker's continuing *decentration*.

- The more *systematic* thinking of this stage is shown in a study by Inhelder & Piaget (1958). This is described in Essential Study 11.3.

AN UNLIKELY EXAMPLE OF FORMAL OPERATIONAL THINKING

**ESSENTIAL STUDY 11.3**

**The Making Coloured Chemicals (MCC) study** (Inhelder & Piaget, 1958)

- Participants were given five containers filled with clear liquid. Four were 'test chemicals', and one was an 'indicator'.

- When the correct combination of one or more test chemicals was added to the indicator, it turned yellow. Participants had to find the right combination.

- Pre-operational children simply mixed the chemicals randomly.

- Concrete operational children were more systematic than this, but they generally failed to test all possible combinations.

- Only formal operational thinkers considered all the alternatives, and systematically varied one factor at a time. Also, they often wrote down all the results, and tried to draw general conclusions about each chemical.

## An Evaluation of Piaget's theory (AO2)

✓ **Major influence:** Piaget's theory has had an enormous impact on our understanding of cognitive development. Some years ago, it was regarded as the major framework or paradigm within child development.

✗ **Declining influence:** It remains a vital source of influence and inspiration, both in psychology and education (see below). But today there are hardly any 'orthodox' Piagetians left (Dasen, 1994). Many fundamental aspects of Piaget's theory have been challenged, and fewer and fewer developmental psychologists now subscribe to his (or other) 'hard' *stage theories*.

✓ • ✗ **Cross-cultural support:** Dasen (1994) cites studies he conducted in remote parts of the central Australian desert with 8- to 14-year-old Aborigines. He gave them conservation-of-liquid, weight and volume tasks, plus a task that tested understanding of spatial relationships. These are described in Essential Study 11.4. According to Dasen, these findings make good sense in terms of Aboriginal culture, where things aren't quantified. Water is vital for survival, but the exact quantity matters little. Counting things is unusual, and number words only go up to five (after which everything is 'many'). By contrast, finding one's way around is crucial: water-holes must be found at the end of each journey, and family members meet up at the end of the day after having split up in order to search for water.

**Conservation and spatial tasks with Aborigines** (CASTA) (Dasen, 1994)

- The tests of conservation were basically the same as used by Piaget.
- Two tests of spatial relationships were used:
    (a) two landscape models, one of which could be turned through 180 degrees. Participants had to locate an object (doll or sheep) on one model, then find the same location on the second model
    (b) a bottle was half-filled with water, then tilted into various positions. A screen hid the water level. Participants were shown outline drawings of the bottle and had to draw in the water level.
- On conservation tasks, Dasen found the same shift from pre-operational to concrete operational thought as Piaget found with Swiss children. But it took place between the ages of 10 and 13 (rather than 5 and 7). A fairly high proportion of adolescents and adults also gave non-conservation answers.
- On the spatial tasks, there was again the same shift from pre- to concrete operational thought as for Swiss children. But they found these tasks easier than the conservation tasks.
- In other words, operational thinking develops *earlier* in the spatial domain. This is the *reverse* of what's found for Swiss children.

✓ • ✗ More cross-cultural support: The few cross-cultural studies of the sensorimotor stage have shown that the sub-stages are universal. Overall, ecological or cultural factors appear not to influence the sequence of stages. But they do affect the rate at which they're attained (Segall *et al.*, 1999). Dasen has argued that only one-third of adolescents and adults actually attains formal operations, and that in some cultures it doesn't 'exist' at all. But formal operational thought can take many forms. According to Segall *et al.* (1999), it's more accurate to argue that formal operational thinking '. . . in effect, scientific reasoning . . . is not what is valued in all cultures . . .'.

✗ Neglect of social factors: Meadows (1995) argues that underlying (implicit in) Piaget's theory is an image of the child 'as scientist'. Children are largely independent and isolated as they construct their knowledge and understanding of the physical world. This excludes the contribution of other people to children's cognitive development. The social nature of knowledge and thought is a basic feature of Vygotsky's theory, to which we now turn.

## VYGOTSKY'S THEORY

Vygotsky outlined a major alternative to Piaget's theory. It was published in the former Soviet Union in the 1920s and 1930s. But it wasn't translated into English until the early 1960s (Vygotsky, 1962).

### Internalisation and the social nature of thinking

- Vygotsky believed that a child's cognitive development doesn't occur in a social vacuum. The ability to think and reason by and for ourselves (*inner speech* or *verbal thought*) is the result of a fundamentally *social* process.
- At birth, we're social beings capable of interacting with others. But we can do little – either practically or intellectually – by or for ourselves.
- Gradually, we become more self-sufficient and independent. By participating in social activities, our abilities become transformed. Cognitive development involves an active *internalisation* of problem-solving processes. This takes place through *mutual interaction* between children and those with whom they have regular social contact (initially the parents, but later friends and classmates).
- This is the reverse of how Piaget (at least initially) saw things. Piaget's idea of the 'child as scientist' is replaced by Vygotsky's 'child as *apprentice*', who acquires the culture's knowledge and skills through graded collaboration with those who already possess them (Rogoff, 1990). According to Vygotsky (1981):

'Any function in the child's cultural development appears twice, or on two planes. First it appears on the social plane, and then on the psychological plane.'

## Box 11.4  Pointing: an example of cultural development from the physical to the social

- At first, a baby's pointing is simply an unsuccessful attempt to grasp something beyond its reach.
- When the mother sees her baby pointing, she takes it as an 'indicatory gesture' that the baby wants something. So she helps it, probably making the gesture herself.
- Gradually the baby comes to use the gesture deliberately. The 'reaching' becomes reduced to movements which couldn't themselves achieve the desired object – even if it were within the baby's reach. The baby cries, looks at the mother, and will eventually speak while pointing.
- The gesture is now directed towards the *mother*, rather than the object. It's become a 'gesture for others', rather than a gesture 'in itself' (Meadows, 1995).

### Scaffolding and the zone of proximal development (ZPD)

- *Scaffolding* refers to the role played by parents, teachers, and others in helping children acquire their knowledge and skills (Wood *et al.*, 1976).
- As the child becomes more familiar with a task, and more competent at it, 'scaffolders' leave more and more for the child to do. Eventually, the child can perform the task successfully on its own.
- In this way, the developing thinker doesn't have to create cognition 'from scratch'. There are others available who've already 'served their own apprenticeship'. Support for the concept of scaffolding comes from a study by Wood *et al.* (1976), described in Essential Study 11.5.

ESSENTIAL STUDY 11.5

**Mothers instructing their children** (MITC) (Wood *et al.,* 1976)

- Wood *et al.* were interested in how mothers of four- and five-year-olds helped them on a construction task.
- Different mothers used instructional strategies which varied in how specific they were. These ranged from (a) general verbal encouragement to (b) direct demonstration of a relevant action.
- No single strategy guaranteed learning. But the most efficient maternal instructors were those who combined general *and* specific interventions according to the child's progress.
- The most useful help is that which is adapted to the learner's successes and failures (Bruner, 1983). For example, using a general instruction initially until the child runs into difficulties. At this point, a more specific instruction or demonstration is given. This approach allows the child considerable autonomy, but also provides carefully planned guidance at the boundaries of its abilities (Vygotsky's *zone of proximal development* or ZPD, see Fig. 11.5, page 279).

- The internalised cognitive skills remain social in two senses:
(a)  as mature learners, we can 'scaffold' ourselves through difficult tasks (self-instruction), as others once scaffolded our earlier attempts
(b)  for most people, the only skills practised to a high level of competence are those offered by their culture. Cognitive potential may be universal, but cognitive expertise is culturally determined (Meadows, 1995).
- Vygotsky's theory predicts that scaffolding processes occur in everyday, naturalistic contexts. There's evidence to support this prediction. Examples are often linked to the transmission across generations of culturally valued skills, such as weaving among the Zinacauteco Mexicans, and American mothers' involvement in their pre-schoolers' development of number (Durkin, 1995).

- The *zone of proximal development* (ZPD) defines those functions that haven't yet matured, but are in the process of maturing (Vygotsky, 1978). These could be called the 'buds' or 'flowers', rather than the 'fruits' of development.
- The actual developmental level describes mental development *retrospectively*, while the ZPD describes it *prospectively*. To understand this distinction, consider Figure 11.5.
- The ZPD may be different for different children. Children with a large ZPD will have a greater capacity for being helped compared with children whose ZPD is small.
- So the actual mental level ('X') relates to what the child can do *now*, while the potential level ('X + 1' or the ZPD) relates to what the child *could* do *in the future* (with the right kind of help).

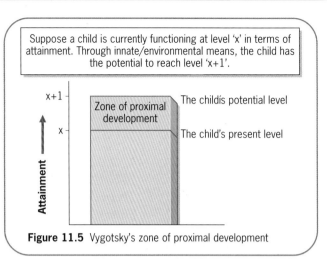

Suppose a child is currently functioning at level 'x' in terms of attainment. Through innate/environmental means, the child has the potential to reach level 'x+1'.

**Figure 11.5** Vygotsky's zone of proximal development

## An Evaluation of Vygotsky's theory (AO2)

✓ Vygotsky's theory clearly 'compensates' for one of the main limitations of Piaget's theory. As Segall *et al.* (1999) put it:

> 'Piaget produced a theory of the development of an "epistemic subject", an idealised, non-existent individual completely divorced from the social environment.'

For Vygotsky, culture (and especially language) plays a key role in cognitive development. The development of the individual cannot be understood (and cannot actually *happen*) outside the context of social interaction.

✓ **Relevance to cross-cultural psychology:** Vygotsky's theory hasn't been tested cross-culturally as Piaget's has. But it has influenced cross-cultural psychology through the development of *cultural psychology* (e.g. Cole, 1990; see Chapter 16). and related approaches. These include 'socially shared cognition' (Resnick *et al.*, 1991) and 'distributed cognition' (Salomon, 1993). According to Segall *et al.* (1999):

> '... cognitive processes are not seen as exclusively individual central processors, but ... are situation specific ... therefore cognition is not necessarily situated "within the head" but is shared among people and settings ... '.

✓ **Stimulus for other theories:** Bruner (e.g. 1966) has helped to extend Vygotsky's ideas – and to apply them to education (see section below). Bruner was influenced by Piaget too, but like Vygotsky (and unlike Piaget), his theory doesn't involve developmental stages. Bruner, like Vygotsky, stresses the role of language and interpersonal communication, and the need for active involvement by expert adults (or more knowledgeable peers) in helping the child to develop as a thinker and problem-solver. Language plays a crucial part in the scaffolding process (see Essential Study 11.5). Bruner also sees instruction as an essential part of the learning process, in both naturalistic and educational settings.

## Applications of Piaget's and Vygotsky's Theories to Education

> **Specification Hint:** The Specification states: 'Application of these theories (e.g. to education)'. 'These theories' refers to those of Piaget and Vygotsky (which are specified in the previous section, i.e. '... including ...'). Although '... (e.g. to education)' allows you to consider applications other than education, this is by far the most obvious area of application. This is the one we discuss below. *Only one area of application is required* (despite 'Applications').

### Applying Piaget's theory to education

Piaget didn't actually advocate a 'theory of instruction' (Ginsberg, 1981). But his theory has three main implications for education (Brainerd, 1983). These are (a) the concept of *readiness*; (b) the *curriculum* (what should be taught); and (c) *teaching methods* (how the curriculum should be taught).

(a) Readiness refers to limits set on learning by a child's current stage of development (see Box 11.5).

(b) Appropriate content would include *logic* (such as transitive inference, as in 'If Adam is taller than Bob, and Bob is taller than Charlie ...': see above), *maths* (numbers), *science* (conservation), and *space* (Euclidean geometry). Teaching materials should consist of concrete objects that children can easily manipulate.

(c) Central to a Piagetian perspective is the view that children learn from actions rather than from passive observation, that is, *self-discovery* or *discovery learning*. Teachers must recognise that each child needs to construct knowledge for itself; deeper understanding comes from *active* learning (Smith *et al.*, 1998).

**Exam Hint:**

Vygotsky addressed education – as did Bruner – very directly, unlike Piaget. It's difficult to know what other applications you could come up with. This difference between Piaget and Vygotsky is an AO2 point worth making in its own right. The question couldn't ask you specifically about education (although it could include the wording '... (e.g. education)'.

### Box 11.5  The role of the teacher in the Piagetian classroom

- It's essential for teachers to assess very carefully each individual child's current stage of cognitive development (this relates to the concept of *readiness*). The child can then be set tasks tailored to its needs, which become *intrinsically* motivating (that is, motivating *in themselves*).
- Teachers must provide children with learning opportunities that enable them to advance to the next developmental step. This is achieved by creating *disequilibrium* (see page 270). Rather than providing the appropriate materials and letting children 'get on with it', teachers should create a proper balance between actively guiding and directing children's thinking patterns, and providing opportunities for them to explore by themselves (Thomas, 1985).
- Teachers should be concerned with the *learning process*, rather than its end product. This involves encouraging children to ask questions, experiment and explore. Teachers should look for the reasoning behind children's answers, especially when they make mistakes.
- Teachers should encourage children to learn from each other. Hearing other (and often conflicting) views can help to break down egocentrism. Peer interaction has both a *cognitive* and a *social value*. As a result, small-group activity is as important as individual work.
- Teachers are the guides in children's process of discovery, and the curriculum should be adapted to each child's individual needs and intellectual level (Smith *et al.*, 1998).

**Some evaluative points (AO2)**

- According to Ginsberg (1981), trying to base a curriculum on the teaching of Piagetian stages is a *misapplication* of his theory. It would be more useful to modify the curriculum in line with what's known about the various Piagetian stages, without allowing them to limit teaching methods.
- Piaget's theory seems to suggest there are definite sequences in which concepts should be taught. For example, different types of conservation appear at different times (see Box 11.3, page 275).

But many traditional schools don't base their teaching on this – or any other – developmental sequences (Elkind, 1976).

- Both Vygotsky and Bruner were unhappy with Piaget's concept of 'readiness'. They proposed a much more active policy of intervention. So instead of waiting until the child is 'ready', Bruner (1966) argued that 'any subject can be taught effectively in some intellectually honest form to any child at any stage of development'.

## APPLYING VYGOTSKY'S THEORY TO EDUCATION

- Vygotsky defines intelligence as the capacity to learn from instruction. He argued that teachers shouldn't play (merely) an *enabling* role (making it easier for the child to achieve). Instead they should guide pupils in paying attention, concentrating and learning effectively. So Vygotsky was advocating a *didactic* role (Sutherland, 1992). By doing this, teachers *scaffold* children to competence.
- Irrespective of the size of children's ZPD, the teacher is responsible for giving them the cues they need, or taking them through a series of steps towards solving a problem.
- Vygotsky rejected any approach which advocated teachers having rigid control over children's learning. Rather (as with Piaget), teachers' control over children's *activities* is what counts. Teachers extend and challenge children to go beyond where they'd otherwise have been. In other words, teachers should help children move closer to their ZPD.
- Vygotsky also believed in *collaborative learning*. As well as being helped by teachers, more advanced children are important in helping less advanced children.

### Some evaluative points (AO2)

- Educators now believe that *group learning* and *peer tutoring* can offer an effective environment for guiding a child through its ZPD. This may be because these settings encourage children to use language, provide explanations and work co-operatively or competitively. All these activities help to produce cognitive change (Pine, 1999).
- The introduction of the National Curriculum and national testing at various ages has returned the UK to the 'teacher-centred' or 'traditional' approach to young children's education. This is consistent with Vygotsky's ideas. The teacher-centred approach was dominant up until the 1960s. But it was then 'revolutionised' by the Piagetian-influenced 'child-centred' or 'progressive' approach. However, as Sutherland (1992) argues, Vygotsky didn't advocate mechanical formal teaching, ' . . . where children go through the motions of sitting at desks and passing exams that are meaningless to them . . . '. On the contrary, he stressed cognitive development rather than procedural learning.

## EXAM **tips** BOX

**Critically consider Piaget's theory of cognitive development.
(24 marks) (30 mins) (600 words minimum) AO1/AO2**

*This essay can be split up into FOUR sections – each about 150 words long. Each section would be worth approx. 6 marks.*

**Section 1:** A **description** of Piaget's theory. This could include brief details of the main ideas (such as assimilation, accommodation, schemas), together with an outline of the four developmental stages. | **AO1**

**Section 2:** This could include a brief description of Piaget's experiments demonstrating egocentrism and conservation, such as: | **AO1**

- SMS (Piaget & Inhelder, 1956)
- CoLQ (Piaget, 1952)

**Section 3:** You should **analyse** and **evaluate** Piaget's theory. You can do this by considering the above studies in the light of subsequent studies, which have questioned Piaget's conclusions by questioning his methodology. | **AO2**

**Section 4:** You can also **analyse** and **evaluate** Piaget's theory by comparing and contrasting it with another theory, such as Vygotsky's. You may also consider the applications of the theory to education. | **AO2**

*Try to answer this question yourself. There's a sample answer on page 315 with which you can compare your essay.*

# Development of measured intelligence

## Defining 'intelligence'

- Intelligence has been conceptualised in several different ways. For example, *biological definitions* see intelligence as related to *adaptation to the environment*. For Piaget (1950), intelligence is:

> ' ... essentially a system of living and acting operations, i.e. a state of balance or equilibrium achieved by the person when he is able to deal adequately with the data before him ... it is dynamic in that it continually adapts itself to new environmental stimuli.'

Piaget is interested in the *qualitative* aspects of intelligence, that is, the nature of intelligence itself (see above).

- Most definitions reflect the *psychometric* ('mental measurement') *approach*. This is concerned with *individual differences* in intelligence, through the use of intelligence (*intelligence quotient/IQ*) tests. By contrast with Piaget, the psychometric approach emphasises the *quantitative* aspects of intelligence.
- The psychometric approach is associated with some of the major *theories* of intelligence, such as those of Spearman (1904, 1967), Burt (1949, 1955), Vernon (1950), Thurstone (1938) and Guilford (1959).
- This approach predominated until fairly recently. Some famous and influential definitions (mainly reflecting the psychometric approach) are shown in Table 11.2.

Table 11.2 Some definitions of intelligence

'It seems to us that in intelligence there is a fundamental faculty, the impairment of which is of the utmost importance for practical life. This faculty is called judgement, otherwise called good sense, practical sense, initiative, the faculty of adapting one's self to circumstances. To judge well, to comprehend well, to reason well ... ' (Binet, 1905)

'An individual is intelligent in proportion as he is able to carry on abstract thinking.' (Terman, 1921)

' ... innate, general, cognitive ability.' (Burt, 1955)

' ... the aggregate of the global capacity to act purposefully, think rationally, to deal effectively with the environment.' (Wechsler, 1944)

' ... the effective all-round cognitive abilities to comprehend, to grasp relations and reason.' (Vernon, 1969)

'Intelligent activity consists in grasping the essentials in a situation and responding appropriately to them.' (Heim, 1970)

' ... the ability to deal with cognitive complexity.' (Gottfredson, 1998)

- The definitions of Terman, Burt, Vernon, and Gottfredson all stress the purely *cognitive* aspects of intelligence. Binet's and Wechsler's are much broader – and perhaps closer to common-sense understanding.
- Heim objects to the use of 'intelligence' as a noun, because it smacks of an 'isolable entity or thing'. So she prefers to talk about 'intelligent activity' rather than 'intelligence'.
- An *operational definition* defines intelligence in terms of tests designed to measure it, that is, 'Intelligence is what intelligence tests measure' (Boring, 1923). Unfortunately, this begs the question as to what intelligence tests *do* measure, and is a *circular* definition (the concept being defined is part of the definition itself).
- Being familiar with different definitions is important because these are reflected in *theories* of intelligence. In turn, these theories are reflected in, and influence the design of, intelligence tests.

## Intelligence tests

### THE STANFORD–BINET TEST

- In 1904 the French Government commissioned Binet and Simon to devise a test which would identify those children who wouldn't benefit from ordinary schooling because of their low intelligence. The result was the Simon–Binet test (1905), generally accepted as the first intelligence test.
- The sample of children used for the development of the test (the *standardisation sample*) was very small. The test was revised in 1908 and 1911 using much larger samples.
- Terman, at Stanford University in California, began adapting the test (in 1910) for use in the USA. It became known as the *Stanford–Binet* test – and is still referred to in this way. The first revision was published in 1916, followed by further revisions in 1937, 1960, 1973 and 1986.
- Before 1960, the Stanford–Binet was designed for individuals up to age 16 (starting at two-and-a-half to three). The upper age was extended to 18 in the 1960 revision. The 1986 version is designed for two- to 23-year-olds. Test items are grouped into four broad areas of intellectual ability: (a) *verbal reasoning*; (b) *abstract/visual reasoning*; (c) *quantitative reasoning*; and (d) *short-term memory*.

### THE WECHSLER TESTS

- Wechsler developed the most widely-used test of adult intelligence: the Wechsler Adult Intelligence Scale (WAIS, 1944, 1958, 1981, 1997).
- The adult test is constructed much like the Wechsler Intelligence Scale for Children (WISC, 1949, 1974, 1991). This is designed for children between five and 15. There's also a Wechsler Pre-School Primary Scale of Intelligence (WPPSI, 1963, 1989), designed for four- to six-and-a-half-year-olds.
- The Wechsler tests produce *three* IQ scores: *verbal*, *performance* and *full* (combined or general) IQs. They're by far the most widely used cognitive assessment instruments today, both in the USA and around the world (Sparrow & Davis, 2000).

### ARMY ALPHA AND BETA TESTS

- The Stanford–Binet and Wechsler tests are *individual* tests, that is, they're given to one person at a time. But *group* tests are administered to several people at once (as in written examinations).
- A major impetus to the development of group testing was America's involvement in World War I. A quick and easy method of selecting over one million recruits was needed, and the result was the *army alpha* and *beta tests*.

## Exam Hint:

The Specification doesn't explicitly require you to know about definitions of intelligence or about specific intelligence tests. But the very fact that there's no single definition that all psychologists agree about, and that there are several (types of) tests, are points that can be used as evaluation (AO2).

For example, if different studies of the role of genetics and/or cultural differences on intelligence test performance use different tests, it's more difficult to compare or combine the resulting findings. Also, the claims (often an assumption made by researchers) that IQ tests actually measure intelligence, and that IQ tests are equally valid in different cultures, are controversial. This is another example of how 'background' knowledge can be used to gain AO2 marks.

*Word of warning:* Remember that you won't be asked a question specifically about IQ tests, but about the role of genetics and environmental factors. To gain AO2 marks, you must make these issues regarding IQ tests *relevant* to the question.

## THE BRITISH ABILITY SCALES (BAS)

- The BAS (Elliot *et al.*, 1979) was designed for use with two-and-a-half to 17-year-olds. Five major 'mental processes' are assessed, including *retrieval and application of knowledge*, and *speed of information processing*.
- Like the Wechsler tests, the BAS gives three IQ scores: *verbal*, *visual* and *overall* (*general*). The aim was to construct a test which would provide a profile of special abilities, rather than merely produce an overall IQ (Richardson, 1991).
- The BAS was revised in 1996, and the upper age limit was extended to 17 years 11 months.

## What do intelligence tests measure?

- IQ tests are one kind of *ability* test. They're designed to measure underlying constructs that aren't a direct result of training (Coolican *et al.*, 1996).
- *Attainment* (or achievement) tests, on the other hand, are designed to assess *specific* school learning, such as reading and comprehension, spelling and numeracy.
- *Aptitude* tests are aimed at measuring *potential* performance (such as logic tests for predicting how good someone would be at computer programming).
- According to Gottfredson (1998), IQ tests are tests of 'mental aptitude rather than accumulated knowledge'. They measure 'pure intelligence'. But this implies that:

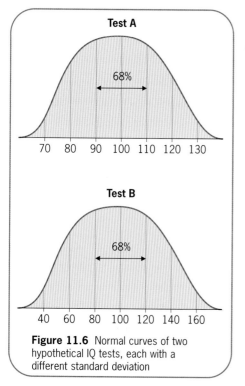

**Figure 11.6** Normal curves of two hypothetical IQ tests, each with a different standard deviation

(a) 'IQ' and 'intelligence' are one and the same. From the psychometric perspective, an individual's score on an intelligence test (his/her IQ) is an accurate measure of his/her intelligence
(b) IQ tests are valid
(c) it's possible to measure someone's potential
(d) IQ tests aren't culturally biased.

### (A) HOW ARE IQ AND INTELLIGENCE RELATED?

- In effect, and implicitly, this defines intelligence *operationally* (see above). But this begs many fundamental questions regarding the *meaning* of the IQ first introduced by Stern in 1912.
- Before 1960, the Stanford–Binet tests calculated IQ by expressing *mental age* (MA) as a ratio of *chronological age* (CA), and multiplying by 100 (so as to produce a whole number). So the first IQ was a *ratio IQ*.
- The Wechsler tests, however, have always used a *deviation IQ*. This expresses the test result as a *standard score*, that is, how many *standard deviations* (SDs) above or below the mean of the testee's age group the score lies.
- All tests are designed to produce a *normal curve*, that is, a symmetrical distribution of IQ scores with a mean of 100. But the SD (or dispersal of scores around the mean) can still differ from test to test. This is shown in Figure 11.6.

## Box 11.6 Demonstrating the difference between intelligence and IQ

- Imagine two tests: A and B. Test A has an SD of 10, and test B has an SD of 20. In both cases, 68% (approximately) of children would be expected to have scores one SD below or above the mean (that is, from 90 to 110 in Test A, and from 80 to 120 in Test B).
- So a particular child might have a score of 110 on Test A and 120 on Test B. But the scores would be telling us the same thing: different IQs, but same intelligence.

- The example in Box 11.6 suggests that (a) intelligence is a *psychological* concept, while (b) IQ is a purely *statistical* concept. It shows that it's possible for the same characteristic (intelligence) to be assigned different values according to which test is used to measure it. So instead of asking 'How intelligent is this individual?', we should ask 'How intelligent is this individual *as measured by this particular test*?'.
- An operational definition of, say, height, is uncontroversial (your height is how far along the tape measure you come). But what intelligence is is a matter of controversy and debate (see the definitions above). Unless we know what it is, we cannot be sure we're measuring it accurately. This is why IQ is an unwarranted 'reduction' of intelligence (see Chapter 17): something very diverse and complex is expressed as a single number.
- Height is measured on an *interval scale*: using metres and centimetres allows us to measure one person's height accurately without knowing anyone else's. But intelligence tests are different. IQ is measured on an *ordinal* scale. This tells us only whether one person is more or less intelligent (higher or lower IQ) than another (it's a *relative* measurement).
- Because IQ is a number, it creates the *impression* that intelligence is being measured in the same way as height. But this is a *false* impression (Ryan, 1972). The BAS *claims* to give 'direct estimates of ability' (that is, it claims to use interval scaling), as if by a dipstick or linear rule. But Richardson (1991) doubts this claim is valid.

## (B) ARE IQ TESTS VALID?

- A test is valid if it measures what it claims to measure. In relation to intelligence tests, the question is 'Do they measure intelligence?'.
- There are different kinds of validity. But probably the most commonly used in relation to psychological tests in general, and IQ tests in particular, is *predictive validity*. This refers to the correlation between (a) the test score and (b) some future criterion measure. The most common and powerful external criterion is *educability* or *educational success*. Occupational success is also important.
- According to Gottfredson (1998) :

> 'Intelligence as measured by IQ tests is the single most effective predictor known of individual performance at school and on the job. It also predicts many other aspects of well-being, including a person's chances of divorcing, dropping out of high school, being unemployed or having illegitimate children.'

- Typically, conventional IQ tests will correlate 0.4–0.6 with school grades. But a test that predicts performance with a correlation of 0.5. still accounts for only 25% of the variation between the performance of different individuals (variation = correlation squared = 0.5 squared = 0.25). This leaves 75% of the variation. So there must be more to school performance than IQ (Sternberg, 1998).

## Box 11.7 What the predictive validity of IQ tests really means

- All the variables (including cognitive ability) that contribute to school success also contribute to performance on IQ tests. So we'd expect a high correlation for this reason alone.
- 'General intelligence' can be called 'school intelligence' – the ability to do well at school (Heather, 1976). The correlation with school performance perhaps makes IQ tests valid tests of *educational prediction*, rather than valid tests of intelligence (Richardson, 1991).
- To the extent that tests measure educability, they're measuring something which is greatly influenced by various social and motivational (that is, non-cognitive) factors. This conflicts with most IQ tests' stated purpose, which is to measure only cognitive ability or potential (Ryan, 1972).

## (C) CAN IQ TESTS MEASURE POTENTIAL?

- According to Ryan (1972), it's logically impossible to measure potential separately from some actual behaviour. Some of the skills that individuals have developed during their lifetime *must be used* when they do an IQ test.

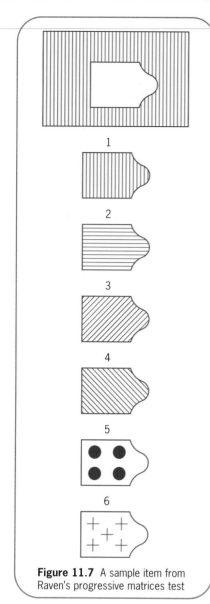

**Figure 11.7** A sample item from Raven's progressive matrices test

- Ryan argues that the notion of 'innate potential' makes no sense.
- Bee (1994) agrees that it's impossible to measure 'basic capacity' or 'underlying *competence*'. All we can ever measure is 'today's *performance*'. According to Bee:

> 'All IQ tests are really achievement tests to some degree. The difference between tests called IQ tests and those called achievement tests is really a matter of degree.'

## (D) ARE IQ TESTS CULTURALLY BIASED?

- There has been much debate over whether it's possible for IQ tests to be either *culture-fair* or *culture-free*. According to Frijda and Jahoda (1966), a *culture-free* test would actually measure some inherent quality or capacity ('intelligence') equally well in all cultures. It's widely agreed that there's no such thing as a culture-free test. But what about a *culture-fair* test? This could be either:

(a) a set of items which are equally unfamiliar to all possible persons in all possible cultures, giving everyone an equal chance of passing (or failing) them, this is what's often understood by a 'culture-free' test. This is virtually impossible (Segall *et al.*, 1999). Or:

(b) multiple sets of items, modified for use in each culture to ensure that each version would contain the same degree of familiarity. This would give members of each culture about the same chance of being successful with their respective versions. This is *theoretically* possible, but very difficult to construct in practice (Segall *et al.*, 1999).

- The emphasis on language has been one of the more obvious sources of bias in traditional IQ tests. Consequently, tests which claim to be culture-fair are often *non-verbal*. A well-known example is *Raven's progressive matrices* (see Figure 11.7).
- Even without any written instructions, you can probably infer what you have to do. However, the very nature of the task is likely to reflect particular cultural experiences. According to Owen and Stoneman (1972), the influence of language is so pervasive that any attempt to devise a culture-fair test by removing 'overt language structures' is doomed to fail. Vernon (1969) rejects the idea of a culture-fair test.
- A major reason that constructing a culture-fair test has proved so problematical could be that the very concept of intelligence is culturally defined. As Bruner (in Gillham, 1975) puts it: 'The culture-free test is the intelligence-free test, for intelligence is a cultural concept.'
- Something which can never be 'built-in' to a test's construction (or translation) is the meaning of the experience of taking an intelligence test. Taking tests of various kinds is a familiar experience for members of Western cultures – both within and outside education. But what about cultures where there's no generally available schooling?
- The very nature or form of the tasks involved in IQ tests (as opposed to the content) has a cultural meaning. This is illustrated in Box 11.8.

## Box 11.8 Can 'intelligent' behaviour be 'foolish' behaviour?

- Glick (1975, in Rogoff & Morelli, 1989) asked members of the Kpelle people to sort 20 familiar objects into groups. They did this by using *functional groupings* (such as knife with orange, potato with hoe), rather than *taxonomic* groupings (such as tools, food, and so on). Glick thought the latter was more appropriate.
- When he challenged their way of classifying, participants often explained that this was how a wise man would do it.
- When the exasperated researcher finally asked 'How would a fool do it?', participants immediately arranged the objects into four neat piles of foods, tools, clothing and utensils (that is, taxonomic groups!).
- The American researcher (Glick) and the non-Western participants (the Kpelle people) simply differed in their beliefs about the intelligent way of doing things.

- Different cultures may promote the development of different abilities. An example is described in Essential Study 11.6.

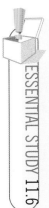

**ESSENTIAL STUDY 11.6**

**The Wirey Intelligence of Zambian children** (WIZ) **study** (Serpell, 1979)

- Serpell predicted that Zambian children would perform better than English children on a task which required them to copy objects using bits of wire.
- This was based on the observation that children all over central and southern Africa are very skilled at constructing wire cars from scraps of wire. This is a popular form of play.
- Serpell also predicted that the English children would perform better when asked to draw the objects.
- Both predictions were supported.
- These findings show that the abstract psychological function of pattern reproduction can be expressed in different ways, This varies according to the demands of the *ecological niche* to which participants' behaviour is adapted (Serpell, 1994).

- As Sternberg (1995) says, we need to take culture into account when considering both the *nature* and *assessment* of intelligence.

## Research into factors associated with the development of measured intelligence

According to Sternberg and Grigorenko (1997), almost all researchers accept that:

(a) both heredity and environment contribute to intelligence

(b) heredity and environment interact in various ways

(c) extremely poor, as well as highly enriched, environments can interfere with the realisation of a person's intelligence, regardless of his/her heredity.

### Genetic factors

#### STUDIES OF IQ STABILITY

- Our genetic inheritance is a constant. So if measured intelligence (an IQ test score) is largely determined by genetic factors, there should be a high degree of stability (or *continuity*) in IQ throughout our lifespan (McGurk, 1975). In other words, our IQ should be pretty much the same at different ages.

- IQ isn't normally used as a measure of intelligence below age two. Instead, a *developmental quotient* (DQ) is used. This assesses a child's developmental rate compared with an 'average' child of the same age (Bayley, 1969). The younger a child is when given a developmental test, the *lower* the correlation between its DQ and later IQ.
- Once IQ is measurable, it becomes a better predictor of adult IQ (the correlation between earlier and later IQ *increases*).
- The stability coefficients reported by some researchers (e.g. Honzik *et al.*, 1948) are impressive. But they're based on large numbers, which tends to obscure *individual differences*.
- McCall *et al.* (1973) found that in 140 middle-class children, the average IQ change between the ages of two-and-a-half and 17 was 28 points. The most 'stable' children changed an average of 10 points. 15% shifted 50 points or more (up or down). One child's IQ increased by 74 points!
- Even where the correlations between IQ at different ages (stability coefficients) are statistically significant, they are low.
- The fluctuations in scores are greater than a simple genetic theory would predict. There's a large amount of convincing evidence that a person's intelligence level can alter, sometimes substantially (Howe, 1997).

## FAMILY RESEMBLANCE STUDIES

- Family resemblance studies examine the correlation in intelligence test scores among people who vary in genetic similarity. If genetic factors influence IQ, then the closer the genetic relationship between two people, the greater the correspondence (or concordance) between their IQs should be.
- Monozygotic (MZ) or identical twins are unique in having exactly the same genetic inheritance: they develop from the same single fertilised egg.
- Dizygotic (DZ) or non-identical (or fraternal) twins develop from two separate fertilised eggs. They're no more alike than ordinary siblings: they share about 50% of their genes.

**Table 11.3** Familial correlations for IQ

| | No. of correlations | No. of pairings | Median correlation | Weighted average |
|---|---|---|---|---|
| Monozygotic twins reared together | 34 | 4672 | 0.85 | 0.86 |
| Monozygotic twins reared apart | 3 | 65 | 0.67 | 0.72 |
| Midparent–midoffspring reared together | 3 | 410 | 0.73 | 0.72 |
| Midparent–offspring reared together | 8 | 992 | 0.475 | 0.50 |
| Dizygotic twins reared together | 41 | 5546 | 0.58 | 0.60 |
| Siblings reared together | 69 | 26 473 | 0.45 | 0.47 |
| Siblings reared apart | 2 | 203 | 0.24 | 0.24 |
| Single parent–offspring reared together | 32 | 8433 | 0.385 | 0.42 |
| Single parent–offspring reared apart | 4 | 814 | 0.22 | 0.22 |
| Half-siblings | 2 | 200 | 0.35 | 0.31 |
| Cousins | 4 | 1176 | 0.145 | 0.15 |
| Non-biological sibling pairs (adopted/natural pairings) | 5 | 345 | 0.29 | 0.29 |
| Non-biological sibling pairs (adopted/adopted pairings) | 6 | 369 | 0.31 | 0.34 |
| Adopting midparent–offspring | 6 | 758 | 0.19 | 0.24 |
| Adopting parent–offspring | 6 | 1397 | 0.18 | 0.19 |
| Assortative mating | 16 | 3817 | 0.365 | 0.33 |

The vertical bar on each distribution indicates the median correlation. The arrow indicates the correlation predicted by a simple polygenic model (that is, the view that many pairs of genes are involved in the inheritance of intelligence) (based on Bouchard & McGue, 1981).

- If genes have any influence on the development of measured intelligence, then MZs should show the greatest concordance for IQ. Any difference between their test scores would have to be attributed to environmental or experiential influences.
- Studies by Erlenmeyer-Kimling and Jarvik (1963), Bouchard and McGue (1981), and others, have supported the 'genetic theory'. In other words, the closer people's genetic similarity, the greater the similarity of their IQ scores. Table 11.3 above presents a summary of Bouchard and McGue's world-wide review of 111 studies reporting IQ correlations between people of varying genetic similarity.
- The last column of Table 11.3 shows that the correlation between cousins (who share approximately 12.5% of their genes) is weaker (0.15) than that for parents and their offspring (0.50: they share roughly 50% of theirs). The strongest correlation of all is for MZs reared together (0.86).
- At first glance, these data suggest that heredity is a major influence on IQ test performance. But as the genetic similarity between people increases, so does the similarity of their environments. In the case of MZs raised together (MZsRT), we cannot tell whether the very high correlation reflects their genetic or their environmental similarity. So, how can we try to disentangle the effects of genetic and environmental factors?

## STUDIES OF SEPARATED TWINS

- Twin studies commonly involve a comparison between MZsRT (same genes, same environment) and those raised apart (MZsRA) (same genes, different environments).
- As Table 11.3 shows, MZsRA are still more similar (correlation of 0.72) than same-sex DZs reared together. This suggests a strong genetic influence (Bouchard *et al*., 1990).
- Not all twin studies involve this comparison between MZsRT and MZsRA. See Essential Study 11.7.

ESSENTIAL STUDY 11.7

**Twins Early Development Study** (TEDS)

- This is an ongoing study, involving more than 15,000 pairs of twins. It's the largest twin study ever carried out in the UK. It's being conducted by researchers at the Institute of Psychiatry in London.
- The basic methodology involves a comparison between MZs and DZs (reared together). The focus is on the three most common childhood psychological problems: communication disorders, mild mental impairment (learning difficulties) and behaviour problems.
- 85–90% of students with learning difficulties who receive support from special education services have reading problems. There seems to be a substantial genetic element to reading disability (Harlaar, in Bignell, 2003).
- Plomin (in Bignell, 2003) is using the TEDS data to look at how children differ in academic achievement. Many studies have examined the influence of home life (especially parental education, income and expectations) or school (teacher skills, class size and peer relations). But relatively few have investigated the role of genetic factors.
- Plomin reports that genetic factors have greater influence on academic achievement than the shared 'environmental' effects that most studies have looked at (see Chapter 17). Predictably, a high proportion of the genetic influence on academic achievement overlaps with IQ scores. But interestingly, half is specific to achievement. Plomin concludes that genetics play a major role in academic achievement. This is highly relevant in relation to the earlier discussion about the validity of IQ tests and their relationship to school success (see page 285).

## An Evaluation of twin studies (AO2)

✗ **Are separated twins truly separated?** In Shields's (1962) and Juel-Nielsen's (1965) studies, some of the 'separated' twins (MZsRA) had been raised in related branches of the parents' families, attended the same schools, and/or played together (Farber, 1981; Horgan, 1993). In Shields's study, excluding these twins reduces the correlation from 0.77 to 0.51. Even if the twins are separated at birth, they've shared the same pre-natal environment for nine months. This alone could account for the observed similarities in IQ (Howe, 1997).

✗ **Are separated twins randomly allocated to their family of rearing?** When twins have to be separated, the agencies responsible for placing them generally try to match the respective families as closely as possible. This could account for high correlations. But when the environments are substantially different, there are marked IQ differences between twins (that is, the correlations are much lower) (Newman *et al.*, 1937).

✗ **Experimenter bias:** In the studies by Newman *et al.* and Shields, the researchers knew which twins were MZsRT and which were MZsRA.

✗ **Biased sample:** Participants in Bouchard *et al.*'s (1990) study were recruited by means of media appeals and 'self-referrals'. Kaprio (in Horgan, 1993) claims that Bouchard *et al.*'s study has attracted people who enjoy publicity and want to be 'famous'. This means they're not typical of twins in general.

✗ **Fabrication of data:** The most widely cited and best-known studies of MZs are those reported by Burt (e.g. 1966). He found correlations between the IQs of 53 pairs, supposedly reared in very different environments. Kamin (1974) and Gillie (1976) noticed several peculiarities in Burt's procedures and data. This led them to question the authenticity of the research. Even Burt's most loyal supporters have conceded that at least some of his data were invented (e.g. Hearnshaw, 1979).

✓ **Evidence for genetic influences is strong:** The limitations of twin studies have undoubtedly led to an *overestimation* of genetic influences. But improved methodologies have produced correlations that are still impressive. According to Plomin and DeFries (1980), these correlations:

'. . . implicate genes as the major systematic force influencing the development of individual differences in IQ.'

✓ **Ethically sound:** Twins aren't separated because psychologists wish to study the relative effects of genetic and environmental factors. These studies are *natural experiments*, in which researchers take advantage of naturally occurring events and situations (see Chapter 6). The same applies to adoption studies.

## Adoption Studies

- Adopted children share *half* their genes, but nothing of their environment, with their biological (natural) parents. They share at least *some* of their environment, but none of their genes, with their adoptive parents.
- One research methodology involves comparing the IQs of children adopted in infancy with those of their adoptive and biological parents. If the correlation between the adopted children's IQs and those of their biological parents was *stronger* than that between the children and their adoptive parents, then this would support the greater influence of genetic factors.
- Munsinger (1975) used this methodology. He found that the average correlation between adopted children and (a) their biological parents, and (b) their adoptive parents was 0.48 and 0.19 respectively.
- By the end of adolescence, adopted children's IQs are only weakly correlated with their adoptive siblings, who share the same environments but are genetically unrelated (Plomin, 1988). This is further support for the role of genetic factors – they seem to become *more* important over the course of development.

 An Evaluation of adoption studies (AO2)

✓ • ✗ **Difficulty in assessing environmental similarity:** It's often difficult in practice to know how similar (or different) the environments of the adoptive and biological parents actually are. This is important because, when assessing the role of genetics, it's assumed that these environments are very similar ('held constant'). When the socio–economic status (SES) of the biological and adoptive parents is roughly equal, the IQs of adopted children tend to be much closer to the biological parents' IQs (Scarr & Weinberg, 1978). This supports the genetic theory. But when the environments are very different (as when children of poor, under-educated parents are adopted by high socioeconomic status parents), substantial increases in IQ scores occur (as in twin studies – see above). In these cases, the correlation between the adopted children's IQ and their adoptive parents' IQ will be higher than with the biological parents'. This, of course, supports the influence of environmental factors. (See Essential Study 11.8.)

**ESSENTIAL STUDY 11.8**

**Transracial Adoption Study** (TRAS) (Scarr & Weinberg, 1976)

- The study involved 101 white families, above-average in intelligence, income and socio–economic status (SES), who had adopted black children.
- If genetics were the only factor influencing the development of measured intelligence, then the average IQ of the adopted children should have been more or less what it was before they were adopted.
- In fact, the adopted children's average IQ was 106 after adoption, compared with an average of 90 before.
- The data also indicated that children adopted within their first year have higher IQs than those adopted later.
- Scarr and Weinberg's finding has been replicated by Schiff *et al.* (1978) and Capron and Duyme (1989).
- Schiff *et al.* studied a group of economically deprived French mothers who'd given up one baby for adoption, while keeping at least one other child. The average IQ of the children adopted into middle-class homes was 110. The average for their siblings who remained with the biological mother was 95.
- Capron and Duyme found that the IQs of French adoptees raised by parents of high SES were about 12 points higher than those of adoptees raised by parents of low SES. This was true regardless of their biological parents' SES.

✓ Helping to distinguish shared and non-shared environments: Plomin and DeFries's Colorado Adoption Project (begun in 1975) is an ongoing study involving over 200 adopted children. By middle childhood, natural mothers and their children who were adopted were just as similar as control parents and their (non-adopted) children on tests of verbal and spatial ability. But the correlation between adoptees' scores and their adoptive parents' scores was almost zero. Plomin & DeFries (1998) see these results as consistent with a growing body of evidence suggesting that the *shared family environment* doesn't make family members more similar. They claim that:

'Rather, family resemblance on such measures [verbal and spatial ability] seems to be controlled almost entirely by genetics, and environmental factors often end up making family members different, not the same.'

It's *non-shared environments* which make family members different (see Chapter 17). Plomin and DeFries's data support the role of both genetic *and* environmental factors.

## Environmental factors

### PRE-NATAL ENVIRONMENTAL INFLUENCES

- Pre-natal non-genetic factors account for the largest proportion of biologically-caused mental retardation or learning difficulties (LDs). IQ is still the main criterion used to diagnose LDs. See Table 11.4.

**Table 11.4** Different categories of mental retardation

| Name | IQ range | Prevalence (proportion of whole population which is retarded) |
|------|----------|--------------------------------------------------------------|
| Mild | 50–70 | 3% (80% of all cases) |
| Moderate | 36–49 | 0.3% (12% of all cases) |
| Severe | 20–35 | 0.04% (7% of all cases) |
| Profound | Below 20 | 0.05% (1% of all cases) |

Based on Carpenter (1997); Gelder *et al.* (1999)

- Known pre-natal *teratogens* (any agent causing abnormalities in the developing foetus) include certain infections (such as maternal rubella or German measles), toxic chemicals in the mother's body (such as heroin, cocaine, alcohol and other drugs), radiation and pollutants. Other toxins are produced by the mother's own faulty metabolism, or are the result of incompatibility between the rhesus factors in the mother's blood and that of her developing foetus (Frude, 1998). (See Figure 11.8.)

- Anxiety has also been found to lead to low-birth-weight babies (because of impaired blood flow to the uterus: Teixeira, 1999). In turn, low birth-weight (prematurity) is associated with neurological impairment, lower IQ and greater problems in school (Hack *et al.*, 1994).

- People with severe or profound LDs (8% of all cases) are more likely to have an identifiable *primary* cause, usually genetic. The most common known autosomal chromosome (not related to the sex chromosomes, pair 23) responsible for mental impairment is Down's syndrome. This is caused by an extra 21st chromosome (three instead of the normal two – trisomy 21), and occurs in one-third of people with IQ below 50 (Carpenter, 1997).

- The most common well-documented single-gene recessive defect is *phenylketonuria* (PKU). This affects 12 people per million. In the UK this is routinely tested for at birth, and a special diet can prevent LDs from developing. But an appreciable minority still isn't put on the special diet within three weeks of birth (Carpenter, 1997). PKU demonstrates the important *interaction* between genetic and environmental factors. It also shows that genes (in this case, a recessive PKU gene inherited from each parent) don't necessarily and inevitably cause a certain behaviour or outcome (LDs, and eventually death). The genes are called the *genotype*, and the behaviour or outcome the *phenotype*.

- *Secondary* (non-genetic) causes include:

(a) *Hypothyroidism:* in its severe form, this used to be called 'cretinism'. One cause is cerebral palsy (see below). Early detection and administering thyroxine within the first three months of life will prevent mental retardation. But many affected children will also be deaf, which can impair intellectual development.

(b) *Cerebral palsy:* this can be congenital (present at birth), as in congenital rubella. But it may also result from post-natal events. About one-third of full-term infants with cerebral palsy have severe LDs. It's much more common in low-birth-weight babies.

(c) *Neural tube abnormalities:* spina bifida is one example, affecting 70–150 per 100,000 live births. Up to 10% will have LDs, and almost all of these will be multiply handicapped.

(d) *Foetal alcohol syndrome (FAS):* this usually involves micro-cephaly (unusually small head

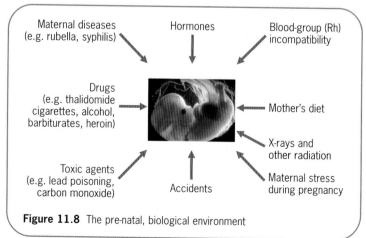

**Figure 11.8** The pre-natal, biological environment

and brain), together with heart defects, short nose and low nasal bridge. FAS children are generally mildly retarded, though some may be moderately retarded. Even those of average intelligence have significant academic and attentional difficulties (Sue *et al.*, 1994 ).

## POST-NATAL ENVIRONMENTAL INFLUENCES

### The effects of malnutrition

ESSENTIAL STUDY 11.9

**Romanian orphans study** (ROS) (Rutter *et al.*, 1998)

- Rutter *et al.* studied 111 institutionalised Romanian children adopted into English families within two years of birth.
- They'd experienced extreme privation, both physically and psychologically, and were all severely malnourished.
- Compared with 42 English adoptees, the Romanian children showed developmental deficiencies in weight, height and head circumference. They were also far slower in reaching developmental milestones.
- But by age four, they showed considerable physical and developmental catch-up, and 'spectacular' cognitive catch-up. Those adopted before six months had a clear advantage over the later-adopted children.
- Rutter *et al.* believe that the malnutrition hasn't had an effect over and above the effects of psychological privation.
- Other studies, however, suggest that periodic or chronic sub-nutrition can adversely affect intellectual development in its own right. For example, children in developing countries given high-quality nutritional supplements in infancy and early childhood have higher IQs and vocabulary scores than non-supplemented children (Pollitt & Gorman, 1994).

### Environmental enrichment (early intervention) studies

- Skeels (1966) followed up a group of children removed from orphanages into more stimulating environments 20 years earlier (Skeels & Dye, 1939). Most of those raised by foster mothers showed significant improvement in IQ. Those who remained in the orphanages had dropped out of high school, or were still institutionalised or not self-supporting.
- Other studies of children raised in orphanages have also shown that environmental enrichment can have beneficial effects. Rutter *et al.*'s ROS study is a striking example (see Essential Study 11.9).
- Hunt (1961) and Bloom (1964) argued that intelligence isn't a fixed attribute. Rather, it depends on, and can be increased by, experience. This led President Johnson (as part of his 'war against poverty') to initiate a number of *intervention programmes*. These were based on the assumption that intelligence could be increased through training, the first being *Operation Headstart* (OH) (1965).
- OH was designed to give culturally disadvantaged preschoolers enriched opportunities in early life. It began as an eight-week summer programme, and shortly afterwards became a full year's preschool project.
- In 1967, two additional *Follow Through* programmes were begun as part of an attempt to involve parents and members of the wider community.
- Early findings indicated that there were significant short-term gains for the children, which generated considerable optimism. But when IQ gains did occur, they disappeared within a couple of years, and the children's educational improvement was minimal.

ESSENTIAL STUDY 11.10

**The Milwaukee Project** (MP) (Heber *et al.*, 1968)

- This is perhaps the most publicised of all the early intervention studies (Clarke & Clarke, 2000).

- Heber *et al.* found that mothers (living in the Milwaukee slum) with IQs below 80 (less than half of all the mothers) accounted for almost 80% of children with similarly low IQs.

- An intensive intervention programme involving 40 poor, mostly black, families began with the birth of their babies. It continued until the children started school at age six. Half the women were given job training and sent to school (the 'experimental group'), while the other half (the 'control group') received neither.

- At age six, the experimental group children had an average IQ of 120.7, compared with 87.2. for the control group. By age 10, these were 104 and 86 respectively. The experimental group was also educationally superior.

- But after age 10, both groups' performance fell below national norms. Over time, the experimental group declined first to the lower levels of the city of Milwaukee, then lower to the level of inner-city schools. When assessed at age 12–14, mean IQs for the experimental and control groups were 100 and 90 respectively.

- Like OH, the MP showed that vigorous and relatively prolonged intervention can make a difference to severely disadvantaged children's cognitive performance. But much of the gain is lost in the years following the end of the programme (Rutter & Rutter, 1992). See Figure 11.9.

**Figure 11.9** IQ performance with increasing age of severely disadvantaged children participating in a broad-ranging intensive intervention programme in the pre-school years.

Data from Garber, 1988, and taken from *Developing Minds. Challenge and Continuity across the Life Span* by Michael Rutter and Marjorie Rutter

## An Evaluation of early intervention studies (AO2)

✗ **Are long-term benefits possible?** The MP was one of the most ambitious pre-school programmes ever attempted. Yet the benefits were only short-lived. This raises the fundamental question of whether there can be any lasting benefits without the whole context of family and other social and school relationships radically changing. Once the programme ended, all the adversities associated with poor social conditions and poor schooling provided an antidote to the earlier intervention (Clarke & Clarke, 2000). In other words, the children and their families 'returned' to exactly the same conditions that had prevailed prior to the programme. (But see the tick below, 'Is there evidence of long-term benefits after all?')

✗ **Do they always provide what children need?** Hunt (1969) argued that OH was inappropriate to the children's needs. It didn't provide them with the skills they'd failed to develop at home during their first four years (and which are developed by most middle-class children).

✗ **How should success be measured?** Hunt also criticised OH for emphasising IQ changes when assessing its effectiveness. If this is taken as the sole or main criterion, then the benefits certainly do seem to be short-lived (Zigler & Styfco, 1993). But critics have argued that measures which reflect social competence, adaptability and emotional health are much better criteria of success (Weinberg, 1989). These tend to develop over a longer period of time (see 'Is there evidence of long-term benefits after all?' below).

✗ **Methodological problems:** According to Bee (2000), children weren't allocated randomly to Headstart or non-Headstart, making it very difficult to interpret the resulting differences.

✓ **Is there evidence of long-term benefits after all?** These criticisms may have been premature. Several reviews looking at OH's *long-term* effects have concluded that the programme has produced lasting changes in children's cognitive abilities. The greatest gains are shown by those with the lowest initial IQs. There's also a *sleeper effect* at work, that is, the impact of intervention programmes is *cumulative* (Collins, 1983). For example, compared with non-participants, children enrolled in intervention programmes:

(a) are less likely to be placed in special education/remedial classes, are slightly less likely to repeat a grade, and slightly more likely to graduate from high school (Darlington, 1991; Haskins, 1989)

(b) tend to score higher on tests of reading, language and maths, with this 'achievement gap' widening between the ages of six and 14 (Collins, 1983)

(c) show better school adjustment than their peers (Zigler & Styfco, 1993)

(d) are more likely to want to succeed academically (Collins, 1982) and function better in school (Bee, 2000).

✓ **What can they tell us about the nature of IQ?:** According to Howe (1997, 1998), evidence that increases in IQ fade over time simply shows that intelligence is *changeable*. Even if most intervention studies had failed to raise children's IQ at all, this wouldn't be conclusive evidence that intelligence was fixed. In view of how little time children actually spend in intervention programmes, it's remarkable that there's any IQ change at all.

## Hothousing

- 'Hothousing' refers to deliberate attempts to speed up children's development.
- Some psychologists believe that accelerated progress *may* occur in some areas. But other skills (such as language) are essentially pre-programmed and hardly affected by early experience (Howe, 1997).
- Parents determined to make their child into a genius or prodigy can pressurise the child with their high expectations and by sending it to an organisation for 'gifted children'. There's no convincing evidence that such organisations are actually effective (Llewellyn-Smith, 1996).
- Children who experience intensive hothousing regimes may miss out on other experiences which may be important for healthy development – if not strictly 'educational' (Howe, 1995). A child who obtains a first-class maths degree from Oxford at the age of 13 (as Ruth Lawrence did in 1985) has clearly achieved something quite remarkable. But he or she may have failed to develop important social skills (such as the ability to make friends), because of an inability to join in 'normal' children's conversations.
- According to Bee (2000), how infants and young children are treated can make a real difference to their cognitive development, regardless of whether they come from poor working-class, or middle-class families. These dimensions of early experience have been the focus of most of the research into environmental effects on IQ.

Ruth Lawrence, who graduated from Oxford University with a first-class maths degree when just 13

- Bee identifies several dimensions of family interaction or stimulation which seem to make a difference. These are described in Box 11.9.

## Box 11.9 Dimensions of family interaction affecting cognitive development

According to Bee (2000), parents of higher-IQ children, or whose IQs show an increase over time, tend to:

- provide interesting and complex physical environments, including play materials that are appropriate for the child's age and developmental level
- be emotionally responsive and involved with their children: smiling when they smile, answering their questions, and generally responding to their cues
- talk to their children often, using language that's diverse, descriptively rich and accurate
- operate within the child's ZPD (see above, page 279) during play and interaction
- avoid excessive restrictiveness, punishment or control, providing opportunities for the child to ask questions (as opposed to giving commands)
- expect their children to do well and develop rapidly, especially academically.

## The interaction between genetic and environmental factors

- Clearly, both genetic and environmental factors can – and do – influence measured intelligence. This relates to the first of Sternberg and Grigorenko's (1997) points (see above, page 287).
- Their second point acknowledges that measured intelligence can be attributed to an *interaction* between both sets of factors. According to Weinberg (1989):

'Genes do not fix behaviour. Rather, they establish a range of possible reactions to the range of possible experiences that environments can provide. Environments can also affect whether the full range of gene reactivity is expressed. Thus, how people behave, or what their measured IQs turn out to be or how quickly they learn, depends on the nature of their environments and on their genetic endowments bestowed at conception.'

### How much does each contribute?

- If we acknowledge that both genetic and environmental factors affect IQ, then we have to ask: *how much* does each contribute?
- The term 'heritability' is used by *behaviour geneticists* (such as Plomin) to refer to the mathematical estimate of how much *variability* in a particular trait is due to genetic variability (Carlson, 1988). Eye colour, for example, is affected almost entirely by heredity and little, if at all, by environmental factors. Hence the heritability of eye colour is close to 100%.
- Early *heritability estimates* (HEs) for IQ of 80% (Jensen, 1969) have been revised more recently down to around 50–60% (Bouchard & Segal, 1988). But to say that the heritability of measured intelligence is 50–60% doesn't mean that 50–60% of measured intelligence is determined by genetic factors. This is because HEs only apply to a *particular population or group of people* at a particular time, and *not* to a single individual. That is, 50–60% (assuming this HE is correct) of the variation in IQ scores within a group of people can be attributed to genetic differences.
- But heritability describes what *is* rather than what could be (Pike & Plomin, 1999). If environmental factors within a population change (such as educational opportunities), then the relative impact of genes and environment will change. Even for a highly heritable trait such as height, environmental changes could make a large difference. Pike and Plomin say that the huge increase in height during the twentieth century is almost certainly due to improved diet.
- As far as intelligence is concerned, heritability of 50% means that environmental factors account for as much variance as genes do (Plomin & DeFries, 1998: see Chapter 17, pages 520–530).

## Box 11.10 Why between-group differences cannot be inferred from within-group differences

**Figure 11.10** Although we can account for within-group differences in terms of genetic factors, between-group differences may be caused by environmental factors (i.e. poor/fertile soil)

- Lewontin (1976) asks us to consider 10 tomato plants grown in poor soil (see Figure 11.10). Their different heights are the result of genetic factors.
- If the same 10 plants were grown in fertile soil, differences in their height would again be due to genetic factors.
- These differences are *within-group* differences.
- But the difference in the *average height* of plants grown in poor and fertile soil (that is, *between-group* differences) is due to the *environmental* differences of the soils.
- So even when the heritability of a trait is high *within* a particular group, differences in that trait *between* groups may have environmental causes (Myers, 1990).

### HOW DO THEY CONTRIBUTE?

- If we accept that genetic and environmental factors *interact*, then the focus shifts from how much they contribute to *how* (in what ways) they exert their influence.
- One way in which this might occur is *cumulative deficit*. Dozens of studies show that children from poor families, or families where the parents are relatively uneducated, have lower IQ scores than those from middle-class families (Bee, 2000). This could reflect either genetic or environmental factors, or both.
- But these social-class differences only appear after the age of two-and-a-half to three, after which they widen steadily. This suggests that the longer a child lives in poverty, the more negative the effects on IQ scores (and other measures of cognitive functioning) become (Duncan, 1993; Smith *et al.*, 1997).
- So the effects of any genetic differences that may be involved to begin with are *accentuated* by environmental factors, especially poverty. Poverty has a significant effect on children's IQ scores *over and above* what the parents' own genes may have contributed (Bee, 2000).
- *Gene–environment interactions* are discussed in Chapter 17 (see pages 527–529).

### THE RACE AND IQ DEBATE

- The false assumption that *between-group differences* can be inferred from *within-group differences* (see Box 11.10) forms a major part of the *hereditarian fallacy* (Gould, 1981).
- In turn, the fallacy is central to the claim that certain racial groups are genetically inferior to others.
- Jensen (1969) published an article called 'How much can we boost IQ and scholastic achievement?'. In it, he reviewed all the literature which compared black and white IQ scores. The basic finding was that 'On average, Negroes test about one standard deviation (15 IQ points) below the average of the white population in IQ'.
- This finding in itself isn't disputed. What's controversial is Jensen's explanation for the racial differences:

'Genetic factors are strongly implicated in the average Negro–white intelligence differences. The preponderance of the evidence is, in my opinion, less consistent with a strictly environmental hypothesis than with a genetic hypothesis . . . '

- Others, including Eysenck (1971) and Herrnstein (1971), agreed with Jensen.
- Some of the evidence on which Jensen based his genetic theory was the apparent failure of compensatory pre-school programmes (such as OH: see above). A fundamental criticism of Jensen is that he based his conclusions about black–white (*between-group*) differences on the HE (of 80%) derived from studies of the white population (that is, *within-group* differences).

## EXAM tips BOX

'... no behaviour is determined solely by culture or solely by biology. The two major classes of behavioural determinants always operate in such an interactive manner that they are difficult to separate ...' (Segall *et al.*, 1999).

**Discuss research into the role of factors associated with the development of measured intelligence. (24 marks) (30 mins) (600 words minimum) AO1/AO2**

*This essay can be split up into FOUR sections – each about 150 words long. Each section would be worth approx. 6 marks.*

*A word of advice: The question doesn't require you to address the quote. It's given as a jumping-off point for your answer. But in the AO2 sections of your essay, you may find it useful to refer to it: many studies can be criticised on the grounds that they emphasise genetic or cultural factors almost to the exclusion of the other. Most psychologists, and behaviour geneticists, would agree with Segall et al. that the interaction between them makes them almost inseparable.*

**Section 1:** A **description** of research into the role of genetics in the development of measured intelligence. This should include an outline of the basic methods used, such as family resemblance, twin and adoption studies, as well as a summary of the major findings of two or three specific studies, such as:

- Bouchard & McGue (1981)
- TEDS (in Bignell, 2003)
- Shields (1962)
- Munsinger (1975).

**AO2**

**Section 2: Analysis** and **evaluation** of the methods used to study the effects of genetics, as described in Section 1. This may include *general limitations* of these methods, and/or examples of these limitations as they apply to *particular studies*. For example, experimenter bias is general, while how this may have affected IQ correlations in Shields's study is specific. Another approach is to consider the role of environmental factors, for example, as demonstrated by:

- TRAS (Scarr & Weinberg, 1976).

*Also, issues regarding the validity of IQ tests, their cultural bias and so on, may be used as analysis and evaluation.*

**AO1**

**Section 3:** A **description** of research into the role of environmental factors in the development of measured intelligence. As with Section 1, you should try to combine an outline of the methods used (such as early intervention/programmes) and specific examples, such as Operation Headstart (OH) and:

- MP (Heber *et al.*, 1968).

*You could also make the distinction between pre- and post-natal environmental influences.*

**AO2**

**Section 4: Analysis** and **evaluation** of the methods used to study the effects of environmental factors. As in Section 2, this may include general and specific limitations. One criticism of OH was its over-emphasis on IQ as a measure of success. This, in turn, relates to more general criticisms of IQ tests (to which you may already have alluded in Section 2). Here the issue regarding the nature of intelligence as a cultural concept may be especially relevant, as shown by WIZ (Serpell, 1979).

**AO1**

*Try to answer this question yourself. There's a sample answer on page 316 with which you can compare your answer.*

- *Environmental* factors which could account for such differences include bias in the tests used to measure intelligence. According to Segall *et al.* (1999), IQ tests are biased against those (such as blacks and other minorities) whose cultural backgrounds differ from that of the test's normative sample (whites). This relates to the earlier discussion of *culture-fair/culture-free tests* (see pages 286–287), and to the *emic–etic distinction* (see Chapter 16, pages 467–468).
- So it's quite possible for individual differences in IQ (within-group differences) to be heavily influenced by genetic factors, while group differences (between-group differences) are largely or entirely due to environmental factors. Jensen's response to this is to appeal to studies which control for environmental factors.
- For example, Shuey (1966) compared middle- and working-class blacks and whites. He found the same average 15-point difference.
- But isn't there more to 'environment' than social class (measured largely in terms of occupation and income)? Given their history of slavery and continuing prejudice and discrimination, surely the *experiences* of working- and middle-class blacks aren't equivalent to that of their white counterparts? According to Bodmer (1972):

> 'Measuring the environment only by standard socioeconomic parameters is . . . like trying to assess the character of an individual by his height, weight and eye colour.'

- By the late 1980s, the gap between average black and white IQ scores had significantly narrowed – to about 7–8 points (Williams & Ceci, 1997). But this trend doesn't seem to have continued into the 1990s.
- Closing of the gap reflects:

(a) increases in educational spending throughout the twentieth century
(b) increased educational attainment by black parents
(c) reduction in the size of black families (Price & Crapo, 1999).

- Although these socioeconomic factors may be important, both genetic and environmental factors can influence the development of IQ. These factors are intertwined, not separate (Segall *et al.*, 1999).

# Development of moral understanding

> Specification Hint: The Specification states: 'Theories of moral understanding and pro-social reasoning (e.g. Kohlberg, Eisenberg) . . . '. Here 'theories' means *one theory of moral understanding* and *one theory of pro-social reasoning*. We've decided to include Piaget's theory as well as these two examples.
>
> The Specification continues: '. . . including the influence of gender (e.g. Gilligan) and cultural variations . . .'. We'll include this here as part of the evaluation of the theories.

## Theories of moral understanding and pro-social reasoning

According to Haste *et al.* (1998), historically four main questions have been asked about moral development:

- How do conscience and guilt develop, acting as sanctions on our misdeeds? This relates to Freud's *psychoanalytic theory* (see Chapters 12 and 18).
- How do we come to understand the basis of rules and moral principles, so that we can make judgements about our own and others' behaviour? This relates to the *cognitive–developmental theories* of Piaget, Kohlberg and Eisenberg.

- How do we learn the appropriate patterns of behaviour required by our culture? This relates to learning theories, including Bandura's *Social Learning Theory* (see Chapters 9, 12 and 18).
- How do we develop the moral emotions that motivate our concern for others? Eisenberg's theory is also relevant here.

The second question has dominated research into moral development for 30 years, through work within the cognitive–developmental theoretical framework. Kohlberg's theory has been the focus of research during this time. But Piaget (1932) pioneered this approach to moral development. What all three theories have in common is the belief that it's the reasons *underlying* behaviour, rather then the behaviour itself, which make it right or wrong.

## PIAGET'S THEORY

- Piaget argued that morality develops gradually during childhood and adolescence.
- These changes are usually referred to as qualitatively different stages. But Piaget explicitly *didn't* use the concept of developmental stages when describing moral development.
- Instead he distinguished between two *types of moral orientation*, namely *heteronomous* and *autonomous* (see below).

### Understanding rules

- To discover how moral knowledge and understanding change with age, Piaget began by looking at children's ideas about the rules of the game of marbles. He believed that the essence of morality lies in rules. Marbles is a game in which children create and enforce their own rules, free from adult influence. In this way, Piaget felt he could discover how children's moral knowledge in general develops.
- Piaget pretended he didn't know the rules. He asked children to explain them to him during the course of a game, where the rules came from, who made them, and whether they could be changed.
- Five- to 9/10-year-olds tended to believe that the rules had always existed in their present form, and that they'd been created by older children, adults or even God. Rules were sacred, and couldn't be changed in any way (an *external law*). Yet they unashamedly broke the rules to suit themselves, and saw nothing contradictory in the idea that *both* players could win.
- Older children (10 and over) understood that the rules were invented by children themselves. They could be changed, but only if all players agreed. The function of rules was to prevent arguments and to ensure fair play. They stuck rigidly to the rules, and discussed the finer points and implications of any changes.
- Piaget called the older child's moral orientation towards co-operation with peers *mutual respect*. This contrasts with the younger child's *unilateral respect* towards adult authority.

### Moral judgement and punishment

- Piaget told children pairs of stories about hypothetical children who'd told lies, stolen or broken something.

According to Piaget, the rules of marbles could be used to study morality, since all morality consists of a system of rules

### Exam Hint:

In any question on moral understanding, you could choose either Piaget or Kohlberg, and draw on the other theory for evaluating the chosen one (AO2). Also, Piaget's and Kohlberg's theories have more in common with each other than either has with Eisenberg's. Again, this can be used for AO2 analysis and evaluation. *Remember, the question cannot ask you specifically about Piaget, Kohlberg or Eisenberg. It can only ask you about theories of moral understanding and/or prosocial reasoning. Similarly, you could be asked about the influence of gender on moral understanding, but not specifically about Gilligan.*

## Box 11.11 Examples of pairs of stories used by Piaget

**Example 1a:** A little boy called John was in his room. He was called to dinner and went into the dining room. Behind the door there was a chair and on the chair there was a tray with 15 cups on it. John couldn't have known that the chair was behind the door and, as he entered the dining room, the door knocked against the tray and the tray fell on the floor, breaking all the cups.

**Example 1b:** One day, a little boy called Henry tried to get some jam out of a cupboard when his mother was out. He climbed onto a chair and stretched out his arm. The jam was too high up, and he couldn't reach it. But while he was trying to get it, he knocked over a cup. The cup fell down and broke.

**Example 2a:** A little girl called Marie wanted to give her mother a nice surprise and so she cut out a piece of sewing for her. But she didn't know how to use the scissors properly and she cut a big hole in her dress.

**Example 2b:** A little girl called Margaret went and took her mother's scissors one day when her mother was out. She played with them for a bit and then, as she didn't know how to use them properly, she made a hole in her dress.

- Piaget asked children who they believed was the naughtier and should therefore be punished more. He was more interested in the children's *reasons* than the answers themselves.
- The younger children (5–9/10) could distinguish an intentional act from an unintentional one. But they still tended to base their judgements on the *severity of the outcome* or the sheer amount of damage done. So John and Marie were typically judged to be naughtier (*objective* or *external responsibility*).
- By contrast, children of 10 and over judged Henry and Margaret to be naughtier. This was because they were both doing something they shouldn't have been. Although the damage they caused was accidental, they considered the motive or intention behind the act to be important in determining naughtiness (*internal responsibility*).
- Younger children believed that naughty people should pay for their crimes. In general, the greater the suffering the better, even though the form of punishment might be quite arbitrary. Such *expiatory* ('paying the penalty for') punishment is seen as decreed by authority and accepted as just because of its source (*moral realism*). So when a child in a class doesn't own up to some misdeed and his or her classmates don't point the finger, younger children see *collective punishment* (the whole class is punished) as fair and just.
- Younger children also often construed some misfortune which happens to someone who's 'got away' with some 'crime' as a punishment for the misdeed (*immanent justice*). For example, a child tells a lie but isn't found out. Later, s/he falls over and breaks an arm. This is punishment for the lie. God (or some equivalent force) is in league with authority figures to ensure that 'the guilty will always be caught in the end'.
- By contrast, older children saw punishment as (a) bringing home to the offender the nature of the offence; and (b) a deterrent to future misbehaviour. They also believed that collective punishment was wrong, and that 'the punishment should fit the crime'. For example, if one child steals another child's sweets, the offender should give his/her own sweets to the victim (based on the *principle of reciprocity*), or be punished in some other appropriate way.
- Older children no longer saw justice as being tied to authority (*moral relativism*), and there was less belief in immanent justice.
- Piaget called young children's morality *heteronomous* ('subject to another's laws or rules'). Older children possess *autonomous morality* ('subject to one's own laws or rules'). They see rules as the product of social agreements, rather than sacred and unchangeable laws (the *morality of co-operation*).
- The change from heteronomous to autonomous morality occurs because of the shift (at about seven) from egocentric to operational thought (see above, pages 272–274). This suggests that cognitive

development is *necessary* for moral development. But moral development lags at least two years behind cognitive development. So other factors must also be involved. One of these is the change from *unilateral respect* (the child's unconditional obedience towards parents and other adults) to *mutual respect* within the peer group (where disagreements between equals have to be negotiated and resolved).

**Table 11.5** Summary of Piaget's theory of moral development

| | Understanding rules | Moral judgement and punishment |
|---|---|---|
| **5–9/10-year-olds:** *Heteronomous moral orientation ('subject to another's laws or rules')* | • **Rules represent an external law**<br>• **Unilateral respect** | • **Objective/external responsibility**<br>**Belief in:**<br>• **expiatory punishment**<br>• **moral realism**<br>• **collective punishment**<br>• **immanent justice** |
| **10-year-olds and above:** *Autonomous moral orientation ('subject to one's own laws or rules')* | • **Mutual respect** | • **Internal responsibility**<br>**Belief in:**<br>• **principle of reciprocity**<br>• **moral relativism**<br>**No longer believe in:**<br>• **collective punishment**<br>• **immanent justice** |

## An Evaluation of Piaget's theory (AO2)

**✗ Gender bias:** Piaget believed that popular girls' games (such as hop-scotch) were too simple compared with boys' most popular game (marbles) to merit investigation. While girls eventually achieve similar moral levels to boys, they're less concerned with legal elaborations. This apparent gender bias is even more evident in Kohlberg's theory (see below).

**✗ Piaget oversimplified children's understanding of intention:** This is much more complex than he believed, and children are capable of applying this understanding to moral decision-making. The pre-school child isn't amoral, as Piaget claimed (Durkin, 1995).

• Piaget's stories (see Box 11.11) make the *consequences* of behaviour explicit rather than the intentions behind it (Nelson, 1980). When three-year-olds see people causing negative consequences, they assume that their intentions are also negative. But when information about intention is made explicit, even three-year-olds can make judgements about them, *regardless* of the consequences. This suggests that the main difference between three-year-olds and older children concerns (a) the ability to separate intentions from consequences, and (b) the use of these separate pieces of information to make moral judgements.
• Armsby (1971) found that 60% of six-year-olds (compared with 90% of 10-year-olds) judged that a child who deliberately breaks a cup is more 'guilty' (and so more deserving of punishment) than one who accidentally breaks a TV set. This suggests that at least some six-year-olds are capable of understanding intention in the sense of 'deliberate naughtiness'.
• According to some *information-processing* theorists (such as Gelman and Baillargeon, 1983), certain developmental changes which Piaget attributed to the increasing complexity and quality of thought are actually the result of increased capacity for the storage and retrieval of information (see Chapter 1). For example, when five-year-olds judge John to be naughtier because he broke more cups, Piaget attributes this to *external responsibility* (see Table 11.5). But it may simply be that they find it easier to remember this detail of the stories. When attempts are made to make it easier

to remember other details, five-year-olds often take intention into account – as well as the amount of damage.

✓·✗ **Cross-cultural support:** The evidence regarding the process of moral development is mixed. But many of the age trends (not necessarily actual ages) Piaget described are supported by later studies. These include cross-cultural data, mainly from Africa (Eckensberger and Zimba, 1997). But based on his idea of a balance between the individual and society, Piaget didn't assume that the developmental changes he observed in his Swiss sample would necessarily be found in other cultures. On the contrary, he claimed that the essential issue was whether the cultural context would allow certain developmental changes to occur (contrast this with his theory of cognitive development: see above, pages 268–277). This is an example of *contextualisation*, which is evident in current cross-cultural research (Eckensberger, 1999). An interesting example is given in Essential Study 11.11.

(see above, pages 268–277)

ESSENTIAL STUDY 11.11

**Lying and truth-telling in China and Canada** (LATTICAC) (Lee *et al.*, 1997)

- Lee *et al.* tested the claim that the understanding of lying is greatly influenced by the social norms and values in which individuals are socialised.
- 120 children from the People's Republic of China and 108 Canadian children (aged seven, nine and 11) were presented with four brief stories. Two of the stories involved a child who intentionally performed a good deed (valued by adults in both cultures), and two involved a child who performed a bad deed (disapproved of by adults in both cultures).
- When the story characters were questioned by a teacher about who committed the act, they either lied or told the truth. The children were asked to evaluate the story characters' deeds and their verbal statements as either 'naughty' or 'good'.
- Overall, the Chinese children rated truth-telling less positively and lie-telling more positively in *pro-social settings* compared with the Canadian children. This indicates that the emphasis on self-effacement and modesty in Chinese culture overrides children's evaluations of lying in certain situations.
- Both groups rated truth-telling positively and lie-telling negatively in *anti-social situations*. This reflects the emphasis in *both* cultures on distinguishing between misdeed and truth/lie-telling.

Lee *et al.*'s results suggest a close link between socio–cultural practices and moral judgement in relation to lying and truth-telling. China is a Communist–collectivist society, which values the community over the individual, and promotes personal sacrifice for the social good (see Chapters 8 and 16). Taking the credit for a good deed is viewed as a violation of both traditional Chinese cultural norms and Communist–collectivist doctrine. In Western culture, 'white lies' and deceptions to avoid embarrassment are tolerated, and concealing positive behaviour isn't explicitly encouraged (especially in the early years). Taking credit for good deeds is an accepted part of individualistic self-promotion in the West – but in China this is seen as a character flaw. Cultural and social factors are key determinants in children's moral development over and above cognitive development (Lee *et al.*, 1997).

## KOHLBERG'S THEORY

- Kohlberg was greatly influenced by Piaget, and they shared the belief that morality develops gradually during childhood and adolescence.
- Also like Piaget, Kohlberg was more interested in people's *reasons* for their moral judgements than the judgements themselves.
- Kohlberg assessed people's moral reasoning through the use of *moral dilemmas*. Typically, these involved a choice between two alternatives, both of which would be considered socially unacceptable. One of the most famous dilemmas concerned 'Heinz'.

### Box 11.12  An example of a moral dilemma

In Europe, a woman was near death from a special kind of cancer. There was one drug that the doctors thought might save her. It was a form of radium that a druggist in the same town had recently discovered. The drug was expensive to make, but the druggist was charging 10 times what the drug cost him to make. He paid $400 for the radium and charged $4,000 for a small dose of the drug. The sick woman's husband, Heinz, went to everyone he knew to borrow the money, but he could only get together about $2,000, which was half of what the drug cost. He told the druggist that his wife was dying and asked him to sell it cheaper or let him pay later. But the druggist said 'No. I discovered the drug and I'm going to make money from it'. So Heinz got desperate and considered breaking into the man's store to steal the drug for his wife.

1  Should Heinz steal the drug? (Why or why not?)

2  If Heinz doesn't love his wife, should he steal the drug for her? (Why or why not?)

3  Suppose the person dying isn't his wife but a stranger. Should Heinz steal the drug for the stranger? (Why or why not?)

4  (If you favour stealing the drug for a stranger) Suppose it's a pet animal he loves. Should Heinz steal to save the pet animal? (Why or why not?)

5  Is it important for people to do everything they can to save another's life? (Why or why not?)

6  Is it against the law for Heinz to steal? Does that make it morally wrong? (Why or why not?)

7  Should people try to do everything they can to obey the law? (Why or why not?)

8  How does this apply to what Heinz should do?

(From Kohlberg, 1984.)

- Kohlberg first started using the Heinz (and other) dilemmas in 1956, with 72 Chicago boys (10–16 years). 58 were followed up at three-yearly intervals for 20 years (Kohlberg, 1984; Colby *et al.*, 1983; Colby & Kohlberg, 1987).
- Based on their answers to the dilemmas, Kohlberg identified six qualitatively different *stages* of moral development. These differ in complexity, with more complex types being displayed by older individuals. The six stages span three *levels* of moral reasoning.
- At the *pre-conventional level*, we don't have a personal code of morality. Instead our moral code is shaped by the standards of adults and the consequences of following or breaking their rules.
- At the *conventional level*, we begin to internalise the moral standards of valued adult role models.
- At the *post-conventional level*, society's values (such as individuals' rights), the need for democratically determined rules, and *reciprocity* (or *mutual action*) are affirmed (stage 5). In stage 6, individuals are guided by *universal ethical principles*, doing what their conscience dictates – even if this conflicts with society's rules.

### Box 11.13 Kohlberg's three levels and six stages of moral development, and their application to the Heinz dilemma

**Level 1: Pre-conventional morality**

*Stage 1 (punishment and obedience orientation):* What's right and wrong is determined by what is and isn't punishable. If stealing is wrong, it's because authority figures say so and will punish such behaviour. Moral behaviour is essentially the avoidance of punishment.

- Heinz *should* steal the drug. If he lets his wife die, he'd get into trouble.
- Heinz *shouldn't* steal the drug. He'd get caught and sent to prison.

*Stage 2 (instrumental relativist orientation):* What's right and wrong is determined by what brings rewards and what people want. Other people's needs and wants are important, but only in a reciprocal sense ('If you scratch my back, I'll scratch yours').

- Heinz *should* steal the drug. His wife needs to live and he needs her companionship.
- Heinz *shouldn't* steal the drug. He might get caught and his wife would probably die before he got out of prison, so it wouldn't do much good.

**Level 2: Conventional morality**

*Stage 3 (interpersonal concordance or 'good boy–nice girl' orientation):* Moral behaviour is whatever pleases and helps others and doing what they approve of. Being moral is 'being a good person in your own eyes and the eyes of others'. What the majority thinks is right by definition.

- Heinz *should* steal the drug. Society expects a loving husband to help his wife regardless of the consequences.
- Heinz *shouldn't* steal the drug. He'll bring dishonour on his family and they'll be ashamed of him.

*Stage 4 (maintaining the social order orientation):* Being good means doing one's duty – showing respect for authority and maintaining the social order for its own sake. Concern for the common good goes beyond the stage 3 concern for one's family: society protects the rights of individuals, so society must be protected by the individual. Laws are accepted and obeyed unquestioningly.

- Heinz *should* steal the drug. If people like the druggist are allowed to get away with being greedy and selfish, society would eventually break down.
- Heinz *shouldn't* steal the drug. If people are allowed to take the law into their own hands, regardless of how justified an act might be, the social order would soon break down.

**Level 3: Post-conventional morality**

*Stage 5 (social contract–legalistic orientation):* Since laws are established by mutual agreement, they can be changed by the same democratic process. Although laws should be respected, since they protect individual rights as well as those of society as a whole, individual rights can sometimes supersede these laws if they become destructive or restrictive. Life is more 'sacred' than any legal principle, and so the law shouldn't be obeyed at all costs.

- Heinz *should* steal the drug. The law isn't set up to deal with circumstances in which obeying it would cost a human life.
- Heinz *shouldn't* steal the drug. Although he couldn't be blamed if he did steal it, even such extreme circumstances don't justify a person taking the law into his own hands. The ends don't always justify the means.

*Stage 6 (universal ethical principles orientation):* The ultimate judge of what's moral is a person's own conscience operating in accordance with certain universal principles. Society's rules are arbitrary and may be broken when they conflict with universal moral principles.

- Heinz *should* steal the drug. When a choice must be made between disobeying a law and saving a life, one must act in accordance with the higher principle of preserving and respecting life.
- Heinz *shouldn't* steal the drug. He must consider other people who need it just as much as his wife. By stealing the drug, he'd be acting in accordance with his own particular feelings, with utter disregard for the values of all the lives involved.

(Based on Rest, 1983; Crooks & Stein, 1991.)

• Both Kohlberg and Piaget saw cognitive development as necessary for, and setting a limit on, the maturity of moral reasoning. Moral reasoning usually lags behind cognitive development. For example, formal operational thought (see above, pages 275–276) is needed to achieve stages 5 and 6, but it cannot guarantee it. Because formal operations are achieved by only a relatively small proportion of people, it's not surprising that only about 15% of people reach stages 5 and 6 (Colby *et al.*, 1983: see Table 11.6).

**Table 11.6** Relationship between Kohlberg's stages and Piaget's types of moral development/stages of cognitive development

| Kohlberg's levels of moral development | Age group included within Kohlberg's developmental levels | Corresponding type of morality (Piaget) | Corresponding stage of cognitive development (Piaget) |
| --- | --- | --- | --- |
| Pre-conventional (stages 1 and 2) | Most nine-year-olds and below. Some over nine | Heteronomous (5–9/10) | Pre-operational (2–7) |
| Conventional (stages 3 and 4) | Most adolescents and adults | Heteronomous (e.g. respect for the law/authority figures) *plus* autonomous (e.g. taking intentions into account) | Concrete operational (7–11) |
| Post-conventional (stages 5 and 6) | 10–15% of adults, not before mid-30s | Autonomous (10 and above) | Formal operational (11 and above) |

## ✗ ✓ An evaluation of Kohlberg's theory (AO2)

✓ **Empirical support:** Kohlberg's *longitudinal* (follow-up) study showed that those who were initially at lower stages had progressed to higher stages. This suggests 'moral progression' (Colby *et al.*, 1983), consistent with the theory. (A major advantage of longitudinal studies is that the participants act as their own controls – the same individuals are compared with *themselves* over time). Based on these findings, Kohlberg argued that stages 1–5 are *universal*, occurring in an *invariant* (fixed) sequence. Rest's (1983) 20-year longitudinal study of men from adolescence to their mid-30s also showed that the stages seem to occur in the order Kohlberg described.

✓ • ✗ **Are the stages universal?** Snarey's (1987) review of 45 studies conducted in 27 different countries provides 'striking support for the universality of Kohlberg's first four stages'. But the results of Kohlberg and Nisan's (1987) study of Turkish youngsters, from both a rural village and a city, over a 12-year period, contradict this conclusion. Their overall scores were lower than Americans', and rural youngsters scored lower than the urban residents. These (and other) findings suggest that cultural factors play a significant part in moral reasoning. According to the socio–cultural approach, what 'develops' is the individual's skill in managing the moral expectations of his/her culture expressed through linguistic and symbolic practices. This contrasts with Kohlberg's cognitive–developmental model, which focuses on individual processes 'inside the head' (Haste *et al.*, 1998).

✗ **Cultural bias:** Stage-6 reasoning is based on supposedly 'universal' ethical principles, such as justice (which is central to Kohlberg's theory), equality, integrity and reverence for life. But these *aren't* universally held (Shweder, 1991; Eckensberger, 1994). For example, South East Asian culture places family loyalty at the centre of its ethical system. Shweder *et al.* (1987) gave the Heinz dilemma to people living in Indian Hindu villages. One very morally sophisticated participant used a high stage of reasoning too far removed from the Western position for it to be scored using Kohlberg's criteria (Shweder, 1990). Conversely, Iwasa (1992) found that Americans and Japanese can give the same emphasis to certain moral principles (such as valuing human life), but for *different reasons*. Americans were concerned to prolong length of life, but the Japanese were concerned to make it purer and cleaner. Hence most Americans thought Heinz *should* steal, while most Japanese thought he *shouldn't*.

✓·✗ Moral reasoning and cultural complexity: Eckensberger (1999) believes that Kohlberg's theory isn't as 'Western-based' (ethnocentric) as some critics have claimed. For example, the highest stages can be found in India, Taiwan and Israel. It seems to be the degree of 'complexity' (industrialisation) – and not 'Westernisation' – that assists the development of higher stages. Nevertheless, cultural psychologists (see Chapter 16) argue that we should be trying to study moral diversity: a focus on justice may be very far removed from some cultures' primary ethical concerns.

✗ Gender bias: According to Gilligan (1982, 1993), because Kohlberg's theory was based on an all-male sample, the stages reflect a male definition of morality. In other words, it's *androcentric* (literally, 'male-centred': see Chapter 16). Men's morality is based on abstract principles of law and justice, while women's is based on principles of compassion and care. In turn, the different 'moral orientations' of men and women rest on a deeper issue, namely how we think about *selfhood*. An ethic of justice (male) is a natural outcome of thinking of people as separate beings who, in continual conflict with each other, make rules and contracts as a way of handling that conflict. A 'female' ethic of caring/responsibility follows from regarding selves as *connected* with one another.

✓·✗ So do females and males 'think differently'? According to Johnston (1988), each sex is competent in each mode, but there are gender-linked preferences. While boys tended to use a justice orientation, they'd also use the care orientation if pressed. Likewise, girls preferred a care orientation, but they also switched easily. Haste *et al*. (1998) believe that Johnston's findings support Gilligan's argument that there's more than one moral 'voice', but not her claim that the 'caring' voice is more apparent among women. Several studies show that sex differences in moral orientation are less important than the kind of dilemmas being considered.

**Studies of Hypothetical and Real-life Dilemmas** (SoHARD) (Walker, 1989)

• Walker studied a large sample of males and females (aged five to 63). Participants were scored for both moral stage and orientation, on both *hypothetical* (such as Heinz) and *personally generated, real-life dilemmas*. The only evidence of sex differences was for adults on real-life dilemmas.

• When asked to produce real-life dilemmas, females reported more *relational/personal ones*. Males reported more *non-relational/impersonal ones*.

• A relational/personal conflict involves someone with whom the participant has a significant and continuing relationship (for example, whether or not to tell a friend her husband is having an affair). A non-relational/impersonal conflict involves acquaintances or strangers (for example, whether or not to correct a shop assistant's error in giving too much change).

• Regardless of gender, relational/personal dilemmas produced a higher level of response than non-relational/impersonal ones did.

• This is the *opposite* of Gilligan's claim that Kohlberg's stages are biased against an ethic of care (Walker, 1996).

• Both females and males tended to use the ethic of care mostly in relational/personal dilemmas, and most people used both orientations to a significant degree. The nature of the dilemma is a better predictor of moral orientation than gender (Walker, 1996).

Walker (1984, 1995) also refuted Gilligan's claim that Kohlberg's scoring system is biased against females, making them more likely to be rated at the conventional level and men at the post-conventional level. He reviewed all the available research evidence relating to sex differences (80 studies, 152 separate samples, and over 10,000 participants), and found that overall the differences were non-significant for all age groups. After controlling for educational or occupational differences favouring men, Walker concluded that there was no evidence of a systematic sex difference in moral-stage scores.

✖ **What do stages of moral development really tell us?** Kohlberg has been criticised for emphasising moral thinking based on quite unusual hypothetical dilemmas. Moral reasoning and behaviour aren't necessarily correlated (Gibbs & Schnell, 1985). What we *say* and what we *do* when faced with a moral dilemma often differ, especially under strong social pressure (see Chapter 5). Moral development research should really look at what people do, rather than what they say they'd do (Mischel & Mischel, 1976).

## EISENBERG'S THEORY

* Kohlberg's concept of moral reasoning is *prohibition-oriented*. In the case of Heinz, for example, one prohibition (stealing) is pitted against another (allowing his wife to die).
* But not all 'moral conflicts' are like this. Eisenberg (1982, 1986; Eisenberg *et al.*, 1991) argues that if we want to understand developmental changes in helping or altruism (see Chapter 9), we need to examine children's reasoning when faced with a conflict between (a) their own needs and (b) others' needs, in a context where the role of laws, rules and the dictates of authority are minimal. This refers *to pro-social moral reasoning*.
* In a series of studies during the 1980s, Eisenberg presented children of different ages (sometimes followed up until early adulthood) with illustrated hypothetical stories. The story character can help another person, but always at some personal cost.

### Box 11.14  A hypothetical story used by Eisenberg to assess pro-social reasoning

> A girl named Mary is going to a friend's birthday party. On her way, she sees a girl who has fallen down and hurt her leg. The girl asks Mary to go to her home and get her parents so the parents can take her to the doctor. But if Mary does run and get the child's parents, she will be late for the birthday party and miss the ice cream, cake and all the games.
>
> **What should Mary do? Why?**

* Based on children's responses to this and other similar dilemmas, Eisenberg identified six stages of pro-social moral reasoning. These are described in Table 11.7.

---

**Table 11.7**  Stages of pro-social moral reasoning

*Level 1 (hedonistic, self-focused orientation):* The individual is concerned with selfish, pragmatic consequences, rather than moral considerations. For example, 'She wouldn't help, because she might miss the party'. What's 'right' is whatever is instrumental in achieving the actor's own ends/desires. Reasons for helping/not helping include direct gain for the self, expectations of future reciprocity, and concern for others whom the individual needs and/or likes.

[This is the predominant mode for pre-schoolers and younger primary-schoolers.]

*Level 2 (needs of others orientation):* The individual expresses concern for the physical, material and psychological needs of others, even though these conflict with his/her own needs. For example, 'She should help, because the girl's leg is bleeding and she needs to go to the doctor'. This concern is expressed in the simplest terms, without clear evidence of self-reflective role-taking, verbal expressions of sympathy, or reference to internalised affect, such as guilt.

[This is the predominant mode for many pre-schoolers and primary-schoolers.]

*Level 3 (approval and interpersonal orientation and/or stereotyped orientation):* Stereotyped images of good and bad persons and behaviours and/or considerations of others' approval/acceptance are used in justifying pro-social or non-helping behaviours. For example, 'It's nice to help' or 'Her family would think she did the right thing'.

[This is the predominant mode for some primary-schoolers and secondary-school students.]

*Level 4a (self-reflective empathic orientation):* The individual's judgements include evidence of self-reflective sympathetic responding, role-taking, concern with others' humanness, and/or guilt or positive affect related to the consequences of one's actions. For example, 'She cares about people', and 'She'd feel bad if she didn't help because she'd be in pain'.

[This is the predominant mode for a few older primary-schoolers and many secondary-school students.]

**Level 4b (transitional level):** The individual's justifications for helping/not helping involve internalised values, norms, duties or responsibilities, or refer to the need to protect the rights and dignity of others. But these aren't clearly or strongly stated. For example, 'It's just something she's learnt and feels'.

[This is the predominant mode for a minority of people of secondary-school age and older.]

**Level 5 (strongly internalised stage):** As for 4b, but internalised values, norms etc. are much more strongly stated. Additional justifications for helping include the desire to honour individual and societal contractual obligations, improve the conditions of society, and belief in the dignity, rights and equality of all human beings. It's also characterised by the wish to maintain self-respect for living up to one's own values and accepted norms. For example, 'She'd feel bad if she didn't help because she'd know she didn't live up to her values'.

[This is the predominant mode for a very small minority of secondary-school students and no primary-schoolers.]

(Based on Eisenberg, 1982, 1986.)

 ## An evaluation of Eisenberg's theory (AO2)

✓ **Theoretical importance and contrast with Kohlberg's theory:**

(a) In a review of her research, Eisenberg (1996) points out that, as predicted, children almost never said they'd help to avoid punishment or out of blind obedience to authority figures, such as adults. This would be expected, given that children are rarely punished for *not* acting in a pro-social way (but *are* for wrongdoing). This contrasts sharply with what's been found for prohibition-oriented moral reasoning (which Kohlberg concentrated on).

(b) For Kohlberg, other-oriented reasoning emerges relatively late. But Eisenberg expected to find it by the pre-school years. Even four-to-five-year-olds often appeared to orient to others' needs, showing what seemed to be primitive empathy. Also, references to empathy-related processes (such as taking the other's perspective and sympathising) are particularly common in pro-social moral reasoning.

(c) Contrary to Kohlberg's claims, even individuals who typically used higher-level reasoning occasionally reverted to lower-level reasoning (such as egotistic, hedonistic reasoning). This was especially likely when they chose not to help, suggesting the role of *situational variables*. These are also implicated in some cross-cultural studies. For example, children raised on Israeli kibbutzim are particularly likely to emphasise reciprocity between people, whereas city children (both Israeli and from the USA) are more likely to be concerned with personal costs for helping others (see Chapter 9).

(d) If individuals' moral reasoning can vary across situations, then the relationship between their typical level of moral reasoning and their actual pro-social behaviour is likely to be weak. This is supported by Eisenberg's research.

(e) One additional factor that Eisenberg's research has revealed is emotion, in particular, *empathy*. Whether or not children help others depends on the *type* of emotional response that others' distress induces in them (rather than *whether or not* they respond emotionally). People (this includes adults) who respond *sympathetically/empathically* (associated with lowered heart rate) are more likely to help than those who experience *personal distress* (associated with accelerated heart rate) (again, see Chapter 9).

(f) According to Eckensberger (1999), emotions (especially positive ones) are increasingly being seen as the basis for moral development. This represents a move away from Kohlberg's theory and a return to Piaget's. Piaget's and Kohlberg's theories are commonly referred to jointly as cognitive–developmental theories, and, as we saw earlier, Kohlberg was very much influenced by Piaget. But instead of seeing morality as a form of cognition, Piaget in fact discussed morality in the context of affects (emotions) and feelings, and mutual respect and empathy were central

(Eckensberger, 1999). In this respect, Eisenberg and Piaget have more in common with each other than either has with Kohlberg.

## EXAM tips BOX

**Critically consider *one* theory of the development of moral understanding. (24 marks) (30 mins) (600 words minimum) AO1/AO2**

*This essay can be split into FOUR sections, each about 150 words long. Each section would be worth about 6 marks.*

*A word of advice: In the Specification, the theories of Kohlberg and Eisenberg are given as examples of 'Development of moral understanding'. So either would do here. However, if the question asked you about a 'theory of pro-social reasoning', only Eisenberg's theory would do.*

**Sections 1 and 2:** A **description** of one theory of the development of moral understanding. It may be useful to begin with the distinction between different kinds of questions that psychologists have asked about morality, and how your chosen theory fits into that context. Whichever theory you choose, you may want to describe the method(s) used to study moral development (Section 1) before summarising the theory itself (Section 2).

With Kohlberg's theory in particular, there are specific studies that you could describe (such as the longitudinal study in Chicago begun in 1956).

**Section 3:** You should **analyse** and **evaluate** the chosen theory (here and in Section 4). This can be done in several ways. For example, you could consider the methods used to gather the evidence for the theory (such as hypothetical moral dilemmas) and how this relates to moral behaviour. Kohlberg's theory in particular has been criticised for its androcentric bias (Gilligan, 1982, 1993), and you could also refer to Walker's research (SoHARD, 1989), which (a) challenges Gilligan and (b) distinguishes between different kinds of moral dilemmas (which is an important way of assessing Kohlberg's methodology).

**Section 4:** You could consider the cross-cultural validity of your chosen theory. This relates to universality of psychological theories. There is relevant evidence relating to both Piaget's and Kohlberg's theories.

You could also compare and contrast your chosen theory with one/both of the other two. For example, Eisenberg's theory is concerned with pro-social moral reasoning, while Kohlberg's is prohibition-oriented.

*Try to answer this question yourself. There's a sample essay on page 317 with which you can compare your essay.*

AO1

↓

AO2

↓

AO2

## PYA4: Cognitive Development

Other possible exam questions:

- Each essay is worth 24 marks and should take 30 minutes to write
- Remember the mark scheme allocates 12 marks for AO1 (knowledge and description) and 12 marks for AO2 (analysis and evaluation).

### DEVELOPMENT OF THINKING

1. **a.** Outline and evaluate any ONE theory of cognitive development. (12 marks)

   **b.** Assess the application of th is theory to education. (12 marks)

2. Critically consider Vygotsky's theory of cognitive development. (24 marks)

## DEVELOPMENT OF MEASURED INTELLIGENCE

**3.** Outline and evaluate research (theories and/or studies) into the role of genetics and/or environmental factors in the development of measured intelligence. (24 marks)

## DEVELOPMENT OF MORAL UNDERSTANDING

**4.** Discuss ONE theory of pro-social reasoning. (24 marks)

**5.** Critically consider the influence of gender OR cultural variations in relation to ONE theory of moral understanding. (24 marks)

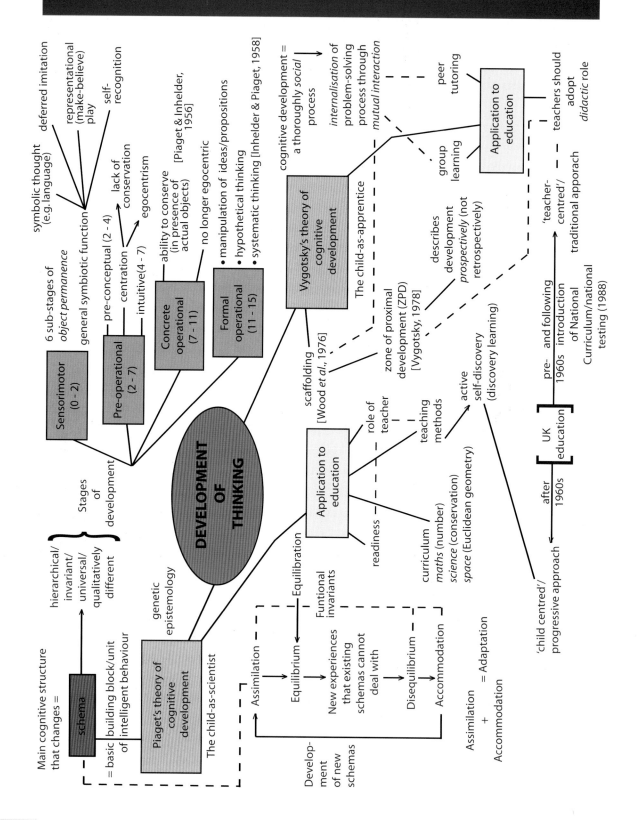

**DEVELOPMENT OF THINKING**

Stages of development

Sensorimotor (0 - 2)
- 6 sub-stages of *object permanence*
- general symbiotic function

symbolic thought (e.g. language)
deferred imitation
representational (make-believe) play
self-recognition

Pre-operational (2 - 7)
- pre-conceptual (2 - 4)
- centration
- intuitive (4 - 7)
- lack of conservation
- egocentrism

Concrete operational (7 - 11)
- ability to conserve (in presence of actual objects) [Piaget & Inhelder, 1956]
- no longer egocentric

Formal operational (11 - 15)
- manipulation of ideas/propositions
- hypothetical thinking
- systematic thinking [Inhelder & Piaget, 1958]

Vygotsky's theory of cognitive development
- The child-as-apprentice

cognitive development = a thoroughly *social* process
*internalisation* of problem-solving process through *mutual interaction*

describes development *prospectively* (not retrospectively)

Application to education
- peer tutoring
- group learning
- teachers should adopt *didactic* role

'teacher-centred'/ traditional approach

scaffolding [Wood *et al.*, 1976]

zone of proximal development (ZPD) [Vygotsky, 1978]

pre- and following introduction of National Curriculum/national testing (1988)

UK education

after 1960s

'child centred'/ progressive approach

Application to education
- role of teacher
- teaching methods
- active self-discovery (discovery learning)
- readiness
- curriculum
  - *maths* (number)
  - *science* (conservation)
  - *space* (Euclidean geometry)

Main cognitive structure that changes =
hierarchical/ invariant/ universal/ qualitatively different

**schema**
= basic building block/unit of intelligent behaviour

Piaget's theory of cognitive development
- The child-as-scientist

genetic epistemology

Equilibration
Funtional invariants

Assimilation → Equilibrium → New experiences that existing schemas cannot deal with → Disequilibrium → Accommodation

Development of new schemas

Assimilation + Accommodation = Adaptation

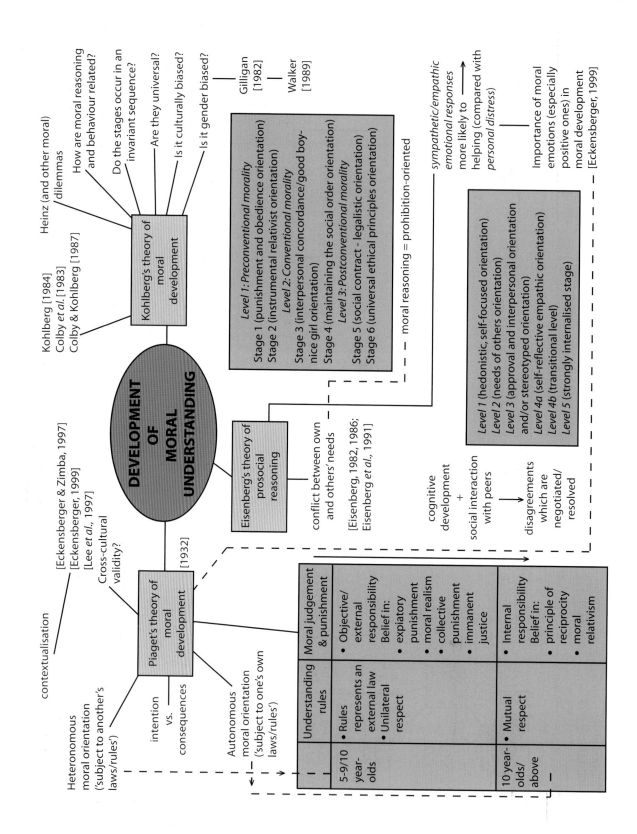

Critically consider Piaget's theory of cognitive development. (24 marks) (30 mins) (600 words minimum)

**Section 1:**

Piaget (1950) was interested in how intelligence changes as children grow (genetic epistemology). Cognitive development occurs through the interaction of innate capacities and environmental events, and children pass through a series of stages. These are hierarchical, invariant, universal and qualitatively different, that is, each stage involves a different type of intelligence. Underlying the stages are functional invariants, most important being assimilation, accommodation and equilibration. Assimilation is the process by which we incorporate new information into existing schemas (the basic building blocks of intelligent behaviour, mental structures which organise past experience). Accommodation involves modifying existing schemas so as to meet the demands of the situation or take in new information. When assimilation is sufficient for the child to deal with most new experiences, it's in a state of equilibrium (produced through equilibration). Otherwise, cognitive disequilibrium results in accommodation. Assimilation and accommodation together constitute adaptation.

The stages of cognitive development are the sensorimotor (0–2 years), pre-operational (2–7 years), concrete operational (7–11 years) and formal operational (11–15 years). A major development within the sensorimotor stage is object permanence. 'Pre-operational' conveys that the child is largely influenced by how things look, rather than by logical principles or operations. The intuitive sub-stage (4–7 years) has probably been investigated more than any other aspect of Piaget's theory, in particular egocentrism and conservation. Both are related to centration, which involves focusing on a single feature of an object or situation. For most logical operations, it's necessary to take several – or all – features into account. So the four-to-seven-year-old is egocentric and is also unable to conserve.

**Section 2:**

According to Piaget, the egocentric child sees the world from its own perspective and fails to appreciate that other people might see things differently. A classic demonstration of this is Piaget and Inhelder's (1956) Swiss mountain scene experiment. The child walks round and explores a 3-D model comprising three mountains of different colours, each with something different on top. The child then sits on one side, while a doll is placed at a different location. The child is then shown 10 pictures taken from different points around the model and is asked to choose the one that represents how the doll sees it. Four-year-olds always chose a picture which matched their own view, while six-year-olds showed some awareness of alternative perspectives. Only seven- and eight-year-olds consistently chose the correct picture.

The classic conservation of liquid quantity experiment (Piaget, 1952) involved beakers of coloured water. The child is asked if two beakers, A and B, contain the same amount of liquid (the pre-transformation question), which they do. In full view of the child, the liquid from B is poured into a taller, thinner beaker, C. The child is asked the questions again (the post-transformation question).

Pre-operational children answered 'No' to the second question, because 'It looks more' or 'It's taller'. This is despite their agreement that none has been spilled or added.

**Section 3:**

Piaget concluded from the Swiss mountain scene experiment that children under seven are bound by the egocentric illusion. That is, they fail to understand that what they see is relative to their own positions, and believe that what they see is how things 'really' are for everybody. But critics see the tasks as an unusually difficult way of presenting a problem to a young child. When it's presented in a way that makes 'human sense' (Donaldson, 1978) even three-and-a-half-year-olds can appreciate the world from another person's viewpoint (Borke, 1975). Gelman (1979) showed that four-year-olds adjust their explanations of things to make them clearer to a blindfold listener and use simpler forms of speech when talking to two-year-olds. Neither finding is consistent with Piaget's claim that four-year-olds are egocentric.

The methodology of Piaget's conservation experiments has also been questioned. Rose and Blank (1974) and Samuel and Bryant (1984) dropped the pre-transformation question, and in both studies six-year-olds were much more likely to show conservation than when asked both questions. The standard form of the task unwittingly 'forces' children to give the wrong answer. Also, according to Piaget, it should make no difference how the transformation happens – or who does it. But McGarrigle and Donaldson's 'Naughty Teddy' experiment shows that it does matter. Pre-operational children showed conservation when the transformation was 'accidental'.

**Section 4:**

Piaget's theory has had an enormous impact on our understanding of cognitive development, and it remains a source of influence in both psychology and education. But many fundamental aspects of his theory have been challenged, and fewer and fewer developmental psychologists accept his (or other) stage theories. Cross-cultural support is mixed. Dasen's (1994) research with Aborigines living in remote parts of the Australian desert found the same shift from pre-operational to concrete operational thought on conservation tasks – but this happened between 10 and 13 years (rather than five and seven). On spatial tasks, the shift occurred much earlier than for Piaget's Swiss sample.

These differences can be explained in terms of the Aborigines' survival needs. But Piaget largely neglected the contextual aspects of children's cognitive development. Underlying Piaget's theory is an image of the child 'as scientist' (Meadows, 1995). Children are largely isolated from other people as they construct their understanding of the physical world. By contrast, the social nature of knowledge and thought is central to Vygotsky's theory of cognitive development. (862 words)

*Note: This is an essay where you could draw diagrams to save you having to describe things, such as the Swiss mountain scene experiment and the conservation experiment.*

# SAMPLE ESSAYS

'... no behaviour is determined solely by culture or solely by biology. The two major classes of behavioural determinants always operate in such an interactive manner that they are difficult to separate ...' (Segall *et al.*, 1999).

Discuss research into the role of factors associated with the development of measured intelligence. (24 marks) (30 mins) (600 words minimum)

### Section 1:

**A01**

According to Sternberg and Grigorenko (1997), almost all researchers accept that both heredity and environment contribute to intelligence, that they interact in various ways, and that extremely poor, as well as highly enriched, environments can interfere with how a person's intelligence develops, regardless of his/her heredity. Family resemblance studies examine the correlation in intelligence test scores (IQ or measured intelligence) among people who vary in genetic similarity. If genetic factors influence IQ, then the closer the genetic relationship between two people, the greater the correspondence (or concordance) between their IQs should be. Monozygotic twins (MZs) should show the greatest concordance of all. Studies by Erlenmeyer-Kimling and Jarvik (1963) and Bouchard and McGue (1981) are consistent with the genetic theory: the closer people's genetic similarity, the greater the similarity of their IQs. But as people's genetic similarity increases, so does the similarity of their environments. One way of trying to disentangle the effects of genetic and environmental factors is to compare MZs raised together (MZsRT) with MZs raised apart (MZsRA). Another comparison involved in twin studies is between MZsRA with same-sex dizygotic twins (DZs). Bouchard and McGue found that the former are still more similar. This suggest a strong genetic influence (Bouchard *et al.*, 1990).

Another way of trying to disentangle the effects of genes and environment is adoption studies. Munsinger (1975), for example, compared the IQs of children adopted as babies with those of their adoptive and biological parents. The average correlation between adopted children and their biological parents was 0.48, compared with 0.19 between the adoptees and their adoptive parents.

### Section 2:

**A02**

One problem with twin studies is that the 'separated' twins aren't always truly separated. For example, in Shields's (1962) and Juel-Nielsen's (1965) studies, some of the separated MZs had been raised in related branches of the parents' families, attended the same schools and/or played together. Even if the twins have been separated at birth, they've shared the same pre-natal environment for nine months. This alone could account for the observed IQ similarities (Howe, 1997). When twins are separated, they're usually placed in families that are as similar as possible, which could account for the high concordance rate. When their respective environments are substantially different, the correlations are much lower (Newman *et al.*, 1937). These and other methodological limitations have undoubtedly led to an overestimation of genetic influences. But twin studies still implicate genes as the major source of IQ differences (Plomin & DeFries, 1980).

One problem with adoption studies is knowing how similar (or different) the environments of the adoptive and biological parents actually are. When their

---

children become much more like their adoptive parents. This was dramatically demonstrated in Scarr and Weinberg's transracial adoption study in the US, and two French studies (Schiff *et al.*, 1978; Capron & Duyme, 1989).

### Section 3:

**A01**

Pre-natal environmental (non-genetic) factors account for the largest proportion of biologically caused mental retardation or learning difficulties. There are several known pre-natal teratogens (agents causing abnormalities in the developing foetus), such as alcohol and hard drugs, and certain toxins which produced by the mother's own faulty metabolism. Post-natal environmental influences on intelligence include malnutrition. Although Rutter *et al.*'s (1998) study of Romanian orphans concluded that malnutrition hadn't had an effect over and above the effects of psychological privation, others suggest that periodic or chronic sub-nutrition can damage intellectual development in its own right (Pollitt & Gorman, 1994).

Studies of children raised in orphanages have shown that environmental enrichment can have beneficial effects (Skeels, 1966; Rutter *et al.*, 1998). Operation Headstart (OH) (1965) was designed to give culturally disadvantaged pre-schoolers enriched opportunities in early life. Early findings indicated significant short-term gains, which generated considerable optimism. But these early IQ gains disappeared within a couple of years, and educational improvement was minimal. The Milwaukee Project (MP) (Heber *et al.*, 1968), an intensive intervention programme involving mainly black families and lasting from birth till the children started school, also showed that relatively prolonged intervention can make a difference to severely disadvantaged children's cognitive performance. But much of the gain is lost in subsequent years (Rutter & Rutter, 1992).

### Section 4:

**A02**

The MP was one of the most ambitious pre-school programmes ever attempted. But if its benefits were only short-lived, we have to ask if there can be lasting benefits without the whole context of family and other social and school relationships radically changing. Once the programme ended, the children and their families returned to exactly the same poor housing, schooling and so on they'd experienced prior to the programme starting. According to Hunt (1969), OH didn't provide the children with the skills they'd failed to develop at home during their early years. It also overemphasised IQ as the criterion of success, overlooking social competence, adaptability and emotional health which are more valid criteria (Weinberg, 1989), and which tend to develop over a longer period. If a longer-term assessment is made, it seems that intervention programmes have produced lasting changes in children's cognitive abilities after all. A 'sleeper effect' means that their impact is cumulative.

Howe (1997) believes that even if most intervention programmes had failed to raise children's IQ, this wouldn't be conclusive evidence that intelligence was fixed (as claimed by the genetic theory). Given how little time children actually spend in intervention programmes, it's remarkable that there's any change in IQ at all. This is even more remarkable if we consider the cultural bias of the standard tests used to measure intelligence. There's also controversy regarding the validity of IQ tests, that is, what they actually measure, and this has

Critically consider *one* theory of the development of moral understanding. (24 marks) (30 mins) (600 words minimum)

A01

### Sections 1 and 2

According to Haste *et al.* (1998), historically four questions have been asked about moral development. One of these concerns how we come to understand the basis of rules and moral principles, so that we can make judgements about our own and others' behaviour. This relates to the cognitive–developmental theories of Piaget, Kohlberg and Eisenberg. This question has dominated research into moral development for 30 years. Piaget (1932) pioneered this approach, but Kohlberg built on Piaget's work and has been the focus of research during this time. Like Piaget, Kohlberg believed that morality develops gradually during childhood and adolescence. Both researchers were also more interested in people's reasons for their moral judgements than the judgements themselves. Kohlberg assessed people's moral reasoning through the use of moral dilemmas. These typically involved a choice between two alternatives, both of which would be considered socially unacceptable. Probably his most famous dilemma concerned Heinz, whose wife was dying from cancer and who could only be saved by a drug which he couldn't afford. The dilemma centres around whether or not he should steal the prohibitively expensive drug in order to save her life.

Kohlberg first started using the Heinz (and other) dilemma in 1956, with 72 Chicago boys (10–16 years), 58 of whom were followed up at three-yearly intervals for 20 years (Kohlberg, 1984; Colby *et al.*, 1983; Colby & Kohlberg, 1987). Based on their answers to the dilemmas, Kohlberg identified six qualitatively different stages of moral development. These differ in complexity, with more complex types being displayed by older individuals. The six stages span three levels of moral reasoning. At the pre-conventional level (most nine-year-olds and younger, and some over nine), we don't have a personal code of morality. Instead our moral code is shaped by the standards of adults and the consequences of following or breaking their rules. At the conventional level (most adolescents and adults), we begin to internalise the moral standards of valued adult role models. At the post-conventional level (10–15% of adults, not before mid-30s), society's values (such as individual rights), the need for democratically determined rules, and reciprocity are affirmed (stage 5). In stage 6, individuals are guided by universal ethical principles, doing what their conscience dictates – even if this conflicts with society's rules.

### Section 3:

According to Gilligan (1982, 1993), because Kohlberg's theory was based on an all-male sample, the stages reflect a male definition of morality (it's androcentric). Men's morality is based on abstract principles of law and justice, while women's is based on principles of compassion and care. But not everyone agrees with Gilligan. Johnston (1988), for example, argues that each sex is competent in each mode, but there are gender-linked preferences. Boys tended to use a justice orientation, but they also switched easily. Haste *et al.* (1998) believe that Johnston's findings support Gilligan's claim that there's more than one moral 'voice', but not her claim that the caring voice is more apparent in women. Several studies have shown that sex differences in moral orientation are less important than the kind of dilemmas used. For example, Walker (1989) studied males and females (aged 5–63) using both hypothetical dilemmas (such as Heinz) and personally generated, real-life dilemmas. The only evidence of sex differences was for adults on real-life dilemmas, with females reporting more relational/personal ones and males more non-relational/impersonal ones. Both sexes tended to use the ethic of care mostly in personal dilemmas, and most people used both orientations. The nature of the dilemmas is a better predictor of moral orientation than gender (Walker, 1996).

### Section 4:

Kohlberg's longitudinal study showed that those who were initially at lower stages had progressed to higher stages. This suggests 'moral progression' (Colby *et al.*, 1983), consistent with the theory. Based on these findings, Kohlberg argued that stages 1–5 are universal, occurring in an invariant (fixed) sequence. Rest's (1983) 20-year longitudinal study of men from adolescence to their mid-30s also showed that the stages seem to occur in the order Kohlberg described. Also, Snarey's (1987) review of 45 studies conducted in 27 different countries provides striking support for the universality of the first four stages. But the results of Kohlberg and Nisan's (1987) 12-year study of Turkish youngsters, from both a rural village and a city, contradict this conclusion. Their overall scores were lower than the Americans', and rural youngsters' scores were lower than the urban youngsters. These findings suggest that cultural factors play a significant part in moral reasoning. According to the socio–cultural approach, what develops is the individual's skill in managing the moral expectations of his/her culture. Kohlberg's theory focuses on what goes on inside the individual's head (Haste *et al.*, 1998). Stage 6 is itself culturally biased, because it's based on supposedly universal ethical principles (such as justice, equality and respect for life) which aren't universally shared (Shweder, 1991; Eckensberger, 1994). But Eckensberger (1999) also believes that Kohlberg's theory isn't as ethnocentric as some have claimed.

(811 words)

**SAMPLE ESSAYS**

# 12

# A2 Module 4:

**Social, Physiological, Cognitive, Developmental and Comparative Psychology**

# Social and personality development

## What's covered in this chapter?

## You need to know about:

**Personality development**

- Psychodynamic (e.g. Freud, Erikson) and social learning (e.g. Bandura; Mischel) explanations of personality development

**Gender development**

- Explanations of the development of gender identity/gender roles (e.g. social learning theories; cognitive–developmental theories)

**Adolescence**

- Research into social development in adolescence, including the formation of identity (e.g. Marcia)
- Research into relationships with parents and peers during adolescence and cultural differences in adolescent behaviour

> **Specification Hint:** The Specification states '... explanations of personality development.' It's important to be aware of how each of these terms is usually defined and what these definitions imply for a study of 'personality development'. Considerations like this can be used as AO2 material. This is where the chapter begins.

## Personality development

### What is personality?

When psychologists use the term 'personality', they're usually trying to describe ways in which people are *different*. According to Bee (2000), 'personality' describes those *enduring individual differences* in how children and adults go about relating to the people and objects in the world around them. However, she believes that we also need to understand the *common developmental patterns* which children experience.

## Personality and development

- If 'development' implies systematic changes associated with age, then some of the theories that are commonly discussed as theories of personality development aren't, strictly speaking, developmental theories at all (e.g. social learning theories). Others (such as psychodynamic theories) stress these common patterns (or stages), with the result that individual differences become overshadowed.

## Temperament vs personality

- According to Bee (2000), the great bulk of research into individual differences in infants' and children's style and manner of interacting with the world has been couched in terms of *temperament* and *not* personality.
- A number of different classifications of temperament have been proposed. The best known are *easy*, *difficult* and *slow-to-warm-up* (Thomas & Chess, 1977), *emotionality*, *activity* and *sociability* (Buss & Plomin, 1984), and *behavioural inhibition* (Kagan & Reznick, 1990). Whichever classification is favoured, it's generally agreed that temperament is genetically determined. However, what we inherit *isn't*, say, a high level of emotionality, but rather a nervous system with a low threshold of arousal.
- Temperamental differences tend to persist through childhood and into adulthood. But the individual's *personality* is the product of an *interaction* between inborn temperament and the environment the child encounters or creates. Temperamental differences between infants and children can influence other people's responses to them, but temperament can also influence what the infant or child *chooses* to experience and how it *interprets* any particular experience (see Chapter 17 on nature–nurture).
- So a child may be born with certain behavioural and emotional tendencies. But its eventual personality depends on the transaction between these and its environment. However, theories of temperament fail to tell us how these inborn individual differences may interact with *common developmental patterns* (the focus of psychodynamic theories).

## Psychodynamic explanations of personality development

- 'Psychodynamic' refers to the active forces within the personality that motivate behaviour, and the inner causes of behaviour, in particular the unconscious conflict between the various personality structures.
- Freud's psychoanalytic theory was the original psychodynamic theory, and all those theories based on his ideas are also psychodynamic. Although all psychodynamic theories are concerned with personality development, this is dealt with most directly and explicitly by Freud (*psychosexual stages*) and Erikson (*psychosocial stages*). Freud's theory (including some of its developmental aspects) is also discussed in Chapter 18 as one of the major theoretical approaches within psychology as a whole.

### FREUD'S PSYCHOANALYTIC THEORY

Freud's theory of personality development is closely related to other aspects of his theory, in particular his accounts of the structure of the personality, and motivation.

### The psychic apparatus

- Freud believed that the personality (or *psychic apparatus*) comprises three parts: the *id*, the *ego* and the *superego*.
- The id:

> ' . . . contains everything that is inherited, that is present at birth, that is laid down in the constitution – above all, therefore, the instincts . . . ' (Freud, 1923)

The wishes and impulses arising from the body's needs build up a pressure or tension (*excitation*), which demand immediate release or satisfaction. Since the *id*'s sole aim is to reduce excitation to a minimum, it's said to be governed by the *pleasure principle*. It is – and remains – the infantile, pre-socialised part of the personality. The two major *id* instincts are sexuality and aggression.

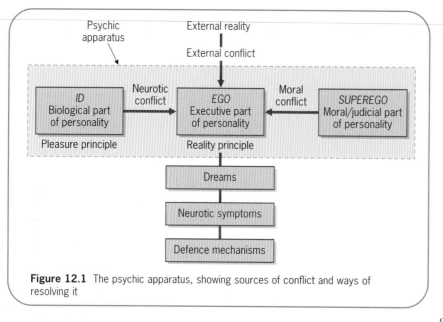

**Figure 12.1** The psychic apparatus, showing sources of conflict and ways of resolving it

- The *ego* is:

' . . . that part of the id which has been modified by the direct influence of the external world . . . ' (Freud, 1923)

It can be thought of as the 'executive' of the personality, the planning, decision-making, rational and logical part of us. It enables us to distinguish between a wish and reality (which the *id* cannot do) and is governed by the *reality principle*. Whereas the *id* demands immediate gratification for our needs and impulses, the *ego* will postpone satisfaction until the appropriate time and place (*deferred gratification*).

'The ego seeks to bring the influence of the external world to bear upon the id and its tendencies . . . For the ego, perception plays the part which in the id falls to instinct. The ego represents . . . reason and common sense, in contrast to the id, which contains the passions . . .' (Freud, 1923)

- Only when the *superego* has developed can we be described as moral beings. It represents the *internalisation* of parental and social moral values:

' . . . it observes the ego, gives it orders, judges it and threatens it with punishment, exactly like the parents whose place it has taken.' (Freud, 1933)

In fact it's the *conscience* which threatens the ego with punishment (in the form of guilt) for bad behaviour. The *ego-ideal* promises the ego rewards (in the form of pride and high self-esteem) for good behaviour. These correspond to the *punishing* and *rewarding parent* respectively.

## Psychosexual development

- Although the *id*, *ego* and *superego* develop within the individual in that order, this isn't strictly part of Freud's developmental theory.
- According to his theory of *infantile sexuality*, sexuality isn't confined to physically mature adults, but is evident from the moment of birth. So babies and young children have sexual experiences and are capable of sexual pleasure. This is derived from the rhythmical stroking or stimulation of any part of the body. However, *different* parts of the body are particularly sensitive at different times during infancy and childhood (the *erogenous zones*), and these become the focus of sexual pleasure (and frustration).
- The sequence of these *psychosexual stages* is determined by *maturation* (biologically programmed). But the crucial factor is how the child is treated by others, especially the parents. Both excessive gratification *and* extreme frustration can result in the individual getting emotionally 'stuck' (*fixated*) at the particular stage at which this occurs, producing associated *adult personality traits*. For example, *anal retentive* traits include parsimony (miserliness) and obstinacy. In this way, Freud was able to explain how individual differences arise from common developmental patterns (see above).

## Box 12.1 Freud's stages of psychosexual development

- **Oral stage (0–1 year)**: The nerve-endings in the mouth and lips are highly sensitive, and the baby derives pleasure from sucking for its own sake (*non-nutritive sucking*). In the earlier *incorporative sub-stage*, the major oral activities are sucking, swallowing and mouthing. In the later biting/aggressive sub-stage, hardening gums and erupting teeth make biting and chewing sources of pleasure.

- **Anal stage (1–3 years)**: The anal cavity and sphincter muscles of the bowel are now the main source of pleasure. In the earlier *expulsion sub-stage*, the child has its first encounter with external restrictions on its wish to defecate where and when it pleases, in the form of 'potty-training'. Parental love is no longer unconditional, but now depends on what the child *does*. In the later *retention sub-stage*, parents come to be seen for the first time as authority figures:

> '. . . by producing them [the contents of the bowels] . . . [the infant] can express his active compliance with his environment, and by withholding them, his disobedience.' (Freud, 1905)

- **Phallic stage (3–5/6 years)**: Sensitivity is now concentrated in the genitals, and masturbation (in both sexes) becomes a new source of pleasure. The child becomes aware of anatomical sex differences ('*phallic*' comes from the Greek word 'phallus' meaning penis), which marks the beginning of the *Oedipus complex*. The name derives from the classical Greek tragedy *Oedipus Rex*, in which Oedipus kills his father and marries his mother. Both boys and girls experience conflicting emotions in relation to their same- and opposite-sex parents. How successfully these emotions are resolved is crucial for future personality development. It's through the resolution of the Oedipus complex that the child's *superego* and sex role are acquired (see text).
- **Latency period (5/6 years–puberty)**: The sexual preoccupations of the earlier years are repressed. This allows the child's energies to be channelled into developing new skills and acquiring new knowledge. In relative terms, the balance between the *id, ego* and *superego* is greater than at any other time in the child's life.
- **Genital stage (puberty–maturity)**: Latency represents the calm before the storm of puberty, which marks the beginning of adolescence. The relative harmony within the child's personality is disrupted by the id's powerful new demands in the form of heterosexual desires (see pages 337–339).

### The Oedipus complex, identification and the superego

- Boys, like girls, take the mother as the first love-object. Starting at about three, a boy's love for his mother becomes increasingly passionate, not wishing to share her with anyone. He's also jealous of his father who already 'possesses' her and wants him out of the way ('dead'), so that he can have the mother all to himself. However, his father is bigger and more powerful than he is, and he eventually becomes afraid that his father will punish him by cutting off his penis (*fear of castration/castration anxiety*). He reaches this conclusion partly as a result of previous punishments for masturbation, and partly based on his observation that females don't have a penis.
- To resolve the dilemma, the boy *represses* (makes unconscious) his desire for the mother and his

hostile feelings for the father, and *identifies* with the father (he comes to act, think and feel as if he were his father). Through this *identification with the aggressor*, boys acquire their *superego* and the male sex role (see next section).

- As for the girl, her Oedipus complex (sometimes referred to as the *Electra complex*) *begins* with the belief that she's already been castrated. She blames her mother for her lack of a penis and experiences *penis envy* (she wants what males have). She eventually realises that this is unrealistic and substitutes the wish for a penis with the wish for a baby. This causes her to turn to her father as a love-object, in the hope that he'll provide her with a (preferably male) baby.

- In order to identify with the mother, the girl must give up her father as a love-object and move *back* to her mother (boys only have to make one 'move', from the mother to the father). However, Freud was much less sure about *why* the girl identifies with the mother than he was about the boy's motive for identifying with the father.

- The stronger the motive, the stronger (or more complete) the identification, which in turn makes for a stronger *superego*. So boys' fear of castration is associated with a strong identification with the father (the 'aggressor') and a strong *superego*. As Freud (1924) says:

'The fear of castration being thus excluded in a little girl, a powerful motive also drops out for the setting up of a superego.'

One suggestion Freud made was that the girl may fear losing the mother's love. To keep the mother 'alive' inside her, she internalises her, becoming the 'good' child her mother would want her to be (*anaclitic identification*). What Freud was quite sure about, however, was that identification with the mother is less complete. The girl's love for her father doesn't have to be as thoroughly abandoned as the boy's for his mother, and her Oedipus complex doesn't have to be so completely shattered (Mitchell, 1974). Consequently, females have a weaker *superego and* their identity as separate, independent persons is also less well developed.

### Box 12.2 Are females morally and sexually inferior to men? (AO2)

- Because a girl's identification with her mother is less complete, she relies more on external authority figures throughout her childhood, and has to be more compliant, less 'naughty' (there's no equivalent of 'boys will be boys'). The boy achieves independence through his strong identification with his father. This is something which the girl will have to try to achieve in adolescence. According to Mitchell (1974):

' . . . Many women, though nominally they leave home, understandably, never make it . . .'

- However, there's little evidence to support this view. For example, Hoffman (1974) reviewed several studies in which children are left alone and tempted to violate a prohibition (such as look round to see a toy placed on a table behind them). There are usually *no* overall gender differences, but, if anything, girls are better able to resist temptation than boys are.

- As noted above, Freud saw women as having to make do with babies as a substitute for a penis. This claim has aroused fierce criticism, particularly from feminist psychologists (see Chapter 16). For example, Horney (1924) and Thompson (1943), both eminent psychoanalysts, argued that what girls (and women) envy is *not* the penis as such, but males' superior social status (the penis is a *symbol* for male privilege). Moreover, it's *men*, not women, who equate lack of a penis with inferiority!

An evaluation of the Oedipus complex

✘ Potential cultural bias: Box 12.2 has considered some of the criticisms of Freud's account of sex differences in morality which follows from his theory of the Oedipus complex ('the central phenomenon of the sexual period of early childhood': Freud, 1924). Another criticism concerns its potential *cultural bias*. Freud assumed that it was a *universal* phenomenon, but even if true for Western cultures, the Oedipus complex may not apply to every culture or to all historical periods (Segall *et al.*, 1990).

**Relationships among the Trobriand Islanders** (RATTI) (Malinowski, 1929)

- Among the Trobriand Islanders of Papua, New Guinea, boys traditionally were disciplined by their maternal uncle (their mother's brother), rather than by their own biological father. It was the uncle's role to guide his nephew through to adulthood (such societies are described as avuncular). However, the father remained the mother's lover. Hence, the two roles (disciplinarian and mother's lover) were adopted by different men, whereas in Viennese society at the time that Freud was proposing his theories, the boy's father played both roles.
- By explaining the boy's hostility towards the father wholly in terms of sexual jealousy, Freud overlooked the possibility that he resented his father's power over him (Segall *et al.*,1990).
- What Malinowski found was that a Trobriand Island boy's relationship with his father was very good, free of the love–hate ambivalence which is central to Freud's Oedipus theory. By comparison, the relationship with the uncle wasn't usually so good.
- However, this doesn't necessarily mean that Malinowski was right and Freud was wrong (Price & Crapo, 1999). Segall *et al.* (1990) suggest that more societies need to be examined, including both Western and avuncular.

✖ **Lack of independent supporting evidence:** Freud cited his case study of Little Hans (1909) as supporting his Oedipal theory. This five-year-old developed a phobia of being bitten by a horse, which Freud interpreted as a fear of castration. A common criticism made of Freud's developmental theory as a whole is that it was based largely on the study of his *adult* patients. This makes the case of Little Hans especially important because he was Freud's only *child* patient. However, Freud saw Hans as a 'little Oedipus', having formulated his theory four years earlier (in *Three Essays on the Theory of Sexuality*, 1905). Hence the case study is biased and provides no *independent* evidence to support Freud. In addition, Hans's therapy was conducted mainly by his own father, a supporter of Freud's ideas! Even more seriously, perhaps, other psychodynamic theorists have provided alternative explanations of Hans's fear of horses, including Bowlby's (1973) reinterpretation in terms of attachment theory (see Chapter 2).

✓ **Support for the belief in the impact of early experience:** According to Bee (2000), attachment research provides a good deal of support for the basic psychoanaytic hypothesis that the quality of the child's earliest relationships affects the whole course of later development. Both Bowlby (1973) and Erikson (1963: see below) regard early relationships as *prototypes* of later relationships. Despite the considerable evidence showing that all types of early privation are reversible (see Chapter 2) and accepting all the criticisms of the Oedipal theory, belief in the impact of early experience is a lasting legacy of Freud's developmental theory.

## ERIKSON'S PSYCHOSOCIAL THEORY

**Specification Hint:** The Specification states 'Psychodynamic (e.g. Freud; Erikson) . . . explanations of personality development'. You're required to know about only *one* psychodynamic explanation. But it's useful to be familiar with psychodynamic alternatives to Freud's theory, especially as many of the criticisms made of Freud come from other psychodynamic theorists, such as Erikson. The comparison and contrast between them that follows can be used as either AO2 material if you're discussing Freud's theory, or AO1 and AO2 material if discussing Erikson's. There's no separate section on 'Evaluation of Erikson's theory' as there is with Freud's.

### Similarities and differences between Erikson and Freud

- Erikson trained as a psychoanalyst under the supervision of Anna Freud, Sigmund Freud's daughter. She was much more interested in child analysis than her father had been, and this in turn influenced Erikson.
- Erikson accepted Freud's *tripartite* theory of the structure of personality (*id*, *ego*, *superego*).
- He also regarded the psychosexual stages of development as basically valid – as far as they went. But for Erikson they didn't go far enough. For Freud, personality development was inseparable from

the development of the sexual instinct. Consequently, once physical/sexual maturation is complete, so is personality development. Hence there are five stages of psychosexual development (see Box 12.1), the last (genital) beginning with puberty and ending with sexual maturity.

- Erikson, together with many other *neo-Freudians* (see Chapter 18) argued that Freud *overemphasised* the role of sexuality and largely neglected the influence of social and cultural factors in development. Since the latter continue to influence development throughout a person's life, what happens to us during the first five or six years is far less crucial (deterministic) in Erikson's theory than it is in Freud's. He identifies eight *psychosocial stages* (the 'Eight Ages of Man' were originally proposed in 1950), the first five of which correspond to Freud's psychosexual stages. These eight stages are shown in Table 12.1.

- According to his *epigentic principle* (based on embryology), it is human nature to pass through a fixed, genetically pre-determined sequence of stages. However, the socio–cultural environment has a significant influence on the psychosocial modalities, the radius of significant relationships and institutions with which the individual interacts, and the nature of the psychosocial crisis at each stage.

**Table 12.1** Comparison between Erikson's and Freud's stages of development (based on Thomas, 1985; Erikson, 1950)

| Number of stage | Name of stage (psycho–social crisis) | Psycho–social modalities (dominant modes of being and acting) | Radius of significant relationships | Human virtues (qualities of strength) | Freud's psycho–sexual stages | Approximate ages (years) |
|---|---|---|---|---|---|---|
| 1 | Basic trust versus basic mistrust | To get. To give in return | Mother or mother-figure | Hope | Oral | 0–1 |
| 2 | Autonomy versus shame and doubt | To hold on. To let go | Parents | Willpower | Anal | 1–3 |
| 3 | Initiative versus guilt | To make (going after). To 'make like' (playing) | Basic family | Purpose | Phallic | 3–6 |
| 4 | Industry versus inferiority | To make things (completing). To make things together | Neighbourhood and school | Competence | Latency | 6–12 |
| 5 | Identity versus role confusion | To be oneself (or not to be). To share being oneself | Peer groups and outgroups. Models of leadership | Fidelity | Genital | 12–18 |
| 6 | Intimacy versus isolation | To lose and find oneself in another | Partners in friendship, sex, competition, co-operation | Love | | 20s |
| 7 | Generativity versus stagnation | To make be. To take care of | Divided labour and shared household | Care | | Late 20s–50s |
| 8 | Ego integrity versus despair | To be, through having been. To face not being. | 'Human-kind', 'my kind' | Wisdom | | 50s and beyond |

From *Comparing Theories of Child Development* 2nd edition by Thomas. © 1985. Reprinted with permission of Wadsworth, a division of Thomson Learning: www.thomsonrights.com, Fax 800 730-2215.

- As Table 12.1 shows, each stage centres around a developmental crisis. This involves a struggle between two opposing or conflicting personality characteristics. The first refers to the positive or functional (*adaptive*) outcome (e.g. trust), and the second to the negative or dysfunctional (*mal-*

*adaptive*) outcome (e.g. mistrust). However, these *aren't* either/or alternatives: every personality represents some mixture of trust and mistrust (and similarly for the other seven stages). Healthy development involves the adaptive quality outweighing the maladaptive (e.g. *more* trust than mistrust), so what matters is achieving the right balance.

- The optimum time for developing a sense of trust, say, is during infancy. But Erikson argued that it's possible to make up for unsatisfactory early experience at a later stage. However, this becomes increasingly difficult, since the individual will be facing *that* stage's conflict as well as the one being carried over. Conversely, a sense of trust acquired during infancy could be shattered, or at least shaken, if the child subsequently suffers deprivation (e.g. parental divorce). Either way, Erikson presents a much less deterministic view of development than Freud.

## Erikson's childhood psychosocial stages

### Basic trust versus basic mistrust (0–1 year)

- The quality of care the baby receives determines how it comes to view its mother in particular, and the world (including other people) in general: is it a safe, predictable, comfortable place to be, or is it full of danger and uncertainty?
- This is linked to the baby's ability to influence what happens to it, and hence to its trust in itself. If the baby's needs are met promptly and its discomforts quickly removed, if it's cuddled, played with and talked to, it develops a sense of the world as safe and of people as helpful and dependable (*trust*).
- But if its care is inconsistent and unpredictable, it develops a sense of *mistrust*, fear and suspicion. These may take the form of apathy or withdrawn behaviour, reflecting a sense of being controlled and unable to influence what happens to it.
- A healthy balance of trust/mistrust allows the baby to accept fear of the unknown as part and parcel of having new experiences.

### Autonomy versus shame and doubt (1–3 years)

- The child's cognitive and muscle systems are maturing, making it more mobile and expanding its range of experiences and choices.
- The child is also beginning to think of itself as a person in its own right, separate from its parents and with a new sense of power. This is the basis for the child's growing sense of *autonomy* or independence.
- The child wants to do everything for itself, and parents have to allow it to exercise these new abilities. At the same time, they must ensure that the child doesn't 'bite off more than it can chew': repeated failures and ridicule from others can induce a sense of *shame* and *doubt*.
- The child must be allowed to do things at its own pace. Parents shouldn't impatiently do things for it 'to save time', or criticise the child for its failures and the inevitable accidents.
- These accidents – and the stage as a whole – may become focused on toilet training. If this is too strict or starts too early, the child may feel powerless to control either its bowels or its parents' actions. This may result in a regression to oral activities (e.g. thumb-sucking), attention-seeking, or a pretence at autonomy by rejecting others' help and becoming very strong-willed.

### Initiative versus guilt (3–6 years)

- Physical, cognitive and social development are all happening very fast, and the child is keen to try out its new abilities and skills. Its sense of *initiative* will be reinforced by being encouraged to express its natural curiosity (such as asking questions), allowed to engage in physical activity and indulge in fantasy and other kinds of play.
- But if parents find the child's questions embarrassing, intellectually difficult or a nuisance, its motor activity dangerous and its fantasy play silly, then the child may come to feel *guilty* about intruding into other people's lives. This may inhibit the child's initiative and curiosity. Erikson believed that this guilt can be exaggerated by the Oedipus complex, but this merely represents one feature of a much wider picture. For Freud, as we noted earlier, it was the core feature of this stage.

*Industry versus inferiority (6–12 years)*

- Industry refers to the child's concern with how things work and how they're made, as well as its own efforts to make things. This is reinforced when the child is encouraged by parents and other adults, such as teachers, who begin to assume a very real significance in the child's life.
- The peer group also assumes increasing importance. Children compare themselves with each other as a way of assessing their own achievements, and unfavourable comparisons can threaten the child's self-esteem. Unsuccessful completion of realistic tasks, not being allowed to make things, and not receiving the necessary guidance and encouragement from adults, can all contribute to a sense of *inferiority*.

*Identity versus role confusion (12–18 years)* is discussed in the last section of this chapter in relation to adolescence. Although in many ways an advance on Freud's developmental theory, Erikson's theory has itself come in for much criticism, including its gender bias (see Chapter 16).

## Social learning explanations of personality development

- Social learning theories (SLTs), such as those of Bandura (1977b) and Mischel (1973), originated in the USA in the 1940s and 1950s. They were an attempt to re-interpret certain aspects of Freud's psychoanalytic theory in terms of *conditoning theory* (classical and operant conditioning: see Chapter 18).
- In the 1960s and 1970s, Bandura and his colleagues tried to make Freud's concept of identification (see above, pages 321–322) more objective by studying it experimentally in the form of *imitation*. More specifically, many of these experiments were concerned with *aggression* (see Chapter 9). But SLT has been applied to many aspects of development, such as gender (see next section of this chapter) and morality (see Chapter 11).
- This focus on *human social behaviour* is one feature that sets SLT apart from conditioning theory (or orthodox learning theory).

> **Specification Hint:** The Specification states '. . . social learning (e.g. Bandura, Mischel)' explanations of personality development. As with psychodynamic approaches, you're required to know about only *one* such theory. We've chosen Bandura's, which is widely accepted as the most influential social learning explanation. One way of evaluating social learning theories in general, and Bandura's in particular, is to compare and contrast it with 'orthodox' learning theory (conditioning theory) from which it's derived. But we've also included a separate section on evaluation, where we return to the questions posed at the beginning of the chapter, namely (a) is it really a developmental theory? and (b) what's meant by personality?

### SOME IMPORTANT SIMILARITIES AND DIFFERENCES BETWEEN SLT AND ORTHODOX LEARNING THEORY

- While SL theorists agree that all behaviour is learned according to the same learning principles, they're interested specifically in *human learning*.
- Although SL theorists agree that we should observe what's observable, they also believe that there are important cognitive or *mediating variables* which intervene between stimulus and response. Without such mediating variables, we cannot adequately explain human behaviour (see Box 12.3).
- SL theorists emphasise *observational learning* or *modelling* (learning through watching the behaviour of others, called *models*). This occurs spontaneously, with no deliberate effort by the learner or any intention by the model to teach anything.
- Observational learning takes place without any reinforcement – mere exposure to the model is sufficient for learning to occur (Bandura, 1965). However, whether the model's behaviour is imitated depends partly on the *consequences* of the behaviour, for both the model and the learner. Reinforcement is important only in so far as it affects *performance* (not the learning itself: see Essential Study 9.2, page 187).

### Reinforcement as information about the future

- Bandura (1977b) challenged Skinner's claim that reinforcements and punishments *automatically* strengthen and weaken behaviour (see Chapter 18). For Bandura:

> 'Reinforcement serves principally as an informative and motivational operation rather than as a mechanical response strengthener.'

- Reinforcement provides the learner with *information* about the likely consequences of certain behaviour under certain conditions. That is, it improves our prediction of whether a given action will lead to pleasant (reinforcement) or unpleasant (punishment) outcomes in the *future*.
- Reinforcement also *motivates* us by causing us to anticipate future outcomes. Our present behaviours are largely governed by the outcomes we *expect* them to have, and we're more likely to try to learn the modelled behaviour if we value its consequences.

### The role of cognitive factors in observational learning

- For Bandura, the learning process is much more complex than it is for Skinner, for whom 'the mind' had no part to play in a scientific psychology (see Chapters 17 and 18). In Bandura's (1974) view:

> '... contrary to mechanistic metaphors, outcomes change behaviour in humans through the intervening influence of thought.'

- Five major cognitive variables that mediate between the modelled behaviour and its imitation (learning versus performance) are described in Box 12.3 (see Chapter 9, page 218–220).

## Box 12.3 Five cognitive/mediating variables influencing the likelihood of learning and/or performance

- **The learner must pay *attention* to the relevant clues and ignore those aspects of the model and the environment that are incidental and irrelevant. Attention can be influenced by:**
  - (a) the model's distinctiveness, attractiveness or power
  - (b) whether or not the model's behaviour has *functional value* for the learner
  - (c) the learner's level of arousal and expectations about the model.
- **A *visual image* or *semantic code* for the modelled behaviour is recorded in memory. Without an adequate coding system, the learner will fail to store what's been seen or heard (see Chapter 1). Whereas infants are largely confined to immediate imitation, older children can defer imitation because of their superior use of symbols (see Chapter 11).**
- ***Memory permanence* refers to devices such as rehearsal and organisation, and use of multiple codes to help retain the stored information over long periods (again, see Chapter 1).**
- ***Reproducing the observed motor activities* accurately usually requires several trials to get the muscular 'feel' of the behaviour. Older children enjoy greater muscular strength and control.**
- ***Motivation* refers to the role of reinforcement, which can be *direct* (as when the child is praised by an adult), *vicarious* (as when a child sees another child being praised), or *self-reinforcement* (as when the child praises itself/feels pleased with itself).**

## ✗✓ An evaluation of Bandura's theory

✗ **Theoretical strengths:** As noted in Box 12.3, *changes* take place in cognitive or mediating processes as children get older. However, Durkin (1995) believes that these processes essentially apply at *any* age, which means that the theory *isn't* a true theory of development. Bandura resists the notion of a general structural reorganisation of the kind proposed by Piaget (see Chapter 11), and so he fails to take account of cognitive *development* (Grusec, 1992). As Bee (2000) points out, SLT can say how a child might acquire a particular behaviour pattern, but it doesn't take into account the underlying developmental changes that are occurring. For example, do three-year-olds and 10-year-olds typically learn the same amount or in the same way from modelling?

> ' . . . Given Bandura's emphasis on cognitive aspects of the modeling process, a genuinely developmental social learning theory could be proposed, although no such theory now exists . . .' (Bee, 2000)

Indeed, the importance of cognitive factors is reflected in Bandura's (1986, 1989) re-naming of SLT as *social cognitive theory*. Other important cognitive processes are those relating to the *self*.

## Box 12.4 Self-concept, self-monitoring, and self-efficacy

- **According to Bandura, children learn both overt behaviour/concrete skills and information, and also abstract skills and information through modelling. Indeed, *abstract modelling* is part of his 'social cognitive theory' (1986, 1989). For example, the 'rule' underlying a model's behaviour can be extracted from observing the behaviour, without the rule being made explicit or articulated. In this way, the child can acquire attitudes, values, expectancies, ways of solving problems, and standards of self-evaluation.**
- **By incorporating (or *internalising*) societal standards into itself, the child can monitor its own behaviours in terms of these standards. This *self-monitoring* ensures that behaviour is regulated even in the absence of reinforcement. Indeed, according to Bandura (1971), 'There is no more devastating punishment than self-contempt', that is, we are our own harshest critics. This mirrors Freud's view of the young child's superego, which is often more punitive than the parents it has replaced (see above, page 320).**
- **Another internalised standard or expectancy is *self-efficacy*. This refers to our belief that we can act effectively and exercise some control over events that influence our life (Bandura, 1977a, 1986). This is crucially important for motivation, since how we judge our own capabilities is likely to affect our expectations about future behaviour. For example, if we feel that a model's actions are within our capabilities, then we may attempt to imitate them. But a low sense of self-efficacy regarding the modelled skill is likely to inhibit us (Durkin, 1995).**

✓ **Theoretical strengths:** One of the strengths of Bandura's SLT (and other versions, such as Mischel's, 1973) is its recognition that behaviour can only be understood by taking the actor's self-concept, self-monitoring, self-efficacy and other mediating variables into account. However, these internal processes *don't* constitute 'personality', a concept which most SL theorists tend to dismiss (Durkin, 1995). Nevertheless, they make the theory far less mechanistic than Skinner's, for example, which focuses entirely on external events. For Bandura (1973):

> ' . . . the environment is only a potentiality, not a fixed property that inevitably impinges upon individuals and to which their behaviour eventually adapts. Behaviour partly creates the environment and the resultant environment, in turn, influences the behaviour.'

This view is called *reciprocal determinism* (Bandura, 1977a, 1986). People are both products *and* producers of their environment (see Chapter 17).

**Critically consider *one* psychodynamic explanation of personality development. (24 marks) (30 mins) (600 words minimum) A01/A02**

*This essay can be split into FOUR sections – each about 150 words long. Each section would be worth approx. 6 marks.*

**Sections 1 and 2:** A **description** of one psychodynamic account of personality development. Whether you choose Freud or Erikson, you'd probably want to begin by briefly explaining what 'psychodynamic' means and how different psychodynamic explanations are related (they all originate from Freud's psychoanalytic theory etc.). Again, whichever theory you choose, you'll need to focus on the strictly developmental parts of the theory (that is, Freud's psychosexual and Erikson's psychosocial stages). However, in doing that you'll need to refer to other aspects of the theory which aren't strictly part of the developmental account (for example, the Oedipus complex ends with the emergence of the *superego*).

A01

**Section 3:** You should **analyse** and **evaluate** your chosen theory. With Freud, the Oedipus complex (that takes place during the phallic stage) is the most controversial part of his developmental theory – and also the most important as far as he was concerned. The male-centred nature of his theory, plus challenges to the universal nature of the Oedipus complex (RATTI – Malinowski, 1929) are two major forms of criticism. When discussing Erikson, it's important to point out the similarities and differences (but especially the differences) between his theory and Freud's.

A02

**Section 4:** Freud's methods for collecting his data (the case study) can be considered here. But the focus should be on the particular case of Little Hans (rather than the method in general). Whichever theory of personality development you may be discussing (including social learning explanations), you should address the issues of what these terms mean and whether the theory in question can truly be considered a theory of personality development.

A02

*A word of advice: It's important to remember that how you answer this – or any other – question doesn't have to be constrained by/limited to the material contained within the corresponding chapter in this book. In other words, you should feel free to take material from other chapters, if you think it will help you answer the question. The watchword is always relevance. Here there's likely to be material from Chapters 16–18 on Perspectives, which you could draw on for AO2 material. But for this 'extra' material to be relevant, you will need to be highly selective.*

*Try to answer this question yourself. There's a sample essay on page 352 with which you can compare your essay.*

# Gender development

**Specification Hint:** The Specification states 'Explanations of the development of gender identity/gender roles ...'. There are many terms that are used to refer to (different aspects of) gender, and 'sex' and 'gender' are often used interchangeably. But these are very different, so we need to begin this section with some key definitions.

## The 'vocabulary' of sex and gender

- Feminist psychologists (e.g. Unger, 1979) distinguish between *sex* and *gender*. *Sex* refers to some biological fact about us, such as a particular genetic make-up, reproductive anatomy and functioning, and is usually referred to by the terms 'male' and 'female'. *Gender*, by contrast, is what culture makes out of the 'raw material' of biological sex. It is, therefore, the social equivalent or social interpretation of sex.
- *Sexual identity* is an alternative way of referring to our biological status as male or female.

A transsexual: gender is more flexible than we might sometimes think

Corresponding to gender is *gender identity*, our classification of ourselves (and others) as male or female, boy or girl, and so on. Sexual and gender identities correspond for most of us, but not in *transsexualism*. Transsexuals are anatomically male or female, but they firmly believe that they belong to the opposite sex. As a result, their biological sexual identity is fundamentally inconsistent with their gender identity.

- *Gender role* (or sex role) refers to the behaviours, attitudes, values, beliefs and so on which a particular society either expects from, or considers appropriate to, males and females on the basis of their biological sex. To be *masculine* (or *feminine*), then, requires males (or females) to conform to their respective gender roles.
- All societies have carefully defined gender roles, although their precise details differ between societies. *Gender* (or sex) *stereotypes* are widely-held beliefs about psychological differences between males and females which often reflect gender roles.
- *Sex typing* refers to our acquisition of a sex or gender identity and learning the appropriate behaviours (adopting an appropriate sex role). Sex typing begins early in Western culture, with parents often dressing their new-born baby boy or girl in blue or pink. Even in infancy's earliest days, our gender influences how people react to us (Condry & Ross, 1985). Indeed, usually the first question asked by friends and relatives of parents with a new-born baby is 'Boy or girl?'.

## Explanations of the development of gender identity/gender roles

**Specification Hint:** The Specification states 'Explanations of . . . (e.g. social learning theories, cognitive-developmental theories)'. 'Explanations' implies that you need to know about *at least two* explanations – but two will do. The examples given in the Specification are the most heavily 'cognitive' (especially the second one). Social learning theory has already been covered in relation to personality development. Even though it would be legitimate to consider other types of explanation (such as biological and biosocial theories), the examples given indicate that you should focus on these more cognitive explanations.

We've included cultural relativism for good measure. This complements the other explanations, but it also gives you a little more variety, especially for evaluating one or more of these cognitive explanations.

It's not always clear which aspect(s) of gender a particular theory is trying to explain. You should try to make this clear in your answer (AO1), and acknowledging that a particular theory doesn't make it clear – or that it may be trying to explain both gender identity and gender role – is valid as analysis and evaluation (AO2).

### SOCIAL LEARNING THEORY

- According to *social learning theory* (SLT), one reason girls and boys learn to behave differently is that they're *treated differently* by their parents and others (*sex typing*). But sex typing isn't, of course, arbitrary. Boys and girls are treated differently in line with parents' expectations and beliefs about how boys and girls *ought to* behave (*gender-role stereotypes*).
- SLT also emphasises the roles of *observational learning* and *reinforcement*. By observing others behaving in particular ways and then imitating that behaviour, children receive reinforcement from 'significant others' for behaviours considered to be *sex-appropriate* (Bandura, 1977b: see above, pages 327–328).

 Research evidence relating to sex-typing

In the 'Baby X' study (Smith & Lloyd, 1978), babies were dressed in unisex snowsuits and given names which sometimes matched their true gender, and sometimes didn't. When adults played with them, they treated the babies according to the gender they believed them to be. This indicates that a person's (perceived) biological make-up becomes part of his/her social environment through others' reactions to it.

✓ When parents (and others) are informed of a child's biological sex, they often react to it according to their gender-role expectations. Thus, girls and boys are often given different toys, have their rooms decorated differently, and are even spoken about in different terms (Rubin *et al.*, 1974).

✗•✓ Karraker *et al.* (1995) found that this strong sex typing of infants at birth has declined, and that there are no differences between mothers and fathers in this respect. However, a consistent and persistent finding is that fathers treat their children in a more gendered way than mothers (Maccoby, 1990). Typically, fathers interact in a more instrumental and achievement-oriented way and give more attention to their sons, while mothers attend equally to sons and daughters (Quiery, 1998).

THE ONE IN PINK LOOKS SO SWEET BUT I'M NOT SO SURE ABOUT THE ONE IN BLUE

✗✓ Research relating to reinforcement of gender-stereotyped behaviour

✓ Sears *et al.* (1957) found that parents allowed sons to be more aggressive in their relationships with other children, and towards themselves, than daughters. For some mothers, 'being a boy' meant being aggressive, and boys were often encouraged to fight back. Although parents believe they respond in the same way to aggressive acts committed by boys and girls, they actually intervene much more frequently and quickly when girls behave aggressively (Huston, 1983).

✓ Parents tend to positively reinforce boys more for behaviours reflecting independence, self-reliance and emotional control. But girls tend to be reinforced for compliance, dependence, nurturance, empathy and emotional expression (Block, 1979). Fathers tend to reinforce these sex-typed behaviours more than mothers do (Kerig *et al.*, 1993).

✗ According to Maccoby and Jacklin (1974), there are *no* consistent differences in the extent to which boys and girls are reinforced for aggressiveness or autonomy. Rather, there appears to be remarkable uniformity in the sexes' socialisation. This is supported by Lytton and Romney (1991), who found very few sex differences in terms of parental warmth, overall amount of interaction, encouragement of achievement or dependency, restrictiveness and discipline, or clarity of communication.

✗✓ Research relating to the imitation of (same-sex) models

✓ Boys are more likely to imitate aggressive male models than are girls (Bandura *et al.*, 1961, 1963: see Ch. 9). Children are also more likely to imitate a same-sex model than an opposite-sex model, even if the behaviour is 'sex-inappropriate'.

✗ Although Bandura *et al.*'s research is often cited, the evidence concerning imitation and modelling is actually inconclusive, and some studies have failed to find that children are more likely to imitate same-sex models than opposite-sex models. Indeed, children have been shown to prefer imitating behaviour that is 'appropriate' to their own sex regardless of the model's (Maccoby & Jacklin, 1974).

✗ While modelling plays an important role in children's socialisation, there's no consistent preference for the same-sex parent's behaviour (Hetherington, 1967). Instead children prefer to model the behaviour of those with whom they have most contact (usually the mother). Also, there's no significant correlation between the extent to which parents engage in sex-typed behaviours and the strength of sex-typing in their children (Smith & Daglish, 1977). However, fathers' adoption of either traditional (sex-typed) or egalitarian attitudes has been found to correlate with four-year-olds' perceptions of sex roles (Quiery, 1998).

✗✓ Research relating to the influence of television

Although parents are important models, SL theorists are also interested in media portrayals of males and females.

✓ A large body of evidence suggests that gender-role stereotypes are portrayed by the media, as well as by parents and teachers (Wober *et al.*, 1987). Moreover, children categorised as 'heavy' viewers of TV hold stronger stereotyped beliefs than 'lighter' viewers (Gunter, 1986) – although no precise measures are taken of the programmes they actually watch (Gunter & McAleer, 1997).

✗ The view that TV can impact upon a passively receptive child audience with messages about sex-role stereotyping, and mould young children's conceptions of gender is oversimplistic. For Gunter and McAleer (1997), children respond selectively to particular characters and events. Their perceptions, memories and understanding of what they've seen may often be mediated by the dispositions they bring with them to the viewing situation.

## COGNITIVE–DEVELOPMENTAL THEORY

- The *cognitive–developmental approach* (Kohlberg, 1969; Kohlberg & Ullian, 1974) emphasises the child's participation in developing both an understanding of gender and gender-appropriate behaviour. Children's discovery that they're male or female causes them to identify with members of their own sex. This discovery happens in the same way as other aspects of the child's cognitive development (see Chapter 11).
- This contrasts with SLT, according to which children learn their gender identity through sex-typing and being reinforced for gender-appropriate behaviour. It's only *after* the child has learned to classify itself as male or female (through sex-typing and differential reinforcement) that it will imitate same-sex models. But as we saw in the previous section, Bandura sees reinforcement (and punishment) as providing children with *information* about when they're behaving in ways that other people consider to be appropriate.
- According to cognitive–developmental theorists, young children acquire an understanding of the concepts *male* and *female* in three stages.
- Once children acquire gender constancy, they come to value the behaviours and attitudes associated with their sex. Only at this point do they identify with the adult figures who possess the qualities they see as being most central to their concepts of themselves as male or female (Perry & Bussey, 1979).

### Box 12.5 Stages in the development of gender identity

- **Stage 1 (Gender labelling or basic gender identity):** This occurs somewhere around age three (Ruble, 1984) and refers to the child's recognition that it's male or female. According to Kohlberg (1969), knowing one's gender is an achievement that allows us to understand and categorise the world. But this knowledge is fragile, and children don't yet realise that boys invariably become men and girls always become women.
- **Stage 2 (Gender stability):** By age four or five, most children recognise that people retain their gender for a lifetime. But children still rely on superficial signs (such as the length of a person's hair) to determine their gender (Marcus & Overton, 1978).
- **Stage 3 (Gender constancy or consistency):** At around age six or seven, children realise that gender is immutable. So, even if a woman has her hair cut very short, her gender remains constant. Gender constancy represents a kind of *conservation* (see Chapter 11) and, significantly, appears shortly after the child has mastered the conservation of quantity (Marcus & Overton, 1978).

✓ **Supporting evidence:** Evidence suggests that the concepts of gender identity, stability and constancy do occur in that order across many cultures (Munroe *et al.*, 1984). A relevant study is described in Essential Study 12.2.

Slaby and Frey's GCS also supports the view that children actively *construct* their gender-role knowledge through purposeful monitoring of the social environment. They engage in *self-socialisation*, rather than passively receiving information (Whyte, 1998).

**ESSENTIAL STUDY 12.2**

**Gender constancy study** (GCS) (Slaby & Frey, 1975)

● ● ● ● ● ● ● ● ● ● ● ● ● ● ● ● ● ● ● ● ● ● ● ● ● ● ● ● ● ● ● ● ● ● ● ● ● ● ● ● ● ● ● ● ● ● ● ● ● ●

- Slaby & Frey divided two- to five-year-olds into 'high 'and 'low' gender constancy.
- The children were then shown a silent film of adults performing simple activities.
- The screen was 'split', with males performing activities on one side and females on the other.
- Children rated as 'high' in gender constancy showed a marked same-sex bias, as measured by the amount of visual attention they gave to each side of the screen.
- This supports Kohlberg's (1969) belief that gender constancy is a *cause* of the imitation of same-sex models, rather than an effect.

✗ **Explanatory limitations:** A major problem for cognitive–developmental theory is that it predicts there should be *little or no* gender-appropriate behaviour *before* gender constancy is achieved. But even in infancy, both sexes show a marked preference for stereotypical male and female toys (Huston, 1983). While such children might have developed a sense of gender identity, they are, as far as cognitive– developmental theory is concerned, some years away from achieving gender stability and constancy (Fagot, 1985).

## GENDER-SCHEMA PROCESSING THEORY

- *Gender schema* (or *schematic processing*) *theory* (GST) addresses the possibility that gender identity *alone* can provide children with sufficient motivation to assume sex-typed behaviour patterns (e.g. Bem, 1985; Martin, 1991).
- Like SLT, this approach suggests that children learn 'appropriate' patterns of behaviour by observation. However, consistent with cognitive–developmental theory, children's active cognitive processing of information also contributes to their sex-typing.
- For example, children learn that strength is linked to the *male* gender-role stereotype and weakness to the *female* stereotype, and that some dimensions (including strength–weakness) are more relevant to one gender (males) than the other (Rathus, 1990). So a boy learns that the strength he displays in wrestling (say) affects others' perceptions of him. Unless competing in some sporting activity, most girls

Jane Couch (the 'Fleetwood Assassin'), women's world welter-weight boxing champion, after winning her sex discrimination case in 1998 against the British Boxing Board of Control over its refusal to grant her a licence to box professionally.

ESSENTIAL AS & A2 Psychology

don't see this dimension as being important. But while boys are expected to compete in sports, girls aren't, and so a girl is likely to find that her gentleness and neatness are more important in the eyes of others than her strength (Rathus, 1990).

- According to GST, then, children learn to judge themselves according to the traits considered to be relevant to their gender. Consequently, their self-concept becomes mixed with the gender schemas of a particular culture, which provide standards for comparison. The theory sees gender identity as being sufficient to produce 'sex-appropriate' behaviour. The labels 'boy' and 'girl', once under-stood, give children the basis for mixing their self-concepts with their society's gender schemas. Children with gender identity will actively seek information about gender schemas, and their self-esteem will soon become influenced by how they 'measure up' to their gender schema (Rathus, 1990).

## CULTURAL RELATIVISM

- This represents the most direct challenge to the biological approach. If gender differences do reflect biological differences, then we'd expect to find the same differences occurring in different cultures. Any differences that exist between cultures with regard to gender roles (*cultural relativism*) support the view that gender roles are *culturally determined.*
- Margaret Mead (1935) claimed that the traits we call masculine and feminine are completely unre-lated to biological sex. Just as the clothing, manner and headdress considered to be appropriate in a particular society, at a particular time, aren't determined by sex, so temperament and gender role aren't biologically but culturally determined.

---

**Key study**

**MEAD'S (1935) STUDY OF THREE NEW GUINEA TRIBES**

Mead studied three New Guinea tribes, who lived quite separately from each other within about a 100-mile radius:

(a) the *Arapesh*, who lived on hillsides, were gentle, loving and co-operative. Boys and girls were reared in order to develop these qualities, which in Western society are stereotypi-cally feminine. Both parents were said to 'bear a child', and men took to bed while the child was born

(b) the *Mundugumor* were riverside dwellers and ex-cannibals. Both males and females were self-assertive, arrogant, fierce and continually quarrelling, and they both detested the whole business of pregnancy and child rearing. Sleeping babies were hung in rough-tex-tured baskets in a dark place against the wall, and when they cried someone would scratch gratingly on the outside of the basket

(c) the *Tchambuli*, who lived on the lakeside, represented the reversal of traditional Western gender roles. Girls were encouraged to take an interest in the tribe's economic affairs, and the women took care of trading and food gathering. Men, on the other hand, were con-sidered sentimental, emotional and incapable of making serious decisions. They spent much of the day sitting around in groups, gossiping and 'preening' themselves.

---

- After she'd studied four other cultures (Samoa, Manus, Iatmul and Bali), Mead (1949) rather dra-matically changed her views about gender roles. From a rather extreme 'cultural determinism', she now concluded that women are 'naturally' more nurturing than men, expressing their creativity through childbearing and childbirth, and are superior in intellectual abilities requiring intuition. While motherhood is a 'biological inclination', fatherhood is a 'social invention' By implication, soci-eties which encourage a gender-role division other than that in which dominant, sexually energetic men live with passive, nurturant women are 'going against nature'. Significantly, by this time she'd given birth to a child of her own (Booth, 1975)!

An evaluation of cultural relativism

**Are there 'natural' differences between the sexes?** A finding which may seem to support Mead in her search for 'natural' differences is that there's no known society in which the female does the fighting in warfare (including the Tchambuli and Arapesh: Fortune, 1939). However, there's more to aggression than warfare. In his study of the Trobriand Islanders (see Essential Study 12.1), Malinowski (1929), reported that, in order to foster their tribe's reputation for virility, groups of women would catch a man from another tribe, arouse him to erection and rape him! This 'gang rape' was carried out in a brutal manner, and the women often boasted about their achievement.

**Can men be aggressive and nurturing at the same time?** According to Wade and Tavris (1994), early researchers assumed that men are naturally aggressive (and women are naturally nurturant). Consequently they often defined nurturing in a way that excluded the altruistic, caring activities of men. For example, men can nurture the family by providing food for mother and child and sometimes by going off to fight in faraway places, sacrificing their lives if necessary, in order to provide a safe haven for their people.

**The cultural content of work:** While most cultures distinguish between 'men's' and 'women's' work and while biological factors undoubtedly play some part in the sexual division of labour, the content of this work varies enormously between cultures. As Hargreaves (1986) observes, in some cultures:

> '. . . men weave and women make pots, whereas in others these roles are reversed; in some parts of the world women are the major agricultural producers, and in others they are prohibited from agricultural activity.'

**Are there only two genders?** Every known culture distinguishes between male and female. Although anatomical sex is universal and unchangeable, gender, as we've seen, is a social invention, and it's gender that gives us a sense of personal identity as male or female (Wade & Tavris, 1994). An even stronger argument for the social construction of gender comes from studies of societies in which gender reversal is relatively commonplace or, more importantly, where there are more than two genders.

## Box 12.6 Are there more than two genders?

- Among the Sakalavas in Madagascar, boys who are thought to be pretty are raised as girls and readily adopt the female gender role. Similarly, the Aleutian Islanders in Alaska raise handsome boys as girls; their beards are plucked at puberty and they're later married to rich men. They too seem to adapt quite readily to their assigned gender role.
- Studies of certain Native American peoples reveal the possibility of more than two basic gender roles. For example, the '*berdache*', a biological male of the Crow tribe, simply chooses not to follow the ideal role of warrior. Instead he might become the 'wife' of a warrior. But he's never scorned or ridiculed by his fellow Crows. (Little Horse in the film *Little Big Man*, starring Dustin Hoffman, was a 'berdache'.)
- The Mohave Indians recognised four distinct gender roles: (i) traditional male; (ii) traditional female; (iii) 'alyha'; and (iv) 'hwame'. The 'alyha' was a male who chose to live as a woman (to the extent of mimicking menstruation by cutting his upper thigh and undergoing a ritualistic pregnancy), and the 'hwame' was a female who chose to become a man.

Julian Clary: just a male who likes to wear make-up, or an androgynous individual?

Western culture has no formally recognised and accepted equivalent of the berdache. However, in recent times, as the economic lives of men and women have become more similar, we've at least *informally* developed some acceptance of berdache-like alternatives. For example, the concept of *androgyny* (Bem, 1974) refers to people who've developed both the 'masculine' and 'feminine' sides of themselves more fully than most. Similarly, the concept of *sexual orientation* implies an awareness that relationships aren't simply an expression of a single inborn norm (Price & Crapo, 1999).

## EXAM tips BOX

**Critically consider explanations of the development of gender identity/gender role. (24 marks) (30 mins) (600 words minimum) AO1/AO2**

*This essay can be split into FOUR sections – each about 150 words long. Each section would be worth about 6 marks.*

*The question requires you to discuss at least two explanations – but two will do. As with all such questions, there's a 'breadth versus depth' trade-off. In other words, if you describe more than two, these won't have to be covered in as much depth/detail as if you cover only two. Also, if you choose only two, you don't have to cover each in exactly the same depth (but there must be a reasonable balance).*

**Section 1:** The question also specifies 'gender identity/gender role'. It's a good idea to begin with a definition of these terms. You might also want to distinguish between gender and sex. The rest of this section can involve a **description** of your chosen explanations.

AO1
↓
AO1

**Section 2:** This could involve a **description** of studies which tend to be supportive of your chosen theories, such as:

* Bandura's experimental studies of imitation of same- and opposite-sex models (Bandura *et al.*, 1961, 1963)
* 'Baby X' experiment (Smith & Lloyd, 1978)
* More naturalistic studies of parents' attitudes and behaviour towards their male and female children (such as Sears *et al.*, 1957)
* Slaby & Frey (1975).

**Section 3:** You should **analyse** and **evaluate** your chosen theories. You can do this by considering other research studies, which aren't supportive of the theories, or which actually contradict the findings of those described in Section 2.

AO2
↓
AO2

**Section 4:** You should continue to **analyse** and **evaluate** the theories. You could do this by comparing and contrasting them with each other and/or with other theories. Cultural relativism is useful here, because it takes the broadest possible view of the influences on gender development, and other theories can be seen from within the context of this explanation. For example, the particular culture determines what the gender stereotypes will be, and hence which behaviours will be sex-typed. The possibility of there being more than two genders also puts all these other theories into perspective.

*Try to answer this question yourself. There's a sample essay on page 353 with which you can compare your essay.*

## Adolescence

* The word 'adolescence' comes from the Latin *adolescere*, meaning 'to grow into maturity'.
* As well as being a time of enormous physiological change, adolescence is also marked by changes in behaviour, expectations and relationships, with both parents and peers.
* In Western, industrialised societies, there's generally no single initiation rite signalling the passage into adulthood. The lack of such initiations into adulthood makes this a more difficult transition than it appears to be in more traditional, non-industrialised societies. Relationships with parents in particular, and adults in general, must be re-negotiated in a way that allows the adolescent to achieve greater independence. This process is aided by changing relationships with peers.
* Historically, adolescence has been seen as a period of transition between childhood and adulthood. But writers today are more likely to describe it as one of *multiple transitions*, involving education,

training, employment and unemployment, as well as transitions from one set of living circumstances to another (Coleman & Roker, 1998).

## Normative and non-normative shifts

- One way of categorising the various transitions involved in adolescence is in terms of normative and non-normative shifts (Hendry & Kloep, 1999; Kloep & Hendry, 1999):

(a) *Normative, maturational shifts*: growth spurt (both sexes), menarche (first menstruation), first nocturnal emissions ('wet dreams'), voice breaking (boys), changes in sexual organs, beginning of sexual arousal, changed romantic relationships, gender role identity, changed relationships with adults, increasing autonomy and responsibility.

(b) *Normative, society-dependent shifts*: change from primary to secondary school, leaving school, getting started in an occupation, acquiring legal rights for voting, purchasing alcohol, driving licence, military service, sex and co-habitation.

(c) *Non-normative shifts*: examples include parental divorce, family bereavement, illness, natural disasters, war, incest, emigration, disruption of peer network, risk-taking behaviours, 'disadvantage' (because of gender, class, regional or ethnic discrimination), physical and/or mental handicap.

- A normative shift may become non-normative, if, say, there are other circumstances that cause a normal developmental 'task' to become more difficult, for example, the onset of puberty occurs unusually early or late.

## Research into social development in adolescence, including the formation of identity

Specification Hint: The Specification states 'Research into social development in adolescence, including the formation of identity (e.g. Marcia). Research into relationships with parents and peers during adolescence and cultural differences in adolescent behaviour'.

You could be asked two different kinds of question corresponding to these two aspects of adolescence, that is (a) social development and (b) relationships with parents and peers, and cultural differences. But there's considerable overlap between them. For example, it's difficult discussing social development without taking relationships and cultural differences into account.

The very concept of 'adolescence', together with social and cultural perceptions and expectations of adolescents, feeds into the adolescent's experience. So it's difficult to separate the individual from the social/cultural (they're really two sides of a coin). This is made very clear in Erikson's theory of identity formation, which we've included here in addition to Marcia's.

When discussing identity formation, the influence of biological factors (puberty) plays a very substantial part. Biological factors, in turn, help to account for individual differences between adolescents in their identity formation.

These are all points that are relevant for AO2 analysis and evaluation. Remember that 'research' refers to both theory and research studies.

### PUBERTY: THE SOCIAL AND PSYCHOLOGICAL MEANING OF BIOLOGICAL CHANGES

#### Puberty and body image

- Puberty is one of the most important adjustments that adolescents have to make (Coleman & Hendry, 1990). Even as a purely *biological* phenomenon, puberty is far from being a simple, straightforward process. All adolescents experience the same bodily changes (depending on their sex, of course!), but the *sequence* of changes may vary within individuals (*intraindividual asynchronies*: Alsaker, 1996). For example, for some girls menstruation may occur very early on in their puberty, while for others it may occur after most other changes (such as growth spurt, breast development) have taken place.

* According to Davies and Furnham (1986), the average adolescent isn't only sensitive to, but also critical of, his/her changing physical self. Because of gender and sexual development, young people are inevitably confronted, perhaps for the first time, by cultural standards of beauty in evaluating their own body image (via the media and the reactions of others). This may produce a non-normative shift in the form of dieting practices, leading to eating disorders (see Chapter 4). Young people may be especially vulnerable to teasing and exclusion if they're perceived by their peers as over- or under-weight (Kloep & Hendry, 1999).

### Gender differences

* Puberty may be a normative, maturational shift. But it may be a more difficult transition for girls than boys. This is because of the *subjective meaning* of bodily change (what it means for the individual), which mirrors the *socio–cultural significance* of puberty (its significance for society).
* According to the *cultural ideal hypothesis* (CIH) (Simmons & Blyth, 1987), puberty will bring boys *closer* to their physical ideal (an increase in muscle distribution and lung capacity produces greater stamina, strength and athletic capacities), while girls move *further away* from theirs.
* Girls begin puberty on average two years ahead of boys. For girls, it's normal to experience an increase in body fat and rapid weight gain, thus making their bodies less like the Western cultural ideal of the thin, sylph-like super-model. In addition, they have to deal with menstruation, which is negatively associated with blood and physical discomfort (Crawford & Unger, 1995).

### The importance of timing

* If the CIH is valid, it follows that *early-maturing boys* will be at an *advantage* relative to their 'on-time' and late-maturing peers (they'll be moving faster *towards* the male ideal). By the same token, *early-maturing girls* will be at a *disadvantage* (they'll be moving faster *away from* the female ideal). Indeed, according to Alsaker (1996):

> ' . . . pubertal timing is generally regarded as a more crucial aspect of pubertal development than pubertal maturation itself.'

In other words, it's not the *fact* of puberty that matters as much as *when* it occurs, and it matters mainly in relation to body image and self-esteem.

### Box 12.7 The falling age of puberty onset

* One in six girls reaches puberty by the age of eight, compared with one in 100 a generation ago. Also, one in 14 eight-year-old boys has pubic hair (an early indicator of puberty), compared with one in 150 of their fathers' generation.
* Bristol University's Institute of Child Health tracked the development of 1,150 children from birth. It's the first study of puberty in Britain for almost 40 years.
* Not only are children starting puberty earlier, but it's lasting longer. The reasons are unclear, but likely causes are higher oestrogen levels in mothers, diet, lifestyle and pollution. There could also be a genetic link, since the mothers of girls who begin puberty earlier also matured earlier.
* Separate research has found that the average age of menarche has fallen below 13 in Britain for the first time. It's now 12 years 10 months, compared with 13 years 6 months in 1969.
* These findings mean that children could be developing sexually before they have the emotional maturity to deal with the possible consequences.

(Based on Peek, 2000)

* Consistent with the CIH is the finding that early-maturing girls and late-maturing boys feel less good about themselves (they have lower self-esteem). Why should this be?
* According to the *deviancy hypothesis* (DH), those who are 'off-time' in physical maturation are socially deviant compared with peers of the same age and sex (Wichstrom, 1998). Since girls begin puberty

on average two years before boys, early-maturing girls are the first to enter this deviant position, followed by late-maturing boys.

- An alternative explanation is the *developmental readiness hypothesis* (DRH) (Simmons & Blyth, 1987). In the case of early/sudden puberty, too little time will have been spent on *ego* development during latency, with early-maturing girls once more being most affected. (This explanation is similar to Coleman's *focal theory*, which is discussed below: see page 345.)

- Wichstrom (1998) maintains that CIH's suggestion that the pubertal girl moves further away from the Western stereotyped female ideal, may *not* be true. *Both* boys and girls move closer to their ideals, provided they don't put on excessive weight.

- The CIH is sensitive to changes in time and context. For example, in Norway there may be less emphasis on stereotypical male stature compared with the USA and UK. Perhaps also the embarrassment and negative affect experienced by American girls when starting their periods and becoming sexually responsive is less among Norwegian girls, because of relatively greater openness about adolescent sexuality (Wichstrom, 1998).

Childhood seems to last for a much shorter time than in previous generations – especially for girls

### Studies of mental disorder

- Several studies have found that *early-maturing girls* score higher on measures of depressive feelings and sadness (e.g. Alsaker, 1992; Stattin & Magnusson, 1990). But this was only true when the measures were taken before or simultaneously with changing schools (Petersen *et al.*, 1991).

- Early-maturing girls have also been reported to have more psychosomatic (psychophysiological) symptoms (e.g. Stattin & Magnusson, 1990), to display greater concerns about eating (e.g. Brooks-Gunn *et al.*, 1989), and to score higher on Offer's psychopathology scale (e.g. Brooks-Gunn & Warren, 1985).

**ESSENTIAL STUDY 12.3**

**The 'Isle of Wight' (IOW) study** (Rutter *et al.*, 1976)

- This involved a large, representative sample of 14- to 15-year-olds (more than 2,000), whose parents and teachers completed a behaviour questionnaire about them.

- More detailed data were obtained from two sub-samples: (i) 200 randomly selected from the total population; (ii) 304 with extreme scores on the teacher/parent questionnaires (suggesting 'deviant' behaviour).

- Those in both sub-samples were given questionnaires and tests and interviewed by psychiatrists. The major findings regarding rates of psychiatric disorder among the adolescents, compared with a sample of 10-year-olds and the adolescents' parents, are shown in Table 12.2.

Table 12.2 Percentage of 10-year-olds, 14- to 15-year-olds, and the latter's parents, displaying psychiatric disorder

|  | 10-year-olds | 14- to 15-year-olds | Adults (parents) |
|---|---|---|---|
| Males | 12.7 | 13.2 | 7.6 |
| Females | 10.9 | 12.5 | 11.9 |

According to Rutter *et al.*:

- there's a rather modest peak in psychiatric disorders in adolescence

- although severe clinical depression is rare, some degree of inner turmoil may characterise a sizeable minority of adolescents. It's not a myth, but it shouldn't be exaggerated either

- a substantial proportion of those adolescents with psychiatric problems had had them since childhood. Also, when problems did first appear during adolescence, they were mainly associated with stressful situations (such as parents' marital discord).

'... adolescent turmoil is fact, not fiction, but its psychiatric importance has probably been overestimated in the past.' (Rutter *et al.*, 1976)

- As far as *early-maturing boys* are concerned, the evidence is much more mixed (Alsaker, 1996). Early maturation is usually found to be advantageous, but it's also been found to be associated with *more* psychopathology (e.g. Petersen & Crockett, 1985), depressive tendencies and anxiety (e.g. Alsaker, 1992).
- In Western societies, some adolescents may display affective disturbances or disorders. But it's a relatively small minority who'll show clinical depression or report 'inner turmoil' (Compas *et al.*, 1995). Instead, the majority worry about everyday issues, such as school and exam performance, finding work, family and social relationships, self-image, conflicts with authority and the future generally (Gallagher *et al.*, 1992).

## ERIKSON'S THEORY: IDENTITY CRISIS

- As we saw earlier (page 324), Erikson (1963) believed that it's human nature to pass through a genetically determined sequence of *psychosocial stages*, spanning the whole lifetime. Each stage involves a struggle between two conflicting personality outcomes, one of which is positive (or *adaptive*), while the other is negative (or *maladaptive*). Healthy development involves the adaptive outweighing the maladaptive.
- The major challenge of adolescence is to establish a strong sense of personal identity. The dramatic onset of puberty, combined with more sophisticated intellectual abilities (see Chapter 11), makes adolescents particularly concerned with finding their own personal place in adult society.
- In Western societies adolescence is a *moratorium*, an authorised delay of adulthood. This frees adolescents from most responsibilities, and helps them make the difficult transition from childhood to adulthood. Although this is meant to make the transition easier, it can also have the opposite effect. Most of the societies studied by cultural anthropologists have important public ceremonies to mark the transition from childhood to adulthood. This is in stark contrast to Western, industrialised nations, which leave children to their own devices in finding their identities. Without a clearly defined procedure to follow, this process can be difficult – both for adolescents and for their parents (see 'generation gap' below).

### Does society create identity crisis?

- The perceived absence of 'rites of passage' in Western society isn't the only problem. For both adolescents and their parents at the beginning of the twenty-first century there's the related lack of consensus as to where adolescence begins and ends, and precisely what adolescent rights, privileges and responsibilities are. For example, the question 'When do I become an adult?' elicits a different response from a teacher, a doctor, a parent or a police officer (Coleman, 1995).
- The 'maturity gap' refers to the incongruity of achieving biological maturity at adolescence without simultaneously being awarded adult status (Curry, 1998). According to Hendry and Kloep (1999):

' . . . young people, as they grow up, find themselves in the trap of having to respond more and more to society's demands in a "responsible" adult way while being treated as immature and not capable of holding sound opinions on a wide range of social matters.'

One possible escape route from this trap is *risk-taking behaviour* (see below).

The Jewish Bar Mitzvah marks the 13-year-old boy's entry into manhood. But to the rest of society, he's still just a teenager.

- As well as having to deal with the question 'Who am I?', the adolescent must also ask 'Who will I be?'. Erikson saw the creation of an adult personality as achieved mainly through choosing and developing a commitment to an occupation or role in life. The development of *ego identity* (a firm sense of who one is and what one stands for) is positive, and can carry people through difficult times.
- When working with psychiatrically disturbed soldiers in World War II, Erikson coined the term *'identity crisis'* to describe the loss of personal identity which the stress of combat seemed to have caused. Some years later, he extended the use of the term to include:

'... severely conflicted young people whose sense of confusion is due ... to a war within themselves.'

## Role confusion

- Failure to integrate perceptions of the self into a coherent whole results in *role confusion*, which, according to Erikson, can take several forms:

(a) *Intimacy:* Fear of commitment to, or involvement in, close relationships, arising from a fear of losing one's own identity. This may result in stereotyped and formalised relationships, or isolation.

(b) *Time perspective:* Inability to plan for the future or retain any sense of time. It's associated with anxieties about change and becoming an adult.

(c) *Industry:* Difficulty in channelling resources in a realistic way into work or study, both of which require commitment. As a defence, the adolescent may find it impossible to concentrate, or become frenetically engaged in a single activity to the exclusion of all others.

(d) *Negative identity:* Engaging in abnormal or delinquent behaviour (such as drug-taking, or even suicide) in an attempt to resolve the identity crisis. This extreme position sets such adolescents apart from the crowd. It's preferable to the loneliness and isolation that come with failing to achieve a distinct and more functional role in life ('a negative identity is better than no identity').

Thrill seeking: a rite of passage into adulthood?

- Related to Erikson's claims about negative identity is *risk-taking behaviour*. Hendry (1999) asks if risk-taking is:

'... part of the psychological make-up of youth – a thrill-seeking stage in a developmental transition – a necessary rite of passage *en route* to the acquisition of adult skills and self-esteem?'

Many teenagers seek out excitement, thrills and risks as earnestly as in their childhood. This may be to escape a drab existence, or to exert some control over their own lives and to achieve *something*.

### Box 12.8 Sex and drugs

- Traditionally, what parents of teenagers have most feared is that their children will engage in (particularly unprotected) sex and (especially hard) drugs. Recent research suggests that they may have good reason to fear the former, but can feel a little less fearful about the latter.
- Figures for 1998 show that the rate of teenage pregnancies is at its highest for almost a decade (47 per 1,000 girls under 18 (101,500) – compared with 45.6 per 1,000 in 1991), with Britain having the highest rate in Europe. Pregnant teenagers are also increasingly likely to opt for abortion.
- Research conducted in Scotland in 1996/1997 found that young people who have sex before the age of 15 often regret it. The researchers conclude that young people need more help to feel in control of their sexual activities, such as relationship and negotiation skills.
- By contrast, a recent survey of 2,600 15- to 16-year-old boys and girls shows that use of illegal drugs among British youngsters has dropped for the first time since the 1960s. An exception is girls in Northern Ireland. Figures for 1999 show a 'startling' turnaround since 1995, when UK teenagers had the highest rates of drug use in the world.
- Certain drugs, such as ecstacy, have acquired a bad name and have gone out of fashion. Nevertheless, drug use is widespread, and heroin use has actually increased. The drug is freely available and cheaper than ever, and the UK has the fastest-growing number of heroin addicts of any country in Europe.
- Recent Scottish research has shown that pre-teens are now experimenting with heroin (5–6% of 11- and 12-year-olds say they've tried some form of heroin, compared with 0% in 1998).
- Also, drug abuse is related to prevalence of sexually transmitted diseases, prostitution, and sexual decision-making (safe sex). Drugs may make people less inhibited and reduce their capacity for decision-making and judgement.

(Based on Boseley, 2000; Khan, 2003; Norton, 2000; Sussman & Ames, 2001; Vasagar, 2000.)

- For some, delinquency may be the solution: it could actually be *adaptive* as a way of facilitating self-definition and expressing autonomy (Compas *et al.*, 1995).
- Such conflict seems to be largely absent in societies where the complete transition to adulthood is officially approved and celebrated at a specific age, often through a particular ceremony. This enables both the individual and society to adjust to change and enjoy a sense of continuity (Price & Crapo, 1999).

### Box 12.9 Initiation into adulthood in non-Western cultures

- Cohen (1964) looked at 45 non-industrialised societies which held adulthood ceremonies. In societies where adult skills were hard and dangerous, or where father–son relationships were weak but men had to co-operate in hard work, male initiation rituals were dramatic and painful. They allowed the boy to prove his manhood to the community – and to himself.
- Sometimes initiation ceremonies are designed to give boys strength, often by associating them with animals or plants. For example, in the Merina of Madagascar, the boy is associated with the banana tree, which bears much fruit resembling the erect penis (an ideal symbol of virility and fertility). The to-be-initiated boy is removed from his mother's home (a symbol of his attachment to her), before being circumcised in the company of men.
- Brown (1963) described 'rites of passage' for girls in 43 societies from all major regions of the world. They most commonly occur where young girls continue to live and work in their mother's home after marriage. But they also sometimes occur even when young women permanently leave home, and here they involve genital operations or extensive tattooing. These dramatically help the girl understand that she must make the transition from dependent child to a woman, who'll have to fend for herself in a male-dominated environment (Price & Crapo, 1999).

- In recent years, infibulation, the most extreme form of female circumcision, has become a global human-rights issue. Its purpose is to preserve the virginity of young girls before marriage, and to tame the disturbing power of women. In many traditional Islamic countries, especially Sudan, Ethiopia and Somalia, millions of young girls continue to undergo painful and risky genital operations.
- Although the act of infibulation may, from a Western perspective, de-individualise and de-personalise women:

> '... it acts as a transition or a rite of passage to a greater female adult collective; one where women hold relatively few advantages in a male-dominated world. It may in fact be one of the few positive status markers for women in traditional Islamic societies ...'
> (Price & Crapo, 1999)

- Segall *et al.* (1999) maintain that tension and some anti-social behaviour are only to be expected in Western societies, because of the much longer adolescent and youth period:

> '... without a clear marking by ritual, no or little productive role or community participation, no childrearing duties, and distance from observing adult activities.'

- However, adolescence in Euro–American societies *isn't* as problem-ridden as the popular stereotype would have it. If any serious problems do arise, they're directly linked to *rapid social change* (Dasen, 1999), with the associated extension of adolescence and youth. Young people aren't given a productive role to play when entering adult society (Segall *et al.*, 1999).
- According to Coleman and Roker (1998), an important trend in adolescence research is an increasing focus on identity development among ethnically diverse populations, such as young black women (e.g. Robinson, 1997) and mixed-race young people (Tizard & Phoenix, 1993). Coleman and Roker believe that notions of identity and identity formation are likely to become more central to the study of adolescence as this life stage becomes longer and more fragmented, and entry into adulthood becomes more problematic.

## Studies of self-esteem: testing Erikson's theory

- Tests of Erikson's theory have typically used measures of self-concept (especially *self-esteem*) as indicators of crisis.
- Girls' dissatisfaction with their appearance begins during puberty, along with a decline in self-esteem (Crawford & Unger, 1995). Comparisons between *early- and late-maturing girls* indicate that dissatisfaction with looks is associated with the rapid and normal weight gain that's part of growing up (Attie & Brooks-Gunn, 1989; Blyth *et al.*, 1981).
- Early maturers have less-positive body images, despite the fact that they date more and earlier. Also, sexual activity is more problematic for adolescent girls (as it is for females in general). There are persisting double standards regarding sex (as reflected in 'slag' and 'stud' for sexually active females and males respectively), together with differential responsibility for contraception and pregnancy (see Box 12.8).
- However, Offer *et al.* (1988) deny that there's any increase in disturbance of the self-image during early adolescence. For Coleman and Hendry (1990), although such disturbance *is* more likely in early than late adolescence, only a very small proportion of the total adolescent population is likely to have a negative self-image or very low self-esteem.
- By contrast, *early-maturing boys* feel more attractive (Tobin-Richards *et al.*, 1983) and tend to be more satisfied with their bodies, looks and muscle development (Blyth *et al.,* 1981; Simmons & Blyth, 1987). However, Alsaker (1996) refers to two studies, which have found a correlation between pubertal boys' *dissatisfaction* with their bodies and the development of pubic and body hair. She asks if this reflects some new image of men in advertisements, and a new trend for men to shave their bodies and be *less* hairy.

OH MY GOD – HOW WILL ANY GIRL FANCY ME NOW...?!

- Most of these (and other similar) studies have been conducted in the USA, UK and other English-speaking countries. But a study of a very large, nationally representative Norwegian sample found that the global self-esteem of both late-maturing boys and girls suffered, while early and on-time maturers (of both sexes) enjoy equally high self-esteem (Wichstrom, 1998).

## MARCIA'S THEORY: IDENTITY STATUSES

- Marcia (1980) extended Erikson's theory by proposing four *statuses* of adolescent identity formation, which characterise the search for identity.
- A mature identity can be achieved only if an individual experiences several *crises* in exploring and choosing between life's alternatives, finally arriving at a *commitment* or investment of the self in those choices.

**Box 12.10 The four identity statuses proposed by Marcia (1980)**

**Table 12.3** Four identity statuses as defined by high/low commitment and high/low crisis

|  |  | Degree of crisis | |
|---|---|---|---|
|  |  | **High** | **Low** |
| Degree of commitment to particular role/values | **High** | *Identity achievement* | *Foreclosure* |
|  | **Low** | *Moratorium* | *Diffusion (or confusion)* |

- **Diffusion/confusion:** the individual hasn't really started thinking about the issues seriously, let alone formulated any goals or made any commitment. (This represents the *least mature* status.)
- **Foreclosure:** the individual has avoided the uncertainties and anxieties of crisis by quickly and prematurely committing to safe and conventional (parental) goals and beliefs. Alternatives haven't been seriously considered.
- **Moratorium:** this is the height of the crisis as described by Erikson. Decisions about identity are postponed while the individual tries out alternative identities, without committing to any particular one.
- **Identity achievement:** the individual has experienced a crisis but has emerged successfully with firm commitments, goals and ideology. (This represents the *most mature* status.)

### An evaluation of Marcia's theory

**Not stages but age-related:** Identity moratorium is a prerequisite for identity achievement, but Marcia doesn't see the four statuses as Erikson-type stages. However, evidence suggests that among 12- to 24-year-old men, they're broadly age-related. For example, Meilman (1979) reported that younger men (12–18) were more likely to experience diffusion or foreclosure, whereas older men were increasingly likely to be identity achievers.

**Mixed empirical support:** In Meilman's study, relatively few men – irrespective of age –

were achieving moratorium. This casts doubt on the validity of the theory. But several longitudinal studies have indicated clear patterns of movement from foreclosure and diffusion to moratorium and achievement (Kroger, 1996).

**✖ Gender bias:** When Marcia's statuses are applied to females, even Marcia himself accepts that they work 'only more or less'. This is an example of *androcentrism*, that is, taking the male experience as the standard and applying it to both men and women. Erikson's theory has been criticised in a similar way (Gilligan, 1982: see Chapters 11 and 16).

## COLEMAN'S FOCAL THEORY: MANAGING ONE CHANGE AT A TIME

- According to Coleman and Hendry (1990), most theories of adolescence help us to understand young people with serious problems and those belonging to minority or deviant groups. However, what's needed is a theory of *normality*.
- The picture that emerges from the research as a whole is that while adolescence is a difficult time for some, for the majority it appears to be a period of relative stability. Coleman's (1980) *focal theory* is an attempt to explain how this is achieved.
- The theory is based on a study of 800 six-, 11-, 13-, 15- and 17-year-old boys and girls. Attitudes towards self-image, being alone, heterosexual and parental relationships, friendships and large-group situations all changed as a function of age. More importantly, concerns about different issues reached a peak at different ages for both sexes.

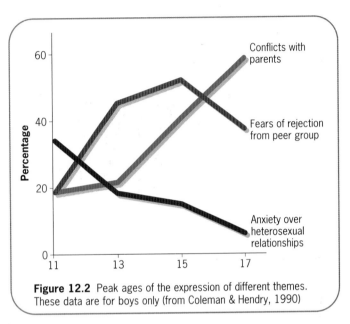

**Figure 12.2** Peak ages of the expression of different themes. These data are for boys only (from Coleman & Hendry, 1990)

- Particular sorts of relationship patterns come into *focus* (are most prominent) at different ages, although no pattern is specific to one age. The patterns overlap and there are wide individual differences.
- Coleman believes that adolescents are able to cope with the potentially stressful changes as well as they do by dealing with one issue at a time. They spread the process of adaptation over a span of years, attempting to resolve one issue first before addressing the next. Because different problems and relationships come into focus and are dealt with at different points during the adolescent years, the stresses resulting from the need to adapt don't all have to be dealt with together.
- Adolescents who, for whatever reason, must deal with *more than one* issue (or normative shift) at a time are the most likely to experience difficulties (Coleman & Hendry, 1990). If normative shifts coincide with non-normative ones, the situation is even more problematic (Hendry & Kloep, 1999).

 **An evaluation of Coleman's focal theory**

**✔ Successfully replicated:** Coleman's original findings have been successfully replicated by Kroger (1985) with large North American and New Zealand samples. Others have successfully tested hypotheses derived from the theory. For example, Simmons and Blyth (1987) predicted that if change (such as puberty):

- occurred at too young an age (causing the individual to be developmentally 'off-time')
- was marked by sharp discontinuity (i.e. sudden change) or
- involved accumulation of significant and temporally close issues (important shifts occurred together)

then adjustment would be more difficult. Their results strongly supported their predictions.

## Research into relationships with parents and peers

### SOCIOLOGICAL APPROACHES: GENERATION GAP

- Sociologists see *role change* as an integral aspect of adolescent development (Coleman, 1995).
- Changing school or college, leaving home and beginning a job all involve a new set of relationships, producing different and often greater expectations. These expectations themselves demand a substantial re-assessment of the self-concept, and *speed up* the socialisation process.
- Some adolescents find this problematic, because of the wide variety of competing socialising agencies (such as the family, mass media and peer group). These often present *conflicting* values and demands (see discussion above of the identity crisis).
- Sociologists also see socialisation as being more dependent on the adolescent's *own generation* than on the family or other social institutions (*auto-socialisation*: Marsland, 1987). As Marsland says:

---

'The crucial meaning of youth is withdrawal from adult control and influence compared with childhood ... '

---

- Young people withdraw into their peer groups, and this withdrawal is (within limits) accepted by adults. What Marsland is describing here is the *generation gap*.
- But what's the evidence for a generation gap? Adolescents and their parents are, by definition, different generations. But does this necessarily mean there's a generation gap, that is, that there'll be conflict between them because they occupy 'different worlds'?

### PARENT–ADOLESCENT RELATIONSHIPS

- According to Hendry (1999):

---

'Adolescence as a transition from childhood to adulthood requires changes from child–parent relationships to young-adult–parent relationships ... '

---

- Failure to negotiate new relationships with parents, or having highly critical or rejecting parents, is likely to make adolescents adopt a negative identity (Curry, 1998).
- Also, parents who rated their own adolescence as stormy and stressful reported more conflict in their relationships with adolescent children, and were less satisified with their family (Scheer & Unger, 1995).
- Parents in general are going through a time of transition themselves, re-appraising their life goals, career and family ambitions, and assessing whether they've fulfilled their expectations as parents.
- However, for most adolescents, relationships with parents become more equal and reciprocal. Parental authority comes to be seen as open to discussion and negotiation (e.g. Coleman & Hendry,

**ESSENTIAL STUDY 12.4**

**Adolescent–parent relationships** (APR) (Hendry *et al.*, 1993)

- In a longitudinal Scottish study, Hendry *et al.* found that parents were chosen in preference to friends when discussing progress and problems at school, and careers, but not necessarily more personal matters.
- Mothers were preferred over fathers as confidantes in all areas except careers and sex (boys) and problems with mothers (both sexes).
- Most girls and nearly half the boys chose to confide in their mother over problems with friends, and nearly half the girls and a third of the boys conveyed doubts about their own abilities to her.
- These figures suggest a disengagement by fathers. Girls tend to be very uncomfortable discussing pubertal issues with their father, and learn almost nothing from him about puberty.
- The mother's role in enforcing family rules brings her into conflict with the children more readily. But she's still seen as being supportive and caring, not 'distanced' like the father.

1990; Hendry *et al.*, 1993). The study described in Essential Study 12.4 also suggests that relationships with mothers and fathers don't necessarily change in the same ways and to the same extent.

- Studies conducted in several countries have found that young people get along well with their parents (e.g. Hendry *et al.*, 1993; Kloep & Tarifa, 1993), adopt their views and values, and perceive family members as the most important 'significant others' in their lives (McGlone *et al.*, 1996).
- Most adolescents who had conflicts with their parents already had poor relationships with them before puberty (Stattin & Klackenberg, 1992).
- Disagreements between young people and their parents are similar everywhere in Europe: Greece (Besevegis & Giannitsas, 1996), Italy (Jackson *et al.*, 1996), Scotland (Hendry *et al.*, 1993), Germany (Fischer *et al.*, 1985), Albania and Sweden (Kloep & Tarifa, 1993). Teenagers have daily quarrels about how long or often they may stay out, how much they should help at home, tidiness of their bedrooms, volume of music, and school achievement.
- According to Jackson *et al.* (1996), disagreements can arise because:

(a) parents expect greater independence of action from their teenagers
(b) parents don't wish to grant as much autonomy as the adolescent demands (with young women having more conflict than young men over independence)
(c) parents and adolescents have different personal tastes and preferences.

- Despite this potential for conflict, evidence suggests that competence as an independent adult can best be achieved within the context of a secure family environment, where exploration of alternative ideas, identities and behaviour is allowed and actively encouraged (Barber & Buehler, 1996). Although detachment and separation from the family are necessary and desirable, young people *don't* have to reject their parents in order to become adults in their own right (see Chapter 2).

## PEER RELATIONSHIPS

- Adolescent *friendship groups* (established around mutual interests) are normally embedded within the wider network of *peer groups* (which set 'norms', provide comparisons and pressures to conform to 'expected' behaviours).
- Friendship groups re-affirm self-image, and enable the young person to experience a new form of intimacy and learn social skills (such as discussing and solving conflicts, sharing and self-assertion). They also offer the opportunity to expand knowledge, develop a new identity, and experiment away from the watchful eyes of adults and family (Coleman & Hendry, 1990).
- Generally, peers become more important as providers of advice, support, feedback and companionship, as models for behaviour and as sources of comparison with respect to personal qualities and skills.
- Peer and friendship groups become important points of reference in social development, and provide social contexts for shaping day-to-day values. But they often *support* traditional parental attitudes and beliefs. Hence peer and friendship groups can work in concert with, rather than in opposition to, adult goals and achievements (Hendry, 1999).

# EXAM tips BOX

**Discuss research into the formation of identity in adolescence. (24 marks) (30 mins) (600 words minimum) AO1/AO2**

*This essay can be split into FOUR sections – each about 150 words long. Each section would be worth about 6 marks.*

**Section 1:** A **description** of research into the formation of identity in adolescence. As research can refer to theory and/or research studies, you could include a brief definition of 'identity' (such as Erikson's), then describe his account of identity crisis as part of his theory of psychosocial development. You could refer to studies of early/late puberty, which demonstrate the inseparability of individual and social/cultural aspects of identity formation. (This could be done here and/or in Section 2.)

AO1

**Section 2:** You could continue your **description** of research into identity formation. You could include Marcia's theory of identity statuses (an extension of Erikson's theory). Studies of mental disorder among adolescents could be described, such as:

* IOW (Rutter *et al.*, 1976).

AO1

**Section 3:** You should **analyse** and **evaluate** the research. In the case of Erikson, you could consider studies of self-esteem (a major way of testing his claims), as well as the androcentric nature of his (and Marcia's) theories. In the case of Marcia, you could consider Meilman's (1979) study.

AO2

**Section 4:** Another way of **analysing** and **evaluating** the research is to put the whole concept of identity and crisis into a cultural context. What features of Western cultures are likely to encourage crisis in adolescents, and what is it about non-Western cultures which make this much less likely? Is adolescence, as we know it, universal, and does our stereotyped image of adolescent turmoil stand up to empirical scrutiny?

AO2

*Try to answer this question yourself. There's a sample essay on page 354 with which you can compare your essay.*

Other possible exam questions:

* Each essay is worth 24 marks and should take 30 minutes to write
* Remember the mark scheme allocates 12 marks for AO1 (knowledge and description) and 12 marks for AO2 (analysis and evaluation).

## PERSONALITY DEVELOPMENT

**1.** Outline and evaluate ONE OR MORE explanations of personality development. (24 marks)

## GENDER DEVELOPMENT

**2. a.** Describe ONE explanation of the development of gender identity/gender role. (12 marks)

**b.** Evaluate the explanation of the development of gender identity/gender role that you described in part (a). (12 marks)

## ADOLESCENCE

**3.** Discuss research into social development in adolescence. (24 marks)

**4.** Critically consider research into cultural differences in adolescent behaviour. (24 marks)

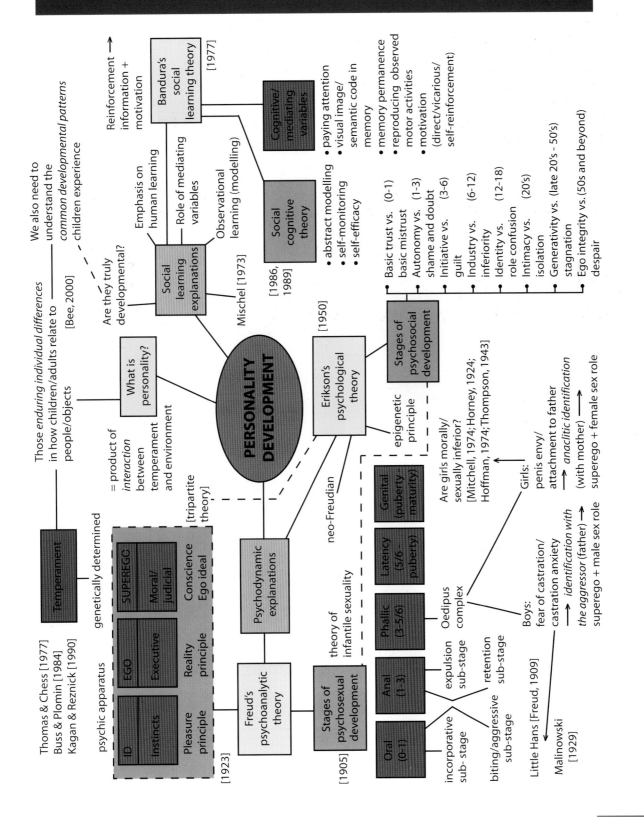

**PERSONALITY DEVELOPMENT**

**What is personality?**

Those enduring individual differences in how children/adults relate to people/objects [Bee, 2000]

= product of *interaction* between temperament and environment

**Temperament**
genetically determined

Thomas & Chess [1977]
Buss & Plomin [1984]
Kagan & Reznick [1990]

**Social learning explanations**

Emphasis on human learning

Role of mediating variables

Observational learning (modelling)

Are they truly developmental?

We also need to understand the *common developmental patterns* children experience

**Bandura's social learning theory** [1977]

Reinforcement → information + motivation

**Cognitive/ mediating variables**

- paying attention
- visual image/ semantic code in memory
- memory permanence
- reproducing observed motor activities
- motivation (direct/vicarious/ self-reinforcement)

**Social cognitive theory** [1986, 1989]

- abstract modelling
- self-monitoring
- self-efficacy

Mischel [1973]

**Erikson's psychological theory** [1950]

**Stages of psychosocial development**

- Basic trust vs. basic mistrust (0-1)
- Autonomy vs. shame and doubt (1-3)
- Initiative vs. guilt (3-6)
- Industry vs. inferiority (6-12)
- Identity vs. role confusion (12-18)
- Intimacy vs. isolation (20's)
- Generativity vs. stagnation (late 20's - 50's)
- Ego integrity vs. despair (50s and beyond)

epigenetic principle

neo-Freudian

**Psychodynamic explanations**

**Freud's psychoanalytic theory** [1923]

psychic apparatus

[tripartite theory]

| ID | EGO | SUPEREGO |
|---|---|---|
| Instincts | Executive | Moral/ judicial |
| Pleasure principle | Reality principle | Conscience Ego ideal |

theory of infantile sexuality

**Stages of psychosexual development** [1905]

| Oral (0-1) | Anal (1-3) | Phallic (3-5/6) | Latency (5/6 - puberty) | Genital (puberty- maturity) |
|---|---|---|---|---|

incorporative sub-stage

biting/aggressive sub-stage

expulsion sub-stage

retention sub-stage

Oedipus complex

Little Hans [Freud, 1909]

Malinowski [1929]

Boys: fear of castration/ castration anxiety → *identification with the aggressor* (father) → superego + male sex role

Girls: penis envy → *attachment to father* → *anaclitic identification* (with mother) → superego + female sex role

Are girls morally/ sexually inferior? [Mitchell, 1974; Horney, 1924; Hoffman, 1974; Thompson, 1943]

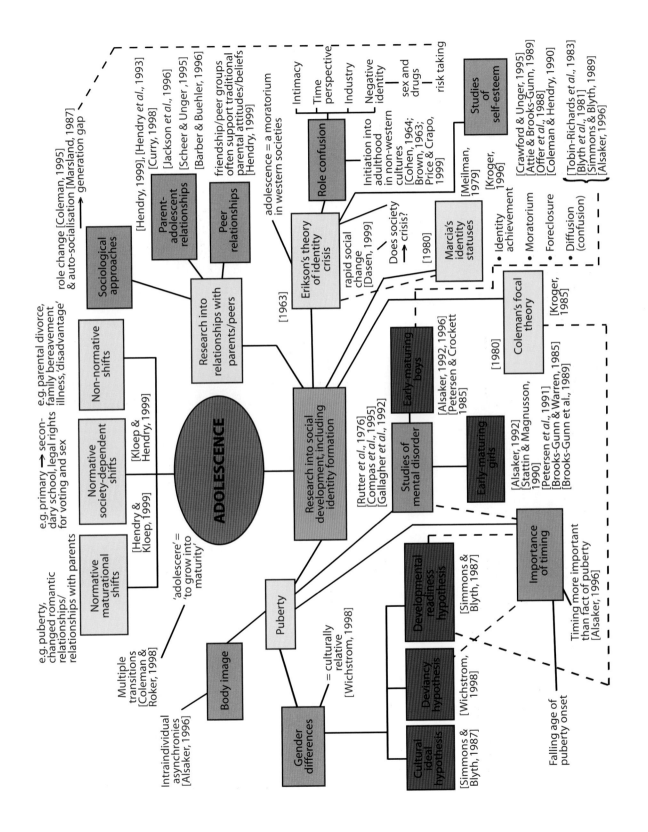

**ADOLESCENCE**

Normative maturational shifts
e.g. puberty, changed romantic relationships/ relationships with parents
[Hendry & Kloep, 1999]

Normative society-dependent shifts
e.g. primary → secondary school, legal rights for voting and sex
[Kloep & Hendry, 1999]

Non-normative shifts
e.g. parental divorce, family bereavement, illness, 'disadvantage'

Multiple transitions [Coleman & Roker, 1998]

'adolescere' = 'to grow into maturity'

Intraindividual asynchronies [Alsaker, 1996]

Sociological approaches
role change [Coleman, 1995] & auto-socialisation [Marsland, 1987] → generation gap

Parent-adolescent relationships
[Hendry, 1999], [Hendry et al., 1993]
[Curry, 1998]
[Jackson et al., 1996]
[Scheer & Unger, 1995]
[Barber & Buehler, 1996]

Peer relationships
friendship/peer groups often support traditional parental attitudes/beliefs [Hendry, 1999]

Research into relationships with parents/peers

Research into social development, including identity formation
[Rutter et al., 1976]
[Compas et al., 1995]
[Gallagher et al., 1992]

Erikson's theory of identity crisis
[1963]

Intimacy
Time perspective
Industry
Negative identity
sex and drugs
risk taking

Role confusion

adolescence = a moratorium in western societies

Initiation into adulthood in non-western cultures
[Cohen, 1964; Brown, 1963; Price & Crapo, 1999]

Does society crisis?
rapid social change [Dasen, 1999]
[Meilman, 1979]
[Kroger, 1996]

[1980]

Marcia's identity statuses
• Identity achievement
• Moratorium
• Foreclosure
• Diffusion (confusion)

Studies of self-esteem
[Crawford & Unger, 1995]
[Attie & Brooks-Gunn, 1989]
[Offer et al., 1988]
[Coleman & Hendry, 1990]
[Tobin-Richards et al., 1983]
[Blyth et al., 1981]
[Simmons & Blyth, 1989]
[Alsaker, 1996]

Coleman's focal theory
[1980]
[Kroger, 1985]

Studies of mental disorder

Early-maturing boys
[Alsaker, 1992, 1996]
[Petersen & Crockett 1985]

Early-maturing girls
[Alsaker, 1992]
[Stattin & Magnusson, 1990]
[Petersen et al., 1991]
[Brooks-Gunn & Warren, 1985]
[Brooks-Gunn et al., 1989]

Importance of timing
Timing more important than fact of puberty [Alsaker, 1996]

Developmental readiness hypothesis
[Simmons & Blyth, 1987]

Deviancy hypothesis
[Wichstrom, 1998]

Cultural ideal hypothesis
[Simmons & Blyth, 1987]

Puberty
= culturally relative [Wichstrom, 1998]

Body image

Gender differences

Falling age of puberty onset

# SAMPLE ESSAYS

Critically consider *one* psychodynamic explanation of personality development. (24 marks) (30 mins) (600 words minimum)

### Sections 1 and 2:

A01

'Psychodynamic' refers to the active forces within the personality that motivate behaviour, as well as the inner causes of behaviour, in particular the unconscious conflict between the various personality structures. Freud's was the original psychodynamic theory, and all those theories based on his ideas (such as Erikson's) are also psychodynamic. Freud's theory of personality development is closely related to other aspects of his psychoanalytic theory. Especially important are his accounts of the structure of the personality (comprising the id, the ego and the superego) and motivation. Although these personality structures develop in this order, this isn't strictly part of Freud's developmental theory. According to his theory of infantile sexuality, sexuality isn't confined to physically mature adults, but is evident from birth, with different parts of the body (erogenous zones) becoming the focus of sexual pleasure – and frustration – at different times. This refers to the psychosexual stages, oral (0–1 years), anal (1–3 years), phallic (3–5/6 years), latency (5/6 years–puberty) and genital (puberty–maturity). Both excessive gratification and frustration can result in the individual becoming fixated at the particular stage (or sub-stage) at which this occurs. In turn, this fixation can result in associated adult personality traits, such as anal expulsive or anal retentive. In this way, Freud was able to explain how individual differences arise from common developmental patterns.

Probably the most important psychosexual stage is the phallic, during which the Oedipus complex arises. The small boy's fear of castration/castration anxiety leads him to repress his desire for the mother and hostile feelings for the father, and to identify with the father. Through this identification with the aggressor, boys acquire their superego and the male sex role. For girls, the Oedipus (or Electra) complex begins with the belief that she's already been castrated. She blames her mother for this and experiences penis envy. For girls to develop their superego and female sex role, they need to identify with the mother. But the girl's motivation for giving up her father as a love-object in order to move back to her mother is much less obvious than the boy's for identifying with his father. As a consequence, girls' identification with their mothers is less complete than boys' with their fathers. In turn, this makes the female superego weaker and their identity as separate, independent persons is less well developed.

### Section 3:

A02

Freud believed that the Oedipus complex was 'the central phenomenon of the sexual period of early childhood'. But there's little evidence to support his claim regarding sex differences in morality (as a result of the female's weaker superego). For example, as measured by children's ability to resist temptation, girls, if anything, are stronger than boys (Hoffman, 1974). According to Horney

(1924) and Thompson (1943), rather than girls wanting a penis, what they really envy is males' superior social status.

Freud assumed that the Oedipus complex is a universal phenomenon, but Malinowski's (1929) study of the Trobriand Islanders showed that where the father is the mother's lover but not the son's disciplinarian (i.e. an avuncular society), the father–son relationship was very good. It seems that Freud over-emphasised the role of sexual jealousy. But this is still only one study, and more societies, both Western and avuncular, need to be examined (Segall *et al.*, 1990). Also, other psychodynamic theorists, such as Erikson (1950) believed that Freud exaggerated the influence of instincts, particularly the sexual instinct, in his account of personality development. Erikson tried to correct this by describing stages of psychosocial development, reflecting the influence of social, cultural and historical factors, but without denying the role of biology.

### Section 4:

A02

Another major criticism of Freud's Oedipal theory is that it was based almost entirely on the case of Little Hans (1909). In fact, Freud's Oedipal theory had already been proposed in 1905, and Little Hans was simply presented as a 'little Oedipus'. Given that this was the only child patient that Freud reported on, and that any theory of development must involve the study of children, Little Hans is a crucially important case study. But it was extremely biased, with Hans's father (a supporter of Freud's theories) doing most of the psychoanalysis, and Freud simply seeing Hans as confirming his Oedipal theory. Quite apart from criticism of the reliability and objectivity of the case study method in general, other psychodynamic theorists have offered alternative interpretations of Hans's horse phobia. These include Bowlby's (1973) re-interpretation in terms of attachment theory.

However, Bee (2000) believes that attachment research provides considerable support for the basic psychoanalytic hypothesis that the quality of the child's earliest relationships affects the whole course of later development. Both Bowlby (1973) and Erikson (1963) see early relationships as prototypes of later relationships. Belief in the impact of early experience is a lasting legacy of Freud's developmental theory.

(778 words)

Critically consider explanations of the development of gender identity and/or gender role. (24 marks) (30 mins) (600 words minimum)

## Section 1:

AO1

'Sex' refers to our biological status as male or female, while 'gender' is what culture makes out of our biological sex (Unger, 1979). So gender identity refers to how we classify ourselves as male or female, boy or girl. Gender role refers to the behaviours, attitudes, values and so on which a particular society either expects from, or considers to be appropriate to, males and females. These expectations are reflected in gender-role stereotypes. Sex typing refers to how we acquire gender identity and adopt a male or female gender role, and this process is central to Social Learning Theory (SLT). According to SLT, boys and girls behave differently because they're treated differently by parents and others. But this sex typing isn't arbitrary. Rather, it's based on expectations and beliefs about how boys and girls ought to behave (gender-role stereotypes). SLT also stresses the role of observational learning and reinforcement. By observing others behaving in particular ways, and then imitating that behaviour, children receive reinforcement for sex-appropriate behaviours (Bandura, 1977). So gender identity and gender role are the result of sex typing and reinforcement.

According to the cognitive-developmental approach (Kohlberg, 1969; Kohlberg & Ullian, 1974), the child first learns to classify itself as male or female. There are three stages in the development of gender identity: gender labelling/basic gender identity (about age three), gender stability (four to five), and gender constancy/consistency (six to seven). Once children have acquired gender constancy, they come to value the behaviours and attitudes associated with their sex. Only then will they identify with/imitate the adult figures who possess the qualities they see as being central to their sense of themselves as male or female.

## Section 2:

AO1

A famous study of sex typing is Smith & Lloyd's (1978) 'Baby X' experiment. Babies were dressed in unisex snowsuits and given names which sometimes matched their true gender and sometimes didn't. When adults played with them, they treated the babies according to which gender they believed they were. When parents (and others) are informed of a baby's biological sex, they often react to it according their gender-role expectations. So boys and girls are often given different kinds of toys, have their rooms decorated differently, and are even spoken about in different terms (Rubin et al., 1974). Other evidence shows that parents tend to positively reinforce boys more for behaviours reflecting independence, self-reliance and emotional control, while girls tend to be reinforced for compliance, dependence and emotional expression (Block, 1979). Fathers tend to reinforce these sex-typed behaviours more than mothers do (Kerig et al., 1993).

Support for cognitive-developmental theory comes from Slaby and Frey's (1975) gender constancy study. High- and low-gender-constancy children (two- to five-year-olds) were shown a silent film, with the screen split, such that males were seen on one side and females on the other. The high-gender-constancy children spent much more time looking at the same-sex adult.

## Section 3:

AO2

Slaby and Frey's findings support Kohlberg's (1969) claim that gender constancy is a cause of children's imitation of same-sex models, rather than an effect (as claimed by SLT). It also supports the view that children actively construct their gender-role knowledge by purposefully monitoring their social environment. They engage in self-socialisation, rather than passively receiving information (Whyte, 1998). However, a major problem for cognitive-developmental theory is its prediction that there should be little or no gender-appropriate behaviour before gender constancy is achieved. But even in infancy, both sexes show a marked preference for stereotypical male and female toys (Huston, 1983). According to the theory, they are far too young to have developed gender stability and constancy, although they might have acquired a sense of basic gender identity. According to gender schema (or schematic processing) theory, it's possible that gender identity alone can provide children with sufficient motivation to assume sex-typed behaviour patterns (Bem, 1985; Martin, 1991). Once children understand the labels 'boy' and 'girl', they have a basis for mixing their self-concepts with their society's gender schemas. They can actively seek information about gender schemas, and their self-esteem will become influenced by how they measure up to these.

## Section 4:

AO2

According to Karraker et al. (1995), the traditionally strong sex-typing of babies at birth has declined, and there are no differences between mothers and fathers in this respect. But Maccoby (1990) argues that a consistent and persistent finding is that fathers do treat their children in a more gendered way than mothers. Typically, fathers give more attention to their sons, while mothers attend equally to sons and daughters (Quiery, 1998). Although parents believe they respond in the same way to their sons' and daughters' aggressive acts, they actually intervene much more often – and quickly – when girls behave aggressively (Huston, 1993). But Lytton and Romney (1991) found very few sex differences in terms of parental warmth, overall amount of interaction, encouragement of achievement or dependency, restrictiveness and discipline, or clarity of communication.

In relation to both SLT and cognitive-developmental theory, what gender roles and gender-appropriate behaviour mean – and how these change over time – are determined by broader cultural factors (cultural relativism: Mead, 1935). These can include how certain terms, such as 'nurturing' and 'aggressive' are defined in relation to males and females (Wade & Tavris, 1994). While every known culture distinguishes between male and female based on biological sex, some societies recognise more than two genders, such as the Mohave Indians who recognise four. This strongly supports the view of gender as socially constructed, and theories of gender development need to address this issue.

(900 words)

# SAMPLE ESSAYS

# SAMPLE ESSAYS

Discuss research into the formation of identity in adolescence. (24 marks) (30 mins) (600 words minimum)

## Section 1:

According to Erikson (1963), it's human nature to pass through a genetically determined sequence of psychosocial stages, spanning the whole lifetime. Each stage involves a struggle between two conflicting personality outcomes, one positive/adaptive, the other negative/maladaptive. Healthy development involves the adaptive outweighing the maladaptive. In the case of adolescence, the major challenge is to establish a strong sense of personal identity, and the struggle is between ego identity (a sense of who one is and what one stands for), and role confusion (failure to integrate perceptions of the self into a coherent whole). Western societies authorise the delay of adulthood (a moratorium) in order to help the adolescent find his/her own personal place in adult society. This is meant to make the transition easier, but it can actually make it more difficult in the absence of public initiation rites and ceremonies. Western, industrialised nations leave young people largely to their own devices in finding their identities, and there's a lack of agreement as to where adolescence begins and ends (Coleman, 1995).

## Section 2:

According to Erikson, role confusion can take several different forms, relating to intimacy, time perspective, industry or negative identity. The last refers to adolescents engaging in abnormal or delinquent behaviour, such as drug-taking, or even suicide, in an attempt to resolve their identity crisis. It's preferable to the loneliness and isolation that come with failing to achieve a distinct and more functional role in life ('a negative identity is better than no identity'). One source of role confusion is the 'maturity gap', that is, being at the same time biologically or sexually mature but still without adult social status. According to Erikson, Coleman and Hendry (1990), and others, puberty is one of the most important adjustments that adolescents have to make, and their changing body image is central to their overall self-image. This may be a more difficult transition for girls than for boys. According to the cultural ideal hypothesis (CIH: Simmons & Blyth, 1987), puberty will bring boys closer to their physical ideal (increased muscle distribution, strength and stamina etc.), while girls move further away from theirs (increased body fat makes them less like the idealised thin super-model).

Marcia's (1980) extension of Erikson's theory proposed four statuses of adolescent identity formation. A mature identity can be achieved only if an individual experiences several crises in exploring and choosing between life's alternatives, before finally making a commitment or investment of the self in these choices.

## Section 3:

Tests of Erikson's theory have typically used measures of self-concept – especially self-esteem – as indicators of crisis, and many studies have been concerned with body image. Girls' dissatisfaction with their appearance begins during puberty, along with lower self-esteem (Crawford & Unger, 1995). This is especially true of early-maturing girls, even though they date more and earlier. Sexual activity is more problematic for these early maturers, because of the double standards regarding sex (which applies to females in general). However, Offer et al. (1988) disagree that there's any increase in disturbance of self-image during early adolescence. According to Coleman and Hendry (1999), although disturbance is more likely in early than late adolescence, this is likely to affect only a very small proportion of all adolescents. Some studies have found that early-maturing boys enjoy increased self-esteem (Tobin-Richards et al., 1983; Blyth et al., 1981; Simmons & Blyth, 1987). But there's also evidence that the development of body and pubic hair can cause boys to feel more dissatisfied with their bodies (Alsaker, 1996).

## Section 4:

Although Marcia's four identity statuses aren't meant to be Erikson-type stages, Meilman (1979) found that they are broadly age-related among 12- to 24-year-old males. In other words, the 18- to 24-year-olds were more likely to be identity achievers, while the 12- to 18-year-olds were more likely to experience diffusion or foreclosure. But relatively few of Meilman's participants were achieving moratorium, which casts doubt on the theory's validity. However, several longitudinal studies have supported the theory (Kroger, 1996). When Marcia's statuses are applied to females, even Marcia himself admits they work 'only more or less'. This demonstrates androcentrism, taking the male experience as the standard and applying it to both genders. Erikson's theory has been criticised on similar grounds (Gilligan, 1982).

According to Coleman and Hendry (1990), most theories of adolescence help us to understand young people with serious problems, and those belonging to minority or deviant groups. What we need is a theory of normality. The picture that emerges from the research as a whole is that, while adolescence is a difficult time for some, for the majority it appears to be a period of relative stability. Coleman's (1980) focal theory tries to explain this by claiming that adolescents are able to cope as well as they do by spreading the process of adaptation over several years, resolving one issue at a time. It's when two or more issues have to be dealt with together that the adolescent is most likely to experience difficulties. Coleman's British study has been successfully replicated with large North American and New Zealand samples (Kroger, 1985). But in traditional societies, where there are public initiation ceremonies that mark the move to adulthood, adolescence as we know it, let alone identity crisis, doesn't exist.

(859 words)

# 13

# A2 Module 4:
Social, Physiological, Cognitive, Developmental and Comparative Psychology

# Evolutionary explanations of human behaviour

## What's covered in this chapter?
### You need to know about:

Human reproductive behaviour
- The relationship between sexual selection and human reproductive behaviour including evolutionary explanations of parental investment (e.g. sex differences, parent–offspring conflict)

Evolutionary explanations of mental disorders
- Evolutionary explanations of human mental disorders including depression (e.g. unipolar and bipolar depression) and anxiety disorders (e.g. phobias and obsessive-compulsive disorder)

Evolution of intelligence
- Evolutionary factors in the development of human intelligence (e.g. ecological demands, social complexity). The relationship between brain size and intelligence (e.g. the adaptive value of large brains, comparative studies across species)

## A brief theory of evolution

Although Darwin published his ground-breaking book called 'The Origin of the Species' in 1859, it was not until the 1970s that psychology took an evolutionary approach to human behaviour. It's helpful to understand the essential features of this theory:

- animals are grouped into species, for example, humans belong to the species Homo sapiens
- within each species, some variation exists. People are not identical to one another in either appearance or behaviour
- many looks and much of behaviour are determined by the individual's genome. The genome consists of DNA strands inherited from their parents (50% from each parent)

- individuals pass on their DNA to their offspring. Offspring are not identical to their parents, since genes can suffer from mutations or not be 'switched on'. Some genes are expressed only if they occur in certain combinations. Thus certain characteristics may 'skip' a generation
- the majority of mutations are harmful and tend to be selected against. However, sometimes a mutation may confer some benefit to the animal
- all animals require resources and often these are limited. Hence there is competition among organisms
- all animals produce more offspring than can possibly survive to adulthood
- some organisms will be more successful in the competition than others. Indeed, some of the mutated variations will have an advantage over other organisms
- since they are more successfully adapted to their environment, successful variants will survive to adulthood, breed more and leave more offspring (the 'survival of the fittest')
- if the variant is sufficiently different, then a new species may occur and natural selection will have led to evolutionary change
- as a consequence of natural selection through this process of adaptation, organisms will become expertly designed, not only in their structure, but also in their behaviours
- since we (humans) have been around in some form or another for about 5 million years by now, we should be fairly well adapted to our environment and reproductive survival; if not for Britain in the early twenty-first century, at least as a hunter-gatherer on the African savannah. (Adapted from Cartwright, 2001.)

Sociobiology (later extended and called evolutionary psychology) is the term used to explain human behaviour through the theory of evolution by natural selection, with the additional consideration of the influence of social factors on behaviour.

## Human reproductive behaviour

### The relationship between sexual selection and human reproductive behaviour including evolutionary explanations of sex differences in parental investment (e.g. sex differences, parent–offspring conflict)

SEXUAL SELECTION

'Thus it is, as I believe, that when the males and females of any animal have the same general habits of life, but differ in structure, colour, or ornament, such differences have been mainly caused by sexual selection; that is, individual males have had, in successive generations, some slight advantage over other males, in their weapons, means of defence, or charms; and have transmitted these advantages to their male offspring.' Darwin, from *The Descent of Man and Selection in Relation to Sex* (1871).

- We've already briefly mentioned Darwin's theory of natural selection. The most successful animals will end up with both physical and behavioural characteristics that will enable them to out-perform rivals. After thousands of years of competitive struggle, our characteristics should be finely tuned for growth, survival and reproduction. However, there are problems.
- Many animals possess some characteristics that don't seem to be of any real benefit. The most cited example is the tail of the (male) peacock. Indeed, the peacock's main predator, the

tiger, finds it a good method to catch it by grabbing the tail. In this way, a shorter tail or no tail would surely have been of greater benefit to peacocks. So why has natural selection resulted in such a long tail? The answer, as with many things, appears to lie with sex. Peacocks must mate frequently in order to be successful. Being eaten is an affordable risk. Peahens need to stay alive in order to rear their young – hence only peacocks have attractive tails. Can a comparison be made with young male drivers and their 'souped-up' cars with lots of unnecessary refinements such as spoilers and alloy wheels?

- **Sexual dimorphism** refers to the different physical characteristics of females and males of the same species. For example, male humans tend to be larger and stronger than females. It's easy to guess that these features may have been beneficial in the past if males went out and hunted for food while women stayed at home and looked after the children, since only females can breast-feed their babies. Thus, these features may have been developed through the process of natural selection. But what about the peacock's tail?
- Darwin suggested that there must be certain features that are selected on the basis of sexual selection. That is, certain features help to make animals attractive to the opposite sex. In other words, peacocks develop their large tails because peahens rather like them (we're still not sure exactly why). It seems that both natural *and* sexual selection play a role in the development of behavioural and physical features.

Can natural selection explain the peacock's tail?

There are actually two types of sexual selection:

- **intra-sexual selection (intra = within):** This refers to the situation where one sex (usually males) competes with the same sex for access to, and matings with, females. This tends to take place prior to mating. An example of this would be stags fighting for access to females in the rutting season. The winner gains the territory and the access to females within it, whereas the loser goes home with a broken antler!
- **inter-sexual selection (inter = between):** This refers to the situation where one sex is very choosy in selecting a sexual partner. It leads to the development of traits that enable animals to attract members of the opposite sex. An example of this would be the display of the peacock in front of a peahen.

Both intra-sexual and inter-sexual selection can also be related to human sexual behaviour.

## PARENTAL INVESTMENT (PI)

- PI refers to any investment that a parent makes which increases the offspring's chance of surviving and which will be at the cost of that parent's ability to invest in other offspring (Trivers, 1972).
- PI includes the provision of resources such as food, energy and time expended obtaining food and maintaining the home or territory; time spent teaching offspring; and risks taken to protect young. In terms of human PI, there is a fundamental asymmetry between the sexes – females have an initial investment in their offspring far greater than that of males because female gametes (eggs) are much more costly to produce than those of males (sperm). Females also nourish the embryo up to birth and this means that a female can have only a limited number of offspring. By contrast, a male can have a virtually unlimited number, provided that he can find females willing to mate with him.
- Trivers (1972) argued that there was an optimum or ideal number of offspring for each parent. A low-investing male could afford many offspring and might favour a 'quantity rather than quality' approach. Females, on the other hand, would prefer quality rather than quantity.
- Thus females generally need to be much choosier about whom they mate with. The criteria for what constitutes a good choice of male will vary considerably from species to species, but the basic point about female choice remains. It must be noted that parental investment involves more than just egg or sperm production and that, in certain species, males do provide a great deal of parental care. For example, male pipefish and male seahorses provide an extraordinary degree of parental care in their offspring, arguably more than females of the same species. The male seahorse has a pouch where it keeps infant seahorses until maturity. In addition, in seahorses, females compete with each other for the attention of males. Female seahorses are brightly coloured, a direct contrast with the dull appearance of the males. Competition appears to be for the sex with the greater PI.
- One way to understand human reproduction is simply to measure the potential offspring production of males and females. This avoids any difficulties associated with measuring PI. The world record for the number of children is 888, fathered by Ismail the Bloodthirsty (1672–1727), an Emperor of Morocco who had a very busy harem, and a Russian woman who had 69 children!
- It seems clear that, in humans, women are the limiting factor in reproduction and this suggests some male–male intrasexual competition and some male–female intersexual competition.
- To be successful, you must pass on your genes. This means, in most cases, that you must have more than two babies who grow up to do the same. There's no imperative to live a long time, particularly if you are male: the time of a single missed psychology lesson would be ample to pass on your genes!

- Men and women enter the evolutionary survival ring with totally different weapons. It would be unrealistic to assume that the same 'fighting' strategies would succeed for both.
- Evolution promotes specialisation. Just as in a tribal village, one person becomes a baker and another becomes the butcher, each to ensure that, by specialising and becoming a master of their trade, their own standard of living is improved, so with males and females. Males produce many, small, mobile gametes (sperm), while females produce few, large and non-mobile gametes (eggs). This puts the ball, or rather the baby, in the female court. In humans it stays there for a while. Pregnancy takes nine months and breast-feeding, or equivalent, a further 3–12 months. Neither of these a male can do; some males may obey the Biblical imperative to go forth and multiply during this time.
- There is a lot of debate about this. For example, if males can afford to be promiscuous it dawns on them that females can be too, so does it make more sense to 'sow your wild oats' with lots of women, in the hope that at least *some* of them mother your children *or* to stick to one woman and watch her like a hawk so you can be *sure* she's mothering only your children?

## SEX DIFFERENCES AND MATE CHOICE

There are a number of characteristics that human males and females appear to value in a potential mate.

**Key study**

- There appear to be marked gender differences in what men and women look for in a potential partner (intersexual selection). Men and women appear to use different criteria when it comes to sexual selection. In a comprehensive study of 37 cultures on six continents and five islands, Buss (1989) found that women value prospective male suitors on a cluster of characteristics related to resource potential. These included good financial prospects, ambition, industriousness, older age and emotional maturity. However, men value potential female partners in terms of fecundity, defined as the ability to produce and care for children. Fecundity is assessed in terms of a preference for youthful looks and physical attractiveness. More specifically, men prefer 'baby face' or infantile features (i.e. large eyes and a small nose) since these are assessed as correlated with attractiveness, fertility and perceptions of few medical problems (Cunningham, 1986). It seems clear that sexual selection can work in a number of ways because sexual signals are seen as providing different sorts of information to potential mates.

- Humans, like many other animals, have developed sexual size dimorphism due to both intra-sexual (male–male) competition and inter-sexual (male–female) competition. Darwin believed that intra-sexual selection would result in special adaptations such as sexual differences in size and shape and the development of different features to deter rivals. Although these are more evident in animals such as stags and elephant seals, where size has been sexually selected, sexual dimorphism also occurs in humans. Men tend to have greater musculature and more facial and body hair than women. Women tend to have a different fat distribution to men, with more on the buttocks and hips. It's most likely that many of these features are the result of sexual selection.

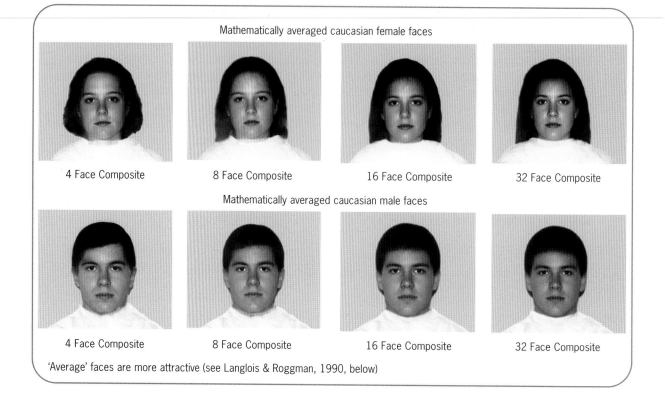

Mathematically averaged caucasian female faces

4 Face Composite    8 Face Composite    16 Face Composite    32 Face Composite

Mathematically averaged caucasian male faces

4 Face Composite    8 Face Composite    16 Face Composite    32 Face Composite

'Average' faces are more attractive (see Langlois & Roggman, 1990, below)

- Inferences concerning social patterns can also be made from relative male–female sizes. In the only pair-bonded ape, the gibbon, there is little size difference. Primate groups where males are larger than females tend to involve multiple matings by successful large males. The larger the male compared to the female, the larger his harem will be, e.g. gorillas.

- Many secondary sexual characteristics are considered to be beautiful by humans. These characteristics are also the result of sexual selection. For example, in humans the ratio of the circumference of the hips to the waist is thought to be an important characteristic. After puberty, women have a greater hip-to-waist ratio than men. Singh (1993) used archival data from the last 50 years to examine these measurements in beauty contest winners and *Playboy* centrefolds. He found that a small waist set against full hips was a consistent feature of female attractiveness, while bust-line, overall body weight and physique varied over the years. He concluded that a larger hip-to-waist ratio was associated with better health status and greater reproductive capacity, hence men's preference for this feature.

- Unsurprisingly, faces play an important part in choosing a mate. A facial configuration close to the population mean is fundamental to attractiveness. Langlois and Roggman (1990) digitised facial images of male and female college students. The faces were averaged together and the composite faces were rated for attractiveness.

**Key study**

- The composite faces were rated as significantly more attractive than the individual faces, if the composites had at least 16 different faces in them. Thus averaged faces are attractive. Langlois and Roggman (1990) also found that individual faces rated extremely attractive when overlayed onto a composite face made of 32 different faces were almost identical. Other researchers have suggested that the symmetry or youthfulness of a face make it attractive. Langlois and Roggman (1990) agree that symmetry, youthfulness or a smile are attributes that can add to facial attractiveness but do not, in themselves, make a face attractive. They believe that 'averageness' is *fundamental and necessary* to facial attractiveness. It seems that 'average' faces are perceived as familiar, more 'face-like' and as the 'best' examples of a category of faces.

But why have these particular features been developed through sexual selection?

* According to evolutionary theory, the mean value of many physical features should be preferred to extreme values because of normalising or stabilising selection. That is, the mean of any distribution is the best solution to any adaptive problem. An obvious example here is height. For example, it's not true that all women prefer extremely tall men. Indeed, most women prefer a partner who is of average height. Like height, people with facial configurations close to the mean of the population for each sex should be preferred.
* Furthermore, humans (and animals) have evolved to perceive and become excited or interested in these particular features. Humans perceive sugar to be sweet only because those ancestors in our past consumed sweet fruits which conveyed them benefits in terms of energy and nutrition. Those ancestors who liked this taste thrived, while others died out. In the same way, faces of women and particular proportions of waists and hips are considered to be beautiful only because our ancestors with such preferences left more and more healthy offspring than the average individual in the population.
* Females tend to be much more choosy in selecting a mate since they have a greater investment in their offspring (Buss & Malamuth, 1996). Women tend to select men who are able to provide for potential offspring through the resources they can bring to any relationship. Men are therefore more competitive with each other (intra-sexual competition) for access to women. This has created a strong demand for men who are able to provide valuable resources, resulting in the characteristics of assertiveness, aggressiveness and sensitivity to hierarchy found in men. In primitive hunting cultures, such men, literally, brought home the bacon!
* Sadalla, Kenrick and Vershure (1987) also report that dominant behaviour in males increases their attractiveness to females. Although male dominance enhanced their sexual attractiveness, it didn't improve their likeability. However, this dominant trait may have arisen as a result of social coercion. For example, a woman who chose a dominant aggressor for a sexual partner may have chosen him in order to stay alive, rather than expressing a personal preference for dominant men.
* According to Cartwright (2001), another factor involved in sexual selection is sexual enthusiasm, that is, the capacity to be sexually aroused. Males appear to have a lower arousal threshold than females. Indeed, some male frog species will mate with anything that vaguely resembles a female frog. Houseflies will mate with a knotted bootlace. One interesting aspect of this is called the 'Coolidge effect' after an incident involving U.S. President Coolidge. When visiting a chicken farm, Mrs Coolidge asked why there was only one cockerel. She was told that the cockerel could copulate many times each day. She asked that the President be told about this! On being informed of this, the President asked if the cockerel always copulated with the same hen. On being told no, it was always with a different hen, he asked that his wife be informed of that! It seems that males can be kept sexually aroused for long periods of time with the continued introduction of different females. It makes evolutionary sense for a male to have multiple partners, each of whom can produce a baby for him. A female, having selected the best 'mate', gains nothing from the sperm of others.

## Research studies that support inter-sexual selection

Regan *et al.* (2000) conducted an experiment at an American university to find out what characteristics men and women look for when finding a partner. Distinctive differences between the sexes were found. Men disliked partners with a low sex drive and also attached greater value to a partner's sexual desirability than the women did. Women placed greater importance on a partner's social position and socioeconomic status. The researchers concluded that this was, in part, because women want a man who can provide for their family in terms of food, protection and material possessions.

Clark and Hatfield (1989) report two studies where 96 university students took part in testing the hypothesis that men were more eager for sex than women. Male and female confederates of average attractiveness approached a potential partner and asked them one of three questions:

- would you go out with me tonight?
- will you come over to my apartment?
- would you go to bed with me?

Results were almost identical for both studies and they found that:

- both men and women were equally willing to go on a date with a person they'd just met
- men were 11 times more likely than women to agree to visit the person's apartment
- while no women agreed to sex, as many as 75% of the men did!

Both these studies support the hypothesis that men and women, through sexual selection, have different strategies when it comes to mate choice. They help to provide answers to the 'who', 'when' and 'how many' questions of sexual behaviour.

## Research study that doesn't support inter-sexual selection

Strassberg and Holty (2003) decided to conduct a study involving personal ads on the Internet. They argued that personal ads provide a rich source of information on relationships, particularly mating strategies. While other research has concentrated on content analyses of naturally occurring ads, Strassberg and Holty placed four 'female seeking male' ads on two large Internet dating bulletin boards. The four ads, each with different key words, were the manipulated independent variable, with the 500 e-mail responses in six weeks being the dependent variable. Contrary to prediction based on previous research, the most popular ad was one in which the woman described herself as 'financially independent . . . successful [and] ambitious', producing over 50% more responses than the next most popular ad, one in which the woman described herself as 'lovely . . . very attractive and slim'. This doesn't support the evolutionary argument for intersexual selection (at least among people using Internet dating).

## Parent–offspring conflict

Trivers (1974) argues that parents endeavour to allocate resources to their offspring in order to ensure that the maximum number of offspring survive. However, conflict occurs when each child wants more resources from the parent than they are prepared to give. For example, with regard to food resources, there are diminishing returns with each increase in consumption. The first piece of food prevents starvation whereas the second simply fills you up more. This also applies to your siblings. It is inevitable that there is competition between siblings for limited parental resources. A parent would allocate resources equally amongst their children whereas children obviously regard themselves as more important than any of their brothers or sisters.

Parent–child conflict over the parent's resource allocation occurs throughout each stage of life. The parent–offspring conflict hypothesis is supported by evidence from Buss (1999), who notes:

- parent-offspring conflict at the time the child is weaned. The child wants to delay the weaning process as long as possible often in contrast to the desires of the parent.
- parents also encourage their children to value their siblings more than they naturally would
- parents punish conflict between siblings and reward co-operation against the child's natural instincts.

# Explanations of human reproductive behaviour and sexual selection

The advantages of sexual selection as seen from the point of view of the choosy partner (typically the female) are explained in the following intersexual selection hypotheses:

## THE 'GOOD TASTE' OR 'RUNAWAY EFFECT' HYPOTHESIS (FISHER, 1930)

- In animal behaviour, females may choose males with exaggerated features simply because such signals indicate the presence of direct fitness benefits that enhance reproductive success. Males may be able to offer females some direct benefits such as a high-quality territory, food, protection, no diseases and healthy sperm. Some male displays may also signal indirect benefits that only occur in the next generation through the success of the offspring (Fisher, 1930). If the male signal and the female preference both have a genetic basis, then these characteristics could become genetically coupled over the generations and their offspring could inherit these genes. A so-called 'runaway effect' will occur where the male trait and the female preference will co-evolve to ever more extreme versions.
- The peacock has a fantastic tail because many generations of peahens have selected on the basis of the best available tail. This trait will continue to become more and more exaggerated since the offspring with this trait will have greater mating success. This runaway effect will only cease when balanced by a natural selection pressure that means the disadvantages of the trait are outweighed by its benefit.
- The interesting point about this hypothesis is that females are choosing males partly on the basis of secondary characteristics that have no direct genetic benefit. The characteristics are valued simply because they have become the fashionable trend or a mark of 'good taste'. For example, a woman selects a man with a fine, deep voice because her male children will be more successful at breeding if they possess this characteristic.

## THE 'GOOD GENES' OR 'HANDICAP PROCESS' HYPOTHESIS (ZAHAVI, 1975)

- An alternative suggestion of female mate preferences that gives rise to indirect fitness benefits is the so-called 'good genes' hypothesis which is based on the handicap process. This suggests that only individuals in prime physical condition can afford to develop costly, secondary characteristics. For example, the long tail of the peacock is actually a handicap in terms of survival since it makes movement and escape from predators more difficult. The peacock that can escape the tiger despite having a massive tail must be worth mating with. It's only particularly strong and robust individuals with healthy genetic constitution that would survive in the face of such serious handicapping and costly traits (Zahavi, 1975). Such displays are costly to the individual and signal to the female that they are high-quality individuals. Low-quality individuals would not be able to maintain such extravagant characteristics. Thus females choose those individuals who thrive with the greatest handicap.
- For example, a woman will select a man not because he has a Porsche or BMW but because he has still managed to feed and clothe himself despite having the financial handicap of having an expensive car. There are a number of studies consistent with the handicap hypothesis of sexual selection, although most relate to non-human animals.

## Evaluation of sexual selection behaviour

✔ **Great explanatory power:** 'The application of sexual selection theory to human behaviour has been the greatest success story in evolutionary psychology, and one of the most fruitful and fascinating developments in the human sciences over the last two decades.' (Miller, 1998). Sociobiology does not justify or excuse all observed behaviour (e.g. rape by males); it just explains why some people may wish to behave the way that they do.

✘ **What counts as investment?** The ideas outlined above concerning parental investment are problematic since it's difficult to quantify the different investments that males and females make in terms of reproduction. Furthermore, the desire to reproduce is not the only factor that's important in relationship choice. Relationships are far more complicated than that.

The male seahorse makes the greater parental investment and females compete for the male's attention

**✘ Child-free women:** It's difficult to see how PI explanations can account for women who choose not to have children or, indeed, men who do make considerable parental investments. Perhaps these individuals are modifying natural urges.

**✘ Unfaithful women:** According to both PI and sexual selection explanations, a woman's mate choice is largely influenced by the resources her partner brings to the relationship. A woman who is unfaithful risks losing these resources for her (future) offspring. The explanations suggest a woman would risk having an affair only if the new partner could offer even greater resources. This doesn't seem a very satisfactory explanation for such behaviour. However, a distinction can be made between life partners and one-night stands. From an evolutionary perspective, the ideal situation for an unfaithful woman is to have a caring partner who will look after the young (thrifty, stay-at-home type). Then she can go and mate with someone who has characteristics that will promote the reproductive success of their children – perhaps an extroverted, good-looking, rich man. Perhaps even the fact that the man is willing to have an affair with a person in a permanent relationship is a sufficient incentive to make him a good gene source. Ridley (1993) found that 20% of UK children are the offspring of males other than their presumed father.

**✘ Gender bias within cultures:** Eagly (1997) criticised the evolutionary explanation for gender-specific mate selection criteria. She suggested that there's a cultural explanation for human mate selection. If females were the dominant gender, then the favoured attributes might be very different. Since it's argued that there aren't any human societies where females socially dominate males, this idea cannot be tested, although Sanday (2002) argues that a matriarchal society exists among the Minangkabau in Sumatra.

**✓ Supportive animal evidence:** In other animal species, this reversal in gender assignment for sexual selection criteria does occur. As mentioned above, this occurs in seahorses. This suggests that the relative level of parental investment by each sex is at the root of sexually dimorphic characteristics valued in potential reproductive partners. The competition will be for the sex with the greater parental investment. Similar patterns have also been found in some bird species.

**✓ Cultural supportive evidence:** The evolutionary perspective on sexual selection makes predictions that are consistent with behavioural patterns observed across different cultures. Generally, the predictions are that women should prefer higher-status mates to help them provide for their offspring and men should prefer younger, highly fertile women. This does indeed appear to be the case. Men in all cultures tend to seek mates near their own age when they themselves are young and seek and find progressively younger women as they age.

**✘ 'The Graduate' problem:** However, contrary to the explanations for mate selection criteria given directly above, teenage males are sometimes attracted to substantially older women (Kenrick & Simpson, 1997). Echoes of this are seen in the film *The Graduate* starring Dustin Hoffman. Such behaviour doesn't readily fit in with ideas of sexual selection and mate choice discussed above.

**Describe and evaluate the extent to which sexual selection can explain human reproductive behaviour. (24 marks) (30 mins) (600 words minimum) AO1/AO2**

*This essay can be split up into FOUR Sections – each about 150 words long. Each section would be worth approx. 6 marks.*

**Section 1:** You could start by **defining** sexual selection, as opposed to natural selection. You might emphasise that the need to reproduce is our main imperative. The distinction between intra-sexual and inter-sexual selection should be made.

A01

**Section 2:** You could **describe** how parental investment (PI) affects sexual selection and how sexual selection (both inter- and intra-sexual) influences human reproductive behaviour in terms of mate choice (what characteristics females reportedly look for in a life partner and contrast these with those of a male), reproductive rates and body dimorphism.

A01

**Section 3:** Here you could **analyse** and **evaluate** material presented above in a positive light. Put forward evidence that supports the argument that sexual selection can explain human reproductive behaviour (see pages x–x).

A02

**Section 4:** Here you could **analyse** and **evaluate** material presented above in a negative light. Put forward evidence that suggests that sexual selection can't explain all aspects of human reproductive behaviour (see page x).

A02

**Remember, the emphasis is on *human* reproductive behaviour – don't mention lots of non-human animals without making the link to human behaviour.**

*Try to answer this question yourself. There's a sample essay on page 383 with which you can compare your essay.*

---

✓ **Support for intra-sexual competition:** More than 90% of all same-sex homicide involves men in their early twenties when mate competition is at its most intense. In addition, male road traffic accident statistics are disproportionately higher for young males compared with all other age and sex groups. Rolls and Ingham (1992) reported the influence of peer pressure from same-sex passenger presence on these figures. Daly and Wilson (1988) suggest such figures support the argument for intra-sexual competition in males.

✓ **Deception and enhancement of characteristics:** There are well-known and well-used techniques to enhance mate attraction. The techniques that males and females use to enhance their attractiveness tend to emphasise the characteristics for which each is valued. Therefore women use make-up and wear clothes that emphasise their shape and figure. In some cases, women may resort to plastic surgery in an attempt to retain their 'youth' and 'beauty'. On the other hand, males may try to exaggerate their resources with demonstrations of wealth such as an expensive car or through gifts. These deceptive gender-specific attraction techniques support the evolutionary explanation of mate selection. Of course, such techniques don't always work and humans are aware of such deceptive techniques.

✓ **Non-human animal evidence:** Male mammals don't normally exceed the female in childcare commitment. The reasons for this are simple: mammals, unlike seahorses or ostriches, don't lay eggs, hence they cannot be given them to hatch out. Neither can they feed the emergent babies. Why not cut male mammals out of society completely, since they contribute so little to childcare? There is a very well-documented animal example of this – hyenas. The social group, which patrols its territory and marks it out with urine is completely female. Males are permitted to enter only if they are needed for mating purposes. Sexual aggression is not unusual in mammals. Males can and do commit rape. They have the strength and equipment needed to enforce their mating intentions. The genetic advantage the act confers to the male is obvious. That it hasn't evolved to be the most common form of sex must mean that the extra investment that males put into courtship is less of a drain on resources than that caused by the damage inflicted by reluctant females. In birds, rape is almost unknown. Female birds are usually larger and more dominant and the males of most species don't have a penis. Co-operative mating and chick-care are consequently the norm. It usually takes two parents to maintain incubating temperature, protect the nest and find enough food for the chicks. Intra-specific competition is very pronounced, with pairs defending territories. Males tend to show most aggression towards other males and females towards other females.

# Evolutionary explanations of mental disorders

## Evolutionary explanations of human mental disorders including depression (e.g. unipolar and bipolar depression) and anxiety disorders (e.g. phobias and obsessive-compulsive disorder)

In Chapter 14 we deal with definitions of mental disorders (see pages 386–430). From this it will be evident that it's not easy to define mental disorders and there are associated problems with all the definitions. Buss (1999) provides a clearer definition of mental dysfunction from an evolutionary perspective: 'Dysfunction occurs when the mechanism is not performing as it was designed to perform in the contexts in which it was designed to perform'. Buss believes that these evolved mechanisms can fail in three ways:

1. the mechanism fails to become active at an appropriate point
2. the mechanism becomes activated at an inappropriate point
3. the mechanism fails to work properly with other mechanisms.

Buss argues that each of these failures can occur because of chance genetic mutations or developmental damage or through a combination of these two.

> Specification Hint: You need to know a minimum of only *two* explanations of both depression and anxiety disorders. Since anxiety disorders is also plural, you need to know about *two* of these disorders.

> Specification Hint: Although the Specification mentions both unipolar and bipolar disorder, they are only mentioned as e.g.s. You need to know only *two* explanations of any form of depression. The examiners can't specifically mention either of the types in the question they ask. We've chosen to deal with both types of depression.

## Depression

- Depression is one of the mood (or affective) disorders. These involve a prolonged and fundamental disturbance of mood and emotions. The depressed person experiences a general slowing down and loss of energy and enthusiasm for life.
- When depression (major depressive disorder) occurs on its own, it's referred to as unipolar disorder.
- Mania (manic disorder) usually occurs in conjunction with depression (when it's called bipolar disorder).
- Bipolar disorder is much less common than unipolar, occurring in fewer than 10 per 1,000, usually before age 50. This compares with unipolar disorder which affects 20–30 men per 1,000, but 40–90 per 1,000 women. The major symptoms of depression are also outlined in Table 14.6 (page 405).

### GENETIC EXPLANATION

We deal in detail with the genetic basis for depression in Chapter 14, page 408. However, to summarise:

- *First-degree relatives* (parents, siblings and children) of severely depressed patients have a higher risk of affective disorders (10–15%) than the general population (1–2%).
- Concordance for bipolar disorder (about 70%) is the same among monozygotic (identical) twins reared together or apart. This compares with 23% for dyzygotic twins (non-identical).
- Adoption studies confirm the importance of genetic factors. The natural parents of adoptees with a bipolar disorder have a higher rate of affective disorder than do natural parents of adoptees without bipolar disorder (Gelder *et al.*, 1999).
- Genetic factors in unipolar disorder seem to be less decisive than in bipolar disorder. Also, there's some evidence that genetic factors are more important in women than in men (Davison & Neale, 2001: but see also Box 14.3, page 407).
- It would seem that there's reasonable evidence to suggest that bipolar disorder, in particular, runs in families. While not denying the role of environmental factors, the overwhelming evidence suggests a genetic explanation. According to the evolutionary argument, a key question thus arises: why have these genes not been naturally selected out of the gene pool? Possible answers to this question are described below.

## ADAPTATIVE VALUE OF DEPRESSION

### Unipolar depression

- Emotions serve many purposes. Feeling sad is an appropriate response to many situations, such as breaking up with a girlfriend or boyfriend. The adaptive nature of sadness is such that it changes our behaviour in the future so that other similar losses are prevented. In other words, we stop doing the things that have led to these losses in the first place. Low mood can also facilitate changes in strategy that are necessary after a loss; it can facilitate submissive behaviour after a loss of status.
- Depression can be viewed as an adaptive response in a similar way. The social homeostasis hypothesis suggests that in a social group with various tensions and hierarchies, depression serves to maintain the stability of the group. That is, a person who 'loses' a social conflict becomes depressed, gives up on the conflict and this helps to prevent further conflict within the group. Thus depression is seen as an act of submission. Not only might this strategy be adaptive for the individual – they will stop themselves from suffering further losses – but it will also be beneficial for group cohesiveness. In ways such as these, depression can be seen to increase the 'fitness' of the person. Fitness is defined as physical and behavioural features that help the person and their offspring survive.

### Bipolar depression

- Many successful people have suffered bipolar disorder. Indeed, the prevalence of mental problems among creatively-gifted people is significantly higher than in the general population (Barron & Harrington, 1981).
- Jamison (1993) reports a number of studies that have examined the link between bipolar disorder and creativity. A 1949 study of 113 German artists, writers and composers found that although two-thirds of the 113 artists and writers were 'psychically normal', there were more suicides and 'insane and neurotic' individuals in the artistic group than could be expected in the general population, with the highest rates of psychiatric abnormality found in poets (50%) and musicians (38%). Similar studies have found a disproportionate occurrence of mental illness, specifically bipolar disorder, in artistic and creative people, including a recent study of individuals over a 30-year period (1960–1990).
- Another recent study was the first to undertake scientific diagnostic inquiries into the relationship

Kurt Cobain: further evidence of the link between creativity and mental disorder?

between creativity and mental disorders in living writers. Almost 50% of the creative writers met the diagnostic criteria for bipolar disorder. This doesn't mean that the majority of artists are bipolar but rather that there's a considerably higher incidence of this disorder among artists than among the general population (Jamison, 1993).

- So how can such genes persist when they cause an illness that severely interferes with function and is fatal in at least 10% of cases? The main possibilities are: (i) the genes are recent mutations, (ii) they're quirks that cause illness only in modern populations, and (iii) they somehow give an advantage that outweighs the disadvantage. The first two possibilities are unlikely in view of the long recognition of this disorder in many societies and the strong selection against it (Goodwin & Jamison, 1990).

- Nesse (1999) suggests that the third possibility has most support. It's suggested that the manic phase of the disorder may be related to creativity. Creativity is the production of new and useful ideas and as such has great adaptive value. Studies on the link between creativity and mental illnesses show that it is exactly the characteristics of the mental disorder that also confer some advantage on afflicted individuals. These advantages extend to the groups to which the creative, mentally-ill individuals belong. The group comprising the most creative personalities will therefore acquire an adaptive advantage that maintains the integrity of the group as a whole, in spite of the vulnerability of the individual.

- Among the creative characteristics most prevalent in bipolar individuals there are some that are specifically related to ability in social intercourse. People with bipolar mood disorders tend to be more emotionally reactive, which gives them greater sensitivity and acuteness. A lack of inhibition permits them unrestrained and unconventional forms of expressions, less limited by accepted norms and customs. This makes them more open to experimentation and risk-taking behaviour and, as a consequence, more assertive and resourceful than most. Sensitivity and lack of inhibition make these subjects warmer and more friendly in social intercourse. Both aptitudes also represent a clear advantage on a professional level, particularly when competition is greater. Being more sociable and less inhibited in expressing themselves, individuals prone to bipolar disorders may manage to spread their ideas with greater ease, allowing their ideas to prevail over others competing for predominance.

- As Gabora (1997) asserts in her paper: 'the bottleneck in cultural evolution is the capacity for innovation'. Groups whose members possess the ability to make innovative mental associations can take advantage from this, even if the ability is linked to maladjusted behaviour at the individual level. Examples deriving from the studies on the relationship between creativity and bipolar disorders are suggestive. The high suicide rate (10% of patients) and the low fertility of bipolar patients, who tend to marry less than the general population and have fewer children than the mean, suggest that, both now and in the past, the carriers of the genetic burden of the disorder must have some compensatory advantage in order for a relatively high percentage of affected individuals (more than 1%) to be maintained in the general population (Wilson, 1994). Creative accomplishment seems to increase sexual attractiveness, and it has been suggested that creativity is a product of sexual selection (Miller, 2001).

### Evaluation of adaptive value of depression

✓ **Case study support:** There does appear to be strong evidence for a positive correlation between bipolar disorder and creativity. This is also demonstrated in the case studies of a number of famous and successful personalities such as Van Gogh and Churchill.

✓ **Research support:** Collectively, these studies above and numerous others have clinically supported the existence of a link between bipolar disorder and creativity.

✓ **Genetic basis:** As outlined above, there's a lot of evidence to support the genetic basis of depression, particularly in bipolar disorders. This supports the adaptive theory of depression.

✗ **Cause and effect problem:** A key question to ask is: is bipolar disorder the result of above-average creativity or is above-average creativity the result of bipolar disorder or are the two a result of some third factor which causes the two effects? At the present time, it appears impossible to answer this question definitely.

✖ **Adaptive value of severe depression:** Although a case can be made for the adaptive value of mild depression, it's difficult to see how severe depression can benefit either an individual or their larger social group.

✖ **Other contributory factors:** It's likely that there are other reasons beyond a purely evolutionary adaptive argument why depression persists in modern-day society. Social and cultural factors must surely play some part in contributing to the development of depression.

## GENOME LAG HYPOTHESIS

* This is also called the 'Exile from Eden' hypothesis and suggests that our genes have not kept pace with the changes in our environment (hence 'genome lag'). Bizarrely enough, this idea was also put forward by Theodore Kaczynski when he stated in an advert in the *New York Times*:

Theodore Kaczynski – the U.S. unabomber – a surprising advocate of the 'Genome Lag' hypothesis

'We attribute the social and psychological problems of modern society to the fact that that society requires people to live under conditions radically different from those under which the human race evolved and to behave in ways that conflict with the patterns of behavior that the human race developed while living under the earlier conditions.' Kaczynski was the infamous U.S.A. 'unabomber' and is now serving four life sentences for killing three people with parcel bombs.

* The environment of evolutionary adaptation (EEA) refers to the period in human evolution (approximately between 10,000 and 3 million years) when our genes were shaped and selected by natural selection to solve survival problems operating then (Cartwright, 2001). Life nowadays is so different that there are bound to be problems and these manifest themselves as mental disorders such as depression and anxiety. Put simply, we have Stone-Age genes in a space-age world.
* A good example of this relates to the human response to stress, specifically the 'fight or flight' response. Many stressors in the modern world are not solved by a simple 'fight or flight' response and thus remain with us and increase the likelihood of a mental disorder developing.
* In terms of relating this explanation to depression, Nesse and Williams (1996) examined data from 39,000 people in five different countries. They found that rates of depression are on the increase, particularly among young people who live in highly developed economies. They suggested that mass communication means that we've become one huge social group. Whereas, in the past, our skills would be compared with our relatively small social group and we could have been the best story-teller or hunter, nowadays we compare ourselves with the best in the world. Such a comparison may lead to depression. This can be seen in the example of mate choice (see above). Two important characteristics are attractiveness and signs of health. When living in small groups of 150, such assessments might be quite easy and accurate. Nowadays the bombardment through the media of 'perfect' figures and highly successful people (models, actors, sports stars) may lead us to be somewhat dissatisfied with our rather ordinary humdrum existences and ordinary-looking partners. Such dissatisfaction could, in turn, lead to depression.

✓ **Modern technological advances:** This hypothesis appears to make sense since technological advances have, indeed, been rapid over the last few centuries. Many behaviours from the time of EEA are not particularly adaptive today and yet remain in our behavioural repertoire.

✗ **Human success:** One problem with this hypothesis is that humans have never been more successful in terms of populating the planet. The world population stands at around 6 billion and is increasing by the second. Despite the 'genome lag', humans are thriving.

✗ **Similarities, not differences:** Crawford (1998) suggests that the environment we find ourselves in today may have changed but the requirements of life aren't actually that different from those faced by early man. We still need to find shelter, food, a mate, have children, make friends, gossip and so on. We're merely using technology to do these things in a different way. For example, the Internet now allows us to chat, gossip and maintain long-distance friendships, work and even find houses, hotels and so on.

✗ **Are mental disorders really disorders?** It could be argued that if disorders have an adaptive value then they shouldn't be classified as disorders. Indeed, some forms of mental disorders may be 'useful' in some way from an individual point of view. If this is accepted, should they still be regarded as 'disorders'? A good example of this would be anti-social personality disorder that's likely to benefit the individual (in some cases) at the risk of causing suffering to others.

✗ **Speculation, not fact:** A major problem with these hypotheses is that they remain hypotheses. They are somewhat speculative and therefore difficult to test. This doesn't mean that they're wrong but further evidence is required to support them.

## Anxiety disorders

- Anxiety disorders are more common than any other form of 'psychopathology'. It's estimated that in the U.S.A. in any 12-month period as many as 7% of the population will suffer from an anxiety disorder. More women than men are affected, and the prevalence is higher among those aged under 45 years than among older people. Phobias are more common in adults than both depression and alcohol-related conditions (Boyd et al., 1990).
- Anxiety is the central feature of a number of disorders such as phobias, generalised anxiety, post-traumatic stress disorder (PTSD) and obsessive–compulsive disorder (OCD). These disorders are marked by considerable emotional distress, high levels of anxiety, frequent fears, persistent worrying and avoidance behaviour in many cases. The main differences between various types of anxiety disorder are in the course of illness and in the situations in which anxiety becomes prominent.

> **Specification Hint:** You need to know a minimum of *two* evolutionary explanations of any two anxiety disorders. We've decided to cover phobias and OCDs.

### THE EVOLUTIONARY BASIS OF ANXIETY

- Anxiety is a normal human emotion and, using an evolutionary perspective, anxiety might be understood as a protective mechanism which was important in guiding the organism away from sources of danger. Anxiety can be seen as an evolved defence. The symptoms of anxiety can be understood as part of the 'fight or flight' response, which is preparing the individual to fight with an aggressor or to flee from harm. Individuals who feel little anxiety and are at the low end of the anxiety distribution should show decreased ability to avoid and escape dangers and increased rates of death and harm. Conversely, individuals who readily experience anxiety should be relatively protected from dangers. Almost every aspect of the 'fight–flight' response – including increased heart rate, sweating, and breathing – matches what's needed in the face of serious danger (Cannon, 1929). For example, fear of heights does seem to cause a 'freezing' response that's probably adaptive in high places.

- Why are people often more anxious than seems useful? The encounter with any potentially dangerous stimulus poses a signal detection problem. Will the reaction to this stimulus result in a benefit or a cost? If anxiety is not associated with any *significant* loss (e.g. time, embarrassment and so on) and a lack of response is costly or fatal, then natural selection will shape the regulation mechanisms to a hair trigger, with many resulting false alarms (Nesse & Williams, 1995). This is called the 'adaptive conservatism hypothesis' of fears. Put simply, it pays to be more anxious than the occasion demands – as the expression goes: 'better safe than sorry'. It's better to over-react to many fire alarms than ignore a real one!
- This evolved defence argument can also be seen in combination with Seligman's theory of 'biological preparedness', i.e. humans are biologically prepared to fear specific objects such as snakes and spiders.

## PHOBIAS

### Biological preparedness (Seligman, 1971)

- A phobia is a type of anxiety disorder where there is a persistent and irrational fear of an object or a situation. It's easy to see how phobias can have adaptive value. For example, it makes sense for us to be afraid of heights since we can't fly!
- Seligman proposed that humans have an evolutionary predisposition (preparedness) to learn to fear certain stimuli more readily than others. Our ancestors who had such phobias were likely to be more successful through natural selection. Indeed Darwin (1877) stated that: 'May we not suspect that the . . . fears of children, which are quite independent of experience, are the inherited effects of real dangers . . . during ancient savage time?' We're not actually born with these fears but we become more readily conditioned to fear them. It's suggested that the fears that we're biologically prepared for include those that were harmful in the EEA, such as fear of darkness and harmful animals such as spiders and snakes. This idea combines evolutionary ideas with conditioning theory. If this idea were correct, we'd expect that most phobias would relate to things harmful to early humans and people would more readily acquire a fear of these objects and situations than other more neutral stimuli. Research studies appear to support both these points.
- Tomarken *et al.* (1989) conducted a study where rhesus monkeys were shown videos of another monkey showing a fear reaction to either a snake or a flower. Monkeys shown a single video of the snake developed a phobia of snakes whereas the monkeys shown the flower developed no such fear of flowers.
- Human studies also show that fear responses are more readily conditioned to objects that were dangerous in the ancestral environment, like snakes, than to objects dangerous only now, like guns (Cook *et al.*, 1986). There are good reasons why this might be so. Any system that's designed to express innate fear with an object will protect an isolated individual on first exposure to a danger. However, it's of limited help with new or novel dangers. A system that requires learning experience in order to protect initially will offer better protection against new dangers, at the cost of learning to fear some stimuli that are not actually dangerous (Staddon, 1983).

 **Evaluation of anxiety disorders and phobias**

✓ **Cognitive sense:** Phobias are obviously easy to explain in evolutionary terms. Many of the most common phobias do relate to the expected adaptive problems faced by our ancestors and there's evidence that these occur across cultures (Buss, 1999). Phobias of cars, guns, knives and electric sockets are extremely rare and yet spider and snake phobias are quite prevalent. This is despite the fact that the former list includes by far the greatest dangers to modern man. However, it's difficult to explain social phobias, such as speaking in public, using this explanation.

✗ **Alternative explanations:** Many phobias can also be readily explained using behavioural or Social Learning Theory (SLT). The best-known research example of behavioural conditioning involved Little Albert (Watson & Rayner, 1920).

✗ **Educated guesswork:** It's not easy to know what were the greatest dangers faced by early humans 500,000 years ago. Arachnophobia (fear of spiders) is a very common phobia and yet only 0.1% of spiders are poisonous. Could such a small number account for our apparent biologically pre-prepared fear of them? Delprato (1980) considers poisonous fungi to have been a greater threat to survival, and yet a mushroom phobia is extremely rare.

**✗ Women and rollercoasters:** Kirkpatrick (1984) reports that women rated a fear of rollercoasters as the most important fear out of 133 different stimuli. It's difficult to use an evolutionary explanation for such fears without suggesting that phobias can develop to recent technological advances. However, then we're left with the difficulty of explaining why other modern dangers (e.g. cars) aren't so feared.

## OBSESSIVE COMPULSIVE DISORDER (OCD)

* Again, we've dealt with the characteristics of these elsewhere on pages 416–417. In summary:
* Obsessions are recurrent, unwanted, intrusive thoughts or images that don't feel voluntarily controlled. They're experienced as morally repugnant or intensely distressing.
* Compulsions are actions which the person feels compelled to repeat over and over again, according to rituals or rules.
* In the UK, OCD is the fourth most common mental disorder, and lifetime prevalence is at least 3% in females and 2% in males.

### Normal distribution theory and fitness benefits

* One of the most common forms of OCD involves 'checking and/or washing'. It would make sense for there to be an optimum level of 'checking and washing' that made good evolutionary sense. Any of our ancestors who frequently checked that they were safe from predators or that their food supplies were secure were likely to survive and increase their chance for reproduction. In addition, those ancestors who didn't frequently check these things may have been less successful in terms of their reproductive 'fitness' and therefore this lack of checking may have been bred out of the gene pool. It may be that people who suffer from OCD merely lie at the upper end of the normal distribution for such 'checking' behaviours.

Why don't people have mushroom phobias?

* By the same token, it's easy to see how frequent washing may have some adaptive benefit (indeed it still does!). Washing helps to reduce infection and disease from micro-organisms and therefore those ancestors who were obsessional about washing may have enhanced their reproductive 'fitness'. At the other end of the scale, those who washed infrequently may have suffered from infection and this could have led to an increased mortality for these individuals. Again, this would have meant that these people and their genes may have been selectively bred out of the gene pool (no doubt, by then, a very clean gene pool!).

* With this argument, OCD may simply be an exaggerated form of behaviour that has some significant fitness benefits.

**✗✓ Evaluation of OCD**

**✓ Cognitive sense:** It makes sense that certain behaviours which lie at the extreme end of the behavioural continuum, such as washing and checking, would have had some adaptive value.

**✗ Environmental factors:** Evolutionary explanations of OCD place too much emphasis on genetic factors and too little on social, environmental factors. The behavioural and SLT approach is also able to present a strong case for the development of OCDs. Of course, it's possible that different forms of OCDs originate in different ways for different people.

## CONCLUSION

- From an evolutionary perspective, explaining mental disorders is no different from explaining other medical disorders. Anxiety is a useful defence, like pain, but can result in disorders characterised by too little as well as too much anxiety. There are different trade-offs associated with each.
- Low mood and depression can be viewed in a similar way. Bipolar disorder results from genetic variation and may also offer fitness advantages as well as disadvantages. Indeed, it could be argued that some of these mental disorders may be perfectly adaptive from an individual point of view.
- As with many physical diseases, mental disorders probably have a wide range of causes and can't be explained by one single explanation. Indeed, the evolutionary theory can be seen as reductionist in this respect (see Chapter 14 for an account of some of these alternative explanations).
- It's probably best to see the cause of mental disorders in terms of an eclectic approach – one in which the best parts of different approaches are combined.

## EXAM tips BOX

**Critically consider evolutionary explanations of depression. (24 marks) (30 mins) (600 words minimum) AO1/AO2**

*This essay can be split up into FOUR Sections – each about 150 words long. Each section would be worth approx. 6 marks.*

**Section 1:** You could briefly **define** evolution and depression. You ought to distinguish briefly between unipolar and bipolar disorders. You could very briefly mention the genetic basis of depression. You should describe the adaptive value of depression theory.

**Section 2:** You need to **analyse** and **evaluate** the adaptive value of depression theory.

**Section 3:** Here you could **describe** the genome lag hypothesis in detail.

**Section 4:** You should **analyse** and **evaluate** the genome lag hypothesis.

*Try to answer this question yourself. There's a sample essay on page 384 with which you can compare your essay.*

AO1
↓
AO2
AO1
AO2

# Evolution of intelligence

**Evolutionary factors in the development of human intelligence (e.g. ecological demands, social complexity); the relationship between brain size and intelligence (e.g. the adaptive value of large brains, comparative studies across species)**

## INTRODUCTION

The most significant features that make humans unique compared with other animals are our high intelligence and 'large' brains.

- There's no universally agreed definition of what intelligence is and hence the measurement of it is extremely problematic. Gross *et al.* (2000) suggest that intelligence can be defined as 'the ability to devise flexible solutions to problems'. It could include:
  - learning
  - the application of learning to new situations
  - thinking, reasoning and original planning.

- A 'large' brain refers to the size of the brain relative to body size. Encephalisation, or the relative size of the brain, is analysed using a measure known as the encephalisation quotient (EQ). EQ is measured by the actual brain mass of a species divided by its 'expected' brain mass based on complicated statistical modelling. The EQ measure is interesting because it allows the quantitative comparison of brain sizes between different species while taking into account body size. For example, elephants have larger brains in terms of actual physical mass than humans. However, after adjusting for body size, humans actually have much 'larger' brains than elephants. Note that the EQ measure is concerned only with size, it does not measure complexity.

- Stephan (1972) provides a comparative anatomy EQ analysis of primate brains. He found that humans are at the very top of the index, with the Lepilemur at the bottom. There's also a large gap between the EQ of modern humans and all present-day non-human primates, even the chimp and other great apes.
- Recent research has concentrated on finding out what evolutionary factors have driven the development of increased human encephalisation. There are a number of factors put forward.

Specification Hint: You need to know a minimum of only *two* evolutionary factors in the development of human intelligence. There's no need to learn more. The examiners can't specifically name any factor since none is mentioned in the Specification. We've dealt with ecological demands (e.g. foraging and diet) and social complexity (the Machiavellian hypothesis) in detail. *Both* of these also deal with the relationship between brain size and intelligence. We've very briefly mentioned other factors that could be included, depending on the nature of the question.

## ECOLOGICAL DEMANDS (E.G. FORAGING AND DIET)

- It's suggested that intelligence may be related to foraging behaviours. Grazing animals can gather their food (e.g. grass) without very many demands on their intellect. They need large guts to break down these foodstuffs whereas primates with smaller guts subsist on a more varied diet but need to be resourceful in finding food. Sometimes, the demands of the diet can make intellectual demands as well.
- Foley and Lee (1991) examined the relationship between brain size and primate feeding strategies, and noted that folivorous diets (leaves) are correlated with smaller brains, while fruit and animal foods (insects, meat) are correlated with larger brains. Animals are more difficult to catch than oranges! Foley and Lee considered the dietary shifts that are found in the fossil record with the advent of humans (genus *Homo sapiens*). *Homo sapiens*, with associated encephalisation, may have been the product of the selection for individuals capable of exploiting these energy- and protein-rich resources as the habitats expanded. This suggests that we, and our large brains, may be the evolutionary result of selection that specifically favoured meat-eating and a high-protein diet, i.e. a carnivorous diet.
- The suggestion that diet may relate to intellect occurs because the process of obtaining food involves a series of activities:
  - **travelling:** finding specific foods can involve travelling over very long distances in order to locate a balanced diet. Many primates have been shown to have cognitive maps to help in this regard. A cognitive map is a mental spatial representation of the environment. This enables them to find and remember where the best food is and the best route to it.
  - **identification:** the more varied the diet, the better an animal has to be at identifying its food. Primates have good colour vision to help in this respect.
  - **extraction:** obtaining food can also be intellectually taxing. After all, ripe fruit appears on a seasonal basis and only on certain trees. Chimps have also been observed using tools to obtain food (see Tool use, page 378). For example, chimps have been seen to use stones to break open nuts and also poke sticks into termite mounds to extract them (Boesch & Boesch, 1984). Hunting is also an ability that requires complex strategies such as planning and co-ordination.

### Male and female brain differences

At birth, a boy's brain is about 15% larger than a girl's, and the head circumference of boys is also larger (2%) than that of girls. A similar pattern is found in adults but it must be remembered that men tend to weigh more than women and that brain size may not be a good measure of intelligence (if this were the case, then elephants would be intellectual giants!). What really matters is the complexity of the cortex. There is evidence of differences in types of intelligence between the sexes. It's well documented that males perform better at visuo-spatial abilities and navigation tasks than females (Voyer *et al.*, 1995). This difference may be related to the roles males and females occupied during human evolution. The male role involved hunting where visuo-spatial abilities (throwing spears at animals) and navigation (tracking animals) would have been beneficial. The female role may have been focused on child rearing and foraging for food near to the home. This 'hunter' hypothesis was suggested by Washburn and Lancaster (1968) and it's argued that these behaviours shaped human nature and separated early humans from their primate relatives and thus may be a possible factor in the development of male brain size. In essence, the demands of hunting caused males to become bigger physically and their brains grew in line with their bodies.

 **Evaluation of ecological demands**

✓ **Correlation of brain size and foraging behaviour:** If the foraging theory is correct, then primates whose diets are very diverse should show more cerebral development than primates with a simpler diet. Milton (1988) compared the brain weight and EQs of both howler monkeys (more leaf-eating diet) and spider monkeys (more fruit-eating diet). Spider monkeys have to cover an area 25 times larger than that of howler monkeys to obtain their food and thus we'd predict they'd have larger brains and EQs. This is exactly what was found, with howler monkeys having roughly half the brain size of spider monkeys.

✗ **Problem of cause and effect:** Foley and Lee (1991) highlighted the difficulty of separating cause and effect in the foraging and diet argument. They stated that: 'increased returns for foraging effort and food processing may be an important prerequisite for encephalization, and, in turn, a large brain is necessary to organize human foraging behaviour' (p 223). Which came first?

✗ **Other factors; not diet alone:** Leonard and Robertson (1994) conclude:

'. . . results imply that changes in diet quality during hominid evolution were linked with the evolution of brain size. The shift to a more calorically dense diet was probably needed in order to substantially increase the amount of metabolic energy being used by the hominid brain. Thus, while nutritional factors alone are not sufficient to explain the evolution of our large brains, it seems clear that certain dietary changes were necessary for substantial brain evolution to take place.'

## SOCIAL COMPLEXITY (MACHIAVELLIAN HYPOTHESIS)

- It's also been suggested that social demands have led to an increase in brain size. Primates are unusual in that they live in complex social

Spider monkeys (EQ = 1.2) have larger brains than howler monkeys (EQ = 0.66)

ONE SKINNY, GRANDE, DOUBLE MOCHA SANS WHIP PLEASE

latte
capuchino
mocha
dark

Coffee

Satisfying the human diet can still be intellectually taxing

groups. The size of groups has increased during the course of hominid evolution. It's estimated that 3 million years ago our australopithecine ancestors lived in groups of about 70 whereas the first *Homo sapiens* (150,000 years ago) lived in groups of about 150. As these groups got bigger, our ancestors found living within them to be more complex. Alliances within the group had to be maintained, social reasoning was developed and bigger memories were needed for this. This idea is called the 'Machiavellian intelligence' hypothesis, after Niccolo Machiavelli (1469–1527), an Italian political theorist who outlined some of the cunning tricks politicians use to obtain and maintain power. The hypothesis suggests that such tricks are not restricted to the political field and that primates also use a mix of cunning and deceit in order to maintain their place in a social group. Such cunning requires considerable intellect. In essence, the complex nature of social groups meant that those animals with greater intelligence were more successful operators in these groups. In turn, these animals had greater reproductive success and this meant that later brain size of the species increased.

- There's evidence that animals (particularly primates and humans) can deceive one another. Byrne and Whiten (1988) report a young baboon who screamed out when a nearby adult found some food. His mother was alerted and on arrival at the scene assumed that the food had been taken from her infant (hence the scream) and she stole the food to give to her infant! Vervet monkeys have been known to give false alarm calls in order to avoid conflict.

## THE 'OUT OF AFRICA' HYPOTHESIS

Anthropological evidence has shown differences in estimated cranial volumes between Asians, Europeans and Africans. Typically, East Asians have more endocranial volume than Europeans, who in turn have slightly more than Africans (Beals *et al.*, 1984). Furthermore, research using Magnetic Resonance Imaging (MRI) brain scans has produced a fairly strong positive correlation (0.44) between brain size and IQ (Rushton & Ankney, 1996). So what might explain these apparent differences? Rushton (1995) supports the 'out of Africa' evolutionary hypothesis for this, suggesting that each group of people had to respond to the different ecological demands placed on them by their respective living environments. These different environments caused, via natural selection, biological differences among populations.

One fairly well accepted view of human origins proposes a beginning in Africa approximately 200,000 years ago, with an African/non-African split about 110,000 years ago, and a European/East Asian split about 40,000 years ago (Stringer & Andrews, 1988). Evolutionary selection pressures were different in the hot savannah where Africans evolved than in the cold arctic where East Asians evolved. According to Rushton (1995), the further north the populations migrated from Africa, the more they encountered cognitively demanding problems of gathering and storing food, gaining shelter, making clothes and raising children during prolonged cold winters. As some from the original African populations evolved into Europeans and East Asians, they did so in the direction of larger brains, greater intelligence, slower rates of maturation, and other traits that differentiate these populations.

It must be noted that this is an extremely controversial area of research. Indeed, Diamond (1997) dismisses such research as both 'loathsome' and 'wrong'. Despite work mentioned by Rushton above there are still arguments about the exact nature of the relationship, if any, between brain size, cranial measurements and IQ. Peters (1993) claimed that research on brain size and IQ is flawed because it does not meet certain criteria such as matching participants for height, weight, age and sex. Furthermore he has claimed that studies of brain size are confounded by systematic bias, including racial bias, over and above normal measurement error.

##  Evaluation of social complexity

✓ **Cortex support:** The cortex is often called 'the grey matter' and it's this that's associated with higher forms of intelligence. It's assumed that the higher the proportion of the cortex to the rest of the brain, the higher the intelligence of the animal. In many non-primate animals this proportion is approximately 35%, in primates it is 50% and in humans it's about 80%. Dunbar (1993) found a strong positive correlation between the size of the cortex and average social group size. This supports the social complexity hypothesis.

✗ **Problem of measuring social complexity:** It's assumed that the larger the group, the more complicated it is to keep track of all group members. However, it doesn't necessarily follow that a larger group size means greater social complexity. Nevertheless, group size is a fairly simple measure in primates.

✗ **The Great Ape problem:** If social factors are an important factor in determining brain size (and hence intelligence), we'd expect that the great apes (chimps, gorillas and orang-utans) would live in the most complex social groups. This doesn't appear to be the case. Orang-utans, reputedly the most intelligent primates and certainly those with the largest brains, favour a solitary existence and some monkeys live in larger groups than gorillas. Baboons also have a higher cortex ratio than gorillas but are considered to be less intelligent.

### GENERAL EVALUATION

✗ **Problem of measuring intelligence:** There's no agreement as to what constitutes intelligence and as such it's very difficult (impossible?) to measure. Furthermore, measuring the intelligence of animals is even more problematic.

✗ **Anthropomorphism:** This is the tendency to view animals as if they were humans. Some psychologists are concerned about anthropomorphism in the types of cognitive ability that research has focused on. The criticism is that it has been targeted too much at finding human abilities in animals. Animals are ranked by how closely their behaviour abilities resemble our own.

### CONCLUSION

While the evolutionary causes of the enlarging human brain themselves are thought to have been due to factors

There are great difficulties measuring the intelligence of animals

that go beyond diet alone (e.g. increasing social complexity), a diet of sufficient quality would nevertheless have been an important prerequisite. That is, diet would have been an important hurdle – or limiting factor – to surmount in providing the necessary physiological basis for brain enlargement to occur within the context of whatever those other primary selective pressures might have been.

## Other theories

There are other theories that have been proposed to explain the origins of human intelligence:

- **Sexual selection:** It's suggested that humans have, for millions of years, chosen partners on the basis of age, health, social status and intelligence. Miller (2000) controversially argued that females chose males on the basis of brain size (and intelligence). Thus the more intelligent males reproduced more successfully and this may have led to an increase in brain size. Female brain growth was maintained by the need to understand the intelligent behaviour of the males and by the daughters of these men with large brains. Miller supports his view by stating that the majority of art, music and literature is produced by young men and functions as a courtship display.
- **Co-evolution of brain tissue (hardware) and language (software):** It's easy to see how advantageous, in the struggle for existence, it would have been to communicate with one another. Those early humans who could convey meaning through grunts would soon have out-reproduced their rivals. This would have continued over and over again, with language (the software) becoming more and more complex. This would only have been possible with a corresponding growth in brain tissue (the hardware). Dawkins (1998) suggests that these two factors would have led to a positive feedback loop. This is where the effect of growth in one thing makes further growth more likely. Both brain tissue and language would have co-evolved.
- **Tool use:** Although some primates have been shown to use tools, it's not essential for their existence. Humans, on the other hand, seem to use tools for almost everything. It's suggested that perhaps tool use can explain the increase in human brain capacity. The argument goes that the more complicated the tools, the more complex the human brain needed to develop and use them. A major problem with this theory is that the sophistication of tools found in various archaeological digs doesn't seem to reflect the known brain size of the hominids found using them. Similarly, brain size has grown only slightly in the last 300,000 years and yet the use of tools has increased at a phenomenal rate.

### CONCLUSION

The evolution of human intelligence was dependent on at least two factors constantly changing over time. That is, the development of the brain to cope with a particular demand (e.g. diet, social group, language and so on) and a subsequent change to that demand. No other species on the planet has changed itself, its environment and its culture so rapidly or drastically. It remains difficult to pin down human intelligence to one particular factor and it may, indeed, be a complex combination of such factors.

## EXAM tips BOX

**Describe and evaluate evolutionary factors in the development of human intelligence. (24 marks) (30 mins) (600 words minimum) AO1/AO2**

*This essay can be split up into FOUR Sections – each about 150 words long. Each section would be worth approx. 6 marks.*

**Section 1:** You could start by defining intelligence and dealing with encephalisation. You should **describe** the foraging and diet argument in the development of human intelligence.

AO1

**Section 2:** You should **analyse** and **evaluate** the foraging and diet argument in terms of the development of human intelligence.

AO2

**Section 3:** You should **describe** the social complexity or Machiavellian hypothesis as a factor in the development of human intelligence. You could (if you wish) include other factors such as sexual selection and tool use. However, the question merely asks for 'factors' (plural) so the two factors already covered would do.

AO1

**Section 4:** You should **analyse** and **evaluate** the social complexity or Machiavellian hypothesis.

AO2

*Try to answer this question yourself. There's a sample essay on page 385 with which you can compare your essay.*

## Sample Essays

## PYA4: Evolutionary explanations of human behaviour – essay questions (all 24 marks – 30 mins)

Other possible exam questions:

* each essay is worth 24 marks and should take 30 minutes to write
* remember, the mark scheme allocates 12 marks for AO1 (knowledge and description) and 12 marks for AO2 (analysis and evaluation).

### HUMAN REPRODUCTIVE BEHAVIOUR

1. Critically consider the relationship between sexual selection and human reproductive behaviour. (24 marks)

2. Describe and evaluate evolutionary explanations of parental investment (e.g. sex differences, parent–offspring conflict). (24 marks)

### EVOLUTIONARY EXPLANATIONS OF MENTAL DISORDERS

3. Outline and evaluate evolutionary explanations of human mental disorders. (24 marks)

4. Critically consider evolutionary explanations of depression (e.g. unipolar and bipolar depression). (24 marks)

5. Describe and evaluate evolutionary explanations of anxiety disorders (e.g. phobias and obsessive-compulsive disorder). (24 marks)

### EVOLUTION OF INTELLIGENCE

6. Describe and evaluate evolutionary factors in the development of human intelligence (e.g. ecological demands, social complexity). (24 marks)

7. Critically consider the relationship between brain size and human intelligence (e.g. adaptive value of large brains, comparative studies across species). (24 marks)

> Specification Hint: Although this is not a particularly popular sub-section of the Specification, there are fewer questions that the examiner can set compared with some of the other sub-sections.

# CHAPTER SUMMARY: revision schema

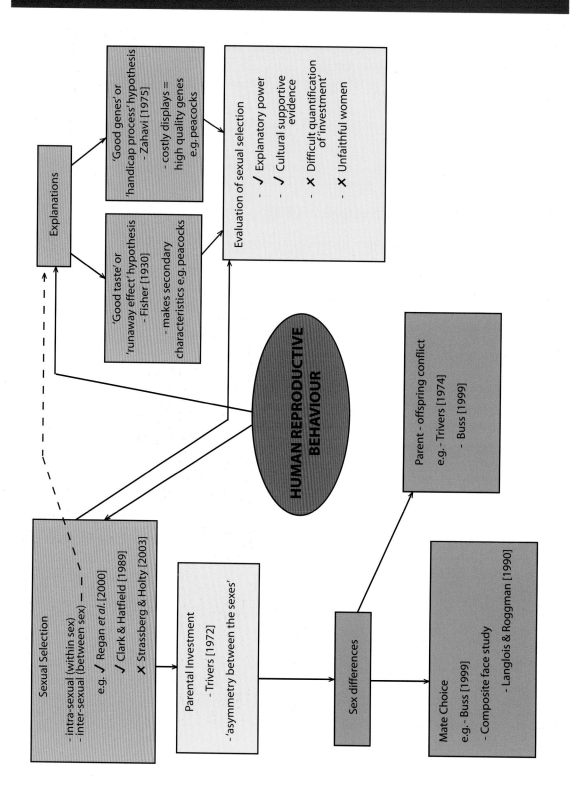

**Explanations**

'Good genes' or 'handicap process' hypothesis - Zahavi [1975]

- costly displays = high quality genes e.g. peacocks

'Good taste' or 'runaway effect' hypothesis - Fisher [1930]

- makes secondary characteristics e.g. peacocks

**Evaluation of sexual selection**

- ✓ Explanatory power
- ✓ Cultural supportive evidence
- ✗ Difficult quantification of 'investment'
- ✗ Unfaithful women

**HUMAN REPRODUCTIVE BEHAVIOUR**

**Sexual Selection**

- intra-sexual (within sex)
- inter-sexual (between sex)

e.g. ✓ Regan et al.[2000]
✓ Clark & Hatfield [1989]
✗ Strassberg & Holty [2003]

**Parental Investment**

- Trivers [1972]
- 'asymmetry between the sexes'

**Sex differences**

**Parent - offspring conflict**

e.g.- Trivers [1974]
- Buss [1999]

**Mate Choice**

e.g.- Buss [1999]
- Composite face study
- Langlois & Roggman [1990]

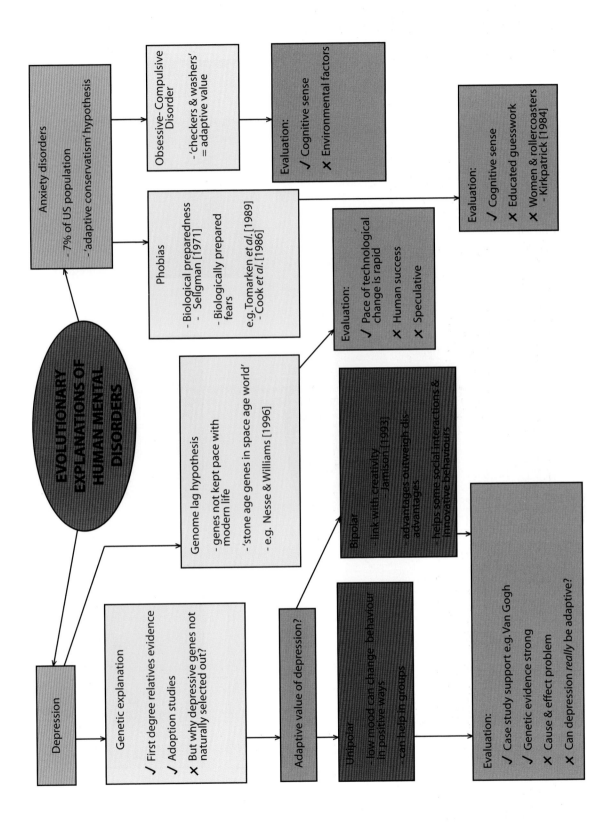

**EVOLUTIONARY EXPLANATIONS OF HUMAN MENTAL DISORDERS**

**Anxiety disorders**

- 7% of US population
- 'adaptive conservatism' hypothesis

**Obsessive-Compulsive Disorder**

- 'checkers & washers' = adaptive value

Evaluation:
✓ Cognitive sense
✗ Environmental factors

**Phobias**

- Biological preparedness - Seligman [1971]
- Biologically prepared fears
e.g. Tomarken et al. [1989]
- Cook et al. [1986]

Evaluation:
✓ Cognitive sense
✗ Educated guesswork
✗ Women & rollercoasters - Kirkpatrick [1984]

**Genome lag hypothesis**

- genes not kept pace with modern life
- 'stone age genes in space age world'
- e.g. Nesse & Williams [1996]

Evaluation:
✓ Pace of technological change is rapid
✗ Human success
✗ Speculative

**Depression**

**Genetic explanation**

✓ First degree relatives evidence
✓ Adoption studies
✗ But why depressive genes not naturally selected out?

**Adaptive value of depression?**

**Unipolar**
- low mood can change behaviour in positive ways
- can help in groups

**Bipolar**
- link with creativity Jamison [1993]
- advantages outweigh disadvantages
- helps some social interactions & innovative behaviours

Evaluation:
✓ Case study support e.g. Van Gogh
✓ Genetic evidence strong
✗ Cause & effect problem
✗ Can depression *really* be adaptive?

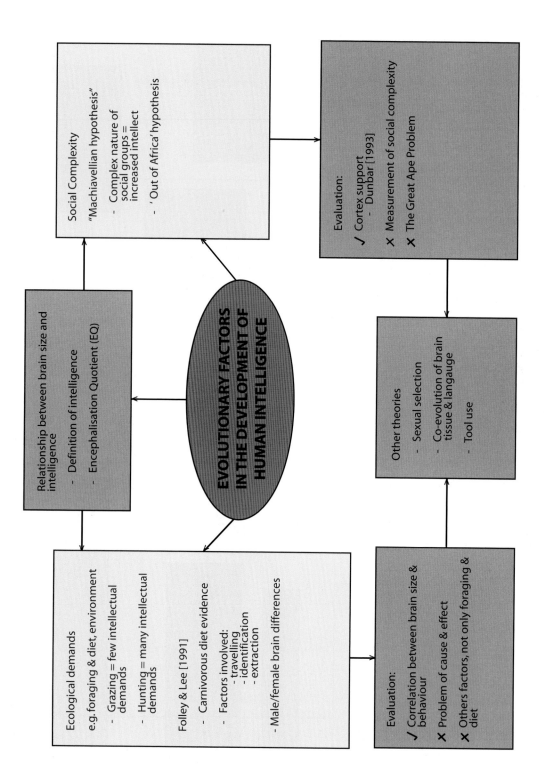

**EVOLUTIONARY FACTORS IN THE DEVELOPMENT OF HUMAN INTELLIGENCE**

Social Complexity

"Machiavellian hypothesis"

- Complex nature of social groups = increased intellect

- 'Out of Africa' hypothesis

Evaluation:

✓ Cortex support
   - Dunbar [1993]

✗ Measurement of social complexity

✗ The Great Ape Problem

Relationship between brain size and intelligence

- Definition of intelligence
- Encephalisation Quotient (EQ)

Other theories

- Sexual selection

- Co-evolution of brain tissue & langauge

- Tool use

Ecological demands

e.g. foraging & diet, environment

- Grazing = few intellectual demands

- Hunting = many intellectual demands

Folley & Lee [1991]

- Carnivorous diet evidence

- Factors involved:
   - travelling
   - identification
   - extraction

- Male/female brain differences

Evaluation:

✓ Correlation between brain size & behaviour

✗ Problem of cause & effect

✗ Others factors, not only foraging & diet

Describe and evaluate the extent to which sexual selection can explain human reproductive behaviour. (24 marks) (30 mins) (600 words minimum) AO1/AO2

### Section 1:

The theory of natural selection suggests that those animals most successful will end up with both physical and behavioural characteristics that enable them to out-perform rivals. Sexual selection is an explanation for why some animals possess characteristics that seem to be of no real benefit, e.g. the peacock's tail. Sexual selection refers to the selection of characteristics or behaviours that are purely beneficial for reproductive success. There are two types: intra-sexual selection refers to the situation where one sex (usually males) competes with the same sex for access to, and matings with, females. Inter-sexual selection refers to the situation where one sex is very choosy in selecting a sexual partner. **AO1**

### Section 2:

Sexual selection competition occurs most when there is a significant difference in the parental investment (PI) of each sex. In terms of human PI, there is a fundamental asymmetry between the sexes – females have a far greater investment in their offspring than males (Trivers, 1972). A low-investing male could afford many offspring and might favour a 'quantity rather than quality' approach. Females, on the other hand, would prefer quality rather than quantity. Thus females generally need to be much choosier about whom they mate with. Indeed, there appear to be marked gender differences in what men and women look for in a potential partner (inter-sexual selection). In a comprehensive study of 37 cultures on six continents and five islands, Buss (1989) found that women value prospective males on characteristics related to resource potential. However, men value potential female partners in terms of fecundity, defined as the ability to produce and care for children. Darwin believed that intrasexual selection would result in special adaptations such as sexual differences in size and shape and the development of different features to deter rivals. Although these are more evident in animals, sexual dimorphism also occurs in humans. Men tend to have greater musculature, more facial and body hair and a different fat distribution from women. Many secondary sexual characteristics are considered to be beautiful by humans. These include a specific hip-to-waist ratio and facial symmetry. These characteristics valued in terms of mate choice are also the result of sexual selection. Sexual selection can also explain differences between the sexes in terms of sexual enthusiasm. **AO1**

### Section 3:

Miller (1998) argued that 'The application of sexual selection theory to human behaviour has been the greatest success story in evolutionary psychology (EP)'.

The evolutionary perspective on sexual selection makes predictions that are consistent with reproductive behavioural patterns observed across different cultures. Generally, the predictions are that women should prefer higher-status mates to help them provide for their offspring and men should prefer younger, highly fertile women. This does indeed appear to be the case. Men in all cultures tend to seek mates near their own age when they themselves are young and seek and find progressively younger women as they age. More than 90% of all same-sex homicide involves men in their early twenties, when mate competition is at its most intense. Daly and Wilson (1988) suggest such figures support the argument for intrasexual competition in males. There are well-known and well-used techniques to enhance mate attraction. The techniques that males and females use to enhance their attractiveness tend to emphasise the characteristics for which each is valued. Therefore women use make-up and wear clothes that emphasise their shape and figure. On the other hand, males may try to exaggerate their resources with demonstrations of wealth such as an expensive car or through gifts. These deceptive gender-specific attraction techniques support the evolutionary explanation of sexual selection. Of course, such techniques don't always work and humans are aware of such deceptive techniques. **AO2**

### Section 4:

However, there are problems with the concept of sexual selection. For example, it's difficult to quantify the different investments that males and females make in terms of reproduction since they are qualitatively different. Furthermore, the desire to reproduce is not the only factor that's important in relationship choice. Relationship choice is not always dominated by the desire to have children. Indeed, significant numbers of women choose not to have children. According to sexual selection explanations, a woman's mate choice is largely influenced by the resources their partner brings to the relationship. A woman who is unfaithful risks losing these resources for their (future) offspring. This explanation suggests a woman would only risk having an affair if the new partner could offer even greater resources. This doesn't seem a very satisfactory explanation for such behaviour. Eagly (1997) criticised the evolutionary explanation for gender-specific mate selection criteria. She suggested if females were the dominant gender, then the favoured attributes might be very different.

Sociobiology only explains why a behavioural pre-disposition exists – it doesn't excuse bad behaviour (male aggression, infidelity). Society/morality modifies the driving forces behind behaviour. It doesn't mean you have to fit in with 'gender' stereotypes, but does explain why they exist and why you may feel happier if you do.

(824 words) **AO2**

# SAMPLE ESSAYS

# SAMPLE ESSAYS

Critically consider evolutionary explanations of depression. (24 marks) (30 mins) (600 words minimum) AO1/AO2

## Section 1:

Depression is an affective disorder involving a prolonged disturbance of mood and emotions. The more common, unipolar disorder involves depression on its own, whereas bipolar disorder also has periods of mania associated with it. Both types of depression appear to have a genetic basis since first-degree relatives of severely depressed patients have a higher risk of affective disorders (10–15%) than the general population (1–2%). In addition, concordance rates for identical twins are far higher than for non-identical twins. Given this genetic basis, according to an evolutionary argument, one might have expected the depressive genes would have been bred out of the gene pool given the idea of the 'survival of the fittest'. The fact that it hasn't suggests that depression may have some adaptive value. In unipolar disorder, depression can be seen as adaptive in that if we feel sad, we will change or adapt our behaviour in an appropriate way. In addition, if we feel sad as a result of social conflict, our feeling of depression may help prevent further conflict and thus help us to prevent suffering from further loss and increase group cohesiveness. Thus depression can be seen to increase the 'fitness' of the individual and the group. In terms of bipolar disorder, it's suggested that innovative, creative thought is associated with the disorder. This may have some compensatory advantage to those individuals. For example, creativity may help with social intercourse, help to develop greater sensitivity, making such individuals warm, friendly and popular. In addition, creativity accomplishment seems to increase sexual attractiveness and thus creativity may be seen as a product of sexual selection.

## Section 2:

There does appear to be strong evidence for a positive correlation between bipolar disorder and creativity. This is supported by case studies of famous personalities such as Van Gogh and Churchill who've had the disorder. There's a lot of evidence to support the genetic basis of depression, particularly in bipolar disorders. So this suggests that the disorder must have some adaptive benefits otherwise the genetic burden would have died out through natural selection. However, it's not clear whether bipolar disorder is the result of above-average creativity or whether above-average creativity is the result of bipolar disorder. Furthermore, it's difficult to use the adaptive explanation for severe depression since it's unclear how it can benefit either an individual or their larger social group. It's likely that there are other reasons why depression persists in modern-day society beyond a purely evolutionary adaptive argument. Social and cultural factors must surely play some part in contributing to the development of depression.

## Section 3:

Another evolutionary explanation for depression is called the genome lag hypothesis which suggests that our genes have not kept pace with the changes in our environment. The environment of evolutionary adaptation (EEA) refers to the period in human evolution (between approximately 10,000 and 3 million years) when our genes were shaped and selected by natural selection to solve survival problems operating then (Cartwright 2001). Life nowadays is so different that there are bound to be problems and these manifest themselves as mental disorders such as depression and anxiety. Put simply, we have Stone-Age genes in a space-age world. A good example of this relates to the human response to stress, specifically the 'fight or flight' response. Many stressors in the modern world are not solved by a simple 'fight or flight' response and thus remain with us and increase the likelihood of a mental disorder developing.  **A01**

## Section 4:

Nesse and Williams provide support for this explanation when they examined data from 39,000 people in five different countries. They found an increase in depression and suggested that the era of mass communication means that we all now live in the same 'social group'. In the EEA we compared ourselves with 150 other people in our group. We could easily find a useful niche or develop a worthwhile skill in such a group. Nowadays we compare ourselves and compete with the best in the world and inevitably we may suffer in comparison and hence fall into depression. The genome lag hypothesis makes sense since there have been huge technological advancements in the last few centuries and many EAA behaviours may no longer be adaptive. However, humans have never been more successful despite this 'genome lag'. Crawford (1998) suggests that if we look at similarities, not differences, then the requirements of life have not actually changed a great deal from those faced by early man.  **A01**

One problem with both explanations outlined is that they remain hypotheses, not theories. They're speculative and as such difficult to test. This doesn't mean that they're inevitably incorrect, but further evidence is needed to support them.  **A02**

(783 words)

Describe and evaluate evolutionary factors in the development of human intelligence. (24 marks) (30 mins) (600 words minimum) AO1/AO2

Section 1:

Intelligence can be defined as the ability to devise flexible solutions to problems. It could include: learning, application of learning to novel situations and thinking, reasoning and original planning. One measure of intelligence is to compare brain size relative to body size; this is called the encephalisation quotient (EQ). One factor in the development of human intelligence is thought to relate to foraging behaviours. Both animal research and human fossil records show that dietary shifts are associated with increased encephalisation. Humans' large brains may be the result of a meat-eating and high-protein diet. The suggestion that diet relates to intelligence occurs because obtaining food requires a series of activities such as travelling, identification and extraction. All of these factors place increased intellectual demands on humans. For example, hunting requires complex strategies such as planning and co-ordination while the extraction of ripe fruit requires the understanding of seasons and a comprehension of the locality of the best trees.

AO1

Section 2:

If the foraging theory is correct, then primates whose diets are very diverse should show more cerebral development than primates with a more simple diet. Milton (1988) compared the brain weight and EQs of both howler monkeys (a more leaf-eating diet) and spider monkeys (a more fruit-eating diet). Spider monkeys have to cover an area 25 times larger than howler monkeys to obtain their food and thus, according to the theory, should have larger brains and EQs. This is exactly what was found, with howler monkeys (EQ = 0.66) having roughly half the brain size of spider monkeys (EQ = 1.2). The main problem with the foraging/diet idea is the difficulty of separating cause and effect. Which came first? The increased brain size which led to greater and more complicated foraging behaviour or did the increased returns for foraging effort and processing lead to an increased brain size? Answers to such questions remain speculative.

A02

Section 3:

Another factor that may have been important in the development of human intelligence was the social demands of group living. Primates are unusual in that they live in complex social groups. The size of groups has increased during the course of hominid evolution. It's estimated that 3 million years ago our australopithecine ancestors lived in groups of about 70 whereas the first *Homo sapiens* (150,000 years ago) lived in groups of about 150. As these groups got bigger, our ancestors found living within them to be more complex. Alliances within the group had to be maintained, social reasoning was developed and bigger memories were needed for this. This idea is called the 'social complexity' or 'Machiavellian intelligence' hypothesis and suggests that primates use a mix of cunning and deceit in order to maintain their place in a social group. Such cunning requires considerable intellect. In essence, the complex nature of social groups meant that those animals with greater intelligence were more successful operators in these groups. In turn, these animals had greater reproductive success and thus brain size increased.

AO1

Section 4:

A major problem with both the factors mentioned is that there's no agreement as to what constitutes intelligence and as such it's very difficult (impossible?) to measure. Furthermore, measuring the intelligence of animals is even more problematic. A possible way to overcome this is to measure the cortex of different animals including humans. The cortex is often called 'the grey matter' and it's this that's associated with higher forms of intelligence. It's assumed that the higher the proportion of the cortex to the rest of the brain, the higher the intelligence of the animal. In many non-primate animals this proportion is approximately 35%, in primates it is 50% and in humans it's about 80%. Dunbar (1993) found a strong positive correlation between the size of the neocortex and mean group size. This supports the social complexity hypothesis. There's another problem associated with the measurement of group size. It's assumed that the larger the group, the more complicated it is to keep track of all group members. However, it doesn't necessarily follow that a larger group size means greater social complexity. Nevertheless, group size is a fairly simple and objective measure in primates. A final criticism of the social complexity argument relates to primate findings. If social factors are important in determining brain size (and hence intelligence), we'd expect that the great apes (chimps, gorillas and orang-utans) would live in the most complex social groups. This doesn't appear to be the case. Orang-utans favour a solitary existence and some monkeys live in larger groups than gorillas. Baboons also have a higher cortex ratio than gorillas but are considered to be less intelligent.

A02

There are a number of other factors that have been proposed to explain the development of human intelligence. These include tool use, sexual selection and the co-evolution of brain tissue through language development. There's a differing amount of support for each of these ideas, which suggests that the development of human intelligence cannot be pinned down to one particular factor. Indeed, it's likely that there may be a complex combination of factors at work.

A02

*(845 words – could leave out final paragraph = 771 words)*

# SAMPLE ESSAYS

# Psychopathology

## What's covered in this chapter?

### You need to know about:

Schizophrenia
- Clinical characteristics of schizophrenia
- Biological (e.g. genetics; biochemistry) and psychological (e.g. social and family relationships) explanations of schizophrenia, including the evidence on which they are based

Depression
- Clinical characteristics of depression (e.g. bipolar disorder; unipolar disorder)
- Biological (e.g. genetics; biochemistry) and psychological (e.g. learned helplessness) explanations of depression, including the evidence on which they are based

Anxiety disorders
- Clinical characteristics of any one anxiety disorder (e.g. post-traumatic stress disorder; phobic disorders; obsessive–compulsive disorder)
- Biological (e.g. genetics; biochemistry) and psychological (e.g. conditioning) explanations of the chosen disorder, including the evidence on which they are based

## Schizophrenia

### The classification and diagnosis of psychological abnormality

- All systems of classification of psychological abnormality stem from the work of Kraepelin. He published the first recognised textbook of psychiatry in 1883.
- Kraepelin claimed that certain groups of symptoms (a *syndrome*) occur together regularly enough to be regarded as having an underlying physical cause (in much the same way as a particular medical disease and its syndrome can be attributed to a biological abnormality).
- He regarded each 'mental illness' as distinct from all others, with its own origins (causes or *aetiology*), symptoms, course and outcome.
- Kraepelin (1896) proposed two major groups of serious mental diseases:

(a) *dementia praecox* (his term for what we now call schizophrenia), caused by a chemical imbalance, and

(b) *manic–depressive psychosis* (now known as bipolar disorder), caused by a faulty metabolism.

IT'S OK, YOU'RE NOT MAD, YOU'RE JUST NEUROTIC!

- This classification helped to establish the *organic* or *somatic* (bodily) nature of mental disorders. It also formed the basis for the *Diagnostic and Statistical Manual of Mental Disorders* (DSM) and the *International Classification of Diseases* (ICD) (Chapter 5: Mental and behavioural disorders).
- DSM is the official classification system of the American Psychiatric Association. It's the 'bible' of American psychiatrists, but it's also used widely throughout the world. DSM was first published in 1952 (DSM-I), and the latest version is DSM-IV (1994).
- ICD is published by the World Health Organization (WHO). Mental disorders were included for the first time in 1948 (ICD-6). The latest version is ICD-10 (1992).
- Both DSM and ICD use the term 'mental disorder'.
- Both DSM and ICD have dropped the traditional distinction between 'neurosis' and 'psychosis' (although ICD-10 retains the term 'neurotic' and DSM-IV still uses 'psychotic').
- 'Psychosis' is the technical term for what the lay person calls 'madness' (Frith & Cahill, 1995). Psychotic symptoms include delusions, hallucinations, passivity experiences and thought disorder. These account for why 'crazy' people are seen as 'out of their head' or 'in another world'. Unlike neurotic symptoms (such as anxiety, including panic attacks and phobias), psychotic symptoms are outside the normal realm of experience. This means that they're also outside our common-sense powers of understanding and empathy.
- Schizophrenia is by far the commonest of the psychoses. It's also considered to be one of the most serious of all mental disorders.
- Both DSM and ICD have introduced explicit operational criteria for diagnosis. For each disorder, there's a specified list of symptoms. All or some of these must be present, for a specified period of time, in relation to age and gender. It's also stipulated what other diagnoses *mustn't* be present, as well as the personal and social consequences of the disorder. The aim is to make diagnosis more reliable and valid, by laying down rules for the inclusion or exclusion of cases.

## Clinical characteristics of schizophrenia

- As we noted above, what we now call schizophrenia Kraepelin originally called *dementia praecox* ('senility of youth'). He believed that the typical symptoms (delusions, hallucinations, attention deficits and bizarre motor activity) were due to a form of mental deterioration which began in adolescence.
- But Bleuler (1911) observed that many patients displaying these symptoms *didn't* go on deteriorating, and that illness often begins much later than adolescence. Consequently, he introduced the term 'schizophrenia' instead (literally 'split mind' or 'divided self') to describe an illness in which 'the personality loses its unity'.
- The lifetime risk of developing schizophrenia is about 1%, affecting males and females in equal numbers. It usually appears in late adolescence/early adulthood (so Kraepelin got that right), and somewhat earlier for men than for women.

**Table 14.1** Schneider's (1959) first rank symptoms of schizophrenia

**Passivity experiences and thought disturbances:**

- *thought insertion* (thoughts are inserted into one's mind from outside and are under external influence)
- *thought withdrawal* (thoughts are removed from one's mind and are externally controlled)
- *thought broadcasting* (thoughts are broadcast to/otherwise made known to others)
- external forces may include the Martians, the Communists and the 'Government'.

**Auditory hallucinations (in the third person):**

- *hallucinatory voices* are heard discussing one's thoughts or behaviour as they occur (a kind of running commentary), or arguing about oneself (or using one's name), or repeating one's thoughts out loud/anticipating one's thoughts
- they're often accusatory, obscene and derogatory, and may order the patient to commit extreme acts of violence
- they're experienced as alien or under the influence of some external source, and also in the light of concurrent delusions (e.g. the voice of God or the Devil: see text below)
- the hallucinations of patients with *organic* psychoses (where there's known brain pathology) are predominantly *visual*.

**Primary delusions:**

- *false beliefs* (incompatible with reality, usually of *persecution* or *grandeur*) held with extraordinary conviction, impervious to other experiences or compelling counter-argument/contradictory evidence
- the patient may be so convinced of their truth that they act on the strength of their belief, even if this involves murder and rape (as in the case of Peter Sutcliffe, the 'Yorkshire Ripper').

- According to Clare (1976), the diagnosis of schizophrenia in the UK relies greatly on Schneider's (1959) *first rank symptoms*.
- Schneider's first rank symptoms (FRSs) are *subjective experiences*, which can only be *inferred* on the basis of the patient's verbal report.
- Slater and Roth (1969) regarded hallucinations as the *least* important of all the major symptoms. This is because they aren't exclusive to schizophrenia, but are found in patients with mania and delusional depression (this is also true of delusions; see below).
- Slater and Roth identified four additional symptoms, which are *directly observable* from the patient's behaviour.

**Table 14.2** Major symptoms of schizophrenia (based on Slater & Roth, 1969)

**Thought process disorder:**

- the inability to keep to the point, being easily distracted/side-tracked (*derailment*)
- in *clang associations* (e.g. 'big', 'pig', 'twig'), words are 'thrown' together based on their sound rather than their meaning; this produces an apparently incoherent jumble of words ('*word salad*')
- also, the inability to finish a sentence, sometimes stopping in the middle of a word (*thought blocking*), inventing new words (*neologisms*), and interpreting language (e.g. proverbs) literally.

**Disturbance of affect:**

- events/situations don't elicit their usual emotional response (*blunting*)
- there's a more pervasive, generalised absence of emotional expression (as in minimal inflection in speech and lack of normal variation in facial/bodily movements used to convey feelings: *flattening of affect*)
- loss of appropriate emotional responses (e.g. laughing/getting angry for no apparent reason, changing mood very suddenly, giggling when given some bad news: *incongruity of affect*).

**Psychomotor disorders:**

- muscles in a state of semi-rigidity (*catalepsy*)
- grimacing of facial muscles, limb twitching, stereotyped behaviours (such as constant pacing up and down), or assuming a fixed position for long periods of time, even several years in extreme cases (*catatonic stupor*).

**Lack of volition:**

- *avolition* (apathy): lack of energy, apparent lack of interest/inability to carry out routine activities (such as grooming, personal hygiene)
- *anhedonia* (inability to experience pleasure): lack of interest in recreational activities, lack of interest in sex
- *asociality* (severe impairment in social relationships): few friends, poor social skills, little interest in being with others.

## SO WHO'S RIGHT — SCHNEIDER OR SLATER AND ROTH?

- According to Claridge and Davis (2003), 'first rank symptoms' imply that:

> ' . . . certain experiences of people clinically labelled "schizophrenic" are so bizarre, incomprehensible, and distant from the normal that we are surely convinced that these must be central to the disorder.'

In other words, FRSs seem to describe the 'fundamental', core, features of schizophrenia.

- But, like Slater and Roth, Bleuler regarded hallucinations and delusions as *accessory* (secondary) symptoms, that is, they are psychological consequences of a more primary, physical process that constitutes the real core.
- Claridge and Davis believe that the DSM and ICD criteria for diagnosing schizophrenia are a confused mix of these views — although there's a bias towards FRSs. They consider this bias to be understandable, since:

> ' . . . Reporting that aliens in outer space are responsible for the thoughts in your head certainly seems more crazy than bemusing your neighbours with your stream of consciousness style of conversation!'

But, unlike most diagnostic categories, there's *no essential* symptom that must be present for a diagnosis of schizophrenia to be made (Davison & Neale, 2001).

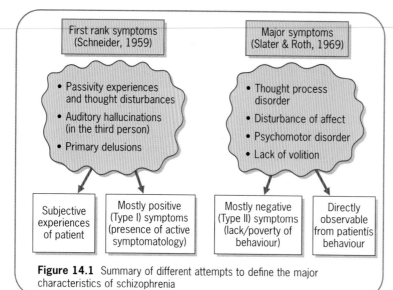

Figure 14.1 Summary of different attempts to define the major characteristics of schizophrenia

POSITIVE AND NEGATIVE SYMPTOMS

## POSITIVE AND NEGATIVE SYMPTOMS

- Most of Schneider's FRSs are what are known as *positive symptoms* (or Type I), that is, excesses or distortions, the *presence of active symptomatology*. They're what define, for the most part, an *acute* episode. Typically, patients have several acute episodes, between which are less severe, but still very debilitating, symptoms.
- Most of Slater and Roth's symptoms are *negative* (Type II) symptoms. They consist of behavioural deficits, *lack of or poverty* of behaviour. These symptoms tend to endure beyond the acute episodes, and have a profound effect on patients' lives. The presence of several negative symptoms is a strong predictor of a poor quality of life two years after leaving hospital (Davison & Neale, 2001).

### An evaluation of the positive/negative distinction

✓ **Important for research:** As we shall see below, the distinction between positive and negative symptoms is very important in relation to research into the causes of schizophrenia. According to Claridge and Davis (2003), currently the most widely quoted research classification is based on this distinction. But despite its popularity, they believe there are several problems with the distinction.

✗ **Are they 'types' or 'states'?** Subjective accounts of psychotic experience suggest that it's doubtful whether negative symptoms define a *type* of schizophrenia. It's more likely that positive and negative symptoms represent alternating *states* occurring at different times within the same individual.

✗ **'Type' or end-state?** If it *does* define a 'type' of schizophrenia, the negative form probably refers to the chronic end-state. Some patients progress into this after years of adaptation to their more acute ('florid') episodes.

✗ **Are negative symptoms unique to schizophrenia?** If a diagnosis of schizophrenia is based on an initial episode which consists solely of negative symptoms, it won't be very convincing. For example, how do negative symptoms differ from those of depression (see below)?

✗ **Ambiguity:** 'Negative symptom' is ambiguous. It could be a way of coping with positive symptoms (say, in the form of social withdrawal). Alternatively, it could be an effect of anti-psychotic medication. Or it could be a manifestation of depression.

✓ **Provides template for understanding variety of schizophrenic symptoms:** Despite these criticisms, the positive/negative distinction (or some elaboration of it) is probably along the right lines as a rough template of how schizophrenic symptoms can vary. It's easily recognisable to psychiatrists and psychologists.

## Varieties of schizophrenia

DSM-IV distinguishes three types of schizophrenia (as initially proposed by Kraepelin). These are *disorganised, catatonic* and *paranoid*. These are described in Table 14.3.

---

**Table 14.3** The three types of schizophrenia as identified by DSM-IV

**Disorganised schizophrenia**

- This is probably the nearest thing to many people's idea about what a 'mad' or 'crazy' person is like (see text above). It's what Kraepelin called *hebephrenic*.
- It's normally diagnosed only in adolescents and young adults.
- Mood is shallow and inappropriate. Thought is disorganised and speech is incoherent. This makes it difficult for the listener to follow.
- Delusions and hallucinations are fleeting and fragmentary, and behaviour is irresponsible, unpredictable, silly or mischievous, childish or bizarre. The person may sometimes become violent (if, for example, s/he is approached while hallucinating).
- The person may become incontinent, and tends to ignore personal appearance and hygiene.

**Catatonic schizophrenia**

- The patient may alternate between extremes such as (a) *hyperkinesis* (hyperactivity) and stupor (a marked reduction of spontaneous movements and activity), or (b) *automatic obedience* ('command automatism') and *negativism* (apparently motiveless resistance to all instructions/attempts to be moved, or doing the opposite of what's asked).
- There may be episodes of apparently purposeless motor activity combined with a dreamlike (*oneroid*) state with vivid scenic hallucinations.
- Other characteristics are *mutism, posturing* (the voluntary assumption of inappropriate and bizarre postures) and *waxy flexibility* (maintenance of the limbs and body in externally imposed positions).
- Onset may be more sudden than other types of schizophrenia. But the patient is likely to have shown previous apathy and withdrawal from reality.

**Paranoid schizophrenia**

- This is dominated by relatively stable, often *paranoid, delusions* (although delusions of *grandeur* are also quite common). These may be accompanied by vivid auditory hallucinations.
- Also common are *ideas of reference*. The patient incorporates unimportant events within a delusional framework, and reads personal significance into other people's trivial actions. For example, they might think that overheard fragments of a conversation, or something on TV or in a magazine, are about them.
- Paranoid schizophrenics also tend to be agitated, argumentative, angry and sometimes violent.
- But in other respects, the patient is less disturbed (the personality is better preserved) than in the other kinds. The person remains emotionally responsive, and s/he is more alert and verbal than other types. Although their language is filled with references to delusions, it *isn't* disorganised.
- It's the most *homogeneous* type, that is, paranoid schizophrenics are more alike than those in other categories.

---

(Based on Gelder *et al.*, 1999; Davison & Neale, 2001.)

---

Other types which have been identified include *simple* and *undifferentiated*.

### Simple schizophrenia

- This often appears during late adolescence, and has a slow, gradual onset.
- The main symptoms are gradual social withdrawal and difficulty in making friends, aimlessness and idleness, blunting of affect, loss of volition and drive, and a decline in academic or occupational performance.
- Such people may become drifters or tramps, and are often regarded by others as idle and 'layabouts'. But there are no major psychotic symptoms as in the other types. Only ICD actually distinguishes this type, which is still used in some countries.

### Undifferentiated (atypical)

- This category is meant to accommodate patients who cannot be easily placed elsewhere, that is, psychotic conditions that meet the general diagnostic criteria for schizophrenia, but which don't conform to any of the sub-types (because of either insufficient or overlapping symptoms).
- *'Residual'* is used when the patient no longer meets the full criteria, but still shows some signs of illness.
- This is a 'supplementary' type used in DSM.

## An evaluation of the sub-types

✘ **Are they really different?** With the possible exception of paranoid, psychiatrists find it very difficult to tell these 'sub-types' apart. Some patients present symptoms of one sub-group at one time, then those of another sub-group later (Gelder *et al.*, 1999). This dramatically reduces the *reliability* of diagnosis (Davison & Neale, 2001).

✘ **Are sub-types 'real' or are they subject to 'external forces?** Catatonic symptoms are much less common now than 50 years ago. This could be because drug therapy works effectively on bizarre motor processes. Alternatively, the apparently high prevalence of catatonic schizophrenia during the early 20th century may have been due to misdiagnosis (Boyle, 1991). There are similarities between it and *encephalitis lethargica* (sleeping sickness). Many cases of the latter may have been diagnosed as catatonic schizophrenia. This was portrayed in the film *Awakenings* (based on the book by Oliver Sacks).

Robin Williams (left) in a scene from *Awakenings*. Patients with sleeping sickness (as portrayed in the film) have often been misdiagnosed with catatonic schizophrenia

✘ **Poor predictive validity:**
Assigning someone to a particular sub-type provides very little information that helps either in treatment or in predicting the outcome of the illness (Davison & Neale, 2001).

## Explanations of schizophrenia

### SOME GENERAL CONSIDERATIONS REGARDING RESEARCH PROBLEMS AND STRATEGIES (AO2) (BASED ON CLARIDGE & DAVIS, 2003)

- Schizophrenia is *heterogeneous* (there are many different symptoms that can be involved, and different sub-types are officially recognised (but see above)). This makes it almost certain that attempts to give a *single* explanation will fail.
- Patients don't just differ from each other (*between*-subject differences). The same patient can show considerable variation on different occasions (*within*-subject differences). For example, individual schizophrenics show enormous day-to-day fluctuations in simple physical responses (such as galvanic skin response/GSR). But most studies take only a single measure. This may be a general problem in any psychological research. But it may be a particular problem in the case of schizophrenia, because what causes this individual instability of function may itself be an important clue to the nature of the disorder.
- People with acute symptoms may be distracted by delusional thoughts about the experimenter. Or they may just not be looking at the computer screen that test stimuli are presented on. A partial solution to this problem is to test people who are taking anti-psychotic medication. But then we cannot be sure whether their performance reflects a genuine feature of the illness or an effect of the drugs!

- This makes the study of schizoid and schizotypal personality disorder (SPD or *schizotypy*) very important. The symptoms of schizophrenia can sometimes appear in a rather muted (toned-down) form. This gave rise to the idea of the *schizophrenic spectrum* (a range of schizophrenia-like disorders). SPD has received the most attention as a possible mild variant of schizophrenia. Diagnostic criteria for SPD include ideas of reference, odd beliefs or magical thinking, unusual perceptual experiences, odd thinking and speech, suspiciousness, inappropriate affect, odd eccentric behaviour or appearance, a lack of close friends, and excessive social anxiety.
- If people high on schizotypy share important characteristics with schizophrenics, then by studying the former it becomes possible to study 'schizophrenia' without the confounding effects of acute mental disturbance or medication. This 'schizotypy strategy' is used to examine possible *mechanisms* involved in psychotic disorder. This includes the *genetics* of schizophrenia (see below).

> **Specification Hint:** The Specification says '... Biological (e.g. genetics, biochemistry) and psychological (e.g. social and family relationships) explanations ..., including the evidence on which they are based'. This requires you to know at least one of each type of explanation, but *one of each type* will do. Some explanations are overlapping, and it's also useful for analysis and evaluation (AO2) to be familiar with other (biological or psychological) explanations. So we've decided to include three biological accounts. These are also helpful for considering explanations of other mental disorders.

## Biological explanations

### IS SCHIZOPHRENIA A NEUROLOGICAL DISORDER?

- When Kraepelin first identified *dementia praecox*, he was convinced that it was a physical disease like any other. The neuropathological changes associated with *general paralysis of the insane* (caused by syphilis) and *Alzheimer's disease* had just been discovered. He expected that similar 'markers' would be found for schizophrenia (and manic–depressive illness).
- The then new CT scan was used for the first time in 1978 to study the brains of chronic schizophrenics (by Johnstone *et al.* at the Clinical Research Centre in Middlesex, England: Gershon & Rieder, 1992). It revealed that chronic schizophrenics show an increase in the size of the lateral cerebral ventricles (the fluid-filled spaces in the middle of the brain). Other X-ray evidence confirmed that there was less brain tissue (especially in the medial temporal lobe). This was subsequently confirmed by MRI scans.
- MRI scans, together with postmortem examinations, also revealed that schizophrenics have a smaller hippocampus. Part of the limbic system is also smaller.
- Gershon and Rieder also cite research which has shown reduced blood flow in the frontal cortex of schizophrenics. This implies decreased neuronal activity.
- Postmortems also show that certain groups of neurons are organised in an abnormal way, or are connected differently, compared with non-schizophrenics.

### An evaluation of the neurological disorder explanation (NDE)

✓ **Evidence for cause rather than effect:** All these differences are found when patients first develop symptoms (and may even precede the onset of symptoms). This suggests that they're *not* the result of being ill for a long time or of medication (Harrison, 1995). Also, these differences don't progress over time, nor is there any evidence of neural scar tissue (*gliosis*) that's normally found in degenerative disorders (such as Alzheimer's and Huntington's). This suggests a *neurodevelopmental disorder*, that is, a failure of brain tissue to develop normally (such as failure of neuronal growth or neuronal connections, or a disturbance in the 'pruning' of neurons that normally takes place between three and 15 years of age) (Gershon & Rieder, 1992).

✗ **The differences between normal and schizophrenic brains are relative:** These differences are only apparent if a group of schizophrenics is compared with a group of non-schizophrenics. That is, no one can yet diagnose schizophrenia in an individual based *solely* on a brain scan or looking down a microscope (Harrison, 1995).

✗ How do such differences arise? Even if we could diagnose schizophrenia just from a brain scan, this wouldn't answer the more fundamental question as to why some people develop these disorders and others don't.

✗ Correlational data: The cognitive and affective abnormalities involved in psychosis are so severe that it's reasonable to expect brain abnormalities to be involved (Frith & Cahill, 1995), but the data are largely *correlational*.

✗ No consistent differences between normal and schizophrenic brains: Individual studies have regularly shown differences between schizophrenics and control samples. But replicable effects *across* studies have remained elusive (Claridge & Davis, 2003). For example, a review by Chua and McKenna (1995) concluded that there was no reliable evidence for gross structural or functional cerebral abnormality that could be said to characterise schizophrenia as a diagnostic category. The only exception was lateral ventricular enlargement. But the degree of enlargement is modest, many patients don't show any enlargement at all, and enlarged ventricles are found in other disorders (such as mania) (Davison & Neale, 2001). Also, enlarged ventricles are more of a vulnerability factor than an immediate cause of the disorder.

✗•✓ No single brain abnormality can explain all symptoms: It's more likely that different brain circuits underlie different clusters of symptoms. For example, people with known abnormalities in their temporal lobe often show schizophrenia-like symptoms. Neuroimaging studies involving schizophrenic patients support this link, and suggest that it's specifically *positive* symptoms that are associated with this dysfunction (Bogerts, 1997). *Negative* symptoms may be related to the *frontal* lobe. Schizophrenics show 'hypofrontality'. This is seen as either (a) reduced activity relative to other brain regions, or (b) failure of the pre-frontal cortex (PFC) and associated structures to be appropriately activated by cognitive tasks (Velakoulis & Pantelis, 1996). Performance deficits on neuropsychological tests of frontal lobe function are much greater in those rated high on negative symptoms (Mattson *et al.*, 1997). This suggests that their core cognitive failure is *indirect*, caused by *motivational* effects (see Table 14.2 above).

## BIOCHEMICAL EXPLANATIONS OF SCHIZOPHRENIA

- *Genetics* may have its effect through body chemistry and related biological processes. So biochemical explanations are *complementary* to genetic theory, not alternatives to it (see below).
- According to the *dopamine hypothesis*, what directly causes schizophrenic symptoms is an excess of the neurotransmitter dopamine. In order to appreciate the dopamine hypothesis (and explanations of other disorders involving neurotransmitters), we need to consider the process of neurotransmission (see Figure 14.2).

### Box 14.1 The process of neurotransmission

- **Information is transmitted in the brain via a combination of electrical impulses and neurotransmitters.**
- *Within* **a nerve cell (or** *neuron***), information is conveyed by electrical impulses. But for transmission** *between* **neurons, transmitters are needed.**
- **When an electrical impulse arrives at the end of the neuron, a neurotransmitter is released into a tiny gap (the** *synaptic gap* **or** *cleft***) between it and the beginning of the next neuron. The first neuron is referred to as the** *pre-synaptic* **neuron, and the second ('receiving') neuron as the** *post-synaptic* **neuron.**
- **The released neurotransmitter attaches to** *post-synaptic receptors***. This action triggers another electrical impulse.**
- **Once it's done its job, the neurotransmitter is then recycled, in one of two ways:**
  - **(a) it may be taken back by the neuron that released it (** *re-uptake* **) or**
  - **(b) it may be broken down chemically in the synaptic gap into simpler compounds by** *monoamine oxidase* **(MAO).**
- **Serotonin (5-HT), norepinephrine (noradrenaline), and dopamine (D2) are major neurotransmitters collectively known as MAO transmitters.**

- The evidence for this hypothesis comes from three main sources:

(a) postmortems on schizphrenics show unusually high levels of dopamine, especially in the limbic system (Iversen, 1979)

(b) anti-schizophrenic drugs (such as chlorpromazine) are thought to work by binding to dopamine receptor sites, that is, they inhibit the ability of the dopamine (D2) receptors to respond to dopamine, thus reducing dopamine activity. They produce side-effects that are similar to the symptoms of Parkinson's disease, which is known to be caused partly by low levels of dopamine in particular nerve tracts

(c) high doses of L-dopa (used in the treatment of Parkinson's disease) can sometimes produce symptoms very similar to the psychomotor disorders seen in certain types of schizophrenia. High doses of amphetamines can induce *amphetamine psychosis* (AP), which closely resembles paranoid schizophrenia and can exacerbate the symptoms of a patient with schizophrenia. Both these drugs are believed to increase the activity of dopamine. Dopamine-containing neurons are concentrated in the basal ganglia and frontal cortex. These areas are concerned with the initiation and control of movement; degeneration of the dopamine system produces Parkinson's disease (see above). Antipsychotics are given to counteract AP.

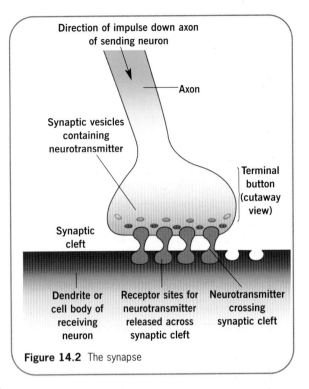

**Figure 14.2** The synapse

Labels in figure: Direction of impulse down axon of sending neuron; Axon; Synaptic vesicles containing neurotransmitter; Terminal button (cutaway view); Synaptic cleft; Dendrite or cell body of receiving neuron; Receptor sites for neurotransmitter released across synaptic cleft; Neurotransmitter crossing synaptic cleft

## An evaluation of biochemical explanations

✗ **Inconclusive evidence:** Overall, the evidence is inconclusive (Lavender, 2000). For example, there's no consistent difference in dopamine levels between drug-free schizophrenics and normals, nor is there any evidence of higher levels of other metabolites indicating greater dopamine activity (Jackson, 1986).

✗ **Cause or effect?** Even if there were evidence of higher dopamine levels, this could just as easily be a *result* of schizophrenia as its cause. If dopamine *were* found to be a causative factor, this might only be *indirect*. For example, abnormal family circumstances give rise to high levels of dopamine which, in turn, trigger the symptoms (Lloyd *et al.*, 1984).

✗ **Dopamine hypothesis couldn't explain all cases:** It's unlikely that any problems with dopamine production/receptivity will prove to be the basic biochemical abnormality underlying all forms of schizophrenia – although it may play a crucial role in some forms (Jackson, 1990). According to Lavender (2000):

> ' . . . if schizophrenia is not a clearly identifiable syndrome but an umbrella term covering a range of symptoms with unclear onset, course, and outcome, then it is obvious that much of the work investigating a specific biological basis will inevitably be inconclusive. So far, this appears to be the case . . . '

As Bentall (1990) argues, perhaps the time has come to concentrate on specific symptoms, before trying to find the biochemical cause(s).

✗ Incomplete explanation: The dopamine hypothesis cannot be a complete explanation. For example, it takes several weeks for antipsychotics gradually to reduce positive symptoms, even though they begin blocking D2 receptors very quickly (Davis, 1978). Their eventual therapeutic effect may be due to the effect this blockade has on *other* brain areas and neurotransmitter systems (Cohen *et al.*, 1997).

✗•✓ Other neurotransmitters implicated: Newer anti-schizophrenic drugs implicate *serotonin*. Serotoninergic neurons are known to regulate dopaminergic neurons in the mesolimbic pathway (MLP: see below and Figure 14.3). So dopamine may be just one piece in a much more complex jigsaw (Davison & Neale, 2001). *Glutamate*, another transmitter found in many parts of the human brain, may also be involved.

✗•✓ Refining the hypothesis: Improved technologies for studying neurochemical factors in humans, plus inconsistent data, have led to the claim that what schizophrenics have is an excess of dopamine *receptors*, or that their D2 receptors are *over-sensitive*. This refined dopamine hypothesis is based on several postmortem and PET scan studies. Having too many – or over-sensitive – receptors is functionally equivalent to having too much dopamine itself, and seems to be associated mainly with *positive* symptoms (Davison & Neale, 2001).

✗•✓ Further refinements: Excess of dopamine located in the *mesolimbic pathway* (MLP) seems to be most relevant to understanding schizophrenia. The therapeutic effects of anti-psychotic drugs on the positive symptoms occur by blocking D2 receptors there. The *mesocortical pathway* (MCP) begins in the same brain region as the MLP, but projects to the pre-frontal cortex (PFC) (see Figure 14.3).

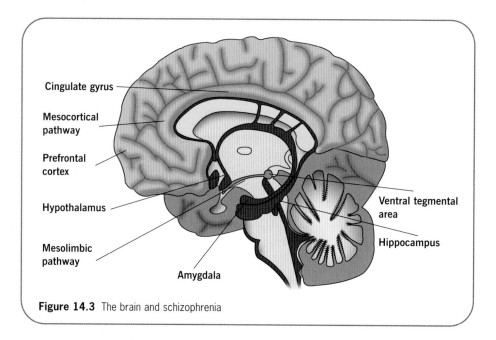

**Figure 14.3** The brain and schizophrenia

The PFC also projects to limbic areas which consist of neurons that are activated by dopamine. These *dopaminergic* neurons in the PFC may be underactive and so fail to exert inhibitory control over dopaminergic neurons in the limbic area. This produces overactivity in the MLP. The PFC is thought to be especially relevant to negative symptoms. Consequently, underactivity of the dopaminergic neurons in this part of the brain may also be the cause of negative symptoms. This proposal has the advantage of explaining how positive and negative symptoms can be present at the same time in the same patient. Also, because anti-psychotics don't have major effects on dopaminergic neurons in the PFC, we'd expect them to be relatively ineffective in treating negative symptoms – and they are (Davison & Neale, 2001).

- As Table 14.4 shows, relatives of patients with schizophrenia (proband or index case) have a greater risk of being diagnosed themselves as the genetic relationship becomes closer. This was confirmed by Kendler *et al.* (1996).

**Table 14.4** Summary of major European family and twin studies of the genetics of schizophrenia (based on Gottesman *et al.*, 1987; Gottesman, 1991)

| Relationship to proband | Percentage with schizophrenia |
|---|---|
| Spouse | 1.00 |
| First cousin | 2.00 |
| Grandchild | 2.84 |
| Niece/nephew | 2.00–2.65 |
| Child | 9.35 |
| – with one schizophrenic parent | 6.00 |
| – with two schizophrenic parents | 46.00 |
| Sibling | 7.30–10.00 |
| Dizygotic (DZ) twin | 12.00–12.08 |
| Monozygotic (MZ) twin | 44.30 |
| Monozygotic twin reared apart (MZRA) | 58.00 |

- As with intelligence (see Chapter 11), *family resemblance studies* confound genetic and environmental influences. In other words, there's no way of telling whether the correlation between the risk of developing schizophrenia and degree of family resemblance/blood tie is caused by the greater genetic similarity or the greater similarity of environments.
- The two major alternative designs, *twin* and *adoption studies*, both face problems of their own. For example, they pre-suppose that schizophrenia is a distinct syndrome which can be reliably diagnosed by different psychiatrists. (This parallels the assumption that IQ tests are valid tests of intelligence: see Chapter 11.)

### Twin studies

**Table 14.5** Concordance rates for schizophrenia for identical (MZ) and non-identical (DZ) twins (based on Rose *et al.*, 1984)

| Study | 'Narrow' concordance* | | 'Broad' concordance* | |
|---|---|---|---|---|
| | %MZs | %DZs | %MZs | %DZs |
| Rosanoff *et al.* (1934); USA (41 MZs, 53 DZs) | 44 | 9 | 61 | 13 |
| Kallmann (1946); USA (174 MZs, 296 DZs) | 59 | 11 | 69 | 11–14 |
| Slater (1953); England (37 MZs, 58 DZs) | 65 | 14 | 65 | 14 |
| Gottesman & Shields (1966); England (24 MZs, 33 DZs) | 42 | 15 | 54 | 18 |
| Kringlen (1968); Norway (55 MZs, 90 DZs) | 25 | 7 | 38 | 10 |
| Allen *et al.* (1972); USA (95 MZs, 125 DZs) | 14 | 4 | 27 | 5 |
| Fischer (1973); Denmark (21 MZs, 41 DZs) | 24 | 10 | 48 | 20 |

* 'Narrow' based on attempt to apply a relatively strict set of criteria when diagnosing schizophrenia. 'Broad' includes 'borderline schizophrenia', 'schizoaffective psychosis', 'paranoid with schizophrenia-like features'.

- As Table 14.5 shows, there's a wide variation in the concordance rate for schizophrenia in different studies, for both MZs and DZs. This suggests that different countries use different criteria for diagnosing schizophrenia.
- By the same token, if the highest concordance rate for MZs is 69% (using a 'broad' criterion), this still leaves plenty of scope for the role of environmental factors. If schizophrenia were totally genetically determined, then we'd expect to find 100% concordance rate for MZs. In other words, if one member of an MZ pair has schizophrenia, the other twin should also have it in every single case. In fact, most diagnosed cases *don't* report a family history (Frith & Cahill, 1995).

- Nevertheless, the average concordance rate for MZs is five times higher than that for DZs (50% and 10% respectively; Shields, 1976, 1978).
- A more precise estimate for the relative importance of genetic and environmental factors comes from studies where MZs reared apart (MZsRA) are compared with MZs reared together (MZsRT). According to Shields (1976, 1978), the concordance rates are quite similar for the two groups, suggesting a major genetic contribution.

## Box 14.2 The equal environments assumption

- Twin studies are based on the *equal environments assumption*:
  (a) MZs aren't treated more similarly than same-sex DZs or
  (b) if they are, this doesn't increase MZs' similarity for the characteristic in question relative to same-sex DZs.
  (This assumption therefore applies to the study of intelligence too.)
- According to Lilienfeld (1995), this assumption has stood up surprisingly well to careful empirical scrutiny. For example, researchers have identified MZs and DZs whose *zygosity* has been misclassified (MZs mistaken for DZs and *vice versa*). If similarity of rearing were the key factor underlying the greater concordance for MZs, then *perceived* zygosity (as opposed to actual zygosity) should be the best predictor of concordance. However, twin similarity in personality and cognitive ability is related much more closely to *actual* than perceived zygosity (Scarr & Carter-Saltzman, 1979).
- Also, the greater similarity in parental rearing for MZs seems to be largely or entirely because of the fact that MZs elicit more similar reactions from their parents (Lytton, 1977). It seems, therefore, that the greater similarity of MZs is a *cause*, rather than an effect, of their more similar parental treatment.

### Adoption studies

- Adoption studies arguably provide the most unequivocal test of genetic influence, because they allow the clearest separation of genetic and environmental factors.
- For example, Heston (1966) studied 47 adults born to schizophrenic mothers and separated from them within three days of birth. As children, they'd been reared in a variety of circumstances, though not by the mother's family. They were compared (average age 36) with controls matched for circumstances of upbringing, but where mothers hadn't been schizophrenic. Five of the experimental group, but none of the controls, were diagnosed as schizophrenic.
- Rosenthal *et al.* (1971) began a series of studies in 1965 in Denmark, which has national registers of psychiatric cases and adoptions. They confirmed Heston's findings, using children separated from schizophrenic mothers, on average at six months.

**Comparing schizophrenic and non-schizophrenic adoptees** (CSANSA) (Kety *et al.,* 1975)

ESSENTIAL STUDY 14.1

- In what's considered to be one of the major schizophrenia adoption studies, Kety *et al.* used a different design from earlier studies.
- Two groups of adoptees were identified: (a) 33 who had schizophrenia, and (b) a matched group who didn't. Rates of disorder were compared in the biological and adoptive families of the two groups of adoptees – the rate was greater among the biological relatives of the schizophrenic adoptees than among those of the controls, a finding which supports the genetic hypothesis. Further, the rate of schizophrenia wasn't increased among couples who adopted the schizophrenic adoptees, suggesting that environmental factors weren't of crucial importance (Gelder *et al.,* 1989).

- The reverse situation was studied by Wender *et al*. (1974), who found no increase among adoptees with normal biological parents but with a schizophrenic adoptive parent. Gottesman and Shields (1976, 1982), reviewing adoption studies, conclude that they show a major role for heredity.

 An evaluation of the genetic theory

**The random placement assumption:** This refers to the assumption that adoptees are placed with parents who are no more similar to their biological parents than by chance. This is crucial when evaluating the results of adoption studies. Rose *et al*. (1984) consider selective placement to be the rule (rather than random placement) and so a major, if not fatal, stumbling block of adoption studies. But Lilienfeld (1995) believes the random placement assumption is largely or entirely warranted.

**Supporting evidence:** Perhaps the most reasonable conclusion is that there's converging evidence, from multiple sources, implicating genetic factors in the aetiology of schizophrenia. Its heritability seems to be comparable to that of any medical condition known to have a major genetic component, such as diabetes, hypertension, coronary artery disease and breast cancer (Lilienfeld, 1995).

**But how is it inherited and what exactly is inherited?** The precise mode of inheritance remains controversial (Frith & Cahill, 1995; Lilienfeld, 1995). The most popular current view is the 'multifactorial' (*polygenic*) model: a number of genes are involved which determine a pre-disposition, which then requires environmental factors to trigger the symptoms of the illness. This is referred to as a *diathesis* (i.e. pre-disposition) *stress model*. Zubin and Spring (1977), for example, claim that what we probably inherit is a degree of *vulnerability* to exhibit schizophrenic symptoms. Whether or not we do will depend on environmental stresses which may include viral infections during pregnancy (especially influenza A), severe malnourishment during pregnancy, birth injury or difficult birth, being born in winter, as well as 'critical life events' (see below).

**The heterogeneity of schizophrenia:** As we saw earlier, there's considerable debate as to whether schizophrenia is a single disorder or whether there are several sub-types. Certainly, there are many different symptoms that count as 'schizophrenic', including the positive/negative distinction. According to Claridge and Davis (2003), individual studies have reported concordance rates for MZs ranging from zero to 90%. Yet 50% is often quoted. Claridge and Davis think this is suspicious:

'... Is it possible that the value of 50 per cent now generally quoted is merely some average of a range of heritabilities for entirely different psychotic disorders, different varieties of schizophrenia, or just illnesses of different severity?'

Heritabilities do vary in proportion to the judged severity among the cases sampled (Gottesman & Shields, 1982). More intriguing – and rather puzzling – is a finding relating to the *same* sets of twins diagnosed on two separate occasions: once according to first rank symptoms (FRSs), then again using broader criteria. On the broader criterion, the concordance rate for MZs was 50%. But on FRSs, it was zero! (Farmer *et al.,* 1987; McGuffin *et al.*, 1987). According to Claridge and Davis (2003):

'... This tends to suggest that, despite their convincingly "psychotic" appearance, first rank symptoms do not tap directly into whatever is inherited in schizophrenia; instead they may indeed be secondary elaborations of some more fundamental (inherited) cognitive pro-cesses, along the lines visualized by Bleuler.'

**The influence of environmental factors:** According to Claridge and Davis (2003):

' ... the contribution of genetic influences is one of the few factual certainties about schiz-ophrenia. Even in the absence of the discovery of specific genes, this is clear from kinship data ... '

But, as the *diathesis–stress model* maintains, any inherited factors can only account for a greater *vulnerability* or likelihood of developing schizophrenia. They don't *guarantee* that the vulnerable individual will actually become schizophrenic. So, just as Claridge and Davis are certain that genetic factors are involved, they're equally certain that the genetic data tell us that environmental factors must also be important. But these can be interpreted as *biological* factors (viral infections, birth complications etc. – see above) or as *social*. For example, Tienari (1991) examined the rate of schizophrenia in Finnish people who'd been adopted and whose biological mothers were schizophrenic. As predicted, having a biological mother with schizophrenia increased the rate of schizophrenia in the adoptees, even if they were adopted by non-schizophrenic families. But the schizophrenic genetics only revealed itself if the adoptive family was psychologically disturbed in some way. So even vulnerable individuals could be protected from schizophrenia if their family of rearing were healthy.

> **Specification Hint:** As we've seen above, the diathesis–stress model incorporates both 'vulnerability' factors (usually taken to mean genetic influences) and 'triggering' factors (usually taken to mean both pre- and post-natal environmental influences). The latter include what's normally understood by 'psychological' So 'psychological explanations' include those which focus on the non-genetic, environmental half of the diathesis–stress model. The Specification gives the example of 'social and family relationships'.

## Psychological explanations

### SOCIAL AND FAMILY RELATIONSHIPS

#### The 'schizophrenogenic mother' and family communication

- Early theorists regarded family relationships as crucial, especially that between mother and son. This view was so popular at the time that the term 'schizophrenogenic mother' was coined. This described the cold, dominant, conflict-inducing parent (Fromm-Reichmann, 1948). She was rejecting, over-protective, self-sacrificing, insensitive to others' feelings, rigid and moralistic about sex, and afraid of intimacy.
- There was little supporting evidence. But the families of schizophrenics differ in some ways from those of non-schizophrenics. For example, they show vague patterns of communication and high levels of conflict (Davison & Neale, 2001). But which is cause and which is effect? Could it be that the abnormal communication and high conflict levels are *caused by* having a schizophrenic in the family?
- Some evidence exists that family relationships may play some part in causing schizophrenia. Goldstein and Rodnick (1975) studied adolescents with behaviour problems and their families over a five-year period. Several developed schizophrenia and related disorders during this period, and abnormal communication did seem to predict the later onset of schizophrenia. However, the parents of manic patients (those with bipolar disorder – see below) also display such deviant communication. So it cannot be a *specific* causal factor in schizophrenia.
- Further evidence comes from the Finnish adoption study by Tienari (1991) referred to above. The adoptive families were classified according to the level of maladjustment they displayed (based on clinical interviews and psychological tests). Adoptees with a biological schizophrenic mother were more severely schizophrenic themselves if reared in a disturbed family. So should we conclude that both a genetic predisposition and a harmful family environment are necessary for schizophrenia (as the diathesis–stress model would maintain)? Again, the disturbed family environment could be a *response* to having a disturbed child (Davison & Neale, 2001).

### LAING AND ANTI-PSYCHIATRY

- During the 1950s and 1960s, several British psychiatrists, notably R.D. Laing, Cooper and Esterson, united in their rejection of the medical model of mental disorder.
- They denied the existence of schizophrenia as a disease entity. Instead, they saw it as a metaphor

for dealing with people whose behaviour and experience fail to conform to the dominant model of social reality. They thus spearheaded the *anti-psychiatry movement* (Graham, 1986).
- In *Self and Others* (1961), Laing proposed the *family interaction model*. Schizophrenia can only be understood as something which takes place *between* people (*not* inside them). To understand individuals we must study not individuals but interactions between individuals (this is the subject-matter of *social phenomenology*).

## ✗✓ An evaluation of the family interaction model

✓ **Supporting evidence:** The family interaction model was consistent with American research, especially that of Bateson *et al.* (1956). This showed that schizophrenia arises within families which use 'pathological' forms of communication, in particular contradictory messages (*double-binds*). For example, a mother induces her son to give her a hug, but when he does she tells him 'not to be such a baby'. This research is, of course, consistent with the studies by Goldstein and Rodnick (1975) and Tienari (1991) described above. Laing and Esterson (1964) presented 11 family case histories, in all of which one member becomes a diagnosed schizophrenic. Their aim was to make schizophrenia intelligible in the context of what happens within the patient's family and, in so doing, to undermine further the disease model of schizophrenia.

✓•✗ **Cause or effect?** As with other correlational evidence, both Bateson *et al.*'s and Laing and Esterson's studies are open to two interpretations. According to Laing and Esterson, it's the family which is 'schizophrenic', and one particularly vulnerable member becomes a scapegoat for the whole family's pathology. Alternatively, the patient is already ill and part of the family's way of dealing with this is to develop abnormal ('schizophrenic') forms of communication. Supporters of biochemical or genetic explanations would argue that there's sufficient data to account for how people become schizophrenic without having to bring family environmental factors into it. But supporters of the diathesis–stress model would claim that only environmental factors (such as disturbed families) can explain how vulnerability is turned into actual schizophrenic illness.

### LABELLING THEORY
- Laing (1967) proposed another model of schizophrenia. The *conspiratorial model* maintains that schizophrenia is a label, a form of violence perpetrated by some people on others. The family, GP, and psychiatrists conspire against the schizophrenic in order to preserve their definition of reality (the *status quo*). They treat schizophrenics as if they were sick and imprison them in mental hospitals, where they're degraded and invalidated as human beings.
- The influence of labelling is demonstrated in a famous experiment by Rosenhan (1973). Rosenhan's aim was to show that psychiatrists are unable to tell the difference between the 'sane' and the 'insane' and that, therefore, psychiatric classification and diagnosis are totally unreliable. But he also discussed the effects of *diagnostic labelling* at great length.
- Rosenhan claims that his results demonstrate dramatically what several authors (such as Scheff, 1966) have claimed, namely that psychiatric (diagnostic) labels tend to become *self-fulfilling prophecies*. Psychiatric labels stick in a way that (other) medical labels don't. More seriously, *everything* the patient says and does is interpreted in accordance with the diagnostic label once it's been applied. For example, after admission the pseudo-patients kept a written record of how the ward was run. This was documented by the nursing staff as 'Patient engages in writing behaviour'. In other words, the writing was seen as a symptom of their pathological behaviour. Rosenhan argues that mental disorder is a purely *social* phenomenon, the consequences of a labelling process.
- According to Scheff (1966), the crucial factor in schizophrenia is the act of assigning a diagnostic label to the individual. This label influences (a) how the person will continue to behave (based on stereotyped ideas of mental illness), and (b) how others will react to them. The labelling process creates a *social role*, which *is* the disorder. Without it, deviant behaviour (or the breaking of *residual rules*) wouldn't become stabilised.
- Residual rules are what's 'left over' after all the formal and obvious ones (about violence, stealing etc.) have been recognised. Examples would be 'Don't report hearing voices' or 'Don't talk to your-

self out loud while walking down a busy street'. Scheff believes it's quite common for people to commit 'one-time violations'. If a 'normal' person is unlucky enough to be caught violating a residual rule, they might be diagnosed as suffering from, say, schizophrenia. Rosenhan's experiment shows how easy it is to 'slip into' the role of psychiatric patient.

**ESSENTIAL STUDY 14.2**

### On being sane in insane places (OBSIIP) (Rosenhan, 1973)

● ● ● ● ● ● ● ● ● ● ● ● ● ● ● ● ● ● ● ● ● ● ● ● ● ● ● ● ● ● ● ● ● ● ● ● ● ● ● ● ● ● ● ● ● ● ● ● ● ● ● ● ● ● ● ● ● ● ● ● ● ●

- Eight psychiatrically 'normal' people (a psychology student, three psychologists, a paediatrician, a psychiatrist, a painter-decorator and a housewife) presented themselves at the admissions offices of 12 different psychiatric hospitals in the USA. They complained of hearing voices saying 'empty', 'hollow' and 'thud' (auditory hallucinations).

- These symptoms, plus their names and occupations, were the only falsification of the truth involved at any stage of the study.

- All eight 'pseudo-patients' were admitted (in 11 cases with a diagnosis of 'schizophrenia', in the other 'manic depression'). Once admitted, they stopped claiming to hear voices.

- They were eventually discharged with a diagnosis of 'schizophrenia (or manic depression) in remission', that is, without signs of illness.

- The only people to have suspected their true identity were some of their 'fellow' patients.

- It took between seven and 52 days (average 19) for them to convince the staff they were well enough to be discharged.

- In a second experiment, members of a teaching hospital were told about the findings of the original study. They were warned that some pseudo-patients would be trying to gain admission during a particular three-month period.

- Each member of staff was asked to rate every new patient as an imposter or not.

- During the experimental period, 193 patients were admitted. 41 of these were confidently alleged to be imposters by at least one member of staff. 23 were suspected by one psychiatrist. A further 19 were suspected by one psychiatrist and one other staff member.

- All were genuine patients.

### ✗✓ An evaluation of labelling theory

✓ **Theoretical significance:** According to Lilienfeld (1995), Rosenhan's OBSIIP:

'. . . provides a sorely-needed reminder of the human mind's propensity to rearrange or reframe facts to achieve consistency with pre-existing beliefs . . . '

This refers to the staff's interpretation of the pseudo–patients' behaviour in terms of the diagnostic label they were given on admission.

✓ **Intuitive appeal:** Most people who've worked for any length of time in a psychiatric setting have witnessed abuses of the diagnostic process. Patients are sometimes given labels that are unjustified (Davison & Neale, 2001).

✗ **More than just a label:** Miller and Morley (1986) argue that the label 'schizophrenic' isn't just a label; there's a reality of some kind behind it. They also believe that it's a mistake to argue for *either* 'labelling' *or* 'mental illness' (it's a false dichotomy).

✗ **Why is the label applied in the first place?** Labelling theory and Rosenhan's study have usefully highlighted how people labelled as mentally ill are treated. But they cannot account for why someone begins to show deviant behaviour in the first place (MacLeod, 1998). Also, if diagnostic labels are really so powerful, why were the genuine patients in Rosenhan's study not deceived by them? The pseudo-patients' actual behaviour seemed to have been more powerful than whatever adverse effects the labels may have exerted on these observers' perceptions (Lilienfeld, 1995).

**✓•✗ Just how sticky are psychiatric labels?** Neisser (1973) supports Rosenhan's claim that psychiatric labels are 'irreversible'. Instead of the pseudo-patients being discharged with a diagnosis of 'normal' or 'normal: initial diagnosis in error', they were given the discharge diagnosis of 'schizophrenia in remission'. It's almost as if the psychiatrist can never be wrong ('heads I win, tails you lose'). But Lilienfeld argues that 'schizophrenia in remission' conveys useful information. Schizophrenia tends to be a chronic disorder, which often recurs after periods of remission. 'In remission' indicates the increased risk of subsequent episodes.

**✗ Historical relativity:** According to MacLeod (1998), labelling theory is an example of a theory that fitted the practices of a particular place and time. For example, it seems to be especially applicable to *involuntary* hospital admissions. When Scheff conducted his research in the 1960s, 90% of all psychiatric admissions were involuntary. When Bean (1979) replicated Scheff's study in the UK, the figure was only 18%. Not only will there be national and cultural differences in admission rates, but the USA figure is likely to have fallen in that time.

**✓•✗ Cultural relativity:** Labelling theory implies that definitions of abnormality will vary across cultures, reflecting different social norms and values. For example, the only difference between the visions of a shaman and the hallucinations of a diagnosed schizophrenic is that shamans are perceived by their culture as wise.

Murphy (1976) studied the Eskimo and Yoruba peoples. Contrary to labelling theory, both cultures have a concept of being crazy that's quite similar to our definition of schizophrenia. The Eskimo's *nuthkavihak* includes talking to oneself, refusing to talk, delusional beliefs and bizarre behaviour. The Yoruba's *were* encompasses similar symptoms. Both cultures also have shamans, but they draw a clear line between their behaviour and that of crazy people.

# EXAM tips BOX

**Describe and evaluate *one* biological (e.g. genetics, biochemistry) explanation of schizophrenia. (30 marks) (40 mins) (800 words minimum) AO1/AO2**

*This essay can be split up into FOUR sections – each about 200 words long. Each section would be worth approx. 7–8 marks.*

**Section 1:** A **description** of the main characteristics of schizophrenia. *A word of warning*: You're only describing the symptoms, sub-types, diagnostic criteria and so on, as these are relevant to describing (AO1) and evaluating (AO2) your chosen biological explanation. For example, the distinction between positive and negative symptoms is important for evaluating both the dopamine hypothesis and the genetic theory, as is the heterogeneity of the disorder.

**AO1**

**Section 2:** A **description** of some of the evidence for your chosen explanation. This can include not just the findings of specific studies, but also an account of the methods used to gather the evidence. So in the case of the genetic theory, you could describe family resemblance, and twin and adoption studies, as well as summarising the results of one or more of these.

**AO1**

**Section 3:** You should **analyse** and **evaluate** your chosen explanation. You might consider the strengths and weaknesses of the methods described in section 2, questioning the conclusions that have been drawn from them. For example, when evaluating the dopamine hypothesis, you could query the logic of inferring that schizophrenia is an effect of too much dopamine, rather than a cause. You could evaluate the findings in terms of the positive/negative symptoms distinction, as well as the general heterogeneity of schizophrenia. For example, because schizophrenia is so diverse, it's unlikely that a single explanation could account for all sub-types and symptoms.

**AO2**

**Section 4:** Your **analysis** and **evaluation** could then extend to considering other explanations. For example, a genetic theory is all very well, but how do genes (even if specific genes for schizophrenia had been identified) make you schizophrenic? A biochemical explanation (such as the dopamine hypothesis) *complements* a genetic one, because genes are expressed through biochemical processes. Also, a 'standard' criticism of biological explanations is that they completely overlook the role of social and cultural influences. This is where the *diathesis–stress model* is so useful for AO2 purposes. The genetic or biochemical evidence may address only the diathesis (predisposition) half of the equation. The other half requires psychological factors. (This applies equally to a question that requires you to describe and evaluate a psychological explanation – and it also applies to other disorders.)

**AO2**

*Try to answer this question yourself. There's a sample answer on page 427 with which you can compare your answer.*

# Depression

## The clinical characteristics of depression

> **Specification Hint:** The Specification states 'Clinical characteristics of depression (e.g. bipolar disorder, unipolar disorder) ... '. You need to know about only one of these. We shall concentrate on unipolar disorder, although it's useful to know how this differs from bipolar.

- Depression is one of the *mood* (or *affective*) *disorders*. These involve a prolonged and fundamental disturbance of mood and emotions.
- When depression (major depressive disorder) occurs on its own, it's referred to as *unipolar disorder*.
- Mania (manic disorder) usually occurs in conjunction with depression (when it's called *bipolar disorder*). But in the rare cases in which mania occurs alone, 'bipolar' is also used. Most patients with mania eventually develop a depressive disorder (Gelder *et al.*, 1999). Strictly, mania on its own and mixed episodes of both mania and depression are called 'Bipolar 1'. 'Bipolar 2' refers to major depression combined with *hypomania* (less extreme than full-blown mania).
- *'Manic–depressive'* refers to both the unipolar and bipolar forms of affective disorder. Bipolar disorder is much less common than unipolar, occurring in fewer than 10 per 1,000, usually before age 50. Each episode lasts about three months (Gelder *et al.*, 1999).

- Bipolar 1 (mixed episodes of mania and depression) is more common than either Bipolar 1 (mania alone) or Bipolar 2 (depression and hypomania). It affects about 1% of the population, usually first appears in the twenties, and occurs equally often in men and women.

## Unipolar (depressive) disorder (UDD)

- Depression represents the complete reverse of mania (see below).
- The depressed person experiences a general slowing down and loss of energy and enthusiasm for life.
- UDD may begin at any time from adolescence onwards, with the average age of onset being the late twenties. The age of onset has decreased over the past 50 years as the prevalence has increased. With treatment, each episode lasts two to three months, but six months or longer if untreated.
- It affects 20–30 men per 1,000, but 40–90 per 1,000 women. One exception to this general rule is that Jewish men and women are about equally likely to be diagnosed with depression. Jewish men are also more likely to be diagnosed with depression than other male groups (Levav *et al.*, 1997).
- About 10% of patients eventually commit suicide (Gelder *et al.*, 1999).

---

**Table 14.6** Symptoms of clinical depression (major depressive disorder) (based on Spitzer *et al.*, 1978)

*In order to be said to be suffering from clinical depression, a person should have experienced a number of the following symptoms together over a period of time.*

**A** Persistent low mood (for at least two weeks)

**plus**

**B** At least five of the following symptoms:
1. Poor appetite or weight loss or increased appetite or weight gain (change of 1lb a week over several weeks or 10lb in a year when not dieting).
2. Sleep difficulty, or sleeping too much.
3. Loss of energy, fatiguability or tiredness.
4. Body slowed down or agitated (not mere subjective feeling of restlessness or being slowed down, but observable by others).
5. Loss of interest or pleasure in usual activities, including social contact or sex.
6. Feelings of self-reproach, excessive or inappropriate guilt.
7. Complaints or evidence of diminished ability to think or concentrate (such as slowed thinking or indecisiveness).
8. Recurrent thoughts of death or suicide, or any suicidal behaviour.

---

- According to Davison and Neale (2001), there's no question that these are the major symptoms of depression. What's controversial is whether a patient with five symptoms for a two-week duration is distinctly different from one who, say, has only three for 10 days. If one twin has been diagnosed with depression, co-twins with fewer than five symptoms for less than two weeks are also likely to be diagnosed with depression. Also, such patients are likely to have recurrences (Kendler & Gardner, 1998). Davison and Neale argue that these findings show that:

> '... depression seems to exist on a continuum of severity, and the DSM diagnostic criteria identify patients at a relatively severe end of the continuum.'

## Manic disorder (mania)

- Mania is a sense of intense euphoria or elation. A characteristic symptom is a 'flight of ideas': ideas come rushing into the person's mind with little apparent logical connection, and there's a tendency to pun and play with words.
- Manics have a great deal of energy and rush around, usually achieving little and not putting their energies to good use. They need very little sleep.
- They may appear excessively conceited ('grandiose ideas' or delusions).
- They display *disinhibition*, which may take the form of a vastly increased sexual appetite (usually

out of keeping with their 'normal' personality), or going on spending sprees and building up large debts.

## ARE THERE DIFFERENT KINDS OF DEPRESSION?

- According to Claridge and Davis (2003), mood disorders and anxiety disorders (see below) have much in common:

(a) they occur much more frequently than other (types of) disorder
(b) their symptoms are much more continuous with normal personality
(c) there's considerable symptom overlap between them (such as a focus on negative and threatening events and stimuli). It's even been proposed that there should be a new DSM category, namely 'Mixed Anxiety–Depression' (MAD). Many patients with severe psychological impairment don't necessarily meet the full diagnostic criteria for either anxiety or depressive disorder
(d) according to DSM, 80–90% of depressed patients have symptoms associated with anxiety disorders (such as poor concentration, sleep disturbance, loss of energy, irritability, health worries and panic attacks). Conversely, 'depressed mood' is an associated feature of all anxiety disorders
(e) stress is an important causal factor in both, as well as a consequence of both.

- The idea that 'depression' may actually comprise a cluster of loosely-connected, distinct disorders has been around since the early 1900s. Claridge and Davis claim there are at least two quite distinct forms of depression:

(a) *melancholic type*, characterised by profound anhedonia (the inability to find pleasure in life), associated with apathy, inactivity, excessive sleeping and severely depressed mood. They cannot feel better even temporarily when something good happens
(b) *agitated type*, characterised by difficulty in recovering from emotionally-stressful events, and obvious signs of anxiety and restlessness.

### Endogenous vs exogenous depression

- A distinction deeply embedded within psychiatric thinking is that between *endogenous* ('from the inside') and *reactive* (or 'exogenous', 'from the outside') depression.
- 'Endogenous' referred to depression arising from biochemical disturbances in the brain. 'Reactive' was seen as being caused by stressful life experiences. These were also classified as psychotic and neurotic depression respectively, implying that the former is much more serious.
- But the distinction is controversial. According to Gelder *et al.* (1999), both types of cause are present in every case, and there appears to be a continuum of severity (as opposed to distinct patterns: see above). Champion (2000) believes that endogenous depression can no longer be defined in terms of the absence of external causes, but by the *presence* of more severe symptoms.

### The heterogeneity of mood disorders

- As with schizophrenia, people with the same unipolar (or bipolar) diagnosis can vary greatly from one another. For example, some bipolar patients experience the full range of symptoms of both mania and depression almost every day (a *mixed episode*). Others have symptoms of only one or the other during any one episode (Davison & Neale, 2001).
- Some depressed patients may be diagnosed as having psychotic features if they're prone to delusions and hallucinations. The presence of delusions seems to be a useful distinction among people with unipolar depression (and this was seen as a characteristic of endogenous depression: see above). Such patients don't respond well to the usual anti-depressants. But they do respond favourably to a combination of anti-depressants and anti-psychotics. This is more severe than depression without delusions, and involves more social impairment and less time between episodes (Coryell *et al.*, 1994).
- According to DSM, both bipolar and unipolar can be sub-diagnosed as *seasonal* if there's a regular relationship between an episode and a particular time of the year (see Chapter 10, page 238).

- In England, a woman is about 40% more likely to be admitted to a psychiatric hospital than a man. However, as in other countries, rates of hospitalisation rise rapidly among the elderly and women outnumber men by 2:1 in the elderly population (75 and over).

## Box 14.3  Are women naturally disposed towards depression?

- A popular and widely-held view is that women are naturally more emotional than men, and so are more vulnerable to emotional upsets. Hormonal fluctuations associated with the menstrual cycle, childbirth, the menopause and oral contraceptives have all been proposed as the mechanism which might account for the sex difference (Cochrane, 1995).
- Cochrane believes that there's no evidence that biochemical or physiological changes involved in the menopause, for example, have any direct effect on psychological functioning. The hormonal changes of the menstrual cycle may not be sufficient on their own to cause clinical depression. But they may tend to reactivate memories and feelings from a previous period of major depression (caused by other factors) (Williams & Hargreaves, 1995).
- According to Callaghan and O'Carroll (1993), some studies suggest that one in 10 women who've just given birth is sufficiently depressed to need medical or psychological help (*mood disorder with post-partum onset/post-natal depression*). But no specific causal hormonal abnormality has been identified. Social factors may be just as important as physical ones, such as her adjustment to a new role and the attention being diverted from her to the baby.
- Hormonal changes cannot explain why the discrepancy in the female/male rates of depression is so large or why only *some* women are affected. One study found that when women who've recently given birth are compared with a sample of non-pregnant women of the same age, depression rates were very similar (8.7 and 9.9% respectively) (Cooper *et al.*, 1988, in Cochrane, 1995). Not only does the risk of depression *not* increase following childbirth; childbirth seems to be good for you!
- Cochrane identifies a number of *non-biological explanations* of women's greater susceptibility to depression:
  (a)  girls are very much more likely to be abused, particularly sexually, than boys, and victims of abuse are at least twice as likely to suffer clinical depression in adulthood as non-victims. Abuse alone could account for the female/male difference in depression
  (b)  a woman's acceptance of the traditional female gender role involves accepting that she'll have relatively little control over her life. This may contribute to *learned helplessness*, which has been used to account for the development of depression (see text below)
  (c)  the female/male difference in the rate of depression is at its greatest between the ages of 20 and 50. Most women will experience marriage, childbearing, motherhood and the 'empty-nest' syndrome during these years. Being a full-time mother (especially of young children) and wife, and not having paid employment outside the home, are increasingly being seen as risk factors for depression. This is especially true if individuals lack an intimate, confiding relationship (Brown & Harris, 1978)
  (d)  Cochrane (1983) argues that depression may be seen as a coping strategy that's available to women. This contrasts with those of men (such as alcohol, drugs and their work). It's more acceptable for women to admit to psychological symptoms, which may represent a means of changing an intolerable situation. But Callaghan and O'Carroll (1993) warn that:

'Unhappiness about their domestic, social, and political circumstances lies at the root of many women's concerns. This unhappiness must not be medicalized and regarded as a "female malady" ...'

- When admission rates for other categories of disorder are taken into account (such as the very similar rates between males and females for schizophrenia), it's depression that contributes most to the high overall rate of treated mental illness among women (Cochrane, 1995). There are no sex differences in the rate of bipolar disorder (Strickland, 1992). But (as we saw above) women are two to three times more likely to be diagnosed with unipolar disorder than men (Williams & Hargreaves, 1995).

## Explanations of unipolar (depressive) disorder

> **Specification Hint:** The Specification states: '... Biological (e.g. genetics, biochemistry) and psychological (e.g. learned helplessness) explanations of depression, including the evidence on which they are based'. As with schizophrenia, you need to know about only *one* explanation of each type. Again, as with schizophrenia, different biological and psychological explanations are overlapping, and it's useful for analysis and evaluation (AO2) to be familiar with more than one. Box 14.3 indicates some of the major (kinds of) explanation of UDD. Although this was looking specifically at gender differences in depression, the points raised can be used for AO2 analysis and evaluation.

## Biological explanations

### THE ROLE OF GENETIC FACTORS

- *First-degree relatives* (parents, siblings and children) of severely depressed patients have a higher risk of affective disorders (10–15%) than the general population (1–2%). This increased risk is even higher among relatives of patients with early onset. But curiously, among first-degree relatives of patients with bipolar disorder, there are more cases of UDD than bipolar disorder (Davison & Neale, 2001).
- Concordance for bipolar disorder (about 70%) is the same among MZs reared together or apart. This compares with 23% for DZs.
- Adoption studies confirm the importance of genetic factors. The natural parents of adoptees with a bipolar disorder have a higher rate of affective disorder than do natural parents of adoptees without bipolar disorder (Gelder *et al.*, 1999).
- Genetic factors in UDD seem to be less decisive than in bipolar disorder. Also, there's some evidence that genetic factors are more important in women than in men (Davison & Neale, 2001: but see Box 14.3 above).

### NEUROCHEMICAL EXPLANATIONS

#### The monoamine hypothesis (MAOH)

- Serotonin (5-HT), norepinephrine (noradrenaline) and dopamine are collectively known as *monoamine oxidase* (MAO) *transmitters*. By far the most studied of these is 5-HT (Claridge & Davis, 2003).
- According to the monoamine hypothesis (MAOH), a depletion of serotonin, noradrenaline and/or dopamine underlies the melancholic symptoms of depression. High levels induce mania.
- The supporting evidence is based largely on working backwards from what's known about the mechanisms of drugs which either induce or reduce depressive symptoms.
- It was discovered in the mid-1950s that depression was a common side-effect of reserpine, one of the first effective drugs for treating high blood pressure. It was known that reserpine reduced the levels of brain 5-HIAA (a chemical produced when 5-HT is broken down).
- Also in the 1950s, tricyclics and monoamine oxidase inhibitors (MAOIs) were found to be effective in relieving depression.
- *Tricyclics* prevent some of the re-uptake of both noradrenaline and serotonin (see Box 14.1, page 394). This leaves more of the transmitter in the synaptic gap, making transmission of the next nerve impulse easier.
- The newest anti-depressants are called *serotonin re-uptake inhibitors* (SRIs), because they act

more selectively on serotonin. (This is why they're sometimes called SSRIs – *specific serotonin re-uptake inhibitors*.) They raise levels of serotonin (5-HT) and have a well-established anti-depressant effect. Examples are fluoxetine (most familiarly marketed as Prozac®). Because SRIs are effective in treating UDD, a stronger link has been established between low levels of 5-HT and depression (Davison & Neale, 2001; Gelder *et al.*, 1999).

- MAOIs prevent the enzyme monoamine oxidase (MAO) from breaking down the neurotransmitters (see Box 14.1). This increases the levels of both 5-HT and noradrenaline in the brain. Like the tri-cyclics, this compensates for the abnormally low levels of these in depressed people.

 An evaluation of the MAOH

✓ **Theoretical importance:** The MAOH is the longest-standing and most persistent biological theory of depression (Claridge & Davis, 2003).

✗ **The delayed benefits of anti-depressants:** It's known that all the main anti-depressants have an immediate effect on the levels of 5-HT and noradrenaline in the brain. But it sometimes take up to 7–14 days for them to have any noticeable effect on patients' symptoms. It seems that by the time the drugs begin to 'work', the neurotransmitter levels have returned to their previous state. So a simple increase in neurotransmitter levels isn't a sufficient explanation for why the drugs alleviate depression (Davison & Neale, 2001).

✓•✗ **Indirect support:** An indirect way of testing the role of 5-HT is to measure concentrations of a particular *metabolite*. This is a by-product of the breakdown of the neurotransmitters found in urine, blood serum and cerebro-spinal fluid (CSF). These are found to be lower in patients with depression, especially in those who commit violent suicide (Claridge & Davis, 2003). But this could be the result of many different kinds of biochemical abnormality. Also, the lower concentrations probably aren't a direct indication of levels of either 5-HT or noradrenaline *in the brain*. Metabolites measured this way could reflect neurotransmitters anywhere in the body (Davison & Neale, 2001).

✗ **Lack of support from more direct measures:** A more direct test comes from experimental depletion studies involving normal participants. When they are given drugs which reduce levels of 5-HT and noradrenaline in the brain, these people *don't* usually experience depressive symptoms (Claridge & Davis, 2003). Nor do the symptoms of unmedicated depressed patients become worse (Delgado, 2000).

## Psychological explanations

### THE INFLUENCE OF CULTURE

- There are an estimated 340 million people world-wide affected by depressive disorders. This makes it the most common of all mental disorders (Lyddy, 2000).
- According to Price and Crapo (1999), various researchers have denied the presence of native con-cepts of depression among groups as diverse as the Nigerians, Chinese, Canadian Inuit (Eskimos), Japanese, Malaysians and the Hopi Native Americans. Price and Crapo ask:

'... If depression, as currently defined in Western culture and psychiatric diagnosis, is not found in non-Western cultures, how do we know that "depression" is not merely a Western folk-concept, analogous to other culture-specific conditions, such as *koro*, *kayak-angst*, *amok*, or *susto*?'

These are all examples of *culture-bound syndromes* (CBSs). A large number of studies have found that, in a wide variety of non-Western cultures, there are apparently unique ways of 'being mad' (Berry *et al.*,1992). In other words, there are forms of abnormality that aren't easily accommodated by the categories of DSM or ICD. For example, *koro* refers to an acute panic/anxiety reaction to the belief, in a man, that his penis will suddenly withdraw into his abdomen. In a woman, the fear is that her breast, labia, or vulva will retract into her body. Koro is reported in south-east Asia, south

China, and India. The assumption made is that mental disorders in the West are *culturally neutral*, and only CBSs show the influence of culture (Fernando, 1991).

- According to Kaiser *et al*. (1998), DSM-IV recognises the vital role of culture in the expression and diagnosis of disorders. It encourages clinicians to keep cultural considerations in mind when assessing patients. In the section dealing with depression, conditions which appear most often in specific cultures are outlined, as well as cultural variations in the manifestation of symptoms. For example, in some cultures people tend to present with *somatic* complaints (such as aches and pains), while in others *affective* symptoms are more common (such as sadness). The task of the clinician is to take the norms of the individual patient's cultural reference group into account, while at the same time avoiding cultural stereotypes (Kaiser *et al*., 1998).

## COGNITIVE EXPLANATIONS

### Beck's theory of depression

- Beck's (1967b, 1987) central idea is that depressed individuals feel as they do because their thinking is dominated by *negative schemas*. This is a tendency to see the world negatively, which is triggered whenever the person encounters new conditions that resemble in some way the conditions in which the schemas were originally learned (usually in childhood and adolescence).
- These negative schemas fuel and are fuelled by certain cognitive biases, which cause the person to misperceive reality. So (a) an *ineptness schema* can make depressed people expect to fail most of the time; (b) a *self-blame schema* makes them feel responsible for all misfortunes; and (c) a *negative self-evaluation schema* constantly reminds them of their worthlessness. The main specific cognitive biases are described in Box 14.4.

### Box 14.4 The main cognitive biases in Beck's theory of depression

- *Arbitrary inference:* a conclusion drawn in the absence of sufficient evidence – or any evidence at all. For example, a man concludes that he's worthless because it's raining the day he's hosting an outdoor party.
- *Selective abstraction:* a conclusion drawn on the basis of just one of many elements in a situation. For example, a worker feels worthless when a product doesn't work, even though she's only one of several people who contributed to making it.
- *Overgeneralisation:* an overall sweeping conclusion drawn on the basis of a single, perhaps trivial, event. For example, a student regards his poor performance in a single class on one particular day as final proof of his worthlessness and stupidity.
- *Magnification and minimisation:* exaggerations in evaluation performance. For example, a man believes that he's completely ruined his car (*magnification*) when he sees a small scratch on the rear bumper. A woman believes herself to be worthless (*minimisation*) despite a succession of praiseworthy achievements.

(Based on Davison & Neale, 2001.)

- Negative schemas, together with cognitive biases or distortions, maintain the *negative triad*. This refers to negative thoughts about the self, the world and the future.

 An evaluation of Beck's theory

✓ **Major cognitive theory:** It's widely agreed that Beck's theory has been the most influential of the cognitive models of depression (that is, the view that depression is caused by how people *think*) (Champion, 2000).

✓ **More general theoretical influence:** Freud saw people as victims of their passions. The *id* is the dominant part of the personality, and the *ego* is able to exert little control over our feelings (see Chapter 12, pages 319–321). But in Beck's theory, the cause–effect relationship is reversed. Our emotional reactions are essentially a function of how we *construe* the world (interpret and predict it). Depressed people see themselves as victims, and Beck sees them as victims of their own illogical self-judgements.

✓ **Do depressed people really think as Beck maintains?** The evidence initially came from Beck's clinical observations (Beck, 1967b). Further support comes from various sources, including self-report questionnaires and laboratory studies of memory and other cognitive processes (Davison & Neale, 2001).

✗•✓ **What's cause and what's effect?** Perhaps the greatest challenge facing any cognitive theory of depression is to show that depressed people's thoughts are the *cause* of their depression rather than the effect. Many experimental studies have shown that a person's mood can be influenced by how s/he construes events. But manipulating people's affect (mood or feeling) has also been shown to change their thinking. Beck (and others) have found that depression and certain kinds of thinking are *correlated*. But a specific causal relationship cannot be determined from such data (as with all correlations: see Chapter 6). Probably the relationship works *both* ways. In recent years, Beck himself has come to this more bi-directional position. There's certainly no unequivocal support for the claim that negative thinking causes depression (Davison & Neale, 2001).

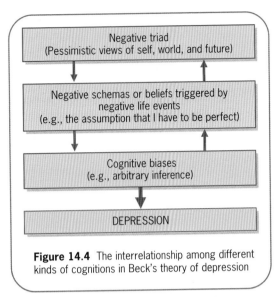

**Figure 14.4** The interrelationship among different kinds of cognitions in Beck's theory of depression

✗•✓ **How to measure cognition?** Recently researchers have recognised that the measure of cognition most widely used in Beck's theory (the Dysfunctional Attitudes Scale) is *multi-dimensional*. That is, it comprises sub-scales that assess different aspects of dysfunctional attitudes (such as a strong need to impress others and a desire to be perfect). These more specific components of dysfunctional thinking may have more success in predicting the subsequent occurrence of depression when they interact with a stressor that's specific to them, for example, a personal failure in someone with a strong need to be perfect (Davison & Neale, 2001).

✓ **Important influence on therapy:** Beck's theory has stimulated considerable research into the treatment of depression. The form of therapy based on cognitive theories in general is called *cognitive behaviour therapy* (CBT). Evidence concerning the effectiveness of Beck's form of CBT can be taken as (indirect) support for the theory it's based on. Beck (1993) reviewed its effectiveness in treating UDD (for which it was originally designed), as well as generalised anxiety disorder, panic disorder and eating disorders. These *outcome studies* show very clearly that CBT is very highly effective. CBT is also being used to treat bipolar disorder, obsessive–compulsive disorder (see below) and schizophrenia, as well as patients with HIV and cancer.

## Learned helplessness theory (LHT)

**Specification Hint:** Strictly, learned helplessness (theory) (one of the examples given) is the original of three related cognitive theories of depression. The other two, which are extensions of the original, are learned helplessness theory grafted on to attribution theory principles, and hopelessness theory. Each of the three counts as a psychological explanation of depression in its own right. So you could choose just one of these. But you probably won't know enough about any particular one. So it's probably safer to treat them as three 'prongs' of the same theory. But in your analysis and evaluation of 'learned helplessness' (AO2), you can look at specific criticisms of each one, as well as overall criticisms that apply to all three.

- The basic premise of *learned helplessness theory* (LHT) is that depression in humans is a form of *learned* helplessness (LH) (Seligman, 1974). This is based on Seligman's experiments with dogs.

**Learned helplessness in dogs** (LHID) (Seligman, 1974)

- Dogs were given inescapable electric shocks.
- Soon after receiving the first shocks, the dogs seemed to give up and passively accept the painful stimulation.
- Later, even though the shocks could now be avoided, the dogs stopped trying. Most of them lay down in a corner and whined.
- A control group, which hadn't received the inescapable shocks, learned the avoidance response relatively easily.

- On the basis of these observations, Seligman proposed that animals acquire a sense of helplessness when confronted with uncontrollable aversive stimulation. Later, this sense of helplessness impairs their performance in stressful situations that *can* be controlled. They seem to lose the ability and motivation to respond effectively to painful stimulation.
- By extension, LH could provide an explanation for at least certain forms of depression in humans. Seligman believed that, like his dogs, many depressed people appear passive in the face of stress. They fail to initiate actions that might allow them to cope. Also, like depressed people, Seligman's dogs lost their appetite and lost weight. They also showed reduced levels of noradrenaline.

 An evaluation of LHT

**Contradictory findings:** By 1978, research with humans began to reveal several inadequacies of LHT. For example, some studies indicated that helplessness sometimes actually *improves* performance. Also, many depressed people blame themselves for their failures, but this is incompatible with the claim that they see themselves as helpless. Finally, the experience of being unable to control the outcome of one particular situation (helplessness) doesn't necessarily lead to clinical depression in most people.

**There's more to depression than helplessness:** The above findings suggest very strongly that LH cannot tell the whole story.

- LHT was revised by Abramson, Seligman and Teasdale in 1978. The major change they proposed was in terms of *attribution theory principles.* When we experience failure, for example, we try to explain it (just as we try to account for our successes) – this is perfectly 'normal'. What's associated with depression is a particular *pattern* of attributions (or *attributional style*), that is, a tendency to make particular kinds of *causal inferences*, rather than others.
- The 'depressed attributional style' is based on three key dimensions, namely *locus* (whether the cause is internal or external, to do with the actor him/herself or some aspect of the situation), *stability* (whether the cause is stable or unstable, a permanent feature of the actor or something transient), and *global* or *specific* (whether the cause relates to the 'whole' person or just some particular feature or characteristic). The depressed person believes that his/her failure:
  - (a) is caused by *internal* factors ('I'm stupid')
  - (b) reflects *stable*, long-term, relatively permanent factors ('I never do well on tests or exams')
  - (c) reflects a *global*, pervasive deficiency, that is, failure applies to all or most aspects of his/her life ('I get everything wrong').

- People diagnosed as clinically depressed are more likely to show this pattern when given, for example, the *Attributional Style Questionnaire* (ASQ) (Seligman *et al.*, 1979).
- But equally important, the person who's *prone* to becoming depressed may also display this attributional style. It's believed to play a mediating role between negative life events and adverse physical and mental health outcomes. When such depression-prone people experience stressors, they're more likely to develop the symptoms of depression, and their self-esteem is shattered (Peterson & Seligman, 1984).

|  | Successes | Failures |
|---|---|---|
| **Depressed** | External Unstable Specific | Internal Stable Global |
| **Non-depressed** | Internal Stable Global | External Unstable Specific |

**Figure 14.5** Attributional styles for success and failure in depressed people (based on Abramson *et al.*, 1978; Abramson & Martin, 1981)

 An evaluation of the attributional theory

✓ **Theoretical value:** This clearly is an improvement on LHT, because it adds cognitive factors that are missing from the latter. There's a vast amount of research into attribution within social psychology, so Abramson *et al.* are drawing on a well-established research area to supplement the idea of helplessness. The concept of attributional style represents a *diathesis*, a predisposition to develop a particular mental disorder under stressful conditions (see the discussion of schizophrenia above, pages 399–401).

✓ **Empirical support:** Seligman *et al.* (1979) gave their ASQ to college students. As predicted by the theory, mildly depressed students more often attributed their failures to personal (internal), global and stable inadequacies than non-depressed students.

✗•✓ **Where does the depressive attributional style come from?** This is a problem faced by most cognitive explanations of psychopathology. In general terms, it's thought to stem from childhood experiences. But there's little empirical support for this claim. However, Rose *et al.* (1994) found that depressive attributional style is related to sexual abuse in childhood, as well as to parental over-protectiveness, harsh discipline and perfectionistic standards.

### Hopelessness theory (HT) (Abramson *et al.*, 1989)

- This is the latest version of the theory. According to HT, some forms of depression (hopelessness depression) are caused by a state of hopelessness, an expectation that desirable outcomes won't occur, or that undesirable ones will occur and that there's nothing the person can do to prevent them (that is, helplessness).
- HT proposes that there may be other diatheses in addition to attributional style. One of these is low self-esteem and a tendency to infer that negative life events will have serious negative consequences.
- Metalsky *et al.* (1993) confirmed the findings of an earlier study (Metalsky *et al.*, 1987), namely, college students who displayed a depressed attributional style in response to poor grades were more likely to experience a persistent depressed mood subsequently. But this pattern was found only among students with low self-esteem, and it was mediated by increased feelings of hopelessness.

 An evaluation of HT

✓ **Supporting evidence:** Apart from Metalsky *et al.*'s research, Davison and Neale (2001) cite a study which found identical results with 12- and 13-year-olds. They cite another study which found that depressive attributional style and low self-esteem predicted the onset of depression in adolescents.

✓ **It can account for more than just depression:** Davison and Neale point out that an advantage of HT is that it can deal directly with the co-occurrence (*comorbidity*) of depression and anxiety disorders (see above, page 406). According to Alloy *et al.* (1990), it's an expectation of helplessness that creates anxiety. When this expectation becomes certain, a syndrome with elements of both depression and anxiety is triggered. If the person believes that negative events are certain and inevitable, hopelessness develops.

✗ **Is it circular?** It could be argued that all HT is saying is that 'hopelessness depression' is caused by 'hopelessness'.

✗✓ **An overall evaluation of helplessness/hopelessness theories**

- Davison and Neale (2001) point out some general problems with all three helplessness-related theories:

✗ **Which type of depression is being explained?** Seligman (1974) was originally trying to explain the similarity between LH and what used to be called reactive depression (see above, page 406). Abramson *et al.* (1989) talk about a hopelessness depression, which refers both to the presumed cause of the depression and to a set of symptoms that don't quite match the DSM criteria.

✗ **Biased samples and inappropriate measures of depression:** Some research has been conducted with clinical populations (people actually diagnosed as having a depressive disorder) (such as Abramson *et al.*, 1978). But many studies have involved college students selected on the basis of the Beck Depression Inventory (BDI) or have simply tried to predict increases in BDI scores. But the BDI wasn't designed to diagnose depression, only to assess its severity among those already diagnosed. Selecting people based on raised BDI scores doesn't produce a group of people that is comparable to those with clinical depression. For example, high scorers have been found to score much lower when re-tested two to three weeks later. Also, the finding that the ASQ can predict BDI scores doesn't necessarily mean that it can predict the onset of actual clinical depression.

✗ **Are the findings specifically about depression?** We've already noted the comorbidity of depression and anxiety. We need to be sure that the theories are truly about depression, rather than about negative affect in general. Depressive attributional style seems to be related to anxiety and general distress, as well as depression.

✗ **Is the depressive attributional style stable?** A key assumption is that the depressive attributional style is a persistent part of the make-up of the depressed person. As a diathesis, it must be 'in place' before the person experiences some stressor. But Hamilton and Abramson (1983) showed that it disappears following a depressive episode.

- Despite these problems, Davison and Neale conclude that these theories have clearly stimulated a great deal of research and theorising about depression. This is likely to continue for many years to come.

## EXAM tips BOX

**Describe and evaluate *one* psychological explanation (e.g. learned helplessness) of depression. (30 marks) (40 mins) (800 words minimum) AO1/AO2**

*This essay can be split up into FOUR sections – each about 200 words long. Each section would be worth approx. 7–8 marks.*

**Section 1:** A **description** of the main characteristics of depression. *A word of warning*: as with schizophrenia, you're only doing this to the extent that it's relevant to describing and evaluating your chosen explanation. For example, you'd expect unipolar and bipolar disorders to be explained in different ways. So you need to make this distinction, then make it clear how your chosen explanation relates to it. You might consider the distinction between reactive (neurotic) and endogenous (psychotic) depression in relation to your chosen explanation.

**Section 2:** A **description** of some of the evidence for your chosen explanation. You might also want to describe some of the methods used to collect this evidence. For example, if you chose learned helplessness, you would want to describe:

* LHID (Seligman, 1974)

which involved experimental studies of dogs, combined with observations about the characteristics of depressed humans. Developments of LHT (the introduction of attribution principles, and hopelessness theory) have been tested using rating scales and the Beck Depression Inventory (BDI) with mainly college students. As we noted in the Specification Hint box, page 411, each of these three theories is, strictly, a separate explanation. But it's probably safer to treat them as three aspects of the same overall theory.

**Section 3:** You should **analyse** and **evaluate** your chosen explanation. If you choose LH, you could consider specific criticisms of each 'mini' theory', as well as criticisms that apply to all three. For example, Seligman's original theory was based on experiments with dogs, so applying this directly to depressed humans was bound to be an incomplete explanation. More generally, the biased samples used to test the later theories, as well as the use of the BDI to select them, represents serious methodological limitations to the evidence.

**Section 4:** Your **analysis** and **evaluation** could then extend to other theories. For example, Beck's theory was intended to explain depression specifically (which LHT clearly wasn't), and it grew out of his clinical work with depressed patients. Arguably, this makes it more valid than theories which were based originally on experiments with dogs (it certainly has more 'face validity'). The attributional style of depressed people represents a diathesis, so you could consider LH in the context of the diathesis–stress model. Biological explanations may account for different diatheses, and social/cultural factors that account for women's greater susceptibility to depression may provide important 'stress' factors.

*Try to answer this question yourself. There's a sample essay on page 428 with which you can compare your essay.*

AO1

↓

AO1

↓

AO2

↓

AO2

## Anxiety disorders

**Specification Hint:** The Specification states 'Clinical characteristics of *one* anxiety disorder (e.g. post-traumatic stress disorder, phobic disorders, obsessive–compulsive disorder) . . .'. While any one of these would do, we've chosen obsessive–compulsive disorder (OCD), partly because treatments overlap to some degree with treatments for depression. In turn, this relates to explanations of OCD.

* Of all forms of psychological distress, emotional disturbances are perhaps the most common (Lilienfeld, 1998), and '. . . Fear is a core emotion in psychopathology' (LeDoux, 1998).
* *Anxiety* (a brooding fear of what might happen) was a central feature of Freud's psychoanalytic theory (LeDoux, 1998: see Chapters 12 and 18). But many psychologists have argued that *fear* is a fundamentally *adaptive reaction* to stressors (specifically, threat), since it increases alertness and

vigilance (see Chapter 3). Fear is generally considered abnormal only when it's disproportionate to objective circumstances. It probably evolved as an alarm signal to warn organisms of potential danger. But some people tend to feel afraid even when there's no (objective) threat present (i.e. anxiety). These 'false alarms' are what we call anxiety disorders.

## Characteristics of obsessive–compulsive disorder (OCD)

- *Obsessions* are recurrent, unwanted, intrusive thoughts or images that don't feel voluntarily controlled. They're experienced as morally repugnant or intensely distressing.
- They mostly have sexual, blasphemous or aggressive themes (see Box 14.5). For example, it's not uncommon for deeply religious people to have repeated blasphemous thoughts, such as 'God doesn't exist', or for caring parents to have thoughts of harming their children.
- Such obsessions are resisted by being ignored or suppressed, or by 'neutralising' them with some other thought or action (Shafran, 1999). These may include compulsions.
- *Compulsions* are actions which the person feels compelled to repeat over and over again, according to rituals or rules.
- Obsessions and compulsions are often related, but they can occur separately (again, see Box 14.5).

### Box 14.5 Obsession without the compulsion (Sutherland, 1976)

An example of an obsession occurring without compulsive behaviour is sexual jealousy. An extreme case is described by Stuart Sutherland in *Breakdown* (1976).

Sutherland was a well-known British experimental psychologist who'd been happily married for several years when his wife suddenly revealed she'd been having an affair (but had no wish to end their marriage). At first, he was able to accept the situation, and found that the increased honesty and communication actually improved their marriage.

But after asking his wife for further details of the affair, he became obsessed with vivid images of his wife in moments of sexual passion with her lover. He couldn't remove these thoughts from his mind, day or night.

Finally, he had to leave his teaching and research duties. It was only after several months of trying various forms of therapy that he managed to reduce the obsessive thoughts sufficiently to be able to return to work.

- When obsessions and compulsions occur together, the latter represent an attempt to counteract the former. For example, compulsive hand-washing may be an attempt to remove the obsessive preoccupation with contamination by dirt or germs, either as agent or victim. The person recognises that the compulsive act is unreasonable and excessive, but it's also seen as purposeful. Their function is to prevent a dreaded event and reduce distress.
- Many patients find the need to perform the compulsion distressing in itself. They're frustrated by the time it takes to complete it 'correctly' and how it interferes with normal social and work functioning.
- Shafran (1999) gives the example of a man obsessed with the thought that he'd contracted AIDS from sitting next to someone who looked unkempt. In response to this, he repeatedly checked his body for signs of illness and washed his hands whenever he had an intrusive image of this person. When outside, he'd continually check around him to see if there were any discarded tissues that might carry the HIV virus. This became so laborious that he stayed indoors for much of the time. Any interruption to the checking and washing resulted in the entire routine starting again.
- Until quite recently, OCD was regarded as a rare disorder (affecting less than 0.5% of the population). But it's now the fourth most common disorder, and lifetime prevalence is at least 3% in females and 2% in males. In the UK, an estimated one to one-and-a-half million people suffer from OCD. According to Claridge and Davis (2003), it's still often under-diagnosed and under-treated in most populations. Between a third and a half of patients experienced their first symptoms during childhood, but it mostly goes unnoticed then.

- It usually begins in early adulthood, but begins earlier in males. Women have more contamination and aggressive obsessions, and tend to display more cleaning rituals. Men's obsessions are more likely to concern symmetry and order, exactness, and sex, and they're most likely to be hoarders.
- Some people have questioned whether OCD should be classified as an anxiety disorder at all. Indeed, in ICD-10 it's listed separately from anxiety disorders. Others have suggested that anxiety is a *product* of the distressing and disabling symptoms (*not* a cause).
- Like other disorders, its clinical features are *heterogeneous*. In other words, individuals with OCD may differ considerably from one another. Any one individual may have one (but typically several) of a variety of symptoms, in varying degrees and combinations. Earlier attempts to deal with this variability led to the identification of 'washers' and 'checkers'. It was thought that all patients fell into one category or the other. But now there are at least four or five primary recognised dimensions: *symmetry and ordering*, *hoarding*, *contamination and cleaning*, *aggressive obsessions and checking*, and *sexual and religious obsessions* (Claridge & Davis, 2003).
- OCD has always been firmly embedded within the 'neurotic' disorders (see above, page 387). This is because of the assumption that patients recognise the excessive and unreasonable nature of their obsessions and compulsions (they have *insight*). But OCD patients display varying degrees of insight. In about 10% of cases, they seem to lack insight altogether. Their thinking begins to resemble delusions (more 'psychotic'). They may be diagnosed as schizophrenic, simply 'psychotic, 'schizo–obsessive subtype', or 'delusional disorder or psychotic disorder not otherwise specified' (Claridge & Davis, 2003). A key factor that distinguishes OCD patients with delusions from psychotics is the clear and logical link between the OCD patient's delusional thoughts and the compulsions they induce (O'Dwyer & Marks, 2000).

## Box 14.6  Body dysmorphic disorder (BDD)

- **Morselli (1886) introduced the term *dysmorphophobia* (from the Greek *dysmorphia*, meaning 'ugliness of the face'). He defined it as the subjective feeling of ugliness and of a physical defect, despite a normal appearance, and an associated feeling of shame.**
- **It was first called *body dysmorphic disorder* in DSM-III-R (1987), and appears in both DSM-IV and ICD-10, where it's classified as a hypochondriacal disorder. But according to Sobanski and Schmidt (2000), some recent researchers have classified it as an 'obsessive-compulsive spectrum disorder'. The characteristic feature is an intense preoccupation with an imagined or real, but minor, defect of physical appearance. This concern becomes so overwhelming that it causes clinically significant distress and impairment in social, occupational and other important areas of functioning.**
- **Any part of the body can be involved, but most commonly anxiety centres on the face and hair abnormalities – like thinning or fear of going bald. Unlike patients with eating disorders (see Chapter 4), BDD patients *don't* have a disturbed body image as a whole.**
- **Their preoccupations are often experienced as repetitive, intrusive thoughts associated with anxiety and distress (as in OCD). Most BDD patients perform ritualised behaviours resembling OCD compulsions, such as mirror-checking, grooming behaviours and compulsive skin-picking.**
- **BDD is treated with a range of treatments, including drugs and psychological therapies. But patients also elect to have cosmetic surgery. Typically, the initial feelings of happiness are replaced by a shifting of their symptoms to another body part, some patients undergoing multiple operations.**

## Explanations of OCD

> **Specification Hint:** The Specification states ' . . . Biological (e.g. genetics, biochemistry) and psychological (e.g. conditioning) explanations of the chosen disorder, including the evidence on which they are based'. As with schizophrenia and depression, you need to know about only *one* explanation of each kind. But, as before, it's useful to be familiar with more than one for purposes of analysis and evaluation (AO2).

## Biological explanations

### BRAIN NEUROPATHOLOGY

- Encephalitis, head injuries and brain tumours are all associated with the development of OCD (Jenike, 1986).
- Several models of OCD all predict, in one way or another, the involvement of the pre-frontal cortex (PFC), the basal ganglia and the limbic system. The basal ganglia comprise the caudate, putamen, globus pallidus and the amygdala. These are linked to the control of motor behaviour. Focus on the basal ganglia is due to their relevance to compulsions, as well as the relationship between OCD and Tourette's Syndrome. The vocal and motor tics characteristic of Tourette's are linked to basal ganglia dysfunction. Tourette's patients also often have OCD (Sheppard *et al.*, 1999).
- The PFC has direct links with the basal ganglia via its connections with the limbic system. It also receives signals *from* these sub-cortical structures. So there are connections between the PFC and the sub-cortical areas which pass through the limbic system.
- According to Saxena *et al.*(1998), the function of all the *direct* pathways between the PFC and basal ganglia is to execute 'pre-packaged' complex responses to 'socio-territorial' stimuli. These refer to things that are highly significant to the organism's survival (such as hygiene, sex, safety, keeping things in order). These need to be performed quickly in order to be adaptive. Also, they must operate to the exclusion of other interfering stimuli.
- The activation of these direct pathways tends to pin or rivet the execution of the behaviour until the attentional need to do so has passed.
- Part of the function of the *indirect* pathways is to inhibit or suppress the direct pathways when it's appropriate to switch to another behaviour. This is something that OCD patients have trouble doing.
- Normally, socio-territorial concerns pass through the direct pathway and are inhibited by the indirect pathway relatively quickly. But in OCD patients, excess activation of the direct pathway causes fixation with these concerns. The indirect pathway is too weak to 'turn off' the signal from the direct pathway. So the socio-territorial concerns are experienced by the individual as repetitive, intrusive obsessions.

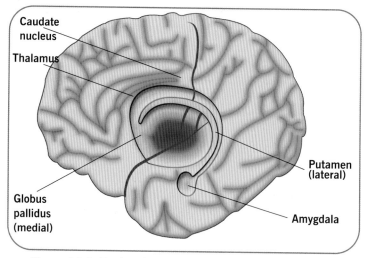

**Figure 14.6** The basal ganglia

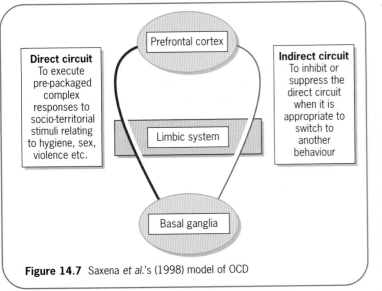

**Figure 14.7** Saxena *et al.*'s (1998) model of OCD

- So Saxena *et al.*'s model proposes a substantial imbalance between the direct and indirect pathway. This causes a response bias towards socio-territorial stimuli. See Figure 14.7.

An evaluation of Saxena *et al.*'s model

✓ **Consistent with neurobiological evidence:** This popular model meshes well with neurobiological evidence from various sources (Claridge & Davis, 2003). For example, brain imaging studies have consistently shown *increased* activity in the PFC (usually involving the right orbito-frontal cortex) in unmedicated OCD individuals (they display 'overheated' frontal lobes). These hyperactive areas tend to become normal when patients receive effective treatment (either drug therapy or behavioural therapy). Rauch *et al.* (1994) stimulated OCD symptoms by presenting patients with stimuli especially selected for them (such as a glove contaminated with household rubbish). This produced increased blood flow in the PFC and certain regions of the basal ganglia. Also, OCD patients have a smaller putamen than controls (Rosenberg *et al.*, 1997).

✓ **Theoretical importance:** The PFC plays an important role in assessing the behavioural significance of biologically important stimuli. So increased frontal lobe activity may relate to obsessional thinking – but not necessarily to compulsions. But the basal ganglia (and cerebellum, which stores behavioural programs such as conditioned responses) may function to control compulsive urges. People with diseases involving pathology of the basal ganglia (such as Parkinson's and Huntington's) often show compulsive symptoms similar to those of OCD patients.

## THE SEROTONIN HYPOTHESIS (SH)

- Abnormal levels of brain serotonin (5-HT) have been proposed as the cause of OCD. The SH is derived largely from the consistent finding that SRI drugs help reduce OCD symptoms. As we saw when discussing depression, SRIs prevent re-uptake of serotonin in the brain, making more available. So it's inferred from their success with OCD patients that OCD must be caused by a *deficiency* of serotonin.
- This has been confirmed by brain imaging studies. Also, there are several case reports of symptom improvement when OCD patients use hallucinogenic drugs (such as LSD). These drugs are potent stimulators of brain 5-HT. Others have reported a worsening of symptoms after patients take 5-HT antagonist drugs, that is, drugs which *reduce* 5-HT levels (Claridge & Davis, 2003).

An evaluation of the SH

✗ **Serotonin not the whole story:** Although 5-HT is clearly important in understanding the causal mechanisms of OCD, it's not the only neurotransmitter likely to be involved. Excessive *dopamine* may also play a part. For example, haloperidol (a dopamine D2 receptor antagonist) has been used for improving treatment response to SRIs. By blocking D2 receptors, the indirect pathway can better counteract the action of the direct pathway (see Saxena *et al.*'s model above) (Claridge & Davis, 2003).

✗ **Limited effectiveness of SRIs:** Many patients are only partially responsive to SRIs. Almost a third don't respond at all. A range of other 5-HT agonists (which increase 5-HT levels) also fail to improve symptoms – and some even make them worse. 5-HT depletion studies have typically shown *no* reversal of the symptom improvement induced by SRIs. This reversal is what we'd expect if OCD really is caused by too little 5-HT. (This reversal effect *is* seen consistently with depressive symptoms: see above.) Nor does 5-HT depletion have any ill-effects on unmedicated OCD patients (Claridge & Davis, 2003).

✖ Faulty logic: Just because drugs such as SRIs increase 5-HT activity and are effective in alleviating the major symptoms of OCD, it doesn't necessarily follow that the disorder is caused by an excess or depletion of that neurotransmitter. This is like saying that because taking an aspirin gets rid of a headache, headaches are caused by a deficiency of acetylsalicyclic acid (Claridge & Davis, 2003). (This same faulty logic applies, of course, to other disorders – see above.) In fact, more and more sophisticated brain imaging techniques are revealing that OCD symptoms could develop without *any* 5-HT involvement at all (Delgado & Moreno, 1998).

## Psychological explanations

### BEHAVIOURAL EXPLANATIONS

- A *behavioural* explanation would see OCD as a way of reducing anxiety. If an obsession induces anxiety, then any compulsive behaviour that alleviates the anxiety should become more likely to occur (through negative reinforcement: e.g. Rachman & Hodgson, 1980).
- Since the compulsion only provides *temporary* relief from anxiety, when it starts to increase again, the person is motivated to repeat the compulsive act.
- Paradoxically, compulsions (as well as avoidance and trying to suppress the obsession) serve to *increase* the frequency of the obsession. As Shafran (1999) says:

'. . . These obsessions subsequently increase the compulsive behaviour, leaving the person trapped in the vicious obsession–compulsion cycle . . .'

- However, this can only account for OCD's *maintenance* – not how it developed in the first place. The *superstition hypothesis* might be more relevant here.

### Box 14.7 The superstition hypothesis

- **Skinner (1948) argued that what we call 'superstition' develops as a result of a chance association between some behaviour and a reinforcer.**
- **In Skinner's experiments, pigeons were given food at regular intervals *regardless* of their behaviour. After a while, they displayed idiosyncratic movements, presumably because these were the movements they happened to be making when the food was given.**
- **This chance reinforcement of behaviour can account for many compulsive rituals (O'Leary & Wilson, 1975). For example, the rituals of soccer players may include being last onto the pitch or wearing only a particular pair of boots. Such behaviours may occur because in the past they were associated with success. If such rituals aren't enacted, anxiety is aroused.**
- **Such chance associations might explain how particular *behaviours* arise. But the development of intrusive *thoughts* are much more difficult for the behavioural model to explain.**

- Rachman and Hodgson's (1980) account explicitly proposed that it's normal for people to have intrusive thoughts. For example, it's been shown that 90% of non-patients have unwanted, intrusive thoughts with the same content as those of people diagnosed with OCD (including the impulse to disrupt a peaceful gathering and to jump in front of an approaching train). However, non-patients can dismiss their obsessions more easily, they experience them less often, and they're less distressed by them (Shafran, 1999). This is related to *interpretation* and *psychological vulnerability* (Salkovskis, 1985: see below).

## COGNITIVE BEHAVIOURAL THEORY

- According to *cognitive behavioural theory* (e.g. Beck, 1976), 'normal' obsessions become abnormal when people interpret the occurrence and content of unwanted intrusive thoughts as indicating that they may be/have been/come to be *responsible* for harm or its prevention (Salkovskis, 1985; Salkovskis *et al.*, 1998).
- Lopatka and Rachman (1995) showed that in a high-responsibility condition, people with checking compulsions had stronger urges to check, experienced greater discomfort, and made higher estimates of the probability of harm, than those in a low-responsibility condition.
- Another interpretation with specific implications for treatment (and which is closely linked to perceived responsibility for harm) is 'thought–action fusion' (TAF) (Rachman, 1993). This involves appraising intrusive thoughts as equivalent to actions. For example, one woman believed that if she had an image of her daughter lying dead, then it was as though she was 'tempting fate' and increasing the chances that her daughter would die. It involves two components:

(a) *likelihood TAF*: the belief that thinking about an unacceptable or disturbing event makes it more likely *actually* to happen
(b) *moral TAF*: interpreting the obsessive thoughts and forbidden actions as morally equivalent. The person feels that his/her unacceptable thoughts, images and impulses are (almost) as bad as the event (e.g. 'Only a wicked mother would have thoughts about harming her child').

- TAF represents a form of *psychological vulnerability*, which increases the likelihood of *misinterpretation* taking place.

 An evaluation of cognitive behavioural theory

✓ **Continuity with normal behaviour:** This currently popular theory sees OCD as an extension or exaggeration of normal behaviour. One of its great strengths is that it can explain OCD symptoms in terms of everyday, 'normal' cognition and behaviour.

(a) Unwanted or intrusive thoughts may be the precursor to or raw material of obsessions. But, more importantly, they're part of everyday cognitive experience. Normal intrusive thoughts in healthy individuals are ideas, impulses and images that interrupt our stream of consciousness. Their *content* is indistinguishable from the obsessional thoughts of people with OCD. But they're less intense, less long-lasting, and less distressing.
(b) Similarly, repetitive behaviours are especially common in childhood. This reflects the young child's strong need for predictability and order. Most normal childhood rituals (often fear-related and observable at night time) have disappeared by puberty. But the *extent* of (developmentally normal) childhood compulsions is highly correlated with anxiety. The more anxious children in all pre-adolescent age-groups engage in more and more intense ritualised behaviours.

So, what is it that turns a normal intrusive thought into an obsession? The answer is *misinterpretation* and *vulnerability*. Misinterpretation may involve seeing some commonplace object or situation as a potential catastrophe, taking an intrusive thought to be much more personally relevant or threatening than it 'really' is. As we saw above, vulnerability is related to TAF.

✓ Theoretical strengths and implications: According to Nieboer (1999), what Rachman calls TAF can be attributed to Freud (1909). Patients with OCD have difficulties distinguishing thoughts from actions. Freud believed that obsessions are defensive psychological responses (that develop during the anal–sadistic stage: see Chapter 12, page 321). Attempts to prevent compulsive behaviour would, at best, produce *symptom substitution* and, at worst, would cause psychotic breakdown. By contrast, Rachman's 'version' of TAF has implications for the origin, maintenance and treatment of OCD, which are *wholly* different from those drawn by Freud (Shafran & Salkovskis, 1999).

## EXAM tips BOX

**Describe and evaluate *one* biological (e.g. genetics, biochemistry) explanation of any one anxiety disorder. (30 marks) (40 mins) (800 words minimum) AO1/AO2**

*This essay can be split up into FOUR sections – each about 200 words long. Each section would be worth approx. 7–8 marks.*

**Section 1:** A **description** of the main characteristics of your chosen anxiety disorder. *A word of warning*: as with the other disorders, you're only describing the main characteristics to the extent that they're relevant to describing and evaluating the chosen explanation. For example, the relationship between obsessions and compulsions in OCD helps to distinguish them from the delusions characteristic of schizophrenia. But obsessions can and do occur separately from compulsions, and some people have questioned whether OCD is really an anxiety disorder at all. Your chosen theory may/may not focus on obsessions and/or compulsions.

**AO1**

**Section 2:** Your **description** of your chosen biological explanation could continue with an outline of the research methods on which it's based. For example, Saxena *et al.*'s model is really based on what's already known about the function of the major brain structures implicated in OCD. The model proposes particular relationships between these different structures to account for obsessions and compulsions. It's quite acceptable to draw diagrams to simplify complex concepts and theories. Here the diagram showing the relationship between direct and indirect pathways in relation to the PFC, basal ganglia and limbic system would be useful, saving you time. *Word of warning*: this shouldn't be a chance to show off your artistic skills, but a labour-saving device. Why use words when you can draw a quick diagram?

**AO1**

**Section 3:** You should **analyse** and **evaluate** your chosen explanation. You can do this by considering the advantages/disadvantages of the methods used to collect the evidence on which the explanation is based, as well as subsequent evidence or the consistency of the explanation with other evidence. For example, is Saxena *et al.*'s theory consistent with neurobiological evidence? In the case of the SH, you could consider the relative ineffectiveness of SRIs with OCD patients, as well as the role of other neurotransmitters.

**AO2**

**Section 4:** Your **analysis** and **evaluation** could continue with consideration of other explanations. Biological explanations fail to account for why particular OCD patients develop the particular obsessions and compulsions they do. A major strength of cognitive behaviour theory (such as Rachman's TAF) is that it explains both obsessions and compulsions in terms of normal cognitions and behaviours. As with other disorders, a useful way of putting your chosen explanation into context is by introducing the diathesis–stress model. TAF represents a form of vulnerability (diathesis), which in turn makes misinterpretation of commonplace events more likely. This could explain how 'normal' events become 'stressful' ones.

**AO2**

*Try to answer this question yourself. There's a sample essay on page 429 with which you can compare your essay.*

# PYA5: Psychopathology

Other possible exam questions:

- Each essay is worth 24 marks and should take 30 minutes to write.
- Remember the mark scheme allocates 12 marks for AO1 (knowledge and description) and 12 marks for AO2 (analysis and evaluation).

## SCHIZOPHRENIA

**1.** Compare and contrast *one* biological and *one* psychological explanation of schizophrenia. (24 marks)

## DEPRESSION

**2. a.** Describe *one* biological (e.g. genetics, bio-chemistry) explanation of depression. (12 marks)

   **b.** Evaluate the evidence on which this explanation is based. (12 marks)

## ANXIETY DISORDERS

**3. a.** Outline the clinical characteristics of any *one* anxiety disorder. (12 marks)

   **b.** Evaluate any *one* explanation of the chosen disorder in part (a). (12 marks)

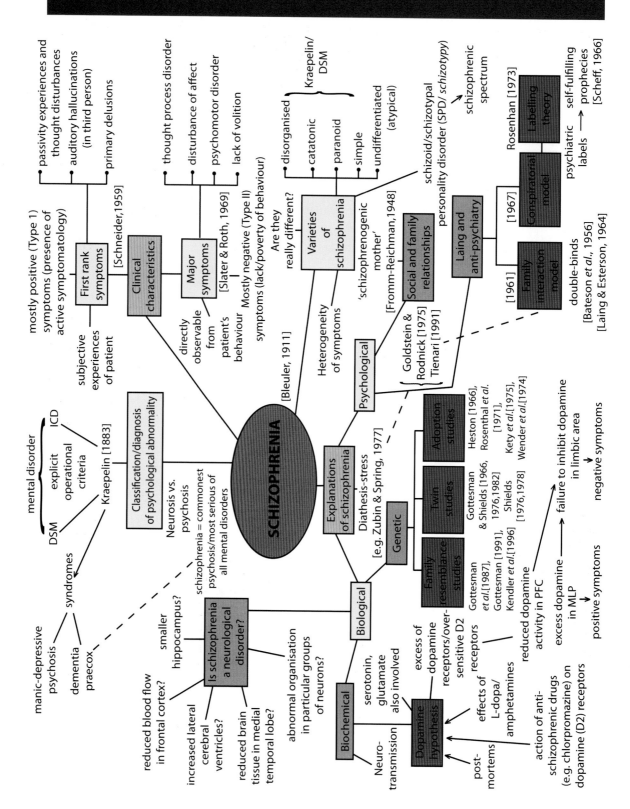

# CHAPTER SUMMARY: revision schema

**SCHIZOPHRENIA** [Bleuler, 1911]

**Clinical characteristics**

subjective experiences of patient

**First rank symptoms** [Schneider, 1959]
- passivity experiences and thought disturbances
- auditory hallucinations (in third person)
- primary delusions

mostly positive (Type 1) symptoms (presence of active symptomatology)

directly observable from patient's behaviour

**Major symptoms** [Slater & Roth, 1969]
- thought process disorder
- disturbance of affect
- psychomotor disorder
- lack of volition

Mostly negative (Type II) symptoms (lack/poverty of behaviour)

**Varieties of schizophrenia**
Are they really different?
- disorganised
- catatonic
- paranoid
- simple
- undifferentiated (atypical)

} Kraepelin/ DSM

schizoid/schizotypal personality disorder (SPD/ schizotypy) → schizophrenic spectrum

**Psychological**

Heterogeneity of symptoms

'schizophrenogenic mother' [Fromm-Reichman,1948]

**Social and family relationships**
Goldstein & Rodnick [1975]
Tienari [1991]

**Laing and anti-psychiatry**

**Family interaction model** [1961]
double-binds [Bateson et al., 1956] [Laing & Esterson, 1964]

**Conspiratorial model** [1967]

Rosenhan [1973]

**Labelling theory** → self-fulfilling prophecies [Scheff, 1966]
psychiatric labels

**Classification/diagnosis of psychological abnormality**

mental disorder
DSM / ICD
explicit operational criteria

Kraepelin [1883] → syndromes
- manic-depressive psychosis
- dementia praecox

Neurosis vs. psychosis
schizophrenia = commonest psychosis/most serious of all mental disorders

**Explanations of schizophrenia**
Diathesis-stress [e.g. Zubin & Spring, 1977]

**Genetic**

**Family resemblance studies**
Gottesman et al.[1987],
Gottesman [1991],
Kendler et al.[1996]

**Twin studies**
Gottesman & Shields [1966, 1976,1982]
Shields [1976,1978]

**Adoption studies**
Heston [1966],
Rosenthal et al. [1971],
Kety et al.[1975],
Wender et al.[1974]

**Biological**

Is schizophrenia a neurological disorder?
- reduced blood flow in frontal cortex?
- smaller hippocampus?
- increased lateral cerebral ventricles?
- reduced brain tissue in medial temporal lobe?
- abnormal organisation in particular groups of neurons?

**Biochemical**
serotonin, glutamate also involved

Neuro-transmission

**Dopamine hypothesis**
- excess of dopamine receptors/over-sensitive D2 receptors
- effects of L-dopa/amphetamines
- post-mortems
- action of anti-schizophrenic drugs (e.g. chlorpromazine) on dopamine (D2) receptors

reduced dopamine activity in PFC

excess dopamine in MLP → failure to inhibit dopamine in limbic area → negative symptoms

positive symptoms

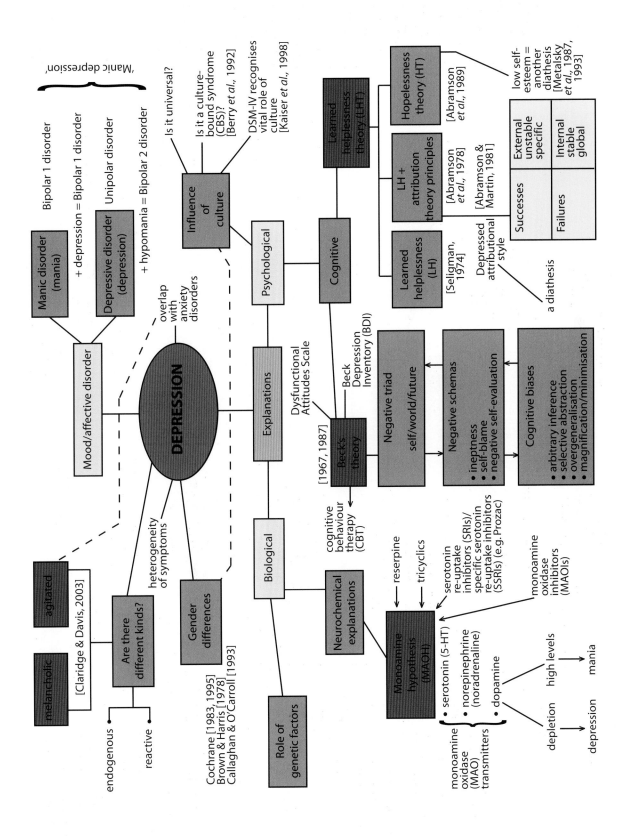

'Manic depression'

Bipolar 1 disorder

Manic disorder (mania)

+ depression = Bipolar 1 disorder

Depressive disorder (depression)

+ hypomania = Bipolar 2 disorder

Unipolar disorder

Mood/affective disorder

overlap with anxiety disorders

Is it universal?

Is it a culture-bound syndrome (CBS)? [Berry et al., 1992]

DSM-IV recognises vital role of culture [Kaiser et al., 1998]

Influence of culture

Psychological

Cognitive

Learned helplessness theory (LHT)

Learned helplessness (LH) [Seligman, 1974]

LH + attribution theory principles [Abramson et al., 1978] [Abramson & Martin, 1981]

Hopelessness theory (HT) [Abramson et al., 1989]

low self-esteem = another diathesis [Metalsky et al., 1987, 1993]

Depressed attributional style

a diathesis

|  | | |
|---|---|---|
| Successes | External unstable specific | Internal stable global |
| Failures | | |

**DEPRESSION**

melancholic

agitated [Claridge & Davis, 2003]

Are there different kinds?

endogenous

reactive

heterogeneity of symptoms

Gender differences

Cochrane [1983, 1995]
Brown & Harris [1978]
Callaghan & O'Carroll [1993]

Explanations

Dysfunctional Attitudes Scale

Beck Depression Inventory (BDI)

Beck's theory [1967, 1987]

Negative triad self/world/future

Negative schemas
• ineptness
• self-blame
• negative self-evaluation

Cognitive biases
• arbitrary inference
• selective abstraction
• overgeneralisation
• magnification/minimisation

cognitive behaviour therapy (CBT)

Biological

Role of genetic factors

Neurochemical explanations

reserpine

tricyclics

serotonin re-uptake inhibitors (SRIs)/ specific serotonin re-uptake inhibitors (SSRIs) (e.g. Prozac)

monoamine oxidase inhibitors (MAOIs)

Monoamine hypothesis (MAOH)
• serotonin (5-HT)
• norepinephrine (noradrenaline)
• dopamine

monoamine oxidase (MAO) transmitters

high levels → mania

depletion → depression

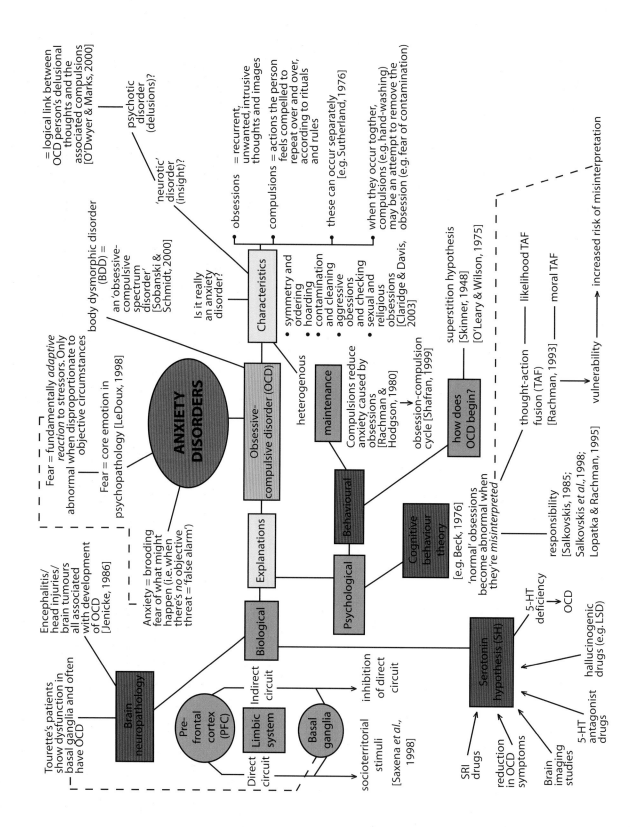

= logical link between OCD person's delusional thoughts and the associated compulsions [O'Dwyer & Marks, 2000]

psychotic disorder (delusions)?

'neurotic' disorder (insight)?

body dysmorphic disorder (BDD) = an 'obsessive-compulsive spectrum disorder' [Sobanski & Schmidt, 2000]

obsessions = recurrent, unwanted, intrusive thoughts and images

compulsions = actions the person feels compelled to repeat over and over, according to rituals and rules

these can occur separately [e.g. Sutherland, 1976]

when they occur togther, compulsions (e.g. hand-washing) may be an attempt to remove the obsession (e.g. fear of contamination)

Characteristics

Is it really an anxiety disorder?

• symmetry and ordering
• hoarding
• contamination and cleaning
• aggressive obsessions
• sexual and religious obsessions [Claridge & Davis, 2003]

superstition hypothesis [Skinner, 1948]
[O'Leary & Wilson, 1975]

thought-action fusion (TAF) [Rachman, 1993]

likelihood TAF

moral TAF

vulnerability ——→ increased risk of misinterpretation

ANXIETY DISORDERS

Fear = fundamentally *adaptive reaction* to stressors. Only abnormal when disproportionate to objective circumstances

Fear = core emotion in psychopathology [LeDoux, 1998]

Obsessive-compulsive disorder (OCD)

heterogenous

maintenance

Compulsions reduce anxiety caused by obsessions [Rachman & Hodgson, 1980]

obsession-compulsion cycle [Shafran, 1999]

how does OCD begin?

Behavioural

Cognitive behaviour theory

[e.g. Beck, 1976]

'normal' obsessions become abnormal when they're *misinterpreted*

responsibility [Salkovskis, 1985; Salkovskis et al., 1998; Lopatka & Rachman, 1995]

Anxiety = brooding fear of what might happen (i.e. when there's *no objective* threat = 'false alarm')

Explanations

Psychological

Encephalitis/ head injuries/ brain tumours all associated with development of OCD [Jenicke, 1986]

Biological

Brain neuropathology

Tourette's patients show dysfunction in basal ganglia and often have OCD

Pre-frontal cortex (PFC)

Limbic system

Basal ganglia

Indirect circuit

inhibition of direct circuit

Direct circuit

socioterritorial stimuli [Saxena et al., 1998]

Serotonin hypothesis (SH)

5-HT deficiency

OCD

hallucinogenic drugs (e.g. LSD)

5-HT antagonist drugs

Brain imaging studies

reduction in OCD symptoms

SRI drugs

## Section 1

The term 'schizophrenia' (Bleuler, 1911) replaced Kraepelin's (1896) 'dementia praecox'. Schizophrenia is by far the commonest of the psychoses, considered to be one of the most serious of all mental disorders. Its diagnosis in the UK relies greatly on Schneider's (1959) first rank symptoms (FRSs), which include auditory hallucinations and primary delusions. But these are subjective experiences. Slater and Roth (1969) regarded hallucinations as the least important of all the major symptoms and added four additional symptoms which are directly observable from the patient's behaviour. These include thought process disorder, disturbance of affect, psychomotor disorders, and lack of volition. DSM and ICD diagnosis of schizophrenia are a mix of these two views. DSM-IV distinguishes three types of schizophrenia: disorganised (hebephrenic), catatonic and paranoid.

Most of Schneider's FRSs are what are known as positive symptoms, that is, excesses or distortions, the presence of active symptoms. Most of Slater and Roth's symptoms are negative, behavioural deficits, lack or poverty of behaviour. This distinction is very important for evaluating research into the causes of schizophrenia. One biological explanation focuses on biochemical processes. According to the dopamine hypothesis, what directly causes schizophrenic symptoms is an excess of the neurotransmitter dopamine. Neurotransmitters, in combination with electrical impulses, transmit information between neurons in the brain. After release across the synaptic gap, the neurotransmitter is recycled, either by being taken back by the neuron that released it (re-uptake) or by being broken down chemically into simpler compounds.

## Section 2

The evidence for the dopamine hypothesis comes from postmortems and what's known about the operation of certain drugs. Postmortems on schizophrenic patients show unusually high levels of dopamine, especially in the limbic system (Iversen, 1979). Anti-schizophrenic drugs (such as chlorpromazine) are thought to work by binding to dopamine receptor sites, that is, they inhibit the ability of the dopamine (D2) receptors to respond to dopamine. This reduces dopamine activity. These anti-schizophrenic drugs also produce side-effects similar to the symptoms of Parkinson's disease, which is known to be caused partly by low levels of dopamine in particular nerve tracts. High doses of L-dopa (used to treat Parkinson's disease) can sometimes produce symptoms very similar to the psychomotor disorders seen in certain types of schizophrenia (especially catatonic). High doses of amphetamines can induce amphetamine psychosis (AP), which closely resembles paranoid schizophrenia and can aggravate the symptoms of a patient with schizophrenia. Both L-dopa and amphetamines are believed to increase the activity of dopamine. Dopamine-containing neurons are concentrated in the basal ganglia and frontal cortex, areas concerned with the initiation and control of movement. Degeneration of the dopamine system produces Parkinson's disease, and anti-psychotic drugs are given to counteract AP.

## Section 3:

Overall, the evidence for the dopamine hypothesis is inconclusive (Lavender,

if there were such evidence, this could just as easily be a result of schizophrenia as its cause. If dopamine were found to be a causative factor, this might only be indirect. For example, abnormal family circumstances give rise to high levels of dopamine, which in turn trigger the symptoms (Lloyd et al., 1984). Also, it's unlikely that any problems with dopamine production or receptivity can be the biochemical abnormality underlying all forms of schizophrenia, although it may be crucial in some forms (Jackson, 1990). Schizophrenia is heterogeneous, comprising many different symptoms and sub-types. Unlike most diagnostic categories, there's no essential symptom that must be present for a diagnosis of schizophrenia to be made (Davison & Neale, 2001). This all makes it implausible for there to be a single explanation that covers all cases. The dopamine hypothesis couldn't be a complete explanation, because it takes several weeks for anti-schizophrenic drugs gradually to reduce positive symptoms – even though they begin blocking D2 receptors very quickly. Newer anti-schizophrenic drugs implicate other neurotransmitters, in particular serotonin. Glutamate may also be involved as part of a much more complex jigsaw (Davison & Neale, 2001).

## Section 4:

A modification of the dopamine hypothesis claims that schizophrenics suffer from an excess of dopamine receptors or that their D2 receptors are over-sensitive. This is functionally equivalent to having too much dopamine itself, and seems to be associated mainly with positive symptoms (Davison & Neale, 2001). According to another modification, the therapeutic effects of anti-schizophrenic drugs on the positive symptoms derive from the blocking of D2 receptors specifically in the mesolimbic pathway (MLP). The mesocortical pathway (MCP) begins in the same brain region as the MLP, but projects to the pre-frontal cortex (PFC), which is thought to be especially relevant to negative symptoms (through underactivity of D2 neurons). This can explain how positive and negative symptoms can occur at the same time in the same patient, as well as why anti-schizophrenic drugs are relatively ineffective in treating negative symptoms (Davison & Neale, 2001).

One strength of biochemical explanations in general is that they can help explain how genetic factors actually make a difference. According to Lilienfeld (1995), perhaps the most reasonable conclusion to draw about genetic explanations is that there's converging evidence implicating genetic factors. The heritability of schizophrenia seems to be comparable to that of any medical condition known to have a major genetic component (such as diabetes, hypertension, and breast cancer). But exactly what is inherited and how this causes actual symptoms is much more controversial. Perhaps biochemical explanations can help to fill this explanatory gap, and in this sense they are complementary to genetic explanations. An excess of dopamine can be thought of a predisposition to exhibit schizophrenic symptoms. Consistent with the diathesis–stress model (e.g. Zubin & Spring, 1977), what we probably inherit is a vulnerability, but this isn't sufficient on its own actually to become schizophrenia. Whether or not we become schizophrenic depends on environmental stresses, which may be biological (such as viral infections during pregnancy) or social (such as having a schizophrenogenic mother: Fromm-Reichmann, 1948). Biochemical explanations, as with genetic ones, can only tell us half the story. (1,002 words)

# SAMPLE ESSAYS

Describe and evaluate *one* psychological explanation (e.g. learned help-lessness) of depression. (30 marks) (40 mins) (800 words minimum)

## Section 1:

A01

Depression is one of the mood or affective disorders, which involve a prolonged and fundamental disturbance of mood and emotions. When depression (major depressive disorder) occurs on its own, it's referred to as unipolar disorder. When it occurs in conjunction with mania, it's called bipolar disorder (the term that's also used in the rare cases when mania occurs on its own). In order to be diagnosed with unipolar (depressive) disorder (UDD), a person should have experienced persistent low mood (for at least two weeks) plus at least five other symptoms, including disturbed sleep, loss of energy, loss of interest or pleasure in usual activities (including social contact or sex), feelings of self-reproach, excessive or inappropriate guilt, and recurrent thoughts of death or suicide, or any suicidal behaviour. Claridge and Davis (2003) distinguish between melancholic and agitated types of depression, and traditionally psychiatrists have distinguished between endogenous (psychotic) and reactive or exogenous (neurotic). The former referred to depression arising from biochemical disturbances in the brain, while the latter was seen as caused by stressful life experiences. Gelder *et al.* (1999) believe that both types of cause are present in every case, and Champion (2000) argues that endogenous depression can no longer be defined in terms of the absence of external causes, but by the presence of more severe symptoms.

## Section 2:

A01

A major cognitive explanation of depression began with Seligman's (1974) experiments with dogs, and is referred to as learned helplessness theory (LHT). Dogs that at first couldn't escape electric shocks soon seemed to give up and passively accept the painful stimulation. Later, even though they could now avoid the shocks, they stopped trying. Seligman called this loss of ability and motivation to respond learned helplessness (LH), and he extended the observation to depressed people. Like Seligman's dogs, many depressed people appear passive when faced with stress, failing to initiate actions that might allow them to cope.

LHT was revised by Abramson, Seligman and Teasdale in 1978. The major change they proposed was in terms of attribution theory principles. When we experience failure, for example, it's quite normal for us to try to explain it (as with our successes). What's associated with depression is a particular pattern of attributions (or attributional style), that is, a tendency to make particular types of causal inferences. Depressed people believe that their failures are caused by internal, stable and global factors, that is, personal characteristics which are relatively permanent and which affect all or most aspects of their life. It's not just the person already diagnosed who's likely to show this attributional style, but also the depression-prone person. When the latter experiences stressors, they're more likely to develop the symptoms of depression and their self-esteem is shattered (Peterson & Seligman, 1984). The latest version of the theory is hopelessness theory (HT) (Abramson *et al.*, 1989). HT proposes that attributional style is only one possible diathesis (predisposition) for developing depression. Another is low self-esteem and a tendency to infer that negative life

## Section 3:

A02

By 1978, research with humans began to reveal the inadequacies of LHT. For example, some studies indicated that helplessness sometimes actually improves performance. Also, many depressed people blame themselves for their failures, which is incompatible with the claim that they see themselves as helpless victims (the human parallel of Seligman's helpless dogs). Finally, the experience of being unable to control the outcome of one particular situation doesn't necessarily lead to clinical depression in most people. For these reasons, Abramson *et al.* introduced their attributional model of depression. This was a clear improvement on LHT, because it adds cognitive factors missing from the latter. Abramson *et al.* were drawing on a very large and well-established body of research into attribution to supplement the idea of helplessness. But while there was supporting evidence for the claim that depressed people have a particular attributional style (Seligman *et al.*, 1979), the question remained as to where the depressive attributional style comes from in the first place. This is a problem faced by cognitive explanations of mental disorders in general. Some support for the latest version, hopelessness theory (HT), comes from a study by Metalsky *et al.* (1993), which confirmed the findings of an earlier study (Metalsky *et al.*, 1987). College students who displayed a depressed attributional style in response to poor grades were more likely to experience a persistent depressed mood subsequently. But this only occurred in the case of students with low self-esteem, and it was mediated by increased feelings of hopelessness.

## Section 4:

A02

Davison and Neale (2001) point out some general problems with all three helplessness-related theories. First, Seligman (1974) was originally trying to explain the similarity between LH and reactive depression. But this is no longer considered to be a distinct form of depression. Abramson *et al.* (1989) talk about a hopelessness depression, which refers both to the presumed cause and to a set of symptoms that don't quite match the DSM criteria. Second, some studies have involved clinical populations (people actually diagnosed as having UDD), while many others have involved college students selected on the basis of the Beck Depression Inventory (BDI) or have simply tried to predict increases in BDI scores. But the BDI wasn't designed to diagnose depression, only to assess its severity among people already diagnosed. These populations are clearly not comparable, so the data from these different studies cannot be pooled. Third, depressive attributional style seems to be related to anxiety and general distress, as well as depression. Unlike Beck's theory, which was specifically intended to explain depression and grew out of his clinical work with depressed patients, LHT was derived from Seligman's laboratory experiments with dogs. This gives Beck's theory more face validity. The latter versions are clearly more valid because they take human cognitive processes into account. HT might be able to help explain why women are so much more likely to become depressed than men, but only by proposing a diathesis (self-esteem) other than attributional style. How the diathesis originates (where it comes from) is likely to reflect social influences and early experiences, such as being victims of child sexual abuse, and the demands and responsibilities associated with traditional female gender roles (Cochrane, 1995). (1,033 words)

A01

## Section 1:

Many psychologists have argued that fear is a fundamentally adaptive reaction to stressors, specifically threat, since it increases alertness and vigilance. Fear is generally considered abnormal only when it's out of proportion to objective circumstances. When people feel afraid even when there's no (objective) threat, it's called anxiety, and these 'false alarms' are what we call anxiety disorders. The fourth most common of all mental disorders is obsessive–compulsive disorder (OCD). Obsessions are recurrent, intrusive thoughts or images that don't feel voluntarily controlled, and they feel morally repugnant or intensely distressing. They mostly have sexual, blasphemous or aggressive themes, and can be 'neutralised' with some other thought or action (Shafran, 1999). These may include compulsions, which are actions the person feels compelled to repeat over and over again, according to rituals and rules. Although obsessions and compulsions are often related in this way, they can occur separately. Some people have questioned whether OCD should be classified as an anxiety disorder at all, and ICD-10 lists it separately from anxiety disorders. Individuals with OCD differ considerably from one another, including how much insight they have regarding the excessive and unreasonable nature of their symptoms. In about 10% of cases, they seem to lack insight altogether, and their thinking begins to resemble psychotic delusions. But a key factor that distinguishes OCD patients from psychotics is the clear and logical link between the former's delusional thoughts and the compulsions they induce (O'Dwyer & Marks, 2000).

A01

## Section 2:

Encephalitis, head injuries and brain tumours are all associated with the development of OCD (Jenike, 1986). Several models of OCD all predict, in one way or another, the involvement of the pre-frontal cortex (PFC), the basal ganglia and the limbic system. The basal ganglia consist of the caudate, putamen, globus pallidus and the amygdala. These are linked to the control of motor behaviour. Focus on the basal ganglia is due to their relevance to compulsions, as well as the relationship between OCD and Tourette's syndrome. The vocal and motor tics characteristic of Tourette's are linked to basal ganglia dysfunction. Tourette's patients also often have OCD (Sheppard et al., 1999). The PFC has direct links with the basal ganglia via its connections with the limbic system. It also receives signals from these sub-cortical structures. So there are connections between the PFC and the sub-cortical areas which pass through the limbic system.

According to Saxena et al. (1998), the function of all the direct pathways between the PFC and basal ganglia is to execute 'pre-packaged' complex responses to 'socio-territorial' stimuli. These refer to things that are highly significant to the organism's survival, such as sex, safety, hygiene and keeping things in order. These need to be performed quickly in order to be adaptive, and they must also operate to the exclusions of other interfering stimuli. When these direct pathways are activated, the behaviour is fixed until the attentional need to

it's appropriate to switch to another behaviour. This is something OCD patients have trouble doing. Excess activation of their direct pathway causes fixation with these socio-territorial concerns, the indirect pathway is too weak to 'turn off' the signal from the direct pathway, and the socio-territorial concerns are experienced by the individual as intrusive obsessions.

A02

## Section 3:

According to Claridge and Davis (2003), Saxena et al.'s model is popular and is consistent with neurobiological evidence from various sources. For example, brain imaging studies have consistently shown increased activity in the PFC (usually involving the right orbitofrontal cortex) in individuals with OCD but who aren't taking medication. Their frontal lobes are 'overheated'. These hyperactive areas tend to become normal when patients receive effective treatment – either drug therapy or behavioural therapy. Rauch et al. (1994) stimulated OCD symptoms by presenting patients with stimuli specially selected for them (such as a glove contaminated with household rubbish). This produced increased blood flow in the PFC and certain regions of the basal ganglia. Also, OCD patients have a smaller putamen (one of the structures making up the basal ganglia) than controls (Rosenberg et al., 1997).

The PFC plays an important role in assessing the behavioural significance of biologically important stimuli. So increased frontal lobe activity may relate to obsessional thinking – but not necessarily to compulsions. But the basal ganglia (and the cerebellum, which stores behavioural programs such as conditioned responses) may function to control compulsive urges. People with diseases that involve pathology of the basal ganglia (such as Parkinson's and Huntingdon's chorea) often show compulsive symptoms similar to those of OCD patients.

A02

## Section 4

One of the strengths of Saxena et al.'s model is that it tries to account for OCD in terms of everyday, 'normal' cognition and behaviour. Also, drawing parallels between OCD patients and others, such as Parkinson's patients whose pathology is well-established, makes it more plausible that the former also suffer from this or similar pathology. But it could be argued that this explanation is insufficient, in that it leaves several fundamental questions unanswered. For example, it (and other biological explanations) fails to account for why particular OCD patients develop the particular obsessions and compulsions they do. As with explanations of schizophrenia, theories of OCD face the problem that the disorder is heterogeneous, that is, there is considerable diversity of symptoms among those diagnosed as having OCD. This suggests that no single explanation can be sufficient. In the case of Saxena et al.'s model, it may have identified some of the crucial underlying brain pathways involved in OCD, but it cannot account for the diversity among patients. It's also possible (as with, for example, the dopamine hypothesis account of schizophrenia) that having OCD may actually produce the brain abnormalities, rather than the other way round. Perhaps Saxena et al. have identified a diathesis, that is, a predisposition or vulnerability towards developing OCD symptoms, but other, psychological, explanations may be needed to account for how vulnerability is converted into actual disorder. (1,003 words)

# SAMPLE ESSAYS

# Treating Mental Disorders

## What's covered in this chapter?

**You need to know about:**

**Biological (somatic) therapies**
- Chemotherapy, ECT and psychosurgery
- Issues surrounding the use of such therapies (e.g. appropriateness and effectiveness)

**Behavioural therapies**
- Behavioural therapies, including those based on classical (e.g. flooding) and operant (e.g. token economies) conditioning
- Issues surrounding the use of such therapies (e.g. appropriateness and effectiveness)

**Alternatives to the biological and behavioural therapies**
- Therapies derived from the psychodynamic model of abnormality (e.g. psychoanalysis; psychodrama)
- Issues surrounding the use of such therapies (e.g. appropriateness and effectiveness)

## Biological (somatic) therapies

Biological therapies ('soma' means 'body' in Greek) derive from the medical model of abnormality. This assumes that altering bodily functioning will be effective in treating certain abnormal behaviours. There are three main biological treatments: chemotherapy, ECT (electro-convulsive shock treatment) and psychosurgery.

### Chemotherapy (drug therapy)

- Approximately 25% of all drugs prescribed by the NHS are for mental health problems. In 1992/1993, spending on psychiatric drugs was £159 million or 5.2% of the NHS drugs budget. Psychiatric drugs modify the working of the brain and affect mood and behaviour (Mind, 2003). People suffering from mental disorders are frequently prescribed more than one drug.
- Drugs work by entering the bloodstream in order to reach the brain. The amount of drug absorbed by the brain depends on the extent to which the drug gets absorbed, excreted or converted into inactive substances. When consumed orally, drugs are

absorbed by the gut and pass into the liver, which breaks down much of the drug. Drugs that are injected into the bloodstream bypass the liver and hence smaller amounts are needed than with oral doses. Slow-acting injections are the exception to this, where release of an appropriate drug can occur over a month or so. Because different people's bodies work in slightly different ways, different doses may be required depending on the individual.

- Drugs affect transmission of chemicals in the nervous system. Some neural transmission occurs when chemicals cross the gaps between nerves. This is called synaptic transmission. These chemicals are called neurotransmitters and have a variety of effects on behaviour. The main neurotransmitters are dopamine, serotonin, acetylcholine, noradrenaline and GABA. Basically, drugs work by either increasing or decreasing the availability of these neurotransmitters and hence modify their effects on behaviour. A drug that blocks the effects of a given neurotransmitter is called an antagonist (meaning 'enemy'). A drug that mimics or increases the effects of a neurotransmitter is called an agonist.

- Drugs can exert their effects in numerous ways, by:

(a) facilitating or inhibiting production of a neurotranmsitter
(b) increasing or decreasing the release of a neurotransmitter or
(c) altering what happens to it after it attaches to the receptor.

Table 15.1 illustrates this.

> **Specification Hint:** For each therapy you need to know:
> - **the use:** Which disorders are treated by this method of therapy?
> - **the mode of action:** How does this therapy work?
> - **issues surrounding the therapy:** When is it appropriate to use this therapy? Is it an effective therapy? Are there any other issues, such as ethical issues, to consider?

**Table 15.1** Some mechanisms of drug action

| Agonistic Drug Effects | Antagonistic Drug Effects |
| --- | --- |
| Drug increases the synthesis of neurotransmitter | Drug blocks the synthesis of neurotransmitter |
| Drug increases neurotransmitter by destroying degrading enzymes | Drug causes the neurotransmitter to leak from the vesicles |
| Drug increases the release of neurotransmitter | Drug blocks the release of the neurotransmitter |
| Drug blocks inhibitory effect on neurotransmitter release | Drug activates autoreceptors and inhibits neurotransmitter release |
| Drug activates or increases the effect of neurotransmitter | Drug is a receptor blocker; it blocks the effect of the neurotransmitter |
| Drug blocks the deactivation of neurotransmitter molecules by blocking degradation or reuptake | |

- It's very easy to get confused about the different medications since there are so many drugs, each with trade names (given by the drugs company) and generic names (the chemical family of the drug) and also the larger chemical family name of the drug. For example:

**Trade name**
Diazepam®

**Generic name**
Valium®

**Chemical family name**
Benzodiazepine

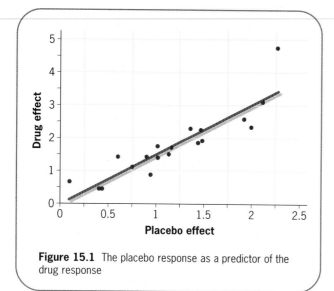

Figure 15.1 The placebo response as a predictor of the drug response

## THE PLACEBO EFFECT

- A placebo is an inactive treatment (e.g. sugar pill) that nevertheless appears to produce some improvement in patients. The placebo effect refers to treatment responses in a placebo group compared with the responses of those patients taking an active treatment (e.g. an active drug). The effects of the active treatment group are then compared with those of the control group taking the placebo.
- It's not unusual for a placebo effect to be found in 50% of patients in any medical study (Schatzberg & Nemeroff, 1999). Obviously, the active treatment has to improve patients by a statistically significant level compared with the placebo control group.
- It's unclear how placebos work, but it's thought that factors such as patient expectations and attitudes and patient production of their own painkillers (endorphins) may play a part in the placebo effect.
- GPs aren't allowed to use placebos except in clinical trials where patients have given their informed consent. Of course, patients in such trials don't know which condition or group they're in (active treatment or control group).
- A controversial analysis of 19 double-blind clinical drug trials involving 2,318 depressed patients concluded that there was a 0.9 correlation between placebo effect and drug effect (see Figure 15.1). Kirsch and Sapirstein (1998) found that the inactive placebos produced improvement that was 75% of the effect of the active drug. Furthermore, the authors concluded that approximately one quarter of the drug response is due to the administration of an active medication, one half is a placebo effect, and the remaining quarter is due to other non-specific factors.

## THE FIVE MAJOR DRUG TYPES ARE:

### Anti-psychotics or neuroleptics (major tranquillisers)

- There are three main families of anti-psychotic drugs: phenothiazines, butyrophenones and dibenzazepines. These drugs work by lowering dopamine activity in the brain.
- The drugs' similar structures mean that they can block D2 dopamine receptors in the brain. Dibenzazepines appear to block D4 receptors. However, they also affect acetylcholine and serotonin.
- Although this dopamine-blocking action occurs within hours, the actual effect takes several weeks. This suggests that secondary adaptive changes in the brain are responsible for the clinical effect.
- These drugs are used to treat schizophrenia, the manic phase of manic depression and other psychotic symptoms.

- The drugs do more than just tranquillise patients and thus the term 'major tranquilliser' can be misleading. The older drugs reduce agitation using a tranquillising effect without causing drowsiness. They can help to relieve voice-hearing, hallucinations, delusions and feelings of paranoia.

✓ **Effectiveness?** They're thought to work for two-thirds of psychotic patients and 80% of schizophrenics (SANE, 2003).

✗ ✓ **Not cures:** The drugs have been shown to reduce the symptoms in carefully controlled trials, but they **do not** cure the illness. Nevertheless, symptom reduction can significantly improve many people's lives.

✓ **Work for positive symptoms, not negative ones:** These drugs reduce 'positive' symptoms (such as hallucinations and delusions) but not 'negative' symptoms (such as blunted emotions or social withdrawal) (see Chapter 14, page 390).

✗ **Side-effects:** The older tranquillisers (e.g. phenothiazines) often cause movement disorders (extra-pyramidal symptoms) such as tremors, slowing of body and facial features, and abnormal body movements. Other anti-muscarinic drugs are taken to control these. Long-term use can lead to permanent neurological damage (tardive dyskinesia) or involuntary movements of the mouth and face. Newer anti-psychotic drugs (e.g. dibenzazepines) seem to be even more effective and have fewer side-effects. The reason for these side-effects is that drugs are blunt instruments and interfere with other brain mechanisms not causing the mental disorder.

✗ **Agents of social control?** It's been claimed that these drugs have been overused to control patients, particularly in institutional settings such as care homes. Their use in such circumstances has been compared to the use of straitjackets in the past. Indeed, they have been called 'pharmacological straitjackets' or 'chemical lobotomies'.

### Anxiolytics or anti-anxiety drugs (minor tranquillisers)

- Anxiolytics are among the most widely prescribed drugs. They're given for anxiety or stress-related symptoms, and occasionally for short-term management of phobias. These drugs are used for only a few weeks at a time to prevent tolerance (more and more of the drug being required) and dependence (the need to keep taking the drug).
- Benzodiazepines are the most commonly used anxiolytics. In 1997, 18 million prescriptions for benzodiazepines were written in the UK. It's estimated that 23% of all adults in Britain in 1984 had taken an anxiolytic drug at some time in their lives (MORI, 1984).
- Benzodiazepines appear to work by inhibiting transmission at GABA synapses. For example, Diazepam increases the effect of GABA which is an inhibitory neurotransmitter and that, in turn, decreases the nerve membrane's excitability. But the correlation between a benzodiazepine's ability to bind to the GABA receptor and its clinical effect is relatively low. This suggests that this isn't a complete account of how the drugs reduce anxiety.
- Buspirone is called a 'second generation' anxiolytic, because it binds to serotonin receptors. It appears to have fewer side-effects (no withdrawal symptoms) but its onset effects are less immediate, and patients may give up taking the drug before it's effective.

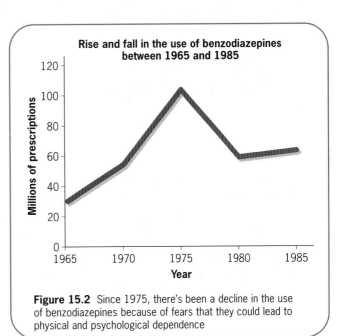

Figure 15.2 Since 1975, there's been a decline in the use of benzodiazepines because of fears that they could lead to physical and psychological dependence

✓ • ✗ **Effectiveness:** Effective in the short term (2–4 weeks) but quickly become less effective and can even produce symptoms they're trying to reduce ('the rebound effect')!

✗ **Side-effects:** Very addictive and so it is essential to monitor patients' tolerance and dependence to the drug. The drugs are poisonous and an overdose can lead to death.

## Anti-depressants

- Unsurprisingly, these drugs are used to relieve persistent low moods and other symptoms of depression.
- Depression is thought to occur because of insufficient amounts of the neurotransmitters serotonin and noradrenaline being produced in the brain. This is quite unlike psychotic illnesses, where there's too much of a neurotransmitter being produced and drugs block their effect.
- When neurotransmitters are released they cross over and stimulate neighbouring nerve cells. To switch off the activation, the neurotransmitters are re-absorbed into the nerves and broken down by monoamine oxide. Depressed people either produce too little neurotransmitter or remove too much of it. Anti-depressant drugs work by either (a) reducing the rate of re-absorption or (b) destroying the enzyme that blocks the amount of neurotransmitter available for the neighbouring cell.
- There are three broad anti-depressant drug types:
  - **MAOIs (monoamine oxidase inhibitors):** Not used greatly today because of the lethal dangers of interaction with other substances including red wine, meat and dairy products. In addition, the drugs' effectiveness has never been clearly established. MAOIs work by inhibiting an enzyme (monoamine oxidase), which destroys the noradrenaline and serotonin neurotransmitters in the brain. Side-effects include drowsiness, trembling and blurred vision.
  - **Tricyclics:** These drugs are extremely toxic and, since they are given to depressed people, there's a chance they may be used in a suicide attempt. Tricyclics work by blocking the re-absorption or re-uptake of both noradrenaline and serotonin neurotransmitters in the brain. This prolongs the neurotransmitters' activity.
  - **SSRI (Selective serotonin re-uptake inhibitors):** These drugs are less sedating and less toxic than tricyclics. However, they're much more expensive than the older drugs. Despite this, they're the most widely used anti-depressants. Prozac® is the best-known SSRI. They work in a similar way to tricyclics by acting only on the neurotransmitter serotonin.

✓ • ✗ **Effective cure?** Unlike the anti-anxiety drugs, anti-depressants often cure the illness. Providing the choice of drug is appropriate, about 75% of patients 'remain free from depression for long periods of their lifetime' (SANE, 2003). However, American research suggests that patients reported a 50% positive response to anti-depressants compared with a 32% response rate to a placebo (AHCPR, 1999).

✓ **Not addictive:** The drugs aren't addictive, and most patients continue to take anti-depressant drugs for six months to avoid the chance of a relapse.

✗ **Tolerance to side-effects:** Most patients develop a tolerance to side-effects during their treatment and the risks can be minimised by a short period when the patient takes a very low dose of the drug.

✗ **Delayed effect:** Although side-effects can occur immediately after taking the drug, the relief of symptoms only becomes apparent after two to four weeks. Some patients thus stop taking the drugs before they work. It's unclear why this effect is delayed, since the effect on the neurotransmitters is immediate.

✗ **Side-effects:** Despite patients developing tolerance to the drugs, side-effects can include nausea, diarrhoea and headaches.

## Anti-manics (mood-stabilising drugs)

These drugs are used to control moods. They're used to treat bipolar affective disorder (manic depression) and severe depression. Lithium is the most common drug that helps to control the mania. It's believed to work by decreasing the levels of noradrenaline and serotonin.

✓ **Effective treatment:** Approximately 75% of patients report positive effects of these drugs. They're also useful as a prophylactic (preventative measure) to reduce the likelihood of further attacks.

✗ **Side-effects:** Lithium is only effective after a couple of days and long-term use can lead to kidney damage. In addition, Lithium is toxic and therefore regular blood tests are required to check that the limits aren't exceeded.

### Stimulants

Stimulants are used to improve mood, alertness and confidence. They're also used to help hyperactive children. You'd think the last thing you'd want to give hyperactive children is a stimulant, but these children do show improvements. Stimulants work by increasing the effect of noradrenaline and serotonin.

✓•✗ **Effectiveness:** Stimulants have been shown to be effective in clinically controlled trials, but it's not recommended to use them on a long-term basis.

✗ **Side-effects:** Patients can become dependent on the drug and develop tolerance to it. These drugs can also have adverse effects on eating and sleeping

## ECT (electro-convulsive therapy)

- ECT is a medical treatment used to treat drug-resistant depressive disorders. ECT tends to be used when drugs and psychotherapy have failed or they cannot be tolerated.
- A course of treatment with ECT usually consists of about 6–12 treatments given several times per week. Nowadays, the patient is given a general anaesthetic and a muscle relaxant that ensures the patient doesn't convulse or feel pain (despite Hollywood's continual portrayal of this!). The patient's brain is then stimulated, using electrodes placed on their head, with a brief, controlled series of electrical pulses. This 110-mv stimulus causes a seizure within the brain that lasts about a minute. After 5–10 minutes, the patient will regain consciousness (APA, 2003).
- There are two types of ECT used. *Unilateral* ECT occurs when only one side of the head is stimulated (the non-dominant hemisphere – the right hemisphere for right-handed people). *Bilateral* ECT involves stimulation on both sides.

Table 15.2 Electro-convulsive therapy: treatments administered in England, 1990–91, 1998–99

|  | **1990–91** | **1998–99** |
|---|---|---|
| All administrations | 105,466 | 65,930 |
| In-patients, ordinary admission | 89,708 | 54,030 |
| Other patients | 15,758 | 11,900 |

Source: Electroconvulsive Therapy: Survey covering the period from January 1990 to March 1999, England. *Statistical Bulletin* 1999/22 (Department of Health)

- There are continuing arguments about the mechanism underlying the effectiveness of ECT. It's suggested that ECT induces changes in various neurotransmitters, including an increased sensitivity to serotonin in the hypothalamus, and an increase in the release of GABA, noradrenaline and dopamine (Sasa, 1999).

✓ **Effectiveness?** ECT can have an immediate beneficial effect. Some patients swear by its effectiveness and others swear at its continued use! Weiner *et al.* (1988) report that ECT produces a substantial improvement in at least 80% of depressed patients, and Sackheim *et al.* (1990) have found this for patients with medically resistant depression. In terms of electrical dosage and placement of the electrodes, it appears that suprathreshold doses (2.5 times the electricity needed to produce a seizure) and bilateral ECT are more effective than low-dose, unilateral ECT (see Figure 15.3 below) (Sackheim *et al.*, 1993).

ECT has changed considerably since its portrayal in the Oscar-winning film *One Flew Over the Cuckoo's Nest*.

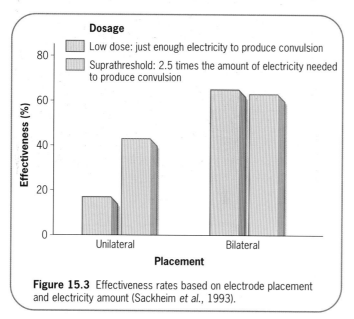

**Figure 15.3** Effectiveness rates based on electrode placement and electricity amount (Sackheim *et al.*, 1993).

✗ Effectiveness? However, a study has shown that, despite the fact that ECT should be used only after other treatments have failed, as many as 18% of people had been offered no other treatment. Also, 78.5% of the people who took part in the study said that they would never have ECT again (UKAN, 1995).

✓•✗ Effectiveness? Geddes *et al.* (2003) reviewed 73 studies using depressed patients and compared ECT with placebo ECT and drug therapy. They showed there was a significant benefit of ECT over the placebo and drug treatments. However, there was a slight increased risk of cognitive impairment in ECT patients, usually involving temporary amnesia.

✓ Side-effects? Some researchers have found no evidence that ECT damages the brain (Weiner, 1984). It's argued that people can have many epileptic seizures and these don't consistently harm the brain so why should ECT? Indeed, ECT-induced seizures take place under far more controlled conditions than epilepsy. Coffey *et al.* (1991), using MRI brain scans, could find no evidence for ECT brain damage.

✗•✓ Method of social control? It's generally agreed that ECT has a troubled history and in the past may have been used to control awkward or troublesome patients. The far stricter guidelines in place today suggest this is unlikely still to occur.

## Psychosurgery

- Psychosurgery or neurosurgery for mental disorder (NMD) is the scientific treatment of mental disorders by means of brain surgery. It's usually used to treat severe, incapacitating non-schizophrenic mood disorders when all other therapeutic attempts have failed.
- Some people consider it ridiculous to think that destruction of brain tissue could lead to an improvement in a mental disorder. Early humans drilled holes in skulls (called 'trepanning') in order to liberate demons, and some people see a comparison with psychosurgery. After all, there's no universally agreed technique for the operation. Most of the operations involve destroying some of the nerve circuits in the limbic system that are largely responsible for control and regulation of emotions.
- The best-known technique involves *stereotactic neurosurgery*. This involves fitting a stereotactic frame to the patient's head and then scanning the brain using computer imaging. With the frame in place, the probe that enters the brain can be accurate to within one millimetre of its desired

target. The probe is inserted in the brain and once in place is heated to 70 degrees Celsius to produce a small lesion (cut) in the brain tissue. The procedure is typically carried out under general anaesthetic and lasts about 90 minutes.

- Stereotactic surgery is now possible without cutting into the head. *Radiosurgery* involves projecting radiation into the brain from several different angles. The so-called 'gamma knife' concentrates radiation into a single point inside the brain, while the surrounding, healthy tissues are spared damage.
- In the UK, psychosurgery is becoming less and less common. Only seven operations occurred in 1999–2000 and just two took place in 2000–2001. There have been over 3,000 operations in total in the UK and these have resulted in one death.

Trepanning: an early form of psychosurgery?

✔ **Effectiveness?** It's very difficult to assess the effectiveness of psychosurgery since the measure of success isn't agreed. Mind (2002) reports a study which suggests that of 42 operations:

- 12 showed some 'significant improvement'
- 22 showed some improvement
- 6 showed no change
- 2 showed some deterioration
- 0 showed significant deterioration.

Patient undergoing an MRI brain scan in preparation for neurosurgery

Nuttin *et al.* (1999) report beneficial effects on patients where a stereotactic operation was performed but *stimulation* of neural cells was administered as opposed to *destruction* of these areas. Behaviour improved in three out of four of the patients and it's concluded that stimulation of brain areas may be a viable alternative to destruction.

✘ **Side-effects:** Unsurprisingly, patients often report headaches that can last up to a week. Other possible effects include confusion, apathy, fits and disinhibition.

✘ **Irreversible effects:** Since the procedure involves the destruction of brain tissue, the results of any operation are irreversible.

✘ **Ethical issues?** Since it's still not clear how psychosurgery works or, indeed, how effective it is, many people think it should be stopped on ethical grounds. However, others believe it is a patient's right to be able to give their informed consent to such a last-chance operation. The mental health charity Mind states that:

'Mind is particularly concerned at the use of an irreversible procedure which carries serious risk when so little is known about its action. Mind is not happy with the continued use of psychosurgery and believes that there should be a rigorous review to determine whether any continued use is justified.' (Mind, 2003)

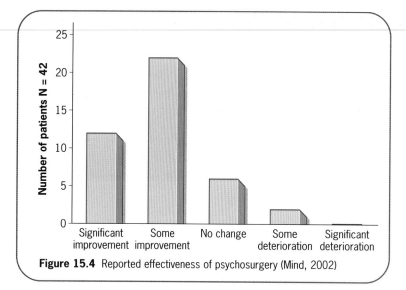

**Figure 15.4** Reported effectiveness of psychosurgery (Mind, 2002)

# EXAM tips BOX

**Discuss the use of and issues surrounding *two or more* biological (somatic) therapies. (40 mins) (800 words minimum) A01/A02**

*This essay can be split up into four sections (each about 200 words per section). You could obviously choose to write about chemotherapy, ECT and/or psychosurgery. We've decided to structure an answer based on ECT and psychosurgery.*

**Section 1:** An **outline** of the use of ECT. This could include:

- what ECT is used for

- the number of treatments.

A description of the way ECT is administered and suggestions as to how it works.

**A01**

**Section 2:** This should include an **evaluation** of ECT in terms of:

- effectiveness: does it work?

- appropriateness: should it be used? This should involve a discussion of side-effects and ethical issues.

**A02**

**Section 3:** An **outline** of the use of psychosurgery. This could include:

- what psychosurgery is used for

- the number of treatments.

A **description** of the way psychosurgery is administered and suggestions as to how it works.

**A01**

**Section 4:** This should include an **evaluation** of psychosurgery in terms of:

- effectiveness: does it work?

- appropriateness: should it be used? This should involve a discussion of side-effects and ethical issues.

**A02**

*Remember, criticisms can be both positive and negative.*

*You could include research studies that support or reject the explanations you've put forward. These studies should not be described in detail but included as evaluative evidence of the explanations.*

*Try to answer this question yourself. There's a sample essay on page 455 with which you can compare your essay.*

# Behavioural therapies

## Behavioural therapies based on classical (e.g. flooding) conditioning

- Behavioural therapy was defined by Wolpe (1958) as 'the use of experimentally established laws of learning for the purposes of changing unadaptive behaviour'. The following behavioural therapies are based on classical conditioning ('learning by association').
- According to classical conditioning theory, a phobia is a reflex acquired to non-dangerous stimuli. The normal fear to a dangerous stimulus such as a poisonous snake becomes generalised to non-poisonous ones as well. If a person were to be exposed to the non-dangerous stimulus over and over again (e.g. non-dangerous snakes) then the phobia would gradually extinguish. Since this is unlikely to occur naturally, behavioural therapy can help by exposing phobics to their fears in a safe and controlled setting.

**Flooding** occurs when the person confronts their fear for a prolonged period of time until the fear itself fades away. Yates (1970) calls this a form of 'forced reality testing'. Flooding can be conducted in reality (*in vivo*) or in imagination (*in vitro*). Flooding using one's imagination is called **implosion**. Some phobias are so strong that implosion is the preferred method.

**Key study**

An example of flooding was reported by Wolpe (1973). He forced a girl with a fear of cars into the back of a car and drove her around for four hours until her fears had subsided. Initially she was hysterical with fear but gradually this subsided.

**Specification Hint:** You need to know a minimum of only *one* behavioural therapy based on classical conditioning (and one for operant conditioning). We've decided to cover two to give a little more choice.

A possible anxiety hierarchy for acrophobia (fear of heights)

- *Systematic desensitisation (SD):* When patients can't cope with flooding, counter-conditioning is sometimes used. Here, a person is trained to substitute a relaxation response for the fear response in the presence of the phobic stimulus.
- The principle of *reciprocal inhibition* suggests that it's impossible to hold two opposite emotions (e.g. fear and anxiety) at the same time. Since relaxation is incompatible with the feeling of fear or anxiety, it helps to counter the fear response ('they cancel each other out': Gross, 2005) when confronted by a phobia.
- Counter-conditioning is used very gradually to introduce the feared stimulus in a step-by-step way and is thus called systematic desensitisation (SD) (Wolpe, 1958). SD involves three steps:

1. training the patient to relax (using deep muscle relaxation or tranquillisers)

2. establishing an anxiety hierarchy of the stimuli involved, and

3. counter-conditioning relaxation as a response to each feared stimulus, beginning first with the least anxiety-provoking stimulus (e.g. toy spider) and then systematically moving on to the next least anxiety-provoking stimulus (e.g. spider in glass box). This continues until all the items listed in the anxiety hierarchy have been dealt with successfully.

An example of SD in practice involves the case of Little Peter (Jones, 1924).

---

**Key study**

## THE CASE OF LITTLE PETER (JONES, 1924)

Peter was a two-year-old living in a charitable institution. Jones was mainly interested in those children who cried and trembled when shown animals (such as frogs, rats or rabbits). Peter showed an extreme fear of rats, rabbits, feathers, cotton wool, fur coats, frogs and fish, although in other respects he was regarded as well adjusted. It wasn't known how these phobias had arisen.

Jones, supervised by John Watson, put a rabbit in a wire cage in front of Peter while he ate his lunch. After 40 such sessions, Peter ate his lunch with one hand and stroked the rabbit (now on his lap) with the other hand. In a series of 17 steps, the rabbit (still in the cage) had been brought a little closer each day, then let free in the room, eventually sitting on Peter's lunch tray. (For further details see Rolls, 2005.)

---

- In summary, SD is a type of counter-conditioning in which a state of relaxation is classically conditioned to a hierarchy of gradually-increasing anxiety-provoking stimuli.

✓ **Effective treatments:** Simple or specific phobias have been quite effectively treated with behaviour therapy (Marks, 1987). Both therapies, but particularly flooding, work relatively quickly.

- Wolpe (1988) claims that behaviour therapy is an extremely effective treatment. He claims: 'alone among the systems of psychotherapy, behaviour therapy yields a percentage of recoveries significantly above the baseline: 80 to 90 percent of patients are either apparently cured or much improved after an average of twenty-five to thirty sessions.'
- Barlow and Lehman (1996) reviewed 12 studies on the efficacy of behavioural methods. They found an average panic-free rate of 77% following behavioural treatment. Also, these were the preferred choice of treatments for their patients.
- Some experts feel that medications such as benzodiazepines actually have an adverse affect on behavioural outcome. This is because the medications suppress the anxiety necessary actually to complete the desensitisation effect (Spiegel & Bruce, 1997).
- When initial treatment involves benzodiazepines, relapse rates are typically around 50% (Marks *et al.*, 1993), compared with much lower relapse rates for behavioural therapies alone.
- In a study by Klosko *et al.* (1990), SD treatment was as good as or better on all measures of outcome at the end of treatment than the most popular drug:
  - SD treatment group: 87% of patients free of panic
  - drug: 50% of patients free of panic
  - placebo condition: 36% of patients free of panic
  - left-on-waiting-list condition: 33% of patients free of panic.

✓ **Cognitive sense:** The therapies developed by Wolpe and others may appear rather obvious and have been applied for years by non-professionals. Once formally stated, however, they can be rigorously applied, tested and improved.

✓ **Patient responsibility for SD therapy:** Since the patient is responsible, with their therapist, for creating their own anxiety hierarchy, they can be seen as in control of their therapy. Furthermore, if the patient finds that too much anxiety is being caused then they can decide to go back down their anxiety hierarchy.

✗ **Ethical issues?** Flooding causes a great deal of anxiety and stress in patients. So-called 'sink or swim' methods such as flooding can also make the symptoms worse. Because of the graded anxiety hierarchy used with SD, it's considered a more ethical form of behaviour therapy.

✗ • ✓ **Impractical method?** It's not always practical for an individual to be desensitised by confronting real situations. Real-life hierarchies in SD can be difficult to arrange and control. In addition, some patients' imaginations may not be vivid enough to produce the desired effect. However, the use of therapies involving imagination means that abstract fears such as fear of failure can be dealt with.

✗ **Restricted application:** These two therapies only work well for minor anxiety disorders such as phobias.

✗ **Are relaxation or an anxiety hierarchy necessary?** It's been claimed that the relaxation techniques used aren't essential for the therapy but merely help the patient to confront their fears. It's exposure to the feared situation that's of paramount importance, not the reciprocal inhibition aspect of the therapy. In addition, the graded anxiety hierarchy merely helps a patient build up to facing their fear but isn't an essential part of the therapy.

> **Specification Hint:** You need to know a minimum of only *one* behavioural therapy based on operant conditioning. We've decided to cover just 'token economies'. There are other therapies based on operant conditioning, but they're not essential for this Specification. Remember the key phrase: 'depth, not breadth.'

## Behavioural therapies based on operant (e.g. token economies) conditioning

- Operant conditioning is also covered elsewhere (see pages 548–550) and can be summarised as 'learning through the consequences of behaviour'.
- Behaviour modification is the application of operant conditioning techniques to modify behaviour. Behaviour-modification programmes are used to help with a number of commonplace behavioural problems such as obesity, smoking and aggression. Perhaps the best-known example of behaviour modification is the use of token economies.

### TOKEN ECONOMIES

- A token economy is a programme for motivating individuals to perform desirable behaviours and to refrain from performing undesirable behaviours.
- In a token economy, a group of individuals can earn *tokens* (token reinforcers) for a variety of desirable behaviours (and lose tokens for undesirable behaviours), and can exchange tokens earned for *back-up reinforcers* (actual reinforcers such as a reinforcing activity).
- There are many advantages to using token reinforcers rather than just providing a reward (such as chocolate):

1. tokens can be given immediately after the desired behaviour has occurred and it doesn't disrupt behaviour

2. tokens can be exchanged for a wide variety of reinforcers and hence satiation is less likely to occur. Satiation occurs when a reinforcer is no longer reinforcing. For example, chocolate will stop being a reinforcer for people when they've eaten too much (they're said to be satiated)

3. tokens work for all individuals since they can be exchanged for different back-up reinforcers. If you chose to use chocolate as a reinforcer, some people wouldn't like chocolate. Using tokens allows individuals to decide on their own appropriate reinforcer

4. tokens can be accumulated towards really valuable goals.

**Figure 15.5** Patients on a psychiatric ward spent more time doing chores when a token economy was being operated (adapted from Ayllon & Azrin, 1965)

A classic example of a token economy involved 44 female psychiatric patients living in a mental institution who had difficulty performing a number of everyday behaviours (Ayllon & Azrin, 1968). The researchers chose to alter a number of simple grooming behaviours, including face-washing, teeth-brushing, bed-making, and dressing properly. A baseline measure of how often these behaviours normally occurred was recorded. Then patients were given a plastic token every time the proper, desired behaviour was performed. The tokens could later be exchanged for food or special privileges such as listening to music, going to the cinema and so on (the back-up reinforcers). The entire life of each patient was controlled as far as possible by this imposed regime. Results showed that the patients significantly increased the frequency of the desired behaviours when they were reinforced with tokens (see Figure 15.5).

✓ **Practical applications:** Token economies (TEs) have been used in psychiatric hospitals, schools, homes for delinquent youths, family homes and various work settings.

✓ **Based on scientifically tested theories:** Behavioural treatments are based on the principles of behaviour therapy and these have been scientifically validated in numerous studies.

✓ **Effectiveness of TEs:** TEs work well with patients who have an obvious and observable disorder, e.g. schizophrenia, and other psychotic patients. However, TEs have also been used for neurotic disorders such as obsessive–compulsive disorders and eating disorders. Marks (1987) concluded that behavioural treatments were the most appropriate therapy for 25% of such patients.

✗ • ✓ **TE Problems:** Behavioural gains may be temporary, but new skills can be learned. The costs of running a TE are high since staff have to monitor behaviour constantly in order to implement the programme and administer the tokens. However, the benefits may outweigh these problems.

✗ **Not a practical approach in psychiatric settings:** Although there's evidence that TEs work in psychiatric settings, TEs haven't been widely applied. Reasons for this include:
- staff resist the approach since it means that they have to interact constantly with the inpatients!
- there's a high initial cost for staffing and the supply of appropriate reinforcers
- patients must learn and adapt to these systems
- TEs are hard to monitor in outpatient settings
- implementation has been restricted by legal rulings and ethical concerns.

✗ **Only work in limited situations with certain people?** It's generally accepted that operant treatments such as TEs work best with people of rather limited intellectual capacity and in situations where the therapist can apply almost total control. This perhaps explains TEs' success with children and in institutionalised settings (Davison & Neale, 1994).

✗ **Treat symptoms not causes?** It's suggested that behavioural treatments concentrate merely on the symptoms of behaviour and don't deal with the underlying causes of the behaviour. However, for many people the causes of the behaviour may be difficult to determine and the main, everyday problem may be their symptoms. Once these disappear, why should the original cause matter?

✗ **Token learning, i.e. not permanent?** It's suggested that behaviour, as a result of extrinsic rewards, is due to an external motivator, not to an innate desire. TEs have been proven to be ineffective. Kazdin and Bootzin (1972), in a review of TE studies, concluded that they don't contribute to permanent behaviour changes. Specifically, removing the reinforcement returns behaviour to its initial level and generalising the reinforced behaviour to other situations doesn't occur.

✗ **TEs reduce intrinsic (internal) interest:** Two studies show that offering token rewards reduces participants' interest in behaviours:

- Lepper *et al.* (1973) found that rewarding children with token rewards can actually reduce their interest in something. They observed pre-school children drawing, and then randomly selected some of the children and asked them to draw some more pictures. These children were promised tokens for the best participants. The rest of the children just drew pictures, without the promise of a token reward. Two weeks later, the drawing behaviour of the children was observed and the researchers found that those who'd been rewarded before drew less, but those who'd never been rewarded still drew at the same rate. Hence the rewards had reduced the children's interest in something that they'd previously enjoyed
- Deci (1971) found similar effects using money as the extrinsic reward. He offered college students money for solving problems, while another group of students just solved the problems without any external reward. Deci found that the unpaid students were more willing than the rewarded students to solve the problems later on in the study.

# EXAM tips BOX

**Outline and evaluate *one or more* behavioural therapies based on operant conditioning. (30 marks) (40 mins) (800 words minimum) AO1/AO2**

*This essay can be split up into four sections (each about 200 words per section). Since we've covered only the minimum amount of information required to meet the Specification, we've covered only token economies.*

**Section 1:** You could give an **outline** of operant conditioning and behaviour therapy. You could explain what a token economy is and describe how TEs work and include their use and application.

**Section 2:** You could **include** a research example using a token economy system (e.g. Ayllon & Azrin, 1965, 1968).

**Section 3:** You could **cover** the main advantages of token economies and give positive criticisms of their use. You should include the appropriateness and effectiveness of TEs.

**Section 4:** You could **cover** the main negative criticisms of the use of token economies. You should again include the appropriateness and effectiveness of TEs.

*Try to answer this question yourself. There's a sample essay on page 456 with which you can compare your essay.*

AO1
↓
AO1
↓
AO2
↓
AO2

---

Rewarding behaviour by giving tokens may suggest to people that the behaviour isn't very interesting in itself (i.e. that's why we need to offer a bribe!). As Kohn (1993) puts it, 'extrinsic rewards turn learning from an end into a means'.

✗ **Social control problem?** The use of TEs can be viewed as a devious or demeaning method of behavioural control. It's often used with children in order to get them to behave in 'socially appropriate' ways. It's a method of 'doing things to people, rather than working with them to develop their behaviour'. However, many patients have reported that they like the implementation of a TE.

---

## Alternatives to the biological and behavioural therapies

### Therapies derived from the psychodynamic model of abnormality (e.g. psychoanalysis; psychodrama)

Therapies derived from the pyschodynamic model of abnormality cover a broad spectrum of treatments, all derived in some respect from Freud's original ideas or those of his followers. The two you need to know are *psychoanalysis* and *psychodrama*.

> **Specification Hint:** You need to know about only *two* therapies from either the psychodynamic (e.g. psychoanalysis, psychodrama) or cognitive–behavioural models of abnormality. Therefore we've covered only psychodynamic therapies. You don't need to learn more and we think they're more interesting than the cognitive–behavioural therapies! If you're asked for one therapy in the exam, it's best to concentrate on psychoanalysis. We've therefore included more information on this particular therapy.

### Psychoanalysis

- Psychoanalysis is derived specifically from Freud's ideas, although most psychoanalytic therapists don't practise the therapy in exactly the same way that he did. We've also covered some of the key principles of psychoanalytic theory on pages 554–558. You'll recall that psychoanalysis places an importance on childhood and repressed impulses and conflicts.
- The goal of psychoanalytic therapy is to try to bring these repressed feelings into conscious awareness ('to make the unconscious conscious') where the patient (called an analysand) can deal with

them. Through gaining 'insight' (see page 446) in this way, the analysand can work through any buried feelings they have.

- There are a number of techniques used by psychoanalytic therapists to help the analysand recover repressed conflicts:

## FREE ASSOCIATION

- Free association involves an analysand lying on the couch and talking about whatever comes to mind, regardless of whether it makes any sense, relates to an earlier point, or is related to their problems.
- The analysand can say absolutely anything, regardless of whether it appears unimportant, embarrassing, shameful or dirty. The therapist usually doesn't react at all and certainly not in a negative way.
- The analysand is relieved of any responsibility for what they say. It's assumed that by using this technique the internal 'censor' of the unconscious will relax so that unconscious material can emerge, at least symbolically.

---

**An example of an instruction given to an analysand during free association:**
*As you talk, various thoughts will occur to you which you like to ignore because of certain criticisms and objections. You'll be tempted to think, 'That is irrelevant or unimportant or nonsensical', and to avoid saying it. Do not give in to such criticism. Report such thoughts in spite of your wish not to do so. Later, the reason for this will become clear. Report whatever goes through your mind. Pretend that you are a traveller, describing to someone beside you the changing views which you see through the train window (Ford & Urban, 1963).*

---

- The analysand's collection of thoughts provides the analyst with clues to help understand their unconscious conflicts.
- Another related technique called *word association* involves single words being presented to the analysand, who has to respond as quickly as possible with the first word that comes to mind. Words thought to be emotionally significant to the analysand are included among common words. The significance of the response is judged subjectively. In addition, some significance is attached to how long it takes the analysand to respond. A long delay in responding suggests that resistance or a censoring of thoughts is occurring.

## DREAM ANALYSIS

- Freud believed that dreams were 'the royal road into the unconscious' that influences so much of our lives.
- He believed that during sleep the *ego* defences are lowered, allowing repressed material to surface, in a disguised, symbolic form. It's disguised in order to stop unacceptable thoughts from waking us up (e.g. dreaming of a lollipop rather than a penis).
- Anxieties and concerns are 'hidden' (the *latent content*) in dreams, whereas the *manifest content* is what is immediately apparent in the dream (what we can recall).
- The analyst guides the analysand in recalling and analysing their dreams, with the goal being to reveal the latent content. For example, a dream of a collapsing bridge (manifest content) might symbolise the analysand's anxiety about their marriage (latent content).

There are a number of therapeutic stages that occur during free association and/or dream analysis:

1. **'Resistance'** involves anything that prevents the progress of the therapy. Resistance can be either conscious (e.g. deliberately changing the subject or arriving late) or unconscious. Any resistance noted by the analyst can provide further clues as to the unconscious conflict experienced by the analysand.

2. **Transference** involves the analysand transferring attitudes from the past toward the therapist.

Analysands respond to the analyst as though they were one of the important people in their past. Freud believed that transference is a vital technique for explaining to analysands the childhood origin of some of their anxieties and fears. The analysand must work through the transference process if success is to be achieved. Analysts encourage transference by remaining in the background as much as possible and revealing little about their own lives and views.

3. **Interpretation** is another technique used in psychoanalysis. This is where the analyst points out and interprets the hidden meanings in what the analysand says and does. The analyst should offer interpretations that the analysand is on the verge of making; they can't be forced on analysands. The analyst may point out what certain reported memories, events or dreams really mean. Interpretation, should help the analysand to re-examine how their present-day behaviour may have evolved from conflicts originating in their childhood. An analysand may show resistance or denial of an interpretation. The analyst may point out why the analysand resists or denies the interpretation, and sometimes the denial is taken as further evidence that the interpretation is correct. An analysand's 'no' may actually be a 'yes'.

4. **Insight** occurs when the analysand gains self-knowledge and understanding into the nature and origin of their neuroses. The analysand understands how the unconscious conflicts they've faced relate to their present-day problems. This can take a considerable time and develop very gradually.

## The appropriateness and effectiveness of psychoanalysis

✗ Difficulties of measuring effectiveness? There's no agreed way of measuring the effectiveness of psychoanalysis. Some studies use analysand self-report, others rely on the analyst to judge the treatment outcome. This is likely to lead to either demand characteristics or a self-serving bias (the analysand exaggerates the success of their treatment). Allied to this problem of measuring outcomes, there are problems of lack of standardised diagnoses and a lack of control over sampling procedures. In addition, it's been claimed that the success of psychoanalysis sometimes only becomes apparent some years after the treatment has ended!

✓・✗ Appropriateness? It's suggested that neurotic analysands (e.g. those with anxiety disorders) are helped more by psychoanalysis than psychotic analysands (e.g. those with severe disorders such as schizophrenia). Even Freud maintained that psychoanalysis wouldn't work with schizophrenics, because such analysands ignore their therapist's insights and are resistant to treatment (Dolnick 1998). If one accepts some biological cause to certain mental disorders such as schizophrenia then it might be considered ridiculous to think that a 'talking cure' can have any effect. Would you treat a broken leg or diabetes with 'talk' therapy or by interpreting the analysand's dreams?

It's also believed that psychoanalysis favours the YAVIS (Young, Attractive, Verbal, Intelligent, Successful) person. Luborsky *et al*. (1993) concludes that psychoanalytic treatment tools are limited by the analysand's capacity to use them.

✗ Scientific status? Psychoanalysis is based on Freudian theory and this has been criticised for its lack of scientific evidence (see page 557). The methods of free association and dream analysis are incapable of being scientifically tested and are based on subjective speculation on the part of the analyst.

✗ Practicalities? Psychoanalysis tends to be costly, time-consuming (several sessions per week) and lengthy (often a number of years).

✗・✓ Studies of effectiveness? One of the most cited studies of the effectiveness of psychoanalysis was that published by Eysenck (1952). Eysenck included patients who'd dropped out of therapy prior to completion and judged the 'success' level at 39%. Bergin (1971) didn't include such patients and arrived at a 91% success rate. However, such data can also be viewed in other ways to obtain other measures of 'success rates' (see Figure 15.6). Eysenck even went on to claim that 'spontaneous remission rates' (people who improve over time without undergoing any treatment) are better than those who undergo psychoanalysis. He stated that: 'the more the psychotherapy, the smaller the recovery rate'.

A more recent review showed that, at the end of psychotherapy, the 'average' patient is better off than 80% of untreated patients (Lambert & Bergin, 1994) and that this beneficial effect is such an effective treatment that it would be unethical to withhold it from patients (Ursano & Silberman, 1994). There are many associated benefits of psychoanalytic therapy. Dossman *et al*. (1997) found in a study of 666 patients that therapy decreased medial visits by 30%, lost work days by 40% and days in hospital by 66%.

## Psychodrama

- 'Psychodrama is a method of psychotherapy in which patients enact the relevant events in their lives instead of simply talking about them.' (Blatner & Blatner, 1988)
- Psychodrama is an active method of group psychotherapy in which past or present experiences are explored.
- The therapeutic techniques were developed by J.L. Moreno after he observed how good children were at dramatising their experiences. Psychodrama can be seen as an extension of natural play.
- Moreno found that his psychiatric patients made surprising progress if they were given opportunities, through the use of drama, to explore their understanding of their own experience. Psychodrama is now practised throughout the world and is used in a wide variety of settings including day centres, patient groups, businesses, schools and mental health centres.

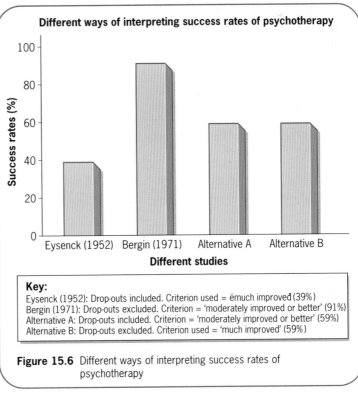

**Figure 15.6** Different ways of interpreting success rates of psychotherapy

Psychodrama: 'The science which explores the truth by dramatic methods' (J.L. Moreno, 1953)

Moreno believed that he was advancing Freud's therapeutic techniques. However, whereas Freud stressed intellectual analysis, Moreno stressed dramatic action.

The basic elements (operational components or tools) of psychodrama are:

1. Director
This is a trained psychodramatist who leads the session. They have three functions:
- producer – provides support to participant and gives direction to the auxiliaries (other group members)
- therapist – helps with exploration of the problem, enabling emotional release (catharsis) to occur. So-called 'repair work' enables behaviour to be changed
- analyst – examines group dynamics and transference processes. Helps the protagonist to identify links between present problems and past difficulties.

2. Protagonist
This is the person who is the focus of the session, whose experiences will be analysed.

3. Auxiliaries (auxiliary *ego*)
Auxiliaries are other group members who play a part in the enactments. They may act out roles such as mother, boyfriend, dog or even inanimate objects such as cuddly toy or television set. Sometimes auxiliaries are asked to role-play a specific aspect of the protagonist, such as the worrier. Auxiliaries are guided by the director to assist the protagonist in the drama. Auxiliaries are an essential ingredient of psychodynamic therapy.

4. Audience
This comprises group members not given a role in the psychodrama. Their role is to act as 'the sounding board of public opinion' (Pitzele, 1992).

5. Stage
This is the physical space in which the drama takes place. Some space is designated as the protagonist's living area during the drama.
There are three distinct phases to psychodrama. They are warm-up, action and sharing:

(a) warm-up
Moreno believed that since we 'warm up' to every event in our lives, a warm-up to a psychodrama session was essential. Psychodrama warm-ups involve cognitive, sensory, verbal, behavioural and physical activities. Warm-ups can involve simple verbal or non-verbal group games. Some psychodramatists use a 'verbal check-in' to try to discover what's been going on in participants' lives at the current time. Warm-ups help to establish trust, confidence and coherence in the group. One

well-known technique used in psychodrama warm-up sessions is the 'empty chair' technique. Here everyone looks at an empty chair and imagines someone sitting there whom they wish to talk to about a particular situation (e.g. one of their children). Each group member takes a turn in reporting who their person is. Any common patterns that emerge will help the director to choose the specific theme for the psychodrama action that follows.

**(b)** action (enactment) phase
- The chosen protagonist will be the focus of the group. A theme will be chosen (e.g. poor relationship with their children) for exploration within the psychodrama. Simple props might be used, such as tables or cushions, to make the situation more realistic. Auxiliaries play the roles of other important people in the scene.
- In the drama there's the chance for the protagonist to re-live important moments in their past and to try to deal with them in more successful ways. In addition, future roles can be practised and conversations that never occurred can be experienced in the here and now. The director needs to ensure that any past traumatic experiences aren't so real that new problems are created. This would have the effect of blocking the therapeutic process.
- A technique often used is that of a 'double'. A double is a role played by one of the auxiliaries who gives voice to possible thoughts and feelings of the protagonist. This can involve emotional support, speaking the unspoken, exaggerating or pointing out contradictions. Again, such a technique helps with analysis of the problem and provides insight.

**(c)** sharing
- This involves group members sharing their views on what they experienced in the drama. This is designed to help release one's emotions. Judgements of the protagonist should be avoided. It's likely that other group members can share their own experiences, and this will help the protagonist deal with and gain insight into the situation.

## Appropriateness and effectiveness of the use of such therapies

✓ **Appropriateness?** It's suitable for people with unresolved issues in their lives, including family and relationship difficulties, for those suffering from anxiety, loss or depression and for those people who want to realise their full potential in life.

Although many clinicians haven't regarded people with mental retardation as suitable candidates for any form of psychotherapy, there are case reports on the effectiveness of individual psychotherapy as well as for group psychotherapy. Psychotherapy for people with mental retardation has been most effective when a directive style with structured sessions is used.

✗ **Effectiveness?** There have been few carefully controlled trials using randomly assigned conditions to assess the effectiveness of psychodrama.

✓ **Flexible and active approach:** Psychodrama is an extremely flexible therapy in that it allows participants the opportunity to try out many different ways of dealing with serious life situations. They can try out new responses to old situations. Its active approach is appealing to people who are put off by the verbal nature of many other therapies. It's a 'doing and showing' rather than 'telling' therapy (Blatner & Blatner, 1991).

✓ **Advantages of group therapy:** There are a number of practical and theoretical advantages to psychodrama group therapy. These include:

- situations that are difficult to deal with in real life can be addressed in a sympathetic and supportive way
- more people can be helped than in an individual therapeutic setting
- the cost of the group therapy is therefore cheaper than individual therapy.

Specific topics (e.g. anger management, bereavement) may be selected which are relevant to all group members, and they may gain support from others in a similar situation. Dayton (1994) states: 'Moreno believed that in a group, each person becomes a therapeutic agent of the other. He viewed the group as rich in healing potential.'

**✘ Risks?** Psychodrama carries a risk of retraumatisation for people who've overcome particularly traumatic experiences in their lives (e.g. those suffering from post-traumatic stress disorder). It can also be rather a frightening therapy for some, although the director should control the drama to avoid this happening. The acting-out of sensitive situations with a (participating) audience can raise ethical issues concerned with confidentiality.

**✘ Ethical issues:** There's no universally agreed code of ethics in psychodrama therapy. There's an ongoing debate as to whether this is required. Some therapists argue that there should be a code as used in other professional therapeutic disciplines. Others such as Lazarus (1994) argue that a rigid set of guidelines would affect the spontaneity and creativity that's an essential part of psychodrama therapy. Nevertheless, since some of the actions that might occur during psychodrama (e.g. affectionate kissing, shouting, chairs being thrown and so on) could be misinterpreted, there's an urgent need for a set of agreed ethical principles (Kellerman, 1992).

## EXAM tips BOX

**Outline and evaluate *one or more* therapies derived from *either* the psychodynamic *or* cognitive-behavioural model of abnormality. (30 marks) (40 mins) (800 words minimum) AO1/AO2**

You could choose to write about both psychoanalysis and psychodrama but we've chosen to concentrate just on psychoanalysis for this **essay**. Here your essay could be split into two sections, each about 400 words long.

**Section 1:** A **description** of what psychoanalysis is, what it's used for and what methods it employs (e.g. free association, dream analysis).

**Section 2:** An **evaluation** of psychoanalysis in terms of its appropriateness, effectiveness, and other issues such as its scientific status and ethical considerations.

*Try to answer this question yourself. There's a sample essay on page 457 with which you can compare your essay.*

**Note:** *We've covered only psychodynamic therapy. Any question will give you a choice of either psychodynamic or cognitive–behavioural therapy.*

AO1
↓
AO2

## Sample essays
## PYA5: Treating mental disorders
## Other possible exam questions:

- Each essay is worth 30 marks and should take 40 minutes to write.
- Try to include synoptic material in your answers.
- Remember, the mark scheme allocates 15 marks for AO1 (knowledge and description) and 15 marks for AO2 (analysis and evaluation).

### BIOLOGICAL (SOMATIC) THERAPIES

1. **a.** Outline the use and mode of action of chemotherapy. (15 marks)

   **b.** Assess the issues surrounding the use of this therapy. (15 marks)

2. Outline and evaluate the use of psychosurgery for the treatment of mental disorders. (30 marks)

3. **a.** Outline the use and mode of action of ECT. (15 marks)

   **b.** Assess the issues surrounding the use of this therapy. (15 marks)

### BEHAVIOURAL THERAPIES

4. 'Behavioural therapies are remarkably effective for treating specific mental disorders but some of the techniques used can be viewed as ethically questionable.'

   Discuss issues relating to the use of behavioural therapies, such as those raised in the quotation above. (30 marks)

5. Outline and evaluate one or more behavioural therapies based on operant conditioning. (30 marks)

6. **a.** Outline any ONE behavioural therapy. (15 marks)

   **b.** Assess the issues surrounding the use of this therapy. (15 marks)

### ALTERNATIVES TO BIOLOGICAL AND BEHAVIOURAL THERAPIES

7. Discuss the issues surrounding the use of therapies derived from *either* the psychodynamic *or* the cognitive–behavioural model of abnormality. (30 marks)

8. **a.** Describe ONE therapy derived from *either* the psychodynamic *or* the cognitive–behavioural model of abnormality. (15 marks)

   **b.** Evaluate the issues surrounding the use of this therapy. (15 marks)

**Note:** We've covered only psychodynamic therapy. Any question will give you a choice of *either* the psychodynamic *or* the cognitive–behavioural therapy.

### COMBINED QUESTIONS

9. Compare and contrast therapies derived from the biological (somatic) and behavioural models of abnormality in the treatment of mental disorders. (30 marks)

10. Compare and contrast therapies derived from the biological (somatic) and *either* the psychodynamic *or* the cognitive–behavioural models of abnormality. (30 marks)

11. Compare and contrast therapies derived from the behavioural and *either* the psychodynamic *or* the cognitive–behavioural models of abnormality. (30 marks)

# CHAPTER SUMMARY: revision schema

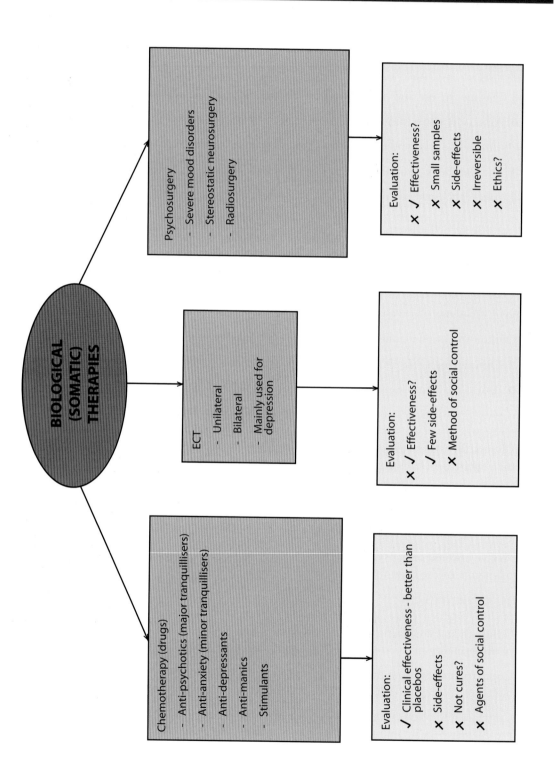

**BIOLOGICAL (SOMATIC) THERAPIES**

Psychosurgery
- Severe mood disorders
- Stereostatic neurosurgery
- Radiosurgery

Evaluation:
- ✗ ✓ Effectiveness?
- ✗ Small samples
- ✗ Side-effects
- ✗ Irreversible
- ✗ Ethics?

ECT
- Unilateral
- Bilateral
- Mainly used for depression

Evaluation:
- ✗ ✓ Effectiveness?
- ✓ Few side-effects
- ✗ Method of social control

Chemotherapy (drugs)
- Anti-psychotics (major tranquillisers)
- Anti-anxiety (minor tranquillisers)
- Anti-depressants
- Anti-manics
- Stimulants

Evaluation:
- ✓ Clinical effectiveness - better than placebos
- ✗ Side-effects
- ✗ Not cures?
- ✗ Agents of social control

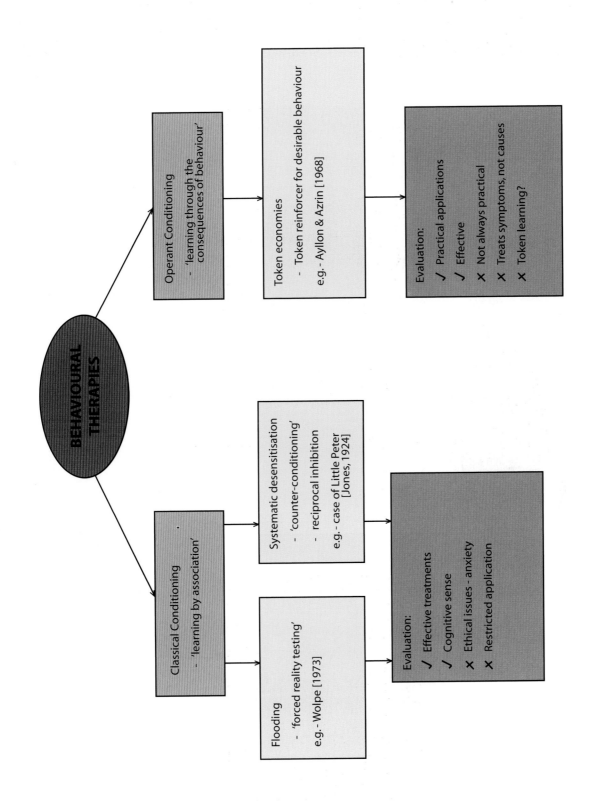

**BEHAVIOURAL THERAPIES**

**Operant Conditioning**
- 'learning through the consequences of behaviour'

**Token economies**
- Token reinforcer for desirable behaviour

e.g.- Ayllon & Azrin [1968]

Evaluation:
✓ Practical applications
✓ Effective
✗ Not always practical
✗ Treats symptoms, not causes
✗ Token learning?

**Classical Conditioning**
- 'learning by association'

**Systematic desensitisation**
- 'counter-conditioning'
- reciprocal inhibition

e.g.- case of Little Peter [Jones, 1924]

**Flooding**
- 'forced reality testing'

e.g.- Wolpe [1973]

Evaluation:
✓ Effective treatments
✓ Cognitive sense
✗ Ethical issues - anxiety
✗ Restricted application

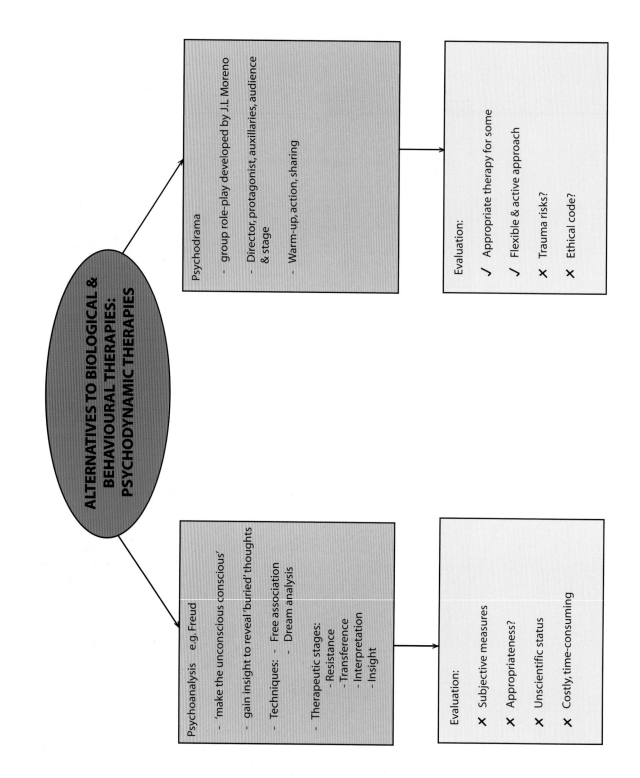

**ALTERNATIVES TO BIOLOGICAL & BEHAVIOURAL THERAPIES: PSYCHODYNAMIC THERAPIES**

Psychodrama

- group role-play developed by J.L Moreno

- Director, protagonist, auxillaries, audience & stage

- Warm-up, action, sharing

Evaluation:

✓ Appropriate therapy for some

✓ Flexible & active approach

✗ Trauma risks?

✗ Ethical code?

Psychoanalysis    e.g. Freud

- 'make the unconscious conscious'

- gain insight to reveal 'buried' thoughts

- Techniques:  -  Free association
               -  Dream analysis

- Therapeutic stages:
  - Resistance
  - Transference
  - Interpretation
  - Insight

Evaluation:

✗ Subjective measures

✗ Appropriateness?

✗ Unscientific status

✗ Costly, time-consuming

(somatic) therapies. (40 mins) AO1/AO2

## Section 1:

Electro-convulsive therapy (ECT) is primarily used to treat people with depression when drugs and psychotherapy have either not been effective or cannot be tolerated by the patient. ECT usually involves about 6–12 treatment episodes given over a period of weeks. There were approximately 65,000 ECT treatments administered in England in 1998–1999.

The patient is given a general anaesthetic and a muscle relaxant to ensure that they don't convulse violently or feel any pain. Electrodes are placed on the patient's head and controlled electrical pulses are passed through the brain. There can be different amounts of electricity provided to produce a seizure, with differing claims as to their effectiveness. There are two types of ECT: unilateral ECT that involves stimulating only one hemisphere of the brain (typically the non-dominant one), whereas bilateral ECT involves stimulation of both hemispheres.

One issue involves arguments as to how ECT works. Perhaps the most plausible explanation is that ECT induces changes in various neurotransmitters including an increased sensitivity to serotonin in the hypothalamus and an increase in the release of GABA, noradrenaline and dopamine (Sasa, 1999). AO1

## Section 2:

ECT does appear to be effective in many cases and can have an immediate beneficial effect. Weiner and Coffey (1988) report that ECT produces a substantial improvement in at least 80% of depressed patients. In terms of electrical dosage and placement of the electrodes, it appears that suprathreshold doses (2.5 times the electricity needed to produce a seizure) and bilateral ECT are more effective than low-dose, unilateral ECT (Sackheim et al., 1993). In support of this, Geddes et al. (2003) reviewed 73 studies using depressed patients and compared ECT with placebo ECT and drug therapy. They showed that there was a significant benefit of ECT over the placebo and drug treatments. However, there are also a number of negative concerns about the effectiveness and use of ECT. One recent study has shown that despite the fact that ECT should be used only after other treatments have failed, as many as 18% of people had been offered no other treatment and 78.5% of the people who took part in the study said that they would never have ECT again (UKAN, 1995).

Two further issues concern possible side-effects and misuse of ECT. Geddes et al. (2003) claimed there was a slight increased risk of cognitive impairment in ECT patients usually involving temporary amnesia, whereas other researchers have found no evidence that ECT damages the brain (Weiner, 1984). After all, ECT-induced seizures do not consistently harm the brain and, furthermore, ECT-induced epileptic seizures take place under far more controlled conditions than epilepsy. Coffey et al. (1991), using MRI brain scans, could find no evidence for ECT brain damage. Another issue involves ECT being (mis-)used as a form of social control. ECT has had a checkered history and may have been used in the past to

---

suggest this is unlikely still to occur.

## Section 3:

Psychosurgery is the scientific treatment of mental disorders by means of brain surgery. It's used to treat severe, incapacitating non-schizophrenic mood disorders. Like ECT, it is used when all other therapeutic attempts have failed. A01

The best-known technique involves stereotactic neurosurgery. This involves fitting a stereotactic frame to the patient's head and then scanning the brain using computer imaging. With the frame in place, the probe that enters the brain can be accurate to within one millimetre of its desired target. The probe is inserted in the brain and once in place is heated to 70 degrees Celsius to produce a small lesion (cut) in the brain tissue. The procedure is typically carried out under general anaesthetic and lasts about 90 minutes A01

Stereotactic surgery is now possible without cutting into the head. Radiosurgery involves projecting radiation into the brain from several different angles. The so-called 'gamma knife' concentrates radiation into a single point inside the brain, while the surrounding, healthy tissues are spared damage. A01

In the UK, psychosurgery is becoming less and less common. Only seven operations occurred in 1999–2000 and just two took place in 2000–2001. There have been over 3,000 operations in total in the UK and these have resulted in one death. A01

## Section 4:

There are a number of important issues associated with the use of psychosurgery. To some, it seems ridiculous to believe that destruction of brain tissue could lead to an improvement in a mental disorder. Early humans drilled holes in skulls (called 'trepanning') in order to liberate demons, and some people see a comparison with psychosurgery. After all, there's no universally agreed technique for psychosurgery. Most of the operations involve destroying some of the nerve circuits in the limbic system that are largely responsible for control and regulation of emotions. A02

Because of the small number of operations performed annually, it's very difficult to assess the effectiveness of psychosurgery, especially since the measure of success is not agreed. Mind (2002) reports a study that suggests that of 42 operations, 34 patients showed an improvement. A02

There are issues involving side-effects and the irreversible nature of psychosurgery. Unsurprisingly, patients often report headaches that can last up to a week. Other possible effects include confusion, apathy, fits and disinhibition. There is also the ethical issue of using an irreversible technique that is somewhat untested and untried. Since it's still not clear how psychosurgery works or indeed how effective it is, many people think it should be stopped on ethical grounds. However, others believe it is a patient's right to be able to give their informed consent to such a last chance operation. The mental health charity Mind states it is unhappy with its continued use. A02

(939 words)

**SAMPLE ESSAYS**

# SAMPLE ESSAYS

Outline and evaluate *one or more* behavioural therapies based on operant conditioning. (30 marks) (40 mins) AO1/AO2

## Section 1:

Operant conditioning can be summarised as 'learning through the consequences of behaviour'. Behaviour modification is the application of operant conditioning techniques to modify behaviour, and the best-known example of this is the use of token economies (TEs).

*AO1*

A token economy is a programme for motivating individuals to perform desirable behaviours and to refrain from performing undesirable behaviours. In a token economy, a group of individuals can earn *tokens* (token reinforcers) for a variety of desirable behaviours (and lose tokens for undesirable behaviours), and can exchange tokens earned for *back-up reinforcers* (actual reinforcers such as a reinforcing activity). TEs are used to help with a number of commonplace behavioural problems such as obesity, smoking and aggression, as well as eating disorders.

*AO1*

## Section 2:

A classic example of a token economy involved 44 female psychiatric patients living in a mental institution who had difficulty performing a number of everyday behaviours (Ayllon & Azrin, 1968). The researchers chose to alter a number of simple grooming behaviours, including face-washing, teeth-brushing, bed-making and dressing properly. A baseline measure of how often these behaviours normally occurred was recorded. Then patients were given a plastic token every time the proper, desired behaviour was performed. The tokens could later be exchanged for food or special privileges such as listening to music, going to the cinema and so on (the back-up reinforcers). The entire life of each patient was controlled as far as possible by this imposed regime. Results showed that the patients significantly increased the frequency of the desired behaviours when they were reinforced with tokens.

*AO1*

## Section 3:

There are many advantages to using token reinforcers rather than just providing a reward (such as chocolate). Tokens can be given immediately after the desired behaviour has occurred and it doesn't disrupt behaviour. Tokens can be exchanged for a wide variety of reinforcers and hence satiation is less likely to occur. Satiation occurs when a reinforcer is no longer reinforcing. For example, chocolate will stop to be a reinforcer for people when they've eaten too much (they're said to be satiated). Tokens work for all individuals since they can be exchanged for different back-up reinforcers. If you chose to use chocolate as a reinforcer, some people would not like chocolate. Using tokens allows individuals to decide on their own appropriate reinforcer. Tokens can be accumulated towards really valuable goals.

*AO2*

There are a number of positive points that can be made about TEs. Token economies have been successfully applied in a number of different settings ranging from psychiatric hospitals, schools, homes for delinquent youths, family homes and various work settings. The TE system is based on the principles of operant conditioning and these have been scientifically validated in numerous experiments and research studies. TEs have also been shown to work well with patients who have an obvious and observable disorder. Behavioural treatments are particularly effective with neurotic disorders such as phobias, obsessive-compulsive disorders and eating disorders. Marks (1987) concluded that behavioural treatments were the most appropriate therapy for 25% of such patients.

*AO2*

## Section 4:

However, there are some negative criticisms associated with TEs. It's claimed that behavioural gains may only be temporary (token economies lead to token learning), but nevertheless it is demonstrated that new skills can be learned. Kazdin and Bootzin (1972), in a review of TE studies, concluded that they don't contribute to permanent behaviour changes. Specifically, removing the reinforcement returns behaviour to its initial level, and generalising the reinforced behaviour to other situations doesn't occur. Practical problems involve the costs of running a TE. These tend to be high since staff have to monitor behaviour constantly in order to implement the programme and administer the tokens. In addition, although there is evidence that TEs work in psychiatric settings, TEs have not been widely applied.

*AO2*

It's also suggested that behavioural treatments concentrate merely on the symptoms underlying behaviour and don't deal with the causes of the behaviour. However, for many people the causes of the behaviour may be difficult to determine and the main, everyday problem may be their symptoms. Once these disappear, why should the original cause matter?

*AO2*

Perhaps surprisingly, it's also been shown that TEs can work to reduce participants' interest in behaviours. Lepper, Greene and Nisbett (1973) observed pre-school children drawing and then randomly selected some of the children and asked them to draw some more pictures. These children were promised tokens for the best participants. The rest of the children just drew pictures without the promise of a token reward. Two weeks later, the drawing behaviour of the children was observed and the researchers found that those who had been rewarded before drew less, but those who had never been rewarded still drew at the same rate. Hence the rewards had reduced the children's interest in something that they had previously enjoyed. Deci (1971) supported these results, using money as the extrinsic reward. Rewarding behaviour by giving tokens may suggest to people that the behaviour is not very interesting in itself (i.e. that's why we need to offer a bribe).

*AO1/AO2*

There is one final ethical consideration involving TEs. The use of TEs can be viewed as a devious or demeaning method of behavioural control. It is often used with children in order to get them to behave in 'socially appropriate' ways. It's a method of 'doing things to people, rather than working with them to develop their behaviour'. However, many patients have reported that they like the implementation of a TE.

*AO2*

(906 words)

Outline and evaluate *one or more* therapies derived from *either* the psychodynamic *or* the cognitive–behavioural model of abnormality. (30 marks) (40 mins) AO1/AO2

Section 1:

Psychoanalysis is a 'talking cure' therapy based on the psychodynamic model of abnormality. The therapy places great importance on childhood and repressed impulses and conflicts. The goal of psychoanalytic therapy is to bring these repressed feelings into conscious awareness ('to make the unconscious conscious') where the patient (called an analysand) can deal with them. Through gaining 'insight' in this way the analysand can work through any buried feelings they have. **A01**

The two main techniques used in psychoanalysis are free association and dream analysis. Free association involves an analysand lying on the couch and talking about whatever comes to mind. The analysand can say absolutely anything regardless of whether it appears unimportant, embarrassing, shameful or dirty. The therapist usually doesn't react at all. It's assumed that by using this technique the internal 'censor' of the unconscious will relax so unconscious material can emerge, at least symbolically. The analysand's collection of thoughts provides the analyst with clues to help understand their unconscious conflicts. **A01**

Word association is a related technique that involves single words being presented to the analysand who has to respond as quickly as possible with the first word that comes to mind. Words thought to be emotionally significant to the analysand are included. The significance of the response is judged subjectively. A long delay in responding suggests that resistance or a censoring of thoughts is occurring. **A01**

Freud believed dreams were 'the royal road into the unconscious' that influences so much of our lives. Freud believed that during sleep the *ego* defences are lowered, allowing repressed material to surface, in a disguised, symbolic form. It's disguised in order to stop unacceptable thoughts from waking us up (e.g. dreaming of a lollipop rather than a penis). Anxieties and concerns are 'hidden' (the latent content) in dreams, whereas the manifest content is what is immediately apparent in the dream (what we can recall). The analyst guides the analysand in recalling and analysing their dreams with the goal being to reveal the latent content. **A01**

Key therapeutic processes that occur during psychoanalysis include transference, interpretation and insight. Transference involves the analysand transferring attitudes from the past toward the therapist. Analysands respond to the analyst as though they were one of the important people in their past. Freud believed that transference is a vital technique for explaining to analysands the childhood origin of some of their anxieties and fears. The analysand must work through the transference process if success is to be achieved. Interpretation is where the analyst points out and interprets the hidden meanings in what the analysand says and does. The analyst should offer interpretations that the analysand is on **A01**

the verge of making. The analyst may point out what certain reported memories, events or dreams really mean. Insight occurs when the analysand gains self-knowledge and understanding into the nature and origin of their neuroses. **A01**

Section 2:

There are a number of problems with psychoanalysis. A key aspect is that there's no agreed way of measuring its effectiveness. Some studies use analysand self-report; others rely on the analyst to judge the treatment outcome. This is likely to lead to either demand characteristics or a self-serving bias. Allied to this problem of measuring outcomes, there are also problems of lack of standardised diagnoses and a lack of control over sampling procedures. In addition, it has been claimed that the success of psychoanalysis sometimes only becomes apparent some years after the treatment has ended! One of the most cited studies of the effectiveness of psychoanalysis was that published by Eysenck (1952). Eysenck included patients who had dropped out of therapy prior to completion and judged the 'success' level at 39%. Bergin (1971) did not include such patients and arrived at a 91% success rate. Eysenck even went on to claim that 'spontaneous remission rates' (people who improve over time without undergoing any treatment) are better than those who undergo psychoanalysis. He stated that: 'the more the psychotherapy, the smaller the recovery rate'. **A02**

A more recent review showed that, at the end of psychotherapy, the 'average' patient is better off than 80% of untreated patients (Lambert & Bergin, 1994) and that this beneficial effect is such an effective treatment that it would be unethical to withhold it from patients (Ursano & Silberman, 1994). There are many associated benefits of psychoanalytic therapy. Dossman *et al.* (1997) found in a study of 666 patients that therapy decreased medical visits by 30%, lost work days by 40% and days in hospital by 66%. **A02**

There are also questions as to how appropriate psychoanalysis is for certain disorders. It's suggested that neurotics (e.g. those with anxiety disorders) are helped more by psychoanalysis than psychotics (e.g. those with severe personality disorders such as schizophrenia). Even Freud maintained that psychoanalysis would not work with schizophrenics because they ignore their therapist's insights and are resistant to treatment (Dolnick, 1998). Indeed, if one accepts some biological cause to certain mental disorders such as schizophrenia then it might be considered ridiculous to think that a 'talking cure' can have any effect. **A02**

Psychoanalysis is based on Freudian theory and this, in turn, has been criticised for its lack of scientific evidence. The methods of free association and dream analysis are incapable of being scientifically tested and are based on subjective speculation on the part of the analyst. In addition, psychoanalysis tends to be costly, time-consuming (several sessions per week) and lengthy (often a number of years). From a practical point of view, this is hardly ideal especially given the controversies outlined above surrounding both its appropriateness and effectiveness. **A02**

*(918 words)*

# SAMPLE ESSAYS

# Perspectives: Issues

## What's covered in this chapter?

### You need to know about:

- **Gender bias** in psychological theories and studies (e.g. alpha/beta bias; androcentrism)
- **Cultural bias** in psychological theories and studies (e.g. ethnocentrism; historical bias; the imposed etic)
- **Ethical issues** involved in psychological investigations using human participants, including the ethics of socially sensitive research
- **The use of non-human animals** in psychological investigations, including constraints on their use and arguments (both ethical and scientific) for and against their use

## Bias in psychological theories and studies

- Mainstream academic psychology models itself on classical, orthodox, natural science (such as physics and chemistry). On this basis, it claims to be objective, unbiased and value-free.
- Collectively, these aims form the *positivist* view of science, or *positivism* (see Chapter 17, page 508).
- As applied to the study of human beings, this view implies that it's possible to study people as they 'really are', without the psychologist's characteristics in any way influencing the outcome of the investigation.
- However, this view of psychology as unbiased and value-free is mistaken. Two major forms of bias, *sexism* and *ethnocentrism*, relate to gender and culture respectively. These permeate a great deal of psychological theory and research studies.

## Gender bias

> **Specification Hint:** The Specification states 'Gender bias in psychological theories and studies (e.g. alpha/beta bias, androcentrism)'. These are just examples, and there's no specific number of biases that you're required to know.

- Not surprisingly, much of the criticism of mainstream psychology regarding its gender bias has come from *feminist psychology*. Wilkinson (1997) defines this as:

'... psychological theory and practice which is explicitly informed by the political goals of the feminist movement.'

- Feminism and feminist psychology can take various forms. But two common themes are (a) the valuation of women as worthy of study in their own right (not just in comparison with men), and (b) recognition of the need for social change on behalf of women (Unger & Crawford, 1996).
- Feminist psychology is openly political. It sets out to challenge the discipline of psychology for its inadequate and damaging theories about women, and for its failure to see power relations as central to social life (Unger & Crawford, 1992). More specifically, it insists on exposing and challenging the operation of male power in psychology. According to Wilkinson (1991):

'Psychology's theories often exclude women, or distort our experience by assimilating it to male norms or man-made stereotypes, or by regarding "women" as a unitary category, to be understood only in comparison with the unitary category "men" ... Similarly, psychology [screens out] ... the existence and operation of social and structural inequalities between and within social groups.'

- Psychology obscures the social and structural operation of male power by concentrating its analysis on people as individuals (*individualism*). Responsibility (and pathology) are located within the individual, to the total exclusion of social and political oppression. By ignoring or minimising the social context, psychology obscures the mechanisms of oppression. For example, the unhappiness of some women after childbirth ('baby blues' or post-natal depression) is treated as a problem in individual functioning (with possible hormonal causes). This distracts attention away from the difficult practical situation many new mothers have to adapt to (Wilkinson, 1997). Another example is the attempts to explain the higher rate of depression (in general) among women (see Box 14.3; page 407).

## Box 16.1 Some major feminist criticisms of psychology

- Much psychological research is conducted on all-male samples. But it then either fails to make this clear, or reports the findings as if they applied equally to women and men.
- Some of the most influential theories within psychology as a whole are based on studies of males only. But they're meant to apply equally to women and men.
- If women's behaviour differs from men's, the former is often judged to be pathological, abnormal or deficient in some way (*sexism*). This is because men's behaviour is taken (implicitly or explicitly) as the 'standard' or norm against which women's behaviour is compared (*androcentrism* – male-centredness, or the *masculinist bias*).
- Psychological explanations of behaviour tend to emphasise biological (and other internal) causes, as opposed to social (and other external) causes. This emphasis on internal causes is called *individualism*. This gives (and reinforces) the impression that psychological sex differences are inevitable and unchangeable. In turn, this reinforces widely-held stereotypes about women and men, contributing to the oppression of women (another form of sexism).
- Heterosexuality (both male and female) is taken (implicitly or explicitly) as the norm. Consequently, homosexuality is seen as abnormal (*heterosexism*).

**Exam Hint:**

There's a fair degree of overlap between these examples of bias. What's really important is that you demonstrate your understanding of what gender bias means in relation to theories and studies. This will involve giving examples of psychological theories and studies that are gender-biased in particular ways. You will need to spell out in what ways they demonstrate the bias(es) you've identified.

## The feminist critique of science

- An even more fundamental criticism of psychology than those listed in Box 16.1 is feminists' belief that scientific investigation itself (whether within psychology or not) is biased.
- As we noted above, scientific enquiry cannot be neutral, completely independent of the value system of the human scientists involved. According to Prince and Hartnett (1993):

> 'Decisions about what is, and what is not, to be measured, how this is done, and most importantly, what constitutes legitimate research are made by individual scientists within a sociopolitical context, and thus science is ideological.'

- Many feminist psychologists argue that scientific method is gender-biased. For example, Nicolson (1995) identifies two major problems associated with the 'objective' study of behaviour for how claims are made about women and gender differences:

(a) The experimental environment takes the individual 'subject's *behaviour*', as opposed to the 'subject' herself, as the unit of study. This ignores the behaviour's *meaning*, including its social, personal and cultural contexts. As a result, claims about gender differences in competence and behaviour are attributed to *intrinsic* qualities (either the product of 'gender role socialisation' or biology) as opposed to *contextual* qualities. This is another example of individualism.

(b) Experimental psychology takes place in a very specific context, which typically works to women's disadvantage (Eagly, 1987). In an experiment, a woman becomes anonymous, stripped of her social roles and the accompanying power and knowledge she might have achieved in the outside world. She's put in this 'strange' environment, and expected to respond to the needs of (invariably) a male experimenter, who's in charge of the situation.

- It's completely invalid to believe that you can study people 'as they really are', removed from their usual sociocultural contexts (that is, in a *decontextualised* way). As Nicolson (1995) says:

> 'Psychology relies for its data on the practices of socialized and culture-bound individuals, so that to explore "natural" or "culture-free" behaviour (namely that behaviour unfettered by cultural, social structures and power relations) is by definition impossible.'

## Some practical consequences of gender bias

- According to Kitzinger (1998), questions about sex differences (and similarities) aren't just scientific questions – they're also highly *political*.
- Answers to some of these questions have been used to keep women out of universities, or to put them in mental hospitals. Others have been used to encourage women to go on assertiveness training courses, or to argue that women should have all the same rights and opportunities as men. In other words, the science of sex differences research is always used for political reasons:

Celia Kitzinger, lesbian feminist psychologist

> 'However much psychologists may think or hope or believe that they are doing objective research and discovering truths about the world they are always influenced . . . by the social and political context in which they are doing their research.' (Kitzinger, 1998).

- For Prince and Hartnett (1993), scientific psychology has *reified* concepts such as personality and intelligence (that is, treating abstract or metaphorical terms as if they are 'things' or entities). This resulted in physical assaults on women such as forced abortions and sterilisations. Between 1924 and 1972, more than 7,500 women in Virginia alone were forcibly sterilised, in particular 'unwed mothers, prisoners, the feeble-minded, children with discipline problems'. The criterion used in all cases was mental age as measured by the Stanford–Binet intelligence test (Gould, 1981: see Chapter 11, page 283).
- According to Gilligan (1993), at the core of her work on moral development in women and girls (see Chapter 11) was the realisation that within psychology (and society at large) 'values were taken as facts'. Psychologists (and other scientists) have a responsibility to make their values explicit about important social and political issues. Failure to do so may (unwittingly) contribute to prejudice, discrimination and oppression. (These considerations are also relevant to a discussion of ethics: see below, pages 471–477).

## The masculinist bias and sexism: a closer look

- As Box 16.1 shows, the masculinist bias (*androcentrism*) and *sexism* are two major criticisms of mainstream psychology made by feminist psychologists.
- Each of these can take different forms, but important examples are (a) taking men as some sort of standard or norm for judging women; and (b) gender bias in psychological theories and research studies.

### THE MALE NORM AS STANDARD

- According to Tavris (1993):

'In any domain of life in which men set the standard of normalcy, women will be considered abnormal, and society will debate woman's "place" and her "nature". Many women experience tremendous conflict in trying to decide whether to be "like" men or "opposite" from them, and this conflict is itself evidence of the implicit male standard against which they are measuring themselves. This is why it is normal for women to feel abnormal.'

- Tavris gives two examples of why it's normal for women to feel abnormal. One relates to mental disorder, and the other relates to explanations of men's and women's behaviour.

(a) In 1985, the American Psychiatric Association proposed two new categories of mental disorder for inclusion in the revised (third) edition of DSM (DSM-III-R, 1987: see Chapter 14). One of these was *masochistic personality*. In DSM-II (1968), this was described as one of the psychosexual disorders, in which sexual gratification requires being hurt or humiliated. It was proposed that this term should be extended, making it a more pervasive personality disorder in which the individual seeks failure at work, at home and in relationships, rejects opportunities for pleasure, puts others first (thereby sacrificing his/her own needs), plays the martyr and so on. This wasn't intended to apply to women exclusively, but these characteristics are associated predominantly with the female role. Caplan (1991) argues that the category represents a way of calling psychopathological the behaviour of women who conform to social norms for a 'feminine woman' (the 'good wife syndrome'). In other words, women who behave as society expects them to were considered to be displaying mascochism (a characteristic of women – not of society). (The category was eventually changed to 'self-defeating personality disorder', and was put in the appendix to DSM-III-R.)

(b) When men have problems (such as drug abuse) and behave in socially unacceptable ways (as in rape and other forms of violence), the causes are looked for in their upbringing. But women's problems are seen as the result of their psyche (mind or personality) or hormones. Explaining women's problems this way is another form of individualism. It implies that it could have been different for men ('they're victims of their childhood'), but not for women ('that's what women are like').

Women are consumers of huge amounts of alpha bias

## THE 'MISMEASURE OF WOMAN' AND ALPHA BIAS

- According to Tavris, the belief that man is the norm and woman is the opposite, lesser or deficient (the problem) constitutes one of three alternative views regarding the 'mismeasure of woman'. (This is meant to parallel Gould's (1981) *The Mismeasure of Man*, a renowned critique of intelligence testing: see Chapter 11).
- This is the view that underpins so much psychological research designed to discover why women aren't 'as something' (moral, intelligent, rational) as men. This is what Hare-Mustin and Maracek (1988) call *alpha bias*.

- Alpha bias underlies the enormous self-help industry. Women consume millions of books and magazines advising them how to become more beautiful, independent and so on. Men, being 'normal', feel no need to 'fix' themselves in corresponding ways (Tavris, 1993).

### Box 16.2  A demonstration of alpha bias

- **Wilson (1994) maintains that the reason 95% of bank managers, company directors, judges and university professors in Britain are men is that men are 'more competitive' and because 'dominance is a personality characteristic determined by male hormones'.**
- **Wilson also argues that women in academic jobs are less productive than men: 'objectively speaking, women may already be over-promoted'. Women who do achieve promotion to top management positions 'may have brains that are masculinised'.**
- **The research cited by Wilson to support these claims comes partly from the psychometric testing industries. These provide 'scientific' evidence of women's inadequacies, such as (compared with men) their 'lack of mathematical and spatial abilities'. Even if women are considered to have the abilities to perform well in professional jobs, Wilson believes they have personality deficits (especially low self-esteem and lack of assertiveness) which impede performance:**

  'These differences [in mental abilities, motivation, personality and values] are deep-rooted, based in biology, and not easily dismantled by social engineering. Because of them we are unlikely to see the day when the occupational profiles of men and women are the same.' (Wilson, 1994)

- Wilson is combining alpha bias with individualism in order to argue that women are 'naturally' deficient in the (male) qualities needed to achieve in certain occupations. He's also assuming that the research he draws on to make his claims isn't itself gender-biased.

## SEXISM IN PSYCHOLOGICAL RESEARCH STUDIES

- The American Psychological Association's Board of Social and Ethical Responsibility set up a Committee on Nonsexist Research. The Committee reported its findings as *Guidelines for Avoiding Sexism in Psychological Research* (Denmark *et al.*, 1988).
- The *Guidelines* maintain that gender bias is found at all stages of the research process:

(a) question formulation
(b) research methods and design
(c) data analysis and interpretation, and
(d) conclusion formulation.

## Box 16.3 Examples of gender bias at each stage of the research process

- *Question formulation:* It's assumed that topics relevant to white males are more important and 'basic' (for example, the effects of TV violence on aggression in boys: see Chapter 9) compared with those relevant to white females, or ethnic minority females or males. The latter are seen as more marginal, specialised, or applied (for example, the psychological correlates of pregnancy or the menopause).
- *Research methods and design:* Surprisingly often, the sex and race of the participants, researchers, and any stooges/confederates who may be involved, aren't specified. Consequently, potential interactions between these variables aren't accounted for. For example, men tend to display more helping behaviour than women in studies involving a young, female stooge 'victim' (again, see Chapter 9). This could be a function of either the sex of the stooge or an interaction between the stooge and the participant – rather than sex differences between the participants (the conclusion that's usually drawn).
- *Data analysis and interpretation:* Significant sex differences may be reported in very misleading ways – because the wrong sorts of comparisons are made. For example:

  "'The spatial-ability scores of women in our sample is significantly lower than those of men, at the 0.01 level''. You might conclude from this that women cannot or should not become architects or engineers. However, "Successful architects score above 32 on our spatial ability tests . . . engineers score above 31 . . . twelve per cent of women and 16 per cent of men in our sample score above 31; eleven per cent of women and 15 per cent of men score above 32". What conclusions would you draw now?' (Denmark *et al*., 1988).

- Conclusion formulation and beta bias: Results based on one sex only are then applied to both. This can be seen in some of the major theories within developmental psychology, notably Erikson's psychosocial theory of development (1950: see Chapter 12), and Kohlberg's theory of moral development (1969: see Chapter 11). These are examples of what Hare-Mustin and Maracek (1988) call *beta bias* (see text below).

(Based on Denmark *et al*., 1988.)

- The principles set out in the *Guidelines* are meant to apply to other forms of bias too – those concerned with race, ethnicity, disability, sexual orientation, and socio–economic status.

## SEXISM IN PSYCHOLOGICAL THEORIES: ALPHA AND BETA BIAS

- Gilligan (1982) gives Erikson's theory (based on the study of males only) as one example of a sexist theory. It portrays women as 'deviants' (alpha bias).
- In one version of his theory, Erikson (1950) describes a series of eight *universal* stages. So, for example, for both sexes, in all cultures, the conflict between identity and role confusion (adolescence) precedes that between intimacy and isolation (young adulthood).
- In another version (Erikson, 1968), he acknowledges that the sequence is *different* for a female. She postpones her identity as she prepares to attract the man whose name she'll adopt, and by whose status she'll be defined. For women, intimacy seems to go along with identity – they come to know themselves through their relationships with others (Gilligan, 1982).
- Despite Erikson's observation of sex differences, the sequence of stages in his psychosocial theory remains unchanged. As Gilligan says:

'Identity continues to precede intimacy as male experience continues to define his [Erikson's] life-cycle concept.'

- Similarly, Kohlberg's (1969) six-stage theory of moral development was based on a 20-year longitudinal study of 84 boys. But he claims that these stages are universal. This represents beta bias.
- When males and females are compared, females rarely attain a level of moral reasoning above Stage 3 ('Good boy–nice girl' orientation). This is supposed to be achieved by most adolescents and adults. This leaves females looking decidedly morally deficient (alpha bias).
- Like other feminist psychologists, Gilligan argues that psychology speaks with a 'male voice', that is, describing the world from a male perspective and confusing this with absolute truth (beta bias).
- The task of feminist psychology is to listen to women and girls who speak 'in a different voice' (Gilligan, 1982; Brown & Gilligan, 1992). Gilligan's work with females has led her to argue that men and women have qualitatively different conceptions of morality (but see Chapter 11). By stressing the *differences* between men and women (an alpha-biased approach), Gilligan is trying to compensate for Kohlberg's theory (which is heavily beta-biased, but also alpha-biased in a different way).

## EXAM tips BOX

Discuss gender bias (e.g. alpha/beta bias, androcentrism) in psychological theories and/or studies. (30 marks) (40 mins) (800 words minimum) AO1/AO2

*This essay can be split up into FOUR sections – each about 200 words long. Each section would be worth 7–8 marks.*

**Section 1:** An **explanation** of what's meant by gender bias, in particular alpha and beta bias, and androcentrism. Related to these are sexism and heterosexism. Some reference to feminist psychology would be useful here in relation to these forms of gender bias.

**Section 2:** You could then give some **examples** of psychological theories and/or research studies which have been cited by feminist psychologists as displaying these biases. You could use Denmark *et al.*'s (1988) *Guidelines for Avoiding Sexism in Psychological Research* as a framework for this section.

**Section 3:** An **analysis** and **evaluation** of the examples given in Section 2 and/or others that weren't included. Freud's, Erikson's and Kohlberg's are amongst the 'meatiest' examples of theories that are gender-biased.

**Section 4:** You could continue your **analysis** and **evaluation** by considering some broader issues. These might include the feminist critique of science, some practical consequences of gender bias, and the 'mismeasure of woman'.

*Try to answer this question yourself. There's a sample essay on pages 489–490 with which you can compare your essay.*

AO1
↓
AO1
↓
AO2
↓
AO2

## Culture bias

- When discussing gender bias, several references were made to culture bias. For example, we noted that Denmark *et al.*'s (1988) *Guidelines* are meant to apply equally to all other major forms of bias, including cultural.
- Ironically, many feminist critics of Gilligan's ideas have argued that women aren't a homogeneous group who speak in a single voice. In other words, not all women are the same. Women speak with a diversity of voices across different ages, ethnic backgrounds, (dis)abilities, class and other social divisions (Wilkinson, 1997).

Specification Hint: The Specification states 'Culture bias in psychological theories and studies (e.g. ethnocentrism, historical bias, the imposed etic)'. As with gender bias, these are just examples and there's no specific number of biases you're expected to know.

## Cross-cultural psychology and ethnocentrism

- According to Smith and Bond (1998), cross-cultural psychology (C-CP) studies *variability* in behaviour among the various societies and cultural groups around the world.
- For Jahoda (1978), an additional goal of C-CP is to identify what's *similar* across different cultures, and so what's likely to be our common human heritage (the *universals* of human behaviour).
- C-CP is important because it helps to correct *ethnocentrism*, that is, the strong human tendency to use our own ethnic or cultural group's norms and values to define what's 'natural' and 'correct' for everyone ('reality': Triandis, 1990).
- Historically, psychology has been dominated by white, middle-class males in the USA. Over the last century, they've enjoyed a monopoly as both the researchers and the 'subjects' of the discipline (Moghaddam & Studer, 1997). They constitute the core of psychology's *First World* (Moghaddam, 1987).

### Box 16.4 Psychology's First, Second and Third Worlds

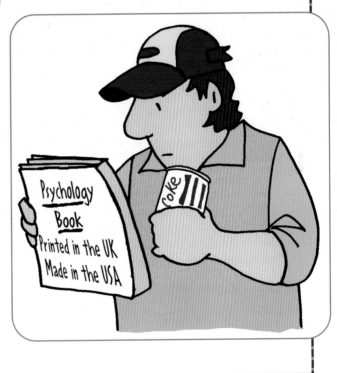

- The USA, the *First World* of psychology, dominates the international arena, and monopolises the manufacture of psychological knowledge. It exports this knowledge to other countries around the globe, through control over books and journals, test manufacture and distribution, training centres and so on.
- The *Second World* countries comprise Western European nations and Russia. These have far less influence in shaping psychology around the world. But, ironically, it's in these countries (such as Germany) that modern psychology has its philosophical and scientific roots (see Chapter 17). The Second World countries find themselves overpowered by American popular culture and by US-manufactured psychological knowledge.
- *Third World* countries are mostly importers of psychological knowledge, first from the USA but also from the Second World countries with which they historically had colonial ties (such as Pakistan and the UK). India is the most important Third World 'producer' of psychological knowledge. But even there most research follows the lines established by the USA and (to a lesser extent) Western Europe.

(Based on Moghaddam & Studer, 1997.)

**Exam Hint:**

There's a fair degree of overlap between these examples of bias. What's really important (as with gender bias) is that you demonstrate your understanding of what culture bias means in relation to theories and studies. This will involve giving examples of psychological theories and studies that are culture-biased in particular ways. You will need to spell out in what ways they demonstrate the bias(es) you've identified.

- According to Moghaddam *et al*. (1993), American researchers and participants:

> ' ... have shared a lifestyle and value system that differs not only from that of most other people in North America, such as ethnic minorities and women, but also the vast majority of people in the rest of the world.'

- Yet the findings from this research, and the theories based upon it, have been applied to *people in general* – as if culture makes no difference. An implicit equation is made between 'human being' and 'human being from Western culture'. This is the *Anglocentric* or *Eurocentric bias*.

- When members of other cultural groups have been studied, they've usually been *compared* with Western samples. The behaviour and experience of the latter are used as the 'standard'. As with androcentrism, it's the failure to acknowledge this bias which creates the misleading and false impression that what's being said about behaviour can be generalised without qualification.
- C-C psychologists *don't* equate 'human being' with 'member of Western culture' because, for them, cultural background is the crucial *independent variable*. Given the domination of First World psychology, this distinction becomes crucial.
- But C-C psychologists also consider the search for universal principles of human behaviour as perfectly valid (and is consistent with the 'classical' view of science: see Chapter 17).

## What is culture?

- Herskovits (1955) defines culture as 'the human-made part of the environment'. For Triandis (1994):

> 'Culture is to society what memory is to individuals. In other words, culture includes the traditions that tell "what has worked" in the past. It also encompasses the way people have learned to look at their environment and themselves, and their unstated assumptions about the way the world is and the way people should act.'

- The 'human-made' part of the environment can be sub-divided into *objective* aspects (such as tools, roads and radio stations) and *subjective* aspects (such as categorisations, associations, norms, roles and values). This allows us to examine how subjective culture influences behaviour (Triandis, 1994). Culture is made by humans, but it also helps to 'make' them. Hence humans have an *interactive* relationship with culture (Moghaddam *et al.*, 1993).
- Much C-C research is actually based on 'national cultures', which often comprise several different sub-cultures. These may be demarcated by religion (as in Northern Ireland), language (as in Belgium), or race (Malaysia and Singapore).
- But such research often fails to provide any more details about the participants than the name of the country (national culture) in which the study was conducted. According to Smith and Bond (1998), when this happens we pay two 'penalties':

(a) When we compare national cultures, we can lose track of the enormous diversity found *within* many of the major nations of the world. Differences found between any two countries might well also be found between carefully selected sub-cultures within those countries.

(b) There's the danger of implying that national cultures are unitary systems, free of conflict, confusion and dissent. This is rarely the case.

## How do cultures differ?

- Definitions of culture such as those above stress what different cultures *have in common*. To evaluate research findings and theories that are culturally biased, it's even more important to consider how cultures *differ* from each other.
- Triandis (1990) identifies several *cultural syndromes*, which he defines as:

> ' . . . a pattern of values, attitudes, beliefs, norms and behaviours that can be used to contrast a group of cultures to another group of cultures.'

## Box 16.5 Three major cultural syndromes used to contrast different cultures

- *Cultural complexity* refers to how much attention people must pay to time. This is related to the number and diversity of social roles that members of the culture typically play. More industrialised and technologically advanced cultures (such as Japan, Sweden and the USA) are more complex in this sense.
- *Individualism–collectivism* refers to whether one's identity is defined by personal choices and achievements (the autonomous individual: *individualism*) or by characteristics of the collective group one is more or less permanently attached to (such as family, tribal or religious group, or country: *collectivism*). People in every culture display both, but the relative emphasis in the West is towards individualism, and in the East towards collectivism. Broadly, capitalist politico–economic systems are associated with individualism, while socialist societies are associated with collectivism.
- *Tight cultures* expect their members to behave according to clearly defined norms, and there's very little tolerance of deviance from those norms. Japan is a good example of a *tight culture*, and Thailand an example of a *loose culture*.

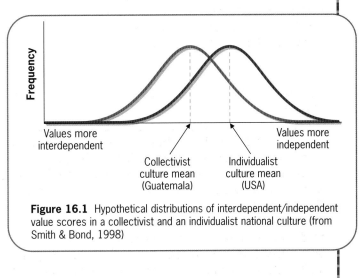

**Figure 16.1** Hypothetical distributions of interdependent/independent value scores in a collectivist and an individualist national culture (from Smith & Bond, 1998)

## The emic–etic distinction

- Research has to begin somewhere and, inevitably, this usually involves an instrument or observational technique rooted in the researcher's own culture (Berry, 1969). These can be used for investigating both C-C differences and universal aspects of human behaviour (the 'psychic unity of mankind').
- The distinction between culture-specific and universal behaviour is related to what C-C psychologists call the *emic–etic distinction* (E–ED). This distinction was first made by Pike (1954).
- The E–ED refers to two approaches to the study of behaviour:

(a) the *etic* looks at behaviour from *outside* a particular cultural system
(b) the *emic* looks at behaviour from the *inside*.

- This derives from the distinction made in linguistics between phon*etics* (the study of universal sounds, independently of their meaning) and phon*emics* (the study of universal sounds as they contribute to meaning).
- 'Etics' refers to culturally general concepts. These are easier to understand because they're common to all cultures. 'Emics' refers to culturally specific concepts, which include all the ways a particular culture deals with etics. It's the emics of another culture that are often so difficult to understand (Brislin, 1993).
- The research tools the 'visiting' psychologist brings from 'home' are an emic for the home culture. But when they're assumed to be valid in an 'alien' culture, and are used to compare the two cultures, they're said to be an *imposed etic* (Berry, 1969).
- Many attempts to replicate American studies in other parts of the world involve an imposed etic. They all assume that the situation being studied has the same meaning for members of the alien culture as it does for members of the researcher's own culture (Smith & Bond, 1998).

- The danger of imposed etics is that they're likely to involve imposition of the researcher's own cultural biases and theoretical framework. These may simply not 'fit' the phenomena being studied, resulting in their distortion. A related danger is ethnocentrism (see above).

### Box 16.6 Intelligence as an imposed etic

- Brislin (1993) gives the example of the concept of intelligence.
- The etic is 'solving problems, the exact form of which hasn't been seen before'. This definition at least recognises that what constitutes a 'problem' differs between cultures.
- But is the emic of 'mental quickness' (as measured by IQ tests, for example: see Chapter 11) universally valid?
- Among the Baganda people of Uganda, for example, intelligence is associated with slow, careful, deliberate thought (Wober, 1974). Nor is quick thinking necessarily a valid emic for all schoolchildren within a culturally diverse country like the USA (Brislin, 1993).

- Psychologists need to adapt their methods to ensure that they're studying the same process in different cultures (Moghaddam *et al.*, 1993). But how do we know that we're studying the same process? What does 'same' mean in this context? For Brislin (1993), this is the problem of *equivalence*.
- The very experience of participating in psychological testing will be strange and unfamiliar to members of non-Western cultures (Lonner, 1990). Even if measures are adapted for use in other cultures, psychologists should be aware that simply being asked to do a test may be odd for some people (Howat, 1999).

## Advantages and limitations of C-C research

It may now seem obvious (almost 'common sense') that psychological theories must be based on the study of people's behaviours from all parts of the world. But it's important to give specific reasons to support this argument.

✔ Highlighting implicit assumptions: C-C research allows investigators to examine the influence of their own beliefs and assumptions, revealing how human behaviour cannot be separated from its cultural context.

✔ Separating behaviour from context: Being able to stand back from their own cultural experiences allows researchers to appreciate the impact of situational factors on behaviour. This makes them less likely (a) to make the fundamental attribution error (FAE), that is, explaining people's behaviour in terms of personal characteristics (individualism), or (b) to use the 'deficit model' to explain the performances of minority group members (alpha bias applied to cultural differences).

✔ Extending the range of variables: C-C research expands the range of variables and concepts that can be explored. For example, people in individualist and collectivist cultures tend to explain behaviour in different ways (the latter are less likely to make the FAE).

✔ Separating variables: C-C research allows the separation of the effects of variables that may be confounded (confused) within a particular culture. For example, studying the effects of TV on school achievement is very difficult using just British or American samples, since the vast majority of these families owns (at least) one TV set! Malinowski's famous test of Freud's Oedipus complex is described below (and in Essental Study 12.1, page 323)

## RELATIONSHIPS AMONG THE TROBRIAND ISLANDERS (RATTI) (MALINOWSKI, 1929)

- According to Freud's theory of the Oedipus complex (see Chapters 12 and 18), little boys become extremely jealous of their fathers over the latter's 'possession of' the mother. At the same time they're also extremely afraid of the father, who's more powerful and in the child's view will punish him by castration if he continues to compete with the father for the mother's affections.

- Among the Trobriand Islanders of the South Pacific, Malinowski found that it's the mother's brother, not the child's father, who's the major authority figure. But the father continues to enjoy a normal sexual relationship with the mother.

- Under these circumstances, sons tend to have a very good relationship with their father, free of the love–hate ambivalence that Freud saw as an inevitable part of the Oedipus complex. But the relationship with the maternal uncle isn't so good.

- This suggests that (a) the Oedipus complex isn't universal (as Freud claimed), and (b) sexual jealousy and rivalry as major components in the whole 'family drama' play a much less important role than Freud believed.

- In most Western families, the father plays both roles – authority figure and mother's lover. But these roles are separated in the Trobriand culture.

✓ Testing theories: Only by conducting C-C research can Western psychologists be sure their theories and research findings are relevant outside their own cultural contexts. For example, Freud's Oedipal theory (as we've just seen), Thibaut and Kelley's (1959) exchange theory of relationships (see Chapter 8) and Sherif *et al.*'s (1961) Robber's Cave field experiment on intergroup conflict (see Gross, 2005) have failed the replication test outside North American settings.

## INTERGROUP CONFLICT IN LEBANON (IGCIL) (DIAB, 1970)

- Diab tried to follow the procedure used by Sherif *et al.* as closely as possible (using a summer-camp setting, with 11-year-old boys, and the same planned stages of group formation, intergroup competition and, finally, group co-operation).

- Two randomly-created groups of nine (Muslims and Christians in each group) developed very different 'cultures'. The 'Friends' were warm and co-operative, while 'Red Genie' were highly competitive, stealing things from each other – not just from the Friends.

- It proved impossible to get the two groups to co-operate in stage three (as Sherif *et al.* had managed to do). When Red Genie lost the tournament, they stole the knives, threatened the Friends with them, and tried forcibly to leave the camp. The study had to be abandoned.

The summer camp is a North American phenomenon (although we could find 'stimulus equivalents' in other cultures). But the formation of friendships rigidly within one's own age group is more characteristic of industrialised societies, compared with traditional cultures, where friendships tend to be extensions of family networks. Such cultural differences help to explain why it's proved so difficult to replicate the Robber's Cave experiment outside North America (Moghaddam *et al.*, 1993).

✗ C-CP versus (trans)cultural psychology: Shweder (1990) makes the crucial distinction between C-CP and *cultural psychology*. C-CP is a branch of experimental social, cognitive and personality psychology, and most of what's been known as C-CP has pre-supposed the categories and models derived from (mostly experimental) research with (limited samples of) Euro-American populations. It has mostly either (a) 'tested the hypothesis' or 'validated the instrument' in other cultures, or (b) 'measured' the social and psychological characteristics of members of other cultures with the methods and standards of Western populations usually assumed as a valid norm. The new 'cultural psychology' (sometimes called trans-cultural: e.g. Bruner, 1990; Cole, 1990) rejects this *universalist* model (Much, 1995).

✓·✗ The 'first' and 'second psychology': Cole (1996) refers to the results of the last 100 years of psychological research, including C-C experimental studies, as the 'first psychology'. We shouldn't discard these results, since:

'Cross-cultural studies, especially when they are sensitive to the local organization of activity, can serve to refute ethnocentric conclusions that "those people" suffer from general cognitive deficits as a consequence of cultural inadequacies . . . '

But Cole advocates a return to the early decades of psychology, particularly Wundt's belief that the methods of natural science could only be applied to the most elementary, universal and therefore *timeless* aspects of human behaviour. Culturally-mediated and historically-dependent 'higher psychological processes' need historical and developmental methods. What Wundt was advocating was:

' . . . the road along which culture is placed on a level with biology and society in shaping individual human natures. The name correctly given to that enterprise is *cultural psychology*, a major late-twentieth-century manifestation of the second psychology.' (Cole, 1996)

## EXAM tips BOX

'While psychologists claim to study "human beings", their theories and research studies in fact apply only to a very small sample of the world's population.'

Critically consider the view that psychology is culture-biased (e.g. ethnocentrism; historical bias; the imposed etic). (30 marks) (40 mins) (800 words minimum) AO1/AO2

*This essay can be split up into FOUR sections – each about 200 words long. Each section would be worth 7–8 marks.*

**Section 1:** An **explanation** of what's meant by culture and a description of the ways in which cultures can differ from each other (such as Triandis's 'cultural syndromes'.)    AO1

**Section 2:** A **definition** of ethnocentrism and the related concept of Anglocentric/Eurocentric bias. This could be put into the context of cross-cultural research and Psychology's First, Second and Third Worlds (Moghaddam & Studer, 1997).    AO1

**Section 3:** A way of **analysing** and **evaluating** the view that psychology is culture-biased is to consider the emic–etic distinction. Intelligence is a good example of an imposed etic. This is crucial for appreciating the *limitations* of cross-cultural research.    AO2

**Section 4:** You could continue your **analysis** and **evaluation** of the view that psychology is culture-biased by considering the *strengths/advantages* of cross-cultural research. You could compare and contrast cross-cultural with (trans)cultural psychology (Cole's first and second psychology).    AO2

*Try to answer this question yourself. There's a sample essay on pages 490–491 with which you can compare your essay.*

# Ethical issues

- One of psychology's unique features is that people are both the investigators and the subject-matter. This means that the 'things' studied in a psychological investigation are capable of thoughts and feelings. Biologists and medical researchers share this problem of subjecting living, sentient things to sometimes painful, stressful or just strange and unusual experiences in the name of science.
- Orne (1962) regards the psychological experiment as primarily a *social situation*, which raises the question of objectivity (see Chapter 17). In a similar way, every psychological investigation can be regarded as an *ethical situation*, raising questions of propriety (what's proper) and responsibility.
- What psychologists can and cannot do is determined by the (possible) effects of the research on those being studied, as much as by what they wish to find out.

> **Specification Hint:** The Specification says 'Ethical issues involved in psychological investigations using human participants, including the ethics of socially sensitive research'. Remember that Ethics has already been discussed in the AS Specification (see Chapter 5). There the focus was on ethical issues surrounding the use of deception, informed consent and the protection of participants from psychological harm, and how these issues arise in the context of social influence research in particular. Also, you needed to know about the ways psychologists deal with these issues, such as through the use of ethical guidelines. This is still relevant here. But the discussion of ethical issues is much broader – both the issues themselves (hence the inclusion of 'socially sensitive research') and the research areas they apply to (you're no longer confined to social influence).

## The ethics of socially sensitive research (SSR)

### WHAT IS SSR?

- According to Sieber and Stanley (1988), SSR refers to:

> ' ... studies in which there are potential social consequences or implications, either directly for the participants in the research or for the class of individuals represented by the research ... '

- Two examples they give are (a) a study that examines the relative merits of day care for infants versus full-time care by the mother, which can have broad social implications, and thus can be regarded as socially-sensitive (see Chapter 2); and (b) studies aimed at examining the relationship between gender and mathematical ability, which can also have significant social implications.
- The American Psychological Association's (APA) *Ethical Principles in The Conduct of Research* (1982) acknowledges the social implications of research as follows:

> 'The scientific enterprise creates ethical dilemmas. Scientific knowledge and techniques that can be used for human betterment can be turned to manipulative and exploitative purposes as well. Just as results of research in atomic physics can be used for the treatment of cancer as well as for destructive weapons, so methods discovered to reduce prejudice towards minority groups, to eliminate troublesome behaviour problems, or to facilitate learning in school may also be used to manipulate political allegiance, to create artificial wants, or to reconcile the victims of social injustice to their fate ... '

In other words, psychological research (like other scientific research) is a 'double-edged sword'. It can be used to benefit those being studied, or against their interests and for the benefit of those with social, economic and political power. There's nothing 'neutral' about research (see above and Chapter 17).

## PROTECTING THE INDIVIDUAL VERSUS HARMING THE GROUP

- The debate about the ethics of psychological research usually focuses on the vulnerability of individual participants, and the responsibility of psychologists to ensure they don't suffer in any way from their participation.
- 'Protection of participants' is one of the specific principles included in the *Ethical Principles For Conducting Research with Human Participants* (BPS, 1990, 1993). These are now incorporated into the *Code of Conduct, Ethical Principles and Guidelines* (BPS, 2000). But the *Ethical Principles* as a whole are designed to prevent any harm coming to participants (the avoidance of overt 'sins': Brown, 1997). According to the *Ethical Principles*:

> 'Participants in psychological research should have confidence in the investigators. Good psychological research is possible only if there is mutual respect and confidence between investigators and participants. Psychological investigators are potentially interested in all aspects of human behavior and conscious experience. However, for ethical reasons, some areas of human experience and behavior may be beyond the reach of experiment, observation or other form of psychological investigation. Ethical guidelines are necessary to clarify the conditions under which psychological research is possible.' (BPS, 2000, para 1.2)

- Sometimes the principles designed to protect individual participants can throw up problems and dilemmas for the researcher. This is especially likely in the case of SSR (and could even be considered a defining feature of SSR). Confidentiality is an example, which is described in Box 16.7 in relation to AIDS.

### Box 16.7 Protecting the individual versus protecting society

- An example of SSR where the conduct of research and the treatment of participants can create ethical dilemmas is investigation of patterns of transmission of AIDS.
- The way in which appropriate research groups are identified (such as waiting outside gay bars) can breach privacy needs.
- Confidentiality can also be a major problem. If a participant reveals that s/he has AIDS, continues to have unprotected sex, and withholds the fact that s/he has AIDS from partners, what is the appropriate role of the researcher? Should they maintain the promise of confidentiality, reveal the information to the authorities, or try to contact the participant's partner(s) directly? (Sieber & Stanley, 1988).
- Melton and Gray (1988) make a strong general case for tipping the balance toward respecting the confidentiality rights of the participant. Ultimately, this approach will protect the integrity of data collected by future researchers. In other words, if individuals from a relatively cohesive research population (such as gay men/lesbians) become aware of breaches of confidentiality, this is likely to be conveyed to other members of their group. As a result, they'll be less willing to participate in other studies or to give truthful information if they do.

- But Brown (1997) argues that formal ethical codes focus too narrowly on risks to the individual participant, in the specific context of the investigation. They neglect broader questions about the risks to the *group* the participant belongs to.
- These groups can include women, ethnic minorities and other sub-cultural groups, as well as non-Western cultures (countries or national cultures). So the different examples of gender and culture bias that we discussed earlier become relevant to a discussion of ethics. To the extent that these biases (and the underlying values and beliefs) are harmful to particular groups, they are ethical issues. In this sense, any comparison between women and men that is made from an alpha bias perspective is *socially sensitive*. Equally, any comparison between blacks and whites is socially sensitive. A much-debated example is the study of racial differences in IQ (see below).

- According to Brown (1997), a core assumption underlying ethical codes is that what psychologists do as researchers (as well as clinicians, teachers, and so on) is basically harmless and inherently valuable. This is because it's based on 'science' (defined as positivism: see Chapter 17). Consequently it's possible for a psychologist to conduct technically ethical research but still do great harm.

- For example, a researcher can strictly follow 'scientific' research methodologies, get technically adequate informed consent from participants (and not breach any of the other prescribed principles), but still conduct research which claims to show the inferiority of a particular group. Because the research is conducted according to 'the rules' (both methodological and ethical), the question of whether it's ethical in the broader sense to pursue such matters is ignored, that is, whether it's ethically acceptable to be doing such research in the first place!

- For example, both Jensen (1969) and Herrnstein (1971) asked questions about the intellectual inferiority of African Americans (see Chapter 11). Yet neither was ever considered by mainstream psychology to have violated psychology's ethics. Individual black participants weren't harmed by being given IQ tests (and might even have found them interesting and challenging). But the way the findings were interpreted and used:

' ... weakened the available social supports for people of colour by stigmatizing them as genetically inferior, thus strengthening the larger culture's racist attitudes. Research ethics as currently construed by mainstream ethics codes do not require researchers to put the potential for this sort of risk into their informed consent documents.' (Brown, 1997)

- Jensen's and Herrnstein's research (highlighted by Herrnstein and Murray in *The Bell Curve* (1994)) has pro-

Nazi scientists conducting 'objective' scientific research

foundly harmed black Americans. Ironically, the book has received much methodological criticism. But only black psychologists (such as Hilliard, 1995; Sue, 1995) have raised the more fundamental question of whether simply conducting such studies might be ethically dubious.

- According to Howe (1997), Herrnstein and Murray, Brand (cited in Richards, 1996) and others, like the Nazi scientists of the 1930s, claim that the study of racial differences is a purely 'objective' and scientific enterprise.

- So psychologists might believe that (a) it's unethical to deceive individual black or female participants about the purposes of some particular study, but (b) it's ethically acceptable to use the results to support the claim that blacks or women are genetically inferior. This narrow view of ethics makes it an ineffective way of guiding research into socially sensitive issues (Howitt, 1991). Formal codes continue to focus narrowly on risks to the individual participant, in the specific context of the investigation. But they neglect questions about the risks to the group:

'As long as research ethics avoid the matter of whether certain questions ethically cannot be asked, psychologists will conduct technically ethical research that violates a more general ethic of avoiding harm to vulnerable populations.' (Brown, 1997)

- The BPS *Code of Conduct* (2000) comprises several sections (apart from the *Ethical Principles*). These include (a) 'Guidelines for psychologists working with animals' (see below), (b) 'Guidelines on advertising the services offered by psychologists', and (c) 'Guidelines for penile plethysmography (PPG) usage'. The last of these refers to the measurement of sexual arousal and involves apparatus being attached to the penis and sexual stimuli being presented. This might be used in the context of assessing paedophilia and sexual dysfunction – so its use is highly sensitive.

## Box 16.8  Guidelines for using PPG (based on BPS, 2000)

- **Responsibility for the supervision of the PPG assessment should rest with a psychologist with up-to-date knowledge of relevant practice, legal issues and research.**
- **Staff who participate at any level should be adequately briefed and have the option of not to be involved if they find the procedure or material distressing.**
- **The PPG should be carried out only in the context of an appropriate range of other assessment and treatment procedures, or in the course of research that's been professionally and ethically approved by the relevant body.**
- **Selection of the stimuli should take into account ethical considerations of how the material was produced or obtained, for example, if it was under abusive circumstances.**
- **Selection of PPG stimuli (content and mode of presentation) should aim to strike an appropriate balance between (a) obtaining the best possible assessment, and (b) risk of exposing the participant to material which may be therapeutically counter-productive if it's outside his/her own suspected or known experience.**
- **The psychologist should brief the participant about the purpose and procedures involved in PPG assessment, including possible results and their interpretation. S/he should explain limits of confidentiality and likely consequences of participation and withdrawal, and check that the participant has understood.**
- **Debriefing should be carried out at the end of each assessment. This should include consideration of the impact of the assessment on the participant, and the need for support and advice.**
- **Stimulus material should be kept secure, and access limited to those using it for professional purposes.**
- **Assessment should only be carried out in appropriate physical conditions, with due regard to the standards of safety, privacy, comfort and current hygiene recommendations.**

## PROTECTING THE INDIVIDUAL VERSUS BENEFITING SOCIETY

- The questions psychologists ask are limited and shaped by the values and biases of individual researchers. The research they carry out is, as we've seen, constrained by ethical considerations. But it's also constrained by considerations of methodology, that is, what it's possible to do, practically, when investigating human behaviour and experience
- For example, in the context of intimate relationships (see Chapter 8), Brehm (1992) claims that, by its nature, the laboratory experiment is extremely limited in the kinds of questions it allows psychologists to explore.
- Conversely, and just as importantly, there are certain aspects of behaviour and experience which could be studied experimentally, but it would be unethical to do so (for example, jealousy between partners). As Brehm says:

> 'All types of research in this area involve important ethical dilemmas. Even if all we do is to ask subjects to fill out questionnaires describing their relationships, we need to think carefully about how this research experience might affect them and their partner.'

- So, what it may be *possible* to do may be *unacceptable*. But, equally, what may be *acceptable* may not be *possible*.
- As we saw earlier, focusing on the protection of individual participants can be detrimental to entire

groups. But by the same token, it may also discourage psychologists from carrying out *socially meaningful* research which may potentially improve the quality of people's lives.

- Such research is something psychologists are obliged to carry out (Brehm calls it the *ethical imperative*). Social psychologists in particular have a two-fold ethical obligation – to individual participants and to society at large (Myers, 1994). This relates to discussion of psychology's *aims* as a science (see Chapter 17). Aronson (1992) argues that psychologists are:

> ' ... obligated to use their research skills to advance our knowledge and understanding of human behaviour for the ultimate aim of human betterment. In short, social psychologists have an ethical responsibility to the society as a whole.'

Talking about the aim of 'human betterment' raises important questions about basic *values*. It opens out the ethical debate in such a way that values must be addressed and recognised as part of the research process (something advocated very strongly by feminist psychologists: see above). An example of how research findings can be used to benefit 'people in general' is given in the Key Study below.

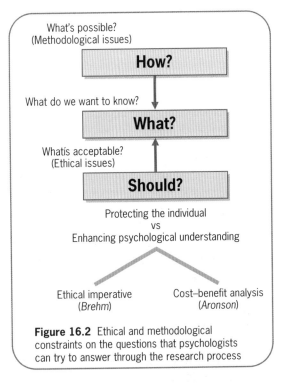

**Figure 16.2** Ethical and methodological constraints on the questions that psychologists can try to answer through the research process

## Key study

### HELPING INCREASED THROUGH TEACHING (HITT) (BEAMAN *ET AL.*, 1978)

- In many bystander intervention studies (such as Latané & Darley, 1970: see Essential Study 9.14, page 214), people are deceived into believing that an 'emergency' is taking place. Many of Latané and Darley's participants were very distressed by their experiences, especially those in the experiment where another participant was supposedly having an epileptic fit. But in a post-experimental questionnaire (which followed a very careful debriefing), they all said they believed the deception was justified and would be willing to participate in similar experiments. None reported anger towards the experimenter.

- Beaman *et al.* built on these earlier experiments. They used a lecture to inform students about how other bystanders' refusals to help can influence both one's own interpretation of an emergency and feelings of responsibility. Two other groups heard either a different lecture or no lecture at all.

- Two weeks later, as part of a different experiment in a different location, the participants found themselves (accompanied by an unresponsive stooge) walking past someone who was slumped over or sprawled under a bike.

- Of those who'd heard the lecture about helping behaviour, 50% stopped to offer help, compared with 25% of those who hadn't.

- This suggests that the results of psychological research can be used to make us more aware of influences on behaviour, making it more likely that we'll act differently, armed with this knowledge, than we might otherwise have done.

- In the case of bystander intervention, this 'consciousness-raising' is beneficial in a tangible way to the person being helped. Being more sensitive to the needs of others, and feeling good about having helped another person, may also be seen as beneficial to the helper.

## THE 'DOUBLE OBLIGATION DILEMMA'

- As we've seen, social psychologists face a dilemma between (a) their obligations to individual participants and (b) to society (the *double obligation dilemma* (DOD)).
- This is greatest when investigating important areas such as conformity, obedience (see Chapter 5) and bystander intervention (Aronson, 1992).
- In general, the more important the issue, (a) the greater the potential benefit for society, and (b) the more likely an individual participant is to experience distress and discomfort. This is because the more important the issue, the more essential the use of *deception* becomes.
- Psychologists want to know how people are likely to behave if they found themselves in that situation *outside* the laboratory. This raises several crucial *methodological* questions (such as experimental and external validity or mundane realism: see Chapters 5 and 6).
- But the key *ethical* issue hinges on the fact that the use of deception (a) contributes enormously (and perhaps irreplaceably) to our understanding of human behaviour (helping to satisfy the obligation to society), and at the same time (b) significantly increases individual participants' distress (detracting from the responsibility to protect individuals). It's worth noting that in Beaman *et al.*'s HITT, participants were deceived both as to the identity of the unresponsive stooge and the apparent victim. But this can be justified in the same way as any use of deception.
- According to Sieber and Stanley (1988):

> 'The likelihood that psychological research will raise socially sensitive issues is great and often unavoidable if useful theory, knowledge, and applications are to be achieved. Restricting psychology to those areas unlikely to raise socially sensitive issues may limit researchers in psychology to examining relatively unimportant problems.'

'Socially important' and 'socially sensitive' seem to go together, two sides of a coin.
- Psychologists are obliged to confront the ethical issues raised by SSR. But equally, as Sieber and Stanley (1988) say:

> ' . . . shying away from controversial topics, simply because they are controversial, is also an avoidance of responsibility'.

### Some proposed solutions to the DOD

- Having accepted that, under certain circumstances, deception is permissible, most psychologists still advocate that it shouldn't be used unless it's considered essential (Aronson, 1992; Milgram, 1992). This is consistent with the BPS *Ethical Principles*.
- Aronson advocates a *cost–benefit analysis* (C–BA), that is, weighing how much 'good' (benefits to society) will derive from doing the research against how much 'bad' will happen to participants. But unfortunately, this comparison is often very difficult to make, because neither the benefits nor the harm are known or calculable. McGhee (2001) identifies several problems faced by any C–BA.

### Box 16.9  Some problems with cost–benefit analysis (McGhee, 2001)

- Both costs and benefits are multiple and subjective, some are immediate, others are longer term, and there are difficulties in 'adding them up'.
- Regarding *multiplicity*, every psychology experiment (like every complex social activity) has many outcomes. It's difficult, if not impossible, to *identify* them, let alone assess them. Even if they can be assessed individually, they need to be *aggregated* in some way, because we're trying to assess the experiment as an overall package. For example, how much is deception 'worth' relative to the 'new data'?
- Ultimately, costs and benefits can be assessed only *subjectively*. Each individual values different kinds of experiences (gains and losses) differently. Indeed, one person's cost might be another's benefit.

- In theory-driven research such as Milgram's (as opposed to applied research), costs tend to be real, while benefits tend to be *potential*.

  'The distress to the participants in Milgram's studies is real but the prospect of reducing the possibility of another Auschwitz is remote – even if extraordinarily desirable.'

- Similarly, although the benefits may outweigh the costs, for individual participants it's mostly all costs (time, effort, stress and occasional humiliation and deception). Any tangible or practical benefits are unlikely to be for them. So the costs are linked to specific people, while the identity of those who will benefit is much less obvious.
- We need to decide *before* a study takes place whether or not it should go ahead. But very often the full range and extent of costs and benefits will only become apparent *retrospectively*.
- Finally, who should have the right to *decide* whether the benefits outweigh the costs?

- Milgram (1992) proposes two compromise solutions to the problem of not being able to obtain informed consent: *presumptive consent* (of 'reasonable people') and *prior general consent*.
- In presumptive consent, a large number of people are asked about how acceptable (or otherwise) they feel an experimental procedure is. These people wouldn't participate in the actual experiment (if it went ahead), but their views could be taken as evidence of how *people in general* would react to participation.
- Prior general consent could be obtained from people who might, subsequently, serve as participants. Before volunteering to join a pool of research volunteers, people would be explicitly told that sometimes partici-

I WOULDN'T MIND BEING DECEIVED BY AN EXPERIMENTER WITH A BUM LIKE THAT!

pants are misinformed about a study's true purpose and sometimes experience emotional stress. Only those who agree would be chosen.
- This is a compromise solution, because people would be giving their 'informed consent' (a) well in advance of the actual study, (b) only in a very general way, and (c) without knowing what specific manipulations/deceptions will be used in the particular experiment they participate in. It seems to fall somewhere between 'mere' consent and full 'informed consent' (and could be called *semi-* or *partially informed consent*).

## EXAM tips BOX

**Discuss issues relating to socially sensitive research.
(30 marks) (40 mins) (800 words minimum) AO1/AO2**

*This essay can be split up into FOUR sections – each about 200 words long. Each section would be worth 7–8 marks.*

**Section 1:** A **definition** of socially sensitive research (SSR), with some examples. Although Sieber and Stanley's (1988) definition just talks about 'social consequences', they clearly mean harmful or negative consequences, a point worth making.

**AO1**

↓

**Section 2:** A **description** of issues (*at least two*) relating to SSR. These may include the protection of individual participants (which ethical codes are designed to ensure), protecting participants versus protecting society, protecting individual participants versus harming the group, and protecting individual participants versus benefiting society. You should illustrate these issues with examples from psychological research. Sieber and Stanley's definition is a broad one, allowing you to draw on research from various parts of the Specification, including social influence research covered in AS, as well as the examples given in this chapter (such as AIDS and intelligence).

**AO1**

↓

**Section 3:** To **analyse** and **evaluate** the issue of protecting individual participants versus protecting society, you could consider how the dilemma might be dealt with and the possible consequences of this. The issue shows that ethical principles such as confidentiality don't operate in isolation from wider (social) considerations. You could examine the second issue (protecting individual participants versus harming the group) more closely by considering Brown's analysis of the relationship between doing ethically proper research (as defined by ethical codes) and harming particular groups.

**AO2**

↓

**Section 4:** You could continue **analysis** and **evaluation** of the issues by considering the double obligation dilemma (DOD). In some ways, this is the central issue in SSR. The more socially important some aspect of human behaviour is, the greater its social sensitivity. If psychologists are obliged to protect individuals, they're equally obliged to carry out socially meaningful research. To avoid the latter because it's socially sensitive is to act irresponsibly.

**AO2**

*Try to answer this question yourself. There's a sample essay on page 492 with which you can compare your essay.*

# The use of non-human animals

## Why do psychologists study non-human animals?

- Experiments that wouldn't be *allowed* for ethical reasons (or would be very impractical if they were) if they involved human participants, are permitted (or have been in the past) using animal subjects. This, of course, begs the question as to the *ethics* of such animal experiments.
- Some examples of animal studies that have been conducted in the past, but which would be totally unethical today, include:

(a) Riesen's (1947) and Blakemore and Cooper's (1970) sensory deprivation experiments (involving chimpanzees and cats respectively)

(b) Harlow and Zimmerman's (1959) study of total social isolation in baby rhesus monkeys (see Chapter 2)

(c) Brady's (1958) 'executive monkey' experiments on stress (see Chapter 3)

(d) Seligman's (1974) study of learned helplessness in dogs (see Chapter 14).

But even if animals aren't subjected to such 'obviously' unethical procedures, greater control can be exerted over the variables under investigation compared with the equivalent human experiment. For example, the Skinner box is an environment totally controlled by the experimenter (see Chapter 18).

Specification Hint: The Specification says 'The use of non-human animals in psychological investigations, including constraints on their use and arguments (both ethical and scientific) for and against their use'.

'Constraints' can be interpreted in different ways, but we take it to refer to both ethical and legal limits to what's allowed (including published Guidelines which mirror the *Ethical Principles* for human research). These overlap, just as the ethical and scientific arguments for and against their use do. Also, the constraints and the for/against arguments overlap. This section will be divided into two main halves, dealing with the constraints and the arguments respectively. But we'll begin by considering why psychologists should want to study non-human animals in the first place.

- There's an underlying *evolutionary continuity* between humans and other species. This gives rise to the assumption that differences between humans and other species are merely *quantitative* (as opposed to *qualitative*). In other words, other species may display simpler behaviour and have more primitive nervous systems than humans, but they're not of a different order from humans. In fact, the mammalian brain (rats, cats, dogs, monkeys and humans all being mammals) is built on similar lines in all these species, and neurons (nerve cells) work in the same way. These similarities of biology are, in turn, linked to behavioural similarities, So, it's argued, studying the simpler cases is a valid and valuable way of finding out about the more complex ones. Skinner's theory of operant conditioning is a good example of this approach (see Chapter 18).
- Compared with humans, non-humans are (mostly) smaller, and, therefore, easier to study in the laboratory. They also have much shorter lifespans and gestation periods. This makes it much easier to study their development, since several generations can be studied in a relatively short time.
- Animal studies can provide useful hypotheses for subsequent testing with human participants. For example, Bowlby's (1969) theory of attachment was partly influenced by Lorenz's (1935) study of imprinting in geese (see Chapter 2). Equally important, animals can be used to test cause-and-effect relationships where the existing human evidence is only correlational (as in smoking and lung cancer). This, of course, raises fundamental ethical questions (see the arguments below for and against animal experimentation).
- The *Guidelines for Psychologists Working with Animals* (BPS, 2000) point out that research isn't the only reason psychologists work with animals (though, not surprisingly, research is what has caused the most controversy and media attention). Animals are sometimes used in practical teaching within psychology degree courses, and increasingly they're being used in various forms of psychological therapy. The latter include companion animal visiting schemes in hospitals or hospices, pet-keeping within prison rehabilitation schemes, and in behaviour therapy for the treatment of specific animal phobias. Psychologists may also be asked for advice on therapy for animals whose behaviour is disordered or inconvenient, and in training animals for commercial purposes (such as appearing in TV commercials).

## Constraints on the use of non-human animals

- The BPS Scientific Affairs Board published its *Guidelines for the Use of Animals in Research* (1985) in conjunction with the Committee of the Experimental Psychological Society. (The *Guidelines* published in 2000 are an updated version of the 1985 document.)
- It offers a checklist of points which researchers should carefully consider when planning experiments with living non-humans. These fall under several headings, including: legislation, choice of species, number of animals, procedures ((a) reward, deprivation and aversive stimulation, (b) isolation and crowding, (c) aggression and predation, (d) fieldwork, (e) anaesthesia, analgesia and euthanasia), procurement of animals, housing and animal care, and final disposal of animals. Researchers have a general obligation to:

' ... avoid, or at least to minimize, discomfort to living animals ... discuss any future research with their local Home Office Inspector and colleagues who are experts in the topic ... seek ... Widespread advice as to whether the likely scientific contribution of the work ... justifies the use of living animals, and whether the scientific point they wish to make may not be made without the use of living animals.' (BPS, 1985)

- The 2000 *Guidelines* state that in all other situations where animals are used (that is, for non-research purposes: see above), ' ... considerations concerning the general care and welfare of therapeutic animals are similar to those ... for experimental animals. In addition, however, a number of specific considerations can be noted ... ' These include issues relating to the temperament and training of the animals, and their need for protection and rest.
- These warnings raise two fundamental questions: (a) how do we know non-humans suffer? and (b) what goals can ever justify subjecting them to pain, suffering and even death?

## Box 16.10  Some criteria for judging animal suffering

- Disease and injury are generally recognised as major causes of suffering. Consequently, research such as Brady's (1958) 'executive monkey' experiments would probably not even be debated in the current climate (Mapstone, 1991).
- Even if we're sure that animals aren't suffering physically, their confinement might cause mental suffering not affecting their external condition (Dawkins, 1980). For example, apparently healthy zoo and farm animals often show bizarre behaviours.
- We must find out about animal suffering by careful observation and experimentation. Different species have different requirements, lifestyles and, perhaps, emotions. So, we cannot just assume that we know about their suffering or wellbeing without studying them species by species (Dawkins, 1980).
- Bateson (1986, 1992) draws on the Institute of Medical Ethics Working Party's report (Haworth, 1992) and proposed criteria for assessing animal suffering. These criteria include:
(a)  possessing receptors sensitive to noxious or painful stimulations, and
(b)  having brain structures comparable to the human cerebral cortex.
Bateson (1992) tentatively concludes that insects probably don't experience pain, whereas fish and octopi probably do. But the boundaries between the presence and absence of pain are 'fuzzy'.

## SAFEGUARDING ANIMAL SUBJECTS

- The very least required of researchers is that the minimum of suffering is caused, both during and following any surgical procedure. This also applies to electric shock and food deprivation, the most objected-to treatments (Gray, 1987).
- Gray claims that food deprivation *isn't* a source of suffering. Rats (the most commonly used experimental subjects in psychology) are either fed once a day when experimentation is over, or maintained at 85% of their free-feeding (*ad lib*) body weight. Both are actually healthier than allowing them to eat *ad lib*.
- Electric shock may cause *some* but not *extreme* pain (based on observation of the animals' behaviour). The permitted level is controlled by the Home Office (HO) Inspectors, who monitor implementation of the Animals (Scientific Procedures) Act (1986). The average level used in the UK is 0.68 milli-amperes, for an average of 0.57 seconds. This produces an unpleasant tickling sensation in humans.
- Procedures causing pain or distress are illegal, unless the experimenter holds an HO licence and relevant certificates. Even then, these procedures should be carried out only if there are no alternative ways of conducting the experiment. Similarly, it's illegal in the UK to perform any surgical or pharmacological (drug-related) procedure on vertebrates (animals with backbones) (or one invertebrate – the octopus) without an HO licence and relevant certification. Such procedures must be performed by experienced personnel.
- The *Guidelines* (1985, 2000) stress the importance of understanding species differences in relation to (a) caging and social environment, (b) the stress involved in marking wild animals for identification or attaching them to radio transmitters, and (c) the duration of food/drink deprivation. Field workers should disturb non-humans as little as possible. Even simple observation of animals in the wild can have marked effects on their breeding and survival.
- The number of animals used in laboratory experiments is declining. For example, in the UK, the

Netherlands, Germany and several other European countries, the numbers have fallen by 50% since the 1970s (Mukerjee, 1997). But the UK still uses approximately three million non-humans a year in experiments (85% of which are mice, rats and other rodents). A sharp rise in genome-related research (see Chapter 17) is threatening to reverse this downward trend (Hawkes, 2000b). But, putting this into perspective, over 700 million non-humans are killed for food every year (*Nursing Times*, 1996).

- The UK, Australia, Germany and several other countries require a utilitarian *cost–benefit analysis* (animal pain, distress and death versus acquisition of new knowledge and the development of new medical therapies for humans) to be performed before any animal experiment can proceed (Mukerjee, 1997; Rowan, 1997). Most non-scientists also seem to perform some kind of (informal) C–BA (Aldhous *et al.*, 1999).

- Despite these safeguards, the very existence of the 1986 Act condones the use of animals. Legally, and explicitly, the Act aims to spare animals 'unnecessary' pain and distress. But, implicitly, the law accepts that some research will involve suffering for the non-human subjects. Under the Act, applications for 'Project Licences' have to say whether they've considered alternatives to using non-humans and, in granting the licence, the Home Secretary must weigh up the likely benefit of the research against the adverse effects on the animals. But there's no remit to consider whether the proposed research is truly necessary (Seymour, 1996). Also, the Medicines Act (1968) requires that all new medicines undergo a range of tests on animals before they can be tested on humans (Lyall, 1993).

- A group of 10 British scientists has called for the Home Office to speed up the process of giving approval for animal experiments. They believe that the procedure is so long-winded that foreign scientists will take all the prizes for medicine, biotechnology and drug research (Hawkes, 2000a). Gray and Blakemore are among them.

## Arguments relating to the use of animals for research

- Some of the points we've just considered in relation to safeguards shade into arguments *for* the use of animal experiments. More accurately, they can be seen as *defending* their use. If the law regulates animal experiments, and if psychologists also regulate themselves (in the form of the *Guidelines*), then isn't this *ethically* sufficient?

- The objection to this argument is that both the 1986 Act and the *Guidelines* make the implicit assumption that some animal suffering, under certain circumstances, can (always) be justified. But can it?

- According to Gray (1987), the main justifications for animal experimentation are (a) *the pursuit of scientific knowledge* and (b) *the advancement of medicine*.

- To justify the use of animals, especially when very stressful procedures are involved, the research must be rigorously designed and the potential results must represent a significant contribution to our knowledge of medicine, pharmacology, biopsychology or psychology as whole. This is (another) safeguard against distressing research being carried out for its own sake, or at the researcher's whim.

- Some knowledge is trivial, and experiments mustn't be done simply because it's possible to do them. In the case of Brady's executive monkey experiments, the medical justification (to discover why business executives develop stomach ulcers) was insufficient to justify their continuation. The monkeys' obvious suffering should have taken precedence over even the combination of gains in scientific and medical knowledge. There are other cases where the scientific justification may be apparent, but the medical justification is much less so. For example, Olds and Milner's (1954) experiments.

### POSITIVE REINFORCEMENT OF RATS' BRAINS (PRORB) (OLDS & MILNER, 1954)

- Olds and Milner found that rats stimulated by an electrode implanted near the septum (part of the limbic system) would make between 3,000 and 7,500 lever-pressing responses (which produced electric shock) in a 12-hour period.

- Olds (1956) reported that one rat stimulated itself more than 2,000 times per hour for 24 consecutive hours. In 1958, he reported that rats which normally press a lever 25 times per hour for food reward will press 100 times per minute for a reward of *electrical self-stimulation of the brain* (ES-SB).

**Figure 16.3** Olds (1956) implanted electrodes in the hypothalami of rats. The rats could trigger an electrical stimulus by depressing a lever. Clearly, the region where the electrode was implanted constitutes some kind of pleasure centre (adapted from J. Olds © 1956. Pleasure centres in the brain. Scientific American, Inc. All rights reserved)

## THE MEDICAL JUSTIFICATION ARGUMENT: A CLOSER LOOK

- This represents the strongest argument for animal experiments. But it's easy to confuse scientific and ethical issues.
- Demonstrating what's been achieved practically from such experiments represents only a *minimum* requirement for their justification. Only if it can be shown convincingly, for example, that many drugs used in the treatment of human diseases (including anti-cancer drugs, AIDS treatments, anti-epileptic and anti-depressant drugs: Green, 1994) have been developed using animals, can the ethical debate begin.
- This is the difference between asking (a) does using animals actually make a difference? Are animal experiments scientifically useful? and (b) is it right that they should be used in this way? Answering 'yes' to the first question only tells half the story. The second question is concerned with the rights of animals, as opposed to the needs of humans.

### Box 16.11 Are animal experiments scientifically useful?

**THE CASE FOR**
- Animal experiments have played a crucial role in the development of modern medical treatments, and will continue to be necessary as researchers seek to alleviate existing illnesses and respond to the emergence of new ones.
- The causes of and vaccines for dozens of infectious diseases (including diphtheria, tetanus, rabies, whooping cough, tuberculosis, poliomyelitis, measles, mumps and rubella) have been determined largely through animal experimentation. This experimentation has also led to the development of antibacterial and antibiotic drugs.
- Animal research has also been vital to areas of medicine, such as open-heart surgery, kidney disease and organ transplantation, diabetes, malignant hypertension and gastric ulcers.
- There are no basic differences between the physiologies of laboratory animals and humans. Both

control their internal biochemistry by releasing the same basic endocrine hormones (see Chapter 3), both send out similar chemical transmitters from neurons in the central and peripheral nervous systems (see Chapters 3 and 14), and both react in the same way to infection or tissue injury. Animal models of disease (see below) are intended to provide a means of studying a particular procedure (such as gene therapy for cystic fibrosis).

## THE CASE AGAINST

- Through genetic manipulation, surgical intervention or injection of foreign substances, researchers produce diseases in laboratory animals that 'model' human diseases. But evolutionary pressures have produced innumerable subtle differences between species. The knock-on effect of applying a stimulus to one particular organ system in the animal's overall physiological functioning is often unpredictable and not fully understood.
- Important medical advances have been delayed because of the misleading results from animal experiments. Cancer research is especially sensitive to physiological differences between species. For example, rats and mice synthesise about 100 times the recommended daily allowance of vitamin C believed to help the (human) body ward off cancer. Penicillin is toxic to guinea pigs, while morphine stimulates cats (the opposite of the human response).
- The stress of handling, confinement and isolation alters an animal's physiology, introducing a variable that makes extrapolating results to humans even more difficult. Laboratory stress can increase animals' susceptibility to infectious disease and certain tumours, as well as influencing hormone and antibody levels.
- Animal experiments to test the safety of drugs are confounded by the fact that tests on different species often produce conflicting results.

(Based on Barnard & Kaufman, 1997; Botting & Morrison, 1997; Mukerjee, 1997; Sawyer, 1996.)

## SPECIESISM: EXTENDING THE MEDICAL JUSTIFICATION ARGUMENT

- Green (1994), Carlson (1992) and many other biopsychologists believe that the potential benefits of animal experiments is sufficient to justify their use.
- According to Gray (1991), most people (both experimenters and animal rights activists) would accept the ethical principle that inflicting pain is wrong. But we're sometimes faced with having to *choose between* different ethical principles. This may mean having to choose between human and animal suffering.
- Gray believes that *speciesism* (discriminating against and exploiting animals because they belong to a particular [non-human] species: Ryder, 1990) is justified. He argues that:

'Not only is it not wrong to give preference to the interests of one's own species, one has a duty to do so.'

Such a moral choice involves establishing a calculus (Dawkins, 1990), which pits the suffering of non-humans against the human suffering which the former will reduce. For Gray (1991):

'In many cases the decision to carry out certain experiments with animals (even if they would inflict pain or suffering) is likely to have the consequence that more people will undergo pain or suffering that might otherwise be avoided.'

- Gray recognises that one of the problems with the pro-speciesism argument is that medical advance may become possible only after extensive development of knowledge and scientific understanding in a particular field. In the meantime, scientific understanding may be the experiment's only realistic, specific objective. It's at this interim stage that the suffering imposed on experimental animals will far outweigh any (lesser) human suffering that's eventually relieved or prevented. This is the core of the decisions that must be made by scientists and ethical committees.

- The speciesism argument also seems to take a special twist when the species in question aren't rats and mice, but our closest evolutionary relatives. In recent years, the ethics debate in relation to animal research has become focused on chimpanzees and other primates. In the process, the scope of the debate has widened to include the idea of equality under the law. One strand of this debate involves psychologists' attempts to teach language to chimpanzees and other great apes. A famous example is described in Box 16.12.

### Box 16.12 Washoe and the Gardners

- In 'Teaching sign language to a chimpanzee', Gardner and Gardner (1969) report their famous research with Washoe, estimated to be between eight and 14 months when she arrived at their laboratory.
- When she was five years old, Washoe was sent away with Roger and Deborah Fouts. The Gardners next saw her 11 years later. When they unexpectedly entered the room Washoe was in, she signed their name, then 'Come, Mrs G', led her to an adjoining room and began to play a game with her which she hadn't been observed to play since she left the Gardners' home (Singer, 1993).

Washoe: no ordinary animal subject. Whether or not she – and other great apes – is capable of language is arguably less important than the ethics of such research

- Observations like this support the argument that non-humans really are capable of language (an extremely interesting and important *scientific* issue). But they also raise crucial *ethical* questions, in particular:

(a) How justifiable is the whole attempt to study language in non-humans, since this involves removing the animals from their natural habitats in which they don't spontaneously use language?
(b) What happens to the animals after they've served their purpose as experimental subjects?

- These kinds of study aren't usually the target for attacks against cruel treatment of animals in psychological research. But they still involve animals that haven't chosen to become involved. Perhaps it's the fact that they're great apes, and not just 'other animals', which makes these ethical questions so fascinating and important.

- This applies equally to the other 'strand' of this wider ethical debate, namely, the several hundred chimpanzee 'veterans' of American research during the 1970s aimed at developing vaccines for hepatitis B and C. Euthanasia was considered at one time, but the AIDS epidemic in the mid-1980s came to their 'rescue'. Once again, because of their genetic similarity to ourselves, they became 'surrogate human beings' (Mahoney, 1998).
- By the mid-1990s, scientists began turning to human volunteers for the initial testing of HIV vaccines. This left large numbers of 'redundant' chimpanzees (which have a lifespan of up to 40 years). A report of the US National Research Council (1997) concluded that they should be given special consideration, on ethical grounds, over other non-humans, and that euthanasia *isn't* an acceptable means of population control (Mahoney, 1998).
- *The Great Ape Project* (GAP) is (a) the title of a book (subtitle: *Equality Beyond Humanity*, edited by Singer and Cavalieri, 1993), (b) a simple but radical idea, namely to extend the 'community of equals' beyond human beings to all great apes (chimpanzees, gorillas and orang-utans), and (c) an organisation, comprising 34 academics and others, set up to work internationally for the immediate inclusion of the great apes within the community of equals. This refers to the moral community within which we accept certain basic moral rights and principles as governing our relationship with each other, and which are enforceable by law.

The central argument of the GAP is that it's ethically indefensible to deny the great apes the basic rights of (a) the right to life, (b) protection of individual liberty, and (c) prohibition of torture (collectively, the *Declaration of Great Apes*).

- Wise (2000), in a book entitled *Rattling the Cage: Towards Legal Rights for Animals*, argues that animals should have full rights under the law. Goodall describes Wise's book as the 'animals' Magna Carta' (Mee, 2000).

- Taylor (2000) considers that Singer has established the basis for a revolution in ethics. Traditional approaches have rested on the belief in the unique value of human life. But Singer insists that this no longer works, and that ethics must be concerned instead with *reducing suffering*. This applies equally to humans and to non-humans.

## EXAM tips BOX

**Describe and evaluate the case *for and against* the use of non-human animals in psychological research. (30 marks) (40 mins) (800 words minimum) AO1/AO2**

*This essay can be split up into FOUR sections – each about 200 words long. Each section would be worth 7–8 marks.*

**Section 1:** A **description** of (some of) the reasons psychologists use non-human animals for research purposes. It would be useful to give some examples of such research. This might continue into Section 2.

**Section 2:** A **description** of the constraints on the use of animals (such as *Ethical Guidelines*, the 1986 Animals Act, and other safeguards).

**Section 3:** An **analysis** and **evaluation** of the case *for* and *against* the use of non-humans. This could begin by considering the limits of these safeguards (including the law). The very existence of these safeguards implies an argument for/in defence of animal experiments, so their limits could represent an argument against.

*Note that the question doesn't distinguish between scientific and ethical arguments (unlike the Specification, which does). To point out that there is a difference – and to explain it – will gain you credit here.*

**Section 4:** A continuation of the **analysis** and **evaluation** of 'for and against' arguments. Speciesism (Ryder, 1990; Gray, 1991) is a powerful extension of the medical justification argument, but this also has its critics. It also assumes a special significance in relation to the great apes. That is, the ethical objections assume much greater force when the non-humans in question are more biologically similar to ourselves.

*Try to answer this question yourself. There's a sample essay on page 493 with which you can compare your essay.*

AO1
↓
AO1
↓
AO2
↓
AO2

## PYA5: Perspectives: Issues

Other possible exam questions:

- Each essay is worth 30 marks and should take 40 minutes to write.
- Remember the mark scheme allocates 15 marks for AO1 (knowledge and description) and 15 marks for AO2 (analysis and evaluation).

There are far fewer possible questions that can be asked in Perspectives.

1.  Discuss TWO OR MORE examples of gender bias (e.g. alpha/beta bias, androcentrism) in psychological theories and/or studies. (30 marks)

2.  Critically consider TWO OR MORE examples of cultural bias (e.g. ethnocentrism; historical bias; the imposed etic) in psychological theories and/or studies. (30 marks)

3.  Discuss ethical issues involved in psychological investigations using human participants. (30 marks)

4.  'Non-human animal research has been a vital component in advancing psychological knowledge. This continues to be the case and outweighs any possible ethical concerns.'

    Critically consider the use of non-human animals in psychology, with reference to the issues raised in the quote above. (30 marks)

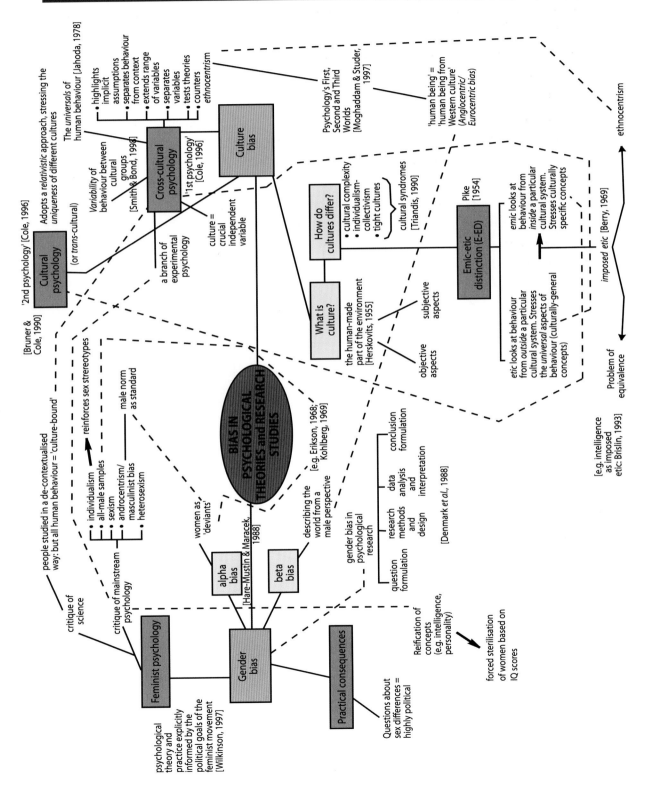

**Cultural psychology** '2nd psychology' [Cole, 1996] [Bruner & Cole, 1990]

Adopts a *relativistic* approach, stressing the *uniqueness* of different cultures

(or *trans-cultural*)

The *universals* of human behaviour [Jahoda, 1978]
- highlights implicit assumptions
- separates behaviour from context
- extends range of variables
- separates variables
- tests theories
- counters *ethnocentrism*

*Variability of behaviour between cultural groups* [Smith & Bond, 1998]

**Cross-cultural psychology** '1st psychology' [Cole, 1996]

a branch of experimental psychology

culture = crucial independent variable

**Culture bias**

Psychology's First, Second and Third Worlds [Moghaddam & Studer, 1997]

'human being' = 'human being from Western culture' (*Anglocentric/ Eurocentric bias*)

ethnocentrism

**How do cultures differ?**
- cultural complexity
- individualism-collectivism
- tight cultures

cultural syndromes [Triandis, 1990]

**What is culture?**

the human-made part of the environment [Herskovits, 1955]

objective aspects

subjective aspects

**Emic-etic distinction (E-ED)**

Pike [1954]

*emic* looks at behaviour from *inside* a particular cultural system. Stresses specific concepts

*etic* looks at behaviour from *outside* a particular cultural system. Stresses the *universal* aspects of behaviour (culturally-general concepts)

*imposed etic* [Berry, 1969]

Problem of equivalence

[e.g. intelligence as imposed etic: Brislin, 1993]

**BIAS IN PSYCHOLOGICAL THEORIES and RESEARCH STUDIES**

[e.g. Erikson, 1968; Kohlberg, 1969]

people studied in a de-contextualised way: but all human behaviour = 'culture-bound'

reinforces sex stereotypes

- individualism
- all-male samples
- sexism
- androcentrism/ masculinist bias
- heterosexism

male norm as standard

critique of science

critique of mainstream psychology

women as 'deviants'

**alpha bias**

**beta bias**

[Hare-Mustin & Maracek, 1988]

describing the world from a male perspective

conclusion formulation

data analysis and interpretation

[Denmark *et al*, 1988]

research methods and design

gender bias in psychological research

question formulation

**Feminist psychology**

**Gender bias**

**Practical consequences**

psychological theory and practice explicitly informed by the political goals of the feminist movement [Wilkinson, 1997]

Questions about sex differences = highly political

Reification of concepts (e.g. intelligence, personality)

forced sterilisation of women based on IQ scores

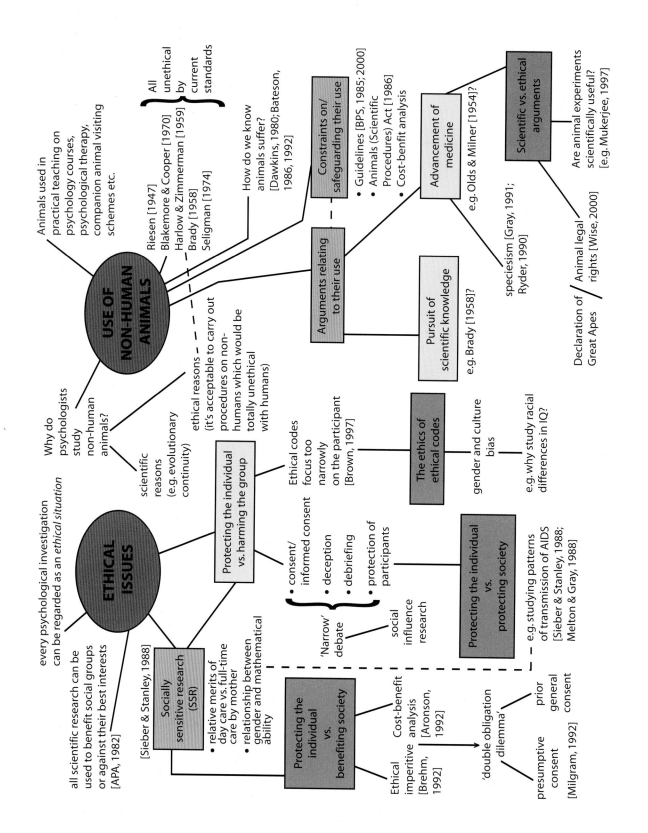

**USE OF NON-HUMAN ANIMALS**

Animals used in practical teaching on psychology courses, psychological therapy, companion animal visiting schemes etc.

Riesen [1947]
Blakemore & Cooper [1970]
Harlow & Zimmerman [1959]
Brady [1958]
Seligman [1974]

} All unethical by current standards

How do we know animals suffer? [Dawkins, 1980; Bateson, 1986, 1992]

Constraints on/ safeguarding their use
• Guidelines [BPS, 1985; 2000]
• Animals (Scientific Procedures) Act [1986]
• Cost-benfit analysis

Advancement of medicine
e.g. Olds & Milner [1954]?

Scientific vs. ethical arguments

Are animal experiments scientifically useful? [e.g. Mukerjee, 1997]

speciesism [Gray, 1991; Ryder, 1990]

Declaration of Great Apes / Animal legal rights [Wise, 2000]

Arguments relating to their use

Pursuit of scientific knowledge
e.g. Brady [1958]?

Why do psychologists study non-human animals?

scientific reasons (e.g. evolutionary continuity)

ethical reasons (it's acceptable to carry out procedures on non-humans which would be totally unethical with humans)

**ETHICAL ISSUES**

every psychological investigation can be regarded as an *ethical situation*

all scientific research can be used to benefit social groups or against their best interests [APA, 1982]

Protecting the individual vs. harming the group

Ethical codes focus too narrowly on the participant [Brown, 1997]

The ethics of ethical codes

gender and culture bias

e.g. why study racial differences in IQ?

• consent/ informed consent
• deception
• debriefing
• protection of participants

} 'Narrow' debate

social influence research

Protecting the individual vs. protecting society

e.g. studying patterns of transmission of AIDS [Sieber & Stanley, 1988; Melton & Gray, 1988]

Socially sensitive research (SSR)
[Sieber & Stanley, 1988]

• relative merits of day care vs. full-time care by mother
• relationship between gender and mathematical ability

Protecting the individual vs. benefiting society

Ethical imperitive [Brehm, 1992]

Cost-benefit analysis [Aronson, 1992]

'double obligation dilemma'

presumptive consent [Milgram, 1992]

prior general consent

Discuss gender bias (e.g. alpha/beta bias, androcentrism) in psychological theories and/or studies. (30 marks) (40 mins) (800 words minimum)

Section 1:

AO1

Mainstream academic psychology models itself on classical, orthodox, natural science (such as physics and chemistry). It claims to be objective, unbiased and value-free. As applied to the study of human beings, positivism implies that it's possible to study people as they 'really are', without the psychologist's characteristics in any way influencing the outcome of the investigation. But this view of psychology as unbiased and value-free is mistaken, and gender bias permeates much psychological theory and empirical research. Much of the criticism of mainstream psychology's gender bias has come from feminist psychologists.

If women's behaviour differs from men's, the former is often judged to be pathological, abnormal or deficient in some way. This is a form of sexism, and also demonstrates alpha bias (Hare-Mustin & Maracek, 1988). Men's behaviour is taken (implicitly or explicitly) as the standard or norm against which women's behaviour is compared and judged. This represents another form of gender bias, namely androcentrism (male-centredness or the masculinist bias). Beta bias (Hare-Mustin & Maracek, 1988) involves formulating a theory based on an all-male sample, and then claiming that it's universally valid, that is, applies equally to women and men. Alternatively, applying the findings of a study which involves males only to women and men illustrates beta bias. Psychological explanations of behaviour tend to emphasise biological and other internal causes, as opposed to social and other external causes. This emphasis on internal causes is called individualism. This gives (and reinforces) the impression that psychological sex differences are inevitable and unchangeable. In turn, this reinforces widely-held stereotypes about women and men, contributing to the oppression of women (another form of sexism). Heterosexuality (both male and female) is taken (implicitly or explicitly) as the norm, with the result that homosexuality (both male and female) is seen as abnormal. This demonstrates heterosexism.

Section 2:

AO1

According to Denmark et al. (1988), gender bias is found at all stages of the research process (question formulation, research methods and design, data analysis and interpretation, and conclusion formulation). As far as question formulation is concerned, it's assumed that topics relevant to white males are more important and 'basic' (for example, the effects of TV violence on aggression in boys) compared with those that are relevant to white females, or ethnic minority females or males. The latter are seen as more marginal, specialised or applied (for example, the psychological correlates of pregnancy or the menopause). In relation to research methods and design, the sex and race of the participants, researchers, and any stooges who may be involved are often left unspecified. This means that potential interactions between these variables aren't accounted for. For example, men tend to display more helping behaviour than

women in studies involving a young, female stooge victim. This could be a function of either the sex of the stooge or an interaction between the stooge and participant, rather than sex differences between participants (the conclusion that's usually drawn).

AO2

Significant sex differences may be reported in very misleading ways, because the wrong sorts of comparisons are made. For example, there may be a significant difference between women and men on a test of spatial ability, which may suggest that women cannot or shouldn't become architects or engineers. But if you're then told that a certain percentage of women score higher than successful architects or engineers do, you'd probably draw very different conclusions. The fact that a higher percentage of men's than women's scores exceed those of successful architects or engineers is almost irrelevant. Conclusion formulation is related to beta bias.

Section 3:

AO2

Two examples of gender-biased theories are Erikson's psychosocial theory of development and Kohlberg's theory of moral development. According to Gilligan (1982), Erikson's theory, based on the study of males only, portrays women as 'deviants'. In one version, Erikson (1950) describes a series of eight universal stages. So, for example, for both sexes, in all cultures, the conflict between identity and role confusions (adolescence) precedes that between intimacy and isolation (young adulthood). But in a later version (Erikson, 1968), he acknowledges that the sequence is different for a female. She postpones her identity as she prepares to attract the man whose name she'll adopt and by whose status she'll be defined. For women, intimacy seems to go hand-in-hand with identity – they come to know themselves through their relationships with others (Gilligan, 1982). Despite Erikson's observations of sex differences, the sequence of stages in his psychosocial theory remains unchanged. As Gilligan says, male experience continues to define Erikson's life-cycle concept. This illustrates beta bias.

Similarly, Kohlberg's (1969) six-stage theory of moral development was based on a 20-year longitudinal study of 84 boys. But he claims that these stages are universal: another example of beta bias. When males and females are compared, females rarely attain a level of moral reasoning above Stage 3 ('Good boy-nice girl' orientation), which is supposed to be achieved by most adolescents and adults. This leaves females looking decidedly morally deficient, and is an example of alpha bias.

Section 4:

AO2

Like other feminist psychologists, Gilligan argues that psychology speaks with a 'male voice, that is, describing the world from a male perspective and confusing this with absolute truth (beta bias). The task of feminist psychology is to listen to women and girls who speak "in a different voice" (Gilligan, 1982; Brown & Gilligan, 1992). Gilligan's work with females led her to argue that women and men have qualitatively different conceptions of morality. By stressing the

SAMPLE ESSAYS

'While psychologists claim to study "human beings", their theories and research studies in fact apply only to a very small sample of the world's population.'

Critically consider the view that psychology is culture-biased (e.g. ethnocentrism; historical bias; the imposed etic). (30 marks) (40 mins) (800 words minimum)

AO1

## Section 1:

Herskovits (1955) defines culture as the human-made part of the environment. This can be sub-divided into objective and subjective aspects, the latter including norms, roles and values. Culture is made by humans, but it also helps to make them, that is, humans have an interactive relationship with culture (Moghaddam et al., 1993). These definitions stress what different cultures have in common (what makes a culture). But to consider the view that psychology is culture-biased, it's even more important to be aware of how cultures differ from each other. Triandis (1990) identifies several cultural syndromes, patterns of values, attitudes, beliefs, norms and behaviours that can be used to contrast different groups of cultures. Three major cultural syndromes are cultural complexity, individualism–collectivism, and tight cultures. More industrialised, technologically advanced cultures (such as Japan and the USA) are more complex in the sense that members play many and diverse social roles. In individualist cultures (mainly Western), individual identity is defined by personal choices and achievements, while in collectivist cultures (mainly non-Western) it's the characteristics of one's family, tribal or religious group that matters. Tight cultures (such as Japan) have little tolerance of deviance from clearly defined norms, unlike loose cultures (such as Thailand).

AO1

## Section 2:

According to Smith and Bond (1998), cross-cultural psychology (C-CP) studies variability in behaviour among the various societies and cultural groups around the world. For Jahoda (1978), an additional goal of C-CP is to identify what's similar across different cultures, and so what's likely to be our common human heritage (the universals of human behaviour). C-CP is important because it helps to correct ethnocentrism (the strong human tendency to use our own ethnic or cultural group's norms and values to define what's 'natural' and 'correct' for everyone ('reality': Triandis, 1990). Historically, psychology has been dominated by white, middle-class males in the USA, who constitute the core of psychology's First World (Moghaddam, 1987). This dominates the manufacture of psychological knowledge, exporting it to other countries around the world through control over books and journals, test manufacture and so on. The

differences between women and men (an alpha-biased approach), Gilligan is trying to compensate for Kohlberg's heavily beta-biased theory.

According to Kitzinger (1998), questions about sex differences aren't just scientific questions, they're also highly political. Answers to some of these questions have been used to keep women out of universities, or to put them in mental hospitals. Others have been used to encourage women to attend assertiveness training courses, or to argue that women should have all the same rights and opportunities as men. In other words, the science of sex differences research is always used for political ends. However much psychologists may hope or believe they're doing objective research and discovering truth about the world, they're always influenced by the social and political context in which they're doing it (Kitzinger, 1998). Gilligan (1993) states that at the core of her work on moral development in females was the realisation that within psychology – and society generally – values were taken as facts. Psychologists (and other scientists) have a responsibility to make their values explicit about important social and political issues. If they fail to do so, they may unwittingly contribute to prejudice, discrimination and oppression.

(1,093 words)

Second World countries comprise Western European nations and Russia, which are overpowered by American popular culture and USA-manufactured psychological knowledge. Third World countries are mostly importers of psychological knowledge, first from the USA but also from the ex-colonial Second World countries (Moghaddam & Studer, 1997).

According to Moghaddam et al. (1993), American researchers and participants have shared a lifestyle and value system that differs both from that of most other people in North America, such as ethnic minorities and women, and the vast majority of people in the rest of the world. Yet the findings from this research, and the theories based on it, have been applied to people in general – as if culture makes no difference. 'Human being' is implicitly equated with 'human being from Western culture'. This is the Anglocentric or Eurocentric bias.

### Section 3:

When members of other cultural groups have been studied, they've usually been compared with Western samples. The behaviour and experience of the latter are used as the standard. As with androcentrism, it's the failure to acknowledge this bias which creates the misleading and false impression that what's being said about behaviour can be generalised without qualification. But research has to start somewhere, and, inevitably, this usually involves an instrument or observational technique that's rooted in the researcher's own culture (Berry, 1969). These can be used for investigating cross-cultural differences and the universal aspects of human behaviour (the 'psychic unity of mankind'). This distinction between culture-specific and universal behaviour is related to what cross-cultural psychologists call the emic–etic distinction (E–ED), first made by Pike (1954). The E–ED refers to two approaches to the study of behaviour. The etic looks at behaviour from outside a particular cultural system, while the emic looks at behaviour from the inside.

Etics are easier to understand because they're common to all cultures, while emics include all the ways a particular culture deals with etics. It's the emics of another culture that are often so difficult to understand (Brislin, 1993). The research tools the 'visiting' psychologist brings from home are an emic for the home culture. But when they're assumed to be valid in an 'alien' culture, and are used to compare the two cultures, they're said to be an imposed etic (Berry, 1969).

### Section 4:

Many attempts to replicate American studies in other parts of the world involve an imposed etic. They all assume that the situation being studied has the same meaning for members of the alien culture as it does for members of the researcher's own culture (Smith & Bond, 1998). The danger of imposed etics is that they're likely to involve imposing the researcher's own cultural biases and

theoretical framework. These may simply not 'fit' the phenomena being studied, resulting in their distortion. A related danger is ethnocentrism. Brislin (1993) gives the example of intelligence. The etic is solving problems which haven't been seen before in exactly that form. But is the emic of 'mental quickness', as measured by IQ tests, universally valid? Among the Baganda people of Uganda, intelligence is associated with slow, careful, deliberate thought (Wober, 1974). Nor is quick thinking necessarily a valid emic for all school children within a culturally diverse country like the USA (Brislin, 1993).

Psychologists need to adapt their methods to ensure that they're studying the same process in different cultures (Moghaddam et al., 1993). But how do we know that we're studying the same process? For Brislin, this is the problem of equivalence. The very experience of participating in psychological testing will be strange and unfamiliar to members of non-Western cultures (Lonner, 1990; Howat, 1999). Cross-cultural psychologists don't equate 'human being' with 'member of Western culture', because for them culture is the crucial independent variable. But they also consider the search for universal principles of human behaviour as perfectly valid and really just a branch of experimental social, cognitive and personality psychology. Most of what's been known as C-CP has presupposed the categories and models derived from research with Euro–American populations. Shweder (1990) makes the crucial distinction between C-CP and (trans)cultural psychology (Bruner, 1990; Cole, 1990) which rejects this universalist model (Much, 1995).

(1,027 words)

A02

A02

# SAMPLE ESSAYS

Discuss issues relating to socially sensitive research. (30 marks) (40 mins) (800 words minimum)

## Section 1:

Sieber and Stanley (1988) define socially sensitive research (SSR) as studies in which there are potential social consequences or implications, either directly for the participants or for the groups represented by the research. One example they give is a study that examines the relative merits of day care for infants versus full-time care by the mother, which can have broad social implications. Another example is research aimed at examining the relationship between gender and mathematical ability. Sieber and Stanley's definition, by implication, refers to harmful or negative potential consequences or implications – this is what makes SSR controversial. The American Psychological Association's 'Ethical Principles in the Conduct of Research' (1982) acknowledges the social implications of research. It states that the scientific enterprise creates ethical dilemmas. The same scientific knowledge and techniques that can be used for human betterment can be used for manipulative and exploitative purposes. For example, methods that have been shown to reduce prejudice towards minority groups may also be used to reconcile the victims of social injustice to their fate. Psychological research (like other scientific research) is a double-edged sword. It can be used to benefit those being studied, or against their interests and for the benefit of those with social, economic and political power. There's nothing neutral about research.

## Section 2:

The debate about the ethics of psychological research usually focuses on the vulnerability of individual participants, and the responsibility of psychologists to ensure they don't suffer in any way from their participation. Protection of participants is one of the specific principles included in the 'Ethical Principles For Conducting Research with Human Participants' (BPS, 1990, 1993, 2000). But the Ethical Principles as a whole are designed to prevent any harm coming to participants – what Brown (1997) calls the avoidance of overt 'sins'. But sometimes the principles designed to protect individual participants can throw up problems and dilemmas for the researcher, and this is especially likely in the case of SSR – and could even be considered a defining feature of SSR. An example is privacy and confidentiality in the context of AIDS research. The way in which appropriate research groups are identified (such as waiting outside gay bars) can breach privacy needs. Also, if a participant reveals that s/he has AIDS, continues to have unprotected sex, and withholds from partners the fact that s/he has AIDS, what is the appropriate role of the researcher? Should they maintain the promise of confidentiality, reveal the information to the authorities, or try to contact the participant's partners directly? (Sieber & Stanley, 1988). This is the issue of protecting the individual versus protecting society.

Consistent with Sieber and Stanley's definition of SSR, Brown (1997) argues that formal ethical codes focus too narrowly on risks to the individual participant and neglect broader questions about the risks to the group the participant belongs to. These groups can include women, ethnic minorities and other sub-cultural groups, as well as entire non-Western national cultures. This issue of

## Section 3:

In relation to protecting the individual versus protecting society, Melton and Gray (1988) make a strong general case for respecting the confidentiality rights of individuals with AIDS. Ultimately, this approach will protect the integrity of data collected by future researchers, that is, if individuals from a relatively cohesive research population (such as gay men/lesbians) become aware of breaches of confidentiality, this is likely to be conveyed to other members of their group, which will make them less willing to participate in other studies or to give truthful information if they do. These are basically pragmatic (expediency) rather than moral/ethical reasons for choosing the confidentiality option, and we could question whether these are 'best' reasons.

To the extent that gender and culture biases are harmful to particular groups, they are ethical issues. In this sense, any comparison between women and men made from an alpha bias perspective (Hare-Mustin & Maracek, 1988) is socially sensitive. Equally, any comparison between blacks and whites is socially sensitive. According to Brown (1997), a core assumption underlying ethical codes is that what psychologists do as researchers is basically harmless and inherently valuable. This is because it's based on 'science'. So a researcher can strictly follow scientific research methodologies, get technically adequate informed consent from participants (and not breach any of the other ethical principles), but still conduct research which is detrimental and potentially harmful to a particular group, such as the intellectual inferiority of blacks compared with whites. The crucial issue is whether it's ethically acceptable to be doing such research in the first place.

## Section 4:

Another issue relating to SSR is protecting the individual versus benefiting society. Not only are psychologists obliged to protect individual participants, they are also obliged to carry out socially meaningful research, that is, research that may potentially improve the quality of people's lives (the ethical imperative: Brehm, 1992). This dual obligation to individual participants and to society can create a dilemma for researchers (the double obligation dilemma/DOD). This is greatest when investigating important areas such as conformity, obedience and bystander intervention. In general, the more important the issue, the greater the potential benefit to society, and the more likely an individual participant is to experience distress and discomfort. This is because the more important the issue, the more essential it becomes to use deception. The key ethical issue hinges on the fact that the use of deception contributes enormously to our understanding of human behaviour (helping to satisfy the obligation to society) and at the same time significantly increases individuals' distress (detracting from the responsibility to protect individuals).

According to Sieber and Stanley (1988), it's almost inevitable that research will raise socially sensitive issues if useful theory, knowledge and applications are to come out of it. If we restrict psychology to areas that are unlikely to raise socially sensitive issues, then research may be confined to relatively unimportant problems. 'Socially important' and 'socially sensitive' seem to be two sides of a coin. Psychologists are obliged to confront the ethical issues raised by SSR. But if they shy away from controversial topics, simply because they're controversial animals in psychological investigations. (30 marks) (40 mins) (800 words minimum)

## Section 1:

Experiments that wouldn't be allowed for ethical reasons, or that would be very impractical if they were, if they involved human participants, are permitted using non-human animals – or at least they have been in the past. This, of course, begs the question as to the ethics of such animal experiments. Some examples of such experiments that wouldn't be permitted today include Harlow and Zimmerman's (1959) study of total social isolation in baby rhesus monkeys, Brady's (1958) executive monkey experiments, and Seligman's (1974) study of learned helplessness. Quite apart from the ethics, greater control can be exerted over the variables under investigation compared with the equivalent human experiment. For example, the Skinner box is an environment that's totally controlled by the experimenter.

Because there's an underlying evolutionary continuity between humans and other species, it's assumed that differences between humans and other species are merely quantitative (as opposed to qualitative). In other words, other species may display simpler behaviour and have more primitive nervous systems than humans, but they're not of a different order. In fact, the mammalian brain (rats, cats, dogs, monkeys and humans are all mammals) is built on similar lines in all these species, and neurons work in the same way. These biological similarities are related to behavioural similarities. So studying the simpler cases is a valid and valuable way of finding out about the more complex ones, as demonstrated by Skinner's theory of operant conditioning.

## Section 2:

Compared with humans, non-humans are mostly smaller and, therefore, easier to study in the laboratory. They have shorter life spans and gestation periods, which makes it easier to study their development – several generations can be studied in a relatively short time. Animal studies also provide useful hypotheses for subsequent testing with humans. For example, Bowlby's (1969) attachment theory was partly influenced by Lorenz's (1935) study of imprinting in geese. Animals can also be used to test cause-and-effect relationships where the existing human evidence is only correlational (as in smoking and lung cancer).

There are several constraints on the use of non-human animals and safeguards to protect them. The BPS Guidelines for the Use of Animals in Research (1985, 2000) offer a checklist of points that researchers must carefully consider when planning experiments with living non-humans. These fall under several headings, including legislation, choice of species, number of animals, and procedures (such as reward, deprivation and aversive stimulation). Researchers are obliged to keep suffering to a minimum, both during and following any surgical procedure. This also applies to electric shock and food deprivation, which are the most objected-to treatments. The permitted level of electric shock is controlled by the Home Office Inspectors, who monitor implementation of the Animals (Scientific Procedures) Act (1986). Procedures causing pain are illegal, unless the experimenter holds a Home Office licence. Even then, these procedures should only be carried out if there are no alternative ways of conducting the experiment.

The number of animals used in laboratory experiments has declined in the UK and other European countries since the 1970s (Mukerjee, 1997), and a cost–benefit analysis must be performed before any experiment can proceed. This involves weighing up animal pain, distress and death against acquisition of new knowledge and the development of new medical therapies for humans. But genome-related research is threatening to reverse this downward trend (Hawkes, 2000). Despite the various safeguards, the very existence of the 1986 Act condones the use of animals. Legally, and explicitly, the Act aims to spare animals 'unnecessary' pain and distress. But implicitly, the law accepts that some research will involve suffering for the non-human subjects. The Home Secretary, in granting 'Project Licences', must perform a cost–benefit analysis. But there's no obligation to consider whether the proposed research is really necessary (Seymour, 1996). Also, the Medicines Act (1968) requires that all new medicines undergo a range of tests on animals before they can be tested on humans (Lyall, 1993). So the law seems to reflect and reinforce the basic assumption that research with non-humans is acceptable, provided certain basic ethical issues are taken into account. There are also more pragmatic reasons for supporting research with non-humans. A group of British scientists – including physiologists and psychologists such as Gray and Blakemore – has called for the Home Office to speed up the process of approving animal experiments. They believe that the procedure is so long-winded that foreign scientists will take all the prizes for medicine, biotechnology and drug research (Hawkes, 2000).

## Section 4:

The very existence of safeguards (including legislation to protect animals) could be seen as implicitly defending the use of animal experiments. If the law regulates such experiments, and if psychologists regulate themselves (in the form of the Guidelines), then isn't this ethically sufficient? The objection to this argument is that both the Act and the Guidelines implicitly assume that some animal suffering, under certain circumstances, can always be justified. But can it? According to Gray (1987), the main justifications for animal experiments are the pursuit of scientific knowledge and the advancement of medicine (the medical justification argument). The latter is the strongest argument. But there's an important distinction between asking whether using animals is scientifically useful (in the development of drugs that can reduce human suffering and save lives), and whether it's right that they should be used in this way. Answering 'yes' to the first question is where the ethical debate begins, not ends. The questions relate to human needs and animal rights respectively. Gray (1991) believes that we sometimes have to choose between human and non-human suffering, in which case choosing to reduce the former is justified. This is an extension of the medical justification argument for speciesism (Ryder, 1990), an extension of the medical justification argument. Not only is it not wrong to favour the needs of one's own species; we have a duty to do so.

The speciesism argument takes a special twist when the species in question isn't rats and mice, but our closest evolutionary relatives: chimpanzees and other primates. The scope of the ethical debate about animal rights in recent years has widened to include the idea of equality under the law (Singer & Cavalieri, 1993; Wise, 2000).

(1,020 words)

# SAMPLE ESSAYS

# Perspectives: Debates

## What's covered in this chapter?

### You need to know about:

- *Free will and determinism*, including definitions of these terms and arguments for and against their existence. The debate in relation to psychological theories and studies (e.g. Freud's and Skinner's theories)

- *Reductionism*, including reductionism as a form of explanation, examples of reductionism in psychological theories and studies (e.g. physiological, machine, experimental), and arguments for and against reductionist explanations

- *Psychology as science*, including definitions/varieties of science, arguments for and against the claim that psychology is a science (e.g. Kuhn's concept of a paradigm; objectivity; and the use of the experimental method)

- *Nature–nurture*, including definitions of the terms, assumptions made about nature and nurture in psychological theories and studies (e.g. Piaget's theory and sociobiology), and different views regarding their relationship (e.g. gene–environment interaction)

## Free will and determinism

Any discussion of psychology's scientific status (see below, pages 508–520) raises fundamental questions about the nature of the person. One of these questions, debated by Western philosophers for centuries, is whether we choose to act as we do, or whether our behaviour is caused by influences beyond our control (*free will* versus *determinism*).

### Defining free will and determinism

- Intuition tells us that people have the ability to choose their own courses of action, and to determine their own behaviour. To this extent, they have *free will*. But this freedom is exercised only within certain physical, political, sociological and other environmental constraints.

- The positivistic, mechanistic nature of scientific psychology (see below) implies that behaviour is *determined* by external (or internal) events or stimuli, and that people are passive responders. To this extent, people *aren't* free.

- *Determinism* also implies that behaviour occurs in a regular, orderly manner, which (in principle) is totally predictable. Things can happen only in the way they do, because everything is caused, and every cause is itself the effect of some other cause. So there's a chain of events that (in principle) stretches back infinitely (Taylor, 1963).
- 'Everything' includes people and their thoughts and behaviour. So a 'strict determinist' believes that thoughts and behaviour are no different from (other) 'things' or events in the world.
- This begs the question of whether thoughts and behaviour are the same *kinds of thing* or *event* as, say, chemical reactions in a test tube or

neurons firing in the brain. We don't usually ask if the chemicals 'agreed' to combine in a certain way, or if the neurons 'decided' to fire. Unless we're trying to be witty, we'd be guilty of *anthropomorphism* (attributing human abilities and characteristics to non-humans or things).
- It's only *people* who can agree and make decisions. These abilities and capacities form part of our concept of a person. This, in turn, forms an essential part of 'everyday' or common-sense psychology. Agreeing and deciding are precisely the kinds of things we do *with our minds* (they're mental processes or events). To be able to agree and make decisions, it's necessary to 'have a mind'. So free will implies having a mind.
- But having a mind *doesn't* imply free will: it's possible that decisions and so on are themselves *caused* (determined), even though they seem to be freely chosen.

## Different meanings of 'free will'

One of the difficulties with the free will versus determinism debate is the ambiguity of the concepts.

### HAVING A CHOICE

- If we have choice, then we could behave differently given the same set of circumstances.
- This contrasts sharply with the earlier definition of determinism, according to which things can only happen as they do, given everything that has happened previously.

### NOT BEING COERCED OR CONSTRAINED

- If someone puts a loaded gun to your head and tells you to do something, your behaviour is clearly not free: you've been *forced* to act this way ('against your will').
- This is usually where the philosophical debate about free will *begins* (and, arguably, you still have the choice as to whether you

do what you're told or not!) This also relates to what James (1890) called *soft determinism* (see below, page 499).

## VOLUNTARY BEHAVIOUR

- 'Involuntary' conveys reflex behaviour (such as the eye-blink response to a puff of air directed at the eye). 'Voluntary' implies 'free' (the behaviour *isn't* reflex or automatic). By definition, most behaviour (both human and non-human) is voluntary. Nor is it usually the result of coercion. So is most behaviour free?
- Penfield's (1947) classic experiments provide convincing evidence for the distinction between voluntary and involuntary behaviour.

> ### Key study
>
> ### STIMULATING THE HUMAN CORTEX (STHC) (PENFIELD, 1947)
>
> - Penfield stimulated the cortex of patients about to undergo brain surgery.
> - The cortical area being stimulated was the same as that which is involved when we normally ('voluntarily') move our limbs. Nevertheless, patients reported feeling that their arms and legs were being moved passively – a very different experience from initiating the movement themselves.
> - This demonstrates that the subjective experience (phenomenology) of the voluntary movement of one's limbs cannot be reduced to the stimulation of the appropriate brain region (otherwise Penfield's patients shouldn't have reported a difference). Doing things voluntarily simply feels different from the same things 'just happening'.

Photograph taken during surgery carried out by Penfield. The numbers refer to the parts of the cortex stimulated

- Delgado (1969) stimulated a part of the primary motor area in a patient's *left* hemisphere. This caused the patient to form a clenched fist with his *right* hand. When the patient was asked to keep his fingers still during the next stimulation, he couldn't do it and commented, 'I guess, Doctor, that your electricity is stronger than my will'.
- Penfield's and Delgado's studies support the claim that having free will is an undeniable part of our subjective experience of ourselves as people. The sense of self is most acute (and important and real for us) when moral decisions and feelings of responsibility for past actions are involved (Koestler, 1967). (The relationship between free will and moral responsibility is discussed further below.)

- One demonstration of people's belief in their free will is *psychological reactance* (Brehm, 1966; Brehm & Brehm, 1981). A common response to the feeling that our freedom is being threatened is the attempt to regain or reassert it. This is related to the need to be free from others' controls and restrictions, to determine our own actions and not be dictated to. A good deal of contrary (resistant) behaviour (otherwise known as 'bloody-mindedness: 'Don't tell *me* what to do!') seems to reflect this process (Carver & Scheier, 1992).
- Similar to this need to feel free from others' control is *intrinsic motivation* or *self-determination* (Deci, 1980; Deci & Ryan, 1987). This refers to people's intrinsic interest in things, such that they

don't need extrinsic incentives for doing them. Engaging in such activities is motivated by the desire for competence.

- So what happens when someone is offered an extrinsic reward for doing something which is already interesting and enjoyable in itself? Lepper *et al.* (1973) found that the activity (children using crayons for drawing) loses its intrinsic appeal, and motivation is reduced (the *paradox of reward*). This has implications for accounts of moral development based on learning theory principles, especially operant conditioning (see Chapters 11 and 18).

## DELIBERATE CONTROL

- Norman and Shallice (1986) define *divided attention* as an upper limit to the amount of processing that can be performed on incoming information at any one time. They propose three levels of functioning, namely *fully automatic processing*, *partially automatic processing* and *deliberate control*. Deliberate control corresponds to free will.
- Driving a car is a sensory-motor skill, which experienced drivers perform more or less automatically. It doesn't require deliberate, conscious control, unless some unexpected event disrupts the performance (such as putting your foot on the brake when there's an obstacle ahead: this is a 'rule of the game'). But on an icy road this can be risky, since the steering wheel has a different 'feel' and the whole driving strategy must be changed. After doing it several times, this too may become a semi-automatic routine:

> 'But let a little dog amble across the icy road in front of the driver, and he will have to make a "top-level decision" whether to slam down the brake, risking the safety of his passengers, or run over the dog. And if, instead of a dog, the jaywalker is a child, he will probably resort to the brake, whatever the outcome. It is at this level, when the pros and cons are equally balanced, that the subjective experience of freedom and moral responsibility arises.'
>
> (Koestler, 1967).

- As we move downwards from conscious control, the subjective experience of freedom diminishes. According to Koestler:

> 'Habit is the enemy of freedom . . . Machines cannot become like men, but men can become like machines.'

- Koestler believes that the second enemy of freedom is very powerful (especially negative) emotions. They result in 'diminished responsibility' and 'I couldn't help it'.

## Why are psychologists interested in the concept of free will?

- As we noted earlier, the philosophical debate about free will and determinism is centuries old. It can be traced back at least to the French philosopher Descartes (1596–1650), whose ideas had a great influence on both science in general and psychology in particular (see below, page 508).
- For much of its history as a separate, scientific discipline, psychology has operated as if there were no difference between natural, physical phenomena and human thought and behaviour. In both cases, determinism (of one kind or another) is the major form of explanation.
- During the period from 1913 to 1956, psychology (at least in the USA) was dominated by behaviourism, Skinner being particularly influential (see Chapter 18). Skinner's beliefs about the influence of mental phenomena on behaviour and free will are discussed on pages 501–502.

## Free will and psychological abnormality

- Definitions of abnormality, and the diagnosis and treatment of mental disorders, often involve implicit or explicit judgements about free will and determinism.
- In a general sense, mental disorders can be seen as the partial or total breakdown of the control people usually have over their thoughts, emotions and behaviours. For example, *compulsive* behaviour is, by definition, behaviour which a person cannot help but do: s/he's 'compelled' to do it. Compulsive hand-washing may be an attempt to deal with the effect of being *obsessed* by thoughts

of germs (see Chapter 14). People may also be *attacked* by panic, or become the victims of thoughts inserted into their mind from outside and which are under external influence (again, see Chapter 14).

- In all these examples, things are happening to, or being done to, the individual, instead of the individual doing them him/herself. Being in control is usually thought of as a major feature of normality. So being judged to have lost control (temporarily or permanently) is a legally acceptable defence in cases of criminal offences.

## Box 17.1 Forensic psychiatry, diminished responsibility and the law

- **Forensic psychiatry deals with assessment and treatment of mentally disturbed offenders. The 1983 Mental Health Act has several clauses providing for the compulsory detention of prisoners in hospital (either while awaiting trial or as part of their sentence).**
- **Psychiatrists, as expert witnesses, can play an important role in advising the court about (a) fitness to plead, (b) mental state at the time of the offence, and (c) diminished responsibility.**
- **The defence of *diminished responsibility* (DR) (for murder) was introduced in England and Wales in the 1957 Homicide Act. This replaced the plea of 'not guilty by reason of insanity', which dates back to 1843.**

Peter Sutcliffe, the 'Yorkshire Ripper', a paranoid schizophrenic but responsible for his crimes

- **If the DR plea is accepted, there's no trial and a sentence of manslaughter is passed. If not, a trial is held and the jury must decide whether the accused (at the time the crime was committed) was suffering from an abnormality of mind. If so, was the abnormality such as to impair substantially his or her responsibility?**
- **Peter Sutcliffe, the 'Yorkshire Ripper', was found guilty of the murder of 13 women and the attempted murder of seven others. This was despite his defence that he heard God's voice telling him to 'get rid' of prostitutes. In finding him guilty of murder, the jury didn't necessarily reject the defence's argument that he was suffering from paranoid schizophrenia (see Chapter 14). Rather, his mental disorder didn't constitute a mental abnormality of sufficient degree substantially to impair responsibility for his actions.**
- **Sutcliffe was sentenced to 20 concurrent terms of life imprisonment, which he served initially in an ordinary prison before being sent to Broadmoor Special Hospital.**

**(Based on Gelder *et al.*, 1989; Prins, 1995.)**

## Free will and moral responsibility

- Underlying the whole question of legal (and moral) responsibility is the presupposition that people are (at least some of the time) able to control their behaviour and choose between different courses of action. How else could we ever be held responsible for any of our actions?
- In most everyday situations, we attribute responsibility, both to ourselves and others, unless we have reason to doubt it. According to Flanagan (1984):

'It seems silly to have any expectations about how people ought to act, if everything we do is the result of some inexorable causal chain which began millennia ago. "Ought", after all, seems to imply "can", therefore, by employing a moral vocabulary filled with words like "ought" and "should", we assume that humans are capable of rising above the causal pressures presented by the material world, and, in assuming this we appear to be operating with some conception of freedom, some notion of free will.'

In other words, we can only hold people (including ourselves, of course) morally (and legally) responsible if we first believe in free will. If all our actions are determined (beyond our control), we couldn't be considered morally or legally responsible for anything we do. In this sense, we'd be no different from non-human animals or physical objects.

YOU'RE TO BLAME FOR ALL THE TROUBLE I'M IN !

Credit Card

## Free will and determinism in psychological theory

### JAMES AND SOFT DETERMINISM

* James was one of the pioneers of psychology as a separate, scientific discipline. In *The Principles of Psychology* (1890), he devoted a whole chapter to the 'will', which he related to attention:

> 'The most essential achievement of the will . . . when it is most "voluntary" is to attend to a different object and hold it fast before the mind . . . Effort of attention is thus the essential phenomenon of will.'

* For James, there was a conflict. Belief in determinism seemed to fit best with the scientific view of the world, while belief in free will seemed to be required by our social, moral, political and legal practices, as well as by our personal, subjective experience (see above). His solution to the conflict was two-fold.

* First, he distinguished between the scientific and non-scientific worlds. Psychology as a science could progress only by assuming determinism. But this doesn't mean that belief in free will must be abandoned in other contexts. So scientific explanation isn't the only useful or valid kind of explanation.

* Second, he drew a further distinction between two kinds of determinism:

William James
(1842–1910)

(a) According to *soft determinism*, the question of free will depends on the *type(s)* of cause(s) our behaviour has, *not* whether it's caused or not caused. (The opposite of 'not caused' is 'random', *not* 'free'). If the immediate (proximate) cause of our actions is processing by a system such as *conscious mental life* (CML), which includes consciousness, purposefulness, personality and personal continuity, then they count as free, rational, voluntary, purposive actions.

(b) According to *hard determinism*, CML is itself caused. This means that the immediate causes are only part of the total causal chain which results in the behaviour we're trying to explain. Therefore, as long as our behaviour is caused at all (that is, not random), there's no sense in which we can be described as acting freely.

### FREUD AND PSYCHIC DETERMINISM

* According to Strachey (1962):

> 'Behind all of Freud's work . . . we should posit his belief in the universal validity of the law of determinism . . . Freud extended the belief (derived from physical phenomena) uncompromisingly to the field of mental phenomena.'

* Similarly, Sulloway (1979) maintains that all of Freud's work in science (and Freud saw himself very much as a scientist) was founded on the strong belief in the principle of cause and effect. All vital phenomena, including psychical (psychological) ones are rigidly and lawfully determined by this principle. This is demonstrated by the importance Freud attached to the technique of *free association*.

### Box 17.2 How 'free' is Freud's 'free association'?

* **'Free association' is a misleading translation of the German '*freier Einfall*'. This conveys much more accurately Freud's intended impression of an uncontrollable 'intrusion' ('*Einfall*') by pre-conscious ideas into conscious thinking.**
* **In turn, this pre-conscious material reflects unconscious ideas, wishes and memories (what Freud was really interested in), since here lies the principal cause(s) of neurotic problems.**
* **It's a great irony that 'free' association should refer to a technique used in psychoanalysis meant to reveal the *unconscious* causes of behaviour (see Chapters 15 and 18). It's because the causes of our thoughts, actions and supposed choices are unconscious (mostly *actively repressed*) that we believe we're free.**
* **Freud's application of this general philosophical belief in causation to mental phenomena is called *psychic determinism*.**

**(Based on Sulloway, 1979.)**

* For Freud, part of what 'psychic determinism' conveyed was that, in the universe of the mind, there are no 'accidents'. No matter how apparently random or irrational behaviour may be (such as 'parapraxes' or 'Freudian slips'), unconscious causes can always account for them. This also applies to hysterical symptoms and dreams.
* As Gay (1988) says, 'Freud's theory of mind is . . . strictly and frankly deterministic'. However:

(a) Freud accepted that true accidents, that is, forces beyond the victim's control (such as being struck by lightning) can and do occur, and aren't unconsciously caused by the victim

(b) one aspect of psychic determinism is *overdetermination*, that is, much of our behaviour has *multiple* causes, both conscious and unconscious. So although our conscious choices, decisions and intentions may genuinely influence behaviour, they never tell the *whole* story

(c) one of the aims of psychoanalysis is to 'give the patient's ego *freedom* to decide one way or another' (Freud, in Gay, 1988).

So therapy rests on the belief that people can change. But Freud saw this potential change as very limited

(d) Freud never actually predicted in advance what choice or decision a patient would make. Nevertheless, he maintained that these aren't arbitrary, and can be understood as revealing personality characteristics (Rycroft, 1966). What Freud often did was to explain his patients' choices, neurotic symptoms, and so on not in terms of causes (the *scientific* argument), but by trying to make sense of them and give them meaning (the *semantic* argument). Indeed, the latter is reflected in the title of, arguably, his greatest book, *The Interpretation of Dreams* (1900) (as opposed to *The 'Cause' of Dreams*).

## SKINNER AND THE ILLUSION OF FREE WILL

- Skinner's and Freud's ideas about human behaviour are diametrically opposed in most respects. However, they shared the fundamental belief that free will is an illusion. But, in keeping with their theories as a whole, their reasons are radically different.
- While Freud focused on 'the mind' (especially unconscious thoughts, wishes and memories), Skinner's *radical behaviourism* eliminates all reference to mental (private) states as part of the explanation of behaviour.
- Skinner doesn't deny that pain and other internal states exist. But they have no 'causal teeth' and hence no part to play in scientific explanations of (human) behaviour (Garrett, 1966).
- Free will (and other 'explanatory fictions') cannot be defined or measured objectively, nor are they needed for successful prediction and control of behaviour (for Skinner, the primary aims of a *science* of behaviour).
- It's only because the causes of human behaviour are often hidden from us in the environment that the myth or illusion of free will survives. (This parallels Freud's argument that we think we have free will only because we're unaware of the unconscious causes of our behaviour.)
- According to Skinner, when what we do is dictated by force or punishment, or by their threat (negative reinforcement), it's obvious to everyone that we're not acting freely. For example, when the possibility of imprisonment stops us committing crimes, there's clearly no choice involved (we know what the environmental causes of our behaviour are). Similarly, it may sometimes be very obvious which positive reinforcers are shaping behaviour (such as a bonus for working overtime).
- But most of the time we're unaware of environmental causes, and it *looks* (and *feels*) as if we're behaving freely. Yet all this means is that we're free of the punishments or negative reinforcements. Our behaviour is still determined by pursuit of things that have been positively reinforced *in the past*. When we perceive others as behaving freely, we're simply ignorant of their reinforcement histories (Fancher, 1996).
- Clearly, Skinner's belief that free will is an illusion conflicts with the need to attribute people with free will if we're to hold them (and ourselves) morally and legally responsible for their actions. Skinner (in *Beyond Freedom and Dignity*, 1971) acknowledges that freedom and dignity are:

'... essential to practices in which a person is held responsible for his conduct and given credit for his achievements.'

But he rejects the notion of 'autonomous man'.
- Skinner equates 'good' and 'bad' with 'beneficial to others' (what's rewarded) and 'harmful to others' (what's punished) respectively. This removes morality from human behaviour. For Skinner, 'oughts' aren't 'moral imperatives' (things we're obliged to do for moral/ethical reasons). Rather, they reflect practical guidelines and rules (Morea, 1990).
- A further consequence of Skinner's rejection of 'autonomous man' is what Ringen (1996) calls the *behaviour therapist's dilemma*. This is closely related to some of the most fundamental ethical issues faced by psychologists as practitioners (or agents of change).

**Box 17.3 The behaviour therapist's dilemma (BTD) (Ringen, 1996)**

- There's a deep tension between two features of modern clinical psychology.
- On the one hand, Skinner (1971) argues that scientific considerations support *radical behaviourism* as the most appropriate framework for understanding and facilitating the development of effective behaviour therapy (including methods based on both classical and operant conditioning: see Chapter 15).
- On the other hand, an increasingly significant ethical and legal constraint on therapeutic practice is the doctrine of *informed consent*. This obliges behaviour therapists (and other practitioners in the helping professions, including psychiatry) to recognise the autonomy of those who come to them for help.
- The BTD describes the tension between these two aspects of modern clinical psychology, namely, that either (a) radical behaviourism is false, or (b) human beings never act autonomously. This involves having to choose between alternatives that many modern behaviour therapists would find difficult to defend.

## EXAM tips BOX

**Discuss the free will and determinism debate with reference to *two or more* psychological theories. (30 marks) (40 mins) (800 words minimum) AO1/AO2**

*This essay can be spilt up into FOUR sections – each about 200 words long. Each section would be worth 7–8 marks.*

**Section 1:** A **description** of the free will and determinism debate. You could define each of the major terms, including some examples of the different meanings of 'free will'. You could also give some reasons for psychologists' interest in the debate.

AO1

↓

**Section 2:** A **description** of how free will and determinism are dealt with by *two or more* psychological theories. Probably Freud and Skinner have the most to say about the debate. But you could include James's theory, in which case you wouldn't be expected to describe each theory in as much detail (the depth/breadth trade-off). This also applies to your analysis and evaluation of your chosen theories (AO2).

AO1

↓

**Section 3:** An **analysis** and **evaluation** of Freud's theory. You might consider Freud's theory of free will in relation to more general aspects of his theory (such as its scientific status – including its refutability – the import- ance of the unconscious and the difficulty of studying it). Alternatively, you might consider more specific aspects, such as the limitations of his theory of psychic determinism.

AO2

↓

**Section 4:** An **analysis** and **evaluation** of Skinner's theory. As with Freud's, you could consider his theory of free will in relation to more general aspects of his theory (such as radical behaviourism, the use of rats and pigeons in his experimental studies, and extreme environmentalism). Alternatively, you might consider more specific aspects, such as the implications of his theory for moral/legal responsibility, and the behaviour therapist's dilemma. You could also compare and/or contrast Freud's and Skinner's theories, or compare and/or contrast either or both with James's. For example, are they soft or hard determinists – and is this a useful/valid distinction to make?

AO2

*Try to answer this question yourself. There's a sample essay on pages 535–536 with which you can compare your essay.*

## Reductionism

### Defining reductionism

- Together with positivism, mechanism, determinism and empiricism, reductionism represents part of 'classical' science (see below, page 508).
- Luria (1987) traces the origins of reductionism to the mid-nineteenth-century view within biology

that an organism is a complex of organs, and the organs are complexes of cells. To explain the basic laws of the living organism, we have to study as carefully as possible the features of individual cells.

- From its biological origins, reductionism was extended to science in general. For example, the properties of a protein molecule could be uniquely determined or predicted in terms of properties of the electrons or protons making up its atoms.
- Consistent with this view is Garnham's (1991) definition of reductionism as:

> ' ... the idea that psychological explanations can be replaced by explanations in terms of brain functioning or even in terms of physics and chemistry.'

- According to its supporters, reductionism's ultimate aim is to account for all phenomena in terms of microphysics. But *any* attempt to explain something in terms of its components or constituent parts may be thought of as reductionist. A useful definition consistent with this broader view is that of Rose *et al.* (1984), for whom reductionism is:

> ' ... the name given to a set of general methods and modes of explanation both of the world of physical objects and of human societies. Broadly, reductionists try to explain the properties of complex wholes – molecules, say, or societies – in terms of the units of which those molecules or societies are composed.'

- Rose (1997) identifies four major types of reductionism (or different meanings of the term).

## Box 17.4  Different meanings of reductionism

- ***Reductionism as methodology:*** This refers to the attempt to isolate variables in the laboratory in order to simplify the living world's enormous complexity, flux and multitude of interacting processes. This is the basis of the experiment, which reflects natural science's attempt to identify cause-and-effect relationships (see Chapter 6).

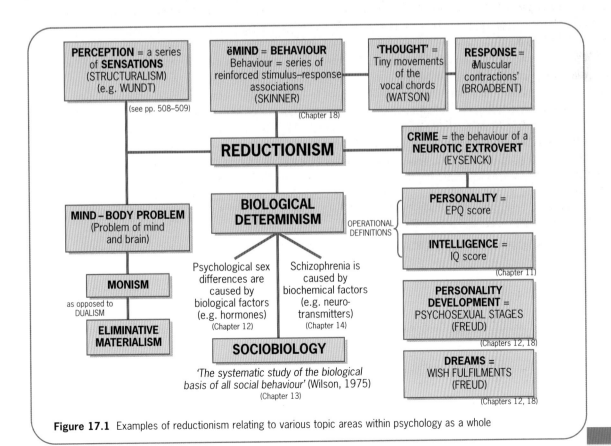

**Figure 17.1** Examples of reductionism relating to various topic areas within psychology as a whole

- *Theory reduction:* This refers to science's aim to capture as much of the world in as few laws or principles as possible. It's related to philosophical reductionism.
- *Philosophical reductionism:* This refers to the belief that because science is unitary, and because physics is the most fundamental of the sciences, ultimately all currently separate disciplines (including psychology) will be 'reduced' to physics (see the quotes from Garnham, 1991, above, and Crick, 1994, below, page 505).
- *Reductionism as ideology:* This refers to the very marked tendency in recent years to identify genes responsible for a whole range of complex human behaviours, including stress, anxiety, depression, personality, homosexuality, intelligence, alcoholism, criminality and violence.

(Based on Rose, 1997.)

- Rose calls the claim that there's a direct causal link between genes and behaviour *neurogentic determinism*. It involves a sequence of (false) assumptions and arguments. One of these is the dichotomy between genetic and environmental causes (or nature and nurture: see below, pages 520–530).

## The mind–body problem

- Perhaps the oldest and most frequently debated example of reductionism is the *mind–body problem* (or the *problem of mind and brain*). Originally a philosophical issue, it continues to be discussed, often passionately, by biologists, neurophysiologists, neuropsychologists, and psychologists in general.
- It's generally agreed that (a) the mind (or consciousness) is a property of human beings (as is walking upright on two legs), and (b) without the human brain there'd be no consciousness. But a 'problem' remains.

### Box 17.5 The problem of the mind–brain relationship

- How can two 'things' be related when one of them is physical (the brain has size, weight, shape, density, and exists in space and time) and the other (the mind) apparently has none of these characteristics?
- How can something non-physical/non-material (the mind) influence or produce changes in something physical (the brain/body)?
- The 'classic' example given by philosophers to illustrate the problem is the act of deciding to lift one's arm. (This example also illustrates the exercise of free will: see Penfield's STHC in Key Study, page 496) From a strictly scientific perspective, this kind of causation should be impossible, and science (including psychology and neurophysiology) has traditionally rejected any brand of *philosophical dualism*. This is the belief in the existence of two essentially different kinds of 'substance' – the physical body and the non-physical mind (see Box 17.6 and Figure 17.2).

- From an evolutionary perspective, could consciousness have equipped human beings with survival value unless it had causal properties (Gregory, 1981), that is, unless it could actually bring about changes in behaviour?
- Our subjective experience tells us that our minds *do* affect behaviour, and that consciousness *does* have causal powers (just try lifting your arm!). But many philosophers and scientists from various disciplines haven't always shared the layperson's common-sense understanding.
- There are many theories of the mind–brain relationship. But most aren't strictly relevant to the debate about reductionism. Box 17.6 and Figure 17.2 summarise most of the major theories, but we've emphasised reductionist approaches, especially as they impinge on psychological theories.

## Box 17.6 Some major theories of the mind–brain relationship

- Theories fall into two main categories: *dualist* (which distinguish between mind and brain) and *monist* (which claim that only mind or matter is real).
- Descartes's seventeenth-century dualist theory first introduced the mind–body problem into philosophy. He claimed that the mind can influence the brain, but not *vice versa*. While *epiphenomenalism* sees the mind as a kind of by-product of the brain (the mind has no influence on the brain), *interactionism* sees the influence as two-way.
- Some major areas of psychological research which seem to involve (one- or two-way) interactions between mind and brain include (a) the effects of psychoactive drugs (see Chapter 15), (b) electrical stimulation of the brain (see Key Study, page 496), (c) Sperry's studies of split-brain patients (see Gross, 2005), and (d) stress (see Chapter 3).
- *Psychophysical parallelists* are dualists who believe there's no mind–brain interaction at all: mental and neural events are merely perfectly synchronised or correlated.
- According to *mentalism/idealism*, only mental phenomena are real. *Phenomenological* theories (such as Carl Rogers's humanistic theory) and *constructionist* explanations of behaviour (see Gross, 2005) have a mentalist 'flavour'.
- Most monist theories take one or other form of *materialism*.
- The *peripheralist* version of materialism is illustrated by Skinner's *radical behaviourism* (see above, pages 501–502 and Chapter 18). During the 1930s, Skinner denied the existence of mental phenomena (as had Watson, the founder of behaviourism). But from 1945, he began to adopt a less extreme view, recognising their existence but defining them as *covert/internal actions*, and subject to the same laws of conditioning as overt, external behaviour. This is a form of reductionism. We also saw earlier, when discussing free will, that Skinner argued that mental events have no explanatory power, that is, they cannot help explain behaviour because they cannot influence behaviour. This is essentially a form of epiphenomenalism.
- *Centralist materialism* (or *mind–brain identity theory*) identifies mental processes with purely physical processes in the central nervous system. It's logically possible that there might be separate, mental, non-physical phenomena. But it just turns out that, as a matter of fact, mental states are identical with physical states of the brain. We are, simply, very complex physico-chemical mechanisms.
- *Eliminative materialism* represents an extreme reductionist form of (centralist) materialism (see text below).

(Based on Flanagan, 1984; Gross, 2003; Teichman, 1988.)

## Reductionist theories of the mind–brain relationship

- What makes eliminative materialism reductionist is the attempt to *replace* a psychological account of behaviour with an explanation in terms of neurophysiology. An example of this approach is Crick's (1994) *The Astonishing Hypothesis: The Scientific Search for the Soul*. According to Crick:

> 'You, your joys and your sorrows, your memories and your ambitions, your sense of personality and free will, are in fact no more than the behaviour of a vast assembly of nerve cells and their associated molecules.'

- But is this a valid equation to make? According to Smith (1994), the mind and brain problem is radically different from other cases of *contingent identity* (identical as a matter of fact) with which it's usually compared (such as 'a gene is a section of the DNA molecule'). What's different is reductionism, and the related issue of exactly what's meant by *identity*.

## Box 17.7 Different meanings of 'identity' relevant to the mind–brain relationship

- It's generally agreed that we cannot have a mind without a brain. But mind states and brain states *aren't* systematically correlated, and the neurophysiological and neurological evidence points towards *token identity*.
- For example, we cannot just assume that the same neurophysiological mechanisms will be used by two different people both engaged in the 'same' activity of reading (Broadbent, 1981). There are many ways that 'the brain' can perform the same task.
- But this is precisely the kind of systematic correlation which mind–brain identity has been taken to imply: whenever a mind state of a certain type occurs, a brain state of a certain type occurs. This is *type identity*.
- Token identity means there must always be a place for an autonomous psychological account of human thought and action.

**(Based on Harré *et al*., 1985.)**

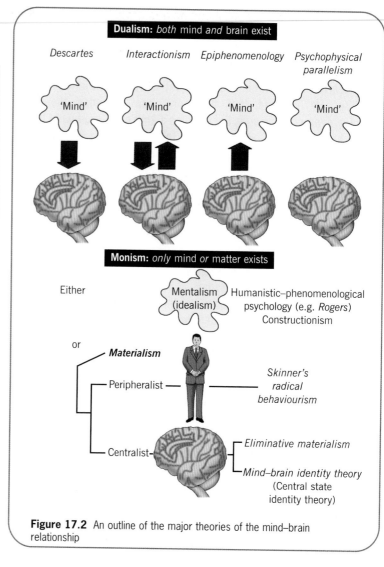

**Figure 17.2** An outline of the major theories of the mind–brain relationship

- According to Penrose (1990), there's a built-in *indeterminacy* in the way individual neurons and their synaptic connections work (their responses are inherently unpredictable). Yet, despite this unpredictability at the level of the individual units or components, the system as a whole is predictable. The 'nervous system' (or sub-systems within it) doesn't operate randomly, but in a highly organised, structured way.
- Consciousness, intelligence (see Chapter 11), and memory (see Chapter 1) are properties of the brain as a system, *not* properties of the individual units. They couldn't possibly be predicted from analysing the units. Instead they 'emerge' from interactions between the units that compose the system (and so are called *emergent properties*). The whole is greater than the sum of its parts (Rose, 1997).

## CAN YOU BE A MATERIALIST WITHOUT BEING A REDUCTIONIST?

- According to Rose (1992):

'The mind is never replaced by the brain. Instead we have two distinct and legitimate languages, each describing the same unitary phenomena of the material world.'

- Rose speaks as a materialist and an *anti-reductionist*. He believes we should learn how to translate between mind language and brain language (although he admits this may be impossibly difficult).

- Most materialists are also reductionists, and *vice versa*. But this isn't necessarily so. Freud, for example, was a materialist who believed that no single scientific vocabulary (such as anatomy) could adequately describe (let alone explain) all aspects of the material world. He believed in the *autonomy of psychological explanation*, that is, mental phenomena need their own language.

- The fact that there are different languages for describing minds and brains (or different *levels of description* or *universes of discourse*) relates to the question of the relevance of knowing, say, what's going on inside our brains when we think or are aware. For Eiser (1994):

> 'The firing of neurons stands to thought in the same relation as my walking across the room (etc.) stands to my getting some coffee. It is absolutely essential in a causal or physical sense, and absolutely superfluous . . . to the logic of the higher-order description. In short, I can accept that it happens, and then happily ignore it.'

- This explains how it's possible to be a materialist and an anti-reductionist at the same time. The brain is necessarily implicated in everything we do, and the mind doesn't represent a different kind of reality (materialism). But we can describe and explain our thinking without having to 'bring our brain into it' (anti-reductionism). Two separate levels of description are involved.

- Belief (or not) in the independence of psychological from neurophysiological explanations of behaviour is crucial to the survival of psychology itself as a separate discipline. According to Hegarty (2000), *psychoneuroimmunology* (see Chapter 3) offers a:

> ' . . . middle ground for mind–body monists and dualists to meet upon. Scientific research has given us insight into the complex realm of psychophysiology – the interface . . . between body and mind and in which the emotions figure large . . .'

## EXAM tips BOX

**Discuss arguments *for and against* reductionism as a form of explanation, using examples from psychological theories and/or studies. (30 marks) (40 mins) (800 words minimum) AO1/AO2**

*This essay can be split up into FOUR sections – each about 200 words long. Each section would be worth 7–8 marks.*

**Section 1:** A **description** of the debate about reductionism, including its origins in biology and how it's been extended to psychology. You could also outline different kinds (or meanings) of reductionism. These might include Rose's four-way classification, namely reductionism as methodology, theory reduction, philosophical reductionism, and reductionism as ideology. The last of these is related to neurogenetic determinism, which allows you to cross-refer to some aspects of the nature–nurture debate (see below, pages 520–531).

**Section 2:** Given psychology's origins in philosophy and physiology, together with the central place of the mind in psychological theory, the mind–body problem (problem of mind and brain) is a focus for the reductionism debate. Some accounts of this problem (such as interactionism and materialism) are especially relevant here. But the emphasis should be on reductionist theories.

**Section 3:** An **analysis** and **evaluation** of arguments *for and against* reductionism. You could take the distinction between token and type identity as your starting point (an argument against eliminative materialism, such as Crick's). Examples from research studies which illustrate the interaction between mind and brain also tend to detract from the claim that your mind is nothing but your brain.

**Section 4:** You could continue your **analysis** and **evaluation** of arguments *for and against* reductionism by considering reductionism as methodology. Any argument for or against the use of scientific method – especially the experiment – is an argument for or against reductionism. So again you can draw on your knowledge of other areas of the Specification here, what makes science in general, and the experiment in particular, 'desirable'. Alternatively, you could consider Penrose's concept of emergent properties, and the related issues of different levels of description/universes of discourse and whether it's possible to be a materialist and anti-reductionist at the same time.

*Try to answer this question yourself. There's a sample essay on pages 536–537 with which you can compare your essay.*

AO1

AO1

AO2

AO2

René Descartes (1596–1650)

# Psychology as science

- Psychology is commonly defined as the *scientific* study of behaviour and cognitive processes (or mind or experience).
- In order to 'unpack' this definition, we need to examine the nature and varieties of science, including the major features of scientific method. This should enable us to address the question of how appropriate it is to use scientific method to study human behaviour and cognitive processes

## Some philosophical roots of science and psychology

- Descartes was mentioned earlier when discussing theories of the mind–brain relationship. He was the first person formally to distinguish between mind and matter (*philosophical dualism*). This had an enormous impact on the development of both psychology as a science and science in general.
- Dualism allowed scientists to treat matter as inert and completely distinct from human beings. This meant that the world could be described *objectively*, without reference to the human observer.
- *Objectivity* became the ideal of science, and was extended to the study of human behaviour and social institutions in the mid-1800s by Comte. He called it *positivism*.
- Descartes also promoted *mechanism*. This is the view that the material world consists of objects which are assembled like a huge machine and operated by mechanical laws. He extended this view to living organisms, including, eventually, human beings. Because the mind is non-material, Descartes believed that (unlike the physical world) it can be investigated only through *introspection* (observing one's own thoughts and feelings). He was also one of the first to advocate *reductionism* (see above).
- *Empiricism* refers to the ideas of the seventeenth- and eighteenth-century British philosophers Locke, Hume and Berkeley. They believed that the only source of true knowledge about the world is sensory experience (what reaches us through our senses or what can be inferred about the relationship between such sensory facts). Empiricism is usually contrasted with *nativism* (or *rationalism*), according to which knowledge of the world is largely innate or inborn (see below, pages 520–522).
- The word *'empirical'* ('through the senses') is often used to mean 'scientific' (hence, 'empirical methods' as an alternative for 'scientific methods'). This implies that what scientists do – and what distinguishes them from non-scientists – is carry out experiments and observations as ways of collecting data ('facts') about the world. Empiricism proved to be one of the central influences on the development of physics and chemistry.

## Empiricism and psychology

Prior to the 1870s, there were no laboratories devoted specifically to psychological research. The early scientific psychologists had trained mainly as physiologists, philosophers, or some combination of these. The two professors who set up the first two psychological laboratories deserve much of the credit for the development of academic psychology. They were Wundt in Germany, and James in the USA (Fancher, 1979).

### WUNDT'S CONTRIBUTION

- Wundt was a physiologist by training and is generally regarded as the 'founder' of the new science of experimental psychology (what he called 'a new domain of science' (1874)). Having worked under the great physiologist Helmholtz, Wundt eventually became professor of 'scientific philosophy' at Leipzig University in 1875. His title illustrated the lack of distinct boundaries between the various disciplines which combined to bring about psychology's development (Fancher, 1979).

- In 1879, Wundt converted his 'laboratory' at Leipzig into a 'private institute' of experimental psychology. For the first time, a place had been set aside for the explicit purpose of conducting psychological research. This is why 1879 is widely accepted as the 'birth date' of psychology as a discipline in its own right. From its modest beginnings, the institute began to attract people from all over the world, who returned to their own countries to establish laboratories modelled on Wundt's.
- Wundt believed that conscious mental states could be scientifically studied through the systematic manipulation of antecedent variables ('events' that precede some other event), as well as through carefully controlled *introspection*.
- Introspection was a rigorous and highly disciplined technique for analysing conscious experience into its most basic elements (*sensations* and *feelings*). Participants were always advanced psychology students, who'd been carefully trained to introspect properly.

Willhelm Wundt
(1832–1920)

- Wundt believed that introspection made it possible to cut through the learned categories and concepts that define our everyday experience of the world. This would expose the 'building blocks' of experience.
- Because of introspection's central role, Wundt's early brand of psychology was called *introspective psychology* (or *introspectionism*). His attempt to analyse consciousness into its elementary sensations and feelings is known as *structuralism*.

## JAMES'S CONTRIBUTION

- James taught anatomy and physiology (A & P) at Harvard University in 1872. By 1875, he was calling his course 'The Relations Between Physiology and Psychology'. In the same year, he established a small laboratory, used mainly for teaching purposes. In 1878, he dropped A & P, and for several years taught 'pure psychology'.
- His view of psychology is summarised in *The Principles of Psychology* (1890). This included discussion of instinct, brain function, habit, the stream of consciousness, the self, attention, memory, perception, emotion and free will (see above).
- *The Principles of Psychology* provided the famous definition of psychology as 'the science of mental life'.
- James became increasingly critical of what psychology could offer as a science. Despite this, he became the first American (in 1894) to bring that country's attention to the recent work of the then little-known Viennese neurologist, Sigmund Freud (Fancher, 1979).
- James proposed a point of view (rather than a theory) that directly inspired *functionalism*. This emphasises the purpose and utility of behaviour (Fancher, 1979).
- Functionalism, in turn, helped to stimulate interest in *individual differences*, since they determine how well or poorly people adapt to their environments. These attitudes made Americans especially receptive to Darwin's (1859) ideas about individual variation, evolution by natural selection, and the 'survival of the fittest'.

## WATSON'S BEHAVIOURIST REVOLUTION

- Watson took over the psychology department at Johns Hopkins University in 1909. He immediately began cutting psychology's ties with philosophy and strengthening those with biology.
- At that time, Wundt's and James's studies of consciousness were still the 'real' psychology. But Watson was doing research on non-human animals and became increasingly critical of the use of introspection.
- In particular, Watson argued that introspective reports were unreliable and difficult to verify. It's impossible to check the accuracy of such reports, because they're based on purely *private* experience to which the investigator has no possible means of access. As a result, Watson redefined psychology in his famous 'behaviourist manifesto' of 1913.

John Broadus Watson
(1878–1958)

**Box 17.8  Watson's (1913) 'Behaviourist manifesto'**

- Watson's article 'Psychology as the behaviourist views it' is often referred to as the 'behaviourist manifesto', a charter for a truly scientific psychology. It was behaviourism which was to represent a rigorous empiricist approach within psychology for the first time.
- According to Watson:

  'Psychology as the behaviourist views it is a purely objective natural science. Its theoretical goal is the prediction and control of behaviour. Introspection forms no essential part of its methods, nor is the scientific value of its data dependent upon the readiness with which they lend themselves to interpretation in terms of consciousness. The behaviourist . . . recognizes no dividing line between man and brute. The behaviour of a man . . . forms only a part of the behaviourist's total scheme of investigation.'

- Three features of the 'manifesto' deserve special mention:
  - (a) psychology must be purely objective, excluding all subjective data or interpretations in terms of conscious experience. This redefines psychology as the 'science of behaviour' (rather than the 'science of mental life')
  - (b) the goals of psychology should be to predict and control behaviour (as opposed to describing and explaining conscious mental states). This goal was later endorsed by Skinner's *radical behaviourism*
  - (c) there's no fundamental (*qualitative*) difference between human and non-human behaviour. If, as Darwin had shown, humans evolved from more simple species, then it follows that human behaviour is just a more complex form of the behaviour of other species (the difference is merely *quantitative* – one of degree). Consequently rats, cats, dogs and pigeons became the major source of psychological data. Since 'psychological' now meant 'behaviour' rather than 'consciousness', non-humans that were convenient to study, and whose environments could be controlled easily, could replace people as experimental subjects.

- In his 1915 presidential address to the American Psychological Association, Watson talked about his recent 'discovery' of Pavlov's work on conditioned reflexes in dogs. He proposed that the conditioned reflex could become the foundation for a full-scale human psychology.
- The extreme environmentalism of Locke's empiricism (see above, page 508) lent itself well to the behaviourist emphasis on learning (through Pavlovian or classical conditioning). Locke had described the mind at birth as a *tabula rasa* ('blank slate'), which was then 'filled in' by experience. Watson, in rejecting the mind as suitable for a scientific psychology, simply swapped mind for behaviour: it's now behaviour that's shaped by the environment.
- According to Miller (1962), empiricism provided psychology with both a *methodology* (stressing the role of observation and measurement) and a *theory*. The theory includes analysis into elements (such as stimulus–response units), and *associationism* (which explains how simple elements can be combined to form more complex ones).
- Behaviourism also embodied positivism, in particular the emphasis on the need for scientific rigour and objectivity. Humans were now conceptualised and studied as 'natural phenomena', with subjective experience, consciousness and other characteristics (traditionally regarded as distinctive human qualities) no longer having a place in the behaviourist world.

## The cognitive revolution

- Academic psychology in the USA and the UK was dominated by behaviourism for the next 40 years. But criticism and dissatisfaction with it culminated in a number of 'events', all taking place in 1956, which collectively are referred to as the 'cognitive revolution'.

## Box 17.9 The 1956 'cognitive revolution'

- At a meeting at the Massachusetts Institute of Technology (MIT), Chomsky introduced his theory of language, Miller presented a paper on the 'magical number seven' in short-term memory (see Chapter 1), and Newell and Simon presented a paper on the logical theory machine (a blueprint for how computers solve problems).
- The first systematic attempt to investigate concept formation (in adults) from a cognitive psychological perspective was reported by Bruner *et al.*
- At Dartmouth College, New Hampshire (the 'Dartmouth Conference'), 10 academics met to discuss the possibility of producing computer programs that could 'behave' or 'think' intelligently. These included McCarthy (who coined the term 'artificial intelligence'/AI), Simon, Newell, Chomsky and Miller.

**(Based on Eysenck & Keane, 2000.)**

- This new way of thinking about and investigating people was called the *information-processing approach*. At its centre is the *computer analogy*, the view that human cognition can be understood by comparing it with the functioning of a digital computer.
- It was now acceptable to study the mind again. But it was conceptualised very differently from how Wundt, James and the other pioneers of the 'new psychology' (prior to Watson's behaviourist revolution) had described and studied it.

## Science, scientism and mainstream psychology

- Despite this major change in psychology after 1956, certain assumptions and practices within the discipline have remained largely unchanged. They're collectively referred to as *mainstream psychology*.
- Harré (1989) refers to the mainstream as the 'old paradigm'. One of the old paradigm's 'unexamined presuppositions' is *scientism*, which Van Langenhove (1995) defines as:

  ' . . . the borrowing of methods and a characteristic vocabulary from the natural sciences in order to discover causal mechanisms that explain psychological phenomena.'

- Scientism maintains that all aspects of human behaviour can and should be studied using the methods of natural science, which claims to be the sole means of establishing 'objective truth'. This can be achieved by studying phenomena:

(a) removed from any particular context ('*context-stripping*' exposes them in their 'pure' form), and
(b) in a *value-free* way (there's no bias on the investigator's part).

  The most reliable way of doing this is through the laboratory experiment. This method provides the greatest degree of control over relevant variables.
- Much research has moved beyond the confines of the laboratory experiment. But the same positivist logic is still central to how psychologists think about and carry out their research. Method and measurement still have a privileged status. According to Smith *et al.* (1995):

  'Whether concerned with mind or behaviour (and whether conducted inside or outside the laboratory), research tends to be constructed in terms of the separation (or reduction) of entities into independent and dependent variables and the measurement of hypothetical relationships between them.'

- Despite the attacks made on the natural sciences model since the mid-1970s, psychology is still to a large extent dominated by it. The most conspicuous effect of this is the dominance of experiments (Van Langenhove, 1995). In turn, this has far-reaching effects on how psychology *pictures* people as more-or-less passive and mechanical information-processing devices, whose behaviour can be split up into variables.

- The dominance of experiments also affects how psychology *deals* with people. In experiments, people aren't treated as single individuals but as interchangeable 'subjects'. There's no room for individualised observations.

## What do we mean by 'science'?

### THE MAJOR FEATURES OF SCIENCE

Most psychologists and philosophers of science would probably agree that for a discipline to be called a science, it must possess certain characteristics. These are summarised in Box 17.10 and Figure 17.3.

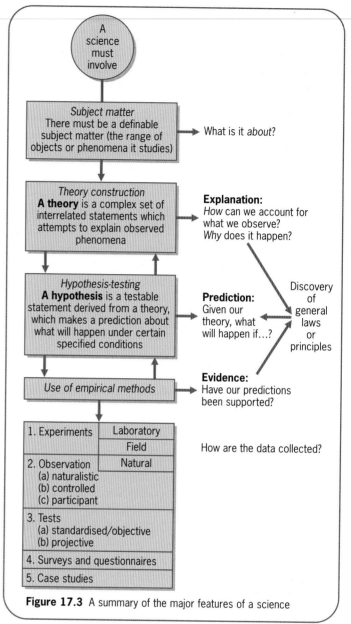

**Figure 17.3** A summary of the major features of a science

## Box 17.10 The major features of science

- *A definable subject matter:* This changed from conscious human thought to human and non-human behaviour, then to cognitive processes, within psychology's first 80 years as a separate discipline.
- *Theory construction:* This represents an attempt to explain observed phenomena, such as Watson's attempt to account for (almost all) human and non-human behaviour in terms of classical conditioning, and Skinner's subsequent attempt to do the same with operant conditioning.
- *Hypothesis-testing:* This involves making specific predictions about behaviour under certain conditions (for example, predicting that by combining the sight of a rat with the sound of a hammer crashing down on a steel bar just behind his head, a small child will learn to fear the rat – as in Watson and Rayner's (1920) famous 'Little Albert' experiment: see Key Study, page 548).
- *Empirical methods:* These are used to collect data (evidence) relevant to the hypothesis being tested.

## WHAT IS 'SCIENTIFIC METHOD'?

- The account given in Box 17.10 and Figure 17.3 of what constitutes a science is non-controversial. But it fails to tell us how the *scientific process* takes place, that is, the sequence of 'events' involved. For example, where does the theory come from in the first place and how is it related to observation of the subject matter? It also fails to tell us the exact relationship between theory construction, hypothesis testing and data collection.
- Collectively, these 'events' and relationships are referred to as (the) *scientific method*. Table 17.1 summarises some common beliefs about both science and scientific method, together with some alternative views.

---

**Table 17.1** Some common beliefs, and alternative views, about 'science' and 'scientific method'

| Common beliefs | Alternative views |
|---|---|
| ● Scientific discovery begins with simple, unbiased, unprejudiced observation (the scientist simply 'samples' the world without any preconceptions, expectations or pre-determined theories). | ● There's no such thing as 'unbiased' or 'unprejudiced' observation. Observation is always selective, interpretative, pre-structured and directed (we must have at least some idea of what we're looking for, otherwise we cannot know when we've found it). |
| ■ From the resulting sensory evidence ('data'/sense-data), generalised factual statements will take shape (we gradually build up a picture of what the world is like based on several separate 'samples'). | ■ 'Data' don't constitute 'facts'. 'Evidence' usually implies measurement, numbers, recordings etc. which need to be interpreted in the light of a theory. Facts don't exist objectively and cannot be discovered through 'pure observation'. For Deese (1972): 'Fact' = Data + Theory. |
| ▲ The essential feature of scientific activity is the use of empirical methods, through which the sensory evidence is gathered (what distinguishes science from non-science is performing experiments etc.). | ▲ Despite the central role of data collection, data alone don't make a science. Theory is just as crucial, because without it data have no meaning (see point above). |
| ▼ The truth about the world (the objective nature of things, what the world's 'really like') can be established through properly controlled experiments and other ways of collecting 'facts' (science can tell us about reality as it is, *independently* of the scientist or the activity of observing it). | ▼ Scientific theory and research reflect the biases, prejudices, values and assumptions of the individual scientist, as well as of the scientific community s/he belongs to. Science *isn't* value-free (see Chapter 16). |
| ◆ Science involves the steady accumulation of knowledge, so that each generation of scientists adds to the discoveries of previous generations. | ◆ Science involves an endless succession of long, peaceful periods ('normal science') and 'scientific revolutions' (Kuhn, 1962: see Table 17.3, page 514). |

---

- The first two common beliefs identified in Table 17.1 are part of the classical view of science (the *inductive* method). Popper (1972) has revised the stages of the scientific process as proposed by the classical view (see Table 17.2).

Table 17.2 Comparison between the classical, inductive view of science and Popper's revised version

| Inductive method | Popper's version |
| --- | --- |
| **Observation and method** | Problem (usually a refutation of an existing theory or prediction) |
| **Inductive generalisation** | Proposed solution or new theory |
| **Hypothesis** | Deduction of testable statements (hypotheses) from the new theory. This relates to the *hypothetico–deductive method*, which is usually contrasted with/opposed to the *inductive method*. In practice, *both* approaches are involved in the scientific process and are complementary |
| **Attempted verification of hypothesis** | Tests or attempts to refute by methods including observation and experiment |
| **Proof or disproof** | Establishing a preference between competing theories |
| **Knowledge** | |

## CAN PSYCHOLOGY BE A SCIENCE IF PSYCHOLOGISTS CANNOT AGREE WHAT PSYCHOLOGY IS?

* We've seen how definitions of psychology have changed during its lifetime. These changes largely reflect the influence and contributions of its major theoretical approaches or orientations (see Chapter 18).
* Each approach rests upon a different image of what people are like, which in turn determines what is important to study, as well as the methods that can be used to study it.
* Consequently, different approaches can be seen as self-contained disciplines, as well as different facets of the same discipline (Kuhn, 1962; Kline, 1988).
* Kuhn argues that a field of study can only legitimately be considered a science if a majority of its workers subscribe to a common, global perspective or *paradigm*. This means that psychology is *pre-paradigmatic*, that is, it lacks a paradigm without which it's still in a state (or stage) of *pre-science*. Whether psychology has, or has ever had, a paradigm, is hotly debated.

Table 17.3 Stages in the development of a science (▲), and their application to psychology (■)

▲ **Pre-science:** No paradigm has evolved, and there are several schools of thought or theoretical orientations.

■ Like Kuhn, Joynson (1980) and Boden (1980) argue that psychology is pre-paradigmatic. But Kline (1988) sees its various approaches as involving different paradigms. Davison and Neale (2001) identify five major paradigms in relation to abnormal psychology, namely the biological, psychoanalytic, humanistic/existential, learning (behaviourist) and cognitive.

▲ **Normal science:** A paradigm has emerged, dictating the kind of research that's carried out and providing a framework for interpreting results. The details of the theory are filled in, and workers explore its limits. Disagreements can usually be resolved within the limits allowed by the paradigm.

■ According to Valentine (1992), behaviourism comes as close as anything could to a paradigm. It provides: (a) a clear definition of the subject-matter (behaviour as opposed to 'the mind'); (b) fundamental assumptions, in the form of the central roles of learning (especially conditioning) and the analysis of behaviour into stimulus–response units, which allow prediction and control; (c) a methodology, with the controlled experiment at its core.

▲ **Revolution:** A point is reached in most established sciences where the conflicting evidence becomes so overwhelming that the old paradigm has to be abandoned and is replaced by a new one (*paradigm shift*). For example, Newtonian physics was replaced by Einstein's theory of relativity. When the paradigm shift occurs, there's a return to normal science.

■ Palermo (1971) and LeFrancois (1983) argue that psychology has already undergone several paradigm shifts. The first paradigm was *structuralism*, represented by Wundt's introspectionism. This was replaced by Watson's *behaviourism*. Finally, *cognitive psychology* largely replaced behaviourism, based on the computer analogy and the concept of information processing (see text above). Glassman (1995) disagrees, claiming there's never been a complete reorganisation of the discipline, as has happened in physics.

- Lambie (1991) believes it's a mistake to equate 'paradigm' with 'approach'. Although theory is an essential part of a paradigm, different theories can coexist within the same overall approach. For example, classical and operant conditioning both form part of 'learning theory' (the basis of the behaviourist approach), and Freud's and Erikson's theories both belong to the psychodynamic approach.
- One of the 'ingredients' that makes a paradigm different from an approach is its *social psychological* dimension. Paradigms refer to assumptions and beliefs held in common by most, if not all, the members of a particular scientific community.

## The scientific study of human behaviour

THE SOCIAL NATURE OF SCIENCE: THE PROBLEM OF OBJECTIVITY

- 'Doing science' is part of human behaviour. When psychologists study what people do, they're engaging in some of the very same behaviours they're trying to understand (such as thinking, perceiving, problem solving, and explaining). This is what's meant by the statement that psychologists are part of their own subject matter. This makes it even more difficult for them to be objective than other scientists. According to Richards (2002):

> 'Whereas in orthodox sciences there is always some external object of enquiry – rocks, electrons, DNA, chemicals – existing essentially unchanging in the non-human world (even if never finally knowable "as it really is" beyond human conceptions), this is not so for psychology. "Doing psychology" is the human activity of studying human activity; it is human psychology examining itself – and what it produces by way of new theories, ideas and beliefs about itself is also part of our psychology.'

- Knowable 'as it really is' refers to objectivity, and Richards is claiming that it may be impossible for any scientist to achieve complete objectivity. One reason for this relates to the social nature of scientific activity. As Rose (1997) says:

> 'How biologists, or any scientists, perceive the world is not the result of simply holding a true reflecting mirror up to nature: it is shaped by the history of our subject, by dominant social expectations, and by the patterns of research funding.'

- Does this mean that 'the truth' only exists 'by agreement'? Does science tell us not about what things are 'really' like, but only what scientists happen to believe is the truth at any particular time?
- According to Richardson (1991), whatever the *logical* aspects of scientific method may be (deriving hypotheses from theories, the importance of refutability, and so on), science is a very *social* business. Research must be qualified and quantified to enable others to replicate it. In this way the procedures, instruments and measures become standardised, so that scientists anywhere in the world can check the truth of reported observations and findings. This implies the need for universally agreed conventions for reporting these observations and findings.
- Collins (1994) takes a more extreme view. He argues that the results of experiments are more ambiguous than is usually assumed, while theory is more flexible than most people imagine:

> 'This means that science can progress only within communities that can reach consensus about what counts as plausible. Plausibility is a matter of social context, so science is a "social construct".'

- Kuhn's concept of a paradigm also stresses the role of agreement or consensus among scientists working within a particular discipline. Accordingly, 'truth' has more to do with the popularity and widespread acceptance of a particular framework within the scientific community than with its 'truth value'. The fact that revolutions do occur (paradigm shifts: see Table 17.3) demonstrates that 'the truth' can and does change.
- But the popularity or acceptability of a theory must have *something* to do with how well it explains and predicts the phenomena in question. In other words, *both* social and 'purely' scientific or rational criteria are relevant.

- However, even if there are widely accepted ways of 'doing science', 'good science' doesn't necessarily mean 'good psychology'. Is it valid to study human experience and behaviour as part of the natural world, or is a different kind of approach needed altogether? After all, it isn't just psychologists who observe, experiment and theorise (Heather, 1976).

## THE PSYCHOLOGY EXPERIMENT AS A SOCIAL SITUATION

To regard empirical research in general, and the experiment in particular, as objective involves two related assumptions:

(a) researchers only influence participants' behaviour (the outcome of the experiment) to the extent that they decide what hypothesis to test, how the variables should be operationalised, what design to use and so on

(b) the only factors influencing participants' performance are the objectively defined variables manipulated by the experimenter.

## EXPERIMENTERS AS PEOPLE: THE PROBLEM OF EXPERIMENTER BIAS

According to Rosenthal (1966), what the experimenter is *like* correlates with what s/he *does*, as well as influencing the participant's perception of/response to the experimenter. This is related to *experimenter bias*.

### Box 17.11 Some examples of experimenter bias

- Experimenter bias has been demonstrated in a variety of experiments, including reaction time, psychophysics, animal learning, verbal conditioning, personality assessment, person perception, learning and ability, as well as in everyday life situations.
- These experiments consistently show that if one group of experimenters has one hypothesis about what it expects to find and another group has the opposite hypothesis, *both* groups will obtain results that support their respective hypotheses.
- These results *aren't* due to the mishandling of data by biased experimenters. Rather, the experimenters' bias somehow creates a changed environment, in which participants actually *behave* differently.
- When experimenters were informed that rats learning mazes had been specially bred for this ability ('maze-bright'), they obtained better learning from their rats than did experimenters told their rats were 'maze-dull' (Rosenthal & Fode, 1963; Rosenthal & Lawson, 1964). In fact, both groups of rats were drawn from the same population and were *randomly* allocated to the 'bright' or 'dull' condition. But crucially, the 'bright' rats actually learned faster. The experimenters' expectations in some way concretely changed the situation (exactly how is unclear).
- In a natural classroom situation, children whose teachers expected them to show academic 'promise' during the next academic year showed significantly greater IQ gains than children who weren't expected to show such promise. The children were in fact *randomly* allocated to the two conditions. But the teachers' expectations produced the predicted improvements, demonstrating a *self-fulfilling prophecy* (Rosenthal & Jacobson, 1968).

(Based on Valentine, 1992; Weisstein, 1993.)

## PARTICIPANTS AS PSYCHOLOGISTS: DEMAND CHARACTERISTICS

- Instead of seeing the person being studied as a passive responder to whom things are done ('subject'), Orne (1962) stresses what the person *does*. This implies a far more active role.
- Participants' performance in an experiment can be thought of as a form of problem-solving behaviour. At some level, they see their task as working out the true purpose of the experiment, and responding in a way that will support (or not, in the case of the unhelpful participant) the hypothesis being tested.

- In this context, the cues which convey the experimental hypothesis to participants represent important influences on their behaviour. The sum total of these cues are called the *demand characteristics* of the experimental situation. They include:

> ' ... the rumours or campus scuttlebutt [gossip] about the research, the information conveyed during the original situation, the person of the experimenter, and the setting of the laboratory, as well as all explicit and implicit communication during the experiment proper.' (Orne, 1962)

- This tendency to identify the demand characteristics is related to the tendency to play the role of a 'good' (or 'bad') experimental participant.

## Key study

### DOING WHATEVER THE EXPERIMENTER ASKS (DWTEA) (ORNE, 1962)

- Orne points out that if people are asked to do five push-ups as a favour, they'll ask 'Why?'. But if the request comes from an experimenter, they'll ask 'Where?'.
- He reports an experiment in which people were asked to add sheets of random numbers, then tear them up into at least 32 pieces. Five-and-a-half hours later, they were still doing it, and the experimenter had to ask them to stop!
- This demonstrates very clearly people's strong tendency to want to please the experimenter, and not to 'upset the experiment'. It's mainly in this sense that Orne sees the experiment as a social situation, where the people involved play different but complementary roles. In order for this interaction to proceed smoothly, each must have some idea of what the other expects.

- The expectations referred to in DWTEA are part of the culturally shared understanding of what science in general, and psychology in particular, involves. Without such shared understandings the experiment couldn't 'happen' (Moghaddam *et al.*, 1993). So not only is the experiment a social situation, but science itself is a *culture-related phenomenon*. This is another sense in which science cannot claim to be completely objective.

What we only do in the name of science!

## THE PROBLEM OF REPRESENTATIVENESS

- Traditional, mainstream experimental psychology adopts a *nomothetic* ('law-like') approach. This involves generalising from limited samples of participants to 'people in general'. This is part of the attempt to establish general 'laws' or principles of behaviour.
- The photograph overleaf of one of Asch's famous conformity experiments (see Chapter 5) captures a fairly typical scene as far as participant characteristics in mainstream psychological research are concerned.
- Asch's experiments were conducted in the 1950s. But very little has changed regarding participant samples. In American psychology (and perhaps to a lesser degree in the UK), the typical participant is a psychology undergraduate. S/he will be mainly white and middle-class (as will the experimenter), obliged to take part in a certain number of studies as a course requirement and receiving 'course credits' for doing so (Krupat & Garonzik, 1994).

What do these participants have in common with each other – and with Asch?

- Mainstream British and American psychology has implicitly equated 'human being' with 'member of Western culture'. Despite the fact that the vast majority of research participants are members of Western societies, the research findings and resulting theories have been applied to 'human beings', as if culture made no difference (they are 'culture-bound' and 'culture-blind': Sinha, 1997).

- This Anglocentric or Eurocentric bias (a form of *ethnocentrism*) is matched by the androcentric or masculinist bias (a form of *sexism*). According to the latter, the behaviour and experience of men are taken as the standard against which women are judged (see Chapter 16).

- As long as these biases remain implicit and go unrecognised (and are reinforced by psychology's claim to be objective and value-free), research findings are seen as providing us with an objective, scientifically valid, account of what 'women/people in general are like'. Once we realise that scientists, like all human beings, have prejudices, biases and values, their research and theories begin to look less objective, reliable and valid than they did before.

## THE PROBLEM OF ARTIFICIALITY

- Criticisms of traditional empirical methods (especially the laboratory experiment) have focused on their *artificiality*. These criticisms include the often unusual and bizarre tasks that people are asked to perform in the name of science (see DWTEA). We cannot be sure that the way people behave in the laboratory is an accurate indication of how they're likely to behave outside it (Heather, 1976).

- What makes the laboratory experiment such an unnatural and artificial situation is the fact that it's almost totally structured by one 'participant' – the experimenter. This relates to *power differences* between experimenters and their 'subjects', which is as much an ethical as a practical issue (see Chapter 16).

- The traditional reference to participants as 'subjects' implies something less than a person, a dehumanised and depersonalised 'object'. According to Heather (1976), it's a small step from reducing the person to a mere thing or object (or experimental 'subject') to seeing people as machines or machine-like ('mechanism' = 'machine-ism' = mechanistic view of people). This way of thinking about people is reflected in the popular definition of psychology as the study of 'what makes people tick'.

The term 'subject' reduces a person to something less than human: man as a machine

## THE PROBLEM OF INTERNAL VERSUS EXTERNAL VALIDITY

- If the experimental setting (and task) is seen as similar (or relevant) enough to everyday situations to allow us to generalise the results, we say the study has high *external* or *ecological validity*. But what about *internal validity*?

- Modelling itself on natural science, psychology attempts to overcome the problem of the complexity of human behaviour by using experimental control (what Rose (1997) calls *reductionism as methodology*: see Box 17.4, page 503). This involves isolating an independent variable (IV) and ensuring that extraneous variables (those other than the IV likely to affect the dependent variable/DV) don't affect the outcome (see Chapter 6). But this begs the crucial question: *how do we know when all the relevant extraneous variables have been controlled?*

## Box 17.12 Some difficulties with the notion of experimental control

- It's relatively easy to control the more obvious *situational variables* (such as noise and temperature). But it's more difficult with *participant variables* (such as age, gender and culture), either for practical reasons (the availability of these groups) or because it isn't always obvious what the relevant variables are. Ultimately, it's down to the experimenter's judgement and intuition: what s/he believes is important (and possible) to control (Deese, 1972).
- If judgement and intuition are involved, then control and objectivity are matters of degree. This is as true of physics as of psychology (see Table 17.1, page 513).
- It's the *variability/heterogeneity* of human beings that makes them so much more difficult to study than, say, chemicals. Chemists don't usually have to worry about how two samples of a particular chemical might be different from each other. But psychologists need to allow for individual differences between participants.
- We cannot just assume that the IV (or 'stimulus' or 'input') is identical for every participant, that it can be defined independently of the participant, or that it exerts a standard effect on everyone. The attempt to define IVs (and DVs) in this way can be regarded as another aspect of reductionism as methodology (see above).
- Complete control would mean that the IV *alone* was responsible for the DV, such that experimenter bias and the effect of demand characteristics were irrelevant. But even if complete control were possible (that is, if we could guarantee the *internal validity* of the experiment), a fundamental dilemma would remain. The greater the degree of control over the experimental situation, the more different it becomes from real-life situations (that is, the more artificial it gets and the *lower* its *external validity*).

- Box 17.12 indicates that, in order to discover the relationships between variables (necessary for understanding human behaviour in natural, real-life situations), psychologists must 'bring' the behaviour into a specially created environment (the laboratory). It's possible there to control the relevant variables in a way that cannot be done in naturally-occurring settings. But in doing so, psychologists have constructed an artificial environment, and the resulting behaviour is similarly artificial. It's no longer the same behaviour they were trying to understand.

# EXAM tips BOX

**Critically consider whether psychology is a science.**
**(30 marks) (40 mins) (800 words minimum) AO1/AO2**

*This essay can be split up into FOUR sections – each about 200 words long. Each section would be worth 7–8 marks.*

**Section 1:** A **description** of the philosophical roots of science and psychology (such as mechanism, empiricism and positivism), together with some of the major historical figures and their 'movements' (such as Wundt, Watson and the cognitive revolution).

*A word of warning: You're only describing these historical details to the extent that they help you to define what a science is and to evaluate psychology's claim to be one.*

**A01**

**Section 2:** A **description** of the major features of science (such as subject matter, theory construction, hypothesis-testing and the use of empirical methods). Related to this is the scientific method. Psychology's claim to be a science must be evaluated in terms of these. Also, you could outline the relationship between scientism and mainstream psychology.

**A01**

**Section 3:** You could begin to **analyse** and **evaluate** psychology's claim to be a science by asking whether psychology conforms to the major features of science and scientific method described above. You could then look more generally at some of the common beliefs and alternative views regarding science/scientific method. To the extent that these alternative views are valid, psychology's claim to be a science is weakened. Psychology also has to contend with issues of representativeness, artificiality and validity, which make it different from the natural sciences.

**A02**

**Section 4:** A second approach to **analysing** and **evaluating** whether psychology is a science is to look at Kuhn's concept of a paradigm. There are conflicting views as to whether psychology is (still) pre-scientific or has already undergone revolutions. This links back to psychology's historical development described in Section 1. A third approach is to focus on the social aspects of science in general, and psychology in particular, which detract from the objectivity demanded by (traditional beliefs about) science.

**A02**

*Try to answer this question yourself. There's a sample essay on pages 538–539 with which you can compare your essay.*

## Nature–nurture

### Nativism, empiricism and interactionism

- *Nativism* is the philosophical theory according to which knowledge of the world is largely innate (inborn). Nature (heredity) is seen as determining certain abilities and capacities.
- Descartes was a nativist who, as we saw earlier, had an enormous impact on science in general, including psychology.
- At the opposite philosophical extreme is *empiricism*. As we saw earlier, this is associated mainly with British philosophers and has probably been even more influential on the development of psychology. A key empiricist was Locke, who believed that at birth the human mind is a *tabula rasa* (blank slate). This is gradually 'filled in' through learning and experience.
- Nativism and empiricism are extreme theories in that they were trying to answer the question 'Is it nature or nurture?' (as if only one or the other could be true). Early psychological theories tended to reflect these extremes, as in Gesell's concept of *maturation* and Watson's *behaviourism*.

## Box 17.13 Gesell and Watson: two extreme viewpoints

- According to Gesell (1925), one of the American pioneers of developmental psychology, *maturation* refers to genetically programmed patterns of change. The instructions for these patterns are part of the specific hereditary information passed on at the moment of conception (Bee, 2000).
- All individuals will pass through the same series of changes (they're *universal*), in the same order (they're *sequential*). Maturational patterns are also 'relatively impervious to environmental influence'.
- Gesell was mainly concerned with babies' psychomotor development (such as grasping and other manipulative skills) and locomotion (such as crawling and walking). These abilities are usually seen as 'developing by themselves', according to a genetically determined timetable. Provided the baby is physically normal, practice or training aren't needed – the abilities just 'unfold'.
- For Watson (1925), environmental influence is all-important (see above and Chapter 18) and human beings are completely malleable:

> 'Give me a dozen healthy infants, well-formed, and my own specialised world to bring them up in and I'll guarantee to take any one at random and train him to become any type of specialist I might select – a doctor, lawyer, artist, merchant-chief and, yes, even beggar-man and thief, regardless of his talents, penchants, abilities, vocations and race of his ancestors.'

- Watson (1928) also claimed that there are no such things as an inheritance of capacity, talent, temperament, mental constitution and character:

> 'The behaviourists believe that there is nothing from within to develop. If you start with the right number of fingers and toes, eyes, and a few elementary movements that are present at birth, you do not need anything else in the way of raw material to make a man, be that man genius, a cultured gentleman, a rowdy or a thug.'

- The concept of maturation continues to be influential within psychology. It explains major biological changes (such as puberty: see Chapter 12), and all stages of theories of development assume that maturation underpins the universal sequence of stages. Examples include Freud's psychosexual theory (see Chapters 12 and 18), Erikson's psychosocial theory (see Chapter 12), and Piaget's theory of cognitive development (see Chapter 11). Watson's extreme empiricism (or *environmentalism*) was adopted in Skinner's *radical behaviourism*, which represents a major model of both normal and abnormal behaviour (see Chapters 9, 15 and 18).

### ARE NATIVISM AND EMPIRICISM MUTUALLY EXCLUSIVE?

- Box 17.13 shows that maturationally determined developmental sequences occur regardless of practice or training. But as Bee (2000) points out:

> 'These powerful, apparently automatic maturational patterns require at least some minimal environmental support, such as adequate diet and opportunity for movement and experimentation.'

At the very least, the environment must be *benign*, that is, it mustn't be harmful in any way, preventing the ability or characteristic from developing.

- More importantly, the ability or characteristic cannot develop without environmental 'input'. For example, the possession of a language acquisition device (LAD) as proposed by Chomsky (1965) must be applied to the particular linguistic data the child is exposed to (its native tongue). This ensures that the child will acquire only *that* language (although it could just as easily have acquired *any* language).

- Another example of the role of the environment involves vision. One of the proteins required for the development of the visual system is controlled by a gene whose action is triggered only by visual experience (Greenough, 1991). So some visual experience is needed for the genetic programme to operate.

- Although every (sighted) child will have some such experience under normal circumstances, examples like these tell us that maturational sequences don't simply 'unfold'. The system appears to be 'ready' to develop along particular pathways, but it requires experience to trigger the movement (Bee, 2000).

- Another way of considering the interplay between nature and nurture is to look at Freud's and Piaget's developmental theories. In both theories, maturation underlies the sequence of stages. But the role of experience is at least as important.

### Box 17.14 Nature and nurture in Freud's and Piaget's developmental theories

- For Freud, it's not the sexual instinct itself that matters, but rather the reactions of significant others (especially parents) to the child's attempts to satisfy its sexual needs. Both excessive frustration and satisfaction can produce long-term effects on the child's personality (such as fixation at particular stages).

- Freud is commonly referred to as an instinct theorist (which suggests he was a nativist). But his concept of an instinct was very different from the earlier view of unlearned, largely automatic (pre-programmed) responses to specific stimuli (based on non-human species). Instead of using the German word '*Instinkt*', Freud used '*Trieb*' ('drive'), which denotes a relatively undifferentiated form of energy capable of almost infinite variation through experience.

- As a biologist, Piaget stressed the role of *adaptation* to the environment. This involves the twin processes of *assimilation* and *accommodation* (which are, in turn, related to (dis-)equilibration).

- These mechanisms are part of human beings' biological 'equipment'. Without them their intelligence wouldn't change, that is, the individual wouldn't progress through increasingly complex stages of development. But the baby actively explores its environment and constructs its own knowledge and understanding of the world. According to Piaget (1970), intelligence consists:

> ' . . . neither of a simple copy of external objects nor of a mere unfolding of structures pre-formed inside the subject, but rather . . . a set of structures constructed by continuous interaction between the subject and the external world.'

- Both Freud's and Piaget's theories demonstrate that:

> 'There is a trade-off in nature between pre-specification, on the one hand, and plasticity, on the other, leading ultimately to the kind of flexibility one finds in the human mind.' (Karmiloff-Smith, 1996)

- Maturation is an example of what Karmiloff-Smith means by 'pre-specification'. *Inborn biases* represent another. For example, very young babies already seem to understand that unsupported objects will fall (move downward), and that a moving object will continue to move in the same direction unless it encounters an obstacle (Spelke, 1991). But these 'pre-existing conceptions' are merely the beginning of the story. What then develops is the result of experience filtered through these initial biases, which constrain the number of developmental pathways that are possible (Bee, 2000).

- According to Bee, no developmental psychologists today would take the 'Is it nature or nurture?' form of the debate seriously. Essentially, every facet of a child's development is a product of some pattern of interaction between the two. But until fairly recently, the theoretical pendulum was well over towards the nurture/environmental end of the continuum. In the last decade or so, there's been a marked swing back towards the nature/biological end. This is partly because of the impact of sociobiology and its more recent offshoot, evolutionary psychology (see Gross, 2005).

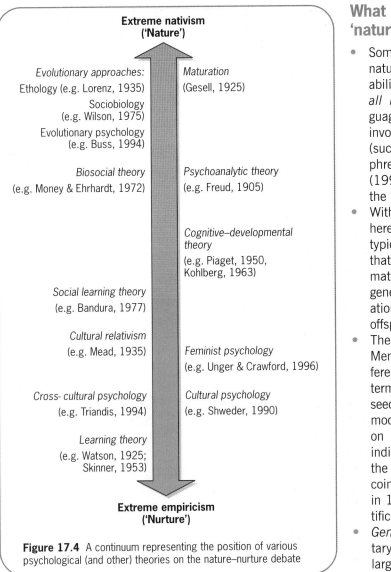

**Figure 17.4** A continuum representing the position of various psychological (and other) theories on the nature–nurture debate

## What do we mean by 'nature'?

- Some examples of the nature–nurture debate involve abilities or capacities *common to all human beings* (such as language and perception). Others involve *individual differences* (such as intelligence and schizophrenia). According to Plomin (1994), it's in the latter sense that the debate 'properly' takes place.

- Within *genetics* (the science of heredity) 'nature' refers to what's typically thought of as inheritance, that is, differences in genetic material (chromosomes and genes) transmitted from generation to generation (parents to offspring).

- The 'father' of genetics, Gregor Mendel (1865), explained the difference between different genes in terms of smooth and wrinkled seeds in garden peas. Similarly, modern human genetics focuses on genetic differences between individuals. This reflects the use of the word 'nature' by Galton, who coined the phrase 'nature–nurture' in 1883 as it's used in the scientific arena (Plomin, 1994).

- *Genes* are the basic unit of hereditary transmission. They consist of large molecules of deoxyribonucleic acid (DNA), extremely complex chemical chains comprising a ladder-like, double helix structure (discovered by Watson and Crick in 1953) (see Fig. 17.5).

- The genes occur in pairs and are situated on the chromosomes, found within the nuclei of living cells. The normal human being inherits 23 pairs of chromosomes, one member of each pair from each parent. The twenty-third pair comprises the sex chromosomes (two Xs in females, and an X and a Y in males) (see Fig. 17.6).

- The steps of the gene's double helix (or 'spiral staircase': Plomin, 1994) consist of four nucleotide bases (adenine, thymine, cytosine and guanine). These can occur in any order on one side of the helix, but the order on the other side is always fixed. So adenine always pairs with thymine, and cytosine always pairs with guanine. Taking just one member of each pair of the 23 pairs of chromosomes, the human *genome* comprises more than three billion nucleotide base pairs (Plomin, 1994).

- Two major functions of genes are *self-duplication* and *protein synthesis*.

## SELF-DUPLICATION

- DNA copies itself by unzipping in the middle of the spiral staircase, with each half forming its complement. That is, when a cell divides, all the genetic information (chromosomes and genes)

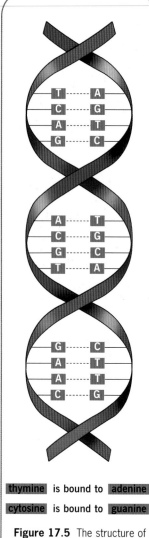

thymine is bound to adenine

cytosine is bound to guanine

**Figure 17.5** The structure of a DNA molecule represented schematically. This shows its double-stranded coiled structure and the complementary binding of nucleotide bases, guanine (G) to cytosine (C) and adenine (A) to thymine (T)

contained within the cell nucleus is reproduced. This means that the 'offspring' cells are identical to the 'parent' cells (*mitosis*). But this process applies only to *non-gonadal* (non-reproductive) cells (such as skin, blood and muscle cells).

- The reproductive (or *germ*) cells (ova in females, sperm in males) duplicate through *meiosis*. Here each cell contains only *half* the individual's chromosomes and genes. Which member of a chromosome pair goes to any particular cell seems to be determined randomly. So the resulting germ cells (*gametes*) contain 23 chromosomes, one of which will be either an X or a Y. When a sperm fertilises an ovum, the two sets of chromosomes combine to form a new individual with a full set of 46 chromosomes.

## PROTEIN SYNTHESIS

- The 'genetic code' was 'cracked' in the 1960s. Essentially, DNA controls the production of *ribonucleic acid* (RNA) within the cell nucleus. This 'messenger' RNA moves outside the nucleus and into the surrounding cytoplasm. Here it's converted by *ribosomes* into sequences of amino acids, the building blocks of proteins and enzymes.
- Genes that code for proteins and enzymes are called *structural* genes, and they represent the basis of modern genetics (Plomin, 1994). The first single-gene disorders discovered in the human species involved metabolic abnormalities caused by mutations (spontaneous changes) in structural genes. A much-cited example is phenylketonuria (see below, page 527).
- Most genes are *regulator* genes. These code for products that bind with DNA itself and serve to regulate other genes. Unlike the structural genes which are 'deaf' to the environment, the regulator genes communicate closely with the environment and change in response to it (Plomin, 1994).

## NEUROGENETIC DETERMINISM: ARE THERE GENES 'FOR' ANYTHING?

- We saw in Box 17.4 (page 503) that several claims have been made in recent years about the discovery of genes 'for' a wide range of complex human behaviours (*reductionism as ideology*: Rose, 1997). This is related to what Rose calls *neurogenetic determinism* (ND), the claim that there's a direct causal link between genes and behaviour. This involves the false assumption that causes can be classified as *either* genetic *or* environmental. There are additional reasons for doubting the validity of ND.
- The phrase 'genes for' is a convenient, but misleading, shorthand used by geneticists. Eye colour, for example, is one of the simpler character-

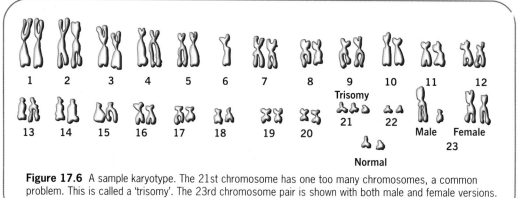

**Figure 17.6** A sample karyotype. The 21st chromosome has one too many chromosomes, a common problem. This is called a 'trisomy'. The 23rd chromosome pair is shown with both male and female versions. In a normal karyotype, only one such pair would be found

istics (or *phenotypes*) from a genetic point of view. But even here the argument for ND is not straightforward. There's a difference in the biochemical pathways that lead to brown and to blue eyes. In blue-eyed people, the gene for a particular enzyme (which catalyses a chemical transformation *en route* to the synthesis of the pigment) is either missing or non-functional for some reason. A gene 'for blue eyes' now has to be re-interpreted as meaning 'one or more genes in whose absence the metabolic pathway that leads to pigmented eyes terminates at the blue-eye stage' (Rose, 1997).

- As we learn more about the human genome, geneticists come to realise that many supposedly 'single-gene disorders' result from different gene mutations in different people. They may show a similar clinical picture (such as high blood cholesterol levels with an increased risk of coronary heart disease). But the gene mutation (and hence the enzyme malfunction) that results in the disorder may be very different in each case.

- This also means that a drug which effectively treats the condition in one person may simply not work in another, whose cholesterol accumulation is caused by *different* biochemical factors (Rose, 1997).

## What do we mean by 'nurture'?

- When the term 'environment' is used in a psychological context, it usually refers to all those *post-natal influences* (or potential sources of influence) lying *outside/external* to the individual's body. These include other people (both members of the immediate family and other members of society), opportunities for intellectual stimulation, and the physical circumstances of the individual's life ('environs' or 'surroundings'). They are implicitly seen as impinging on a passive individual, who is *shaped* by them (see Fig. 17.7).

- On all three counts (the environment is post-natal, outside the individual, and acting on a passive individual), this view seems inadequate.

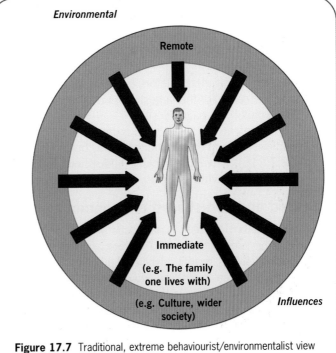

**Figure 17.7** Traditional, extreme behaviourist/environmentalist view of the environment as a set of external, post-natal influences acting upon a purely passive individual

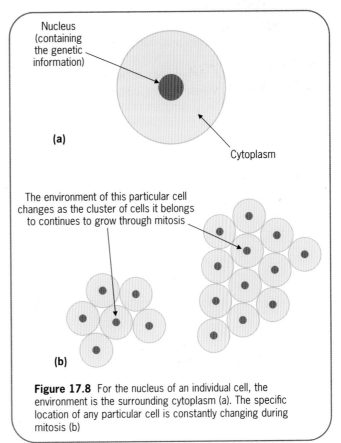

**Figure 17.8** For the nucleus of an individual cell, the environment is the surrounding cytoplasm (a). The specific location of any particular cell is constantly changing during mitosis (b)

- Even if the view of the passive individual were valid, influences begin *pre-natally* and can be analysed at the level of the *individual cell*. During mitosis, the specific location of any particular cell is continually changing as the cluster of cells it belongs to constantly grows. At an even more micro level, the cell nucleus (which contains the DNA) has as its environment the cell cytoplasm (see Fig. 17.8).
- Pre-natal, non-genetic factors (such as the mother's excessive alcohol consumption during pregnancy) account for the largest proportion of biologically-caused learning difficulties and lowered IQ (see Chapter 11, page 292).
- The environment *doesn't* exist independently of the individual (that is, objectively). Not only do people's environments influence them, but people make their own environments (Scarr, 1992: see Box 17.15). A way of thinking about how people do this is through the concept of *non-shared environments*, which, in turn, is related to *gene–environment correlation*.

## Shared and non-shared environments

- When the environment is discussed as a set of (potential) influences that impinge on the individual, it's often broken down into factors such as overcrowding, poverty, socioeconomic status (SES), family break-up, marital discord and so on. In studies of intelligence, for example, children are often compared in terms of these environmental factors, so that those from low SES groups are commonly found to have lower IQs than those from high SES groups (see Chapter 11).
- When families are compared in this way, it's assumed that children from the same family will all be similarly and equally affected by those environmental factors (*shared environments*). In fact, they're often extremely varied in personality, abilities and psychological disorders. This observation is most striking when two adopted children are raised in the same family: they're usually no more alike than any two people chosen at random from the general population (Plomin, 1996; Rutter & Rutter, 1992).
- This substantial within-family variation *doesn't* mean that family environment is unimportant. Rather, as Plomin (1996) puts it:

> 'Environmental influences in development are doled out on an individual-by-individual basis rather than a family-by-family basis.'

In other words, differences between children growing up together is exactly what we'd expect to find. This is because it's the *non-shared environment* (N-SE) which has a greater impact on development than the shared environment.

- Different children in the same family have different experiences. For example, Dunn and Plomin (1990) found that how parents respond differently to their different children (*relative differences*) is likely to be much more influential than the overall characteristics of the family (*absolute differences*). So it may matter very little whether children are brought up in a home that's less loving or more punitive than average. But it may matter considerably that one child receives less affection or more punishment than his/her sibling. These findings imply that:

> '. . . the unit of environmental transmission is not the family, but rather micro-environments within families.' (Plomin & Thompson, 1987)

### GENE–ENVIRONMENT CORRELATIONS

- The concept of N-SE helps explain how the environment influences development, and is far more useful than the original 'Is it nature or nurture?' (see above). But we need to understand the processes by which N-SEs arise:

(a) *why* do parents treat their different children differently, and
(b) *how* do children in the same family come to have different experiences?

- In trying to answer these questions, psychologists and behaviour geneticists (see below and Chapter 11) have stressed the role of *genetic differences*. A major example of this approach is the concept of *gene–environment correlation*.

## Box 17.15 Gene–environment correlations

**Plomin *et al.* (1977) identified three types of gene–environment correlations:**

- *Passive:* Children passively inherit from their parents environments that are correlated with their genetic tendencies. For example, parents who are of above-average IQ are likely to provide a more intellectually stimulating environment than lower-IQ parents.
- *Reactive:* Children's experiences derive from other people's reactions to their genetic tendencies. For example, babies with a sunny, cheerful disposition/temperament are more likely to elicit friendly reactions than miserable or 'difficult' babies (see Key Study, page 529). It's widely accepted that some children are easier to love (Rutter & Rutter, 1992). Similarly, aggressive children tend to experience aggressive environments, because they tend to evoke aggressive responses in others (see Chapter 9).
- *Active:* Children construct and reconstruct experiences consistent with their genetic tendencies. Trying to define the environment independently of the person is futile, since every person's experience is different. According to Plomin (1994):

> 'Socially, as well as cognitively, children select, modify and even create their experiences. Children select environments that are rewarding or at least comfortable . . . Children modify their environments by setting the background tone for interactions, by initiating behaviour, and by altering the impact of environments . . . they can create environments with their own propensities . . . '

**Plomin refers to children's selection and modification of their environments as *niche-picking* and *niche-building* respectively.**

## GENE–ENVIRONMENT INTERACTIONS

- Genetically speaking, *phenylketonuria* (PKU) is a simple characteristic. It's a bodily disorder caused by the inheritance of a single recessive gene from each parent. Normally, the body produces the amino acid phenylalanine hydroxylase which converts phenylalanine (a substance found in many foods, particularly dairy products) into tyrosine. But in the presence of the two recessive PKU genes, this process fails and phenylalinine builds up in the blood, depressing the levels of other amino acids. As a result, the developing nervous system is deprived of essential nutrients. This leads to severe mental retardation and, without intervention, eventual death.
- The relationship between what the child inherits (the two PKU genes – the *genotype*) and the actual signs and symptoms of the disease (high levels of phenylalanine and mental retardation – the *phenotype*) appears to be straightforward, direct and inevitable. In other words, given the genotype, the phenotype will occur.
- But a routine blood test soon after birth can detect the presence of the PKU genes. An affected baby will be put on a low-phenylalanine diet, which prevents the disease from developing. In other words, an environmental intervention will prevent the phenotype from occurring. As Jones (1993) put it:

> '[The] nature [of children born with PKU genes] has been determined by careful nurturing and there is no simple answer to the question of whether their genes or their environment is more important to their well-being.'

- If there's no one-to-one relationship between genotype and phenotype in the case of PKU, it's highly likely that there'll be an even more complex interaction in the case of intelligence, certain mental disorders, personality and so on. Two examples of such an interaction are *cumulative deficit* (see Chapter 11, page 297) and *facilitativeness*.

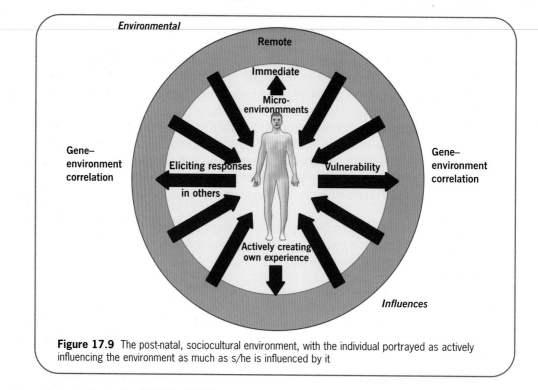

**Figure 17.9** The post-natal, sociocultural environment, with the individual portrayed as actively influencing the environment as much as s/he is influenced by it

- According to Horowitz (1987, 1990), a highly *facilitative* environment is one in which the child has loving and responsive parents, and is provided with a rich array of stimulation. When different levels of facilitativeness are combined with a child's initial *vulnerabilities/susceptibilities*, there's an interaction effect. For example, a *resilient* child (one with many protective factors and a few vulnerabilities) may do quite well in a poor environment. Equally, a *non-resilient* child may do quite well in a highly facilitative environment. Only the non-resilient child in a poor environment will do really poorly (see Figure 17.10).
- This interactionist view is supported by a 30-year longitudinal study carried out on the Hawaiian island of Kanuai.

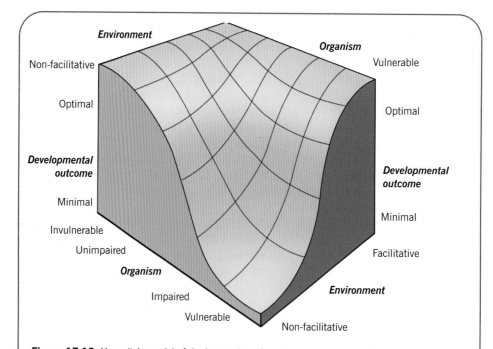

**Figure 17.10** Horowitz's model of the interaction of a child's environment with protective factors and vulnerabilities. The surface of the curve illustrates the level of a developmental stage, such as IQ or social skills. According to this model, if a low-birthweight child is reared in a poor environment, then it's likely that child will do less well than other children reared with a different combination of vulnerabilities and environment

## CHILDREN OF THE GARDEN ISLAND (COGI) (WERNER, 1989)

- Starting in 1955, Werner and her colleagues studied all of the nearly 700 children born on Kanuai in a given period. They were followed up at the ages of two, 10, 18 and 31–32.

- Werner became interested in 72 'high-risk'/'vulnerable' children. They had been exposed before the age of two to four or more of the following risk factors: reproductive stress (either difficulties during pregnancy and/or during labour and delivery), and discordant and impoverished home lives (including divorce, uneducated, alcoholic or mentally disturbed parents).

- Despite their early exposure to these risk factors, these children went on to develop healthy personalities, stable careers and strong interpersonal relationships.

- As babies, these resilient children were typically described as 'active', 'affectionate', 'cuddly', 'easy-going' and 'even-tempered', with no eating or sleeping habits causing distress to their carers. These are all temperamental characteristics which elicit positive responses from both family members and strangers.

- There were also environmental differences between the resilient and non-resilient children. Resilient children had smaller family size, at least two years between themselves and the next child, and a close attachment to at least one carer (relative or regular baby-sitter). They also received considerable emotional support from outside the family, were popular with their peers and had at least one close friend. School became a refuge from a disordered household.

- 62 of the resilient children were studied after reaching their 30s. As a group, they seemed to be coping well with the demands of adult life. 75% had received some college education, nearly all had full-time jobs and were satisfied with their work. According to Werner:

'As long as the balance between stressful life events and protective factors is favourable, successful adaptation is possible. When stressful events outweigh the protective factors, however, even the most resilient child can have problems.'

## Behaviour genetics and heritability

### BEHAVIOUR GENETICS

- According to Pike and Plomin (1999), 'Behaviour geneticists explore the origins of individual differences . . . in complex behaviours'. More specifically, they try to quantify how much of the *variability* for any given trait (such as intelligence or schizophrenia) can be attributed to (a) genetic differences between people (*heritability*), (b) shared environments, and (c) N-SEs. The heritability of intelligence was discussed in Chapter 11, as were twin and adoption studies, the two major methods used in behaviour genetics.

- If genetic factors are important for a particular trait, identical twins (MZs) will be more similar than non-identical twins (DZs). To the extent that twin similarity cannot be attributed to genetic factors, the shared environment is implicated. Any differences *within* MZ pairs can be attributed to the N-SE. Because adopted siblings are genetically unrelated to their adoptive family members, similarities between them is a direct measure of shared environmental influence (Pike & Plomin, 1999).

- The effects of a shared environment seem to *decrease* over time. In a 10-year longitudinal study of over 200 pairs of adoptive siblings, Loehlin *et al.* (1988) found that the average correlation for IQ at age 18 was close to zero.

- This finding actually supports the role of *non-genetic* factors in behavioural development, as does behaviour genetics in general (Plomin, 1995). For example, the concordance rate of MZs for schizophrenia is 40%. This means that most pairs are *discordant* for diagnosed schizophrenia (see Chapter 14). This cannot be explained in genetic terms. But 20 years ago the message from behaviour genetics research was that genetic factors play the major role. Today the message is that these same data provide strong evidence for the importance of environmental as well as genetic factors (Plomin, 1995).

## HERITABILITY

- According to Ceci and Williams (1999), *heritability* is one of the most controversial concepts in psychology. It tells us what proportion of individual differences within a population (*variance*) can be attributed to genes.
- But this *doesn't* mean that 'biology is destiny'. Indeed, as we've seen, behaviour genetics has helped confirm that environmental factors generally account for as much variance in human behaviour as genes do (Plomin & DeFries, 1998). Even when genetic factors have an especially powerful (and known) effect (as in PKU), environmental interventions can often fully or partly overcome the genetic 'determinants'.

### Box 17.16 Some 'facts' about heritability

- The degree of heritability (or *heritability estimate*/$h2$) isn't set in stone. The relative influence of genes and environment can change. For example, if environmental factors were made almost identical for all members of some hypothetical population, any differences in, say, their intelligence would then have to be attributed to genetics. Heritability would be closer to 100% than 50%.
- But equating the environment would probably reduce the size of differences observed among individuals. If all children enjoyed the best environment possible, they'd probably differ much *less* than if some had been given the worst possible environment.
- Within the *same* population, $h2$ will differ depending on which trait is being measured. For example, it's higher for IQ than for most aspects of personality.
- $h2$ will also differ for the *same* trait when assessed in *different* populations.
- $h2$ will tend to be higher in a good environment than a poor one. This is because the former provides the necessary resources for the biological potential to be realised.
- $h2$ is a way of explaining what makes people different, *not* the relative contribution of genes and environment to any one *individual's* make-up.
- The explanation of individual differences *within* groups bears no relation to the explanation of differences *between* groups (see Chapter 11, page 297).

(Based on Ceci & Williams, 1999; Plomin & DeFries, 1998.)

- According to Plomin (1995):

' ... It is time to put the nature–nurture controversy behind us and to bring nature and nurture together ... in order to understand the processes by which genotypes become phenotypes.'

Similarly, Ceci and Williams (1999) conclude thus:

'The battle today seems more over the specific genetic and environmental mechanisms than over whether genes or environments matter.'

## EXAM tips BOX

**(a)** Explain what is meant by the nature–nurture debate. **(5 marks)**

**(b)** Discuss *two or more* examples of the nature–nurture debate in psychology. **(25 marks) (40 mins) (800 words minimum) AO1/AO2**

*This essay can be split into FIVE sections – each about 160 words long. The first (which addresses part (a)) is worth 5 marks, the other four are worth 6–7 marks each.*

**Section 1:** An **explanation** of what is meant by the nature–nurture debate. You could point out that there are different ways in which the debate has been framed during its long history, that is, different questions asked about the relationship between nature and nurture (heredity/environment). You could also outline what each of the components involves.

**Section 2:** Perhaps the easiest option is to choose two examples of psychological research where the nature–nurture debate is prominent and which you have already covered in detail elsewhere on the Spec. (and which are included in this book). These might be the development of measured intelligence (Chapter 11) and schizophrenia (Chapter 14). In the case of measured intelligence, you need to give a **description** of the issues, methods and (some of the) conclusions regarding the influence of genes and environment.

**Section 3:** An **analysis** and **evaluation** of the issues, methods and conclusions described in Section 2. This might include, for example, considering the strengths and limitations of twin studies. But you could also draw on some of the issues raised in this chapter, such as the distinction between shared and non-shared environments and the related concepts of gene–environment correlation and interaction. Werner's COGI is relevant here. Discussion of heritability is also particularly relevant to the intelligence debate.

**Section 4:** A **description** of some of the issues, methods and (some of the) conclusions concerning the influence of genes and environment in relation to schizophrenia.

**Section 5:** An **analysis** and **evaluation** of the issues, methods and conclusions described in Section 4. There may be some overlap with Section 3 here (for example, considerations of the strengths and limitations of twin studies and/or adoption studies), in which case you should just refer back to the earlier part of your essay (repeating the same point – however valid it may be – will not gain you any extra marks and will use up precious time). Particularly relevant to schizophrenia are the diathesis–stress model, reductionism as ideology, and neurogentic determinism.

*Note that 'examples' here could mean psychological theories. You could take two or more of Freud's, Piaget's, Gesell's and Watson's theories as illustrating the nature–nurture debate. You could also 'mix and match' these with the examples of intelligence and schizophrenia (or other mental disorders).*

*Try to answer this question yourself. There's a sample essay on pages 539–540 with which you can compare your essay.*

AO1

AO1

AO2

AO1

AO2

## PYA5: Perspectives: Debates

Other possible exam questions:

- Each essay is worth 30 marks and should take 40 minutes to write.
- Remember, the mark scheme allocates 15 marks for AO1 (knowledge and description) and 15 marks for AO2 (analysis and evaluation).
- There are far fewer possible questions that can be asked in Perspectives.

**1. a.** Explain what is meant by the terms 'free will' and 'determinism'. (6 marks)

   **b.** Describe and evaluate the arguments for and against the existence of free will and determinism in psychology. (24 marks)

**2. a.** Briefly describe some examples of reductionism in psychological theories and studies. (5 marks)

   **b.** Describe and evaluate the case for reductionist explanations in psychology. (25 marks)

**3.** Discuss the arguments for and against the claim that psychology is a science. (30 marks)

**4.** Critically consider the nature–nurture debate in psychology. (30 marks)

# CHAPTER SUMMARY: revision schema

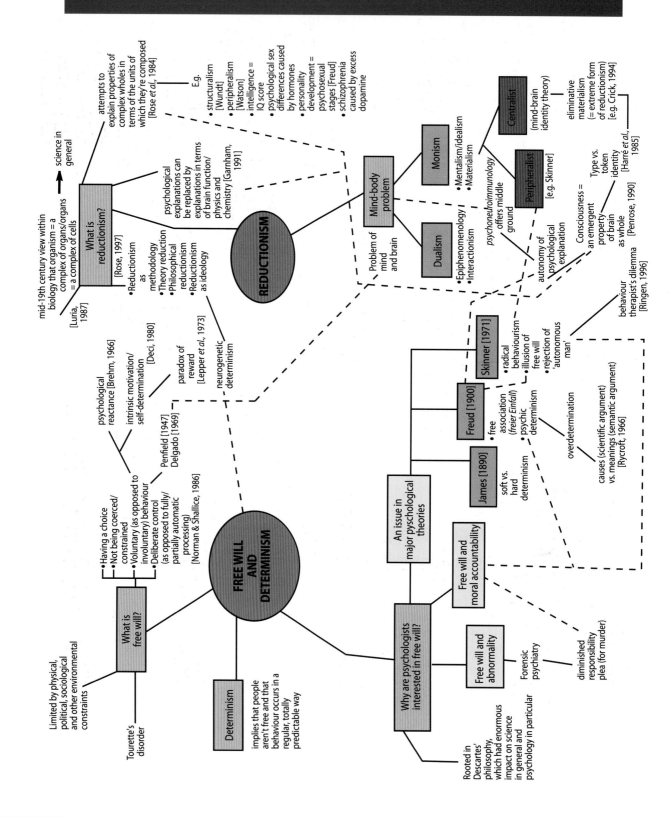

**REDUCTIONISM**

**What is reductionism?**

attempts to explain properties of complex wholes in terms of the units of which they're composed [Rose et al., 1984]

mid-19th century view within biology that organism = a complex of organs/organs = a complex of cells [Luria, 1987]

science in general

[Rose, 1997]
• Reductionism as methodology
• Theory reduction
• Philosophical reductionism
• Reductionism as ideology

psychological explanations can be replaced by explanations in terms of brain function / physics and chemistry [Garnham, 1991]

E.g.
• structuralism [Wundt]
• peripheralism [Watson]
• intelligence = IQ score
• psychological sex differences caused by hormones
• personality development = psychosexual stages [Freud]
• schizophrenia caused by excess dopamine

**Mind-body problem**

Problem of mind and brain

**Monism**
• Mentalism/idealism
• Materialism

**Dualism**
• Epiphenomenology
• Interactionism

*psychoneuroimmunology* offers middle ground

autonomy of psychological explanation

Consciousness = an emergent property of brain as whole [Penrose, 1990]

**Centralist** (mind-brain identity theory)

eliminative materialism (= extreme form of reductionism) [e.g. Crick, 1994]

**Peripheralist** [e.g. Skinner]

Type vs. token identity [Harré et al., 1985]

behaviour therapist's dilemma [Ringen, 1996]

**FREE WILL AND DETERMINISM**

**What is free will?**

• Having a choice
• Not being coerced/constrained
• Voluntary (as opposed to involuntary) behaviour
• Deliberate control (as opposed to fully/partially automatic processing) [Norman & Shallice, 1986]

Limited by physical, political, sociological and other environmental constraints

Tourette's disorder

psychological reactance [Brehm, 1966]

intrinsic motivation/self-determination [Deci, 1980]

paradox of reward [Lepper et al., 1973]

neurogenetic determinism

Penfield [1947]
Delgado [1969]

**Determinism**

implies that people aren't free and that behaviour occurs in a regular, totally predictable way

**An issue in major psychological theories**

**James [1890]**
soft vs. hard determinism

**Freud [1900]**
• free association (*freier Einfall*)
• psychic determinism

**Skinner [1971]**
• radical behaviourism
• illusion of free will
• rejection of 'autonomous man'

overdetermination

causes (scientific argument) vs. meanings (semantic argument) [Rycroft, 1966]

**Why are psychologists interested in free will?**

Rooted in Descartes' philosophy, which had enormous impact on science in general and psychology in particular

**Free will and moral accountability**

**Free will and abnormality**

Forensic psychiatry

diminished responsibility plea (for murder)

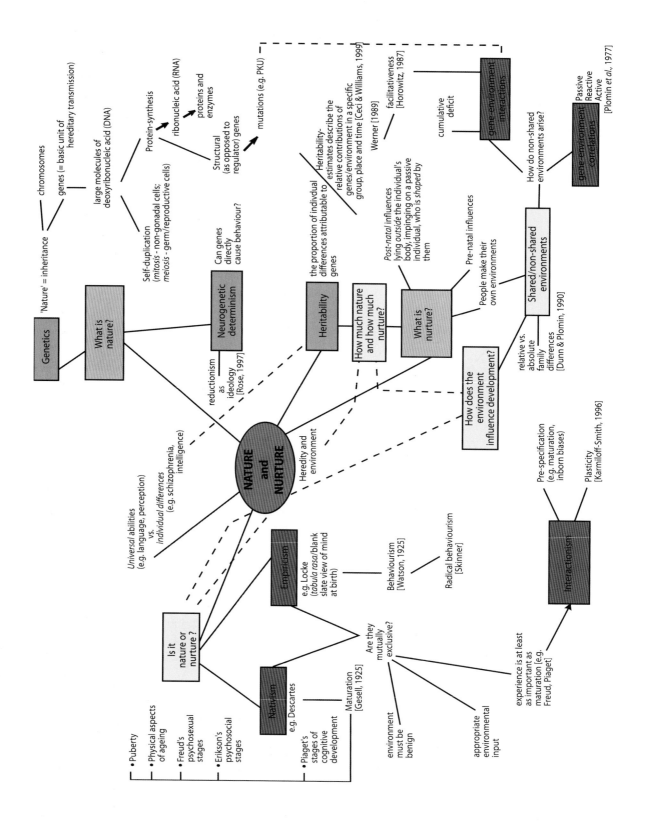

Discuss the free will and determinism debate with reference to *two or more* psychological theories. (30 marks) (40 mins) (800 words minimum)

A01

### Section 1:

The free will and determinism question has been debated by Western philosophers for centuries. Intuition tells us that we have the ability to choose our actions, that is, we determine our own behaviour (we have free will). But this freedom is constrained by physical, social, political and other factors. But according to positivistic, mechanistic, scientific psychology, behaviour is determined by external events, and so people aren't free. Determinism also implies that things can only happen as they do because everything is caused and every cause is itself the effect of some other cause. This includes people and their thoughts and behaviour, which are no different from other 'things' or events.

Both free will and determinism are ambiguous concepts. Free will can mean having a choice (implying that things could have been different from the way they turn out), not being coerced or constrained (as in having a gun to your head), voluntary behaviour (as opposed to involuntary or reflex), and deliberate control (as opposed to automatic behaviour). The voluntary nature of behaviour is illustrated by Penfield's (1947) classic experiments in which he stimulated the cortex of conscious patients undergoing brain surgery, and Delgado's (1969) stimulation of a patient's motor cortex. A demonstration of people's belief in their free will is psychological reactance (Brehm, 1966). Norman and Shallice (1986) proposed three levels of divided attention: fully automatic processing, partially automatic processing, and deliberate control. Deliberate control corresponds to free will, and as we move downwards from conscious control, so the subjective experience of freedom diminishes (Koestler, 1967).

### Section 2:

Psychologists are interested in the concepts of free will and determinism for a variety of reasons. Definitions of abnormality, and the diagnosis and treatment of mental disorders, often involve judgements about free will and determinism. Also, the assumption that people have free will underlies the whole question of legal and moral responsibility.

A01

Some of the most influential theories in the whole of psychology have given considerable attention to the debate, including those of Freud and Skinner. According to Strachey (1962), Freud believed in the universal validity of the law of determinism, which he extended from physical to mental phenomena. Freud saw himself very much as a scientist, and all his work in science was founded on the strong belief in the principle of cause and effect. Psychical or psychological phenomena are rigidly and lawfully determined by this principle (psychic determinism) (Sulloway, 1979). Part of what 'psychic determinism' conveyed was that there are no accidents. That is, however random or irrational

behaviour may appear to be (such as parapraxes or Freudian slips), unconscious causes can always account for them. This also applies to hysterical symptoms and dreams.

Skinner, like Freud, saw free will as an illusion. For Skinner, this is because free will, like all other references to mental (private) states, has no part to play in the explanation of behaviour (radical behaviourism). It's an 'explanatory fiction'. Free will cannot be defined or measured objectively, nor is it needed for successful prediction and control of behaviour – the primary aims of a science of behaviour. It's only because the causes of human behaviour are often hidden from us in the environment that the myth or illusion of free will survives. When what we do is dictated by force or punishment, or by negative reinforcement, it's obvious that we're not acting freely. But most of the time we're unaware of environmental causes, and we feel as if we're behaving freely. But all this means is that we're free of the punishments or negative reinforcements. Our behaviour is still determined by past positive reinforcements.

A02

### Section 3:

Freud's belief in determinism is, ironically, demonstrated by the importance he attached to the psychoanalytic technique of free association. 'Free association' is a misleading translation of the German 'freier Einfall', an uncontrollable 'intrusion' by pre-conscious ideas into conscious thinking. In turn, this pre-conscious material reflects unconscious material. It's because the causes of our thoughts, actions and supposed choices are unconscious (and so, by definition, unknown to us) that we believe we're free. This parallels Skinner's belief that we think we're free because we're often ignorant of the environmental causes of our behaviour (especially the past positive reinforcements that we're pursuing now). According to Gay (1988), Freud's theory of mind is 'strictly and frankly deterministic'. But Freud accepted that true accidents can and do occur, that is, forces beyond the victim's control (such as being struck by lightning). One aspect of our behaviour is overdetermination. Much of our behaviour has multiple causes, both conscious and unconscious. So although our conscious choices, decisions and intentions may genuinely influence behaviour, they never tell the whole story. Freud believed that the unconscious causes are the more important and interesting part of the story, but there's still room for some degree of freedom.

One of the aims of psychoanalysis is to give the patient's ego freedom to decide one way or another. So therapy rests on the belief that people can change, although Freud saw this change as very limited. Freud often explained his patients' choices, neurotic symptoms and so on not in terms of causes (the scientific argument), but by trying to make sense of them and give them meaning (the semantic argument). This is reflected in the title of arguably his greatest book, the 'Interpretation (not Cause) of Dreams (1900)'.

# SAMPLE ESSAYS

# SAMPLE ESSAYS

Discuss arguments *for and against* reductionism as a form of explanation, using examples from psychological theories and/or studies. (30 marks) (40 mins) (800 words minimum)

A01

### Section 1:

Together with positivism, mechanism, determinism and empiricism, reductionism represents a part of 'classical' science. Luria (1987) traces the origins of reductionism to the mid-nineteenth-century view within biology that an organism is a complex of organs, and the organs are complexes of cells. To explain the basic laws of the living organism, we have to study as carefully as possible the features of individual cells. From its biological origins, reductionism was extended to science in general. For example, the properties of a protein molecule could be determined or predicted in terms pf properties of the electrons or protons making up its atoms. Consistent with this view, Garnham (1991) defines reductionism as the idea that psychological explanations can be replaced by explanations in terms of brain functioning or even physics and chemistry. Supporters of reductionism see its ultimate aim as accounting for all phenomena in terms of microphysics. But any attempt to explain something in terms of its components or constituent parts is reductionist. This could include complex wholes such as molecules or societies (Rose *et al.*, 1984).

Rose (1997) identifies four different meanings of the term. Reductionism as methodology refers to the attempt to isolate variables in the laboratory in order to simplify the living world's enormous complexity, flux and interactions. This is the basis of the experiment, which reflects natural science's attempt to identify cause-and-effect relationships. Theory reduction is related to philosophical reductionism, the belief that because science is unitary and, because physics is the most fundamental science, ultimately all currently separate disciplines (including psychology) will be explained in terms of physics. Reductionism as ideology refers to the tendency to identify genes responsible for a whole range of complex human behaviours (including depression, personality, homosexuality, intelligence and criminality).

A01

### Section 2:

Perhaps the oldest example of reductionism is the mind–body problem (or the problem of mind and brain). This was originally a philosophical issue, but it continues to be discussed by biologists, neurophysiologists, neuropsychologists, and psychologists in general. It's generally agreed that the mind or consciousness is a property of human beings, as is walking upright on two legs, and that without the human brain there'd be no consciousness. But how can something non-physical (the mind) produce changes in something physical (the brain)? From a strictly scientific perspective, it should be impossible for us to raise our arm simply by willing it. But Penfield's (1947) classic experiment involving conscious patients undergoing brain surgery suggests very strongly that doing

A02

### Section 4:

Skinner's belief that free will is an illusion conflicts with the need to attribute people with free will if we're to hold them – and ourselves – morally and legally responsible for their actions. Skinner himself acknowledges this in 'Beyond Freedom and Dignity' (1971), but he rejects the idea of 'autonomous man'. Skinner equates 'good' and 'bad' with 'beneficial to others' (what's rewarded) and 'harmful to others' (what's punished) respectively. 'Oughts' aren't 'moral imperatives'; that is, things we're obliged to do for moral or ethical reasons, but reflect practical guidelines and rules (Morea, 1990). A further consequence of Skinner's rejection of 'autonomous man' is the 'behaviour therapist's dilemma' (Ringen, 1996). This refers to having to choose between the belief in radical behaviourism as the most appropriate framework for behaviour therapy, and the doctrine of informed consent (based on people's ability to act autonomously). For both Freud and Skinner, belief in determinism seems to fit best with the scientific view of the world. But James (1890) argued that this conflicts with a belief in free will required by our social, moral, political and legal practices – something which Skinner deals with directly (even if not very satisfactorily). James's solution to this conflict is, first, to distinguish between the scientific and non-scientific worlds (psychology as a science has to assume determinism, but we can accept free will in other contexts), and, second, to distinguish between soft and hard determinism. According to soft determinism, the question of free will depends on the types of cause our behaviour has. If the immediate cause is conscious mental life (CML), then our actions are free. But according to hard determinism, CML is itself caused, and as long as our behaviour is caused at all (isn't random), we cannot be described as acting freely.

(1,178 words)

this voluntarily feels very different compared with the experience of having the same part of your brain electrically stimulated.

There are many theories of the mind–brain relationship, which fall into two broad categories: dualist or monist. Most theories aren't strictly relevant to the debate about reductionism. Centralist materialism (or mind–brain identity theory) identifies mental processes with purely physical processes in the central nervous system. It's logically possible that there might be separate, mental, non-physical phenomena. But it just turns out that, as a matter of fact, mental states are identical with physical states of the brain. We are just very complex physico–chemical machines. Eliminative materialism is an extreme reductionist form of (centralist) materialism.

A02

### Section 3:

What makes eliminative materialism reductionist is the attempt to replace a psychological account of behaviour with an explanation in terms of neurophysiology. An example of this is Crick's (1994) claim that everything we are, our joys and sorrows, memories and ambitions, our sense of personality and free will, are no more than the behaviour of a vast assembly of nerve cells. But according to Smith (1994), the mind and brain problem is radically different from other cases of contingent identity (identical as a matter of fact) with which it's usually compared (such as a gene is a section of the DNA molecule). What's different is reductionism, and the related issue of exactly what's meant by identity. Mind states and brain states aren't systematically correlated, and the neurophysiological evidence points towards token identity. For example, we cannot just assume that the same neurophysiological mechanisms will be used by two different people both engaged in the 'same' activity of reading (Broadbent, 1981). 'The brain' can perform the same tasks in many different ways. But mind–brain identity is usually taken to imply that whenever a certain type of mind state occurs, a certain type of brain state also occurs (type identity). Token identity means there must always be a place for an independent psychological account of human thought and actions (Harré et al., 1985).

A02

### Section 4:

According to Penrose (1990), there's a built-in indeterminacy in the way individual neurons and their synaptic connections work, that is, their responses are inherently unpredictable. But despite this unpredictability at the level of individual units or components, the system as a whole is predictable. The 'nervous system', or sub-systems within it, don't operate randomly, but in a highly organised, structured way. Consciousness, intelligence and memory are properties of the brain as a system, not of the individual units. They couldn't possibly be predicted from analysing the units that compose the system. Instead they 'emerge' from interactions between the units that compose the system (and so are called emergent properties). The whole is greater than the sum of its parts (Rose, 1997).

According to Rose (1992), the mind is never replaced by the brain. Instead, there are two distinct and valid languages, each describing the same material phenomena. Rose is speaking as both a materialist and an anti-reductionist. Although most materialists are also reductionists, and *vice versa*, this isn't necessarily so. For example, Freud was a materialist who believed that no single scientific vocabulary (such as anatomy) could adequately describe (let alone explain) all aspects of the material world. He argued for the autonomy of psychological explanation – mental phenomena need their own language. The brain is necessarily implicated in everything we do, and the mind doesn't represent a different kind of reality (materialism). But we can describe and explain our thinking without having to 'bring our brain into it' (anti-reductionism). This is because two separate levels of description, or universes of discourse, are involved. This is crucial to the survival of psychology as a separate discipline. Psychoneuroimmunology represents a middle ground between materialists and anti-reductionists, the interface between body and mind (Hegarty, 2000).

(1,025 words)

# SAMPLE ESSAYS

# SAMPLE ESSAYS

Critically consider whether psychology is a science. (30 marks) (40 mins) (800 words minimum)

### Section 1:

A01

Descartes's seventeenth-century philosophical dualism allowed scientists to treat matter as inert. This meant that the world could be described objectively, without reference to the human observer. Objectivity became the ideal of science, and was extended to the study of human bahaviour and social institutions by Comte in the mid-1800s. He called it positivism. Descartes had also promoted mechanism, the view that the material world consists of objects which are assembled like a huge machine and operated by mechanical laws. He extended this view to living organisms, including human beings. Because the mind is non-material, it can only be investigated through introspection. He was also an early advocate of reductionism.

Empiricism refers to the ideas of the seventeenth- and eighteenth-century British philosophers Locke, Hume and Berkeley. For them, the only source of true knowledge about the world is sensory experience. The word 'empirical' has come to mean 'scientific'. This implies that what scientists do, and what distinguishes them from non-scientists, is carry out experiments and observations as ways of collecting data ('facts') about the world. Empiricism proved to be one of the major influences on the development of the natural sciences. Wundt, a German physiologist, is generally regarded as the founder of the new science of experimental psychology (in 1879). He used introspection to analyse consciousness into its elementary sensations and feelings (structuralism). The American psychologist Watson rejected what Wundt and other introspectionists were doing and founded behaviourism (1913). For psychology to become a true science, it had to limit itself to what could be studied objectively, namely behaviour (as opposed to mind or consciousness). Academic psychology in the USA and UK was dominated by behaviourism for the next 40 years. But dissatisfaction with it culminated in the 'cognitive revolution' of 1956. Central to this information-processing approach was the computer analogy. It was now acceptable again to study the mind, although in a rather different way from how Wundt had gone about it.

### Section 2:

A01

Most psychologists and philosophers of science would probably agree that for a discipline to be called a science, it must possess certain characteristics. These include a definable subject matter (what it's about), theory construction (explanations of why observed phenomena happen), hypothesis testing (predictions derived from theories), and the use of empirical methods to collect evidence relating to the hypothesis. This is all aimed at trying to establish general laws or principles. But this fails to tell us how the scientific process actually works in practice. For example, where does the theory come from in the first place, and what is the exact relationship between theory construction, hypothesis testing and data collection? Accounts of the scientific process are referred to as the scientific method. The classical view of the scientific method is induction (or the inductive method), which was revised by Popper (1972) as the hypothetico–deductive method. In practice, both approaches are used.

A02

Understanding how science works is crucial for assessing psychology's claim to be a science and what this means. According to Van Langenhove (1995), one of mainstream academic psychology's 'unexamined presuppositions', is scientism, the borrowing of methods and a vocabulary from the natural sciences in order to discover causal mechanisms that explain psychological phenomena. Scientism maintains that all aspects of human behaviour can and should be studied using the methods of natural science, which claims to be the sole means of establishing objective truth. This involves context-stripping and studying behaviour in a value-free way. The most reliable way of doing this is through the laboratory experiment, which provides the greatest degree of control over relevant variables.

### Section 3:

A great deal of psychological research now takes place outside the laboratory. But according to Smith et al. (1995), whether the research is concerned with mind or behaviour and whether it's conducted inside or outside the laboratory, it tends to be constructed in terms of separation of behaviour into independent and dependent variables and the measurement of hypothetical relationships between them (what Rose (1997) calls reductionism as methodology). The natural sciences model (including the inductive method) has been attacked since the mid-1970s. For example, there's no such thing as unbiased observation, data aren't the same as facts ('fact' = data + theory: Deese, 1972), scientific theory and research reflect the biases, values and assumptions of individual scientists, and science involves quiet periods (normal science) and revolutions (Kuhn, 1962). But despite these and other criticisms, psychology is still dominated by the natural sciences model to a large extent. The most conspicuous effect of this is the continued dominance of experiments (Van Langenhove, 1995). In turn, this has far-reaching effects on how psychology pictures people as more or less passive and mechanical information-processing devices, whose behaviour can be split up into variables. The dominance of experiments also affects how psychology deals with people. In experiments, people aren't treated as single, unique individuals, but as interchangeable 'subjects'.

A01

Mainstream psychology, therefore, seems to be modelling itself on an outdated view of what natural science involves. But even if this view were still valid, psychology would face unique problems as a science. These include representativeness (generalising research findings to 'people in general' when participants are typically white, middle-class students attending Western universities), artificiality (generalising research findings to the 'real world' when they're based on 'unnatural' laboratory situations), and internal versus external

(a) Explain what is meant by the nature–nurture debate (5 marks).

(b) Discuss *two or more* examples of the nature–nurture debate in psychology (25 marks). (30 marks) (40 mins) (800 words minimum)

AO1

### Section 1:

The nature–nurture (or heredity–environment) debate concerns the causes of (usually) human abilities and capacities. Nativism is the philosophical theory, according to which knowledge of the world is largely inborn or innate. Nature (heredity) is seen as determining certain abilities and capacities, such as language, perception and psychomotor abilities, which unfold through the biological process of maturation (Gesell, 1925). Environmental influences are negligible and learning plays little if any part. Empiricism represents the opposite philosophical extreme. According to the seventeenth-century English philosopher Locke, the mind at birth is a '*tabula rasa*' or blank slate, which is gradually 'filled in' through learning and experience. Watson's behaviourism (1913) embodies this extreme environmentalist approach. These philosophical theories, and the early psychological theories associated with them, appeared to be answering the question 'Is it nature or nurture?'. But the debate is as much concerned with individual differences as with general abilities or capacities. It becomes most heated when it focuses on intelligence or mental disorders (such as schizophrenia), and the questions asked are 'How much does each contribute?' and 'How does each contribute?'.

AO1

### Section 2:

Family resemblance studies show that relatives of patients with schizophrenia have a greater risk of being diagnosed themselves as the genetic relationship becomes closer (Kendler *et al.*, 1996). But, as with the study of intelligence, these studies confound genetic with environmental influences. In other words, there's no way of telling whether the correlation between the risk of developing schizophrenia and degree of family resemblance (blood tie) is due to the greater genetic similarity or the greater similarity of environments. The two major alternative designs, twin and adoption studies, are aimed at disentangling the effects of nature and nurture. The average concordance rate for monozygotic (identical) twins/MZs is five times higher than that for dizygotic (non-identical) twins/DZs (Shields, 1976, 1978). But a more precise estimate for the relative importance of genetic and environmental factors comes from studies where MZs reared apart (MZsRA) are compared with MZs reared together (MZsRT). According to Shields, the concordance rates are quite similar for the two groups, suggesting a major genetic contribution. Adoption studies allow the clearest separation of genetic and environmental factors. Gottesman and Shields (1976, 1982) in a review of adoption studies (such as Heston, 1966; Rosenthal *et al.*, 1971; Kety *et al.*, 1975) concluded that they show a major role for heredity.

---

validity (in trying to control relevant variables, the resulting behaviour may bear little resemblance to what the psychologist was originally interested in).

AO2

### Section 4:

Definitions of psychology have changed during its lifetime, largely reflecting the influence of its major theoretical orientations (structuralism, behaviourism, cognitive psychology, psychodynamic and so on). Each approach rests upon a different image of what people are like, what it's important to study and how to study it. Kuhn (1962) argues that a field of study can only legitimately be regarded as a science if most of its workers subscribe to a common perspective or paradigm. Kuhn believes that psychology is still pre-paradigmatic, while others believe it's already experienced scientific revolutions (Wundt's structuralism being replaced by Watson's behaviourism, in turn replaced by the information-processing approach: Palermo, 1971; LeFrancois, 1983). The crucial point here is: can psychology be considered a science if psychologists disagree about what to study and how to study it?

One of the factors that makes a paradigm different from a theoretical approach is its social–psychological dimension. According to Richards (2002), one reason it may be impossible for any scientist to achieve complete objectivity is the social nature of scientific activity. How scientists perceive the world is shaped by the history of their discipline, dominant social expectations and patterns of research funding (Rose, 1997). The fact that scientific revolutions (paradigm shifts: Kuhn, 1962) occur shows that 'the truth' can and does change. Even if there are widely-accepted ways of 'doing science', 'good science' doesn't necessarily mean 'good psychology'. Is it valid to study human experience and behaviour as part of the natural world, or is a different kind of approach needed altogether? As Heather (1976) says, it isn't just psychologists who observe, experiment and theorise. Psychologists are part of their own subject-matter, which makes objectivity even more unattainable than in other sciences, as well as making psychology unique.

(1,189 words)

Section 3:

A02

The concordance rates for schizophrenia vary widely between studies conducted in different countries, suggesting that different criteria are used for its diagnosis. Both twin and adoption studies also presuppose that schizophrenia is a distinct syndrome which can be reliably diagnosed by different psychiatrists. There is reason to doubt both. The highest concordance rate for MZs is 69% (Rose *et al.*, 1984), which still leaves plenty of scope for the role of environmental factors. If schizophrenia were totally genetically determined, then we'd expect to find 100% concordance rate for MZs, that is, if one member of an MZ pair has schizophrenia, the other twin should also have it in every single case. But most diagnosed cases don't report a family history (Frith & Cahill, 1995). Rose *et al.* consider selective placement to be the rule in adoption studies (rather than random placement, that is, the assumption that adoptees are placed with parents no more similar to their biological parents than by chance). This would be a major stumbling block for adoption studies, but Lilienfeld (1995) believes the random placement assumption is warranted. The heritability of schizophrenia is comparable to that of medical conditions such as diabetes and hypertension, but the precise mode of inheritance remains controversial (Frith & Cahill; Lilienfeld, 1995). According to the diathesis–stress model (Zubin & Spring, 1977), what we inherit is a vulnerability towards schizophrenic symptoms, but whether or not we actually display them depends on environmental stressors.

Section 4:

A01

According to Gesell (1925), maturation refers to genetically programmed patterns of changes. The instructions for these patterns are part of the specific hereditary information passed on at the moment of conception (Bee, 2000). All individuals will pass through the same series of changes, in the same order, making maturational patterns universal and sequential. They're also relatively impervious to environmental influence. Gesell was mainly concerned with babies' psychomotor development (such as grasping and other manipulative skills) and locomotion (crawling and walking). These abilities 'develop by themselves' according to a genetically determined timetable. Provided the baby is physically normal, practice or training are unnecessary – they just 'unfold'. For Watson (1925), environmental influence is all-important and human beings are completely malleable. Famously, Watson claimed to be able to train anyone to

become anything. He also claimed (1928) that there's no such thing as an inheritance of capacity, talent, temperament or anything else. Despite the influence of behaviourism, the concept of maturation is still influential within psychology, explaining major biological changes such as puberty, and all stages theories of development assume that it underlies the universal sequence of stages (such as Freud's psychosexual theory, Erikson's psychosocial theory and Piaget's theory of cognitive development). Watson's extreme environmentalism was adopted in Skinner's radical behaviourism.

Section 5:

A02

Crawling or walking may appear to need no practice or training, but they require some environmental support, such as adequate diet and opportunity for movement and experimentation (Bee, 2000). At the very least, the environment must be benign (not harmful in any way). But there must also be environmental 'input'. For example, the possession of a language acquisition device (LAD) as proposed by Chomsky (1965) must be applied to the particular linguistic data the child is exposed to (its native tongue). Both Freud's and Piaget's developmental theories illustrate the interplay between nature and nurture. Freud (e.g. 1905) is often referred to as an instinct theorist (implying that he was a nativist), but it wasn't the sexual instinct itself that matters, but rather how significant others (especially the parents) react to the child's attempts to satisfy its sexual needs. Both excessive frustration and satisfaction can produce long-term effects on the child's personality. For Piaget (1970), intelligence is neither a simple copy of external objects nor a simple unfolding of pre-formed (inherited) structures. Rather, it consists of a set of structures that are constructed through continuous interaction between the child and its environment. Both theories demonstrate what Karmiloff-Smith (1996) describes as a trade-off between pre-specification (such as maturation and inborn biases) and plasticity (the capacity for learning and change). According to Bee (2000), no developmental psychologists today would take the 'Is it nature or nurture?' form of the debate seriously, because every facet of a child's development is a product of some pattern of interaction between nature and nurture.

(1,103 words)

# Perspectives: Approaches

## What's covered in this chapter?
## You need to know about:

- In the exam, you're required to apply your knowledge and understanding of any two theoretical/methodological approaches (e.g. biological/medical; behavioural; psychodynamic) to a novel situation or psychological phenomenon as described in the stimulus material

## Introduction

- These approaches might be selected from any number within psychology or related disciplines (e.g. sociology). Indeed, there are a number of different theoretical/methodological approaches that can be applied to novel situations or psychological phenomena. An approach is a way of addressing the problem of explaining behaviour that a number of people would agree with.

- Since human behaviour is so complicated and difficult to explain, no single approach can easily explain every behaviour. You should choose the most appropriate approach for the particular behaviour described. In the exam, you're expected to know **two** approaches in detail and be able to apply them to the given stimulus material behaviour. There are any number of different approaches you could use, but the three most popular ones are:
  - biological/medical approach
  - behavioural approach (including the Social Learning Theory approach)
  - psychodynamic approach.

You'll have covered aspects of these approaches in the other areas of the Specification. This is where the synoptic part of the Specification comes in. Nevertheless, we'll cover the important aspects of these approaches again here.

## The Biological Approach
### Definition of biological approach

An approach to behaviour that emphasises bodily events and changes associated with actions, feelings and thoughts.

## Outline of the Biological Approach

- **Nature argument:** The biological approach is very much on the side of 'nature' in the nature–nurture debate (see page 520). It emphasises the importance of genes and neurophysiology.
- **Importance of human genes:** Genes are the basic units of heredity. Genes influence physical characteristics and, in combination with the environment, can influence psychological characteristics or traits. Traits are characteristics of an individual that remain consistent across time and situations. Some characteristics are highly heritable (e.g. height) while others are less so (e.g. table manners), because the latter are primarily determined by upbringing. **Heritability** refers to an estimate of the proportion to which a trait can be attributed to genetic differences within a group (Tavris & Wade, 1997). It's been estimated that 50–80% of intelligence, measured by IQ tests, is attributable to hereditary factors.
- **Importance of neurophysiology:** Neurophysiology refers to the workings of the brain and nervous system and its influence on human behaviour. However, it's not the physiological processes within the human body that are of central importance, but what these processes can tell us about human behaviour. Humans are restricted in their behaviours by what they can physically do (e.g. we can't fly unaided) and, in addition, our physiology determines the extent and nature of our learning capabilities.
- **Psychological is also physiological:** All human thoughts and behaviours must have a physiological origin. For example, you could explain all behaviours in terms of internal physiological actions (but see Reductionism, Chapter 17, pages 504–509).
- **Heritable traits are modified by the environment:** To use the example of height again, a malnourished child may not grow as tall as they have the potential to do.
- **Chemical messengers:** You don't have to know much about the brain or nervous system (thankfully!) to explain how the biological approach addresses human behaviour. However, there are three chemical messengers that operate throughout the body, and which would be useful to learn. A simplified account of them is on the next page.

### EXAM tips BOX

Remember, marks are awarded for how well you engage with the stimulus material. Although we can outline each approach in general, you must apply your knowledge to the specific behaviour in the stimulus material. Note that for this Perspectives question you have 40 minutes in total. This means that you only have about eight minutes for each six-mark answer. You'll see that you don't need to know everything about each approach! There simply won't be time in the exam.

Remember that this part of Perspectives is assessed through the use of stimulus material questions. A particular behaviour will be described and your task is to explain the behaviour using two approaches. The format of the questions will always be the same. They will be:

(a) Describe how *the subject presented in the stimulus material* might be explained by two different approaches. (6 + 6 marks)

(b) Assess one of these explanations of *the subject presented in the stimulus material* in terms of its strengths and limitations. (6 marks)

(c) How might *the subject presented in the stimulus material* be investigated by one of these approaches? (6 marks)

(d) Evaluate the use of this method *of investigating the subject material* presented in the stimulus material. (6 marks)

Note: The words in italics will be replaced by whatever stimulus material they are describing. This will make the questions easier to understand.

There will be two stimulus material questions and you have to answer one of these.

In part (b) you must assess one of the explanations you wrote about in part (a). You can switch to the other approach for parts (c) and (d) but you must not switch approaches between parts (c) and (d). Part (d) asks you 'to evaluate the use of this method'. You don't *have* to include *both* strengths and limitations (either would suffice) although both would be preferable.

1. **Neurotransmitters:** These have been shown to affect certain behaviours. They exist in the brain, spinal cord, peripheral nerves and certain glands. Table 18.1 outlines some of the better-known neurotransmitters and their effects on behaviour. It would be very impressive if you could mention the particular neurotransmitter that's implicated in the particular behaviour included in any stimulus material. Abnormal behaviours can occur when someone has too much or too little of these neurotransmitters (see psychopathology, Chapter 14, page 394).

2. **Endorphins:** Another group of chemical messengers which reduce pain and promote pleasure. They play a role in appetite, sexual pleasure, mood, learning and memory. Endorphin levels increase when someone is in pain, stress or fearful. They seem to act as the body's natural painkiller.

Physiological explanation: a comprehensive explanation of human behaviour?

3. **Hormones:** These are released in the bloodstream and are chemical substances secreted by various glands that affect the functioning of other organs (see the effects of stress hormones – Chapter 3). There are a number of different types of hormones but some of the effects include: increased energy levels, memory improvement, control of biological rhythms (see Chapter 10), sexual arousal and so on. The most important sex hormones are testosterone in men and oestrogen in women.

(Note: There is an overlap between neurotransmitters and hormones, e.g. noradrenaline is both a neurotransmitter and a hormone.)

**Table 18.1** Well-known neurotransmitters and their effects on behaviour

| Neurotransmitter | Behavioural effects |
| --- | --- |
| Serotonin | Sleep, appetite, sensory perception, pain suppression, mood |
| Dopamine | Voluntary movements, learning, memory and emotion<br>Schizophrenia |
| Acetylcholine | Muscle actions, cognitive functioning, memory, emotion, drinking, behavioural inhibition |
| Noradrenaline | Stress, learning, memory, eating, dreaming, emotion, depression, arousal |
| GABA | Sleep, movements and eating disorders |

## ✘✔ Strengths and limitations of biological approach

✔ **Highly scientific approach:** The bio-psychological approach is highly scientific in its methods (see below).

✔ **Objective supporting evidence:** Studies that have examined different areas of the brain have shown that specific areas of the brain are implicated in certain types of behaviour. For example, speech production is located in Broca's area in the left frontal lobe.

✔ **Practical applications:** The biological approach has been successfully used in a number of practical applications, from the use of drugs to treat mental disorders (see page 430) to the development of the most appropriate types of shift patterns for 24-hour workers.

✔ **Humans as physiological machines:** All thoughts, actions and behaviours are physiological in origin – we are physiological machines and therefore physiological processes must play an important role.

✘ **Limited knowledge:** Each passing decade appears to be called 'the decade of the brain', when we discover more about the brain and exactly how physiological functions relate to psychological behaviours. Although advancements are made, progress remains slow because of the complexities involved.

✘ **Reductionist approach:** The biological approach has been criticised for reducing complex behaviours to simple biological explanations. Most bio-psychologists now recognise the importance of environmental and cognitive factors in explaining much human behaviour.

✘ **Deterministic approach:** Related to the last point, the emphasis on heritability of behaviour can lead people to ignore or underplay the importance of good environmental circumstances. It might suggest that behaviour is largely predetermined at birth. However, it's worth noting that 'environmentalism' is also a deterministic approach.

## Methods used with the biological approach

- **Clinical/anatomical methods:** These allow us to study the effects of brain injury on behaviour. This might involve brain damage through illness (tumour) or accidental damage (e.g. caused by car accidents). Anatomical methods have been used to examine brain physiology during postmortems. It seems reasonable that brain damage found during a postmortem might explain any behavioural deficits evident during the person's lifetime.
- **Invasive methods:** These involve studies where areas of the brain have been surgically removed or destroyed (Lashley, 1929). These are usually conducted on animals. In addition, during brain operations areas can be electrically stimulated to see the effect on behaviour. Since there are no pain receptors in the brain, some brain operations on humans are conducted under local anaesthetic. These allow the patient to report any feelings, memories or thoughts that are produced by the stimulation (Penfield, 1958) (see Key Study, page 496).
- **Non-invasive methods:** There are a number of different methods available:
  - **the electroencephalogram (EEG):** this involves an electrical recording device (electrodes) that's strapped to the scalp to record electrical brain activity. It records the electrical potential of numerous neurons and has been used widely, particularly in sleep studies
  - **brain scanning techniques:** there are numerous scanning techniques available, all of which have a different acronym (CAT, PET, fMRI). All of the techniques allow us to 'see' inside the brain and provide images of the brain. Patients undergoing scans can be asked to perform different tasks or produce different thoughts. Those areas of the brain that are most active at these times are thought to be implicated in that behaviour. However, a major drawback is that patients have to remain still while the scans take place
  - **adoption or twin studies:** these studies help to discover the effects of genetics and environment. Adoption studies are useful since the children share half their genes with each biological parent but not their environment, and their environment with their adoptive parents but not their genes. Correlations can be made between the children's traits and behaviours compared to both their

biological parents and adoptive parents. Twin studies use a similar method. Monozygotic (identical) twins can be compared with non-identical (dizygotic) twins. It's assumed that if identical twins are more alike than non-identical twins, then this increased similarity must be due to genetics (see Chapters 11 and 14).

 ## Evaluation of the methods used with the biological approach

✓ **Scientific, experimental methods:** The methods used adopt a scientific approach. They involve objective measures and the studies are well-controlled. In addition, they use the latest scientific, medical techniques.

✗ **Damage doesn't necessarily relate to function:** Damage to a particular part of the brain doesn't necessarily explain loss of a particular ability. The damaged area might be controlled by another undamaged area or the damage might have affected other related areas.

✗ **Low ecological validity:** Biological methods often involve removing the individual from the environment where they perform their behaviour into a laboratory situation. This then becomes an artificial situation and it makes the results less worthwhile.

✗ **Twin studies:** Identical twins may experience more similar environments than non-identical twins (i.e. people may treat them more alike). This can lead to heritability estimates of behaviour being inflated (but see Chapter 14).

✗ **Non-human animal studies:** Using invasive brain techniques such as lesions (cutting) or ablations (removal) on animals has been questioned on ethical grounds (see page 478). There's also the problem of generalising findings obtained from animals to human behaviour.

✗ **Inaccurate environmental measures:** It's very difficult to measure environmental influences (e.g. peer pressures), so their possible contribution to a particular behaviour (e.g. intelligence) may be under- or over-estimated. This, of course, means that the influence of genes on the same trait may be similarly inaccurate.

## EXAM tips BOX

**Stimulus material: 'One for the road'**

Kate was a very popular 'girl about town' who had lots of friends. She always used to go down the pub for a drink after work and was always the last to leave. Unfortunately, she did not always watch how much she had to drink before driving home and always enjoyed 'one for the road'. One day, she was stopped by the police who had noticed her erratic driving. She was later prosecuted for drink-driving and lost her licence.

(a) Describe how the biological approach might try to explain drink-driving. (6 marks)*

(b) Assess one of these explanations of drink-driving in terms of its strengths and limitations. (6 marks)

(c) How might one of these approaches investigate Kate's drink-driving behaviour? (6 marks)

(d) Evaluate the use of this method of investigating Kate's drink-driving behaviour. (6 marks)

*In the real exam, the question will ask you to describe any two approaches and will be worth 6 + 6 marks.

Try to answer this question yourself. There's a sample essay on pages 562–563, with which you can compare your essay.

## The essential biological approach

(a[1]) Summary of approach:

- nature argument
- importance of human genes
- importance of neurophysiology
- psychological is also physiological – all thoughts/behaviours must have a biological cause
- heritable traits are modified by the environment
- chemical messengers:
  - neurotransmitters
  - endorphins
  - hormones.

(b) Evaluation:

Strengths of approach:
- highly scientific approach
- objective supporting evidence
- practical applications
- humans as physiological machines.

Weaknesses of approach:
- limited knowledge
- reductionist approach
- deterministic approach.

(c) Methods used:

- clinical/anatomical methods
- invasive methods
- non-invasive methods:
  - EEG
  - brain scanning methods
  - adoption or twin studies.

(d) Strengths of methods:

- scientific, experimental
- objective measures
- advanced techniques.

Weaknesses of methods:

- damage doesn't necessarily relate to function
- twin studies: still difficulties separating nature and nurture effects
- animal studies – ethical and scientific issues?
- inaccurate environmental measures.

[1] a, b, c, d refer to questions in exam.

# The Behavioural Approach

## Definition of behaviourism

An approach that emphasises the study of objectively-observable behaviour and the role of the environment as a determinant of human (and other animal) behaviour (Tavris & Wade, 1997).

The two psychologists most closely associated with this approach are J.B. Watson and B.F. Skinner.

## Outline of behavioural approach

- **Humans are born blank slates:**
  Behaviourists believe that all knowledge and learning are acquired through the senses. Humans are born as 'blank slates' ('*tabula rasa*'). The role of instincts and hereditary factors is largely ignored. Watson believed that a person's achievements were limited only by their environmental restrictions. Behaviourism takes the side of nurture in the nature–nurture debate.

- **All behaviour is learned through the environment:**
  Behaviourists believe that behaviour is determined primarily by experiences within the environment. Skinner regarded 'free will' as an illusion and argued in favour of determinism (see page 494). Learning is the key to behaviour and is defined as any relatively permanent change in behaviour that occurs as a result of experience. Behaviourists claim that 'experience is the greatest teacher, providing the link between past and future and enabling the organism to adapt to changing circumstances in order to survive and thrive' (Tavris & Wade, 1997). A basic form of learning is called conditioning, which involves associations between stimuli in the environment and responses to these stimuli (see below).

- **All behaviour is observable:**
  Behaviourists stress the importance of dealing with behaviours that are directly observable. External events dictate the occurrence of behaviour, and external events can be observed and measured in an objective (unbiased) way.

- **Humans and animals learn in similar ways:**
  The laws of learning apply to both humans and animals. Examining the way animals learn in the lab can therefore help us to understand the ways humans learn in their environment. There are two main types of learning, classical conditioning and operant conditioning:

  - **Classical conditioning:** This was first discovered by Ivan Pavlov, a Russian physiologist studying the salivation reflex in dogs. He noticed that his laboratory dogs salivated to the sound of the footsteps of the person who came to feed them. The dogs had learnt by association ('conditioned') to salivate to the sound of footsteps! Pavlov found that he could condition his dogs to salivate to other things that he paired with the presentation of food, including bells, lights and buzzers. Pavlov believed that classical conditioning was the basis of all human and animal learning.

  - A definition of classical conditioning is the process by which a previously neutral stimulus acquires the capacity to elicit a response through association with a stimulus that already elicits a similar response (Tavris & Wade, 1997).

  - There are a number of confusing terms associated with classical conditioning. The term 'conditioned' can be understood as 'learned' so an unconditioned stimulus (UCS) is an unlearned one, i.e. it produces a reflex without the need for learning. An unconditioned response (UCR) is an unlearned one, i.e. it's produced by an UCS without the need for learning and so on. A stimulus that's repeatedly paired with an unconditioned stimulus (UCS) becomes a conditioned stimulus (CS), and a response that's learned during conditioning is called a conditioned response (CR).

  - Classical conditioning is best demonstrated in Figure 18.1 on page 548.

    *Just remember:*
    *Conditioned = learned*
    *Unconditioned = unlearned!*

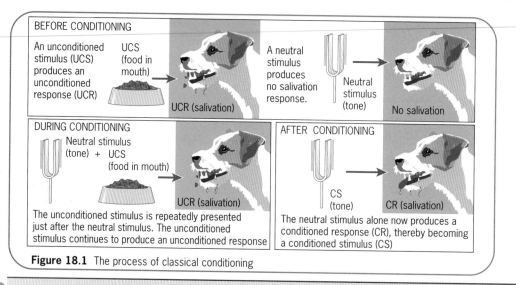

**Figure 18.1** The process of classical conditioning

---

**Key study**

## THE CASE OF LITTLE ALBERT (WATSON & RAYNER, 1920)

Albert B.'s mother was a wet-nurse in a children's hospital. Albert was described as 'healthy from birth', and 'on the whole stolid and unemotional'. When he was about nine months old, his reactions to various stimuli were tested – a white rat, a rabbit, a dog, a monkey, masks with and without hair, cotton wool, burning newspapers, and a hammer striking a four-foot steel bar just behind his head. Only the last of these frightened him, so this was designated the UCS (and fear the UCR). The other stimuli were neutral, because they *didn't* produce fear.

When Albert was just over eleven months old, the rat and the UCS were presented together: as Albert reached out to stroke the animal, Watson crept up behind the baby and brought the hammer crashing down on the steel bar! This occurred seven times in total over the next seven weeks. By this time, the rat (the CS) *on its own* frightened Albert, and the fear was now a CR. Watson and Rayner had succeeded in deliberately producing in a baby a phobia of rats.

The CR transferred spontaneously to the rabbit, the dog, a sealskin fur coat, cotton wool, Watson's hair, and a Santa Claus mask. But it didn't generalise to Albert's building blocks or to the hair of two observers (so Albert was showing discrimination).

Five days after conditioning, the CR produced by the rat persisted. After ten days it was 'much less marked', but it was still evident a month later (for further details see Rolls, 2005).

---

Skinner taught us more than just the techniques for 'pulling habits out of rats'

There are five major conditioning processes. These are summarised as follows:

- **acquisition:** the first stage of learning, when a response is established (acquired) and strengthened. Watson demonstrated how phobias are acquired using learning principles with the case of Little Albert
- **extinction:** the diminishing of a learned (conditioned) response. It occurs when a UCS no longer follows a CS
- **spontaneous recovery:** the reappearance, after a set period, of the extinguished CR
- **generalization:** the tendency for other stimuli like the CS to elicit a similar response
- **discrimination:** the ability to distinguish between a CS and other stimuli that don't precede a UCS.
- **Operant conditioning:** Through operant conditioning, the organism (human and animal) associates its behaviour with **consequences**. They become more likely to repeat behaviours that are rewarded

(reinforced) and less likely to repeat behaviours that are punished. It's called operant conditioning because the behaviour *operates* on the environment to produce a reward or punishment. A **reinforcer** is defined as any behaviour that strengthens the behaviour that follows it. Thus, reinforcers vary from one individual to another. For some, chocolate is a reinforcer (reward), whereas for others it might be a punishment (someone who dislikes the taste).

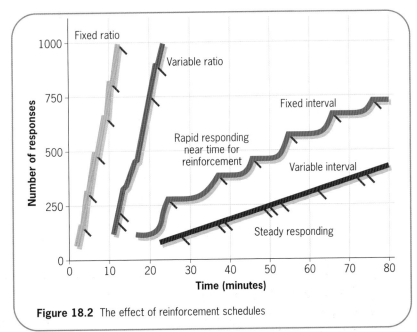

**Figure 18.2** The effect of reinforcement schedules

- Skinner is the psychologist most closely associated with operant conditioning. He elaborated on Edward Thorndike's *Law of Effect* which states that 'rewarded behaviour is likely to recur'. Skinner developed a 'behavioural technology' that enabled him, using the principles of operant conditioning, to teach pigeons and rats all kinds of unusual behaviours. In 1944, during World War II, Skinner trained pigeons to guide bombs. Pigeons were conditioned to keep pecking a target that would hold a missile onto a target. The pigeons pecked reliably but Project Pigeon was discontinued (because of another top secret project – radar!).
- **Primary and secondary reinforcers: Primary reinforcers** are those that satisfy a biological need (e.g. hunger, thirst). **Secondary reinforcers** are stimuli that gain their reinforcing power through association with a primary reinforcer (e.g. money is a secondary reinforcer which can be used to purchase food). Primary reinforcers are particularly effective reinforcers of behaviour. I'd do many things for money but I'd do anything if I was starving!
- **Schedules of reinforcement:** There are various ways of giving reinforcement (see Fig. 18.2). Reinforcement can be continuous (reward given every time a response is made) or intermittent (reward given sometimes). **Intermittent schedules** include:

  ■ **fixed ratio (FR) schedule:** reinforcement is given after a fixed number of responses. Examples here could be workers on a production line who get paid on a piecework basis or authors who get paid per chapter!

  ■ **variable ratio (VR) schedule:** reinforcement is given after a variable number of responses. Examples here could be fishing and gambling. You never know when you're going to land the big one! Gamblers know that slot machines are set at a particular level to pay off in favour of the casino, but the more coins you put in, the greater your chance of a pay-off

■ **fixed interval (FI) schedule:** reinforcement is given after a fixed amount of time has passed. These are less common with human behaviour, but workers might check their online bank account more often at the end of the month, when their wages are due to be paid in. They won't check again for a month

■ **variable interval (VI) schedule:** reinforcement is given after a variable amount of time has passed. If a worker didn't know when their wages were going to be paid into their bank account, they'd check their account fairly consistently.

## Strengths and limitations of the behavioural approach

✔ **Very scientific approach:** Behaviourism is a scientific approach using objective, experimental methods in the lab. All behaviour is observable and measurable. The laws of learning have been experimentally tested and there's a great deal of experimental support.

✔ **The law of parsimony:** This suggests that if two opposing theories or approaches claim to explain the same behaviour, then the simpler of the two should be preferred. Behaviourism comprises a few simple rules and yet is applied to many different behaviours both normal and abnormal.

✔ **Everyday, practical applications:** The behaviourist approach is successfully applied in numerous areas of life. Merely nodding and maintaining eye contact with someone you're listening to could be a reinforcer, suggesting to them that what they're saying is interesting. Schools use gold stars as secondary reinforcers. Praise, applause and money are other examples used all the time to shape and maintain appropriate behaviours. Other applications involve the use of programmed learning, training of guide dogs, child-rearing practices, behavioural therapies and advertising campaigns.

✔ **Long-lasting, influential approach:** It's difficult to argue with many of the assumptions of behaviourism. Indeed, it's argued that some aspects of behaviourism apply to all the other approaches. The environment must play at least some part in determining our behaviour! The scientific nature of behaviourism has also helped to enhance the status of psychology as a scientific discipline.

✔ **Positive approach:** With its emphasis on the environmental influences, behaviourism suggests that behaviour can be changed. It adopts a positive, optimistic view of human behaviour. Alter the environmental situation and behavioural change will occur.

✔ **Predict and promote behaviour:** The behaviourist approach can be used to predict how people will behave in certain situations. Suitable environments can be created to promote socially appropriate behaviour (e.g. road layouts, classrooms and prison buildings!).

✘ **Largely ignores innate behaviours:** Many critics of behaviourism state that there must be some biological influence on behaviour. The influence of genetics and physiological processes isn't given enough weight.

✘ **Ethics – use of animals in labs:** The use of animals in controlled lab conditions is ethically questionable (see page 478). Can the use of rats and pigeons be justified?

✘ **Low ecological validity:** Experiments conducted in the lab are criticised for demonstrating artificial learning, not real-life learning or behaviour.

✘ **Reductionist approach:** Behaviourism has been criticised for reducing complex behaviours to simple stimulus-response (S-R) links. Except for radical behaviourists, many behaviourists now recognise the importance of cognitive factors in explaining much human behaviour. Skinner maintained to his death that 'cognitive science' was a throwback to introspectionism.

✘ **Humans are different from animals:** Human behaviour is far more complex than animal behaviour. The laws of learning derived from animal studies cannot adequately explain the enormous variety of human behaviour.

**✗** Deterministic approach: If we're merely the products of our environment, then individuals are regarded as passive organisms. Our lives are determined by the environment and there is no such thing as 'free will' (see pages 494–502). This is sometimes seen as a pessimistic, and simply mistaken, view of human behaviour.

**✗•✓** Conditioning can't account for novel behaviours: It's been argued that creative or novel behaviour can't be explained using a behaviourist approach. However, behaviourists argue that such behaviour is probably an unusual combination of previously learned patterns of behaviour.

**✗•✓** Behavioural control: Behaviourism has been accused of being a dangerous approach since it offers the possibility of controlling people's behaviour through manipulation of the environment. Behaviourists argue that society should use the principles of learning to achieve humane goals.

The behaviourist approach has many everyday practical applications

## Methods used with behavioural approach

- It's no surprise, given the scientific approach of the behaviourists, that research methods adopted are also scientific. It's perhaps worth making the distinction between methodological (methods associated with it) and philosophical (overall philosophical approach) behaviourism. Most psychologists would admit to being the former (but not necessarily the latter). This demonstrates the behaviourist influence on psychology as a whole.
- Given the fact that humans are thought to learn in similar ways to other animals, behaviourists often conduct studies using animals and then generalise their findings to human behaviour. It's easier and more practical to study animals in the lab than humans.
- The laws of learning and reinforcement schedules were developed under very strictly controlled lab situations, but it's not always possible to do this with human behaviours. Nevertheless, any behaviours would need to be monitored in a carefully controlled environment. Behaviourists would need to be clear which reinforcers are operating in any situation, and learning responses would have to be carefully operationalised and measured accurately.
- Accurate, objective observation would play an important part since all behaviour is observable. Cognitions or thought processes can be discounted.

**✗✓** Evaluation of the methods used in the behavioural approach

**✓** Scientific methods: The methods used by behaviourists have the advantage of being highly controlled. Carefully controlled experiments are highly regarded in science (but see Chapters 16 and 17).

**✓** Objective measurements: Behaviourists observe behaviour using objective measurements. Objectivity is an important requirement in science. In addition, behavioural measures are precisely defined or operationalised. This is another important requirement of the scientific method.

**✓** Replication: Because of the methods used, precise replication of any behavioural study should be possible. Replication is an important requirement in science.

**✗** Low ecological validity: Usually, the more highly controlled a study is, the more artificial the situation is. Lab experiments tend to be low in ecological validity, meaning that findings may not relate to real life.

IT'S POURING WITH RAIN, WE'VE JUST LOST 5–0 AND I'M ABOUT TO BE BEATEN UP. I'M NOT QUITE SURE WHAT THE POSITIVE REINFORCER IS HERE

✗ **Non-human animal studies:** It's not clear whether one can generalise the findings of animal studies to human behaviour. Is there really little difference between humans and animals? What about the importance of language and the effect this has on human learning and behaviour?

✗ **Quantification problem:** Not all behaviours can be quantified easily. A good example is whether a book should be judged by the number of words in it rather than the quality of the material. The fewer words, the better?

✗ **Impractical methods?** It's not always easy to conduct behavioural studies through carefully controlled observation. Can you really observe what the reinforcer is for the behaviour of trainspotting? Don't you have to ask trainspotters what they get out of it? What feelings do they have when they see a different train?

✗ **Reductionist approach:** The attempt to explain all behaviour using a strictly behavioural approach has led to criticisms that it reduces behaviour to an over-simplistic level of explanation.

✓ **Social Learning Theory:** This was an extension of Learning Theory, suggesting that behaviour isn't always learned directly but learned and maintained through observation (imitation of others) and positive and negative consequences it has for them. Seeing others being rewarded and punished for their behaviour and copying this is called vicarious learning. The Social Learning Theory approach has been covered in greater detail in Chapter 9 (also see Chapter 12).

> **Specification Hint:** The Social Learning Theory approach is a good one to use since it's likely that any behaviours described in the stimulus material will be ones that might have been learnt through observation and imitation. You can choose to present the Social Learning Theory as a second approach in itself *or* as an extension to behaviourism. If you use it as an extension to behaviourism, you should emphasise that it's a *neo–behaviourist approach*.

## EXAM tips BOX

**Stimulus material: Football hooliganism**

Andy is a season-ticket holder at a Premiership club. He has a respectable job and is regarded as a 'good family man'. However, he has a number of arrests for football hooliganism. He often travels to home and away games with his friends and always seems to get involved in trouble.

(a) Describe how the behavioural approach might try to explain Andy's football hooliganism. (6 marks)*

(b) Assess one of these explanations of football hooliganism in terms of its strengths and limitations. (6 marks)

(c) How might one of these approaches investigate Andy's football hooliganism? (6 marks)

(d) Evaluate the use of this method of investigating Andy's football hooliganism. (6 marks)

*In the real exam, the question will ask you to describe any two approaches and will be worth 6 + 6 marks.*

*Try to answer this question yourself. There's a sample essay on pages 563–564 with which you can compare your essay.*

# The essential behavioural approach

(a[1]) Summary of approach:

- humans are blank slates at birth ('*tabula rasa*')
- all behaviour is learned and determined from the environment (S-R psychology)
- all behaviour is observable
- humans and animals are only quantitatively different and learn in same way:
  — classical conditioning: ('*learning by association*'): a simple form of learning where a neutral stimulus is paired with a stimulus (UCS) that automatically produces a response (UCR) and in time the neutral stimulus (CS) alone elicits that response (CR); e.g. food – salivation – bell/food – salivation
  — operant conditioning: ('*learning by reinforcement*'): behaviour is shaped by its consequences (reward/punishment).

(b) Evaluation

Strengths of approach:
- very scientific, objective and experimental, both observable and measurable
- simple rules effectively applied to many different behaviours – the 'law of parsimony' ('economical' theories are superior)
- everyday, practical applications (e.g. schools, therapies, child rearing, advertising)
- long-lasting, influential approach enhanced psychology as a science
- can both predict and promote behaviour.

Weaknesses of approach:
- largely ignores innate behaviours
- ethics – use of animals in labs
- low ecological validity: lab experiments demonstrate artificial learning
- reductionist approach: over-simplified approach which reduces complex behaviours to S-R links
- humans are different from animals
- ignores internal thought (cognitive and conscious) processes
- deterministic and pessimistic view
- can't account for novel behaviours
- behavioural control: ethical problem.

(c) Methods used:

- only observable behaviour should be studied – scientific, (lab) experiments
- animal studies because: laws of learning are universal; there's only a very small qualitative difference between humans and animals; animals more practical and ethical to test in lab
- accurate, objective measures used.

(d) Strengths of methods:          Weaknesses of methods

Strengths of methods:
- scientific methods: cause and effect
- highly controlled experiments
- objective measurements
- replication possible.

Disadvantages of methods:
- low ecological validity
- quantification problem
- difficult to operationalise and measure thoughts, beliefs and attitudes.

NOTE: Can use SLT and call it neo–behaviourism as an additional **OR** the same approach.

[1] a, b, c, d refer to questions in exam.

# The Psychodynamic Approach

## Definition of psychodynamic approach

Psychological approaches, originating with Freud's theory of psychoanalysis, that emphasises unconscious energy dynamics within the individual (Tavris & Wade, 1997).

## Outline of psychodynamic approach

- Sigmund Freud is generally recognised as one of the most influential thinkers of the twentieth century.
- The psychodynamic approach arises from Freud's theory of personality development (see Chapter 12). The assumptions common to Freud's original theory of psychoanalysis are:
  - **the developmental approach:** Freud emphasised the importance of early childhood experiences for later personality and emotional development
  - **the crucial importance of the unconscious:** Freud believed that a large part of the mind isn't accessible to the conscious and that the unconscious is the source of motivation
  - **instinctual drives motivate and regulate behaviour even in childhood:** The source of these drives is psychic energy. According to Freud, the personality is made up of three systems:

    - **the** *id*: this is present at birth: the source of all psychological energies and instincts. The *id* works according to the **pleasure principle** – the new-born infant is all 'id'. The pleasure principle seeks to reduce tension, avoid pain and obtain pleasure. The id contains two groups of instincts: the life or sexual instincts called the '**libido**', and the death or aggressive instincts called '**thanatos**'. Within this system, energy can be shifted or transformed, but the amount of energy always remains the same. Energy that builds up in the id must be released in one way or another
    - **the** *ego*: during the first year of life, some of the child's id becomes part of the ego. The *ego* functions according to the **reality principle**. It represents reality and reason.
    - **the** *superego*: the last part of the personality to develop. It's the voice of morality or the conscience.
  - **the defence mechanisms:** the ego deals with reality and the conflict between the id and the superego. Sometimes, when the anxiety becomes overwhelming, the ego protects itself by blocking or distorting the impulses in a more acceptable and less threatening form. The techniques for doing

If you asked most 'lay' people to name one psychologist, they would name Sigmund Freud

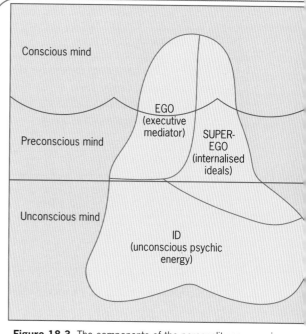

**Figure 18.3** The components of the personality as conscious or unconscious processes

this are called the ego defence mechanisms. Some of the best-known ones are:

- **repression (motivated forgetting)** occurs when a threatening idea or emotion is blocked from consciousness. For example, someone with a strong fear of spiders may not be able to recall the initial incident that led to a fear of spiders. They've repressed the traumatic event (see Chapter 1).
- **denial:** blocking external events from conscious awareness ('I'm not angry with him'). For example, some people may deny that they're alcoholics
- **displacement:** the redirection of an emotion (particularly anger) towards a substitute target. For example, someone who's unable to have children may redirect their love onto their cat or dog. Someone who's frustrated by their boss at work may go home and kick their dog or cat
- **turning against oneself:** a special form of displacement where the person becomes their own substitute target. It's been suggested that depression is the result of anger that we've refused to acknowledge
- **regression:** a reversion to a previous psychological phase when one is faced with stress. For example, a child may start to suck their thumb again or wet their bed. This relates to the psychosexual stages of development outlined below

I THOUGHT THAT WOMEN DIDN'T LIKE ME – BUT NOW I REALISE IT'S JUST A REACTION FORMATION

- **projection:** the tendency to see one's own unacceptable desires in other people. Anna Freud called this 'displacement outward' and is the complete opposite of 'turning against oneself'. For example, when someone goes on and on about the lack of morality in the world today, you wonder whether the lack of morality lies in themselves. It's echoed in the Shakespearean phrase in Hamlet: 'The lady doth protest too much, methinks'
- **reaction formation:** changing an unacceptable impulse into its opposite. The best example of this is when children aged about 11 years say how disgusting the opposite sex are, when you know they really like them
- **humour:** another way of defending against fear. Perhaps this is why jokes about sexual performance are so frequently told by men
- **rationalisation:** the distortion of facts – this helps to make an event less threatening.

I'M REALLY ENJOYING THE FREEDOM OF HAVING NO BOYFRIEND, AND DAVE WAS UGLY ANYWAY....

An example of rationalisation?

There are a great many defence mechanisms. One way to summarise them is to see them all as a combination of denial or repression with various kinds of rationalisations.

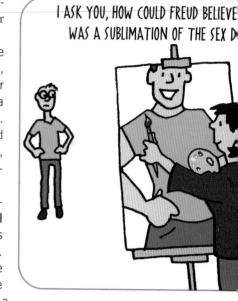

I ASK YOU, HOW COULD FREUD BELIEVE
WAS A SUBLIMATION OF THE SEX D

- **sublimation:** a positive defence mechanism. This is the transformation of an unacceptable impulse (e.g. sex, anger) into a socially acceptable or productive form. For example, someone who's particularly hostile might be a very successful football player or businesswoman. Someone who's particularly anxious might make a good personnel officer or scientist (e.g. well-organised, planner). Freud believed that all positive, creative activities were sublimations of the sexual drive

- **personality development:** Freud believed that personality develops through a fixed series of **psychosexual stages**. Each one of these is marked by different areas of the body that give us pleasure (erogenous zones). Any behavioural difficulties associated with each stage (e.g. weaning, toilet training) can result in people becoming fixated at that particular stage. Fixation at a particular stage leads to long-term effects in our personality

- **the oral stage:** (0–1 year): the focus of pleasure here is the mouth. The most common activities are sucking and biting. Frustration with suckling or inappropriate weaning can result in an oral-passive character. Oral-passive people tend to retain an interest in oral gratifications such as eating, drinking and/or smoking. Pleasure is gained through the mouth. Alternatively, people can develop an oral-aggressive personality. This occurs if their weaning has caused a great deal of upset. Oral-aggressive personalities have a life-long desire to bite on things such as pencils or chewing gum. They are also verbally aggressive and sarcastic

- **the anal stage** (1–3 years): the major concern here is control of bodily wastes, and the focus of pleasure is the anus. Remember, toilet training is an important part of this stage. People who become fixated at this stage (wait for it!) become either (a) anal expulsives (sloppy, disorganised and generous to a fault) through lax toilet training regimes; or (b) if the toilet training is too strict, an anal-passive personality (clean, perfectionist, stubborn)

- **the phallic stage** (3–5/6 years): the important part of this stage is the Oedipus Complex for boys and the Electra Complex for girls. The Oedipus Complex was named after the Greek legend of Oedipus who unknowingly killed his father and married his mother. It's believed that children unconsciously desire their opposite-sex parent and view the same-sex parent as a rival. Boys realise that their fathers are far more powerful than themselves and fear they might remove their penises (they've already done it to girls). This castration anxiety causes boys to repress their desires for their mother and identify with their fathers (i.e. if you can't beat

Freud believed that children identify with the same sex parent to overcome threatening rivalry 'em, join 'em!). This is how boys develop their sense of gender identity. Girls suffer from penis envy, believing they've already been castrated. Their desire to have a child from their father results in them identifying with their mother. A male child can be thought of as their surrogate penis (see Chapter 12).

- the **latency period** (5/6 years to puberty): very little happens here. Children are so engrossed in play (primarily with their own peers) that sexuality is dormant
- **genital stage:** (puberty onwards): puberty begins and the components of the personality come together in adult genital sexuality.

- Freud's theory of psychosexual development is extremely important because in one single framework we can see how physical, cognitive, emotional, social, sexual and personal development arise. However, he has been criticised for over-emphasising the physical/sexual aspects of this.
- It's evident that, according to these stages, if you're frustrated or over-indulged in some way, then you'll have problems later in life. These problems lead to certain characteristics or personality types.

## Strengths and limitations of psychodynamic approach

✓ **Large impact on psychology:** The psychodynamic approach has been called the thumb on the hand of psychology – connected to the other fingers but set apart from them. Freudian ideas have had an immense impact on psychology and twentieth-century thought. Surely we all recognise aspects of defence mechanisms we've employed in the past (and will use in the future).

✓ **Importance of childhood:** Many psychologists now accept the importance of childhood on later life and development. They may not agree on the psychosexual stages, but place value on childhood experiences in shaping the later personality.

✓ **Importance of the unconscious:** Again, many psychologists recognise that the unconscious does play some part in determining our behaviour. Freud was one of the first to recognise this.

✓ **Wide applications:** Freudian ideas have found favour in diverse fields beyond psychology, such as literary criticism and art (symbolism). Freudian terms are used in everyday language (e.g. 'you're in denial'). Would this have happened with an approach that lacks merit?

✓ **Therapeutic applications:** The psychodynamic approach has been developed into therapy. Many people claim to have benefited from such therapies, although their effectiveness is still an area of dispute within psychology.

✓ **Neurological support for Freud:** There's an increasing body of neurological data using advanced brain scanning techniques that appear to support Freud's ideas of unconscious drives (Tallis, 2002).

✗•✓ **Over-emphasis on sex as a motivating force?** Can it really be true that so much seems to derive from the expression or repression of the sex drive? Freud managed to see the importance of sexuality in an age of very little obvious sexuality. Today, much behaviour is influenced by sexuality. Much of our behaviour is sexually motivated (particularly, I recall, when you're 17 years old!) and sex is seen in many aspects of today's society, from newspapers, television, advertising and so on. However, perhaps Freud took his ideas too far and didn't expect the sexual liberation of today's society. Ironically, Freud contributed to the permissive attitudes to sex we experience today.

✗ **Sexist approach:** Horney (1973) criticised Freud for his view of female inferiority and the idea of penis envy. Freud's theory is criticised as being 'phallocentric'. Horney believed that since men lack 'the wonderful womb, they fear and envy women and therefore force women into an inferior status' (Tavris & Wade, 1997).

✗•✓ **Unscientific approach:** A common criticism is that the psychodynamic approach can't be falsified. It's a 'heads I win, tails you lose' situation. It's impossible to refute the psychodynamic approach since the methods adopted are unscientific and open to interpretation. They're very subjective. The psychodynamic approach explains everything retrospectively but predicts very little. A good scientific theory should be able to make predictions about behaviour. Freud believed that scientific techniques weren't appropriate to investigate repression or dreams. However, some psychologists have argued it is possible to test the psychodynamic approach using traditional methods such as lab experiments. For example, Levinger and Clark (1967) tested the idea of repression using word recall of emotionally-charged words.

✗ Reductionist approach: The attempt to explain all behaviour using a strictly psychodynamic approach has led to criticisms that it reduces behaviour to an over-simplistic level of explanation.

## Methods used with the psychodynamic approach

Since much behaviour can't be explained at 'face value', it's important to tap into the unconscious to try to find out the motivation behind behaviour. Clinical methods which involve 'making the unconscious conscious' include:

- **free association:** this involves the uninhibited expression of thought associations. The analyst often begins such episodes by saying 'Tell me what comes to mind'. Sometimes situations might be described and patients asked what they think of immediately. For example, an analyst might ask how they'd react to a phone call that reveals the death of a particular relative. The associations people make are supposed to reveal aspects of the unconscious. To aid this process, patients in psychoanalysis recline on a couch with the analyst sitting behind them taking notes and sometimes suggesting interpretations of the unconscious material
- **word association:** this is where people are given a word or phrase and have to pair it with the first thing that comes to mind. For example, an analyst might suggest words such as 'father' and see what the unconscious reveals
- **dream analysis:** Freud considered analysis of dreams 'the royal road to . . . the unconscious'. The content of dreams is hidden in symbolism and imagery. The *manifest content* of a dream is the reported censored content and the hidden or 'real' meaning behind it is the *latent content*. By interpreting dreams closely, Freud believed he was capable of finding desires that his patients didn't want to face. The meanings of symbols are related to the actual context of the dream and therefore don't always hold constant. For example, a dream of entering a tunnel or climbing the stairs might be seen as symbolic of sexual intercourse. Similarly, a sword might be interpreted as a penis symbol. However, as Freud stated, sometimes a cigar is merely a cigar!
- **Freudian 'slips':** not a technique as such since Freudian slips (literally 'slips of the tongue') occur so infrequently. Nevertheless, Freud believed they can reveal inner, unconscious thoughts. It's reported that at a dinner at Oxford University a toast to 'our dear old Queen' was accidentally changed to 'our queer old Dean'. For a slip to be Freudian, the speaker would have had to be unaware of the slip and the thought should have been repressed. Either way, the Dean of Faculty was not amused!
- **hypnosis:** a technique used initially by Freud but later dropped when he discovered that people didn't recall information that they'd 'uncovered' during hypnosis
- **case study method:** Freud used case studies and anecdotes to illuminate his theory. This involves the detailed analysis and reporting of an individual or small group.

### ✗✓ Evaluation of methods used with the psychodynamic approach

✓ • ✗ Effectiveness of methods? Some people swear by these methods, arguing that they are the only methods available to us to try to uncover the unconscious. Freud saw himself as an archaeologist of the mind, scraping away layers of the conscious. Others argue that his methods reveal nothing and psychoanalysis is a fraudulent waste of time, money and effort. It's likely that this difference of opinion will continue for many years to come.

✓ Rich detail: The use of case studies provides rich, detailed information on an individual basis.

✗ Subjective nature of interpretation: What guarantee do we have that the things that do come to mind during free association or dreaming have any meaning in the sense of uncovering the unconscious?

**✗ Long-term and time-consuming:** In psychoanalysis, patients often see their analyst a couple of times per week for an hour a day. This can continue for several years. The attempt to understand and reveal the motives behind behaviour is a time-consuming (and hence costly) process.

**✗ Require intelligent and highly motivated individuals:** The psychodynamic methods are only really appropriate for articulate people with good verbal skills. After all, they need to try to tap into their unconscious thoughts and feelings. This 'talking cure' approach is not suitable for all individuals.

**✗ Case study bias?** Freud used clinical evidence from only his patient case studies. A major problem is that with this method the analyst will inevitably influence the patient's views on their behaviour. There's no second opinion to support any findings.

## EXAM tips BOX

**Stimulus material: Jim's Life of Grime**

Jim is 32 years old and has been involved in petty crime for a number of years. His parents went through a messy divorce when he was six years old. His Dad is now in prison for grievous bodily harm. Jim works as an occasional refuse collector but is not popular since he appears angry with his workmates and is disrespectful towards his boss. He has low self-esteem and generally leads a disorganised day-to-day existence.

(a) Describe how the psychodynamic approach might try to explain Jim's behaviour. (6 marks)*

(b) Assess one of these explanations of Jim's behaviour in terms of its strengths and limitations. (6 marks)

(c) How might one of these approaches investigate Jim's behaviour? (6 marks)

(d) Evaluate the use of this method of investigating Jim's behaviour. (6 marks)

*In the real exam, the question will ask you to describe any two approaches and will be worth 6 + 6 marks.

Try to answer this question yourself. There's a sample essay on pages 564–565 with which you can compare your essay.

## The essential psychodynamic approach

(a[1]) Summary of approach:

- developmental approach: oral, anal, phallic, latent, genital. Personality and behaviour are shaped by conflicts which occur at these different stages
- importance of unconscious – the source of motivation
- instinctual drives: *id* – basic desires; *ego* – reality manager; *superego* – conscience
- Defence mechanisms.

Research: can explain abnormal behaviours, memory, personality development.

(b) Evaluation

Strengths of approach:
- large impact on psychology
- importance of childhood on later life
- importance of unconscious
- wide applications
- therapeutic applications
- neurological support.

Weaknesses of approach:
- over-emphasis on sex?
- sexist approach
- unscientific approach? Explains everything, predicts very little
- reductionist approach?

(c) Methods used:

Goal is to make the unconscious conscious. Achieved through:
- free association: uninhibited expression of thought associations
- word association
- dream analysis: 'the royal road to . . . the unconscious' – symbolism: latent and manifest content
- Freudian slips: all we say and do has a cause – even slips of the tongue
- hypnosis: used at first by Freud but later less popular
- case study method.

(d) Strengths of methods

- effectiveness of methods?
- rich detail gained.

Weaknesses of methods

- subjective, interpretative
- long-term and time-consuming
- requires intelligent and motivated individuals
- case study bias?

[1] a, b, c, d refer to questions in exam.

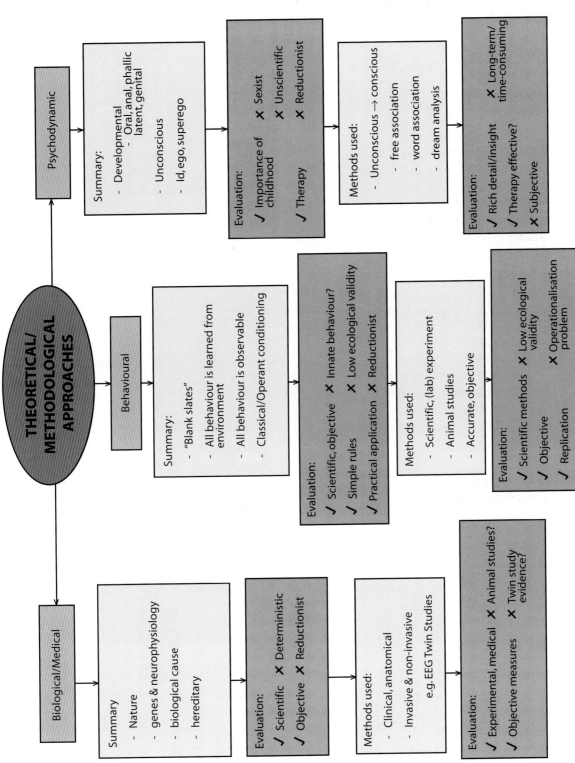

**THEORETICAL/ METHODOLOGICAL APPROACHES**

## Psychodynamic

Summary:
- Developmental
  - Oral, anal, phallic latent, genital
- Unconscious
- Id, ego, superego

Evaluation:
- ✓ Importance of childhood ✗ Sexist ✗ Unscientific ✗ Reductionist
- ✓ Therapy

Methods used:
- Unconscious → conscious
  - free association
  - word association
  - dream analysis

Evaluation:
- ✓ Rich detail/insight ✗ Long-term/ time-consuming
- ✓ Therapy effective?
- ✗ Subjective

## Behavioural

Summary:
- "Blank slates"
- All behaviour is learned from environment
- All behaviour is observable
- Classical/Operant conditioning

Evaluation:
- ✓ Scientific, objective ✗ Innate behaviour?
- ✓ Simple rules ✗ Low ecological validity
- ✓ Practical application ✗ Reductionist

Methods used:
- Scientific, (lab) experiment
- Animal studies
- Accurate, objective

Evaluation:
- ✓ Scientific methods ✗ Low ecological validity
- ✓ Objective ✗ Operationalisation problem
- ✓ Replication

## Biological/Medical

Summary
- Nature
- genes & neurophysiology
- biological cause
- hereditary

Evaluation:
- ✓ Scientific ✗ Deterministic
- ✓ Objective ✗ Reductionist

Methods used:
- Clinical, anatomical
- Invasive & non-invasive
  e.g. EEG Twin Studies

Evaluation:
- ✓ Experimental, medical ✗ Animal studies?
- ✓ Objective measures ✗ Twin study evidence?

# SAMPLE ESSAYS

Example examination questions

You have about 40 minutes to answer this question and it's worth 30 marks – this works out at just over seven minutes per approach for question (a) and seven minutes for each other part of the question.

We've produced some sample answers for each of the *three* approaches we've covered. For the part (a) question, we've covered just *one* approach each time in our answer but in the exam you'd have to cover *two*. Here, perhaps more than ever, there are many different ways of gaining top marks.

## STIMULUS MATERIAL: 'ONE FOR THE ROAD'

Kate was a very popular 'girl about town' who had lots of friends. She always used to go down the pub for a drink after work and was always the last to leave. Unfortunately, she did not always watch how much she had to drink before driving home and always enjoyed 'one for the road'. One day, she was stopped by the police who had noticed her erratic driving. She was later prosecuted for drink-driving and lost her licence.

(a) Describe how the biological approach might try to explain drink-driving. (6 marks)*

(b) Assess one of these explanations of drink-driving in terms of its strengths and limitations. (6 marks)

(c) How might one of these approaches investigate Kate's drink-driving behaviour? (6 marks)

(d) Evaluate the use of this method of investigating Kate's drink-driving behaviour. (6 marks)

## SAMPLE ANSWER: USING THE BIOLOGICAL APPROACH

(a) Describe how the biological approach might try to explain drink-driving.*
(6 marks – A01)

Kate's behaviour may be described in terms of the biological model as being the result of genetic inheritance. It's been suggested that alcoholism is genetically caused, which may explain the excessive manner of Kate's drinking habits. Perhaps there is a history of alcoholism in Kate's family. Indeed, Kate's family may be more susceptible to the effects of alcohol than other families. Kate may have some dysfunction with the neurotransmitter acetylcholine that has been implicated in both drinking behaviour and behavioural inhibition. Kate sounds like a very outgoing person and perhaps she finds it difficult to modify her (drinking) behaviour. Alcohol is likely to lead to a reduced anxiety level. This would mean she would be less concerned about her alcohol levels when setting out to drive home.

(This is enough for one approach – in the exam you have to cover two.)

*In the real exam, the question will ask you to describe any two approaches and will be worth 6 marks.

(b) Assess one of these explanations of drink-driving in terms of its strengths and weaknesses.
(6 marks – A02)

The biological approach is a highly scientific approach that uses objective measures to research and test its claims. There is a wealth of supporting studies that appear to show that certain traits are inherited and alcoholism would be one of these. Although heritability levels vary for different behaviours, it's likely that heritability of alcoholism is quite high. There are certainly studies that demonstrate different biological tolerance levels for consumption of alcohol. Alcoholism does appear to run in families but it's unlikely that drink-driving does to the same (or any) extent. Nevertheless, since we're all physiological machines the biological explanation for drink-driving in terms of reduced anxiety levels and the possible effect of faulty neurotransmitters must play a part in this behaviour. After all, no-one would argue that there's a biological effect of drinking; the question of interest is whether there's a biological cause.
Unfortunately, the biological approach has been criticised for only describing the processes of a behaviour rather than explaining it. The biological approach is therefore often seen as reductionist, in that it only accounts for physical processes in a certain behaviour, rather than explaining the reasons and motivations behind a certain behaviour, in this case, excessive drinking of alcohol. Related to this is the argument that the biological approach does not consider any psychological factors, that is, mental processes; it only accounts for physiological, and furthermore does not consider the interaction between the two forms of process.

(c) How might one of these approaches investigate Kate's drink-driving behaviour?
(6 marks – A02)

In a biological analysis of drink-driving, the bio-psychologist might first investigate Kate using non-invasive methods such as brain-scanning techniques. They might investigate which areas of the brain are most active when she's been drinking and see if these match any other mood states, thus allowing a comparison of the two. In addition, bio-psychologists might investigate Kate's family history to see if there is any evidence of heavy alcohol consumption among her relatives. It's possible that genetic tests might be made to investigate any genetic predisposition for alcoholism. In terms of a link to drinking behaviour, bio-psychologists have previously conducted invasive studies on animals to determine the physiological effects of alcohol on the body. Bio-psychologists might even give Kate precise measures of alcohol and ask her to drive on a driving simulator in order to measure and assess the precise effects that the alcohol has on driving behaviour. If Kate has any brothers or sisters, it might be possible to try to untangle the relative influence of environment or genetics on drink-driving behaviour.

**(d) Evaluate the use of this method of investigating Kate's drink-driving behaviour.**

(6 marks – A02)

The methods suggested above for investigating Kate's drink-driving behaviour largely involve scientific, laboratory methods. These involve a high level of control and reduce the possibility of confounding variables affecting results. However, they could be said to lack ecological validity since they don't truly replicate Kate's usual drinking circumstances (e.g. being in a pub environment with friends). According to other approaches, factors such as her being in the pub environment are crucial in attempting to explain her behaviour, although a biological explanation may consider such factors irrelevant, as the emphasis is on internal physiological processes. Nevertheless, most bio-psychologists would accept that the environment is likely to affect Kate's biological processes, as her mood would be altered and certain hormonal changes would be evident with this.

It can be argued in favour of the laboratory experiment that it allows objective measurements to be taken, for example of Kate's brain activity. However, this doesn't necessarily explicitly explain her behaviour, merely describes it and allows the psychologist to infer reasons for Kate's behaviour based on what the medical reports imply.

## Stimulus material: Football Hooliganism

Andy is a season-ticket holder at a Premiership club. He has a respectable job and is regarded as a 'good family man'. However, he has a number of arrests for football hooliganism. He often travels to home and away games with his friends and always seems to get involved in trouble.

(a) Describe how the behavioural approach might try to explain Andy's football hooliganism. (6 marks)*

(b) Assess one of these explanations of football hooliganism in terms of its strengths and limitations. (6 marks)

(c) How might one of these approaches investigate Andy's football hooliganism? (6 marks)

(d) Evaluate the use of this method of investigating Andy's football hooliganism. (6 marks)

## Sample answer: using the behavioural approach

**(a) Describe how the behavioural approach might try to explain football hooliganism.***

(6 marks – A01)

Behaviourism explains football hooliganism as behaviour that's learned and determined by the environment. Behaviourism focuses on objectively observable behaviour, rather than any internal processes. Behaviourists might propose three ways by which ordinary, peaceful football fans come to behave in such anti-social ways:

- classical conditioning involves learning by association, simply learning to associate the opposition's fans' taunts with aggressive behaviour. The stimulus (taunting) is followed by the response (fighting). The aggressive behaviour occurs as an automatic behaviour in response to the taunting. Andy has acquired this learning through experience and the process of discrimination ensures that his aggressive behaviour is restricted to hooliganism at football matches

- operant conditioning is learning by consequence; behaviour that is reinforced tends to be repeated as a reward is gained. In this case the reward is social approval of others also involved so the individual feels part of the group and is not socially rejected. Behaviour that is not reinforced or is punished tends to be extinguished. Andy can see no reward for ignoring the taunts and may actually be punished by his mates with social disapproval and ridicule if he doesn't respond aggressively

- Social Learning Theory, a form of behaviourism, proposes that people learn by observation and imitation, a process known as modelling. Andy may copy other fans' aggressive behaviours if he sees them being reinforced for their behaviour. For example, an aggressive hooligan may be reinforced by peer approval.

*(This is enough for one approach – in the exam you have to cover two.)*

**In the real exam, the question will ask you to describe any two approaches and will be worth 6 + 6 marks.*

**(b) Assess one of these explanations of football hooliganism in terms of its strengths and weaknesses.**

(6 marks – AO2)

Behaviourism is a scientific approach that uses objective, experimental methods. Learning theories have been examined in the lab and have been shown to apply in any number of situations, and football hooliganism is unlikely to be any different. Behaviourism has a number of practical applications and can both predict and control behaviour. Given the environmental factors that could be shown to influence Andy, it's likely that football hooliganism is the obvious behavioural end result.

However, behaviourism is a reductionist approach that ignores internal thought (cognitive and conscious) processes and any innate factors that may cause an individual to behave anti-socially at a football match. Behaviour is seen as determined entirely by the environment, not by free will. Surely, if Andy really wanted to behave at a match, he could? One of the main criticisms of behaviourism is that it reduces complex human behaviour to simple stimulus–response links. Although behaviourism is promoted as an approach to explain

# SAMPLE ESSAYS

# SAMPLE ESSAYS

all human behaviour, much of the background research has been conducted using animals in lab settings. Can Andy's episodes of football hooliganism really be compared to a pigeon pecking a disk for food?

### (c) How might one of these approaches investigate Andy's football hooliganism?
(6 marks – AO2)

A behaviourist would try to assess and measure the reinforcement Andy gets from acts of football hooliganism. Ideally, a behaviourist would be likely to test his or her explanation through the use of lab experiments because behaviourists believe that only observable behaviours count, and because they feel it is possible to reduce behaviour to simple cause-and-effect relationships. In this case, a behaviourist could observe Andy's behaviour as a result of a taunting stimulus. Perhaps Andy's behavioural responses could be measured in a lab situation when shown incidents from football matches or Andy could actually be observed at football matches. Accurate, objective observation would play an important part in any such study. Behaviourists would need to be clear what reinforcers were operating on Andy in the football-match situation, and learning responses would have to be carefully operationalised and measured accurately.

### (d) Evaluate the use of this method of investigating Andy's football hooliganism.
(6 marks – AO2)

An advantage of using an experimental, lab approach is that one can demonstrate cause-and-effect relationships under highly controlled conditions. This is important in order to be able to exclude any confounding variables from the study. However, this means that other factors that may influence Andy's behaviour (e.g. referee decisions, score or weather) may be overlooked. Laboratory experiments also tend to be quick, easy and cheap to conduct, so are an effective way of gaining scientific results. On the negative side, laboratory experiments are low in ecological validity as any lab stimulus cannot possibly replicate the passion involved in a football match. Demand characteristics in the lab situation may mean that Andy's results cannot be generalised. This limits their relevance. A lab study of football hooliganism is somewhat impractical; it might be preferable to observe Andy's behaviour at an actual football match. This method brings its own problems with a lack of control. A further problem concerns the operationalisation of behaviour. How easy would it be to observe which reinforcers are operating on Andy or indeed to measure Andy's level of football hooliganism?

## STIMULUS MATERIAL: LIFE OF GRIME

Jim is 32 years old and has been involved in petty crime for a number of years. His parents went through a messy divorce when he was six years old. His Dad is now in prison for grievous bodily harm. Jim works as an occasional refuse collector but is not popular since he appears angry with his workmates and is disrespectful towards his boss. He has low self-esteem and generally leads a disorganised day-to-day existence.

### (a) Describe how the psychodynamic approach might try to explain Jim's behaviour. (6 marks)*

### (b) Assess one of these explanations of Jim's behaviour in terms of its strengths and limitations. (6 marks)

### (c) How might one of these approaches investigate Jim's behaviour? (6 marks)

### (d) Evaluate the use of this method of investigating Jim's behaviour. (6 marks)

## SAMPLE ANSWER: USING THE PSYCHODYNAMIC APPROACH

### (a) Describe how the psychodynamic approach might try to explain Jim's behaviour.
(6 marks – AO1)

In terms of the psychodynamic approach, it is suggested that all behaviours have roots in childhood experiences. Jim's early experiences as a child should be considered. A psychodynamic approach might explain Jim's petty criminal activity as occurring as a result of an under-developed superego (conscience). Jim's id impulses are dominant and he wants immediate gratification of pleasure. He gains pleasure through acquiring stolen property. His ego cannot balance out the competing demands of his id and superego. There appear to be a number of defence mechanisms to try to cope with this conflict. Jim appears to have repressed his parents' messy divorce and also to be in denial about his father's imprisonment. His low self-esteem might be interpreted as the defence mechanism of 'turning against himself'. Finally, his disorganised approach to life could be indicative of Jim being fixated in the anal stage and being characterised as an 'anal expulsive' personality.

*(This is enough for one approach – in the exam you have to cover two.)*

*\*In the real exam, the question will ask you to describe any two approaches and will be worth 6 + 6 marks.*

### (b) Assess one of these explanations of Jim's behaviour in terms of its strengths and weaknesses.
(6 marks – AO2)

The psychodynamic approach has been highly influential in the field of psychology, with its emphasis on the importance of the unconscious and childhood processes affecting later development. It appears that Jim's childhood experiences may have played a part in his adult behaviour. Evidence to support the psychodynamic explanation can be seen in Jim's repression of his parents' divorce and his denial of his father's imprisonment. The explanation does seem able to account for much of Jim's behaviour.

However, the subjective nature of the psychodynamic approach is a weakness. Although Jim's behaviour can be explained in psychodynamic terms, it could equally well be explained in other ways such as the social learning approach. The psychodynamic approach is impossible to disprove and relies too much on interpretation to be regarded as a truly scientific approach. The approach can be seen as reductionist in that it reduces behaviour to instinctual drives and problems in childhood. There may be a number of other factors that explain Jim's behaviour which are not accounted for (e.g. poverty).

**(c) Analyse how one of these approaches might investigate Jim's behaviour.**

(6 marks – AO2)

It's most likely that Jim's behaviour would be investigated using an individual case study approach. Jim would probably visit a psychodynamic therapist on a number of occasions for a few months. Each session would last about an hour and involve Jim lying on a couch, with the therapist sitting out of view, making notes. A number of methods might be used to try to determine the root cause of Jim's behaviour. Methods would involve making Jim's unconscious conscious. In free association, Jim would be given time alone with the therapist, who would allow Jim to explore his thoughts and feelings without interruption. Although prompts may be given at the beginning of the session, Jim would be encouraged to express all thoughts immediately they came to mind. Occasionally the therapist might offer some interpretations of the reported material. This method might be coupled with word association, in which the therapist would suggest a series of words to Jim, to which Jim would respond by uttering the first thought or word that entered his head. From the nature of Jim's responses, there might be clues given which reveal aspects of Jim's unconscious.

**(d) Evaluate the use of this method of investigating Jim's behaviour.**

(6 marks – AO2)

It's obviously a difficult task to try to make the unconscious conscious. If this process is necessary to explain Jim's behaviour then free association and dream analysis might be two methods of achieving this. However, these methods rely to a large extent on subjective interpretation of reported material. How can we be sure that these methods do actually reveal the unconscious? Dream analysis is somewhat subjective; another therapist might make an alternative interpretation from the same material and evidence, showing that the method is not fully reliable. There might also be a question mark over Jim's capacity fully to understand the methods used. The 'talking cure' approach is not appropriate for all individuals, and favours articulate and highly-motivated individuals. It seems likely that Jim does not fall into either category. The effectiveness of these methods for explaining behaviour has been questioned. Jim may find that the therapy does him more harm than good and it may be that the methods are a waste of time, effort and money. There's also a danger that the therapist might influence Jim's views of his behaviour in a biased way. With no second opinion to rely on, Jim may become very confused as to why he behaves the way he does.

# SAMPLE ESSAYS

# A2 Exams and Coursework

## Psychology Specification A: The A2 Exams

Unlike the AS course, the A2 papers contain options and you only have to cover certain areas of the Specification and as a result will only be able to answer specific questions in the exams.

There are three units in the A2 course. They are:

## PYA 4: The options paper (15% of the A Level)

You have to answer **three** questions in 90 minutes. Questions must cover at least **two** different sections within the Specification. The sections are:

### SECTION A: SOCIAL PSYCHOLOGY

1. Social cognition (see Gross *et al.* (2000) pages 176–207).
2. Relationships (see pages 152–183).
3. Pro- and anti-social behaviour (see pages 183–233).

### SECTION B: PHYSIOLOGICAL PSYCHOLOGY

4. Brain and behaviour (see Gross *et al.* (2000) pages 272–303).
5. Biological rhythms: sleep and dreaming (see pages 234–268).
6. Motivation and emotion (see Gross *et al.* (2000) pages 331–362).

### SECTION C: COGNITIVE PSYCHOLOGY

7. Attention and pattern recognition (see Gross *et al.* (2000) pages 363–392).
8. Perceptual processes and development (see Gross *et al.* (2000) pages 393–432).
9. Language and thought (see Gross *et al.* (2000) pages 433–468).

### SECTION D: DEVELOPMENTAL PSYCHOLOGY

10. Cognitive development (see pages 268–317).
11. Social and personality development (see pages 318–354).
12. Adulthood (see Gross *et al.* (2000) pages 538–572).

## Section E: Comparative Psychology

13. Determinants of animal behaviour (see Gross *et al.* (2000) pages 573–609).

14. **Animal cognition (see Gross *et al.* (2000) pages 610–645).**

15. Evolutionary aspects of human behaviour (see pages 355–385).

Thus there are a total of 15 questions on the paper, of which you have to answer **three**. We've only covered the Essential (most popular) sections outlined in pink above. To cover the other sections you could use Gross *et al.* (2000) *Psychology: A New Introduction for A2 Level* (2nd edition) (London: Hodder & Stoughton).

The PYA4 exam is worth 30% of the A2 mark (15% of the overall A Level). In other words, each essay is worth 5% of your final A Level grade. Each essay in this paper is marked out of 24.

## PYA 5: The synoptic paper (20% of the A Level)

You have to answer three questions in two hours, one from each section.

## Section A: Individual differences

You're required to answer *ONE* question from THREE on:

- Issues in the classification and diagnosis of psychological abnormality (see Gross *et al.* (2000) pages 674–701).
- **Psychopathology (see pages 386–429).**
- **Treating mental disorders (see pages 430–457).**

## Section B: Perspectives: Issues and Debates

You're required to answer *ONE* question from four on:

**Issues**

**Two questions on: gender bias, cultural bias, human ethical issues, the use of non-human animals (see pages 458–493).**

**Debates**

**Two questions on: free will and determinism, reductionism, psychology as science, nature–nurture (see pages 494–540).**

Again, we've only covered the Essential (most popular) sections (in blue above).

## Section C: Perspectives: Approaches

Here you have to apply your knowledge of any two theoretical/methodological approaches to a novel situation or psychological phenomenon presented in the stimulus material. You're given two sets of short answer questions and have to answer *one* of these. While the stimulus material will change from exam to exam, the basic questions will remain the same.

## PYA6: Coursework (15% of the A Level)

You have to submit a project brief to demonstrate that you have thought through the design and analysis of your investigation. This is worth 12 marks. Copies of the project brief can be found in the Specification available from AQA (www.aqa.org.uk).

You also have to produce a report of one psychological investigation. This shouldn't be more than 2,000 words in length, excluding the project brief, tables, figures, references and appendices (see page 572 for more details on Coursework).

## WHAT IS 'SYNOPTICITY'?

Unsurprisingly, synopticity is assessed in PYA5: The Synoptic Paper! 'Synopticity' is defined as 'affording a general view of the whole' and addresses aspects of psychology that you may have covered elsewhere in the A Level Specification. The AQA Specification states that synopticity is: 'Having an understanding and critical appreciation of the breadth of theoretical and methodological approaches, issues and debates in Psychology'. In practice, this means that your answers should make links between different psychological approaches (e.g. biological, behavioural, psychodynamic etc.), different psychological issues and debates (e.g. ethics, culture bias, reductionism etc.) and different psychological methods (e.g. experiments, observations, field studies etc.).

You'll see that, in reality, it's very difficult to write an answer on PYA5 that doesn't involve a synoptic element. However, examiners stress the importance of including as much synopticity in your answers as possible. Synopticity should be included in AO1 and AO2.

## HOW THE MARKS ARE AWARDED IN THE EXAMS

The Specification requires you to demonstrate two main assessment objectives (AO1 and AO2). These are:

| AO1: Knowledge and understanding | Knowledge and understanding of psychological theories, terminology, concepts, studies and methods in all areas of the Specification and to communicate this knowledge and understanding in a clear and effective manner. |
| --- | --- |
| AO2: Analyse and evaluate | Analyse and evaluate psychological theories, concepts, studies and methods in all areas of the Specification and to communicate this knowledge and understanding in a clear and effective manner. |

In addition, the Quality of Written Communication is assessed in both A2 exams. There are a total of 4 possible marks in both PYA4 and PYA5. You need to:

* select and use an appropriate style of writing for the subject matter
* organise the information correctly and use appropriate vocabulary
* write legibly and use correct spelling, grammar and punctuation
* in addition, the meaning must be clear.

The answers in PYA4 are marked out of 24 whereas the answers for PYA5 are marked out of 30. In summary, in PYA4 these are as follows:

## PYA4: The options paper

### AO1: Knowledge and understanding

In 24-mark questions, there is a maximum of 12 marks allocated to knowledge and understanding (description). The marks are allocated as follows:

| 12-mark questions | Mark allocation |
|---|---|
| 12–11 | Content is accurate and well-detailed. Descriptions are coherent and there is substantial evidence of breadth and depth and a balance between them is achieved. |
| 10–9 | Content is slightly limited, although accurate and well-detailed. Descriptions are coherent and there is evidence of breadth and depth but a balance is not always achieved. |
| 8–7 | Content is limited although accurate and reasonably detailed. Descriptions are reasonable and there is some evidence of breadth and/or depth. |
| 6–5 | Content is limited and while descriptions are generally accurate, they lack detail. The answer is reasonably constructed and shows some evidence of breadth and/or depth. |
| 4–3 | Content is basic, rudimentary and sometimes flawed. Content is only sometimes focused and relevant. |
| 2–0 | Content is weak, muddled and shows incomplete understanding. Psychological aspects are just discernible. The answer may be wholly or mainly irrelevant. |

### AO2: Analyse and evaluate

In 24-mark questions, there is a maximum of 12 marks allocated to analysis and evaluation. The marks are allocated as follows:

| 12-mark questions | Mark allocation |
|---|---|
| 12–11 | Evaluation is informed and thorough. Material is used in a highly effective manner and shows evidence of appropriate selection and coherent elaboration. |
| 10–9 | Evaluation is slightly limited. Material is used in an effective manner and shows evidence of appropriate selection and coherent elaboration. |
| 8–7 | Evaluation is reasonable but limited. Material is used in an effective manner and shows coherent elaboration. |
| 6–5 | Evaluation is reasonable but limited. Material is used in a reasonably effective manner and shows some evidence of elaboration. |
| 4–3 | Evaluation is minimal, superficial and rudimentary. Material is of a restricted nature. |
| 2–0 | Evaluation is weak, muddled and incomplete. Psychological content of material is just discernible and may be wholly or mainly irrelevant. |

## PYA5: The synoptic paper

### AO1: KNOWLEDGE AND UNDERSTANDING (DESCRIPTION)

In 30-mark questions, there is a maximum of 15 marks allocated to knowledge and understanding (description). The marks are allocated as follows:

| 15 marks | Mark allocation |
| --- | --- |
| 15–13 | Content is accurate and well-detailed. Material is presented coherently and shows substantial evidence of breadth and depth. There's clear evidence of the range of synoptic possibilities suggested by the question. |
| 12–10 | Content is slightly limited, although accurate and well-detailed. Material is presented coherently and shows substantial evidence of breadth and depth, although not always a balance between them.<br>There's slightly limited evidence of the range of synoptic possibilities suggested by the question. |
| 9–7 | Content is limited, although accurate and reasonably detailed. Material presented is reasonably constructed and there's evidence of breadth and/or depth.<br>There's limited evidence of the range of synoptic possibilities suggested by the question. |
| 6–4 | Content is sometimes focused, but basic and lacking detail.<br>There's little evidence of the range of synoptic possibilities suggested by the question. |
| 3–0 | Content is weak, muddled and incomplete. Content is just discernible but mainly inaccurate. Answer may be wholly or mainly irrelevant.<br>There's little or no evidence of the range of synoptic possibilities suggested by the question. |

### AO2: ANALYSE AND EVALUATE

In 30-mark questions, there is a maximum of 15 marks allocated to analysis and evaluation. The marks are allocated as follows:

| 15 marks | Mark allocation |
| --- | --- |
| 15–13 | Evaluation is informed and thorough. Material is used in a highly effective manner and shows appropriate selection and coherent elaboration.<br>There's clear evaluation of the range of synoptic possibilities suggested by the question. |
| 12–10 | Evaluation is informed but slightly limited. Material is used in an effective manner and shows coherent elaboration.<br>There's slightly limited evaluation of the range of synoptic possibilities suggested by the question. |
| 9–7 | Evaluation is reasonable but limited. Material is used in a reasonably effective manner and shows some elaboration.<br>There's limited evaluation of the range of synoptic possibilities suggested by the question. |
| 6–4 | Evaluation is minimal, superficial and rudimentary. Material is used in a minimally effective manner and shows little evidence of elaboration.<br>There's minimal evaluation of the range of synoptic possibilities suggested by the question. |
| 3–0 | Evaluation is weak, muddled and incomplete. Material is not used in an effective manner and may be wholly or mainly irrelevant.<br>There's little or no evaluation of the range of synoptic possibilities suggested by the question. |

# Terms used in the exam questions

There are a number of (injunctions) terms that are used in exam questions. They relate to either AO1, AO2 or both AO1 and AO2. They are:

## AO1 TERMS: KNOWLEDGE AND UNDERSTANDING (DESCRIPTION)

*Define*: explain what is meant by a particular term

*Describe*: show knowledge of the topic

*Explain*: show understanding of the topic

*Outline/state*: offer a brief description of the topic

## AO2 TERMS: ANALYSE AND EVALUATE

*(Critically) analyse*: demonstrate understanding through a consideration of the different components of the topic

*(Critically) assess*: present an appraisal through a judgement of strengths and weaknesses of the topic

*To what extent*: present an appraisal through a judgement of strengths and weaknesses of the topic

*(Critically) evaluate*: make an informed judgement of the value of the topic

## AO1 AND AO2 TERMS: KNOWLEDGE AND UNDERSTANDING (DESCRIPTION)/ANALYSE AND EVALUATE

*Compare and contrast*: consider both the similarities and differences between the topics

*Critically consider*: show knowledge and understanding of the topic including strengths and limitations of the material cited

*Discuss*: describe and evaluate a topic area

## PYA6: Coursework (15% of total A Level)

What coursework involves and what needs to be done for the A2 assessment.

### OBJECTIVES

- To give direct experience of some of the methods used by psychologists to collect and analyse data.
- To understand the difficulty encountered when carrying out research and the problems associated with interpreting results and drawing conclusions from these results.

### INTRODUCTION

Progress in science depends on active communication between research workers in the same, and in related, fields. It's therefore essential to describe the results of empirical research as accurately and as effectively as possible. Some general advice on writing experimental reports is given below, including some of the conventions which apply to scientific reporting.

Replicability is essential in scientific enquiry. In principle, it should be possible for someone else to repeat your experiment. Report-writing skills are one of the main skills that psychologists have to learn.

### PURPOSE OF A COURSEWORK WRITE-UP

Put simply, it is the place in which you tell a story of your study:

- what was done
- why it was done
- what was found
- what it means.

This should be done clearly and concisely. The aim is to be explicit and avoid ambiguity. The reader will then be able to repeat the study in all its essential procedural features. Sometimes quite similar studies report different results. In order to work out why this happened, one needs full information about *what* was done. If you treat replicability as a goal, you will succeed with your coursework write-up.

REMEMBER: When in doubt, spell it out!

### SETTING OUT YOUR REPORT

There's no single correct way to set out scientific reports. In many cases it would be foolish to impose a rigid format since for some areas of psychology this could be quite impractical. The format suggested below should be taken as a guide for A2. If you divide your report into sections and give them clear headings, you'll assist the reader (and the marker) to understand your report without difficulty.

- TITLE
- ABSTRACT
- INTRODUCTION
- METHOD

- RESULTS
- DISCUSSION
- REFERENCES
- APPENDICES

## A2 Requirements

Candidates must produce *one* piece of coursework drawn from any area of the AS or A2 specification.

Data can be collected and analysed in groups of four candidates or fewer but the write-up must be each individual's own work. The appropriate method must be one of those covered in the Specification, namely, laboratory, field and natural experiments, surveys, observational studies and correlational research. The results must involve appropriate inferential statistics.

Candidates must complete a project brief form before starting any data collection, to check that ethical guidelines are being adhered to and to help with their planning of the coursework. Marks are awarded for the project brief form, up to a maximum of 12 marks. Copies of the psychology project brief proposal forms are available from AQA (www.aqa.org.uk).

## Suggested titles for coursework

Here are some suggested titles for coursework. Always be aware of ethical issues and associated safety issues when approaching participants. If children (less than 16 years of age) take part in any study, written informed consent must be obtained from them *and* their parents or guardian.

### Developmental Psychology

Because of the greater likelihood of ethical issues arising with this module, AQA advises that candidates should not select investigations from this area. However, some possible suggestions include:

- Is there sex-role stereotyping in British television adverts?
- Can Piagetian conservation experiments be replicated/modified?
- Is there a correlation between self-estimated IQ and gender and/or self-esteem?

### Individual Differences

Again, this module is one that is likely to have ethical issues associated with it, so care must be taken over the choice of an investigation from this area. However, some possible suggestions include:

- Is there an association between fear rating and experienced trauma? (questionnaire study)

### Social Psychology

- Who gets helped the most: men or women? (Male and female experimenters need to drop a pile of books.)
- Are women car drivers more compliant than male drivers?
- Will more women drivers than men stop for a pedestrian at a zebra crossing?
- Does the amount of violent television watched correlate with aggressive behaviour?
- Do smokers and non-smokers differ in their attitudes to smoking?
- What do people look for in a partner?
- Does the order of presentation of positive and negative traits affect overall personal evaluation?

### Physiological Psychology

- Does a placebo affect vigilance of psychomotor tasks? (Caffeine can be used as an apparent stimulant; both groups consume decaffeinated coffee; but one group is told that they have drunk caffeine.)
- Does invasion of personal space affect pulse rate?
- Do pheromones/scents affect pulse rate? (Some perfumes/aftershaves use pheromones, e.g. musk oil.)
- Do relaxation tapes work? (Relaxation tapes versus white noise; measure pulse rate or galvanic skin response to assess level of relaxation/stress.)
- Is there evidence of circannual rhythms in humans? (e.g. birth dates).
- Does grooming hair affect pulse rate or galvanic skin response? (In some animals it is supposed to be relaxing – is it the same in humans?)

### Cognitive Psychology

- Does listening to Mozart enhance problem-solving ability?
- Does self-esteem affect the time taken to extract embedded figures? (A hidden shape located within a complex figure.)
- Does perceptual set affect participants' interpretation of Leeper's Lady?
- Is perception of the Moon Illusion affected by context? (e.g. with or without horizon.)
- Are words or images remembered best?

- Does context affect memory recall?
- Do 'leading' questions affect eye-witness testimony?
- Is there a correlation between STM capacity and age in children? (STM capacity increases until age of 11 when magic number 7 is reached.)
- Is it true that the more bizarre the image, the better the recall?
- Are high-schema-expectancy items recalled better than low-expectancy items? (People recall items they expect to see in certain situations (e.g. desk in classroom) – these are high-expectancy items. They are less likely to remember items not usually in a given situation.)
- Is it easier to recall 'doodles' which are given an explanation or those which are not? (It is suggested that nonsense drawings are better recalled if they are given a thematic label that explains them.)
- Is recall affected by the state one is in during learning and subsequent recall? (Test of state-dependent recall.) Does current mood dictate recall of memories matching mood?
- Sleep and memory – is interference greater after a day's activity or a night's sleep? Does sleep help to consolidate memory?
- Does using a story to link unrelated words improve recall? (Use of narratives to aid recall of word lists.)
- Does similarity of interference tasks affect recall?
- Do a balancing task and reading use the same central processor? Manual balancing task for each hand while 'shadowing' prose. Do these two tasks draw on resources from the same processor? If so, reading aloud using the right hand to balance a rod will be harder than using the left hand and reading aloud.
- Are word lists recalled better than picture lists while participants 'shadow' prose? (Again, are there separate processors for different inputs/sense modalities? If so, recall of pictures will not be affected by shadowing, whereas learning and recall of words will.) [Caution: proper controls needed because images are better remembered than words.]

### Comparative Psychology

A visit to the local zoo may be needed here!

- Is there a dominance hierarchy in any herd species? (e.g. horses, zebras.)
- Is there a pecking order when feeding? (Based on age, weight, size, breeding etc.)
- Do certain primates favour particular hands?
- Do individuals in larger groups spend less time scanning? (Group size and vigilance (scanning behaviour) either humans or non-humans.)
- Is it possible to show latent learning in rodents?
- Is there an optimum group size for communication? (Optimum group size in humans is three, therefore communication should be greatest in groups of this size.)
- Do friends co-operate more than strangers? Or males more than females? Use the Prisoner's Dilemma strategy game.

## How to write your coursework

The report should be similar to a journal article. The report write-up should be no longer than 2,000 words, excluding tables, figures and appendices. It is usual to write up coursework in continuous prose, in the past tense, and to avoid colloquialisms. The report should have the following sub-headings:

### TITLE

This should be precise enough to give the reader a good idea of the topic you are investigating.

### TABLE OF CONTENTS

This is optional, but is best included, along with page numbers.

### ABSTRACT (APPROXIMATELY 150 WORDS)

This is a summary of your coursework and informs the reader whether it is worth reading any further! Obviously, the examiner will read on regardless! The abstract should include approximately two sentences from each of the other sections in your report: the theoretical background, the aim and hypothesis, the design method and participants, a brief outline of the results, the conclusion and suggestions for future research. Although the abstract comes first, it's usually best to leave the write-up till the end.

## INTRODUCTION (APPROXIMATELY 600 WORDS)

This answers **why** you carried out the study. It should include general theoretical background, identifying the main theories, controversies and investigations of the chosen topic. It's important to concentrate on relevant material. This section is very much like a 'funnel' whereby it starts off with a broad perspective and should lead on to the more precise aims and hypothesis under study.

### AIMS

The overall aim(s) of the study should be mentioned.

### HYPOTHESES

The precise experimental/alternative hypothesis should be included, along with the null hypothesis. These should be as precise as possible and unambiguous as possible. A justification of the direction of the hypothesis should be included (i.e. one-tailed or two-tailed).

The minimum acceptable level of significance should be stated; this is normally 5% ($p \leq 0.05$).

## METHOD (APPROXIMATELY 600 WORDS)

This covers what you did. All details of the method should be reported so that other researchers can replicate the study if they wish to. Materials used in the study, such as questionnaires, observation checklists and standardised instructions, should be included in the appendices. The method is split into several sub-sections.

### DESIGN

There are no hard-and-fast rules about what goes in the design section and what goes in the procedure section. The design section should cover:

- the choice of method such as laboratory experiment, observation and so on
- the type of design you used (e.g. repeated/independent measures or matched pairs)
- the choice of observational technique (if applicable) (e.g. time or event sampling)
- the identification of variables such as the independent variables, dependent variables and extraneous variables
- ethical considerations.

### PARTICIPANTS

This is where you describe your sample. This section should cover:

- the target population described in terms of relevant variables such as age, gender, socio–economic groups and so on
- the method you used to obtain your sample (e.g. random, opportunity and so on)
- the actual sample, in terms of how many participants there were, how they were selected and recruited, and described in terms of any relevant variables outlined above
- were participants naïve as to the purpose of the study? Did any participants refuse to take part or subsequently drop out?
- how participants were allocated to conditions.

### APPARATUS/MATERIALS

This section should include a description of any technical equipment involved and how it was used. The main point of this section is relevance. Only include materials that are directly relevant to the investigation, not trivial inclusions such as 'pencil and paper' (although this may be crucial to some studies!). Include relevant mark schemes for any tests or questionnaires in the appendix.

## STANDARDISED PROCEDURE

The aim of this section is to allow precise replication of your study. It's a step-by-step description of exactly how your study was conducted. You need to describe what happened in the order it happened. You ought to include details of where the study took place, any standardised instructions and debriefing procedures. If the instructions are lengthy, then it may be better to place them in an appendix. Try not to repeat information that has appeared elsewhere in your method section.

## CONTROLS

Sometimes this information is included in the design section. Controls to be mentioned would include counter-balancing, random allocation of participants to groups, single- or double-blind procedures, control of extraneous variables, and what steps were taken to avoid bias in the sampling or experimental procedures.

## RESULTS

This covers what you found and it's where you present the data you've collected. It needs to be presented clearly so that others can evaluate your work. The section should be written in connected prose with the support of tables and/or figures (graphs) which are referred to in your text. The main features of this section are described in more detail below.

There's an art in tabulating your data. If you organise yourself fully before you run your study, there should be no need to write out your raw data more than once. *Don't* insert it in the body of the text, but possibly in an appendix. Tables and figures in the text will typically be very abbreviated or summary versions of the raw data. Each summary table should be clearly headed.

Don't include any names of the participants in answer sheets or on questionnaires. Names should be treated as confidential information. One example answer sheet, questionnaire and so on should be included in the appendix.

### Descriptive statistics

Descriptive statistics are essential and give the reader a chance to 'eyeball' the data. You should try to summarise your results in the most appropriate graphical form. You could include numerical statistics such as measures of central tendency (mean, mode or median), measures of dispersion (range, standard deviation). Your aim must be to present the key findings in the most straightforward manner. Sometimes the choice of graph is a difficult one. Don't be tempted to include a number of graphs of the same data. Label tables and figures clearly so that the reader understands what the values represent (always specify measurement units), and number these tables and figures so that they can be easily referred to in the text. Tables should be numbered and titled above the table; figures and graphs below. Labels on axes should be unambiguous. Do not insert too much information. Make sure the figure makes optimum use of the space available. Join points on line plots with straight lines and not meandering curves. Try to make figures (graphs, histograms etc.) as visually pleasing as your teacher's (not easy perhaps!). Don't label figures or tables 'Figure to show . . . '. Use a simple but informative title about the variables displayed. Describe the key features briefly in the text, where appropriate. Don't provide both a table and a figure of the same data; this is wasteful of time and space. Decide which works best and choose that one!

### Inferential statistics

When statistical tests or analyses on the data are conducted, you should state clearly why you chose a particular test and what it tests for. This should be in terms of whether the data involve repeated or independent measures or correlational data. Calculations should not appear in the body of the text but should be shown clearly in an appendix so that a reader can follow them easily if necessary. Be clear about the outcome of the statistical analyses. In the main text, summarise the key findings and cite test statistics. You should include a statement on the observed and critical table values of the test, the significance level and whether the test was one-tailed or two-tailed. You must show that you understand what the results of your statistical tests mean. Do the results mean that you accept or reject your null hypothesis? Don't attempt to interpret the results at this stage; leave that to the discussion section.

## DISCUSSION (APPROXIMATELY 600 WORDS)

This covers what you think the results mean. The discussion section is worth the most marks and is split into four sub-sections (which should be clearly marked as such).

### Explanation of findings

This must begin with a clear description of the key findings. The findings should be stated in psychological terms in relation to the aims/hypotheses identified earlier. What bearings do your findings have upon the original hypotheses? State what your most important finding is and explain what this illustrates. *All* results are results. You must never ignore or dismiss findings that don't fit with previous findings. Science would not progress if scientists dismissed every finding that they weren't looking for. You should show why you obtained the results you did and what they show. A good researcher will themselves act as a participant before conducting a study. Alternatively, you may have conducted a pilot study. Reports by the participants themselves can be most informative. Often they give information about possible sources of error in the design or procedure. Also, participants tend to adopt different strategies, changing course in the middle of a study. They may not do what you want or expect them to do and such information can be included in the Discussion section either here in the 'Explanation of findings' section or in the 'Limitations and modifications' section (or both).

### Relationship to background research

This is where you account for and discuss your results in terms of previous research findings. You should refer back to the relevant research studies mentioned in your introduction. Mention any aspects of your design that may account for any differences in your findings and previous ones. If your results support previous reviewed work, then this section may be quite short although it's still worth emphasising any design or procedural differences that there may be.

### Limitations and modifications

Don't sidestep embarrassing findings or paradoxical results. If the study went 'wrong', try to locate possible sources of error. These might include measurement techniques, poor sampling, lack of controls and/or poor procedures. Even the best-designed study is likely to have some flaws or could have been conducted in a better way. Outline what was done, what was intended (this may not be the same) and how things might have been improved or modified.

### Implications and suggestions for further research

Questions to consider in this section include: If you were to repeat the study, would you alter the methodology in any way, and why? What further experiments are suggested to you by this experiment and its findings? Can you think of better ways of testing the hypotheses? Do you think that standard studies in the literature might be improved? Are there any other applications or implications that arise as a result of your findings?

When making suggestions for further research, do so only if they arise directly out of your results. Try to be precise with your suggestions and do not make general statements such as 'A lot more work needs to be done in this area'. Specific suggestions such as using more participants, eliminating confounding variables such as background environmental noise and improving standardised instructions are fine provided you have demonstrated that some of these factors have affected your findings in some way.

## CONCLUSION (APPROXIMATELY 50 WORDS)

Finally, you might end this section with a paragraph that recapitulates the key findings and conclusions which can be drawn from the study.

## REFERENCES

You should cite *only* authors' names and dates of publications in the text. You should list *all* references that you have cited in the text. The purpose of a reference list is to enable others to research the references. Thus, if in doubt, give as much information as possible.

Use the following standard format for your list of references:

i. **Journal articles:** author's name(s) and initial(s), year of publication, title of article (lower case preferred), *title of journal* (in full), *volume number*, page numbers. For example:

Shepard, R.N. & Metzler, J. (1971) Mental rotation of three-dimensional objects. *Science, 171*, 701–703.

ii. **Books:** author's name(s) and initial(s), year of publication, *title of book* (initial capitals for key words), place of publication, publisher. For example:

Gross, R. & Rolls, G. (2003) *Essential AS Psychology*. London: Hodder & Stoughton.

iii. **Chapters in books.** Combine aspects of (i) and (ii) by giving the author of the chapter and his/her chapter title first followed by 'In A. Smith (Ed.) ...', etc. For example:

Cohen, G. (1982) Theoretical interpretations of visual asymmetries. In J.G. Beaumont (Ed.), *Divided Visual Field Studies of Cerebral Organisation*. London: Academic Press.

iv. **Websites:** author's name(s), initial(s), year of publication, *title of website*, place of publication, publisher, available from: (Date accessed). For example:

Fink, M. (1990) *Max Fink discusses ECT.* Available from: http://www.psycom.net/ depression.central.ect.html (Accessed 15 March 2004).

## APPENDICES

As mentioned earlier, you should provide appendices containing the full instructions given to subjects, the raw data, and calculations for statistical analyses. In addition, if you've generated lists of words or other stimulus materials for use in your study they should be included as an appendix. The different information should be put in numbered appendices so that you can refer to them easily in your text. This isn't a rough-work section and all information should be presented clearly and unambiguously. It's perhaps unfortunate that such sections don't appear in published journal articles.

## GENERAL CONSIDERATIONS AND STYLE

This kind of report-writing is somewhat specialised. Clear and lucid descriptions are required and unsupported personal opinions and over-generalisations should be avoided. Only those conclusions warranted by your results should be drawn, and where speculations are made these should be made clear to the reader. You should write in connected prose throughout the report; *never* let it degenerate into a series of notes. It's preferable to write in the third person, past tense. This, along with many of the other points made in these notes, are conventions of scientific writing. Try to avoid slang, stereotyped phrases; these are often vague and ambiguous. However, reports do require imagination and creativity; they needn't be dull and tedious. Remember that it's doubtful that we ever 'prove' anything in psychology. Results may support a hypothesis, but 'prove' is definitely a word to avoid.

## ARE YOU COMPLETELY CONFUSED?

If you've never written a practical before, this information will probably be confusing or even terrifying. Don't worry; read through these notes a few times before you write your coursework report and discuss them with other members of the class.

On the following page, there's a coursework checklist designed to help you with the details required in a coursework write-up.

## A2 level psychology coursework checklist

Before you start your coursework, you should fill in the Psychology Project Brief Proposal Form. Your teacher should have a copy or you can get one from the examining board (www.aqa.org.uk).

The checklist that follows is designed to help with the details required in a coursework write-up. Follow the order of items in each section. Required length is 2,000 words.

[Mark allocations are shown in brackets]

# Coursework checklist

## TITLE
A short, precise title but more than three words. [ ]

## CONTENTS
All pages numbered. [ ]
Contents listed in appropriate scientific style. [ ]

## B          ABSTRACT (3)
Aim of the investigation. [ ]
One sentence about one relevant Research. [ ]
Method: e.g. Experiment/Observation? [ ]
Independent Design/Repeated Measures? [ ]
Sampling: e.g. Opportunist/Random? [ ]
Participants: number, age & gender. [ ]
Independent and Dependent variables (if relevant)[ ]
Result (including values of statistical analysis). [ ]
Level of Significance (e.g. $p \leq 0.05$). [ ]
Experimental or Alternative Hypothesis. [ ]
Hypotheses accepted or rejected. [ ]
Final sentence: Implication for behaviour. [ ]

## INTRODUCTION (10)
C1 (5)  Background psychological literature. [ ]
          Relevant research discussed concisely. [ ]
C2 (3)  Background linked to the aims with [ ]
          Reasons and some detail of method. [ ]
C3 (2)  Experimental/Alternative hypothesis. [ ]
          Null hypothesis. One-two-tail test? [ ]

## METHOD (4)
**D (a) Design**
Experiment/Observation/Questionnaire? [ ]
Independent Design/Repeated Measures? [ ]
Explanation of the design. [ ]
Independent & Dependent variables (if relevant) [ ]
Extraneous variables. [ ]
Removing bias e.g. Counter-balancing. [ ]
Any assumptions to be stated. [ ]
Conventional level of significance as 0.05. [ ]

**D (b) Participants**
Target population. [ ]
Sampling: e.g. Opportunist/Random. [ ]
Age range. [ ]
Numbers of each gender. [ ]
Allocation to conditions. [ ]
Did any decline or drop out? [ ]
Naïve. [ ]

**D (c) Materials**
Description and explanation. [ ]
Refer to Appendix page number. [ ]
Diagram of materials and location (if necessary). [ ]

**D (d) Procedure**
Explain the investigator's role. [ ]
Describe the participant's role. [ ]
Consent from and briefing of the participants. [ ]
Standardised instructions (refer to appendix). [ ]

Debriefing of and thanks to participants. [ ]

## RESULTS (8)
E1 (4) Draw up a summary table of data. [ ]
State result with calculated and critical values. [ ]
Level of significance. (0.05). No. of participants. [ ]
Give basic facts from graph(s) (e.g. range). [ ]
State in which appendix the raw data is listed [ ]
and where the statistical analysis is found.
Give a full justification of the choice of test. [ ]
E2 (4) Raw data in appendix (labelled). [ ]
Pooled data (where applicable in the appendices).[ ]
Relevant tables with full headings. [ ]
Statistical analysis in full (in appendix). [ ]
Relevant graph/s: Frequency plot of raw data/ [ ]
Bar chart/Scattergram/Pie chart etc. [ ]
Check headings and labels. [ ]
Analysis of graphs (e.g. trend/range of responses).[ ]

## DISCUSSION (12)
F1 (3) Outcome in terms of hypotheses including [ ]
result, critical value and level of significance. [ ]
Comment on the graphs related to the result. [ ]
F2 (3) Result linked to background literature and[ ]
research that agrees or disagrees with this result. [ ]
Be specific and quote research names from C1/2. [ ]
F3 (3) Possible sources of error. [ ]
Include any uncontrolled variables. [ ]
Be critical of any design fault. [ ]
Limitations (actual and possible). [ ]
Corresponding modifications. [ ]
F4 (3) Implications of further research. [ ]
Possible gender/age/cross-cultural issues. [ ]
Suggestions thoroughly discussed. [ ]
Research in terms of everyday behaviour. [ ]

## CONCLUSION
Key findings and conclusion. [ ]

## REFERENCES (2)
Sources quoted in conventional style. [ ]
Include all research names mentioned in C1/2. [ ]
In alphabetical order of surnames. [ ]
Include statistical textbook, computer
package and websites. [ ]

## APPENDICES
Number and title each appendix. [ ]
Diagram of materials/apparatus if relevant. [ ]
Standardised instructions. [ ]
Copy of test/questionnaire/survey. [ ]
Consent form (if necessary).
Raw data/Pooled data. [ ]
Statistical analysis: workings in full. [ ]
Graph/Scattergram/Pie chart (Supastat or Excel). [ ]
Reporting style (past tense, no pronouns). [ ]
Quality of language (use 'spellcheck'). [ ]

## AQA Specification A A2 Exam Summary

| Exam Unit | Time | Requirement | Sections | % of A Level |
|---|---|---|---|---|
| PYA4 | 1½ hours | **Three** essay questions from at least **two** sections | • Social Psychology<br>• Physiological Psychology<br>• Developmental Psychology<br>• Cognitive Psychology<br>• Comparative Psychology | 15% |
| PYA5 | 2 hours | **Three** questions, one from each section | • Individual differences<br>• Perspectives: Issues and Debates<br>• Perspectives: Approaches | 20% |
| PYA6 | n/a | Project brief and one investigation report | • Drawn from any area of the Specification | 15% |

**Key exam tips**

1. Make a revision timetable and try to stick to it.
2. Employ psychology: The optimum learning time is about 20 minutes. Reward yourself at the end of your revision sessions.
3. Revise with friends: Discuss revision strategies and topics with your friends. Share your difficulties with others – they might be able to solve some of the problems.
4. Start with the easiest topics: This will give you confidence and help you move through the material more quickly.
5. Know the Specification content. Questions can only be set from the Specification. If it's not on the Specification, it won't be in the exam. This is the 'Essential' ethos of this book.
6. Know the format of each of the exam papers. Remember the allocation of AO1 and AO2 marks.
7. Choose your questions carefully. Many students may have covered the bare minimum of topics for each exam. Make sure you answer the topic question you've learned. The questions appear in the exam in the order they are in the Specification. Therefore you should be able to work out which questions you're going to answer beforehand.
8. Answer the question. Don't waffle. It's quality, not quantity, that counts. Make sure all of your answers are relevant.
9. Time allocation: Allocate your time appropriately in the exam. Don't be tempted to spend more time on your favourite answers. The first few marks are the easiest to obtain; always answer the correct number of exam questions.
10. Practise exam questions: 'Practice makes perfect.' Remember that there are a limited number of questions that can be asked. The more past paper questions you practise, the better your examination technique will be. If you're fortunate, you may even have practised a question that comes up in the exam.

Finally, remember, examiners mark to the standard of a 'notional 17-year-old' – they don't expect perfect answers.

We hope you succeed and that this book has helped.

Good luck.

Be organised and you will remember more . . .

Suggestions for AS/A2 REVISION in PSYCHOLOGY

| RESOURCES: | used at student's discretion | | | | | |
|---|---|---|---|---|---|---|
| SPECIFICATION | TEACHING NOTES | SUMMARY OF NOTES | PAST EXAM QUESTIONS | ESSAY EXAMPLES | ESSAY PLANS/CARDS/ SPIDERGRAMS |
| AS/A2 AQA Selected paragraphs Know them well | TEXTBOOKS *Essential AS & A2 Psychology* (Gross & Rolls) | Plus: Your own notes from textbook | Summarise your notes into 15 bullet points per sub-section | Use past papers available from www.aqa.org.uk | Share with friends. Use sample answers from *Essential AS & A2* textbook | Make your own to summarise topics and possible exam questions |

- **ESSAY QUESTION**    Interpret the wording carefully.
- **INTRODUCTION**    *If* necessary, explain how you are interpreting the question.
  Some answers don't require an introduction.
- **DEFINITION**    Give a definition of the topic *if* relevant to the question.
- **RESEARCH EXAMPLES**    Support your answer with psychological research.
  Research names are not always vital and dates less so.
- **ASSESSMENT OBJECTIVE 1**    Identify clearly where you made DESCRIPTIVE AO1 points.
- **ASSESSMENT OBJECTIVE 2**    Identify clearly where you made EVALUATIVE AO2 points.
  It may help the balance of your answer to re-phrase some AO1 material into AO2. For example, rather than merely describing research, you state how it supports or rejects a particular explanation.
- **BREADTH AND DEPTH**    For top marks, both AO1 and AO2 are required.
- **COHERENCE**    Stay relevant to the question with a range of research and some detail.
- **CONCLUSION**    One sentence is better than nothing! Make some *new* AO2 comment.

(Adapted from Larcombe, 2003)

# 18-Mark (Part C) Exam Questions

## Introduction:

All the exam questions below are derived from the AS Exam Tips Boxes throughout the book. If you feel you could answer all the questions below then you'll be **brilliantly** prepared for the AS exam. Don't forget you'll have a choice of questions in the exam, so, with luck, **two** of them from each section topic should come up in some form or another and you'll have to tackle **one**.

You can think of the answer as writing three paragraphs, each about 100–130 words long. The first one could comprise the description (AO1) and is worth 6 marks. The final two paragraphs could comprise the commentary (analysis and evaluation (AO2)) and are worth 12 marks. You can, of course, mix the description and commentary throughout the three paragraphs – just remember the mark allocations for AO1 (6) and AO2 (12).

*Some examiners recommend you concentrate on writing just the AO2 commentary (analysis and evaluation) in your answer since the AO1 (description) will inevitably appear when you have to describe briefly the theories and/or studies you choose to analyse and evaluate. We've included most of the Part c questions you could be asked, but we haven't tried to cover every possibility. All the Part c questions which follow are worth 18 marks.*

## Cognitive Psychology: Human Memory

1. Briefly describe and evaluate research into the nature of short-term and long-term memory (e.g. encoding, capacity and duration).

2. Outline and evaluate the multi-store model (MSM) of memory.

3. Give a brief account of **one** alternative to the multi-store model (MSM) of memory and consider its strengths and limitations.

4. Give a brief account of **one** alternative to the multi-store model (MSM) of memory and consider its strengths and limitations.

5. Consider psychological research into explanations of forgetting in short-term memory.

6. Consider psychological research into explanations of forgetting in long-term memory.

7. To what extent is there psychological evidence to support the idea of repression in forgetting?

8. Briefly describe and evaluate research into the role of emotional factors in memory.

9. '*There are so many factors that influence memory that we cannot be sure that any memories are not merely biased reconstructions.*' To what extent does psychological research support this view of reconstructive memory?

10. To what extent has psychological research shown eyewitness testimony to be unreliable?

## Developmental Psychology: Attachments

1. Consider psychological research into individual differences in attachment.

2. Give a brief account of one psychological explanation of attachment and consider its strengths and limitations.

3. Give a brief account of and evaluate Bowlby's maternal deprivation hypothesis.

4. To what extent does psychological research show that deprivation is harmful to children's development?

5. Consider psychological research into the effects of privation on children's development.

6. '*While going out to work may benefit mothers of young children, the children themselves may suffer compared with those whose mothers stay at home.*' To what extent does psychological research support this view of the effects of day care on children's social development?

## Physiological Psychology: Stress

1. To what extent does stress play a role in cardiovascular disorders?

2. Consider research into the effects of stress on the immune system.

3. Consider psychological research into the role of life events as a source of stress.

4. Consider psychological research into the effects of workplace stressors.

5. To what extent have the effects of stress been shown to be modified by personality?

6. Give a brief account of psychological methods of stress management and consider their strengths and limitations.

## Individual Differences: Abnormality

1. Outline and evaluate the different attempts to define abnormality.

2. Briefly describe and evaluate the biological (medical) approach to abnormality.

3. Give a brief account of the psychodynamic approach to abnormality and assess its strengths and limitations.

4. Give a brief account of the behavioural model of abnormality and consider its strengths and limitations.

5. Outline and evaluate the cognitive approach to abnormality.

6. 'Anorexia nervosa is a biological rather than a psychological disorder.' Assess to what extent research supports the view that anorexia nervosa (AN) is caused by biological factors.

7. Outline and evaluate psychological approaches as explanations of AN.

## Social Psychology: Social Influence

1. Consider psychological research into majority influence (conformity).

2. Give a brief account of psychological explanations of conformity and consider their strengths and limitations.

3. Give a brief account of psychological explanations of obedience and consider their strengths and limitations.

4. To what extent can use of deception in social influence research studies be justified?

5. To what extent can ethical guidelines ensure that the major ethical issues involved in research with human participants are properly dealt with?

It's worth answering these Part c questions yourself using the textbook material and *then* comparing your answer with the SAs that follow. Ensure your answers:

• Are about the same number of words (could you write them in 18 mins?).
• Are divided up into the same AO1 (6 marks – one-third of essay) and AO2 format (12 marks – two-thirds of essay).

# COGNITIVE PSYCHOLOGY: HUMAN MEMORY

Briefly describe and evaluate research into the nature of short-term and long-term memory (e.g. encoding, capacity and duration). (18 marks)

### First paragraph: Description:

AO1: worth 6 marks

The main differences between STM and LTM relate to encoding, capacity and duration. STM tends to favour 'acoustic' coding whereas long-term memory tends to favour 'semantic' coding (Baddeley, 1966). STM has a limited capacity of 7 +/– 2 words (Jacobs, 1887) whereas LTM is regarded as having an infinite capacity. STM duration is very short (<18 seconds – Peterson & Peterson, 1959) whereas LTM can last a lifetime (Bahrick, 1975). Another key difference is that rehearsal is vital for STM whereas it is not essential for maintenance in LTM. People also tend to be aware of information in their STM whereas this is not necessarily the case with LTM.

*Note: It's not possible to describe all the studies supporting STM/LTM differences in the time available. Evidence to support these differences can come in later paragraphs.*

### Second and third paragraphs:

AO2: 12 marks

Many of the studies that demonstrate STM/LTM differences are robust, reliable and easily replicable. Evaluation of the research will cover encoding and duration differences.

Baddeley demonstrated that acoustically similar words are recalled less well than acoustically dissimilar words in a STM task and that semantically similar words are recalled less well in a LTM task. However, the STM difference was quite small (64% to 71%), suggesting semantic coding does occur in STM (as does some visual). Also, we can recall holiday places, smells, tastes and faces extremely well from LTM, suggesting that LTM can, and does, use more than merely semantic coding.

The Peterson and Peterson STM duration study used nonsense trigrams that students had to remember for differing time periods whilst completing a distractor task. Criticisms of this study are that nonsense syllables lack ecological validity in that they do not represent everyday memories. Furthermore, the sample of students may not be representative of the wider population and third, the distractor task introduced another cognitive processing task that, although preventing rehearsal, might also have led to some interference. However, it has to be accepted that a 'number counting' distractor task would be least likely to interfere with a 'letter recall' task. The Bahrick (1975) study testing 440 participants on their recall of high school friends demonstrated the duration of LTM. This study used everyday, real-life memories of a large and diverse age sample and as a result the findings of very long-term memories (VLTM) were ecologically valid and important. However, the study inevitably lacked some important controls such as whether participants had 'refreshed' their memories in the intervening period since school by reminiscing with friends or by viewing their old yearbook. To be fair, Bahrick did try to examine this influence.

*Note: Two different characteristics of STM and LTM along with analysis and evaluation of the relevant research have been covered.*

---

## [Second question]

AO1: worth 6 marks

### First paragraph: Description:

Atkinson and Shiffrin (1968) believed there were three components of memory (sensory memory, STM and LTM). Sensory memory processes only about 1/20th of the information received through the senses – it is the 'gatekeeper of information'. The information selected is passed onto the STM that has a limited capacity (+/– 2 magic 7) and duration (30 seconds). Through rehearsal, information is transferred from STM to LTM. The longer information is rehearsed in STM the more likely it is that information will be transferred from STM to LTM for more permanent storage. Information in STM not rehearsed will be quickly forgotten.

*A diagram of the multi-store model would be appropriate but the description is essential.*

### Second and third paragraphs:

AO2: 12 marks

Experiments support the multi-store model by demonstrating differences between STM and LTM with respect to encoding, duration and capacity. They demonstrate that STM favours acoustic encoding (semantic in LTM) and has a far smaller capacity and duration than LTM (Baddeley, 1966). These findings are robust and replicable both within a laboratory and in a more real-life setting. The serial position curve study (Murdock, 1962) strongly supports the notion of two separate stores with the primacy effect demonstrating LTM (through acoustic rehearsal) and the recency effect demonstrating STM. Work in the clinical field also gives weight to the STM/LTM distinction. Studies such as KF (Shallice & Warrington, 1970) whose LTM was fine but STM was poor support this idea of dual stores. However, the MSM does not explain how KF's LTM can remain normal with STM so poor since *all* information is supposed to be processed through STM. Since case studies deal with 'one-off' situations this evidence must be treated with caution.

However, the MSM is criticised for being over-simplified, passive and a linear ('one-way') model. It is argued that it is not rehearsal itself that is important but what we do with the information (Bekerian & Baddeley, 1980). For example, the model does not easily explain flashbulb memories. Researchers have suggested that the LTM (episodic, semantic and procedural) and STM (working-memory model) are split into several different, not unitary, stores. Studies have shown that LTM is actively involved in all aspects of memory and also demonstrate the two-way flow of information between the STM and LTM and hence challenge the idea that STM contains only new information (Morris *et al*, 1985).

*Note: We've written one paragraph supporting the model and one criticising it. You could choose to write two paragraphs either supporting OR rejecting the model.*

---

# EXAM QUESTIONS

# SAMPLE ANSWERS (SAs)

Give a brief account of ONE alternative to the multi-store model (MSM) of memory and consider its strengths and limitations. (18 marks)

First paragraph: Description:
AO1: worth 6 marks

Baddeley and Hitch (1974) proposed that the STM should be replaced by a system that allows several pieces of information to be processed and interrelated concurrently (hence 'working memory' title). They argued that STM was far more complex than just a 'stopping-off' station for information to transfer to LTM. The components are: the central executive, in overall charge, which is an attentional system of limited capacity allocating resources to the other 'slave' systems. These are the articulatory loop (a verbal rehearsal system or inner voice), the visuo-spatial sketch pad (a visual rehearsal system or inner eye) and, later, the primary acoustic store or phonological store (auditory system or inner ear).

Note: A diagram of the working memory model would be appropriate but the description is essential.

Second and third paragraphs:
AO2: 12 marks

There are a number of positive points that can support the working-memory model. Psychologists generally accept that STM is better viewed as comprising a number of different processing systems and is more realistic in explaining how memory works in everyday life. Each of the components is supported by experimental evidence, for example, dual task studies (Baddeley, 1973). The model is supported by physiological evidence from PET scans where different brain areas have been shown to be active during different STM processing tasks. These areas correspond to the model's components. Such studies involve 'normal' patients and evidence can be more easily generalised than those using case studies. Nevertheless, brain-damaged patients who suffer selective deficits to their STM also support the model (e.g. KF's motorcycle accident mainly affected only verbal information – Warrington & Shallice, 1970).

Weaknesses of the model include the fact that we know least about the most important aspect of the model, namely, the central executive store. Since its precise function is unknown it has been argued that this is as inappropriate as one single STM store. Also, the capacity of the central executive has never been measured. A further criticism is that the model does not explain changes in processing ability that occur as the result of practice or time. Much of the evidence to support the model has been confined to the laboratory and it may therefore fail in what it claims to do, that is, explain memory in real-life settings. Even Baddeley stated: 'We have a long way to go before we can be sure of the details of the model'.

Note: We've chosen the Working Memory model here as an alternative to the MSM and written one paragraph supporting the model and one criticising it. You could choose to write two paragraphs either supporting OR rejecting the model.

---

Give a brief account of ONE alternative to the multi-store model (MSM) of memory and consider its strengths and limitations. (18 marks)

First paragraph: Description:
AO1: worth 6 marks

Craik and Lockhart (1972) Levels of Processing (LOP) approach stated that memory should not be viewed as a 'structural' model but rather a process – it's not where information goes that's important but what we do with it. They see memory as the by-product of the processing of information: the durability of the memory is a function of the depth of processing. They believe that stimuli are processed through a series of levels that become progressively more complex. The simplest level is 'visual' (analysing material by the shape of the word), 'acoustic' (analysing material according to its sound) and 'semantic' (analysing material by its meaning). The level used depends on both the nature of the stimulus and the processing time available.

Second and third paragraphs:
AO2: 12 marks

The LOP approach changed the direction of memory research from searching for simple models to looking for complex processes. Experimental work supports the superiority of semantic processing. Craik and Tulving's (1975) experiment demonstrated that words that are semantically encoded by participants are significantly better recalled than acoustically or visually processed ones. These results have also been supported by experiments by Hyde and Jenkins (1973). The LOP approach also makes 'cognitive sense'. Imagine trying to learn all your AS material by sound or visual analysis; you have to understand the meaning of the material to process it deeply and hence recall it later.

The LOP approach is too simplistic and descriptive rather than explanatory. It presents a circular argument in that there is no independent way of measuring depth. The model predicts that deep processing will lead to better retention and, in turn, better retention is taken as evidence for deeper processing. Another criticism is that depth of processing may not be the only factor influencing retention. Tyler et al (1979) showed that difficult anagrams were later recalled better than simple anagrams. The LOP approach would suggest they should be recalled equally well since they were processed at the same semantic level. However, this criticism may have been answered to some extent since later research extended 'depth' to include 'organisation', 'distinctiveness', 'elaboration' and 'effort'.

Note: We've chosen the Levels of Processing model here as the alternative to the MSM. Although we've tried to stick to the three-paragraphs format, description (AO1), 'for' and 'against' paragraphs (AO2), inevitably sometimes AO1 and AO2 come into each of the different paragraphs. This doesn't matter. Just ensure that one-third of the material you present is descriptive (AO1 = 6 marks) and two-thirds analysis and evaluation (AO2 = 12 marks).

Consider psychological research into explanations of forgetting in short-term memory. (18 marks)

First paragraph: Description:                                    AO1: worth 6 marks

The trace decay theory suggests that stimuli create nerve cell activity in the brain but it may not be strong enough to create a structural neural change. Thus, a memory trace or engram would be encoded in STM but would not have made a permanent trace in the LTM. Metabolic processes degrade the trace (unless it is maintained by repetition and rehearsal), which means the memory rapidly fades from STM. Whilst trace decay focuses on time, displacement theory focuses on capacity. STM has a capacity of $7 +/- 2$ and therefore in order to hold more information, old information has to be displaced or 'pushed out'. This old information is thus forgotten.

Second and third paragraphs:                                  AO2: 12 marks

Displacement theory is supported by Waugh and Norman's serial probe task where 16 digits are presented at a rate of either one or four per second. One of the digits (the probe) is repeated and participants must report the digit that followed this probe. When the probe is given near the end of the list, recall is good; but when it is near the beginning, recall is poor. This supports displacement theory since it is assumed that later ones displace the earlier probe. However, this finding can also support decay theory since the earlier the probe is in the list the more time it has to decay. To further support decay theory, they used the different presentation rate conditions and found that the faster the list was presented, the better the recall. Although Shallice (1967) later confirmed these findings, it was found that elapsed time (decay) was less influential than number of subsequent items (displacement). One criticism is that decay and displacement cannot be easily separated.

Peterson and Peterson's STM duration study supports the decay theory since they demonstrated that information was largely lost from STM after an 18-seconds delay. However, the rehearsal prevention task (counting backwards) may have interfered or displaced the original material, thus questioning support for decay theory. Reitman (1971) cleverly overcame this problem by using a 'tonal attention' intervening task. She obtained similar results supporting decay theory without the associated problems of interference or displacement. All of these studies are laboratory-based and most often involve rather meaningless lists to learn. The value of such results to everyday memory can be questioned.

Note: The question asks for explanations so you have to include at least TWO: trace decay and displacement. A more difficult question could ask you how much research into forgetting has revealed about the nature of STM and LTM. You'd have to deal with STM/LTM differences (see earlier) and then evaluate studies that demonstrate these such as Waugh and Norman (1965), Murdock (1965) and Babrick et al. (1975).

Consider psychological research into explanations of forgetting in long-term memory. (18 marks)

First paragraph: Description:                                    AO1: worth 6 marks

Interference occurs because memories interfere with and disrupt one another. In retroactive interference, new memories can disrupt old memories. Proactive interference is when old memories disrupt new memories. Retrieval failure is another explanation of LTM. It suggests that failure to recall memories occurs because there are insufficient cues or clues to help locate the memory. This explanation suggests that the memory is not accessible at a particular point in time. The 'tip of the tongue' phenomenon, state- and context-dependent studies demonstrate retrieval-failure forgetting.

Second and third paragraphs:                      AO2: 12 marks (some AO1)

Many experiments using meaningless word lists and nonsense syllables and the paired associate word technique have demonstrated interference in the laboratory (Keppel & Underwood, 1962). However, these procedures (and thus the findings) do not seem to apply to everyday life. Interference theory seems to explain laboratory studies that involve learning compressed in time but not learning that occurs in 'real life' with more meaningful material (Solso, 1995). It would seem from interference experiments that the more material we try to remember, the more likely there is to be interference. However, experts in a particular field with great pre-existing knowledge (and thus the greater likelihood of interference effects) tend to suffer from less interference when they try to learn new relevant information than a 'novice'.

There are numerous studies that support the idea of retrieval-failure forgetting. Godden and Baddeley (1975) found evidence for context-dependent retrieval with their study of divers recalling and learning information underwater or on dry land. However, Fernandez and Glenberg, despite trying to replicate context-dependent studies, have never found reliable evidence for such claims. Goodwin (with alcohol) and Darley (with marijuana) have also found state-dependent effects, although the ethical stance of such studies has been questioned. Ucros (1989) with a meta-analysis of the effect of mood on retrieval found rather weak support for it. Support cited for retrieval-failure theory of forgetting comes from both within and outside the laboratory. Indeed, returning to one's old school, tasting or smelling something one has not experienced for years often appears to trigger 'long-lost' memories and this led Eysenck to conclude that 'it seems probable that this (retrieval failure) is the main reason for forgetting in LTM'.

# SAMPLE ANSWERS (SAs)

## To what extent is there psychological evidence to support the idea of repression in forgetting? (18 marks)

**First paragraph:**  **Description: AO1: worth 6 marks**

Freud claimed that some forgetting is motivated and the mechanism for this is repression. Freud believed that we forget things that are a source of anxiety and/or guilt. These memories are not lost (i.e. they are inaccessible) but they are no longer in the conscious mind (i.e. they are inaccessible). Freud used the example of 'Freudian slips' to explain this. This refers to a situation when one word is 'accidently' replaced with another. Freud claimed that this was due to an unresolved conflict and that 'innocent forgetting' simply did not exist.

**Second and third paragraphs:**  **AO2: 12 marks (some AO1)**

Much of Freud's claims were based on clinical case studies. Also in support of Freud's theory, Parkin claimed that repression could be related to psychogenic amnesia caused by severe emotional shock (as opposed to physical trauma or disease). Parkin claimed that repression was beneficial to sufferers of post-traumatic stress disorder (PTSD) and presented clinical studies to demonstrate this. It has also been suggested that 'recovered memories' of sexual abuse from childhood are evidence of repression. However, this is a highly controversial area with serious moral and ethical implications and there has been conflicting evidence to support these claims.

One of the major criticisms of repression is that there is very little scientific, quantitative data to support it. However, some argue that this is because it is difficult and often unethical to study the effects of emotional stress. Despite this, Kline argues that you can adequately demonstrate repression in the laboratory. He told participants that they had failed a test and asked them to recall questions from the test at a later date. He found relatively poor recall scores for those given the negative feedback of failing the test compared to those participants given their correct scores. However, Eysenck disputed these results by pointing out that similar poor recall scores were present in participants given 'success feedback'. Eysenck believed that poor recall was due to the high state of arousal in that particular participant, not the negative feedback. However, other laboratory research has reported evidence of repression (Levinger & Clark, 1961).

Overall, Freud's theory was largely derived from rather subjective case studies and findings cannot be generalised because they concern individuals. Also, there is far more scientific and reliable evidence to support other theories of forgetting such as retrieval-cue failure and interference.

*Note: You don't have to provide a balanced argument – you can take one side or the other.*

## Briefly describe and evaluate research into the role of emotional factors in memory. (18 marks)

**First paragraph: Description:**  **AO1: worth 6 marks**

Emotional factors do appear to influence memory; some seem to minimise forgetting and others seem to increase it. State-dependent studies that investigate physiological factors present at encoding and recall have shown that good moods can reduce forgetting. McCormick and Mayer supported this with regard to happy memories. According to Freud, anxiety-provoking memories are deliberately forgotten or repressed and thus increase forgetting. An extremely detailed and vivid memory of an event or incident is called a 'flashbulb' (FB) memory and these are more likely if the event is personally and emotionally significant. FB memories thus reduce forgetting.

**Second and third paragraphs:**  **AO2: 12 marks (some AO1)**

Freud reported case studies that he believed demonstrated motivated forgetting. However, such case studies lack objectivity and findings cannot be generalised to a wider population. Studies of patients with psychogenic amnesia support the idea of severe emotional trauma causing forgetting (Parkin, 1993) as do studies that report 'recovered' memories of child abuse (Williams, 1994). Due to ethical considerations, experimental evidence of repression is difficult. But Levinger and Clark (1961) showed that emotionally-charged words were more difficult to recall than neutral ones. However, the poorer recall of the emotional words could have been because they were more difficult to visualise than the neutral words!

Conway et al. (2003) support the existence of FB memory since 75% of Americans had near-perfect recall of the September 11th 2001 tragedy. However, they've only tested FB memories up to one year later. Brown and Kulik's (1977) 'racial relevance' findings also support the idea that emotionally-arousing events cause unforgettable memories. However, other studies question the accuracy of FB memories. Wright (1993) found people reporting inaccurate memories for the Hillsborough tragedy but it can always be claimed that events not remembered do not fit the criteria required for a FB memory (e.g. unexpected, emotionally and personally significant). It has also been claimed that FB memories are not forgotten because they are repeated over and over again. Repeated rehearsal of any memory aids recall and emotional factors do not play a significant part in FB memories.

It would seem that emotional factors can help remembering and in some cases they can increase forgetting.

*Note: A difficult question since so much information could be included. Note that some AO1 appears in the last two paragraphs and some AO2 occurs in the first paragraph. This doesn't matter – it's perhaps a little artificial for us to separate them out. We've done this to try to aid clarity. You can mix description and analysis & evaluation throughout the paragraphs. Just remember the proportion of marks available for AO1(6) and AO2 (12).*

## To what extent has psychological research shown eyewitness testimony to be unreliable? (18 marks)

### First paragraph: Description:
A01: worth 6 marks

There are numerous studies that question the accuracy of EWT. Loftus has shown consistently with numerous experimental studies that EWT can be influenced by people's willingness to make their memories fit their schemas. Loftus and Palmer (1974) showed the effect of changing a single verb on witness statements of the speed of a crashing car. Using the verb 'smashed into' led to a faster speed estimate (41 mph) than use of the verb 'contacted' (32 mph). Loftus (1975) also provides evidence that the style of questioning used with eyewitnesses can actually distort memories. Eyewitnesses asked about a car passing a barn on a country road were later more likely to report having seen a barn when, in fact, the barn did not exist.

### Second and third paragraphs:
A02: 12 marks (also some A01 included)

Criticisms of many of these studies are that they are low in ecological validity in that they do not take place in real-life situations and that the emotional effects associated with seeing such incidents may affect memory recall and that this is unlikely to be replicated in the laboratory setting. In addition, most of the studies used students as participants so there are questions as to the generalisation of the findings. Other factors such as race, clothing and social influence have been shown to affect the accuracy of EWT.

However, Baddeley questions whether EWT research is so clear-cut. He argues that research does not prove destruction of the memory trace but merely interference with its retrieval. This suggests that reconstructive questioning of witnesses is all-important. Yuille and Cutshall (1986), using witnesses to a real-life serious crime (in contrast to Loftus' methodology), found memories to be accurate, detailed and not easily distorted: in essence, EWT can be very reliable. Foster et al. (1994) also found memories for real-life crimes to be more accurate than simulations. In summary, it is suggested EWT can be inaccurate if misleading information concerns insignificant details and if witnesses have little reason to distrust it.

---

## 'There are so many factors that influence memory that we cannot be sure that any memories are not merely biased reconstructions.' To what extent does psychological research support this view of reconstructive memory? (18 marks)

### First paragraph: Description:
A01: worth 6 marks

Bartlett (1932) was one of the first psychologists to question the accuracy of memory and to suggest that all memories are reconstructed based on prior knowledge and experiences (schemas). He claimed that remembering is an active process which involves 'effort after meaning', that is, making the past more coherent to fit in with existing knowledge. Schemas are an important factor in memory reconstruction since they allow people to interpret their world and events in a simplified and stereotyped way. This can also lead to inaccurate memory reconstructions.

### Second and third paragraphs:
A02: 12 marks (also some A01 included)

Bartlett's (1932) classic study into the 'War of the Ghosts' supports the reconstructive nature of memory by showing that reproductions of an unfamiliar story are altered in significant ways. For example, the reproductions are shortened and made more coherent (intrusions, omissions and normalisation) from the cultural viewpoint of the participant. However, the methodology employed by Bartlett was questionable. The analysis of the story reproductions was subjective and the stories used were culturally unfamiliar and, as such, do not represent everyday memories. Allport and Postman (1947) also support the reconstructive nature of memory with their study demonstrating the effect of racial stereotyping. Both of these studies are exceptionally old and the Allport and Postman, in particular, may not be so valid today.

EWT is a particular aspect of memory where research predominantly supports the view that memory is reconstructive. Loftus has conducted numerous studies which illustrate this. However, again there are criticisms of her work in that most of it involved laboratory experiments using film clips of incidents rather than real-life events. A contrasting view is that of Yuille and Cutshall (1989) who, using a real-life shooting incident, showed that memories are not so easily reconstructed, even when using misleading questions. Further support from Wynn and Logie (1998) using real-life events suggests that memories are very accurate and not subject to reconstruction, and the accuracy of flashbulb memories is not easily explained using the reconstructive idea of memory.

Note: You could choose to answer this question using EWT research exclusively. There is certainly enough information in EWT to do this successfully. However, this answer predominantly deals with Bartlett, schemas and related research.

# EXAM QUESTIONS

●●●●●●

# SAMPLE ANSWERS (SAs)

## DEVELOPMENTAL PSYCHOLOGY: ATTACHMENTS

Consider psychological research into individual differences in attachments. (18 marks)

First paragraph: Description:

AO1: worth 6 marks

Ainsworth *et al.* (1971, 1978) devised the Strange Situation, a method for studying attachments in one-year-olds. This consists of eight episodes, involving the baby, its mother, and a female stranger. They were most interested in the baby's reunion behaviours. Ainsworth *et al.* identified three types of attachment. 70 per cent were classified as securely attached (Type B). They became upset when the mother left the room, and wanted her to comfort them as soon as she returned. 15 per cent were classified as anxious-avoidant (Type A). These babies were indifferent towards their mother, and barely reacted when she returned. 15 per cent were anxious-resistant (Type C). They became quite distressed when the mother left, but when she returned they showed ambivalence towards her. Many other studies have been conducted using the Strange Situation, including cross-cultural studies.

Second and third paragraphs:

AO2: worth 12 marks

Ainsworth *et al.*'s study is the most important in all of attachment research. But the sample was small. However, several more recent studies, using larger samples, have supported their original claim that the mother's sensitivity determines whether the baby is securely or insecurely attached (van Ijzendoorn & Schuengel, 1999). Cross-cultural studies using the Strange Situation have shown important differences, both within and between cultures. For example, Van Ijzendoorn and Kroonenberg (1988) reviewed the research. They found that although Type B is the most common type, Type C in Israel and Japan. This suggests that the Strange Situation may not be equally valid as a way of measuring attachment in different countries.

Attachment types are often regarded as fixed characteristics of the child. But if the family's circumstances change (such as the mother's stress levels), the child's attachment type can change. This couldn't happen if attachment style were a fixed characteristic. Also, a child's attachment to its mother may be different from attachment to its father. It could be securely attached to one but not to the other. This shows that attachments are a feature of unique relationships, rather than characteristics of the child. The Strange Situation has also been criticised as highly artificial (it lacks ecological validity). And surely it's unethical for psychologists deliberately to expose babies to stress, even if this sometimes happens in real life.

Give a brief account of *one* psychological explanation of attachment and consider its strengths *and* limitations. (18 marks)

First paragraph: Description:

AO1: worth 6 marks

According to Bowlby (1969, 1973), newborn human babies are completely helpless. So they're genetically programmed to behave towards their mothers (or mother-figures) in ways that ensure their survival. These species-specific behaviours include cuddling, looking, smiling and crying. Babies use them to shape and control their caregivers' behaviour. Mothers are also genetically programmed to respond to the baby's attachment behaviours. There's a critical period for attachment formation (Bowlby, 1951). Mothering is useless for most children after 12 months, and for all children after two-and-a-half to three years. Generally, attachment behaviours are more evident when the child is distressed, unwell, afraid or in unfamiliar surroundings. Babies also display monotropy, a strong innate tendency to become attached to one particular adult female. This attachment to the mother-figure is unique.

Second and third paragraphs:

AO2: worth 12 marks

Bowlby's theory was opposed to 'cupboard theories' of attachment such as learning theory. He rejected learning theory's claim that attachments are based on the baby's need for food by drawing on Lorenz's (1935) study of imprinting in goslings, and Harlow's (1959) study of contact comfort in rhesus monkeys. Their research showed the importance of instinct, but we can't necessarily apply these findings to humans. However, Schaffer and Emerson's (1964) longitudinal study of Scottish babies also contradicted the learning theory explanation. They showed that babies were often attached to people who weren't involved in their physical care, and often the main carer wasn't the baby's main attachment figure. But these attachment figures included fathers, and this seems to contradict Bowlby's monotropy theory.

Also, babies and young children display a wide range of attachment behaviours towards various attachment figures other than their mothers. That is, mothers aren't special or unique as implied by monotropy. Schaffer and Emerson also showed that it's quite common for young children to form multiple attachments (it's the 'rule'). Although Bowlby accepted that this can happen, he thought it was the exception rather than the rule. Bowlby also believed that fathers aren't of any direct emotional importance to the baby. Their main role is to provide emotional and financial support to the mother. But Schaffer and Emerson's findings suggest that fathers are attachment figures in their own right.

Give a brief account of and evaluate Bowlby's maternal deprivation hypothesis. (18 marks)

### First paragraph: Description:

A01: worth 6 marks

Bowlby's maternal deprivation hypothesis (MDH) is based on two of the central elements from his attachment theory. First, there's a critical period for the development of attachments. For most children, if they haven't formed an attachment during their first year, it will be too late to form one later on. For all children, this becomes impossible after two-and-a-half to three years. Second, monotropy refers to the innate tendency to become attached to one particular female adult (not necessarily the biological mother). The attachment to her is the first to develop, and is the child's strongest attachment. This makes it unique. Specifically, the MDH claims that if the mother-baby attachment were broken in the first years of life, the child's emotional and intellectual development would be seriously and permanently harmed.

### Second and third paragraphs:

A02: worth 12 marks

The MDH was based largely on studies of children raised in orphanages and other institutions (such as Goldfarb, 1943; Spitz, 1945, 1946; and Spitz & Wolf, 1946). According to these researchers, and Bowlby, in all these institutions the common factor was lack of maternal care. This was the crucial harmful influence on the children growing up in them. This is what Bowlby later called maternal deprivation. But these studies had some serious methodological weaknesses. For example, in Goldfarb's study the children who were raised in institutions and those who were raised by foster parents weren't randomly assigned to these two 'conditions' (as would happen in a true experiment). It's possible that the latter were more 'desirable' in various ways, which is why they were fostered in the first place. This makes it difficult to make direct comparisons between the two groups.

Also, the institutionally-reared children lived in almost complete social isolation for their first year. All the institutions involved were extremely unstimulating environments, and this lack of stimulation (social and intellectual) could have been responsible for the children's poor development, in addition to, or even rather than, the lack of maternal care (maternal deprivation). Also, as Rutter (1981) points out, maternal 'deprivation' refers to loss of a mother-figure. Strictly speaking, the children raised in institutions suffered maternal 'privation', because they lacked the opportunity to form an attachment with anyone in the first place. Deprivation and privation refer to very different types of early experience, with very different types of effect. Studies of institutionally-raised children provide evidence for the effects of privation (not just maternal), rather than deprivation.

---

To what extent does psychological research show that deprivation is harmful to children's development? (18 marks)

### First paragraph: Description:

A01: worth 6 marks

Deprivation refers to the loss, through separation, of an attachment figure. Short-term deprivation usually lasts days or weeks, such as when a child goes into a residential nursery, or stays with foster parents, while its mother goes into hospital. Or the child might go into hospital itself. Long-term deprivation includes the death of a parent, and separation through parental divorce. Another example is day care. According to Bowlby (1969, 1973), children become distressed when separated from their mothers, which was illustrated by Robertson and Robertson's (1969) study of John. He displayed the three components of distress, namely protest, despair and detachment. According to Schaffer (1996), most children are adversely affected by parental divorce, but most are resilient enough to adapt eventually (Hetherington & Stanley-Hagan, 1999). One important effect of long-term deprivation is separation anxiety.

### Second and third paragraphs:

A02: worth 12 marks

John became increasingly distressed as his stay in the residential nursery went on. But the Robertsons and Bowlby disagreed as to the exact cause of his distress. For the Robertsons, John suffered bond disruption. In his mother's absence, there was no one to take her place. For Bowlby, it was loss of his mother that was crucial (that is, John suffered maternal deprivation). But Robertson and Robertson (1989) argue that they provided clear evidence that a young child's separation from his mother triggers a sequence of psychological reactions likely to have long-term effects. The children they fostered in subsequent studies showed much less distress than John, and good-quality substitute care should always involve a 'substitute mother'. Nevertheless, they concluded that separation is always dangerous and should be avoided if possible.

Apart from the quality of the substitute care, the degree of distress is affected by several factors. For example, separation will probably be most distressing between the ages of 12–18 months (Maccoby, 1980); for boys (although there are wide differences between boys and between girls); if there have been any behaviour problems (such as aggression) before separation, and if the child hasn't been separated from the mother before. Similarly, the nature, severity and duration of the effects of divorce are influenced by several factors. These include continuity of contact with the non-custodial parent, the financial status/lifestyle of the custodial parent, and whether the custodial parent remarries and the nature of the resulting stepfamily. So it may not be separation (short- or long-term) itself that's harmful, but factors associated with it.

# SAMPLE ANSWERS (SAs)

Consider psychological research into the effects of privation on children's development. (18 marks)

### First paragraph: Description:

A01: worth 6 marks

Privation refers to the failure to develop an attachment to any individual. This is often associated with children growing up in institutions. The effects are mainly long-term, and a major example is affectionless psychopathy, the inability to care and have deep feelings for other people. The early studies of children raised in institutions (such as Goldfarb, 1943) on which Bowlby based his maternal deprivation hypothesis, actually show the effects of privation. Hodges and Tizard's (1989) longitudinal study of children raised in institutions for at least their first two years provides evidence both for and against the view that the effects of early privation are reversible. Case studies of children who've endured extreme early privation (such as the Czech twins studied by Koluchova, 1972, 1991) are also relevant.

### Second and third paragraphs:

A02: worth 12 marks

Bowlby et al.'s (1956) study of TB sanatorium children was originally discussed in relation to deprivation. The children who'd spent time in a sanitorium before the age of four weren't any more likely to show affectionless psychopathy than a control group. But they did show more signs of emotional disturbance. Bowlby admitted that factors other than separation were responsible for this disturbance, including illness and death in their families. Some of the sanitorium children may have suffered privation. Hodges and Tizard's data for the 16-year-olds who'd spent their early years in institutions suggests that there may be a critical period for developing attachments with peers later in life (so supporting Bowlby). But they also showed that early privation may not prevent the formation of attachments to adoptive parents later on (so contradicting Bowlby).

However, longitudinal studies like that of Hodges and Tizard suffer from the problem of participant drop-out. It's unclear how representative the 16-year-olds were of the original sample. It's also unclear what determined whether the institutional children were adopted or returned to their biological families. This is important, because only the adopted children successfully developed attachments with their parents. However, at each point in the study the children were compared both with themselves (at earlier ages) and with a matched control group. Koluchova's study of the Czech twins supports the findings of other studies involving children who suffer extreme privation and then are 'rescued'. That is, it's possible to reverse the effects of prolonged early privation, which doesn't predestine them to a life of severe handicap (Clarke & Clarke, 2000).

---

'While going out to work may benefit mothers of young children, the young children themselves may suffer compared with those whose mothers stay at home.' To what extent does psychological research support this view of the effects of day care on children's social development? (18 marks)

### First paragraph: Description:

A01: worth 6 marks

Day care includes all types of non-maternal care of children who normally live with their parent(s). Examples include crèches, day nurseries, childminders and nannies. One view of the harmful effects of day care on children's social development is that such children are more likely to develop insecure attachments to their mothers. According to Bowlby, children whose mothers go out to work suffer maternal deprivation. Belsky and Rovine (1988) reported evidence that compared with 'home-reared' babies, those who'd been in day care for at least four months before their first birthday, and for more than 20 hours per week, were more likely to develop insecure attachments. Several other studies have shown that children who were in day care as babies are as self-confident and emotionally well-adjusted as those who weren't (Clarke-Stewart, 1989).

### Second and third paragraphs:

A02: worth 12 marks

Bowlby's attachment theory, and his maternal deprivation hypothesis, have both influenced the still widely-held view that children should be cared for by their own mothers. Any criticisms of Bowlby's theories weaken the argument that day care is non-normative. But most modern British and American mothers with school-age children go out to work. So shared childcare is actually the norm, and has always been shared (Scarr, 1998). Belsky and Rovine's findings were based on the Strange Situation. But this is an inappropriate technique to use with children in day care. It assumes that repeated separations from the mother are stressful for the child. But day-care children are used to such separations. What looks like indifference to the mother (implying insecure attachment) may just be independence and self-reliance (Clarke-Stewart, 1989).

Day care doesn't necessarily weaken attachments to the mother. Provided the day care is stable and of a reasonable quality, children don't suffer any ill effects. They might actually benefit from it (Schaffer, 1996). Where the quality of the day care is poor, children are likely to be rated lower on social and emotional development. However, the quality of day care chosen by parents is correlated with their personal characteristics or circumstances. For example, children from families with single working mothers or low income are more likely to experience low-quality care. So we can't be sure whether it's the quality of day care or parental circumstances which influence children's development. This confusion between the two variables has led to an overestimation of the effects of day care (Scarr, 1988).

## PHYSIOLOGICAL PSYCHOLOGY: STRESS

To what extent does stress play a role in cardiovascular disorders? (18 marks)

First paragraph: Description: 

A01: worth 6 marks

Selye (1956) defined stress as the non-specific response of the body to any demand made upon it. This response reflects the General Adaptation Syndrome (GAS), the body's defence against stress. The body responds in the same way to any stressor, whether it's environmental (such as extreme temperature or electric shock) or arises from within the body itself. The GAS comprises three stages, alarm reaction, resistance and exhaustion. By this last stage, the body's resources are becoming depleted, and psychophysiological disorders develop. These include cardiovascular disorders such as high blood pressure/BP (hypertension), coronary artery disease (CAD), and coronary heart disease (CHD). Friedman and Rosenman (1974) found evidence for the role of individual differences in men's ways of dealing with stressful situations. They concluded that men who displayed Type A behaviour (TAB) were far more likely to develop CHD than other men.

Second and third paragraphs: 

A02: worth 12 marks

Selye's concept of stress as a non-specific bodily response was based upon his observations of hospital patients. But research into the GAS involved mainly rats' responses to stressors. So it hasn't been tested directly with human beings. Nevertheless, it helps to account for the physiology of stress. For example, the alarm reaction involves the fight-or-flight response (FOFR), which is a well-established reaction to stressful situations. This is also crucial to the evolutionary explanation of how stress makes us ill. Most modern-day stressors have a much greater psychological element than those faced by our ancestors. Stress is more likely to be chronic, which involves repeated episodes of increased heart rate and BP, causing plaque formation within the cardiovascular system. Selye has been criticised for largely ignoring the psychological aspects of stress.

Friedman and Rosenman's American study of TAB showed how psychological factors (personality) can produce physiological effects (CHD). It was a long-term study involving a very large sample. All the participants were free of heart disease at the start, and the researchers were able to separate out the effects of risk factors (such as smoking) from the effects of personality. But the measures used to assess Type A and Type B behaviour have been criticized. Also, their results can't be generalised to women, since their sample was all-male. Their basic findings have been replicated in other countries. But most Type A men don't develop CHD, and many Type Bs do. Also, their evidence is only correlational. There's no evidence to support their claim that personality actually causes CHD.

---

Consider research into the effects of stress on the immune system. (18 marks)

First paragraph: Description: 

A01: worth 6 marks

The immune system is a collection of billions of cells which travel through the bloodstream. They move in and out of tissues and organs, defending the body against foreign bodies (antigens), such as bacteria, viruses and cancerous cells. The main types of immune cells are white blood cells (leucocytes). When we're stressed, the immune system's ability to fight off antigens is reduced. This is why we're more susceptible to infections. The immunosuppressive effects of stress were demonstrated by Kiecolt-Glaser et al.'s (1984) study of medical students facing important exams, and in Schliefer et al.'s (1983) study of men whose wives had died from breast cancer. Riley's (1981) study of tumour development in mice implanted with cancer cells also demonstrates the immunosuppressive effects of stress.

Second and third paragraphs: 

A02: worth 12 marks

There are always important ethical issues raised by experiments with non-humans which involve subjecting them to painful or life-threatening procedures. In Riley's experiment, not only were the high-stress condition rats deliberately subjected to stress, but they developed large tumours before being killed. There are also scientific issues. In particular, what can studies of mice placed on rotating turntables tell us about the immunosuppressive effects of stress in humans? However, studies using human participants are broadly consistent with Riley's results. In Kiecolt-Glaser et al.'s study, blood samples from the medical students were analysed for the amount of leucocyte activity: specifically, how much natural killer-cell activity. These help fight off viruses and tumours.

Kiecolt-Glaser et al.'s study was a natural experiment. The exams would have happened anyway, and all the participants volunteered for the study. So there are no ethical problems raised by the study, unlike Riley's. Also, the medical students were compared with themselves when the two blood samples were taken (prior to and on the first day of the exams). This controls for important participant variables, such as personality. But we can't be sure that it was exam stress alone which caused the change in immune function. Nevertheless, different stressors, including exams, death of spouse, caring for relatives with Alzheimer's disease (Kiecolt-Glaser et al., 1995) have all been shown to be involved in reduced immune function.

# SAMPLE ANSWERS (SAs)

Consider psychological research into the role of life events as a source of stress. (18 marks)

First paragraph: Description:
A01: worth 6 marks

Life events include changes which happen to most people, such as leaving school and marriage, and much less common ones, such as imprisonment and being fired at work. Holmes and Rahe (1967) constructed an instrument for measuring stress, which they defined as the amount of change a person has to deal with during a particular period of time. Their Social Readjustment Rating Scale (SRRS) comprises 43 life events, each given a life-change unit (LCU) score. They found that the higher someone's overall LCU score (how many life events they'd experienced during the previous year), the more likely they were to show symptoms of both physical and psychological illness. The greater the stress, the more serious the illness. They claimed that stress actually makes us ill.

Second and third paragraphs:
A02: worth 12 marks

Holmes and Rahe's SRRS was the first attempt to measure stress objectively and to examine its relationship to illness. It assumes that any change is stressful. But the list of life events is largely negative, especially those with the highest LCU scores (such as death of spouse). So, the SRRS may be confusing 'change' with 'undesirability'. Some of the life events could refer to positive or negative change, and there's no reference to the problems of old age, or natural or man-made disasters. Also, it seems that only those life events classified as uncontrollable are correlated with later illness. By definition, most of the 43 life events aren't everyday occurrences. This is in contrast with Kanner et al.'s (1981) hassles scale, which includes traffic jams, bad weather and financial worries.

Kanner et al. found that daily hassles were correlated with undesirable psychological symptoms. Also, hassles were a more powerful predictor of both physical and psychological symptoms than the SRRS's life events. Delongis et al. (1982) confirmed these findings, but they also reported a correlation between life events and physical symptoms for the 2–3 years prior to the study. Instead of life events causing illness, it could be that some life events are early signs of an illness that's already developing (Penny, 1966). Studies like Rahe et al.'s (1970) study of navy personnel are often correlational, so we cannot be sure what's cause and what's effect. Also, participants are often asked to recall both their illnesses and the stressful life events that occurred during the preceding year. Retrospective studies like this often produce unreliable data.

Consider psychological research into the effects of workplace stressors. (18 marks)

First paragraph: Description:
A01: worth 6 marks

Some occupations are more stressful than others. Four of the most stressful are nursing, social work, teaching and the emergency services. Nurses have to deal constantly with patients' pain, anxiety and death, and give emotional support to relatives, and are often in the front line when major incidents occur. Brady's (1958) executive monkey experiment was designed to throw light on the effects of stress in business executives who are under constant pressure to 'perform'. This fits the common-sense view that too much stress is what is harmful. However, Marmot et al.'s (1997) study of British civil servants shows that the opposite can also be true. Those civil servants in the lowest grades were at a much higher risk of developing coronary heart disease (CHD) than those in the highest grades, and this was related to the low job-control or decision latitude.

Second and third paragraphs:
A02: worth 12 marks

Weiss's (1972) replication of Brady's experiment (using rats) suggested that control is harmful if it involves having to be constantly vigilant. Indeed, human executives and air-traffic controllers have the highest incidence of stomach ulcers of any US occupational groups. The latter especially have to be constantly vigilant. Similarly, quantitative overload involves having too much to do, and having to be excessively quick or productive. This is associated with anxiety and frustration, as is qualitative overload, where the work is too difficult or demands excessive attention. However, underload can also be stressful and harmful to health. Not having enough to do (quantitative underload) is associated with boredom, low job satisfaction and lack of commitment. Qualitative underload involves underusing one's skills and abilities.

Apart from being unethical, Brady's and Weiss's experiments can only suggest why stress is harmful for humans. However, Marmot et al.'s large-scale study of civil servants shows fairly convincingly that having little control over one's work can have potentially life-threatening consequences. They found that low job-control or decision latitude was a greater contributor to CHD than various established risk factors (such as smoking, obesity, lack of exercise and so on). This applied more-or-less equally to men and women. While British civil servants may not be representative of workers in general, a study of male workers in the Czech Republic replicated the findings of Marmot et al.'s study. It is possible that low job-control may have different effects on health in different occupations, but Marmot et al.'s large and well-controlled study points strongly to control as a crucial factor in general.

## To what extent have the effects of stressors been shown to be modified by personality? (18 marks)

AO1: worth 6 marks

First paragraph: Description:

Friedman and Rosenman's (1974) study of Type A behaviour (TAB) was intended to provide evidence for the role of non-physiological factors in coronary heart disease (CHD). They showed how psychological factors, in the form of personality, can have physiological effects (CHD). TAB describes a typical way of reacting to life in general, and work-related situations in particular, such that Type A men have a greater chance of developing CHD compared with other types. More recent research has suggested that specific Type A characteristics, in particular hostility, may be a better predictor of CHD than TAB as a whole. Type C personalities, who tend to suppress their anger, are cancer-prone (Temoshok 1987). Women diagnosed with breast cancer showed significantly more emotional suppression than those with non-life-threatening breast disease (Greer & Morris, 1975).

AO2: worth 12 marks

Second and third paragraphs:

Friedman and Rosenman's study has been criticised on many counts. For example, the sample was all male, so the results don't necessarily apply to women, and the two measures of TAB produced different scores for some men, so they might have measured different things. Also, hostility specifically seems to be a better predictor of CHD than TAB as a whole. However, their basic findings have been replicated outside the US, and their results suggest that the harmful effects of stressors can be mediated through psychological factors. It's how people perceive and react to stressors that's (potentially) dangerous to health.

Greer et al. (1979) investigated how women with breast cancer use coping mechanisms. Women who either used denial or showed a 'fighting spirit' were significantly more likely to be free of cancer five years later than those who either showed 'stoic acceptance' or 'gave up'. A follow-up at 15 years confirmed the improved prognosis (Greer et al., 1990). These findings lend scientific support to the advice to 'think positively', and it might be possible to teach people such strategies (Hegarty, 2000). But personality or coping mechanisms can only have an indirect effect on cancer through their effect on the immune system. Also, personality interacts with gender. For example, women are less likely than men to display TAB, which may reflect the male gender role. This, in turn, implies the role of culture. Women are also less hostile than men.

---

## Give a brief account of psychological methods of stress management and consider their strengths *and* limitations. (18 marks)

AO1: worth 6 marks

First paragraph: Description:

Formally, stress management (SM) refers to a range of techniques, both psychological and physiological, used deliberately by professionals, singly or in combination, to help people reduce their stress levels. Psychological examples include stress inoculation training/SIT (Meichenbaum, 1976), and increasing hardiness (Kobasa, 1979, 1982). SIT attempts to reduce stress through changing cognitions. The individual's self-defeating internal dialogue is first identified, then s/he is helped to make positive, coping statements, and finally is guided through increasingly threatening situations. Hardiness can be increased in three ways. Focusing involves helping people to identify the physical signs of stress; reconstructing past stressful situations helps to make a more realistic assessment of different stressors; and compensation through self-improvement is about taking on challenges that we can meet in the face of unavoidable stressors.

AO2: worth 12 marks

Second and third paragraphs:

SIT, like other forms of cognitive restructuring, is a practical application of cognitive psychology. It's based on a widely held belief that our emotional responses and behaviour are largely determined by the way we think. So if you can change the thoughts which normally produce stress reactions, you can reduce people's stress levels. Meichenbaum believes that people sometimes find things stressful because they think about them in catastrophising ways. This is an extreme example of the view that it's how people interpret events or situations that makes them stressful. Meichenbaum (1997) believes that SIT's 'power-of-positive-thinking' approach can successfully change people's behaviour. Some behaviourist psychologists believe that focusing on internal thoughts is unscientific, but it's proved successful, especially in reducing exam nerves and the anxiety associated with severe pain.

Increasing hardiness is a practical application of Kobasa's theory of personality. Hardy people have high internal locus of control (Rotter, 1966). Research shows that events seen as uncontrollable are the most stressful. So helping people to gain control should help reduce their stress levels. In turn, locus of control is related to learned helplessness (Seligman, 1975; Miller & Norman, 1979). Psychological methods don't suffer from some of the disadvantages of physiological methods, such as the side-effects of anxiolytic drugs, or the need for biofeedback's specialised equipment. But perhaps SIT or increasing hardiness are effective not because of the specific techniques involved, or the underlying theory, but simply the attention and support given by the therapist. By contrast, physiological methods are more likely to work because of the specific physiological changes they induce. But even here, psychological factors still play a part.

# SAMPLE ANSWERS (SAs)

## INDIVIDUAL DIFFERENCES: ABNORMALITY

Outline and evaluate the different attempts to define abnormality. (18 marks)

### First paragraph: Description:

A01: worth 6 marks

The 'statistical infrequency' definition of abnormality refers to behaviour that is statistically or numerically infrequent in a given population. Specific characteristics can be measured and plotted on a 'normal' distribution. Anybody who deviates from the average is classified as 'abnormal'. The 'deviation from social norms' definition regards abnormality as any behaviour that deviates from accepted norms or rules within society. It would include any behaviour that 'is beyond the bounds of social acceptability'. The 'failure to function adequately' definition is applied to people who cannot live a 'normal' life. They do not experience 'normal' emotions and/or display everyday behaviours. The 'deviation from ideal mental health' definition involves a comparison between a person's thoughts and behaviours with a list of 'normal', desirable or ideal characteristics. The further people are from these ideals the more abnormal they are.

### Second and third paragraphs:

A02: worth 12 marks

The 'statistical infrequency' definition fails to distinguish between desirable and undesirable behaviour. Statistically speaking, many extremely gifted individuals could be classified as 'abnormal' using this definition. The use of the term 'abnormal' in such cases is inappropriate. It has also been shown that as many as 50% of Americans suffer from a mental disorder during their lifetime and thus such behaviours are not really that 'statistically infrequent'. The knowledge that men are less likely to report mental problems than females also suggests that the prevalence rate for mental disorders reflects reporting levels rather than the true incidence of any disorder. The 'deviation from social norm' definition reflects the 'norms' of a particular culture. Such norms change across and within cultures over time. The definition fails to account for the fact that it can be beneficial to break social norms as in the case of the suffragettes. 'Conforming neurotics' are individuals who conform so strictly to social norms that they become neurotic about following them. Paradoxically, their adherence to social norms makes them abnormal!

The main problems with the 'failure to function adequately' definition of abnormality is that there are individuals who carry on functioning within society perfectly well and yet must be suffering from a mental disorder. Such individuals would include Harold Shipman who managed to continue working as a GP despite being a serial killer. To a certain extent, all the definitions can be considered as arbitrary and subjective definitions with many problems attached. There is no single 'perfect' definition. There is little objective evidence to support one definition over another. The concept of 'abnormality' can be viewed as a social construction within a particular culture.

*Note: You do not have to cover all the definitions, although you should include at least TWO. You could also include the cross-cultural problems that psychologists have encountered with their attempts to define abnormality.*

---

Briefly describe and evaluate the biological (medical) approach to abnormality. (18 marks)

### First paragraph: Description:

A01: worth 6 marks

The Biological (Medical) Model assumes that abnormality has a physiological cause related to the physical structure or functioning of the brain. Genetic factors are believed to play a part in the development of mental disorders that appear to 'run in the family'. Biochemical explanations propose that many disorders can be explained by neurotransmitter imbalances. Infections are also implicated in many mental disorders. It's also assumed that, like physical illnesses, mental illnesses can be diagnosed accurately by examining patient symptoms. It follows that treatments based on this model involve physical, invasive techniques involving drugs, electro-convulsive therapy and psychosurgery.

### Second and third paragraphs:

A02: worth 12 marks

Objective, scientific evidence to support the biological model includes brain scans of people who have been found to suffer from mental dysfunction due to physical brain damage such as a tumour. Kendler *et al.* (1985) found supporting evidence for a genetic component to mental disorder. They found that relatives of schizophrenics were 18 times more likely to develop the illness than matched controls. Neurotransmitter imbalances (excess dopamine) have also been detected in the brains of schizophrenics. Barr *et al.* (1990) found evidence that mothers who developed flu whilst pregnant were more likely subsequently to develop schizophrenia. This suggests a possible correlational link between the infection and the disorder. The successful use of physical treatments including drugs and the objective clinically controlled tests of their effectiveness also provide evidence to support the biological approach.

One of the main problems with such physiological evidence is that it could be the *effect* of mental disorder rather than the *cause*. Is an excess of dopamine the *result* of schizophrenia or the *cause* of it? Studies on animals suggest it is more likely to be the latter. However, it remains uncertain whether animals are actually experiencing a particular disorder in a similar way to humans and whether such findings can be generalised. The reliability of psychiatric diagnosis using the biological approach has been questioned by Rosenhan (1973). He showed that psychiatrists could not reliably distinguish between the 'sane and insane'. Although the use of deception in this study has been criticised, the study highlights the lack of objective tests used within the biological approach. Psychiatrists have to rely on patient self-report of their symptoms and these could well be unreliable. The biological approach has also been criticised for being reductionist and ignoring patient thoughts, feelings and experiences. It's suggested that other environmental factors must contribute to the development of mental disorders and these are largely ignored by the biological approach.

*Note: There is a wealth of information that could be included here. Evaluation of the medical approach could also include a consideration of whether it is a humane approach, whether it labels people and results in the stigmatising of vulnerable individuals.*

Give a brief account of the behavioural model of abnormality and consider its strengths and limitations. (18 marks)

**First paragraph: Description:** AO1: worth 6 marks

The behavioural model suggests that abnormal behaviour, like all behaviour, is learnt through the processes of classical and operant conditioning. Classical conditioning involves 'learning through association' whereas operant conditioning involves 'learning through the consequences of behaviour'. Abnormal behaviours are the result of faulty learning. The approach suggests that what is learnt can be unlearnt through the implementation of the same conditioning principles. The approach concentrates on present, observable behaviour. The patient's history is not important and the original cause of the illness is not examined. Only the patient's symptoms are treated since these represent the problem. The goal of behavioural therapy is to replace maladaptive behaviours with more appropriate ones.

**Second and third paragraphs:** AO2: worth 12 marks

The behavioural approach can be experimentally tested in the laboratory and is thus supported by a large amount of scientific evidence. The concentration on observable behaviours, not mental processes, means that the approach is easily tested empirically. The concept of using reinforcement (rewards and punishments) to modify behaviour is widespread and often effective. Watson and Raynor's (1920) study on Little Albert shows support for the model. However, this study is one of the most ethically dubious studies in psychology. Little Albert was not protected from harm and it appears unlikely that *informed* consent was gained prior to the study. Behavioural therapy (e.g. systematic desensitisation) and behaviour modification (e.g. token economies) have proved successful in treating patients with obsessive–compulsive disorders and phobias and thus provide support for the approach. However, they are less successful with more serious disorders such as schizophrenia. Critics also claim that such treatments only deal with the symptoms of the illness. The underlying causes remain and thus the symptoms are likely to reappear. However, behaviourists would argue that the symptoms *are* the problem.

The behavioural approach is a simple, mechanistic model and it is argued that it does not take into account the complexity of human behaviour. The influence of thoughts and emotions are largely ignored with this approach. Many behaviourist principles have been developed by studying animals' behaviour in the laboratory. Two problems arise here. There is the ethical debate of using animals in research and it is arguable whether animal findings can be applied to the more complex human behaviour. There are also ethical concerns regarding behavioural treatments. Behavioural treatments have been given without consent and punishments to lessen certain behaviours have involved pain and discomfort for patients. Indeed, behavioural techniques are sometimes used as a form of 'social control' to manipulate people's behaviour.

---

Give a brief account of the psychodynamic approach to abnormality and assess its strengths *and* limitations. (18 marks)

**First paragraph: Description:** AO1: worth 6 marks

The psychodynamic approach suggests that mental illness is caused by psychological forces. These forces remain 'unconscious' and explain why people do not know the reasons for their behaviour. According to Freud, there are three parts to the personality: the id (a person's basic instinctual drives), the ego (their 'reality manager') and the superego (their conscience). There is a perpetual conflict between the ego and superego and it is balanced by the ego. When this balance is not achieved, abnormal behaviour occurs. Conflict is particularly marked during childhood when the personality is still developing and thus childhood experiences play a vital part in adult development. Distressing events in childhood can be repressed (placed in the unconscious) only to re-emerge in adulthood. Freudian psychoanalysis is a 'talking cure' and concentrates on making the 'unconscious conscious'. It's assumed that re-experiencing past conflicts helps people to deal with them in the present.

**Second and third paragraphs:** AO2: worth 12 marks

Freud was the first to recognise the importance of psychological factors on the development of mental disorders. This, along with his emphasis on the influence of childhood, is widely accepted today. In addition, the idea of the unconscious having some effect on conscious behaviour attracts much support. The therapy seeks to treat the whole person and is therefore not reductionist. Psychodynamic therapeutic practice is extensive and widespread. The psychodynamic approach has been influential and long-lasting. Its influence extends beyond the narrow constrains of psychology into film, literature and the arts. It is suggested that an unimportant theory would have been dismissed many years previously.

The main criticism of the psychodynamic approach is that it cannot be scientifically tested. Evidence 'recovered' from the unconscious can support the approach and any evidence that is not forthcoming can be claimed still to be in the unconscious! The predominant use of case studies ensures that such findings cannot be easily generalised. Indeed, the majority of Freud's patients were middle-class, Viennese women – not a particularly representative sample. Evidence to support the approach is often reported by the therapists themselves and thus could be open to interpretative bias. It is generally accepted that Freud exaggerated the effectiveness of his psychodynamic therapy for his own patients. Eysenck (1952) in a comprehensive review of 7000 cases claimed that the therapy does more harm than good.

Although influential, evidence to support the psychodynamic approach remains weak and questionable.

*Note: You do not have to consider evidence that both supports and rejects the approach. You could choose to evaluate the approach from one viewpoint. Although a fairly balanced answer is provided above, it is perhaps easier to find evidence to reject the approach.*

# EXAM QUESTIONS

# SAMPLE ANSWERS (SAs)

Outline and evaluate the cognitive approach to abnormality. (18 marks)

First paragraph: Description:                                        A01: worth 6 marks

The cognitive model concentrates on the disturbed thought processes of individuals. It's not one's life circumstances that affect people, but the way that individuals perceive and evaluate these circumstances and events. It's assumed that thought affects behaviour – healthy thoughts lead to healthy behaviour and *vice versa*. Unhealthy individuals make 'cognitive errors'. Without thinking, they look at the negative aspects of life ('the glass is always half-empty rather than half-full'). The model explains how cognitive processes can be faulty. The approach assumes that thoughts can be monitored and altered. Therapy involves cognitive restructuring. Individuals must talk about their irrational cognitions and try to challenge their self-defeating negative thoughts. The model assumes that a cognitive change will lead to behaviour change.

Second and third paragraphs:                                        A02: worth 12 marks

A strength of the cognitive approach is that it concentrates only on current thought processes, it doesn't delve into the past to sort out problems. This is a strength because often details to do with the past are unclear. Research evidence to support the cognitive model is strong and many people who suffer from anxiety disorders and/or depression do report irrational thinking. Indeed, the cognitive model is an extremely popular and successful approach favoured within NHS practice. This may be because it empowers the individual to take responsibility for their own cognitions.

Limitations of the approach include the fact that it underplays physiological and environmental influences on a person's behaviour. Arguably, it's too simplistic to concentrate entirely on cognitive processes. Another limitation is that since thoughts cannot be objectively measured or observed, the approach relies too much on patient self-report. As a result, the approach has been claimed to be unscientific. The blame for any disorder rests with the individual since it's a result of their faulty thinking. This may also be unfair given that many people's unfortunate life circumstances are beyond their control. Indeed, given these circumstances, a person's depressive thoughts might be a perfectly rational response to the situation they find themselves in!

---

*'Anorexia nervosa is a biological rather than a psychological disorder.'* Assess to what extent research supports the view that anorexia nervosa (AN) is caused by biological factors. (18 marks)

First paragraph: Description:                                        A01: worth 6 marks

The biological explanation assumes that anorexia nervosa (AN) has a physiological cause related to the physical structure or functioning of the brain. Genetics, bio-chemistry and brain damage have been implicated in AN causation.

Second and third paragraphs:            also A01: 6 marks and A02: 12 marks

Genetic factors are believed to play a part in the development of AN as shown by Holland *et al.* (1988). Looking at twins (where at least one had AN) they found a 56% concordance rate in MZs (identical twins) and only 5% in DZs (non-identical twins) brought up in the same environment. Biochemical explanations propose that AN can be explained by neurotransmitter imbalances. Noradrenaline has been shown to increase appetite in animals and hypothalamic dysfunction has also been associated with eating disorders in animals. Tumours of the hypothalamus can cause hyperphagia (excessive over-eating) and obesity. This has been clearly demonstrated in both animals and humans. It's also been suggested that a blood-flow deficiency in the brain responsible for perception and appetite could cause AN and explain the mismatch between their actual and perceived appearance. All of this evidence provides strong support for the biological explanation of AN.

There are some problems with this evidence. If AN was caused entirely by genetic factors, then the MZ concordance rate should be nearer to 100%. In addition, twins do not just share the same genes, they often share the same environment. Therefore you could argue that the 56% MZ rate might be *entirely* due to their similar upbringing. The small sample size (25 pairs) also weakens the claims of the Holland *et al.* (1988) study. As many as 15,000 pairs of twins would be needed for a definitive study. The lack of AN in relatives of Western immigrants who have gone on to develop AN also questions the biological link and suggests a social-cultural explanation. The dramatic increase in AN over the past 20 years and the higher incidence of AN in social classes I and II (McClelland & Crisp, 2001) is also difficult to explain using a biological argument. Any supporting evidence that involves animal research may not be applicable to humans and such findings cannot always be generalised.

*Note: The three-paragraph format doesn't work so well here. The first paragraph is very short and AO1 marks are included in the other paragraphs. The 'three paragraphs' approach is not compulsory!*

*You could use evidence for other approaches (e.g. behavioural, psychodynamic) to evaluate the biological approach, but the link must be made explicitly.*

*You could be asked a similar question about BN. Some of the same material could be included, although the Kendler et al. (1991) study refers to BN and comprised a very large sample size.*

## SOCIAL PSYCHOLOGY: SOCIAL INFLUENCE

Consider psychological research into majority influence (conformity). (18 marks)

### First paragraph: Description:

**A01: worth 6 marks**

Majority influence or conformity is yielding to group pressure. It's the influence a group has over an individual. We conform with the expectations of our peers, but we're often unaware of it at the time. Sherif (1935) concluded that when people are faced with an ambiguous situation, they're more likely to conform. But Asch (1951) argued that the true test of conformity is to see if people will agree with others who give the wrong answer when the answer is obvious. Using what's come to be called the Asch paradigm, Asch found a 32 per cent conformity rate on the critical trials in a line-matching task, that is, where all the stooges agreed on the same wrong answer. He saw this figure as remarkably high, considering the unambiguous nature of the task. He conducted several subsequent studies to identify the specific factors that accounted for such high conformity.

*Note: You could draw a diagram to show the line-matching task used by Asch.*

### Second and third paragraphs:

**A02: worth 12 marks**

Control participants who performed Asch's line-matching task individually hardly ever made mistakes. So conformity could be measured objectively. The Asch paradigm has become the standard method for studying conformity, and has been used in several replications, in both Western and non-Western countries. Some American and British replications have found similar conformity rates to Asch, but others have found lower rates. This suggests the role of social and political influences. In his later experiments, Asch found that it wasn't the size of the majority that mattered. The crucial factor was whether or not the stooges agreed with each other, that is, whether they were unanimous. So if one of the stooges (a dissenter) gave a different answer from the rest, naïve participants resisted group pressure more easily.

Generally, people in Western cultures, such as the US and the UK, are less likely to conform than people in non-Western countries, such as Japan and Africa. This suggests that conformity has different meanings in different cultures. Crutchfield (1954) considered the Asch paradigm to be uneconomical and time-consuming, since only one naïve participant is tested at a time. Crutchfield's use of separate booths with light panels allowed several participants to be tested at once. The Asch paradigm has also been criticised for being both highly artificial and unethical – some participants reported feeling quite stressed on the critical trials, and Asch deceived them regarding the experiment's true purpose. Moscovici and Faucheux (1972) reinterpreted Asch's findings in terms of minority influence.

---

Outline and evaluate psychological approaches as explanations of AN. (18 marks)

### First paragraph: Description:

**A01: worth 6 marks**

The psychodynamic approach assumes that AN has a psychological origin. Childhood experiences and the conflict in the personality (id, ego and superego) play an important part in the development of AN. It's suggested that adolescents don't want to grow up and they become fixated at the oral stage when they were totally dependent on their parents. AN is an unconscious desire to remain dependent on their parents. Eating and sex are symbolically related. A refusal to eat represents a refusal of sexuality. This often occurs in reality with young girls suffering from amenorrhoea. According to the behavioural approach, AN is a learnt behaviour which follows classical and operant principles. Eating is associated with anxiety since it makes people overweight (classical conditioning). To reduce these feelings of anxiety, the adolescent stops eating. The reward of feeling good about themselves from not eating is sometimes also reinforced by praise from others (operant conditioning).

### Second and third paragraphs:

**A02: worth 12 marks**

Support for the psychodynamic approach to AN comes from case studies of anorexics who were abused as children (Romans et al., 2001). The desire to destroy their bodies and prevent sexual maturation may be a reaction to this. It's difficult to generalise findings from 'one-off' case studies and there are many anorexics who don't report such abuse. Tyrka et al., (2002) found that 'perfectionism' was a predictor of AN onset. This also supports the idea that girls who cannot achieve perfection shrink from the demands of being an adult. It's difficult to test the psychodynamic explanation objectively. After all, the unconscious, by definition, cannot be measured and many of the ideas remain untested. Other support comes from patients who accept the psychodynamic explanation for AN but it's claimed that some have done so due to the demand characteristics of their therapist. Further, psychodynamic explanations cannot account for the increase in AN over recent years.

The behavioural approach appears to make 'cognitive sense' and the principles of conditioning have been shown to apply to all forms of human behaviour. These principles have been empirically tested and can be applied to AN. Groesz et al.'s (2001) study provides support for the social learning approach. They found that women with greater 'body dissatisfaction' were likely to develop an eating disorder. They concluded that this 'dissatisfaction' was fuelled by the media preoccupation with the 'slender beauty ideal'. However, many of these studies do not take account of possible biological influences. The behavioural approach cannot fully explain why all dieters do not develop AN (are dieters really conditioned differently?) and why anorexics continue to starve themselves when there would appear to be little reward for doing so.

*Note: You could be asked a similar question about BN. Some of the same material could be included, especially since the Tyrka et al. (2002) study investigated both AN and BN. However, you must refer to the specific eating disorder mentioned in the question.*

# EXAM QUESTIONS

# SAMPLE ANSWERS (SAs)

Give a brief account of psychological explanations of conformity and consider their strengths *and* limitations. (18 marks)

First paragraph: Description:                                      **A01: worth 6 marks**

Deutsch and Gerard (1955) distinguished between informational social influence (ISI) and normative social influence (NSI). They felt this distinction was crucial for understanding conformity. Underlying ISI is the basic need to be confident that our ideas and beliefs are correct (a need for certainty). This makes us feel in control of our lives. When we're unsure about something, or in unfamiliar or ambiguous situations, we tend to seek other people's opinions. This is related to a type of conformity called internalisation or true conformity. Underlying NSI is the need to be accepted by other people. We want them to like us and respect us, and other people have the power to reward us or punish us by rejecting us. This is related to a different type of conformity called compliance.

Second paragraph:                                                 **A02: worth 12 marks**

ISI seems to have been the motive underlying conformity in Sherif's experiment. His participants had to estimate how far a light moved which was, in fact, stationary. There couldn't be a right or wrong answer, so the task was ambiguous. Similarly, when Asch made the comparison lines more similar, the task became harder because it was more ambiguous. If we conform because of ISI, it's very likely that we really believe the majority opinion – we're 'converted' to their view. This is internalisation or true conformity. Other people help us 'define social reality'. But it's not just anyone who can do this (Brown, 1988). We're influenced by others' opinions in an ambiguous situation only if we see ourselves as sharing important characteristics with them, such as being fellow psychology students (Abrams *et al.*, 1990).

NSI seems to have been the motive underlying conformity in most of Asch's experiments. In post-experimental interviews, many of his participants who'd conformed on the critical trials said they knew the stooges' answer was wrong. But if they gave the correct answer, they risked being laughed at by the majority – a form of rejection. They said they didn't want to look stupid or be the odd-one-out. So what they said publicly and what they believed privately were different. This is compliance. It's a compromise solution when our own and other people's opinions conflict. But we experience conflict only if we disagree with others whom we regard as being like us in some relevant way (they're also psychology students: Abrams *et al.*, 1990).

Give a brief account of psychological explanations of obedience and consider their strengths *and* limitations. (18 marks)

First paragraph: Description:                                      **A01: worth 6 marks**

Milgram originally believed the 'Germans are different' explanation of obedience. But his research convinced him that this was false, and that both specific and more general factors are involved. Most people would have behaved like his obedient participants did, so the explanation lies in aspects of the situation itself, rather than in individual – or national – characteristics. Similarly, Zimbardo *et al.*'s (1973) prison simulation experiment shows the power of social situations on people's behaviour. In both experiments, the authority figure possessed highly visible symbols of their power and status. This makes it more difficult to disobey them. According to Milgram (1974), when we obey we come to see ourselves as the instrument or agent of the authority figure's wishes (the agentic state). We give up personal responsibility for our actions (the autonomous state).

Second and third paragraphs:                                      **A02: worth 12 marks**

Milgram's experimenter always wore a grey lab coat (white would have implied 'scientist' rather than 'authority figure'), and the prison guards carried handcuffs, wore reflector sunglasses and so on. In Bushman's (1984) naturalistic study, a stooge wearing a firefighter uniform was obeyed more often than a stooge dressed in ordinary clothes. This shows the power of uniforms on people's perception of authority figures. Another feature of the situation in Milgram's experiments relates to how participants got 'sucked into their role' ('foot-in-the-door'). The original advert made no mention of punishment, but through a series of small steps participants found themselves giving electric shocks as punishment to a learner. Escaping from the situation proved harder than getting into it.

Milgram's participants were more likely to obey if they couldn't see for themselves the effects of their behaviour. Obedience rates dropped when they were in the same room as the victim or held his arms down on the shock plate, as well as when the experimenter wasn't physically present to give his instructions. Under these conditions, there was a shift away from the agentic to the autonomous state. For Milgram, obedience always involves the agentic state, regardless of who the authority figure is and their orders or instructions. It's useful to have a single explanation for a variety of behaviours, but wasn't he just assuming that his participants, and Nazis war criminals such as Eichmann, were all influenced by the same agentic state? Also, these explanations are based on experiments which Orne and Holland (1968) argue lack both experimental and ecological validity.

## To what extent can use of deception in social influence research studies be justified? (18 marks)

First paragraph: Description:                                    AO1: worth 6 marks

Deception involves either not telling participants the (whole) truth about the purpose of the study, or telling them that it's about something quite different from its true purpose. For example, Milgram's adverts asked for volunteers for a study of learning and memory. Obedience was never mentioned, but neither were electric shock or even punishment. In Asch's conformity experiments, participants were told the experiment was concerned with perceptual judgement. No reference was made to conformity. Related to this is deception regarding the identity of the other people involved. The learner in Milgram's experiments was introduced as Mr Wallace, another participant, when he was really an actor playing the role of participant. In Asch's experiments, all but one of the group were stooges, also pretending to be other participants. Crucially, Milgram's participants were also deceived about the electric shock.

Second and third paragraphs:                                   AO2: worth 12 marks

Most people would agree that it's unethical to lie to or deceive someone in everyday life. In the context of psychological research in general, and social influence research in particular, deception is considered to be ethically unacceptable because it prevents participants from giving their informed consent. If you don't know the true purpose of the study for which you're volunteering (consenting), or exactly what's going to happen, it's always possible that you wouldn't have volunteered in the first place. The researcher has got you there 'under false pretences'. Milgram's participants gave their consent for a study of learning and memory, not for a study of obedience. Similarly, Asch's consented to a study of perceptual judgement, not conformity.

However, in post-experimental interviews most of Asch's participants were very positive about the experimental procedure. Milgram had lengthy debriefing sessions with each participant individually, and he sent them a detailed account of the procedure and results, plus a follow-up questionnaire. Most of those who returned it said they were glad/very glad they'd participated, and many said they learned something valuable about themselves and advocated more research like it. Milgram took this to be the crucial justification for using deception. If they didn't object, why should anyone else? Also, participants had to believe the shocks were real, otherwise we couldn't generalise the results to real-life obedience situations. Sometimes deception is necessary if participants are to behave in a 'realistic' way. But social influence researchers face a greater risk of harming participants' self-image compared with other areas of psychological research.

## To what extent can ethical guidelines ensure that the major ethical issues involved in research with human participants are properly dealt with? (18 marks)

First paragraph: Description:                                    AO1: worth 6 marks

Deception, consent/informed consent, protection of participants from psychological harm, and withdrawal from the investigation, all refer to participants' rights. Milgram's participants were deceived about the true purpose of his obedience experiments, which required them to be deceived about the true identity of the learner and the reality of the electric shock. Asch also deceived his participants about the true purpose of his conformity experiments. Deception prevents participants giving their informed consent. This amounts to being tricked into taking part. Baumrind (1964) accused Milgram of exposing his participants to extreme stress and conflict. Part of his experimental procedure involved pressurising them into carrying on with the experiment, which made it difficult for them to exercise their right to withdraw. In Zimbardo et al.'s prison study, this was almost impossible – although they did give their informed consent.

Second and third paragraphs:                                   AO2: worth 12 marks

While Milgram's, Asch's and Zimbardo et al.'s experiments have all been criticised for being unethical, they've also helped to identify the major ethical issues that all psychologists today must consider when planning and conducting their research. Without the social influence research there might not be an 'ethical debate' at all. An ethics committee of the American Psychological Association (APA) investigated Milgram's (1963) experiment and judged it to be ethically acceptable. But there were no formal, written ethical guidelines at this time. The various sets of guidelines published by the APA and the British Psychological Society (BPS), such as the BPS 'Ethical Principles' (1993), are at least partly a consequence of social influence research. They represent the responsibilities of psychologists to their participants.

The Principles state that ethical guidelines are necessary for clarifying the conditions under which psychological research is acceptable. So there are certain criteria that have to be met before a particular procedure can go ahead, and certain safeguards that must be put in place to protect participants' rights. For example, if the researcher decides that deception is necessary, participants should be debriefed as soon as possible after the experiment. This involves revealing the true purpose of the study, and reassuring those who've suffered emotional distress. The Principles should be followed by anyone conducting any kind of psychological research, including AS/A level students. Although ethical guidelines cannot guarantee that every participant will be completely protected from harm, they help to ensure that psychologists consider major ethical issues, which should help reduce risk to participants.

# EXAM QUESTIONS

# SAMPLE ANSWERS (SAs)

Research Methods Answers:

*Note: In Research Methods (unlike the other Units) only the first answer will count. If the question asks for 'one limitation of repeated measures design . . .' do not give two limitations since only the first one will be marked. You are wasting your time. Even if the second answer is correct, it cannot be credited. Remember the 'mark a minute' rule. For a 6-mark question you should write for 6 minutes.*

## Question One:

**1a i.** There will be no (significant) difference between the exam performance of students who revise whilst listening to music and students who revise in silence. *(2 marks)*

**ii.** The experimental/alternative hypothesis would be directional since previous research suggests that a negative effect of listening to music is the most likely outcome. *(1 + 2 marks)*

**b i.** Opportunity or self-selected sampling: *(1 mark)*

**ii.** Advantage: it is the easiest method of sampling in order to obtain a sufficient number of participants. *(1 mark)*

Disadvantage: The sample is likely to be unrepresentative of the target population (biased) and therefore findings cannot easily be generalised. *(1 mark)*

**c.** Repeated measures design:

Advantages: Fewer participants are needed than with independent or matched-pairs design since participants take part in both conditions of the study. *(2 marks)*

Disadvantages: There are possible order effects. That is, the order in which the conditions are undertaken affects the results through practice, fatigue or boredom. Any difference may be due to order effects and not the independent variable (listening to background music whilst revising or silence). *(2 marks)*

**d.** The mean. This is appropriate to use with interval data. In addition, the mode (History = 47, Psychology = 47) and median (History = 65, Psychology = 65) are not suitable to describe the data. They illustrate no difference between the two exam scores when there clearly is a difference (as shown by the mean). *(1 + 2 marks)*

**e.** The data in Table 1 seem to show a marked difference between the History exam performance and Psychology exam performance. This difference appears to be the result of the manipulation of the IV (revising with music or in silence).

It would appear to confirm that listening to music whilst working does have a negative effect on exam performance and thus confirms earlier research findings.

However, the data also show distinct individual differences and variation. There is some overlap between the History and Psychology scores. The table does not state how the pairs of scores are related. It might be that some students actually performed better in the History exam than the Psychology exam. This cannot be ascertained from the Table as it is currently set out.

Finally, the study suffered from a lack of control of confounding variables and therefore the data in Table 1 need to be treated with caution. These could include the exam difficulty, amount of revision given to each subject, the marking of the scripts and so on. *(6 marks)*

**f.** The participants were not 'protected from harm'. The researchers were aware that listening to music may have a negative effect on exam performance and yet participants were not warned of this in advance. It could be that participants' later History performances may be affected by their results. The results may also have damaged their self-esteem. Participants may not have left the study feeling as good as when they started the study. The researchers could have dealt with this by briefing the participants fully about the study and gaining informed consent before they agreed to take part. *(3 marks)*

**g.** The design could have been improved by using a stratified sample rather than an opportunity sample. The stratified sample could have been selected on the basis of academic ability and identified different ability bands or strata. This could have important consequences for the study. It may be that different academic abilities are more or less affected by background music.

A matched-pairs design might also be favoured instead of a repeated-measures design. The use of a matched-pairs design means that participants are less likely to guess the aim of the study and results are less likely to be affected by demand characteristics. In this study it is likely that participants could guess that the researchers were expecting them to perform poorly in the History exam (background music condition) and they may have acted accordingly. A matched-pairs design would also help to overcome order effects in the study. Since all the participants sat the History exam in the afternoon they may have been more tired by this time and this might explain the findings. If participants sat just one of the exams there would be no order effects. *(3 + 3 marks)*

## Question Two:

**2a.** Two disadvantages of a correlation are:

- You cannot determine cause and effect with a correlation.
- Correlations work only with linear (straight line) relationships. *(2 + 2 marks)*

b. There will be a significant positive correlation between intelligence score and GCSE exam performance. (2 marks)

c. Random sampling is where every member of the target population has an equal chance of being selected. The easiest way to do this would be to allocate a number to everyone on the school register and then select numbers from a random-number table which would match the numbers (and names) on the registers. (1 + 2 marks)

d. Two advantages are:

• Once the correlation has been found, predictions can be made about one variable from the other.

• It shows both the strength and the relationship of the correlation (2 + 2 marks)

e. A scattergraph (or scattergram). (1 mark)

f. It shows a strong, positive correlation. (2 marks)

g. Standard deviation is a measure of dispersion. It indicates the variability or spread of scores from the mean. The larger the standard deviation, the larger the spread of scores. (2 marks)

h. There is no mention that informed consent was obtained from the participants prior to the study. The researchers should have explained all details of the study prior to the commencement of the study. The researchers could have dealt with this by telling participants the purpose and procedure of the study beforehand in order to gain their informed consent. They do not appear to have gained informed consent to ask their school for their GCSE results.

The lack of debriefing is an ethical issue. It is particularly important in this case since participants were given an invalid IQ test. Participants may have been affected by their IQ results and thus a thorough debriefing is essential to explain their results. (3 + 3 marks)

i. The design could have been improved if the researchers had used a pilot study to test the procedures and methodology that they were planning to employ. This might have highlighted the fact that their 'homemade' IQ test was not a valid measure of intelligence.

The design could also have been improved with a larger sample size. A random sample ensures a sample that is selected in an unbiased way, but does not guarantee an unbiased sample. With only 10 students in the sample, there is a high chance of anomalous results affecting the findings. (3 + 3 marks)

# EXAM QUESTIONS

# Essential Glossary

*This includes the terms mentioned in the Specification. As such, you could be asked about them in part (a) and/or part (b) questions. They're set out in alphabetical order by Module Section. It's worth learning them all (hard luck)!*

## 10.1 Cognitive Psychology

**Alternatives to the MSM (Multi-Store Model):** These include the Working Memory model (Baddeley & Hitch 1974) and the Levels of Processing approach (Craik & Lockhart 1974).

**Eyewitness testimony:** Refers to the reported memory that people have for criminal incidents that they have seen. This often involves visual identification of an individual. Research has concentrated on the accuracy of such accounts and the common errors that are made. It also includes the role of leading questions (e.g. Loftus and Palmer's 1974 SCCS study) and the reconstructive nature of many of these accounts.

**Flashbulb (FB) memories:** Memories that can be vividly recalled in such detail that they are almost like 'photographic' memories (hence the name). They are usually about public events (e.g. September 11th 2001) or personal events (e.g. death of a family member). The recalled event tends to be unexpected and emotionally significant. People can often recall where they were and what they were doing when they heard the news. Conway *et al.*'s (2003) 9/11 study investigated the nature of FB memories.

**Forgetting:** The inability to recall or recognise material which has been previously stored in memory. A distinction can be made between:

- Material that was placed in memory and which has now disappeared (lack of availability)
- Material that's still in memory but can't be recalled (lack of accessibility).

Forgetting in STM can be through displacement or trace decay whereas forgetting in LTM can be by interference or retrieval failure.

**Long-term memory:** A place for storing information for a longer period of time. It has an unlimited capacity. The duration of LTM can be a lifetime. LTM favours semantic encoding (on the basis of meaning).

**Memory:** This can mean (1) the system of retaining information, (2) the actual storage system, or (3) the material that's been retained.

**Reconstructive memory:** This suggests that memory does not work like a camera but is prone to inaccuracies and interpretations based on prior experiences. Memory is influenced by schemas. Schemas are ready-made expectations that help us to interpret and understand our world. Bartlett's (1932) WAROG study was one of the first to investigate the reconstructive nature of memory.

**Repression:** A technique proposed by Freud which involves the pushing out of painful memories into the unconscious (i.e. motivated forgetting). The memory is too anxiety-provoking for it to remain in the conscious. Repression is thus a 'defence mechanism' to protect the conscious mind. However, this repressed memory may reappear in other ways such as in dreams or 'Freudian slips'. Although impossible to prove and difficult to test scientifically, Levinger and Clark's (1961) ECW study provides some experimental support for repression.

**Short-term memory:** A temporary place for storing information received through the senses where it receives little processing. It has a limited capacity although this can be increased by chunking. STM duration is limited to about 30 seconds. STM favours acoustic encoding.

**The Multi-Store Model (MSM):** A model of memory first proposed by Atkinson and Shiffrin in 1969. It suggests that memory is split into two different stores (STM and LTM). With rehearsal, information flows from one store to the other. The greater the rehearsal, the more chance the information will be stored permanently in LTM. Support for this STM/LTM distinction comes from capacity and duration studies, clinical case studies (KF) and the serial position effect. Criticisms of the model suggest it's over-simplified, rehearsal alone doesn't always lead to LTM transfer and that the linear direction of the model is incorrect.

## 10.2 Developmental Psychology

**Attachment:** A relatively permanent emotional tie to a particular individual.

**Cognitive development:** Changes in the child's ability to think, reason and understand. This can be assessed by teachers' ratings, academic achievement (for example, SATs), or specialised tests (such as intelligence tests). Children from low-income families may benefit academically from day care more than other children.

**Cross-cultural variations in attachment:** The *patterns* of attachment type (secure, anxious-avoidant, anxious-resistant) that exist both between and within cultures.

**Day care:** All varieties of non-maternal care of children who normally live with their parents or close relatives. Examples include crèches, day nurseries, childminders ('out-of-home' facilities), (non-resident) nannies, and grandparents ('in-the-home' arrangements). It *excludes* foster care and institutional (residential) care.

**Deprivation:** The loss (through separation) of an attachment figure (usually the mother-figure). This can be *short-term* (for example, when the child goes into care while the mother is in hospital) or *long-term* (as in divorce or the death of a parent). The most common (short-term) effect of deprivation is distress.

**Insecure attachment:** A relationship with another person in which the attachment figure is either treated with *indifference* and much like a stranger (anxious-avoidant: Type A); or shown *ambivalence* following a period of separation (anxious-resistant: Type C). In neither case does the attachment figure provide a sense of security and safety.

**Institutionalisation:** The fact of growing up in an institution (such as an orphanage or residential nursery) or the effects of such an upbringing. Institutionalisation is associated with privation.

**Privation:** In relation to attachment, the absence of an attachment figure or the lack of opportunity to form an attachment. More generally, the lack of particular kinds of stimulation. Privation is usually associated with children raised in institutions and/or under conditions of extreme hardship. The most common (long-term) effect is developmental retardation (such as affectionless psychopathy).

**Secure attachment (Type B):** A (usually) long-term relationship with another person, who provides a sense of security and comfort at times of stress, and separation from whom causes distress and sorrow.

**Separation:** Disruption to the relationship with an attachment figure. This can be short-term/temporary (as when a child's mother goes into hospital) or long-term/permanent (as in parental divorce or death).

**Social development:** Changes in the child's social relationships, in particular, its ability to become attached to a mother-figure. In relation to day care, it is claimed that children experiencing day care are more likely to develop *insecure attachments*.

# 11.1 Physiological Psychology

**Cardiovascular disorders:** Disorders/diseases of the heart and the circulatory system. Examples include high blood pressure/BP (hypertension), coronary artery disease (CAD), and coronary heart disease (CHD).

**General Adaptation Syndrome (GAS):** According to Selye, the body's defence against any stressor, either environmental or arising from within the body itself. It consists of the alarm reaction (*shock* and *countershock phases*), resistance and exhaustion.

**Immune system:** A collection of (billions of) cells, produced mainly in the spleen, lymph nodes, thymus and bone marrow, which travel through the bloodstream, defending the body against antigens (such as bacteria, viruses and cancerous cells). The major type of immune cells are white blood cells (leucocytes).

**Life changes:** Events that require us to adapt. In Holmes and Rahe's Social Readjustment Rating Scale (SRRS), the degree of stress (that is, change) associated with particular life events is measured in Life Change Units (LCUs). Death of spouse, divorce and marital separation are rated as being the most stressful. Change in sleeping habits, Christmas, and minor violations of the law are rated as being the least stressful.

**Physiological approaches to stress management:** Formal attempts to reduce the effects of stress, such as the use of psychotherapeutic drugs (in particular, *anxiolytic* – anxiety-reducing – drugs), and biofeedback (which helps patients control their BP, heart rate, muscle tension and other *autonomic functions*).

**Psychological approaches to stress management:** Both formal and informal attempts to reduce the effects of stress. *Formal* attempts include stress inoculation training (SIT), a form of cognitive restructuring and increasing hardiness. *Informal* attempts refer mainly to coping strategies/mechanisms, such as problem-focused and emotion-focused helping (Lazarus and Folkman).

**Sources of stress:** The different kinds of stressors which can induce a stress response. These include environmental 'insults' (such as electric shock and excessive heat or cold), life changes (such as death of spouse) and workplace stressors (such as work overload and role conflict).

**Stress:** (a) An environmental event or situation (a stressor) which induces a stress-response in us; (b) our response to a stressor, in particular the physiological/bodily responses (such as the General Adaptation Syndrome/GAS); (c) interaction between an individual and their environment, in particular the belief that they don't possess the resources needed to deal with the demands of a situation. But people differ in what makes them feel stressed, how much stress they feel and how they try to deal with it.

**Stress management:** (a) A range of techniques used deliberately by professionals to help people reduce their stress levels. These can be psychological (as in cognitive restructuring and increasing hardiness) or physiological (as in the use of psychotherapeutic drugs and biofeedback). This is *formal* stress management. (b) *Informal* stress management involves what we do spontaneously in our attempts to reduce stress, such as when we use coping strategies/mechanisms.

**Stressors:** An environmental event or situation which we feel unable to deal with and which induces a stress response.

**Workplace stressors:** Stressors which are either common to many occupations (such as work overload/underload, role ambiguity/conflict, job insecurity/redundancy), or which are related to the nature of the particular occupation (such as nurses having to deal constantly with suffering and death, and air traffic controllers having to be vigilant for long periods).

## 11.2 Individual Differences

**Abnormality:** Since abnormality can take many different forms, there is no single feature that encompasses the term. Generally, abnormality can be defined as *deviating from the norm or average* but it is difficult to determine this norm or average. Attempts to define abnormality include: statistical infrequency, deviation from social norms, failure to function adequately and deviation from ideal mental health.

**Anorexia nervosa** *(literally means 'nervous loss of appetite')*: Primarily a female eating disorder characterised by a refusal to maintain normal body weight (<85% normal weight). Accompanied by an intense fear of being overweight, a distortion of body image and a general, evident physical decline with the cessation of menstruation (amenorrhoea), dry, cracking skin and constipation. In some cases AN can be fatal. Depression and low self-esteem are also common.

**Behavioural model of abnormality:** This approach isn't associated with mental disorders but with maladaptive behaviour. It assumes that all behaviour is learnt through the process of classical and operant conditioning and thus can be unlearnt using the same principles. Treatment involves behaviour therapy and behaviour modification. This approach is scientifically tested and proven to be effective for less serious disorders.

**Biological (medical) model of abnormality:** An approach which assumes that abnormal behaviour has an underlying physical cause. Diagnosis involves the identification of symptoms. Studies into genetic inheritance, biochemistry and infection support this approach. Treatment involves invasive techniques such as drugs, ECT and psychosurgery. There is considerable scientific evidence to support this approach, although it is argued that it treats the symptoms rather than the root cause of any illness.

**Bulimia nervosa** *(literally means 'ox hunger')*: Primarily a female eating disorder characterised by periods of binge eating frequently followed by purging (expulsion of food). Accompanied by an intense fear of being fat, the physical effects are not obvious but include the deterioration of tooth enamel and digestive tract damage. BN is rarely fatal.

**Clinical characteristics:** This refers to the symptoms displayed by individuals which help in the diagnosis of patients. The list of symptoms is gained through observation, examination and self-report.

**Cognitive model of abnormality:** Assumes that abnormal behaviour is caused by an individual's disturbed thoughts. It assumes that thoughts affect behaviour. Individuals make 'cognitive errors' such as magnifying failures and minimising successes. Therapy involves cognitive restructuring. Irrational and negative thoughts need to be replaced by rational and positive ones. This approach is both modern and popular.

**'Deviation from ideal mental health':** This definition concentrates on the 'normal' characteristics people should possess for ideal mental health. This list includes positive self-esteem, autonomy and resistance to stress. If people do not possess these characteristics they are said to be abnormal. Limitations of this include the subjective nature of the over-demanding criteria. Indeed, based on the criteria proposed by Jahoda (1958) most people might be classified as abnormal!

**'Deviation from social norms':** Abnormality is seen as any behaviour that violates the social norms within a society. Social norms are unwritten rules for acceptable behaviour (i.e. how one ought to behave). This definition has limitations in that it can be subjective and norms change over time and vary across cultures.

**Eating disorders:** A term that applies to psychological and physical illnesses that are associated with harmful eating patterns or behaviour. The most well-known of these are anorexia nervosa and bulimia nervosa.

'Failure to function adequately': This definition involves a list of behaviours that prevent a person from coping with their day-to-day life. This list includes personal distress, unpredictability and mal-adaptive behaviour. The more of these indicators a person has, the more abnormal they are seen to be. One limitation is that some people who would be classified as abnormal (e.g. Harold Shipman) appear to function adequately in society.

Psychodynamic model of abnormality: Assumes that mental disorders are psychological in origin. Childhood experiences and the conflict in the personality (id, ego and superego) play an important part in the development of mental disorders. Traumatic events are placed in the unconscious through repression. The goal of psychodynamic therapy is to make the 'unconscious conscious'. This is achieved through insight and is a 'talking cure'. The psychodynamic model remains controversial and is difficult to evaluate scientifically.

Psychological models of abnormality: This is an 'umbrella' term to refer to any approach which explains abnormal behaviour with the exception of the biological (medical) model. It includes the psychodynamic, behavioural and cognitive models.

Statistical infrequency: This definition of abnormality defines any behaviour that is statistically rare as abnormal. It has the advantage of being objective but fails to distinguish between statistically rare desirable and undesirable behaviour. It is also difficult to measure all behaviours and to determine the 'cut-off' point for normality. When is behaviour sufficiently rare as to be defined as 'abnormal'?

## 12.1 Social influence

**Conformity (majority influence):** Yielding to group pressure. It is the influence that a group has over an individual (hence, 'majority influence'). The group consists of the individual's peers (that is, they are all of equal status).

**Deception:** Misleading research participants about the true purpose of a research study. This can be done through telling them that the study is concerned with one thing (such as the effects of punishment on learning), when it's really about something else (such as obedience, as in Milgram's experiments). Participants can also be deceived if certain information is *withheld*. Deception, therefore, prevents participants from giving their informed consent.

**Ecological (external) validity:** Being able to generalise the findings of a study beyond the particular laboratory setting in which they were collected. This includes more naturalistic ('real-life') situations. Also called mundane realism.

**Ethical guidelines:** Formal, written documents which provide a framework within which psychologists should carry out their research. For example, the *Ethical Principles* published by the British Psychological Society (BPS) help determine what's an acceptable psychological investigation.

**Ethical issues:** Considerations that relate to the welfare and wellbeing of participants in psychological research. Major issues, which have been highlighted by research into social influence, include deception, informed consent, protection of participants from psychological harm, and withdrawal from the investigation.

**Experimental (internal) validity:** The belief of participants in an experiment that the experimental situation is real. For example, the teacher-participants in Milgram's obedience studies believed that they were actually administering electric shocks to the learner (Mr Wallace), and that he, like them, was a volunteer. Also called experimental realism.

**Informed consent:** Agreeing to participate in psychological research (giving your consent) in the full knowledge of the true purpose of the research. If participants have been deceived to any degree then they haven't given informed consent.

**Minority influence:** The ability of the numerical minority to change the views of the majority. As in majority influence, all the individuals involved are of equal status.

**Obedience to authority:** Complying with the demands or instructions of an authority figure. By definition, this figure has greater power in the particular situation or setting in which they make their demands.

**Protection of participants from psychological harm:** One of the ethical issues highlighted by social influence research in particular. The harm may be physical and/or psychological. Ethical guidelines are designed to help define what is acceptable research. Researchers must consider the consequences of their research *for the participants*, whose psychological wellbeing, health, values and dignity mustn't be threatened in any way.

**Social influence:** The various ways in which other people affect what we do and think. In conformity, other people's influence is indirect and often we're unaware of it. The people concerned are of equal status to us (our peers), and they affect us by example. This also applies to minority influence. But in obedience, someone with greater power or authority than us tries directly to influence our behaviour by giving us orders or instructions.

# 12.2 Research Methods

*There aren't any questions that ask you to define Research Methods terms. You'll have to understand the meaning of the terms in relation to the particular research described in the Stimulus Material. However, the following terms are mentioned in the Specification.*

*(Note: Unlike the other Sections, the terms are set out in Specification order and not alphabetical order. We think that grouping them like this makes more sense.)*

**Quantitative research methods:** Techniques that lend themselves to the collection of numerical and statistical data. Experimental methods would be examples of this.

**Qualitative methods:** Techniques that lend themselves to the collection of non-numerical data (e.g. the written or spoken word). Interviews and naturalistic observations would be examples of this.

**Experiments:** A situation where the independent variable is deliberately manipulated to find the effects on the dependent variable, whilst controlling extraneous variables.

- **Laboratory experiments:** An experiment that occurs in a carefully controlled environment, usually a laboratory.
- **Field experiments:** An experiment that takes place in the real world as opposed to a laboratory. The IV is still manipulated by the experimenters.
- **Natural experiments:** An experiment that takes place in the real world and where the IV occurs naturally. There is no manipulation of the IV.

**Investigations using correlational analysis:** A method of data analysis which allows the strength of the relationship between two (or more) co-variables to be measured.

**Naturalistic observations:** A study where an observer objectively records the behaviour of participants in their natural environment.

**Questionnaires:** Written methods of data collection. They can involve open or closed questions. Surveys tend to involve a large sample of participants.

**Interviews:** A verbal method of data collection that involves the researcher asking questions in a face-to-face way. They can vary from very structured (formal) to unstructured (informal).

**Aims:** An outline of the general purpose of the research study. A statement of *why* the research study is taking place.

**Hypotheses:** These are predictions made about the possible outcomes of a study that is yet to be conducted. A statement of *what* is expected to happen.

- **Experimental/alternative hypothesis:** The prediction made before the study takes place that an IV will have an effect on the DV. There are two types: directional (one-tailed) and non-directional (two-tailed).
- **Directional (one-tailed) hypothesis ($H_1$):** This hypothesis states the direction of any difference that is expected. In correlations, the hypothesis is predicted as being either positive or negative.
- **Non-directional (two-tailed) hypothesis ($H_1$):** The prediction that there will be a significant difference between the results of the two conditions (or a correlation between the variables). It does not predict the direction that difference (or correlation) will take.

**Experimental design:** A procedure used in experiments that allows for the control of participant variables. Without this control, the experimental results would be jeopardised. There are three types: independent-groups design, repeated-measures design and matched-pairs design.

- **Independent-groups design:** Different participants are randomly allocated to the different experimental conditions.

- **Repeated-measures design:** The same participants are tested in all the experimental conditions. They 'repeat' all the conditions.
- **Matched-participants (or pairs) design:** The same as independent-groups design except that similar participants are randomly allocated to the different experimental conditions. They are previously 'matched' on whatever criteria are judged to be important for the study. This might include age and sex.

**Independent variable (IV):** The variable that is directly manipulated by the experimenter to see the effect it has on the dependent variable (DV)

**Dependent variable (DV):** The variable that is measured by the experimenter. So-called because changes in this variable are *dependent* on the IV.

**Extraneous variables:** Anything, other than the IV, which might have an effect on the DV. Extraneous variables should be controlled.

**Confounding variables:** Extraneous variables that aren't controlled, and which can adversely affect or 'confound' results.

**Operationalisation:** The appropriate way to define or measure the variable in question. For example, can you operationalise 'good' driving in terms of the number of accidents you've had?

**Pilot studies:** Small scale 'practice' investigations that allow the researcher to check all aspects of their research. Appropriate improvements can then be made to the 'real' study.

**Reliability:** Means consistency. Research should be consistent over time and across different researchers. In other words, the research should be repeatable, replicable and the same (or similar) results should be obtained. If this occurs, the research is reliable.

**Validity:** Means accuracy. Is the research measuring what it is supposed to be measuring?

- **Internal validity:** Refers to whether the research is accurate *within* the confines of the experimental setting. The research must not be affected by investigator effects or demand characteristics. If results can be directly attributed to the manipulation of the IV, then the research is internally valid.
- **External (ecological) validity:** Refers to whether the research results are accurate and can thus be generalised *beyond* the confines of the experimental setting.

**Participants:** The people who take place in the research study. They form the sample.

**Random sampling:** A technique where every member of the population has an equal chance of being selected. The simplest way to do this is to draw names out of a hat.

**Demand characteristics:** Refers to the situation where participants try to guess the purpose of the study and amend their behaviour accordingly. They act according to what they feel are the 'demands' of the study or experiment.

**Investigator effects:** This refers to the process whereby a researcher inadvertently influences the results of the study. This could be due to physical characteristics of the researcher affecting respondents' answers or behaviour.

**Measures of central tendency:** These are data values that represent the typical mid-point value of a set of scores. They're 'averages' and the most commonly used measures are the mean, median and mode.

- **Mean:** The arithmetic average obtained by adding up all the scores and dividing by the number of scores. Most appropriate with interval/ratio data.
- **Median:** The middle value when scores are placed in rank order. Most appropriate with ordinal data.
- **Mode:** The value that occurs most frequently. Most appropriate with nominal data.

Measures of dispersion: These are measures of the variability or spread of scores. They include the range and standard deviation.

- Range: The difference between the highest and lowest scores.
- Inter-quartile range: The spread of scores for the middle 50% of the scores.
- Standard deviation: A measure of the distribution of scores around the mean. A large SD suggests a wide scatter of scores, a small SD suggests that scores are close to the mean.

Positive correlation: Where one variable increases, the other variable increases (e.g. ice cream sales increase as temperature increases). It is expressed from 0 (no correlation) to +1 (perfect positive correlation).

Negative correlation: Where one variable increases, the other variable decreases (e.g. raincoat sales decrease as temperature increases). It is expressed from 0 (no correlation) to −1 (perfect negative correlation).

Histograms: A type of graph used for frequency data. The area of each column is proportional to the number of cases it represents. The X axis must involve continuous data and is divided into appropriate intervals.

Bar charts: A type of graph used to present discrete (non-continuous) or nominal data visually.

Scattergraphs: A type of graph used to plot correlations. Allows any clear relationship between two variables to be seen at a glance. So-called because the scores are 'scattered' across the graph.

# References

Abrams, D., Wetherell, M., Cochrane, S., Hogg, M.A. & Turner, J.C. (1990) Knowing what to think by knowing who you are: Self-categorization and the nature of norm formation. *British Journal of Social Psychology, 29*, 97–119.

Abramson, L.Y., Metalsky, G.I. & Alloy, L.B. (1989) Hopelessness depression: A theory-based subtype of depression. *Psychological Review, 96*, 358–372.

Abramson, L.Y., Seligman, M.E.P. & Teasdale, J.D. (1978) Learned helplessness in humans: Critique and reformulation. *Journal of Abnormal Psychology, 87*, 49–74.

Adam, K. (1980) Sleep as a restorative process and a theory to explain why. *Progress in Brain Research, 53*, 289–305.

AHCPR (1999) Treatment of Depression – Newer Pharmacotherapies. Summary, Evidence Report/Technology Assessment: No. 7, March. Rockville, MD: Agency for Health Care Policy and Research: http://www.ahrq.gov/clinic/epcsums/deprsumm. htm

Ainsworth, M.D.S. (1967) *Infancy in Uganda: Infant Care and the Growth of Love*. Baltimore, MD: Johns Hopkins University Press.

Ainsworth, M.D.S., Bell, S.M.V. & Stayton, D.J. (1971) Individual differences in strange-situation behaviour of one-year-olds. In H.R. Schaffer (Ed.) *The Origins of Human Social Relations*. New York: Academic Press.

Ainsworth, M.D.S., Blehar, M.C., Waters, E. & Wall, S. (1978) *Patterns of Attachment: A Psychological Study of the Strange Situation*. Hillsdale, N.J: Lawrence Erlbaum Associates Inc.

Alberge, D. (1999) Dancers take lessons in eating. *The Times*, 18 August.

Aldhous, P., Coghlan, A. & Copley, J. (1999) Let the people speak. *New Scientist, 162* (2187), 26–31.

Allen, L. & Santrock, J. (1993) *The Contexts of Behavior Psychology*. Madison, WI: Brown & Benchmark Press.

Alloy, L.B., Kelly, K.A., Mineka, S. & Clements, C.M. (1990) Comorbidity in anxiety and depressive disorders: A helplessness/hopelessness perspective. In J.D. Maser & C.R. Cloninger (Eds) *Comorbidity in Anxiety and Mood Disorders*. Washington, D.C.: American Psychiatric Press.

Allport, G.W. & Postman, L. (1947) *The Psychology of Rumour*. New York: Holt, Rinehart & Winston.

Alsaker, F.D. (1992) Pubertal timing, overweight, and psychological adjustment. *Journal of Early Adolescence, 12*, 396–419.

Alsaker, F.D. (1996) The impact of puberty. *Journal of Child Psychology and Psychiatry, 37* (3), 249–258.

American National Association of Anorexia Nervosa and Associated Disorders: www.anad.org.

American Psychiatric Association (1952) *Diagnostic and Statistical Manual of Mental Disorders*. Washington, D.C.: American Psychiatric Association.

American Psychiatric Association (1968) *Diagnostic and Statistical Manual of Mental Disorders* (2nd edition). Washington, D.C.: American Psychiatric Association.

American Psychiatric Association (1980) *Diagnostic and Statistical Manual of Mental Disorders* (3rd edition). Washington, D.C.: American Psychiatric Association.

American Psychiatric Association (1987) *Diagnostic and Statistical Manual of Mental Disorders* (3rd edition, revised). Washington, D.C.: American Psychiatric Association.

American Psychiatric Association (1994) *Diagnostic and Statistical Manual of Mental Disorders* (4th edition). Washington, D.C.: American Psychiatric Association.

American Psychological Association (1982) *Ethical Principles in Conduct of Research with Human Participants.* Washington, D.C.: American Psychological Association.

Anderson, C. & Bushman, B. (2001) Effects of Violent Video Games . . . A Meta-Analytic Review. *Psychological Science*, Sept., 353–359.

Anderson, C.A. (1987) Temperature and aggression: Effects on quarterly, yearly, and city rates of violent and nonviolent crime. *Journal of Personality & Social Psychology, 52 (6)*, 1161–1173.

Anderson, C.A. (1989) Temperature and aggression: Ubiquitous effects of heat on the occurrence of human violence. *Psychological Bulletin, 106*, 74–96.

Anderson, C.A., Anderson, K.E. & Deuser, W.E. (1996) Examining the affective aggression framework: Weapon and temperature effects on aggressive thoughts, affect and attitudes. *PSPB, 22*(4), 366–376.

Andersson, M. (1994) *Sexual Selection.* Princeton, NJ: Princeton University Press.

Anokhin, P. K. (1973) The forming of natural and artificial intelligence. *Impact of Science on Society*, Vol. XXIII, 3.

APA (2003): www.apa.org

Argyle, M. (1983) *The Psychology of Interpersonal Behaviour* (4th edition). Harmondsworth: Penguin.

Argyle, M. (1987) *The Psychology of Happiness.* London: Methuen.

Armsby, R.E. (1971) A re-examination of the development of moral judgement in children. *Child Development, 42*, 1241–1248.

Aronson, E. (1992) *The Social Animal* (6th edition). New York: Freeman.

Asch, S.E. (1951) Effect of group pressure upon the modification and distortion of judgements. In H. Guetzkow (Ed.) *Groups, Leadership and Men.* Pittsburgh, PA: Carnegie Press.

Aschoff, J. (1960) Exogenous and endogenous components in circadian rhythms. *Cold Spring Harbor Symposia on Quantitative Biology*, Vol.XXV. *Biological Clocks.* New York: Cold Spring Harbor Press, 11–28.

Aschoff, J. (1981) A survey on biological rhythms. In J. Aschoff (Ed.) *Biological Rhythms*, Vol.4, *Handbook of Behavioral Neurobiology.* New York: Plenum Press.

Aschoff, J., Hoffman, K., Pohl, H. & Wever, R. (1975) Re-entrainment of circadian rhythms after phase-shifts of the zeitgeber. *Chronobiologia, 11*, 23–78.

Aschoff, J. & Wever, R. (1962) Spontanperiodik des Menschen bei Ausschluss aller Zeitgeber. *Natuurwissenschaften, 49*, 337–342. see also: http://www.talkaboutsleep.com/sleepbasics/ history.htm

Aschoff, J. & Wever, R. (1981) The circadian system in man. In J. Aschoff (Ed.) *Biological Rhythms*, Vol.4, *Handbook of Behavioural Neurology.* New York: Plenum Press.

Atkinson, R.C. & Shiffrin, R.M. (1968) Human memory: a proposed system and its control processes. In K.W. Spence & J.T. Spence (Eds) *The Psychology of Learning and Motivation*, Vol.2. London: Academic Press.

Atkinson, R.C. & Shiffrin, R.M. (1971) The control of short-term memory. *Scientific American, 224*, 82–90.

Attie, I. & Brooks-Gunn, J. (1989) Development of eating problems in adolescent girls: A longitudinal study. *Developmental Psychology, 25*, 70–79.

Ayllon, T. & Azrin, N.H. (1965) The measurement and reinforcement of behavior of psychotics. *Journal of the Experimental Analysis of Behavior, 8*, 357–383.

Ayllon, T. & Azrin, N.H. (1968). *The Token Economy: A Motivational System for Therapy and Rehabilitation.* New York: Appleton-Century-Crofts.

Baddeley, A.D. (1966) The influence of acoustic and semantic similarity on long-term memory for word sequences. *Quarterly Journal of Experimental Psychology, 18*, 302–309.

Baddeley, A.D. (2001) Is working memory still working? *American Psychologist, 56*, 861–864.

Baddeley, A.D., Grant, S., Wight, E. & Thomson, N., (1973) Imagery and Visual Working in P.M.A. Rabbitt & S. Darnit (Eds) *Attention & Performance V*, London: Academic Press.

Baddeley, A.D. & Hitch, G. (1974) Working memory. In G.H. Bower (Ed.) *Recent Advances in Learning and Motivation*, Vol.8. New York: Academic Press.

Baddeley, A.D., Thomson, N. & Buchanan, M. (1975) Word length and the structure of short-term memory. *Journal of Verbal Learning and Verbal Behavior, 14*, 575–589.

Bahrick, H.P., Bahrick, P.O. & Wittinger, R.P. (1975) Fifty years of memory for names and faces: A cross-sectional approach. *Journal of Experimental Psychology: General, 104*, 54–75.

Baillargeon, R. (1987) Object permanence in 3½- and 4½-month-old infants. *Developmental Psychology, 33*, 655–664.

Bandura, A. (1965) Influence of model's reinforcement contingencies on the acquisition of imitative responses. *Journal of Personality & Social Psychology, 1*, 589–595.

Bandura, A. (1971) *Social Learning Theory*. Englewood Cliffs, NJ: Prentice-Hall.

Bandura, A. (1973) *Aggression: A Social Learning Analysis*. London: Prentice-Hall.

Bandura, A. (1974) Behaviour theory and models of man. *American Psychologist, 29*, 859–869.

Bandura, A. (1977a) Self-efficacy: Toward a unifying theory of behaviour change. *Psychological Review, 84*, 191–215.

Bandura, A. (1977b) *Social Learning Theory* (2nd edition). Englewood Cliffs, NJ: Prentice-Hall.

Bandura, A. (1986) *Social Foundations of Thought and Action*. Englewood Cliffs, NJ: Prentice-Hall.

Bandura, A. (1989) Social cognitive theory. In R. Vasta (Ed.) *Six Theories of Child Development*. Greenwich: JAI Press.

Bandura, A. & Ribes-Inesta, E. (1976) *Analysis of Delinquency and Aggression*. Hillsdale, NJ: Lawrence Erlbaum Associates, Inc.

Bandura, A., Ross, D. & Ross, S. (1961) Transmission of aggression through imitation of aggressive models. *Journal of Abnormal and Social Psychology, 63*, 575–582.

Bandura, A., Ross, D. & Ross, S. (1963) Imitation of film-mediated aggressive models. *Journal of Abnormal and Social Psychology, 66*(1), 3–11.

Barber, B.K. & Buehler, C. (1996) Family cohesion and enmeshment: Different constructs, different effects. *Journal of Marriage and The Family, 58* (2), 433–441.

Barlow, D.H. & Lehman, C.L. (1996) Advances in the psychosocial treatment of anxiety disorders: Implications for national health care. *Archives of General Psychiatry, 53*, 727–735.

Barnard, N.D. & Kaufman, S.R. (1997) Animal research is wasteful and misleading. *Scientific American*, February, 64–66.

Baron, R. (1977) *Human Aggression*. New York: Plenum.

Baron, R. & Byrne, D. (1997) *Social Psychology*. Boston, MA: Allyn and Bacon.

Baron, R.A. (1979) Aggression and heat: the long hot summer revisited. In A. Baum, J.E. Singer & S. Valins (Eds) *Advances in Environmental Psychology*. Hillsdale, NJ: Erlbaum.

Baron, R.A. & Bell, P.A. (1976) Aggression and heat: the influence of ambient temperature, negative affect, and a cooling drink on physical aggression. *Journal of Personality and Social Psychology, 33*, 245–255.

Baron, R.A. & Bell, P.A. (1977) Sexual arousal and aggression by males: Effects of type of erotic stimuli and prior provocation. *Journal of Personality & Social Psychology, 35*(2), 79–87.

Barongan, C. & Hall, G. (1995) The influence of misogynist rap music on sexual aggression against women. *Psychology of Women Quarterly, 19*, 195–207.

Barr, C.E., Mednick, S.A. & Munk-Jorgenson, P. (1990) Exposure to influenza epidemics during gestation and adult schizophrenia: A forty-year study. *Archives of General Psychiatry, 47*, 869–874.

Barron, F. & Harrington, D.M. (1981) Creativity, intelligence and personality. *Annual Reviews of Psychology*, 32: 439–476.

Bar-Tal, D. & Saxe, L. (1976) Perception of similarity and dissimilarity in attractive couples and individuals. *Journal of Personality & Social Psychology, 33*, 772–781.

Bartlett, F.C. (1932) *Remembering*. Cambridge: Cambridge University Press.

Bateson, G., Jackson, D., Haley, J. & Weakland, J. (1956) Toward a theory of schizophrenia. *Behavioural Science, 1*, 251–264.

Bateson, P. (1986) When to experiment on animals. *New Scientist*, **109** (14960), 30–32.

Bateson, P. (1992) Do animals feel pain? *New Scientist, 134* (1818), 30–33.

Batson, C., Dyck, J., Brandt, J., Batson, J., Powell, A., McMaster, M., & Griffitt, C. (1988) Five studies testing two new egoistic alternatives to the empathy–altruism hypothesis. *Journal of Personality & Social Psychology, 55*, 52–77.

Batson, C.D. (1987) Prosocial Motivation: Is it ever truly altruistic? *Advances in Experimental Social Psychology, 20*, 65–122.

Batson, C.D., Duncan, B.D., Ackerman, P., Buckley, T. & Birch, K. (1981) Is empathic emotion a source of altruistic motivation? *Journal of Personality & Social Psychology, 40*, 290–302.

Baumrind, D. (1964) Some thoughts on the ethics of research: After reading Milgram's behavioural study of obedience. *American Psychologist, 19*, 421–423.

Baydar, N. & Brooks-Gunn, J. (1991) Effects of maternal employment and child-care arrangements on preschoolers' cognitive and behavioural outcomes. *Developmental Psychology, 27*, 932–945.

Bayley, N. (1969) *Bayley Scales of Infant Development*. New York: Psychological Corporation.

Beaman, A.L., Barnes, P.J., Klentz, B. & Mcquirk, B. (1978) Increasing helping rates through information dissemination: Teaching pays. *Personality and Social Psychology Bulletin*, 4, 406–411.

Bean, P. (1979) Psychiatrists' assessments of mental illness. *British Journal of Psychiatry*, 135, 122–128.

Beck, A.T. (1967a) *Cognitive Therapy and the Emotional Disorders*. New York: International Universities Press.

Beck, A.T. (1967b) *Depression: Causes and Treatment*. Philadelphia: University of Philadelphia Press.

Beck, A.T. (1987) Cognitive models of depression. *Journal of Cognitive Psychotherapy: An International Quarterly*, 1, 5–37.

Beck, A.T. (1993) Cognitive therapy: Past, present and future. *Journal of Consulting & Clinical Psychology*, 61(2), 194–198.

Bee, H. (1994) *Lifespan Development*. New York: HarperCollins.

Bee, H. (2000) *The Developing Child* (9th edition). Boston: Allyn & Bacon.

Bekerian, D.A. & Baddeley, A. D. (1980) Saturation advertising and the repetition effect. *Learning and Verbal Behaviour*, 19, 17–25.

Bellur, R. (1995) Interpersonal attraction revisited: Cross-cultural conceptions of love. *Psychology Review*, 1, 24–26.

Belsky, J. & Rovine, M.J. (1988) Non-maternal care in the first year of life and the infant–parent attachment. *Child Development*, 59, 157–167.

Bem, S.L. (1974) The measurement of psychological androgyny. *Journal of Consulting and Clinical Psychology*, 42 (2), 155–162.

Bem, S.L. (1985) Androgyny and gender schema theory: A conceptual and empirical integration. In T.B. Sonderegger (Ed.) *Nebraska Symposium on Motivation*. Lincoln, NE: University of Nebraska Press.

Bentall, R. (Ed.) (1990) *Reconstructing Schizophrenia*. London: Routledge.

Bentley, E. (2000) *Awareness*. London: Routledge.

Bergin, A.E. (1971) The evaluation of therapeutic outcomes. In A.E. Bergin & S.L. Garfield (Eds) *Handbook of Psychotherapy and Behavior Change*. New York: Wiley.

Berkowitz, L. (1983) The experience of anger as a parallel process in the display of impulsive, 'angry' aggression. In R. Geen & E. Donnerstein (Eds) *Aggression: Theoretical and empirical reviews*, Vol.1. New York: Academic Press.

Berkowitz, L. (1984) Some Effects of Thoughts on anti- and pro-social influences of Media Events: A cognitive-neoassociation. *Psychological Bulletin*, 95, 410–427.

Berkowitz, L. & Alioto, J.T. (1973) The meaning of an observed event as a determinant of its aggressive consequences. *Journal of Personality & Social Psychology*, 28, 206–217.

Berry, J.W. (1969) On cross-cultural compatibility. *International Journal of Psychology*, 4, 119–128.

Berry, J.W., Poortinga, Y.H., Segall, M.H. & Dasen, P.R. (1992) *Cross-Cultural Psychology*. Cambridge: Cambridge University Press.

Berscheid, E., Dion, K., Hatfield, E. & Walster, G.W. (1971) Physical attractiveness and dating choice: A test of the matching hypothesis. *Journal of Experimental and Social Psychology*, 7, 173–189.

Berscheid, E. & Walster, E.M. (1974) Physical attractiveness. In L. Berkowitz (Ed.) *Advances in Experimental Social Psychology*, Volume 7. New York: Academic Press.

Berscheid, E. & Walster, E.M. (1978) *Interpersonal Attraction* (2nd edition). Reading, MA: Addison-Wesley.

Besevegis, E. & Giannitsas, N. (1996) Parent–adult relations and conflicts as perceived by adolescents. In L. Verhofstadt-Deneve, I. Kienhorst & C. Braet (Eds) *Conflict and Development in Adolescence*. Leiden: DSWO Press.

Bickman, L. (1974) Clothes make the person. *Psychology Today*, 8(4), 48–51.

Bierhoff, H. (1996) Pro-social behaviour. In M. Hewstone, W. Stroebe & G.M. Stephenson (Eds) *Introduction to Social Psychology*. London: Blackwell.

Bignell, S. (2003) The Mother of all twin studies. *The Psychologist*, 16 (7), 366.

Binet, A. & Simon, T. (1905) New methods for diagnosis of the intellectual level of subnormals. *L'Année Psychologique*, 14, 1–90.

Blackman, J. & Hornstein, H. (1977) Newscasts and the social actuary. *Public Opinion Quarterly*, 41, 295–313.

Blakemore, C. & Cooper, G.F. (1970) Development of the brain depends on the visual environment. *Nature*, 228, 447–448.

Blatner, A. & Blatner, A. (1988) *Foundations of Psychodrama* (3rd edition). New York: Springer.

Blatner, A. & Blatner, A. (1991) Imaginative interviews: A psychodramatic warm-up for developing role-playing skills. *Journal of Group Psychotherapy, Psychodrama, and Sociometry*, 44, 115–120.

Blau, P.M. (1964) *Exchange and Power in Social Life*. New York: Wiley.

Bleuler, E. (1911) *Dementia Praecox or the Group of Schizophrenias* (J. Avikin, trans.). New York: International University Press.

Block, J. (1979) Another look at sex differentiation in the socialisation behaviours of mothers and fathers. In F. Denmark & J. Sherman (Eds) *Psychology of Women: Future Directions of Research*. New York: Psychological Dimensions.

Bloom, B.S. (1964) *Stability and Change in Human Characteristics*. New York: Harcourt Brace Jovanovich.

Blyth, D.A., Simmons, R.G., Bulcroft, R., Felt, D., Vancleave, E.F. & Bush, D.M. (1981) The effects of physical development on self-image and satisfaction with body-image for early adolescent males. *Research in Community and Mental Health*, 2, 43–73.

Boden, M. (1980) Artificial intelligence and intellectual imperialism. In A.J. Chapman & D.M. Jones (Eds) *Models of Man*. Leicester: British Psychological Society.

Bodmer, W.F. (1972) Race and I.Q.: The genetic background. In K. Richardson & D. Spears (Eds) *Race, Culture and Intelligence*. Harmondsworth: Penguin.

Boesch, C. & Boesch, H. (1984) Mental map in wild chimpanzees: an analysis of hammer transports for nut cracking. *Primates*, 25, 160–170.

Bogerts, B. (1997) The temperolimbic system theory of positive schizophrenic symptoms. *Schizophrenia Bulletin*, 23, 423–435.

Booth, T. (1975) *Growing Up in Society*. London: Methuen.

Boring, E.G. (1923) Intelligence as the tests test it. *New Republic*, 6, June, 37.

Borke, H. (1975) Piaget's mountains revisited: Changes in the egocentric landscape. *Developmental Psychology*, 11, 401–419.

Boseley, S. (2000) Study reveals teenage regrets over first sex. *The Guardian*, 5 May, 11.

Botting, J.H. & Morrison, A.R. (1997) Animal research is vital to medicine. *Scientific American*, February, 67–79.

Bouchard, T.J., Lykken, D.T., McGue, M., Segal, N.L. & Tellegen, A. (1990) Sources of human psychological differences: The Minnesota study of twins reared apart. *Science*, 250, 223–228.

Bouchard, T.J. & McGue, M. (1981) Familial studies of intelligence: A review. *Science*, 212, 1055–1059.

Bouchard, T.J. & Segal, N.L. (1988) Heredity, environment and IQ. In *Instructor's Resource Manual* to accompany G. Lindzay, R. Thompson & B. Spring *Psychology* (3rd edition). New York: Worth Publishers.

Bower, T.G.R. & Wishart, J.G. (1972) The effects of motor skill on object permanence. *Cognition*, 1, 28–35.

Bowlby, J. (1951) *Maternal Care and Mental Health*. Geneva: World Health Organisation.

Bowlby, J. (1969) *Attachment and Loss, Volume 1: Attachment*. Harmondsworth: Penguin.

Bowlby, J. (1973) *Attachment and Loss*. Volume 2: *Separation*. Harmondsworth: Penguin.

Bowlby, J., Ainsworth, M., Boston, M. & Rosenbluth, D. (1956) The effects of mother– child separation: A follow-up study. *British Journal of Medical Psychology*, 29, 211.

Boyanowsky, E.O., Calvert, J., Young, J. & Brideau, L. (1981) Toward a thermo-regulatory model of violence. *Journal of Environmental Systems*, 1, 81–87.

Boyd, J.H., Rae, D.S., Thompson, J.W., Burns, B.J., Bourdon, K., Locke, B.Z. & Regier, D.A. (1990) Phobia: prevalence and risk factors. *Social Psychiatry & Psychiatric Epidemiology*, 25(6), 314–323.

Boyle, M. (1991) *Schizophrenia: A Scientific Delusion?* New York: Routledge.

Bradley, L.A. (1995) Chronic benign pain. In D. Wedding (Ed.) *Behaviour and Medicine* (2nd edition). St. Louis, MO: Mosby-Year Book.

Brady, J.V. (1958) Ulcers in executive monkeys. *Scientific American*, 199, 95–100.

Brainerd, C.J. (1983) Modifiability of cognitive development. In S. Meadows (Ed.) *Development of Thinking*. London: Methuen.

Brehm, J.W. (1966) *A Theory of Psychological Reactance*. New York: Academic Press.

Brehm, S.S. (1992) *Intimate Relationships* (2nd edition). New York: McGraw-Hill.

Brehm, S.S. & Brehm, J.W. (1981) *Psychological Reactance: A Theory of Freedom and Control*. New York: Academic Press.

Briere J. & Conte, J. (1991) Self reported amnesia for abuse in adults molested as children. *Journal of Traumatic Stress*. 6, 21–31.

Brislin, R. (1993) *Understanding Culture's Influence on Behaviour*. Orlando, FL.: Harcourt Brace Jovanovich.

British Psychological Society (1990) Ethical principles for conducting research with human participants. *The Psychologist, 3* (6), 269–272.

British Psychological Society (1993) Ethical principles for conducting research with human participants (revised). *The Psychologist, 3*(6) 269–272.

British Psychological Society (1993) Ethical principles for conducting research with human participants (revised). *The Psychologist, 6*(1), 33–35.

British Psychological Society (2000) *Code of Conduct, Ethical Principles and Guidelines.* Leicester: BPS.

British Psychological Society & The Committee of the Experimental Psychological Society (1985) *Guidelines for the Use of Animals in Research.* Leicester: BPS.

Brooks-Gunn, J., Attie, H., Burrow, C., Rosso, J.T. & Warren, M.P. (1989) The impact of puberty on body and eating concerns in athletic and non-athletic contexts. *Journal of Early Adolescence, 9,* 269–290.

Brooks-Gunn, J. & Warren, M.P. (1985) The effects of delayed menarche in different contexts; Dance and non-dance students. *Journal of Youth and Adolescence, 14,* 285–300.

Brown, J.K. (1963) A cross-cultural study of female initiation rites. *American Anthropologist, 65,* 837–853.

Brown, L.M. & Gilligan, C. (1992) *Meeting at the Crossroads: Women's Psychology and Girls' Development.* Cambridge, MA: Harvard University Press.

Brown, L.S. (1997) Ethics in psychology: Cui bono? In D. Fox & I. Prilleltensky (Eds) *Critical Psychology: An Introduction.* London: Sage.

Brown, R. (1986) *Social Psychology: The Second Edition.* New York: Free Press.

Brown, R. & Kulik, J. (1977) Flashbulb memories. *Cognition, 5,* 73–99.

Brown, R. & McNeill, D. (1966) The 'tip-of-the-tongue' phenomenon. *Journal of Verbal Learning and Verbal Behaviour, 5,* 325–337.

Brown, R.J. (1988) Intergroup relations. In M. Hewstone, W. Stroebe & G.M. Stephenson (Eds) *Introduction to Social Psychology* (2nd edition). Oxford: Blackwell.

Bruner, J.S. (1966) *Towards a Theory of Instruction.* Cambridge, MA: Harvard University Press.

Bruner, J.S. (1983) *Child's Talk: Learning to Use Language.* Oxford: Oxford University Press.

Bruner, J.S. (1990) *Acts of Meaning.* Cambridge, MA: Harvard University Press.

Bryan, J.H. & Test, M.A. (1967) Models and helping: naturalistic studies in aiding behaviour. *Journal of Personality & Social Psychology, 6,* 400–407.

Bulik C.M., Wadt T.D., & Kendler K.S. (2001) Characteristics of Monozygotic twins discordant for bulimia nervosa. *International Journal of Eating Disorders, 29,* 1–10.

Burt, C. (1949) The structure of the mind: A review of the results of factor analysis. *British Journal of Educational Psychology, 19,* 110–11, 176–199.

Burt, C. (1955) The evidence for the concept of intelligence. *British Journal of Educational Psychology, 25,* 158–177.

Burt, C. (1966) The genetic determination of differences in intelligence: A study of monozygotic twins reared together and apart. *British Journal of Psychology, 57,* 137–153.

Bushman, B. (2001) The Impact of Violent Television Programs and Movies: www.extension.iastate.edu/families/media/qa.bushman.html

Bushman, B.J. (1995) Moderating role of trait aggressiveness in the effects of violent media on aggression. *Journal of Personality & Social Psychology, 69,* 950–960.

Bushnell, J.A., Wells, J.E., McKenzie, J.M., Hornblow, A.R. Oakley, Browne, M.A. & Joyce, P.R. (1994) Bulimia co-morbidity in the general population and in the clinic. *Psychological Medicine, 20,* 605–611.

Buss, A.H. & Plomin, R. (1984) *Temperament: Early Developing Personality Traits.* Hillsdale, NJ: Erlbaum.

Buss, D. (1989) Sex difference in human mate preferences: Evolutionary hypotheses tested in 37 cultures. *Behavioral and Brain Sciences, 12,* 1–49.

Buss, D. (1999) *Evolutionary Psychology.* Needham Heights, MA: Allyn and Bacon.

Buss, D.M. (1988) The evolutionary biology of love. In R.J. Sternberg & M.L. Barnes (Eds) *The Psychology of Love.* New Haven, CT: Yale University Press.

Buss, D.M. (1989) Sex differences in human mate preferences: Evolutionary hypotheses tested in 37 cultures. *Behavioural and Brain Sciences, 12,* 1–49.

Buss, D.M. & Malamuth, N. (Eds) (1996) *Sex, Power, Conflict: Evolutionary and Feminist Perspectives.* Oxford: Oxford University Press.

Byrne, R. & Whiten, A. (Eds) *Machiavellian Intelligence: Social Expertise and the Evolution of Intellect in Monkeys, Apes, and Humans.* New York: Oxford University Press.

Callaghan, P. & O'Carroll, M. (1993) Making women mad. *Nursing Times*, 89, 26–29.

Campbell, S.S. & Murphy, P.J. (1998) Extraocular circadian phototransduction in humans. *Science*, 279, 396.

Cannon, W.B. (1927) The James-Lange theory of emotions: A critical examination and an alternative theory. *American Journal of Psychology*, 39, 106–124.

Cannon, W.B. (1929) *Bodily Changes in Pain, Hunger, Fear and Rage* (2nd edition). New York: Appleton-Century-Crofts.

Caplan, P. (1991) Delusional dominating personality disorder (DDPD). *Feminism & Psychology*, 1(1), 171–174.

Capron, C. & Duyme, M. (1989) Assessment of effects of socioeconomic status on IQ in full cross-fostering study. *Nature, 340,* 552–554.

Carlsmith, J.M. & Anderson, C.A. (1979) Ambient temperature and the occurrence of collective violence: A new analysis. *Journal of Personality & Social Psychology*, 37, 337–344.

Carlson, N.R. (1988) *Foundations of Physiological Psychology*. Boston: Allyn & Bacon.

Carlson, N.R. (1992) *Foundations of Physiological Psychology* (2nd edition). Boston: Allyn & Bacon.

Carlson, N.R. (2001) *Foundations of Physiological Psychology* (8th edition). Boston, MA: Allyn & Bacon.

Carlson, N.R., Buskist, W. & Martin, G.N. (2000) *Psychology: The Science of Behaviour* (European edition). Harlow: Pearson Education Ltd.

Carpenter, P. (1997) Learning Disability. In L. Rees, M. Lipsedge & C. Ball (Eds) *Textbook of Psychiatry*. London: Arnold.

Cartwright, J. (2001) *Evolutionary Explanations of Human Behaviour*. London: Routledge.

Cartwright, R.D., Lloyd, S., Knight, S. & Trenholme, I. (1984) Broken Dreams: A Study of the Effects of Divorce and Depression on Dream Content. *Psychiatry*, 47, 251–259.

Carver, C.S. & Scheier, M.F. (1992) *Perspectives on Personality* (2nd edition). Boston: Allyn & Bacon.

Ceci, S.J. & Williams, W.M. (1999) *The Nature–Nurture Debate: The Essential Readings*. Oxford: Blackwell.

Champion, L. (2000) Depression. In L. Champion & M. Power (Eds) *Adult Psychological Problems: An Introduction* (2nd edition). Hove: Psychology Press.

Charlton, T. (2000) TV is not bad for you – official. *Observer*, 29 October.

Chen, T., Chen, S., Hsieh, P. & Chiang, H. (1997) Auditory effects of aircraft noise on people living near an airport. *Archives of Environmental Health*, 52, 45–50.

Chisolm, K., Carter, M.C., Amers, E.W. & Morison, S.J. (1995) Attachment security and indiscriminately friendly behaviour in children adopted from Romanian orphanages. *Development & Psychopathology, 7,* 283–294.

Chomsky, N. (1965) *Aspects of the Theory of Syntax*. Cambridge, MA: MIT Press.

Chua, S.E. & McKenna, P.J. (1995) Schizophrenia – a brain disease? A critical review of structural and functional cerebral abnormality in the disorder. *British Journal of Psychiatry*, 166, 563–582.

Cialdini, R.B., Schaller, M, Houlihan, D., Arps, K., Fultz, J. & Beaman, A.L. (1987) Empathy-based helping: is it selflessly or selfishly motivated? *Journal of Personality & Social Psychology*, 52, 749–758.

Clare, A. (1976) What is schizophrenia? *New Society*, 20 May, 410–412.

Claridge, G. & Davis, C. (2003) *Personality and Psychological Disorders*. London: Arnold.

Clark, R.D. & Hatfield, E. (1989) Gender differences in receptivity to sexual offers. *Journal of Psychology & Human Sexuality*, 2, 39–55.

Clarke, A. & Clarke, A. (2000) *Early Experience and the Life Path*. London: Jessica Kingsley.

Clarke, D. (2001) *Pro- and anti-social behaviour*. London: Routledge.

Clarke, M. (Ed.) (1991) *Pro-social Behaviour*. London: Sage Publications.

Clarke-Stewart, K.A. (1989) Infant day care: Maligned or malignant? *American Psychologist*, 44, 266–273.

Clarke-Stewart, K.A. (1991) A home is not a school. *Journal of Social Issues*, 47, 105–123.

Clore, G.L. & Byrne, D.S. (1974) A reinforcement-affect model of attraction. In T.L. Huston (Ed.) *Foundations of Interpersonal Attraction*. New York: Academic Press.

Cobb, A. (1993) *Safe and effective? Mind's views on psychiatric drugs, ECT and psychosurgery*. London: Mind Publications.

Cochrane R. (1977) Mental illness in immigrants in the UK. *Social Psychiatry*, 12, 23–35.

Cochrane, R. (1983) *The Social Creation of Mental Illness*. London: Longman.

Cochrane, R. (1995) Women and depression. *Psychology Review*, 2, 20–24.

Coffey, C.E., Weiner, R.D., Djang, W.T., Figiel, G.S., Soady, S.A.R., Patterson, L.J., Holt, P.D., Spritzer C.E. & Wilkinson, W.E. (1991) Brain anatomic effects of ECT: A prospective magnetic resonance imaging study. *Archives of General Psychiatry*, **115**, 1013–1021.

Cohen, C.E. (1981) Person categories and social perception: Testing some boundaries of the processing effects of prior knowledge. *Journal of Personality and Social Psychology, 40*, 441–452.

Cohen, F. & Lazarus, R. (1979) Coping with the stresses of illness. In G.C. Stone, F. Cohen & N.E. Ader (Eds) *Health Psychology: A Handbook*. San Francisco, CA: Jossey-Bass.

Cohen, G., Eysenck, M. & Le Voi, M. (1996) *Memory: A Cognitive Approach*. London. Open University Press.

Cohen, R.M., Nordahl, T.E., Semple, W.E., Andreason, P. *et al.* (1997) The brain metabolic patterns of clozapine and fluphenazine-treated patients with schizophrenia during a continuous performance task. *Archives of General Psychiatry, 54*, 481–486.

Cohen, S., Tyrrell, D.A.J. & Smith, A.P. (1991) Psychological stress and susceptibility to the common cold. *New England Journal of Medicine, 325*, 606–612.

Cohen, Y.A. (1964) *The Transition from Childhood to Adolescence: Cross-Cultural Studies in Initiation Ceremonies, Legal Systems, and Incest Taboos*. Chicago: Aldine.

Colby, A. & Kohlberg, L. (1987) *The Measurement of Moral Judgement*. New York: Cambridge University Press.

Colby, A., Kohlberg, L., Gibbs, J. & Lieberman, M. (1983) A longitudinal study of moral development. *Monographs of the Society for Research in Child Development, 48* (1–2, Serial No. 200).

Cole, M. (1990) Cultural psychology: A once and a future discipline? In J.J. Berman (Ed.) *Nebraska Symposium on Motivation: Cross-Cultural Perspectives*. Lincoln, NE: University of Nebraska Press.

Cole, M. (1996) *Cultural Psychology: A Once and Future Discipline*. Cambridge, MA: Harvard University Press.

Coleman, J.C. (1995) Adolescence. In P.E. Bryant & A.M. Colman (Eds) *Developmental Psychology*. London: Methuen.

Coleman, J.C. & Hendry, L.(1990) *The Nature of Adolescence* (2nd edition). London: Routledge.

Coleman, J.C. & Roker, D. (1998) Adolescence. *The Psychologist, 11* (12), 593–596.

Coleman, J.C. (1980) *The Nature of Adolescence*. London: Methuen.

Collett, P. & O'Shea, G. (1976) Pointing the way to a fictional place: a study of direction-giving in England and Iran. *European Journal of Social Psychology, 6*, 447–458.

Collins, H. (1994) *Times Higher Education Supplement*, 30 September, 18.

Collins, R.C. (1983) Headstart: An update on program effects. *Newsletter of the Society for Research in Child Development*. Summer, 1–2.

Compas, B.E., Hinden, B.R. & Gerhardt, C.A (1995) Adolescent development: Pathways and processes of risk and resilience. *Annual Review of Psychology, 46*, 265–293.

Condry, J.C. & Ross, D.F. (1985) Sex and aggression: The influence of gender label on the perception of aggression in children. *Child Development, 56*, 225–233.

Conrad, R. (1964) Acoustic confusion in immediate memory. *British Journal of Psychology, 55*, 75–84.

Conway, A. R., Skitka, L.J., Hemmerich, J. & Kershaw, T. (2003) Flashbulb memory of Sept 11th 2001 (Personal Correspondence. Paper submitted to Psychological Science).

Conway, M.A., Anderson, S.J., Larsen, S.F., Donnelly, C.M., McDaniel, M.A., McClelland, A.G.R. & Rawles, R.E. (1994) The formation of flashbulb memories. *Memory and Cognition, 22*, 326–343.

Cook, E.W., Hodes, R.L. & Lang, P.J. (1986) Preparedness and phobia: Effects of stimulus content on human visceral conditioning. *Journal of Abnormal Psychology, 95*, 195–207.

Cook, T.D., Kendziersky, D. & Thomas, A. (1982) The implicit assumptions of television: An analysis of the 1982 NIMH Report on Television and Behavior. *Public Opinion Quarterly, 47*, 161–201.

Cooke, P. (1993) TV Causes Violence? Says Who?, *The New York Times*, 14 August.

Coolican, H. (1999) *Research Methods and Statistics in Psychology* (3rd Ed) London: Hodder & Stoughton.

Coolican, H., Cassidy, T., Chercher, A., Harrower, J., Penny, G., Sharp, R., Walley, M. & Westbury, T. (1996) *Applied Psychology*. London: Hodder & Stoughton.

Cooper, C. & Faragher, B. (1993) Psychological stress and breast cancer: the interrelationship between stress events, coping strategies and personality. *Psychological Medicine, 23*, 653–662.

Cooper, R.S., Rotimi, C.N. & Ward, R. (1999) The puzzle of hypertension in African-Americans. *Scientific American, 253*, 36–43.

Coryell, W., Winokur, G., Shea, T., Maser, J.W., Endicott, J. & Akiskal, H.S. (1994) The long-term stability of depressive subtypes. *American Journal of Psychiatry, 151*, 199–204.

Craik, F.I.M. & Lockhart, R. (1972) Levels of processing. *Journal of Verbal Learning and Verbal Behaviour, 11*, 671–684.

Craik, F.I.M. & Tulving, E. (1975) Depth of processing and retention of words in episodic memory. *Journal of Verbal Learning and Verbal Behaviour, 12*, 599–607.

Craik, F.I.M. & Watkins, M.J. (1973) The role of rehearsal in short-term memory. *Journal of Verbal Learning and Verbal Behaviour, 12*, 599–607.

Crawford, C. (1998) The theory of evolution in the study of human behaviour: An introduction and overview. In C. Crawford & D.L. Krebs (Eds) *Handbook of Evolutionary Psychology: Ideas, Issues and Applications.* Hillsdale, NJ: Lawrence Erlbaum Associates, Inc.

Crawford, C.B. (1989) The theory of evolution: Of what value to psychology? *Journal of Comparative Psychology, 103*, 4–22.

Crawford, M. & Unger, R.K. (1995) Gender issues in psychology. In A.M. Colman (Ed.) *Controversies in Psychology.* London: Methuen.

Crick, F. (1994) *The Astonishing Hypothesis: The Scientific Search for the Soul.* London: Simon & Schuster.

Crick, F. & Mitchison, G. (1983) The function of dream sleep. *Nature, 304*, 111–114.

Crooks, R.L. & Stein, J. (1991) *Psychology: Science, Behaviour and Life* (2nd edition). London: Holt, Rinehart & Winston Inc.

Crutchfield, R. S. (1954) A new technique for measuring individual differences in conformity to group judge-ment. *Proceedings of the Invitational Conference on Testing Problems*, 69–74.

Cumberbatch, G. (1997) Media violence: Science and common sense. *Psychology Review, 3*, 2–7.

Cunningham, M. (1986) Measuring the physical in physical attractiveness: Quasi-experiments on the sociobi-ology of female facial beauty. *Journal of Personality & Social Psychology, 50*, 925–935.

Curry, C. (1998) Adolescence. In K. Trew & J. Kremer (Eds) *Gender & Psychology.* London: Arnold.

Czeisler, C.A., Duffy, J.F., Shanahan, T.L., Brown, E.N., Mitchell, J.F., Rimmer, D.W., Ronda, J.M., Silva, E.J., Allan, J.S., Emens, J.S., Dijk, D. & Kronauer, R.E. (1999) Stability, Precision, and Near-24-Hour Period of the Human Circadian Pacemaker. *Science, 284* (5423), 2177–2181.

Czeisler, C., Moore-Ede, M. & Coleman, R. (1982) Rotating shift-work schedules that disrupt sleep are improved by applying circadian principles. *Science, 217*, 460–463.

Czeisler, C.A., Kronauer, R.E., Allan, J.S., Duffy, J.F., Jewett, M.E., Brown, E.N. & Ronda, J.M. (1989) Bright light induction of strong (type O) resetting of the human circadian pacemaker. *Science, 244*, 1328–1333.

Daly, M. & Wilson, M. (1988) *Homicide.* New York: Aldine de Gruyter Hawthorne.

Darley, C.F., Tinklenberg, J.R., Roth, W.T., Hollister, L.E. & Atkinson, R.C. (1973) Influence of marijuana on storage and retrieval processes in memory. *Memory and Cognition, 1*, l96–200.

Darley, J. & Batson, C. (1973) From Jerusalem to Jericho: A study of situational and dispositional variables in helping behaviour. *Journal of Personality & Social Psychology, 27*, 100–108.

Darley, J.M. & Latané, B. (1968) Bystander intervention in emergencies: Diffusion of responsibility. *Journal of Personality & Social Psychology, 8*, 377–383.

Darlington, R.B. (1991) The long-term effects of model preschool programs. In L. Ogagaki & R.J. Sternberg (Eds) *Directors of Development.* Hillsdale, NJ: Erlbaum.

Darwin. C. (1859) *On The Origin of Species by Means of Natural Selection.* London: John Murray.

Darwin, C. (1871) *The Descent of Man and Selection in Relation to Sex.* London: John Murray.

Darwin, C. (1877) A Biographical Sketch of an Infant. *Mind, 2*, 285–294.

Dasen, P.R. (1994) Culture and cognitive development from a Piagetian perspective. In W.J. Lonner & R.S. Malpass (Eds) *Psychology and Culture.* Boston: Allyn & Bacon.

Dasen, P.R. (1999) Rapid social change and the turmoil of adolescence: A cross-cultural perspective. *World Psychology, 5*.

Davies, E. & Furnham, A. (1986) Body satisfaction in adolescent girls. *British Journal of Medical Psychology, 59*, 279–288.

Davis, J.M. (1978) Dopamine theory of schizophrenia: A two-factor theory. In L.C. Wynne, R.L. Cromwell & S. Matthysse (Eds), *The Nature of Schizophrenia.* New York: Wiley.

Davison, G.C. & Neale, J.M. (1994) *Abnormal Psychology* (6th edition). New York: Wiley.

Davison, G.C. & Neale, J.M. (2001) *Abnormal Psychology* (8th edition). New York: John Wiley & Sons Inc.

Dawkins, M.S. (1980) The many faces of animal suffering. *New Scientist*, November 20.

Dawkins, M.S. (1990) From an animal's point of view: Motivation, fitness and animal welfare. *Behavioural and Brain Sciences, 13*, 1–9.

Dawkins, R. (1989) *The Selfish Gene.* Oxford: Oxford University Press.

Dawkins, R. (1998) *Unweaving the Rainbow.* London: Penguin.

Dayton, T. (1994) *The Drama Within: Psychodrama and Experiential Therapy*. Deerfield Beach, FL: Health Communications Inc.

De Koninck, J. & Koulack, D. (1975) Dream Content and Adaptation to a Stressful Situation. *Journal of Abnormal Psychology*, 84, 250–260.

de Munck, V.C. (1998) Lust, love, and arranged marriages in Sri Lanka. In V.C. de Munck (Ed.) *Romantic Love and Sexual Behaviour: Perspectives from the Social Sciences*. Westport, CT: Paraeger.

Deci, E. (1971) Effects of externally mediated rewards on intrinsic motivation. *Journal of Personality & Social Psychology*, 18, 105–115.

Deci, E.L. (1980) *The Psychology of Self-determination*. Lexington, MA: D.C. Health.

Deci, E.L. & Ryan, R.M. (1987) The support of autonomy and the control of behaviour. *Journal of Personality & Social Psychology*, 53, 1024–1037.

Deese, J. (1972) *Psychology as Science and Art*. New York: Harcourt Brace Jovanovich.

Delgado, J.M.R. (1969) *Physical Control of the Mind*. New York: Harper & Row.

Delgado, P.L. (2000) Depression: a case for a monoamine deficiency. *Journal of Clinical Psychiatry*, 61 (Suppl. 6), 7–11.

Delgado, P.L. & Moreno, F.A. (1998) Different roles for serotonin in anti-obsessional drug action and the pathophysiology of obsessive–compulsive disorder. *British Journal of Psychiatry*, 173 (Suppl. 35), 21–25.

DeLongis, A., Coyne, J.C., Dakof, G., Folkman, S. & Lazarus, R.S. (1982) The impact of daily hassles, uplifts and major life events to health status. *Health Psychology*, 1, 119–136.

Delorme, M.-A., Lortie-Lussier, M. & De Koninck, J.D. (2002) Stress and Coping in the Waking and Dreaming States During an Examination Period. *Dreaming*, 12(4), December, 171–183.

Delprato, D. (1980) Hereditary determinants of fears and phobias. *Behaviour Therapy*, 11, 79–103.

Dement, W. (1960) The effect of dream deprivation. *Science*, 131, 1705–1707.

Dement, W. (1978) *Some Must Watch While Some Must Sleep*. New York: W.W. Norton.

Dement, W. & Kleitman, N. (1957) The relation of eye movements during sleep to dream activity: an objective method for the study of dreaming. *Electroencephalography & Clinical Neurophysiology*, 9, 673–690.

Dement, W. & Wolpert, E.A. (1958) The relation of eye movements, body motility and external stimuli to dream content. *Journal of Experimental Psychology*, 55, 543–553.

Denmark, F., Russo, N.F., Frieze, I.H. & Sechzer, J.A. (1988) Guidelines for Avoiding Sexism in Psychological Research: A report of the *ad hoc* committee on non-sexist research. *American Psychologist*, 43(7), 582–585.

Deutsch, M. & Gerard, H.B. (1955) A study of normative and informational social influence upon individual judgements. *Journal of Abnormal & Social Psychology*, 51, 629–636.

Diab, L.N. (1970) A study of intragroup and intergroup relations among experimentally produced small groups. *Genetic Psychology Monographs*, 82, 49–82.

Diener, E. (1980) Deindividuation: The absence of self-awareness and self-regulation in group members. In P.B. Paulus (Ed.) *The Psychology of Group Influence*. Hillsdale, NJ: Lawrence Erlbaum.

Diener, E., Fraser, S.C., Beaman, A.L. & Kelem, R.T. (1976) Effects of Deindividuating Variables on Stealing among Halloween Trick-or-treaters. *Journal of Personality & Social Psychology*, 33(2), 178–183.

Dion, K.K., Berscheid, E. & Walster, E. (1972) What is beautiful is good. *Journal of Personality & Social Psychology*, 24, 285–290.

Dodd, D. (1985) Robbers in the classroom: A deindividuation exercise. *Teaching of Psychology*, 12, 89–91.

Dolnick, E. (1998) *Madness on the Couch – Blaming the Victim in the Heyday of Psychoanalysis*. New York: Simon & Schuster.

Donaldson, M. (1978) *Children's Minds*. London: Fontana.

Donnerstein, E. & Wilson, D.W. (1976) Effects of noise and perceived control on ongoing and subsequent aggressive behavior. *Journal of Personality & Social Psychology*, 34, 774–781.

Dossman, R., Kutter, P., Heinzel, R. & Wurmser, L.(1997) The long-term benefits of intensive psychotherapy. A view from Germany. In S. Lazar (Ed.) *Psychoanalytic Inquiry Supplement, Intensive Dynamic Psychotherapy: Making the Case in an Era of Managed Care*. USA: The Analytic Press.

Dovidio, J.F., Piliavin, J.A., Gaertner, S.L., Schroeder, D.A. & Clark, R.D. (1991) The arousal: Cost–reward model and the process of intervention. In M. Clarke (Ed.), *Pro-social Behaviour*. London: Sage Publications.

Duck, S. (Ed.) (1982) *Personal Relationships 4: Dissolving Personal Relationships*. London: Academic Press.

Duck, S. (1988) *Relating to Others*. Milton Keynes: Open University Press.

Duck, S. (1999) *Relating to Others* (2nd edition) Buckingham: Open University Press.

Duck, S. (2001) Breaking up: The dissolution of relationships. *Psychology Review*, 7(3), 2–5.

Dunbar, R. (1993) Co-evolution of neo-cortical size, group size and language in humans. *Behavioural & Brain Sciences, 16*, 681–735.

Duncan, G. (1993) Economic deprivation and childhood development. Paper presented at the biennial meetings of the Society for Research in Child Development, New Orleans, April.

Dunn, J. & Plomin, R. (1990) *Separate Lives: Why siblings are so different.* New York: Basic Books.

Durkin, K. (1995) *Developmental Social Psychology: From Infancy to Old Age.* Oxford: Blackwell.

Dworetzky, J.P. (1981) *Introduction to Child Development.* St Paul, MS: West Publishing Co.

Eagles, J.M., Andrew, J.E., Johnston, M.I., Easton, E.A. & Millar, H.R. (2001) Season of birth in females with anorexia nervosa in Northern Scotland. *International Journal of Eating Disorders, 30* (2); 167–175.

Eagly, A.H. (1987) *Sex Differences in Social Behaviour: A Social Role Interpretation.* Hillsdale, NJ: Erlbaum.

Eagly, A.H. (1997) Sex differences in social behavior: Comparing social role theory and evolutionary psychology. *American Psychologist, 52*, 1380–1383.

Eastman C.I., Young, M.A., Fogg, L.F., Liu, L. & Meaden, P.M. (1998) Bright light treatment of winter depression: a placebo-controlled trial. *Archives of General Psychiatry, 55*, 883–889.

Eckensberger, L.H. & Zimba, R. (1997) The development of moral judgement. In J.W. Berry, P.R. Dasen & T.S. Saraswathi (Eds) *Handbook of Cross-Cultural Psychology, Volume 2: Basic Processes and Human Development.* Boston: Allyn & Bacon.

Eckensberger, L.H. (1994) Moral development and its measurement across cultures. In W.J. Lonner & R.S. Malpass (Eds) *Psychology and Culture.* Boston: Allyn & Bacon.

Eckensberger, L.H. (1999) Socio-moral development. In D. Messer & S. Millar (Eds) *Exploring Developmental Psychology: From Infancy to Adolescence.* London: Arnold.

Eisenberg, N. (1982) The development of reasoning regarding prosocial behaviour. In N. Eisenberg (Ed.) *The Development of Prosocial Behaviour.* New York: Academic Press.

Eisenberg, N. (1986) *Altruistic Emotion, Cognition and Behaviour.* Hillsdale, NJ: Erlbaum.

Eisenberg, N. (1996) In search of the good heart. In M.R. Merrens & G.C. Brannigan (Eds) *The Developmental Psychologists: Research Adventures across the Life Span.* New York: McGraw-Hill.

Eisenberg, N., Miller, R.A., Shell, R., McNalley, S. & Shea, C. (1991) Prosocial development in adolescence: A longitudinal study. *Developmental Psychology, 27*(5), 849–857.

Eiser, J.R. (1994) *Attitudes, Chaos and the Connectionist Mind.* Oxford: Blackwell.

Elkind, D. (1976) *Child Development and Education: A Piagetian Perspective.* Oxford: Oxford University Press.

Elliot, C.D., Murray, D.J. & Pearson, L.S. (1979) *British Ability Scales.* Slough: National Foundation for Educational Research.

Ellis, N.C and Hennelley R.A. (1980) A bilingual word-length effect: implications for intelligence testing and the relative ease of mental calculation in Welsh and English. *British Journal of Psychology, 71*, 43–52.

Erikson, E.H. (1950) *Childhood and Society.* New York: Norton.

Erikson, E.H. (1963) *Childhood and Society* (2nd edition). New York: Norton.

Erikson, E.H. (1968) *Identity: Youth and Crisis.* New York: Norton.

Erlenmeyer-Kimmling, L. & Jarvik, L.F. (1963) Genetics and intelligence: A review. *Science, 142*, 1477–1479.

Eron, L.D., Huesmann, L.R., Lefkowitz, M.M. & Walder, L.D. (1972) Does television violence cause aggression? *American Psychologist, 27*, 253–263.

Evans, G.W., Bullinger, M. & Hygge, S. (1998) Chronic noise exposure and physiological response: A prospective study of children living under environmental stress. *Psychological Science, 9*, 75–77.

Evans, G.W., Hygge, S. & Bullinger, M. (1995) Chronic noise and psychological stress. *Psychological Science, 6*, 333–338.

Evans, G.W. & Maxwell, L. (1997) Chronic noise exposure and reading deficits: The mediating effects of language acquisition. *Environment & Behavior, 29*, 638–656.

Eysenck, H. (1952) The effects of psychotherapy: an evaluation. *Journal of Consulting Psychology, 16*, 319–324.

Eysenck, H.J. (1952) The effects of psychotherapy: an evaluation. *Journal of Consulting Psychology, 16*, 319–324.

Eysenck, H.J. (1971) *Race, Intelligence and Education.* London: Temple-Smith.

Eysenck, H.J. & Wilson, G.D. (1973) (Eds) *The Experimental Study of Freudian Theories.* London: Methuen.

Eysenck, M. (1998) Memory. In M. Eysenck (Ed.) *Psychology: An integrated approach.* Harlow: Longman.

Eysenck, M.W. (1986) Working memory. In G. Cohen, M.W. Eysenck & M.A. Le Voi (Eds) *Memory: A Cognitive Approach.* Milton Keynes: Open University Press.

Eysenck, M.W. & Keane, M.T. (2000) *Cognitive Psychology: A Student's Handbook* (4th edition). Hove: Psychology Press.

Fagot, B.I. (1985) Beyond the reinforcement principle: Another step toward understanding sex-role development. *Developmental Psychology, 21*, 1091–1104.

Fancher, R.E. (1979) *Pioneers of Psychology*. New York: Norton.

Fancher, R.E. (1996) *Pioneers of Psychology* (3rd edition). New York: Norton.

Farber, S.L. (1981) *Identical Twins Reared Apart*. New York: Basic Books.

Farmer, A.E., McGuffin, P. & Gottesman, I.I. (1987) Twin concordance for DSM-III schizophrenia: Scrutinizing the validity of the definition. *Archives of General Psychiatry, 44*, 634–641.

Fearn, N. (1999) Anorexia via TV. *The Independent*, 27 May.

Feldman, R.E. (1967) Honesty toward a compatriot and foreigner: Field experiments in Paris, Athens and Boston. In W.W. Lambert & R. Weisbrod (Eds) *Comparative Perspectives on Social Psychology*. Boston, MA: Little, Brown.

Felipe, N.J. & Sommer, R. (1966) Invasion of personal space. *Social Problems, 14*, 206–214.

Felson, R.B. (1996) Mass Media Effects on Violent Behaviour. *Annual Review of Sociology, 22*, August, 103–128.

Fernandez, A. & Glenberg, A.M. (1985) Changing environmental context does not reliably affect memory. *Memory and Cognition, 13*, 333–345.

Fernando, S. (1991) *Mental Health, Race and Culture*. London: Macmillan, in conjunction with MIND.

Festinger, L. (1954) A theory of social comparison processes. *Human Relations, 7*, 117–140.

Festinger, L., Pepitone, A. & Newcomb, T. (1952) Some consequences of de-individuation in a group. *Journal of Abnormal & Social Psychology, 47*, 382–389.

Fichter, M.M. & Pirke, K.M. (1995) Starvation models and eating disorders. In G. Szmulker, C. Dare & J. Treasure (Eds) *Handbook of eating disorders: Theory, treatment and research*. Chichester: Wiley.

Field, A.E., Camargo, C.A., Taylor, C.B., Berkey, C.S. & Colditz, G.A. (1999) Relation of peer and media influences to the development of purging behaviors among preadolescent and adolescent girls. *Archives of Pediatrics and Adolescent Medicine, 153*, 1184–1189.

Fink, M. (2002) *Electroshock – Healing Mental Illness*. Oxford: Oxford University Press.

Fischer, A., Fuchs, W. & Zinnecker, J. (1985) Jugenliche und Erwachsene '85. In *Jugenwerk der Deutschen Shell (Ed.) Arbeitsbericht und Dukumentation*, Vol.5. Leverskusen: Leske und Budrich.

Fisher, R.A. (1930) *The Genetical Theory of Natural Selection*. Oxford: Clarendon Press.

Fiske, A.P. (1991) *Structures of Social Life: The four elementary forms of human relations: Communal sharing, authority ranking, equality matching, market pricing*. New York: Free Press.

Flanagan, C. Psychology Review, Vol. 9, No.1. Exam Corner (pp. 6–8).

Flanagan, O.J. (1984) *The Science of the Mind*. Cambridge, MA.: MIT Press.

Fletcher, G. (2002) *The New Science of Intimate Relationships*. Oxford: Blackwell.

Foley, R.A & Lee, P.C. (1991) Ecology and energetics of encephalization in hominid evolution. In A.Whiten & E.M. Widdowson (Eds) *Foraging Strategies and Natural Diet of Monkeys, Apes, and Humans*. Oxford: Science Publications.

Ford, D.H. & Urban, H.R. (1963) *Systems of Psychotherapy: A Comparative Study*. New York: Wiley.

Fortune, R. (1939) Arapesh warfare. *American Anthropologist, 41*, 22–41.

Foster, R.A., Libkuman, T.M., Schooler, J.W. & Loftus, E.F. (1994). Consequentiality and eyewitness person identification. *Applied Cognitive Psychology, 8*, 107–121.

Foulkes, D. (1967) Nonrapid eye movement mentation. *Experimental Neurology, Supplement 4*, 28–37.

Frankenhauser, M. (1983) The sympathetic–adrenal and pituitary–adrenal response to challenge: Comparison between the sexes. In T.M. Dembroski, T.H. Schmidt & G. Blumchen (Eds) *Behavioural Bases of Coronary Heart Disease*. Basle: S. Karger.

Freud, S. (1900/1976) *The Interpretation of Dreams*. Pelican Freud Library (4) Harmondsworth: Penguin.

Freud, S. (1901) *Psychopathology of Everyday Life*. Translation by A. A. Brill (1914). London: Fisher Unwin.

Freud, S. (1905/1977) *Three Essays on the Theory of Sexuality*. Pelican Freud Library (7). Harmondsworth: Penguin.

Freud, S. (1909/1977) *Ananlysis of a Phobia in a Five-year-old Boy*. Pelican Freud Library (8) Harmondsworth: Penguin.

Freud, S. (1910) The origin and development of psychoanalysis. *American Journal of Psychology, 21*, 181–218.

Freud, S. (1915) *Repression*. In Freud's Collected Papers, Vol. IV. London: Hogarth.

Freud, S. (1923/1984) *The Ego and the Id*. Pelican Freud Library (11). Harmondsworth: Penguin.

Freud, S. (1924) The passing of the Oedipus complex. In E. Jones (Ed.) *Collected Papers of Sigmund Freud*, Vol.5. New York: Basic Books.

Freud, S. (1933) *New Introductory Lectures on Psychoanalysis*. New York: Norton.

Friedman, M. & Rosenman, R.H. (1974) *Type A Behaviour and Your Heart*. New York: Harper Row.

Frijda, N. & Jahoda, G. (1966) On the scope and methods of cross-cultural psychology. *International Journal of Psychology, 1*, 109–127.

Frith, C. & Cahill, C. (1995) Psychotic disorders: Schizophrenia, affective psychoses and paranoia. In A.A. Lazarus & A.M. Colman (Eds) *Abnormal Psychology*. London: Longman.

Fromm, E. (1962) *The Art of Loving*. London: Unwin Books.

Fromm-Reichmann, F. (1948) Notes on the development of treatment of schizophrenics by psychoanalytic psychotherapy. *Psychiatry, 11*, 263–273.

Frude, N. (1998) *Understanding Abnormal Psychology*. Oxford: Blackwell.

Fulton, J.F., & Bailey, P. (1929) Tumors in the region of the third ventricle: Their diagnosis and relation to pathological sleep. *Journal of Nervous & Mental Diseases, 69*, 1–25.

Gabora, L. (1997) The origin and evolution of culture and creativity. *Journal of Memetics – Evolutionary Models of Information Transmission, 1*: http://jomemit.cfpm.org/voll/gabora_l.html

Gallagher, M., Millar, R., Hargie, O. & Ellis, R. (1992) The personal and social worries of adolescents in Northern Ireland: Results of a survey. *British Journal of Guidance and Counselling, 30* (3), 274–290.

Gardner, R.A. & Gardner, B.T. (1969) Teaching sign language to a chimpanzee. *Science, 165* (3894), 664–672.

Garner, D.M., Garfinkel, P.E., Schwartz, D. & Thompson, M. (1980) Cultural expectations of thinness in women. *Psychological Reports, 47*, 483–491.

Garnham, A. (1991) *The Mind in Action*. London: Routledge.

Garrett, R. (1996) Skinner's case for radical behaviourism. In W. O'Donohue & R.F. Kitchener (Eds) *The Philosophy of Psychology*. London: Sage.

Gay, P. (1988) *Freud: A Life for our Time*. London: J.M.Dent & Sons.

Geddes, J. & UK ECT Review Group (2003) Efficacy and safety of electroconvulsive therapy in depressive disorders: A systematic review and meta-analysis *The Lancet, 361*(9360), 799–808.

Geen, R.G.& O'Neal, E.C. (1969) Activation of cue-elicited aggression on general arousal. *Journal of Personality and Social Psychology, 11*, 289–292.

Gelder, M., Gath, D. & Mayon, R. (1989) *The Oxford Textbook of Psychiatry* (2nd edition). Oxford: Oxford University Press.

Gelder, M., Mayou, R. & Geddes, J. (1999) *Psychiatry* (2nd edition). Oxford: Oxford University Press.

Gelman, R. & Baillargeon, R. (1983) A review of some Piagetian concepts. In J.H. Flavell & E.M. Markman (Eds) *Handbook of Child Psychology: Cognitive Development, Volume 3*. New York: Wiley.

Gelman, R. (1979) Preschool thought. *American Psychologist, 34*, 900–905.

Gerbner, G. & Gross, L. (1976) Living with television: The violence profile. *Journal of Communication, 26*(2) 173–199.

Gergen, K.J., Gergen, M.M. & Barton, W.H. (1973 October) Deviance in the dark. *Psychology Today*, 129–130.

Gershon, E.S. & Rieder, R.O. (1992) Major disorders of mind and brain. *Scientific American, 267*(3), 88–95.

Gesell, A. (1925) *The Mental Growth of the Preschool Child*. New York: Macmillan.

Gibbs, J.C. & Schnell, S.V. (1985) Moral development 'versus' socialisation. *American Psychologist, 40*, 1071–1080.

Gillham, W.E.C. (1975) Intelligence: The persistent myth. *New Behaviour*, 26 June, 433–435.

Gillie, O. (1976) Pioneer of IQ fakes his research. *The Sunday Times*, 29 October, H3.

Gilligan, C. (1982) *In a Different Voice: Psychological Theory and Women's Development*. Cambridge, MA: Harvard University Press.

Gilligan, C. (1993) Letter to Readers (Preface). *In a Different Voice*. Cambridge, MA: Harvard University Press.

Ginsberg, H.P. (1981) Piaget and education: The contributiuons and limits of genetic epistemology. In K. Richardson & S. Sheldon (Eds) *Cognitive Development to Adolescence*. Milton Keynes: Open University Press.

Glanzer, M. & Cunitz, A.R. (1966) Two storage mechanisms in free recall. *Journal of Verbal Learning and Verbal Behavior, 5*, 351–360.

Glassman, W.E. (1995) *Approaches to Psychology* (2nd edition). Buckingham: Open University.

Godden, D. & Baddeley, A.D. (1975) Context-dependent memory in two natural environments: On land and under water. *British Journal of Psychology, 66*, 325–331.

Goldfarb, W. (1943) The effects of early institutional care on adult personality. *Journal of Experimental Education, 12*, 106–129.

Goldstein, A.P., Sprafkin, R.P., Gershaw, N.J. & Klein, P. (1998) *Skillstreaming the Adolescent*. Champaign, IL: Research Press.

Goldstein, M.J. & Rodnick, E. (1975) The family's contribution to the aetiology of schizophrenia: Current status. *Schizophrenia Bulletin, 14*, 48–63.

Goodwin, D.W., Powell, B., Bremer, D. Hoine, H. & Stern, J. (1969) Alcohol and recall: State dependent effects in man. *Science, 163*, 1358.

Goodwin, F.K. & Jamison, K.R. (1990) *Manic–Depressive Illness*. New York: Oxford University Press.

Gottesman, I. (1991) *Schizophrenia Genesis*. New York: W.H. Freeman.

Gottesman, I., McGuffun, P. & Farmer, A.E. (1987) Clinical genetics as clues to the "real" genetics of schizophrenia. *Schizophrenia Bulletin, 13*, 23–47.

Gottesman, I. & Shields, J. (1976) A critical review of recent adoption, twin and family studies of schizophrenia: Behavioural genetics perspectives. *Schizophrenia Bulletin, 2*, 360–398.

Gottesman, I. & Shields, J. (1982) *Schizophrenia: The Epigenetic Puzzle*. Cambridge: Cambridge University Press.

Gottfredson, L.S. (1998) The General Intelligence Factor. *Scientific American Presents: Exploring Intelligence, 9*(4), 24–29.

Gould, S.J. (1981) *The Mismeasure of Man*. Harmondsworth: Penguin.

Graham, C.A. (2002) Methods for obtaining menstrual cycle data in menstrual synchrony studies: Reply to Schank (2001). *Journal of Comparative Psychology*, September 2002, 313.

Graham, H. (1986) *The Human Face of Psychology*. Milton Keynes: Open University Press.

Gray, J.A. (1987) The ethics and politics of animal experimentation. In H. Beloff & A.M. Colman (Eds) *Psychology Survey, No.6*. Leicester: British Psychological Society.

Gray, J.A. (1991) On the morality of speciesism. *The Psychologist, 4*(5), 196–198.

Green, D.J. & Gillette, R. (1982) Circadian rhythm of firing rate recorded from single cells in the rat suprachiasmatic brain slice. *Brain Research, 245*, 198–200.

Green, S. (1987) *Physiological Psychology*. London: Routledge.

Green, S. (1994) *Principles of Biopsychology*. Sussex: Lawrence Erlbaum Associates.

Greenough, W.T. (1991) Experience as a component of normal development: Evolutionary considerations. *Developmental Psychology, 27*, 11–27.

Greer, S. & Morris, T. (1975) Psychological attributes of women who develop breast cancer: A controlled study. *Journal of Psychosomatic Research, 19*, 147–153.

Gregory, R.L. (1981) *Mind in Science*. Harmondsworth: Penguin.

Griffiths, M.D. (1999) All but connected (Online relationships). *Psychology Post, 17*, 6–7.

Griffiths, M.D. (2000) Cyberaffairs: A new era for psychological research. *Psychology Review, 7*(1), 28–31.

Groesz, L.M., Levine, M.P. & Murnen, S.K. (2001) The effect of experimental presentation of thin media images on body dissatisfaction: a meta-analytic review. *International Journal of Eating Disorders, 31* (1), 1–16.

Gross, R. (2003) *Themes, Issues and Debates in Psychology* (2nd edition). London: Hodder & Stoughton.

Gross, R.D. (2005) *Psychology: the Science of Mind and Behaviour* (5th edition). London: Hodder Arnold.

Gross, R., McIlveen, R., Coolican, H., Clamp, A. & Russell, J. (2000) *Psychology: A New Introduction for A Level* (2nd edition). London: Hodder & Stoughton.

Grusec, J.E. (1992) Social learning theory and developmental psychology: The legacies of Robert Sears and Albert Bandura. *Developmental Psychology, 28*, 776–786.

Guilford, J.P. (1959) Three faces of intellect. *American Psychologist, 14*, 469–479.

Gulevich, G., Dement, W.C. & Johnson, L. (1966) Psychiatric and EEG observations on a case of prolonged (264 hours) wakefulness. *Archives of General Psychiatry, 15*, 29–35.

Gunter, B. (1986) *Television and Sex-Role Stereotyping*. London: IBA and John Libbey.

Gunter, B. & McAleer, J.L. (1997) *Children And Television – The One-Eyed Monster?* (2nd edition). London: Routledge.

Gupta, U. & Singh, P. (1982) Exploratory study of love and liking and types of marriage. *Indian Journal of Applied Psychology, 19*, 92–97.

Hack, M., Taylor, C.B., Klein, N., Eiben, R., Schatschneider, C. & Mercuri-Minich, N. (1994) School-age outcomes in children with birth weight under 750 g. *The New England Journal of Medicine, 331*, 753–759.

Hall, E.T. (1959) *The Silent Language*. New York: Doubleday.

Hall, E.T. (1966) *The Hidden Dimension*. Garden City, New York: Doubleday & Co.

Hamilton, E.W. & Abramson, L.Y. (1983) Cognitive patterns and major depressive disorder: A longitudinal study in a hospital setting. *Journal of Abnormal Psychology, 92,* 173–184.

Hare, P.A. & Hare, J.R. (1996) *J. L. Moreno*. London: Sage Publications.

Hare-Mustin, R. & Maracek, J. (1988) The meaning of difference: Gender theory, post-modernism and psychology. *American Psychologist, 43,* 455–464.

Hargreaves, D., Molloy, C. & Pratt, A. (1982) Social factors in conservation. *British Journal of Psychology, 73,* 231–234.

Hargreaves, D.J. (1986) Psychological theories of sex-role stereotyping. In D.J. Hargreaves & A.M. Colley (Eds) *The Psychology of Sex Roles*. London: Harper & Row.

Harlow, H.F. (1959) Love in infant monkeys. *Scientific American, 200,* 68–74.

Harlow, H.F. & Zimmerman, R.R. (1959) Affectional responses in the infant monkey. *Science, 130,* 421–432.

Harré, R. (1989) Language games and the texts of identity. In J. Shotter & K.J. Gergen (Eds) *Texts of Identity*. London: Sage.

Harré, R., Clarke, D. & De Carlo, N. (1985) *Motives and Mechanisms: An Introduction to the Psychology of Action*. London: Methuen.

Harrison, P. (1995) Schizophrenia: A misunderstood disease. *Psychology Review, 2(2),* 2–6.

Hartmann, E.L. (1973) Sleep requirements: Long sleepers, short sleepers, variable sleepers, and insomniacs. *Psychosomatics, 14,* 95–103.

Haskins, R. (1989) Beyond metaphor: The efficacy of early childhood education. *American Psychologist, 44,* 274–282.

Haste, H., Markoulis, D. & Helkama, K. (1998) Morality, wisdom and the life span. In A. Demetriou, W. Doise & C. van Lieshout (Eds) *Life-Span Developmental Psychology*. Chichester: John Wiley & Sons Ltd.

Hawkes, N. (2000a) Scientists seek more animal test freedom. *The Times,* 13 June, 10.

Hawkes, N. (2000b) Second rise in animal experiments. *The Times,* 24 July, 6.

Haworth, G. (1992) The use of non-human animals in psychological research: The current state of the debate. *Psychology Teaching, 46–54,* New Series, No.1.

Hearnshaw, L.S. (1979) *Cyril Burt: Psychologist*. London: Hodder & Stoughton.

Hearold, S. (1986) A synthesis of 1,043 effects of television on social behavior. In G. Comstock (Ed.) *Public communication and behavior,* Vol.1. New York: Academic Press.

Heather, N. (1976) *Radical Perspectives in Psychology*. London: Methuen.

Heber, R., Dever, R.B. & Conry, R.J. (1968) The influence of environmental and genetic variables on intellectual development. In H.J. Prehm, L.J. Hamerlynck & J.E. Crosson (Eds) *Behavioural Research in Mental Retardation*. Eugene: University of Oregon Press.

Hegarty, J. (2000) Psychologists, doctors and cancer patients. In J. Hartley & A. Branthwaite (Eds) *The Applied Psychologist* (2nd edition). Buckingham: Open University Press.

Heim, A. (1970) *Intelligence and Personality – Their Assessment and Relationship*. Harmondsworth: Penguin.

Hendry, L.B. & Kloep, M. (1999) Adolescence in Europe – an important life phase? In D. Messer & S. Millar (Eds) *Exploring Developmental Psychology: From Infancy to Adolescence*. London: Arnold.

Hendry, L.B. (1999) Adolescents and society. In D. Messer & F. Jones (Eds) *Psychology and Social Care*. London: Jessica Kingsley.

Hendry, L.B., Shucksmith, J., Love, J.G. & Glendenning, A. (1993) *Young People's Leisure and Lifestyles*. London: Routledge.

Hennighausen, K., Enkelmann, D. Wewezer, C. & Remschmidt, H. (1998) Body image distortion in Anorexia Nervosa – is there really a perceptual deficit? *European Child and Adolescent Psychology, 8(3),* 200–7.

Herrnstein, R.J. (1971) IQ. *Atlantic Monthly,* September, 43–64.

Herrnstein, R.J. & Murray, C. (1994) *The Bell Curve: Intelligence and Class Structure in American Life*. New York: Free Press.

Herskovits, M.J. (1955) *Cultural Anthropology*. New York: Knopf.

Heston, L.L. (1966) Psychiatric disorders in foster-home-reared children of schizophrenic mothers. *British Journal of Psychiatry, 122,* 819–825.

Hetherington, E.M. (1967) The effects of familial variables on sex-typing, on parent–child similarity, and on initiation in children. In J.P. Hill (Ed.) *Minnesota Symposium on Child Psychology,* Vol.1. Minneapolis, MN: University of Minnesota Press.

Hetherington, E.M. & Stanley-Hagan, M. (1999) The adjustment of children with divorced parents: A risk and resiliency perspective. *Journal of Child Psychology & Psychiatry, 40(1),* 129–140.

Hewstone, M., Stroebe, W. & Stephenson, G.M. (Eds) (1996) *Introduction to Social Psychology*. Oxford: Blackwell.

Hicks, D.J. (1965) Imitation and retention of film-mediated aggressive peers and adult models. *Journal of Personality and Social Psychology*, 2, 97–100.

Hilliard, A.G. (1995) The nonscience and nonsense of the bell curve. *Focus: Notes from the Society for the Psychological Study of Ethnic Minority Issues*, 10–12.

Hobson, J.A. & McCarley, R.W. (1977) The brain as a dream state generator: An activation-synthesis hypothesis of the dream process. *American Journal of Psychiatry*, *134*, 121.

Hobson, J.A. (1989) Sleep. New York: Scientific American Library.

Hobson, J.A. (1994) *The Chemistry of Conscious States: How the Brain Changes Its Mind*. Boston, MA: Little, Brown Co.

Hodges, J. & Tizard, B. (1989) Social and family relationships of ex-institutional adolescents. *Journal of Child Psychology & Psychiatry*, 30, 77–97.

Hoffman, L.W. (1974) Effects of maternal employment on the child: A review of the Research. *Developmental Psychology*, 10, 204–228.

Hofling, K.C., Brotzman, E., Dalrymple, S., Graves, N. & Pierce, C.M. (1966) An experimental study in the nurse–physician relationship. *Journal of Nervous & Mental Disorders, 143*, 171–180.

Hofstede, G. (1980) *Culture's Consequences: International Differences in Work-related Values*. Beverly Hills, CA: Sage.

Hofstede, G. (1983) Dimensions of national cultures in fifty countries and three regions. In J. Deregowski, S. Dzuirawiec & R. Annis (Eds) *Explications in Cross-Cultural Psychology*. Lisse, Netherlands: Swets & Zeitlinger.

Hogg, M.A. & Vaughan, G.M. (1998) *Social Psychology* (2nd edition). London: Prentice-Hall.

Holland, A.J., Sicotte, N. & Treasure, J. (1988) Anorexia nervosa: Evidence for a genetic basis. *Journal of Psychosomatic Research, 32*, 561–572.

Holloway, S., Tucker, L. & Hornstein, H. (1977) The effects of social and non-social information on intepersonal behaviour of males. The news makes news. *Journal of Personality & Social Psychology*, 35, 514–522.

Holmes, P. & Karp, M. (1991) *Psychodrama, Inspiration and Technique*. London: Routledge.

Holmes, T.H. & Rahe, R.H. (1967) The social readjustment rating scale. *Journal of Psychosomatic Research, 11*, 213–218.

Homans, G.C. (1974) *Social Behaviour: Its Elementary Forms* (2nd edition). New York: Harcourt Brace Jovanovich.

Honzik, M.P., McFarlane, H.W. & Allen, L. (1948) The stability of mental test performance between two and eighteen years. *Journal of Experimental Education*, 17, 309–324.

Horgan, J. (1993) Eugenics revisited. *Scientific American*, June, 92–100.

Horne, J. (1978) A review of the biological effects of sleep deprivation in man. *Biological Psychology*, 7, 55–102.

Horne, J. (1988) *Why we sleep*. Oxford: Oxford University Press.

Horney, K. (1924) On the genesis of the castration complex in women. *International Journal of Psychoanalysis*, *v*, 50–65.

Horney, K. (1973) *Feminine Psychology*. New York: W.W. Norton.

Horowitz, F.D. (1987) *Exploring Developmental Theories: Towards a Structural/behavioural Model of Development*. Hillsdale, NJ: Erlbaum.

Horowitz, F.D. (1990) Developmental models of individual differences. In J. Colombo & J. Fagan (Eds) *Individual Differences in Infancy: Reliability, Stability, Predictability*. Hillsdale, NJ: Erlbaum.

Howat, D. (1999) Social and cultural diversity. *Psychology Review*, 5(3), 28–31.

Howe, M. (1995) Hothouse tots: Encouraging and accelerating development in young children. *Psychology Review*, 2, 2–4.

Howe, M. (1997) *IQ in Question: The Truth about Intelligence*. London: Sage.

Howe, M. (1998) Can IQ change? *The Psychologist*, 11(2), 69–71.

Howitt, D. (1991) *Concerning Psychology: Psychology Applied to Social Issues*. Milton Keynes: Open University Press.

Huesmann, L.R. (1982) Television violence and aggressive behavior. In D. Pearl, L. Bouthilet & J. Lazar (Eds) *Television and Behavior: Ten Years of Scientific Programs and Implications for the 80s*. Washington, DC: U.S. Government Printing Office.

Huesmann, L.R. & Eron, L.D. (Eds) (1986) *Television and the aggressive child: a Cross-national Comparison.* New York: Erlbaum.

Hunt, J. McVicker (1961) *Intelligence and Experience.* New York: Ronald Press.

Hunt, J. McVicker (1969) Has compensatory education failed? Has it been attempted? *Harvard Educational Review, 39,* 278–300.

Huston, A.C. (1983) Sex-typing. In E.M. Hetherington (Ed.) *Socialisation, Personality and Social Development.* New York: Wiley.

Huston, M. & Schwartz, P. (1995) Lesbian and gay male relationships. In J.T. Wood & S. Dock (Eds) *Understanding Relationship Processes 6: Under-studied Relationships: Off the Beaten Track.* Thousand Oaks, CA: Sage.

Hyde, T.S. & Jenkins, J.J. (1973) Recall for words as a function of semantic, graphic and syntactic orienting tasks. *Journal of Verbal Learning and Verbal Behaviour, 12,* 471–480.

Ickes, W. & Duck, S. (2000) Personal Relationships and Social Psychology. In W. Ickes & S. Duck (Eds) *The Social Psychology of Personal Relationships.* Chichester: John Wiley & Sons Ltd.

Ingham, R. (1978) *Football Hooliganism: The Wider Context.* London: Inter-Action Imprint.

Inhelder, B. & Piaget, J. (1958) *The Growth of Logical Thinking.* London: Routledge & Kegan Paul.

Iversen, L.L. (1979) The chemistry of the brain. *Scientific American, 241,* 134–149.

Iwao, S. (1993) *The Japanese woman: Traditional Image and Changing Reality.* New York: Free Press.

Iwasa, N. (1992) Postconventional reasoning and moral education in Japan. *Journal of Moral Education, 21*(1), 3–16.

Jackson, H.F. (1986) Is there a schizotoxin? A critique of the evidence of the major contender – dopamine. In N. Eisenberg & D. Glasgow (Eds) *Current Issues in Clinical Psychology, Volume 5.* Aldershot: Gower.

Jackson, H.F. (1990) Biological markers in schizophrenia. In R.P. Bentall (Ed.) *Reconstructing schizophrenia.* London: Routledge.

Jackson, S., Cicogani, E. & Charman, L. (1996) The measurement of conflict in parent–adolescent relationships. In L. Verhofstadt-Deneve, I. Kienhorst & C. Braet (Eds) *Conflict and Development in Adolescence.* Leiden: DSWO Press.

Jacobs, J. (1887) Experiments on 'prehension'. *Mind, 12,* 75–79.

Jahoda, G. (1978) Cross-cultural perspectives. In H. Tajfel & C. Fraser (Eds) *Introducing Social Psychology.* Harmondsworth: Penguin.

Jahoda, M. (1958) *Current Concepts of Positive Mental Health.* New York: Basic Books.

James, W. (1890) *The Principles of Psychology.* New York: Henry Holt & Co.

Jamison, K. (1993) *Touched with Fire.* New York: Simon & Schuster.

Jankowiak, W.R., Fischer, E.F. (1992) A cross-cultural perspective on romantic love. *Ethnology, 31,* 149–155.

Jeffery, C.R. (1990) *Criminology: An Interdisciplinary Approach.* Englewood Cliffs, NJ: Prentice-Hall.

Jenike, M.A. (1986) Theories of aetiology. In M.A. Jenike, L. Baer & W.E. Minichiello (Eds) *Obsessive–compulsive disorders.* Littleton, MA: PSG Publishing.

Jensen, A. (1969) How much can we boost IQ and scholastic achievement? *Harvard Educational Review, 39,* 1–23.

Johnson, J. *et al.* (2002) The effects of media violence on society, *Science, 295,* 2468.

Johnson, J.H. & Sarason, I.G. (1978) Life stress, depression and anxiety: Internal/external control as a moderator variable. *Journal of Psychosomatic Research, 22,* 205–208.

Johnson, R.D. & Downing, L.L. (1979) Deindividuation and valence of cues: Effects on prosocial and anti-social behavior. *Journal of Personality & Social Psychology, 37,* 1532–1538.

Johnston, A., DeLuca, D., Murtaugh, K. & Diener, E. (1977) Validation of a laboratory play measure of child aggression. *Child Development, 48,* 324–327.

Johnston, D.K. (1988) Adolescents' solutions to dilemmas in fables: Two moral orientations – two problem-solving strategies. In C. Gilligan, J.V. Ward & J.M. Taylor (Eds) *Mapping the Moral Domain.* Cambridge, MA: Harvard University Press.

Jones, S. (1993) *The Language of the Genes.* London: Flamingo.

Josephson, W. (1987) Television violence and children's aggression: Testing the priming, social script, and disinhibition predictions. *Journal of Personality & Social Psychology, 53,* 882–890.

Jouvet, M. (1967) Mechanisms of the states of sleep: a neuropharmacological approach. *Research Publications of the Association for the Research in Nervous and Mental Diseases, 45,* 86–126.

Joy, L.A., Kimball, M. & Zabrack, M.L. (1986) Television exposure and children's aggressive behaviour. In

T.M. Williams (Ed.) *The Impact of Television: A Natural Experiment Involving Three Towns*. New York: Academic Press.

Joynson, R.B. (1980) Models of man: 1879–1979. In A.J. Chapman & D.M. Jones (Eds) *Models of Man*. Leicester: British Psychological Society.

Judd, J. (1997) Working mothers need not feel guilty. *Independent on Sunday*, 27 November, 5.

Juel-Nielsen, N. (1965) Individual and environment: A psychiatric and psychological investigation of monozygous twins raised apart. *Acta Psychiatrica et Neurologica Scandinavia (Suppl. 183)*.

Kagan, J., Kearsley, R. & Zelago, P. (1978) *Infancy: Its Place in Human Development*. Cambridge, MA: Harvard University Press.

Kagan, J., Reznick, J.S. (1990) The temperamental qualities of inhibition and lack of inhibition. In M. Lewis & S.M. Miller (Eds) *Handbook of Developmental Psychopathology*. New York: Plenum Press.

Kaiser, A.S., Katz, R. & Shaw, B.F. (1998) Cultural Issues in the Management of Depression. In S.S. Kazarian & D.R. Evans (Eds) *Cultural Clinical Psychology: Theory, Research, and Practice*. New York: Oxford University Press.

Kamin, L.J. (1974) *The Science and Politics of IQ*. Potomac, MD: Lawrence Erlbaum Associates.

Kanner, A.D., Coyne, J.C., Schaefer, C. & Lazarus, R.S. (1981) Comparison of two modes of stress measurement: Daily hassles and uplifts versus major life events. *Journal of Behavioural Measurement*, 4, 1–39.

Karmiloff-Smith, A. (1996) The connectionist infant: Would Piaget turn in his grave? *Society for Research in Child Development Newsletter*, Fall, 1–2 and 10.

Karraker, K.H., Vogel, D.A. & Lake, M.A. (1995) Parents' gender-stereotyped perceptions of newborns: The eye of the beholder revisited. *Sex Roles*, 33 (9/10), 687–701.

Kazdin, A. & Bootzin, R. (1972) The token economy: An evaluative review. *Journal of Applied Behavior Analysis*, 5, 359–360.

Kellermann, P.F. (1992) *Focus on Psychodrama: The Therapeutic Aspects of Psychodrama*. London: Jessica Kingsley Publishers.

Kelley, H.H. & Thibaut, J.W. (1978) *Interpersonal relations: A Theory of Interdependence*. New York: Wiley.

Kendler, K.S. & Gardner, C.O. (1998) Boundaries of major depression: An evaluation of DSM-IV criteria. *American Journal of Psychiatry*, 155, 172–177.

Kendler, K.S. Masterson, C.C. & Davis, K.L. (1985) Psychiatric illness in first-degree relatives of patients with paranoid psychosis, schizophrenia, and medical controls. *British Journal of Psychiatry*, 147, 524–531.

Kendler, K.S., Karkowski, L.M. & Prescott, C.A. (1996) Age of onset in schizophrenia and risk of illness in relatives. *British Journal of Psychiatry*, 169, 213–218.

Kendler, K.S., Maclean, C., Neale, M., Kessler, R., Heath, A. & Eaves, L. (1991) The genetic epidemiology of bulimia nervosa. *American Journal of Psychiatry*, 148, 1627–1637.

Kenrick, D. (1991) Proximate altruism and ultimate selfishness. *Psychological Inquiry*, 2, 135–137.

Kenrick, D.L. & McFarlane, S.W. (1986) Ambient temperature and horn honking: A field study of the heat/aggression relationship. *Environment & Behaviour*, 18, 179–191.

Kenrick, D.T. & Simpson, J.A. (Eds) (1997) *Evolutionary Social Psychology*. Mahwah, NJ: Lawrence Erlbaum.

Kephart, W.M. (1967) Some correlates of romantic love. *Journal of Marriage and The Family*, 29, 470–474.

Keppel, G. & Underwood, B.J. (1962) Pro-active inhibition in short-term retention of single items. *Journal of Verbal Learning and Verbal Behaviour*, 1, 75–121.

Kerckhoff, A.C. & Davis, K.E. (1962) Value consensus and need complementarity in mate selection. *American Sociological Review*, 27, 295–303.

Kerckhoff, A.C. (1974) The social context of interpersonal attraction. In T.L.Huston (Ed.) *Foundations of Interpersonal Attraction*. New York: Academic Press.

Kerig, P.K., Cowan, P.A. & Cowan, C.P. (1993) Marital quality and gender differences in parent–child interaction. *Developmental Psychology*, 29 (6), 931–939.

Kety, S.S., Rosenthal, D., Wender, P.H., Schulsinger, F. & Jacobson, B. (1975) Mental illness in the biological and adoptive families of adoptive individuals who have become schizophrenic. In R.R. Fieve, D. Rosenthal & H. Bull (Eds) *Genetic Research in Psychiatry*. Baltimore: Johns Hopkins University Press.

Keys, A., Brozek, J., Henschel, A., Michelsen, O. & Taylor, H.L. (1950) *The Biology of Human Starvation*. Minneapolis, MN: University of Minneapolis Press.

Khan, S. (2003) New wave of heroin sucks in pre-teens. *The Observer*, 6 July, 6.

Kiecolt-Glaser, J.K., Garner, W., Speicher, C.E., Penn, G.M., Holliday, J. & Glaser, R. (1984) Psychosocial modifiers of immunocompetence in medical students. *Psychosomatic Medicine*, 46, 7–14.

Kiecolt-Glaser, J.K., Marucha, P.T., Malarkey, W.B., Mercado, A.M. & Glaser, R. (1995) Slowing of wound healing by psychological stress. *The Lancet, 346,* 1194–1196.

King, D.P. & Takahashi, J.S. (2000) Molecular genetics of circadian rhythms in mammals. *Annual Review of Neuroscience, 23,* 713–742.

Kirkpatrick, D.R. (1984) Age, gender and patterns of common-sense fears among adults. *Behaviour Research & Therapy, 22,* 141–150.

Kirsch, I. & Sapirstein, G. (1998) Listening to Prozac but hearing placebo: A meta-analysis of antidepressant medication. *Prevention & Treatment,* Vol.1, Article 2a.

Kitzinger, C. & Coyle, A. (1995) Lesbian and gay couples: Speaking of difference. *The Psychologist, 8,* 64–69.

Kitzinger, C. (1998) Challenging gender biases: Feminist psychology at work. *Psychology Review, 4*(3), 18–20.

Kline, P. (1972) *Fact and fantasy in Freudian theory.* London: Methuen.

Kline, P. (1988) *Psychology Exposed.* London: Routledge.

Kline, P. (1989) Objective tests of Freud's theories. In A.M. Coleman & J.G. Beaumont (Eds.), *Psychology Survey No.7.* Leicester: British Psychological Society.

Kloep, M. & Hendry, L.B. (1999) Challenges, risks and coping in adolescence. In D. Messer & S. Millar (Eds) *Exploring Developmental Psychology: From Infancy to Adolescence.* London: Arnold.

Kloep, M. & Tarifa, F. (1993) Albanian children in the wind of change. In L.E. Wolven (Ed.) *Human Resource Development.* Hogskolan: Ostersund.

Klosko, J.S., Barlow, D.H., Tassinari, R. & Cerny, J.A. (1990) A comparison of alprazolam and behavior therapy in treatment of panic disorder. *Journal of Consulting and Clinical Psychology, 58,* 77–84.

Kobasa, S. (1979) Stressful life events, personality and health: An inquiry into hardiness. *Journal of Personality & Social Psychology, 37,* 1–11.

Kobasa, S. (1986) How much stress can you survive? In M.G. Walraven & H.E. Fitzgerald (Eds) *Annual Editions: Human Development, 86/87.* New York: Dushkin.

Koestler, A. (1967) *The Ghost in the Machine.* London: Pan.

Kohlberg, L. & Nisan, M. (1987) A longitudinal study of moral judgement in Turkish males. In A. Colby & L. Kohlberg (Eds) *The Measurement of Moral Judgement.* New York: Cambridge University Press.

Kohlberg, L. & Ullian, D.Z. (1974) Stages in the development of psychosexual concepts and attitudes. In R.C. Van Wiele (Ed.) *Sex Differences in Behaviour.* New York: Wiley.

Kohlberg, L. (1966) A cognitive-developmental analysis of children's concepts and attitudes. In E.E. Maccoby (Ed.) *The Development of Sex Differences.* Stanford, CA: Stanford University Press.

Kohlberg, L. (1969) Stage and sequence: The cognitive developmental approach to socialisation. In D.A. Goslin (Ed.) *Handbook of Socialisation Theory and Research.* Chicago: Rand McNally.

Kohlberg, L. (1984) *Essays on Moral Development: The Psychology of Moral Development, Volume 2.* New York: Harper & Row.

Kohn, A. (1993) Rewards versus learning: A response to Paul Chance. *Phi Delta Kappan, 74,* 783–787.

Koluchova, J. (1972) Severe deprivation in twins: A case study. *Journal of Child Psychology & Psychiatry, 13,* 107–114.

Koluchova, J. (1991) Severely deprived twins after 22 years observation. *Studia Psychologica, 33,* 23–28.

Kraepelin, E. (1896) Dementia Praecox (trans.). In J. Cutting & M. Shepherd (Eds) *The Clinical Routes of the Schizophrenia Concept.* Cambridge: Cambridge University Press.

Kremer, J. (1998) Work. In K. Trew & J. Kremer (Eds) *Gender and Psychology.* London: Arnold.

Kroger, J. (1985) Separation-individuation and ego identity status in New Zealand university students. *Journal of Youth & Adolescence, 14,* 133–147.

Kroger, J. (1996) *Identity in Adolescence: The Balance Between Self and Other* (2nd edition). London: Routledge.

Krupat, E. & Garonzik, R. (1994) Subjects' expectations and the search for alternatives to deception in social psychology. *British Journal of Social Psychology, 33,* 211–222.

Kuhn, T.S. (1962) *The Structure of Scientific Revolutions.* Chicago: University of Chicago Press.

Kurdek, L. (1991) The dissolution of gay and lesbian relationships. *Journal of Social & Personal Relationships, 8,* 265–278.

Kurdek, L. (1992) Relationship stability and relationship satisfaction in cohabiting gay and lesbian couples: A prospective longitudinal test of the contextual and interdependence models. *Journal of Social & Personal Relationships, 9,* 125–142.

Laing, R.D. (1959) *The Divided Self – An Existential Study in Sanity & Madness.* Pelican Books.

Laing, R.D. (1961) *Self and Others.* London: Tavistock.

Laing, R.D. (1967) *The Politics of Experience and the Bird of Paradise.* Harmondsworth: Penguin.

Laing, R.D. & Esterson, A. (1964) *Sanity, Madness and the Family.* London: Tavistock.

Lambe, E.K., Katzman, D.K., Mikulis, D.J., Kennedy, S.H. & Zipursky, R.B. (1997). Cerebral grey matter volume deficits after weight recovery from anorexia nervosa. *Archives of General psychiatry, 54,* 537–542.

Lambert, M.J. & Bergin, A.E. (1994) The effectiveness of psychotherapy. In A. Bergin & S. Garfield (Eds), *Handbook of Psychotherapy & Behavior Change* (4th edition). New York: John Wiley & Sons.

Lambie, J. (1991) The misuse of Kuhn in psychology. *The Psychologist, 4*(1), 6–11.

Langlois, J.H. & Roggman, L.A. (1990) Attractive faces are only average. *Psychological Science, 1,* 115–121.

Larcombe, J. (2003) Personal correspondence.

Lashley, K.S. (1929) *Brain Mechanisms and Intelligence.* Chicago: University of Chicago Press. Reprinted in Dover edition (1963) with Introduction by D.O. Hebb.

Latané, B. & Darley, J. (1968) Group inhibition of bystander intervention in emergencies. *Journal of Personal & Social Psychology, 10,* 215–221.

Latané, B. & Darley, J.M. (1970) *The Unresponsive Bystander: Why Doesn't He Help?* New York: Appleton-Century-Crofts.

Latané, B. & Darley, J.M. (1976) Help in a crisis: Bystander response to an emergency. In J.W. Thibaut & J.T. Spence (Eds) *Contemporary Topics in Social Psychology.* Morristown, NJ: General Learning Press.

Latané, B., Nida, S.A. & Wilson, D.W. (1981) The Effects of Group Size on Helping Behavior. In J.P. Rushton & R.M. Sorrentino (Eds) *Altruism and Helping Behavior.* Hillsdale, NJ: Erlbaum.

Lavender, T. (2000) Schizophrenia. In L. Champion & M. Power (Eds) *Adult Psychological Problems: An Introduction* (2nd edition). Hove: Psychology Press.

Lazarus, A.A. (1994) How certain boundaries and ethics diminish effectiveness. *Ethics & Behavior, 4,* 255–261.

Lazarus, R.S. & Folkman, S. (1984) *Stress, Appraisal, and Coping.* New York: Springer.

Le Bon, G. (1995) *The Crowd: A Study of the Popular Mind.* London: Transaction Publishers. (Original work published in 1895.)

LeDoux, J.E. (1998) *The Emotional Brain: The Mysterious Underpinnings of Emotional Life.* New York: Simon & Schuster.

Lee, K., Cameron, C.A., Xu, F., Fu, G. & Board, J. (1997) Chinese and Canadian children's evaluations of lying and truth telling: Similarities and differences in the context of pro- and antisocial behaviours. *Child Development, 68,* 924–934.

Lee, S.G. (1969) Spirit Possession among the Zulu. In J. Beattie and J. Middleton (Eds) *Spirit Mediumship and Society in Africa.* New York: Africana.

LeFrancois, G.R. (1983) *Psychology.* Belmont, CA: Wadsworth Publishing Co.

Leonard, W.R. & Robertson, M.L. (1994) Evolutionary perspectives on human nutrition: the influence of brain and body size on diet and metabolism. *American Journal of Human Biology, 6,* 77–88.

Lepper, M.R., Greene, D. & Nisbett, R.E. (1973) Undermining children's intrinsic interest with extrinsic reward: A test of the overjustification hypothesis. *Journal of Personality & Social Psychology, 28,* 129–137.

Levav, I., Kohn, R., Golding, J.M. & Weissman, M.M. (1997) Vulnerability of Jews to major depression. *American Journal of Psychiatry, 154,* 941–947.

Levine, R. V., Sato, S., Hashimoto, T. & Verma, J. (1995) Love and marriage in eleven cultures. *Journal of Cross-Cultural Psychology, 67,* 69–82.

Levinger, G. & Clark, J. (1967) Emotional factors in the forgetting of word associations. *Journal of Abnormal & Social Psychology, 62,* 99–105.

Lewontin, R. (1976) Race and Intelligence. In N.J. Block & G. Dworkin (Eds) *The IQ Controversy: Critical Readings.* New York: Pantheon.

Lewy, A.J., Wehr, T.A., Goodwin, F.K., Newsome, D.A. & Markey, S.P. (1980) Light suppresses melatonin secretion in humans. *Science, 210,* 1267–1269.

Liebert, R.M. & Baron, R.A. (1972) Short term effects of television aggression on children's aggressive behavior. In G.A. Comstock, E.A. Rubinstein & J.P. Murray (Eds) *Television and Social Behavior*, Vol.2, Television and Social Learning. Washington, D.C.: United States Government Printing Office.

Light, P. (1986) Context, conservation and conversation. In M. Richards & P. Light (Eds) *Children of Social Worlds.* Cambridge: Polity Press.

Light, P., Buckingham, N. & Robbins, A.H. (1979) The conservation task as an interactional setting. *British Journal of Educational Psychology, 49,* 304–310.

Light, P. & Gilmour, A. (1983) Conservation or conversation? Contextual facilitation of inappropriate conservation judgements. *Journal of Experimental Child Psychology, 36*, 356–363.

Lilienfeld, S.O. (1995) *Seeing Both Sides: Classic Controversies in Abnormal Psychology*. Pacific Grove, CA.: Brooks/Cole Publishing Co.

Lilienfeld, S.O. (1998) *Looking into Abnormal Psychology: Contemporary Readings*. Pacific Grove, CA: Brooks/Cole Publishing Co.

Lippa, R. (1994) *Introduction to Social Psychology* (2nd edition). Belmont, CA: Wadsworth Inc.

Llewellyn-Smith, J. (1996) Courses for gifted children are often 'a waste of time'. *The Sunday Telegraph*, 5 September, 8.

Lloyd, P., Mayes, A., Manstead, A.S.R., Meudell, P.R. & Wagner, H.L. (1984) *Introduction to Psychology – An Integrated Approach*. London: Fontana.

Loehlin, J.C., Willerman, L. & Horn, J.M. (1988) Human behaviour genetics. *Annual Review of Psychology, 39*, 101–133.

Loftus, E.F. (1975) Leading questions and the eyewitness report. *Cognitive Psychology, 1*, 560–572.

Loftus, E.F., Miller, D.G. & Burns, H.J. (1978) Semantic integration of verbal information into visual memory, *Journal of Experimental Psychology, 4*(1), 19–31.

Loftus, E.F. & Palmer, J.C. (1974) Reconstruction of automobile destruction: An example of the interaction between language and memory. *Journal of Verbal Learning and Verbal Behavior, 13*, 585–589.

Lombroso, C. (1911) *Crime and its remedies*. Boston, MA: Little, Brown. See www.epub.org.br/cm/n01/frenolg/lombroso.htm.1/10/99

Lonner, W. (1990) An overview of cross-cultural testing and assessment. In R. Brislin (Ed.) *Applied Cross-Cultural Psychology*. Newbury Park, CA: Sage.

Lopatka, C. & Rachman, S. (1995) Perceived responsibility and compulsive checking: An experimental analysis. *Behaviour Research and Therapy, 33*, 673–684.

Lorenz, K.Z. (1935) The companion in the bird's world. *Auk, 54*, 245–273.

Lott, A.J. & Lott, B.E. (1974) The role of reward in the formation of positive interpersonal attitudes. In T. Huston (Ed.) *Foundations of Interpersonal Attraction*. New York: Academic Press.

Lovelace, V.O. & Huston, A.C. (1983) Can television teach pro-social behaviour?, *Prevention in Human Services, 2*(1–2), 93–106.

Luborsky, L., Diguer, L., Luborsky, E., McLellan, A.T., Woody, G. & Alexander, L. (1993) Psychological health as predictor of the outcomes of psychotherapy, *Journal of Consulting & Clinical Psychology, 61*.

Luria, A.R. (1987) Reductionism. In R.L. Gregory (Ed.) *The Oxford Companion to the Mind*. Oxford: Oxford University Press.

Lyall, J. (1993) Animal rites. *Nursing Times, 89*(10), 18–19.

Lyddy, F. (2000) Depression: The state of the disorder. *The Psychologist, 13*(8), 414–415.

Lytton, H. & Romney, D.M. (1991) Parents' differential socialisation of boys and girls: A meta-analysis. *Psychological Bulletin, 109*, 267–296.

Lytton, H. (1977) Do parents create, or respond to, differences in twins? *Developmental Psychology, 13*, 456–459.

Maccoby, E.E. (1990) Gender and relationships: A developmental account. *American Psychologist, 45*, 513–520.

Maccoby, E.E. & Jacklin, C.N. (1974) *The Psychology of Sex Differences*. Stanford, CA: Stanford University Press.

MacLeod, A. (1998) Therapeutic interventions, in M. Eysenck (Ed.) *Psychology: An Integrated Approach*. Harlow: Addison Wesley/Longman Ltd.

Mahoney, J. (1998) Mates past their prime. *Times Higher Educational Supplement*, 25 September, 18.

Maier, S.F. & Seligman, M.E.P. (1976) Learned helplessness: Theory and evidence. *Journal of Experimental Psychology: General, 105*, 3–46.

Malinowski, B. (1929) *The Sexual Life of Savages*. New York: Harcourt Brace Jovanovich.

Mapstone, E. (1991) Special issue on animal experimentation. *The Psychologist, 4*(5), 195.

Marcia, J.E. (1980) Identity in adolescence. In J. Adelson (Ed.) *Handbook of Adolescent Psychology*. New York: Wiley.

Marcus, D.E. & Overton, W.F. (1978) The development of cognitive gender constancy and sex-role preferences. *Child Development, 49*, 434–444.

Marks, I. (1987) *Fears, Phobias and Rituals*. Oxford: Oxford University Press.

Marks, I.M., Swinson, R.P., Basoglu, M., Kuch, K., Noshirvani, H., O'Sullivan, G., Lelliott, P.T., Kirby, M., McNamee, G., Sengun, S. & Wickwire, K. (1993) Alprazolam and exposure alone and combined in panic disorder with agoraphobia: A controlled study in London and Toronto. *British Journal of Psychiatry, 162,* 776–787.

Marmot, M., Bosma, H., Hemingway, H., Brunner, E. & Stansfield, S. (1997) Contribution of job control and other risk factors to social variation in health disease incidence. *The Lancet, 350,* 235–239.

Marmot, M.G. and Theorell, T. (1988) Social clan and cardiovascular disease: the contribution of work. *International Journal of Health Services,* 18, 659–674.

Marsland, D. (1987) *Education and Youth.* London: Falmer.

Martin, C.L. (1991) The role of cognition in understanding gender effects. *Advances in Child Development and Behaviour, 23,* 113–149.

Maslow, A. (1954) *Motivation and Personality.* New York: Harper & Row.

Maslow, A. (1968) *Towards a psychology of being (2nd Ed).* New York: Van Nostrand Reinhold.

Maslow, A.H. (1943) A theory of human motivation. *Psychological Review, 50,* 370–396.

Matthews, K.E, & Cannon, L.K. (1975) Environmental noise level as a determinant of helping behavior. *Journal of Personality & Social Psychology, 32,* 571–577.

Mattson, D.T., Berk, M. & Lucas, M.D. (1997) A neuropsychological study of prefrontal lobe function in the positive and negative subtypes of schizophrenia. *Journal of Genetic Psychology, 158,* 487–494.

McCall, R.B., Applebaum, M.I. & Hogarty, P.S. (1973) Developmental changes in mental test performance. *Monographs of the Society for Research in Child Development,* 36 (3, Whole No. 150).

McClelland, L. & Crisp, A. (2001) Anorexia nervosa and social class. *International Journal of Eating Disorders,* 29 (2), 150–156.

McClintock, M. & Stern, K. (1998) Regulation of Ovulation by Human Pheromones. *Nature, 12,* March, 177–179.

McClintock, M.K. (1971) Menstrual synchrony and suppression. *Nature, 291,* 244–245.

McClintock, M.K. (1988) On the nature of mammalian and human pheromones, olfaction and taste. *XII Annals of the New York Academy of Sciences, 855,* 390–392.

McCloskey, M., Wible, C.G. & Cohen, N.J. (1988) Is there a special flash-bulb memory mechanism? *Journal of Experimental Psychology: General, 117,* 171–181.

McCloskey, M. & Zaragoza, M.S. (1985) Misleading post-event information and memory for eents: Arguments and evidence against memory impairment hypotheses. *Journal of Experimental Psychology: General, 114,* 1–16.

McGarrigle, J. & Donaldson, M. (1974) Conservation accidents. *Cognition, 3,* 341–350.

McGhee, P. (2001) *Thinking Psychologically.* Basingstoke: Palgrave.

McGlone, F., Park, A. & Roberts, C. (1996) *Relative Values.* Family Policy Studies Centre: BSA.

McGuffin, P., Farmer, A. & Gottesman, I.I. (1987) Is there really a split in schizophrenia? *British Journal of Psychiatry, 150,* 581–592.

McGurk, H. (1975) *Growing and Changing.* London: Methuen.

Mead, M. (1935) *Sex and Temperament in Three Primitive Societies.* New York: Dell.

Mead, M. (1938–49) *The Mountain Arapesh*: 3 volumes. Reprinted by Transaction Publishers (2002). Garden City, NY: Natural History Press.

Mead, M. (1949) *Male and Female: A Study of the Sexes in a Changing World.* New York: Dell.

Meadows, S. (1995) Cognitive Development. In P.E. Bryant & A.M. Colman (Eds) *Developmental Psychology.* London: Longman.

Mee, B. (2000) We'll see you in court. *The Independent on Sunday,* 21 May, 9–12.

Meichenbaum, D. (1976) Towards a cognitive therapy of self-control. In G. Schwartz & D. Shapiro (Eds) *Consciousness and Self-Regulation: Advances in Research.* New York: Plenum Publishing Co.

Meichenbaum, D. (1997) The evolution of a cognitive-behaviour therapist. In J.K. Zeig (Ed.) *The Evolution of Psychotherapy: The Third Conference.* New York: Brunner/Mazel.

Meilman, P.W. (1979) Cross-sectional age changes in ego identity status during adolescence. *Developmental Psychology, 15,* 230–231.

Melton, G.B. & Gray, J.N. (1988) Ethical Dilemmas in AIDS Research: Individual Privacy and Public Health. *American Psychologist, 43* (1), 60–64.

Mendel, G. (1865) Versuche uber Pflanzenhybriden [Experiments in plant hybrisation]. *Verhandlungen des Naturs – Forschunden Vereines in Bruenn, 4,* 3–47.

Messner, S. (1986) Television Violence and Violent Crime: An aggregate analysis. *Social Problems, 33*(3), 218–235.

Metalsky, G.I., Halberstadt, L.J. & Abramson, L.Y. (1987) Vulnerability and invulnerability to depressive mood reactions: Toward a more powerful test of the diathesis-stress and causal mediation components of the reformulated theory of despression. *Journal of Personality & Social Psychology, 52,* 386–393.

Metalsky, G.I., Joiner, T.E., Hardin, T.S. & Abramson, L.Y. (1993) Depressive reactions to failure in a natural setting: A test of the hopelessness and self-esteem theories of depression. *Journal of Abnormal Psychology, 102,* 101–109.

Milavsky, J. R., Kessler, R. C., Stipp, H. H. & Rubens, W. S. (1982) *Television and Aggression: A Panel Study.* New York: Academic Press.

Miles, D.R. & Carey, G. (1997) Genetic and environmental architecture of human aggression. *Journal of Personality & Social Psychology, 72,* 207–217.

Miles, L.E.M., Raynal, D.M.& Wilson, M.A. (1977) Blind man living in normal society has circadian rhythms of 24.9 hours. *Science, 198,* 421–423.

Milgram, S. (1963) Behavioural study of obedience. *Journal of Abnormal & Social Psychology, 67,* 391–398.

Milgram, S. (1970) The experience of living in cities. *Science, 167 (3924),* 1461–1468.

Milgram, S. (1974) *Obedience to Auithority.* New York: Harper & Row.

Milgram, S. (1992) *The Individual in a Social World* (2nd edition). New York: McGraw-Hill.

Miller, E. & Morley, S. (1986) *Investigating Abnormal Behaviour.* London: Erlbaum.

Miller, G. (1969) Psychology as a means of promoting human welfare. *American Psychologist, 24,* 1063–1075.

Miller, G.A. (1956) The magical number seven, plus or minus two: some limits on our capacity for processing information. *Psychological Review, 63,* 81–97.

Miller, G.A. (1962) *Psychology: The Science of Mental Life.* Harmondsworth: Penguin.

Miller, G.F. (1998) How mate choice shaped human nature: A review of sexual selection and human evolution. In C. Crawford & D. Krebs (Eds) *Handbook of Evolutionary Psychology: Ideas, Issues, and Applications.* Hillsdale, NJ: Lawrence Erlbaum.

Miller, G.F. (2000) *The Mating Mind: How Sexual Choice Shaped the Evolution of Human Nature.* New York: Doubleday.

Miller, G.F. (2001) The Mating Mind: How Sexual Choice Shaped the Evolution of Human Nature. *Psychology, 12*(8).

Miller, J.G., Bersoff, D.M. & Harwood, R.L. (1990) Perceptions of social responsibilities in India and in the USA: moral imperatives or personal decisions. *Journal of Personality & Social Psychology, 58,* 33–47.

Mills, J. & Clark, M.S. (1980) 'Exchange in communal relationships' (Unpublished manuscript).

Milton, K. (1988) Foraging Behavior and the Evolution of Primate Cognition. In R. Byrne & A. Whiten (Eds) *Machiavellian Intelligence: Social Expertise and the Evolution of Intellect in Monkeys, Apes, and Humans,* 285–305. New York: Oxford University Press.

Mind 2002: http://www.mind.org.uk/information/factsheets/P/psychosurgery/Psychosurgery.asp# Introduction

Mischel, W. (1973) Toward a cognitive social learning reconceptualisation of personality. *Psychological Review, 80,* 252–283.

Mischel, W. & Mischel, H.N. (1976) A cognitive social learning approach to morality and self-regulation. In T. Lickona (Ed.) *Moral Development and Behaviour: Theory, Research and Social Issues.* New York: Holt, Rinehart & Winston.

Mitchell, J. (1974) *Psychoanalysis and Feminism.* Harmondsworth: Penguin.

Moghaddam, F.M. & Studer, C. (1997) Cross-cultural psychology: The frustrated gadfly's promises, potentialities and failures. In D. Fox & D. Prilleltensky (Eds) *Critical Psychology: An Introduction.* London: Sage.

Moghaddam, F.M. (1987) Psychology in the Three Worlds: As reflected by the crisis in social psychology and the move towards indigenous Third World Psychology. *American Psychologist, 42,* 912–920.

Moghaddam, F.M. (1998) *Social Psychology: Exploring Universals Across Cultures.* New York: W.H. Freeman & Co.

Moghaddam, F.M., Taylor, D.M. & Wright, S.C. (1993) *Psychology in Cross-Cultural Perspective.* New York: W.H. Freeman & Co.

Moore, C. & Frye, D. (1986) The effect of the experimenter's intention on the child's understanding of conservation. *Cognition, 22,* 283–298.

Morea, P. (1990) *Personality: An Introduction to the Theories of Psychology.* Harmondsworth: Penguin.

MORI (1984): www.mind.org.uk

Morris, P.E., Tweedy, M. & Gruneberg, M.M. (1985) Interest, knowledge and the memorising of soccer scores. *British Journal of Psychology*, 76, 415–425.

Morselli, E. (1886) Sulla dismorfofobia e sulla tafefobia. *Bolletino della R Accademia di Genova*, 6, 110–119.

Moscovici, S. & Faucheux, C. (1972) Social influence, conforming bias and the study of active minorities. In L. Berkowitz (Ed.) *Advances in Experimental Social Psychology*, Volume 6. New York: Academic Press.

Moscovici, S., Lage, E. & Naffrechoux, M. (1969) Influence of a consistent minority on the responses of a majority in a colour perception task. *Sociometry*, 32, 365–380.

Much, N. (1995) Cultural psychology. In J.A. Smith, R. Harre & L. Van Langenhove (Eds) *Rethinking Psychology*. London: Sage.

Mukerjee, M. (1997) Trends in animal research. *Scientific American*, 63, February.

Munroe, R.H., Shimmin, H.S. & Munroe, R.L. (1984) Gender understanding and sex-role preference in four cultures. *Developmental Psychology*, 20, 673–682.

Munsinger, H. (1975) The adopted child's IQ: A critical review. *Psychological Bulletin*, 82, 623–659.

Murdock, B.B. (1962) The serial position effect in free recall. *Journal of Experimental Psychology*, 64, 482–488.

Murphy, J. (1976) Psychiatric labelling in cross-cultural perspective. *Science*, 191, 1019–1028.

Murstein, B.I. (1972) Physical attractiveness and marital choice. *Journal of Personality & Social Psychology*, 22, 8–12.

Murstein, B.I. (1976) The stimulus-value-role theory of marital choice. In H. Grunebaum & J. Christ (Eds) *Contemporary Marriage: Structures, Dynamics and Therapy*. Boston: Little Brown.

Murstein, B.I. (1987) A clarification and extension of the SVR theory of dyadic pairing. *Journal of Marriage and The Family*, 49, 929–933.

Murstein, B.I. & MacDonald, M.G. (1983) The relation of 'exchange orientation' and 'commitment' scales to marriage adjustment. *International Journal of Psychology*, 18, 297–311.

Murstein, B.I., MacDonald, M.G. & Cereto, M. (1977) A theory of the effect of exchange orientation on marriage and friendship. *Journal of Marriage and The Family*, 39, 543–548.

Myers, D.G. (1990) *Exploring Psychology*. New York: Worth Publishers.

Myers, D.G. (1994) *Exploring Social Psychology*. New York: McGraw-Hill.

Myers, D.G (1998) *Psychology* (5th edition). New York: Worth Publishers.

Neisser, U. (1973) Reversibility of psychiatric diagnosis. *Science*, 180, 1116.

Nelson, S.A. (1980) Factors influencing young children's use of motives and outcomes as moral criteria. *Child Development*, 51, 823–829.

Nemeth, C., Swedund, M. & Kanki, G. (1974) Patterning of the minority's reponses and their influence on the majority. *European Journal of Social Psychology*, 4, 53–64.

Nesse, R. (1999) Testing evolutionary hypotheses about mental disorders. In S.C. Stearns (Ed.) *Evolution in Health and Disease*, 260–266. Oxford: Oxford University Press.

Nesse, R.M. & Williams, G.C. (1995) *Evolution and Healing: The New Science of Darwinian Medicine*. London: Weidenfeld and Nicolson.

Nesse, R.M. & Williams, G.C. (1996) *Why We Get Sick*. New York: Vintage.

Newman, H.H., Freeman, F.N. & Holzinger, K.J. (1937) *Twins: A study of Heredity and Environment*. Chicago, ILL: University of Chicago Press.

Newson, E. (1995) Video violence and the protection of children. *Psychology Review*, 1(2), 2–6.

Nicolson, P. (1995) Feminism and psychology. In J.A. Smith, R. Harré & L. Van Langenhove (Eds) *Rethinking Psychology*. London: Sage.

Nieboer, R. (1999) Bridging the gap. Letter, *The Psychologist*, 12(8), 385.

Nobles, W.W. (1976) Extended self: Rethinking the so-called Negro self-concept. *Journal of Black Psychology*, 2, 99–105.

Norenzayan, A, & Levine, R.V. (1994) Helping in 18 international cities. Paper presented at the Annual meeting of the Western Psychological Association, Kona, Hawaii.

Norman, D.A. & Shallice, T. (1986) Attention to action: Willed and automatic control of behaviour. In R.J. Davison, G.E. Schwartz & D. Shapiro (Eds) *The Design of Everyday Things*. New York: Doubleday.

Norton, C. (2000) Rate of teenage pregnancies is highest for nearly a decade. *The Independent*, 29 March, 12.

Nursing Times (1996) *Nursing Times*, 92 (5), 27.

Nuttin, B., Cosyns, P., Demeulemeester, H., Gybels, J. & Meyerson, B. (1999) Electrical stimulation in anterior limbs of internal capsules in patients with obsessive compulsive disorders, *The Lancet*, 354, 1526.

O'Dwyer, A.-M. & Marks, I. (2000) Obsessive-compulsive disorder and delusions revisited. *British Journal of Psychiatry*, 176, 281–284.

O'Leary, K.D. & Wilson, G.T. (1975) *Behaviour Therapy; Application and Outcome*. Englewood Cliffs, NJ: Prentice-Hall.

Offer, D., Ostrov, E., Howard, K.I. & Atkinson, R. (1988) *The Teenage World: Adolescents' Self-Image in Ten Countries*. New York: Plenum Press.

Olds, J. (1956) Pleasure centres in the brain. *Scientific American*, October, 105–106.

Olds, J. & Milner, P. (1954) Positive reinforcement produced by electrical stimulation of the septal area and other regions of the rat brain. *Journal of Comparative & Physiological Psychology*, 47, 419–427.

Orne, M.T. (1962) On the social psychology of the psychological experiment: with particular reference to demand characteristics and their implications. *American Psychologist*, 17, 776–783.

Orne, M.T. & Holland, C.C. (1968) On the ecological validity of laboratory deceptions. *International Journal of Psychiatry*, 6, 282–293.

Oswald, I. (1980) Sleep as a restorative process: human clues. *Progress in Brain Research*, 53, 279–288.

Owen, L. & Stoneman, C. (1972) Education and the Nature of Intelligence. In D. Rubinstein & C. Stoneman (Eds) *Education for Democracy* (2nd edition). Harmondsworth: Penguin.

Pagel, J.F., Vann, B.H. & Altomare, C.A. (1995) Reported Association of Stress and Dreaming: Community Background Levels and Changes with Disaster (Hurricane Iniki). *Dreaming*, 5, 43–50.

Paik, H. & Comstock, G (1994) The effects of television violence on anti-social behaviour: a meta-analysis. *Communication Research*, 21, 516–546.

Palermo, D.S. (1971) Is a scientific revolution taking place in psychology? *Psychological Review*, 76, 241–263.

Parkin, A.J. (1993) *Memory: Phenomena, Experiment and Theory*. Oxford: Blackwell.

Paulescu, E., Frith, C.D. & Frackoviak, R.S.J. (1993) The neural correlates of the verbal component of working memory. *Nature*, 362, 342–345.

Peek, L. (2000) One in six girls now reaches puberty aged 8. *The Times*, 19 June, 3.

Penfield, W. (1947) Some observations on the cerebral cortex of man. *Proceedings of the Royal Society*, 134, 349.

Penfield, W. (1958) *The Excitable Cortex in Conscious Man*. Liverpool: Liverpool Press.

Penny, G. (1996) Health Psychology. In H. Coolican *Applied Psychology*. London: Hodder & Stoughton.

Penrose, R. (1990) *The Emperor's New Mind*. Oxford: Oxford University Press.

Peplau, L.A. (1982) Research on homosexual couples: An overview. *Journal of Homosexuality*, 8, 3–8.

Peplau, L.A. (1991) Lesbian and gay relationships. In J.C. Gonsiorek & J.D. Weinrich (Eds) *Homosexuality: Research Implications for Public Policy*. London: Sage.

Perry, D.G. & Bussey, K. (1979) The social learning theory of sex differences: Imitation is alive and well. *Journal of Personality & Social Psychology*, 37, 1699–1712.

Petersen, A.C. & Crockett, L. (1985) Pubertal timing and grade effects on adjustment. *Journal of Youth & Adolescence*, 14, 191–206.

Petersen, A.C., Sarigiani, P.A. & Kennedy, R.E. (1991) Adolescent depression: Why more girls? *Journal of Youth & Adolescence*, 20, 247–271.

Peterson, C. & Seligman, M.E.P. (1984) Causal explanations as a risk factor for depression: Theory and evidence. *Psychological Review*, 91, 347–374.

Peterson, L.R. & Peterson, M.J. (1959) Short-term retention of individual verbal items. *Journal of Experimental Psychology*, 58, 193–198.

Phillips, J.L. (1969) *The Origins of Intellect: Piaget's Theory*. San Francisco: W.H. Freeman.

Piaget, J. (1932) *The Moral Judgement of the Child*. London: Routledge & Kegan Paul.

Piaget, J. (1950) *The Psychology of Intelligence*. London: Routledge & Kegan Paul.

Piaget, J. (1952) *The Child's Conception of Number*. London: Routledge & Kegan Paul.

Piaget, J. (1970) Piaget's theory. In P.H. Mussen (Ed.) *Carmichaels' Manual of Child Psychology* (3rd edition), Volume 1. New York: Wiley.

Piaget, J. & Inhelder, B. (1956) *The Child's Conception of Space*. London: Routledge & Kegan Paul.

Pike, A. & Plomin, R. (1999) Genetics and development. In D. Messer & S. Millar (Eds) *Exploring Developmental Psychology: From Infancy to Adolescence*. London: Arnold.

Pike, K.L. (1954) Emic and etic standpoints for the description of behaviour. In K.L. Pike (Ed.) *Language in Relation to a Unified Theory of the Structure of Human Behaviour*. Glendale, CA: Summer Institute of Linguistics.

Piliavin, J.A., Dovidio, J., Gaertner, S. & Clark, R.D. (1981) *Emergency Intervention*. New York: Academic Press.

Piliavin, J.A. & Piliavin, I.M. (1972) Effect of Blood on Reactions to a Victim. *Journal of Personality & Social Psychology, 23*(3), 353–361.

Piliavin, I.M., Rodin, J., & Piliavin, J.A. (1969) Good samaritanism: an underground phenomenon? *Journal of Personality & Social Psychology, 13,* 289–299.

Pine, K. (1999) Theories of cognitive development. In D. Messer & S. Millar (Eds) *Exploring Developmental Psychology: From Infancy to Adolescence.* London: Arnold.

Pippard, J. (1992) Audit of electroconvulsive therapy in two National Health Service Regions. *British Journal of Psychology, 160,* 621–637.

Pitzele, M.S. (1992) Moreno's Chorus: The Audience in Psychodrama. *Journal of The British Psychodrama Association, 7*(1).

Plomin, R, & DeFries, J.C. (1980) Genetics and intelligence: Recent data. *Intelligence, 4,* 15–24.

Plomin, R. & DeFries, J.C. (1998) The genetics of cognitive abilities and disabilities. *Scientific American,* May, 62–69.

Plomin, R. & Thompson, R. (1987) Life-span developmental behavioural genetics. In P.B. Baltes, D.L. Featherman & R.M. Lerner (Eds) *Life-Span Development and Behaviour, Volume 8.* Hillsdale, NJ: Erlbaum.

Plomin, R. (1988) The nature and nurture of cognitive abilities. In R.J. Sternberg (Ed.) *Advances in the Psychology of Human Intelligence, Volume 4.* Hillsdale, NJ: Erlbaum.

Plomin, R. (1994) *Genetics and Experience: The Interplay Between Nature and Nurture.* Thousand Oaks, CA: Sage.

Plomin, R. (1995) Genetics and children's experiences in the family. *Journal of Child Psychology and Psychiatry, 36,* 33–68.

Plomin, R. (1996) Nature and nurture. In M.R. Merrens & G.C. Brannigan (Eds) *The Developmental Psychologists: Research Adventures across the Life Span.* New York: McGraw-Hill.

Plomin, R., DeFries, J.C. & Loehlin, J.C. (1977) Genotype-environment interaction and correlation in the analysis of human behaviour. *Psychological Bulletin, 84,* 309–322.

Pollitt, E. & Gorman, K.S. (1994) Nutritional deficiencies as developmental risk factors. In C.A. Nelson (Ed.) *The Minnesota Symposia on Child Development, Volume 27.* Hillsdale, NJ: Erlbaum.

Popper, K. (1972) *Objective Knowledge: An Evolutionary Approach.* Oxford: Oxford University Press.

Postmes, T. & Spears, R. (1998) Deindividuation and anti-normative behavior: A meta-analysis. *Psychological Bulletin, 123,* 238–259.

Prentice-Dunn, S. & Rogers, R.W. (1982) Effects of public and private self-awareness on deindividuation and aggression. *Journal of Personality & Social Psychology, 43,* 503–513.

Price, W.F. & Crapo, R.H. (1999) *Cross-Cultural Perspectives in Introductory Psychology* (3rd edition). Belmont, CA: Wadsworth Publishing Company.

Prince, J. & Hartnett, O. (1993) From 'psychology constructs the female' to 'females construct psychology'. *Feminism & Psychology, 3*(2), 219–224.

Prins, H. (1995) *Offenders, Deviants or Patients?* (2nd edition). London: Routledge.

Quiery, N. (1998) Parenting and the family. In K. Trew & J. Kremer (Eds) *Gender & Psychology.* London: Arnold.

Rachman, S. (1993) Obsessions, responsibility and guilt. *Behaviour Research & Therapy, 31,* 793–802.

Rachman, S. & Hodgson, R. (1980) *Obsessions and Compulsions.* New York: Prentice Hall.

Rack, P. (1982) *Race, culture and mental disorder.* London: Tavistock.

Rahe, R.H., Mahan, J. & Arthur, R. (1970) Prediction of near-future health-change from subjects' preceding life changes. *Journal of Psychosomatic Research, 14,* 401–406.

Ralph, M.R., Foster, R.G., Davis, F.C. & Menaker, M. (1990) Transplanted suprachiasmatic nucleus determines circadian period. *Science,* Feb. 23, 247 (4945), 975–978.

Rathus, S.A. (1990) *Psychology* (4th edition). New York: Holt, Rinehart, Winston.

Rauch, S.L., Jenike, M.A., Alpert, N.M., Bare, L., Breiter, H.C.R. *et al.* (1994) Regional cerebral blood flow measured during symptom provocation in obsessive-compulsive disorder using oxygen-15 labelled carbon dioxide and positron emission tomography. *Archives of General Psychiatry, 51,* 62–70.

Rechtschaffen, A. (1999) cited in W.C. Dement *The Promise of Sleep.* London: Macmillan.

Rechtschaffen, A., Bergmann, B.M., Everson, C.A., Kushida, C.A. & Gilliland, M.A. (1989) Sleep deprivation in the rat: I. Conceptual issues. *Sleep, 12*(1), 1–4.

Regan, P., Levin, L., Sprecher, S., Christopher, S. & Cate, R. (2000) Partner Preferences: What characteristics do men and women desire in their short-term sexual and long-term romantic partners? *Journal of Psychology & Human Sexuality, 12*(3), 1.

Reicher, S.D. (1987) Crowd behaviour as social action. In J.C. Turner, M.A. Hogg, P.J. Oakes, S.D. Reicher & M.S. Wetherell (Eds) *Rediscovering the Social Group: A Self-Categorization Theory*. Oxford: Basil Blackwell.

Reifman, A.S., Larrick, R.P. & Fein, S. (1991) Temper and temperature on the diamond: the heat–aggression relationship in major league baseball. *Journal of Personality & Social Psychology*, 38, 580–585.

Reitman, J.S. (1971) Mechanisms of short-term memory. *Cognitive Psychology*, 2, 185–195.

Resnick, L., Levine, J. & Teasley, S. (Eds) (1991) *Perspectives on Socially Shared Cognition*. Washington, D.C.: American Psychological Association.

Rest, J. (1983) Morality. In J.H. Flavell & E.M. Markman (Eds) *Handbook of Child Psychology, Volume 3*. New York: Wiley.

Richards, G. (1996) Arsenic and old race. *Observer Review*, 5 May, 4.

Richards G. (2002) *Putting Psychology in its Place: A Critical Historical Overview* (2nd edition). Hove: Routledge.

Richards, M.P.M. (1995) The International Year of the Family – family research. *The Psychologist*, 8, 17–20.

Richardson, K. (1991) *Understanding Intelligence*. Milton Keynes: Open University Press.

Riesen, A.H. (1947) The development of visual perception in man and chimpanzee. *Science*, 106, 107–108.

Riley, V. (1981) Psychoneuroendocrine influence on immuno-competence and neoplasia. *Science, 212*, 1100–1109.

Ringen, J. (1996) The behaviour therapist's dilemma: Reflections on autonomy, informed consent, and scientific psychology. In W. O'Donohue & R.F. Kitchener (Eds) *The Philosophy of Psychology*. London: Sage Publications.

Robertson, J. & Robertson, J. (1967–73) Film Series, *Young Children in Brief Separation:* No. 3 (1969). John, 17 months, 9 days in a residential nursery. London: Tavistock.

Robertson, J. & Robertson, J. (1989) *Separation and the Very Young*. London: Free Association Books.

Robinson, L. (1997) Black adolescent identity and the inadequacies of Western psychology. In J. Roche & S. Tucker (Eds) *Youth in Society*. London: Sage.

Rockman, H. (1994) Matchmaker, matchmaker, make me a match: The art and conventions of Jewish arranged marriages. *Sexual & Marital Therapy*, 9, 277–284.

Rogoff, B. & Morelli, G. (1989) Perspectives on children's development from cultural psychology. *American Psychologist*, 44, 343–348.

Rogoff, B. (1990) *Apprenticeship in Thinking: Cognitive Development in Social Context*. New York: Oxford University Press.

Rolls, G. (2005) Classic case studies in Psychology. Hodder & Stoughton, UK.

Rolls, G.W. & Ingham, R. (1992) *Safe and Unsafe: a Comparative Study of Younger Drivers*. Basingstoke: AA Foundation for Road Safety Research.

Romans, S.E., Gendall, K.A., Martin, J.L. and Mullen, P.E. (2001) Child sexual abuse and later disordered eating: A New Zealand epidemiological study. *International Journal of Eating Disorders*, 29 (4), 380–392.

Rose, D.T., Abramson, L.Y., Hodulik, C.J., Halberstadt, L. & Gaye, L. (1994) Heterogeneity of cognitive style among depressed inpatients. *Journal of Abnormal Psychology*, 103, 419–429.

Rose, S. (1992) *The Making of Memory: From Molecule to Mind*. London: Bantam Books.

Rose, S. (1997) *Lifelines: Biology, Freedom, Determinism*. Harmondsworth: Penguin.

Rose, S., Lewontin, R.C. & Kamin, L.J. (1984) *Not in our Genes: Biology, Ideology and Human Nature*. Harmondsworth: Penguin.

Rose, S.A. & Blank, M. (1974) The potency of context in children's cognition: An illustration through conservation. *Child Development*, 45, 499–502.

Rosenberg, D.R., Keshavan, M.S., O'Hearn, K.M., Seymour, A.B., Birmaher, B. *et al.* (1997) Frontostriatal measurement in treatment-naïve children with obsessive-compulsive disorder. *Archives of General Psychiatry*, 54, 824–830.

Rosenberg, M.J. (1969) The conditions and consequences of evaluation apprehension. In R. Rosenthal & R.L. Rosnow (Eds) *Artifact in Behavioral Research*. New York: Academic Press.

Rosenhan, D.L. (1973) On Being Sane in Insane Places. *Science* 179, 250–258.

Rosenhan, D.L. & Seligman, M.E. (1989) *Abnormal Psychology*. New York: Norton.

Rosenthal, D., Wender, P.H., Kety, S.S., Welner, J. & Schulsinger, F. (1971) The adopted away offspring of schizophrenics. *American Journal of Psychiatry*, 128, 307–311.

Rosenthal, R. (1966) *Experimenter Effects in Behavioural Research*. New York: Appleton-Century-Crofts.

Rosenthal, R. & Fode, K.L. (1963) The effects of experimenter bias on the performance of the albino rat. *Behavioural Science*, 8, 183–189.

Rosenthal, R. & Jacobson, L. (1968) *Pygmalion in the Classroom: Teacher Expectation and Pupils' Intellectual Development*. New York: Holt.

Rosenthal, R. & Lawson, R. (1964) A longitudinal study of the effects of experimenter bias on the operant learning of laboratory rats. *Journal of Psychiatric Research*, 2, 61–72.

Rotton, J. (1993) Ubiquitous errors: Reanalysis of Anderson's (1987) Temperature and aggression. *Psychological Reports*, 73, 259–271.

Rowan, A.N. (1997) The benefits and ethics of animal research. *Scientific American*, 64–66, February.

Rubin, J.Z., Provenzano, F.J. & Luria, Z. (1974) The eye of the beholder: Parents' views on sex of newborns. *American Journal of Orthopsychiatry*, 44, 512–519.

Rubin, Z. (1973) *Liking and Loving*. New York: Holt, Rinehart & Winston.

Ruble, D.N. (1984) Sex-role development. In M.C. Bornstein & M.E. Lamb (Eds) *Developmental Psychology: An Advanced Text*. Hillsdale, NJ: Erlbaum.

Russell, M.J., Switz, G.M. & Thompson., K. (1980) Olfactory influences on the human menstrual cycle. *Pharmacology, Biochemistry. & Behavior*, 13, 737–738.

Rutter, M. (1981) *Maternal Deprivation Reassessed* (2nd edition). Harmondsworth: Penguin.

Rutter, M. (and the English and Romanian Adoptees (ERA) study team) (1998) Developmental catch-up, and deficit following adoption after severe global early privation. *Journal of Child Psychology & Psychiatry*, 39(4), 465–476.

Rutter, M., Graham, P., Chadwick, D.F.D. & Yule, W. (1976) Adolescent turmoil: Fact or fiction? *Journal of Child Psychology & Psychiatry*, 17, 35–56.

Rutter, M. & Rutter, M. (1992) *Developing Minds: Challenge and Continuity across the Life Span*. Harmondsworth: Penguin.

Ryan, J. (1972) IQ – the illusion of objectivity. In K. Richardson & D. Spears (Eds) *Race, Culture and Intelligence*. Harmondsworth: Penguin.

Rycroft, C. (1966) Introduction: Causes and Meaning. In C. Rycroft (Ed.) *Psychoanalysis Observed*. London: Constable & Co. Ltd.

Ryder, R. (1990) Open reply to Jeffrey Gray. *The Psychologist*, 3, 403.

Sachs, C.J. & Chu, L.D. (2000) The association between professional football games and domestic violence in Los Angeles county. *Journal of Interpersonal Violence*, 15, 1192–1201.

Sackheim, H.A., Prudic, J. & Devanand, D.P. (1990) Treatment of Medication resistant depression with electro-convulsive therapy. In A. Tasman, S.M. Goldfinger & C.A. Kaufman (Eds) *Review of Psychiatry*, Vol.9. Washington, D.C.: American Psychiatric Press, Inc.

Sackheim, H.A., Prudic, J., Devanand, D.P., Kiersy, J.E., Fitzsimons, L., Moody, B.J., McElhiney, M.C., Coleman, E.A. & Settembrino, J.M. (1993) Effects of stimulus intensity and electrode placement on the efficacy and cognitive effects of electroconvulsive therapy. *New England Journal of Medicine*, 328(12), 882–883.

Sadalla, E.K., Kenrick, D.T. & Vershure, B. (1987) Dominance and heterosexual attraction. (1987). *Journal of Personality & Social Psychology*, 52, 730–738.

Saegert, S.C., Swap, W. & Zajonc, R.B. (1973) Exposure context and interpersonal attraction. *Journal of Personality & Social Psychology*, 25, 234–242.

Salkovskis, P.M. (1985) Obsessional-compulsive problems: A cognitive-behavioural analysis. *Behaviour Research & Therapy*, 23, 571–583.

Salkovskis, P.M., Forrester, E. & Richards, C. (1998) Cognitive-behavioural approach to understanding obsessional thinking. *British Journal of Psychiatry* (Supplement, 35), 53–63.

Salomon, G. (Ed.) (1993) *Distributed Cognitions: Psychological and Educational Considerations*. Cambridge: Cambridge University Press.

Samuel, J. & Bryant. P. (1984) Asking only one question in the conservation experiment. *Journal of Child Psychology & Psychiatry*, 25, 315–318.

Sanday, P. (2002) *Women at the Center: Life in a Modern Matriarchy*. New York: Cornell University Press.

SANE (2003): www.sane.org.uk

Sasa, I.K. (1999) Mechanism underlying the therapeutic effects of ECT on depression. *Japanese Journal of Pharmacology*, 80(3), 185–189.

Savin, H.B. (1973) Professors and psychological researchers: conflicting values in conflicting roles. *Cognition*, 2(1), 147–149.

Sawyer, L. (1996) ... Or an abomination. *Nursing Times*, 92(5), 28.

Saxena, S., Brody, A.L., Schwartz, J.M. & Baxter, L.R. (1998) Neuroimaging and frontal-subcortical circuitry in obsessive-compulsive disorder. *British Journal of Psychiatry, 173* (Suppl. 35), 26–37.

Scarr, S. (1992) Developmental theories for the 1990s: Development and individual differences. Child Development, 63, 1–19.

Scarr, S. (1998) American child care today. *American Psychologist, 53*(2), 95–108.

Scarr, S. & Carter-Saltzman, L. (1979) Twin method: Defence of a critical assumption. *Behaviour Genetics, 9,* 527–542.

Scarr, S. & Thompson, W. (1994) Effects of maternal employment and nonmaternal infant care on development at two and four years. *Early Development & Parenting, 3*(2), 113–123.

Scarr, S. & Weinberg, R.A. (1976) IQ test performance of black children adopted by white families. *American Psychologist, 31,* 726–739.

Scarr, S. & Weinberg, R.A. (1978) The influence of 'family background' on intellectual attainment. *American Sociological Review, 43,* 674–692.

Schaffer, H.R. & Emerson, P.E. (1964) The development of social attachments in infancy. *Monographs of the Society for Research in Child Development, 29* (Whole No. 3).

Schaffer, H.R. (1971) *The Growth of Sociability.* Harmondsworth: Penguin.

Schaffer, H.R. (1996) *Social Development.* Oxford: Blackwell.

Schaffer, R. (1998) Deprivation and its effects on children. *Psychology Review, 5*(2), 2–5.

Schatzberg, A.F. & Nemeroff, C.B. (1999) *Textbook of Psychopharmacology.* Washington, D.C.: American Psychiatric Press Inc.

Scheer, S.D. & Unger, D.G. (1995) Parents' perceptions of their adolescence – implications for parent–youth conflict and family satisfaction. *Psychological Reports, 76* (1), 131–136.

Scheff, T.J. (1966) *Being Mentally Ill: A Sociological Theory.* Chicago: Aldine Press.

Schiff, N., Duyme, M., Dumaret, A., Stewart, J., Tomkiewicz, S. & Feingold, J. (1978) Intellectual status of working-class children adopted early into upper-middle-class families. *Science, 200,* 1503–1504.

Schliefer, S.J., Keller, S.E., Camerino, M., Thornton, J.C. & Stein, M. (1983) Suppression of lymphocyte stimulation following bereavement. *Journal of the American Medical Association, 250,* 374–377.

Schneider, D.J. (1959) *Clinical Psychopathology.* New York: Grune & Stratton.

Schroeder, D.A., Dovidio, J.F., Sibicky, M.E., Matthews, L.L. & Allen, J.L. (1988) Empathic concern and helping behavior: Egoism or altruism? *Journal of Experimental Social Psychology, 24,* 333–353.

Schroeder, D.A., Penner, L., Dovidio, J.F. & Piliavin, J.A. (1995) *The psychology of helping and altruism: Problems and puzzles.* New York: McGraw-Hill.

Sear, D.O. (1986) College sophomores in the laboratory: influences of a narrow database on psychology's view of human nature. *Journal of Personality and Social Psychology, 51,* 515–530.

Sears, R.R., Maccoby, E.E. & Levin, H. (1957) *Patterns of Child Rearing.* New York: Harper & Row.

Sebrechts, M.M., Marsh, R.L. & Seaman, J.G. (1989) Secondary memory and very rapid forgetting. *Memory and Cognition, 17,* 693–700.

Segall, M.H., Dasen, P.R., Berry, J.W. & Poortinga, Y.H. (1990) *Human Behaviour in Global Perspective: An Introduction to Cross-Cultural Psychology.* New York: Pergamon.

Segall, M.H., Dasen, P.R., Berry, J.W. & Poortinga, Y.H. (1999) *Human Behaviour in Global Perspective: An Introduction to Cross-Cultural Psychology* (2nd edition). Needham Heights, MA: Allyn & Bacon.

Seligman, M.E.P. (1971) Phobias and preparedness. *Behavior Therapy, 2,* 307–320.

Seligman, M.E.P. (1974) Depression and learned helplessness. In R.J. Friedman & M.M. Katz (Eds) *The Psychology of Depression: Contemporary Theory and Research.* Washington, D.C.: Winston-Wiley.

Seligman, M.E.P. (1975) *Helplessness: On Depression, Development and Death.* San Francisco: W.H. Freeman.

Seligman, M.E.P., Abramson, L.Y., Semmel, A. & Von Beyer, C. (1979) Depressive attributional style. *Journal of Abnormal Psychology, 88,* 242–247.

Selye, H. (1956) *The Stress of Life.* New York: McGraw-Hill.

Serpell, R.S. (1979) How specific are perceptual skills? A cross-cultural study of pattern reproduction. *British Journal of Psychology, 70,* 365–380.

Serpell, R.S. (1994) The cultural construction of intelligence. In W.J. Lonnen & R.S. Malpass (Eds) *Psychology and Culture.* Boston, MA: Allyn and Bacon.

Seymour, J. (1996) Beastly dilemmas. *Nursing Times, 92*(5), 24–26.

Shafran, R. (1999) Obsessive–compulsive disorder. *The Psychologist, 12*(12), 588–591.

Shafran, R. & Salkovskis, P.M. (1999) The safe hands of Dr Freud? Letter, *The Psychologist, 12*(10), 487.

Shallice, T. (1967) Paper presented at NATO symposium on short-term memory. Cambridge, England. Cited in A.D. Baddeley (1976) *The Psychology of Memory*. New York. Harper & Row.

Shallice, T. & Warrington, E.K. (1970) Independent functioning of verbal memory stores: A neurophysiological study. *Quarterly Journal of Experimental Psychology, 22,* 261–269.

Shapiro, C.M., Bortz, R. & Mitchell, D. (1981) Slow-wave sleep: A recovery period after exercise. *Science, 214,* 1253–1254.

Shaver, P.R., Collins, N. & Clark, C.L. (1996) Attachment styles and internal working models of self and relationship patterns. In G.J.O. Fletcher & J. Fitness (Eds) *Knowledge structures in close relationships: A social psychological approach*. Mahwah, NJ: Lawrence Erlbaum Associates.

Shepard, R.N. (1967) Recognition memory for words, sentences and pictures. *Journal of Verbal Learning and Verbal Behaviour, 6,* 156–63.

Sheppard, D.M., Bradshaw, J.L., Purcell, R. & Pantelis, C. (1999) Tourette's and comorbid syndromes: Obsessive-compulsive and attention deficit hyperactivity disorder. A common aetiology? *Clinical Psychology Review, 19,* 531–552.

Sheridan, C.L. & King, R.G. (1972) Obedience to authority with an authentic victim. *Proceedings of the 80th Annual Convention, American Psychological Association, 7* (1) 165–166.

Sherif, M. (1935) A study of social factors in perception. *Archives of Psychology, 27,* Whole No. 187.

Sherif, M., Harvey, O.J., White, B.J., Hood, W.R. & Sherif, C.W. (1961) *Intergroup Conflict and Co-operation: The Robber's Cave Experiment*. Norman, OK: University of Oklahoma Press.

Sherry, J.L. (2001) The effects of violent video games on aggression: A meta-analysis. *Human Communication Research, 27*(3), 409–431.

Shields, J. (1962) *Monozygotic Twins Brought Up Apart and Brought Up Together*. London: Oxford University Press.

Shields, J. (1976) Heredity and environment. In H.J. Eysenck & G.D. Wilson (Eds) *Textbook of Human Psychology*. Lancaster: MTP.

Shields, J. (1978) Genetics. In J.K. Wing (Ed.) *Schizophrenia – Towards a New Synthesis*. London: Academic Press.

Shuey, A. (1966) *The Testing of Negro Intelligence*. New York: Social Science Press.

Shweder, R.A. (1990) Cultural psychology: What is it? In J.W. Stigler, R.A. Shweder & G. Herdt (Eds) *Cultural Psychology*. Cambridge: Cambridge University Press.

Shweder, R.A. (1991) *Thinking Through Cultures: Expeditions in Cultural Psychology*. Cambridge, MA: Harvard University Press.

Shweder, R.A., Mahapatra, M. & Miller, J.G. (1987) Culture and moral development. In J. Kagan & S. Lamb (Eds) *The Emergence of Morality in Young Children*. Chicago: University of Chicago Press.

Sieber, J.E. & Stanley, B. (1988) Ethical and Professional Dimensions of Socially Sensitive Research. *American Psychologist, 43* (1), 49–55.

Siegel, L. (1992) *Criminology*. St Paul, Minn.: West Publishing Co.

Siffre, M. (1975) Six months alone in a cave. *National Geographic*, March, 426–435.

Sigall, H. & Landy, D. (1973) Radiating beauty: Effects of having a physically attractive partner on person perception, *Journal of Personality & Social Psychology, 28,* 218–224.

Silverman, L.T. & Sprafkin, J.N. (1980) The effects of Sesame Street's prosocial spots on cooperative play between young children. *Journal of Broadcasting, 24,* 135–147.

Simmons, R.G. & Blyth, D.A. (1987) *Moving into Adolescence: The Impact of Pubertal Changes and School Context*. New York: Aldine de Gruyter.

Simon, H.A. (1974) How big is a chunk? *Science, 183,* 482–488.

Simpson, J.A., Campbell, B. & Berscheid, E. (1986) The association between romantic love and marriage: Kephart (1967) twice revisited. *Personality & Social Psychology Bulletin, 12,* 363–372.

Singer, P. & Cavalieri, P. (Eds) (1993) *The Great Ape Project: Equality beyond Humanity*. London: Fourth Estate.

Singer, P. (1993) The rights of ape. *BBC Wildlife Magazine, 11*(6), 28–32.

Singh, D. (1993) Adaptive significance of female physical attractiveness: Role of waist-to-hip ratio. *Journal of Personality & Social Psychology, 65,* 293–307.

Sinha, D. (1997) Indigenising psychology. In J.W. Berry, Y.H. Poortinga & J. Pandey (Eds) *Handbook of Cross-Cultural Psychology* (2nd edition), *Volume 1*. Boston: Allyn & Bacon.

Sirois-Berliss, M. & De Koninck, J. (1982) Menstrual Stress and Dreams: Adaptation or Interference? *The Psychiatric Journal of the University of Ottawa, 7,* 77–86.

Skeels, H.M. (1966) Adult status of children with contrasting early life experiences. *Monographs of the Society for Research in Child Development, 31* (Whole No. 30.)

Skeels. H.M. & Dye, H.B. (1939) A study of the effects of differential stimulation on mentally retarded children. *Proceedings of the American Association of Mental Deficiency, 44*, 114–136.

Skinner, B.F. (1948) Superstition in the pigeon. *Journal of Experimental Psychology, 38*, 168–172.

Skinner, B.F. (1971) *Beyond Freedom and Dignity*. New York: Knopf.

Slaby, R.G. & Frey, K.S. (1975) Development of gender constancy and selective attention to same-sex models. *Child Development, 46*, 839–856.

Slamecka, N.J. (1966) Differentiation versus unlearning of verbal associations. *Journal of Experimental Psychology, 71*, 822–828.

Slater, E. & Roth, M. (1969) *Clinical Psychiatry* (3rd edition). London: Bailliere Tindall & Cassell.

Smith, C. & Lloyd, B.B. (1978) Maternal behaviour and perceived sex of infant. *Child Development, 49*, 1263–1265.

Smith, C.U.M. (1994) You are a group of neurons. *The Times Higher Educational Supplement*, 27 May, 20–21.

Smith, J.A., Harré, R. & Van Langenhove, L. (1995) Introduction. In J.A. Smith, R. Harré & L. Van Langenhove (Eds) *Rethinking Psychology*. London: Sage.

Smith, J.R., Brooks-Gunn, J. & Klebanov, P.K. (1997) Consequences of living in poverty for young children's cognitive and verbal ability and early school achievement. In G.J. Duncan & J. Brooks-Gunn (Eds) *Consequences of Growing Up Poor*. New York: Russell Sage Foundation.

Smith, P.B. & Bond, M.H. (1998) *Social Psychology across Cultures* (2nd edition). Hemel Hempstead: Prentice Hall Europe.

Smith, P.K. & Daglish, L. (1977) Sex differences in parent and infant behaviour in the home. *Child Development, 48*, 1250–1254.

Smith, P.K., Cowie, H. & Blader, M. (1998) *Understanding Children's Development* (3rd edition). Oxford: Blackwell.

Snarey, J.R. (1987) A question of morality. *Psychology Today*, June, 6–8.

Sobanski, E. & Schmidt, M.H. (2000) Body dysmorphic disorder: A review of the current knowledge. *Child Psychology & Psychiatry Review, 5*(1), 17–24.

Solms, M. (2000) Freudian Dream Theory Today. *The Psychologist, 13*(12).

Solso, R.L. (1995) *Cognitive Psychology* (4th Ed.) Boston: Allyn & Bacon.

Sparrow, S.S. & Davis, S.M. (2000) Recent advances in the assessment of intelligence and cognition. *Journal of Child Psychology & Psychiatry, 41*(1), 117–131.

Spearman, C. (1904) General intelligence, objectively determined and measured. *American Journal of Psychology, 15*, 201–293.

Spearman, C. (1967) The doctrine of two factors. In S. Wiseman (Ed.) *Intelligence and Ability*. Harmondsworth: Penguin. (Original work published 1927).

Spelke, E.S. (1991) Physical knowledge in infancy: Reflections on Piaget's theory. In S. Carey & R. Gelman (Eds) *The Epigenesis of Mind: Essays on Biology and Cognition*. Hillsdale, NJ: Erlbaum.

Spiegel, D.A. & Bruce, T.J. (1997) Benzodiazepines and exposure-based cognitive behavior therapies for panic disorder: Conclusions from combined treatment trials. *American Journal of Psychiatry, 154*, 773–781.

Spitz, R.A. & Wolf, K.M. (1946) Anaclitic depression. *Psychoanalytic Study of the Child, 2*, 313–342.

Spitz, R.A. (1945) Hospitalism: An enquiry into the genesis of psychiatric conditions in early childhood. *Psychoanalytic Study of the Child, 1*, 53–74.

Spitz, R.A. (1946) Hospitalism: A follow-up report on investigation described in Vol. 1, 1945. *Psychoanalytic Study of the Child, 2*, 113–117..

Spitzer, R.L., Endicott, J. & Robins, E. (1978) Research diagnostic criteria: Rationale and reliability. *Archives of General Psychiatry, 35*, 773–782.

Stack, S. (1987) Celebrities and suicide: A taxonomy and analysis, 1948–1983. *American Sociological Review, 52*, 401–402.

Staddon, J.R. (1983) *Adaptive behavior and learning*. New York: Cambridge University Press.

Starbuck, M. (1998) A practical guide to evaluation. *Psychology Review, 4*, 3, 8–10.

Stattin, H. & Klackenberg, G. (1992) Family discord in adolescence in the light of family discord in childhood. Paper presented at Conference Youth – TM, Utrecht.

Stattin, H. & Magnusson, D. (1990) *Pubertal Maturation in Female Development*. Hillsdale, NJ: Erlbaum.

Stephan, F.K. & Zucker, I. (1972) Circadian rhythms in drinking behaviour and locomotor activity of rats are eliminated by hypothalamic lesion. *Proceedings of the National Academy of Sciences, 69*, 1583–1586.

Stephan, H. (1972) Evolution of primate brains: a comparative anatomical investigation. In R. Tuttle (Ed.) *The Functional and Evolutionary Biology of Primates*. Chicago: Aldine Atherton.

Stern, K. & McClintock, M.K. (1998) Regulation of ovulation by human pheromones. *Nature, 392*, 177–178.

Stern, W.C. & Morgane, P.I. (1974) Theoretical view of REM sleep function: Maintenance of catecholamine systems in the central nervous system. *Behav. Biol., 11*, 1–32.

Sternberg, R.J. (1988) Triangulating love. In R.J. Sternberg & M.L. Barnes (Eds) *The Psychology of Love*. New Haven, CT: Yale University Press.

Sternberg, R.J. (1995) Intelligence and cognitive styles. In S.E. Hampson & A.M. Colman (Eds) *Individual Differences and Personality*. London: Longman.

Sternberg, R.J. (1998) How intelligent is intelligence testing? *Scientific American Presents: Exploring Intelligence, 9*(4), 12–17.

Sternberg, R.J. & Grigorenko, E. (Eds) (1997) *Intelligence, Heredity and Environment*. New York: Cambridge University Press.

Strachey, J. (1962–1977) Sigmund Freud: A sketch of his life and ideas. (This appears in each volume of the Pelican Freud Library, originally written for the *Standard Edition of the Complete Psychological Works of Sigmund Freud*, 1953–1974). London: Hogarth Press.

Strassberg, D.S. & Holty, S. (2003) An Experimental Study of Women's Internet Personal Ads. *Archives of Sexual Behavior, 32*(3), 253–260.

Strickland, B.R. (1992) Women and Depression. *Current Directions in Psychological Science, 1*, 132–135.

Sue, D., Sue, D. & Sue, S. (1994) *Understanding Abnormal Behavior* (4th edition). Boston: Houghton Mifflin.

Sue, S. (1995) Implications of the Bell curve: Whites are genetically inferior in intelligence? *Focus: Notes from the Society for the Psychological Study of Ethnic Minority Issues*, 16–17.

Sulloway, F.J. (1979) *Freud, Biologist of the Mind: Beyond the Psychoanalytic Legend*. New York: Basic Books.

Sussman, S. & Ames, S.L. (2001) *The Social Psychology of Drug Abuse*. Buckingham: Open University Press.

Sutherland, S.N. (1976) *Breakdown*. London: Weidenfeld & Nicolson.

Sutherland, S.N. (1992) *Cognitive Development Today: Piaget and his Critics*. London: Paul Chapman Publishing.

Szasz, T.S. (1962) The myth of mental illness. *American Psychologist, 15*, 113–118.

Tallis, F. (2002) Science supports Dr Freud. *Sunday Times*, 10 February.

Tavris, C. (1993) The mismeasure of woman. *Feminism & Psychology, 3*(2), 149–168.

Tavris, C. & Wade, C. (1997) *Psychology in Perspective* (2nd edition). New York: Longman.

Taylor, R. (1963) *Metaphysics*. Englewood Cliffs, NJ: Prentice-Hall.

Taylor, R. (2000) The Singer revolution. *Philosophy Now, 28*, August/September, 10–13.

Teichman, J. (1988) *Philosophy and the Mind*. Oxford: Blackwell.

Teixeira, J.M.A. (1999) Association between maternal anxiety in pregnancy and increased uterine artery resistance index: Cohort based study. *British Medical Journal, 318* (7177), 153–157.

Temoshok, L. (1987) Personality, coping style, emotions and cancer: Towards an integrative model. *Cancer Surveys, 6* , 545–567 (Supplement).

Terman, L. (1921) In symposium: Intelligence and its measurement. *Journal of Educational Psychology, 12*, 127–133.

Terman, M, Terman, J.S. & Ross, D.C. (1998) A controlled trial of timed bright light and negative air ionization for treatment of winter depression. *Archives of General Psychiatry, 55*, 875–882.

Thibaut, J.W. & Kelley, H.H. (1959) *The Social Psychology of Groups*. New York: Wiley.

Thomas, A. & Chess, S. (1977) *Temperament and Development*. New York: Brunner/Mazel.

Thomas, R.M. (1985) *Comparing Theories of Child Development* (2nd edition). Belmont, CA: Wadsworth Publishing Company.

Thompson, C. (1943) 'Penis envy' in women. *Psychiatry, 6*, 123–125.

Thurstone, L.L. (1938) Primary mental abilities. *Psychometric Monographs, No.1*.

Tienari, P. (1991) Interaction between genetic vulnerability and family environment: The Finnish adoptive family study of schizophrenia. *Acta Psychiatrica Scandinavica, 84*, 460–465.

Tizard, B. & Phoenix, A. (1993) *Black, White or Mixed Race?* London: Routledge.

Tobin-Richards, M.H., Boxer, A.M. & Petersen, A.C. (1983) The psychological significance of pubertal change: Sex differences in perceptions of self during early adolescence. In J. Brooks-Gunn & A.C. Petersen (Eds) *Girls at Puberty: Biological and Psychological Perspectives*. New York: Plenum.

Tomarken, A.J., Mineka, S. & Cook, M. (1989) Fear-relevant selective associations and covariation bias. *Journal of Abnormal Psychology, 98*, 381–394.

Triandis, H. (1990) Theoretical concepts that are applicable to the analysis of ethnocentrism. In R.W. Brislin (Ed.) *Applied Cross-Cultural Psychology*. Newbury Park, CA; Sage.

Triandis, H. (1994) *Culture and Social Behaviour*. New York: McGraw-Hill.

Triandis, H.C., Kashima, Y., Shimada, E. & Villareal, M. (1986) Acculturation indices as a means of conforming cultural differences. *International Journal of Psychology, 21*, 43–70.

Trivers, R.L. (1972) Parental Investment and Sexual Selection. In B. Campbell (Ed.) *Sexual Selection and the Descent of Man*. Chicago: Aldine-Atherton.

Turnbull, C.M. (1972) *The Mountain People*. New York: Simon & Schuster.

Tyler, S.W., Hertel, P.T., McCallum, M.C. and Ellis. H. (1979) Cognitive effect and memory. *Journal of Experimental Psychology*: Human Learning and Memory, 5 (6), 607–617.

Tyrka, A.R., Waldron, I., Graber, J. and Brooks-Gunn, J. (2002) Prospective predictors of the onset of anorexic and bulimic syndromes. *International Journal of Eating Disorders, 32*, 282–90.

Ucros, C.G. (1989) Mood state-dependent memory: A meta-analysis. *Cognition and Emotion, 3*, 139–167.

UKAN (1995): United Kingdom Advocacy Network ECT Survey.

Unger, R. (1979) *Female and Male*. London: Harper & Row.

Unger, R. & Crawford, M. (1992) *Women and Gender: A Feminist Psychology*. New York: McGraw-Hill.

Unger, R. & Crawford, M. (1996) *Women and Gender: A Feminist Psychology* (2nd edition). New York: McGraw-Hill.

Ursano, R. & Silberman, E.K. (1994) Psychoanalysis, psychoanalytic psychotherapy, and supportive psychotherapy. In E. Hales, S.C. Yudofsky & J. Talbott (Eds) *The American Psychiatric Press Textbook of Psychiatry* (2nd edition). Washington, D.C.: American Psychiatric Press.

Valentine, E.R. (1992) *Conceptual Issues in Psychology* (2nd edition). London: Routledge.

Van Ijzendoorn, M.H. & Kroonenberg, P.M. (1988) Cross-cultural patterns of attachment: a meta-analysis of the strange situation. *Child Development, 59,* 147–156.

Van Langenhove, L. (1995) The theoretical foundations of Experimental Psychology and its alternatives. In J.A. Smith, R. Harré & L. Van Langenhove (Eds) *Rethinking Psychology*. London: Sage.

Velakoulis, D. & Pantelis, C. (1996) What have we learned from functional imaging studies in schizophrenia? The role of prefrontal, striatal and temporal areas. *Australian & New Zealand Journal of Psychiatry, 30*, 195–209.

Vernon, P.E. (1950) The hierarchy of ability. In S. Wiseman (Ed.) *Intelligence and Ability*. Harmondsworth: Penguin.

Vernon, P.E. (1969) *Intelligence and Cultural Environment*. London: Methuen.

Vygotsky, L.S. (1962) *Thought and Language*. Cambridge, MA: MIT Press (originally published 1934).

Vygotsky, L.S. (1978) *Mind in Society*. Cambridge, MA: Harvard University Press.

Vygotsky, L.S. (1981) The genesis of higher mental functions. In J.V. Wertsch (Ed.) *The Concept of Activity in Soviet Psychology*. Armonk, NY: Sharpe.

Wade, C. & Tavris, C. (1994) The longest war: Gender and culture. In W.J. Lonner & R.S. Malpass (Eds) *Psychology and Culture*. Boston, MA: Allyn & Bacon.

Wade, T., Martin, N.G. & Tiggemann, M. (1998). Genetic and environmental risk factors for weight and shape concerns characteristic of bulimia nervosa. *Psychological Medicine, 28*, 761–72.

Walker, L.J. (1984) Sex differences in the development of moral reasoning: A critical review. *Child Development, 55*, 677–691.

Walker, L.J. (1989) A longitudinal study of moral reasoning. *Child Development, 60*, 157–166.

Walker, L.J. (1995) Sexism in Kohlberg's moral psychology? In W.M. Kurtines & J. Gewirtz (Eds) *Moral Development: An Introduction*. Needham Heights, MA: Allyn & Bacon.

Walker, L.J. (1996) Is one sex morally superior? In M.R. Merrens & G.C. Brannigan (Eds) *The Developmental Psychologists: Research Adventures across the Life Span*. New York: McGraw-Hill.

Walster, E., Aronson, E., Abrahams, D. & Rottman, L. (1966) The importance of physical attractiveness in dating behaviour. *Journal of Personality & Social Psychology, 4*, 508–516.

Walster, E., Walster, G.W. & Berscheid, E. (1978) *Equity Theory and Research*. Boston, MA: Allyn & Bacon.

Watson, J.B. (1913) Psychology as the behaviourist views it. *Psychological Review, 20*, 158–177.

Watson, J.B. (1925) *Behaviourism*. New York: Norton.

Watson, J.B. (1928) *Psychological Care of the Infant and Child*. New York: Norton.

Watson, J.B. (1930) *Behaviorism*. New York: W.W. Norton.

Watson, J.B. & Rayner, R. (1920) Conditioned emotional responses. *Journal of Experimental Psychology, 3*, 1–14.

Waugh, N.C. & Norman, D.A. (1965) Primary memory. *Psychological Review*, 72, 89–104.

Wayforth, D. & Dunbar, R.I.M. (1995) Conditional mate choice strategies in humans – evidence from lonely hearts advertisements. *Behaviour*, 132, 755–779.

Webb, W.B. & Cartwright, R.D. (1978) Sleep and dreams. *Annual Review of Psychology*, 29, 223–252.

Wechsler, D. (1944) *The Measurement of Adult Intelligence* (3rd edition). Baltimore: Williams & Wilkins.

Wechsler, D. (1958) *The Measurement and Appraisal of Adult Intelligence* (4th edition). Baltimore: Williams & Wilkins.

Wechsler, D. (1974) *Wechsler Intelligence Scale for Children*. New York: Psychological Corporation.

Wechsler, D. (1989) *Wechsler Preschool and Primary Scale of Intelligence* (revised edition). San Antonio, TX: The Psychological Corporation.

Wechsler, D. (1991) *Wechsler Intelligence Scale for Children* (3rd edition). San Antonio, TX: The Psychological Corporation.

Weinberg, R. (1989) Intelligence and IQ: Landmark issues and great debates. *American Psychologist*, 44, 98–104.

Weiner, R.D. (1984) Does electroconvulsive therapy cause brain damage? *The Behavioral & Brain Sciences*, 7, 1–22.

Weiner, R.D. & Coffey, C.E. (1988) Indications for use of electroconvulsive therapy. In A.J. Frances & R.E. Hales (Eds) *Review of Psychiatry*, Vol.7. Washington, D.C.: American Psychiatric Press Inc.

Weisberg, R. (1992) *Creativity, Beyond the Myth of Genius*. New York: W.H. Freeman.

Weiss, J.M. (1972) Psychological factors in stress and disease. *Scientific American*, 226, 104–113.

Weisstein, N. (1993) Psychology constructs the female; Or, the fantasy life of the male psychologist (with some attention to the fantasies of his friend, the male biologist and the male anthropologist). *Feminism & Psychology*, 3(2), 195–210.

Wender, P.H., Rosenthal, D., Kety, S.S., Schulsinger, F. & Welner, J. (1974) Crossfostering: A research strategy for clarifying the role of genetic and experiential factors in the aetiology of schizophrenia. *Archives of General Psychiatry*, 30, 112–128.

Werner, E.E. (1989) Children of the Garden Island. *Scientific American*, April, 106–111.

Weston, K. (1991) *Families We Choose*. New York: Columbia University Press.

Whiting, B.B. & Whiting, J.W. (1975) Children of 6 countries: a psychological analysis. Cambridge, MA: Harvard University Press.

Whyte, J. (1998) Childhood. In K. Trew & J. Kremer (Eds) *Gender & Psychology*. London: Arnold.

Wichstrom, L. (1998) Self-concept development during adolescence: Do American truths hold for Norwegians? In E. Skoe & A. von der Lippe (Eds) *Personality Development in Adolescence: A Cross National and Life Span Perspective*. London: Routledge.

Wiegman, O., Kuttschreuter M. & Baarda, B. (1992) A Longitudinal Study of the Effects of Television Viewing on Aggressive and Prosocial Behaviors. *British Journal of Social Psychology*, 31(2), June, 147.

Wilkinson, S. (1991) Feminism & psychology: From critique to reconstruction. *Feminism & Psychology*, 1(1), 5–18.

Wilkinson, S. (1997) Feminist psychology. In D. Fox & D. Prilleltensky (Eds) *Critical Psychology: An Introduction*. London: Sage.

Williams, J.M.G. & Hargreaves, I.R. (1995) Neuroses: Depressive and anxiety disorders. In A.A. Lazarus & A.M. Colman (Eds) *Abnormal Psychology*. London: Longman.

Williams, L.M. (1994). Recall of childhood Trauma: A prospective study of women's memories of childhood abuse. *Journal of Consulting and Clinical Psychology*, 62, 1167–76.

Williams, P. (2000) 'Soon we won't relate to each other in person at all.' *The Independent on Sunday*, 16 January, 12.

Williams, W.M. & Ceci, S.J. (1997) Are Americans becoming more or less alike? Trends in race, class, and ability differences in intelligence. *American Psychologist*, 52, 1226–1235.

Wilson, D.R. (1994) Evolutionary epidemiology. *Integrative Psychiatry*, 10, 6–12.

Wilson, G. (1994) Biology, sex roles and work. In C. Quest (Ed.) *Liberating Women from Modern Feminism*. London: Institute of Economic Affairs, Health & Welfare Unit.

Wilson, H.C. (1992) A critical review of menstrual synchrony. *Psychoneuroendocrinology*, 17, 565–591.

Winch, R.E. (1958) *Mate Selections: A Study of Complementary Needs*. New York: Harper.

Winton, F., Corn, T., Huson, L.W., Franey, C., Arendt, J. & Checkley, S.A. (1989) Effects of light treatment upon mood and melatonin in patients with SAD. *Psychological Medicine*, 19(3), 585–590.

Wise, S. (2000) *Rattling the Cage: Towards Legal Rights for Animals*. London: Profile Books.

Wober, J.M., Reardon, G. & Fazal, S. (1987) *Personality, Character Aspirations and Patterns of Viewing Among Children*. London: IBA Research Papers.

Wolpe, J. (1958) *Psychotherapy by reciprocal inhibition*. Stanford, CT: Stanford University Press.

Wolpe, J. (1973) *The Practice of Behaviour Therapy* (2nd edition). New York: Pergamon Press.

Wolpe, J., with Wolpe, D. (1988) *Life Without Fear*. New Harbinger Publications.

Wood, D.J., Bruner, J.S. & Ross, G. (1976) The role of tutoring in problem-solving. *Journal of Child Psychology & Psychiatry*, 17, 89–100.

Wood, W., Wong, F.Y. & Chachere, J.G. (1991) Effects of media violence on viewers' aggression in unconstrained social interaction. *Psychological Bulletin*, 109(3), 371–383.

Woods, J. (1990) The Good Freud Guide. Guardian, 25th August.

World Health Organization (1992) *The ICD-10 Classification of Mental and Behavioural Disorders: Clinical Descriptions and Diagnostic Guidelines*. Geneva: WHO.

Wright, D.B. (1993) Recall of the Hillsborough disaster over time: Systematic biases of 'flashbulb' memories. *Applied Cognitive Psychology*, 7, 129–138.

Wundt, W. (1874) *Grundzuge der Physiologischen Psychologie*. Leipzig: Engelmann.

Wynder, E. & Graham, E. (1950) Tobacco smoking as a possible etiological factor in bronchiogenic carcinoma. *Journal of American Medical Association*, 143, 329–336.

Wynn, T. (1988) Tools and the evolution of human intelligence. In R.W. Byrne & A. Whiten (Eds) *Machiavellian intelligence*. Oxford: Oxford University Press.

Wynn, V.E. & Logie, R.H. (1998) The veracity of long-term memories – did Bartlett get it right? *Applied Cognitive Psychology*, 12, 1–20.

Yamazaki, S., Numano, R., Abe, M., Hida, A., Takahashi, R., Ueda, M., Block, G.D., Sakaki, Y., Menaker, M. & Tei, H. (2000) Resetting central and peripheral circadian oscillators in transgenic rats. *Science*, 288, 682–685.

Yates, A.J. (1970) *Behaviour Therapy*. New York: Wiley.

Yip, A. (1999) Same-sex couples. *Sociology Review*, 8(3), 30–33.

Yuille, J.C. & Cutshall, J.L. (1986) A case study of eyewitness testimony of a crime. *Journal of Applied Psychology*, 71, 291–301.

Zahavi, A. (1975) Mate selection – A selection for a handicap. *Journal of Theoretical Biology*, 53, 205–214.

Zeifman, D. & Hazan, C. (2000) A process model of adult attachment formation. In W. Ickes & S. Duck (Eds) *The Social Psychology of Personal Relationships*. Chichester: John Wiley & Sons Ltd.

Zhdanova, I.V., Wurtman, R.J., Lynch, H.J., Ives, J.R., Dollins, A.B., Morabito, C., Matheson, J.K. & Schomer, D.L. (1995) Sleep-inducing effects of low doses of melatonin ingested in the evening. *Clin. Pharmacol. Ther.*, 57, 552–558.

Zigler, E. & Styfco, S.J. (1993) Using research and theory to justify and inform Head Start expansion. Social Policy Report. *Society for Research in Child Development*, 7(20), 1–21.

Zillman, D. (1983) Arousal and aggression. In R. Geen & E. Donnerstein (Eds) *Aggression: Theoretical and Empirical Reviews*. New York: Academic Press.

Zimbardo, P.G. (1970) The human choice: Individuation, reason, and order vs. deindividuation, impulse and chaos. In W.J. Arnold & D. Levine (Eds) *Nebraska Symposium on Motivation*, Vol.17. Lincoln, NE: University of Nebraska Press.

Zimbardo, P.G., Haney, C., Banks, W.C. & Jaffe, D. (1973) The mind is a formidable jailer: A Pirandellian prison. *The New York Times Magazine*, 8 April, 122, 38–60.

Zubin, J. & Spring, B. (1977) Vulnerability – a new view of schizophrenia. *Journal of Abnormal Psychology*, 86, 103–126.

# Index

This index is in word by word order. Hypotheses, models, studies and theories can be found listed alphabetically under the relevant main heading (eg. 'studies') as well as having individual main entries. Revision schemas are listed alphabetically under 'schemas (revision)'.